简明汉英词典

修订版

A Concise Chinese-English Dictionary

Revised Edition

编 著 者　《简明汉英词典》编写组

中文修订　赖汉纲　　田万湘

　　　　　许德楠　　张　维

英文修订　王　还　王升印

商 务 印 书 馆

The Commercial Press

2002 · Beijing

目　　录
Contents

出　版　说　明

随着改革开放的进一步深化以及全球一体化进程的加快,中国与世界各国的交往越来越密切和频繁,而在这种交往中,汉语和英语是两个使用人数最多的语种,不仅愈来愈多的中国人在学习英语,很多外国人也正在努力学习汉语。因此,中外广大读者急需一部简明易读的汉英词典,为求解、翻译、作文打开一扇方便之门。我馆出版的《简明汉英词典》便是这样一部词典。自1982年问世以来,该词典赢得了国内外读者的喜爱,销量一直很好。

然而,20世纪最后20年里,社会的进步和科技的发展带来了人们语言上的巨大变化,汉语语言中涌现出大量的新词新义和新用法,《简明汉英词典》的修订因而显得十分重要。本书原作者系北京语言文化大学的教授,他们不仅拥有丰富的对外汉语教学经验,而且对语言有着特殊的敏感性,因此本次修订的主要工作仍请他们承担。

本词典在原来20 000词条的基础上,又增加了3 000多条反映新时代风貌的词语及示例,特别突出经济、法律、科技、生活等方面的语汇;根据国家的最新规定,对个别汉字和注音进行了订正,删除了一些不常用的词条,并为附录作了必要的补充及调整。

本书的英文翻译由北京语言文化大学的王还教授亲自主持,此外我们还特地聘请了英美文学研究专家朱虹女士为本书进行审定。

　　本次修订仍保留了原版的特色,强调了词典的语用功能,保留了词性标注和语法注释,特别适合对外汉语教学及汉英对译的需要。

商务印书馆编辑部
2001 年 12 月

Publisher's Note

As China steps up its reforms and opens the door wider, and as peoples all over the world are increasingly interconnected, China's ties with the rest of the world have also multiplied by leaps and bounds. In countless communications and exchanges, Chinese and English—two languages that are used by the largest numbers of people on earth—have been playing an important role. Nowadays, not only are more and more Chinese people studying English, but the number of non-natives now studying the Chinese language is also on the rise. Students of either language would need a handy dictionary of Chinese/English for vocabulary building, translation, or writing. *A Concise Chinese-English Dictionary* published by our publishing house answers just such a need and has sold well since its first publication in 1982.

Social developments as well as scientific and technological advances in the last two decades of the twentieth century have brought about significant changes to the Chinese language. Many new definitions and new uses of terms have cropped up, calling for a revision of the existing *A Concise Chinese-English Dictionary*. The original compilers of this dictionary are professors from the Beijing Language and Culture University who are not only experienced in teaching Chinese to non-native speak-

ers, but are also experts in the study of the Chinese language. To their hard work we owe the latest revision of this dictionary.

In the course of revision, 3,000 terms and examples have been added to the existing 20,000 entries, consisting mainly of newly emerged terms in the fields of economy, law, science and technology as well as everyday life. Besides the above, the phonetic symbols for a handful of Chinese characters as well as the ideograph for certain characters have been modified in accordance with newly promulgated regulations, while a handful of obsolete characters have been deleted. The appendices have also been revised.

Professor Wang Huan of the Beijing Language and Culture University supervised the entire translation of the entries into English. We have also acquired Zhu Hong, research professor of English Literature, to give the whole work a final polish.

This latest revision maintains the special features of the original version, with emphasis on the functional aspect of language. It likewise preserves all the indicators for the parts of speech and the grammatical notes, with the objective of making this dictionary particularly useful to teachers and students of either Chinese or English, and as a reference for translation from Chinese into English and vice versa.

Editorial Department
The Commercial Press
December 2001

前　言

　　《简明汉英词典》主要供外国朋友学习汉语使用，同时也供我国的翻译工作者、英语教师及学习英语的学生参考。共收近20 000 词条（包括成语、熟语、结构、格式等），单字条目（即打头字）3 065 个。收词以一般词语为主，适当兼顾一些常用的专业词语，特别注意多收报刊杂志及日常生活中广泛使用的新词汇。

　　编者总结留学生汉语教学工作的经验，在 1976 年 7 月本院铅印的《汉英》、《汉法》两部小词典的基础上，进行了修订，并参考外国留学生以及各方面提来的意见，增加了词条、注释（特别是常用虚词的注释）、例句和附录。因水平有限，缺点在所难免，欢迎读者多提建议，以便再版时修订补充。

　　本书编辑工作的负责人是钟棬。汉语编辑有：（按姓氏笔画排列）王笑湘、田万湘、龙世辉、许德楠、张维、余云霞、李培元、孟凯、郝恩美、赵桂玲、黄文彦、董树人、赖汉纲。先后参加汉语编写工作的还有：王正娃、王向明、白舒荣、祁学义、关立勋、任宣知、李明、李辉、李忆民、李延祜、李润新、陈忠、陈不同、胡书经、贾颖、彭庆生、蔡日英。英语编辑有：王还、吕炳洪、麦秀闲、林诗仲。参加英语翻译工作的还有：王华明、姜南方、黄大备。全部英语翻译由王还定稿。加拿大朋友商慧民（Sandra Sachs）参加了英语译稿的修改工作。许孟雄也修改了部分英语译稿。在我院学习的部分留学生，给予我们热情的协助；院内外各单位和许多同志给予

我们大力支持，在此谨向他们表示诚挚的谢意。

《简明汉英词典》编写组

1979 年 12 月

Foreword

Wang Xiaoxiang, Tian Liegan, Xu Liegan, Zhang Weier Liu Yuxing, Li Fayuan, Meng Pei, Hao Jiany, Zhao Zhiliang, Huang Wei en, Wen Chunmei and teachers who had participated in the Wang Zhenya, Wang Xiangzhu, Hai Shifang, Qi Zheng, Gu Zhi ... Ren Kuanli, Lu Ming, Lü Hui, Bi Youn

This dictionary is intended mainly for non-native speakers of the Chinese language, and we hope that it may also be useful to translators, teachers and students of English. It contains some 20,000 entries (including words, set phrases, common sayings, various constructions and structures) with 3,065 main entry characters. The entries are primarily everyday words in current usage though familiar terms in science and technology are also included. Special care has been taken to incorporate new words that appear frequently in the media and in daily life.

This dictionary has been compiled on the basis of the *Chinese-English Dictionary* and the *Chinese-French Dictionary* published by our Institute in July 1976 for restricted circulation. In later revisions, more entries, usage notes (especially the usage of function words), examples and appendices have been added. In compiling this dictionary, the editors have made the advantage of the Institute's experience in teaching Chinese to foreign students and taken into consideration the suggestions of students and experts there. As mistakes and lapses are inevitable, we welcome comments and suggestions that would be helpful towards revisions in future editions.

Zhong Qin is responsible for organizing the compilation of this dictionary. The Chinese editors (arranged in order of stroke number of their names) are: Wang Xiaoxiang, Tian

Wanxiang, Long Shihui, Xu Denan, Zhang Wei, Yu Yunxia, Li Peiyuan, Meng Kai, Hao Enmei, Zhao Guiling, Huang Wenyan, Dong Shuren, Lai Hangang. Others who had participated are Wang Zhengwa, Wang Xiangming, Bai Shurong, Qi Xueyi, Guan Lixun, Ren Xuanzhi, Li Ming, Li Hui, Li Yimin, Li Yanhu, Li Runxin, Chen Zhong, Chen Butong, Hu Shujing, Jia Ying, Peng Qingsheng and Cai Riying. The English editors are Wang Huan, Lü Binghong, Mai Xiuxian and Lin Shizhong. Others who took part in the translation are Wang Huaming, Jiang Nanfang and Huang Dabei. The entire English translation was finalized by Wang Huan. Acknowledgement is gratefully made to our Canadian friend Sandra Sachs who gave us very valuable help in polishing the English translation. Xu Mengxiong read a part of the translation and made suggestions. We also wish to acknowledge the support of many organizations and the valuable assistance of experts and students. To each and all, we extend our sincere thanks.

A Concise Chinese-English Dictionary
Compiling Group
December 1979

说　明
Explanatory Notes

一、词条
I. The Entries

分读音、汉字、释义三个方面加以说明。

Each entry consists of three parts: the symbolized pronunciation, the Chinese character and the definition in English.

读音　Pronunciation

1. 词条按《汉语拼音方案》字母次序排列。有关《汉语拼音方案》同国际音标、威托玛式音标等的对照情况参见附录(一)。

1. The symbols used in this dictionary for indicating pronunciation are those of the Chinese Phonetic Alphabet. The entries have been arranged alphabetically according to the Chinese Phonetic Alphabet. For a comparison of the Chinese Phonetic Alphabet, the International Phonetic Alphabet, and the Wade system, see Appendix I.

2. 音同调不同的汉字，按阴平(第一声)、阳平(第二声)、上声(第三声)、去声(第四声)、轻声的次序排列。同音同调的按汉字笔画多少排列，少的在前，多的在后。

2. Characters having the same sound but different tones are arranged in order of tones: 1st, 2nd, 3rd, 4th and neutral. Characters having the same sound and the same tone are arranged according to the number of strokes, characters having fewer strokes preceding those having more strokes.

3. 同音同形的单音词，作一条处理，如("白"(形)(副))；由于所注词性不同，释义不同，不致发生混淆。

3. Monosyllabic words represented by the same character and having

the same pronunciation are combined in one entry, e. g. 白(形) white, (副) in vain. The user will not find this confusing since they differ in part of speech and definition.

4. 轻声是独立的一个声调,发轻声的单音词或有一个音节读轻声的词均单独处理,如助词"过"在轻声"guo"音序下见;名词"大意 dàyi"与形容词"大意 dàyì"分两条。轻声的音高变化见"变调"。

4. The neutral tone is treated as a separate tone equivalent to the other 4 tones. Monosyllabic words having a neutral tone or words having one syllable pronounced in the neutral tone are dealt with as separate items, e. g. the particle 过 is listed under guo in the neutral tone; the noun 大意 (dàyi) and the adjective 大意 (dàyi) are listed as two separate entries. For the change in the pitch of the neutral tone, see the entry 变调.

5. 读音儿化的,标"(～儿)";书写时经常带"儿"字的,词条收"儿",如"一块儿"。读音因儿化而发生的变化情形,见"儿化",各词条不一一标出。

5. Those words pronounced with a retroflex "r" are marked "(～儿)". If the written form always has 儿, e. g. 一块儿, the entry is printed that way. For the modification of speech sounds due to the retroflex "r", see the entry 儿化.

6. 某些变调规则,如第三声音节因后随音节声调的不同而变为第二声或半三声,参见"变调"条,各词均标原调。"不"的变调见"不"条。"七""八"变调带方音性质,本词典不收。某些词重叠后读音略有变化,因普遍性不大,亦未作特殊处理。

6. For certain rules regarding changes of tone, e. g. the change from a 3rd tone to a 2nd tone or semi 3rd tone due to the difference in tone of the character following it, see the entry 变调. All entries are marked in their original tones. The changes of tones of 不 are explained under the respective entry. This dictionary does not indicate the changes in tone of 七 and 八 because they are dialectal changes. Some characters change slightly in pronunciation after reduplication. These are not dealt with because they are regional.

7. 词条拼音分写连写按以下原则处理:

7. The principles having to do with the joining or separation of syllables in phonetic transcription are as follows:

（1）词条凡标注词性的,拼音连写。

（1）Entries with the parts of speech stated are transcribed with syllables joined.

（2）大于词的,拼音分写,分写原则以词为单位。在成语、熟语中划词适当体现古汉语的特点。

（2）Entries which are phrases are transcribed with the syllables separated, each word forming a unit. In set phrases and common sayings, classical Chinese is taken into consideration in the division into words.

（3）动宾结构的拼写,中间以"＝"号隔开,如"打架 dǎ＝jià"。（见 19 页动宾结构）。

（3）The phonetic transcription of the V-O (verb-object) construction is separated by the sign ＝, e. g. 打架 dǎ＝jià (see V-O construction, P. 19).

（4）动补结构的拼写,中间以"∥"号隔开,如"打开 dǎ∥kāi"。（见 19 页动补结构）。

（4）The phonetic transcription of the V-C (verb-complement) construction is separated by the sign ∥, e. g. 打开 dǎ∥kāi (see V-C construction, P. 19).

（5）格式是由一些常用在一起互相呼应的词组成的,拼音以词为单位分写,如"除了…以外 chúle…yǐwài"。

（5）Structures are made up of words which are often used together. Whether they are transcribed with the syllables joined or separated, each word forms a unit, e. g. 除了…以外 chúle…yǐwài.

8. 例句英译文中的人名、地名一概用《汉语拼音方案》标注。

8. Names of persons and places in the English translation of examples are all written in the Chinese Phonetic Alphabet.

汉字　Chinese characters

1. 本词典兼用"笔画查字法"和"部首查字法"。具体查检方法见《笔画

查字表》和《部首查字表》。

1. This dictionary adopts both the "Stroke Index" and the "Radical Index" systems. Instructions for each index are to be found at the beginning of the index.

2. 本词典中汉字，凡有简体字者，全部用简体字。词典正文的打头字如有繁体，繁体字加括号排在打头字后；如果只是一个词的某一个义项有繁体的问题，则在这一义项号码后列繁体，如"表"（名）（2）后列繁体"錶"。

2. All characters which have simplified forms are given in simplified forms in this dictionary. Those of the main entry characters in the text of the dictionary which have original complex forms, have the complex forms placed in brackets after the main entry characters. In the case where only in one definition of a character does it have a complex form, the complex form is placed after this particular definition, e. g. 表（名）（2）（錶）.

3. 同汉字又同音同调的词条，按词在前、词组在后的原则排列，如"贷款（名）"条在前，"贷款"（动宾结构）条在后。

3. Entries having the same characters and the same pronunciations and tones are arranged with word preceding phrase, e. g. 贷款 as a noun precedes 贷款 as V-O construction.

4. 为方便读者，本词典附有《繁简体字对照表》。

4. For the convenience of the user, this dictionary lists simplified characters and their original complex forms in Appendix 3.

释义　Definitions

1. 词条释义尽量先给英语等同词。等同词不足以表达汉语词条的特殊含义或用法的，适当加注。

1. For each entry word, an English equivalent is provided. If such an equivalent is not enough to convey the particular meaning or usage of the entry word, some explanation is given.

2. 有两种以上词性的词按实词在前、虚词在后的原则注释。同一词性下的义项排列顺序为：本义在前，引申义在后；常用的在前，次常用的在后。

2. For a word used as more than one part of speech, definitions are given with notional word preceding function word. The definitions of a word under one part of speech are so arranged that the original meaning precedes the figurative meaning, and the more frequently used meaning precedes the less frequently used meaning.

3. 释义后的例句和搭配以帮助读者掌握用法为主要着眼点。只用于书面语的词，标〈书〉；多见于书面语的，在释义中说明。纯属日常口语的词语，标〈口〉。

3. The examples which follow the definition are mainly intended to help the user grasp the usage of the word. Words used only in written language are marked 〈书〉; where words are usually used in written language, that is indicated in the definition. Words used only in spoken language are marked 〈口〉.

二、语法
II. Grammar

词典在确定词条、词性，注释用法以及举例时不可避免地要牵涉到语法。关于汉语语法，目前大家看法很不一致。为方便词典使用者，现将本词典的语法规律及术语，从分词、词组、句子三个方面加以说明。

The determination of which entries shall be included in a dictionary and of the part of speech of each word, writing usage notes and giving examples are all questions having a lot to do with grammar. Views on Chinese grammar are still very divergent. For the convenience of the user, there follows a note on the grammatical principles which govern this dictionary and the grammatical terminology under the three headings: words, phrases and sentences.

词 Words

1. 本词典划词以现代汉语为标准。在现代汉语中不能独立作词运用

的字,一律不注词性,不释义。有的虽不能自由运用,但在某些固定词组或习惯组合中仍有生命力,具有独立含义,本词典标注词性,释义,并加"◇"号以示区别。

1. Whether a character is a word or not, is decided by its function in modern Chinese. Neither the part of speech nor definition (English equivalent) is given for those characters which cannot function independently as words in modern Chinese. Characters which cannot stand on their own as words but which still have independent meaning in certain set phrases are treated as words and the sign ◇ is added to indicate which these are.

2. 词分实词、虚词两大类。

2. Chinese words can be classified into two categories: notional words and function words.

实词包括:名词、代词、动词、助动词、形容词、数词、量词。另有词头、词尾两个附类。

Notional words include: nouns, pronouns, verbs, auxiliary verbs, adjectives, numerals and measure words. Prefixes and suffixes are also included in this category.

虚词包括:副词、介词、连词、助词、叹词、象声词。

Function words include: adverbs, prepositions, conjunctions, particles, interjections and onomatopoeic words.

3. 名词内有时间词及方位词两个附类。本词典一律注"(名)"。这两个名词附类的最大特点是可作状语(如"咱们现在屋里谈吧")。

3. Nouns denoting time and nouns of locality are also included in the category of nouns and are marked (名). Their distinguishing feature is that they can function as adverbial adjuncts, e.g. 咱们现在屋里谈吧.

4. 代词分人称代词(如"我""咱们""人家 rénjia"),疑问代词(如"什么""哪儿""哪 nǎ"),指示代词(如"这""那""每")和其他代词(如"其他""其余")。本词典一律注"(代)"。

4. Pronouns are divided into personal pronouns, such as 我,咱们,人家 (rénjia); interrogative pronouns such as 什么,哪儿,哪 (nǎ); demonstrative

pronouns such as 这，那，每 and other pronouns such as 其他，其余. They are all marked（代）.

5. 动词有及物、不及物之分，本词典一律注"（动）"。

5. Both transitive and intransitive verbs are marked（动）.

6. 形容词一般兼有能作谓语又能作定语的特性，但有部分形容词只作定语不作谓语用（即非谓形容词），另有一部分又只作谓语不作定语用（即非定形容词），本词典一律注"（形）"，读者应注意词条后的用法注释和搭配与例句，以免用错。

6. In general, an adjective can serve either as a predicate or as an attributive, but some adjectives can serve only as attributives（non-predicate adjectives）; whereas others can serve only as predicates（non-attributive adjectives）. They are all marked（形）. The user can learn their usages from usage notes and examples.

7. 量词分名量及动量两大类，都标"（量）"。本词典正文中部分名词条后标注了常用名量（如"椅子——〔把 bǎ〕"）。附录（十一）列出常用名量与动量共 164 个，供读者参考。许多名词可借作量词使用（如"一杯酒""一坛酒""一瓶酒""洒了一桌子酒""溅了一地酒"等等），诸如此类的纯属临时借用性质，本词典一律不标"（量）"。

7. Measure words are divided into noun measure words and verb measure words. They are all marked（量）. Following some nouns, their specific measure words are given, e. g. 椅子〔把 bǎ〕. 135 common noun and verb measure words are listed in Appendix 11 for the user's reference. Many nouns can be used as measure words（e. g. 一杯酒，一坛酒，一瓶酒，洒了一桌子酒，溅了一地酒，etc.）; all such nouns which can be used as measure words are not marked（量）.

8. 词头、词尾不是能独立运用的词，但还没有发展到词的形态变化成分的地步。

8. Prefixes and suffixes are not words but on the other hand, they are not quite the same as the affixes of some other languages.

9. 助词分结构助词（"的""得""地"）、语气助词（如"吗""呢""吧"

"啊")、时态助词("了""着""过")和其他助词(如"罢了""而已")。本词典一律注"(助)"。

9. Particles：structural particles（的，得，地），modal particles（吗，呢，吧，啊），aspect particles（了，着，过）and other particles such as 罢了，而已，are all marked（助）.

10. 确定词性

10. The determination of parts of speech

确定词性时对以下几个方面进行综合考察，即：一类词与其他词类的词的组合，词在句子中的功能，词的意义和词的变化（如重叠形式等）。

In determining the parts of speech of the words the following points are taken into consideration：the word's collocations with words of different parts of speech, the function of the word in the sentence, the meaning of the word and the morphological changes in the word（e. g. reduplication, etc. ）.

(1) 动词与名词：

(1) Verbs and nouns：

① 同形同音但明显是两个词，一动一名的，当然要注两个词性，如"锁"（动）：把箱子锁上；（名）：一把锁。

①Two words made up of the same character and having the same pronunciation，one being a noun, the other a verb, are put in one entry and marked with both parts of speech, e. g. 锁（动）lock：把箱子锁上；（名）lock：一把锁.

②动词一般都可作主语、宾语，不能因此给动词都兼注"(名)"。动词一般还可作定语，也不能因此都兼注"(形)"。

② Verbs in general can function as the subject or the object of a sentence，but we have not marked every verb（名）. Verbs can also function as attributives，but they have not been marked（形）.

③ 从词源看是"(动)"，但现代汉语中已可受名量修饰（至少可受"种""项""套""宗"等名量修饰），也可受一般形容词和名词修饰的，兼注"(名)"，如"斗争(动)(名)"；"教育(动)(名)"。

③ Sometimes, judging from its etymology, a word is a verb, but in

modern Chinese it can be modified by a noun measure word (at least by 种，项，套，宗，etc.) and can also be modified by an ordinary adjective or noun. In this case, it is marked both (动) and (名), e. g. 斗争(动)(名)，教育(动)(名).

(2) 名词与形容词：

(2) Nouns and adjectives：

名词一般可作定语，本词典不以此给名词兼注"(形)"，如"文化(名)"，但例子中可以有"文化生活"。只有可受副词"很""不"等修饰的，才兼注"(形)"，如"科学(名)(形)""文明(名)(形)"。

Nouns in general can function as attributives, but we do not mark them (形), e. g. in the entry 文化(名) there may be an example 文化生活. Only those nouns which can be modified by the adverbs 很，不，etc. , are marked both (名) and (形), e. g. 科学 (名) (形)，文明(名)(形).

(3) 形容词与副词：

(3) Adjectives and adverbs：

① 同音同形但明显是两个词，一形一副，意义不同的，当然注两个词性，如"白"(形)：白衣服；(副)：白跑一趟。

① Two words made up of the same character and having the same pronunciation, yet having two entirely different meanings, one as adjective and the other as adverb, are put in one entry and marked with both parts of speech, e. g. 白(形) white：白衣服；(副) in vain：白跑一趟.

② 汉语形容词常作状语，倘若意义不变，不算兼"(副)"，如"积极(形)：积极工作"，这里"积极"是形容词作状语。

② Adjectives can generally function as adverbial adjuncts, so, if the meaning remains the same, an adjective is not marked (副) when it functions as an adverbial adjunct, e. g. 积极(形)：积极工作.

(4) 副词与连词：

(4) Adverbs and conjunctions：

只能用在句子谓语前的是副词，如"就""才""很""尚且"；只能用在主语前的是连词，如"但是""否则""然而"。可在主语前也可在谓语前的，按以下

标准划分：用了这个词的句子能单独成立的注"（副）"，如"尤其""难道"；不能单独成立的注"（连）"，如"即使""宁可""于是"。

Words which can only be used before the predicate of a sentence are adverbs, e. g. 就，才，很，尚且；words which can only be used before the subject of a sentence are conjunctions, e. g. 但是，否则，然而. Words which can be used both before the predicate and before the subject are determined by the following principle：if a clause containing the word can be an independent sentence，then the word is an adverb, e. g. 尤其，难道；if not, it is a conjunction，e. g. 即使，宁可，于是.

（5）助动词：

（5）Auxiliary verbs：

仅仅看是否用在动词前这一条，尚不足以确定某词是否为助动词，因为副词（如"懒得"）与一些动词（如"喜欢"）都可占据这个地位。助动词除了上述条件，还要能单独回答问题，受"不"修饰，不能带名词、代词作的宾语。这样，助动词（如"可以""应该"等）就同动词、副词划清了界线。

The fact that a word can be used before a verb does not ensure that it is an auxiliary verb，because some adverbs（e. g. 懒得）and some verbs（e. g. 喜欢）can also be so used. An auxiliary verb must be able to form the answer to a question standing by itself，must be able to be qualified by 不，and cannot take an object made up of a noun or pronoun. In these ways，auxiliary verbs（e. g. 可以，应该）are distinguished from verbs and adverbs.

（6）某些重叠形式：

（6）Reduplications：

① 各类词符合规律的重叠形式，不另出词条，如有"马虎（形）"，但不收"马马虎虎（形）"。

① The regular reduplications of words of different parts of speech are not included as separate entries. Thus 马虎（形）is an entry, and there is no entry for 马马虎虎（形）.

② 重叠形式如果同未重叠时的词义、用法，尤其是语法功能有差别，则另出词条，如"晃悠（动）"之外，另出"晃晃悠悠（形）"；"支吾（动）"之外，另出

"支支吾吾(形)"。

② If the reduplication of a word has a different meaning, usage and especially grammatical function from the word, then it is included as a separate entry, e.g. 晃悠(动),晃晃悠悠(形);支吾(动),支支吾吾(形).

词组　Phrases

本词典在释义及用法注释中提到的词组有两种:结构和词组。结构有下列四种:

In the definitions and usage notes in this dictionary there are two kinds of phrases mentioned: constructions and phrases. There are four kinds of constructions:

1. 动宾结构:

1. Verb-object (V-O) constructions:

动宾结构由一个动词加一个作它的宾语的词(多为名词)构成。有时这个宾语前可用数量词,动词可带"了"(或"着""过"),重叠时只重叠动词部分,等等。本词典词条中常用的动宾结构占有一定的数量。

A V-O construction is made up of a verb and its object (usually a noun). This object can take a numeral plus measure word, and the verb can take 了 or 着 or 过. When reduplicated, only the verb is reduplicated and not the object. The V-O constructions which are entries in this dictionary have been included because they are very frequently used.

2. 动补结构:

2. Verb-complement (V-C) constructions:

动补结构由一个动词加一个作它的结果补语(或趋向补语)的词构成。这个补语常可加"得"或"不"转为可能式,时态助词"了"要用在整个结构的后面而不在动补之间,无重叠形式,等等。本词典词条中常用的动补结构占有一定的数量。

A V-C construction is made up of a verb and its resultative or directional complement. A 得 or 不 can be added between the verb and its complement to form the potential form. If the aspect particle 了 is used, it must be

placed after the complement and not after the verb. Such a construction cannot be reduplicated. The V-C constructions which are entries in this dictionary have been included because they are very frequently used.

3. 介宾结构：

3. Preposition-object (P-O) constructions：

介宾结构由一个介词加一个作它的宾语的词（多为名词）构成，一般在句中作状语用。

A P-O construction is formed by a preposition and its object (usually a noun) and is often used as an adverbial adjunct.

4. 主谓结构：

4. Subject-predicate (S-P) constructions：

原为主谓结构的一些组合有些已固定为词，如"气馁（形）"，"地震（名）"等。小部分结合较为松散，如"军用""民办"等，虽收作词条，但拼音分写，不注词性。主谓结构在句中可作主语、谓语、定语等。

Some S-P constructions have already become words, e. g. 气馁（形），地震（名）. Others, such as 军用 and 民办 are included as entries but are not considered to be words so their phonetic transcriptions do not have the syllables joined.

词组有名词词组和动词词组。以名词为中心的词组，一般是名词及其定语，在句中作用相当于一个名词的，叫名词词组。以动词为中心的词组，一般是动词及其状语，在句中作用相当于一个动词的，叫动词词组。此外，在用法注释中有时提到词或词组，其中词组则与前面说到的词往往起同一作用。

Phrases include nominal phrases and verbal phrases. A phrase with a noun as its core, usually a noun and its attributive, functioning as a noun in a sentence is known as nominal phrase. A phrase with a verb as its core, usually a verb and its adverbial adjunct, functioning as a verb in a sentence, is known as verbal phrase. Moreover, in usage notes, sometimes "a word or phrase" is used and the "phrase" here usually has the same function as the "word" mentioned before.

句子 Sentences

本词典的句法体系
Syntax

1. 句子分类　Classification of sentences

单句分类　Classification of simple sentences

复句分类（略）　Classification of compound sentences（omitted）

（1）单句按构成分类　Classification of simple sentences according to their structure

（2）单句按作用分类　Classification of simple sentences according to their function

2. 句子成分　Sentence components

（1）主语　subject　　　　（2）谓语　predicate

（3）宾语　object　　　　（4）定语　attributive

（5）状语　adverbial adjunct　　（6）补语　complement

① 情态补语　descriptive complement

② 结果补语（及其可能式）　resultative complement（and its potential form）

③ 趋向补语（及其可能式）　directional complement（and its potential form）

④ 程度补语　complement of degree

⑤ 动量补语　complement of verb measure word

⑥ 时量补语　complement of time

1. 句子分类（单句分类）

1. Classification of sentences（of simple sentences）

（1）按构成分类

（1）Classification according to their structure

①主谓句

① Subject-predicate sentence

a. 动词谓语句

a. sentence with a verb-predicate

电灯灭了。

他是学生。

中国人民已经掌握了自己的命运。

张老师教我们汉语。（双宾语句　a sentence with double objects）

烈马挣开缰绳逃脱了。（连动句　sentence with a series of verbs）

教练员勉励运动员创造出更优异的成绩。（兼语句　pivotal sentence）

晚霞把天都映红了。（"把"字句　the 把 sentence）

树被大风刮倒了。（被动句　the 被 sentence）

衣服洗干净了。（意义上的被动句　sentence passive in meaning）

门前停着一辆小汽车。（存现句　sentence showing existence, emergence）

b. 形容词谓语句

b. sentence with an adjective-predicate

这把刀真快。

消息十分确切。

c. 名词谓语句

c. sentence with a noun-predicate

今天星期六。

您老人家多大岁数了？

d. 主谓谓语句

d. sentence with a S-P construction as its predicate

他们俩脾气不对头。

② 无主句

② Sentence without a subject

下雨了。

③ 独词句

③ One-word sentence

　　　　小心!

　　　　注意!

(2) 按作用分类

(2) Classification according to their function

① 陈述句(略)

① declarative sentence (omitted)

② 疑问句

② interrogative sentence

a. 用"吗"的疑问句

a. question using 吗

　　　　你每天都在食堂吃饭吗?

b. 正反疑问句

b. affirmative＋negative question

　　　　你有没有《简明汉英词典》?

　　　　他参加不参加比赛?

c. 选择疑问句

c. alternative question

　　　　你去北京还是去上海?

d. 用疑问代词的疑问句

d. question using an interrogative pronoun

　　　　这是谁的雨衣?

　　　　你假期都干什么了?

e. 用"是不是"的疑问句

e. question using 是不是

　　　　客人是不是到齐了?

f. 用"呢"的疑问句

f. question using 呢

　　　　我的帽子在这儿,你的呢?

　　　　你们都同意了,小王呢?

③ 祈使句

③ imperative sentence

请勿吸烟!

小声点儿!

④ 感叹句

④ exclamatory sentence

嘿! 这活儿干得多棒!

2. 句子成分

2. Sentence components

(1) 主语 除名词、代词可作主语外,动词、形容词、数量词以及各种结构也都可作主语。

(1) Subject Besides nouns and pronouns which can serve as subject, verbs, adjectives, numerals plus measure words, and the various constructions can also function as subject.

(2) 谓语 汉语的单句按谓语的特征分为动词谓语句、形容词谓语句、名词谓语句和主谓谓语句四大类(见第 18 页)。

(2) Predicate The simple sentences in Chinese are divided into sentence with a verb-predicate, sentence with an adjective-predicate, sentence with a noun-predicate and sentence with a S-P construction as its predicate (see page 18).

(3) 宾语 除名词、代词可作宾语外,动词、形容词、数量词以及主谓、动宾结构等也都可作宾语。

(3) Object Besides nouns and pronouns which can serve as object, verbs, adjectives, numerals plus measure words and S-P and V-O constructions can also function as object.

(4) 定语 除名词、代词、形容词、数量词可作定语外,动词及各种结构也都可作定语。

(4) Attributive Besides nouns, pronouns, adjectives and numerals plus measure words which can serve as attributive, verbs and various constructions can also function as attributive.

(5) 状语 除副词、介宾结构可以作状语外,名词(特别是时间词和方

位词)、形容词、动词、动宾结构等也常作状语：

(5) Adverbial adjunct　Besides adverbs and P-O constructions which can serve as adverbial adjunct, nouns (especially nouns denoting time and nouns of locality), adjectives, verbs and V-O constructions can also function as adverbial adjunct：

> 刚睡醒　(副词 adverb)
>
> 为人民服务　(介宾结构 P-O construction)
>
> 晚上把稿子写完　(时间词 noun denoting time)
>
> 大家炕上坐吧。　(方位词 noun of locality)
>
> 积极工作　(形容词 adjective)
>
> 躺着看书　(动词 verb)
>
> 凭什么下这样的结论?　(动宾结构 V-O construction)

(6) 补语　补语有下列六种

(6) Complement

① 情态补语　形容词、主谓结构等可以作情态补语。情态补语一般加"得"与前面的动词、形容词等连接,有时也用"个"来连接：

① Descriptive complement　Adjectives, S-P constructions, etc. can serve as descriptive complement. In general, a descriptive complement is connected with the verb or adjective by 得 or sometimes by 个：

> 这人长得漂亮。
>
> 汽车开得不快。
>
> 他唱得没有你好。
>
> 笑得肚子疼。
>
> 打了个落花流水。

动宾结构带情态补语时,要重复动词部分,然后再加"得"和情态补语：

When a V-O construction takes a descriptive complement, the verb must be repeated before 得 and the complement：

> 打球打得可好了。
>
> 说话说得不清楚。

② 结果补语

② resultative complement

　　在足球赛中，我们两个队踢平了。

可能式 potential form：礼堂坐得下 3000 人。

　　汽车有毛病，再也开不快了。

③ 趋向补语

③ directional complement

　　寄来一封信

　　从国外回来

　　打河里游过去

可能式 potential form：你明天回得来吗？——回不来。

　　怎么想也想不起来了。

④ 程度补语

④ complement of degree

　　心里透亮多了。

　　冷极了

　　碍事得很

　　差远了

⑤ 动量补语

⑤ complement of verb measure word

　　把足球场平整一下。

　　刷了两遍

　　去过三次

⑥ 时量补语

⑥ complement of time

　　坐一会儿

　　参观了两个小时

　　雪整整下了一夜。

三、凡例
III. Printing Conventions

1. 词类简称表

1. Abbreviations of parts of speech

（名）	míng	名词	noun
（代）	dài	代词	pronoun
（动）	dòng	动词	verb
（助动）	zhùdòng	助动词	auxiliary verb
（形）	xíng	形容词	adjective
（数）	shù	数词	numeral
（量）	liàng	量词	measure word
		（头）tóu	词头	prefix
		（尾）wěi	词尾	suffix
（副）	fù	副词	adverb
（介）	jiè	介词	preposition
（连）	lián	连词	conjunction
（助）	zhù	助词	particle
（叹）	tàn	叹词	interjection
（象声）	xiàngshēng	象声词	onomatopoeic word

2. 简略符号表

2. Marks

◇　"◇"表示虽不能自由运用,但在某些固定词组或习惯组合中具有独立词义的非自由词。

◇　denotes that the word though cannot be used freely, still has a meaning of its own in certain set phrases or common sayings.

～　在词条行文及举例中,～代表词目词,如"步调"(名):～一致|统一～。"(～儿)"表示该词读时儿化。

～　is used in the article to represent the headword, e. g. 步调(名):～

一致,统一～.

（～儿）indicates that the word should be pronounced with a retroflexed 儿.

〈书〉　只用于书面语。

〈书〉　indicates that the word is only used in written language.

〈口〉　只用于日常口语。

〈口〉　indicates that the word is only used in colloquial speech.

笔画查字表
Stroke Index

　　本表所列汉字按笔画多少排列；笔画少的在前，多的在后。同笔画的字，则按第一笔横(一)、竖(丨)、撇(丿)、点(丶)、横折(乛)、竖折(乚)先后排列。

　　The Chinese characters in this index are arranged in order of the number of strokes, characters with fewer strokes preceding those with more strokes. Characters with the same number of strokes are arranged in order of the first stroke as follows：一,丨,丿,丶,乛,乚.

　　"一 丨 丿 丶 乛 乚"以外的笔形按下面的办法处理：

　　Apart from "一 丨 丿 丶 乛 乚", all other strokes are dealt with as follows：

1. (㇀ ㇏) 　　　　　equivalent to (一)
2. (亅 ㇈) 　　　　　equivalent to (丨)
3. (㇇ 一 ノ) 　　　　equivalent to (丿)
4. (丶 、 ㇔) 　　　　equivalent to (丶)
5. (フ ㇆ ㇌ ㇠ 乁 乙 乛) equivalent to (乛)
6. (亅 乚 く 乚 ㇉) 　　equivalent to (乚)

乡　722

四画

〔一〕
丰　190
王　682
井　337
开　352
夫　194
天　649
元　813
无　697
云　818
专　875
扎　821,831
艺　786
木　451
五　701
支　854
厅　655
不　47
太　638
犬　542
区　536
历　393
友　803
歹　118
尤　800
匹　490
厄　164
车　73
巨　345
牙　755
屯　672
戈　212
比　31
互　269
切　525
瓦　675

〔丨〕
止　858
少　578,579
日　554

中　864,867
内　462
水　619
见　309

〔丿〕
手　607
午　702
牛　469
毛　427
气　512
升　588
天　765
长　69,837
仁　551
什　585
片　490,492
仆　502
化　271
仇　86
币　33
仍　554
仅　329
斤　328
爪　840
反　175
介　326
父　197
从　102
今　328
凶　742
分　186,189
乏　171
公　219
仓　61
月　817
氏　600
勿　703
风　190
欠　520
匀　818
乌　696
勾　223,224
凤　193

〔丶〕
六　411

文　692
方　178
闩　617
火　285
为　685,689
斗　152
忆　786
计　296
订　147
户　269
讣　197
认　552
讥　289
冗　556
心　734

〔乛〕
尺　82
引　791
丑　86
巴　9
孔　366
队　157
办　18
予　810
劝　542
双　617
书　611

〔乚〕
以　783
允　819
幻　276

五画

〔一〕
玉　811
刊　356
末　448
未　690
示　600
击　289
打　109,110
巧　524
正　849
扑　502

扒　9,477
功　221
扔　554
去　539
甘　204
世　601
艾　3
古　226
节　323
本　29
术　615
札　832
可　361
丙　44
左　895
厉　394
石　122,596
右　807
布　55
龙　412
戊　703
平　496
灭　441
轧　832
东　148

〔丨〕
卡　352,514
北　26
占　835
凸　666
卢　413
业　770
旧　341
归　238
目　451
旦　122
且　525
叮　145
叶　770
甲　302
申　582
号　253,256
电　142
田　651
由　800

叭　9
只　854,858
史　600
兄　743
叫　319
另　408
叹　641
凹　7
囚　535
四　626

〔丿〕
生　588
失　593
矢　600
乍　832
禾　257
丘　535
付　197
仗　838
代　118
仙　715
仟　516
们　434
仪　781
白　13
仔　884
他　637
斥　83
瓜　229
丛　104
令　409
用　798
甩　617
印　793
乐　386,817
尔　168
句　345
匆　102
册　63
犯　177
外　676
处　92,93
冬　149
鸟　468
务　703

包　20
饥　289

〔丶〕
主　871
市　601
立　394
玄　748
闪　570
兰　381
半　18
汁　855
汇　281
头　663,666
汉　252
宁　468,469
穴　750
它　637
讨　643
写　733
让　546
礼　391
训　753
必　33
议　786
讯　753
记　297
永　797

〔乛〕
司　623
尼　464
民　441
弘　264
阡　516
辽　401
加　300
召　840
皮　488
边　36
孕　819
圣　592
对　157
矛　428

〔乚〕
出　87
奶　456

奴 472	厌 761	岁 633	全 540	米 436	驰 82
发 169	在 823	回 279	会 282,371	灯 134	〔乚〕
台 638	百 14	岂 508	杀 567	汗 252	收 606
纠 340	有 803	则 828	合 257	污 696	妁 304
母 451	存 106	刚 207	兆 840	江 312	如 557
幼 807	而 167	网 682	企 509	池 82	妇 198
丝 623	页 770	肉 557	众 868	汤 641	好 254,256
六画	夸 371	〔丿〕	爷 768	忏 69	她 637
	夺 162	年 466	伞 564	忙 426	妈 421
〔一〕	灰 278	朱 870	创 96,97	兴 739,741	牟 450
邦 20	达 109	先 716	肌 290	宇 810	红 264
式 601	列 403	丢 148	肋 388	守 609	纤 716
迁 808	死 625	舌 579	朵 162	字 887	约 816
刑 739	成 77	竹 871	杂 821	安 4	级 293
动 149	夹 301,302	迁 516	危 684	讲 313	纪 297
扛 358	轨 240	乔 523	旬 752	讳 282	巡 752
寺 626	邪 733	迄 513	旭 747	军 350	**七画**
吉 292	划 271,272	伟 688	旮 201	许 747	
扣 369	迈 423	传 94,877	负 197	讹 164	〔一〕
考 359	毕 34	乒 496	各 215	论 417	寿 610
托 672	至 860	休 744	名 443	农 471	弄 471
老 384	〔丨〕	伍 702	多 160	讽 193	麦 423
巩 222	此 101	伎 297	争 847	设 580	玖 341
执 855	师 594	伏 194	色 566	访 181	玛 422
扩 375	尘 74	优 799	〔丶〕	诀 348	形 740
扪 433	尖 304	延 756	壮 879	〔乛〕	进 331
扫 566	劣 403	件 310	冲 84,85	寻 752	戒 327
地 131,138	光 236	任 553	冰 43	那 455	吞 672
扬 762	当 123,125	伤 571	庄 878	迅 753	远 815
场 70,71	吁 746	价 303	庆 534	尽 329,331	违 686
耳 168	早 827	伦 417	亦 786	导 126	韧 554
共 222	吐 668	份 189	齐 505	异 787	运 819
芍 578	吓 715	华 271	交 315	孙 634	扶 195
亚 755	虫 84	仰 763	次 101	阵 846	抚 196
芝 855	曲 537,538	仿 180	衣 780	阳 763	坛 640
朽 745	团 669	伙 286	产 68	阶 321	技 298
朴 502	同 659	伪 688	决 348	阴 790	坏 274
机 289	吊 144	自 884	充 83	防 179	抠 367
权 540	吃 81	伊 780	妄 683	戏 709	扰 546
过 243,247	因 789	血 734,751	闭 34	羽 810	扼 164
再 822	吸 705	向 726	问 694	观 233	拒 346
协 732	吗 422	似 601,627	闯 97	欢 274	找 840
西 705	屹 786	后 265	羊 763	买 423	批 487
压 754	帆 172	行 252,740	并 44	驮 674	扯 74
		舟 869	关 231	驯 753	

走	890	芭	9	足	891	佣	799	亩	451	究	340
抄	72	苏	628	邮	801	低	135	况	373	穷	534
坝	12	杆	205	男	457	你	464	床	97	灾	822
贡	223	杜	154	困	375	住	873	库	370	良	399
攻	221	杠	209	吵	73	位	690	庇	35	证	851
赤	83	材	58	串	96	伴	19	疗	401	启	509
折	579,842	村	106	呐	456	身	582	吝	406	评	498
抓	875	杏	742	呗	28	伺	627	应	793,795	补	46
扳	16	极	293	员	813	佛	194	冷	389	初	91
抡	417	杞	509	听	655	伽	201	这	843	社	581
扮	19	杨	763	吩	188	近	333	序	747	诅	892
抢	522	求	535	吻	694	彻	74	辛	736	识	598
孝	731	匣	710	吹	98	彷	481	弃	514	诈	832
坎	356	更	217,218	呜	696	返	177	冶	769	诉	629
坍	639	束	615	吭	365	余	808	忘	683	罕	252
均	351	豆	152	吼	265	希	705	闰	560	诊	845
抑	787	两	400	吧	13	坐	896	闲	717	诋	137
抛	482	丽	395	囵	159,672	谷	227	间	305,310	词	100
投	664	医	780	别	42	妥	674	闷	432,433	译	787
坟	188	否	194	岗	209	含	250	判	480	〔乛〕	
坑	365	还	248,275	帐	838	邻	404	兑	159	君	351
抗	358	歹	305	财	58	岔	66	灶	828	灵	406
抖	152	来	378	囮	268	肝	205	灿	61	即	293
护	269	连	396	〔丿〕		肛	208	灼	881	层	64
壳	361	〔丨〕		钉	146,147	肚	154	弟	139	屁	490
志	861	志	640	针	844	肘	870	汪	682	尿	468
块	371	步	56	牡	451	肠	70	沐	452	尾	688
抉	348	卤	413	告	211	龟	239	沥	395	迟	82
扭	470	坚	305	我	695	免	438	沙	568	局	344
声	590	肖	731	乱	416	狂	373	汽	514	改	201
把	10,12	旱	252	利	394	犹	802	沦	417	张	836
报	24	盯	146	秃	666	角	317,348	洶	743	忌	298
拟	464	呈	78	秀	745	删	570	泛	178	陆	412,414
抒	612	时	597	私	624	条	652	沧	62	阿	1,164
却	543	助	873	每	431	卵	416	沟	223	孜	882
劫	324	县	719	兵	43	岛	127	没	429,448	陈	75
芽	755	里	392	估	225	刨	24,482	沉	74	阻	892
花	270	吃	787	体	648	迎	794	怀	273	附	198
芬	188	呆	117	何	259	饭	178	忧	800	坠	880
苍	62	呕	475	但	122	饮	792,793	怅	71	忍	552
芳	179	园	813	伸	582	系	298,709	快	372	劲	333,338
严	757	旷	373	佃	143	〔丶〕		忸	470	甬	798
芦	413	围	686	作	895	言	757	完	678	鸡	290
劳	383	呀	755,756	伯	46	冻	150	宏	265	驱	537
克	363	吨	159	伶	406	状	879	牢	384	驳	46

饱	22	泡	483	隶	395	贰	168	甚	587	砂	568
饲	627	注	873	录	414	奏	891	荆	335	砚	762
〔丶〕		泣	514	居	344	春	98	革	213	砍	356
变	37	泌	437	届	327	帮	20	荏	65	面	439
京	334	泥	464	刷	616	玷	143	荤	727	耐	457
享	725	沸	185	屈	537	珍	845	巷	119	耍	616
庞	481	沼	840	弧	268	玲	406	带	63	牵	516
店	143	波	45	弥	435	珊	570	草	307	残	60
夜	770	泼	499	弦	717	玻	45	茧	65	轴	870
庙	441	治	862	承	79	毒	153	茶	277	轻	529
底	137	怯	526	孟	435	型	741	荒	427	鸦	755
疟	473	怙	270	陋	413	拭	604	茫	126	皆	321
疙	212	性	742	陌	449	挂	230	荡	555	〔丨〕	
郊	316	怕	477	孤	225	封	192	荣	283	背	26,27
废	184	怜	397	降	314,725	持	82	荤	794	战	835
净	338	怪	231	函	251	拷	359	荧	228	点	141
盲	426	学	750	限	720	拱	222	故	268	虐	473
放	181	宝	22	虱	595	项	727	胡	791	临	404
刻	363	宗	888	驾	303	垮	371	荫	395	竖	615
育	811	定	147	艰	306	挎	371	荔	457	省	591
闸	832	宠	85	驻	874	城	79	南	766	削	728,750
闹	461	审	587	驼	674	挟	733	药	40	尝	70
郑	851	官	233	〔乚〕		挠	460	标	369	是	604
券	543	空	365,366	妹	432	政	852	枯	150	盼	481
卷	347	帘	397	姑	225	赴	198	栋	722,727	眨	832
单	120	实	598	姐	325	挡	125	相	65	哇	676
炖	160	试	603	姓	742	挺	656	查	15	哄	264,265
炒	73	诗	595	始	600	括	376	柏	832	哑	755
炊	98	肩	305	叁	564	拴	617	栅	411	显	718
炕	359	房	180	参	60,64	拾	599	柳	874	冒	428
炎	758	诙	279	线	721	挑	652,653	柱	604	星	739
炉	413	诚	78	练	399	垛	163	柿	381	昨	895
沫	449	衬	76	组	892	指	859	栏	469	昭	839
浅	519	视	604	绅	583	垫	143	柠	301	畏	691
法	172	祈	507	细	709	挣	848,852	枷	615	毗	489
泄	734	话	273	织	855	挤	296	树	46	趴	477
沽	225	诞	123	终	866	拼	494	勃	765,767	胃	691
河	260	诡	240	绊	19	挖	675	要	717	贵	241
沾	833	询	752	经	334	按	6	咸	684	界	327
沮	345	该	201	贯	235	挥	279	威	676	虹	265
泪	388	详	725			挪	473	歪	759	虾	710
油	802	诧	66	**九 画**		拯	848	研	876	思	624
泗	536	〔乛〕		〔一〕		某	450	砖	390	蚂	422
沿	758,762	建	310	契	514			厘	267	虽	631
		肃	629					厚	488	品	495
								砒			

咽	756,762	段	156	狡	318	逆	465	穿	94	娃	675
骂	422	偎	759	狠	262	总	888	窃	526	姨	781
勋	752	便	39,492	贸	429	炼	399	客	364	娇	317
哗	270,271	俩	395	怨	816	炽	83	冠	234,235	怒	472
咱	825	贷	119	急	294	炯	339	诬	696	怠	120
响	725	顺	621	饶	546	炸	832	语	810	垒	388
哈	248	修	744	饺	318	炮	482,483	扁	37	绑	20
哆	162	俏	524	饼	44	炫	749	袄	8	绒	555
咳	766	俚	392			烂	382	祖	892	结	321,324
咳	248,361	保	22	〔丶〕		剃	649	神	586	绕	546
哪	453,456	促	105	弯	678	洼	675	祝	874	绘	282
哟	797	侮	702	孪	416	洁	324	祠	100	给	215,296
炭	641	俭	307	将	312,314	洪	265	误	704	绚	749
峡	710	俗	629	奖	314	洒	562	诱	807	络	419
罚	172	俘	195	哀	2	柒	504	诲	282	绝	349
峥	848	信	738	亭	656	浇	316	说	622	绞	318
贱	311	皇	277	亮	400	浊	882			统	661
贴	654	泉	542	度	154	洞	150	〔𠃌〕			
骨	227	鬼	240	迹	298	测	64	郡	351	十 画	
幽	800	侵	526	庭	656	洗	708	垦	365		
		追	880	疮	96	活	284	退	671	〔一〕	
〔丿〕		俊	351	疯	192	派	479	既	298	耕	218
钝	160	盾	160	疫	788	洽	515	屋	696	耗	257
钞	72	待	119	疤	9	染	545	昼	870	耙	12,477
钟	867	律	415	咨	883	浏	409	屏	499	艳	762
钢	208	很	262	姿	883	洋	763	屎	600	泰	639
钥	768	须	746	亲	527,534	洲	869	费	185	珠	870
钦	526	舢	570	音	791	浑	283	陡	152	班	16
钩	223	叙	747	飒	562	浓	471	逊	753	素	629
卸	734	剑	311	帝	139	津	329	眉	430	匿	465
缸	208	逃	643	施	595	恒	263	孩	249	蚕	61
拜	16	食	599	闺	240	恢	279	陛	35	顽	679
看	356	盆	486	闻	693	恍	278	除	91	盏	834
矩	345	胚	484	阁	213	恫	150	险	719	匪	184
氢	530	胆	122	差	64,66,67	恬	651	院	816	捞	383
怎	829	胜	592	养	764	恰	514	架	303	栽	822
牲	591	胖	482	美	432	恼	460	贺	261	捕	47
选	749	脉	424	姜	313	恨	262	盈	794	捂	702
适	605	胎	638	进	31	举	345	勇	798	振	846
秒	441	匍	502	叛	481	觉	319,349	柔	557	载	822,825
香	724	勉	438	送	628	宣	748	矜	329	赶	205
种	867,869	狭	710	类	388	室	605	骁	728	起	509
秋	535	狮	595	迷	436	宫	222	骄	316	盐	759
科	360	独	153	前	517	宪	721	骆	419	捎	577
重	84,868	狰	848	酋	536	突	666	骇	250	捍	252
复	198			首	609			〔𠃍〕			

捏	468	核	260	哺	47	秤	80	颂	628	凉 399,401
埋	423,424	样	764	哽	218	租	891	胰	782	站 836
捉	881	根	216	晌	573	秧	762	脍	372	剖 501
捆	375	栩	747	剔	646	积	290	脆	106	竞 338
捐	347	索	636	晕	818,820	秩	863	脂	855	部 56
损	634	哥	212	蚜	755	称	76	胸	743	旁 481
捌	9	速	630	畔	481	秘	437	胳	212	旅 415
都	151,152	逗	152	蚯	253	透	665	脏	826	畜 93,747
哲	843	栗	395	蚊	694	笔	33	胶	317	阅 817
逝	605	酌	882	哨	579	笑	731	脑	461	羞 745
捡	307	配	485	哩	395	笋	634	脓	471	瓶 499
挫	107	翅	83	哭	369	债	833	逛	238	拳 542
挎	415,418	辱	559	哦	475	借	327	狼	382	粉 189
换	276	唇	99	恩	166	值	857	逢	193	料 403
挽	680	夏	715	唤	276	倚	785	鸵	674	益 788
热	547	砝	172	唁	762	倾	530	留	409	兼 306
恐	366	砸	821	哼	262,263	倒	127,128	衮	468	烤 359
捣	127	破	500	啊	1	倘	642	皱	870	烘 264
壶	269	原	814	唉	2,3	俱	346	饿	165	烦 174
捅	661	套	644	唆	634	倡	72	〔丶〕		烧 578
挨	2	逐	871	罢	12	候	267	凌	406	烟 756
耻	82	烈	404	峭	524	俯	196	凄	504	烩 283
耿	218	殊	612	峰	193	倍	27	恋	399	烙 386
耽	122	殉	753	圆	814	健	311	桨	314	递 139
恭	222	顾	229	觊	299	臭	87	浆	313	涝 386
莽	427	轿	320	峻	351	射	581	衰	616	酒 341
莲	397	较	320	贼	829	息	706	衷	867	涉 581
莫	449	顿	160	贿	283	倔	350	高	209	消 728
荷	260	毙	35	赃	826	徒	667	席	707	浩 257
获	287	致	863	〔丿〕		徐	747	准	881	海 249
晋	333	〔丨〕		钱	519	殷	791	座	897	涂 667
恶	164	柴	68	钳	519	舰	311	症	848,852	浴 811
真	845	桌	881	钻	893	般	17	病	44	浮 195
框	374	虔	519	钾	302	航	253	疾	295	涣 276
桂	241	监	306	铁	654	途	667	疼	645	涤 136
栖	504	紧	330	铃	406	拿	453	痂	301	流 410
桎	863	逍	728	铅	517	釜	196	疲	489	润 560
档	126	党	125	铆	428	耸	627	痉	338	浪 382
株	870	逞	80	缺	543	爹	145	脊	296	浸 333
桥	523	晒	569	氧	764	舀	766	效	732	涨 837,838
桃	643	晓	731	特	644	爱	3	离	390	烫 642
桅	687	昧	82	牺	706	豺	68	紊	694	涩 567
格	213	唠	384	造	828	豹	25	润	143	涌 798
桩	878	鸭	755	乘	79	奚	706	瓷	100	悄 523
校	319,731	晃	278	敌	136	颁	17	资	883	悍 252

梅 281	验 762	捐 519	辆 401	〔丿〕	舵 163
悦 817	骏 351	探 641	〔丨〕	铜 661	斜 733
害 250	〔乚〕	据 346	虚 746	铡 832	盒 261
宽 372	娱 809	掘 350	雀 544	铣 708	鸽 212
家 301	娘 467	掺 68	堂 641	铤 657	欲 812
宴 762	娓 689	职 857	常 70	铭 446	彩 59
宾 43	能 463	基 291	眺 653	铲 69	领 408
窍 524	绢 347	勘 356	睁 848	银 791	脚 318
窄 833	绣 745	聊 401	眯 435	矫 318	脖 46
容 556	绥 632	娶 539	眼 760	甜 651	脸 398
宰 822	继 299	著 874	悬 748	梨 391	脱 673
案 6		菱 407	野 769	犁 391	象 727
请 533	**十一画**	勒 387,388	啪 477	移 781	够 224
朗 382		黄 277	啦 378	透 685	猜 57
诸 870	〔一〕	萌 434	晦 283	笨 30	猪 871
诺 474	彗 283	萝 418	晚 680	笼 412	猫 404
读 154	球 536	菁 689	啄 882	笛 137	猫 427
扇 570,571	琐 636	菜 60	畦 507	笙 591	猖 69
诽 184	理 392	菊 345	距 346	符 196	猛 435
袜 676	捧 486	菠 46	趾 860	第 140	祭 299
祖 640	堵 154	营 795	啃 365	笤 653	馄 284
袖 745	措 107	乾 519	啰 418	敏 442	馅 721
被 28	描 440	萧 729	跃 818	做 897	〔丶〕
课 364	掐 456	梦 435	略 416	借 733	凑 104
冥 446	掩 759	梗 218	蛊 227	袋 120	减 307
谁 618	捷 325	梅 431	蚯 535	悠 800	毫 253
调 144,652	排 478	检 307	蛀 875	偿 71	烹 486
冤 813	掉 145	梳 612	蛇 580	偶 475	麻 421
谅 401	捞 413	梯 646	累 388,389	傀 375	痊 542
谆 880	赦 581	桶 662	唱 72	偷 662	痒 764
谈 640	推 669	救 341	患 276	您 468	痕 262
〔乛〕	堆 157	副 199	唾 674	售 611	康 358
剥 21,45	掀 716	票 494	唯 687,689	停 656	庸 797
恳 365	授 611	酝 820	啤 489	偏 490	鹿 414
展 834	捻 467	酗 747	啥 568	躯 537	盗 129
剧 346	教 317,320	硅 240	啐 106	皑 3	章 837
弱 561	掏 642	硕 623	崎 507	兜 151	竟 338
陵 407	掐 514	奢 579	崭 834	皎 318	商 572
陶 643	掠 416	爽 618	逻 418	假 302,304	旌 336
陷 721	掂 140	聋 412	崩 30	徘 479	旋 750
陪 484	培 484	袭 708	崇 85	得 130,133	望 684
通 657	接 321	盛 80,592	崛 350	衔 718	率 415,617
难 458,460	掷 863	匮 37	婴 794	盘 480	阉 756
预 811	掸 122	雪 751	赊 579	船 96	阎 759
桑 565	控 367	辅 197	圈 347,540	舷 718	阐 69

着	839,840,844,882
盖	203
眷	348
粘	467,834
粗	104
粒	395
断	156
剪	308
兽	611
焊	252
焕	276
烽	193
焖	434
清	531
添	650
鸿	265
淋	405
淹	756
渠	538
渐	311
混	284
渊	813
渔	809
淘	643
淳	99
液	770
淤	808
淡	123
淀	143
深	583
涮	617
涵	251
婆	500
梁	399
渗	588
情	532
惬	526
惜	706
惭	61
悼	129
惧	346
惟	687
惆	86
惊	335

惦	143
惋	680
惨	61
惯	235
寄	299
寂	300
宿	630
窒	863
窑	765
密	437
谋	450
谎	278
谐	733
祷	127
祸	287
谒	770
谓	691
谚	762
谜	436

〔フ〕

逮	118,120
敢	206
屠	668
弹	123,640
堕	163
随	632
蛋	123
隆	412
隐	792
颇	500
颈	337
骑	508

〔乚〕

婚	283
姊	587
欸	165,166
婉	680
绪	747
绰	100
绳	591
维	687
绵	437
绷	31
综	888

绿	415
巢	73

十二画

〔一〕

琵	489
琴	528
琳	405
琢	882,895
斑	17
替	649
揍	891
款	373
塔	637
搭	109
越	818
趁	76
趋	537
超	72
提	136,646
堤	136
博	46
揭	322
喜	708
揣	94
插	65
揪	340
搜	628
煮	873
援	815
搀	68
裁	59
搁	212
搓	107
搂	412
搅	318
壹	781
握	696
揉	557
斯	625
期	504
欺	505
联	398
散	564

惹	547
葬	826
募	452
董	149
葡	502
敬	339
葱	102
落	378,386,419
朝	73,839
辜	226
葵	374
棒	20
棱	389
棋	508
椰	768
植	857
森	567
焚	189
椅	785
棵	360
棍	241
棉	438
棚	486
棕	888
棺	234
椰	382
椭	674
惠	283
逼	31
棘	295
酣	250
酥	629
厨	92
硬	796
硝	729
确	544
硫	411
雁	762
殖	858
裂	404
雄	743
暂	825
雅	755
翘	524

〔丨〕

辈	28
悲	26
紫	884
凿	827
辉	279
敞	71
赏	573
掌	837
晴	533
暑	614
最	893
量	399,401
鼎	147
喷	485
喋	145
晶	336
喇	377
遇	812
喊	252
遏	165
晾	401
景	337
践	311
跋	10
跌	145
跑	483
遗	782
蛙	675
蛛	871
喝	257,261
喂	691
喘	96
嗖	628
喉	265
啼	647
喽	412
喧	748
嵌	520
幅	196
帽	429
赋	199
赌	154
赎	613
赐	102

赔	484
黑	261

〔丿〕

铸	875
铺	502,503
链	399
铿	365
销	729
锁	636
锄	92
锅	241
锈	746
锉	107
锋	193
锐	560
掰	13
短	155
智	863
毯	641
氮	123
鹅	164
剩	593
稍	578
程	80
稀	706
税	620
筐	373
等	134
筑	875
策	64
筛	569
筒	662
筵	759
答	109,110
筋	329
傲	8
牌	479
堡	24
集	295
焦	317
傍	20
储	93
奥	8
遁	160
街	323

惩	80	渺	441	缆	381	幕	452	暖	473	毁	281
循	752	湿	596	缉	292	蓖	35	盟	435	舅	343
舒	612	温	692	骗	492	蓬	486	歇	732	鼠	614
逾	809	渴	363	骚	566	蓄	748	暗	6	催	105
番	172	溃	375	〔乚〕		蒙	434,435	照	840	傻	568
释	605	湍	669	媒	431	蒸	848	畸	292	像	728
腊	378	溅	311	絮	747	献	721	跨	371	躲	162
腌	756	滑	271	嫂	566	禁	329,333	跳	654	魁	374
脾	489	渡	155	媚	432	楷	356	踩	163	微	685
腋	770	游	802	缄	306	想	725	跪	241	愈	812
腔	521	滋	883	缅	439	槐	274	路	414	遥	766
腕	682	渲	750	缓	275	楼	412	跟	217	腻	465
鲁	413	愤	190	缔	140	概	203	遣	520	腰	765
猩	739	慌	277	编	36	赖	380	蜗	695	腼	439
猴	265	惰	163	缘	815	剽	493	蛾	164	腥	739
飓	347	愕	165			甄	845	蜂	193	腮	562
然	545	愣	390	**十三画**		酬	86	蜕	671	腹	200
馇	269	惶	278			感	206	嗅	746	鹏	486
馊	628	愧	375	〔一〕		碍	4	嗨	248	腾	645
馋	68	愉	809	瑟	567	碘	142	嗤	82	腿	671
〔丶〕		割	212	瑞	560	碑	26	嗓	565	肆	789
装	878	寒	251	瑰	240	碉	144	署	614	猿	815
蛮	424	富	199	魂	284	碎	634	置	863	触	93
就	342	寓	812	肆	627	碰	487	罪	894	解	325
敦	159	窜	105	摄	582	碗	680	罩	842	煞	568
痧	490	窝	695	摸	446	尴	205	幌	278	雏	92
痢	395	窗	96	填	651	雷	388	〔丿〕		〔丶〕	
痛	662	窘	339	搏	46	零	407	错	107	酱	315
童	661	扁	184	塌	637	雾	704	锚	428	痴	82
竣	351	遍	39	鼓	227	雹	22	锣	418	痰	640
阑	381	雇	229	摆	15	辐	196	锤	98	廉	398
阔	376	裤	370	携	733	输	613	锥	880	新	737
善	571	裙	544	搬	17	〔丨〕		锦	331	韵	820
羡	721	幂	437	摇	765	督	152	锯	347	意	788
普	503	谢	734	搞	211	频	495	锰	435	豢	277
粪	190	谣	765	搪	642	鉴	311	矮	3	誉	646
尊	894	谦	517	摊	639	睦	452	辞	100	粮	399
奠	143	〔丁〕		聘	496	瞄	441	稗	16	数	614,615
道	129	属	614	斟	845	睫	325	稠	86	煎	306
遂	634	屡	415	蒜	630	睡	621	颖	670	塑	630
曾	64	强	521,522	勤	528	嗜	605	愁	86	慈	100
港	209	粥	869	靴	750	嗑	257	筹	86	煤	431
滞	863	疏	612	靶	12	嘻	250	签	517	满	424
湖	269	隔	214	蓝	381	鄙	33	简	308	漠	449
渣	832	登	134	墓	452	愚	809	筷	372	源	815

滥 382	截 325	嘘 596	漱 616	增 831	墨 449
滔 642	誓 605	嘛 423	漂 493,494	撰 878	〔丿〕
溪 707	境 339	嘀 137	漫 426	聪 102	镇 846
溜 409	摘 833	赚 878	滴 136	鞋 733	镑 347
滚 241	墒 573	骷 369	演 761	鞍 5	镐 211
滂 481	摔 616	〔丿〕	漏 413	蕃 172	镣 20
溢 789	撇 494	锹 523	慢 426	蔬 613	靠 359
溶 556	聚 347	锻 156	慷 358	蕴 820	稻 130
溺 466	暮 452	镀 155	寨 833	横 263	黎 391
慑 582	蔓 426	舞 702	赛 563	槽 63	稿 211
慎 588	蔑 441	舔 651	寡 230	橡 728	箱 724
塞 562,567	斡 696	稳 694	察 66	樟 837	篓 412
窥 374	熙 707	熏 752	蜜 437	敷 194	箭 312
窟 369	蔚 691	算 630	寥 402	飘 493	篇 492
谨 331	兢 336	管 234	寤 842	醋 105	篆 878
裸 419	模 447,450	舆 809	褐 261	醉 894	僵 313
福 196	榜 20	僧 567	谰 381	磕 360	躺 642
谩 425	榨 832	鼻 31	谱 503	磊 388	僻 490
谬 446	歌 212	魄 501	〔乛〕	磅 20,482	德 131
〔乛〕	遭 826	魅 432	隧 634	碾 467	艘 628
群 544	醉 321	貌 429	翠 106	震 846	磐 480
殿 143	酷 370	膀 482	凳 135	霉 431	膝 707
辟 490	酿 467	鲜 717	骡 418	〔丨〕	〔丶〕
障 838	酸 630	疑 782	〔乚〕	瞌 360	熟 613
叠 145	斯 625	馒 424	嫩 463	瞒 424	摩 447
〔乚〕	碟 145	〔丶〕	嫡 137	题 647	褒 21
媾 225	碱 309	裹 243	熊 744	暴 25	瘪 42
媳 708	碳 641	敲 523	缥 493	瞎 710	瘤 411
媲 490	磋 107	豪 253	缩 635	瞑 446	瘫 640
嫌 718	磁 100	膏 211		嘻 768	凛 405
嫁 304	愿 816	遮 842	**十五画**	嘶 625	颜 759
缝 193,194	需 746	腐 197		嘲 73	毅 789
缠 68	辗 834	瘦 611	〔一〕	嘹 402	糊 269
剿 319	〔丨〕	辣 378	撑 467	影 795	遵 895
	雌 101	竭 325	撕 625	踢 646	憋 42
十四画	颗 360	韶 578	撒 562	踏 637	潜 519
	嘈 63	端 155	撅 348	脚 82	澎 486
〔一〕	暖 4	旗 508	撩 401	踩 59	潮 73
静 339	踌 86	精 336	趣 540	踪 888	潭 640
碧 35	踊 798	歉 520	趟 642	蝶 145	潦 402
熬 7	蜻 532	弊 35	撑 77	蝴 269	鲨 568
墙 522	蜡 378	熄 707	撮 107	蝎 732	潺 68
嘉 302	蜘 855	熔 556	播 46	蝗 278	澄 80,135
摧 106	蜷 542	潇 729	撞 879	嘿 262	懂 149
赫 261	蜿 678	漆 505	撤 74	嘱 873	憔 524

懊	8	瞟	494	激	292	歉	630	鹰	794	〔丿〕	
憧	84	踹	94	懒	381	簇	105	癣	490	籍	295
憎	831	嘴	893	懈	734	繁	174	糨	315	〔丶〕	
额	164	蹄	647	褶	843	斸	250	鳖	42	魔	448
翩	492	踩	557	〔丁〕		徽	279	瀑	503	糯	474
褥	559	蟒	427	壁	35	朦	435	襟	329	灌	236
褴	381	螃	482	避	35	膜	566	〔丁〕		〔丁〕	
遣	520	器	514	〔乚〕		臆	789	戳	99	譬	490
〔丁〕		噪	828	缴	319	臃	797				
憨	250	罹	391			鳄	165	十九画		二十一画	
熨	820	鹦	794	十七画		〔丶〕					
慰	691	赠	831			糜	436	〔一〕		〔一〕	
劈	488,490	默	450	〔一〕		癌	3	攒	825	蠢	99
履	415	黔	519	戴	120	辫	40	警	338	蘼	12
〔乚〕		〔丿〕		壕	254	赢	795	蘑	448	露	413,414
嬉	707	镜	339	擦	57	槽	827	攀	479	霹	488
缭	402	赞	826	罄	534	檫	358	〔丨〕		二十二画	
		篝	224	鞠	344	懦	474	曝	25		
十六画		篮	381	藏	62	豁	284,288	蹲	159	〔一〕	
		篡	105	薮	441	〔丁〕		蹭	64	蕻	836
〔一〕		篓	391	檄	708	臀	672	蹬	134	蘘	460
操	62	盥	236	檀	640	翼	789	〔丿〕		〔丿〕	
擅	571	儒	558	礁	317	孟	428	簸	46	镶	725
燕	762	翱	8	磷	405	骤	870	〔丶〕		〔丶〕	
薪	738	邀	765	霜	618			颤	69	瓤	545
薄	22,46	衡	263	霞	711	十八画		靡	436		
颠	140	膨	486	〔丨〕				癜	749	二十三画	
噩	165	膳	571	瞧	524	〔一〕		瓣	20		
薅	253	雕	144	瞬	622	藕	475	爆	25	〔一〕	
橱	92	鲸	337	瞪	135	鞭	37	〔丁〕		攥	350
橘	345	〔丶〕		瞭	403	覆	200	疆	313	攮	893
整	848	磨	447,450	曙	614	〔丨〕				〔丿〕	
融	556	瘾	792	蝗	642	瞻	834	二十画		罐	236
瓢	493	瘸	543	螺	418	蹦	31				
醒	741	凝	469	蟋	707	蹚	641	〔丨〕		二十四画	
磺	278	辨	39	赡	571	〔丿〕		耀	768		
霓	464	辩	39	〔丿〕		镰	398	蠕	558	〔一〕	
霍	288	糖	642	镣	403	翻	173	嚼	317	矗	94
霎	569	燎	402	穗	634	鳏	234	嚷	545,546		
〔丨〕		燃	545	黏	467	〔丶〕		巍	685		
餐	60	濒	43								

部首查字表
Radical Index

　　本词典部首共 174 个,按笔画数目排列,同笔画数目的按—(横)丨(竖)丿(撇)、(点)乛(折)五种笔形顺序排列。

　　查字时,先按要查的字的部首在《部首目录》里查出页码,然后查《查字表》。《查字表》内,同一部首的字按除去部首笔画以外的画数排列。

　　对于难查的字,解决的办法是:(1)部首难于决定的字分收在几个部首内,如:"志"分收在部首"士"和"心"两处,"功"分收在部首"工"和"力"两处。(2)部首不明显的字,一般按起笔(即书写时的第一笔)的笔形收入—丨丿、乛(包括乙乛乚丨乚等)五个单笔部首内。并为难查字备有笔画索引附于《查字表》后。

Explanatory Note

　　This dictionary uses 174 radicals, arranged according to number of strokes. Radicals with the same number of strokes are placed in order of first strokes as follows:—丨丿、乛.

　　To look up a character, the user should first find the page number in the "Table of Radicals" according to the radical of the character and then find the character under the page number in the "Radical Index". Characters with the same radicals are arranged in order of the number of strokes, excluding the strokes in the radical.

　　To help find characters the radical of which the user may not be sure, they are placed under more than one radical, e. g. 志 is under both 士 and 心, 功 under both 工 and 力, etc. Some characters which don't seem to have any radical are placed under the five single stroke radicals:—丨丿、乛 (including 乙乛乚丨乚 etc.) according to their first strokes when written and there is a Stroke Index for Characters of Dubious Radicals at the end of the "Radical Index".

（一）部首目录
Table of Radicals

（二）查字表
Radical Index

九画		单	120	舍	580	兢	336	衰	616
做	897	典	141	命	446			衷	867
偕	733	**七画**		**八画**		**几(几)部**		高	209
偿	71	养	764	拿	453			离	390
偶	475	前	517	**九画**		几	289,296	旁	481
傀	375	酋	536	盒	261	**一画**		**九画**	
偷	662	首	609	**十画**		凡	174	毫	253
停	656	**八画**		舒	612	**二画**		烹	486
偏	490	真	845			凤	193	商	572
假	302,304	益	788	**勹部**		**五画**		率	415,617
十画		兼	306			壳	361	**十画**	
傲	8	**九画**		**一画**		秃	666	就	342
傍	20	黄	277	勺	578	**六画**		**十二画**	
储	93	兽	611	**二画**		咒	870	裹	243
十一画		**十画**		勿	703	凯	355	豪	253
催	105	普	503	匀	818	凭	499	膏	211
傻	568	奠	143	勾	223,224	**十二画**		**十三画**	
像	728	尊	894	**三画**		凳	135	褒	21
十二画		曾	64	句	345			**十五画**	
僧	567	**十二画**		匆	102	**亠部**		赢	795
十三画		與	809	包	20				
僵	313			**四画**		**一画**		**冫部**	
僻	490	**人(入)部**		旬	752	亡	682		
十四画				**七画**		**二画**		**一画**	
儒	558	人	548	匍	502	六	411	习	707
		入	559	**九画**		**三画**		**四画**	
八(丷)部		**一画**		够	224	市	601	冲	84,85
		个	214			玄	748	冰	43
八	9	**二画**		**儿部**		**四画**		次	101
二画		介	326			交	315	决	348
分	186,189	从	102	儿	166	亦	786	**五画**	
公	219	今	328	**二画**		产	68	冻	150
三画		以	783	元	813	充	83	况	373
兰	381	仓	61	允	819	**五画**		冷	389
半	18	**三画**		**三画**		亩	451	冶	769
只	854,858	丛	104	兄	743	弃	514	**六画**	
四画		令	409	**四画**		**六画**		净	338
并	44	**四画**		光	236	变	37	**八画**	
关	231	全	540	先	716	京	334	凌	406
共	222	会	282,371	充	83	享	725	凄	504
兴	739,741	合	257	**五画**		夜	770	准	881
五画		企	509	克	363	**七画**		凋	143
兑	159	众	868	兑	159	弯	678	凉	399,401
兵	43	伞	564	**八画**		哀	2	**九画**	
弟	139	**五画**		党	125	亭	656	凑	104
六画		余	808	**九画**		亮	400	减	307
卷	347	含	250	兜	151	帝	139	**十三画**	
具	346	**六画**		**十二画**		**八画**		凛	405

十四画			
凝	469		
冖部			
二画			
冗	556		
三画			
写	733		
四画			
军	350		
五画			
罕	252		
七画			
冠	234,235		
八画			
冥	446		
冤	813		
十画			
幂	437		

讠部			
二画			
计	296		
订	147		
认	197		
认	552		
讥	289		
三画			
讯	753		
讨	643		
让	546		
训	753		
议	786		
记	297		
四画			
讲	313		
讳	282		
许	747		
论	164		
论	417		
讽	193		
设	580		
访	181		
诀	348		
五画			
证	851		

评 498	**十画**	阻 892	部 56	赖 380	**八画**
讯 892	谢 734	附 198	**九画**	**十三画**	能 463
识 598	谣 765	**六画**	鄙 33	劈 488,490	
诈 832	谦 517	陋 413			**又(ㄡ)部**
诉 629	**十一画**	陌 449	**凵部**	**力部**	
诊 845	谨 331	降 314,725			又 806
诋 137	谩 425	限 720	**二画**	力 393	**一画**
词 100	谬 446	**七画**	凶 742	**二画**	叉 64,66
译 787	**十二画**	陡 152	**三画**	办 18	**二画**
六画	谰 381	陛 35	击 289	劝 542	支 854
试 603	谱 503	除 91	凸 666	**三画**	友 803
诗 595	**十三画**	险 719	出 87	功 221	反 175
诙 279	遣 520	院 816	凹 7	加 300	劝 542
诚 78		**八画**	**六画**	务 703	双 617
话 273	**卩(㔾)部**	陵 407	画 272	幼 807	**三画**
诞 123		陶 643	函 251	**四画**	圣 592
诡 240	**一画**	陷 721	**七画**	动 149	对 157
询 752	卫 689	陪 484	幽 800	劣 403	发 169
该 201	**三画**	**九画**	**十画**	**五画**	**四画**
详 725	印 793	堕 163	凿 827	劫 324	戏 709
诧 66	**四画**	随 632		助 873	观 233
七画	仰 763	隆 412	**刀(⺈)部**	男 457	欢 274
语 810	危 684	隐 792		努 472	**六画**
诬 696	**五画**	**十画**	刁 143	劲 333,338	取 538
误 704	却 543	隔 214	刀 126	**六画**	叔 612
诱 807	即 293	**十一画**	**一画**	势 602	受 610
诲 282	**六画**	障 838	刃 552	**七画**	变 37
说 622	卷 347	**十二画**	**二画**	勃 46	艰 306
八画	**七画**	隧 634	切 525	勋 752	**七画**
请 533	卸 734		分 186,189	勉 438	叙 747
诸 870		**阝(在右)部**	**三画**	勇 798	**八画**
诺 474	**阝(在左)部**		召 840	**九画**	难 458,460
读 154		**二画**	**四画**	勘 356	**十一画**
诽 184	**二画**	邦 20	危 684	**十一画**	叠 145
课 364	队 157	邪 733	负 197	勤 528	
谁 618	**三画**	那 455	争 847		**廴部**
调 144,652	阡 516	**三画**	色 566	**厶部**	
谅 401	**四画**	邮 801	**五画**		**四画**
谆 880	阵 846	邻 404	龟 239	**三画**	延 756
谈 640	阳 763	**四画**	免 438	去 539	**六画**
九画	阶 321	郁 811	初 91	台 638	建 310
谋 450	阴 790	郊 316	**六画**	**四画**	
谎 278	防 179	郑 851	兔 668	牟 450	**工部**
谐 733	**五画**	**五画**	券 543	**五画**	
谒 770	陆 412,414	郡 351	**九画**	县 719	工 218
谓 691	阿 1,164	**六画**	象 727	**六画**	**二画**
谚 762	陈 75	都 151,152	剪 308	叁 564	左 895
谜 436			**十一画**	参 60,64	巧 524

狡	318	**二画**		店	143	闸	69	沸	185	淹	756
狠	262	饥	289	庙	441	**九画**		沼	840	渐	311
七画		**四画**		底	137	阑	381	波	45	渠	538
狼	382	饭	178	废	184	阔	376	泼	499	混	284
八画		饮	792,793	**六画**				治	862	渊	813
猜	57	**五画**		度	154	**氵部**		**六画**		渔	809
猪	871	饯	310	庭	656			洼	675	淘	643
猫	404	饱	22	**七画**		**二画**		洁	324	淳	99
猫	427	饲	627	席	707	汁	855	洪	265	液	770
狷	69	**六画**		座	897	汇	281	洒	562	淤	808
猛	435	饶	546	**八画**		汉	252	浇	316	淡	123
九画		饺	318	康	358	**三画**		浊	882	淀	143
猩	739	饼	44	庸	797	汗	252	洞	150	深	583
猴	265	**七画**		**十画**		污	696	测	64	涮	617
十画		饿	165	廉	398	江	312	洗	708	涵	251
猿	815	**八画**		**十一画**		池	82	活	284	渗	588
		馄	284	腐	197	汤	641	派	479	**九画**	
夕部		馅	721	**十五画**		**四画**		洽	515	港	209
		九画		鹰	794	汪	682	浏	409	湖	269
夕	705	馈	269			沐	452	洋	763	渣	832
三画		馒	628	**门部**		沥	395	洲	869	滞	863
名	443	馋	68			沙	568	浑	283	渺	441
岁	633	**十一画**		门	433	汽	514	浓	471	湿	596
多	160	馒	424	**一画**		沦	417	津	329	温	692
五画				闩	617	汹	743	**七画**		渴	363
罗	418	**丬部**		**二画**		泛	178	涝	386	溃	375
八画				闪	570	沧	62	酒	341	湍	669
梦	435	**三画**		**三画**		沟	223	涉	581	溅	311
		壮	879	闭	34	没	429,448	消	728	滑	271
夂部		**四画**		问	694	沉	74	浩	257	渡	155
		状	879	闯	97	**五画**		海	249	游	802
二画		**六画**		**四画**		沫	449	涂	667	滋	883
处	92,93	将	312,314	闰	560	浅	519	浴	811	渲	750
冬	149			闲	717	法	172	浮	195	**十画**	
务	703	**广部**		间	305,310	泄	734	涣	276	满	424
三画		广	238	闷	432,433	沽	225	涤	136	漠	449
各	215	**三画**		**五画**		河	260	流	410	源	815
四画		庄	878	闸	832	沾	833	润	560	滥	382
条	652	庆	534	闹	461	泪	388	浪	382	滔	642
五画		**四画**		**六画**		沮	345	浸	333	溪	707
备	26	床	97	闺	240	油	802	涨	837,838	溜	409
六画		库	370	闻	693	泅	536	涩	567	滚	241
复	198	庇	35	阁	213	沿	758,762	涌	798	滂	481
七画		应	793,795	**七画**		泡	483	**八画**		溢	789
夏	715	序	747	阅	817	注	873	清	531	溶	556
		五画		**八画**		泣	514	添	650	溺	466
饣部		庞	481	阉	756	泌	437	鸿	265	**十一画**	
				阎	759	泥	464	淋	405	潇	729

望	684	杞	509	栗	395	楷	356	**车部**		或	286
八画		杨	763	桎	863	槐	274			**五画**	
琵	489	**四画**		柴	68	楼	412	车	73	战	835
琴	528	枉	682	桌	881	概	203	**一画**		咸	717
琳	405	林	404	档	126	**十画**		轧	832	威	684
琢	882,895	枝	855	株	870	模	447,450	**二画**		**六画**	
斑	17	杯	25	桥	523	榜	20	轨	240	栽	822
九画		枢	612	桃	643	寨	833	军	350	载	822,825
瑟	567	柜	240	桅	687	榨	832	**四画**		盏	834
瑞	560	杳	766	格	213	**十一画**		转	876,878	**八画**	
瑰	240	果	243	桨	314	横	263	斩	834	裁	59
十二画		枣	828	桩	878	槽	63	轮	417	**十画**	
疆	165	枚	430	校	319,731	橡	728	软	559	截	325
		板	17	核	260	樟	837	轰	263	**十三画**	
韦部		采	59	样	764	**十二画**		**五画**		戴	120
		松	6	案	6	橱	92	轴	870	**十四画**	
三画		枪	520	根	216	橘	345	轻	529	戳	99
韧	554	枫	192	栩	747	**十三画**		**六画**			
		构	224	桑	565	橄	708	载	822,825	**比部**	
木部		杰	324	**七画**		檀	640	晕	818,820		
		枕	846	梗	218			轿	320	比	31
木	451	**五画**		梨	391	**犬部**		较	320	**二画**	
一画		标	40	梅	431			**七画**		毕	34
本	29	某	450	检	307	犬	542	辅	197	**五画**	
未	690	荣	555	梳	612	**三画**		辆	401	毗	489
末	448	枯	369	梯	646	状	879	**八画**		皆	321
术	615	栋	150	渠	538	**六画**		辈	28	**六画**	
札	832	查	65	梁	399	哭	369	辉	279	毖	35
二画		相	722,727	桶	662	臭	87	**九画**			
朽	745	柏	15	**八画**		**九画**		辐	196	**瓦部**	
朴	502	栅	832	棒	20	献	721	输	613		
朱	870	柳	411	棱	389			**十画**		瓦	675
杀	567	柱	874	棋	508	**歹部**		辗	834	**四画**	
机	289	柿	604	椰	768					瓮	695
朵	162	亲	527,534	植	857	歹	118	**戈部**		**六画**	
杂	821	栏	381	森	567	**二画**				瓷	100
权	540	柒	504	椅	785	列	403	戈	212	瓶	499
三画		染	545	棵	360	死	625	**一画**		**九画**	
杆	205	柠	469	棍	241	**三画**		戊	703	甄	845
杠	209	枷	301	棘	295	歼	305	**二画**			
杜	154	架	303	集	295	**五画**		划	271,272	**止部**	
材	58	树	615	棉	438	残	60	成	77		
村	106	柔	557	棚	486	**六画**		戏	709	止	858
杏	742	**六画**		棕	888	毙	35	**三画**		**一画**	
束	615	框	374	棺	234	殊	612	戒	327	正	849
条	652	桂	241	椰	382	殉	753	我	695	**二画**	
极	293	栽	822	椭	674	**八画**		**四画**		此	101
床	97	栖	504	**九画**		殖	858			**三画**	

步	56	**六画**	永 797	贿 283	牧 452	**攵部**
四画		晋 333	**三画**	赃 826	物 703	
武 702		晒 569	求 535	资 883	**五画**	**二画**
歧 507		晓 731	尿 468	**七画**	牵 516	收 606
肯 364		晃 278	**四画**	赊 579	牲 591	**三画**
五画		晌 573	录 414	**八画**	**六画**	攻 221
歪 676		晕 818,820	隶 395	赋 199	特 644	改 201
六画		**七画**	**五画**	赌 154	牺 706	孜 882
耻 82		晦 283	泉 542	赎 613	**七画**	**四画**
		晚 680	**六画**	赏 573	犁 391	败 16
支部		**八画**	泰 639	赐 102	**十一画**	放 181
十画		晴 533	浆 313	赔 484	靠 359	**五画**
敲 523		替 649	**十一画**	**九画**		政 852
		暑 614	黎 391	赖 380	**手部**	故 228
日部		量 399,401		**十画**	手 607	**六画**
日 554		暂 825	**贝部**	赚 878	**五画**	致 863
一画		晶 336		赛 563	拜 16	敌 136
旦 122		智 863	**二画**	**十二画**	**六画**	效 732
旧 341		晾 401	则 828	赞 826	拿 453	**七画**
二画		景 337	负 197	赠 831	拳 542	赦 581
早 827		普 503	**三画**	**十三画**	**八画**	教 317,320
旮 201		曾 64	贡 223	赡 571	掌 837	救 341
旭 747		**九画**	财 58		掰 13	敏 442
旬 752		暖 473	员 813	**见部**	**十一画**	敢 206
三画		暗 6	**四画**	见 309	摩 447	**八画**
旱 252		**十画**	责 828	**二画**	**十五画**	散 564
时 597		暮 452	败 16	观 233	攀 479	敬 339
旷 373		暖 4	货 287	**四画**		敞 71
四画		**十一画**	质 862	规 239	**毛部**	敦 159
旺 684		暴 25	贩 178	觅 436	毛 427	**九画**
昙 640		**十三画**	贪 639	视 604	**三画**	数 614,615
昔 706		曙 614	贫 495	**五画**	尾 688	**十一画**
杳 766		**十五画**	贬 37	觉 319,349	**七画**	敷 194
昆 375		曝 25	购 224	**六画**	毫 253	**十二画**
昌 69			贮 873	觊 299	**八画**	整 848
明 444		**曰(日)部**	贯 235	舰 311	毯 641	
昏 283		**四画**	账 838			**片部**
易 787		者 843	**五画**	**牛(牜牛)部**	**气部**	片 490,492
昂 7		**五画**	贰 168	牛 469	气 512	**四画**
五画		冒 428	贱 311	**二画**	**五画**	版 18
春 98		**八画**	贴 654	牟 450	氢 530	**八画**
是 604		最 893	贵 241	**三画**	**六画**	牌 479
显 718			贷 119	牡 451	氧 764	
星 739		**水(氺)部**	贸 429	告 211	**八画**	**斤部**
昨 895		水 619	费 185	**四画**	氮 123	斤 328
昭 839		**一画**	贺 261			
			六画			
			贼 829			

一画		
斥	83	
四画		
所	635	
斧	196	
欣	737	
七画		
断	156	
八画		
斯	625	
九画		
新	737	

爪(爫)部

爪	840
三画	
妥	674
四画	
采	59
觅	436
受	610
爬	477
乳	559
六画	
舀	766
爱	3
奚	706

父部

父	197
二画	
爷	768
四画	
斧	196
爸	12
六画	
釜	196
爹	145

月(月)部

月	817
二画	
有	803
肌	290
肋	388

三画

肝	205
肛	208
肚	154
肘	870
肖	731
肠	70
四画	
肤	194
肺	185
肯	364
肾	587
肿	867
胀	838
朋	486
股	227
肮	7
育	811
肩	305
肥	184
胁	733
服	195
五画	
胡	268
胚	484
背	26,27
胆	122
胃	691
胜	592
胖	482
脉	424
胎	638
六画	
胰	782
脍	372
脊	296
脆	106
脂	855
胸	743
胳	212
脏	826
胶	317
脑	461
朗	382
胀	471
能	463
七画	
脚	318

脖	46
脸	398
望	684
脱	673
八画	
期	504
腊	378
朝	73,839
腌	756
脾	489
腋	770
腔	521
腕	682
九画	
腻	465
腰	765
腼	439
腥	739
腮	562
腹	200
鹏	486
腾	645
腿	671
十画	
膏	211
膀	482
十一画	
膝	707
十二画	
膨	486
膳	571
十三画	
朦	435
臊	566
臆	789
臃	797
臀	672

欠部

欠	520
二画	
次	101
欢	274
四画	
欧	475
软	559
欣	737

炊	98
七画	
欲	812
欷	165,166
八画	
款	373
欺	505
九画	
歇	732
十画	
歌	212
歉	520

风部

风	190
五画	
飒	562
八画	
飓	347
十一画	
飘	493

殳部

殳	
四画	
殴	475
五画	
段	156
六画	
殷	791
殷	17
九画	
毁	281
殿	143
十一画	
毅	789

文部

文	692
二画	
齐	505
三画	
斋	406
六画	
虔	519
紊	694

八画

斑	17

方部

方	178
四画	
放	181
房	180
五画	
施	595
六画	
旅	415
旁	481
七画	
旌	336
旋	750
十画	
旗	508

火部

火	285
一画	
灭	441
二画	
灰	278
灯	134
三画	
灶	828
灿	61
灼	881
灾	822
灵	406
四画	
炖	160
炒	73
炊	98
炕	359
炎	758
炉	413
五画	
荧	794
炼	399
炽	83
炭	641
炯	339
炸	832

炮	482,483
炫	749
烂	382
六画	
烤	359
耿	218
烘	264
烦	174
烧	578
烟	756
烩	283
烙	386
烫	642
七画	
焊	252
焕	276
烽	193
焖	434
八画	
焚	189
九画	
煤	431
十画	
熄	707
熔	556
十一画	
熨	820
十二画	
燎	402
燃	545
十五画	
爆	25

斗部

斗	152
六画	
料	403
七画	
斜	733
九画	
斟	845
十画	
斡	696

灬部

四画

杰 324	三画	七画	**示部**	碱 309	眺 653
五画	社 581	悬 748	示 600	碳 641	睁 848
点 141	四画	患 276	六画	磋 107	眷 348
六画	视 604	悠 800	票 494	磁 100	眯 435
烈 404	祈 507	您 468	祭 299	十画	眼 760
热 547	五画	八画	八画	磕 360	七画
七画	祖 892	惹 547	禁 329,333	磊 388	鼎 147
烹 486	神 586	惠 283	**石部**	磬 480	八画
八画	祝 874	悲 26	石 122,596	磅 20,482	睦 452
煮 873	祠 100	惩 80	三画	碾 467	瞄 441
焦 317	七画	九画	岩 758	十一画	睫 325
然 545	祷 127	想 725	矾 174	磺 278	督 152
九画	祸 287	感 206	矿 374	磨 447,450	睡 621
蒸 848	九画	愚 809	码 422	十二画	十画
照 840	福 196	愁 86	四画	礁 317	瞌 360
煞 568	**心部**	愈 812	研 759	磷 405	瞒 424
煎 306	心 734	意 788	砖 876	**龙部**	瞎 710
十画	一画	慈 100	砒 488	龙 412	瞑 446
熬 7	必 33	十画	砂 568	三画	十一画
熙 707	三画	愿 816	砚 762	垄 412	瞟 494
熏 752	志 861	十一画	砍 356	六画	瞭 403
熊 744	忐 640	憋 42	五画	聋 412	十二画
十一画	忘 683	慭 250	砝 172	袭 708	瞧 524
熟 613	忍 552	慰 691	砸 821	**业部**	瞬 622
十二画	四画	**聿(⺻)部**	破 500	业 770	瞪 135
燕 762	态 639	四画	六画	七画	十三画
户部	忠 866	肃 629	硅 240	凿 827	瞻 834
户 269	怂 627	隶 395	硕 623	**目部**	**田部**
三画	念 467	九画	七画	目 451	田 651
启 509	忽 267	肆 627	硬 796	二画	甲 302
四画	五画	肄 789	硝 729	盯 146	申 582
肩 305	思 624	十画	确 544	三画	由 800
所 635	怎 829	肇 842	硫 411	盲 426	电 142
房 180	怨 816	**毋(母)部**	八画	四画	二画
五画	急 294	一画	碍 4	相 722,727	亩 451
扁 37	总 888	母 451	碘 142	省 591	男 457
六画	怒 472	三画	碑 26	看 356	三画
扇 570,571	急 120	每 431	碉 144	盾 160	备 26
八画	六画	四画	碎 634	盼 481	四画
扉 184	恐 366	贯 235	碰 487	眨 832	畏 691
雇 229	恶 164	五画	碗 680	眉 430	毗 489
礻部	恩 166	毒 153	九画	六画	胃 691
一画	息 706		碧 35		界 327
礼 391	恋 399		碟 145		思 624
	恳 365				五画
					留 409

癖 749	窝 695	**五画**	**九画**	**九画**	蜂 193
	窗 96	皲 870	聪 102	题 647	蜕 671
立部	窘 339	**六画**		颜 759	
	八画	颇 500	**臣部**	额 164	**八画**
立 394	窥 374			**十画**	靖 532
一画	窟 369	**矛部**	**二画**	颠 140	蜡 378
产 68			卧 696	**十三画**	蜘 855
四画	**衤部**	矛 428		颤 69	蜷 542
亲 527,534		**四画**	**西(覀)部**		蜿 678
竖 615	**二画**	柔 557		**虍部**	蜜 437
飒 562	补 46	矜 329	西 705		
五画	初 91	**十二画**	**三画**	**二画**	**九画**
站 836	**三画**	蟊 428	要 765,767	虎 269	蝶 145
竞 338	衬 76		**四画**	**三画**	蝴 269
六画	**四画**	**耒部**	栗 395	虐 473	蝎 732
章 837	袄 8		**五画**	**四画**	蝗 278
竟 338	**五画**	**四画**	票 494	虔 519	**十画**
七画	袜 676	耕 218	**十二画**	**五画**	蟒 427
童 661	祖 640	耗 257	覆 200	虚 746	融 556
竣 351	袖 745	耙 12,477			螃 482
八画	被 28		**页部**	**虫部**	**十一画**
意 788	**七画**	**老部**			螳 642
九画	裤 370		页 770	虫 84	螺 418
竭 325	裙 544	老 384	**二画**	**二画**	蟋 707
端 155	**八画**	考 359	顶 146	虬 595	蟊 428
	裸 419		顷 533	**三画**	**十四画**
穴部	**九画**	**耳部**	**三画**	虹 265	蠕 558
	褐 261		项 727	虾 710	**十五画**
穴 750	**十画**	耳 168	顺 621	虽 631	蠢 99
二画	褥 559	**二画**	须 746	蚂 422	
究 340	褴 381	取 538	**四画**	**四画**	**缶部**
穷 534	**十一画**	**三画**	顽 679	蚕 61	
三画	褶 843	闻 693	顾 229	蚜 755	**三画**
空 365,366	**十三画**	**四画**	顿 160	蚯 253	缸 208
帘 397	襟 329	耻 82	颁 17	蚊 694	**四画**
四画		耸 627	颂 174	**五画**	缺 543
突 666	**疋(⺪)部**	耽 218	预 811	蛊 227	**十一画**
窃 526		耿 122	**五画**	蚯 535	罄 534
穿 94	**六画**	**五画**	硕 623	蛙 875	**十七画**
五画	蛋 123	聋 412	领 408	蛇 580	罐 236
窍 524	**七画**	职 857	颇 500	蛋 123	
窄 833	疏 612	聊 401	颈 337	**六画**	**舌部**
容 556	**九画**	**六画**	**七画**	蛙 675	
六画	疑 782	联 398	频 495	蛛 871	舌 579
窒 863		**七画**	颏 670	蛮 424	**一画**
窑 765	**皮部**	聘 496	**八画**	**七画**	乱 416
七画		**八画**	颗 360	蜗 695	**二画**
窜 105	皮 488	聚 347		蛾 164	舍 580
					五画
					甜 651

三画		踩	163	欲	812	**青部**		齿	82	**二画**	
辱	559	跪	241	**十画**						勒	387,388
唇	99	路	414	糵	284,288	青	528	**佳部**		**四画**	
豕部		跟	217			**六画**				靴	750
		七画		**豸部**		静	339	**二画**		靶	12
家	301	踌	86			**其部**		难	458,460	**六画**	
四画		踊	798	**三画**				**三画**		鞋	733
象	727	**八画**		豺	68	其	506	雀	544	鞍	5
六画		踢	646	豹	25	**一画**		售	611	**八画**	
豢	277	踏	637	**七画**		甚	587	**四画**		鞠	344
七画		踟	82	貌	429	**三画**		集	295	**九画**	
豪	253	踩	59	**角部**		基	291	雁	762	鞭	37
卤部		踪	888			**四画**		雄	743	**骨部**	
		九画		角	317,348	斯	625	雅	755		
卤	413	踹	94	**六画**		期	504	焦	317	骨	227
里部		蹄	647	触	93	欺	505	雇	229	**五画**	
		蹂	557	解	325	**雨(⻗)部**		**五画**		骷	369
里	392	**十一画**		**言部**				雏	92	**鬼部**	
二画		蹦	31			雨	810	**六画**			
厘	390	蹚	641	言	757	**三画**		雌	101	鬼	240
重	84,868	蹩	42	**六画**		雪	751	**八画**		**四画**	
四画		**十二画**		誉	646	**五画**		雕	144	魂	284
野	769	蹲	159	**七画**		雷	388	**金部**		魁	374
五画		蹭	64	誓	605	零	407			**五画**	
量	399,401	蹬	134	**十二画**		雾	704	金	328	魅	432
童	661	**身部**		警	338	雹	22	**五画**		魄	501
足(⻊)部				**十三画**		**六画**		鉴	311	**十一画**	
		身	582	譬	490	需	746	**鱼部**		魔	448
足	891	**三画**		**辛部**		**七画**				**食部**	
二画		射	581			震	846	鱼	809		
趴	477	**四画**		辛	736	霉	431	**四画**		食	599
四画		躯	537	**五画**		**八画**		鲁	413	**七画**	
距	346	**六画**		辜	226	霓	464	**六画**		餐	60
趾	860	躲	162	**六画**		霍	288	鲜	717	**音部**	
跃	818	**八画**		辞	100	霎	569	**七画**			
五画		躺	642	辟	490	**九画**		鲨	568	音	791
践	311	**采部**		**七画**		霜	618	**八画**		**二画**	
跋	10			辣	378	霞	711	鲸	337	章	837
跌	145	**一画**		**九画**		**十三画**		**九画**		竟	338
跑	483	番	172	辨	39	霾	12	鳄	165	**四画**	
六画		释	605	辩	39	霸	413,414	**十画**		韵	820
跨	371	**谷部**		**十画**		霹	488	鳏	234	**五画**	
跳	654			辫	40	**齿部**		**革部**		韶	578
		谷	227	**十二画**							
		四画		瓣	20	齿		革	213		

麻部	五画	九画	黑部	四画	鼻部
	磨　447,450	魔　448		默　450	
	六画			黔　519	鼻　31
麻　421	縻　436	鹿部	黑　261	鼠部	三画
四画	八画		三画		鼾　250
摩　447	靡　436	鹿　414	墨　449	鼠　614	九画

（三）难查字笔画索引
Stroke Index for Characters of Dubious Radicals

（字右边的号码指词典正文的页码）

The number on the right of the character is the page number in the body of the dictionary

二画		世　601	头　663,666	兆　840	卑　25
刁　143	无　697	本　29	司　623	农　471	周　869
乃　456	专　875	戊　703	民　441	**七画**	肃　629
三画	支　854	平　496	出　87	严　757	隶　395
干　203,207	牙　755	东　148	发　169	求　535	承　79
才　57	屯　672	卡　352,514	**六画**	束　615	**九画**
丈　838	中　864,867	北　26	考　359	来　378	奏　891
与　809	内　462	凸　666	亚　755	串　96	甚　587
丸　678	午　702	且　525	再　822	卵　416	巷　727
及　292	升　588	甲　302	死　625	**八画**	咸　717
亡　682	长　69,837	申　582	成　77	奉　193	威　684
义　786	氏　600	电　142	夹　301,302	武　702	歪　676
已　783	为　685,689	由　800	至　860	表　40	临　404
也　769	尺　82	史　600	师　594	其　506	幽　800
刃　552	丑　86	凹　7	曲　537,538	直　856	拜　16
习　707	巴　9	生　588	网　682	丧　565	香　724
乡　722	予　810	乍　832	肉　557	事　602	重　84,868
四画	书　611	甩　617	年　466	枣　828	将　312,314
丰　190	以　783	乐　386,817	朱　870	非　183	叛　481
井　337	**五画**	册　63	乔　523	果　243	举　345
开　352	末　448	玄　748	乒　496	畅　71	**十画**
夫　194	未　690	半　18	行　252,740	垂　98	艳　762
	击　289				

哥 212	**十二画**	就 342	聚 347	**十五画**	**十七画**
乘 79	棘 295	**十三画**	翰 696	靠 359	戴 120
高 209	鼎 147	鼓 227	兢 336	**十六画**	囊 460
十一画	舒 612	赖 380	舞 702	噩 165	蠹 94
爽 618	释 605	**十四画**	疑 782	整 848	
够 224					

A

ā

ā

阿 ā

另见 ē

阿尔法射线 ā'ěrfǎ shèxiàn 【名】alpha ray

阿飞 āfēi 【名】a young person who dresses and behaves in a bizarre and rowdy fashion

阿拉伯数字 Ālābó shùzì Arabic numeral

阿姨 āyí 【名】*form of address used by a young person or child for any woman one generation his senior*

啊 ā 【叹】*in conversation affirms the truth of the statement of the other party* yes：你是说这儿要盖一个图书馆吗？——～，下月就动工了。Are you saying that a library will be built here? —Yes, construction work will start next month. 他是不是没买到票？——～，白跑了一趟。Do you mean he didn't get a ticket after all? —True. Just a waste of time.

另见 á；à；a

á

啊 á 【叹】*demands an answer or asks a rhetorical question* hey；what：～? 这是怎么回事? Hey!

What's this all about? ～? 还早哇? 都七点啦! What! Still early? It's already seven o'clock!

另见 ā；à；a

à

啊 à 【叹】❶ *expresses consent* well；yes：～，就这么办吧! Well, let's do it this way, then! or Okay, so be it! ❷ *expresses realization* oh；aha：～，原来是这么回事。So that's what it is! ❸ *expresses admiration* oh：～，天晴了。The weather is clearing. ～，这片牡丹开得多好哇! How pretty these peonies are!

另见 ā；á；a

a

啊 a 【助】❶ *used at the end of a sentence to emphasize exclamation, agreement, interrogation, command, entreaty, etc.*：多好看的花儿～! What pretty flowers! 行～，就这么办吧! All right, let's do it this way. or Okay, so be it! 咱们什么时候出发～? When are we going to leave? 等等我～! Hey, wait for me! ❷ *used after a clause, phrase or word to mark an exclamation followed by a pause drawing attention to what is to follow*：自从你开

了家公司～,咱们的日子越过越好啦! Since you set up a company, our lives are getting better and better. 你～,真有办法! How resourceful you are! ❸ *used after each item of an enumeration*:高粱～,玉米～,都长得很好。the sorghum, corn, etc. are all growing well. Note: *the pronunciation of* 啊 *often becomes* ya,wa,na, *or* nga *according to the final of the preceding character. The written form of* 啊 *may remain unchanged, or be changed into* 呀, 哇 *or* 哪:

The finals of the preceding characters	The pronunciations of 啊	The written forms
a,o,e,i,ü	a····→ia	呀
u,ao,ou	a····→ua	哇
-n	a····→na	哪
-ng	a····→nga	啊

另见 ā;á;à。

āi

哎 āi 【叹】❶ *expresses surprise or dissatisfaction* well:～! 人都到哪儿去啦? Well! Where is everybody? ～! 你怎么弄得这么乱了? Damn it! Why did you make such a mess? ❷ *used to remind sb. of sth.* hey:～,别忘了通知他一声! Hey! Don't forget to tell him about it!

哎呀 āiyā 【叹】*expresses surprise* oh; oh my:～,这里的变化真大呀! My! How this place has changed! ～,好大的风啊! Oh! It's blowing hard!

哎哟 āiyō 【叹】*expresses surprise or pain* good gracious; oh dear:～,车开走了! Oh no! The bus has left! ～,真疼啊! Ouch! That really

hurts!

哀 āi

哀悼 āidào 【动】mourn for (the dead); lament or grieve over (sb.'s death); express one's condolences (on the death of sb.)

哀求 āiqiú 【动】entreat; implore; beseech

哀思 āisī 【名】grief; mourning (for someone who has died):寄托(or 表达)～ express one's grief

哀叹 āitàn 【动】sigh sorrowfully

哀乐 āiyuè 【名】funeral music; dirge

唉 āi 【叹】*response to someone calling* yes; all right; OK:快来呀, 小王! ——～,来了! Hurry up, Xiao Wang! — All right! I'm coming! 另见 ài。

挨 āi 【动】❶ by turns; one by one; in sequence:这位医生～家～户给小孩儿打预防针。The doctor went door to door, giving inoculations to the children. ❷ be close to; get near to; be next to:你～我坐吧! You sit here beside me! 体育馆紧～着公园。The gymnasium is next to the park. 另见 ái。

挨次 āicì 【副】(do sth.) in sequence or one after the other; by turns; in succession

挨个儿 āigèr 【副】one by one; one after another:大家～走进礼堂。All filed into the auditorium, one after another.

挨近 āijìn 【动】be close by; come close to

ái

挨 ái 【动】❶ suffer; undergo:

～批评 be criticized ～冻 suffer from cold ～揍 be beaten up ❷ live (e.g. a hard life); go through: 病床上躺了三个月，日子真难～呀! I was laid up in bed for three months. What a drag! 也作"捱"。
另见 āi

挨打 ái＝dǎ suffer a beating; be spanked

挨饿 ái＝è suffer from hunger; starve

挨骂 ái＝mà be given a good scolding

皑（皚）ái

皑皑 ái'ái 【形】〈书〉(of frost or snow) dazzlingly white: 白雪～ an expanse of white snow

癌 ái 【名】cancer

癌变 áibiàn 【动】canceration

癌扩散 ái kuòsàn metastasis of cancer

癌细胞 áixìbāo 【名】cancer cell

癌症 áizhèng 【名】cancer

ǎi

矮 ǎi 【形】❶ short in stature: 小王比老张～多了。Xiao Wang is much shorter than Lao Zhang. ❷ (of hills, houses, etc.) low: 一堵～墙 a low wall ❸ (of grades in school) less advanced: 弟弟比哥哥～两班。The younger brother is two grades behind the older one.

矮小 ǎixiǎo 【形】(of stature or house) short and small

ài

艾 ài

艾滋病 àizībìng 【名】AIDS

唉 ài 【叹】expresses sorrow or pity: ～,这只小羊羔恐怕活不成了! What a shame! This little lamb is probably going to die. ～,多好的一个杯子打破了! Too bad! This nice glass is broken.
另见 āi

爱（愛）ài 【动】❶ love: ～祖国 love one's country 干一行～一行 love whatever work you're doing 他很～他的女儿。He loves his daughter dearly. ❷ like; be fond of: ～打球 like ball games ～听音乐 be fond of music ❸ be apt to; be liable to: 铁～生锈。Iron rusts easily. 这一带～刮风。It is often windy here. 他～激动。He tends to be excitable.

爱称 àichēng 【名】pet or affectionate name; term of endearment

爱戴 àidài 【动】love and support: 老村长深受乡亲们的～。The village chief is deeply revered by the villagers.

爱抚 àifǔ 【动】caress

爱国 ài＝guó love one's country; be patriotic

爱国者 àiguózhě 【名】patriot

爱国主义 àiguózhǔyì 【名】patriotism

爱好 àihào 【动】be fond of; like: ～游泳 be fond of swimming ～美术 have a liking for art 【名】hobby; interest: 共同的～ a common interest 特殊的～ one's own special interest

爱护 àihù 【动】cherish; give full attention to; devote loving care to: ～公共财物 take good care of public property ～青年一代 devote loving care to the younger generation

爱面子 àimiànzi be anxious to keep up appearances; be intent on sav-

ing face

爱莫能助 ài mò néng zhù　be willing to help, but unable to do so

爱慕 àimù 【动】love; adore; admire

爱情 àiqíng 【名】love

爱人 àiren 【名】❶ husband or wife ❷ fiancé or fiancée

爱惜 àixī 【动】treasure (sth.); cherish (sth.); hold (sth.) dear; use sparingly: ～时间 make the best use of one's time ～人力物力 use manpower and materials sparingly ～集体荣誉 cherish the good name of the collective ～每一粒粮食. Do not waste the least bit of grain.

爱心 àixīn 【名】compassion; loving care

爱憎分明 ài zèng fēnmíng　be clear about whom or what to love or hate; to have one's heart in the right place

碍（礙） ài 【动】hinder; obstruct: ～手～脚 stand in the way of 有～交通 obstruct traffic 东西放在这儿吧,～不着谁. Just leave your things here. They won't be in anyone's way.

碍事 ài=shì ❶ hinder; be in the way: 柜子放在这儿～得很. If you put the cupboard here, it'll be in our way. 你们干你们的,不碍我的事. You go ahead with your work. It won't bother me. ❷ be of consequence; serious (*usu. used in an interrogative or negative sentence*): 他的病～不～? ——不～. Is his illness serious or not? — No.

暖（暖） ài

暧昧 àimèi 【形】❶ ambiguous; equivocal ❷ dubious; shady

ān

安 ān 【动】❶ fix; install: ～电灯 install lights ～煤气管道 lay a gas pipe-line ❷ force sth. upon sb.: ～赃 incriminate sb. by planting stolen goods in his house ～罪名 bring false charges against ❸ ◇ be satisfied; be contented with (life, work, etc.): ～于现状 be satisfied with things as they are 【形】◇ safe; secure: 转危为～ be out of danger; emerge from danger; extricate (oneself) from a dangerous situation

安插 ānchā 【动】place sb. in a job or position; plant: ～亲信 plant one's own men (in key positions) ～一段故事情节 insert an anecdote (e.g. in a talk)

安定 āndìng 【形】stable; settled; secure: ～的生活 secure livelihood 社会秩序很～. The society is stable. 【动】reassure; stabilize: ～人心 reassure the public 把情绪～下来 set one's mind at ease

安顿 āndùn 【动】find a place for; arrange for; help settle down

安放 ānfàng 【动】put in a certain place

安分 ānfèn 【形】well-disciplined; law-abiding

安分守己 ān fèn shǒu jǐ　abide by the law and behave oneself; accept one's lot; know one's place

安家落户 ān jiā luò hù　settle down in a place; make one's home in a place

安静 ānjìng 【形】quiet; calm; peaceful and serene

安居 ān jū　live in peace

安居乐业 ān jū lè yè　live and work in peace and contentment: 由于生产发展,这里的人们都～. As a result

of the development of production, people here live and work in peaceful contentment.

安乐 ānlè 【形】peaceful and happy

安乐死 ānlèsǐ 【名】euthanasia

安理会 Ānlǐhuì 【名】*short for* 安全理事会 the Security Council

安眠药 ānmiányào 【名】sleeping pill

安民告示 ān mín gàoshi notice to reassure the public (in the past, e.g. after a war)

安宁 ānníng 【形】❶ (of a place, society, etc.) in good order; peaceful; free from disturbances ❷ (of state of mind) free from worry; be at ease; relaxed

安排 ānpái 【动】arrange; plan: ～时间 arrange a schedule ～生活 arrange one's daily life 把工作～好 plan the work well 【名】arrangement: 一项合理的～ a rational arrangement 作出具体～ make concrete arrangements 人事～ arrangements concerning personnel

安培 ānpéi 【量】ampere

安全 ānquán 【形】safe; secure: 超速行车不～。When driving, it is not safe to exceed the speed-limit. 【名】safety; security: 注意交通～ pay attention to traffic safety

安全带 ānquándài 【名】〔条 tiáo〕seat belt; safety belt

安全岛 ānquándǎo 【名】safety island; pedestrian island

安全灯 ānquándēng 【名】safety lamp; safelight

安全理事会 Ānquán Lǐshìhuì the Security Council (of the United Nations)

安全门 ānquánmén 【名】emergency exit

安全系数 ānquán xìshù safety factor (coefficient)

安身 ān = shēn try to find a place to settle down (*usu. in adverse circumstances*); take shelter

安危 ānwēi 【名】safety or danger; safety

安慰 ānwèi 【动】comfort; console

安稳 ānwěn 【形】calm and steady

安息 ānxī 【动】rest in peace (R.I.P.)

安详 ānxiáng 【形】serene; composed; peaceful: ～的面容 serene expression 举止～ behave with composure

安心 ān = xīn ❶ be content and not anxious to make any change: 工作很～ work contentedly at one's job (not looking for greener pastures) ～学习 keep one's mind on one's studies and not be distracted ❷ compose oneself: 安下心来休养。Don't worry. Just rest. ❸ have (bad) intentions: 黄鼠狼给鸡拜年，没安好心。When the weasel pays the hen a New Year's call, you bet he has no good intentions. 他安的什么心? I wonder what he is up to.

安逸 ānyì 【形】leisurely and comfortable; easy

安营扎寨 ān yíng zhā zhài make camp; encamp; pitch camp: 登山运动员在山脚下～,做好登山准备。The mountaineers pitched camp at the foot of the mountain and got ready to climb.

安置 ānzhì 【动】arrange; put sth. in its place; find a place for: 把东西～好 put things in their proper places 乡政府正在研究～复员军人的工作。The township government is considering how best to place the exservicemen in jobs.

安装 ānzhuāng 【动】fix; install; assemble 【名】installation

鞍 ān 【名】◇ saddle

鞍马 ānmǎ 【名】(gymnastics) horse

鞍子 ānzi 【名】saddle

àn

岸　àn　【名】bank（of a river）；shore；coast

岸然　ànrán　【形】in a solemn manner

按　àn　【动】❶ press；push down：～电钮 press a button ～图钉 push in a drawing pin ❷ ◇ hold sth. back；put aside：～下不提 leave（a matter）for later discussion ❸ suppress；control：～不住心头怒火 can barely contain one's anger 【介】in accordance with：～制度办事 act in accordance with the rules ～计划完成了任务 fulfil the task in accordance with the plan ～顺序排列 arrange in order ～节气说，现在该穿棉衣了。It's the time of year when we usually put on warm clothes.

按兵不动　àn bīng bù dòng　keep the troops in readiness，but do not send them into action；be on the alert，but make no move（often applies to occasions when action should have been taken）

按部就班　àn bù jiù bān　（act）in accordance with the prescribed order；keep to conventional ways of doing things：麦收时节必须连夜突击，不能～地干。During the wheat harvest，we should work round the clock，and not stick to routine.

按键　ànjiàn　【名】a push-button key

按劳分配　àn láo fēnpèi　to each according to his work；distribution according to work

按摩　ànmó　【动】massage

按捺　ànnà　【动】control；restrain：～不住急切的心情 cannot restrain one's impatience

按钮　ànniǔ　【名】a push button；a switch

按期　ànqī　【副】on the agreed date；on schedule

按时　ànshí　【副】at the scheduled or prescribed time；（complete a plan，etc.）on schedule

按说　ànshuō　【副】ordinarily；normally；as a rule：～北京的冬天见不到葡萄，可是今年市场上却有卖的。You don't usually see grapes in Beijing during the winter，but there are some on the market this year.

按需分配　àn xū fēnpèi　to each according to his need；distribution according to need

按语　ànyǔ　【名】comment；（editor's or author's）introduction or introductory remarks

按照　ànzhào　【介】according to；in line with；in accordance with：～预定方案施工 carry out construction in accordance with the original plan 这件事应该～大家的意见去做。In this case，let's act according to the opinion of the majority.

案　àn　【名】◇ ❶ case（usu. legal）❷ record；file：备～ keep a record of the matter 有～可查 be on file

案底　àndǐ　【名】criminal records

案犯　ànfàn　【名】offender

案件　ànjiàn　【名】case；legal case

案例　ànlì　【名】case

案情　ànqíng　【名】the facts of a case；case

案头　àntóu　【名】on one's desk

案子　ànzi　【名】❶ a long wooden board put up as a table：乒乓球～ table-tennis table ❷ case（usu. legal）

暗　àn　【形】❶ dark；dim ❷ secret；hidden

暗藏　àncáng　【动】hide；conceal

暗淡　àndàn　【形】dim；dull（colour）；dismal；bleak：～的色彩 dull colour 前景～ bleak prospects

暗地里　àndìli　【名】secretly；behind sb.'s back；inwardly；on the sly：～勾结 secretly work hand in glove with ～来往 make secret contacts 躲在～放冷枪 shoot from a concealed point of vantage

暗害　ànhài　【动】do some secret injury to (sometimes fatally)

暗号　ànhào　【名】secret sign；password

暗礁　ànjiāo　【名】hidden rocks；submerged reef

暗杀　ànshā　【动】assassinate

暗示　ànshì　【动】hint；insinuate；imply 【名】hint；implication；insinuation

暗室　ànshì　【名】dark room

暗算　ànsuàn　【动】plot against

暗锁　ànsuǒ　【名】a built-in lock

暗无天日　àn wú tiān rì　(fig.) complete darkness；utter darkness；total absence of justice

暗指　ànzhǐ　【动】hint at；imply

暗中　ànzhōng　【名】❶ in the dark：猎人躲在～观察森林里的情况。The hunter, hiding in the shadow, observed what was going on in the forest. ❷ in secret；secretly：这项调查必须～进行。The investigation must be carried out secretly.

暗自　ànzì　【副】inwardly；secretly：～高兴 be secretly delighted

āng

肮（骯）āng

肮脏　āngzāng　【形】dirty；filthy

áng

昂　áng

昂奋　ángfèn　【形】exuberant；spirited；with great spirit

昂贵　ángguì　【形】very expensive；costly

昂然　ángrán　【形】upright and unafraid

昂首　áng = shǒu　with one's head held high；hold one's head up

昂首阔步　áng shǒu kuò bù　stride forward with head held high：运动员们～走进赛场。The athletes strode into the arena, proud and high-spirited.

昂扬　ángyáng　【形】high-spirited：斗志～ have high morale

āo

凹　āo　【形】concave；hollow

凹版　āobǎn　【名】intaglio

凹面镜　āomiànjìng　【名】concave mirror

凹透镜　āotòujìng　【名】concave lens

凹陷　āoxiàn　【动】cave in, sink

熬　āo　【动】boil；cook in water；stew：～白菜 boiled cabbage ～豆腐 boiled bean curd
另见 áo

áo

熬　áo　【动】❶ cook；decoct：～粥 cook porridge ～药 decoct medicinal herbs ❷ endure；pull through：他终于从一场重病中～过来了。He was seriously ill but finally pulled through.
另见 āo

熬煎　áojiān　【动】suffer

熬夜　áo = yè　stay up all night or far into the night；burn the midnight candle

翱 áo

翱翔 áoxiáng 【动】〈书〉soar；wheel in the air；hover

ǎo

袄（襖） ǎo 【名】〔件 jiàn〕lined or padded jacket or coat

ào

傲 ào

傲慢 àomàn 【形】haughty；impudent；arrogant

傲气 àoqì 【名】arrogance【形】arrogant

奥 ào

奥林匹克运动会 Àolínpǐkè yùndònghuì the Olympic Games

奥妙 àomiào 【形】abstruse and subtle

奥运会 Àoyùnhuì 【名】short for 奥林匹克运动会

懊 ào

懊悔 àohuǐ 【形】regretful；remorseful 【动】regret

懊恼 àonǎo 【形】annoyed；vexed

懊丧 àosàng 【形】dismayed；dispirited；downcast；dejected；昨天丢了个钱包，越想越～。Yesterday, I lost my wallet. The more I think about it, the more I am depressed.

B

bā

八 bā 【数】eight
八卦 bāguà 【名】the Eight Tri-grams
八仙桌 bāxiānzhuō 〔张 zhāng〕square table
八月 bāyuè 【名】August
八月节 Bāyuèjié 【名】the Mid-Autumn Festival

巴 bā
巴不得 bābude 【动】〈口〉earnestly hope; wish anxiously; be very anxious (to do sth.): 他病好了，～马上回去上班。Now that he is well, he can't wait to get back to work.
巴结 bājie 【动】〈口〉fawn on; flatter; toady to: 奴才～主子。Underlings fawn on their bosses.
巴士 bāshì 【名】bus
巴掌 bāzhang 【名】palm (of the hand)

扒 bā 【动】❶ cling to; hold on to: 孩子～着窗户往外看。Holding on to the windowsill, the children looked out. ❷ dig (out): 把埋在雪里的汽车～出来 dig out the car buried in the snow ❸ pull down; demolish: ～了草房盖砖房 pull down the adobe house to build a brick one ❹ part; pull apart: ～开草丛捉蟋蟀 part the grass to catch a

cricket ❺ take off; strip: ～羊皮 skin a sheep 他们把鞋袜一～就下田了。They took off their shoes and socks and set to work in the paddy field.
另见 pá

叭 bā 【象声】snap; crack; rap: ～的一声枪响，一个人倒下去了。There was the crack of a rifle shot and a man dropped down.

芭 bā
芭蕾舞 bālěiwǔ 【名】ballet

疤 bā 【名】scar
疤痕 bāhén 【名】scar

捌 bā 【数】eight (*complicated form of* 八 *used in cheque-writing etc. to avoid alteration*)

bá

拔 bá 【动】❶ pull out; draw: ～草 pull out weeds ～牙 extract a tooth ～剑 unsheath a sword ❷ destroy or seize (military posts): ～掉敌人炮楼 wipe out the enemy gun emplacement
拔除 báchú 【动】uproot; eradicate
拔刀相助 bá dāo xiāng zhù come to sb.'s rescue without hesitation
拔河 báhé 【名】tug of war
拔尖儿 bájiānr ❶ be outstanding;

be among the best：他的学习成绩在全班是～的。He is one of the best students in his class. ❷ stand out among the crowd

拔节 bá=jié jointing；elongating

拔苗助长 bá miáo zhù zhǎng try to help seedlings grow by pulling them (*fig.*) spoil things by undue haste 也作"揠(yà)苗助长"。

跋 bá 【名】postscript (to a book)

跋扈 báhù 【形】domineering；bullying；bossy

跋山涉水 bá shān shè shuǐ scale mountains and ford streams；undertake a long, hard journey：勘探队员们～，不畏艰险，为国家寻找地下宝藏。Prospectors make long, difficult journeys, braving all hardships, to discover the earth's treasures for the country.

跋涉 báshè 【动】cross land and water；make a difficult journey

bǎ

把 bǎ 【动】❶ hold：～着方向盘 hold the steering wheel 手～手地教 show sb. how to do sth. by guiding his hand ❷ guard：～门 guard the door 【名】handle：车～ handle-bar 【量】❶ *for nouns* ① *for anything with a handle*：一～斧子 an axe 一～镰刀 a sickle 一～椅子 a chair ② handful：一～花生 a handful of peanuts 摘两～豆角 pick two handfuls of beans ③ *for some abstract nouns, if used with a numeral, only* 把 *can be used*：出(一)～力 do one's share 大家加(一)～劲儿，这活儿一会儿就干完了。Let's pull together and get the job done. ❷ *for any action done with the hand*：拉他一～ give him a hand up 一～抓住

他的手 grasp him by the hand 【介】 *used to indicate how a thing or person is disposed of, dealt with or affected. The object of* 把 *is in general the thing or person disposed of or affected*：他～灯关了。He turned off the light. 请你～登山经验介绍介绍。Please tell us your experiences in mountaineering. 他～书放在书架上了。He put the book on the shelf. 你能～这本书借给我吗？Could you lend me this book? 请你～这封信贴上邮票寄出去。Please put a stamp on this letter and post it. Note：❶ *the main verb is usu. transitive and the verb or the verb plus the complement etc. which follows it can affect the object of* 把：他～那件事忘了。He's forgotten the matter. 小林昨天踢球，～脚踢坏了。Xiao Lin hurt his ankle yesterday while playing soccer. *Verbs which, though transitive, have nothing to do with the disposal of things can't be used in a* 把 *sentence, e. g.* 有、在、赞成、知道、进、*etc.* ❷ *since the object of* 把 *is to be disposed of, it usually represents sth. or sb. specific or generic*：请～那几个杯子拿过来。Please hand me those cups over there. (*It is ungrammatical to say*：请～几个杯子拿过来。) 昨天我～衣服都洗了。Yesterday I washed (my) clothes. (*It is understood that the clothes were "mine", and therefore specific articles of clothing*.) 他总～三声读成一声 He always mispronounces 3rd tones as 1st tones. ❸ *the verb of a* 把 *sentence cannot stand by itself. It is either reduplicated, or takes an object, complement or a particle* 了、着、*etc. to show the result of the action or the effect on the object*：我要～这件衣服洗洗。I want to wash this dress.

老林抽烟的时候~衬衫烧了个洞。Lao Lin burnt a hole in his shirt while smoking. 他 ~ 药 吃 了。He has taken his medicine. 我~那篇文章看了三遍。I've read that article three times. ❹ *if there is an adverbial adjunct of time，an adverb of negation，or an auxiliary verb，it must be placed before* 把：我今天晚上要~这篇文章写完。I must finish writing this article tonight. 不~情况搞清楚，就不能下结论。If you haven't grasped the situation, don't draw any conclusions. *there are two kinds of* 把 *sentences where the function of disposal isn't obvious*：① *where the main verb is intransitive or the predicate consists of an adjective instead of a verb，the whole sentence has a causative implication*：他还没回来，可~同伴们急坏了。He wasn't back yet, and his friends became extremely anxious. 他说了个笑话，~我肚子都笑疼了。He told a joke, and I laughed until my sides ached. ② *where* ~ *is used before the verb，with nothing following the verb，to show a momentary，sudden action.* 把……… *can only form a subordinate clause，and there must，therefore，be a main clause following*：他~外衣一脱，就打球去了。He flung off his jacket and rushed to play ball. 他~头一扬，就走过去了。He threw back his head and strode off. *the idea conveyed by a* 把 *sentence can also be conveyed by an ordinary sentence in many cases*：你能借给我这本书吗? Could you lend me that book? 请你介绍介绍登山经验。Please tell us your experiences in mountaineering. 他忘了那件事了。He's forgotten that matter. *there are other sentences，owing to the*

complicated construction after the verb，which cannot be turned into ordinary sentences：请你~这封信贴上邮票寄出去。Please put a stamp on this letter and post it. 他~书放在书架上了。He put the book on the shelf. 【助】 *used after measure words or numerals such as* 个、丈、百、千，*etc. to show an approximate number；no other numeral may be added in front*：个~月 over a month 百~人 more than 100 people 丈~高 over 10 feet high

另见 bà

把柄 bǎbǐng 【名】 handle；sth. (shortcoming, mistake, etc.) that may be taken advantage of and used against sb.：让人抓住了~ give sb. sth. which can be used against one ~落在对方手里。The evidence against（him）has fallen into the hands of（his）opponent.

把持 bǎchí 【动】 control；retain one's grip on（*derog.*）：~某些部门 have complete control over some departments 不能让他一个人~大权。He is not to take a grip on everything all by himself.

把关 bǎ = guān guard the pass；check that sth. is in accordance with principles and rules：修建地铁，每一道工序都有人~。In building the subway, the quality of every step in the process of construction is guaranteed. 对产品要把好质量关。The quality of products must be guaranteed.

把门 bǎ = mén guard a gate：把好门 guard the door 那个大机关，有人~。There is a guard at the door of that big office.

把势 bǎshi 【名】〈口〉❶ Wushu；martial arts：练~ practise martial arts ❷ a person skilled in a particular trade：车~ cart-driver 花儿~

a man who cultivates flowers 干庄稼活儿，他可是个好～。He is a highly skilled farmer. 也作"把式"。

把守 bǎshǒu 【动】guard；defend；～关口 guard the pass 分兵～ divide the army to defend (the passes)

把手 bǎshou 【名】handle；knob；hand-grip

把头 bǎtou 【名】hirer of contract labour

把握 bǎwò 【动】grasp；seize (*usu. refers to abstract matters*)：～时机 seize the chance ～事物的本质 grasp the essence of a matter 【名】one's certainty of being successful：～不大 be not quite sure 没什么～ be not certain 有～提前完成生产计划。It's certain that the production plan will be completed ahead of schedule. 不做无～之事。Don't take action unless you know what you're doing.

把戏 bǎxì 【名】❶ (in old times) juggling；acrobatics ❷ trick：鬼～ a cheap trick

把兄弟 bǎxiōngdì 【名】sworn brothers

靶 bǎ 【名】target

靶子 bǎzi 【名】target；butt

bà

坝（壩）bà 【名】dam；dike；embankment

把 bà 【名】❶ handle：茶壶～儿 handle of a tea-pot 刀～儿 handle of a knife 镐～ pick-handle ❷ stem of a flower，leaf or fruit：梨～儿 the stem of a pear
另见 bǎ

爸 bà 【名】dad；pa

爸爸 bàba 【名】dad；papa

耙 bà 【名】harrow 【动】draw a harrow over (a field)：～地 draw a harrow over the field
另见 pá

罢（罷）bà 【动】❶ stop；cease：～教 teachers' strike ❷ dismiss：～了官 have an official dismissed from his post ❸ ◇ finish；be through with：听～ finish listening 说～ finish speaking

罢工 bà＝gōng strike；go on strike

罢官 bà＝guān dismiss an official from his post

罢课 bà＝kè student strike

…罢了 …bàle 【助】*used at the end of a sentence，equivalent to "that's all"；usu. in conjunction with* 只是,不过,无非,*etc.* (*usu. in written language*)：我只是做了我应该做的事～。I just did my duty，that's all. 我不过业余爱画儿笔画儿～，哪儿算得上画家！I just dabble a little in my spare time. I can hardly be called an artist.

罢免 bàmiǎn 【动】remove from office；dismiss sb. from his post

罢免权 bàmiǎnquán 【名】the right of recall

罢市 bà＝shì shop keepers' strike

罢休 bàxiū 【动】give up；stop；let the matter drop

霸 bà 【名】◇ ❶ bully ❷ hegemony 【动】◇ tyrannize over

霸道 bàdao 【形】overbearing；high-handed

霸权 bàquán 【名】hegemony

霸权主义 bàquánzhǔyì 【名】hegemonism

霸王 bàwáng 【名】overlord；bully

霸占 bàzhàn 【动】forcibly occupy

霸主 bàzhǔ 【名】❶ the most pow-

erful of the feudal princes of the Spring and Autumn period in Chinese history ❷ overlord

ba

吧 ba【助】*used at the end of a sentence* ❶ *indicates entreaty*, *suggestion*, *command*, *etc.*：这个任务交给我～! Please entrust me with this task. 明天咱们去博物馆～! How about going to the museum tomorrow? 快走～! Please go at once. 让我们为祖国的繁荣富强努力奋斗～。Let's work for the prosperity, well-being and strength of our motherland. ❷ *indicates estimation or conjecture*, *sometimes in the form of a question*：今年收成不错～! There will probably be a good harvest this year, don't you think? 他走了吗? ——大概走了～。Has he gone? — Probably. 十几天以前～,他曾给我来过一封信。I suppose it was more than ten days ago that he wrote to me. ❸ *indicates agreement*：好～, 明天谈～! All right, let's talk it over tomorrow! 行, 就这么办～! Good, let's do it this way. ❹ *indicates a pause* ① *shows a dilemma by citing two opposite cases*：这种药材很难培育,温度高了～,不行;温度低了～,也不行。It is very difficult to cultivate this medicinal herb. If the temperature is too high or too low, it won't grow properly. ② *gives an illustration*：参观的人真多,拿今天来说～,就有五千人。The place is certainly swarming with visitors. Today, for example, there were 5000. ❺ *indicates that things have turned out just as expected*：你看,我猜着了～。See, just as I guessed!

bāi

掰 bāi【动】break into two or tear off with both hands

bái

白 bái【形】❶ white：～衬衣 white shirt ～花 white flower ❷ plain; clean; unused：～卷儿（turn in a) blank examination paper【副】❶ in vain; to no avail：～忙了一天 busy over nothing for a whole day 我去找他没找到,～跑了一趟。I went but didn't find him, so I made the trip in vain. *This "白" can be reduplicated into "白白".* ❷ get sth. for nothing：～吃 eat without paying; eat free of charge ～给我也不要。I don't want it even if it is free. 不买票想～看电影,那怎么行呢! You want to see the film without buying a ticket. That's not right.

白班儿 báibānr【名】day shift (antonym of 夜班 night shift)

白璧无瑕 bái bì wú xiá flawless white jade

白菜 báicài【名】〔棵 kē〕Chinese cabbage

白痴 báichī【名】❶ idiocy ❷ idiot

白费 báifèi【动】waste：～力气 waste energy ～唇舌 waste one's breath 时间～了。Time was wasted.

白花花 báihuāhuā【形】gleaming white; shining white：～的大米 gleaming white rice

白话 báihuà【名】◇ ❶ empty words：他空口说～。He's all talk. ❷ modern written Chinese; vernacular：～文 writings in the vernacular

白金 báijīn【名】platinum

白酒 báijiǔ 【名】white spirit distilled from grains such as sorghum, maize, etc.

白开水 báikāishuǐ 【名】plain boiled water

白兰地 báilándì 【名】brandy

白领 báilǐng 【名】white collar

白茫茫 báimángmáng 【形】(of snow, cloud, fog) an endless whiteness

白皮书 báipíshū 【名】white paper; white book

白热化 báirèhuà 【动】be at a white heat

白日作梦 báirì zuò mèng daydream

白色 báisè 【名】❶ white colour ❷ reactionary; counter-revolutionary

白色恐怖 báisè kǒngbù white terror

白手起家 bái shǒu qǐ jiā start from scratch; build up from nothing: 我们村～，建了一个农具修配厂。Our village built a farm-tool repair shop starting from scratch.

白薯 báishǔ 【名】sweet potato

白糖 báitáng 【名】powdered sugar

白天 báitiān 【名】day-time

白条 báitiáo 【名】an IOU; a written acknowledgement of debt

白头偕老 báitóu xié lǎo live to ripe an old age in conjugal bliss

白血球 báixuèqiú 【名】white blood cell; white corpuscle

白银 báiyín 【名】silver

白昼 báizhòu 【名】daytime

白字 báizì 【名】incorrectly written or mispronounced character

bǎi

百 bǎi 【数】❶ hundred ❷ ◇ many

百般 bǎibān 【副】in a hundred-and-one ways; in every possible way: ～劝解 persuade in every possible way ～抵赖 try to deny by every possible means

百病 bǎibìng all sorts of diseases

百发百中 bǎi fā bǎi zhòng hit the bull's eye every time; shoot with great accuracy

百废俱兴 bǎi fèi jù xīng an overall revival of all the neglected tasks

百分比 bǎifēnbǐ 【名】percentage

百分点 bǎifēndiǎn 【名】a percentage point

百分率 bǎifēnlǜ 【名】percentage

百分数 bǎifēnshù 【名】percentage

百分之百 bǎi fēn zhī bǎi a hundred percent; absolutely; out and out

百分制 bǎifēnzhì 【名】hundred-mark system

百花齐放，百家争鸣 bǎi huā qí fàng, bǎi jiā zhēng míng let a hundred flowers bloom and a hundred schools of thought contend

百货 bǎihuò 【名】general merchandise

百货公司 bǎihuò gōngsī department store

百科全书 bǎikēquánshū 【名】encyclopaedia

百孔千疮 bǎi kǒng qiān chuāng a hundred holes, a thousand scars; riddled with a thousand gaping wounds; heavily damaged (and hard to repair) 也作"千疮百孔"。

百里挑一 bǎi lǐ tiāo yī one in a hundred

百炼成钢 bǎi liàn chéng gāng be toughened and hardened into steel; become hardened like steel after long tempering: 他是～的缉毒战士。He is a hardened fighter in combating drug trafficking.

百年大计 bǎi nián dàjì a fundamental task crucial for generations to come; a matter of vital and lasting importance; a vital matter of both immediate and long-range concern: 在施工过程中，要做到"～，质量第一"。In the course of construc-

tion，we should put quality first as a matter of vital and lasting importance. 教育事业是～。Education is a cause of paramount importance with lasting benefits.

百万 bǎiwàn 【数】million

百闻不如一见 bǎi wén bùrú yī jiàn better to see once than to hear a hundred times；one picture is worth a thousand words；seeing is believing

百姓 bǎixìng 【名】common people；the masses

百业 bǎiyè 【名】all business and enterprise：～兴旺 all business and enterprise are flourishing

百战百胜 bǎi zhàn bǎi shèng a hundred battles, a hundred victories；come out victorious in every battle；be invincible

百折不挠 bǎi zhé bù náo undeterred by repeated setbacks；搞科学研究要有～的精神。Scientific research demands a spirit of tenacity.

佰 bǎi 【数】hundred (*complicated form of* 百)

柏 bǎi 【名】◇ cypress
柏树 bǎishù 【名】〔棵 kē〕cypress
柏油 bǎiyóu 【名】pitch；tar

摆（擺） bǎi 【动】❶ put；place；arrange：把展品～在桌子上 arrange the exhibits on the table 儿童商店的橱窗里～着各式各样的玩具。All kinds of toys are displayed in the windows of the children's store. ❷ present；set forth：～理由 present reasons 把各方面的意见都～一～ set all the opinions on the table ❸ sway；swing；wave：～手 wave one's hand ❹ put on；assume：～威风 put on airs ～老资格 put on the airs of a veteran 【名】pendulum：这个钟的～坏了。Some-

thing is wrong with the pendulum of this clock.

摆布 bǎibù 【动】manipulate (sb. or sth.)；order about：任人～ allow oneself to be ordered about 不受别人～ not allow oneself to be pushed around

摆动 bǎidòng 【动】oscillate；swing

摆渡 bǎidù 【名】ferry 【动】ferry

摆放 bǎifàng 【动】place；put

摆架子 bǎi jiàzi put on airs；assume airs；be pretentious：好(hào)～ be fond of putting on airs 摆官僚架子 put on official airs 不要～。Don't put on airs.

摆弄 bǎinòng 【动】twiddle；fiddle with (sth.)；play with：～闹钟 fiddle with the alarm clock 他一回家就～收音机。As soon as he gets home，he begins fiddling with the radio.

摆平 bǎipíng 【动】❶ strike a balance；be fair to ❷ revenge；get even with

摆设 bǎishè 【动】furnish and decorate (a room)

摆设 bǎishe 【名】ornaments；furnishings (in a room)

摆事实，讲道理 bǎi shìshí，jiǎng dàolǐ present the facts and reason things out

摆摊子 bǎi = tānzi ❶ set up a stall：老王在街上摆了个小摊子。Lao Wang set up a street stall. ❷ maintain a large staff：企业刚开办，别把摊子摆得太大。Since the business is just started，we must not maintain a large staff.

摆脱 bǎituō 【动】get rid of；break away from；free oneself from；shake off：～困境 extricate oneself from a predicament ～旧习惯的束缚 cast off the burden of old customs 无法～ can't rid oneself of ～不开 cannot free oneself from

摆样子 bǎi = yàngzi do sth. for

show; keep up appearances

bài

败（敗）

bài 【动】❶ ①lose; (*as opp. to* 胜): 这场球赛，甲队胜了，乙队~了。In this match, Team A won and Team B lost. 立于不~之地 remain invincible 胜不骄，~不馁 be neither overwhelmed by victory, nor discouraged by defeat ② defeat; beat: 大~敌军 utterly defeat the enemy troops ❷ ①fail (*as opp. to* 成): 不计成~ not care whether one will succeed or not; to strive, and be oblivious to the outcome 成~在此一举。Success or failure rides on what we do now. ②spoil; ruin: 成事不足，~事有余 unable to achieve anything, but good at spoiling things ❸ wither: 枯枝~叶 withered twigs and leaves 这盆菊花儿且开不~呢! This pot of chrysanthemums won't fade for a long time.

败北 bàiběi 【动】be defeated

败坏 bàihuài 【动】corrupt; undermine; degenerate: ~名誉 damage one's reputation 道德~ morally degenerate

败家 bài = jiā squander a family fortune

败家子 bàijiāzǐ 【名】(~儿) spendthrift; wastrel

败局 bàijú 【名】losing battle

败类 bàilèi 【名】dregs (of society); scum

败露 bàilù 【动】(of a plot) be exposed; be uncovered

败落 bàiluò 【动】decline; be on the decline

败诉 bàisù 【动】lose a lawsuit

败退 bàituì 【动】retreat defeated

败仗 bàizhàng 【名】lost battle; defeat

败阵 bài = zhèn be defeated (on the battlefield); be beaten (in a contest): 败下阵来 be defeated on the battlefield or in a contest

拜

bài 【动】❶ visit ❷ respectfully request (sb. to teach one)

拜倒 bàidǎo 【动】(*fig.*) bow; prostrate oneself; fall on one's knees

拜访 bàifǎng 【动】pay a visit; call on

拜会 bàihuì 【动】make an official visit; pay a call

拜见 bàijiàn 【动】pay a formal visit

拜年 bài = nián pay a New Year's visit; wish sb. a Happy New Year

拜寿 bài = shòu offer (an elderly person) birthday congratulations

拜堂 bài = táng (of bride and groom) perform the wedding ceremony

拜托 bàituō 【动】entrust

稗

bài

稗子 bàizi 【名】barnyard grass

bān

扳

bān 【动】pull; turn (bar, switch, shift gears)

扳子 bānzi 【名】〔把 bǎ〕wrench; spanner

班

bān 【名】❶ class: 甲~ Class A 研究生进修~ postgraduate research class 平行~ classes of the same grade ❷ shift; duty: 日~ day-shift 夜~ night-shift ❸ (mil.) squad: 他是这个~的班长。He is the leader of this squad. 【量】❶ class; squad: 一~学生 a class of students 两~战士 two squads of soldiers ❷ (of people) bunch: 咱们村里这~年轻人真不错。This bunch of young people in our village is really nice.

❸ *for regularly scheduled train*, *bus*, *etc*.：我乘三点的那～汽车走。I'm leaving on the three o'clock bus.

班车　bānchē　【名】scheduled bus

班次　bāncì　【名】classes（in a school）

班底　bāndǐ　【名】the core；the life and soul（of an organization）

班机　bānjī　【名】scheduled flight

班级　bānjí　【名】grades and classes in a school

班门弄斧　Bān mén nòng fǔ　wield an axe at the door of Lu Ban（a famous carpenter in ancient China）；show off one's meagre skill in the presence of an expert

班长　bānzhǎng　【名】❶ monitor（of a class）❷ squad leader

班主任　bānzhǔrèn　【名】teacher in charge of a class

班子　bānzi　【名】a group of people organized for a specific purpose

班组　bānzǔ　【名】teams and groups

般 bān　【助】as；like：兄弟～的友谊 fraternal friendship 暴风雨～的掌声 a storm of applause

般配　bānpèi　【形】match；matchable：这位女士和这位先生很～。This lady and this gentleman are well matched. 她的上衣和裙子太不～。Her jacket and skirt don't match at all.

颁（頒）bān

颁布　bānbù　【动】issue；promulgate：～宪法 promulgate a constitution ～法令 issue a decree

颁发　bānfā　【动】❶ award：～奖状 award a certificate of merit ～证书 award a certificate ❷ issue；promulgate：～命令 issue an order

颁行　bānxíng　【动】issue for enforcement

斑 bān

斑白　bānbái　【形】（of hair）grizzled；grey

斑点　bāndiǎn　【名】stain；spot

斑马　bānmǎ　【名】zebra

斑马线　bānmǎxiàn　【名】zebra crossing

搬 bān　【动】❶ remove；move；take away：把箱子～走 move the trunk away ～掉障碍物 remove the obstacles 把话剧～上银幕 adapt a stage drama for the screen ❷ move；move house：～进新建的宿舍楼 move into a newly-built residential building ❸ copy slavishly：死～教条 slavishly follow dogma

搬家　bān = jiā　move house：～公司 removal firm；removal company

搬弄是非　bānnòng shìfēi　tell tales；gossip（behind people's backs）in order to sow discord

搬起石头打自己的脚　bān qǐ shítou dǎ zìjǐ de jiǎo　lift a rock only to drop it on one's own foot；intend to do injury to sb. else, and wind up hurting oneself instead；hoist with his own petard 也说"搬起石头砸自己的脚"。

搬迁　bānqiān　【动】move

搬运　bānyùn　【动】convey；transport

bǎn

板 bǎn　【名】board；plank；plate：把木头锯成～ saw the timber into planks 金属～ metal plate 【动】be unsmiling；put on a serious expression：～着面孔 keep a long face

板报　bǎnbào　【名】〔张 zhāng〕blackboard newspaper

板擦儿　bǎncār　【名】〔个 gè〕chalk-eraser

板凳　bǎndèng　【名】〔条 tiáo、个 gè〕stool；wooden bench

板结 bǎnjié 【形】(of soil) hard-packed

板书 bǎnshū 【动】write on the blackboard 【名】writing on the blackboard

板子 bǎizi 【名】〔块 kuài〕board; plank

版 bǎn 【名】❶ (printing) plate ❷ edition; printing ❸ (of a newspaper) page

版本 bǎnběn 【名】(of books) edition

版画 bǎnhuà 【名】〔张 zhāng、幅 fú〕engraving; print; block print

版面 bǎnmiàn 【名】❶ layout of a printed sheet ❷ a printed sheet

版权 bǎnquán 【名】copyright

版权页 bǎnquányè 【名】copyright page

版税 bǎnshuì 【名】royalty (on books)

版图 bǎntú 【名】domain; territory

bàn

办 (辦) bàn 【动】❶ do; handle; manage; attend to: ～手续 go through the formalities 这件事你～得了～不了? Can you handle the matter or not? ❷ run; set up; start; found: ～电视大学 run a university which uses television teaching 大～农业 go in for agriculture in a big way ❸ punish; bring to justice: 首恶必 ～。The principal criminals must be punished.

办案 bàn = àn handle a legal case

办报 bàn = bào run a newspaper

办不到 bàn bu dào not feasible; can't be done: 你想一手遮天、～! You think you can block out the sky with one hand (deceive the whole world)? It can't be done!

办法 bànfǎ 【名】way; method; means

办公 bàn = gōng do office or administrative work

办公室 bàngōngshì 【名】office

办公自动化 bàngōng zìdònghuà automated office work

办理 bànlǐ 【动】attend to; deal with; handle

办事 bàn = shì take care of one's affairs; do business

办事处 bànshìchù 【名】office

办事员 bànshìyuán 【名】a clerk

办学 bàn = xué run a school

半 bàn 【数】❶ half ① *when used without a whole number, it is placed before the measure word or the noun which does not need a measure word*: ～公斤苹果 half a kg. of apples ～年 half a year ② *when used with a whole number, it is placed after the measure word or the noun which does not need a measure word*: 两岁～的孩子 a two-and-a-half year old child 一天～的时间 one day and a half ❷ in the middle of: ～山腰 half-way up the mountain ❸ *plus a measure word used in a negative sentence forms an emphatic negative expression*: ～点儿希望也没有。It's utterly hopeless. ❹ semi: ～机械化 semi-mechanization ～旧的衣服 half-worn clothing 门～开着。The door stood ajar.

半…半… bàn… bàn… *with two words or morphemes with contrary meanings, indicates the co-existence of opposite qualities*: 半明半暗 half-light and half-dark; dim 半真半假 partly true and partly false 半文半白 half classical and half colloquial 半信半疑 half believing, half doubtful (somewhat suspicious)

半辈子 bànbèizi 【名】half a lifetime

半边天 bàn biān tiān half the sky

(referring to the women of new China)：充分发挥～的作用 give full scope to women's abilities 妇女能顶～。Women hold up half the sky.

半成品　bànchéngpǐn　【名】partly finished product

半大不小　bàn dà bù xiǎo　adolescent；quite a grown-up

半导体　bàndǎotǐ　【名】transistor；semiconductor

半岛　bàndǎo　【名】peninsula

半吊子　bàndiàozi　【名】an unreliable person

半封建　bàn fēngjiàn　semi-feudalism

半工半读　bàn gōng bàn dú　part work，part study

半价　bànjià　【名】half price

半截　bàn jié　half (of sth.)；～烟卷儿 half of a cigarette 他话说了～儿。He stopped what he was saying halfway through.

半斤八两　bàn jīn bā liǎng　six of one and half-a-dozen of the other；There is not much to choose between the two. (derog.)

半径　bànjìng　【名】radius

半路　bànlù　【名】midway；halfway

半票　bànpiào　【名】a half-price ticket

半三声　bànsānshēng　【名】half-third tone (in Putonghua)

半生　bànshēng　【名】half of one's life-time

半天　bàntiān　【名】quite a while；a long time：我给你解释了这么～，你还不明白。I have spent such a long time explaining it to you, but you still do not understand. 我等了～，他才来。I waited for quite a long time before he turned up.

半途　bàntú　【名】halfway；midway

半途而废　bàn tú ér fèi　give up halfway；leave sth. unfinished：这项试验一定要搞到底，不能～。We must carry the experiment through to the end, and not give up halfway.

半夜　bànyè　【名】mid-night；in the middle of the night

半元音　bànyuányīn　【名】semi-vowel

半圆　bànyuán　【名】semicircle

半月刊　bànyuèkān　【名】semimonthly (a periodical)；fortnightly

半殖民地　bàn zhímíndì　semi-colony

扮 bàn　【动】❶ be dressed up as sb.：女～男装 a woman dressed up as a man ❷ play the part of；act：在这出戏里他～个老工人。He played the part of a veteran worker in the play.

扮演　bànyǎn　【动】play the part of；play (a role in a play, etc.)

伴 bàn　【名】(～儿) companion：我要去南京，想找个～。I'm going to Nanjing and want someone to keep me company. 【动】keep (sb.) company；accompany

伴唱　bànchàng　【动】accompany with singing 【名】a sung accompaniment (e.g. to a dance)

伴侣　bànlǚ　【名】companion

伴随　bànsuí　【动】accompany；follow；follow in sb.'s wake (often followed by 着)：孩子们～着欢乐的乐曲，跳起舞来。Accompanied by cheerful music, the children began to dance.

伴舞　bànwǔ　【动】background dancing

伴奏　bànzòu　【动】(of musical instrument) accompany；to the accompaniment of

拌 bàn　【动】mix

拌嘴　bàn = zuǐ　bicker；squabble；quarrel

绊（絆） bàn　【动】catch (one's foot on sth.)；trip over；stumble over

绊倒　bàn//dǎo　stumble and fall

绊脚石　bànjiǎoshí　【名】stumbling block；obstacle；impediment：骄傲自满是进步的～。Complacency is a stumbling block to progress.

瓣　bàn　【名】（～儿）❶ petal：这种花有几个～? How many petals has this flower? ❷ segment；section；clove：蒜～ garlic clove【量】（～儿）segment；section：三～橘子 3 segments of a tangerine 把苹果切四～ cut the apple into quarters

bāng

邦　bāng

邦交　bāngjiāo　【名】diplomatic relations

帮（幫）　bāng　【动】help；assist：～妈妈洗衣服 help mother do the washing 互～互学 help and learn from each other【名】❶ side（of a car, boat, shoe, etc.）：车～ the sides of a cart 船～ the sides of a boat 鞋～ the upper of a shoe ❷ band；gang；clique：边境山区常有马～来往。Caravans often come to the mountain areas along the border.【量】（of people）group：一～孩子 a group of children

帮会　bānghuì　【名】secret society；underworld gang

帮忙　bāng = máng　help；lend a (helping) hand

帮腔　bāng = qiāng　❶ choral accompaniment ❷ back；support（sb.）；chime in

帮手　bāngshou　【名】helper；assistant

帮凶　bāngxiōng　【名】accomplice

帮助　bāngzhù　【动】help；aid；assist【名】help；assistance

bǎng

绑（綁）　bǎng　【动】tie；bind

绑架　bǎngjià　【动】kidnap

榜　bǎng　【名】list of names posted on a notice-board or wall（e.g. of successful candidates）

榜样　bǎngyàng　【名】example；model；pattern

bàng

棒　bàng　【名】◇ stick；club；cudgel【形】（physically）strong；skillful：～小伙子 strong young fellow 他小提琴拉得真～。He plays the violin very well.

棒槌　bàngchui　【名】❶ a wooden club used to beat clothes in washing ❷ a layman（a term used in theatrical circles）

棒球　bàngqiú　【名】〔个 gè〕❶ baseball ❷ baseball game

棒子　bàngzi　【名】❶ stick；club；cudgel ❷ maize；corn

傍　bàng

傍晚　bàngwǎn　【名】evening；nightfall

磅　bàng　【量】pound
另见 páng

磅秤　bàngchèng　【名】〔台 tái〕scales（for weighing）

镑（鎊）　bàng　【名】pound（unit of money）

bāo

包　bāo　【名】❶（～儿）package；

packet：纸～ parcel wrapped in paper ❷ swelling；bump；lump：腿上起了个～。He has got a bump on his leg.【动】❶ wrap：把东西～起来 wrap things up 纸～不住火。You cannot wrap fire in paper, i.e. You can't conceal facts. ❷ take responsibility for the whole thing：这些活儿我们组～了。Our group will do all the work. ❸ assure；guarantee：～你满意。I guarantee you satisfaction. ❹ book all the tickets (for a film, play, etc.)；charter：我们公司今天～了一场电影。Our company has bought out all the tickets for today's film.【量】pack；packet；package；bundle：一～点心 a package of cakes

包办 bāobàn 【动】take everything on oneself；run the whole show；keep everything in one's own hands

包庇 bāobì 【动】shield or harbour (a wrong-doer)

包产 bāochǎn 【动】make a production contract

包袱 bāofu 【名】❶ bundle wrapped in cloth：手里提着一个～ with a cloth-wrapped bundle in one's hand ❷ (fig.) mental burden：背思想～ be spiritually weighed down

包干儿 bāo = gānr be responsible for a task until it is completed；take on full responsibility for a task：剩下的这点儿活儿，我们俩～了。Just leave all the unfinished work to the two of us.

包工 bāo = gōng contract for a construction project

包裹 bāoguǒ 【名】parcel；package

包含 bāohán 【动】contain；embody

包涵 bāohan 【动】be tolerant towards；not too exacting (used apologetically to request tolerance towards one's weaknesses)

包伙 bāo = huǒ get or supply all meals at a fixed rate (e.g. by week or month)；board

包括 bāokuò 【动】include；embrace；contain：语言教学～听、说、读、写四个方面。Language teaching includes four aspects: listening, speaking, reading and writing. 本学期上课时间为二十周，其中～复习和考试。There will be twenty weeks of class this term, including review and exams. 我们村子有七百亩土地，～新修的梯田在内。Our village has seven hundred mu of land, including the newly terraced fields.

包揽 bāolǎn 【动】～生意 undertake the whole thing：do all the business

包罗万象 bāoluó wànxiàng all-embracing；all-inclusive；comprehensive

包围 bāowéi 【动】surround；encircle；besiege

包销 bāoxiāo 【动】have exclusive selling rights；be the sole agent for

包扎 bāozā 【动】❶ dress (a wound) ❷ wrap up；pack up

包子 bāozi 【名】stuffed steamed bun

包装 bāozhuāng 【动】wrap up；pack 【名】packing

包租 bāozū 【动】rent；hire；charter

剥 bāo 【动】peel；skin

另见 bō

褒 bāo

褒贬 bāobiǎn 【动】estimate；appraise：不加～ make no comment；neither praise nor blame ～人物 make a critical appraisal of sb.

褒贬 bāobian 【动】blame；speak ill of：有意～ spread gossip with malicious intent ～别人 speak ill of others

褒义词 bāoyìcí 【名】word which is laudatory or complimentary

báo

雹 báo 【名】◇ hailstone

雹子 báozi 【名】hailstone

薄 báo 【形】❶ thin：～纸 thin paper ～棉衣 thin cotton-padded clothes ❷（fundamentally）weak：数学底子～ weak in mathematics 解放初咱们的工业底子～。In the early post-liberation years, the industrial foundation of our country was weak. ❸ poor；not fertile：土质～ poor soil
另见 bó

bǎo

饱（飽）bǎo 【形】❶ full ❷ （of eating）full；having eaten one's fill

饱和 bǎohé 【形】saturated

饱经风霜 bǎo jīng fēngshuāng weather-beaten；toughened by a long experience of the hardships of life：他是一位～的老人。He is an old man who has survived the ups and downs of life.

饱满 bǎomǎn 【形】❶ well filled-out；plump：颗粒～ plump grains （of wheat, rice, etc.）❷ full （of vigour, etc.）：精神～ energetic

饱食终日，无所用心 bǎo shí zhōngrì, wú suǒ yòng xīn eat three square meals a day and do nothing

宝（寶）bǎo 【名】treasure

宝贝 bǎobèi 【名】❶ treasure；treasured object ❷（of children）darling

宝岛 bǎodǎo 【名】a precious island；a treasure island

宝贵 bǎoguì 【形】valuable；precious

宝剑 bǎojiàn 【名】〔把 bǎ〕double-edged sword

宝库 bǎokù 【名】treasure-house

宝石 bǎoshí 【名】precious stone；gem

宝塔 bǎotǎ 【名】〔座 zuò〕pagoda

宝藏 bǎozàng 【名】❶ treasure-trove ❷ ore deposits

宝座 bǎozuò 【名】throne

保 bǎo 【动】❶ defend；protect：～家卫国 protect one's home and defend one's country ❷ keep；retain：～住冠军称号 keep the championship title ❸ assure：～你能看上这出戏。I will make sure that you see this play. ～你不出危险。Rest assured there is no danger.

保安 bǎo'ān 【动】❶ ensure public security ❷ ensure safety

保镖 bǎobiāo 【名】bodyguard

保藏 bǎocáng 【动】preserve；keep：～历史文物 preserve historic cultural relics

保持 bǎochí 【动】keep；maintain；preserve：～清洁 keep clean ～记录 hold a record ～优良传统 preserve good traditions ～清醒的头脑 keep a cool head

保存 bǎocún 【动】keep；preserve；conserve：～资料 preserve reference material ～实力 conserve one's strength 这张珍贵的照片，她一直～着。She has preserved this precious photograph through thick and thin.

保单 bǎodān 【名】warranty

保底 bǎo = dǐ set no minimum quota：上不封顶，下不～。Set neither a maximum nor a minimum quota.

保管 bǎoguǎn 【动】❶ keep；take care of：～粮食 take care of grain ～文件 be in charge of documents ～图书 take care of books ❷ be certain；be sure：天天坚持锻炼，～身

体好。You will certainly keep fit if you exercise every day.【名】keeper

保护 bǎohù 【动】protect; safeguard: ～幼苗 protect the young seedlings ～人民利益 safeguard the interests of the people ～现场 preserve the scene (of a crime or accident) undisturbed

保护伞 bǎohùsǎn 【名】(*fig.*) protective umbrella

保护色 bǎohùsè 【名】❶ protective colouration (of animal or insect) ❷ camouflage

保健 bǎojiàn 【名】health protection; health care

保健操 bǎojiàncāo 【名】setting-up exercises; fitness exercises

保龄球 bǎolíngqiú 【名】bowling ball

保留 bǎoliú 【动】❶ retain; maintain; reserve: ～自己的意见 reserve one's opinion 这座古建筑还～着当年的面貌。This ancient building has preserved its original appearance. ❷ not give away; keep: 他收藏的大部分国画都献给了博物馆，自己只～了一小部分。He donated the bulk of his collection of Chinese paintings to the museum and kept only a few pieces for himself. 老师傅毫无～地把技术传授给徒弟。The old worker passed on his skills to his apprentices without holding anything back.

保留剧目 bǎoliú jùmù repertory; repertoire

保密 bǎo = mì keep secret; maintain secrecy

保姆 bǎomǔ 【名】woman employed to take care of a child or do housework

保全 bǎoquán 【动】save; preserve: 幸亏及时抢救，这孩子的腿才～下来了。Thanks to a timely rescue, the child's leg was saved.

保人 bǎorén 【名】❶ guarantor ❷ bail

保墒 bǎo = shāng keep or preserve moisture in the topsoil

保守 bǎoshǒu 【动】guard; keep: ～机密 keep a secret 【形】conservative: 思想 ～ be conservative in one's thinking 计划订得一点儿也不 ～。The plan was in no way conservative.

保送 bǎosòng 【动】send (sb.) on recommendation (e.g. to college)

保卫 bǎowèi 【动】defend; safeguard

保险 bǎoxiǎn 【形】❶ safe; secure: 打井时戴上安全帽比较～。It's safer to wear a protective helmet when drilling a well. ❷ be bound to; be sure to; guarantee: 把工作交给他，～能干好。If he is given the job, he is sure to do it well. 【名】insurance: 社会～ social insurance

保险公司 bǎoxiǎn gōngsī insurance company

保险丝 bǎoxiǎnsī 【名】fuse

保险箱 bǎoxiǎnxiāng 【名】safe; strong-box

保养 bǎoyǎng 【动】❶ take care of (one's health) ❷ maintain; keep in good repair

保育员 bǎoyùyuán 【名】nursery school teacher

保障 bǎozhàng 【动】secure; ensure; guarantee; safeguard: ～公民权利 guarantee citizens' rights 发展经济，～供给 develop the economy and ensure supplies 【名】security; guarantee: 安全是增产的～。Safety is the best guarantee of a rise in production.

保证 bǎozhèng 【动】pledge; guarantee; assure; ensure: ～按期完工 make a pledge to complete a task on schedule 【名】guarantee: 团结是我们事业胜利的～。Unity is the best guarantee of the victory of our cause.

保值　bǎo = zhí　protect the buying power of the currency

保质保量　bǎo zhì bǎo liàng　guarantee both quality and quantity

保重　bǎozhòng　【动】(hope a person will) look after (himself)

堡 bǎo

堡垒　bǎolěi　【名】fortification；fortress；fort；stronghold

bào

报（報）

bào　【动】❶ report；announce；declare；～捷 report victory ～信儿 give information ～时 (clock) strike the hours；tell the correct time ～上级批准 report sth. to a higher level for approval ❷ ◇ respond；～以热烈的掌声 respond with warm applause 【名】❶〔份 fèn，张 zhāng〕newspaper；读书看～ read books and papers ❷ telegram；发～ send a telegram 收～ receive a telegram

报案　bào = àn　report a case to the security authorities

报表　bàobiǎo　【名】forms for reporting statistics，etc.；report forms

报仇　bào = chóu　revenge；avenge

报仇雪恨　bào chóu xuě hèn　avenge oneself and cancel out one's hatred

报酬　bàochou　【名】reward；remuneration

报答　bàodá　【动】requite；repay

报到　bào = dào　report (for duty)；report in person；check in

报道　bàodào　【动】report；cover；～消息 report news 【名】report；写了一篇～ write a news report 也作"报导(dǎo)"

报废　bàofèi　【动】report (to the person in charge) that sth. is no longer usable

报复　bàofù　【动】retaliate；get even (with sb.)【名】retaliation

报告　bàogào　【动】report；tell (a piece of news)【名】report (written or oral)；talk；speech

报告文学　bàogào wénxué　reportage

报关　bàoguān　【动】declare sth. at customs

报话机　bàohuàjī　【名】radiotelephone

报警　bàojǐng　【动】❶ report to the police ❷ give an alarm

报警器　bàojǐngqì　【名】an alarm

报刊　bàokān　【名】newspapers and periodicals；the press

报考　bàokǎo　【动】enter oneself for an examination

报名　bào = míng　enter one's name (for sth.)

报幕　bào = mù　announce items to be performed

报社　bàoshè　【名】newspaper office

报数　bào = shù　number off

报头　bàotóu　【名】masthead (of a newspaper)

报喜　bào = xǐ　announce good news；report success

报销　bàoxiāo　【动】claim payment or refund

报章　bàozhāng　【名】newspapers；～杂志 newspapers and magazines

报账　bào = zhàng　render an account；apply for reimbursement

报纸　bàozhǐ　【名】〔份 fèn，张 zhāng〕❶ newspaper ❷ newsprint

刨 bào　【动】plane

另见 páo

刨床　bàochuáng　【名】〔台 tái〕planer

刨子　bàozi　【名】〔把 bǎ〕(carpenter's) plane

抱

bào　【动】❶ hold or carry in the arms；embrace；hug；～着一大捆麦子 carry a big sheaf of wheat in one's arms 把孩子～起来 take a child up in one's arms ❷ cherish；

harbour; hold: ～着远大的理想 cherish great ideals ～着乐观主义的态度 take an optimistic attitude

抱不平 bàobùpíng 【动】be outraged and impelled to take action by an injustice committed against another person: 为他 ～ defend him against an injustice 打～ defend sb. against an injustice

抱负 bàofù 【名】lofty aim; ideal

抱愧 bàokuì 【动】feel ashamed

抱歉 bàoqiàn 【形】feel sorry; be apologetic

抱屈 bàoqū 【动】feel wronged

抱头鼠窜 bào tóu shǔ cuàn cover one's head and scurry off like a frightened rat: 警方赶到, 暴徒～. When the police arrived, the ruffians fled helter-skelter.

抱怨 bàoyuàn 【动】complain; grumble

豹 bào 【名】〔只 zhī〕leopard

暴 bào 【形】❶ sudden and violent; fierce ❷ short-tempered

暴病 bàobìng 【名】sudden attack of a serious illness

暴跌 bàodiē 【动】steep fall (in price)

暴动 bàodòng 【动】resort to insurrection 【名】insurrection

暴发户 bàofāhù 【名】upstart; parvenu

暴风雪 bàofēngxuě 【名】snowstorm

暴风雨 bàofēngyǔ 【名】storm

暴风骤雨 bào fēng zhòu yǔ violent storm (*often used to describe the surging up of revolutionary mass movements*)

暴君 bàojūn 【名】tyrant; despot

暴力 bàolì 【名】violence; force

暴利 bàolì 【名】fabulous profits; extravagant profits

暴露 bàolù 【动】expose; unmask; reveal; lay bare

暴露无遗 bàolù wú yí completely exposed; completely unmasked

暴乱 bàoluàn 【名】riot

暴跳如雷 bào tiào rú léi stamp with rage; stamp about in a frenzy

暴徒 bàotú 【名】ruffian

暴行 bàoxíng 【名】atrocity; savage act; outrage

暴雨 bàoyǔ 【名】rainstorm; torrential downpour

暴躁 bàozào 【形】short-tempered; irascible

暴政 bàozhèng 【名】tyranny

曝 bào

曝光 bào = guāng ❶ expose to the light ❷ expose to the public: 这件事在社会上曝了光。This incident became known to the public.

爆 bào 【动】explode; burst

爆发 bàofā 【动】erupt; break out; burst: 火山 ～ 了。The volcano erupted. ～战争了。War broke out. 全场～出雷鸣般的掌声。The entire hall burst into thunderous applause.

爆冷门 bào lěngmén produce an unexpected winner

爆裂 bàoliè 【动】explode

爆满 bàomǎn 【动】fill to capacity; have a full house

爆破 bàopò 【动】blow up; explode

爆炸 bàozhà 【动】explode

爆炸物 bàozhàwù 【名】explosive

爆竹 bàozhú 【名】fire-cracker

bēi

杯 bēi 【名】◇ cup

杯子 bēizi 【名】〔个 gè〕cup

卑 bēi 【形】◇ low; lowly; mean

卑鄙 bēibǐ 【形】despicable; con-

temptible；mean；base

卑鄙无耻　bēibǐ wúchǐ　utterly shameless；base and shameless

卑躬屈膝　bēi gōng qū xī　cringing；subservient；obsequious 也作"卑躬屈节"。

卑贱　bēijiàn　【形】❶ of low rank or humble position；lowly ❷ despicable；contemptible；ignoble

卑劣　bēiliè　【形】（of persons，behaviour）sordid；abject；base；mean

卑微　bēiwēi　【形】lowly；humble

背　bēi　【动】carry on one's back：～枪 carry a. rifle on one's back ～背包 carry a knapsack on one's back

另见 bèi

背包　bēibāo　【名】knapsack；rucksack

背包袱　bēi bāofu　be spiritually weighed down：这次考试没考好，不要～。Though your examination result is not satisfactory，you mustn't let it weigh on your mind. 工作取得了成绩，可不能背上骄傲自满的包袱。You shouldn't let conceit keep you from further achievements.

悲　bēi　【形】sad；grieved

悲哀　bēi'āi　【形】sorrowful；grieved

悲惨　bēicǎn　【形】miserable；tragic

悲愤　bēifèn　【形】grieved and indignant

悲观　bēiguān　【形】pessimistic

悲剧　bēijù　【名】❶ tragedy ❷ sad event

悲伤　bēishāng　【形】sorrowful

悲痛　bēitòng　【形】grieved；distressed；sorrowful

悲壮　bēizhuàng　【形】sad but heroic and stirring：～的诗篇 sad but stirring poetry ～的乐曲 sad but stirring music ～的事迹 heroic and stirring deed

碑　bēi　【名】〔块 kuài、座 zuò〕stone tablet；stele；monument

碑文　bēiwén　【名】inscription on a memorial tablet

běi

北　běi　【名】north

北边　běibiān　【名】north；to the north

北冰洋　Běibīngyáng　【名】the Arctic Ocean

北斗星　běidǒuxīng　【名】the Dipper；the Plough

北伐战争　Běifá Zhànzhēng　the Northern Expedition against the Imperialists and the Northern Warlords（1926—1927）

北方　běifāng　【名】the northern part of；north

北极　běijí　【名】North Pole

北极圈　běijíquān　【名】the Arctic Circle

北极星　běijíxīng　【名】Polaris；the North star；the polestar

北京　Běijīng　【名】capital of the People's Republic of China

北京时间　Běijīng shíjiān　Beijing time

北京猿人　Běijīng Yuánrén　Peking Man（sinanthropus Pekinensis）

北美洲　Běiměizhōu　【名】North America

bèi

备（備）　bèi　【动】❶ ◇ have；be equipped with：万事俱～，只欠东风。Everything is ready except what is most crucial. ❷ prepare；get ready：～料 get the materials ready ～而不用 get sth. ready in

case one may need it in the future
❸ ◇ prepare for; be on guard against; 以～万一 prepare for all eventualities ❹ ◇ all; in all possible ways; 关怀～至 show every possible concern for ～受欢迎 be warmly welcomed

备案 bèi'àn 【动】 put on record; enter (a case) in the records

备耕 bèi = gēng prepare for ploughing and sowing

备荒 bèi = huāng be prepared against natural disasters; be prepared in case of famine

备件 bèijiàn 【名】 spare parts

备考 bèikǎo 【名】 additional information (on a form)

备课 bèi = kè (of teachers) prepare lessons

备料 bèi = liào ❶ get the materials ready ❷ prepare feed (for livestock)

备取 bèiqǔ 【动】 be on the waiting list

备忘录 bèiwànglù 【名】 memorandum; aide-memoire; written reminder

备用 bèiyòng 【动】 reserve; spare

备战 bèi = zhàn ❶ prepare for war ❷ be prepared against war

备注 bèizhù 【名】 comments on information (on a form)

背 bèi 【名】 ❶ (of person) back ❷ (of thing) back; 刀～儿 the back of a knife 椅～儿 the back of a chair 【动】 ❶ recite; learn by heart; 这首诗他能～出来。 He can recite this poem by heart. ❷ ◇ with its back towards; ～山面水 with the hill behind and the river in front ❸ turn away; ～过身去 turn around 把脸～过去 turn one's face away
另见 bēi

背道而驰 bèi dào ér chí (of two things) tend in opposite directions; 这种思想是和时代的要求～的。 This notion runs counter to the mood of the times.

背风 bèi = fēng ❶ out of the wind; 这里向阳而且～。 This spot faces the sun and is out of the wind. ❷ leeward

背光 bèi = guāng with one's back to the light

背后 bèihòu 【名】 behind; at the back; behind sb.'s back

背景 bèijǐng 【名】 ❶ background; setting ❷ backdrop

背离 bèilí 【动】 deviate; depart from

背面 bèimiàn 【名】 back; wrong side; reverse side

背叛 bèipàn 【动】 betray

背书 bèi = shū recite a lesson; learn a text by heart

背诵 bèisòng 【动】 recite; say by heart

背心 bèixīn 【名】 〔件 jiàn〕 vest

背信弃义 bèi xìn qì yì perfidious; treacherous

背影 bèiyǐng (～儿) 【名】 a view of sb.'s back

背约 bèiyuē go back on one's word, breach an agreement

背着 bèizhe 【动】 behind (sb.'s) back; ～人干坏事 do sth. bad behind people's backs 你们俩嘀咕什么? 干吗～大家? What are you two whispering about? Why do things behind others' backs?

倍 bèi 【量】 ...-time; ...-fold

倍加 bèijiā 【副】 extra; ～赞扬 give extra praise to ～爱护 take extra care of

倍数 bèishù 【名】 multiple

倍塔射线 bèitǎ shèxiàn 【名】 beta ray

倍增 bèizēng 【动】 double; increase

被 bèi 【名】〔床 chuáng〕quilt

【介】 *used in a passive sentence to introduce the agent*：他～电话铃惊醒了。He was wakened by the ringing of the telephone. 书～小李借走了。The book was borrowed and taken away by Xiao Li. Note：❶ *sometimes the agent need not be mentioned*：阴谋～揭穿了。The plot was exposed. ❷ *if there is an auxiliary verb or adverb, it must be placed before* 被：他们没有～困难吓倒。They were not daunted by difficulties. 他一定能～选为代表。I'm sure he will be elected a delegate. ❸ *the main verb in a* 被 *sentence must take some element after it*：山坡上的石板路～雨水冲得干干净净。The stone path of the mountain slope was washed very clean by the rain.

被乘数 bèichéngshù 【名】multiplicand

被除数 bèichúshù 【名】dividend

被单 bèidān 【名】〔条 tiáo〕sheet; bedsheet

被动 bèidòng 【形】passive

被动式 bèidòngshì 【名】passive form; passive voice

被告 bèigào 【名】the accused; the defendant

被告人 bèigàorén 【名】the defendant; the accused

被告席 bèigàoxí 【名】(of court) dock

被害人 bèihàirén 【名】victim; injured party

被减数 bèijiǎnshù 【名】(maths.) minuend; number from which another number is subtracted

被里 bèilǐ 【名】the inner cotton lining of a quilt

被面 bèimiàn （～儿）【名】the covering of a quilt

被迫 bèi pò be forced; be compelled：法西斯侵略者～宣布无条件投降。The fascists were forced to declare an unconditional surrender.

被…所… bèi...suǒ... "所" *is used with* "被" *to emphasize the passive voice*：小王的父亲是一位被大家所尊敬的学者。Xiao Wang's father is a scholar highly respected by all who know him. 这个新产品的优越性已经被越来越多的事实所证明。More and more facts demonstrate the superiority of this new product.

被选举权 bèixuǎnjǔquán 【名】the right to be elected

被子 bèizi 【名】〔床 chuáng〕quilt; cotton-padded quilt

辈（輩）bèi 【名】❶ generation ❷ life; lifetime

辈子 bèizi 【名】 *must take a numeral or* 这 *or* 那 *before it* ❶ lifetime ❷ generation

bei

呗（唄）bei 【助】❶ *indicates forced agreement*：你一定要去，就去～! Since you insist on going, well, go. 他既然那么喜欢这张画儿，就给他～! If he is that fond of this painting, well, give it to him. ❷ *indicates that sth. is very obvious*：不会做就学着做～. If you don't know how to do it, well, learn how. 雪是谁扫的? ——我弟弟～! Who has shovelled the snow? —My younger brother. (Who else could it be!)

bēn

奔 bēn 【动】◇run quickly; hurry：东～西跑 run hither and thither 列车在飞～。The train is flying

past.

另见 bèn

奔波 bēnbō 【动】 be on the go; be busy running about

奔驰 bēnchí 【动】 gallop; speed

奔放 bēnfàng 【形】 (of feelings or style of writing) bold and unrestrained

奔赴 bēnfù 【动】 rush to; hasten to: ～前线 hurry to the front

奔流 bēnliú 【动】 flow at a great speed

奔忙 bēnmáng 【动】 be busy rushing about

奔跑 bēnpǎo 【动】 run

奔腾 bēnténg 【动】 ❶ gallop ❷ surge forward

奔走 bēnzǒu 【动】 ❶ run: ～相告 run around to tell each other (the news) ❷ bustle about with a certain purpose: 四处～ rush purposefully here and there

běn

本 běn 【名】 ❶ root or stem of a plant ❷ root or source of things: 这个办法只能治标，不能治～。 This way, you can only treat the symptoms but not reach the heart of the problem. ❸ (～儿) notebook: 他买了个～。 He bought an exercise book. ❹ ◇ edition: 合订～ bound volume (of consecutive issues of periodicals, newspapers, etc.) 精装 ～ deluxe edition 影印～ photostated edition ❺ (of business) capital 【形】 ❶ one's own: ～校 our school ～厂 our factory ～单位 our unit ❷ present; current: ～世纪 this century ～月 this month ～周 this week 【量】 for books, etc.: 两～工作手册 two handbooks 【副】 originally; at first: 他～想来看你，因为忙没有来成。 He had wanted to come and see you, but he had no time.

本部 běnbù 【名】 headquarters: 校 ～ the main campus

本地 běndì 【名】 local; native

本分 běnfèn 【名】 one's duty

本国 běnguó 【名】 one's own country

本行 běnháng 【名】 one's own profession; one's line

本科 běnkē 【名】 undergraduate course

本科生 běnkēshēng 【名】 undergraduate

本来 běnlái 【形】 original *usu. used attributively or adverbially, but not as a predicate or complement*: 几年没回家，我的家乡不是～的样子了。 I've been away for a couple of years, and my hometown has changed from its original appearance. ～的计划被否定了。 The original plan has been turned down. 【副】 as a matter of course: 当天的工作～就应该当天做完。 A day's work should be finished at the end of the day as a matter of course. 你看他在台上那个紧张的样子。——～嘛，台下有那么多眼睛瞧着他。 He looks so nervous on the platform! —How can you blame him with so many eyes staring at him?

本利 běnlì 【名】 principal and interest

本领 běnlǐng 【名】 skill; ability; capability; know-how

本名 běnmíng 【名】 original name; first name

本末倒置 běn mò dàozhì put the cart before the horse; confuse cause and effect: 看问题要抓住本质，如果只强调非本质的东西，就会～，得出错误的结论。 If you put focus on nonessentials, you put the cart before the horse and will arrive at the wrong conclusion.

本能 běnnéng 【名】 instinct

本钱 běnqián 【名】capital

本人 běnrén 【代】❶ oneself：～简历 one's curriculum vitae 毕业证书让～来领。Everybody should come and receive his diploma in person. 这个计划，老李～也认为应该修改。Lao Li himself thought this plan should be revised. ❷ me or I （when referring to oneself in speaking）

本色 běnsè 【名】intrinsic character；true qualities

本身 běnshēn 【代】itself：这收音机～没有毛病，大概是插销接触不良。There's nothing wrong with the radio itself. Perhaps something is wrong with the connection.

本事 běnshi 【名】ability；skill

本土 běntǔ 【名】native land

本位 běnwèi 【名】❶ standard：金～gold standard ❷ one's own department or unit：应该做好～工作。One ought to do one's own job well.

本位货币 běnwèi huòbì the basic monetary unit of a country's currency

本位主义 běnwèizhǔyì 【名】departmental chauvinism

本息 běnxī 【名】capital and interest

本相 běnxiàng 【名】true colours

本心 běnxīn 【名】true intention；real intention

本性 běnxìng 【名】natural character；disposition

本义 běnyì 【名】original meaning；literal sense

本意 běnyì 【名】original intention

本着 běnzhe 【介】according to；based on（equivalent to 按照 or 根据，its object is usu. an abstract noun such as 精神，原则）：我们～节约的精神办一切事业。We must be frugal in managing our enterprises. ～实事求是的态度进行科学分析。One must make a scientific analysis in line with the principle of seeking truth from facts.

本质 běnzhì 【名】innate character；intrinsic quality；essence

本子 běnzi 【名】〔本 běn〕note-book；exercise book

bèn

奔 bèn 【动】❶ go straight；head for：～向前方 march forward 他顺着小河直～扬水站。He followed the stream and came right to the pumping station. ❷ approach（the age of fifty, sixty, etc.）：她是～六十岁的人了，可是精力仍然很充沛。She is getting on for sixty and still quite energetic.

另见 bēn

奔头 bèntou 【名】prospects；prospective achievements：有～have prospects in view 没～have no prospects

笨 bèn 【形】❶ stupid ❷ clumsy ❸（of a thing, building, etc.）heavy；cumbersome and lacking in grace

笨蛋 bèndàn 【名】stupid fellow；clumsy person

笨手笨脚 bèn shǒu bèn jiǎo clumsy

笨重 bènzhòng 【形】❶ cumbersome；heavy and awkward to carry ❷ heavy and arduous

笨拙 bènzhuō 【形】clumsy；stupid

bēng

崩 bēng 【动】❶ collapse；crumble：山～地裂。The mountain crumbled and the earth cracked. ❷ break down；burst：车胎～了。The tire blew out. 两个人谈～了。The talks between the two broke down. ❸ be hit by sth. exploding：

放鞭炮～了手。The firecracker exploded in his hand as he was lighting it.

崩溃 bēngkuì【动】collapse；crumble

崩裂 bēngliè【动】crack；burst apart

崩塌 bēngtā【动】crumble；collapse

绷（綳）bēng【动】stretch
tight：请你把绳子～紧。Please pull the rope tight. 这件上衣太小了，～在身上很不舒服。The jacket is too tight, it's uncomfortable.
另见 běng

绷带 bēngdài【名】bandage：几卷～ several rolls of bandage 这位伤员头上缠着～。The soldier's head was bandaged.

běng

绷（綳）běng【动】〈口〉
tighten：～着脸不说话 keep a face and remain speechless
另见 bēng

bèng

迸 bèng【动】burst forth；spurt

迸发 bèngfā【动】burst out；burst forth

迸裂 bèngliè【动】burst；split；burst open

蹦 bèng【动】bounce；jump；hop

bī

逼 bī【动】❶ force；threaten；press：你简直是～我表态。You are simply forcing me to take a stand. ❷ extort：～债 extort payment of a debt ～供 extort a confession

逼近 bījìn【动】gain on；close in on

逼迫 bīpò【动】force；compel；con-

strain

逼上梁山 bī shàng Liángshān be driven to revolt；be forced to do sth.

逼问 bīwèn【动】question closely；force sb. to answer

逼真 bīzhēn【形】❶ life-like；vivid ❷ distinct；clear

bí

鼻 bí【名】◇ nose

鼻孔 bíkǒng【名】nostril

鼻腔 bíqiāng【名】nasal cavity

鼻涕 bítì【名】nasal mucus；snot

鼻音 bíyīn【名】nasal sound；nasal

鼻子 bízi【名】nose

bǐ

匕 bǐ

匕首 bǐshǒu【名】〔把 bǎ〕dagger

比 bǐ【动】❶ compete：我们要～干劲～贡献。We ought to compete both in our spirit of dedication and in the results achieved. ❷ make a gesture (with one's hand)：他用手～了一下说："那些树苗有这么高了。"Gesturing with his hand, he said："The saplings are this tall." ❸ follow (a pattern) usu. takes 着：～着纸样裁衣服 cut the cloth according to the pattern ❹ draw an analogy here 比 is followed by 作，为 or 成：人们常把见识少、眼光短浅的人，～成"井底之蛙"。There is a well-known analogy between a frog at the bottom of a pond and a person with tunnel vision. ❺ to (used in giving scores in competition)：十一～～七 11 to 7 甲队以二～一取胜。Team A won by 2 to 1. ❻ compare：不怕不识货，就怕货～货。

Don't worry about consumer information, just compare and you'll see the difference.【名】(maths.) ratio：一与三之～ in the ratio of 1：3【介】❶ *indicates comparison*：他～我小三岁。He is three years younger than I. 他跑得不～我快。He doesn't run faster than I do. 这个农场今年～去年多开垦了三千亩荒地。This farm reclaimed 3000 more *mu* of wasteland this year than last. 今天～昨天冷得多。It's much colder today than yesterday. ❷ — *plus measure word or noun which doesn't need a measure word used both before and after* 比 *to mean "more and more"*：产量一年～一年高。The output gets bigger every year. 生活一天～一天好。Life is getting better every day.

比比皆是 bǐbǐ jiē shì　many；(of thing, person, etc.) such as can be found everywhere：这个山区充分利用水力发电，几年的工夫，小水电站就～。This mountainous area has made full use of waterpower, and the whole place has become dotted with small hydroelectric power stations in just a few years.

比不上 bǐ bu shàng　cannot be compared with；no match for：我的英语水平～他。My English is no match for his.

比得上 bǐ de shàng　can be compared with；comparable：我的手艺哪儿～他呀！How can my workmanship be compared to his!

比方 bǐfang【名】example；analogy：打个～ give an example 拿学游泳作～ take swimming for example 这不过是个～。This is just an analogy.【连】for example：他很喜欢读鲁迅的小说，～说，《阿Q正传》、《故乡》等。He likes to read Lu Xun's stories, *The True Story of Ah Q, My Old Home*, and so on, for example.

比画 bǐhua【动】gesticulate, also 比划 bǐhua

比价 bǐjià【名】❶ price relations；parity；rate of exchange ❷ compare bids or prices

比较 bǐjiào【动】compare；make a comparison：把这两个方案～一下 make a comparison between these two proposals 和去年同期～，形势有很大发展。Compared with the same period last year, there has been great progress.【副】comparatively：～简单 fairly simple ～成熟 relatively mature ～习惯 quite accustomed to

比例 bǐlì【名】❶ proportion ❷ ratio ❸ scale

比例尺 bǐlìchǐ【名】scale (e.g. on a map)

比例税制 bǐlì shuìzhì proportional tax

比拟 bǐnǐ【动】❶ compare；draw a parallel ❷ metaphor or simile

比如 bǐrú【连】for example；for instance；such as：中国古代有许多重要发明，～指南针、造纸、印刷术、火药等。In ancient China, there were many important inventions, such as the compass, paper-making, printing, gunpowder, and so on.

比赛 bǐsài【动】compete；have a match：～足球 have a football match【名】match；contest；competition：象棋～ chess match 摩托车～ motorcycle race 跳伞～ parachuting contest

比索 bǐsuǒ【名】peso (currency)

比喻 bǐyù【动】compare one thing to another；draw an analogy【名】metaphor；simile

比值 bǐzhí【名】ratio；rate

比重 bǐzhòng【名】❶ specific gravity ❷ proportion

彼 bǐ【代】❶ that；those；the

other；another ❷ one's opposite

彼岸　bǐ'àn　【名】❶ the other shore ❷ nirvana

彼此　bǐcǐ　【代】each other；one another：不分～（of two people）share everything ～一样（of two things）much alike ～呼应（of two things）go together 我们～之间应该互相帮助。We should help each other.

彼一时，此一时　bǐ yī shí, cǐ yī shí　times have changed：～，不要拿老眼光看问题。Times have changed. Don't look at things from an outdated perspective. 也作"此一时，彼一时"。

笔（筆）　bǐ　【名】〔枝 zhī〕❶ pen；pencil；writing brush ❷（of a Chinese character）stroke：“中”字有四～。"中" has four strokes. 这个字少写了一～。One stroke is missing from this character. 【量】for money or things to do with writing：一～钱 a sum of money 记下一～账 keep an account 写一～好字 write a good hand 写信的时候替我带上一～。Please give him my regards when you write.

笔触　bǐchù　【名】style and characteristic of writing or painting

笔调　bǐdiào　【名】writing style

笔杆　bǐgǎn　【名】〔枝 zhī〕❶ holder for a writing brush；pen-holder ❷ pen

笔杆子　bǐgǎnzi　【名】❶ penholder ❷ pen：耍～ wield the pen ❸ an effective writer：他是我们单位的～。He is the most effective writer of our unit.

笔耕　bǐgēng　【动】write

笔画　bǐhuà　【名】stroke of a Chinese character

笔迹　bǐjī　【名】handwriting（as it can be identified as being that of a particular person）

笔记　bǐjì　【名】notes；memorandum

笔记本　bǐjìběn　【名】〔本 běn〕notebook

笔尖　bǐjiān　【名】(～儿) pen-nib

笔录　bǐlù　【名】record；notes 【动】take down

笔名　bǐmíng　【名】pen name

笔墨　bǐmò　【名】pen and ink；(fig.) writing；words

笔试　bǐshì　【名】written examination

笔顺　bǐshùn　【名】order of strokes in writing a Chinese character

笔挺　bǐtǐng　【形】very straight；trim

笔筒　bǐtǒng　【名】pen container

笔误　bǐwù　【名】slip of the pen 【动】make a slip in writing

笔译　bǐyì　【名】written translation 【动】translate (in writing)

笔者　bǐzhě　【名】author

笔直　bǐzhí　【形】perfectly straight；upright：～的路 straight road

鄙　bǐ

鄙薄　bǐbó　【动】despise；scorn

鄙视　bǐshì　【动】despise；disdain；look down upon

币（幣）　bì

币值　bìzhí　【名】value of a currency

币制　bìzhì　【名】currency system；monetary system

必　bì　【副】❶ certainly；surely：我三点～到。I will be there at three. 骄兵～败。An army swollen with pride is bound to lose. ❷ must；have to：～读书目 list of required readings

必不可免　bì bù kě miǎn　unavoidable

必不可少　bì bù kě shǎo　absolutely necessary；indispensable；essential

必定　bìdìng　【副】(usu. in written

language) ❶ *indicates certainty*：有全队的配合, 这场球我们～胜利。If we pull together, we are bound to win this ball game. 这几棵花总不见阳光, ～长不好。These flowers will certainly not grow since they never get any sunshine. ❷ *indicates sureness regarding one's conjecture*：我看那个小伙子～是中学生, 不会是工人。I'm sure that young man is a high school student and not a worker.

必将 bìjiāng 【副】will certainly; surely will：这个建议～引起一场争论。This suggestion will certainly lead to an argument.

必然 bìrán 【形】inevitable; be bound to：～结果 inevitable result ～规律 inexorable law 新生力量～战胜腐朽力量。The newly emerging forces are bound to defeat what is corrupt and moribund.

必然王国 bìrán wángguó realm of necessity

必然性 bìránxìng 【名】inevitability; certainty; necessity

必修课 bìxiūkè 【名】compulsory subject; required course

必须 bìxū 【助动】must; have to; be obliged to：～刻苦学习 must study hard ～马上出发 must start at once Note: *the negative form of* 必须 *is* 无须 *or* 不必.

必需 bìxū 【动】necessary; indispensable：～的日用品 daily necessities 石油是发展工业所～的。Petroleum is indispensable in developing industry. 把资金用在最～的地方。Use the funds where they are most needed.

必需品 bìxūpǐn 【名】necessities

必要 bìyào 【形】essential; necessary：～的措施 necessary measure 进一步讨论是～的。A further discussion on the matter is necessary. ～的时候可以再调两个人来。We can

have two more people transferred here if necessary.

必要性 bìyàoxìng 【名】necessity

必由之路 bì yóu zhī lù road one must follow or take; the only road to; the only way

必争之地 bì zhēng zhī dì hotly contested territory (e.g. in a battle)

毕(畢) bì

毕竟 bìjìng 【副】❶ after all 同"究竟"jiūjìng【副】：他～是个老演员, 舞台经验就是丰富。After all, he is a veteran actor. He has lots of experience on the stage. 个人的力量～是有限的。After all, individual strength is limited. ❷ after all; in the end *indicates reluctance*：他虽然不太愿意, 但～把这个任务接受下来了。Although he was unwilling, he accepted the task after all.

毕生 bìshēng 【名】all one's life; lifelong; life-time

毕业 bì＝yè finish school; graduate

毕业证书 bì yè zhèngshū diploma

闭(閉) bì 【动】shut; close

闭关自守 bì guān zì shǒu closed-door (policy)

闭路电视 bìlùdiànshì 【名】closed-circuit TV

闭门羹 bìméngēng 【名】closed door; (of a visitor) find the door closed because the host is not at home：吃～ be refused entry

闭门造车 bì mén zào chē make a cart behind closed doors; (*fig.*) divorce oneself from reality, and do things without considering the actual conditions

闭目塞听 bì mù sè tīng close one's eyes and stop one's ears; (*fig.*) be out of touch with reality

闭幕 bì＝mù ❶ the curtain falls ❷ (of a conference, etc.) close; conclude

闭塞　bìsè　【形】cut off from the outside world; secluded; out of touch with current affairs; 你可能想不到，这里以前是个很～的地方。You probably won't believe it, but this was a rather secluded spot before. 快来谈谈有什么消息，我病了几天，仿佛很～。Please come and tell me the news. I was ill for a few days and feel rather out of touch. 那里至今交通还很～。Transportation and communication facilities are quite primitive there even now.

庇　bì

庇护　bìhù　【动】(of wrong-doer) shelter; shield; put under one's protection

陛　bì

陛下　bìxià　【名】His (Her, Your) Majesty

毙 (斃)　bì　【动】❶ die ❷ kill; shoot

毙命　bì = mìng　be done for; lose one's life (derog.)

蓖　bì

蓖麻　bìmá　【名】castor-oil plant

碧　bì　【形】◇ emerald green; green or blue

碧绿　bìlǜ　【形】jade green

弊　bì　【名】◇ corrupt practice; drawback; disadvantage; 有百～而无一利。It has a hundred drawbacks and not a single advantage.

弊病　bìbìng　【名】malpractice; corrupt practice; abuse

弊端　bìduān　【名】malpractice; abuse

壁　bì　【名】◇ wall; wall-like structure

壁报　bìbào　【名】wall newspaper

壁橱　bìchú　【名】built-in wardrobe; closet

壁画　bìhuà　【名】fresco; mural

壁垒　bìlěi　【名】❶ fortified barrier ❷ rival camps confronting each other; two sharply opposed sides

壁毯　bìtǎn　【名】tapestry for covering walls

避　bì　【动】avoid; evade; shun; eschew

避而不谈　bì ér bù tán　evade the issue

避讳　bìhuì　【动】regard sth. as taboo; avoid the mention of

避开　bì // kāi　evade; steer clear of; ～敌人的正面火力，从侧面攻上去 steer clear of the enemy's frontal fire, and attack from the flank

避雷器　bìléiqì　【名】lightning conductor

避雷针　bìléizhēn　【名】lightning rod

避免　bìmiǎn　【动】avoid; avert; shun; ～片面性 avoid one-sidedness ～了一场事故 have averted an accident 资本主义的经济危机是无法～的。Economic crisis under capitalism is unavoidable.

避难　bì = nàn　take refuge; seek asylum

避暑　bì = shǔ　avoid the summer heat; take a summer holiday; go to a summer resort for the summer holidays

避孕　bì = yùn　practise contraception; birth control

避重就轻　bì zhòng jiù qīng　❶ shirk the heavy work and choose the light; 工作中要勇于挑重担，不要～。In one's work, one should shoulder the heavy loads of one's own accord, and not try to shift them to others while keeping the light ones for oneself. ❷ avoid the important

and dwell on the trivial

biān

边（邊） biān 【名】❶ side; rim; border; margin: 马路两～ both sides of the road 宽～草帽 a straw hat with a broad brim 无～的草原 boundless grass lands 手～没有现成的材料。I have no material ready at hand. ❷ (maths.) side ❸ *used to show location*: 上～ above 下～ below 里～ inside 外～ outside 前～ in front of 后～ behind; at the back of 这～ this side 那～ that side 哪～ which side 左～ left 右～ right 东～ east 西～ west 南～ south 北～ north

边…边… biān... biān... ... while...; ... as... 见"一边…一边…"

边防 biānfáng 【名】frontier defence

边防军 biānfángjūn 【名】frontier force

边疆 biānjiāng 【名】border area; frontier; frontier region

边界 biānjiè 【名】border; borderline; boundary line

边境 biānjìng 【名】border; frontier

边境贸易 biānjìng màoyì frontier trade

边区 biānqū 【名】border area — revolutionary base area in the countryside on the borders of several adjacent provinces, established by the Chinese Communist Party during the Democratic Revolution and the Anti-Japanese War: 陕甘宁～ Shanxi-Gansu-Ningxia Border Area 晋察冀～ Shanxi-Chahar-Hebei Border Area

边音 biānyīn 【名】(phonetics) lateral (sound)

边缘 biānyuán 【名】brink; verge; edge

边缘科学 biānyuán kēxué frontier science

边远 biānyuǎn 【形】distant; remote

编（编） biān 【动】❶ weave; plait; braid: ～草帽 weave a straw hat ～席子 weave a mat ❷ organize; arrange: ～成五个组 organize into five groups ～队 organize into teams ❸ compile; write; compose: ～电影剧本 write a film script ～词典 compile a dictionary ❹ cook up; fabricate: 胡～ sheer fabrication 这话是～出来的。This remark is a fabrication.

编号 biānhào 【名】serial number

编号 biān = hào number; give a number to

编辑 biānjí 【动】edit; compile 【名】editor; compiler

编辑部 biānjíbù 【名】editorial board

编剧 biān = jù write a play, scenario, etc.

编码 biānmǎ 【名】coding

编目 biānmù 【名】catalogue

编目 biān = mù make a catalogue of

编排 biānpái 【动】arrange; lay out

编审 biānshěn 【动】read and edit 【名】copy editor; senior editor

编写 biānxiě 【动】❶ compile: ～教科书 compile a text-book ～汉语教材 compile Chinese teaching materials ❷ compose; write

编造 biānzào 【动】❶ organize; work out; make: ～预算 make a budget ～名册 compile a list of names ❷ fabricate; make up: ～的理由 fabricated justifications

编者 biānzhě 【名】editor; compiler

编者按 biānzhě àn editor's note

编织 biānzhī 【动】knit; weave; braid; plait

编制 biānzhì 【动】❶ weave; plait: 这种笆筐是用竹子～的。This kind

of basket is woven out of bamboo.
❷ work up;draw up:～十年规划 draw up a ten-year plan【名】establishment of an organization;the number of staff and the allocation of their work:本单位～已满。This unit is already fully staffed.

编著 biānzhù【动】compile;write

编纂 biānzuǎn【动】compile（often referring to voluminous writings）:～百科全书 compile an encyclopaedia

鞭 biān【名】whip

鞭策 biāncè【动】spur on;urge on:要经常～自己，努力学习外语。Always push yourself harder to learn a foreign language.【名】spur:你们的表扬，是对我的鼓励和～。Your commendation is an encouragement and spur to me.

鞭笞 biānchī【动】whip;flog;lash

鞭炮 biānpào【名】fire-crackers;a string of small fire-crackers

鞭子 biānzi【名】〔杆 gǎn、条 tiáo〕whip

biǎn

贬（貶）biǎn【动】❶ devaluate ❷ censure;depreciate

贬低 biǎndī【动】depreciate;disparage;belittle

贬义 biǎnyì【名】derogatory meaning

贬义词 biǎnyìcí【名】word which is derogatory in meaning

贬值 biǎn=zhí（of currency）devaluate;depreciate

扁 biǎn【形】flat

扁担 biǎndan【名】〔条 tiáo〕carrying-pole;shoulder-pole

扁桃腺 biǎntáoxiàn【名】tonsil

匾 biǎn【名】❶ a horizontal board with a painted inscriptioı ❷ a round and shallow bamboo basket

匾额 biǎn'é【名】a horizontal inscribed board

biàn

变（變）biàn【动】❶ change;alter;become different:老张的老习惯没～，还抽烟斗。Lao Zhang hasn't changed his old habit;he still smokes a pipe. 这条街大～了,～得我都不认识了。This street has changed so much that I don't recognize it any more. ❷ become;turn into:枫叶到秋天就～红了。In autumn,the maple leaves turn red. ❸ alter;change（sth. into sth. else）:～消费城市为生产城市 turn a consumer city into a productive one

变本加厉 biàn běn jiā lì become aggravated;intensify

变成 biàn // chéng become;change into;transform:把沙漠～良田 transform a desert into fertile farm-land

变电站 biàndiànzhàn【名】substation

变调 biàn=diào change of tones *when two syllables are pronounced consecutively, one will sometimes change its tone . The rules for the tone change are as follows*:❶ *when a 3rd tone is followed by a 1st, 2nd, 4th or neutral tone, it changes into a semi-third tone, that is, the full 3rd tone minus its terminal rising part（In this dictionary, it is still marked as a 3rd tone）, e.g.* 小说,祖国,请进,喜欢 ❷ *when a 3rd tone is followed*

by another 3rd tone, the first changes into the 2nd tone (In this dictionary, it is still marked as a 3rd tone) e.g. 表演 ❸ *a neutral tone varies its pitch with the tone of the preceding syllable; it is pronounced in a lower pitch if it follows a 1st, 2nd or 4th tone and in a higher pitch if it follows a 3rd tone*

变动 biàndòng 【动】change 【名】change

变法 biàn=fǎ reform

变革 biàngé 【动】transform 【名】transformation

变更 biàngēng 【动】alter;change

变卦 biàn=guà suddenly change a decision or one's mind (*derog.*): 我是前天和他约好今天来吃晚饭的,他不会~吧! The day before yesterday he promised to come to supper today. Could he have changed his mind?

变化 biànhuà 【动】change 【名】change

变幻 biànhuàn 【动】change irregularly

变幻莫测 biànhuàn mò cè changeable and unpredictable;capricious: 高山地区气候~。 The weather in mountainous areas is very changeable and unpredictable.

变换 biànhuàn 【动】change (one for another)

变节 biàn=jié be a turn-coat; become a traitor

变脸 biàn=liǎn turn hostile suddenly

变卖 biànmài 【动】sell off (one's property)

变迁 biànqiān 【动】change gradually: 各种语言的语音总在不断~。 The speech sounds of all languages are gradually but constantly changing. 【名】vicissitude;change: 大自然的~ the gradual changes of Nature 一座古城的~ the gradual changes of an ancient city

变色 biàn=sè ❶ change colour; discolour: 有的金鱼经过日照就会~。 Some goldfish changes colour after exposure to sunlight. ❷ ◇ one's face changes colour due to anger: 勃然~ flare up

变色镜 biànsèjìng 【名】light-sensitive glasses

变色龙 biànsèlóng 【名】chameleon, usually political chameleon (opportunist)

变速器 biànsùqì 【名】gearshift

变速运动 biàn sù yùndòng motion with variable velocity

变态 biàntài 【名】❶ metamorphosis ❷ abnormal

变天 biàn=tiān ❶ change in the weather: 要~啦,快把麦子收起来吧! A storm is coming. Let's get the wheat covered quickly! ❷ (of reactionary forces) stage a come-back

变通 biàntōng 【动】accommodate; fall in with; change methods; do sth. in another way

变相 biànxiàng 【形】in a disguised form (usu. referring to negative things): ~剥削 disguised exploitation ~贪污 corruption in a disguised form

变心 biàn=xīn cease to be faithful (usually in a romantic relationship)

变形 biàn=xíng change form

变压器 biànyāqì 【名】(electr.) transformer

变异 biànyì 【名】variation

变质 biàn=zhì go bad; deteriorate; degenerate: 蜕化~ degenerate 药物~了。 The medicine has gone bad.

变种 biànzhǒng 【名】❶ variation; mutation ❷ (*fig.*) variant (of an ideology or theory) (*derog.*): 机会主义的~ variant of opportunism

便 biàn 【副】〈书〉同 "就" jiù
❶，❸，❿，⓫，⓬ then; no sooner
than...;thereupon
另见 pián

便道 biàndào 【名】side-walk; pavement

便饭 biànfàn 【名】〔顿 dùn〕informal
meal;potluck

便服 biànfú 【名】informal dress;
plain clothes;civilian clothes

便笺 biànjiān 【名】(informal)
note;notepaper

便捷 biànjié 【形】nimble

便利 biànlì 【形】convenient; 交通~
very convenient transportation ~
条件 convenient conditions 【动】fa-
cilitate; for the convenience of;
accommodate: 售货员送货上门,~
当地居民。The shop assistants sell
goods from door to door for the
convenience of the local people.

便秘 biànmì 【名】constipation

便条 biàntiáo 【名】short note
(written on a slip of paper)

便携式 biànxiéshì 【形】portable

便宴 biànyàn 【名】informal dinner

便衣 biànyī 【名】❶ civilian clothes
❷ plain-clothes policeman

便于 biànyú 【动】be easy to; be
convenient for: ~携带 easy to carry ~查阅 easy to look up (in a
book, dictionary, etc.) 为了~青少
年学习,他们编了一套《自然科学小丛
书》。They have compiled a collection of *Elementary Readings on
the Natural Sciences* to help young
people in their studies.

便装 biànzhuāng 【名】informal
dress;civilian clothes

遍 biàn 【形】all over; widespread: 走~全国 travel all over the
country 【动】spread everywhere:
我们的朋友~天下。We have friends
all over the world. 【量】time: 从头

到尾看了一~ read once from be-
ginning to end 一~又一~地讲解
explain again and again

遍布 biànbù 【动】be found everywhere

遍地 biàndì 【名】all over the place

遍及 biànjí 【动】extend everywhere;reach every place

遍体鳞伤 biàn tǐ línshāng　with the
body covered with wounds; be
beaten black and blue

辨 biàn 【动】distinguish; discriminate

辨别 biànbié 【动】distinguish; discriminate; differentiate: ~ 好坏
differentiate the good from the
bad ~方向 take one's bearings

辨明 biànmíng 【动】distinguish between: ~是非 distinguish between
right and wrong ~真伪 distinguish
between truth and falsehood

辨认 biànrèn 【动】recognize; make
out;identify: 这是谁的笔迹,你~得
出 来 吗? Whose hand-writing is
this? Can you identify it?

辩(辯) biàn 【动】argue;dis-
pute

辩白 biànbái 【动】try to justify;
make an excuse

辩驳 biànbó 【动】argue and refute

辩护 biànhù 【动】❶ justify;speak in
defence of (*usu*. 为 or 替⋯辩护):
不要为自己的缺点~。Don't try to
justify your mistakes. ❷ (law) defend

辩护权 biànhùquán 【名】right of
defence

辩护士 biànhùshì 【名】apologist

辩解 biànjiě 【动】argue; explain
away

辩论 biànlùn 【动】debate;argue

辩证 biànzhèng 【形】dialectical

辩证法 biànzhèngfǎ 【名】dialectics

辩证唯物主义　biànzhèng wéiwùzhǔyì

dialectical materialism

辫(辮) biàn

辫子　biànzi　【名】〔条 tiáo〕❶ braid；queue ❷ (*fig.*) fact that may be used against sb.

biāo

标(標) biāo　【动】write a punctuation or other mark：～个句号 put a period there ～上号码 number sth.【名】◇ the trivial part or outward sign of sth. (*as opp. to* 本)：治～不治本。This will only give temporary relief. It will not effect a radical cure.

标榜　biāobǎng　【动】brag about；give favourable publicity to；style or present (oneself as)

标本　biāoběn　【名】specimen；sample

标兵　biāobīng　【名】❶ marker；person posted at a point to indicate a position ❷ (*fig.*) a model；an example to be followed：树立～ single out sb. (or a certain unit) as a model (to be followed by the masses)

标点　biāodiǎn　【名】punctuation

标点符号　biāodiǎn fúhào　punctuation marks

标记　biāojì　【名】mark；sign

标价　biāojià　【名】price marked on sth.

标价　biāo = jià　mark the price on (sth.)

标明　biāomíng　【动】clearly indicate or state

标签　biāoqiān　【名】label；tag

标枪　biāoqiāng　【名】javelin

标题　biāotí　【名】heading；headline

标新立异　biāo xīn lì yì　❶ express unconventional ideas for shock effect (*derog.*)：爱显示自己的人，遇

事总好 (hào) ～。Show-offs never miss an opportunity to draw attention to themselves with some outrageous proposal. ❷ be original and do things creatively：我们要敢于～，做前人没有做过的事。We should be innovative and do things never before attempted.

标语　biāoyǔ　【名】〔条 tiáo〕slogan

标志　biāozhì　【动】mark；show (*often followed by* 着)：蒸汽机～着工业革命的开始。The steam engine marked the beginning of the industrial revolution.【名】marking；symbol：地图上有各种不同的～。There are symbols designating many different things on a map.

标致　biāozhi　【形】(women) beautiful

标准　biāozhǔn　【名】standard；criterion：合乎～ up to the standard 达到～ reach the standard 政治～和艺术～ political criteria and artistic criteria【形】standard：～时间 standard time 他普通话说得很～。He speaks putonghua correctly.

标准化　biāozhǔn huà　【动】standardize

标准音　biāozhǔnyīn　【名】standard pronunciation

标准语　biāozhǔnyǔ　【名】standard speech

biǎo

表 biǎo　【名】❶〔张 zhāng〕table；chart；form：统计～ statistical table 填一张～ fill in a form ❷ (錶)〔块 kuài〕watch；meter：他买了块～。He bought a watch. ❸ thermometer：小孩发烧了，先试试～。The child seems to have a fever, let's first take his temperature.【动】express；show：～决心 express one's determination 深～敬意 show one's

profound respect（for sb.）

表白 biǎobái 【动】indicate；explain oneself

表层 biǎocéng 【名】outer layer；surface

表尺 biǎochǐ 【名】rear sight

表达 biǎodá 【动】express

表弟 biǎodì 【名】son of one's father's sister or mother's brother or sister（younger than oneself）

表哥 biǎogē 【名】son of one's father's sister or mother's brother or sister（older than oneself）

表格 biǎogé 【名】form；table；chart

表姐 biǎojiě 【名】daughter of one's father's sister or mother's brother or sister（older than oneself）

表决 biǎojué 【动】put to the vote；vote

表决权 biǎojuéquán 【名】the right to vote；the vote

表里不一 biǎo lǐ bù yī one is not what one professes to be

表里如一 biǎo lǐ rú yī what one says and does corresponds with what is in one's mind；one's inner and outer selves are in harmony

表露 biǎolù 【动】show；reveal：大家都～出轻松愉快的神情。Everybody looked cheerful and happy.

表妹 biǎomèi 【名】daughter of one's father's sister or mother's brother or sister（younger than oneself）

表面 biǎomiàn 【名】surface；appearance；outside：物体～ surface of an object【形】exterior；ostensible；superficial：不要～地看问题。Don't look at things superficially.

表面化 biǎomiànhuà 【动】become overt；come out into the open

表面性 biǎomiànxìng 【名】superficiality

表明 biǎomíng 【动】make clear；demonstrate；indicate

表皮 biǎopí 【名】（biol.）epidermis

表情 biǎoqíng 【名】facial expression

表示 biǎoshì 【动】❶ express；show：～支持 express one's support ～欢迎 extend a welcome to ❷ indicate：红色信号灯～车辆不能通行。The red traffic light indicates that vehicles must stop.【名】expression；indication：友好的～ expression of friendship

表叔 biǎoshū 【名】father's first cousin（male）from the maternal line

表率 biǎoshuài 【名】good example

表态 biǎo = tài make public one's stand；clarify one's stand

表现 biǎoxiàn 【动】❶ express；show；display：～出优秀的品质（of persons）show fine qualities 他无私的精神～在各个方面。His selflessness is revealed in everything he does. 她～得很坚强。She displayed a very strong character. ❷ show off：好（hào）～ like to show off 自我～ self-expression 【名】expression；manifestation：他在工作中的～很好。He makes a very good showing in his work.

表兄 biǎoxiōng 【名】同"表哥"

表演 biǎoyǎn 【动】❶ perform；act：～歌舞 give a song and dance performance ～体操 give a gymnastic display ❷ demonstrate：～新操作方法 demonstrate new techniques ❸ reveal（one's character）（derog.）：这个家伙～得很充分。This fellow has fully revealed his true nature.【名】performance；exhibition；demonstration：射击～ shooting exhibition 乒乓球～赛 exhibition table tennis match

表扬 biǎoyáng 【动】praise；commend

表语 biǎoyǔ 【名】（gram.）predicative

表彰 biǎozhāng 【动】honorable

mention;commend

biē

憋

憋　biē　【动】❶ hold back;restrain:～了一口气 hold one's breath 把～了多年的心里话说了出来 pour out what one has bottled up inside for years ❷ choke;stifle:心里～得慌 feel suffocated;feel very much depressed ～得透不过气来 so stifling that one can hardly breathe

憋闷　biēmen　【形】dejected;depressed

憋气　biēqì　【形】❶ short of breath;suffocating ❷ feel angry and depressed;dejected

bié

别

别　bié　【动】❶ ◇ leave;make one's departure;depart:临～赠言 parting words of advice to sb. 久～重逢 meet again after a long separation ❷ pin things together;clip things together:把两张表格～在一起 clip the two forms together 他胸前～着一枚纪念章。He is wearing a badge pinned on his chest. ❸ tuck:腰里～着一枝手枪 He is wearing a pistol tucked into his belt.【副】don't 同"不要"bùyào【副】:～客气。Please don't stand on ceremony. ～生气了。Please don't go on being angry.
另见 biè

别出心裁　bié chū xīncái　have an original idea;unique;original and different 也作"独出心裁"。

别处　biéchù　【名】elsewhere;other place

别的　biéde　【代】other

别管　biéguǎn　【连】no matter,同"不

管"bùguǎn, *but less frequently used*:～刮风下雨,你就按约定的时间去。Never mind the weather, just leave at the appointed time.

别号　biéhào　【名】another name

别具匠心　bié jù jiàng xīn　with marked ingenuity;show originality

别具一格　bié jù yī gé　have a peculiar style;be unique

别开生面　bié kāi shēng miàn　create a new form;break new ground 在这个话剧里,演员说各地不同的方言,真是～。The characters in this play speak different dialects just as in real life. This is certainly something new.

别名　biémíng　【名】another name

别人　biérén　【代】another person;others

别墅　biéshù　【名】villa

别有用心　bié yǒu yòng xīn　with ulterior motives

别针　biézhēn　【名】pin;safety pin

别致　biézhì　【形】novel and unusual;unique and ingenious:天坛的建筑结构很～。The architectural structure of the Temple of Heaven is unique.

别字　biézì　【名】incorrectly written or mispronounced character

蹩

蹩　bié

蹩脚　biéjiǎo　【形】inferior in skill or quality;poor and incompetent

biě

瘪（癟）

瘪（癟）　biě　【形】shrivelled;flat (tyre)

biè

别（彆）

别（彆）　biè
另见 bié

别扭 bièniu 【形】〈口〉❶ disagreeable；wretched；morose；eccentric：这天儿真～，一会儿下雨，一会儿出太阳。The weather is really disagreeable；one minute the sun is shining, the next it is raining again. 这个抽屉很～，不好开。This drawer is very stubborn；it doesn't open easily. 老张因为病老不好，心里很～。Lao Zhang feels awful because his illness isn't getting any better. 老李太不爱说话，不了解他的人认为他很～。Lao Li is a man of few words, and those who don't really know him think him a bit odd. ❷ be at odds；be at cross-purposes：他们俩老闹～。Those two are often at cross-purposes. 你怎么老跟我别别扭扭的？Why on earth are you always at odds with me？❸ (of speech, writing) awkward：这句话有点儿～。This sentence is a bit awkward.

bīn

宾(賓) bīn 【名】◇ guest：～朋满座 full of guests and friends

宾馆 bīnguǎn 【名】guest house

宾客 bīnkè 【名】guest

宾语 bīnyǔ 【名】(gram.) object

宾至如归 bīn zhì rú guī　make guests feel at home

宾主 bīnzhǔ 【名】guest and host

濒(瀕) bīn

濒于 bīnyú 【动】be on the verge of (misfortune)；be on the brink of：～破产 verge on bankruptcy ～灭亡 be on the brink of collapse or extinction

bīng

冰 bīng 【名】ice【动】make very cold；ice；refrigerate

冰雹 bīngbáo 【名】hailstone

冰川 bīngchuān 【名】glacier

冰刀 bīngdāo 【名】(ice) skates

冰点 bīngdiǎn 【名】freezing point

冰雕 bīngdiāo 【名】carved ice；ice sculpture

冰棍儿 bīnggùnr 【名】〔根 gēn〕ice-stick；ice lolly

冰冷 bīnglěng 【形】ice-cold

冰凉 bīngliáng 【形】(of a thing) icycold；very cold

冰淇淋 bīngqílín 【名】ice-cream

冰球 bīngqiú 【名】ice-hockey

冰山 bīngshān 【名】iceberg

冰糖 bīngtáng 【名】sugar candy；rock candy

冰天雪地 bīng tiān xuě dì　icy and snowy field；all covered with ice and snow

冰箱 bīngxiāng 【名】〔个 gè〕ice-box；refrigerator

冰鞋 bīngxié 【名】〔只 zhī、双 shuāng〕skates

冰雪 bīngxuě 【名】ice and snow

冰镇 bīngzhèn 【动】put ice around；refrigerate

兵 bīng 【名】❶ soldier：当～ be a soldier ❷ ◇ weapon；arms：短～相接 fight at close quarters ❸ ◇ army；troops：～分两路 divide an army into two contingents ❹ ◇ war；fighting：胜败乃～家常事。Losing battles is as ordinary an experience to a general as is winning them.

兵工厂 bīnggōngchǎng 【名】arsenal

兵荒马乱 bīng huāng mǎ luàn　turmoil and chaos caused by war

兵力 bīnglì 【名】force；military

strength

兵马俑 bīngmǎyǒng 【名】wood or clay figures of warriors and horses buried with the dead

兵团 bīngtuán 【名】army corps

兵役 bīngyì 【名】military service

兵役法 bīngyìfǎ 【名】military service law

兵员 bīngyuán 【名】soldiers; troops

兵种 bīngzhǒng 【名】any combatant branch of the military services; arm

bǐng

丙 bǐng 【名】*used to represent "third" according to old Chinese tradition*

饼（餅）bǐng 【名】〔张 zhāng〕cake; pastry

饼干 bǐnggān 【名】〔块 kuài〕biscuit

bìng

并 bìng 【动】merge; combine: 三步～作两步走 walk three steps in two (walk quickly) 两个小组～成一个大组。Two small groups were combined into one big group. 【副】❶ abreast; side by side; simultaneously: 车辆不得～行。Vehicles are not allowed to drive two abreast. 两项工程齐头～进。Two construction projects were carried on simultaneously. ❷ *used before a negative to indicate that things are not as one might think*: 这个句子虽然比较复杂，但～不难懂。This sentence is a bit involved but not hard to understand. 昨天下了一夜雪，可是～不太冷。It snowed last night, but it isn't too cold. 【连】*basically similar in meaning and usage to* 并且:

我们认真讨论了这个问题，～得出了明确的结论。We discussed the matter very carefully and arrived at a conclusion. Note：并 *cannot connect two clauses*.

并存 bìngcún 【动】coexist

并发症 bìngfāzhèng 【名】(med.) complication

并驾齐驱 bìng jià qí qū run neck and neck; can well stand side by side with

并肩 bìngjiān 【副】shoulder to shoulder; side by side

并举 bìngjǔ 【动】promote or carry on simultaneously

并立 bìnglì 【动】exist side by side

并列 bìngliè 【动】put...on a par with...; parallel; be in juxtaposition with

并排 bìngpái 【副】side by side; alongside; abreast

并且 bìngqiě 【连】and *used to connect verbs, auxiliary verbs, verbal constructions or clauses only*: 代表们讨论～通过了大会的决议。The deputies discussed and passed the resolution. 我们应该～能够生产更多的石油。We ought to and can produce more petroleum. 他把一个孤儿养大，～把自己的医术传给了他。He brought up the orphaned child, and taught him his knowledge of medicine. Note：*sometimes used in conjunction with* 不但: 海面上起风了，不但天变冷了，～天空也昏暗起来。The wind rose over the sea and it not only became cold, but the sky turned dark and cloudy.

并吞 bìngtūn 【动】annex; gobble up

并行 bìngxíng 【动】go side by side

并重 bìngzhòng 【动】regard both as equally important; attach equal importance to

病 bìng 【名】❶ disease; illness

❷ problem；weakness ❸ fault；defect：语～ language mistake 这是个～句。This is a faulty sentence.【动】fall ill；be taken ill；他着凉了，～了三天。He was ill for three days with a cold.

病虫害 bìngchónghài 【名】plant diseases and insect pests

病床 bìngchuáng 【名】〔张 zhāng〕hospital bed

病毒 bìngdú 【名】virus

病房 bìngfáng 【名】sick-room；ward

病根 bìnggēn 【名】(～儿)(lit.) cause of a disease；(fig.) root of the trouble

病故 bìnggù 【动】die of illness

病号 bìnghào 【名】sick person

病假 bìngjià 【名】sick-leave

病菌 bìngjūn 【名】germ which causes disease

病理学 bìnglǐxué 【名】pathology

病历 bìnglì 【名】case history

病情 bìngqíng 【名】patient's condition

病人 bìngrén 【名】sick person；patient

病入膏肓 bìng rù gāohuāng the disease beyond cure；(fig.) beyond all hope；beyond remedy

病态 bìngtài 【名】physiologically or psychologically abnormal；(in a) morbid (state of mind)

病危 bìngwēi 【动】be critically ill

病症 bìngzhèng 【名】disease

bō

拨（撥） bō 【动】❶ set；poke；move with finger etc.；turn；～电话号码 dial a telephone number 把钟～一下 set a clock 用针～刺 poke with a needle (e.g. to remove a sliver) ～正航向 set the course right ❷ set aside；assign；allocate；～给你们研究所两名大学生。Two graduates are to be assigned to your institute.【量】group；batch；分～参观，半个小时一～ visit in batches at half-hour intervals

拨付 bōfù 【动】appropriate (a sum of money)

拨款 bō = kuǎn allocate funds

拨乱反正 bō luàn fǎn zhèng restore order and return to the right path

拨弄 bōnòng 【动】❶ stir up；fiddle with ❷ provoke；stir up ❸ manipulate

波 bō 【名】wave

波长 bōcháng 【名】wave-length

波动 bōdòng 【名】fluctuation 【动】undulate；fluctuate

波及 bōjí 【动】involve；affect；～范围很广 extensively affected 这次地震～周围几个城市。This earthquake affected several cities in the vicinity.

波澜壮阔 bōlán zhuàngkuò on a magnificent scale；surge forward with tremendous momentum

波浪 bōlàng 【名】wave

波涛 bōtāo 【名】huge wave；billow

波涛汹涌 bōtāo xiōngyǒng billowing waves

波折 bōzhé 【名】setback

玻 bō

玻璃 bōli 【名】〔块 kuài〕glass (material)

剥 bō 【动】peel；skin

另见 bāo

剥夺 bōduó 【动】❶ expropriate ❷ deprive；～政治权利 deprive sb. of political rights

剥削 bōxuē 【动】exploit 【名】exploitation

剥削阶级 bōxuē jiējí exploiting class

剥削者 bōxuēzhě 【名】exploiter

菠 bō

菠菜 bōcài 【名】spinach

菠萝 bōluó 【名】〔个 gè〕pineapple

播 bō

【动】❶ sow ❷ broadcast (by radio)

播发 bōfā 【动】broadcast

播送 bōsòng 【动】broadcast (by radio)

播音 bō = yīn broadcast (by radio)

播音员 bōyīnyuán 【名】announcer

播种 bō = zhǒng sow seeds

播种机 bōzhǒngjī 【名】〔台 tái、架 jià〕seeder; seeding machine

播种 bōzhòng 【动】plant by sowing seeds (e.g. as opp. to planting seedlings)

bó

伯 bó

【名】uncle

伯父 bófù 【名】uncle, one's father's elder brother

伯母 bómǔ 【名】aunt, wife of one's father's elder brother

驳（駁） bó

【动】refute

驳斥 bóchì 【动】refute

驳船 bóchuán 【名】〔只 zhī〕barge; lighter

驳倒 bó//dǎo succeed in refuting

驳回 bóhuí 【动】reject (e.g. an appeal)

勃 bó

勃然 bórán 【副】❶ vigorously：～兴起 rise up vigorously (as a new force) ❷ (flare up) excitedly：～大怒 fly into a rage

脖 bó

脖子 bózi 【名】neck

博 bó

博爱 bó'ài 【名】fraternity; universal brotherhood; universal love

博得 bódé 【动】win (praise, applause, etc.)

博览会 bólǎnhuì 【名】fair; international exhibition

博士 bóshì 【名】doctor (of chemistry, philosophy, etc.); Ph. D.

博士后 bóshìhòu 【名】post-doctoral; post-doctorate

博物馆 bówùguǎn 【名】museum

博学 bóxué 【形】learned; knowledgeable; erudite

搏 bó

搏斗 bódòu 【动】wrestle; fight hand-to-hand

薄 bó

【形】◇ thin; slight; small; little：～礼 humble gift 【动】◇ despise; belittle：厚此～彼 favour one and slight the other 另见 báo

薄利 bólì 【名】small profits：～多销 small profits but quick turnover

薄弱 bóruò 【形】weak; vulnerable

bò

簸 bò

簸箕 bòji 【名】dustpan

bǔ

补（補） bǔ

【动】❶ mend; patch; repair：～衣服 mend clothes 修桥～路 build bridges and repair roads 拆东墙～西墙 borrow from Peter to pay Paul ❷ fill; supply; make up for：～上个名额 add one person to make up a quota 取人之长，～己之短 overcome one's own shortcomings by learning from the strong points of others ❸ nourish;

～血 build up one's blood ～～身体 build up one's health by good nutrition

补偿 bǔcháng 【动】compensate

补偿贸易 bǔcháng màoyì compensation trade

补充 bǔchōng 【动】make up; supplement

补丁 bǔding 【名】patch (clothing)

补给 bǔjǐ 【动】(mil.) supply

补角 bǔjiǎo 【名】supplementary angles

补救 bǔjiù 【动】remedy

补课 bǔ = kè make up for missed lessons; redo sth. which was not properly done

补台 bǔ = tái help sb. out; come to one's aid

补贴 bǔtiē 【动】subsidize 【名】subsidy

补习 bǔxí 【动】take or give supplementary classes after school or work

补药 bǔyào 【名】tonic

补语 bǔyǔ 【名】(gram.) complement

补正 bǔzhèng 【动】supplement and correct

补助 bǔzhù 【动】subsidize; help 【名】subsidy; allowance

补足 bǔzú 【动】supply what is lacking; make up a deficiency

捕 bǔ 【动】catch

捕风捉影 bǔ fēng zhuō yǐng chase after the wind and catch at shadows; make groundless judgements; speak or act on hearsay evidence

捕获 bǔhuò 【动】succeed in catching; capture

捕捉 bǔzhuō 【动】catch

哺 bǔ

哺乳动物 bǔ rǔ dòngwù mammal

哺育 bǔyù 【动】nurture

bù

不 bù 【副】❶ *used as a negative answer to a question using* 吗 *or* 吧 *or to an affirmative-negative question inquiring about a habitual, future or willed action. It is usu. followed by some additional comments*：你每天都在食堂吃饭吗？——～, 我有时也回家吃饭。Do you always eat at the dining-hall? —No, sometimes I eat at home. 你去不去看篮球？——～, 不去。Are you going to watch the basketball game? —No, I'm not. 他不去工厂吧？——～, 他去。He isn't going to the factory, is he? —Yes, he is. 他们请他主持明天的会, 他到底干不干？——～, 他不干。They went to ask him to preside over the meeting tomorrow. Did he say he would? — No, he wouldn't. ❷ *used to form the negative of a stative verb*：～是 is not ～像 is not like ～知道 does not know ～属于 does not belong to ～喜欢 does not like ❸ *used to form the negative of an active verb when it expresses a habitual, future or willed action*：他从来～抽烟。He never smokes. 词典我现在～用, 你先用吧。I am not using the dictionary now; you may have it. 他们今天也许～去看戏了。They are probably not going to the theatre today. 我怎么说他也～听。No matter what I said, he wouldn't listen. ❹ *used to form the negative of an adj., adv. or auxiliary verb*：～热 not hot ～科学 not scientific ～应该 ought not to ～可能 not possible ～太好 not very good ～常来 not come often ❺ *inserted between a verb and its resultative or directional complement to form the neg-*

ative potential form：吃～完 cannot eat up 看～清楚 cannot see clearly 解决～了 (liǎo) cannot solve 进～去 can not enter 想～起来 cannot recall ❻ *used before certain words or phrases showing indefinite quantity, to emphasize smallness of quantity or brevity of time*：坐了～一会儿 sit for a little while 用～多少 won't need much 他来了～几天就走了。He was here for only a few days, and then left. Note：*before a 4th tone, or a 4th tone which has turned into a neutral tone*, 不 *is pronounced in the 2nd tone, e. g.* 不去 (bú qù), 不是 (búshi). *In this dictionary, all instances of* 不 *are marked in the original tone, except when it is pronounced in the neutral tone when there is no tone mark*]

不安 bù'ān 【形】uneasy; perturbed; worried

不卑不亢 bù bēi bù kàng neither haughty nor humble

不比 bùbǐ 【动】unlike; different from：老大爷，您～年轻人，这种力气活儿还是让我们干吧! Grandpa, you aren't as young as we are. Leave the hard work to us.

不必 bùbì 【副】need not; not have to：～担心 need not worry ～客气 make yourself at home ～张罗。There is no need to bother.

不变价格 bù biàn jiàgé fixed price

不便 bùbiàn 【形】❶ inconvenient；交通～ poor transportation 行动～ move with difficulty ❷ inappropriate：他工作很忙，我～再去麻烦他。He is very busy with his work, it's inappropriate for me to put him to more trouble.

不…不… bù...bù... ❶ *used with two words of opposite meanings, this expression indicates an in-between state, which in a positive sense may mean just right for the purpose*：不冷不热 neither cold nor hot 不死不活 neither dead nor alive 不卑不亢 neither overbearing nor servile 他的毛笔字写得不好不坏。His brush-writing is just so-so. 这件衣服不肥不瘦正合适。This dress fits perfectly. It is neither too tight nor too loose. ❷ *cites two examples of sth., leaving others unstated*：不吃不喝 consume neither food nor drink 不吵不闹 not make any fuss at all 对孩子们的事情不能采取不闻不问的态度。One mustn't take an indifferent attitude towards any concern of the children. ❸ *the first* 不... *is the condition of the second* 不...：不破不立 no construction without destruction 不塞不流 no flowing without cessation 不止不行 no motion without rest 不见不散。Neither of us must leave until the other comes. ❹ *used to make an emphatic negative form of a two-character word*：不清不楚 not clear 不慌不忙 leisurely 不折不扣 hundred percent; completely 不知不觉 unawares 不理不睬 take no heed at all 不言不语 say not a word 不干不净 not clean

不曾 bùcéng 【副】never yet *negative of* "曾经", *usu. used in conjunction with* 过：他～来过。He has never been here. 这次科学考察的规模是过去～有过的。A scientific investigation on this scale is something which has never been done.

不成文法 bùchéngwénfǎ 【名】unwritten law

不辞劳苦 bù cí láokǔ spare no pains; take pains

不错 bùcuò 【形】❶ not bad; pretty good：字写得还～。The handwriting is not bad. 这种新产品很～。This new kind of product is pretty good. ❷ yes; that's right (in re-

ply)：～,我是这个意思。Yes, this is what I mean.

不打自招 bù dǎ zì zhāo confess without being pressed; make a voluntary confession

不但 bùdàn 【连】not only *used in conjunction with* 并且、而且、也、还, *etc.*：他～那样说了,并且也那样做了。(他～那样说了,而且也那样做了。)He didn't just say he would do it, he actually did it. 这首诗～我喜欢,他也很喜欢。I am not the only one who likes this poem, he likes it too. 他～能说汉语,还能说英语。He can speak not only Chinese but also English.

不当 bùdàng 【形】unsuitable; improper

不得不 bùdébù 【副】have to; be compelled to：天气突然变了,他们～改变原来的施工计划。The weather suddenly changed, and they had to alter their work-schedule. 时间到了,我～走了。Time was up and I had to go.

不得了 bùdéliǎo 【形】❶ disastrous; appalling：易燃物品如果保管不好,发生事故可～! If flammable goods are not properly stored, disastrous accidents can happen. ❷ terribly; very much *used after* 得 *as a complement of degree*：高兴得～ terribly happy 急得～ be very much worried

不得已 bùdéyǐ 【形】act against one's will; have to; have no alternative but to：不到万～的时候,他是不会缺席的。He won't be absent unless he absolutely couldn't help it. 实在～,她只好放弃了这次参观的机会。She had no alternative but to give up the chance to visit.

不等式 bùděngshì 【名】(maths.) inequality

不定 bùdìng 【副】not sure; not certain (*always followed by an inter-rogative word or phrase*)：他～到哪儿去了呢! Who knows where he is gone to! 明天他还～来不来呢! We are not certain whether or not he will come tomorrow.

不动产 bùdòngchǎn 【名】realty; real estate; real property

不冻港 bùdònggǎng 【名】ice-free port; open port

不动声色 bù dòng shēngsè be composed; stay calm and collected; poker-faced

不断 bùduàn 【副】unceasingly; uninterruptedly; continuously：～前进 march on without cease 今天～(地)有人给他打电话。Today a lot of people have kept on telephoning him.

不对 bùduì 【形】unhealthy; abnormal; odd; 脸色～ sick or unhealthy appearance 神情有点儿～。There is something odd about his expression.

不法 bùfǎ 【形】unlawful

不妨 bùfāng 【副】no harm (in doing so); no harm (in trying)：这种药对高血压很有效,你～吃吃看。This medicine is helpful in treating high blood pressure. Why not try it? 他也许在办公室,～打个电话问问。Perhaps he is in his office. There's no harm in phoning to find out.

不甘 bùgān 【动】not be resigned to：～落后 not be resigned to lagging behind ～示弱 not be resigned to being outshone ～失败 not be resigned to failure

不攻自破 bù gōng zì pò collapse of its own accord

不共戴天 bù gòng dài tiān refuse to share the same sky (with one's enemy)；(*fig.*) feel irreconcilable hatred for sb.

不顾 bùgù 【动】have no regard for; regardless of；他～一切冲进烈火抢救国家财产。Regardless of his

own danger, he dashed into the fire to save state property.

不管 bùguǎn 【连】同"不论", usu. used in colloquial speech：～困难多大,都阻挡不住我们前进的步伐。Whatever the difficulties, they will not prevent us from forging ahead. ～做什么工作,都要认真负责。Whatever we do, we should go about it conscientiously. ～远不远,他都要去。He is determined to go, whether it's close or far.

不管三七二十一 bù guǎn sān qī èrshí yī regardless of anything; in spite of anything; come what may：～,先干了再说！Let's pitch in regardless.

不过 bùguò 【连】only; but; except that：这篇文章写得不错,～长了点儿。This article is not bad; it is just a bit long. 担子是重了点儿,～我相信你挑得起来。Your load is really heavy but I believe you can carry it. 【副】merely：我～随便说说罢了,你倒当起真来了。I just said it casually. How can you take it so seriously? 我～是劝劝你,并没有别的意思。I was merely giving advice, that's all.

不寒而栗 bù hán ér lì tremble with fear

不好意思 bù hǎoyìsi ❶ feel embarrassed; shy：听到同学的夸奖,他反而有点儿～了。He felt a little embarrassed at being so highly praised by his fellow students. ❷ feel it impolite (to do sth.)：有问题不要～问。Don't hesitate to ask questions if you have any. 大家都约我去,我～推辞。Since everyone is asking me to go, I find it hard to refuse.

不和 bùhé 【形】not on good terms with; at variance with

不及 bùjí 【动】not be as good as,同"不如", but less frequently used：我的枪法～他。My marksmanship is not as good as his. 这个～那个。

This one is not as good as the other one.

不及物动词 bùjíwùdòngcí 【名】intransitive verb

不即不离 bù jí bù lí keep sb. at arm's length; be half-hearted; be lukewarm

不济 bùjì 【动】be no good

不假思索 bù jiǎ sīsuǒ without thinking

不见得 bù jiàn dé may not; it is improbable that; not likely to：这本书他看是看了,但～看懂了。He did read this book, but he may not have understood it. 你说他明天一定来,我看～。You think that he will certainly come tomorrow? But I think it unlikely.

不结盟 bù jiéméng nonalignment：～国家 nonaligned countries

不解 bùjiě 【动】do not understand; be puzzled

不禁 bùjīn 【副】involuntarily; spontaneously; unintentionally：他激动得～流下了眼泪。He was so moved that he couldn't help shedding tears. 看到杂技演员的精彩表演,观众～拍手叫好。After seeing the acrobats' excellent performance, the spectators spontaneously clapped and shouted "bravo".

不仅 bùjǐn 【连】not only, 同"不但"：他们～提前完成了生产任务,而且还支援了兄弟单位。They not only filled their work quota ahead of time, but also helped their fellow workers in other units. ～要优质高产,而且要低消耗。Not just high production and good quality but also low consumption of raw materials is absolutely necessary. 也说"不仅仅"。

不久 bùjiǔ 【名】❶ near future：我～就要出差去。I'm leaving very soon on business. ❷ not long (after a certain period of time or an occur-

rence in the past)：你刚走～,他就回
来了。He came back not long after
you left.

不咎既往 bù jiù jì wǎng forgive past
misdeeds; irrespective of one's
past

不拘小节 bù jū xiǎojié defy trivial
conventions

不拘一格 bù jū yī gé without being
confined by a rigid pattern

不堪 bù kān ❶ unbearable; revolt-
ing：～入耳 unbearable to hear ～
入目 unbearable to see ❷ can't end-
ure：～一击 can't withstand a
blow ～其苦 can't endure the hardship ❸ indicates high degree (used
after words expressing negative
states)：疲惫～ extremely fatigued
狼狈～ extremely embarrassed; extremely awkward

不堪入目 bù kān rù mù most un-
sightly; disgusting; revolting

不堪设想 bù kān shèxiǎng too
dreadful to think of; unimaginable
(e.g. unimaginably grave consequences)

不可避免 bù kě bìmiǎn unavoidable;
inevitable

不可多得 bù kě duō dé hard to
come by; seldom encountered

不可告人 bù kě gào rén (ulterior
motives that) will not stand exposure to the light of day

不可救药 bù kě jiù yào incorrigible;
incurable; beyond help or remedy;
beyond cure

不可开交 bù kě kāi jiāo awfully (often used after 得 as a complement)：
忙得～ be up to one's eyes in
(work) 吵得～ be locked in violent
argument; quarrel hotly

不可磨灭 bù kě mómiè indelible; in-
effaceable

不可偏废 bù kě piānfèi do not emphasize one thing at the expense
of the other

不可思议 bù kě sīyì unimaginable;
inconceivable

不可调和 bù kě tiáohé irreconcilable; implacable

不可一世 bù kě yī shì consider oneself without peer; be insufferably
arrogant：当年的希特勒真是气势汹
汹,～,但最后也逃脱不了覆灭的下场。
Hitler was at one time so overbearing and insufferably arrogant,
but he couldn't escape defeat in
the end.

不可知论 bùkězhīlùn 【名】agnosti-
cism

不可终日 bù kě zhōng rì so worried
that one feels unable to survive
the day; in a desperate situation

不可阻挡 bù kě zǔdǎng irresistible

不客气 bù kèqi phrase used to indicate that thanks are unnecessary：
谢谢您! ——～! Thank you. —
Don't mention it.

不快 bùkuài 【形】unhappy; an-
noyed

不愧 bùkuì 【动】be worthy of：他～
劳动模范的称号。He is quite wor-
thy of the title "model worker". 不
愧 often takes 是 or 为 (wéi) after
it：我们的民族～为伟大的民族。Our
people is worthy of being called a
great people. 老王～为 (wéi) 我们学
习的榜样。Lao Wang deserves to
stand as a model for us to follow.

不劳而获 bù láo ér huò be idle and
profit by others' toil; reap without
sowing：～的寄生虫 parasites who
enjoy the fruits of other people's
labour

不力 bùlì 【形】be ineffective; in-
competent：领导～ fail to exercise
effective leadership 办事～ prove
incompetent in one's work

不利 bùlì 【形】❶ adverse; disadvantageous; unfavourable：～因
素 unfavourable factors ～条件 adverse conditions ～于工作的开展

unfavourable for the carrying out of the work 这种灯光对眼睛～。Such light is harmful to one's eyes. ❷ unsuccessful：出师～（in war or sports）lose the first battle

不良 · bùliáng 【形】bad；unhealthy

不了了之 bù liǎo liǎo zhī　let（a matter）take its own course（due to incompetence）；end up with nothing definite：这个问题一定要认真处理，不能～. This matter must be dealt with seriously, and must not be allowed to take its own course.

不料 bùliào 【副】unexpectedly；beyond one's expectation：多年不见的老朋友，～在北京遇见了。Old friends who had not seen each other for many years, met unexpectedly in Beijing. 正要进行足球赛，～下起雨来。It began to rain unexpectedly when the football game began.

不伦不类 bù lún bù lèi　neither fish nor fowl：翻译时应该注意两种语言的特点，否则就会弄出一些～的句子来。In doing translation, one should pay attention to the differences between the two languages；otherwise one is bound to make the translation neither fish nor fowl.

不论 bùlùn 【连】no matter usu. followed by 谁,什么,怎么,多么,…还是… etc. and often used in conjunction with 都 or 也：～天气多么冷,他也坚持锻炼身体。No matter how cold it is, he persists in doing physical exercise.

不满 bùmǎn 【动】be dissatisfied；be discontented：～现状 be dissatisfied with the present state of affairs 【形】dissatisfied；discontented：～的表情 look dissatisfied 显出～的神色 wear a dissatisfied expression

不毛之地 bù máo zhī dì　barren land

不免 bùmiǎn 【副】unavoidable；

bound to：她第一次上讲台，～有些紧张。It was the first time she had stood before a class, and it was only natural for her to be a little nervous. 工作中～会遇到一些困难。One is bound to meet with difficulties in one's work.

不谋而合 bù móu ér hé　happen to coincide with；see eye to eye

不偏不倚 bù piān bù yǐ　without bias or favour；impartial

不平 bùpíng 【形】indignant in the face of injustice

不平等条约 bù píngděng tiáoyuē　unequal treaty；unjust treaty

不求甚解 bù qiú shèn jiě　do not seek to understand things thoroughly

不求有功，但求无过 bù qiú yǒu gōng, dàn qiú wú guò　do not attempt praiseworthy actions；simply attempt to avoid blame

不屈 bùqū 【动】be unyielding

不屈不挠 bù qū bù náo　unswerving；unyielding

不然 bùrán 【连】otherwise，同"要不" yàobù ❶：学了外语要常常用，～就会忘。Try to use what you have learned in a foreign language as often as possible；otherwise you will forget it. 可惜明天我有事，～我倒很想跟你们去长城。Sorry I am engaged tomorrow；otherwise I would go with you to the Great Wall.

不忍 bùrěn 【形】can't endure；can't bear（due to sympathy）：这个小学生知道自己错了，哭得很伤心，老师～再责备他。The little boy knew that he had misbehaved and cried bitterly, so the teacher couldn't bear to scold him anymore.

不容 bùróng 【动】not allow；not tolerate

不容置疑 bùróng zhì yí　no doubt；beyond a doubt

不如 bùrú 【动】be not as good as；

论分析问题的能力,我～他。I am not as good as he in analysing problems. Note: *sometimes the word or phrase which tells in which respect one is outshone comes at the end*: 姐姐～妹妹爽快。The elder sister is not as frank as the younger one. 这种自行车～那种销路广。This kind of bicycle doesn't sell as well as the other kind. 【连】*introduces the best course of action*: 材料没准备齐,～晚几天再开工。The materials aren't ready yet. We'd better wait a few days before we start construction.

不入虎穴,焉得虎子 bù rù hǔxué, yān dé hǔzǐ How can you catch tiger cubs without entering the tiger's lair? (*fig.*) You can't get something for nothing.

不三不四 bù sān bù sì ❶ dubious; shady: ～的人 a shady-looking character ❷ neither fish nor fowl: 这首诗翻得～,既不像诗又不像散文。The translation of this poem is very badly done; it is neither poetry nor prose.

不善 bùshàn 【形】be bad at; be no good at; be unskilful at

不甚了了 bù shèn liǎoliǎo do not quite understand

不声不响 bù shēng bù xiǎng quiet; mute

不胜枚举 bù shèng méi jǔ too numerous to mention; can't be counted

不时 bùshí 【副】(*usu. in written language*) time and again; now and then: 战士们～地回过头来向欢送的人群招手。The soldiers turned back and waved again and again to the people who were seeing them off. 从窗口～传出愉快的笑声。Now and then we could hear hearty laughter from outside the window.

不是…而是… bùshì… érshì… (*usu.*

in written language) not…but…: 我们不是没有想办法,而是还没有想出好办法来。It isn't that we haven't tried to find a way out. We just haven't found a good one yet. *in colloquial speech* 而 *is often omitted*: 昨天你看见的不是她,(而)是她姐姐。The person you saw yesterday was not her, but her elder sister.

不是…就是… bùshì… jiùshì… ❶ either…or… (where there are only two alternatives): 从中国到日本去,不是坐飞机就是坐轮船。One can travel from China to Japan either by air or by sea. 他不是星期六来,就是星期日来。He is coming either on Saturday or Sunday. ❷ *illustrates a state of affairs by citing two examples, leaving others unstated*: 他每天晚上不是看书就是做练习,学习可努力了。He works really hard, either reading or doing homework every evening.

不舒服 bùshūfu 【形】unwell; indisposed

不送气音 bùsòngqìyīn 【名】unaspirated sound

不速之客 bù sù zhī kè uninvited guest; gate crasher

不同 bù tóng different

不外 bùwài 【动】nothing but; only: 常来往的～几个老朋友。The only people he sees often are a few old friends. 课间休息时,同学们～是打打乒乓球、做做早操。During the break, the students don't have much to do except playing ping-pong or do the morning exercises.

不惜 bùxī 【动】not hesitate (to do sth.) whatever the cost; at all costs ～工本 spare no expense ～采取造谣栽赃的手段 be so mean as to resort to rumourmongering and framing 为了正义的事业,他不惜牺牲一切。For a right-

eous cause, he will not hesitate to give up everything.

不相上下 bù xiāng shàng xià　on a par; be roughly the same

不像话 bù xiàng huà　shocking; bad beyond description: 简直太～了! It's downright shocking! 这份草稿乱得～, 得重抄一遍。 The manuscript is in terrible shape. It has to be recopied.

不屑 bùxiè 【动】disdain（to do sth.）; scorn（to do sth.）; feel it beneath one's dignity（to do sth.）: ～一驳 disdain to refute sth. not worth an argument ～一顾 scorn to take even a glance at（sth. or sb.）

不行 bù xíng ❶ will not do; not allowed: 你不去可～。 You simply have to go. 这本书今天不还～。 This book must be returned today. ❷ do not know how to; be no good at: 我跳舞～, 唱歌还可以。 I don't know how to dance at all, but I can sing a little. 他搞电这一行（háng）是～的。 He knows nothing about electricity. ❸ hopeless: 眼看病人～了。 The patient is hopeless. 这盆花叶子都掉了, ～了。 This flowering plant has lost all its leaves; it is dying. ❹ not up to the standard; not satisfactory: 这块布质量不错, 那块～。 This material is not bad; that is of rather poor quality. ❺ used after 得 as a complement of degree: 他已经醉得～了。 He is dead drunk.

不幸 bùxìng 【形】unfortunate

不朽 bùxiǔ 【动】immortal

不锈钢 bùxiùgāng 【名】stainless steel

不许 bù xǔ　do not allow; do not permit

不宣而战 bù xuān érzhàn　start an undeclared war

不学无术 bù xué wú shù　ignorant; does not study and knows nothing;

ignorant and not willing to learn

不言而喻 bù yán ér yù　matter of course; it goes without saying

不要 bùyào 【副】used in imperative sentences, do not（do sth.）: ～随地吐痰! Don't spit in public! ～着急。 Don't hurry. Take it easy.

不要紧 bù yàojǐn ❶ it doesn't matter; never mind; it's not serious: 路远～, 我们都有自行车。 Never mind the distance, we all have our bikes. ❷ used in the first clause of a compound sentence to indicate that an event may seem of little consequence, but in fact has the bad effect shown in the second clause. It is a very colloquial expression.: 他这一喊～, 把我吓了一跳。 He might have thought it was all right for him to shout, but he startled me.

不一而足 bù yī ér zú　（of similar cases）numerous

不遗余力 bù yí yú lì　do one's utmost; spare no pains

不义之财 bù yì zhī cái　ill-gotten wealth

不翼而飞 bù yì ér fēi　fly without wings;（fig.）disappear suddenly

不用 bù yòng　need not: ～客气 make yourself at home; don't stand on ceremony 这本书我有, 你～买了。 I've got a copy of the book, you don't need to buy one.

不由得 bùyóude 【副】can't help（doing sth.）: 听说小王受了伤, 她～流下泪来。 When she heard that Xiao Wang had been injured, she couldn't help breaking into tears. 她脚下一滑, 几乎跌倒, ～叫了一声。 As she slipped and almost fell she couldn't suppress a startled cry.

不由自主 bù yóu zì zhǔ　involuntarily; cannot restrain oneself; be tempted to

不约而同 bù yuē ér tóng　by coinci-

dence; do sth. in concert without previous arrangement; agree without previous consultation

不在话下 bù zài huà xià be nothing to (sb.); think nothing of (sth.); 这几道数学题对他来说～! These few mathematical problems are nothing to him.

不择手段 bù zé shǒuduàn by hook or by crook; by fair means or foul; unscrupulously

不知所措 bù zhī suǒ cuò at a loss; do not know what to do

不止 bùzhǐ 【动】be more than; 有这种意见的～我们。We are not the only people who think as much. 这个问题我们讨论过～一次了。We have discussed this problem more than once.

不只 bùzhǐ 【连】not only, 同"不但"; 这里～有现代化的大型工厂，也有乡镇办的中小型工厂。There are not just big modern factories here, but small township ones as well. 这孩子是在西安长大的,～没坐过轮船,也没见过海。This child grew up in Xi'an and has not been on a steamboat nor has ever he seen the sea.

不致 bùzhì 【副】not likely to (involve certain undesirable result); 事前有准备,问题发生时就～手忙脚乱了。If you are prepared beforehand, you will not be thrown into confusion should anything unforeseen occur.

不置可否 bù zhì kě fǒu decline to comment; be noncommittal; refuse to say yes or no

不着边际 bù zhuó biānjì off the point; entirely irrelevant; wide of the mark

不自量力 bù zì liàng lì not be aware of one's own limitations

不足 bùzú 【形】be insufficient; be inadequate; ～之处 drawbacks; limitations 准备～。The preparations (you have made) are inadequate. 【动】❶ less than (in number); ～四岁 not quite four years old ～两千人 less than two thousand people ❷ cannot; ～为凭 cannot be taken as proof ～为训 cannot serve as an example to follow

不足道 bùzúdào 【动】not worth mentioning; of no consequence; 我们现在这点儿成绩太～了。What we have accomplished now is not worth mentioning.

不足为奇 bù zú wéi qí not at all surprising; entirely to be expected

布 bù 【名】cotton cloth 【动】❶ spread; disseminate; 天空～满阴云。The sky is overcast with dark clouds. 农业技术站遍～全省。Agrotechnical stations are found all over the province. ❷ deploy; spread out; ～防 deploy troops for safe purposes 沿路都～上了岗哨。Sentinels were posted all along the road.

布告 bùgào 【名】notice (on a bulletin board)

布景 bùjǐng 【名】(stage) scenery; setting; decor

布局 bùjú 【名】overall arrangement; layout

布匹 bùpǐ 【名】cotton cloth (general term)

布鞋 bùxié 【名】〔只 zhǐ、双 shuāng〕cloth shoe

布置 bùzhì 【动】❶ get (a place) ready for a certain purpose; ～会场 get the place ready for the meeting ～房间 arrange a room ❷ make arrangements for work or some activity; ～学习 make arrangements for study 把下半年的工作～一下 make arrangements for the latter half of the year's work

步　bù　【名】❶ step：迈开大～ stride ❷ step；stage：工作分两～进行。The work will be carried out in two stages.

步兵　bùbīng　【名】infantry

步步为营　bù bù wéi yíng　fortifications are erected every time the troops make an advance；(*fig.*) advance cautiously

步调　bùdiào　【名】step；pace：～一致 keep in step 统一～ at a uniform pace

步伐　bùfá　【名】length and quickness of steps of drilling soldiers：～很整齐 with a uniform stride 加快前进的～ quicken one's pace 跟上时代的～ keep pace with the times

步话机　bùhuàjī　【名】〔个 gè、只 zhī〕walkie-talkie

步枪　bùqiāng　【名】〔支 zhī、杆 gǎn〕rifle

步人后尘　bù rén hòu chén　follow in sb.'s footsteps；follow suit (*derog.*)

步行　bùxíng　【动】be on foot

步骤　bùzhòu　【名】steps；procedure

部　bù　【名】❶ part；section：上～ upper part 北～ northern part 腹～ abdomen ❷ ministry；board：外交～ the Ministry of Foreign Affairs 财政～ the Ministry of Finance ❸ (mil.) headquarters；command：团～ regimental headquarters 【量】*for books*, *films*, *etc.*：一～彩色故事片 a colour feature film 这～词典是一册，那～是上下两册。This dictionary is one volume, while the other is in two volumes.

部队　bùduì　【名】unit；army；armed forces

部分　bùfen　【名】part；section

部件　bùjiàn　【名】parts or component parts

部落　bùluò　【名】tribe

部门　bùmén　【名】department

部首　bùshǒu　【名】(of Chinese characters) radical

部署　bùshǔ　【动】arrange；dispose；deploy：～兵力 deploy troops for battle 【名】arrangement；disposition

部位　bùwèi　【名】position；place；location

部下　bùxià　【名】troops or officers under a commander

部长　bùzhǎng　【名】minister (of a ministry)

C

cā

擦　cā　【动】❶ wipe；scrub；erase；clean：～黑板 wipe the blackboard ～机器 clean the machine ～汗 wipe away the sweat ❷ rub；scratch：手上～破了点儿皮 just a scratch on the hand ❸ put on；spread：～鞋油 apply shoe polish ❹ brush；shave：～肩而过 brush past sb.

擦拭　cāshì　【动】clean；rub

擦音　cāyīn　【名】(phonetics) fricative

cāi

猜　cāi　【动】guess；conjecture

猜测　cāicè　【动】guess

猜忌　cāijì　【动】be suspicious of and resent

猜谜　cāi = mí　give the answer to a riddle

猜想　cāixiǎng　【动】guess；conjecture

猜疑　cāiyí　【动】suspect

cái

才　cái　【名】◇ ability；talent：真～实学 real ability and solid learn-ing【副】(纔) ❶ used after a word or phrase expressing time to indicate that the time is late or has been long. No 了 is used at the end of the sentence even with a past event：昨天他一直忙到十二点～睡。Yesterday he was kept up until midnight. 老马现在～开始学外语。Lao Ma has only just begun to study a foreign language. 那场雨夜里很晚～停。The rain didn't stop until very late that night. ❷ indicates that one event precedes another and often implies a slow or leisurely manner：他总是等人都走了，～最后离开。He always stays until everyone else has left. 他把屋子收拾干净了，～坐下来看书。He sat down to read only after he had tidied up the room. ❸ used after a phrase with a numeral to indicate a large quantity：去参观的人很多，五辆车～够。Five buses were needed to take everybody to the exhibition. 我叫了他三四声他～听见。I had to call him 3 or 4 times before he heard me. ❹ used before a verb to indicate the immediate past：这座楼～盖好，人还没搬进去呢。This building is just finished and nobody has moved in yet. 他～回来，又出去了。He left again right after he returned. ❺ used before a word or phrase expressing time or quantity to indicate that the time is ear-

ly or the quantity small：现在～五点，等一会儿再去。It's only five o'clock now；we'd better wait a few minutes before we go. 这个孩子～四岁。This child is only four. ❻ *used in the second clause of a compound sentence to indicate that the condition stated in the first clause is a necessary condition and the second clause expresses the result or conclusion*：听了他的解释，我～知道是怎么回事。Only after I had heard his explanation did I understand what it was all about. 必须深入群众，～能了解群众。One must have close contact with the masses before one can understand them. 在这个城市，"火车头队"～是最好的足球队。Of all the football teams in this city, the *Locomotive* is easily the best. 咱们讨论讨论怎样～能加快速度。Let's discuss how we can work faster. *Sometimes the second clause is as simple as* 才行，才好 *etc. What it refers to is either the idea expressed in the first clause*：要解决这个难题，看来得老张亲自出马～行。Only Lao Zhang can fix this tough problem. Note：*or is one alternative in a situation where a choice is involved*：又是橘子又是苹果的，叫我先尝哪一样～好呢？There are both oranges and apples available here, and I can't decide which to have first. 您这么客气，我真不知说什么～好。You are so kind. I really don't know what to say. ❼ *used in conjunction with* 呢 *to form a very colloquial exclamatory sentence* ① *expresses the strong conviction of the speaker*：屋子里哪儿热呀，外面～热呢。You think it's hot in this room？Just try going outside！他画的那张画～好呢！That painting of his is what I call a masterwork. ② *shows one's own attitude or one's estimate of another's attitude, delivered in a determined tone, usu. in the negative*：我～不相信他的话呢。I'll be damned if I believe him！这么重要的事，他们～不会不管呢。Of course they won't be able to leave such an important matter unattended to！③"才怪呢"*used at the end of a sentence to indicate that the case is exactly opposite to what goes before* 才怪呢：这么重要的事，他们不管～怪呢。They do not take care of such an important matter？Not a chance！这本小说小李爱看～怪呢。That book is awfully dull；I bet Xiao Li won't enjoy it！

才干 cáigàn 【名】ability；competence；capability：这人很有～。He is a man of great ability.

才华 cáihuá 【名】literary or artistic talent：～横溢 overflowing with talent ～出众 possess exceptional talent

才能 cáinéng 【名】knowledge and ability：他是一个很有领导～的人。He has great leadership ability.

才子 cáizǐ gifted scholar

材 cái

材料 cáiliào 【名】material；stuff；data

财(財) cái 【名】wealth

财宝 cáibǎo 【名】money and valuables

财产 cáichǎn 【名】property；assets：一笔～ an assets

财产权 cáichǎnquán 【名】property right

财富 cáifù 【名】wealth；riches：物质～ material wealth 精神～ spiritual wealth

财经 cáijīng 【名】finance and economics

财会 cáikuài 【名】finance and ac-

counting

财力 cáilì 【名】financial resources；financial capability

财贸 cáimào 【名】finance and trade

财迷 cáimí 【名】person with an obsessive desire for money；money-grubber【形】obsessed by a craving for money

财神 cáishén 【名】money god

财团 cáituán 【名】consortium；financial group

财务 cáiwù 【名】financial affairs

财物 cáiwù 【名】money and property

财源 cáiyuán 【名】financial resources

财政 cáizhèng 【名】finance

财主 cáizhu 【名】moneybags

裁 cái 【动】cut（cloth，paper，etc.）：～纸 cut paper ～衣服 cut out material for clothing

裁减 cáijiǎn 【动】cut down；dismiss

裁剪 cáijiǎn 【动】cut out（a dress）

裁决 cáijué 【动】rule；make a ruling；hand down a verdict【名】verdict；ruling

裁军 cái = jūn disarmament

裁判 cáipàn 【动】❶ judge；decide ❷ referee【名】referee

cǎi

采 cǎi 【动】❶ pick；pluck；gather：～茶 pick tea 上山～药 climb the mountain to gather medicinal herbs ❷ collect；gather：～矿样 collect mineral samples ❸ mine；extract：～煤 mine coal

采伐 cǎifá 【动】fell（timber）

采访 cǎifǎng 【动】cover（news）；be on assignment（for a newspaper）

采购 cǎigòu 【动】purchase

采购员 cǎigòuyuán 【名】purchasing agent

采集 cǎijí 【动】collect；gather：～植物标本 collect plant specimens ～民歌 collect folk songs

采掘 cǎijué 【动】excavate

采矿 cǎi = kuàng 【动】mine；extract（coal，etc.）from a mine

采买 cǎimǎi 【动】select and purchase【名】purchasing agent

采纳 cǎinà 【动】adopt；accept；take（sb.'s advice）：～合理化建议 accept suggestions 我们提的方案被～了。Our project has been approved.

采取 cǎiqǔ 【动】adopt；take；follow：～预防措施 take preventive measures ～中西医结合的方法进行治疗 adopt the method of combining traditional Chinese medicine with modern medicine

采用 cǎiyòng 【动】employ；adopt；use

采摘 cǎizhāi 【动】pluck；pick

彩 cǎi 【名】◇ ❶ coloured silk ❷ variety；splendour

彩礼 cǎilǐ 【名】wedding gifts given by the bridegroom to the bride's family

彩排 cǎipái 【名】dress rehearsal

彩旗 cǎiqí 【名】〔面 miàn〕coloured flag；streamer

彩色 cǎisè 【名】colour

彩色电视 cǎisè diànshì colour television

彩色胶卷 cǎisè jiāojuǎn colour film

彩色片 cǎisèpiàn 【名】〔部 bù〕colour film

彩霞 cǎixiá 【名】rose-coloured cloud

踩 cǎi 【动】trample；tread；step on：脚～两只船 sit on the fence；double-deal 不要～庄稼！Don't step on the crops!

cài

菜　cài　【名】❶ vegetable；greens ❷ (of food) dish；course

菜单　càidān　【名】menu

菜篮子　càilánzi　【名】basket for vegetables；non-staple food；～工程 the "vegetable basket" project；project to enhance vegetable supply

菜市场　càishìchǎng　【名】food market

菜园　càiyuán　【名】vegetable garden

菜站　càizhàn　【名】wholesale vegetable market

菜子儿　càizǐr　【名】vegetable seed

cān

参（參）　cān　【动】◇ ❶ join；take part ❷ consult；refer：～看 read for reference

另见 cēn

参观　cānguān　【动】visit (place, exhibition, etc.)

参加　cānjiā　【动】❶ join；take part in；participate；attend：～一个旅游团 to join a tour group；to go on a package holiday ～宴会 attend a banquet 工人～工厂管理。Workers take part in the management of the factory. ❷ offer；give (opinion)：大家正商量怎么过元旦，你也～点儿意见吧！We are trying to decide how to celebrate New Year. You better come up with a few ideas.

参军　cān＝jūn　join the army

参考　cānkǎo　【动】consult；refer to：他写这篇文章～了不少资料。He consulted a great deal of reference material while writing this article. 这些意见仅供～。These suggestions are just for your reference.

参谋　cānmóu　【动】offer advice：会场怎么布置，请你帮助～～。Would you give us your advice on the arrangement at the meeting place? 【名】staff officer

参谋长　cānmóuzhǎng　【名】chief of staff

参数　cānshù　【名】parameter

参与　cānyù　【动】take part in；join；be a party to

参阅　cānyuè　【动】consult；read sth. for reference：此书可～。This book can be used for reference.

参赞　cānzàn　【名】(of an embassy) counsellor

参战　cān＝zhàn　participate in war

参照　cānzhào　【动】refer to；consult：以上办法，可～实行。The work should be carried out with reference to above recommended methods.

参照物　cānzhàowù　【名】reference

参政　cān＝zhèng　participate in government and political affairs

餐　cān　【名】◇ meal：一顿美～ a delicious meal 【动】◇ eat：饱～一顿 have a square meal 【量】*for meals*

餐车　cānchē　【名】dining car

餐巾　cānjīn　【名】table napkin

餐具　cānjù　【名】tableware

餐厅　cāntīng　【名】❶ large dining hall ❷ restaurant

餐饮业　cānyǐnyè　【名】food and beverage line；restaurants and bars

cán

残（殘）　cán　【形】◇ ❶ incomplete；deficient：～品 defective goods ❷ remaining：～匪 a remaining handful of bandits ～枝败叶 decaying branches and withered leaves ～冬 the last few days of

winter ❸ deformed; maimed; injured: 身～志不～ physically disabled but spiritually wholesome; broken in body but not in spirit

残暴　cánbào　【形】brutal; cruel; ruthless; merciless

残兵败将　cán bīng bài jiàng　a routed army and a beaten general; remnants of a completely defeated army

残存　cáncún　【动】(of a few people, houses, etc.) survive (a disaster, war, etc.)

残废　cánfèi　【名】cripple; physically disabled person 【动】be physically disabled

残害　cánhài　【动】❶ mutilate ❷ murder; slaughter

残疾　cánjí　【名】physical disability; deformity

残疾人　cánjírén　【名】disabled person

残局　cánjú　【名】❶ final phase (e.g. of a chess game) ❷ situation after the failure of an undertaking

残酷　cánkù　【形】❶ cruel; brutal; merciless: 压榨的手段十分～。The oppression was brutal to the extreme. ❷ harsh; fierce; bitter: 他经受过～环境的磨练。He has been tempered in a harsh environment.

残缺不全　cán quē bù quán　incomplete; mutilated

残忍　cánrěn　【形】brutal; cruel; merciless

残杀　cánshā　【动】slaughter; kill brutally; massacre

残余　cányú　【名】remnants; remains; vestiges

蚕(蠶) cán　【名】silkworm

蚕豆　cándòu　【名】broad bean

蚕茧　cánjiǎn　【名】silkworm cocoon

蚕食　cánshí　【动】nibble (e.g. at another country's territory)

蚕丝　cánsī　【名】silk

惭(慚) cán

惭愧　cánkuì　【形】ashamed; abashed

cǎn

惨(慘) cǎn　【形】❶ miserable; wretched; pitiful: ～不忍睹 so horrible that one could hardly bear 他晚年的遭遇很～。He was miserable in his old age. ❷ to a serious degree; disastrous; crushing: 这场球咱们队输得很～。Our team suffered a crushing defeat in this match.

惨案　cǎn'àn　【名】massacre; tragedy

惨白　cǎnbái　【形】ghostly pale

惨剧　cǎnjù　【名】tragic event

惨痛　cǎntòng　【形】bitter; grievous; painful: ～的教训 a bitter lesson

惨无人道　cǎn wú réndào　cruel and inhuman

惨重　cǎnzhòng　【形】devastating; disastrous; heavy; serious; grievous: 损失～ heavy losses 遭到～的失败 suffer a crushing defeat

càn

灿(燦) càn

灿烂　cànlàn　【形】bright; magnificent; splendid: 阳光～ bright sunshine 光辉～的未来 a bright and glorious future

cāng

仓(倉) cāng　【名】granary; storehouse

仓储　cāngchǔ　【动】keep grain, goods, etc. in a storehouse

仓促　cāngcù　【形】hasty; hurried: ～应战 put up a last-minute resist-

ance 时间～。Time is pressing. 他走得很～，来不及跟你告别了。He left in haste and could not say goodbye to you.

仓皇　cānghuáng　【形】scared and hasty; in a flurry; in haste: 神色～ panic-stricken 敌人～逃命。The enemy fled in panic.

仓库　cāngkù　【名】ware-house; store

苍（蒼）cāng

苍白　cāngbái　【形】❶ (of complexion) pale ❷ (of hair) grey

苍苍　cāngcāng　【形】❶ grizzled: 鬓发～ grey-haired ❷ 同"苍茫": 海山～ a vast expanse of hazy mountains and seas

苍翠　cāngcuì　【形】dark green

苍劲　cāngjìng　【形】(of trees, paintings of trees, calligraphy) vigorous and bold: ～挺拔的青松 sturdy and upright pines 笔法～有力 vigorous and bold handwriting

苍老　cānglǎo　【形】(of looks or voice) aged; old

苍茫　cāngmáng　【形】boundless and indistinct; vast and hazy: ～大地 a vast area of land 暮色～ deepening shades of dusk

苍蝇　cāngying　【名】〔只 zhǐ〕fly

沧（滄）cāng

沧海一粟　cānghǎi yī sù　a drop in the ocean: 地球与整个太阳系相比，只不过是～。Compared with the solar system as a whole, the earth is just a speck of dust.

沧桑　cāngsāng　【名】(short for 沧海桑田) the seas change into mulberry fields and mulberry fields into seas; the world is changing all the time: 饱经～ have seen much of the world; have seen the vicissitudes of life

藏 cáng

藏　cáng　【动】hide

藏身　cángshēn　【动】hide oneself

藏书　cángshū　【名】collection of books

藏污纳垢　cáng wū nà gòu　shelter evil people and countenance evil practices: 旧上海的外滩是个～的地方。The Bund of old Shanghai used to be a den of iniquity. 也作"藏垢纳污"。

cāo

操　cāo　【动】◇ hold; grasp: ～枪 hold a rifle 【名】drill; exercise: 出～ turn out for drill 做～ do physical exercises 课间～ exercise during the class-break

操办　cāobàn　【动】orchestrate

操场　cāochǎng　【名】sports-ground; playground

操持　cāochí　【动】manage; handle: ～家务 manage house-hold affairs 安排住房的事，请你～一下。Will you please take care of arranging accommodation?

操劳　cāoláo　【动】work painstakingly; do sth. industriously

操练　cāoliàn　【动】drill

操心　cāo = xīn　worry about; be concerned over

操演　cāoyǎn　【动】drill; demonstrate

操之过急　cāo zhī guò jí　act with undue haste; be too hasty

操纵　cāozòng　【动】❶ control; operate: 远距离～ remote control ❷ manipulate; rig: 幕后～ pull strings; manipulate from behind the scenes ～市场 rig the market

操纵台　cāozòngtái　【名】control

panel

操作 cāozuò 【动】operate (a machine)

操作规程 cāozuò guīchéng operating regulations

cáo

嘈 cáo

嘈杂 cáozá 【形】noisy

槽 cáo 【名】❶ trough；manger ❷ groove

槽床 cáochuáng 【名】troughstand

槽牙 cáoyá 【名】〔颗 kē〕molar

cǎo

草 cǎo 【名】〔棵 kē、株 zhū〕grass；straw 【形】careless；rough；sloppy (usu. handwriting)：他写的字太～了。His handwriting is rather sloppy.

草案 cǎo'àn 【名】draft (of a plan, resolution, proposal,etc.)

草包 cǎobāo 【名】❶ straw bag or sack；packing mat ❷ a sack loaded with straw ❸ a good-for-nothing (derog.)

草草 cǎocǎo 【副】hastily；hurriedly；carelessly：～了事 get through sth. in a perfunctory way ～收兵 withdraw troops in haste；give up before fully completing a task ～地看了一遍 glance over (sth.) roughly

草地 cǎodì 【名】lawn；grasslands

草稿 cǎogǎo 【名】manuscript；draft (of an article, drawing, etc.)

草绿 cǎolǜ 【形】grass green

草帽 cǎomào 【名】〔顶 dǐng〕straw hat

草木皆兵 cǎo mù jiē bīng　see an enemy behind every tree；(fig.) be plagued by imaginary fears

草拟 cǎonǐ 【动】draft

草坪 cǎopíng 【名】lawn

草签 cǎoqiān 【动】initial：双方～了协定。Both parties initialed an agreement.

草书 cǎoshū 【名】rapid cursive style of writing；grass writing

草率 cǎoshuài 【形】rash；careless；perfunctory：～从事 act rashly 处理得很～ deal with sth. in a careless manner 这个决定太～。This decision is too hasty.

草图 cǎotú 【名】sketch (drawing or designing)

草鞋 cǎoxié 【名】〔只 zhī、双 shuāng〕straw sandal

草原 cǎoyuán 【名】steppe；prairie；grasslands

草字 cǎozì 【名】cursive calligraphy

cè

册 cè 【名】pamphlet；booklet：记分～ (teacher's) markbook 【量】for books volume；copy

册子 cèzi 【名】〔本 běn〕pamphlet；booklet

厕(廁) cè

厕所 cèsuǒ 【名】toilet；lavatory

侧(側) cè 【名】side；flank：铁路两～都是稻田。There are paddy fields on both sides of the railway. 【动】incline：～耳细听 tilt one's head and listen carefully ～着身子躺着 lie on one's side

侧面 cèmiàn 【名】side；profile

侧视图 cèshìtú 【名】side view

侧翼 cèyì 【名】(mil.) flank

侧影 cèyǐng 【名】profile；silhouette

侧重 cèzhòng 【动】lay emphasis on (one aspect)

测(測)　cè　【动】survey

测绘　cèhuì　【动】survey and draw（a map）

测控　cèkòng　【动】monitor

测量　cèliáng　【动】survey

测试　cèshì　【动】test；try out

测验　cèyàn　【动】test；check 【名】test

策　cè　【名】◇ plan；scheme；strategy：出谋划 ～ mastermind a scheme；give counsel【动】◇ whip；spur：～马前进 spur a horse on

策动　cèdòng　【动】incite；instigate

策反　cèfǎn　【动】foment rebellion within the enemy camp

策划　cèhuà　【动】hatch（a plot）；plot

策略　cèlüè　【名】tactics

策源地　cèyuándì　【名】source；place of origin

cēn

参(參)　cēn

另见 cān

参差不齐　cēncī bù qí　uneven；not uniform：山坡上的树长得～。Trees of varying heights grow on the slope. 他们的英语水平～。Their proficiency in English varies from one to another.

céng

层(層)　céng　【名】layer；stratum【量】layer；storey

层出不穷　céng chū bù qióng　emerge in an endless stream；emerge one after another

层次　céngcì　【名】❶（of speech or writing）arrangement of ideas ❷ administrative level

曾　céng　【副】indicates that an event has happened before（usu. in written language）：你我似 ～ 相识。It seems we have met before. 他～听过这位物理学家的学术报告。He once attended a lecture by this physicist.

曾经　céngjīng　【副】indicates that sth. happened before、and cannot be modified by a negative adverb. the verb following it often takes "过"：王先生～当过我的英语老师。Mr. Wang was once my English teacher. 我～到桂林参观过一次。I have visited Guilin once.

cèng

蹭　cèng　【动】❶ rub；brush；scrape：～破了腿 scrape one's knee ❷ brush by：他 ～ 了一身灰。He brushed against sth. and got dust all over himself. 小心 ～ 上油漆！Watch out for the wet paint! ❸ move at a snail's pace：一步～一步往前～ drag along at a snail's pace

chā

叉　chā　【名】❶ fork ❷（～儿）"×"（usu. used to indicate errors or to cross out sth.）【动】❶ spear：～鱼 spear fish ❷ interlace：～着手 with hands clasped；with folded hands；with interlaced fingers

另见 chǎ

叉子　chāzi　【名】〔把 bǎ〕fork

差　chā　【名】difference

另见 chà；chāi

差别　chābié　【名】difference；gap；disparity：城乡之间现在是有～的。There is, at present, a disparity between the city and the country.

差错　chācuò 【名】mistake；error；slip：她当邮递员已经十几年了，从未出过一次～。She had delivered letters for over ten years and never made a mistake.

差额　chā'é 【名】(of accounts) balance

差额选举　chā'é xuǎnjǔ multi-candidate election

差价　chājià 【名】price difference

差距　chājù 【名】gap (between the more advanced and those lagging behind)

差异　chāyì 【名】difference；dissimilarity：～很大 a great difference 两者之间有～。There is a difference between the two.

插　chā 【动】❶ stick in；insert：把花～在花瓶里 arrange flowers in a vase 运动场周围～满了彩旗。Coloured banners have been placed all around the sports-ground. ❷ insert；interpose：～了一句话 put in a word 这个新来的同学～到三年级二班。This new student has been assigned to class two of the third year.

插班　chā = bān classify a student from another school according to his level

插翅难飞　chā chì nán fēi even with wings (he) couldn't escape

插话　chāhuà 【名】a remark interjected

插话　chā = huà interrupt while sb. is speaking；interject

插曲　chāqǔ 【名】❶ interlude ❷ the song or songs from a film or play, not including the theme song ❸ a side issue；an event irrelevant to the proceedings

插手　chā = shǒu ❶ take part；lend a hand：我很想帮忙，可是插不上手。I'm willing to help, but I don't know how. ❷ meddle；get one's hands on (derog.)：这是他们的家庭纠纷，别人不用～。This is a family quarrel, and nobody should butt in.

插头　chātóu 【名】plug

插图　chātú 【名】illustration in a book

插销　chāxiāo 【名】❶ bolt ❷ electric plug

插秧　chā = yāng transplant rice shoots

插秧机　chāyāngjī 【名】〔台 tái〕rice-transplanter

插嘴　chā = zuǐ put in a word；interrupt sb.'s speech；interject

插座　chāzuò 【名】socket (for a plug)

chá

茬　chá 【名】(～儿) roots and stubble left in the field after reaping 【量】crop

茶　chá 【名】❶ tea (plant) ❷ tea (beverage)

茶杯　chábēi 【名】〔个 gè〕tea cup

茶点　chádiǎn 【名】tea served with pastries；refreshments

茶馆　cháguǎn 【名】(～儿) tea-house

茶壶　cháhú 【名】〔把 bǎ〕tea pot

茶会　cháhuì 【名】tea party

茶具　chájù 【名】tea-set

茶盘　chápán 【名】tray for a tea-set

茶水　cháshuǐ 【名】drink (e.g. tea, water, etc.)

茶叶　cháyè 【名】tea leaves

查　chá 【动】❶ check ❷ investigate ❸ look up

查办　chábàn 【动】investigate and punish：撤职～ dismiss from office and prosecute

查点　chádiǎn 【动】check the number or amount of：～人数 make a

head count ～货物 stock-taking

查对 cháduì 【动】verify；check：～数目 verify the figures ～资料 check the information

查封 cháfēng 【动】check and seal up

查看 chákàn 【动】inspect；examine

查收 cháshōu 【动】check and accept

查问 cháwèn 【动】inquire

查询 cháxún 【动】investigate；make an inquiry

查阅 cháyuè 【动】read for information；consult（books）

查账 chá＝zhàng　check accounts

查证 cházhèng 【动】investigate and verify；check

察

chá 【动】◇ ❶ observe；notice；see ❷ look over；inspect；examine

察访 cháfǎng 【动】go about and make inquiries；engage in fact-finding：四处～ make inquiries everywhere 公安干警经过细心～，终于替他找到了失散多年的亲人。After painstaking inquiry, the public security officers and men found the family member with whom he had lost contact for many years.

察觉 chájué 【动】realize；sense

察看 chákàn 【动】look over；examine

察言观色 chá yán guān sè guess sb.'s intentions by studying his words and facial expression

chǎ

叉

chǎ 【动】separate；spread apart：～开腿 spread one's legs apart；straddle
另见 chā

chà

岔

chà 【动】❶（of a road）fork ❷ stagger（e. g. alternation office hours）

岔路 chàlù 【名】fork（in a road）

岔子 chàzi 【名】trouble；mishap

刹

chà
另见 shā

刹那 chànà 【名】in the twinkling of an eye；in a flash

诧（詫）

chà

诧异 chàyì 【形】be perplexed

差

chà 【动】❶ short of：～一道工序。Thére is one more step in the work process. ～五分钟汽车就要开了。The bus will be leaving in five minutes. ❷ fall short of；differ from：丝毫不～ not the least bit different；without the slightest discrepancy；(of calculation) without the slightest error 我们的成绩虽不小，但离要求还～得很远。We have achieved a measure of success, but we still fell short of expectations. 我把日子记～了。I got the date wrong. 【形】poor；not up to standard：效果～ poor results 质量～ poor quality
另见 chā；chāi

差不多 chàbuduō 【形】❶ more or less the same；nearly；almost：他们俩年纪～。The two of them are about the same age. 这两条铁路～一样长。The two railway routes are more or less the same length. 我和他～三年没见面了。He and I haven't seen each other for nearly three years. 水～要开了。The water is almost boiling. ❷ nearly complete；nearly finished（cannot

be used as an attributive)：这个电视机修得～了。The repairs on this television set are just about finished. 人到得～了，开始干吧。The people are almost all here. Let's start. ❸ almost used up；not much left (cannot be used as an attributive)：水泥用得～了，赶快去拉。The cement is almost used up. We'd better go and get more. ❹ general；common；average (used only as an attributive)：这种物理常识，～的中学生都懂。Any middle school student knows it, since it is simply a common-sense principle of physics. 中国～的大城市他都去过。He has been to almost all the big cities of China.

差劲儿 chàjìnr 【形】〈口〉poor (in quality)；no good；worthless：这活儿干得有点儿～。This work has been poorly done.

差(一)点儿 chà(yi)diǎnr 【副】nearly；barely；by a hair's breadth indicates that sth. nearly took place or just barely took place and implies either thankfulness or regret ❶ when the event referred to is sth. undesirable, both 差(一)点儿 and 差(一)点儿没 indicate that sth. nearly happened but in fact did not：我今天早上～迟到。I was almost late this morning. 我今天早上～没迟到。I was almost late this morning. ❷ when the event referred to is sth. desirable, 差(一)点儿 together with 就 indicates that sth. didn't take place though it had seemed possible：我～(就)赶上火车了。I nearly caught the train. 差(一)点儿没 indicates that sth. barely took place：我～没赶上火车。I just barely caught the train.

chāi

拆 chāi 【动】❶ take apart；tear open：～信 open a letter ～开包裹 open a parcel 把枪～开 disassemble a gun ❷ demolish；tear down；dismantle：～房子 demolish a house 伤口已经～线了。The stitches closing the wound have already been taken out.

拆除 chāichú 【动】 dismantle；demolish；remove：～旧房屋 demolish old houses ～工事 dismantle the defence works

拆穿 chāichuān 【动】expose；reveal；unmask：～阴谋 expose a plot ～谎言 expose a lie

拆毁 chāihuǐ 【动】destroy；break down；tear down

拆迁 chāiqiān 【动】have an old building pulled down and its occupants moved elsewhere

拆散 chāi // sǎn break up (e.g. a set)

拆散 chāi // sàn break up (e.g. a family)

拆台 chāi = tái undermine；disrupt；cut the ground out from under sb.'s feet

拆卸 chāixiè 【动】take apart；dismantle；disassemble

拆字 chāi = zì glyphomancy

差 chāi 【名】errand；mission
另见 chā；chà

差旅费 chāilǚfèi 【名】allowances for an business trip

差遣 chāiqiǎn 【动】send (sb.) (on a mission)

差事 chāishi 【名】assignment；errand

chái

柴　chái　【名】firewood

柴火　cháihuo　【名】firewood

柴油　cháiyóu　【名】diesel oil

柴油机　cháiyóujī　【名】〔台 tái〕diesel engine

豺　chái　【名】jackal

豺狼　cháiláng　【名】jackals and wolves;（*fig.*）cruel and evil people

chān

掺（摻）　chān　【动】mix; blend：水泥里～点儿沙子 add some sand to the cement

搀（攙）　chān　【动】❶ support or help sb. by placing one's hand under the person's elbow：乘务员～着老大娘上了火车。The conductor helped the old woman onto the train. ❷ 同"掺"chān

搀扶　chānfú　【动】give one's arm to（an aged person or an invalid）; support

搀和　chānhuo　【动】mix; blend 也作"掺和"。

搀假　chān = jiǎ　adulterate

搀杂　chānzá　【动】mix in（sth. which should not be there）也作"掺杂"。

chán

馋（饞）　chán　【形】❶ greedy; gluttonous ❷ ◇ covet：眼～ with covetous eyes

缠（纏）　chán　【动】❶ wind; twine：～线球 wind yarn into a ball ❷ bother; pester：他被事务性工作～住了。He has been tied up with routine work. 小明～着爷爷带他去动物园。Xiǎo Míng is pestering his grandfather to take him to the zoo.

缠绵　chánmián　【形】〈书〉❶（of illness or feelings）be entangled in; be in the grips of ❷ sweet and charming

缠绕　chánrào　【动】❶ wind; twine ❷ worry; harass

潺　chán

潺潺　chánchán　【象声】gurgling and babbling; purling

chǎn

产（産）　chǎn　【动】❶ give birth to：～卵 lay eggs ❷ produce; yield：～粮 produce grain 沿海盛～鱼虾。The coastal waters abound in fish and prawns.

产地　chǎndì　【名】the place where a thing is produced

产妇　chǎnfù　【名】lying-in woman

产科　chǎnkē　【名】obstetrical department; maternity department

产量　chǎnliàng　【名】yield; output

产品　chǎnpǐn　【名】product

产权　chǎnquán　【名】property right

产生　chǎnshēng　【动】❶ produce; give rise to; engender：他对原有结论～了怀疑。He had doubt about the original conclusion. ❷ nominate; elect：每个小组～一个代表。Each group nominates one representative.

产物　chǎnwù　【名】products; outcome

产销　chǎnxiāo　【动】production and marketing

产业　chǎnyè　【名】❶ property; es-

tate ❷ industrial (*attrib. only*)

产业工人　chǎnyè gōngrén　industrial worker

产值　chǎnzhí　【名】output value

铲（鏟）chǎn　【名】shovel; spade【动】❶ shovel; ～煤 shovel coal ～土 shovel earth ❷ scrape even; level (with a spade); ～草 clear away weeds with a spade 把地～平 level the ground with a shovel

铲除　chǎnchú　【动】uproot; eradicate; root out; ～杂草 root out the weeds ～陋习，树立新风 do uproot bad customs and encourage new practices

铲土机　chǎntǔjī　【名】〔台 tái〕spading machine

铲子　chǎnzi　【名】〔把 bǎ〕spade

阐（闡）chǎn

阐明　chǎnmíng　【动】explain; expound; ～观点 explain a point of view ～科学道理 expound scientific theory

阐述　chǎnshù　【动】elaborate; explain; expound; 把道理～清楚 explain the reason clearly

chàn

忏（懺）chàn

忏悔　chànhuǐ　【动】show repentance; repent

颤（顫）chàn　【动】quiver; vibrate

颤动　chàndòng　【动】quiver; vibrate

颤抖　chàndǒu　【动】tremble

chāng

昌　chāng

昌盛　chāngshèng　【形】prosperous; flourishing

猖　chāng

猖獗　chāngjué　【形】wild; unbridled; unrestrained; ～一时 run wild for a time

猖狂　chāngkuáng　【形】rampant; wild; ～反扑 desperate counter-attack

cháng

长（長）cháng　【形】long 【名】❶ length; 这座桥全～五百米。The overall length of this bridge is 500 metres. 这块木板的～是宽的二倍。The length of this plank is twice its width. ❷ ◇ strong point; forte; 一技之～ be skillful in something 取～补短 overcome one's shortcomings by learning from the strengths of others 另见 zhǎng

长波　chángbō　【名】(of a radio) long wave

长城　Chángchéng　【名】the Great Wall

长处　chángchù　【名】merit; strong point

长此以往　cháng cǐ yǐ wǎng　if things go on like this

长度　chángdù　【名】length

长短　chángduǎn　【名】❶ length ❷ right and wrong; strong and weak points

长方形　chángfāngxíng　【名】rectangle

长工　chánggōng　【名】regular farmhand

长久　chángjiǔ　【形】for a long time; lasting

长年累月　cháng nián lěi yuè　year after year; 这些珍贵资料，是他～收集起来的。These valuable materials

were collected by him over the years.

长跑 chángpǎo【名】long-distance running

长篇大论 chángpiān dàlùn long-winded tirade；lengthy speech or piece of writing (*usu. derog.*)

长篇小说 chángpiān xiǎoshuō〔本 běn、部 bù〕novel

长期 chángqī【名】long-term

长驱直入 cháng qū zhí rù push forward unopposed；1949 年，解放大军 ～，直取南京。In 1949, the Liberation Army pushed forward meeting no opposition and liberated Nanjing.

长生 chángshēng【形】live long；～ 不老 long-lived

长寿 chángshòu【形】long-lived

长途 chángtú【名】long distance

长途电话 chángtú diànhuà long distance call；trunk call

长线 chángxiàn【名】(of products) be in oversupply

长线产品 chángxiàn chǎnpǐn products of oversupply

长于 chángyú【动】be good at；～外 语 be good at foreign languages ～ 数学 be good at mathematics

长远 chángyuǎn【形】long-range；long-term；～利益 long-term interests ～目标 long-range objective ～ 规划 long-range plan

长治久安 cháng zhì jiǔ ān lasting peace and stability

长足 chángzú【形】by leaps and bounds；～的进步 rapid progress 取 得了～的发展 have made progress by leaps and bounds

场（場）cháng【名】level ground；open space（threshing ground）【量】*for the duration of sth*.：一～大雨 a heavy rain 一～争 论 a debate 一～大病 a serious illness 哭了一～ a fit of crying

另见 chǎng

场院 chángyuàn【名】threshing floor；threshing ground

肠（腸）cháng【名】intestines

肠胃病 chángwèibìng【名】stomach trouble

肠炎 chángyán【名】enteritis

肠子 chángzi【名】intestines

尝（嘗）cháng【动】taste；have a taste of

尝试 chángshì【动】try；attempt

常 cháng【形】◇ ❶ common；ordinary；universal：～人 ordinary people ～理 a universal principle of logic ❷ constant：～绿植物 evergreens【副】often；frequently：～来 ～往 come and go frequently 医疗 队～到农村巡回医疗。The medical team often goes to the countryside and travels around to visit patients.

常备 chángbèi【形】ever prepared

常备不懈 cháng bèi bù xiè maintain constant vigilance；be always prepared

常备军 chángbèijūn【名】standing army；regular army

常常 chángcháng【副】often；frequently

常规 chángguī【名】convention；routine

常规武器 chángguī wǔqì conventional weaponry

常规战争 chángguī zhànzhēng conventional war

常轨 chángguī【名】normal practice

常见病 chángjiànbìng【名】common disease

常例 chánglì【名】common practice

常年 chángnián【名】all year round

常情 chángqíng【名】reason；sense：人之～ reason；sense

常任　chángrèn　【形】permanent；standing：～理事 permanent member of a council ～理事国 permanent member state of a council

常识　chángshí　【名】common sense

常态　chángtài　【名】normal state

常务　chángwù　【形】day-to-day business：～委员 member of the standing committee ～副市长 managing vice-mayor

常务委员会　chángwù wěiyuánhuì　standing committee

常用　chángyòng　【形】in common use：～词语 everyday expressions

偿（償）　cháng　【动】◇ make up；compensate；pay back

偿付　chángfù　【动】pay back

偿还　chánghuán　【动】compensate；pay back

chǎng

厂（廠）　chǎng　【名】factory

厂房　chǎngfáng　【名】factory building；factory workshop

厂矿　chǎngkuàng　【名】factories and mines

厂史　chǎngshǐ　【名】the history of a factory

厂长　chǎngzhǎng　【名】director of a factory

场（場）　chǎng　【名】❶ site；spot：事件发生时，他不在～。He was not there when it happened. ❷ stage or playing ground：今天赛乒乓球，你上～吗? Are you taking part in the table tennis match today? ❸ (of drama) scene：这个话剧共四幕七～。There are four acts and seven scenes in this play. 【量】*for sports and recreation*：一～电影 a showing of a movie 一～足球赛 a football match

另见 cháng

场地　chǎngdì　【名】a stretch of level ground

场合　chǎnghé　【名】occasion

场面　chǎngmiàn　【名】❶ (of drama, film, novel) scene；event ❷ a particular occasion in real life ❸ Chinese opera orchestra

场所　chǎngsuǒ　【名】place (*used for a specific purpose*)；area

敞　chǎng　【动】open：～一会儿门 leave the door open for a moment 瓶子～着口儿 The bottle has been left uncorked. 【形】open；not enclosed：这个院子太～，连个围墙也没有。This courtyard is too open. It doesn't even have a proper wall around it.

敞开　chǎngkāi　【动】❶ open wide：～窗户 throw open the windows ❷ free and unrestricted：～价格 set no limits on prices；non-controlling prices

敞亮　chǎngliàng　【形】spacious and bright

敞篷车　chǎngpéngchē〔辆 liàng〕open car；convertible

chàng

怅（悵）　chàng

怅惘　chàngwǎng　【形】〈书〉depressed；dispirited

畅（暢）　chàng

畅快　chàngkuài　【形】happy and carefree

畅所欲言　chàng suǒ yù yàn　speak one's mind freely；get things off one's chest：在小组会上，大家～，对工作提出了不少建议。During the group meeting, we all voiced our

opinions freely, making a lot of suggestions.

畅谈　chàngtán　【动】talk freely

畅通　chàngtōng　【动】unimpeded

畅想　chàngxiǎng　【动】give free rein to one's imagination

畅销　chàngxiāo　【动】(of merchandise) sell very well

畅行　chàngxíng　【动】advance unimpeded

畅游　chàngyóu　【动】swim unrestrained

倡　chàng

倡导　chàngdǎo　【动】take the lead in advocating sth.

倡议　chàngyì　【动】propose 【名】proposal

倡议书　chàngyìshū　【名】written proposal

唱　chàng　【动】❶ sing：～支山歌 sing a folk song ～戏 sing in an opera ❷ ◇ read out aloud：～票 call out the names of those voted for when counting ballots

唱段　chàngduàn　【名】(of Chinese opera) aria

唱对台戏　chàng duìtáixì　(of two theatrical troupes) put on rival performances；(fig.) set oneself up against；take an opposing stand

唱反调　chàng fǎndiào　strike a discordant note；wilfully speak or act contrary to

唱高调　chàng gāodiào　be bombastic；use high-sounding language

唱机　chàngjī　【名】gramophone；phonograph

唱片　chàngpiàn　【名】〔张 zhāng〕gramophone record；放～ play a record

唱腔　chàngqiāng　【名】(of Chinese opera) melody of an aria

chāo

抄　chāo　【动】❶ copy；transcribe：～文件 make a copy of the document ～书 copy (a passage) from a book ❷ plagiarize ❸ search and confiscate ❹ take (a short cut)：～近路 take a short cut ❺ grab：～起铲子把煤铲到炉子里去 grab a shovel and shovel the coal into the stove ❻ fold (one's arms)：～着手 fold one's arms ❼ outflank；thwart：～敌人的后路 outflank the enemy and attack from the rear

抄获　chāohuò　【动】search (a place) and seize (e.g. stolen goods)

抄家　chāo = jiā　search sb.'s house and confiscate his property

抄录　chāolù　【动】copy (sth.) down

抄袭　chāoxí　【动】❶ plagiarize；copy ❷ follow blindly (in another's footsteps)：不能生吞活剥地～别国的经验。We cannot blindly adopt the practices of other countries. ❸ (of troops) take a detour and surprise the enemy

抄写　chāoxiě　【动】make a clear copy of；copy

钞(鈔)　chāo

钞票　chāopiào　【名】banknote

超　chāo　【动】❶ surpass；overtake；exceed：～车 overtake the car in front 赶～世界先进水平 catch up with and surpass the international level ❷ transcend；go beyond；be above：～越个人得失 transcend personal considerations ❸ super-；ultra-；extra-：～短波 ultra-short wave ～高压 superhigh pressure

超产　chāo = chǎn　overfulfill the

planned quota

超出　chāochū　【动】go beyond；exceed：～范围 overstep the bounds ～规定 overstep the regulations ～预算 exceed the budget

超导体　chāodǎotǐ　【名】superconductor

超额　chāo＝é　overfulfill

超过　chāo∥guò　surpass；overtake；outstrip：在百米赛跑中小王一下子就～好几个人。Xiao Wang outstripped several runners in the 100 metre race. 今年他们的粮食产量～了历史最高水平。Their grain output this year is higher than at any other time in its history.

超级　chāojí　【形】super-

超级大国　chāojí dàguó　super-power

超级市场　chāojí shìchǎng　【名】supermarket

超阶级　chāo jiējí　transcending classes；above classes

超龄　chāo＝líng　over-age

超然　chāorán　【形】stand aloof

超声波　chāoshēngbō　【名】ultrasonic wave

超音速　chāoyīnsù　【名】supersonic speed

超越　chāoyuè　【动】transcend；surmount；exceed；surpass

超支　chāo＝zhī　overspend

超重　chāo＝zhòng　（of goods）overweight

cháo

巢　cháo　【名】nest；den

巢穴　cháoxué　【名】den；lair（also fig.）

朝　cháo　【名】dynasty：明～ the Ming dynasty 【动】face（usu. in colloquial speech）：他家的大门～南。The gate of his house faces south. 【介】towards：隔着窗户～外看 gaze

out through the window 农业必须～着机械化的方向发展。Agriculture must be mechanized. Note：朝 when used before a monosyllabic word of locality，such as 东，西，上，下，前，后，doesn't take 着. 另见 zhāo

朝代　cháodài　【名】dynasty

嘲　cháo

嘲弄　cháonòng　【动】mock；ridicule

嘲笑　cháoxiào　【动】ridicule；jeer

潮　cháo　【名】tide 【形】damp；moist

潮流　cháoliú　【名】trend；tide

潮湿　cháoshī　【形】damp

潮水　cháoshuǐ　【名】tide

chǎo

吵　chǎo　【动】❶ quarrel ❷ make a noise；disturb 【形】noisy

吵架　chǎo＝jià　quarrel

吵闹　chǎonào　【动】❶ make a lot of noise ❷ make a fuss；wrangle

吵嚷　chǎorǎng　【动】make a racket

吵嘴　chǎo＝zuǐ　quarrel；bicker

炒　chǎo　【动】stir-fry

炒股　chǎo＝gǔ　speculate on stocks

炒面　chǎomiàn　【名】❶ stir-fried noodles ❷ stir-fried flour（with water added，eaten as a kind of porridge）

炒鱿鱼　chǎo yóuyú　sack；fire；give sb. the sack

chē

车（車）　chē　【名】〔辆 liàng〕vehicle 【动】❶ shape；turn：这个零件～得很光。This part has been turned on a lathe until it is smooth

and shiny. ❷ pump water by using a waterwheel：这里早就不用水车～水了。This place has long since abandoned the use of the waterwheel for pumping water.

车床　chēchuáng　【名】〔台 tái〕lathe

车次　chēcì　【名】a train's number

车灯　chēdēng　【名】〔盏 zhǎn〕general name for lights on a vehicle

车工　chēgōng　【名】turner；lathe operator

车祸　chēhuò　【名】〔起 qǐ〕traffic accident：出了～。A traffic accident occurred.

车间　chējiān　【名】workshop

车辆　chēliàng　【名】vehicles；traffic

车轮　chēlún　【名】wheel

车牌　chēpái　【名】licence plate

车票　chēpiào　【名】〔张 zhāng〕train or bus ticket

车水马龙　chē shuǐ mǎ lóng　an endless stream of horses and carriages；(fig.) heavy traffic；bustling traffic

车厢　chēxiāng　【名】railway carriage；coach (of a train)

车站　chēzhàn　【名】❶ railway station ❷ bus stop

车子　chēzi　【名】〔辆 liàng〕vehicle

chě

扯　chě　【动】❶ pull：～住他不放 keep a tight hold on him ❷ tear：～破了衣服 tear one's clothes ❸ gossip；chat：胡～ talk nonsense 东拉西～ babble

扯皮　chěpí　【动】haggle over trifles；argue back and forth

chè

彻(徹)　chè

彻底　chèdǐ　【形】thorough；thoroughgoing：问题解决得很～。The problem is completely settled. 他的病得到～的治疗。His illness is completely cured.

彻头彻尾　chè tóu chè wěi　out-and-out；downright：～的伪君子 out-and-out hypocrite

彻夜　chèyè　【名】throughout the night

撤　chè　【动】❶ dismiss；remove (from office) ❷ withdraw；retreat

撤除　chèchú　【动】remove；dismantle

撤防　chèfáng　【动】withdraw a garrison

撤换　chèhuàn　【动】dismiss and replace

撤回　chèhuí　【动】❶ withdraw；pull back ❷ (of document, etc.) withdraw from circulation

撤军　chè = jūn　pull back troops

撤离　chèlí　【动】withdraw from

撤退　chètuì　【动】withdraw；evacuate；retreat

撤销　chèxiāo　【动】abolish

撤职　chè = zhí　remove from office；dismiss sb. from his post

chén

尘(塵)　chén

尘埃　chén'āi　【名】dust

尘土　chéntǔ　【名】dust

沉　chén　【动】❶ sink (as opp. to 浮)：船～了。The boat sank. ❷ subside；sink；settle：～下心来 settle down (to one's work, etc.) 把脸一～ put on a long face 地基下～。The foundation has subsided. 沙发的弹簧坏了，一坐就～下去。The springs of the sofa are broken；it sags under your weight.【形】❶ heavy：这块石板太～了。This slab

of stone is very heavy. ❷ *indicates a high degree*：天阴得很～。The sky is heavy with clouds. 他睡得真～。He is fast asleep.

沉甸甸 chéndiāndiān 【形】heavy：～的手袋 heavy handbag 心里～的。Feel heavy at heart.

沉淀 chéndiàn 【动】precipitate 【名】precipitate；sediment

沉淀物 chéndiànwù 【名】sediment

沉寂 chénjì 【形】dead silent

沉浸 chénjìn 【动】immerse（*usu. fig.*）：～在幸福的回忆之中 be immersed in happy recollections ～在节日的欢乐中 be caught up in the rejoicing of the festival

沉静 chénjìng 【形】❶ quiet；silent：夜深了，四周逐渐～下来了。As the night deepens, a quiet settles over the scene. ❷ calm；serene；placid：性格～ placid temperament

沉闷 chénmèn 【形】❶（of weather or atmosphere ）oppressive；depressing：天气～ depressive weather 气氛～。The atmosphere is rather oppressive. ❷ depressed；in low spirits；reserved；introverted

沉没 chénmò 【动】submerge

沉默 chénmò 【形】❶ taciturn；reticent：他平时比较～，近几天话却多起来了。He is usually reticent, but has become quite communicative these last few days. ❷ silent：会场出现了短暂的～。A momentary silence fell in the meeting.

沉默寡言 chénmò guǎ yán taciturn；reticent；of few words

沉溺 chénnì 【动】indulge in；be immersed in；get bogged down in

沉睡 chénshuì 【动】sleep soundly

沉思 chénsī 【动】ponder；contemplate；think deeply

沉痛 chéntòng 【形】❶ feeling of profound grief；deeply grieved：心情～ with a feeling of profound grief 无比～ with great sorrow ～哀

悼 sorrowfully mourning ❷ bitter；serious；deeply felt：～的教训 bitter lesson

沉稳 chénwěn 【形】❶ steady：性格～ steady character ❷ be fast asleep：孩子睡得很～。The child is fast asleep.

沉重 chénzhòng 【形】heavy（*usu. used with abstract nouns*）：～的负担 heavy burden 病情～ seriously ill 侵略者遭到～的打击。The invaders were dealt a heavy blow.

沉住气 chén zhù qì keep one's head；keep cool

沉着 chénzhuó 【形】cool；composed

沉醉 chénzuì 【动】be dead drunk；be intoxicated

陈（陳） chén 【形】old；stale：～货 stock which has gone stale；old stock ～酒 old mellow wine 【动】◇ station；mass：～兵百万 station troops one million strong

陈词滥调 chén cí làn diào platitude；cliché；hackneyed phrase

陈腐 chénfǔ 【形】（of views, opinions）stale；antiquated；outworn

陈旧 chénjiù 【形】outdated；outmoded；stale：设备～ outdated equipment ～的式样 outmoded style ～的观念 old-fashioned view

陈列 chénliè 【动】exhibit；display

陈列馆 chénlièguǎn 【名】exhibition hall

陈设 chénshè 【动】display；arrange；set out：会客厅里～着几扇精致的屏风。The sitting room is furnished with a few exquisite screens. 【名】furnishings：房间里的～朴素大方。The room is furnished simply and in good taste.

陈述 chénshù 【动】state；recount：～理由 state one's reasons ～意见 state one's views

陈述句 chénshùjù 【名】declarative

sentence

chèn

衬（襯）　chèn　【动】❶ put sth. underneath；line：～上一张纸 put a sheet of paper underneath ❷ serve as a contrast

衬衫　chènshān　【名】〔件 jiàn〕shirt

衬托　chèntuō　【动】serve as a foil；serve as a contrast or background：绿叶～着红花 with green leaves setting off the red flowers

衬衣　chènyī　【名】〔件 jiàn〕shirt

称（稱）　chèn　【动】suit；fit；match：～了他的心愿 be in accordance with his wishes 这件上衣他穿起来很～身。This jacket fits him well.

另见 chēng

称心　chèn = xīn　to one's liking；just as one wishes

称职　chèn = zhí　be competent at one's job

趁　chèn　【介】趁（着）plus its object forms an adverbial adjunct which means "at an opportune moment" or "take an opportunity"：我们～这次到农村去劳动的机会，访问了农民家庭。While doing physical labour in the countryside we took the opportunity to visit some farmers' families. ～（着）天没黑，赶快回去吧! We'd better go back while it's still light.

趁便　chènbiàn　【副】when it is convenient：她上班～买了点东西。She did some shopping on her way to work.

趁火打劫　chèn huǒ dǎ jié　loot a burning house；fish in troubled waters

趁机　chènjī　【副】take advantage of

趁热打铁　chèn rè dǎ tiě　strike while the iron is hot

趁早　chènzǎo　【副】❶ while there is yet time；as early as possible；before it is too late：我们应该～把计划订出来。We should draw up the plan as soon as possible. ❷ might as well：他肯定不在家，你～别去。He is definitely not at home. You might as well not go.

chēng

称（稱）　chēng　【动】❶ call；style as：他～得上英雄。He deserves to be called a hero. 收音机又～无线电。A "radio" is also called a "wireless". ❷ ◇ say；state：连声～好 keep saying "good" over and over again ❸ weigh；scale：～体重 weigh oneself 把肉～一～ have the meat weighed

另见 chèn

称霸　chēng = bà　dominate；play the tyrant；seek hegemony

称号　chēnghào　【名】title

称呼　chēnghu　【动】call；address (sb.)：工人们都亲切地～厂长为老高。The workers address their director affectionately as Lao Gao. 【名】form of address

称颂　chēngsòng　【动】pay tribute to；praise

称王称霸　chēng wǎng chēng bà　lord it over；rule supreme；act like an overlord；be domineering

称谓　chēngwèi　【名】title；appellation

称兄道弟　chēng xiōng dào dì　be on intimate terms

称赞　chēngzàn　【动】praise

称作　chēngzuò　【动】call：有的地区把马铃薯～土豆。In some places the potato is called *tudou*.

撑 chēng 【动】❶ prop up；support：～起帐篷 put up a tent 你不舒服就去休息一下吧，别硬～着干了。Go take a break if you don't feel well. Don't try to stick it out. ❷ punt；pole（a boat）：～船 pole a boat ❸ open：～开伞 open an umbrella ❹ stuff or fill to the bursting point：少装点，别把口袋～破了。Don't fill the sack too much or it will burst. 少吃点儿，别～着。Be careful and don't overeat.

撑竿跳 chēnggāntiào 【名】polevault

撑腰 chēng = yāo support；back up；bolster：有群众给我们～，还怕什么！With grass-root support what have we to fear!

chéng

成 chéng 【动】❶ turn into；become：解放后工农～了国家的主人。Since Liberation, the workers and peasants have become the masters of their country. 积水～河。Water accumulates and becomes a river. ❷ ◇ help to bring about：～人之美 help to bring a good thing about ❸ be successful：买书的事，他一说就～了。He clinched the matter of book-buying by putting in a word. ❹ all right（interj.）：～，就那么办吧！All right, that's settled. ❺ "成" is often used as a complement of result to indicate change or completion：锣鼓声、口号声交织～一支嘹亮的进行曲。The sounds of drums and gongs and slogans blended into a resounding march. 这本小说已经翻译～阿拉伯文了。This novel has already been translated into Arabic. 这条河上已经建～了两座桥了。Two bridges have already been

built over this river. 【形】capable；competent：你可真～，一个人挑这么重的担子。You must be very capable to be able to shoulder such heavy responsibilities all by yourself. 【量】one-tenth：这个村子今年早稻产量比去年增加了一～。The yield of this year's early rice for this village is ten percent greater than last year.

成败 chéngbài 【名】success or failure

成倍 chéngbèi 【副】（increase）by several times；several-fold

成本 chéngběn 【名】production costs

成材 chéng = cái ❶ grow into useful timber ❷ become a person of worth：自学～ self-improvement through self-study 受了那么多教育，他还不～。In spite of much education, he is still worthless.

成分 chéngfèn 【名】❶ composition；ingredient：化学～ chemical composition 药的主要～ the main ingredient in the medicine ❷ class status

成风 chéng = fēng become a common practice

成功 chénggōng 【动】succeed 【形】successful

成规 chéngguī 【名】rut；set rules；established practice

成果 chéngguǒ 【名】result；accomplishment

成婚 chénghūn 【动】get married

成活 chénghuó 【动】survive：～率 survival rate

成绩 chéngjì 【名】achievement；school record

成家 chéng = jiā ❶ (of a man) get married ❷ become an authority or expert

成见 chéngjiàn 【名】prejudice

成交 chéngjiāo 【动】strike a bargain；close a business deal：～额

volume of business

成就 chéngjiù 【名】accomplishments；achievements 【动】achieve

成立 chénglì 【动】❶ set up；found；establish：～工会 establish a trade union ❷ be tenable：这个论点能～。This argument holds water.

成龙配套 chéng lóng pèi tào link up the parts to form a complete system：这个地区的排灌系统已经～。A complete irrigation system has been constructed in this area. 也作 "配套成龙"。

成名 chéng=míng make a name for oneself

成年 chéngnián 【动】come of age；～人 an adult 【副】all year round；year after year：～在野外作业 engage in field work all year round

成批 chéngpī 【形】in batches；groups of；one group after another：～的产品 batches of products ～运送 send in batches ～生产 serial production；mass production

成品 chéngpǐn 【名】finished product

成千上万 chéng qiān shàng wàn thousands：每天都有～的人参观出土文物展览。Every day thousands of people visit the exhibition of new archaeological finds.

成人 chéngrén 【名】adult

成人 chéng=rén be grown up；become full-grown

成人教育 chéngrén jiàoyù adult education

成熟 chéngshú 【动】mature；ripe：这种水稻生长期短，～得早。This strain of rice takes only a short period to mature. 【形】mature；ripe：条件不～。Conditions are not yet ripe.

成套 chéngtào 【形】in a complete set：～家具 a suite of furniture ～设备 a complete set of equipment

成天 chéngtiān 【副】all day long；

all the time：他～乐呵呵的。He's jolly all day long.

成为 chéngwéi 【动】become；prove to be；turn into：他现在已经～熟练工人了。He has become a skilled worker. 这一带可以开垦～商品粮基地。This area can be reclaimed and made into a commodity grain base.

成效 chéngxiào 【名】effect

成心 chéngxīn 【形】purposely；intentionally

成语 chéngyǔ 【名】idiom；idiomatic expression

成员 chéngyuán 【名】member

成长 chéngzhǎng 【动】grow up；grow to maturity：新栽的白杨树正在茁壮～。The newly planted aspen trees are growing well. 一代新人正在～。The younger generation is growing up.

呈 chéng 【动】❶〈书〉show；appear：湖水～绿色。The water in the lake looks green. ❷ offer；present；submit：～交 present (sth. to a superior)～阅 submit for perusal 谨～ respectfully submit

呈报 chéngbào 【动】submit a report：～上级审批 submit (sth.) for approval

呈递 chéngdì 【动】present；submit：～国书 present credentials ～公文 submit documents

呈现 chéngxiàn 【动】appear；present：～出一片欣欣向荣的景象 present a picture of prosperity

诚(誠) chéng

诚惶诚恐 chéng huáng chéng kǒng〈书〉with awe and respect

诚恳 chéngkěn 【形】sincere；earnest：待人很～ treat others with sincerity ～地接受意见 sincerely accept the criticisms of others

诚然 chéngrán 【副】(usu. in writ-

ten language）❶ indeed；really；truly；小朋友都喜欢熊猫,熊猫也~可爱。Children are fond of pandas, which are truly lovable. ❷ be sure, 同"固然" gùrán

诚实 chéngshí 【形】honest

诚心 chéngxīn 【名】sincerity

诚意 chéngyì 【名】sincerity；earnestness

诚挚 chéngzhì 【形】sincere

承 chéng 【动】〈书〉❶ assume；bear；undertake：~制各式服装 undertake to make all kinds of clothes ❷ be indebted to：~贵国政府热情接待 feel indebted to your government for the kind hospitality accorded ❸ continue：~前启后 serve as a link between past and future

承包 chéngbāo 【动】contract：~工程 undertake contracted projects ~下来 have undertaken（sth.）by contract 把商店~下来 to manage a store by contract

承包商 chéngbāoshāng 【名】contractor

承包制 chéngbāozhì 【名】contracting out system

承担 chéngdān 【动】bear；assume；undertake：~任务 undertake the task ~义务 fulfill an obligation

承当 chéngdāng 【动】bear；take：~责任 bear the responsibility（for sth.）

承诺 chéngnuò 【动】promise to undertake

承认 chéngrèn 【动】❶ recognize；admit；acknowledge：~错误 acknowledge one's mistake 大家都一致~他是环境保护方面的专家。We all admit that he is an expert in environmental protection. ❷ extend（diplomatic）recognition

承上启下 chéng shàng qǐ xià （of writing）connect what preceded sth. with what follows：这一段文字,在全篇文章中起着~的作用。This paragraph of the article serves as a link to what preceded.

承受 chéngshòu 【动】bear；withstand；sustain；support：~一百公斤的压力 bear the weight of one hundred kilograms ~住各种考验 withstand various ordeals

承袭 chéngxí 【动】❶ follow（e. g. tradition）❷ inherit（e. g. a title）

承运 chéngyùn 【动】undertake the transportation of（goods）

承重 chéngzhòng 【动】load-bearing：~墙 bearing wall

城 chéng 【名】❶ city wall ❷ city；town

城郊 chéngjiāo 【名】outskirts；suburb

城楼 chénglóu 【名】tower above a city gate

城区 chéngqū 【名】the city proper；urban area

城市 chéngshì 【名】city

城乡 chéngxiāng 【名】city and countryside

城乡差别 chéngxiāng chābié the difference between town and country

城镇 chéngzhèn 【名】city and town

乘 chéng 【动】❶ ride（usu. in written language）：~车 ride in a car or train ~船 go by boat ~飞机 travel by air ❷ take advantage of；avail oneself of：~势 take advantage of the situation ❸ multiply：三~三等于九。Three times three is nine.

乘法 chéngfǎ 【名】（maths.）multiplication

乘方 chéngfāng 【名】（maths.）❶ involution ❷ power

乘风破浪 chéng fēng pò làng brave wind and waves：远洋货轮~在海上

航行。The ship is at sea, braving wind and waves.

乘机　chéngjī　【副】jump at the chance; seize an opportunity (*used as an adverbial adjunct*): ～破坏 jump at the chance to cause trouble ～捣乱 seize the opportunity to create a disturbance ～逃脱 seize the chance to escape

乘积　chéngjī　【名】(maths.) product

乘客　chéngkè　【名】passenger

乘凉　chéng = liáng　enjoy the cool air

乘人之危　chéng rén zhī wēi　take advantage of the misfortune of others

乘胜前进　chéng shèng qiánjìn　march forward in triumph

乘数　chéngshù　【名】(maths.) multiplier

乘务员　chéngwùyuán　【名】crew (esp. of a train)

乘虚而入　chéng xū ér rù　take advantage of a weak point: 身体太弱了,疾病就会～。One has no resistance to disease, when the body is weakened.

盛　chéng　【动】❶ dish out; ladle out: ～饭 fill a bowl with rice ～汤 ladle out soup ❷ contain; hold: 缸里～着水。The crock is filled with water. 这个仓库～不了那么多粮食。This granary cannot hold that much grain.
另见 shèng

程　chéng

程度　chéngdù　【名】❶ level; degree: 文化～ level of education 觉悟～ level of political consciousness ❷ degree; extent: 破坏的～ the extent of the damage 今天不太冷,到不了结冰的～。It isn't very cold today; it won't reach the freezing point.

程控电话　chéngkòng diànhuà　program control telephone

程式　chéngshì　【名】(chem., maths.) formula; equation

程式化　chéngshìhuà　【动】stylize

程序　chéngxù　【名】procedure: ～法 procedural law ～教学 programmed instruction or learning

惩（懲）　chéng　【动】punish; discipline

惩办　chéngbàn　【动】punish

惩处　chéngchǔ　【动】punish; penalize

惩罚　chéngfá　【动】punish

惩前毖后　chéng qián bì hòu　learn from past mistakes in order to avoid future ones

惩治　chéngzhì　【动】punish

澄　chéng
另见 dèng

澄清　chéngqīng　【形】clear; transparent: 碧绿～的湖水 green, clear water of the lake 【动】clear up; clarify: ～事实 clarify the facts 把问题～一下 clear up the matter
另见 dèngqīng

chěng

逞　chěng　【动】❶ show off; exhibit; flaunt: ～威风 flaunt one's power ～英雄 play the hero ❷ give free rein to: ～凶 act brutally

逞能　chěng = néng　show off one's ability

逞强　chěng = qiáng　flaunt one's strength

逞凶　chěngxiōng　act violently

chèng

秤　chèng　【名】〔个 gè、杆 gǎn〕

steelyard; scale

秤盘 chèngpán 【名】〔个 gè〕the pan or dish of a steelyard

chī

吃 chī 【动】❶ eat ❷ have one's meal at：～食堂 eat in a dining-hall ～馆子 eat in a restaurant ❸ depend on certain things for one's living：靠山～山，靠水～水。Those living on a mountain make their living from the mountain; those living near the water make their living from the water. ❹ wipe out; annihilate (usu. of warfare and chess)：这一仗～掉了敌人一个团。In this battle, an enemy regiment was wiped out. 我～了他好几个棋子儿。I've taken several of his chess pieces. ❺ absorb; soak up：这块地不～水。Water simply runs off this land. ❻ suffer; receive：～了一拳 receive a blow

吃不开 chī bu kāi be unpopular：过去的这套做法，现在已经～了。The whole methods of working in the past are leading us up a blind alley.

吃不消 chī bu xiāo be unable to stand：你的病刚好，就急着上工地，恐怕～吧！You won't be able to stand the strain of work at the construction site, since you've only just recovered from your illness.

吃大锅饭 chī dàguōfàn eat from the same pot (referring to equalitarian form of remuneration)

吃得开 chī de kāi be popular; be well-received：这种小型拖拉机在山区可～啦！Small tractors like this are very popular in the mountain areas.

吃得消 chī de xiāo be able to bear up against sth.：深水作业必须身体

好才～。One needs to be strong to work in deep water.

吃饭 chī∥fàn make a living：王大爷靠这门手艺～。Grandpa Wang makes a living by his skill. 山区水利化改变了靠天～的局面。With water conservation, the people of the mountain area are no longer at the mercy of Nature.

吃紧 chījǐn 【形】be critical

吃劲 chījìn 【形】entail much effort

吃惊 chī∥jīng be startled; get a shock or fright; be flabbergasted：令人～ startling 吃了一惊 get a shock

吃苦 chī∥kǔ endure hardships：能～ be able to endure hardships ～在前，享受在后 be the first to bear hardships and the last to enjoy comforts 他吃过很多苦。He has gone through countless hardships.

吃苦耐劳 chī kǔ nài láo be able to stand wear and tear

吃亏 chī∥kuī get the worse of it; suffer losses; suffer reverses：不按科学办事的人，总是要～的。If you don't play by the rules, you'll fail. 他在学习上进步不大，是吃了骄傲自满的亏。Self-conceit prevents him from making progress in his studies.

吃老本 chī lǎoběn live off one's past glory; rest on one's laurels

吃力 chīlì 【形】strenuous; laborious：～地走着 make one's way laboriously 顶风骑车很～。It's hard to bicycle against the wind. 他学习外语不觉得～。He has no difficulty in studying foreign languages.

吃透 chī∥tòu have a thorough grasp

吃香 chīxiāng 【形】be very popular

吃一堑，长一智 chī yī qiàn, zhǎng yī zhì a fall into the pit, a gain in your wit：这次比赛失败，教训很大，真是～。We've learned a lesson from

our loss in this match. It is indeed a case of "a fall into the pit, a gain in your wit".

吃重　chīzhòng　【形】❶ arduous ❷ need or use great effort：完成这个课题，他觉得～。He found the job demanding. 【动】carrying capacity

哧　chī　【象声】giggling

嗤　chī
嗤之以鼻　chī zhī yǐ bí　turn up one's nose at

痴　chī　【形】silly；foolish；stupid；dull
痴呆　chīdāi　【形】mentally retarded
痴心　chīxīn　【名】infatuation
痴心妄想　chīxīn wàngxiǎng　wishful thinking；hope vainly for

chí

池　chí　【名】◇ pool；pond
池塘　chítáng　【名】pond

驰（馳）　chí
驰骋　chíchěng　【动】〈书〉gallop
驰名　chímíng　【动】become well-known（not referring to persons）

迟（遲）　chí　【形】❶ ◇ slow；tardy：～～不决 slow at reaching a decision ❷ late：他来～了。He came late.
迟到　chídào　【动】arrive late
迟钝　chídùn　【形】slow-witted
迟缓　chíhuǎn　【形】slow
迟误　chíwù　【动】delay
迟延　chíyán　【动】delay
迟疑　chíyí　【动】hesitate

持　chí　【动】❶ ◇ hold；grasp：

～枪 hold a gun　手～棍棒 hold a stick ❷ keep；maintain：～慎重态度 have a cautious attitude（towards sth.）～不同意见 hold a differing opinion ❸ ◇ manage；run：勤俭～家 run one's home frugally
持家　chíjiā　【动】keep house
持久　chíjiǔ　【形】lasting；persistent；protracted
持久战　chíjiǔzhàn　【名】protracted war
持平　chípíng　【形】fair；unbiased；even with；even out；equal to
持续　chíxù　【动】carry on；sustain；continue
持之以恒　chí zhī yǐ héng　in a persistent way；persevere：学习要～。One must persevere with one's studies.

踟　chí
踟蹰　chíchú　【动】〈书〉hesitate as to where to go

chǐ

尺　chǐ　【名】〔把 bǎ〕ruler【量】measurement of length（1/3 of a metre）
尺寸　chǐcùn　【名】size；dimensions；measurements
尺度　chǐdù　【名】criterion
尺子　chǐzi　【名】〔个 gè，把 bǎ〕ruler

齿（齒）　chǐ　【名】◇ tooth
齿轮　chǐlún　【名】cogwheel；gear
齿龈　chǐyín　【名】(phy.) gum

侈　chǐ
侈谈　chǐtán　【动】engage in glib talk

耻　chǐ　【名】◇ shame；disgrace
耻辱　chǐrǔ　【名】shame
耻笑　chǐxiào　【动】sneer at；laugh at

chì

斥 chì 【动】◇ scold；blame

斥责 chìzé 【动】rebuke；denounce

赤 chì 【形】❶ red (*rarely used*) ❷ ◇ absolutely sincere：一片～心 utter devotion 【动】bare：～脚 barefoot ～背 barebacked

赤膊上阵 chì bó shàng zhèn go into battle stripped to the waist；(*fig.*) come out into the open

赤胆忠心 chì dǎn zhōng xīn utter devotion

赤道 chìdào 【名】the equator

赤金 chìjīn 【名】pure gold；solid gold

赤裸裸 chìluǒluǒ 【形】❶ naked ❷ barefaced；undisguised

赤贫 chìpín 【名】❶ extreme poverty ❷ the utterly destitute

赤手空拳 chì shǒu kōng quán with one's bare hands；unarmed：这个青年曾经～地和豹子搏斗过。This young man once fought a leopard with his bare hands.

赤卫队 chìwèiduì 【名】Red Guards

赤字 chìzì 【名】financial deficit

炽(熾) chì

炽热 chìrè 【形】scorching heat

翅 chì 【名】◇ wing

翅膀 chìbǎng 【名】wing

chōng

充 chōng 【动】play the part；pose as：～行 (háng) 家 pretend to be an expert ～好汉 pose as a hero

充斥 chōngchì 【动】fill up；flood；glut (*derog.*)：～舞台 the stage was filled with... ～市场 the market was glutted with...

充当 chōngdāng 【动】act as；pose as；play the part of：～不光彩的角色 play the disgraceful part of ～辩护士 act as an apologist for

充电 chōng = diàn charge (a battery)

充耳不闻 chōng ěr bù wén plug one's ears and refuse to listen；(*fig.*) turn a deaf ear to

充分 chōngfèn 【形】full；ample；abundant (usu. for sth. abstract)：～的时间 ample time ～的信心 full of confidence 在工作中，要～调动群众的积极性。In any kind of work, the masses must be fully mobilized. 准备工作做得很～。Ample preparations have been made.

充公 chōng = gōng confiscate

充满 chōngmǎn 【动】❶ (of light or gaseous substances) be filled with；fill to the brim；be full of：～阳光 full of sunshine ❷ be imbued with：～豪情 imbued with lofty sentiments ～团结战斗的气氛 filled with militant solidarity

充沛 chōngpèi 【形】full of (energy)

充其量 chōngqíliàng 【副】at most；at best：这个大厅～只能容一千人。This hall can hold one thousand people at most.

充实 chōngshí 【形】rich；substantial：内容～ rich in content 技术力量很～ have a large and competent staff of technicians 【动】strengthen；enrich；substantiate：～领导班子 strengthen the leading body ～基层 strengthen organizations at the grass-roots level

充数 chōng = shù merely make up the number：我唱得不好，参加合唱队不过是充个数。I'm a poor singer. I'm joining the choir just to fill in the numbers.

充血 chōngxuè 【动】hyperemia；congestion

充裕　chōngyù　【形】ample；plentiful；well off：经济 ～ financially well off：～的时间 plenty of time

充足　chōngzú　【形】abundant；quite sufficient：～ 的经费 sufficient funds：～的理由 ample reason 光线 ～ full of light

冲　chōng　【动】❶ infuse（usu. with boiling water）：～茶 make tea ～藕粉 make a porridge using lotus root powder ❷ flush；rinse：把杯子用开水 ～ rinse the cups with boiling water 大水～垮了石坝，～不垮我们改天换地的决心。The flood may wash away the dyke, but it cannot wash away our determination to transform Nature. ❸（衝）dash；rush；charge：～ 入敌阵 charge the enemy position ～出重围 break through the encirclement ❹ soar to；shoot up：凯歌～云霄。The air is filled with a paean of victory. 战斗机～上云层。Fighter planes soar into the sky. 另见 chòng

冲刺　chōngcì　【动】spurt；sprint：向终点 ～ make a dash towards the tape

冲淡　chōngdàn　【动】dilute

冲动　chōngdòng　【形】excited

冲锋　chōngfēng　【动】charge forward

冲锋陷阵　chōngfēng xiàn zhèn　storm and shatter（the enemy position）；charge（the enemy position）：他在与破坏森林的斗争中敢于冲锋陷阵 He does not hesitate to throw himself into the fight against deforestation.

冲昏头脑　chōng hūn tóunǎo　be carried away（by success）；（one's success）goes to one's head

冲击　chōngjī　【动】❶ pound；batter；lash：洪水～着堤坝。The flood waters pounded at the dam. ❷ attack fiercely；charge boldly：向敌人猛烈 ～ charge the enemy boldly

冲击波　chōngjībō　【名】blast wave；shock wave

冲破　chōngpò　【动】break through；breach：～ 封锁线 break through the blockade ～ 牢笼 break out of prison ～ 重重阻力 break through countless barriers

冲刷　chōngshuā　【动】wash and brush clean

冲天　chōngtiān　【形】soaring；towering；boundless：～的干劲 boundless enthusiasm 怒气 ～ towering rage

冲突　chōngtū　【动】clash；conflict

冲洗　chōngxǐ　【动】❶ flush；rinse；wash：～地板 wash the floor ❷ develop：～胶卷 develop a roll of film

冲账　chōng=zhàng　strike a balance

冲撞　chōngzhuàng　【动】collide；offend

憧　chōng

憧憬　chōngjǐng　【动】〈书〉long for；look forward to：～着美好的未来 look forward to a bright future

chóng

虫（蟲）　chóng　【名】〔条 tiáo、个 gè〕insect；worm

虫害　chónghài　【名】insect pest

重　chóng　【动】repeat；duplicate：今天的晚会，你们俩准备的节目 ～ 了。The two of you have prepared the same item for this evening's performance. 东西买 ～ 了。Two lots of the same stuff have been bought by mistake. 【量】layer：万～山 undulating mountains 冲破一 ～ 又一 ～ 困难 overcome one difficulty after another 【副】again；once more；repeatedly：～写一遍

write it once more ～返前线 go back to the front again
另见 zhòng

重版 chóngbǎn 【动】be republished 【名】republication

重重 chóngchóng 【形】layer upon layer；pile upon pile：～难关 one difficulty after another ～阻力 full of obstacles 顾虑～ filled with misgivings

重重叠叠 chóngchóngdiédié 【形】overlapping；one on top of another

重蹈覆辙 chóng dǎo fù zhé follow the same old catastrophic road：要从过去的错误中吸取教训，以免～。One should learn from past mistakes so as to avoid falling into the same old trap.

重叠 chóngdié 【动】duplicate；reduplicate；overlap

重复 chóngfù 【动】repeat；reiterate

重合 chónghé 【动】coincide

重婚 chónghūn 【动】(commit) bigamy

重建 chóngjiàn 【动】rebuild

重申 chóngshēn 【动】reiterate；restate；reaffirm

重围 chóngwéi 【名】encirclement

重新 chóngxīn 【副】anew；again；afresh：～布置 rearrange ～考虑 reconsider 他又～讲了一遍。He explained it once again.

重整旗鼓 chóng zhěng qí gǔ rally forces again (after a defeat)；begin all over again

崇 chóng

崇拜 chóngbài 【动】worship；adore

崇高 chónggāo 【形】lofty；sublime：～的理想 lofty ideal ～的形象 sublime image 享有～的威望 enjoy high prestige

崇敬 chóngjìng 【动】respect；respect and admire

崇山峻岭 chóng shān jùn lǐng lofty mountains and high hills

崇尚 chóngshàng 【动】advocate；uphold

chǒng

宠（寵） chǒng 【动】treat with undue care and affection

宠爱 chǒng'ài 【动】treat with undue care and affection

宠儿 chǒng'ér 【名】child of fortune

宠物 chǒngwù 【名】pet

chòng

冲（衝） chòng 【形】❶ forceful；dynamic；powerful：水流得很～。Water flows with great force. 咱们的妇女队长干活儿可～了。Our woman team leader works with great vigour. ❷ (of smells) strong；powerful：烟味很～。The tobacco smells strong. 【动】❶ face (e.g. direction)：工厂的大门～东。The gate of the factory faces east. ❷ punch：这个零件是冲床～的。This part was manufactured on a punch press. 【介】face；turn towards：汽车～着那片树林驶去。The car turned towards the woods. 她～他笑了笑。She smiled at him.
另见 chōng

冲床 chòngchuáng 【名】〔台 tái〕punching machine

冲压 chòngyā 【动】stamping

冲压机 chòngyājī 【名】〔台 tái〕another name for 冲床

chōu

抽 chōu 【动】❶ take out (from in between)：从书架上～出一本书来 take out a book from the book

shelf ❷ sprout；ear：高粱～穗了。The sorghum is coming into ear. ❸ draw up (by pumping, etc.)：～水 pump water ❹ whip；thrash：用鞭子～牲口 whip the draught animal ❺ shrink：这种布下水也不～。This cloth doesn't shrink in the wash. ❻ smash (in table-tennis, badminton, tennis)

抽查　chōuchá　【动】make a spot check；selective examination

抽调　chōudiào　【动】(e. g. cadres) select for transfer

抽空　chōu = kòng　manage to find time：～写封回信 manage to answer a letter　～学点儿外语 find time to study a foreign language

抽泣　chōuqì　【动】sob

抽身　chōu = shēn　try to get away (e. g. from one's work)：尽量～去一趟 try one's best to get away and go there 这几天忙，没有抽出身来看你。I have been very busy the last few days and couldn't get away to come and see you.

抽水机　chōushuǐjī　【名】〔台 tái〕water pump

抽税　chōu = shuì　levy a tax

抽屉　chōuti　【名】〔个 gè〕drawer (in a desk or table)

抽象　chōuxiàng　【形】abstract

抽烟　chōu = yān　smoke (a cigarette)

chóu

仇　chóu　【名】hatred；enmity；animosity

仇敌　chóudí　【名】enemy；foe

仇恨　chóuhèn　【动】hate

仇人　chóurén　【名】enemy

仇视　chóushì　【动】be hostile to

惆　chóu

惆怅　chóuchàng　【形】〈书〉disconso-late；depressed；melancholy：心情～ feel melancholy

绸（綢）　chóu　【名】silk

绸缎　chóuduàn　【名】silks and satins

酬　chóu

酬金　chóujīn　【名】monetary reward；remuneration

酬劳　chóuláo　【动】reward；remunerate

酬谢　chóuxiè　【动】thank with a gift

稠　chóu　【形】(of liquids) thick

稠密　chóumì　【形】(of population) dense

愁　chóu　【动】worry

愁苦　chóukǔ　【形】distressed

愁眉苦脸　chóu méi kǔ liǎn　despair written all over sb.'s face；a distressed expression

筹（籌）　chóu

筹办　chóubàn　【动】make preparations for the setting up of：～夜校 take steps to set up a night school

筹备　chóubèi　【动】prepare；arrange：建新厂的工作正在～。Steps are being taken to set up a new factory.

筹划　chóuhuà　【动】plan

筹集　chóují　【动】try to collect

踌（躊）　chóu

踌躇　chóuchú　【动】hesitate

chǒu

丑（醜）　chǒu　【形】ugly

丑恶　chǒu'è　【形】loathsome；despicable

丑化　chǒuhuà　【动】vilify

丑剧　chǒujù　【名】(fig.) farce

丑角　chǒujué　【名】(of Chinese op-

era) clown；comic character

丑类 chǒulèi 【名】infamous lot

丑陋 chǒulòu 【形】ugly

丑态 chǒutài 【名】disgusting manner

丑态百出 chǒutài bǎi chū act like a buffoon；cut a ridiculous figure

丑闻 chǒuwén 【名】scandal

chòu

臭 chòu 【形】smelly；stinking
另见 xiù

臭架子 chòu jiàzi pretentious airs：放下～,甘当小学生 throw off one's pretentious airs and be willing to learn

臭名远扬 chòu míng yuǎn yáng notorious；infamous

臭名昭著 chòu míng zhāozhù infamous；notorious

臭味相投 chòuwèi xiāng tóu birds of a feather (derog.)

臭氧 chòuyǎng 【名】ozone

臭氧层 chòuyǎngcéng 【名】ozone layer

chū

出 chū 【动】❶ go out；depart from：～轨 be derailed 小李～国了。Xiao Li has gone abroad. 我刚～门，就碰上老张了。I was no sooner out than I met Lao Zhang. ❷ put forth；issue：～布告 put up a notice ～题目 set a topic；set an examination paper ～主意 think of a way out 有多大力～多大力 give your best efforts ❸ produce；publish：这里～石油。This place produces petroleum. 这个厂～的收音机很有名。The radios turned out by this factory are well known. 唐朝～了不少诗人。There were plenty of poets in the

Tang dynasty. 这个出版社今年～了不少新书。This publishing house has published a lot of new books this year. ❹ happen；occur：机器～故障了。Something has gone wrong with the machine. ～危险了。An accident has happened. ～了问题怎么办？What if an accident happens? ❺ emerge；break forth：小孩～疹子了。The child has broken out with measles. 果树～芽了。The fruit trees have come out in bud. 他～了一身汗。He perspired all over. ❻ appear：天上～虹了。A rainbow appeared. Note: ❶ 出 is used as a complement after a verb，indicates movement outward：从银行取～一笔款子 draw a sum of money from the bank 他一脚把球踢～场外。He kicked the ball beyond the sports ground. 小程刚跑～门，就跌了一跤。No sooner had Xiao Cheng run out of the door than he tripped and fell. (same as 出来 or 出去 as a complement ① but speaker's position is irrelevant. An object is necessary) ② indicates appearance：提～问题 put forward a question 这种要求太过分了,实在说不～口。This is asking too much and I simply can't bring myself to make it. 呈现～一片欢乐景象。A festive scene appeared (before one's eyes). ③ indicates identification：我听不～说话的是谁。I can't identify the voice. 大家都看～他有些着急。Everybody could see that he was very anxious. ④ indicates achieving a result：我答不～这道题。I cannot answer that question. 他在平凡的工作中作～了不平凡的成绩。He has made extraordinary achievements in an ordinary job. (same as 出来 as a complement after a verb ②③④，though an object is necessary) ❷ as a comple-

ment after an adj. indicates more than necessary, more than there was originally or more than there actually is：我们只要二十把铁锹，怎么多～三把？ We only need twenty shovels. Why are there three too many? 这孩子长得真快，一年不见，又高～了一头。 How fast this child has grown! I haven't seen him for a year and he has grown a head taller. 那件大衣要再长～两寸就好了。 I wish that coat were two inches longer. (*same as* 出来 *as a complement after an adj. except that it must be followed by a numeral plus a measure word*) 【量】 (齣) *for drama, etc.*：一～好戏 an excellent play

出版 chūbǎn 【动】publish

出版社 chūbǎnshè 【名】publishing house

出版物 chūbǎnwù 【名】publication

出殡 chū=bìn hold a funeral

出兵 chū=bīng send an army into battle

出岔子 chū chàzi run into trouble; go wrong：小心～。 Be careful or it will go wrong.

出差 chū=chāi be out on official business

出产 chūchǎn 【动】produce; manufacture

出超 chūchāo 【动】have an export surplus

出丑 chū=chǒu be disgraced; look ridiculous

出处 chūchù 【名】(of a quotation) source

出典 chūdiǎn 【名】source (of a quotation or allusion)

出动 chūdòng 【动】❶ go into action; set out：待命～ waiting for orders to set out 咱们全体～大扫除。 Let's get busy and do a general cleaning. ❷ (of troops) dispatch; send out：～两翼部队，增援主力部队 send out troops on both flanks to support the main force

出尔反尔 chū ěr fǎn ěr go back on one's word; be inconsistent

出发 chūfā 【动】set out; start off：队伍～了。 The troops have set out.

出发点 chūfādiǎn 【名】starting point; point of departure

出风头 chū fēngtou show off; seek the limelight

出乎意料 chūhū yìliào contrary to one's expectations：～的事故 unexpected accident 早晨天还很晴朗，中午突然下起大雨，真是～。 It was sunny this morning, but suddenly at noon it began to rain. It was really unexpected.

出工 chū=gōng go to work

出海 chū=hǎi put to sea

出击 chūjī 【动】launch an attack

出嫁 chūjià 【动】(of girls) be married

出价 chū=jià bid; offer a price

出界 chū=jiè (sports) go out-of-bounds; outside

出境 chū=jìng leave a country; (visa) exit

出口 chūkǒu 【动】❶ speak：～伤人 speak with a sting in one's words ～成章。 Words flow from one's mouth as from the pen of a master. ❷ export：～税 export duty ～成套设备 export complete units of machinery 【名】exit：体育馆的～ the exit of a gymnasium 火车站～ the exit of a railway station

出口贸易 chūkǒu màoyì export trade

出口商 chūkǒushāng 【名】exporter

出来 chū // lái come out (*towards the direction of the speaker*)：把款子从银行取～ draw a sum of money from the bank 快～看，放烟火了! Come! The fireworks have started! 月亮～了。 The moon has risen. 问题又～了。 Another problem

has come up. Note：❶出来 *is used as a complement after a verb*：① *indicates movement outward*：小程刚跑出门来，就跌了一跤。No sooner had Xiao Cheng run out than he tripped and fell. (*same as* 出 *as a complement after a verb* ① *but towards the direction of the speaker. An object is optional*) ② *indicates appearance*：把问题提～ put forward the problem 这个主意是他想～的。It was he who thought of this idea. 他脸上显出高兴的样子来。A happy look appeared on his face. ③ *indicates identification*：二十年没见你，我差点儿认不～了。I haven't seen you for twenty years, I hardly recognize you. 你看得～这是谁的字吗？Can you identify this handwriting? ④ *indicates achieving a result*：这道题我答不～。I can't give an answer to that question. 本领是练～的。Skill comes from practice. 这片草地让人走出一条路来了。A trail through the meadow has been trampled down by passers-by. (*same as* 出 *as a complement after a verb* ② ③ ④, *but an object is optional*) ❷ *as a complement after an adj. to indicate more than is necessary, more than there was originally or more than there is actually*：我们只要二十把铁锹，这三把是多～的。We only need twenty shovels and these three are extra ones. 那件大衣要再长出两寸来就好了。I wish that coat were two inches longer. (*same as* 出 *as the complement following an adj., but may or may not be followed by a numeral plus a measure word*)

出类拔萃　chū lèi bá cuì　(of a person's ability or character) stand out among others; stand out from the common herd

出力　chū＝lì　exert oneself; con-tribute one's strength：出一把力 do one's bit 为边疆的建设事业～ do one's part for the undertaking of building the border area 排练这个节目，他出了不少力。He has done a lot toward rehearsing this item.

出笼　chūlóng　【动】❶ (of cooking) come out of the steamer：刚～的包子 hot stuffed buns just out of the steamer ❷ come out into the open; come forth; emerge (*derog.*)

出路　chūlù　【名】outlet; way out：生活～ way of making a living 工厂正为产品寻找～。The factory is searching for a market for its products.

出马　chūmǎ　【动】go into action

出卖　chūmài　【动】❶ offer for sale ❷ betray：～民族利益 betray national interests

出面　chū＝miàn　(act) in the name of：～调停 act as a mediator 由领导～解决 settle some problem in the name of the leadership

出名　chū＝míng　become famous; famous

出没　chūmò　【动】appear and disappear：～无常 come and go unpredictably 这里是野兽经常～的地方。This is the place haunted by wild animals.

出谋划策　chū móu huà cè　give advice and make suggestions; mastermind a plot (*usu. derog.*)：在幕后～ mastermind a plot from behind the scenes

出纳　chūnà　【名】❶ cashier ❷ the work of receiving and paying out money

出品　chūpǐn　【动】manufacture; make; produce 【名】manufactured product; produce

出其不意　chū qí bù yì　catch sb. unawares; take sb. by surprise：～地袭击敌人 take the enemy by surprise

出奇　chūqí　【形】extraordinary；exceptional（*usu. used as an adverbial adjunct or a complement*）：今天～地热。It's unusually hot today. 他算账真是快得～。He is exceptionally fast at sums.

出奇制胜　chū qí zhì shèng　defeat（the enemy）by a surprise attack：尖刀班～，捣毁了敌人指挥部。The bayonet squad made a surprise attack and wiped out the enemy's command post.

出气　chū = qì　vent one's anger on sb./sth.；vent one's spleen

出勤　chūqín　【动】be present at work；attendance（rate）

出去　chū // qù　go out（*not in the direction of the speaker*）：咱们～散散步，好吗？Shall we go out for a walk? 雪太大了，出不去门了。The snow is too heavy and we can't go out. Note：出去 *is used as a complement after a verb, indicates movement outward*：他从屋里跑～了。He ran out of the room. 主人很热情，一直把客人送出大门去。The host saw the guest to the door. 他一脚把球踢出场外去了。His kick sent the ball out of the sports ground. 消息已经传～了。The news has spread. 门太小，整台机器抬不～。The door is too small, and the machine can't be taken out assembled.（*same as* 出 *as a complement after a verb* ① *but not towards the speaker. An object is optional.*）

出让　chūràng　【动】sell（one's own things）

出人头地　chū rén tóu dì　stand out among one's fellows（*usu. derog.*）

出入　chūrù　【动】come in and go out：这里开个门，～就方便了。Make a door here. It will be convenient for coming and going. 【名】divergence；difference；discrepancy：这块地的产量跟大家估计的没多少～。There is not much discrepancy between the actual yield of this land and our estimate. 你们俩对这个问题的看法～很大。You two have very different views on that question.

出色　chūsè　【形】outstanding；remarkable；distinguished：～的骑手 outstanding horseman 他的学习成绩很～。He has a distinguished record as a student.

出身　chūshēn　【动】❶ come from（a certain kind of family）：～贫农 come from a poor peasant family ❷ be originally（a profession）：他是工人～的干部。He is a cadre who was originally a worker. 【名】class origin；family background：他的～很苦。He comes from a poor family.

出神　chū = shén　❶ lost in thought：～地望着 watch while lost in thought ❷ spellbound：听得出了神 listen spellbound

出生　chūshēng　【动】be born

出生入死　chū shēng rù sǐ　go through fire and water；brave countless dangers

出世　chūshì　【动】be born

出售　chūshòu　【动】offer for sale

出台　chū = tái　❶ appear on the stage ❷ enforcement of a new policy or law

出头　chū = tóu　❶ make a public appearance；(do sth.) in the name of ❷ raise one's head；free oneself（from oppression, etc.）❸ slightly over；...odd：这小伙子刚二十～。This young man is twenty-odd years old.

出头露面　chū tóu lù miàn　make a public appearance；be in the limelight：他是一个不爱～的人。He doesn't like being in the limelight.

出土　chū = tǔ　❶ be unearthed ❷ break through the earth

出息　chūxi　【名】(of persons) 有～ promising 没～ not very promising

出席　chūxí　【动】be present (at a meeting, etc.)

出现　chūxiàn　【动】appear; emerge; arise

出线　chū=xiàn　qualify for the next round of competitions

出以公心　chū yǐ gōngxīn　act out of concern for the public interest; act without selfish motives; 领导人必须～, 为大多数人谋利益。Leading members must act without selfish motives and in the interests of the majority.

出诊　chūzhěn　【动】(of doctors) make a house call

出资　chūzī　【动】provide funds or capital

出走　chūzǒu　【动】run away; flee

出租　chūzū　【动】rent out (sth.)

出租汽车　chūzū qìchē　taxi; taxicab

初　chū　【名】◇ beginning: 完好如～ in as good condition as before 【形】❶ early: ～冬 early winter ～夏 early summer ～愿 original intention ❷ for the first time; first: ～学 begin to learn ～诊 consult (a particular doctor) for the first time 红日～升 the newly-risen sun 【头】for the first ten days of the lunar month: ～一 the first day of the lunar month ～十 the tenth day of the lunar month

初步　chūbù　【形】preliminary; initial; tentative: ～的意见 tentative opinion ～设想 tentative assumption

初出茅庐　chū chū máolú　just out on his own; be young and inexperienced

初等　chūděng　【形】❶ elementary; primary: ～数学 elementary mathematics ❷ primary: ～教育 primary education

初稿　chūgǎo　【名】first draft

初级　chūjí　【形】elementary

初年　chūnián　【名】first few years (of a period)

初期　chūqī　【名】initial stage

初中　chūzhōng　【名】junior middle school

chú

除　chú　【动】❶ get rid of; eliminate: ～草 weed 为民～害 get rid of the things which are harmful to the people ❷ (maths.) divide: 六～以二得三。6 divided by 2 is 3.

除法　chúfǎ　【名】(maths.) division

除非　chúfēi　【连】similar in meaning to 只有 which indicates that what follows it is a necessary condition and often used in conjunction with 才, 否则, etc.: ～你去请他, 他才会来, 否则他不会来。He will only come at your invitation; otherwise he won't come. Note: one part of such a sentence can be omitted without affecting the meaning: ～你去请他, 他才会来。He will come only at your personal invitation. ～你去请他, 否则他不会来。You must invite him, otherwise he won't come. ～你去请他, 他不会来。Unless you go and ask him; he won't come. Note: the clause with 除非 may be placed after the other clause: 他不会来, ～你去请他。He won't come unless you go and ask him. 要解决这个山区的用电问题, ～修个水电站。The problem of electricity for this mountain area cannot be solved except by constructing a hydro-electric power station.

除开　chúkāi　【连】except, 同"除了",

but less frequently used

除了 chúle 【连】❶ except *often used in conjunction with* 都：这个博物馆一星期一(不开放)，每天都开放。This museum is open every day except Monday. ～深秋和冬天(没有花)，这里漫山遍野都是鲜花。Except in late autumn and winter, the mountains and fields are always carpeted with flowers. 那条山路，～他(熟悉)，谁也不熟悉。No one is familiar with the trail over that mountain except him. ❷ besides *usu. in conjunction with* 还 *or* 也：这个旧书店，～(有)中文书，还有许多外文书。This secondhand bookstore, in addition to Chinese books, has a large stock of foreign books. 住在这条街上，～方便，也很安静。Living in this street, we enjoy quiet as well as convenience. Note：除了 *can also be said as* 除了…以外 *or* 除了…之外 *without affecting the meaning*，*e.g.*：那条山路，除了他(熟悉)以外，谁也不熟悉。住在这条街上，除了方便之外，也很安静。

除了…以外 chúle...yǐwài 见"除了"
除了…之外 chúle...zhīwài 见"除了"
除去 chúqù 【连】except；besides 同 "除了" *but less frequently used*
除数 chúshù 【名】(maths.) divisor
除外 chúwài 【动】be excepted
除夕 chúxī 【名】New Year's Eve

厨 chú
厨房 chúfáng 【名】kitchen
厨师 chúshī 【名】chef

锄(鋤) chú 【名】hoe：一把～ a hoe 【动】❶ hoe：～地 hoe the field ❷ get rid of：～草 weed with a hoe ～奸 eliminate the traitors
锄头 chútou 【名】〔把 bǎ〕hoe

雏(雛) chú

雏形 chúxíng 【名】microcosm

橱 chú 【名】wardrobe；cabinet
橱窗 chúchuāng 【名】show-window

chǔ

处(處) chǔ 【动】❶ get along with：～得来 able to get along with 他们～得很好。They get along with one another very well. ❷ exist；be in (a position, etc.)：～在一个新的时期 be in a new era ❸ ◇ punish：～以极刑 inflict the death penalty upon (sb.)
另见 chù
处罚 chǔfá 【动】punish：～犯罪分子 punish a criminal 严加～ mete out severe punishment 受～ be punished
处分 chǔfèn 【名】punishment；disciplinary action：最严厉的～ the most severe punishment 给予警告～ issue a warning as a form of discipline 【动】punish：因为违反工作纪律，他受了～。He was punished for violating discipline.
处境 chǔjìng 【名】the circumstances (one finds oneself in)
处决 chǔjué 【动】execute；put to death
处理 chǔlǐ 【动】❶ deal with；handle；manage：严肃～ deal with in a serious way ～日常事务 handle routine matters 正确～人民内部矛盾 handle contradictions among the people correctly ❷ sell at a reduced price
处理机 chǔlǐjī 【名】〔台 tái〕processor：文字～ word processor
处理品 chǔlǐpǐn 【名】goods sold at reduced prices
处女 chǔnǚ 【名】virgin
处女地 chǔnǚdì 【名】virgin land

处女作　chǔnǔzuò　【名】maiden work

处世　chǔshì　【动】deal with people and affairs：这个人不大会～。This guy is out of touch with the ways of the world.

处事　chǔshì　【动】deal with affairs；handle

处死　chǔsǐ　【动】execute death sentence

处心积虑　chǔ xīn jī lǜ　have all along nurtured schemes to；be bent on (derog.)

处于　chǔyú　【动】be in (a position or situation)：～优势 get the upper hand ～水深火热之中 be in the depths of misery

处置　chǔzhì　【动】❶ deal with；manage；handle：～得当 handle appropriately 合理地～ deal with sth. in a reasonable way ❷ punish

储(儲)　chǔ

储备　chǔbèi　【名】reserve supply：粮食的～充足 store an adequate reserve supply of grain 【动】reserve；lay by；store up：～物资 have goods stored up 把种子～起来 have seeds laid by

储备粮　chǔbèiliáng　【名】grain reserve

储藏　chǔcáng　【动】❶ save and preserve ❷ deposit：这一带地下～着大量的石油。There is a large underground oil deposit in this area.

储藏量　chǔcángliàng　【名】reserves

储藏室　chǔcáng shì　【名】storeroom

储存　chǔcún　【动】lay in；store：把白菜～起来 lay in Chinese cabbages 西红柿～得很好。The tomatoes stored well.

储蓄　chǔxù　【动】deposit (money)：把节余的钱～起来 deposit the surplus money 【名】savings；deposits：人民的～年年有增长。The amount of people's savings keeps rising

every year.

chù

处(處)　chù　【名】❶ place：住～ dwelling place 各～ various places 心灵深～ in (one's) heart of hearts ❷ department；office：借书～ (of a library) circulation desk 秘书～ office of the secretariat 问事～ inquiry desk

另见 chǔ

处处　chùchù　【副】everywhere；in all respects：～洋溢着节日气氛。A festival atmosphere prevails everywhere. 他～关心同事。He shows concern for his colleagues in every possible way.

处所　chùsuǒ　【名】place；location

畜　chù

另见 xù

畜力　chùlì　【名】animal power

触(觸)　chù　【动】❶ touch：～礁 strike a reef ❷ touch；stir；move：～到了痛处 touch (him) to the quick

触电　chù = diàn　get an electric shock

触动　chùdòng　【动】❶ touch：有电危险，请勿～。Danger! Live wire! Don't touch! ❷ move；touch；stir：他的一番话～了姑娘的心事。His words stirred the girl's memories.

触犯　chùfàn　【动】violate；offend

触及　chùjí　【动】touch

触角　chùjiǎo　【名】(of an insect) feeler；antenna

触景生情　chù jǐng shēng qíng　the sight arouses deep feelings

触觉　chùjué　【名】the sense of touch

触目惊心　chù mù jīng xīn　shocking；ghastly (sight)；horrifying

触怒　chùnù　【动】enrage；infuriate

矗 chù

矗立 chùlì 【动】tower；rise；stand tall and upright：人民英雄纪念碑～在天安门广场上。The Monument to the People's Heroes towers over Tian'anmen Square.

chuāi

揣 chuāi

【动】❶ (of hands) put in (e.g. pockets, sleeves)：～着手 put one's hands in one's sleeves ❷ keep sth. in one's pockets：把东西～起来 put sth. in one's pocket
另见 chuǎi

chuǎi

揣 chuǎi

另见 chuāi

揣测 chuǎicè 【动】guess

揣度 chuǎiduó 【动】conjecture；surmise：暗暗～ secretly surmise ～对方的心理 make conjectures as to what is on the mind of the other party

揣摩 chuǎimó 【动】try hard to figure out；weigh and consider：他是怎么想的，我一直～不透。I've tried, but I can't figure out what was on his mind.

chuài

踹 chuài

【动】kick with the sole of one's foot

chuān

川 chuān

【名】◇ ❶ river：名山大～ famous mountains and big rivers 百～归大海。All rivers flow in-to the sea. ❷ plain：八百里平～ a vast eight hundred *li* plain 荒滩变成米粮～。Wild and desolate land has been turned into grain fields.

川流不息 chuān liú bù xī　stream past in an endless flow：宽阔的林阴道上，汽车～。Automobiles speed in an endless stream along the boulevard.

chuān

穿 chuān

【动】❶ wear；put on：～衣服 put on one's clothes；get dressed ～鞋 put on one's shoes ❷ penetrate；pierce：凿～ tunnel through；cut through 机翼被子弹～了一个洞。The wing of the aeroplane has been pierced by a bullet. ❸ pass through：～针 thread a needle ～过一片草地 cross a stretch of grassland 火车～山洞。The train passed through the tunnel.

穿插 chuānchā 【动】❶ do alternately：舞蹈、诗歌朗诵～表演。Dances and recitations of poems are performed alternately. ❷ (of a play or novel) subplots；interlude

穿戴 chuāndài 【名】what one wears：不要过分讲究～。Don't be too fussy about clothes.

穿孔 chuān = kǒng　perforate

穿梭 chuān = suō　shuttle；move rapidly back and forth：工地上人来车往如～一般。People and vehicles move rapidly back and forth on the construction site.

穿着 chuānzhuó 【名】dress；apparel：～朴素大方 dressed simply and in good taste

chuán

传（傳） chuán

【动】❶ pass on；hand down：～球 pass the ball 唐代诗人白居易的诗，～下来的近三千首。Of all the poems by Bai Juyi,

a Tang dynasty poet, about three thousand have been handed down. ❷ spread: 远处～来了悦耳的歌声。 The pleasant sound of singing can be heard in the distance. ❸ (law) issue a summons: ～讯 summon sb. to appear before a court ❹ transmit; conduct: ～热 transmit heat ～电 conduct electricity
另见 zhuàn

传播 chuánbō 【动】propagate; disseminate: 广泛～ spread widely ～先进经验 disseminate advanced experience

传播媒介 chuánbō méijiè the media

传布 chuánbù 【动】spread; disseminate: 胜利的消息很快～开来。The news of victory spread quickly.

传达 chuándá 【动】transmit; relay; pass on: ～上级指示 pass on the instructions of a higher level organization ～文件精神 communicate the gist of the documents 【名】the transmitting of information: 我没参加会议,只听了～。 I didn't attend the meeting. I only heard a report on it.

传达室 chuándáshì 【名】janitor's office

传单 chuándān 【名】〔张 zhāng〕handbill; leaflet

传导 chuándǎo 【动】conduct (heat electricity)

传递 chuándì 【动】hand down; deliver; pass on: ～情报 transmit information ～消息 convey news

传感器 chuángǎnqì 【名】sensor; transducer

传呼 chuánhū 【动】notify sb. to receive a phone call: ～电话 neighbourhood telephone service

传呼机 chuánhūjī 【名】pager; beeper

传家宝 chuánjiābǎo 【名】family heirloom: 勤俭节约是我们的～。 The practice of hard work and

frugality is a cherished part of our tradition.

传媒 chuánméi 【名】 *short for* 传播媒介

传奇 chuánqí 【名】❶ legend: ～式的英雄 legendary heroes ❷ (in the Tang and Sung dynasties) short stories; (in the Ming and Qing dynasties) verse dramas

传染 chuánrǎn 【动】infect; communicate (disease)

传人 chuánrén 【名】descendant

传神 chuánshén 【形】vivid; graphic; lifelike; expressive: 他画的马很～。 The horse he painted is very lifelike. 这一段描写可谓～之笔。 This descriptive passage is very vivid indeed.

传声筒 chuánshēngtǒng 【名】 ❶ megaphone; loud hailer ❷ mouthpiece; one who parrots another

传授 chuánshòu 【动】(of knowledge) teach; impart; pass on: ～经验 pass on one's experience ～技术 impart one's skill to another ～知识 pass on one's knowledge to sb. else

传说 chuánshuō 【动】it is said: ～他又立了一大功。 It is said that he has made another outstanding achievement. 【名】lore: 民间～ folklore

传送 chuánsòng 【动】deliver (message); convey (news)

传颂 chuánsòng 【动】sb.'s praises are being sung everywhere; be on everyone's lips: 这位厂长的开创精神,广为～。 Praise for this factory director's spirit of enterprise is on everybody's lips.

传统 chuántǒng 【名】tradition; conventions: 优良～ fine tradition 革命～ revolutionary tradition ～剧目 a traditional opera or drama ～观念 traditional views

传闻 chuánwén 【名】hearsay

传阅 chuányuè 【动】pass around or

circulate (for perusal)：～文件 pass the document around for everybody to read 互相～ circulate it to everyone 这个通知请各班～。Please pass the circular around to all the classes.

传真 chuánzhēn 【名】facsimile；无线电～ radio facsimile ～照片 telephotograph

船 chuán 【名】〔只 zhī、条 tiáo〕boat；ship；vessel

船舶 chuánbó 【名】ships and vessels

船舱 chuáncāng 【名】cabin (of a ship)

船队 chuánduì 【名】fleet

船帆 chuánfān 【名】sail

船坞 chuánwù 【名】dock；ship-yard

船员 chuányuán 【名】〔名 míng〕(ship's) crew

船长 chuánzhǎng 【名】captain

船只 chuánzhī 【名】ships and boats

chuǎn

喘 chuǎn 【动】gasp；pant

喘气 chuǎn = qì ❶ gasp；pant；他累得直～。He is so exhausted he is gasping for breath. 他气管炎一犯，就有点喘不过气来。He gasps for breath whenever he gets an attack of bronchitis. ❷ take a short break；休息一会儿，喘口气再干。Let's take a breather before we go on.

喘息 chuǎnxī 【动】❶ gasp for breath；～未定 before one has a chance to catch one's breath ❷ breathing spell；respite；他们在比赛中乘胜进攻，不给对手以～的机会。They pushed on in the flush of victory, allowing no breathing space for their opponents.

chuàn

串 chuàn 【动】❶ string together；～讲课文 explain the text word by word and clause by clause from beginning to end ❷ collude with；conspire；～供 doctor the evidence to make each other's confessions tally ❸ get things messed up；电话～线 get a wrong number when telephoning 字写得很密，容易看～行 (háng)。The lines are so close together that it is easy to skip a line when one reads. ❹ go from place to place；～亲戚 go and see one's relatives ～门儿 drop in on sb. 【量】string；cluster；一～珠子 a string of beads 一～钥匙 a bunch of keys

串联 chuànlián 【动】establish ties with；contact 也作"串连"。

串通 chuàntōng 【动】collude with；work hand in glove with

chuāng

创(創) chuāng
另见 chuàng

创伤 chuāngshāng 【名】❶ wound；trauma ❷ damage；医治战争的～ heal the wounds of war 心灵的～ a wound to one's psyche

疮(瘡) chuāng 【名】sore

疮疤 chuāngbā 【名】scar

窗 chuāng 【名】window

窗户 chuānghu 【名】window

窗口 chuāngkǒu 【名】wicket；window (e.g. for selling tickets)

窗帘 chuānglián 【名】window curtain

窗台 chuāngtái 【名】windowsill

chuáng

床 chuáng 【名】〔张 zhāng〕bed 【量】for quilt, bedding：他家新做了两～被子。They have just had two quilts made.

床单 chuángdān 【名】〔条 tiáo〕bedsheet

床铺 chuángpù 【名】bed (esp. one made of board)

床位 chuángwèi 【名】bed or berth (in hospital, hotel, ship, train, etc.)

chuǎng

闯（闖）chuǎng 【动】force one's way in or out; dash：为技术革命～出一条新路 break a new path for revolution in technology 你怎么连门也不敲就往里～? Why did you rush in without knocking?

闯祸 chuǎng = huò precipitate a disaster; lead to trouble

闯将 chuǎngjiàng 【名】(in war) a daring general；(fig.) a person who dares to innovate or make revolution：技术革新的～ a trail blazer in the technological revolution

闯劲儿 chuǎngjìnr 【名】the spirit of an innovator：他有一股～。He has the spirit of an innovator.

chuàng

创（創）chuàng 【动】initiate; inaugurate
另见 chuāng

创办 chuàngbàn 【动】set up; found; establish：～刊物 start a publication ～学校 found a school

创汇 chuàng = huì bring in foreign exchange

创见 chuàngjiàn 【名】original idea：他对甲骨文的研究很有～。He has lots of original ideas about the research into oracle bone inscriptions.

创建 chuàngjiàn 【动】found; create; establish

创举 chuàngjǔ 【名】pioneering undertaking

创刊 chuàngkān 【动】launch (a magazine or newspaper)

创立 chuànglì 【动】set up; originate; found：～一个学会 set up a learned society

创设 chuàngshè 【动】❶ found; set up ❷ create (conditions)：政府为青少年～了有利的学习条件。The Government has created favourable study conditions for young people.

创始 chuàngshǐ 【动】initiate; originate

创始人 chuàngshǐrén 【名】founder

创收 chuàngshōu 【动】generate income

创新 chuàngxīn 【动】create sth. new; blaze new trails：勇于～ boldly create something new 要有～精神。One must be bold to bring forth new ideas.

创业 chuàngyè 【动】start an undertaking or enterprise; do pioneering work：披荆斩棘，艰苦～ brave all difficulties and do pioneering work

创议 chuàngyì 【名】proposal

创意 chuàngyì 【名】originality; creativity

创造 chuàngzào 【动】create; bring about：～条件 create conditions ～新记录 set a new record 【名】creation

创造力 chuàngzàolì 【名】creative power

创造性 chuàngzàoxìng 【名】creativity

创作 chuàngzuò 【动】 create 【名】 creative work

chuī

吹 chuī 【动】❶ blow；puff：～气 blow；breathe out ～哨 blow a whistle ～笛子 play a flute ❷ blow：风～雨打 be exposed to wind and rain ❸ boast；brag：你别～了，我不信你有那么大力气。Stop bragging! I don't believe you're that strong. ❹ fall through：这件事算～啦! The arrangement has fallen through.

吹风 chuī=fēng ❶get in a draught：刚出了汗别～。Don't get in a draught. You've just been perspiring. ❷ dry（hair）：只理发不～ a dry cut ❸ let out information in an informal way：这事还没正式通知，先给大家吹吹风。It has not been officially released, so this is just a hint.

吹鼓手 chuīgǔshǒu 【名】 trumpeter（*usu. fig.*）

吹毛求疵 chuī máo qiú cī find fault with；split hairs

吹牛 chuī=niú boast；brag 也说“吹牛皮”。

吹捧 chuīpěng 【动】 lavish praise on；flatter

吹嘘 chuīxū 【动】 brag

炊 chuī

炊事员 chuīshìyuán 【名】 cook；member of the kitchen staff

chuí

垂 chuí 【动】❶ droop；hang down；dangle：杨柳低～。The branches of the willow droop gracefully. ❷ ◇ hand down；be-queath：名～千古。His name will go down in history.

垂死挣扎 chuísǐ zhēngzhá put up a last-ditch struggle

垂头丧气 chuí tóu sàng qì crestfallen；dejected；despondent；in low spirits：工作中受到些挫折不可能～。Don't be discouraged when you meet with setbacks.

垂危 chuíwēi 【动】 close to death：病已～ critically ill 他生命～。His life is hanging in the balance.

垂涎 chuí=xián 〈书〉covet：～欲滴 be unable to hide one's greed；hanker after

垂涎三尺 chuí xián sān chǐ with one's mouth watering for

垂直 chuízhí 【动】 perpendicular

锤（鎚）chuí 【名】 hammer 【动】 hammer

锤炼 chuíliàn 【动】❶ hammer into shape；steel and temper ❷（of writing）polish：～词句 improve the wording

锤子 chuízi 【名】〔把 bǎ〕hammer

chūn

春 chūn 【名】❶ ◇ spring：温暖如～ as warm as spring ❷ ◇ life；vitality：妙手回～（of a doctor）with the skill to bring the dying back to life 病树前头万木～。Facing a decaying tree, thousands of trees burst with life.

春播 chūnbō 【名】 spring sowing 【动】 sow in the spring

春风 chūnfēng 【名】 spring breeze

春风满面 chūnfēng mǎn miàn 见“满面春风” mǎn miàn chūnfēng。

春耕 chūngēng 【名】 spring ploughing 【动】 plough in the spring

春光 chūnguāng 【名】 the splendour of spring；the sights of spring：～

明媚 the enchanting sights of spring 大好～ the splendid sights of spring

春季 chūnjì 【名】the spring season

春假 chūnjià 【名】spring holiday

春节 chūnjié 【名】Spring Festival

春雷 chūnléi 【名】spring thunder；(*fig.*) inspiring news

春联 chūnlián 【名】〔副 fù〕New Year couplets

春色 chūnsè 【名】the beautiful scenery of spring；(*fig.*) an atmosphere of prosperity, etc.；～满园 the garden is bursting with spring vegetation；(*fig.*) a scene of prosperity

春天 chūntiān 【名】spring

春游 chūnyóu 【动】spring outing

春种 chūnzhòng 【动】spring sowing

chún

纯（純） chún 【形】pure；unmixed：～毛的料子 pure wool fabric：～蓝 pure blue

纯粹 chúncuì 【形】unadulterated；absolute；pure：他说的是～的北京话。He speaks pure Beijing dialect. 他说这话～是开玩笑。He is simply joking.

纯度 chúndù 【名】degree of purity

纯洁 chúnjié 【形】pure；clean and honest：思想～ ideological purity

纯洁性 chúnjiéxìng 【名】purity

纯熟 chúnshú 【形】skilful；fluent；well-versed：～的写作技巧 highly skilled in writing 技术～ highly skilled

纯正 chúnzhèng 【形】❶ pure：酒味～。The wine has a pure taste. ❷ pure and upright；pure：动机～。His motives are straightforward and pure.

唇 chún 【名】lip

唇齿相依 chún chǐ xiāng yī as dependent on each other as lips and teeth：我们两国是山水相连、～的邻邦。We are neighbours sharing common rivers and mountains, and as dependent on each other as lips and teeth.

唇齿音 chúnchǐyīn 【名】labiodental

唇舌 chúnshé 【名】arguments used in convincing or dissuading：费了很多～，才把他说服。It took me a lot of arguing to convince him. 别白费～了。You might as well save your breath.

唇亡齿寒 chún wáng chǐ hán when the lips are gone the teeth will be exposed to the cold；(*fig.*) (two countries which are) so closely related that they have common interests and share the same fate

淳 chún

淳厚 chúnhòu 【形】pure and simple；honest and kind：风俗～ simple unpretentious ways

淳朴 chúnpǔ 【形】simple and honest；unsophisticated：他那～的性格给人留下很深的印象。His ingenuousness left a deep impression on others.

chǔn

蠢 chǔn 【形】stupid

蠢蠢欲动 chǔnchǔn yù dòng waiting for a chance to cause trouble

蠢动 chǔndòng 【动】❶ wriggle ❷ create trouble

chuō

戳 chuō 【动】❶ poke；thrust；jab；stab：笔尖把纸～破了。The pen-nib poked a hole in the paper.

❷ sprain：他打排球把手～了。He sprained his finger while playing volleyball.

戳穿　chuōchuān　【动】❶ thrust through；puncture ❷ lay bare；expose：～谎言 expose a lie 阴谋诡计被～。The plot has been exposed.

chuò

绰（綽）chuò

绰号　chuòhào　【名】nick-name

cí

词（詞）cí　【名】❶ words；words of a song：他问得我没～儿回答。His question left me speechless. 这支歌是老王作的～。Lao Wang wrote the words for this song. ❷ classical poetry conforming to a definite pattern with lines of unequal length：宋～ poems of this kind，written in the Sung dynasty 填～ compose poems of this kind ❸ word

词典　cídiǎn　【名】〔本 běn、部 bù〕dictionary 也作"辞典"。
词根　cígēn　【名】the root of a word
词汇　cíhuì　【名】vocabulary
词句　cíjù　【名】words and sentences
词类　cílèi　【名】part of speech
词素　císù　【名】morpheme
词头　cítóu　【名】prefix
词尾　cíwěi　【名】suffix
词性　cíxìng　【名】part of speech
词序　cíxù　【名】word order
词语　cíyǔ　【名】words and phrases
词藻　cízǎo　【名】flowery language；rhetoric 也作"辞藻"。
词组　cízǔ　【名】group of words；phrase

祠 cí

祠堂　cítáng　【名】ancestral temple；ancestral hall

瓷 cí　【名】porcelain

瓷器　cíqì　【名】porcelain；china-ware

辞（辭）cí　【名】a special form of long classical Chinese poem 【动】❶ ◇ take leave of：不～而别 go away without taking leave ❷ shirk；evade：不～辛苦 spare no effort 粉身碎骨，在所不～ readily give one's life for（sth. or sb.）❸ resign；dismiss（sb. from his post）

辞别　cíbié　【动】say good-bye；bid farewell
辞典　cídiǎn　【名】〔本 běn、部 bù〕dictionary 同"词典"。
辞行　cíxíng　【动】say good-bye（before going on a long journey）
辞藻　cízǎo　【名】同"词藻"。
辞章　cízhāng　【名】poetry and prose
辞职　cí = zhí　resign

慈 cí

慈爱　cí'ài　【形】loving；kind：～的祖母 loving grandmother
慈悲　cíbēi　【形】merciful
慈善　císhàn　【形】charitable
慈善家　císhànjiā　【名】philanthropist
慈祥　cíxiáng　【形】（of elderly people）kindly；amiable：～的老人 kindly old person ～的笑容 kindly smile

磁 cí　【名】magnetism

磁场　cíchǎng　【名】magnetic field
磁带　cídài　【名】〔盘 pán〕magnetic tape
磁疗　cíliáo　【名】magnetotherapy
磁盘　cípán　【名】magnetic disk
磁石　císhí　【名】magnet
磁铁　cítiě　【名】magnet
磁性　cíxìng　【名】magnetism

雌 cí 【形】(of plants or animals) female

cǐ

此 cǐ 【代】❶ this：～人 this person ～地 this place ❷ now；here：由～往西 go west from here 就～告别。I'm leaving now.

此地无银三百两 cǐ dì wú yín sānbǎi liǎng According to legend, a man put a sign over the spot where he had buried his money："300 taels of silver are not here." (fig.) a transparent lie；(fig.) a guilty person gives himself away by protesting his innocence

此后 cǐhòu 【连】henceforth；hereafter

此刻 cǐkè 【名】now；at this moment

此起彼伏 cǐ qǐ bǐ fú rise and fall；recur：欢呼声～ resounding cheers 也作"此起彼落"。

此外 cǐwài 【连】besides this：菜田里只种着黄瓜、西红柿，～再没有别的了。There are only cucumbers and tomatoes in the vegetable field. There is nothing else. 我们剧团在城里演了六场，～还到附近农村演了两场。Our troupe gave six performances in town and two performances in the nearby villages.

cì

次 cì 【形】inferior；second-rate；of poor quality：这种产品比较～。This product is of poor quality. 【名】order；sequence：顺～入场 enter (the sports field) in a certain order 【数】◇second；next：～日 the next day ～子 the second son 【量】time：初～ the first time 次 can be made into a compound measure word with another measure word or noun：架 ～ flight 人 ～ per person (used e. g. in calculating number of admissions to an exhibition)

次第 cìdì 【名】order；sequence

次品 cìpǐn 【名】seconds；product not up to the required standard

次数 cìshù 【名】number of times

次序 cìxù 【名】order；sequence

次要 cìyào 【形】next in importance

刺 cì 【动】❶ prick ❷ irritate ❸ stab (a person)【名】thorn；small bone of a fish

刺刀 cìdāo 【名】〔把 bǎ〕bayonet

刺耳 cì'ěr 【形】ear-piercing；irritating or unpleasant to the ear：录音机坏了，发出～的声音。This tape-recorder must be broken. It makes a horrible noise. 你的话让人听着真～。Your words are jarring to the ears.

刺骨 cìgǔ 【形】cut to the bone；piercing

刺激 cìjī 【动】❶ stimulate ❷ stimulate；spur on：需要～～他，让他振作起来。He needs to be encouraged to pull himself together. ❸ give sb. a shock 【名】shock：这件事对他是一个很大的～。This came as a great shock to him.

刺杀 cìshā 【名】a bayonet charge：练～ do bayonet-drill 【动】assassinate

刺探 cìtàn 【动】detéct

刺绣 cìxiù 【名】embroidery

刺眼 cìyǎn 【形】dazzling；hard on the eyes：光线太强，真～。The light is dazzlingly bright. 这件衣服怪里怪气的，让人看了觉得～。That outfit looks funny. It's hard on the eyes.

赐(賜) cì

赐予 cìyǔ 【动】 bestow...on

cōng

从(從) cōng
另见 cóng

从容 cōngróng 【形】❶ calm and unhurried; confident and controlled: ~就义 meet one's death unflinchingly 举止~ move about in a calm and collected manner ❷ (of time, etc.) ample: 时间~ ample time

从容不迫 cōngróng bù pò take one's time and act calmly: 指挥员要沉着镇静,~。A commander must always keep his cool.

匆 cōng

匆匆 cōngcōng 【形】hurried: 来去~ come and go in a hurry

匆促 cōngcù 【形】hasty; hurried; in a rush: 时间~,来不及细谈了。There isn't much time left, so I can't explain in detail.

匆忙 cōngmáng 【形】in a hurry: 他走得很~,没能跟同学们一一告别。He left in a hurry and couldn't say good-bye to his schoolmates.

葱 cōng 【名】scallion

葱葱 cōngcōng 【形】(of vegetation) green: 草木~ the lush green of trees and grass

葱绿 cōnglǜ 【形】pale yellowish-green: ~的田野 a pale green field

葱郁 cōngyù 【形】luxuriantly green: 山上是~的竹林。The bamboo on the hill is a lush green.

聪(聰) cōng

聪明 cōngmíng 【形】intelligent; clever; bright

cóng

从(從) cóng 【动】◇ ❶
join: ~军 join the army ❷ adopt: 一切~简 get something done with the least fuss 【介】❶ *indicates the starting point*: ~一数到十 count from one to ten ~1950 年他就住在北京。He has been living in Beijing since 1950. 新作息时间~下星期开始实行。The new work schedule will start next week. 一轮红日~波涛中升起。A bright red sun is rising out of the sea. ~第一段至第五段由你翻译。Please translate paragraph one to five. ~到中国以来,我交了不少中国朋友。I've made a lot of friends since I came to China. ❷ *indicates the original state of a change*: ~棉花织成布要经过多少辛勤劳动啊! It certainly takes a great deal of work to turn cotton into cloth! 他~睡梦中醒来时,天已大亮。By the time he awoke from his dream, it was already broad daylight. ❸ *indicates the source of sth. or the place from which a person has come*: 王老师是~上海调来的。Teacher Wang was transferred here from Shanghai. 这个消息是~报纸上看到的。I learned this from the newspaper. 正确的理论只能~实践中来。A correct theory can only be derived from practice. ❹ pass by: 河水~桥下流过。The river flowed by under the bridge. 汽车~我身边开过去。The car passed me by. ❺ *indicates the reason for or cause of sth.*: ~说话的声音就听出是老王。You can tell by his voice that it is Lao Wang. 我们应~长远利益着想。We must consider things while keeping long-term interests in mind. 【副】 *used before a nega-*

tive word, *equivalent to* 从来:他~不计较个人得失。He is never concerned about personal gain. 我~没离开过这个地方。I've never been away from here.

另见 cōng

从长计议 cóng cháng jìyì take time to consider sth.; talk sth. over at length:这件事应~,不宜操之过急。We must talk this matter over at length. We mustn't be too hasty.

从…出发 cóng…chūfā proceed from; proceed on the basis of:从实际出发 proceed on a realistic basis 从人民的利益出发 proceed on the basis of the interests of the people

从此 cóngcǐ 【连】 from then on; from now on; henceforth

从…到… cóng…dào… ❶ *applies to time or space*:暑假从七月十五日放到八月十五日。Summer vacation starts on July 15th and lasts till Aug. 15th. *sometimes*, 从 *can be omitted*:(从)北京到天津120公里。It is 120 km. from Beijing to Tianjin. (从)下午四点半到六点是体育锻炼时间。4:30 p.m. to 6 p.m. is the time for exercise. ❷ *indicates a process or range*:从无到有 start from scratch 从弱到强 from weakness to strength 从不懂到懂 from layman to expert 从城市到农村 from the city to the countryside 从内地到边疆 from inland to the border

从而 cóng'ér 【连】(*usu. in written language*) *used to introduce a clause of result or purpose in a compound sentence with a common subject for both clauses, the first clause indicating the condition, means or cause*:他们改进了方法,~提高了工作效率。They improved their working method, raising efficiency. 制定远景规划,能

使广大群众看到远大目标,~激发群众的积极性。A long-range plan will provide a perspective and stimulate enthusiasm.

从犯 cóngfàn 【名】accessory; accomplice

从简 cóngjiǎn 【动】simplify

从军 cóngjūn 【动】join the army

从…看来 cóng…kànlái ❶ *indicates evidence of conclusion*:从展览会上的展品看来,这个国家的工业发展很快。You can see from the exhibits that the industry of this country has developed very fast. 从实验结果看来,他的假设是正确的。The results of the experiments showed that his assumption was correct. ❷ *indicates a certain point of view*:从营养学的观点看来,蔬菜对于人的健康非常重要。From the point of view of nourishment, vegetables are essential to people's health. *Note*:从…看来 *can also be said as* 从…来看

从来 cónglái 【副】always; at all times (*forms emphatic affirmative or negative, often used in conjunction with* 也,就 *etc.*):这种事我~也没听说过。I have never heard of such a thing! 他~不吸烟。He has never smoked.

从略 cónglüè 【动】omit; leave out:引文~。The quotation is omitted here.

从…起 cóng…qǐ *applies to time or space, meaning* 从…开始:从1976年起,这个计划就开始实行了。This plan was implemented in 1976. 京广铁路从北京起,到广州止。The Jing-Guang Railway starts from Beijing and ends in Guangzhou. "从" *can be omitted sometimes*:(从)小学三年级起开设英语课。English is taught from the third grade on.

从前 cóngqián 【名】formerly; be-

fore：几年没见，他的脾气还跟～一样。I haven't seen him for several years，but he remains his same old self.

从事 cóngshì【动】engage in；be taken up with；go in for：～各种活动 engage in various activities ～体育工作 work in the field of athletics

从属 cóngshǔ【动】be subordinated to

从头 cóngtóu【副】from the beginning

从业 cóngyè【动】pursue an employment

从业员 cóngyèyuán【名】employees in commerce and the service trades

从政 cóngzhèng go into politics；take up governmental posts；go into civil service

从中 cóngzhōng【副】thereby；therefrom

丛（叢）cóng【名】❶ bush；shrubbery ❷ a group of people or things

丛刊 cóngkān【名】books published in a series on a specific topic

丛林 cónglín【名】jungle；bush

丛生 cóngshēng【动】grow up in profusion

丛书 cóngshū【名】同"丛刊"

còu

凑 còu【动】❶ assemble；put together；crowd together：～在一起 crowd together ～钱 pitch in money（to make up a figure）❷ take advantage of；happen by chance：～机会 make use of an opportunity ❸ move close to：～上去搭话 go and put in a word 两人往一块儿～了。The two of them

moved closer together.

凑合 còuhe【动】❶ gather together：大家往一块儿～～。Let's all get together. ❷ make do（with sth.）：这支钢笔不太好，但还能～着用。This pen doesn't work very well，but it will do it. ❸ piece together；patch together：他要箱子是为了装工具，找点旧木头～一个就行了。He just wants a case to hold tools，so get some old boards and knock one together.

凑巧 còuqiǎo【形】happen to；by coincidence；as luck would have it：真～，刚说到你，你就来了。What a coincidence! We were just talking about you and here you are! Speak of the devil!

凑热闹 còu rènào❶ take part in and join the fun：我们正打扑克，你也来凑个热闹吧。We're playing cards. Come and join us. ❷ trouble；bother：你们这儿很忙，我不来～了。I won't butt in，since you are all so busy.

凑数 còu = shù make up the number（with the incompetent or unqualified）

cū

粗 cū【形】❶ thick：大厅里的柱子很～。The pillars in the hall are very thick. ❷（of sb.'s voice）rough：～声～气 with a gruff voice ～嗓子 a rough voice ❸ rough；coarse；crude：这活儿干得太～了。This work is crudely done. ❹ careless；negligent：～～一想 on first thought（about sth.）❺ rude；vulgar；unrefined：～话 vulgar language ❻ slightly；roughly：～知一二 merely have a rough idea of sth. ～具规模 begin to take shape

粗暴 cūbào【形】（of person，

speech, behaviour) rough; rude

粗笨 cūbèn 【形】(of person, furniture, etc.) clumsy; heavy

粗糙 cūcāo 【形】(of material) rough; coarse; (of work) crude; slipshod

粗放 cūfàng 【形】free and easy：～经营 extensive farming

粗犷 cūguǎng 【形】❶ boorish; rough ❷ straightforward and uninhibited：～的性格 of straightforward, unsophisticated character

粗粮 cūliáng 【名】coarse grain

粗鲁 cūlǔ 【形】crude 也作"粗卤"。

粗略 cūlüè 【形】rough; not detailed; sketchy：～的估计 a rough estimate 这本书我～地看了一遍。I just took a quick glance through this book.

粗浅 cūqiǎn 【形】superficial; simple; shallow：～的道理 the simple truth 谈一点儿～的认识。I'll give you my superficial impressions.

粗细 cūxì 【名】❶ diameter：钢管~不等。The steel pipes vary in diameter. ❷ degree of care (in doing sth.)：不能光看快慢, 还要看活儿的～。Don't just look for speed. Workmanship is important.

粗心 cūxīn 【形】careless

粗野 cūyě 【形】(of person, manners) rude; crude

粗枝大叶 cū zhī dà yè crude and careless

粗制滥造 cū zhì làn zào roughly made

粗壮 cūzhuàng 【形】❶ (of person's build) sturdy; thick-set：身材~ sturdily built ❷ (of a person's voice) resonant：～的嗓音 loud and resonant voice

cù

促 cù 【动】promote; spur;

urge：把生产～上去 promote production

促成 cùchéng 【动】help bring into being

促进 cùjìn 【动】promote; accelerate：改革有力地～了生产力的发展。Reform brought about great development in the productive forces.

促使 cùshǐ 【动】cause; impel; precipitate：经常召开学习经验交流会, 可以～同学们互相学习, 取长补短。Regular exchanges would encourage students to learn from others.

促膝谈心 cù xī tán xīn sit together and have a heart-to-heart talk

促销 cùxiāo 【动】promote sale

醋 cù 【名】vinegar

簇 cù 【量】(of flowers) bunch

簇新 cùxīn 【形】brand-new

簇拥 cùyōng 【动】cluster round (sb.)

cuàn

窜(竄) cuàn 【动】(of bandits, etc.) flee

窜犯 cuànfàn 【动】(of a gang of bandits) carry out a raid

窜扰 cuànrǎo 【动】(of a gang of bandits) engage in harassment

窜逃 cuàntáo 【动】(of a gang of bandits) flee

篡 cuàn 【动】usurp

篡夺 cuànduó 【动】usurp

篡改 cuàngǎi 【动】tamper with; revise (*derog.*)

cuī

催 cuī 【动】urge

催促 cuīcù【动】press for

催化剂 cuīhuàjì【名】catalyst

催泪弹 cuīlèidàn【名】tear-gas grenade

催眠 cuīmián【动】hypnotize

摧 cuī【动】destroy；devastate；ravage

摧残 cuīcán【动】cause serious damage to（culture, economics, people's abilities, etc.）

摧毁 cuīhuǐ【动】smash to pieces；completely destroy；shatter

摧枯拉朽 cuī kū lā xiǔ crumble as easily as dead wood：以～之势，破获了贩毒分子的老巢。With an invincible force they destroyed the drug-traffickers' den.

cuì

脆 cuì【形】❶ fragile ❷ crisp ❸ clear；well-enunciated

脆弱 cuìruò【形】（of character）weak

啐 cuì【动】spit

翠 cuì

翠绿 cuìlǜ【形】jade green；bright green

cūn

村 cūn【名】village

村落 cūnluò【名】hamlet；village

村民 cūnmín【名】villager

村舍 cūnshè【名】cottage

村镇 cūnzhèn【名】villages and country towns

村庄 cūnzhuāng【名】village

村子 cūnzi【名】village

cún

存 cún【动】❶ ◇ survive；exist ❷ preserve；keep；～粮食 store up grain 他很直爽，心里有话～不住。He is quite outspoken, and would not keep anything to himself. ❸ place（sth.）for safe-keeping；deposit：～车 park one's bicycle ～行李 check in one's luggage ❹ remain as the balance in an account：支出六千元，尚～一千元。The accounts show a balance of 1,000 yuan after paying out 6,000. ❺ cherish；harbour：～着很大希望 cherish high hopes

存车处 cúnchēchù【名】parking place（for bicycles）

存放 cúnfàng【动】put aside for safekeeping

存活 cúnhuó【动】survive：～率 survival rate

存货 cúnhuò【名】goods in stock or in storage

存货 cún = huò　stock goods

存款 cúnkuǎn【名】deposit；savings

存款 cún = kuǎn　deposit money（in a bank）

存栏 cúnlán【动】livestock on hand

存亡 cúnwáng【名】survival or extinction

存心 cúnxīn【副】on purpose；deliberately

存心 cún = xīn　have（a certain）intention

存衣处 cúnyīchù【名】cloakroom

存在 cúnzài【动】exist；be：我们工作中还～不少缺点。There are still plenty of shortcomings in our work.

存折 cúnzhé【名】deposit book；passbook

cùn

寸　cùn　【量】*measurement of length* (1/30 metre)

寸步不离　cùn bù bù lí　never separated from not even by an inch

寸步难行　cùn bù nán xíng　difficult to move even a step

寸土必争　cùn tǔ bì zhēng　fight for every inch of land

寸土不让　cùn tǔ bù ràng　will not give up even an inch of land

cuō

搓　cuō　【动】rub the palms of one's hands together or rub the palm of one's hand against sth.; ～手 rub one's hands ～绳子 make rope by twisting hemp between the palms of one's hands

磋　cuō
磋商　cuōshāng　【动】discuss; consult

撮　cuō　【动】hold between the fingers 【量】pinch
撮合　cuōhé　【动】bring (two parties) together

cuò

挫　cuò　【动】◇ ❶ frustrate ❷ subdue; lower
挫败　cuòbài　【动】thwart; frustrate
挫伤　cuòshāng　【动】❶ bruise ❷ discourage; dampen (sb.'s enthusiasm, etc.)
挫折　cuòzhé　【名】setback

措　cuò
措辞　cuò = cí　choose the proper words to express the meaning; wording
措施　cuòshī　【名】measure; step
措手不及　cuò shǒu bù jí　be caught unprepared; 打他个 ～ catch him unprepared 准备工作要周到些，免得临时 ～。Exhaustive preparations should be made so that we will not be caught unprepared.

锉（銼）　cuò　【名】〔把 bǎ〕file 【动】file
锉刀　cuòdāo　【名】〔把 bǎ〕file

错（錯）　cuò　【名】(～儿) mistake; error; wrong; 他没 ～，都怪我。I'm completely to blame. It has nothing to do with him. 放心吧！出不了～。Don't worry. It will be all right. 【形】❶ wrong; mistaken; erroneous; ～字 the wrong character 走～了路 take the wrong road ❷ bad; poor (*usu. used in the negative*); 他演这个角色准～不了。He will be excellent in that role. 【动】❶ stagger; arrange alternately; 要把合唱队和篮球队活动的时间～开。Make sure the schedules for the chorus and the basketball practice don't conflict. ❷ pass each other going in opposite directions; ～车 (of trains speeding in opposite directions) pass each other at a place where the track is double
错案　cuò'àn　【名】misjudged case
错别字　cuòbiézì　【名】wrongly written or pronounced character
错处　cuòchù　【名】wrong act; error in conduct
错怪　cuòguài　【动】blame sb. wrongly; 我～了你，很对不起。I've been wrong in blaming you. I'm very sorry.
错过　cuòguò　【动】miss (an opportunity)

错觉　cuòjué　【名】illusion

错乱　cuòluàn　【形】in disorder；deranged

错落　cuòluò　【形】strewn at random

错位　cuòwèi　【动】dislocation

错误　cuòwù　【名】mistake；error

错综复杂　cuòzōng fùzá　complex；intricate：～的案件 a very complex case 这个问题～，要慎重处理。It is a complicated problem. Handle carefully.

D

dā

搭 dā 【动】❶ put up；pitch；build：～帐篷 pitch a tent ～桥 put up a bridge；build a bridge ❷ hang over；put over：肩上～了条毛巾 throw a towel over one's shoulder 把衣服～在椅背上。Put one's clothes over a chair. ❸ join together：不要把两根电线～在一起。Don't let the two wires touch each other! 前言不～后语。What you are saying contradicts your previous words. ❹〈口〉add；throw in：他一个人忙不过来,把我也～上吧! He can't handle it alone; I better lend a hand. ❺〈口〉co-ordinate；go together：米饭不太够,烙点儿饼～着吃吧。There isn't enough rice, let's throw in a few pancakes. ❻ carry；lift up：这个柜子两个人～不动。Two people can't carry this wardrobe. ❼ take（ship, vehicle, etc.）：～汽车 take a bus ～两点钟的轮船 take the two o'clock boat

搭伴 dā = bàn （～儿）（travel）together；in company：去看戏的时候,咱们可以～走。We can go together to the theatre. 你去延安吗? 咱们搭个伴儿吧! Are you going to Yan'an too? Let's go together.

搭伙 dā = huǒ ❶ join as partner ❷ eat regularly in（a mess etc.）

搭救 dājiù 【动】rescue

搭配 dāpèi 【动】arrange（in pairs or groups）；co-ordinate；combine：这些动词常与哪些词～? What words are usually used in collocation with these verbs? 布置工作时,强弱劳动力要合理～。When assigning workers to tasks, see that the strong and the weak are matched suitably.

答 dā
另见 dá

答应 dāying 【动】❶ answer；reply；respond：他在门外喊了几声,没人～。He stood outside the door and called several times, but there was no answer. ❷ promise；agree：赵大爷～给他们讲家史。Uncle Zhao has agreed to tell them the history of his family.

dá

打 dá 【量】dozen
另见 dǎ

达（達）dá 【动】◇ ❶ reach；attain：不～目的,决不罢休。We will never give up until our goal is achieved. 这条铁路长～三千公里。This railway extends 3,000 km. ❷ express；convey：词不～意。That word fails to convey（your）meaning.

达成 dá // chéng reach；conclude；

achieve：～协议 reach agreement

达到 dá // dào　reach；achieve；attain：～目的 achieve the aim ～国际水平 reach international standards ～高中程度 reach senior high school level 要求达得到达不到? Can you meet the requirements or not?

答 dá 【动】◇ answer；reply：～题 answer questions

另见 dā

答案 dá'àn 【名】answer to a question；solution to a problem

答辩 dábiàn 【动】defend one's own idea or opinion 【名】defence of one's idea or opinion

答词 dácí 【名】(on a formal occasion) speech in reply (e.g. response to a toast)

答复 dáfù 【动】reply (formally)【名】formal reply

答谢 dáxiè 【动】reciprocate；express appreciation

答疑 dáyí 【动】(of a teacher) answer questions

dǎ

打 dǎ 【动】❶strike；hit；beat：～鼓 beat a drum ～人 strike sb. ❷attack；fight：～碉堡 attack a stronghold ～敌人 fight the enemy ❸tie up：～行李 tie up one's luggage ❹knit；weave：～毛衣 knit a sweater ～草鞋 weave straw-sandals ❺write；draw：～草稿 write a draft ～了个问号 put a question mark here ❻sink；dig；bore：～个洞 dig a hole ～一眼井 dig (or sink) a well ❼hoist；raise：～伞 hold up an umbrella；put up an umbrella ❽give out；send；emit：～炮 fire a gun ～个电报 send a telegram ❾get in；collect：～了两万斤粮食 get in 20,000 *jin* of grain ❿fetch；

gather in；get：～饭 take out food (e.g. a cooked meal from a dining-hall) ⓫catch；hunt：～鸟 shoot a bird ～鱼 catch fish ⓬buy：～张车票 buy a (train, bus, etc.) ticket ～油 buy cooking oil ⓭play：～乒乓球 play table tennis ～扑克 play cards ～太极拳 do t'ai chi ch'uan (or shadow boxing) ⓮break；smash：碗～了。The bowl is broken. ⓯lay：～基础 lay a foundation ⓰do；engage in：～游击wage guerrilla warfare ～短工 be hired as a day labourer ⓱calculate；estimate：这个会就～着有二百人参加吧! Let's presume that 200 people will attend the meeting. 我们系连走读生～在内,准备招三百名新生。Our department will enroll 300 new students, including day students. 【介】from；since：你～哪儿来? Where did you come from? ～去年春节以后,我就没见到他。I haven't seen him since Spring Festival last year.

另见 dá

打靶 dǎ = bǎ　practise shooting；rifle practice；target practice

打败 dǎ // bài　defeat；beat：～侵略者 defeat the aggressors 把对手～defeat one's rival

打扮 dǎban 【动】dress up；deck out；make up：六一儿童节那天,孩子们都～得非常漂亮。On June 1st, Children's Day, the children are all dressed up. 【名】style of dress：他的～像个农民。He dresses like a farmer.

打包 dǎ = bāo　bale；pack：～机 baling press

打保票 dǎ bǎopiào　guarantee

打抱不平 dǎ bàobùpíng　speak up for sb. who has been wronged；stand up to a bully in defense of sb.

打草惊蛇 dǎ cǎo jīng shé　beat the

grass and frighten away the snake; (*fig.*) give away secrets by acting rashly, thus putting the enemy on guard：为了将这伙暗藏的敌人一网打尽，先要摸清他们的内部情况，但不要～。In order to wipe out our secret enemies, we must ascertain the true situation. We must not, however, put the enemy on guard by acting rashly.

打岔 dǎ=chà interrupt (a conversation or work)：你别～,让他讲下去。Don't interrupt. Let him continue his speech. 你们别跟他～,他正忙着写总结呢! Don't interrupt him. He is busy writing a summary of his work.

打场 dǎ=cháng thresh (grain)

打成一片 dǎ chéng yī piàn become one with; merge with; identify oneself with; be one with：干部要和群众～。Cadres should be one with the masses.

打倒 dǎ//dǎo overthrow; down with

打的 dǎ=dī hire a taxi; take a taxi

打电报 dǎ diànbào send a telegram

打电话 dǎ diànhuà make a telephone call

打动 dǎdòng 【动】(of emotions) move; touch；～人心 touch (sb.) to the heart 这一番话～了他的心。What she said touched him to the heart.

打赌 dǎ=dǔ bet

打断 dǎduàn 【动】interrupt; break；～思路 interrupt sb.'s train of thought 狼的腿被～了。The wolf's leg was broken by the beating. 谈话被～了。The conversation was interrupted.

打哆嗦 dǎ duōsuo tremble; shiver

打工 dǎ=gōng work as a temporary worker

打官腔 dǎ guānqiāng talk like a bureaucrat; stall with official jargon：要真心实意地帮助群众解决困难,不要～。Let's help people with their problems and not spew jargon.

打官司 dǎ guānsi go to law (against sb.)

打火机 dǎhuǒjī 【名】〔个 gè〕cigarette lighter

打击 dǎjī 【动】hit; strike; attack; deal a blow (to, at)：～敌人 attack the enemy; deal a blow at the enemy 不能～群众的积极性。We shouldn't pour cold water on the enthusiasm of the masses. 【名】blow：一个毁灭性的～ an annihilating blow

打击乐 dǎjīyuè 【名】percussion music

打假 dǎ=jiǎ crack down on counterfeit goods and forgeries

打架 dǎ=jià fight; come to blows; engage in a brawl

打江山 dǎ jiāngshān fight for sovereignty over territory; seize political power by force

打交道 dǎ jiāodao ❶ have dealings with; have contact with; negotiate with (a person)：跟老王打过几次交道,我觉得他很热情。I had dealings with Lao Wang and found him cordial. ❷ have contact with; engage in; do (sth.)：这位工人整年跟钻机～,打井的经验非常丰富。This worker operates a drilling machine all the year round, so he has plenty of expertise in sinking wells.

打搅 dǎjiǎo 【动】❶ disturb; interrupt：大家都忙着工作,我不去～了。They are all busy working, so I won't butt in. ❷ trouble; bother (as an apology)：～了您半天,我该走了。I've taken up a great deal of your time. I must be going.

打井 dǎ=jǐng sink a well

打开 dǎ//kāi ❶ open; unfold; turn

on; untie: ~抽屉 open a drawer ~书 open a book ~箱子 open a box ~包袱 untie a bundle ❷ make a beginning; break (the ice); make (a breach); widen (one's outlook); ~僵局 break the deadlock 打不开局面 be unable to make a beginning

打垮 dǎ//kuǎ crush; completely defeat

打雷 dǎ=léi thunder

打量 dǎliang【动】take the measure (of sb.); look sb. up and down: 张大娘把那个小伙子上下~了一下说: "你是刚到这里的吧!" Aunt Zhang looked the young fellow up and down and said: "You're a newcomer, aren't you?"

打猎 dǎ=liè go hunting

打埋伏 dǎ máifu ❶ lie in ambush; set an ambush; ambush ❷ keep under cover; hold sth. back: 他的话里打下不少埋伏,没有把意思全说出来。There's a lot which he has left unsaid.

打喷嚏 dǎ pēntì sneeze

打破 dǎ//pò break; smash: ~情面 do not spare sb.'s sensibilities ~沉默 break the silence ~清规戒律 break with outmoded rules and conventions

打破常规 dǎ pò chángguī break away from convention

打破记录 dǎ pò jìlù break a record

打破沙锅问到底 dǎ pò shāguō wèn dào dǐ 璺,a crack in pottery, is pronounced in the same way as "问". If a pottery pot (沙锅) is broken (打破), it will crack (璺) straight across (到底). So we can say 打破沙锅问(with 问 replacing 璺)到底 to mean keep asking (问) till one gets to the bottom of the matter.

打气 dǎ=qì ❶inflate (tyre); pump up: 自行车已经打足气了。The tyres

of the bicycle were already fully inflated. ❷ bolster (up); encourage; cheer up

打前站 dǎ qiánzhàn act as an advance party

打球 dǎ=qiú play a ball game

打趣 dǎqù【动】make fun of

打入冷宫 dǎ rù lěnggōng be out of favour; relegate; consign to the back; put aside: 这些资料还有参考价值,不能~。The material is still valuable and should not be put aside and forgotten.

打扫 dǎsǎo【动】clean up

打闪 dǎ=shǎn (of lightning) flash

打手 dǎshou【名】hatchet man

打水 dǎ=shuǐ fetch water

打算 dǎsuàn【动】intend; plan: 星期日我~去看一个老朋友。I plan to go and see an old friend on Sunday.【名】plan; intention: 在新的一年里,你有什么~? What plans do you have for the coming year?

打听 dǎtīng【动】inquire; ask: ~一件事 ask about something ~一个人 inquire about someone ~~消息 ask for news 我跟您~一下,去十三陵怎么走? Excuse me, could you show me the way to the Ming Tombs?

打通 dǎ//tōng ❶ open up; break through; get through: 隧道~了。The tunnel has been opened up through the last bit of earth. ❷ dispel (sb.'s doubts, etc.)

打退堂鼓 dǎ tuìtánggǔ beat a retreat; back out before sth. is finished: 不要遇到一点儿困难就~。Don't back out the moment you run up against a difficulty.

打响 dǎ//xiǎng ❶open fire: 一场缉毒战~了。A battle against drug trafficking was launched. ❷ (fig.) win initial success; make a good start; get off to a good start: 头一

步打不响,下一步就不好办了。A set-back in the beginning will make the next step harder.

打消　dǎxiāo　【动】dispel; give up; remove; get rid of (abstract things):～顾虑 dispel misgivings ～了学戏的念头 give up the idea of training for an acting career 疑虑完全～了。All his misgivings have been dispelled.

打掩护　dǎ yǎnhù　❶ provide cover for:替战友～ to cover one's comrade-in-arms ❷ protect; shield (evil persons or things):不要替他的错误行为～。Don't cover up for his mistakes.

打仗　dǎ = zhàng　fight; fight a battle

打招呼　dǎ zhāohu　❶ greet sb. (by word or gesture):小玲在街上碰到我,老远就～。When Xiao Ling saw me in the street, she waved to me from afar. ❷ inform; let (sb.) know:你哪天来我家玩儿,先跟我打个招呼。Please let me know ahead of time when you're coming over. 事情处理完了,向上级打个招呼就可以,不必写书面报告。Just let your boss know when the job is done, no need to put it down on paper.

打折扣　dǎ zhékòu　sell at a discount; fall short of requirements

打针　dǎ = zhēn　have or give an injection

打主意　dǎ zhǔyi　think of a plan; mastermind a plan; think of a way out:你去不去南方,打定主意了吗? Have you made up your mind whether or not to go to the south? 要节约,先从设计上～。If we want to cut down production costs, we must first look to good design.

打字　dǎ = zì　type; type-write

打字机　dǎzìjī　【名】〔架 jià〕typewriter

dà

大　dà　【形】❶ big; great:团结起来力量～。In unity, there is strength. ❷ (of age, area, size, etc.) big; large; great:你多～了? How old are you? 这间屋子有那间屋子两个～。This room is twice the size of that one. ❸ more than half; most:大部分 the greater part of sth. ～半个西瓜 the greater part of a water-melon ❹ the eldest:～哥 the eldest brother ❺ ◇ 大 increases the distance in time from the present by one day or one year:～后天 2 days after tomorrow ～前天 2 days before yesterday ～前年 3 years ago ～后年 2 years after next ❻ greatly; fully; in a big way; on a large scale:～笑 laugh heartily ～红 scarlet; bright red 你们有果园,可以～养蜜蜂。You've got an orchard and can go in for beekeeping on the large scale. ❼ used after 不 not very; seldom:她不～会唱歌。She is not very good at singing. 老李星期日不～出门。Lao Li seldom goes out on Sundays. used before certain negative expressions beginning with 不 quite; completely:～不相同 quite different 对我这种想法他～不以为然。He completely disapproved of my idea.

另见 dài

大半　dàbàn　【名】for the most part; the greater part; most:这些书有一～是哲学方面的著作。These books are, for the most part, works of philosophy. 工程已完成一～了。The greater part of the project has been completed.【副】very likely; probably:天气闷热,～要下雨。It's so suffocatingly hot that it's likely

to rain.

大本营 dàběnyíng 【名】❶ head-quarters ❷ centre of certain sorts of activities

大便 dàbiàn 【名】stool 【动】move the bowels

大不了 dàbuliǎo 【形】❶ even if worst comes to worst：今天晚上我一定要把这本书看完，～晚睡一会儿。I must finish this book. If worst comes to worst, it will only mean I'll stay up a bit late tonight. ❷ (*usu. used in the neg.*) serious：我只是有点儿头痛，没什么～的病。I just have a slight headache, nothing serious.

大材小用 dà cái xiǎo yòng wasting talent on trivial tasks；use a steam-engine to crack a nut

大车 dàchē 【名】〔辆 liàng〕cart

大吃一惊 dà chī yī jīng be startled；be greatly shocked；be astounded

大吹大擂 dà chuī dà léi blow a loud blast on the trumpet；(*fig.*) make a big noise；talk big；brag；to blow one's own trumpet

大大 dàdà 【副】greatly；enormously；to a great degree：～促进了工农业生产 greatly promote industrial and agricultural production 学习成绩～提高 make great progress in one's studies

大…大… dà...dà... *placed before two related nouns，verbs or adjectives to give an exaggerated meaning to sth.*：大风大浪 strong wind and big waves 大摇大摆 swagger 大吃大喝 make a pig of oneself 大红大绿 loud colours

大胆 dàdǎn 【形】bold；daring

大刀阔斧 dà dāo kuò fǔ make a snap decision；bold and resolute；drastic：他在工作中一向是～，雷厉风行。He is bold and resolute in his work. 这篇文章太长了，你就～地删吧! This article is too long；you

had better shorten it drastically.

大道 dàdào 【名】〔条 tiáo〕❶ broad road ❷ (*fig.*) the path leading to a bright future

大地 dàdì 【名】the earth

大豆 dàdòu 【名】soybean

大都 dàdū 【副】mostly；for the most part：这个书架上的书，～是散文和诗歌。The books on this book-shelf are mostly collections of essays and poems.

大多 dàduō 【副】mostly；mainly：这个池塘里养的～是鲤鱼。The fish in this pool are carp for the most part.

大多数 dàduōshù 【名】majority

大发雷霆 dà fā léitíng burst into a rage

大方 dàfang 【形】❶ generous；liberal ❷ natural and poised：举止～ behave with grace and ease 在掌声中她大大方方地走上讲台 Amid warm applause, she went up to the platform with great natural poise. ❸ (of fashion, colour, pattern, etc.) in good taste；tasteful：样式美观～ a pattern which is in good taste

大方向 dàfāngxiàng 【名】general orientation；main direction

大放厥词 dà fàng jué cí talk a lot of drivel

大概 dàgài 【形】general；rough：～的内容 a rough idea of the content ～的印象 general impression 【副】approximately；about；probably：参观摄影展览的～有五六万人。Approximately 50-60 thousand people visited the photography exhibition. ～是因为激动的缘故，他竟不知说什么才好。Probably due to emotion, he was at a loss for words.

大纲 dàgāng 【名】general outline

大哥大 dàgēdà 【名】〔个 gè〕cellular telephone；wireless telephone；mobile phone (popular name for

移动电话 yídòng diànhuà)

大功告成 dà gōng gào chéng the task is accomplished

大公无私 dà gōng wú sī selfless

大规模 dà guīmó large scale；massive；extensive：举行～的庆祝活动 hold mass celebrations ～地开展卫生运动 launch a public health movement on a large scale

大锅饭 dàguōfàn 【名】food prepared in a large canteen cauldron

大国沙文主义 dàguó shāwénzhǔyì chauvinism

大国主义 dàguózhǔyì 【名】同"大国沙文主义"

大海捞针 dà hǎi lāo zhēn look for a needle in a haystack

大好 dàhǎo 【形】very good；excellent：～时光 the best years（of one's life）～河山 beautiful rivers and mountains（of a country）形势～。The situation is excellent.

大会 dàhuì 【名】assembly；conference；rally；congress

大伙儿 dàhuǒr 【代】all；everybody

大计 dàjì 【名】a question of fundamental importance

大家 dàjiā 【代】all；everybody：这些书报～可以随便看。These books and newspapers are for everybody to read freely. ～对工作都充满了信心。We all have great faith in the success of our work. Note：① *when a certain person or certain persons are mentioned in a sentence which also contains* 大家，大家 *does not include this person or these persons. e.g.*：他们要到外地去了，～都来欢送。They are leaving and we have all come to see them off. ② 大家 *is often placed after* "你们"，"我们"，"咱们" *or* "他们" *as an appositive*：明天去公司参观，咱们～都可以去。We can all join in tomorrow's visit to the company.

大街 dàjiē 【名】〔条 tiáo〕street

大节 dàjié 【名】matter of principle；main principles guiding one's conduct

大捷 dàjié 【名】great victory

大惊小怪 dà jīng xiǎo guài make a fuss over

大局 dàjú 【名】general situation；overall situation

大军 dàjūn 【名】a huge army；large force

大快人心 dà kuài rénxīn to the great satisfaction of the masses

大款 dàkuǎn 【名】money bag；tycoon

大理石 dàlǐshí 【名】marble

大力 dàlì 【副】energetically；vigorously：～宣传 conduct propaganda energetically ～推广 energetically popularize ～提倡 make strenuous efforts to promote

大力士 dàlìshì 【名】a man of unusual physical strength

大量 dàliàng 【形】a large number；a great quantity；a great deal：～投产 large scale production ～涌现 come forward in great numbers 图书馆有～的外文参考书。The library contains a large number of foreign language reference books.

大陆 dàlù 【名】continent

大陆架 dàlùjià 【名】continental shelf

大陆性气候 dàlùxìng qìhòu continental climate

大乱 dàluàn 【形】in great disorder

大米 dàmǐ 【名】rice

大民族主义 dà mínzúzhǔyì chauvinism of a majority nationality toward a minority nationality

大名鼎鼎 dàmíng dǐngdǐng （of a person）famous；well-known；celebrated

大拇指 dàmǔzhǐ 【名】thumb

大难临头 dà nàn lín tóu a disaster has befallen（sb.）

大脑 dànǎo 【名】cerebrum

大娘 dàniáng 【名】❶ auntie; aunt ❷ respectful form of address for an elderly woman

大排档 dàpáidàng 【名】a market stall; a roadside stall; foodstalls of various kinds

大炮 dàpào 【名】〔门 mén〕❶ cannon ❷ 见"放大炮"fàng dàpào ❸ one who likes to express radical views

大批 dàpī 【形】large quantities, numbers or amounts; a lot: ~货物 a large amount of goods ~图书 a large number of books ~地生产插秧机 produce rice-transplanters in large numbers

大气 dàqì 【名】air; atmosphere

大气层 dàqìcéng 【名】atmosphere

大气压 dàqìyā 【名】atmospheric pressure

大秋 dàqiū 【名】September and October, when corn and sorghum are harvested

大人 dàren 【名】grown-up; adult

大厦 dàshà 【名】〔座 zuò〕big building; edifice

大赦 dàshè 【动】amnesty; general pardon

大声 dàshēng 【名】in a loud voice

大声疾呼 dà shēng jí hū cry out a warning; sound a grave warning

大失所望 dà shī suǒ wàng greatly disappointed

大使 dàshǐ 【名】ambassador

大使馆 dàshǐguǎn 【名】embassy

大势所趋 dà shì suǒ qū general trend of history; the general, inevitable trend of development of events

大势已去 dà shì yǐ qù the game is up; (of a situation) hopeless; irretrievable

大是大非 dà shì dà fēi questions of principle; fundamental issues of right and wrong; ~分得清 draw clear distinctions concerning fundamental issues of right and wrong

大手大脚 dà shǒu dà jiǎo be wasteful; spend money or use things extravagantly: 一切开支都要精打细算,不能~。Be very careful of all expenditures; don't be extravagant or wasteful.

大肆 dàsì 【副】recklessly; wantonly; frantically: ~活动 bustle about ~宣扬 frantically propagandize ~吹嘘 recklessly boast; feverishly advertise

大踏步 dàtàbù 【副】with great strides

大体 dàtǐ 【形】on the whole; in general; in the main; roughly: ~的情况就是如此。That, roughly, is the situation. 我们的意见~一致。Our opinions are, on the whole, the same. 这件工作~上安排好了。The arrangements for this job have, in the main, been made. 【名】fundamental principle; main principle; what is of paramount importance: 顾大局, 识~。Grasp the overall situation and hold on to essentials.

大庭广众 dà tíng guǎng zhòng in front of everybody; openly; in public

大同小异 dà tóng xiǎo yì similar in essentials but differing in minor respects; mostly alike except for slight differences

大团圆 dàtuányuán 【名】❶ happy reunion ❷ happy ending (of a novel etc.)

大腕儿 dàwànr 【名】master hand; star

大无畏 dàwúwèi 【形】utterly fearless; dauntless

大西洋 Dàxīyáng 【名】the Atlantic Ocean

大显身手 dà xiǎn shēnshǒu fully display one's skill; give full play to one's abilities: 运动员们在比赛场上~。The athletes displayed their

skill fully in the games.

大写 dàxiě 【名】❶ the complicated Chinese character for a numeral (e.g. in cheque-writing 叁 instead of 三) ❷ capital (letter)【动】❶ write the complicated Chinese character for a numeral ❷ capitalize

大型 dàxíng 【形】large size; large scale; full-length (*usu. used attributively*)

大选 dàxuǎn 【名】general election

大学 dàxué 【名】〔所 suǒ〕university

大言不惭 dà yán bù cán boast shamelessly

大洋 dàyáng 【名】❶ ocean ❷ silver dollar

大洋洲 Dàyángzhōu 【名】Oceania

大爷 dàye 【名】❶ father's elder brother ❷ a respectful form of address for a man not too much older than one's father

大衣 dàyī 【名】〔件 jiàn〕overcoat

大义凛然 dàyì lǐnrán inspire awe due to one's defiance of death for a just cause

大意 dàyì 【名】general idea

大意 dàyi 【形】careless

大有可为 dà yǒu kě wéi there are bright prospects; there is plenty of opportunity for development of one's abilities: 中草药的研究工作～。 Research on traditional Chinese medicinal herbs holds out bright prospects for the future.

大有文章 dà yǒu wénzhāng there's a great deal behind all this; there's more to it than meets the eye

大有作为 dà yǒu zuòwéi there is plenty of room to fully develop one's talents and to make a contribution: 你那么能写文章,去报社工作,一定～。 You will have every chance to develop your talents if you work for a newspaper since

you are so good at writing.

大约 dàyuē 【副】about; approximately; probably; 同"大概":他现在还没来,～不来了。 Since he hasn't come yet, he probably won't come. ～有几万人听过他的报告。 Tens of thousands of people have heard his report. 这个会～要两小时。 This meeting will last about two hours.

大跃进 dàyuèjìn 【名】❶ a great leap forward ❷ The Great Leap Forward; the 1958 mass movement

大张旗鼓 dà zhāng qí gǔ on a grand scale; in a big way; pomp and circumstance

大致 dàzhì 【形】rough; main; general: 我只能谈谈水库工地施工的～情况。 I can only give you a rough idea of the work on the reservoir construction site. 那些画报我～翻了一下。 I just leafed through those magazines. 他们哥儿俩的模样～相像。 The two brothers are spitting images of each other.

大众 dàzhòng 【名】the masses; the people

大众化 dàzhònghuà 【动】suit sth. to the tastes, needs, educational level, etc. of the masses; popularize

大篆 dàzhuàn 【名】Chinese script at the time of the Zhou dynasty (1046 B.C.–221 B.C.)

大自然 dàzìrán 【名】Nature

dāi

呆 dāi 【动】stay (at a place)【形】stupid; foolish

呆板 dāibǎn 【形】rigid; wooden (face); inflexible

呆头呆脑 dāi tóu dāi nǎo idiotic

呆滞 dāizhì 【形】dull; idle

呆子 dāizi 【名】idiot

dǎi

歹　dǎi 【形】bad；evil

逮　dǎi 【动】catch
另见 dài

dài

大　dài
另见 dà

大夫 dàifu 【名】doctor；medical man

代　dài 【名】❶ dynasty；historical period：汉～ the Han dynasty ❷ generation：老一～ older generation 年轻的一～ younger generation 【动】take the place of；act for others；act on behalf of：～主任 acting director ～课 take over a class for another teacher 请～我买一张电影票。Please buy a movie ticket for me.【量】generation：一～新人 a new generation

代办 dàibàn 【名】chargé d'affaires 【动】do or act for another

代办处 dàibànchù 【名】office of the chargé d'affaires

代表 dàibiǎo 【名】representative；deputy；delegate：工农兵～ worker-peasant-soldier representatives 全国人民代表大会 deputy of the National People's Congress 【动】represent；stand for；act on behalf of：～了人民的利益 represent the interests of the people 他～全组介绍了学习经验。He represented his group and talked about their study experience.

代表权 dàibiǎoquán 【名】representation

代表团 dàibiǎotuán 【名】delegation；mission

代表性 dàibiǎoxìng 【名】the quality of being representative of；typical

代词 dàicí 【名】pronoun

代沟 dàigōu 【名】generation gap

代管 dàiguǎn 【动】manage sth. for sb.；act for others；act as an agent：车间主任外出期间，他的工作请你～一下。Please take charge of the workshop director's work when he is out.

代号 dàihào 【名】code name，number or letter（which symbolizes sth.）

代价 dàijià 【名】price；cost

代劳 dàiláo 【动】do sth. for sb.；我想买几个信封，如果你去邮局，请～一下。I want to buy some envelopes. If you go to the post-office, could you please get me some? 这事我愿意～。I am willing to do it（for you）.

代理 dàilǐ 【动】act on sb.'s behalf；act for；take（sb.'s）place：～部长 acting minister 主任去省里开会，工作暂由老张～。Lao Zhang will act for the director who is away at a meeting in the provincial capital.

代理人 dàilǐrén 【名】❶ temporary head of an institution or department ❷ agent ❸ one who is being used to perform acts for the benefit of someone else

代数 dàishù 【名】algebra

代替 dàitì 【动】replace；displace；substitute

代销 dàixiāo 【动】act as a commissioned agent（e.g. for the state）：这个小饭馆～香烟、邮票。This little eatery acts as a commissioned agent for the sale of cigarettes and stamps.

代言人 dàiyánrén 【名】spokesman

代用 dàiyòng 【动】substitute

代用品 dàiyòngpǐn 【名】substitute

带（帶） dài 【名】❶（～儿）band；tape；lace；belt：鞋～ shoelace ❷ tyre：自行车外～ bicycle tyre 【动】❶ take；bring；carry：～着挎包 carry a knapsack 别忘了～字典。Don't forget to bring a dictionary with you. ❷ do sth. by the way or incidentally：你路过他家的时候，请给他～一封信。When you pass his house, please give him this letter. 你去商店买东西，顺便给我～一包烟。Since you're going to the store, please buy me a package of cigarettes. 他到上海开会～探亲，要去三个星期。He is going to Shanghai to attend a meeting and will also see his parents, so he will be away for three weeks. ❸ take；lead：老师～着学生下乡劳动。The teacher took the students to work in the countryside. 难忘的回忆把他～到了战火纷飞的年代。Unforgettable memories took him back to the war years. ❹ bear；with：～日历的手表 a calendar watch 这是刚摘下来的玫瑰，还～着露水呢！Here are some roses I've just picked, still wet with dew. ❺ have；contain：满脸～笑 a face wreathed in smiles 这种梨～点酸味。This pear tastes a bit sour. ❻ drive；spur on；lead to action：他工作热情、积极肯干，把全组都～起来了。His enthusiasm and energy at work spurred on the whole group. ❼ look after；bring up；raise：～孩子 look after children；bring up a child ～徒弟 train an apprentice

带电 dài = diàn electrified：～作业 live-wire work

带动 dàidòng 【动】drive；bring along；spur on：这些机器全靠电力～。These machines are completely run on electricity. 在村长的～下，村民们全部投入了抗旱斗争。Spurred on by the village head, all the villagers plunged into combatting the drought.

带劲 dàijìn 【形】❶（～儿）energetic；forceful；with great energy；in high spirits：小学生排着队，唱着歌，走得可～啦！The school children formed lines and marched along with great energy, singing as they went. ❷ with great interest；interesting：别叫他了，他看小说看得正～呢！Don't interrupt him. He is absorbed in reading a novel. 这场赛马可真～！The horse race was really interesting!

带领 dàilǐng 【动】❶ take (a person) ❷ lead

带路 dài = lù lead the way；serve as a guide

带头 dài = tóu take the lead；set an example；take the initiative：处处～ take the lead all the time 起模范～作用 set an example ～抢重活干 take the lead in doing the hardest work 这项工作请你带个头。Please take the lead in doing this work.

带子 dàizi 【名】〔条 tiáo〕ribbon；strap

贷（貸） dài 【动】lend；borrow；loan（between an institution and a bank or government, or between governments）

贷款 dàikuǎn 【名】〔笔 bǐ〕loan

贷款 dài = kuǎn loan a sum of money

待 dài 【动】❶ treat；deal with：～人热情诚恳 treat people warmly and with sincerity ❷ ◇ wait for；await：上述问题暂不作决定，～时机成熟，再予解决。We won't make any decision for the time being；we'll wait until the time is ripe. 此种产品的质量尚～提高。The quality of this product requires further

improvement.

待命　dàimìng　【动】await orders

待遇　dàiyù　【名】❶ treatment；manner of dealing with people：~平等 equal treatment 政治~ political status ❷ pay；wages；salary：~优厚 excellent pay

怠 dài

怠工　dàigōng　【动】sabotage；slow down

怠慢　dàimàn　【动】❶ slight；receive (sb.) without due attention ❷ *used as an apology for not having properly entertained a visitor*

袋 dài 【名】bag

袋子　dàizi　【名】bag

逮 dài

另见 dǎi

逮捕　dàibǔ　【动】arrest

戴 dài 【动】put on；wear：~帽子 put on one's hat ~手套 put on one's gloves ~纪念章 wear a badge ~手表 wear a watch ~眼镜 wear glasses Note："穿" *is not used in these expressions*.

dān

担（擔）dān 【动】❶ carry with a shoulder-pole：~水 carry water ~着两筐土 carry two baskets of earth ❷ take on；shoulder；undertake；assume（responsibility）：不论多艰巨的工作，我们也要~起来。No matter how hard the task, we must take it on.

另见 dàn

担保　dānbǎo　【动】assure；vouch for

担保人　dānbǎorén　【名】guarantor

担当　dāndāng　【动】take on；undertake；assume：我们决心把这项试验工作~起来。We are determined to

undertake the experiment. 这么珍贵的文物，如果弄坏了，这个责任可~不起呀！These historical objects are so valuable, we can't assume responsibility should they be damaged.

担风险　dān fēngxiǎn　take risks；run risks：不怕~ not be afraid to take risks 你这项投资不会担很大风险。You won't take too much risk in this investment.

担负　dānfù　【动】bear；shoulder；take on；undertake：~任务 take on a task ~费用 bear an expense ~重要工作 take on important work

担架　dānjià　【名】〔副 fù〕stretcher

担任　dānrèn　【动】hold the post of；undertake；take charge of：~班长 be the squad leader 他~什么职务？What post does he hold? 历史课由谁~? Who will be in charge of the history course?

担心　dān＝xīn　worry；be anxious；feel uneasy：别为他~，他不会迷路的。Don't be worried about him. He won't lose his way. 他骑车的技术很好，你担什么心? He rides a bicycle very well. What are you worried about?

担忧　dān＝yōu　be worried

单（單）dān 【名】❶ ◇（~儿）sheet：被~ top sheet 褥~ bottom sheet ❷ sheet (of paper)：货~ inventory sheet 【形】❶ one；single（*as opp. to* 双 *or* 多）：~人床 single bed ~音节词 a monosyllabic word ~项练习 a drill on one item ❷ odd（number）：~日 on odd days ~号 odd numbers ❸（of clothing）singlelayered：~裤 unlined trousers【副】❶ alone；separately：这些书要~放着。These books must be put in a separate place. 这几个学生程度比较高，要~开一个班。Those students are more advanced in

their studies. We should have a separate class for them. ❷ only; solely (*cannot be used before numerals*)：～凭热情不行，还要有科学态度。Mere enthusiasm isn't enough; you must also have a scientific attitude. ❸ *about the same as* 偏，*with an emotional implication of discontent or bad luck*：别人都来了，~他没来，他还是第一个发言呢！Everybody else is here except him and he is giving the first speech! 你怎么早不来晚不来，~在他出去的时候来找他？Why have you come to see him at the very moment when he is out? Note; *as an adverb,* 单 *in* ❷ *and* ❸ *can be reduplicated as* 单单 *for emphasis*

单薄 dānbó 【形】❶ thinly (clad)：他穿得很~。He is thinly clad. ❷ thin; weak：人力 ~ shortage of manpower 他身子骨儿很~。He is thin and weak. ❸ poor; scanty：内容~ poor in content
单产 dānchǎn 【名】per unit yield
单程 dānchéng 【名】one-way trip
单纯 dānchún 【形】❶ simple; uncomplicated：思想~ simple-minded 问题并不那么~。The problem is not so simple. ❷ single; alone; merely：他的任务很~，只管贴商标。His job is to do a single operation; applying the trademark. 在生产中不要 ~ 地追求数量。Don't strive merely for quantity of production.
单纯词 dānchúncí 【名】simple word; single-morpheme word
单词 dāncí 【名】word (*as opp. to phrase or sentence*)
单刀直入 dān dāo zhí rù speak out without beating about the bush; come straight to the point：他~，一下子指出了问题的要害。He didn't beat about the bush, but came straight to the heart of the problem.

单调 dāndiào 【形】monotonous; dull
单独 dāndú 【形】alone; by oneself
单方面 dān fāngmiàn one-sided; unilateral
单干 dāngàn 【动】work on one's own
单杠 dāngàng 【名】❶ (of gymnastics) horizontal bar ❷ horizontal bar (event in gymnastics competition)
单季稻 dānjìdào 【名】single cropping of rice
单价 dānjià 【名】unit price
单晶硅 dānjīngguī 【名】single crystal silicon
单晶体 dānjīngtǐ 【名】monocrystal
单据 dānjù 【名】〔张 zhāng〕bill; receipt; voucher
单枪匹马 dān qiāng pǐ mǎ single-handed; all by oneself：他~绿化了一座荒山。He afforested an uncultivated mountainside all by himself. 做工作要依靠广大群众，~是不能成功的。Everybody must pull together, nothing can be achieved single-handedly.
单亲 dānqīn 【名】single parent：~家庭 single-parent family
单身 dānshēn 【名】single; unmarried; (be) away from one's family
单数 dānshù 【名】❶ odd number ❷ singular number
单位 dānwèi 【名】❶ unit of measurement ❷ organization; unit of an organization; work unit
单位面积 dānwèi miànjī unit area
单行本 dānxíngběn 【名】article in pamphlet form; reprint
单一 dānyī 【形】single; unitary
单衣 dānyī 【名】〔件 jiàn〕unlined jacket
单元 dānyuán 【名】❶ suite of rooms; flat ❷ unit (of lessons)
单子 dānzi 【名】❶ bed sheet ❷ list; bill form

耽 dān

耽搁　dānge　【动】❶ stop；stay：他还要在县城多～几天。He will stay in town for a few more days. ❷ delay：这事情很重要，可别～了。This matter is important and must not be delayed.

耽误　dānwu　【动】delay；hold up；spoil sth. because of delay：～时间 lose time ～功课 miss one's class 别把病～了。Get medical treatment in time.

dǎn

胆（膽） dǎn　【名】❶ gall-bladder ❷ ◇ courage；bravery：～大心细 brave but careful ❸ bladder-like inner container：球～ rubber bladder of a ball 暖瓶～ glass liner of a thermos bottle

胆敢　dǎngǎn　【副】dare

胆固醇　dǎngùchún　【名】cholesterol

胆量　dǎnliàng　【名】courage；boldness

胆略　dǎnlüè　【名】courage and wisdom

胆怯　dǎnqiè　【形】timid；cowardly

胆小如鼠　dǎn xiǎo rú shǔ　timid as a mouse

胆战心惊　dǎn zhàn xīn jīng　tremble with fear

胆子　dǎnzi　【名】courage；bravery；spunk：～大 bold；brave 好大的～！You've got a lot of nerve!

掸（撣） dǎn　【动】dust；wipe off

掸子　dǎnzi　【名】〔把 bǎ〕duster

dàn

石 dàn　【量】measurement for

grain（100 litres）

另见 shí

旦 dàn

旦夕　dànxī　【名】〈书〉this morning or evening；in a very short time

但 dàn　【连】but，同“但是”（usu. in written language）：他喜欢买书，～不是藏书家。He is fond of buying books, though not a bibliophile.

但是　dànshì　【连】but often used in conjunction with 虽然：虽然学校有个游泳池，～他还是愿意到河里去游泳。Although there is a swimming pool at the school, he prefers to go swimming in the river. 他的话虽然不多，～讲得很透彻。His words were few, but his exposition was clear-cut. 这个词好懂，～不好用。It is easy to understand this word, but difficult to use it.

但愿　dànyuàn　【动】if only；wish for sth.（though it is not likely to happen）：～如此。I wish it were true. ～能下一场透雨，旱象就可以解除了。If it would only rain heavily, the drought would be over. ～这消息不是真的。I wish this news were not true.

担（擔） dàn　【名】◇ a load to be carried；a carrying-pole with its two loads：货郎～ a load of goods carried by a pedlar 【量】❶ for things which can be carried on a shoulder pole：一～粮食 two baskets of grain（carried on a shoulder pole）❷ picul：一百市斤为一～。One hundred jin equals one picul.

另见 dān

担子　dànzi　【名】〔副 fù〕❶ a carrying-pole with its two loads：他挑着一副～。He is carrying a load on his shoulder using a shoulder pole.

❷(*fig.*)burden；task：你肩上的～可不轻啊！You have a heavy burden on your shoulders!

诞(誕) dàn

诞辰 dànchén 【名】(of a revered person)birthday

诞生 dànshēng 【动】be born

淡 dàn 【形】❶ thin；light；weak(*as opp. to* 浓)：～茶 weak tea ～酒 light wine 天高云～。The sky is high, the clouds are pale. ❷ not salty(*as opp. to* 咸)：这菜太～了。This dish is too bland. ❸light；pale(colour)(*as opp. to* 深 or 浓)：～绿 light green 颜色有点儿～。The colour is somewhat too light.

淡薄 dànbó 【形】❶(of feelings, interest, etc.)weak：老王对篮球的兴趣～了。Lao Wang's interest in basketball has begun to weaken. ❷(of impressions)dim；hazy：童年的印象已经～了。His memories of childhood have already faded.

淡化 dànhuà 【动】cause to fade out；cause to sink into oblivion；bring into oblivion

淡季 dànjì 【名】slack season

淡漠 dànmò 【形】❶indifferent；apathetic：对人～ treat people with indifference ❷ dim；faint：这件事在我的记忆里已经～了。The event has already faded in my memory.

淡水 dànshuǐ 【名】fresh water

淡雅 dànyǎ 【形】(of colour)light, subdued, and in good taste：这块绸子的花色很～。Both the colour and pattern of this printed silk are very subdued and in good taste.

弹(彈) dàn 【名】◇ bullet：每～必中(zhòng)。Every shot hit the target.

另见 tán

弹坑 dànkēng 【名】(shell)crater

弹片 dànpiàn 【名】shell fragment

弹丸 dànwán 【名】pellet；shot；～之地 a ting spot；a tiny little place

弹药 dànyào 【名】ammunition

蛋 dàn 【名】egg

蛋白 dànbái 【名】❶ egg white ❷ protein

蛋白质 dànbáizhì 【名】protein；albumen

蛋糕 dàngāo 【名】〔块 kuài〕cake

蛋黄 dànhuáng 【名】yolk

氮 dàn 【名】nitrogen

氮肥 dànféi 【名】nitrogenous fertilizer

dāng

当(當) dāng 【动】❶ be；become；work(or serve)as：小宏说他长大要～天文学家。Xiao Hong says that when he grows up, he wants to be an astronomer. 他既～官，又～老百姓。He remains one of the common people while serving as an official. ❷ take；accept(job, responsibility, etc.)：敢做敢～ dare to do sth. and dare to take responsibility for it 【介】in sb.'s presence；to sb.'s face；facing：～着大家说说 speak up in the presence of everyone 【象声】(嘡)clang：铁锤～～响。A hammer clangs.

另见 dàng

当场 dāngchǎng 【名】on the spot；then and there：～表演 give performances then and there ～捕获 catch or arrest sb. on the spot；catch sb. redhanded

当初 dāngchū 【名】in the beginning；in the past；originally；at the time when something happened in the past：～这里是一片荒地，现在建

成工人新村了。Originally this area was wasteland; now it has become a new residential area for workers. ～他们俩结婚的时候,就决定在边疆安家落户了。It was when they got married that they decided to settle down near the border.

当代 dāngdài 【名】present age

当…的时候 dāng...de shíhòu *used at the beginning of a sentence as an adverbial adjunct* when; at the time (at which something happens): 当气温降到摄氏零度的时候,水就会结冰。When the temperature goes down to 0˚C., water will freeze. 当燕子飞来的时候,已是阳春三月了。By the time the swallows come back, it is already lovely March weather.

当地 dāngdì 【名】that place (a specific place mentioned before): ～盛产大米。Rice abounds there. 他是～人。He is a native of that place.

当机立断 dāng jī lì duàn make a prompt decision

当家 dāng = jiā manage household affairs

当家作主 dāng jiā zuò zhǔ be master in one's own house

当今 dāngjīn 【名】now; nowadays; at present

当局 dāngjú 【名】the authorities

当面 dāng = miàn to sb.'s face; in sb.'s presence; face-to-face: 请把钱～点清。Please count the money in my presence. 有意见～提,不要背后议论。You should be forthright about your opinions. Please don't gossip.

当年 dāngnián 【名】❶ in those years or days; at that time ❷ prime of life: 他正在～,熬几夜不算什么。He is in his prime; burning the midnight candle is no big deal.
另见 dàngnián

当前 dāngqián 【名】present; current; now; today; ～的任务 the present task ～国内外形势如何? How is the present situation at home and abroad? 【动】be faced with; be confronted with

当权 dāng = quán be in power

当然 dāngrán 【形】of course; 代表大会的决议,我们～要执行。We must, as a matter of course, carry out the resolutions of the conference. 你喜欢旅行吗? ——那～啰! Do you like to travel? — Of course I do! 他做了那么多好事,～应该受到表扬。Of course he should get merit for his good deeds. 这件事很难办,～,也不是一定办不成。This is a difficult problem, of course we are not saying that it is absolutely impossible.

当仁不让 dāng rén bù ràng view something as one's obligation; do what is right and not shirk responsibility; 他在荣誉面前从不伸手,但在艰巨任务面前却～。He never seeks credit for himself, but is always ready to take on arduous tasks.

当时 dāngshí 【名】at that time; then; in those days; 这篇反映工人生活的作品是他 1952 年写的,～他在工厂工作。He wrote about the life of workers in 1952. At that time, he was in a factory.
另见 dàngshí

当事人 dāngshìrén 【名】person directly concerned

当头一棒 dāng tóu yī bàng a blow on the head; severe warning; an abrupt warning intended to bring sb. to his senses

当务之急 dāng wù zhī jí pressing matter at the moment; pressing obligation; high priority task

当先 dāngxiān 【动】take the lead

当心 dāngxīn 【动】take care; look out; be careful; ～路滑! Watch

your step. The road is slippery. ～点儿，别洒了酒。Be careful not to spill the wine.

当选 dāngxuǎn 【动】be elected

当政 dāngzhèng 【动】be in power；be in office

当之无愧 dāng zhī wú kuì be worthy of；deserving：这个青年工人被评为先进生产者，是～的。This young worker was commended as an advanced worker and he deserved the honour.

当中 dāngzhōng 【名】❶ in the middle；in the centre：坐在～的是我们的老队长。The man sitting in the middle is our old team leader. ❷ among：领导干部要生活在群众～。Leading cadres should live among the masses. 这班学生～，有不少文体活动的积极分子。Among these students，there are many who are active in sports and the arts.

当众 dāngzhòng 【副】in front of everybody

dǎng

挡（擋） dǎng 【动】❶ block；keep off；hold back：一条大河～住了去路。A big river blocks the way. 这么薄的棉衣在高山上～不住寒风。Such a thinly padded coat cannot ward off the cold mountain wind. ❷ cover；obscure：飘过来一片云彩～住了月亮。A cloud drifted by and covered the moon.

挡箭牌 dǎngjiànpái 【名】shield (*used only fig.*)；excuse；pretext

党（黨） dǎng 【名】❶ political party ❷ ◇ gang

党籍 dǎngjí 【名】party membership

党纪 dǎngjì 【名】party discipline

党派 dǎngpài 【名】political parties and groups

党徒 dǎngtú 【名】gangster；member of a reactionary political party

党羽 dǎngyǔ 【名】member of a gang；gangster

党员 dǎngyuán 【名】party member

dàng

当（當） dàng 【动】❶ equal to；match：他干活儿来，一个人～两个人。He can do the work of two. 要抓紧时间，一天～两天用。Hurry up. Make the day twice as long. ❷ think，同"以为" yǐwéi：我他不来了，谁知他来得比谁都早。I thought that he would not show up，but he was the first to do so. ❸ treat as；regard as；take for；look upon as：死马也要～活马医 treat a dead horse as if it were still alive — make every effort to remedy a hopeless situation 【形】◇ proper；right：用词不～ inappropriate choice of words 以上意见～否，请批示。Whether the above is appropriate，please comment.

另见 dāng

当年 dàngnián 【名】the same year：这些树苗～就长到五尺高了。Those saplings grew to five feet within the year. 这条公路年初动工，～冬天就完工了。Construction of the highway was started at the beginning of the year，and completed by the end of that same year.

另见 dāngnián

当时 dàngshí 【名】just at that moment；at once；immediately：缝纫部可以～为顾客剪裁服装。The dressmaking department can cut out dresses for customers on the spot. 火车票～就能买，用不着预购。You can get the train ticket right at the time. It is not necessary to book a ticket.

另见 dāngshí

当天 dàngtiān 【名】the same day; that day; ～的工作,～完成。Don't put off until tomorrow what you can do today. 剧团来到山区,～晚上就为村民演出。On the evening that they arrived in the mountain district, the troupe performed for the villagers.

当真 dàngzhēn 【形】true; 这消息可～? Is the news true? 【副】really; 他答应借给我的那本书,今天～送来了。Today he really brought me the book just as he said he would.

当真 dàng = zhēn believe sth. to be true; take seriously; 他是跟你开玩笑,你可别～呀! He was just joking; don't take it seriously!

当作 dàngzuò 【动】treat as; regard as; take as; look upon as; 别把我～外人。Don't treat me like an outsider! Don't treat me as a guest. 这个剧本可以～教材。This play can be used as a textbook.

荡(蕩) dàng 【动】swing; sway; ～秋千 swing; play on a swing ～桨 pull an oar

荡涤 dàngdí 【动】〈书〉clean up

荡漾 dàngyàng 【动】(of water) ripple

档(檔) dàng

档案 dàng'àn 【名】archives; records; files

dāo

刀 dāo 【名】〔把 bǎ〕knife; sword

刀具 dāojù 【名】tool

刀口 dāokǒu 【名】the edge of a knife

刀片 dāopiàn 【名】〔片 piàn〕razor-blade

刀枪 dāoqiāng 【名】swords and spears

刀刃 dāorèn 【名】edge of a knife or sword

刀山火海 dāo shān huǒ hǎi a mountain of swords and a sea of flames; (fig.) immense dangers and difficulties

刀子 dāozi 【名】〔把 bǎ〕knife

dǎo

导(導) dǎo 【动】◇ divert; guide; ～淮入海 divert the Huai River into the sea

导弹 dǎodàn 【名】〔枚 méi〕missile

导电 dǎo = diàn conduct electricity

导购 dǎogòu 【动】guided shopping

导管 dǎoguǎn 【名】conduit

导航 dǎoháng 【动】pilot; guide

导火线 dǎohuǒxiàn 【名】❶ (of a shell or mine) fuse ❷ event which is the direct cause of another, usually disastrous

导论 dǎolùn 【名】introduction (to a book)

导热 dǎo = rè conduct heat

导师 dǎoshī 【名】tutor; teacher

导体 dǎotǐ 【名】conductor

导线 dǎoxiàn 【名】❶ (electr.) lead; (conducting) wire ❷ (of a shell or mine) fuse

导言 dǎoyán 【名】foreword; introduction

导演 dǎoyǎn 【动】direct (a film or play) 【名】(of film or play) director

导游 dǎoyóu 【动】guide (a tour) 【名】a guide; a travel guide; a tourist guide

导致 dǎozhì 【动】bring about; cause; lead to; result in; 理论上的错误必然～实践上的失败。Errors in theory inevitably result in failures in practice.

岛（島）dǎo 【名】〔个 gè〕island

岛国 dǎoguó 【名】island nation

岛屿 dǎoyǔ 【名】islands

捣（搗）dǎo 【动】❶ pound (with a mortar & pestle, etc.); beat; smash：～药 pound medicinal herbs ～米 pound rice (to husk it) ❷ smash; destroy：直～匪巢 break through to the bandits' den

捣鬼 dǎo = guǐ play an under-handed trick

捣毁 dǎohuǐ 【动】crush; destroy

捣乱 dǎo = luàn ❶ sabotage ❷ make trouble; create a disturbance; stir up a riot

倒 dǎo 【动】❶ fall; topple：摔～ fall over 撞～ knock sth. over ～在床上睡着了 flop down and fall a-sleep immediately 墙～了。The wall has collapsed. 任何困难也压不～我们。No difficulties can ever daunt us. ❷ be overthrown; topple; collapse：～台 be overthrown; fall from power ❸ change; shift：～一下手 (of merchandise, etc.) change hands ～班 change shifts (e.g. in a factory) 另见 dào

倒闭 dǎobì 【动】close down; go bankrupt

倒车 dǎo = chē change trains, buses, etc.

倒伏 dǎofú 【动】(of crops) lodge

倒霉 dǎo = méi out of luck; bad luck; get into trouble

倒牌子 dǎo páizi bring discredit on; fall into disrepute

倒手 dǎo = shǒu (of merchandise) change hands

倒塌 dǎotā 【动】collapse; fall down

祷（禱）dǎo

祷告 dǎogào 【动】pray

dào

到 dào 【动】❶ arrive; reach; get to：他今天下午～北京。He will arrive in Beijing this afternoon. 从图书馆借来的书～期了。The book from the library is due. ～昨天他还没有回来。Up to yesterday, he hadn't come back. ❷ go to：～祖国最需要的地方去。Go where the country needs you most. 他经常～我家来。He often drops in at my house. Note：到 *is used after another verb as a complement* ① *indicates getting to a certain place through the action expressed by the verb*：这种新麦种已推广～全国。This new strain of wheat has been popularized throughout the country. 我坐船只坐～南京，然后坐火车。I'll travel by boat to Nanjing, and then I'll travel on by train. ② *indicates duration of an action*：坚持～胜利 persist till victory 工作～深夜 work into the night ③ *indicates the degree of the action*：这个水浇地今年已扩大～三百亩。The irrigated area has been expanded to 300 *mu* this year. 我们一定要把非生产人员压缩～最低限度。We must reduce the number of support staff to the minimum. ④ *indicates the sphere or the object effected by the action*：我们已经估计～了可能出现的困难。We've taken into account all possible difficulties. 这个问题关系～群众生活，必须注意。This concerns people's welfare and merits close attention. ⑤ *indicates a gain*：地质队找～了一个铝土矿。The geological prospecting team has

found a deposit of bauxite. 他买～了一本汉英词典。He bought a Chinese-English dictionary. 在这一个月的学习中，我学～了不少东西。I've learned a lot during this month of study.

到处 dàochù 【副】in all places; everywhere: 这种草药～都能采到。This medicinal herb can be gathered everywhere. 屋顶上、田野里，～都是厚厚的雪。Rooftops and fields were all blanketed by snow.

到达 dàodá 【动】reach

到底 dàodǐ 【副】❶ after all; as a result: 经过医生们的努力，孩子的生命～抢救过来了。Through the doctor's efforts, the child's life was finally saved. 我劝了半天，他～也没去。I spent a long time trying to persuade him, but in the end he didn't go. ❷ 同"究竟" jiūjìng 【副】❶：你～是开玩笑，还是真的？Are you joking after all, or is it true? ❸ 同"究竟"【副】❷：～是突击队，这么快就干完了。They are, after all, shock troops, so their task was completed very quickly.

到底 dào∘dǐ to the end: 将调查工作进行～ carry the investigation through to the end 实验～成功了。The experiment has succeeded, after all.

到手 dào∘shǒu succeed in getting

到头 dào∘tóu to the end

到头来 dàotóulái 【副】 *indicates that after elaborate efforts, the situation isn't any better, or the person concerned has still got nowhere*: 争论了好几天，～还得按这个意见做。After a lot of arguing we still had to follow this suggestion in the end. 不要跟他谈了，～你也说不服他。Don't waste your time talking to him because you won't be able to convince him anyway. 搞阴谋诡计的人，～都没有好下场。In

the end, mischief will bring its own punishment.

到位 dào∘wèi pass (a ball) accurately; be at the ready

到…为止 dào...wéizhǐ until; till: 到目前为止，学习计划已经完成一半了。Up to now, we have completed half of the study plan. 从今天开始到下星期三为止，每天下午都有篮球比赛。Starting today till next Wednesday, there will be a basketball match every afternoon.

倒

dào 【动】❶ turn upside down; invert: 第四页～数第二行 the second line from the bottom on p. 4 这个瓶塞儿不紧，千万别～过来。The bottle is not properly corked. Don't overturn it. 箱子里有药水，不要～着放。There are bottles of tonic in the box. Don't leave it upside down. ❷ pour; tip: ～茶 pour tea 把米从口袋里～出来 empty the rice from the bag 他把心里话都～出来了。He poured out everything that was on his mind. ❸ go backward; reverse: ～车 back one's car 【副】❶ *indicates that sth. brings about an effect which is exactly opposite to what ought to be the case* 同"反而" fǎn'ér: 都春天了，～下起雪来了。It's spring already, yet it is snowing. 你这一帮忙，事情～不好办了。You've come to help, but you've created more problems. 我们以为这么走能近一点，没想到～远了。We thought this was a shortcut, but we've ended up the long way around. ❷ *indicates that some favourable feature has been discovered unexpectedly*: 那所房子从外面看不怎么样，里面～挺讲究。That house doesn't impress from the outside, but it is beautifully furnished inside. 这本小说～挺有意思

的。I didn't expect this novel to be so interesting. 别看他八十多了，身体～一点毛病没有。Though he is over eighty, he is as sound as a bell. ❸ *indicates that one admits a certain favourable point but with the intention of pointing out a drawback*：他说的那地方风景～是不错，就是太远了。The place he mentioned does have beautiful scenery, but it is too far. 老王干活～非常细致，不过有点慢。Lao Wang works very meticulously indeed, but he's a bit slow. ❹ *indicates impatience and the desire to hurry someone along*：你～快点走啊！Please walk faster! 你～说话呀，去还是不去？Will you please answer me? Are you going or not? ❺ *indicates friendly sarcasm*：你时间抓得～紧，吃饭还看书！You certainly know how to make full use of your time; reading even while you eat! 他～真会找人，有你帮他翻译，当然快了。He certainly knows where to look for help! With you doing the translation, of course he works fast! 你说得～容易，事情哪有那么简单！It is easy for you to talk, but things are actually not that simple! ❻ *indicates that the facts are not as someone might think*：我自己～用不着，歌本是替我姐姐买的。In fact I don't need it. I bought the songbook for my sister. 这个电影我～很想看，你有票吗？I'd like to see that movie as a matter of fact. Have you got a ticket? 他～愿意试试，让他去吧！He'd like to try, you know. Let him have a go at it. ❼ *indicates doubt about sb.'s ability to do sth.*：我～想听听他这样做的理由。I'd like to hear what he has to say for his own behavior!（He may not be able to justify himself.）你～说说这本书好在哪儿？You just tell me why you think this book is good!（I think that you will not be able to give me reasons.）另见 dǎo

倒打一耙 dào dǎ yī pá make unfounded charges when one is at fault oneself
倒挂 dàoguà 【动】hang upside down; (of price) be upside down
倒计时 dào jìshí count down; countdown
倒立 dàolì 【动】stand on one's head; handstand
倒退 dàotuì 【动】reverse; go backwards; retrogression
倒行逆施 dào xíng nì shī go against the trend; act against principles of social justice：暴君～只能加速自己的灭亡。Despotism will bring about its own down fall.
倒置 dàozhì 【动】(*usu. in written language*) ❶ place or put upside down：小心轻放，请勿～！Handle with care! This side up! ❷ invert：轻重～ got one's priorities wrong

悼 dào
悼词 dàocí 【名】memorial speech
悼念 dàoniàn 【动】mourn; grieve over

盗 dào 【名】burglar; thief 【动】steal
盗版 dàobǎn 【名】pirated edition
盗匪 dàofěi 【名】burglars and bandits
盗卖 dàomài 【动】illegally sell (public property)
盗窃 dàoqiè 【动】steal；～犯 thief
盗用 dàoyòng 【动】usurp

道 dào 【名】❶ road; way; path ❷ ◇ way; method; reason：以其人之～，还治其人之身 deal with a man as he deals with others; pay him back in his own coin 讲得头头是～

speak impressively and well; speak with all the facts at his fingertips ❸ (～儿) line: 铅笔～ a pencil line 划了两条红～ draw two red lines 【动】◇ say; speak; talk: 说长～短 idle chatter; random talk; gossip 【量】*for things in the form of a line*: 一～防线 a line of defence 三～数学题 three mathematics questions 杯子裂了一～缝。The cup is cracked.

道白　dàobái　【名】(of Chinese operas) dialogue

道德　dàodé　【名】morality; moral integrity

道具　dàojù　【名】theatre property; props

道理　dàolǐ　【名】the whys and wherefores; reason

道路　dàolù　【名】road; way

道貌岸然　dàomào ànrán　be sanctimonious (*usu. used in sarcastic remarks*): ～的伪君子 a hypocrite who poses as a man of high morals

道歉　dào = qiàn　apologize

道听途说　dào tīng tú shuō　hearsay

道谢　dào = xiè　thank (sb.); express gratitude (to sb.)

道义　dàoyì　【名】morality and justice

稻

稻　dào　【名】◇ ❶ paddy: 双季～ two crops of rice a year ❷ unhusked rice

稻草　dàocǎo　【名】〔根 gēn〕rice straw

稻谷　dàogǔ　【名】rice in the husk

稻田　dàotián　【名】paddy field

稻种　dàozhǒng　【名】rice seed

稻子　dàozi　【名】❶ rice (unhusked) ❷ rice plant

dé

得

得　dé　【动】❶ get; obtain; gain;

两个球队～分一样，打成了平局。The two teams wound up with the same score, tying the match. ❷ (*colloq.*) be finished; ready: 饭做～了。Dinner is ready.

另见 de; děi

得病　dé = bìng　be ill; fall ill

得不偿失　dé bù cháng shī　the loss outweighs the gain

得逞　déchěng　【动】accomplish or succeed in (an evil act)

得宠　dé = chǒng　find favour with sb.; be in the grace of; be sb.'s favourite

得寸进尺　dé cùn jìn chǐ　reach out for a yard after getting an inch; give him an inch and he'll take an ell

得当　dédàng　【形】proper; suitable; fitting: 安排～ arrange properly 处理～ handle properly

得到　dé // dào　get; gain; obtain; receive: ～一面奖旗 get a banner as a reward ～一个学习的机会 be given an opportunity to study ～群众的拥护 win the support of the masses

得道多助，失道寡助　dé dào duō zhù, shī dào guǎ zhù　a just cause enjoys support while an unjust cause loses support

得法　défǎ　【形】do sth. in the proper way; have the knack (of doing sth.): 使用～ use properly 果树管理～，结的果子就多。If fruit trees are properly tended, they will bear more fruit.

得救　déjiù　【动】be saved

得力　délì　【形】capable; efficient; competent: ～助手 capable assistant; right-hand man ～干部 an efficient cadre 领导很～。The leadership is very capable.

得人心　dé rénxīn　be popular; win popular approval: 大～ win the support of the masses 最～ be the most popular with the masses 办事

不公的人不～。Unjust administrators lose the support of the people.

得胜 dé=shèng win victory

得失 déshī 【名】❶ gain and loss ❷ advantages and disadvantages

得势 dé=shì be in power; be in favour; get the upper hand

得手 dé=shǒu ❶ (of matter, things) go smoothly; come off; (of tools, etc.) suits one nicely: 这把铁锹用起来很～。This spade suits me very nicely. ❷ succeed (in accomplishing sth.)

得数 déshù 【名】answer (to a maths question); result

得体 détǐ 【形】(of words or behaviour) proper; appropriate: 话说得很～ speak in terms appropriate to the occasion

得天独厚 dé tiān dú hòu (of environment, nature, etc.) be richly endowed by nature; enjoy exceptional advantages

得闲 déxián 【形】have leisure

得心应手 dé xīn yìng shǒu handle easily and with great efficiency; perform with facility; attain high proficiency: 他画起山水画儿来～。He paints landscapes with great facility.

得以 déyǐ 【动】bring about; manage to; be able to; contrive to: 理想～实现。One's ideal has been achieved. 由于进行了深入的调查,问题才～澄清。The matter is now clarified, thanks to a thorough investigation.

得意 déyì 【形】elated; exulting

得意忘形 déyì wàng xíng have one's head turned by success: 他这个人哪,有了一点成绩就～。His head is easily turned by even a small achievement.

得意洋洋 déyì yángyáng very proud and satisfied; immensely proud;

elated; self-satisfied

得志 dézhì 【动】achieve one's ambition

得主 dézhǔ 【名】winner; holder: 金牌～ medalist; medal holder

得罪 dézuì 【动】offend

德

德 dé 【名】❶ moral character; virtue; moral excellence: ～、智、体全面发展 develop morally, intellectually and physically in an all-round way ❷ ◇ heart; mind: 一心一～ be united in purpose; be of one mind ❸ ◇ kindness; favour or act of kindness: 感恩戴～ be deeply indebted to sb. for his kindness

德才兼备 dé cái jiān bèi have both ability and integrity

德高望重 dé gāo wàng zhòng be of noble character and enjoy high prestige

德行 déxíng 【名】moral conduct

德育 déyù 【名】an education that develops character

de

地

地 de 【助】 *used after an adj., noun, onomatopoeic word or a phrase to form an adverbial adjunct*: 胜利～完成了任务 accomplish the task successfully 老老实实～向群众学习 sincerely learn from the masses 聚精会神～听课 listen to the lecture attentively 溪水潺潺～流着。The brook gurgles along.

另见 dì

的

的 de 【助】❶ *used after a modifier* ① *indicates a possessive or a qualifying or descriptive word or phrase*: 可爱～中国 beautiful China 绿油油～麦田 brilliantly green wheat fields 获得了独立～民族 newly independent nations 群众～意见

the opinions of the masses ② *where the modifier is a personal pronoun or noun indicating a person who is in fact the receiver of the action*: 他请我～客. He treated me (to a dinner, etc.). 大家在开小李～玩笑. The joke is on Xiao Li. ③ *where the modifier is a person's name or personal pron. and the headword is the name of a post or role, the two together indicate who is assigned the post or plays the role*: 今天开会是老张～主席. Lao Zhang will preside over the meeting today. 今天演《白毛女》,谁～喜儿? In today's performance of *The White-Haired Girl*, who is to play Xi Er? ❷ *used to form a construction in which the headword is understood*: ① *indicating a certain type of person or thing*: 这架钢琴是中国制造～. This piano is made in China. 那两件衬衫,蓝～是他～,白～是我～. Of the two shirts, the blue one is his and the white one is mine. 他是新来～. He is a newcomer. 我不爱吃甜～. I'm not fond of sweet things. ② *indicates certain circumstances or a certain state of affairs*: 外边敲锣打鼓～,什么事? They are beating the drums and gongs out there. What's it all about? 他的脸晒得黑红黑红～. His face is perfectly tanned. ③ *used after a personal pronoun, which is the same as or stands for the subject, to form the object, indicating non-interference*: 你们讨论你们～,我不参加了. You just go on with your discussion. I won't join in. 叫小林睡他～吧,别叫醒他. Let Xiao Lin sleep. Don't wake him. ④ *with the same verb or verbal construction both before and after* 的. *Several such phrases in parallel indicate a lot of people doing differ-

ent things at the same time.*: 操场上打球～打球,跑步～跑步,人真不少. There are lots of people on the playground, some playing ball and others running. ⑤ *a phrase with the same adj. both before and after* 的 *combined with another similar phrase composed of an adj. opposite in meaning, indicates inappropriateness*: 这几篇文章,深～深,浅～浅,做教材都不合适. Some of these essays are too difficult while others are too easy, none of them are suitable as teaching material. 这几双鞋,大～大,小～小,我都不能穿. Some of the shoes are too big and others too small. None of them fits me. ⑥ *used after the verb in a sentence to put emphasis on the agent, time, place, manner, etc. of the action*: 是这位大夫给我看～病. It was this doctor who treated me. 他前年去～西藏. It was the year before last that he went to Tibet. 我在北京买～手表. It was in Beijing that I bought my wrist watch. 水这么急,他们到底怎么过～河? The currents are so rapid, I wonder how they crossed the river. ⑦ *used after nouns or phrases expressing similar things to indicate other things of the same kind*: 这厨柜里瓶瓶罐罐～,什么都有. The kitchen cabinet is full of bottles and jars and what not. 小孩儿们到了博物馆,问这问那～,兴趣可大啦! The children asked about this and that at the museum and were very interested. 【语气助词】 ❶ *puts emphasis on the agent, time, place, manner, aim, etc. of the action*: 这趟车是八点零五分开～. It was at 8:05 that the train left. 电烙铁是从她那儿借～. It was from her that I borrowed the iron. 他是到法国去学习～. He

went to France to study. ❷ *when the verb of the sentence takes an auxiliary verb or the potential form of a resultative complement，的 stresses possibility，probability，certainty，etc.*：我们的目的是一定能够达到～。Our goal is certainly attainable. 你不要担心，明天他会来～。Don't worry，I'm sure he'll come tomorrow. ❸ *used at the end of a declarative sentence to stress the truth of a fact*：她是很了解我～。She knows me very well. 这套科学杂志我曾收藏过～，可惜已经不全了。I did once have a whole set of this science magazine. It's a pity it is no longer complete.

另见 dí

…的话 …dehuà 【助】*used at the end of a conditional clause as an extra indication that it is conditional*：你能来～，我一定陪你游览北京的名胜。if you come，I will take you sight-seeing in Beijing. Note: *if there is a conjunction of condition，…的话 is optional*：要是你对这个问题有兴趣（～），欢迎你参加我们的讨论。If you are interested in this question，you are welcome to join the discussion.

…的时候 …de shíhou　*when；at the time of used after a word or phrase to form an adverbial adjunct of time*：休息～我来找你。I'll drop in on you during the break. 我总在下雨～才想起该买把雨伞。I think of buying an umbrella only when it rains. 咱们等玉兰花开～去一次颐和园。Let's go to the Summer Palace when the magnolias are in bloom.

得 de　【助】❶ *used between a verb and its complement of result or directional complement to indicate possibility*：听～懂 listen and be able to understand 办～到 can

do（sth.）；（sth.）can be done 拿～出办法来 can come up with a solution（*The negative is formed by replacing* 得 *with* 不.）❷ *used after a verb or an adj. to connect it with a descriptive complement or a complement of degree*：这个电影好～很。This film is awfully good. 雪下～很大。It snowed very heavily. 他说～大家都笑了。His remarks made everybody laugh. ❸ *used after certain verbs to show possibility*（*usu. in the sense of being harmful or harmless to the agent*）：这种蘑菇吃～；那种有毒，吃不～。This kind of mushroom is edible；that kind is poisonous. 我晚上喝不～茶，喝了就睡不着觉。I cannot drink tea in the evening. It keeps me awake. 这孩子长得真快，半年前的衣服都穿不～了。This child is growing really fast. His clothes of six months ago don't fit him any more.

另见 dé；děi

…得慌 …de huang　*used after a word expressing an uncomfortable feeling to indicate a very high degree of that feeling*：难受～ very uncomfortable 屋子里烟太大了，呛～。There is too much smoke in the room and it's quite suffocating. 今天下午闷～，是不是要下雨啦？It's extremely sultry this afternoon. I wonder if it is going to rain.

děi

得 děi　【动】need：修建这样的大桥，至少～两年。A bridge like this will take at least two years to complete. 【助动】❶ must；have to；ought to：时间紧迫，我～马上回去。Time is running out. I get back at once. ❷ will；will certainly be；be

sure to：电影七点钟开演，不快走，就～迟到。The film begins at seven o'clock. If we don't hurry we'll be late. *The negative of* 得 is 不用,不会,*not* 不得.

另见 dé；de

dēng

灯（燈）dēng 【名】〔盏 zhǎn〕lamp；light

灯光 dēngguāng 【名】❶ lamp light ❷ illumination（e. g. of a stage）

灯火 dēnghuǒ 【名】lights in general

灯火辉煌 dēnghuǒ huīhuáng brightly illuminated

灯笼 dēnglong 【名】lantern

灯谜 dēngmí 【名】riddles written on a lantern（as a game during Spring Festival）

灯泡 dēngpào 【名】（～儿）〔个 gè〕light bulb

灯塔 dēngtǎ 【名】light-house；beacon

灯头 dēngtóu 【名】socket for a light bulb

灯罩 dēngzhào 【名】（～儿）lamp shade

登 dēng 【动】❶ step on；tread；脚～在凳子上 rest one's foot on a stool ❷ press down with the foot；pedal（a bicycle）；operate（a treadle sewing-machine）：～三轮儿 pedal a pedicab ～水车 push a water wheel with one's feet ❸ mount；ascend；climb；scale：～上顶峰 climb to the top of a mountain ～上北海的白塔 climb up to the White Tower in Beihai Park ❹ publish；record：～广告 advertize（e. g. in a newspaper）～消息 publish news（in a newspaper）

登报 dēng＝bào publish in a newspaper

登场 dēng＝chǎng go on stage（to give a performance）

登峰造极 dēng fēng zào jí （of skill，learning，etc.）reach the peak of perfection；plumb the depths

登记 dēngjì 【动】enrol；register：～簿 register；registry

登陆 dēng＝lù land（from a ship）

登山 dēng＝shān climb a mountain

登载 dēngzǎi 【动】carry（in the papers）

蹬 dēng 【动】同"登" dēng ❶ ❷

děng

等 děng 【名】class；grade；rank：一～品 top-quality goods 二～功 second-class merit 特～英雄 special class（combat）hero 【动】wait（for）；await；when...：～他半天,他才来。We had been waiting for him for a long time when he finally arrived. ～大家来齐了,我们就出发。We'll set out when everyone has arrived.【代】❶ *used after* 我,你 *or a noun denoting a person to indicate plural number*（*only in written language*）：我～八人 eight of us 张华～五人 Zhang Hua and four others ❷ *and so on*；*and so forth*（*at the end of a sentence*，*can be reduplicated as* 等等）：他买了许多水果,如苹果、橘子等等。He bought a lot of fruit，such as apples，tangerines，etc. ❸ *used to end an enumeration*：代表团访问了北京、上海、天津、武汉、广州～五大城市。The delegation visited the five big cities of Beijing，Shanghai，Tianjin，Wuhan，and Guangzhou.

等次 děngcì 【名】grade；class

等待 děngdài 【动】wait（for）；await：～命令 wait for orders；await instructions 耐心～ wait pa-

tiently ~时机 await a favourable opportunity; wait for a chance

等到 děngdào 【连】when (*placed at the beginning of a sentence to indicate the moment when an action is completed*): ~他们赶来，汽车已经开走了。When they arrived, the bus had already left.

等分 děngfèn 【名】(maths.) (divide into) equal parts

等号 děnghào 【名】sign of equation

等候 děnghòu 【动】wait; await; expect (*used of persons, news, etc., but not abstract nouns*): ~客人 expect a visitor ~通知 await information ~上级命令 wait for instructions from a higher level; await orders

等级 děngjí 【名】❶ grade; rank; class; level: 这种商品分好几个~。This kind of merchandise is classified into several grades. ❷ social stratum; rank; status: ~观念 the concept of (social) status

等价 děngjià 【名】equal value

等价交换 děngjià jiāohuàn exchange of equal value

等价物 děngjiàwù 【名】objects of equal value

等量 děngliàng 【名】equal quantity

等量齐观 děng liàng qí guān be regarded as equal (in value, merit) (*usu. used in the negative*): 这两件事差得太远了，不能~。These two things are poles apart. They cannot be mentioned in the same breath.

等式 děngshì 【名】equation

等同 děngtóng 【动】equate: 把两类不同性质的问题~起来是不对的。These are entirely different issues and shouldn't be lumped together.

等闲 děngxián 【形】〈书〉ordinary; unimportant; (regard sth.) casually: 切不可~视之。We mustn't treat this matter lightly.

等于 děngyú 【动】❶ be equal to; be equivalent to: 二加二~四。Two plus two is four. ❷ be the same as; be like: 这个定理你懂了，但并不~掌握了。You may understand this theorem, it doesn't mean you can apply it.

dèng

凳 dèng 【名】◇ stool; bench

凳子 dèngzi 【名】〔个 gè〕stool; bench

澄 dèng 【动】(of liquid) settle
另见 chéng

澄清 dèngqīng 【动】(of liquid) settle; become clear
另见 chéngqīng

瞪 dèng 【动】❶ open (one's eyes) wide: ~起眼睛 open one's eyes wide ❷ stare; glare at sb.: ~他一眼 give him a dirty look

dī

低 dī 【形】low: ~声讲话 speak in a low voice ~水平 low level (e.g. of knowledge) ~年级 (of schooling) lower grade 飞机飞得很~。The plane is flying very low. 【动】bow; hang: 把头~下来 hang one's head; bow or lower one's head

低产 dīchǎn 【名】low-yield

低潮 dīcháo 【名】❶ low tide; ebbtide ❷ at a low ebb

低沉 dīchén 【形】❶ overcast: ~的天空给人一种窒息的感觉。One feels oppressed by such a overcast sky. ❷ (of voice) low, deep in pitch: ~的声调 a deep voice ~的歌声 song sung in a deep voice ❸ low in spirits; downcast (*as opp. to* 高

昂)：这几天他的情绪有些～。He has been somewhat downcast recently. 那首古诗的调子有点～。The tone of that classical poem is somewhat gloomy.

低档 dīdàng 【形】❶ low gear ❷ low grade

低调 dīdiào 【名】low-key

低估 dīgū 【动】underestimate；underrate：节约原材料是一项重要措施，不能～它的作用。The economical use of raw materials is a very important measure. Don't underestimate its role.

低谷 dīgǔ 【名】at an all time low

低级 dījí 【形】❶ low-grade；elementary；on a low level：～阶段 an elementary stage；a lower stage ❷ vulgar；low：～趣味 vulgar interests；bad taste

低劣 dīliè 【形】inferior；low grade

低落 dīluò 【动】be downcast：情绪～ be downcast；be in low spirits 士气～。The morale of the troops is sagging.

低三下四 dī sān xià sì servile；abject：一副～的奴才相。Scrape and bow with fawning looks.

低烧 dīshāo 【名】low fever

低声下气 dī shēng xià qì meek and subservient；servile

低头 dī = tóu yield；succumb：他在任何困难面前都不～。He never gives up in the face of difficulties.

低温 dīwēn 【名】low temperature

低下 dīxià 【形】low；lowly；humble

低压 dīyā 【名】❶ low pressure ❷ low voltage ❸ low atmospheric pressure ❹ diastolic pressure

堤 dī 【名】dam；dike

堤岸 dī'àn 【名】bank；embankment

堤坝 dībà 【名】dam；dike

堤防 dīfáng 【名】dyke；embankment

堤堰 dīyàn 【名】embankment；dyke

提 dī
另见 tí

提防 dīfang 【动】guard against

滴 dī 【动】drip 【量】drop

滴滴涕 dīdītì 【名】D.D.T.

滴水成冰 dī shuǐ chéng bīng water turns into ice instantly as it drips

dí

的 dí
另见 de

的确 díquè 【副】indeed；certainly：这部电影～好。This film is certainly a good one. ～，这个意见值得考虑。You are right. This opinion is worth considering. 这只鼎的的确确是商代的遗物。This *ding* is really a genuine relic of the Shang dynasty.

的士 díshì 【名】taxi

敌（敵） dí 【名】◇ enemy；foe：分清～友 draw a distinction between friends and enemies 【动】◇ resist；hold back；withstand：寡不～众。A handful cannot hold back a large opposing force.

敌对 díduì 【形】hostile；adverse；antagonistic

敌后 díhòu 【名】behind the enemy lines

敌寇 díkòu 【名】enemy

敌情 díqíng 【名】the enemy's situation；the state of the enemy forces

敌人 dírén 【名】enemy

敌视 díshì 【动】be hostile to；regard as an enemy

敌手 díshǒu 【名】rival

敌意 díyì 【名】hostility

涤（滌） dí

涤荡　dídàng　【动】〈书〉wipe out；clean up

涤纶　dílún　【名】dacron；terylene

笛　dí　【名】❶ flute ❷ ◇ whistle

笛子　dízi　【名】〔枝 zhī〕flute

嘀　dí

嘀咕　dígu　【动】❶ talk in whispers；talk in a low voice：你们俩～什么呢？What are you two whispering about？❷ have misgivings about sth.；have sth. on one's mind；be indecisive：拿定主意就行了，别心里老～。Just make up your mind and don't have second thoughts about it.

嫡　dí

嫡亲　díqīn　【名】blood relations

嫡系　díxì　【名】closest ties of relationship (e.g. one's relationship with one's own troops)

dǐ

诋（詆）dǐ

诋毁　dǐhuǐ　【动】vilify；slander

抵　dǐ　【动】❶ support；sustain ❷ ◇ resist；withstand：～敌 resist the enemy ❸ ◇ compensate；make good：～命 a life for a life ❹ ◇ mortgage；mortgage sth. as security for a loan ❺ be equal to：一个～两个。One can do the work of two. ❻〈书〉reach；arrive at：他十五日～京。He arrived in Beijing on the 15th.

抵偿　dǐcháng　【动】compensate (for loss)；make amends

抵触　dǐchù　【动】conflict；contradict：～情绪 feeling of antagonism 两种意见互相～。The two interpretations contradict each other.

抵达　dǐdá　【动】reach；arrive

抵挡　dǐdǎng　【动】withstand；resist；keep off

抵抗　dǐkàng　【动】resist；oppose；withstand

抵赖　dǐlài　【动】refuse to admit (guilt)；deny (facts)

抵消　dǐxiāo　【动】offset；cancel out；counterbalance

抵押　dǐyā　【动】mortgage　【名】mortgage：～品 security

抵御　dǐyù　【动】resist；withstand；stand up against

抵债　dǐ＝zhài　pay a debt in kind or by labour

抵制　dǐzhì　【动】resist；oppose；reject；boycott：～会议的召开 boycott the meeting

抵罪　dǐ＝zuì　be punished for a crime

底　dǐ　【名】❶ bottom；base：壶～ the bottom of a kettle ❷ end (of a year，month)：八月～ the end of August ❸ the ins and outs of；the cause；(get to) the bottom of sth.：摸摸～ try to find out what the real situation is 露了～。The inside story was revealed. ❹（～儿）rough draft or sketch；copy as a record；original manuscript：这篇稿子我留了个～。I have kept a copy of the draft of this article. ❺ end：干到～ carry sth. through to the end ❻ background；ground：白～红花 red flowers on a white background

底层　dǐcéng　【名】ground floor (BrE)；first floor (AmE)；bottom

底稿　dǐgǎo　【名】manuscript

底价　dǐjià　【名】upset price；base price；bid and offered price

底牌　dǐpái　【名】one's last card；trump card

底片　dǐpiàn　【名】〔张 zhāng〕(of photograph) negative

底数 dǐshù 【名】base number; truth

底细 dǐxi 【名】the ins and outs of; the details of

底下 dǐxia 【名】❶ underneath; under; below; beneath; 桌子～ under the table ❷ later; next; afterward; 第二节课上完了,～我们干什么? The second class is over. What do we do next?

底子 dǐzi 【名】❶ sole of a shoe ❷ foundation; grounding; 他日文～很好,稍加复习就能用。He has a good grounding in Japanese. With a bit of brush up, he'll be able to use the language adequately. ❸ a rough draft or sketch; 画画儿的时候,先打个～。When you draw a picture, it's a good idea to make a rough sketch first.

dì

地 dì 【名】❶ earth; land ❷ farmland; field; 下～干活儿 work in the fields 这个村子有一一千亩。This village has 1000 *mu* of land. ❸ floor; 水泥～ cement floor 花砖～ tile floor ❹ distance (used after *li*); 走了四十里～。He walked a distance of 40 *li*.
另见 de

地板 dìbǎn 【名】(wooden) floor

地步 dìbù 【名】❶ condition; situation; plight (usu. unfavourable); 敌人陷于孤立的～。The enemy was in an isolated position. ❷ extent; 他到了不可挽救的～。He has exceeded all bounds and refused to mend his ways. 他刻苦学习到了废寝忘食的～。He studies so diligently that he forgets to eat and sleep.

地产 dìchǎn 【名】landed property; real estate

地大物博 dì dà wù bó (generally of a country) vast territory and abundant resources

地带 dìdài 【名】region; zone

地道 dìdào 【名】tunnel

地道 dìdao 【形】❶ pure; real; 她说的北京话很～。She speaks with a pure Beijing accent. 这是地地道道的龙井茶。It is genuine Longjing tea. ❷ up to standard; fine; 这活儿干得很～。This is a job well done. 景德镇的瓷器真～。The porcelain made in Jingdezhen is superb.

地点 dìdiǎn 【名】locality; place

地洞 dìdòng 【名】tunnel; cave

地方 dìfāng 【名】❶ (of administration) district; local; 要注意发挥中央和～的积极性。We should take care to mobilize the initiative of both the central and the local authorities. ❷ local; of that place; 他一到乡下,就同～上的群众打成一片。When he went to the countryside, he soon became integrated with the local people.

地方 dìfang 【名】❶ area; place; 他是什么～的人? Where does he come from? 到祖国最需要的～去。We will go to the part of our country where we are most needed. ❷ place; part of; 他的意见有对的～,也有不对的～。His view is correct in some places, but wrong in others.

地方戏 dìfāngxì 【名】local opera

地基 dìjī 【名】❶ ground ❷ foundation

地窖 dìjiào 【名】cellar

地雷 dìléi 【名】mine (weapon)

地理 dìlǐ 【名】geography

地理学 dìlǐxué 【名】geography

地面 dìmiàn 【名】❶ the earth's surface; ground; 河床比～低两米。The river bed is two metres below the level of the land surrounding it. ❷ covering; ground; pavement; floor-covering; 浴室的～是瓷砖铺的。The bathroom floor is

covered with glazed tiles.

地膜 dìmó 【名】agro-plastic film (for covering young plants)

地盘 dìpán 【名】sphere of influence

地皮 dìpí 【名】land for building; ground

地痞 dìpǐ 【名】local ruffian

地平线 dìpíngxiàn 【名】horizon

地壳 dìqiào 【名】the earth's crust

地勤 dìqín 【名】(of the air force) ground duty

地球 dìqiú 【名】the earth

地球仪 dìqiúyí 【名】world globe

地区 dìqū 【名】district; area; zone

地势 dìshì 【名】geographic features (of an area)

地毯 dìtǎn 【名】〔块 kuài〕carpet

地铁 dìtiě 【名】short for 地下铁道: 坐～ travel by subway

地头 dìtóu 【名】edge of a field

地头蛇 dìtóushé 【名】local tyrant; local bully

地图 dìtú 【名】〔张 zhāng〕map

地位 dìwèi 【名】social position; rank; status

地下 dìxià 【名】❶ underground; subterranean: ～岩层 subterranean strata ～城市 underground city ❷ underground; secret: ～工作 (do) underground work 转入～ go underground

地下室 dìxiàshì 【名】basement

地下水 dìxiàshuǐ 【名】subterranean water

地下铁道 dìxià tiědào subway; underground railway; metro

地下 dìxia 【名】on the ground: 茶杯掉在～了。The cup fell on the floor (or ground). ～很干净。The floor is very clean.

地线 dìxiàn 【名】(electr.) ground wire

地形 dìxíng 【名】terrain; topography

地狱 dìyù 【名】hell

地域 dìyù 【名】region; district; area; territory: 部队进入集结～。The troops have entered the assembly area.

地震 dìzhèn 【名】earthquake

地址 dìzhǐ 【名】address

地质 dìzhì 【名】geology

地质学 dìzhìxué 【名】geology

地租 dìzū 【名】land rent

弟 dì 【名】younger brother

弟弟 dìdi 【名】younger brother

弟媳 dìxí 【名】younger brother's wife

弟兄 dìxiong 【名】brothers

帝 dì 【名】◇ ❶ emperor ❷ short for 帝国主义

帝国 dìguó 【名】empire

帝国主义 dìguózhǔyì 【名】imperialism

帝王 dìwáng 【名】emperors and kings

帝王将相 dì wáng jiàng xiàng emperors and kings, generals and ministers

帝制 dìzhì 【名】imperial system

递(遞) dì 【动】❶ hand over; pass; give: ～了个眼色 wink at sb. 把钳子～给我。Hand me a pair of pliers, please. ❷ successively; in sequential order: ～补 fill vacancies in turn

递减 dìjiǎn 【动】decrease by degrees

递交 dìjiāo 【动】present; deliver

递进 dìjìn 【动】advancing or increasing in successive stages: 这三个并列的句子意思上是～的。These three clauses build up the meaning step by step.

递送 dìsòng 【动】send; deliver by messenger

递增 dìzēng 【动】increase progressively：每年～百分之十 increase 10 per cent a year.

第 dì 【头】prefix for ordinal numbers：～十页 page ten ～五个五年计划 the fifth Five-Year Plan

第二次世界大战 Dì'èr Cì Shìjiè Dàzhàn the Second World War

第二信号系统 dì'èr xìnhào xìtǒng second signal system（Pavlovian psychology）

第二职业 dì'èr zhíyè moonlighting；second job

第纳尔 dìnà'ěr 【名】dinar（currency）

第三产业 dìsān chǎnyè tertiary industry；the service sector

第三者 dìsānzhě 【名】a third party

第一把手 dìyī bǎ shǒu person who is in a position of primary responsibility；first in command

第一次世界大战 Dìyī Cì Shìjiè Dàzhàn the First World War

第一流 dìyī liú first-class；first-rate：～的文学作品 a literary work of the first rank 这个木刻展览的展品都是～的。All the items in the exhibition of wood-cuts are first-rate.

第一手材料 dìyī shǒu cáiliào first-hand material；original material

第一线 dìyī xiàn front line；forefront；at the forefront：生产～ the front lines of production 斗争～ the forefront of the struggle 教学～ at the front lines of teaching（i.e. in the classroom）

第一信号系统 dìyī xìnhào xìtǒng first signal system（Pavlovian psychology）

缔（締）dì

缔结 dìjié 【动】conclude（a treaty）

缔约 dì＝yuē sign a treaty

缔造 dìzào 【动】create；found

diān

掂 diān 【动】weigh in the hand：你～一～这包糖有多重？Pick up this bag of candy and see how heavy it is! 我～着不轻。When I weigh it in my hand, it feels heavy.

掂量 diānliang 【动】❶ weigh in the hand ❷ estimate；consider；weigh up：大家～一下这么办行不行？Let's see whether we can do it this way.

颠（顛）diān 【动】totter；fall；tumble

颠簸 diānbǒ 【动】bump；reel

颠倒 diāndǎo 【动】❶ turn upside down；invert；transpose：这两个字～过来意思就不同了。Transpose these two characters, and the meaning will be different. 把一了的历史再～过来。Set the record straight. ❷ be confused：神魂～ be in a confused state of mind due to infatuation（with sb. or sth.）

颠倒黑白 diāndǎo hēi bái call white black and black white；confuse right and wrong

颠倒是非 diāndǎo shìfēi confuse truth and falsehood

颠覆 diānfù 【动】subvert；overthrow

颠来倒去 diān lái dǎo qù repetitive；same thing in different words（derog.）

颠沛流离 diānpèi liúlí wandering about homeless；leading a vagrant life

颠扑不破 diān pū bù pò irrefutable；indisputable：～的真理 irrefutable truth

颠三倒四 diān sān dǎo sì（of speech, actions, etc.）incoherent；confused

diǎn

典 diǎn

典范 diǎnfàn 【名】model to be followed

典故 diǎngù 【名】fable from which a saying is derived

典礼 diǎnlǐ 【名】ceremony

典型 diǎnxíng 【名】❶ model；typical example；type：抓住先进～，推动全面工作。Using exemplary workers to drum up the over-all performance. ❷（in literature or art）a type；a typical character：他们塑造了一个农民英雄的～。They created a heroic image of a peasant rebel. 【形】typical：老张是个～的北方人。Lao Zhang is a typical northerner.

点（點） diǎn 【动】❶ make a dot：～个逗号 make a comma ❷ drip：～眼药 put eye-drops in one's eyes ❸ dibble；plant in holes：～花生 dibble peanuts；plant peanuts in holes ～豆子 plant beans in holes ❹ count；check the number（of sth.）：～人数 count the number of people ～一～货 take an inventory of goods ❺ point out；hint：经你这么一～，我就明白了。I understand, now that you have pointed it out. ❻ kindle；light：～灯 light a lamp ～炉子 light a stove 【名】❶（～儿）a drop of liquid：雨～ raindrops 水～ drops of water ❷（～儿）spot；dot；speck；blot：泥～ a speck of dirt 墨～ a spot of ink ❸（～儿）point；decimal point 二•五：two point five (2.5) ❹（geometry）point：两～成一直线。A line is formed by connecting two points. ❺ point；aspect：突破一～ make a breakthrough in one aspect (of a prob-

lem) ❻ an appointed time；a fixed time：到～了，快走吧！Time is up. Let's go. ❼（～儿）（of Chinese characters）dot 【量】❶（～儿）a little；a bit；some：一～小事 a mere trifle 吃～东西 have something to eat ❷ piece；item；point：两～意见 two opinions, ideas or suggestions 三～注意事项 three points to pay attention to ❸ o'clock：四～三刻 a quarter to five（o'clock）五～钟 five o'clock

点播 diǎnbō 【动】order a special item to be broadcasted

点菜 diǎn=cài order dishes

点滴 diǎndī 【形】(fig.) in very small drops

点火 diǎn=huǒ ❶ light a fire；kindle：～放炮 fire a gun ❷ (fig.) stir up trouble；cause mischief；arouse；incite

点名 diǎn=míng ❶ call the roll；roll-call ❷ name：～批评 criticise sb. by name 他～要你去。He named you as the person he wanted.

点破 diǎnpò 【动】with a few words expose sth. hidden

点燃 diǎnrán 【动】kindle

点头 diǎn=tóu give a nod

点心 diǎnxin 【名】cake；pastry

点缀 diǎnzhuì 【动】embellish；adorn；decorate：油绿的秧苗，把大地～得十分美丽。The earth, adorned with green seedlings, looks very beautiful. 【名】sth. merely for show：虽然客人都不大会喝酒,吃饭的时候总得有几瓶酒做～。Though nobody will drink much, there must be a few bottles of wine at the dinner simply for show.

点子 diǎnzi 【名】❶ a drop of liquid；spot：油～ grease spot ❷ idea；method：会出～ be good at coming up with ideas 他～很多。

He's full of ideas. ❸key point；key-link；这话说到～上了。This remark goes to the heart of the matter.

碘 diǎn 【名】iodine

碘酒 diǎnjiǔ 【名】tincture of iodine

diàn

电（電）diàn 【名】❶ electricity ❷ ◇ telegram；cable：急～ an urgent telegram 新华社～ a Xinhua News Agency dispatch 【动】get an electric shock：当心，别～着你。Be careful not to get a shock.

电报 diànbào 【名】〔份 fèn〕telegram；cable

电表 diànbiǎo 【名】meter for measuring electricity

电冰箱 diànbīngxiāng 【名】refrigerator

电波 diànbō 【名】electrical wave

电唱机 diànchàngjī 【名】record-player

电车 diànchē 【名】〔辆 liàng〕tram；trolley bus

电池 diànchí 【名】〔节 jié〕(electr.) battery

电传 diànchuán 【名】telex

电磁场 diàncíchǎng 【名】electric magnetic field

电磁感应 diàncí gǎnyìng electro-magnetic induction

电灯 diàndēng 【名】〔盏 zhǎn〕electric light

电动 diàndòng 【形】electric；power-operated

电动机 diàndòngjī 【名】〔台 tái〕electric motor

电镀 diàndù 【动】electroplate 【名】electroplating

电饭煲 diànfànbāo 【名】electric rice cooker

电饭锅 diànfànguō 【名】electric cooker

电工 diàngōng 【名】electrician

电工学 diàngōngxué 【名】electrical engineering

电焊 diànhàn 【动】weld using an electric arc welder 【名】electric arc welding

电荷 diànhè 【名】electric charge

电话 diànhuà 【名】telephone

电汇 diànhuì 【动】telegraphic transfer

电机 diànjī 【名】generator；motor

电极 diànjí 【名】electrode

电解 diànjiě 【动】electrolysis

电缆 diànlǎn 【名】cable

电离 diànlí 【名】ionization

电力 diànlì 【名】electric power

电量 diànliàng 【名】〔库仑 kùlún〕total electric charge

电疗 diànliáo 【动】electrotherapy

电铃 diànlíng 【名】electric bell

电流 diànliú 【名】electric current

电炉 diànlú 【名】electric furnace；electric fire；electric stove；hot plate

电路 diànlù 【名】electric circuit

电脑 diànnǎo 【名】electronic brain；electronic computer

电钮 diànniǔ 【名】switch；button

电气化 diànqìhuà 【动】electrify

电容 diànróng 【名】electric capacity

电扇 diànshàn 【名】electric fan

电视 diànshì 【名】television；T. V.

电视机 diànshìjī 【名】〔架 jià，台 tái〕TV set

电视剧 diànshìjù 【名】TV drama；TV play

电视塔 diànshìtǎ 【名】〔座 zuò〕television tower

电视台 diànshìtái 【名】television station

电台 diàntái 【名】radio station

电梯 diàntī 【名】elevator；lift

电文 diànwén 【名】content of a telegram

电线 diànxiàn 【名】wire；cable

电讯　diànxùn　【名】（telegraphic）dispatch

电压　diànyā　【名】〔伏特 fútè〕electric pressure；voltage

电唁　diànyàn　【动】send a message of condolence by telegram

电影　diànyǐng　【名】film；motion picture

电影放映机　diànyǐng fàngyìngjī　movie projector

电影摄影机　diànyǐng shèyǐngjī　cine-camera

电影院　diànyǐngyuàn　【名】cinema

电源　diànyuán　【名】（electr.）mains；power source；power supply

电子　diànzǐ　【名】electron

电子管　diànzǐguǎn　【名】electron tube

电子计算机　diànzǐ jìsuànjī　〔台 tái〕electronic computer

电阻　diànzǔ　【名】（electr.）resistance

电钻　diànzuàn　【名】electric drill

佃　diàn

佃户　diànhù　【名】tenant

佃农　diànnóng　【名】a peasant who rented land；tenant-farmer

佃租　diànzū　【名】rent

店　diàn　【名】shop；store

店铺　diànpù　【名】〔个 gè，家 jiā〕shop；store

店员　diànyuán　【名】shop-assistant

玷　diàn

玷辱　diànrǔ　【动】humiliate

玷污　diànwū　【动】sully

垫（墊）　diàn　【动】❶ put sth. under sth. else to raise it or make it even higher；把枕头～高一点儿 put sth. under a pillow to make it higher ❷ fill sth. up to make it thicker or level；level；把

这一段路～平 level this part of the road ❸ advance money to sb.，expecting to be repaid soon；你没带钱,我先给你～上。Let me put down the money as you don't have any with you. 【名】（～儿）pad；cushion；mat；草～ grass mat 椅～ cushion for a chair

垫付　diànfù　【动】pay for sb. and expect to be repaid later

垫子　diànzi　【名】cushion

惦　diàn　【动】remember；think of

惦记　diànjì　【动】remember；have（sb. or sth.）constantly on one's mind

惦念　diànniàn　【动】remember；have（sb.）constantly on one's mind；miss

淀（澱）　diàn

淀粉　diànfěn　【名】starch

奠　diàn　【动】❶ lay（a foundation）❷ make offerings（to the spirits of the dead）

奠定　diàndìng　【动】lay（a foundation）

奠基　diànjī　【动】lay a foundation

殿　diàn　【名】hall；palace

殿下　diànxià　【名】Your（His, Her）Highness

diāo

刁　diāo　【形】artful；sly

刁滑　diāohuá　【形】sly and deceitful

刁难　diāonàn　【动】make trouble or difficulties for sb.；成心～人 deliberately make things difficult for sb.

凋　diāo

凋零　diāolíng　【形】withered and desolate

凋落　diāoluò　【动】wither

凋谢　diāoxiè　【动】wither

碉　diāo

碉堡　diāobǎo　【名】fortification

雕　diāo　【名】◇ carving【动】carve

雕刻　diāokè　【动】carve；engrave【名】carving；engraving

雕漆　diāoqī　【名】carved lacquerware

雕塑　diāosù　【动】sculpt【名】sculpture

雕琢　diāozhuó　【动】chisel and carve

diào

吊　diào　【动】❶ hang；suspend：门前～着两盏红灯。There were two red lanterns hanging over the door. ❷ lift up or let down with a rope，etc.：把水泥～上去 lift up the bucket of cement

吊车　diàochē　【名】〔台 tái〕crane

吊儿郎当　diào'erlángdāng　【形】take a careless and casual attitude toward everything（one's appearance，work，etc.）

吊环　diàohuán　【名】❶（of gymnastics）rings ❷ rings（event in gymnastic competition）

吊唁　diàoyàn　【动】offer condolences to

钓（釣）　diào　【动】angle；fish with a rod and line

钓饵　diào'ěr　【名】bait；lure

钓钩　diàogōu　【名】fishhook；wiles

调（調）　diào　【动】❶ transfer；shift；move；dispatch：新～来一个干部。A new cadre has been transferred here. 他～到工厂工作去了。He was transferred to a factory. ❷ allot；allocate：～来一批钢材。A batch of rolled steel was allocated to us. ❸ exchange：～一～位子。Let's trade seats. 【名】❶（～儿）melody：这个歌～很好听。This song has a very pleasing melody. ❷（music）key signature；C ～ the key of C ❸（～儿）accent：他说话带点四川～。He speaks with a slight Sichuan accent. ❹ tone；intonation

另见 tiáo

调包　diào bāo = bāo same as 掉包 diàobāo

调兵遣将　diào bīng qiǎn jiàng deploy forces

调拨　diàobō　【动】allot and deliver

调查　diàochá　【动】investigate【名】investigation

调动　diàodòng　【动】❶ transfer；shift；move：～队伍 move troops ～工作 transfer sb. to another post ❷ bring into play；arouse；mobilize：～一切积极因素 bring all positive factors into play【名】transfer；change：一项人事～ a transfer of personnel

调度　diàodù　【动】（of trains，buses，etc.）dispatch【名】dispatcher

调号　diàohào　【名】tone mark（for a Chinese character）

调虎离山　diào hǔ lí shān lure the tiger out of the mountains；lure one's opponent away from his base

调换　diàohuàn　【动】exchange；change；swap：我们俩～一个值班时间吧！Would you mind changing shifts with me?

调集　diàojí　【动】concentrate；assemble

调配　diàopèi　【动】allot；distribute

调遣　diàoqiǎn　【动】send or dispatch（to different places）

调运　diàoyùn　【动】allocate and ship

调值 diàozhí【名】(phonetics) tone pitch

调子 diàozi【名】tune；tone；air；melody

掉 diào【动】❶ drop；fall；～眼泪 shed tears 苹果从树上～下来了。The apples are falling from the tree. ❷ lose；be missing：这段译文～了几个字。Several words are missing from the translation of this paragraph. ❸ turn；wag；把汽车～过头来。Turn the car around. ❹ fade；lose；～色 (colour) fade ～分量 lose weight ❺ *used as a complement after certain verbs* be done with sth.；...away：扔 ～ throw sth. away 把脸上的汗擦～ wipe the sweat from one's face 跑不 ～ be unable to get away

掉包 diào＝bāo stealthily substitute one thing for another

掉队 diào＝duì fall behind：长途行军几百里，没有一个人～。In a long march of several hundred *li*, no one dropped out. 跟上形势，不要～。Keep up with the developing situation and don't fall behind.

掉价 diào＝jià fall in price；fall into disfavour

掉头 diào＝tóu make a U-turn

掉以轻心 diào yǐ qīng xīn let down one's guard；adopt a casual attitude；treat sth. lightly

diē

爹 diē【名】father；dad

跌 diē【动】❶ fall down；stumble：～了一跤 trip and fall down ❷ fall；reduce：药价～了不少。The price of various medicines has dropped.

跌倒 diēdǎo【动】fall；tumble

跌价 diē＝jià fall in price

跌跤 diē＝jiāo ❶ trip and fall；stumble ❷ make a mistake, and so suffer a setback

跌落 diēluò【动】drop；fall

dié

喋 dié

喋喋不休 diédié bù xiū keep muttering

叠 dié【动】❶ pile；overlap：～假山 pile up rocks to make a decorative hill ～床架屋 pile one bed on top of another or build one house on top of another；needless duplication ❷ fold：～衣服 fold clothes 把信～ 起来装在信封里 fold the letter and put it into an envelope

碟 dié【名】(～儿) plate；dish

碟子 diézi【名】〔个 gè〕dish；saucer

蝶 dié

蝶泳 diéyǒng【名】(of swimming) butterfly stroke

dīng

丁 dīng【名】❶ (～儿) small cubes (of vegetables or meat) ❷ *used to represent "fourth" according to old Chinese tradition*

丁当 dīngdāng【象声】tinkle；jingle

丁香 dīngxiāng【名】❶lilac ❷clove

叮 dīng【动】❶ (mosquito, etc.) bite ❷ enjoin：临走我又～他一句，叫他千万别忘了。Before I left, I repeated what I had said and begged him not to forget it for the world. 你再去～～他，看他有什么意见。Please try to question

him closely as to whether he has any objections.

叮咛　dīngníng　【动】repeatedly enjoin

叮嘱　dīngzhǔ　【动】repeatedly enjoin

盯　dīng　【动】gaze；stare；keep a close watch on：我紧～着师傅的手，看他怎么操作。I watched the master-worker's hands very closely to see how he operated the machine. 也作"钉"。

钉（釘）　dīng　【名】nail；tack 【动】❶ follow closely and persistently；watch closely：大刘～住对方的前锋，使他没有投篮的机会。Da Liu watched the forward of the rival team so closely that the fellow could hardly get a chance to shoot. ❷ urge；press；remind：这事你～着点儿，让他抓紧办。Will you press him a little on the matter and ask him to do it quickly? ❸ 同"盯"dīng

另见 dìng

钉梢　dīng = shāo　shadow；trail；follow closely (e.g. a spy) 也作"盯梢"。

钉子　dīngzi　【名】〔根 gēn〕nail

dǐng

顶（頂）　dǐng　【名】top；peak；summit：头～ top of the head 山～ mountain top；hill-top 屋～ roof 【动】❶ carry on the head：朝鲜老大娘～着水罐请我们喝水。The Korean old woman carried a pitcher of water on her head and offered us a drink. ❷ prop up；support：拿杠子～上门 prop a pole against the door (to keep it closed) ❸ go against：他～

着雨出去了。Braving the rain, he went out. ❹ retort：他的话说得不对，我就～了他几句。What he said was wrong, so I made a sharp rejoinder. ❺ be equivalent to：他力气大，一个～俩。He is enormously strong, the equal of two men. ❻ take sb.'s place；replace；substitute for：今天我～他的班。I am taking his shift today. ❼ push from below；prop up：嫩芽顶土～起来了。The sprouts have pushed through the earth. 【量】for caps，mosquito-nets，etc.：一～帽子 a cap or hat 【副】〈口〉most；very；extremely：～好 best 我～喜欢打网球。I am extremely fond of playing tennis.

顶点　dǐngdiǎn　【名】❶ (maths.) vertex ❷ summit；top

顶端　dǐngduān　【名】top；apex

顶风　dǐng = fēng　against the wind：～骑车 cycle against the wind

顶峰　dǐngfēng　【名】peak；summit：攀登科学～ scale the heights of science 咱们不爬到～决不下来。We won't stop until we get to the top.

顶尖　dǐngjiān　【名】tip

顶替　dǐngtì　【动】take on someone's identity (by forging or assuming his name)

顶天立地　dǐng tiān lì dì　(fig.) of gigantic stature；upright and high-minded；heroic；indomitable：～的英雄汉 a hero of indomitable spirit

顶用　dǐngyòng　【形】be of use；efficient；serve the purpose very well：这种抽水机真～，一天就把这么一大片地都浇完了。How useful this kind of water pump is! In one day it has irrigated such a vast expanse of land! 我去不～，还是你亲自去一趟吧！My going won't be of any use. You had better go yourself.

顶住　dǐng // zhù　stand up to；hold out against；withstand：把门～ hold the door closed (by propping

something against it)：～歪风邪气 stand up against evil winds and bad tendencies

顶撞 dǐngzhuàng 【动】rebut with rude remarks

顶罪 dǐng = zuì　bear the blame for sb. else；make a scapegoat of

鼎 dǐng　【名】an ancient cooking vessel；tripod

鼎鼎大名 dǐngdǐng dà míng　of great repute；illustrious

鼎立 dǐnglì　【动】keep equilibrium among three rival powers

dìng

订（訂） dìng　【动】❶ conclude；draw up (a contract)：～条约 conclude a treaty　～计划 work out (or draw up) a plan ❷ subscribe；book (tickets，etc.)：～报纸 subscribe to a newspaper　～杂志 subscribe to a magazine ❸ bind (a book)；staple together：把这几本杂志～起来 bind these magazines

订单 dìngdān　【名】〔个 gè、张 zhāng、份 fèn〕order form；order for goods

订户 dìnghù　【名】subscriber (to a newspaper，etc.)

订婚 dìng = hūn　be engaged to marry

订货 dìng = huò　order goods

订金 dìngjīn　【名】deposit；earnest

订立 dìnglì　【动】conclude (a treaty，contract)

订阅 dìngyuè　【动】subscribe to (a newspaper，etc.)

订正 dìngzhèng　【动】correct；revise；amend

钉（釘） dìng　【动】nail (down)；drive a nail into：～两个钉子 drive a few nails 几块木板～了一个箱子 nail boards together to

make a box
另见 dīng

定 dìng　【动】❶ calm down：～一一神再说。Calm down，and then speak. ❷ fix；set；decide：拿～主意 make up one's mind 出发的时间已经～了。The time for departure is fixed. 【副】◇ sure；certainly；definitely：～能成功 bound to succeed

定案 dìng'àn　【名】final verdict on a case or the final draft (of a plan for a project)

定案 dìng = àn　pass the final verdict on a case

定额 dìng'é　【名】quota

定购 dìnggòu　【动】order (goods)

定规 dìngguī　【名】rules and regulations

定货 dìng = huò　同"订货" dìng = huò

定价 dìngjià　【名】fixed price

定居 dìngjū　【动】settle down

定局 dìngjú　【名】inevitable outcome；conclusion；foregone conclusion：这场足球赛，谁胜谁负已成～。The outcome of this football game is a foregone conclusion. 【动】make a final decision；settle finally：事情还没有～，先不要公布。The matter is not yet settled. It should not be made public.

定礼 dìnglǐ　【名】betrothal gifts (from the bridegroom to the bride's family)

定理 dìnglǐ　【名】〔条 tiáo〕theorem

定量 dìngliàng　【名】ration；allowance；quota

定量 dìng = liàng　(chem.) determine the amounts of elements or the percentage of components

定律 dìnglù　【名】〔条 tiáo〕law (of nature)

定论 dìnglùn　【名】conclusion；final verdict

定名 dìng = míng　choose a name for；be named

定期 dìng = qī ❶ fix the date ❷ at regular intervals

定时 dìngshí 【形】regular; fixed time

定时炸弹 dìngshí zhàdàn 〔颗 kē〕time-bomb

定位 dìngwèi 【动】orientate 【名】fixed position

定息 dìngxī 【名】fixed rate of interest on capital paid to the capitalists for a given period of time by the Chinese government after the introduction of joint state-private ownership

定向 dìngxiàng 【形】directional; oriented

定型 dìng = xíng become fixed and unchangeable (in nature, quality, etc.)

定义 dìngyì 【名】definition

定语 dìngyǔ 【名】(gram.) attribute

定员 dìngyuán 【名】a fixed number of people, e.g. the passenger capacity of a train, the limit of the number of personnel in an organization

定罪 dìng = zuì convict sb. (of a crime); declare sb. guilty

diū

丢 diū 【动】❶ lose; be missing; 我的钢笔不知～在哪儿了。I don't know where I've left my pen. ❷ throw away; cast away; toss away; 把菜叶～给小兔吃 toss down cabbage leaves to feed rabbits ❸ put (or lay) aside; cast aside; 这件事可以～开不管。This matter can be put aside.

丢掉 diūdiào 【动】throw away

丢盔卸甲 diū kuī xiè jiǎ throw away one's shield and armour; fly pellmell

丢脸 diū = liǎn lose face; be disgraced

丢人 diū = rén lose face; be disgraced

丢三落四 diū sān là sì always losing and forgetting things; forgetful; careless; scatter-brained; 他这个人马马虎虎, 总好 (hào) ～的。He is careless and scatter-brained, always losing and forgetting things.

丢失 diūshī 【动】lose

dōng

东(東) dōng 【名】east

东北 dōngběi 【名】❶ northeast ❷ northeast China; the Northeast

东边 dōngbiān 【名】the east side

东道国 dōngdàoguó 【名】host country

东道主 dōngdàozhǔ 【名】host or hostess

东方 dōngfāng 【名】❶ the east ❷ the East; Asia

东南 dōngnán 【名】southeast

东山再起 Dōngshān zài qǐ stage a comeback

东…西… dōng…xī… here… there…; 东张西望 look around; glance this way and that; look in all directions 东奔西跑 run to and fro; bustle about 东拼西凑 (of an organization, composition, etc.) knock together 东倒西歪 lie about in disorder 东拉西扯 ramble on; talk randomly 东一句西一句 speak incoherently 东一群西一伙 be in straggling groups

东西 dōngxi 【名】❶ thing; 他上街买～去了。He's out shopping. 这几天我眼睛不好, 看～有些模糊。There is something wrong with my eyes. I can't see things clearly. 病人吃～了没有? Has the patient eaten anything? ❷ (of a person or animal, implying liking or dislike) crea-

ture：你这糊涂～! What a muddle-headed creature you are! 松鼠这小～真可爱。What a lovely thing a little squirrel is!

冬 dōng 【名】winter

冬瓜 dōngguā 【名】〔个 gè〕winter melon

冬季 dōngjì 【名】winter season

冬眠 dōngmián 【名】hibernation 【动】hibernate

冬天 dōngtiān 【名】winter

冬装 dōngzhuāng 【名】winter clothes

dǒng

董 dǒng

董事 dǒngshì 【名】director；trustee

董事会 dǒngshìhuì 【名】board of directors（in an enterprise）

董事长 dǒngshìzhǎng 【名】chairman of the board of directors

懂 dǒng 【动】understand

懂得 dǒngde 【动】understand

懂事 dǒngshì 【形】sensible；(of a child) be perceptive and understanding beyond one's years

dòng

动（動） dòng 【动】❶ move：坐好别～。Sit still. Don't move! ❷ act；get moving：只要群众一起来，事情就好办。Once the masses are mobilized, matters will be readily solved. ❸ use：凡事都要～脑筋想一想。We should always use our heads and think things out. ❹ *used as a complement after a verb* be moved：螺丝拧不～了。The screw can't be turned. 这顶帐篷一个人搬得～。One person can carry

this tent.

动笔 dòng = bǐ start writing；set pen to paper

动宾结构 dòng bīn jiégòu verb-object construction

动兵 dòng = bīng send soldiers to fight；resort to arms

动补结构 dòng bǔ jiégòu verb-complement construction

动不动 dòngbudòng 【副】at every move；on every occasion；apt to（*indicates the displeasure of the speaker towards the situation described，usu. used with* 就）：她～就发脾气。She is apt to lose her temper. 这个孩子～就哭，太娇气了。This child is spoiled, and cries easily.

动产 dòngchǎn 【名】movable property

动词 dòngcí 【名】verb

动荡 dòngdàng 【动】be unstable

动工 dòng = gōng begin the construction

动画片 dònghuàpiàn 【名】〔部 bù〕cartoon (film)

动机 dòngjī 【名】motive；intention

动静 dòngjing 【名】❶ signs of activity；stir：院子里静悄悄的，一点儿～也没有。It was quiet in the courtyard. There were no signs of activity. ❷ movement；happenings：前沿的士兵密切注意着敌人的～。The soldiers at the front kept a close watch on the enemy's movements.

动力 dònglì 【名】motive force

动量 dòngliàng 【名】momentum

动乱 dòngluàn 【名】turmoil

动脉 dòngmài 【名】artery

动能 dòngnéng 【名】(phys.) kinetic energy

动怒 dòng = nù flare up；lose one's temper

动气 dòng = qì get angry；take offence

动人　dòngrén　【形】moving；touching：这个剧本情节十分～。The plot of this play is very moving.

动身　dòng = shēn　begin a journey；set out

动手　dòng = shǒu　❶ touch（with the hand）：请勿～! Please don't touch! ❷ start work；set to work：大家一齐～,不一会儿就把那片甘蔗收完了。Everybody set to work together, and the harvesting of the sugar-cane was soon finished. 图纸有了,我们马上就～吧! We have the blueprint. Let's get to work right away. ❸ raise a hand to strike；strike out at sb.

动态　dòngtài　【名】tendency；general trend of affairs

动弹　dòngtan　【动】move

动听　dòngtīng　【形】attractive；moving；pleasant to the ear：～的歌声 singing which is pleasant to the ear ～的词句 fine words

动武　dòng = wǔ　use force；start a fight

动物　dòngwù　【名】animal

动物学　dòngwùxué　【名】zoology

动物园　dòngwùyuán　【名】zoo

动向　dòngxiàng　【名】trend；tendency；direction：思想～ ideological tendency；the direction of one's thinking

动心　dòng = xīn　be attracted by；one's desire to have sth. is aroused：使他～的是那位姑娘的性格好。What attracted him was the girl's personality.

动摇　dòngyáo　【动】❶ waver；vacillate：走社会主义道路毫不～ never waver from the socialist road ❷ shake：环境再艰苦也～不了这些青年建设新山村的决心。However hard the conditions may be, they can't shake the young people's determination to transform the mountain village.

动议　dòngyì　【名】motion

动用　dòngyòng　【动】employ；draw on（resources, funds, etc.）：这是一批防汛物资,不能随便～。These are flood control materials. Don't use them without permission.

动员　dòngyuán　【动】mobilize；rally：开个～大会 hold a mobilization meeting ～起来讲究卫生,减少疾病。Get mobilized, pay attention to hygiene and reduce disease.

动作　dòngzuò　【名】action；movement

冻(凍)　dòng　【动】❶ freeze：河水～冰了。The river is frozen. 天寒地～。It is cold, and the ground is frozen. ❷ feel very cold；freeze；suffer frostbite：这几天没戴手套,手都～了。I haven't worn gloves these last few days, and my hands are frost-bitten. 寒流来了,真～得慌。The cold wave has arrived. It is freezing. 【名】(～儿) jelly：肉～ jellied meat 鱼～ jellied fish

冻疮　dòngchuāng　【名】chilblain

冻结　dòngjié　【动】❶（of liquid）freeze；congeal ❷ freeze；block：～资金 freeze funds 人员～ personnel freeze（preventing increase or transfer）

冻伤　dòng//shāng　frostbite

栋(棟)　dòng　【量】for buildings

栋梁　dòngliáng　【名】(fig.) pillars of the state

恫　dòng

恫吓　dònghè　【动】frighten；scare

洞　dòng　【名】cave；hole

洞察　dòngchá　【动】see through clearly；have penetrating insight

洞口　dòngkǒu　【名】entrance to a

cave

洞穴　dòngxué　【名】cave

dōu

都　dōu　【副】usu. precedes a predicate ❶ all；both refers to what goes before it：他们全家～住在农村。Their whole family lives in the countryside. 姐妹俩～八十多岁了。Both of the sisters are over eighty. 一连几个星期日天气～不好。The weather has been bad several Sundays in a row. 老师布置的作业你～做完了吗？Have you finished all the homework assigned by the teacher? ❷ all refers to all the causes or reasons，usu. in a sentence without a subject：～是他把开会的时间记错了，害得我们白跑一趟。It's all because he got the time of the meeting wrong that we made a useless trip. 你看，要带的东西忘记拿了，～怨你老催我。See, I've forgotten what I wanted to take along. It's all because you hurried me. （都 must be stressed in ❶ and ❷）❸already：柳梢～绿了，可见春天已经来了。It must be spring, the tips of the willow branches have turned green. ～八点了，你怎么还不走？It's already eight o'clock. Why are you still here? 时间真快，这孩子～这么大了。How time flies! He is such a big child now! 火车～要开了，赶快上车吧！The train is about to leave. Let's get on. ❹ used as an emphatic expression serving to indicate that what goes before it is an extreme or hypothetical instance of sth.：学过三年英语的，翻译这本小说～很困难。Three years of English is hardly enough to translate this novel. 普通数学他～没学过，怎么能学高等数学呢？He hasn't even

learned basic mathematics. How can he learn advanced mathematics? 她待我比亲姐姐～好。She treats me even better than a sister would. ❺ used in conjunction with an interrogative pron. to indicate that there is no exception or that the case is extreme：我们这儿谁～会骑自行车。Everybody here can ride a bicycle. 我怎么想～想不起来了。No matter how hard I tried, I couldn't remember. 他不舒服了，什么～不想吃。He is ill and doesn't want to eat anything. ❻ used in a question with an interrogative pron. to indicate that the persons or things in the expected answer are presumable in the plural number. It can be used before the subject as well as before the predicate of a sentence. 都 must not be used in the answer：三个星期的假期你～干什么了？What have you done in your three-week holiday? 老张一个星期里～哪几个晚上在家？On which evenings of the week is Lao Zhang at home? ～（有）谁参加了昨天的招待会？Who went to the reception yesterday? （都 in ❸、❹、❺、❻ must be pronounced in the neutral tone）

另见 dū

兜　dōu　【名】(～儿) pocket；bag：布～ cloth bag 这种上衣有两个～。This style of jacket has two pockets. 【动】❶ wrap up (in a piece of cloth or the like)：手绢儿里～着几个梨。Here are a few pears, wrapped up in this handkerchief. ❷ go round；circle：～抄敌军 encircle the enemy 说话要直截了当，别～圈子。When speaking, come straight to the point. Don't beat about the bush. ❸ canvass；solicit：～主顾 try to win customers ❹〈口〉

take responsibility for sth.；take upon oneself：你们别管，有什么事我～着。If anything goes wrong, I'll take the responsibility. It has nothing to do with you.

兜揽　dōulǎn　【动】canvass；solicit：～生意 solicit business

兜售　dōushòu　【动】try to sell；peddle；hawk

兜子　dōuzi　【名】pocket；bag

dǒu

斗　dǒu　【名】peck【量】*measurement of capacity*（10 litres）
另见 dòu

斗笠　dǒulì　【名】〔顶 dǐng〕hat with a wide brim made of bamboo leaves or strips of bamboo

斗篷　dǒupeng　【名】〔件 jiàn〕cloak；cape

抖　dǒu　【动】❶ shake：把衣服上的土～掉 shake the dust off one's clothes ❷ tremble；shiver；quiver：浑身直～ tremble all over

抖动　dǒudòng　【动】tremble；shake

抖擞　dǒusǒu　【动】stir up；rouse；enliven：精神～ full of energy；in high spirits

陡　dǒu　【形】steep；precipitous：悬崖～壁 precipice；cliff 山路很～。The mountain road is very steep.【副】◇ suddenly；abruptly：天气～变。The weather changed suddenly.

陡坡　dǒupō　【名】steep slope

陡峭　dǒuqiào　【形】steep；abrupt（slope）

dòu

斗（鬥）　dòu　【动】❶ struggle against；fight ❷（of cock-fighting, etc.）hold a fight：～蛐蛐儿 hold a cricket-fight ❸ fight；contest：～智 battle of wits 你～不过他。You're not his match.
另见 dǒu

斗争　dòuzhēng　【动】❶ struggle against ❷ make great efforts；fight【名】struggle

斗争性　dòuzhēngxìng　【名】fighting spirit

斗志　dòuzhì　【名】fighting will

斗志昂扬　dòuzhì ángyáng　with a strong fighting will

豆　dòu　【名】〔粒 lì、颗 kē〕bean

豆腐　dòufu　【名】〔块 kuài〕bean-curd

豆浆　dòujiāng　【名】bean-curd milk

豆角儿　dòujiǎor　【名】bean or pea pod

豆子　dòuzi　【名】〔粒 lì、颗 kē〕bean

逗　dòu　【动】❶ attract；charm：这孩子很～人喜欢。This is a very charming child. ❷ tease：姐姐拿着玩具～小明玩儿。Her elder sister is holding a toy out of reach and teasing Xiao Ming.【形】funny：这个笑话～极了。This joke is very funny.

逗号　dòuhào　【名】comma

逗留　dòuliú　【动】tarry；stop；stay

dū

都　dū
另见 dōu

都城　dūchéng　【名】capital

都会　dūhuì　【名】metropolis

都市　dūshì　【名】同"都会"

督　dū

督促　dūcù　【动】supervise and urge

dú

毒 dú 【名】poison：蛇～ snake venom 这种植物有～。This plant is poisonous.【动】poison：老鼠被～死了。The rat was poisoned.【形】poisonous；vicious；malevolent；malicious：心～手辣 vicious heart and sinister tactics 伏天的太阳真～。The sun is at its fiercest during the dog-days.

毒草 dúcǎo 【名】❶ poisonous weeds ❷ (fig.) harmful speech or piece of writing

毒贩 dúfàn 【名】dealer of drugs

毒害 dúhài 【动】injure (ideologically)；poison (a person's thinking)

毒化 dúhuà 【动】poison；infect

毒计 dújì 【名】venomous scheme

毒辣 dúlà 【形】vicious；murderous

毒瘤 dúliú 【名】cancer；malignant tumour

毒品 dúpǐn 【名】narcotic drug

毒气 dúqì 【名】poisonous gas

毒气弹 dúqìdàn 【名】〔发 fā、枚 méi〕gas shell；gas bomb

毒蛇 dúshé 【名】〔条 tiáo〕poisonous snake

毒手 dúshǒu 【名】murderous means

毒素 dúsù 【名】poisonous element；poison

毒刑 dúxíng 【名】torture

毒性 dúxìng 【名】toxicity

毒药 dúyào 【名】poison；poisonous drug

独（獨） dú 【形】❶ single；alone：～来～往 come and go alone；keep oneself to oneself 无～有偶。Though it is rare, it comes in pairs. ❷ only；solely

独霸 dúbà 【动】dominate exclusively；monopolize

独白 dúbái 【名】monologue；soliloquy

独裁 dúcái 【动】exercise dictatorship 【名】dictatorship

独裁者 dúcáizhě 【名】dictator

独唱 dúchàng 【名】solo 【动】sing a solo

独出心裁 dú chū xīncái 见"别出心裁" bié chū xīncái

独词句 dúcíjù 【名】a one-word sentence

独当一面 dú dāng yī miàn be on one's own in dealing with a job

独断独行 dú duàn dú xíng go one's own way；decide and act arbitrarily (derog.) 也作"独断专行"。

独家 dújiā 【名】by oneself；exclusive：～新闻 an exclusive news report ～采访 scoop ～经营 engage in a line of business without competition

独立 dúlì 【动】❶ stand alone：一棵青松～山巅。A pine-tree stands alone on the mountain peak. ❷ (of a country) be independent：宣布～ declare independence ～国家 an independent country ❸ independent；on one's own (often used as an adverbial adjunct)：～思考 think independently；think things out for oneself ～工作的能力 the ability to work on one's own

独立王国 dúlì wángguó independent kingdom；a district or institution that assumes illegal independence from the central government

独立性 dúlìxìng 【名】independence；independent spirit

独立自主 dúlì zìzhǔ act independently and keep the initiative in one's own hands：新中国一贯奉行～、自力更生的方针。New China has consistently adhered to the policy of being independent, and relying on her own efforts.

独木桥 dúmùqiáo 【名】bridge made of a single log

独幕剧　dúmùjù　【名】one-act play

独生子　dúshēngzǐ　【名】only son

独生子女　dúshēng zǐnǚ　only child

独树一帜　dú shù yī zhì　fly one's own colours；take a course or line of one's own：针刺麻醉在世界医学上真可谓～的创举。Acupuncture anaesthesia is a new contribution to the world's practice of medical science. 也作"别树一帜"。

独特　dútè　【形】special；original；unique：有 ～ 见解 have original views 苏州园林具有 ～ 的风格。Landscape-gardening in Suzhou has a unique style.

独一无二　dú yī wú èr　unique；unparalleled；unmatched：中国的熊猫在世界上是 ～ 的。The panda is an animal found uniquely in China.

独资　dúzī　【名】exclusively with one's own investment

独自　dúzì　【副】alone；by oneself：～散步 take a walk alone ～沉思 be by oneself and think deeply

独奏　dúzòu　【名】solo performance on any musical instrument 【动】play a solo

读（讀）　dú　【动】❶ read；read aloud：我～一句,请你们跟着一句。I'm going to read this aloud sentence by sentence. Please read it after me. ❷ read（book、article、etc.）：这篇文章你～过没有? Have you read this article? 这本书可以一～。This book is worth reading. ❸ attend school：他初中已经～完了,该上高中了。He has completed junior high school, and should move on to senior high.

读本　dúběn　【名】reader；school textbook

读书　dú = shū　❶ read a book ❷ study ❸ attend school

读物　dúwù　【名】reading material

读者　dúzhě　【名】reader

读者来信　dúzhě láixìn　reader's letters

dǔ

堵　dǔ　【动】❶ block up；stop up；plug up：两辆卡车把路～上了。These two trucks are blocking the road. ❷ feel suffocated；be frustrated：他满肚子委屈,心里～得慌。He has a deep sense of having been unjustly treated, and feels terribly depressed. 【量】for walls：一～墙 a wall

堵塞　dǔsè　【动】block；jam；stop；choke

赌（賭）　dǔ　【动】gamble；bet

赌博　dǔbó　【名】gambling 【动】gamble

赌气　dǔ = qì　（behave）obstinately（because one's wishes have been frustrated）；cut one's nose to spite one's face

赌徒　dǔtú　【名】gambler

赌咒　dǔ = zhòu　swear

赌注　dǔzhù　【名】stake（in gambling）

dù

杜　dù

杜鹃　dùjuān　【名】❶ cuckoo ❷ azalea

杜绝　dùjué　【动】completely eradicate；put an end to

杜撰　dùzhuàn　【动】fabricate（a story）

肚　dù　【名】abdomen；belly

肚子　dùzi　【名】abdomen；belly

度　dù　【动】（of time）spend；pass：欢～佳节 joyously celebrate a

festival ～假 spend one's holidays 【名】 limit；extent；degree：清晰～ visibility 发言以十五分钟为～。When making your speech, keep to a 15-minute time limit. 【量】❶ time；occasion：这个话剧曾两～在北京公演。This play has already been performed publicly twice in Beijing. 一年一～的中秋节又要来到了。This year's annual Moon Festival is approaching. ❷ degree *unit of measure for angles*，*temperature*，*etc.*：北纬三十八～ latitude 38°N. 摄氏零下五～ -5°C. ❸ *unit of measure for electricity*：一～电 one kilowatthour

度过 dùguò 【动】 spend；pass：～暑假 spend one's summer holidays 我们愉快地～了春节。We celebrated Spring Festival with great gaiety.

度假 dù=jià go on a holiday；vacation

度量 dùliàng 【名】 tolerance：～大 tolerant；broad-minded ～小 petty；narrow-minded

度量衡 dùliànghéng 【名】 measurements of length, capacity and weight

度数 dùshù 【名】 number of degrees

渡 dù 【动】 ferry

渡船 dùchuán 【名】 ferry boat

渡口 dùkǒu 【名】 ferry landing

镀（鍍） dù 【动】 plate

镀金 dù=jīn ❶ gild ❷ study or do sth. just to acquire surface polish

duān

端 duān 【动】 carry or hold sth. level with one or both hands underneath it：～饭 hold a bowl of rice 把锅～起来 lift or carry a pot (using both hands) 【名】 end；ex-

tremity：竹竿的两～ the two ends of a bamboo pole

端午节 Duānwǔjié 【名】 Dragon Boat Festival (the 5th day of the 5th lunar month)

端详 duānxiáng 【动】 scrutinize；examine

端正 duānzhèng 【形】 ❶ upright；regular：五官～ have regular features 小学生在课堂上端端正正地坐着。The pupils are sitting up straight in their seats. ❷ proper；correct：品行～ of honourable character and correct behaviour；respectable 【动】 correct；rectify；straighten：～态度 set right one's attitude towards sth.

端庄 duānzhuāng 【形】 (of appearance, behaviour) dignified and respectable

duǎn

短 duǎn 【形】 short；brief：～袖 short sleeves 时间太～。The time is too short. 【动】 lack；run short of：快开会了，还～老张一个人。It's time for the meeting. Lao Zhang is the only one missing.

短兵相接 duǎn bīng xiāng jiē fight hand-to-hand；fight at close quarters：～的搏斗 hand-to-hand combat ～的斗争 struggle at close quarters ～的辩论 argue face-to-face

短波 duǎnbō 【名】 short wave

短处 duǎnchu 【名】 shortcoming；weak point；defect

短促 duǎncù 【形】 pressed (for time)；of short duration

短工 duǎngōng 【名】 farm labourer hired by the day

短路 duǎnlù 【动】 short circuit

短命 duǎnmìng 【形】 short-lived

短跑 duǎnpǎo 【名】 sprint；dash

短篇小说 duǎnpiān xiǎoshuō short

story

短评 duǎnpíng 【名】short review

短期 duǎnqī 【名】short-term; short period

短缺 duǎnquē 【动】be short of; shortage

短少 duǎnshǎo 【动】be short of; lack; be deficient in

短途 duǎntú 【名】short distance

短小精悍 duǎnxiǎo jīnghàn ❶（of persons）short but well-built; small but capable ❷（of articles, speech, etc.）short and pithy; short but to the point

短语 duǎnyǔ 【名】phrase

短暂 duǎnzàn 【形】momentary

duàn

段 duàn 【量】❶ section of sth.; part of sth.：两～木头 two logs 这一～公路正在翻修。This section of the road is under repair. ❷ duration; distance：一～时间 a period of time 从学校到公园还有一一～路呢！It's some distance from the school to the park. ❸ part of sth.：一～话 a passage from a speech 这篇文章共九～。This article contains a total of nine paragraphs.

段落 duànluò 【名】paragraph; section

断（斷）duàn 【动】❶ break; snap：绳子～了。The rope is broken. ❷ break off; cut off; discontinue; stop：～了联系 lose contact with ～电 cut off electricity ❸ decide; judge：～案 settle a lawsuit 【副】〈书〉（used only before a negative word）absolutely; decidedly：～无此理 absolutely untenable; doesn't hold water at all ～～不信 absolutely unbelievable; to be discredited outright

断层 duàncéng 【名】fault

断定 duàndìng 【动】form a judgement; conclude

断断续续 duànduànxùxù 【形】intermittent; off-and-on：这篇论文他～地写了半年。He has been writing this thesis off-and-on for half a year.

断绝 duànjué 【动】❶ break off; cut off; sever：～关系 break off（or sever）relations ～来往 break off communication（between two persons）～交通 shut down transportation; the traffic was obstructed ❷ stop; cut off（supplies）：粮食～ run out of grain

断裂 duànliè 【动】crack; split; snap

断气 duàn = qì breathe one's last

断然 duànrán 【形】flatly; categorically; absolutely：采取～措施 take drastic measures ～拒绝 flatly refuse; flatly reject（proposals, demands, requests, etc.）

断送 duànsòng 【动】forfeit; lose; ruin：～了性命 forfeit one's life ～了前途 forfeit one's future; forfeit the future of（a nation, country, etc.）

断言 duànyán 【动】say with certainty

断章取义 duàn zhāng qǔ yì quote out of context; garble（a quotation, statement, etc.）：对这篇报告要全面理解，不能～。One must not quote this speech out of context.

断肢再植 duàn zhī zài zhí rejoin a severed limb

锻（鍛）duàn 【动】◇ forge

锻工 duàngōng 【名】❶ forging（of metals）❷ forger

锻件 duànjiàn 【名】forging

锻炼 duànliàn 【动】❶ train physically ❷（of persons）temper; steel

锻压 duànyā 【动】forge and stamp

锻造 duànzào 【动】forge

duī

堆 duī【动】pile up；heap up；stack；粮食～成山。The grain is heaped up as high as a mountain.【名】heap；pile；stack；土～ a mound of earth 草～ a hay-stack 成～成～的大白菜 heap upon heap of cabbages【量】pile；heap；一～煤 a heap of coal

堆积 duījī【动】pile up；accumulate

堆砌 duīqì【动】(of language) load with fancy phrases

duì

队（隊） duì【名】❶ group；team：篮球～ a basketball team ❷ a row of people；line：排成一列横～ line up side by side；line up shoulder to shoulder 站好～ stand in an even line；form an even line【量】team；column；line：一～民兵 a file of militiamen

队伍 duìwu【名】troops；rank；contingent

队形 duìxíng【名】(mil.) formation

队员 duìyuán【名】member of a team

队长 duìzhǎng【名】group leader；team leader

对（對） duì【动】❶ treat：你不能这样～他。You can't treat him like this. ❷ compare (to see if two things are the same)：～号入座 find one's seat according to the number on the ticket 听完报告，我跟他～了～笔记。After the report, I compared my notes with his. ❸ mix (usu. liquids)：茶太浓了，～点儿开水。The tea is too strong. Pour in some hot water, please. ❹ adjust：

～～表 adjust one's watch 照相要～好距离。One must adjust the camera for distance before taking a photo. ❺ face：我们学校的大门～着广场。The gate of our school faces a square. 把枪口～准敌人。Aim your gun at the enemy.【形】correct；right：他的意见很～。His opinion is quite correct. 你这话说得不～。That remark of yours is not correct.【量】(～儿) pair：一～枕头 a pair of pillows 一～鸽子 a pair of pigeons【介】❶ forms a P-O construction used as an adverbial adjunct ① indicates movement or action towards a person or place or one's attitude towards sb.：他～我笑了笑。He smiled at me. 老张～待人非常诚恳。Lao Zhang is very sincere towards other people. ② indicates the object of some action：这孩子～连环画有很浓厚的兴趣。This child is very much interested in picture-story books. 大家～他的发言有各种不同的反映。The reaction to his talk was varied. ③ indicates the person or thing which is the object of a certain effect：他的经验～我们很有帮助。His experience is very helpful to us. 这是～神经衰弱比较有效的药。This medicine has proved efficacious for neurasthenia. ❷ forms a P-O construction used as a modifier：他～国内外形势的分析很透彻。His analysis of the national and international political situation was very thorough. 感谢你们～我的关心。Thank you all very much for your kindness to me.

对比 duìbǐ【动】compare；contrast：两相～，悬殊甚大。Seen side by side, the contrast between the two is striking.【名】contrast：今昔～ contrast the new with the old 形成鲜明的～ form a striking contrast

对比度 duìbǐdù 【名】contrast

对比色 duìbǐsè 【名】contrast colours

对不起 duì bu qǐ ❶ (used as an apology) I'm sorry; excuse me: ~、耽误你半天时间。Sorry to have taken up so much of your time. 把你的新书弄脏了, 真~。I'm very sorry to have gotten your new book dirty. ❷ let sb. down; be unworthy of; fail to live up to: 如果不好好学习, 就~父母对我的培养。If I don't study hard, I will fail to live up to the education given me by my parents.

对策 duìcè 【名】counter-measure

对称 duìchèn 【形】symmetrical

对答 duìdá 【动】answer; reply

对答如流 duìdá rú liú answer fluently; respond with ready answers

对待 duìdài 【动】treat; deal; approach; handle: 正确~失足青年。Treat properly young people who've made a slip. 他以满腔热情~穷亲戚。He treats his poor relatives with great warmth and considerateness.

对得起 duì de qǐ live up to; be worthy of

对等 duìděng 【形】of the same rank, quality, etc.; on an equal footing; equal to: ~的交换条件 make an exchange on an equal footing

对方 duìfāng 【名】opposite side; the other party

对付 duìfu 【动】❶ deal with; tackle; cope with: 这匹烈马很不好~。This high-spirited horse is hard to control. 这个复杂的局面, 你~不了。You can't handle such a complex situation. ❷ make do; get by: 他学了半年汉语, 现在能~着看《人民日报》了。He has studied Chinese for half a year; now he can just manage to read the *People's Daily*. 我

的旧工作服补一补, 还能~着穿。I can still make do with my old overalls, if I have them mended.

对话 duìhuà 【动】engage in a dialogue 【名】dialogue

对号 duì = hào check the number

对号入座 duì hào rù zuò sit in the right seat as numbered

对讲机 duìjiǎngjī 【名】〔个 gè, 副 fù〕walkie-talkie two-way radio

对角 duìjiǎo 【名】(maths.) opposite angles

对角线 duìjiǎoxiàn 【名】〔条 tiáo〕(maths.) diagonal line

对抗 duìkàng 【动】oppose; resist; antagonise

对抗性 duìkàngxìng 【名】antagonism

对口 duìkǒu 【形】speak or sing alternately; fit in nicely with

对口相声 duìkǒu xiàngsheng 【名】comic dialogue; cross talk

对立 duìlì 【动】oppose; counterpose; be antagonistic to each other: 情绪~ antagonistic feelings 不要把这两种学术观点人为地~起来。Don't deliberately set the two differing academic points of view against each other.

对立面 duìlìmiàn 【名】opposite sides

对联 duìlián 【名】〔副 fù〕couplet

对流 duìliú 【动】convection

对门 duìmén 【名】the house opposite 【动】(of two houses) face each other

对面 duìmiàn 【名】❶ opposite; across the way: 我家的~就是汽车站。Opposite my house is a bus stop. 图书馆在教学大楼~。The library is opposite the classroom building. ❷ directly (i. e. from right in front of): 一辆卡车从~开过来。A truck is heading straight for us. ~走过来一个人。Someone is coming right towards us. 【副】face to face: 他们俩~坐着。The

two of them were sitting face to face.

对牛弹琴 duì niú tán qín play the lute to a cow; cast pearls before swine; (*fig.*) appeal to an unappreciative audience

对手 duìshǒu 【名】❶ opponent ❷ match

对台戏 duìtáixì 【名】rival performance; rival show

对头 duìtóu 【形】❶ correct; right; proper; 想法～ correct ideas 方法不～。 The method is incorrect. ❷ normal; right; 这孩子脸色不～, 恐怕是病了。This child doesn't look right. Perhaps he's ill. ❸ get on well with sb.; be on good terms with sb. (*usu. in the negative*); 他们两人脾气不～。Those two are temperamentally incompatible.

对头 duìtou 【名】adversary; enemy

对外贸易 duì wài màoyì foreign trade

对虾 duìxiā 【名】prawn

对象 duìxiàng 【名】❶ target; object; 研究的～ object of study ❷ boy-friend or girl-friend; fiancé or fiancée

对于 duìyú 【介】同 "对" 【介】❶ ②, ③; ❷

对照 duìzhào 【动】contrast with; compare with

对折 duìzhé 【动】reduce to half the price; give a 50% discount

对证 duìzhèng 【动】check; verify

对症下药 duì zhèng xià yào suit the medicine to the disease; (*fig.*) suit one's methods to the situation; 对待少年罪犯, 必须～。In dealing with juvenile delinquints, one must suit one's methods to the situation.

对质 duìzhì 【动】confrontation (in court)

对峙 duìzhì 【动】stand facing each other; be at a stalemate

对子 duìzi 【名】antithetical couplet; a pair of antithetical phrases; a pair (of persons)

兑 duì 【动】cash

兑付 duìfù 【动】cash

兑换 duìhuàn 【动】exchange

兑现 duìxiàn 【动】❶ get cash for ❷ realize

dūn

吨(噸) dūn 【量】*measure of weight* ton

吨公里 dūngōnglǐ 【量】ton kilometer

吨位 dūnwèi 【名】tonnage

敦 dūn

敦促 dūncù 【动】urge

敦厚 dūnhòu 【形】honest and simple

敦实 dūnshi 【形】solid

蹲 dūn 【动】❶ squat on one's heels ❷ sit idle and do nothing; 大家都很忙, 我在家里怎么能～得住呢? How can I stay at home and do nothing when everyone else is so busy?

蹲点 dūn = diǎn go to a particular place at the grass-roots level to help improve the work and sum up experience; 县长正在一个小村子～。The county head is currently working in a small village to gain grassroots experience.

dùn

囤 dùn 【名】grain receptacle; bin

另见 tún

炖 dùn 【动】stew

盾 dùn 【名】shield

盾牌 dùnpái 【名】shield

钝（鈍） dùn 【形】blunt

钝角 dùnjiǎo 【名】(maths.) obtuse angle

顿（頓） dùn 【动】❶ pause ❷ pause of the writing brush to reinforce the beginning or end of a stroke in Chinese calligraphy 【量】 *for meal，beating，scolding，etc.*： 一～饭 a meal 我批评了他一～。I gave him a piece of my mind.

顿号 dùnhào 【名】 punctuation mark ("、") used between parallel words or short phrases

顿开茅塞 dùn kāi máo sè be suddenly enlightened

顿时 dùnshí 【副】(*usu. in written language*) immediately；suddenly； at once：好消息～传遍了全村。The good news spread through the village. 会场上～沸腾起来了。The meeting hall was in an uproar.

遁 dùn

遁词 dùncí 【名】subterfuge

duō

多 duō 【形】❶ numerous；many； much：人～力量大。More people means more energy. 近来雨下得不 ～。It hasn't rained much recently. ～种树很有好处。Planting more trees is very beneficial. *when used as an attrib. in the absence of any other adverbial adjunct，it must take* 很：山里有很～ 铁矿石。There is plenty of iron ore in the mountain. ❷ *used as*

the complement of an adj. or a phrase to indicate a large difference：这样说比那样说清楚～了。 Putting it this way is much clearer than putting it the other way. 这样 说比那样说清楚得～。It is much clearer putting it this way than the other way. 小李现在能吃苦～了。 Xiao Li can endure hardship much better than before. ❸ *used as the resultative complement of a verb to indicate that sth. is frequent or excessive*（了 *is necessary at the end of the sentence*）：院子里树种～了， 屋子很暗。There are too many trees in the courtyard, and the rooms are rather dark. 这种活儿干 ～了，自然就熟练了。If you do this kind of work more often，you'll naturally become skillful at it. ❹ *used as an adverbial adjunct in conjunction with a numeral plus measure word to show comparison*： 采用良种以后，每亩小麦～产了五十 斤。After an improved variety of seed was adopted，the average output of wheat per *mu* was increased by 50 catties. 今天去的人比 昨天多，要～开一辆车。There are more people going today than yesterday and we need one more bus. 【动】*indicates more than there was originally or more than is needed*： ～一个人就～一分力量。If we have one more person, we have that much more strength. 这个字写错 了，～了一笔。You've written this character wrong. There is one stroke too many. 【数】*when used after a numeral indicates approximate number and means " more than"*：一百～块钱 over a hundred *yuan* 二十～间屋子 more than twenty rooms 一万～人 over ten thousand people Note：*when the number represented by* 多 *is less*

than one，多 *is placed after the measure word or noun which doesn't take a measure word*：两年～ more than two years 三个～月 more than 3 months 五米～长 over 5 metres long 【副】❶ *indicates an inquiry about degree*：这座山有～高? How high is this mountain? 你女儿～大了? How old is your daughter? ❷ 没多 *when used before certain adjectives means " not very"*：这个箱子没～重。This trunk isn't very heavy. 小陈参加工作没～久，对业务已经很熟悉了。It didn't take Xiao Chen very long to master the ins and outs of the business. ❸ 同"多半"❶ *for the most part（usu. in written language）*：那片树林里～是杨树。Most of the trees in that forest are poplars. 近来夜间～有雨。It has rained mostly at night recently.

多半 duōbàn 【副】❶ *the greater part；most；mostly；more often than not*：同学们～都游泳去了，只有少数在操场练太极拳。Most of the students went swimming. Only a few were doing t'ai chi ch'uan on the sports-ground. ❷ *probably；most likely*：你看，这所房子～就是咱们要找的那所。Look，this is probably the house we are looking for.

多边 duōbiān 【名】multilateral：～会谈 multilateral talks ～贸易 multilateral trade

多边形 duōbiānxíng 【名】polygon

多才多艺 duō cái duō yì versatile；gifted in many ways

多此一举 duō cǐ yī jǔ do sth. which is unnecessary or superfluous

多的是 duōdeshì 【形】abundant；a lot of；a great deal（*used only as a predicate*）：我们家乡花生～。My home-town is in an area where peanuts grow abundantly.

多多益善 duō duō yì shàn the more，the better

多发病 duōfābìng 【名】disease with a high incidence

多方 duōfāng 【副】in many ways；with various devices

多亏 duōkuī 【动】*indicates that owing to someone's help or some favourable condition，a misfortune is avoided or some advantage is gained*：我们在深山中没有迷路，～了这位老大爷。We didn't get lost in the mountains，thanks to the directions of this old man. 【副】luckily，同"幸亏"xìngkuī：～消防队来得快，才避免了一场火灾。Fortunately，the fire brigade arrived in time，so a serious fire was prevented.

多么 duōme 【副】*indicates a high degree* ❶ *used in an exclamatory sentence*：这位外国朋友汉语说得～流利啊! How fluently this foreigner speaks Chinese! 当年修这条水渠是～不容易! How difficult it was to build the tunnel then! ❷ *used in a compound sentence in conjunction with* 不管 *or* 不论：不管天气～冷，他总是坚持骑自行车上班。No matter how cold it was，he always went to work by bike.

多媒体 duōméitǐ 【名】multimedia

多面手 duōmiànshǒu 【名】a person who is skilled in many areas；a versatile person

多少 duōshǎo 【副】more or less：你们不要笑，他说得～有点儿道理。Don't laugh. There is something in what he says. 把你们的菜子～匀给我们几斤。Please spare us a few *jin* of your vegetable seeds. Note：*sometimes* 多少 *can be reduplicated as* 多多少少

多少 duōshao 【数】❶ *used in asking questions about quantity，with the measure word optional*：你们学校有～（个）学生? How many students are there in your school?

他走了～天了? How many days has he been away? ❷ *when* 多少 *is used twice it indicates that the quantity is the same each time*：你们能来～人就来～吧! Send as many people as possible! 纸需要～领～. Go and fetch as much paper as you need. ❸ *indicates a large quantity* ① *used in an exclamatory sentence*：有～人来参加交易会啊! What a lot of people attended the trade fair! 取得今天的成就他花了～精力啊! What a lot of energy he had spent to be where he is today! ② *used in a negative sentence to indicate a small quantity*：夜已经很深了，街上没有～人了。It was very late at night, and there weren't many people in the streets. 用不了～时间，大坝就可以合龙了。It won't be long before the two parts of the dam are joined together.

多时　duōshí　【形】a long time

多数　duōshù　【名】majority

多谢　duōxiè　【动】many thanks

多心　duō = xīn　distrustful；prone to be suspicious；oversensitive：他这个人就是心直口快，你可别～。He is an outspoken man，don't take his words personally.

多样　duōyàng　【形】various

多疑　duōyí　【形】suspicious；skeptical

多义词　duōyìcí　【名】a word with more than one meaning

多余　duōyú　【形】superfluous

多种经营　duō zhǒng jīngyíng　a diversified economy

咄　duō

咄咄逼人　duōduō bī rén　（of manner）domineering and unsparing of others' feelings

咄咄怪事　duōduō guài shì　monstrous absurdity

哆　duō

哆嗦　duōsuo　【动】tremble

哆哆嗦嗦　duōduosuōsuō　【形】trembling；shivering

duó

夺（奪）　duó　【动】❶ take by force；seize；rob：～权 seize（political）power 民警把坏人手里的刀子～下来了。The policeman seized the knife from the hooligan. ❷ strive for；win：～高产 strive for high yields

夺标　duóbiāo　【动】win the championship

夺得　duódé　【动】take by force or skill

夺目　duómù　【形】dazzling

夺取　duóqǔ　【动】❶ seize；capture：～敌人的阵地 capture an enemy position ❷ win；score：～新的胜利 score new victories ～冠军 win the championship

duǒ

朵　duǒ　【量】*for flowers or clouds*

躲　duǒ　【动】❶ hide：～在树后边 hide behind a tree ❷ avoid；dodge；evade：～车 get out of the way of a bus；dodge a car ～雨 take shelter from the rain

躲避　duǒbì　【动】❶ hide；stay away ❷ avoid；evade；try to elude：渔船为了～台风，纷纷返航。In order to avoid the typhoon, the fishing-boats returned to harbour one after another.

躲藏　duǒcáng　【动】hide

躲躲闪闪　duǒ duǒ shǎn shǎn　❶

dodge; avoid ❷ be evasive; hedge; prevaricate

躲开 duǒ // kāi stay away; get out of the way

躲债 duǒ = zhài avoid creditors

duò

剁 duò 【动】chop; hack

垛 duò 【动】pile up 【名】stack

舵 duò 【名】rudder

舵手 duòshǒu 【名】helmsman

堕(墮) duò

堕落 duòluò 【动】go down hill; degenerate

堕入 duòrù 【动】fall into

堕胎 duò = tāi abortion

惰 duò

惰性 duòxìng 【名】❶ (chem.) inert ❷ (phys.) inertia ❸ laziness：这个人～很大。He is a very lazy man.

跺 duò 【动】stamp (one's foot)

跺脚 duò = jiǎo stamp one's foot

E

ē

阿 ē

另见 ā

阿谀奉承 ēyú fèngcheng　curry favour with；flatter and fawn on；toady

é

讹（訛） é 【动】extort；blackmail：~人 blackmail sb.【名】◇ error：以~传~ spread a falsehood

讹诈 ézhà 【动】blackmail；extort；intimidate：~钱财 extort money under false pretences 战争~ blackmail with the threat of war

蛾 é 【名】moth

蛾子 ézi 【名】moth

鹅（鵝） é 【名】〔只 zhī〕goose

额（額） é 【名】◇ ❶ forehead ❷ quota；a fixed number or amount ❸ a horizontal board with inscriptions（on the top of building, etc.）

额头 étóu 【名】forehead

额外 éwài 【形】extra；additional；added：~开支 extra expenses ～负担 added burden ～的要求 additional demands

ě

恶（惡） ě

另见 è

恶心 ěxin 【动】❶ feel nausea；feel sick ❷ nauseate；disgust：~人 disgusting 这种吹吹拍拍的作风,真让人~。This toadying really makes people sick.【形】nauseating；disgusting：真~! How disgusting! ～得要死。It makes one sick!

è

厄 è

厄运 èyùn 【名】misfortune

扼 è

扼杀 èshā 【动】strangle；smother：～新生力量 smother rising forces

扼要 èyào 【形】concise；to the point：简单 brief and to the point ～地介绍情况 give a brief introduction；introduce briefly

恶（惡） è 【名】◇ evil；vice；wickedness 【形】◇ ❶ ferocious；fierce；vicious：～狼 a ferocious wolf 一场~战 a fierce battle

❷ evil；wicked；bad：～人先告状。It is often the guilty party who files the suit.

另见 é

恶霸　èbà　【名】local tyrant；local despot

恶毒　èdú　【形】vicious；malicious；sinister：手段～ vicious means；base means

恶感　ègǎn　【名】resentment；hostility

恶贯满盈　è guàn mǎn yíng　(of a person) have committed innumerable crimes and finally reached the day of retribution

恶棍　ègùn　【名】rough-neck；scoundrel；villain

恶果　èguǒ　【名】evil result；disastrous effect

恶狠狠　èhěnhěn　【形】fierce；ferocious：～的样子 a ferocious expression ～地训人 scold sb. severely；give sb. a good scolding

恶化　èhuà　【动】worsen；deteriorate；take a turn for the worse：关系～ a deterioration in relations 病人的病情～了。The patient's condition has deteriorated. 形势～了。The situation has taken a turn for the worse.

恶劣　èliè　【形】very bad；evil；unfavourable；undesirable：品质～ bad character 行为～ unsavoury conduct ～的环境 adverse circumstances；unfavourable conditions

恶魔　èmó　【名】demon；devil；evil spirit

恶人　èrén　【名】evil person

恶习　èxí　【名】bad habit

恶性　èxìng　【名】malignant；lethal

恶意　èyì　【名】malice

恶作剧　èzuòjù　【名】practical joke；mischievous trick；mischief；prank

饿（餓）è　【形】hungry：～极了 feel very hungry；be as hungry as a wolf 我一点儿也不～。I do not feel hungry at all. 【动】starve；be left to go hungry：～了一顿 made to skip a meal

愕　è

愕然　èrán　【形】(usu. in written language) startled；stunned；astounded：听到这个意外的消息,我不禁为之～。I was stunned by the unexpected news.

遏　è

遏止　èzhǐ　【动】check；hold back；stop：不可～的洪流 irresistible tide

遏制　èzhì　【动】contain；keep within limits：～对方的行动 restrain a rival faction from doing sth.

噩　è

噩耗　èhào　【名】sad news of the death of a beloved or respected person

噩梦　èmèng　【名】nightmare

鳄（鰐）è

鳄鱼　èyú　【名】crocodile

ē̄

欸　ē̄　【叹】used to attract sb.'s attention, but only among people familiar with each other：～,你快来! Hey, come here quickly! ～,昨天说的那个事你可别忘了! Hey, you mustn't forget what we talked about yesterday.

另见 é；ě；è

é̄

欸　é̄　【叹】used to express surprise：～,你怎么走哇? Oh! Why do you want to go away? ～,都三月了,

怎么下起雪来了? Why, it's March and it's snowing!

另见 ē; ế; è

ě

欸 ě 【叹】 *used to express disapproval*: ～, 你这话可不对呀! Well, I'm afraid you shouldn't have said that! ～, 完全不是那么回事! Now, you've got it completely wrong!

另见 ē; ế; è

è

欸 è 【叹】 *used to express one's response to a person calling or one's agreement to a request*: 老张! ——～, 我这就来。Lao Zhang! — Yes, I'm coming! 请你把这个录音机给他们送去! ——～, 好吧! Please take this tape recorder to them! — All right!

另见 ē; ế; ě

éi

欸 éi 【叹】 *another pronunciation of* 欸 ế

另见 ěi; èi

ěi

欸 ěi 【叹】 *another pronunciation of* 欸 ě

另见 éi; èi

èi

欸 èi 【叹】 *another pronunciation of* 欸 è

另见 éi; èi

ēn

恩 ēn 【名】 favour or kindness from above

恩赐 ēncì 【动】 bestow (favour, charity, etc.)

恩惠 ēnhuì 【名】 special gift or kindness; special favour

恩将仇报 ēn jiāng chóu bào return evil for good; repay kindness with ingratitude

恩情 ēnqíng 【名】 great kindness

恩人 ēnrén 【名】 benefactor

恩怨 ēnyuàn 【名】 feelings of gratitude or bitterness (towards a person)

ér

儿(兒) ér 【名】◇ son: 一—女 a son and a daughter 【尾】❶ *diminutive*: 小孩～ child 小碗～ a small bowl 冰棍 ～ popsicle ❷ *makes a verb or an adj. into a noun*: 盖～ cover 亮～ light 尖～ tip 蛋黄 ～ yolk of an egg ❸ *changes the meaning of a word*: 信——信～ letter — piece of information 头——头～ head — leader 眼——眼～ eye — hole (*for change in the pronunciation of* 儿, 见 "儿化")

儿歌 érgē 【名】〔首 shǒu〕song for children; nursery rhyme

儿化 érhuà 【动】 *in "Putonghua" and some other Chinese dialects, there is a phonetic phenomenon — the retroflex ending "r". This ending must not be pronounced separately, but causes the preceding syllable to be retroflexed, e.g. the retroflexed "那儿" should be pronounced "nàr", not "nà' ér". The rules for pronunciation changes*

due to the retroflex ending are roughly as follows: ❶ *to* -a,-o,-e, -u:"r" *is added directly*, *e.g.*: huā -r — huār,cuò -r—cuòr,gē -r — gēr,tù -r —tùr. ❷ *to* -ai,-an,-ei,-en;"r" *is added after the final* i *or* n *has been dropped*, *e.g.*: pái -r — pár, wán -r — wár,wèi -r — wèr,fēn -r— fēr. ❸ "i" *of* zhi,chi,shi,ri,zi,ci,si *is changed into* "er", *e.g.*: shì -r — shèr,cì -r — cèr. ❹ *to* -in,-un;"er" *is added after the final* n *has been dropped*, *e.g.*: xìn -r — xièr,dūn -r — duēr. ❺ *to* -i,-ü;"er" *is added directly*, *e.g.*: jī -r — jiēr, qǔ -r — quēr.

儿科 érkē 【名】paediatrics

儿女 érnǚ 【名】son and daughter

儿孙 érsūn 【名】descendants

儿童 értóng 【名】children

儿童节 Értóngjié 【名】Children's Day

儿童团 értóngtuán 【名】Children's Corps (organization of children in Revolutionary Base Areas before the Liberation of 1949)

儿童文学 értóng wénxué literature for children

儿媳妇 érxífu 【名】daughter-in-law

儿戏 érxì 【名】trifling matter

儿子 érzi 【名】son

而 ér 【连】*connects words* (*verbs*), *adjectives and auxiliary verbs*), *phrases or clauses*, *mostly used in written language* ❶ *expresses co-ordination*: 一个美丽～动人的神话 a beautiful and moving myth 万里长城雄伟～壮观。The Great Wall is impressive and magnificent. ❷ *similar to* "but" *or* "yet": 紧张～有秩序 under great tension, yet in a very orderly fashion 现在北方还是遍地冰雪,～海南岛早已春暖花开。While the north is still snow-bound, spring has come to

Hainan Island and flowers are in bloom. ❸ *connects cause and effect*, *aim and means or manner and action*: 为胜利～高兴 be elated over a victory 为提高生产～钻研技术 master technical skills to help boost production 汽车急驰～去。The car drove away at a great speed. ❹ *further*; *in addition*: 凡是原来有基础～又有发展前途的手工业,应该继续发展。Those handicrafts which are rooted in the past and have a promising future are to be carried on. 掌握外语是很重要的,～要学好一种外语,非下苦功夫不可。It's very important to master a foreign language, and in order to master it, you must work hard at it. ❺ *indicates change from one state to another*: 由小 ～ 大 from small to big 由近～远 from near to far 自上～下 from top to bottom

而后 érhòu 【副】同"然后"(*usu. in written language*)

而今 érjīn 【名】now; at present; nowadays

而且 érqiě 【连】moreover; in addition; but also, *often in conjunction with* 不但: 一切产品不但求数量多,～求质量好。Not only quantity but quality is also required of all products. 不但全体职工,～大部分家属都参加了义务劳动。Not only all staff members and workers but most of their family members went to take part in voluntary labour. 读书是学习,使用也是学习,～是更重要的学习。Reading is learning; practice is also learning and an even more important part of learning. Note:而且 *can also connect two adjectives*: 勇敢 ～ 机智 courageous and quick-witted 高～陡 high and steep

而已 éryǐ 【助】that is all; nothing more; only; just: 开个玩笑～,何必

认真? It's just a joke. Don't take it too seriously. 如此～,岂有他哉! That's all there is to it!

ěr

尔(爾) ěr

尔后 ěrhòu 【名】〈书〉thereafter; subsequently: 他先发表了几篇论文, ～又有专著出版。He published several papers, followed by a book.

尔虞我诈 ěr yú wǒ zhà mutual suspicion and deception; each trying to cheat and outwit the other

耳 ěr 【名】ear

耳朵 ěrduo 【名】〔只 zhī〕ear

耳光 ěrguāng 【名】box on the ear

耳环 ěrhuán 【名】〔只 zhī、副 fù〕earring

耳机 ěrjī 【名】earphones

耳鸣 ěrmíng 【名】buzzing in the ears; tinnitus

耳膜 ěrmó 【名】eardrum

耳目 ěrmù 【名】❶ ears and eyes: ～不灵 ill-informed ❷ one who spies for another

耳目所及 ěr mù suǒ jí what one has heard and seen; information within one's grasp

耳目一新 ěr mù yī xīn find everything fresh and new; a pleasant change in the atmosphere or appearance of a place: 归国华侨一踏上祖国的大地, 就觉得～。On returning to China, overseas Chinese find everything fresh and new.

耳旁风 ěrpángfēng 【名】sth. what goes in at one ear and out at the other: 你怎么总是把我的话当做～? Why do you always turn a deaf ear to what I say? 也作"耳边风"。

耳濡目染 ěr rú mù rǎn be influenced by one's surroundings; be influenced by what one constantly hears and sees

耳闻 ěrwén 【动】hear of; learn about

耳闻目睹 ěr wén mù dǔ see and hear for oneself

耳语 ěryǔ 【动】whisper

èr

二 èr 【数】two 见"两"liǎng

二重性 èrchóngxìng 【名】dual character or nature; duality: 商品具有～, 一方面它有使用价值, 另一方面它有价值。All commodities have a dual nature: they have use-value on the one hand and monetary value on the other. 也作"两重性"。

二七大罢工 Èr Qī Dà Bà Gōng The Great Strike of February 7th, 1923, staged by the Beijing-Hankou Railway workers

二手 èrshǒu 【形】second-hand: ～车 second-hand car ～货 second-hand goods; used goods

二氧化碳 èryǎnghuàtàn 【名】carbon dioxide

二元论 èryuánlùn 【名】dualism

二月 èryuè 【名】February

二者必居其一 èr zhě bì jū qí yī either one or the other

贰(貳) èr 【数】two (the complicated form of 二) 见"捌"bā

F

fā

发（發）fā 【动】❶ send out; issue；dispatch：～通知 send out a notice ～电报 send a telegram ❷ discharge；shoot；emit：～炮 fire a gun ～光 emit light ～亮 shine ❸ distribute；deliver：～枪 issue rifles ～工资 pay out wages ～传单 distribute leaflets ❹ show；express：～议论 express opinions ❺ come into existence；burst out：～病 suffer an attack of a chronic illness ～大水。A flood occurred. ❻ feel (usu. an uncomfortable feeling)：～痒 itch；feel itchy ～麻 have pins and needles 腿～软 feel weak in the knees 他嗓子～干。His throat felt dry. ❼ exhibit a certain characteristic：～红 turn red ～潮 become damp ❽ ◇ show or express (one's feelings)：～笑 laugh ❾ (of foodstuffs) rise or expand after fermentation or soaking：把面～好 allow dough to rise fully【量】(for ammunition)：两～子弹 two bullets 几千～炮弹 several thousand shells

发榜 fā=bǎng publish a list of successful candidates or applicants

发报机 fābàojī 【名】〔台 tái〕telegraph transmitter

发表 fābiǎo 【动】❶ publish；issue：～演说 make a speech 充分～意见 give full expression to one's opinions ～声明 issue a statement ❷ publish：～文章 publish an article ～作品 publish (one's) work

发布 fābù 【动】issue；release；publish officially：～新闻 release news

发财 fā=cái make a fortune；get rich

发愁 fā=chóu worry

发出 fā // chū ❶ produce；emit；give out：～香味儿 emit a fragrant smell 天车～隆隆的响声。The crane made a rumbling sound. ❷ issue；announce：～命令 issue an order ～号召 issue a call；call on (the people to do sth.) ❸ send out；deliver：～信件 send a letter ～稿件 send off a manuscript

发达 fādá 【形】developed；flourishing：肌肉～ have well-developed muscles 工业～ flourishing industry ～的国家 a developed country

发呆 fā=dāi stupefied

发电 fā=diàn generate electricity

发电厂 fādiànchǎng 【名】power plant

发电机 fādiànjī 【名】〔台 tái〕generator

发电量 fādiànliàng 【名】generated energy

发电站 fādiànzhàn 【名】power-station

发动 fādòng 【动】❶ launch：～进攻 launch an attack ～战争 start a war ❷ mobilize；rouse：～群众搞好环境

卫生。Mobilize the residents to improve the environment. ❸ start a vehicle or machine：这种拖拉机很容易～。This kind of tractor is easy to start. 汽车～了。The car started.

发动机 fādòngjī 【名】〔台 tái〕motor

发抖 fādǒu 【动】shiver；shake；tremble：冻得浑身～ shiver all over with cold 气得～ tremble with anger

发放 fāfàng 【动】provide；grant；issue：～贷款 grant a loan ～通行证 issue a pass

发奋 fāfèn 【动】rouse oneself；bestir oneself：～学习 put all one's energies into one's studies ～工作 put all one's energies into one's work

发愤图强 fāfèn tú qiáng work with a will to make the country strong 也作"奋发图强"。

发疯 fā=fēng lose one's senses；be out of one's mind

发号施令 fā hào shī lìng issue orders；order people about（*often derog.*）：要发动群众，只靠少数人～是什么也干不成的。We must mobilize the masses；nothing will be accomplished by just a few people ordering others about.

发还 fāhuán 【动】return；give back：老师把改好的作业～给学生。The teacher returned the homework which he had corrected to the students.

发慌 fā=huāng flustered

发挥 fāhuī 【动】❶ bring into play；give scope to：～创造性 give full scope to creativity ～了巨大作用 play a big role in 充分～集体力量 bring collective strength into play ❷（of idea, theme, etc.）develop；express；elaborate；air：借题～ seize a pretext to air one's opinion 这篇文章还要改写，把中心思想充分～

一下。The article is to be rewritten in order to develop the theme fully.

发火 fā=huǒ ❶ catch fire；ignite ❷（of bullets）go off：打了十几发子弹，有一发没有～。Ten rounds were fired, but one failed to go off. ❸ get angry；be enraged；lose one's temper：急得直～ be provoked to anger 他有点儿～了。He was a little angry.

发家致富 fā jiā zhì fù build up a family fortune

发酵 fā=jiào ferment

发觉 fājué 【动】find；realize；discover：经他一提醒，我才～自己认错人了。Not until he told me did I realize that I had been mistaken about（the identity of）the man.

发掘 fājué 【动】excavate；unearth；explore：～宝藏 excavate ore ～历史文物 unearth historic cultural relics ～潜力 explore the latent potential of sb. or sth.

发刊词 fākāncí 【名】inaugural statement in first issue of a periodical

发狂 fā=kuáng go mad

发愣 fā=lèng be stupefied

发霉 fā=méi mould；become mildewed

发明 fāmíng 【动】invent 【名】invention

发明家 fāmíngjiā 【名】inventor

发难 fānàn 【动】be the instigator of a revolt

发怒 fā=nù flare up；fly into a rage

发脾气 fā píqi fly into a rage

发票 fāpiào 【名】〔张 zhāng〕invoice

发起 fāqǐ 【动】❶ initiate；sponsor：这次义务劳动是校长～的。The voluntary work project was initiated by the headmaster. ❷ start；launch：～总攻 launch a general attack ～冲锋 charge forward

发起人 fāqǐrén 【名】sponsor

发球 fā = qiú （of sports） serve a ball

发人深省 fā rén shēn xǐng thought-provoking；provide food for thought；provocative：院长的话语重心长，～。 The director's words were of great significance, and made one think. 这篇杂文中有不少～的东西。 There is much food for thought in this essay. 也作"发人深醒"。

发烧 fā = shāo have a fever；have a temperature

发烧友 fāshāoyǒu 【名】a fanatic

发射 fāshè 【动】shoot；fire；launch （e.g. a man-made satellite）

发生 fāshēng 【动】happen；occur；take place；arise；crop up：要防止意外事件 ～ prevent accidents ～了问题。 Problems arose. ～了冲突。 Conflicts occurred. 芦沟桥事变～在1937年7月。 The Lugouqiao Bridge Incident took place in July, 1937.

发誓 fā = shì take an oath；swear

发现 fāxiàn 【动】❶ discover；find out：～规律 discover the law of ... ～古代青铜器 discover ancient bronze vessels ❷ find；notice：～机器有故障，要及时排除。 If you find anything wrong with the machine, you should fix it at once. 【名】discovery；find：考古新 ～ new archaeological finds 一项重大的 ～ an important discovery

发泄 fāxiè 【动】give vent to；vent

发行 fāxíng 【动】publish；distribute

发芽 fā = yá germinate

发言 fā = yán give a speech；speak （at a meeting）

发言权 fāyánquán 【名】the right to speak

发言人 fāyánrén 【名】spokesman

发炎 fā = yán inflame

发扬 fāyáng 【动】develop；foster；bring into play：～光荣传统 devel-op the glorious tradition ～成绩，纠正错误 add to your achievements and correct your mistakes

发扬光大 fāyáng guāngdà carry for-ward；give full play to；foster and enhance

发音 fāyīn 【名】pronunciation

发音 fā = yīn pronounce

发育 fāyù 【动】develop gradually by a process of growth and change

发源 fāyuán 【动】originate；have its origin in；have as its source：长江 ～ 于青海省沱沱河。 The Changjiang River has the Tuotuo River of Qinghai Province as its source. 真知不一定都～于个人的直接经验。 Not all knowledge neces-sarily originates from direct per-sonal experience.

发源地 fāyuándì 【名】place of ori-gin；source

发展 fāzhǎn 【动】❶ develop；ex-pand：～国民经济 develop the na-tional economy ～组织 expand an organization 语言总是在不断地 ～着。 Languages are always develop-ing. ❷ （in order to expand an or-ganization） take in；recruit：～会员 recruit a new member ～新党员 take new members into the party

发展中国家 fāzhǎn zhōng guójiā de-veloping countries

发作 fāzuò 【动】❶ break out；show the effects of：酒性 ～ begin to show the effects of alcohol 旧病～ a recurrence of an old illness ❷ lose one's temper：他非常气愤，只是当着众人的面不好 ～。 He was furi-ous, but restrained himself in the presence of others.

fá

乏 fá 【形】tired；weary：人困马 ～。 Both the men and the horses

were tired out. 走了几十里路,觉得有点儿~。He was a bit tired from walking dozens of miles.

乏力　fá lì　feeble

乏味　fáwèi　【形】dull；insipid；语言~ insipid language

罚(罰)　fá　【动】punish

罚不当罪　fá bù dāng zuì　the punishment is not in keeping with the crime

罚款　fákuǎn　【名】fine

罚款　fá = kuǎn　fine；punish by a levying fine

罚球　fá = qiú　free throw or penalty kick

fǎ

法　fǎ　【名】❶ law；海洋~ maritime law　依~惩办 punish according to law ❷ method；way；写~ method of writing（e.g. a composition, a character）作 ~ way of doing （sth.） ❸ technique；style；枪 ~ marksmanship　笔 ~（of writing, painting or calligraphy）style

法案　fǎ'àn　【名】proposed law

法办　fǎbàn　【动】be dealt with according to law

法宝　fǎbǎo　【名】sth. with magical powers；effective weapon

法定　fǎdìng　【形】legal；statutory

法定货币　fǎdìng huòbì　legal tender

法定人数　fǎdìng rénshù　quorum

法规　fǎguī　【名】laws and regulations

法家　Fǎjiā　【名】the Legalist School

法郎　fǎláng　【名】franc（currency）

法令　fǎlìng　【名】law；statute；decree

法律　fǎlǜ　【名】law

法律顾问　fǎlǜ gùwèn　legal adviser

法盲　fǎmáng　【名】a person ignorant of the law；legally illiterate

法人　fǎrén　【名】legal person

法庭　fǎtíng　【名】court room

法网　fǎwǎng　【名】（fig.）meshes of the law；web of justice

法西斯　fǎxīsī　【名】fascist

法西斯主义　fǎxīsīzhǔyì　【名】fascism

法医　fǎyī　【名】a legal medical expert

法院　fǎyuàn　【名】law court；court building

法则　fǎzé　【名】law（of nature）

法治　fǎzhì　【名】the rule of law

法制　fǎzhì　【名】legality；the legal system

法子　fǎzi　【名】method；way；means

砝　fǎ

砝码　fǎmǎ　【名】weight（used in old-fashioned scales）

fān

帆　fān　【名】sail

帆布　fānbù　【名】canvas

帆船　fānchuán　【名】〔只 zhī〕sail boat；junk

番　fān　【量】❶ kind；别有一~风味 have a flavour of a different kind 他完全是一~好意。He did it out of good will. ❷ for actions which take time or effort：下了一~苦功 put in a lot of painstaking effort 一~话说得他心服口服。He was completely convinced by the talk. 费了他 一 ~ 心思。He racked his brains.（In ❶, ❷, the numeral preceding 番 can only be 一.）❸ -fold；times；产量翻了一~。The output was doubled.

番号　fānhào　【名】（mil.）the number designating a unit

蕃　fān

蕃茄 fānqié 【名】tomato

翻 fān 【动】❶ turn over; turn upside down: 车～了 the car turned over 人仰马～ the bodies of men and horses littered the ground (*fig.*) thrown into a chaotic state; out of control ❷ rummage: ～乱了 rummage about ❸ turn (pages): ～到第 50 页 turn to p. 50 把书一开。Open your books. ❹ climb over: ～山越岭 climb over mountains and hills; cross one mountain after another ❺ translate; interpret: 把文件～成英文 translate the document into English ❻ turn hostile to; quarrel with sb.: 他们两个人闹～了。The two of them had a falling out. 他一句话把老王惹～了。His remark provoked Lao Wang into a fit of temper. ❼ increase twofold; double: 产量～几番。The output has increased several times over.

翻案 fān = àn reverse a verdict

翻版 fānbǎn 【名】❶ pirated edition ❷ duplicate; sth. different in form but the same in essence

翻番 fān = fān increase by specified times; increase ... fold

翻滚 fāngǔn 【动】❶ roll: 麦浪～ a rolling sea of wheat 波涛～。The waves rolled without stopping. 开水在壶里～。The boiling water bubbled furiously in the kettle. ❷ turn over; tumble: 小孩在沙坑里～着玩。The children tumbled about in the sand pit.

翻江倒海 fān jiāng dǎo hǎi over-turn a river and empty the sea; (*fig.*) accomplish sth. requiring great strength; take a lot of trouble over sth.; overwhelming 也作"倒海翻江"。

翻来覆去 fān lái fù qù ❶ toss from side to side: 他～睡不着。He tossed and turned, unable to sleep. ❷ (constant) change: 别老是～拿不定主意。Don't keep changing your mind. ❸ again and again; repeatedly: 这封信他～地看了好几遍。He read the letter over and over again.

翻脸 fān = liǎn suddenly turn hostile; have a falling out with sb.: ～不认人 suddenly turn against a friend 两人吵翻了脸。The two had a falling out.

翻然悔悟 fānrán huǐwù be aware of and correct one's errors or misdeeds

翻砂 fānshā 【名】(mech.) casting

翻身 fān = shēn ❶ turn over (e. g. in bed) ❷ free oneself from oppression or exploitation; be liberated ❸ thoroughly change the backward state of things: 打好农业～仗 work hard to thoroughly change the backward state of agriculture

翻腾 fānténg 【动】seethe; surge; rise: 波浪～。The waves are rolling. 四海～。The four seas are surging. (*fig.*) There are revolutionary uprisings everywhere.

翻腾 fānteng 【动】❶ think about again and again; turn (sth.) over in one's mind: 这些问题一直在我脑子里～着。I've been turning these problems over and over in my mind. ❷ rummage: 抽屉刚整理好，别～乱了。I've just tidied up this drawer. Don't rummage through it.

翻天覆地 fān tiān fù dì (of social change) such a tremendous change is taking place that as if heaven and earth are turned upside down 也作"地覆天翻"。

翻箱倒柜 fān xiāng dǎo guì rummage in chests and cupboards; overturn things in a thorough

search

翻新　fānxīn　【动】❶（*usu. of clothes*，*etc.*）mend；make over；～补旧 make over and patch old (clothes) ❷ the new emerges out of the old：花样 ～ innovations in style；playing new tricks (*derog.*)

翻修　fānxiū　【动】rebuild：～ 房屋 have the houses rebuilt ～马路 reconstruct a road

翻译　fānyì　【动】translate；interpret 【名】translator；interpreter

翻译本　fānyìběn　【名】translation

翻译片　fānyìpiàn　【名】〔部 bù〕dubbed film

翻印　fānyìn　【动】reprint；reproduce

翻阅　fānyuè　【动】glance through；leaf through

fán

凡　fán　【副】同"凡是"（*usu. in written language*）

凡士林　fánshìlín　【名】vaseline

凡是　fánshì　【副】all that … (*must be placed at the beginning of a sentence*，*usu. in conjunction with* 都)：～损害公共利益的行为，都应该制止。Any conduct harmful to the public interest must not be permitted.～天气晴朗的晚上都可以看见那颗星。On any fine night, one can see that star.

矾（礬）　fán　【名】alum

烦（煩）　fán　【形】❶ vexed；irritated；annoyed：真让人 ～ 得慌。It's really very annoying. ❷ impatient：你可别嫌～，这事比较啰嗦。Please don't be impatient；this is a rather complicated matter. ❸ ◇wordy：要言不～ a concise but witty statement 【动】trouble（*polite way of asking a favour*）：电视机坏

了，～ 您修理一下。Something is wrong with the T. V. set. Would you be so kind as to repair it?

烦闷　fánmèn　【形】unhappy；worried；upset

烦恼　fánnǎo　【形】worried；vexed；out of sorts：令人～ vexing 自寻～ fret needlessly；worry oneself for nothing

烦扰　fánrǎo　【动】perturb；bother

烦琐　fánsuǒ　【形】undue insistence on forms or details：～的事务工作 tedious and trivial daily routine 也作"繁琐"。

烦琐哲学　fánsuǒ zhéxué　scholasticism

烦躁　fánzào　【形】irritable

繁　fán　【形】❶ complicated ❷ numerous

繁多　fánduō　【形】various；numerous（*can only be used as the predicate*）：品种 ～ of many varieties 名目～ various pretexts

繁华　fánhuá　【形】（of towns and streets) full of shops and bustling people；prosperous and bustling：～ 的街道 busy streets 这一带越来越 ～ 了。This district is getting more and more prosperous and bustling.

繁忙　fánmáng　【形】busy；fully occupied（with all sorts of work)：工作 ～ be busy with all sorts of work

繁荣　fánróng　【形】flourishing；prosperous；booming：经济～。The economy is thriving. 市场～。The market is booming.【动】make sth. flourish：～ 文 化 make culture flourish ～经济 bring about a prosperous economy

繁荣昌盛　fánróng chāngshèng　thriving and prosperous：祖国日益～。Our country is growing more prosperous every day.

繁体字　fántǐzì　【名】a complex character, of which there is also a sim-

plified equivalent (e.g. 體 is the 繁体字 of the simplified character 体)

繁星　fánxīng　【名】a host of stars

繁杂　fánzá　【形】(of affairs) numerous and diverse

繁殖　fánzhí　【动】breed; multiply

繁重　fánzhòng　【形】(of duties or responsibilities) too many and heavy

fǎn

反　fǎn　【形】inverse; in an opposite direction (as opp. to 正):～比例 inverse proportion 把衣服穿～了 wear one's coat inside out 【动】❶ oppose; be against; resist:～侵略 resist against aggression ❷ ◇ turn over:～败为胜 turn defeat into victory ～守为攻 turn defense into offense 【副】同"反而":他不但不支持我,～把我批评了一顿。He not only gave me no support, on the contrary, he sharply criticized me.

反比　fǎnbǐ　【名】(maths.) inverse ratio

反比例　fǎnbǐlì　【名】inverse ratio; inverse proportion

反驳　fǎnbó　【动】rebut; refute; confute

反差　fǎnchā　【名】contrast

反常　fǎncháng　【形】unusual; abnormal; strange; perverse:～的现象 an unusual phenomenon 气候～。The weather is peculiar. 他的态度～。His attitude is strange.

反衬　fǎnchèn　【动】set off; show in contrast

反倒　fǎndào　【副】同"反而", but more colloquial:小刘受了表扬～不好意思起来了。When Xiao Liu was praised, he was embarrassed, much to our surprise.

反动　fǎndòng　【形】reactionary

反动派　fǎndòngpài　【名】reactionary (person)

反对　fǎnduì　【动】oppose; be against; object to:～非正义战争 oppose an unjust war 遭到大多数人的～ encounter opposition from the majority 对这项决议有～的没有? Are there any objections to this resolution?

反而　fǎn'ér　【副】indicates that a state of affairs results in a certain effect contrary to what might have been expected:这么近的路,你开汽车去～比走路慢。The place is so close that if you go there by car, it will actually take longer than if you walk. 广州在南京的南面,～没有南京热。Guangzhou is south of Nanjing, but contrary to what one might suppose, it is not as hot.

反复　fǎnfù　【动】❶ repeatedly; again and again; over and over again:～思考 think a lot about sth. ～实践 repeatedly try out in practice ～较量 repeatedly match strength with each other ❷ go back on one's word; have a relapse:已经达成协议,不应该再～了。An agreement has been reached, and there shouldn't be any more changes. 一年之内他的病～了好几次。He has had several relapses within the past year. 【名】relapse; reversal; setback:这场斗争还会出现～。There will be setbacks in this struggle.

反复无常　fǎnfù wúcháng　inconsistent; capricious

反感　fǎngǎn　【形】repugnant 【名】repugnance

反戈一击　fǎn gē yī jī　turn round and strike; turn round and hit back

反攻　fǎngōng　【动】counter-attack; counter-offensive

反光镜　fǎnguāngjìng　【名】reflector

反话 fǎnhuà 【名】remark implying a meaning opposite to what it says; irony; sarcasm

反悔 fǎnhuǐ 【动】repent; go back on one's word

反击 fǎnjī 【动】strike back; launch a counter-attack; ～侵略者 strike back against aggressors 进行有力的 ～ deal a vigorous counter-blow

反抗 fǎnkàng 【动】resist; revolt against

反馈 fǎnkuì 【动】feedback

反面 fǎnmiàn 【名】❶ back; wrong side ❷ negative (as opp. to 正面)：～角色 villain (in a play, etc.)，的典型 a stock character of a negative kind ❸ the other side of a matter or problem：看问题,不仅要看它的正面,而且还要看它的～。In considering a problem, we should look at its less obvious side, as well as at what is immediately apparent; When considering a problem, we should take into account the negative as well as the positive aspects.

反面教材 fǎnmiàn jiàocái negative example which may serve as a lesson from which sth. positive may be learned

反面人物 fǎnmiàn rénwù (in literary and artistic works) villain; negative character; negative role

反扑 fǎnpū 【动】(of a cornered enemy or animal) counter-attack; attack in retaliation

反其道而行之 fǎn qí dào ér xíng zhī do exactly the opposite

反切 fǎnqiè 【名】a traditional method, pre-dating phonetic transcription, of indicating the pronunciation of a Chinese character by using two other characters. The first has the same initial as the given character and the second the same final and tone (e. g. the pronunciation of 塑 is given as 桑故切 or 桑故反,indicating that the initial of 塑 is s,as in 桑 and the final is ù,as in 故).

反射 fǎnshè 【动】reflect

反思 fǎnsī 【动】introspect

反弹 fǎntán 【动】rebound

反问 fǎnwèn 【动】❶ answer a question with a question：老王问我喜欢不喜欢这个话剧,我～他一句:"你呢?" Lao Wang asked me whether I liked the play. I responded by asking:"Did you?" ❷ make an emphatic statement using a rhetorical question：～语气 the tone of one's voice when asking a rhetorical question

反问句 fǎnwènjù 【名】rhetorical question

反响 fǎnxiǎng 【名】response; repercussions (arising from a speech, action, etc.)：这个激动人心的讲话,在群众中引起了强烈的～。The stirring speech evoked a strong response from the masses.

反省 fǎnxǐng 【动】engage in self-examination; introspect; 停职～ be relieved of one's duties in order to engage in self-examination and consider one's errors

反义词 fǎnyìcí 【名】antonym

反应 fǎnyìng 【名】reaction：化学～ chemical reaction 热核～ thermonuclear reaction 药物～ allergic reaction (to a certain medicine) ～灵敏 (of a measuring device, etc.) react sensitively 【动】react; 对他的报告普遍 ～ 良好。The audience generally reacted well to his report.

反应堆 fǎnyìngduī 【名】reactor

反映 fǎnyìng 【动】❶ reflect; mirror; depict：这个画展大部分题材是～草原牧民生活的。The exhibition of paintings mostly portrays the life of the nomadic people on the

prairie. ❷ report; make known (to the leadership): 把情况如实 ～ 上去 report true conditions or circumstances to a higher level 向领导 ～自己的意见。Let the leadership know one's opinions. 【名】response; reaction: 大家对这部电影的 ～ 很好。People responded very favourably to the film.

反映论　fǎnyìnglùn　【名】(phil.) Theory of Reflection

反正　fǎnzhèng　【副】❶ *indicates that the result remains unchanged whatever may happen*, *usu. in conjunction with* 无论 *or* 不管: 无论你怎么说，～ 我不同意。Put it any way you like, I still won't agree to it. 你说吧，～ 你说我说一样。You'd better tell them, it doesn't make any difference whether you tell them or I tell them. ❷ *stresses the truth of a fact*, *under any of the following conditions*: ① *when the details are not clear*: 他的孩子究竟多大我不清楚，～ 不超过二十岁。I don't know how old his child is, but certainly not over twenty. ② *when the individual situations are different*: 他们家一个弹钢琴的，一个拉小提琴的，一个唱歌的，～ 都是搞音乐的。In their family, one plays the piano, another the violin, and the third is a singer; in short they are all musicians. ③ *when a decision is made as a result of a circumstance which won't change*: 这本词典 ～ 我不用，你拿去用吧！I don't use this dictionary anyway, you might as well take it and use it. 咱们看电影去吧！～ 今天晚上没事。Let's go to a movie, we haven't got anything to do this evening anyway.

反证　fǎnzhèng　【动】furnish counter-evidence 【名】counter-evidence; disproof

反之　fǎnzhī　【连】❶ equivalent to; 如果与此相反: 按照正确的政策办事，我们就胜利；～，就失败。Whenever we followed a correct policy, we were successful; otherwise we failed. ❷ vice versa: 农业发展了，可以促进工业的发展；～，工业发展了，又可以促进农业的发展。When agriculture is developed, it will hasten the development of industry, and vice versa.

反殖　fǎn＝zhí　anti-colonialism

反作用　fǎnzuòyòng　【名】❶ (phys.) reaction ❷ (produce) an effect opposite to what was intended

反作用力　fǎnzuòyònglì　【名】(phys.) reaction; the force of a reaction

返　fǎn　【动】return

返工　fǎn＝gōng　do (a poorly done job) over again: 这段墙砌得不合要求，要 ～。This part of the wall was not built according to specifications, and must be redone.

返航　fǎnháng　【动】(ship) make a return voyage; (aeroplane) make a return flight

返回　fǎnhuí　【动】return; go back

返青　fǎnqīng　【动】(of winter crops or transplanted seedlings) resume growth

返销　fǎnxiāo　【动】resell to the original producer

fàn

犯　fàn　【动】❶ violate; commit an offense against ❷ attack; invade: 警惕一切 ～ 我领空之敌。Be alert to all possible invasions of our airspace. 人不～我，我不～人，人若～我，我必 ～ 人。We will not attack unless we are attacked; if we are attacked, we will certainly counterattack. ❸ have a recur-

rence of（e.g. an old illness）; commit（an error）:～错误 commit an error 心里直～嘀咕 be puzzled and suspicious（about sth.）他的心脏病～了。He had an attack of recurrent heart trouble.【名】convict; criminal: 盗窃～ a convicted thief

犯案　fàn＝àn　be found out and brought to justice

犯病　fàn＝bìng　have an attack of an illness

犯不上　fàn bu shàng　it won't pay; it is not worthwhile

犯不着　fàn bu zháo　同"犯不上"

犯得上　fàn de shàng　it is worthwhile（esp. in rhetorical question）

犯得着　fàn de zháo　同"犯得上"

犯法　fàn＝fǎ　break the law

犯规　fàn＝guī　（of sports）foul

犯人　fànrén　【名】convict; prisoner

犯罪　fàn＝zuì　commit a crime; commit an offence

饭（飯）fàn　【名】（cooked）rice; meal

饭店　fàndiàn　【名】hotel; restaurant

饭馆　fànguǎn　【名】（～儿）restaurant

饭盒　fànhé　【名】lunch-box

饭量　fànliàng　【名】appetite; the amount of food one can consume

饭厅　fàntīng　【名】dining hall

饭桶　fàntǒng　【名】good-for-nothing（person）

饭碗　fànwǎn　【名】rice bowl;（fig.）livelihood

泛　fàn　【动】❶ ◇ float:～舟湖上 go boating on the lake ❷ be suffused with; spread: 脸上～起红晕 with one's face flushed ～出香味 emit a good smell

泛泛　fànfàn　【形】not thoroughgoing; superficial:～地一说 talk generally ～之交 casual acquaint-ance

泛滥　fànlàn　【动】be in flood; overflow;（of ideas, usually derogatory）spread unchecked; run rampant: 洪水～ be in flood ～成灾 disaster caused by flooding 决不允许赌博之风到处～。Gambling should not be allowed to spread unchecked.

泛指　fànzhǐ　【动】make a general reference; in a general sense（as opp. to 专指）:"江湖"过去～四方各地。The term "rivers and lakes" in old days meant in general all corners of the country.

范（範）fàn

范畴　fànchóu　【名】category

范例　fànlì　【名】model; example; pattern

范围　fànwéi　【名】scope; limits; range: 活动～ the physical area within which an activity is carried on ～很广 extensive in scope; wide-ranging 这个问题在小组～内进行了酝酿。This question was discussed within the confines of the group.

范文　fànwén　【名】model essay

贩（販）fàn　【动】peddle; buy goods and sell them at a higher price

贩毒　fàn＝dú　traffic in narcotics; drug trafficking

贩卖　fànmài　【动】peddle; traffic in; sell:～毒品 traffic in narcotics

贩运　fànyùn　【动】（of merchant's goods）transport in order to sell

贩子　fànzi　【名】trader; monger

fāng

方　fāng　【名】❶ direction ❷ side; party: 我～ our side 一～有难,八～支援。When a problem ari-

ses, help pours in from all quarters. ❸ ◇ method；way：想～设法 try in a hundred and one ways 领导有～ exercise good leadership ❹ (～儿) prescription：请医生开个～ ask the doctor to write a prescription ❺ (maths.) power：3 的 3 次～是 27。The third power of three is 27.【形】square：这块木头是～的。This piece of wood is square.【量】❶ *for square objects*：一～砚台 one ink-stone 两～图章 two seals ❷ *short for* 平方米 *or* 立方米：一～土 a cubic metre of earth【副】❶ ◇ 同 "正" zhèng：血气～刚 be in the flower of one's youth ❷〈书〉just：年～二十。He has just turned twenty.

方案 fāng'àn 【名】❶ plan；program；project：建厂～ plan for the construction of a factory 作战～ battle-plan ❷ scheme；schema：汉语拼音～ the scheme for the Chinese Phonetic Alphabet

方便 fāngbiàn 【形】❶ convenient：阅览室词典多，在那儿学习很～。There are a lot of dictionaries in the reading room. You'll find them very handy if you go there to study. 我家就住在商场旁边，买东西很～。I live just by the market, it's very convenient for shopping. ❷ proper；suitable：你们现在正开会，我呆在这儿不～。Since you are having a meeting, it would be awkward for me to stay.【动】do sth. for the convenience of sb.；facilitate：～群众 do sth. for the convenience of the people ～顾客 do sth. for the convenience of the customers

方便面 fāngbiànmiàn 【名】〔包 bāo〕instant noodles

方才 fāngcái 【名】同 "刚才" gāngcái，*but not as frequently used*

方程 fāngchéng 【名】equation

方程式 fāngchéngshì 【名】equation

方法 fāngfǎ 【名】method；way；means

方法论 fāngfǎlùn 【名】methodology

方面 fāngmiàn 【名】respect；aspect；side：技术～的问题 technical problem 各～的例子 all kinds of examples 优势在我们～。Our side has the superior position.

方式 fāngshì 【名】way；fashion；pattern：斗争～ method of struggle 工作～ way of working

方位 fāngwèi 【名】❶ direction ❷ position and direction

方位词 fāngwèicí 【名】(gram.) word of locality；localizer

方向 fāngxiàng 【名】❶ bearing；direction (N., S., E., W.)：在森林里迷失了～ lose one's way in the forest ❷ direction；orientation：队伍朝西山的～前进。The contingent marched in the direction of the Western Hills.

方向盘 fāngxiàngpán 【名】steering wheel

方兴未艾 fāng xīng wèi ài on the rise；be in the ascendant

方言 fāngyán 【名】dialect

方圆 fāngyuán 【名】neighbourhood；surrounding area：～几百里都是平原。In this area, the plains extend for hundreds of *li*. ～左近的几个学校都是先进单位。The neighboring schools in this area are all model units.

方针 fāngzhēn 【名】guiding principle；orientation；guideline

芳 fāng

芳香 fāngxiāng 【形】fragrant

fáng

防 fáng 【动】guard against；prevent：～盗 guard against robbery ～潮 moisture-proof【名】◇

defense：布～ deploy troops for purposes of defense

防暴 fáng = bào violence prevention guard against violence：～警察 riot police

防备 fángbèi 【动】guard against；take precautions against：把羊圈关好，～羊群跑掉。Close the gate of the pen properly to prevent the sheep from getting away.

防毒 fáng = dú take precautions against poisoning

防范 fángfàn 【动】be on guard；keep watch：严加～ take strict precautions against ～ 坏人破坏捣乱 be on guard against bad elements making trouble and engaging in sabotage

防腐 fáng = fǔ anti-corrosive

防腐蚀 fáng fǔshí anti-corrosive

防洪 fáng = hóng flood prevention

防护堤 fánghùdī 【名】embankment

防护林 fánghùlín 【名】sand and windbreak；shelterbelt

防患未然 fáng huàn wèi rán take preventive measures；take preventive measures against possible calamities：汛前加固堤坝，是～的必要措施。It is necessary to strengthen the dike before the water rises.

防火 fáng = huǒ ❶ prevent fire ❷ fireproof

防空 fáng = kōng （measures for） protection in the event of an airraid

防涝 fáng =' lào take measures to prevent waterlogging

防守 fángshǒu 【动】guard；defend

防水 fáng = shuǐ be waterproof

防微杜渐 fáng wēi dù jiàn check evil before it has a chance to spread；nip sth. evil in the bud

防伪 fángwěi 【动】anti-forging

防卫 fángwèi 【动】defend and guard against

防务 fángwù 【名】defence

防线 fángxiàn 【名】line of defence

防汛 fáng = xùn take measures to prevent a river from flooding

防疫 fáng = yì prevent an epidemic

防御 fángyù 【动】protect against

防震 fáng = zhèn ❶ shock-proof ❷ make preparations in case of earthquakes

防止 fángzhǐ 【动】prevent；guard against

防治 fángzhì 【动】prevent and cure

妨 fáng

妨碍 fáng'ài 【动】hamper；impede：～交通 impede traffic 在阅览室里，不要大声说话，以免～别人。Keep quiet in the reading-room and don't disturb others.

房 fáng 【名】〔间 jiān〕❶ house：瓦 ～ house with a tiled roof ❷ room：一间～ one room

房产 fángchǎn 【名】house property

房地产 fángdìchǎn 【名】real estate

房东 fángdōng 【名】owner of a house；landlord or landlady of a house

房间 fángjiān 【名】room

房屋 fángwū 【名】houses；buildings

房子 fángzi 【名】〔间 jiān〕house；building

房租 fángzū 【名】(house) rent

fǎng

仿 fǎng 【动】imitate；copy；pattern after

仿佛 fǎngfú 【动】❶ seem；as if：我～在哪儿见过他。I seem to have seen him somewhere before. 听着《黄河大合唱》，我～又回到了当年的岁月。Listening to the Yellow River Cantata，I seem to be back in time. ❷ be more or less the same；be alike：样子相～ look alike 内容相

~。The contents are more or less the same.

仿古 fǎnggǔ 【动】model after an antique; follow the ancient style of

仿宋体 fǎngsòngtǐ 【名】an imitation of Song Dynasty block-printed characters, characterized by strokes of an even thickness, often used in modern printing

仿效 fǎngxiào 【动】imitate; copy; follow suit

仿造 fǎngzào 【动】make sth. from a model

仿照 fǎngzhào 【动】imitate; follow; copy: 我这件上衣是 ~ 他的那件做的。This jacket of mine is patterned after his.

仿制 fǎngzhì 【动】同"仿造"

访(訪) fǎng 【动】◇ ❶ visit; call on: ~友 visit a friend 人民来 ~ visit by a citizen to the authorities concerned (usu. to lodge a complaint) ❷ seek out; inquire after; try to obtain: 明察暗 ~ investigate both openly and secretly

访问 fǎngwèn 【动】❶ interview (by a newspaper reporter) ❷ visit (a place)

纺(紡) fǎng 【动】spin

纺织 fǎngzhī 【动】spin and weave; textile

纺织品 fǎngzhīpǐn 【名】textiles

fàng

放 fàng 【动】❶ let go; set free; release: 把鸽子 ~ 了 set the dove free 经过教育, 把俘虏 ~ 了 release P.O.W.s after re-education ❷ let oneself go: ~开胆子干吧! Go on! Don't be afraid to do it. ~开嗓子唱 sing as loud as you like ❸ let

out; let off: ~气 let out air (e.g. from a tyre) ❹ put (cattle, etc.) out to pasture; graze: ~牛 graze cattle ~羊 graze sheep ❺ send out; radiate: 永 ~ 光辉 shine forever ❻ shoot; let off: ~枪 shoot a rifle ~炮 fire a cannon ❼ set off; let off: ~鞭炮 let off firecrackers ❽ expand; make larger: ~了几张照片 enlarge some photographs 把袖子 ~ 长了一寸 lengthen the shirt sleeves by an inch ❾ ◇ bloom; open: 鲜花怒 ~。The flowers are in full bloom. ❿ leave alone; lay aside: 这件事不急, 先一一 ~ 再说。The matter is not urgent. Let's put it aside for the moment. ⓫ put; place: 把书 ~ 在桌子上。Put the book on the table. ⓬ add; put in: 菜里少 ~ 一点儿盐。Don't put too much salt in the dish you are cooking. 箱子里已经 ~ 满了东西。This suitcase is already full. ⓭ readjust (attitudes, behaviour, etc.) to a certain extent: 态度 ~ 谦虚些 be a little more modest ~慢速度 slow down a bit

放大 fàng // dà enlarge

放大镜 fàngdàjìng 【名】magnifying glass

放大炮 fàng dàpào (fig.) speak with a sharp tongue; brag: 他又在会上~了。He spoke sharply at the meeting again. 这个人言过其实, 就会吹牛皮~。This chap likes to exaggerate and is good at nothing but boasting.

放胆 fàng=dǎn act boldly and confidently

放荡 fàngdàng 【形】dissolute

放飞 fàngfēi 【动】release (a bird) to nature

放风 fàng=fēng let in fresh air; let prisoners out for exercise; spread word

放虎归山 fàng hǔ guī shān let the ti-

ger go back to the mountain；(*fig.*) release an enemy whom one has captured, and so breed calamity for the future 也作"纵虎归山"。

放还 fànghuán 【动】release

放火 fàng = huǒ commit arson；set fire to

放假 fàng = jià give sb. a holiday；begin a vacation；have a holiday

放空炮 fàng kōngpào talk big；brag：说到做到，不～。Live up to your commitments, and don't promise what you can't deliver.

放宽 fàngkuān 【动】relax (a rule, restriction, etc.)

放牧 fàngmù 【动】turn (cattle, etc.) out into the fields to graze

放弃 fàngqì 【动】abandon；give up；renounce (an opportunity, opinion, idea, etc.)；～个人意见 withdraw one's opinion ～休息时间 give up one's time for rest ～原则 forsake one's principles

放任 fàngrèn 【动】let go unchecked；not interfere with：对错误的行为，不能～不管。One should not let bad behaviour go unchecked.

放任自流 fàngrèn zìliú let things drift；take a laissez-faire attitude toward：对孩子要加强教育，不能～。One must be strict in bringing up children. They should not be left to follow their own path completely.

放哨 fàng = shào stand sentry

放射 fàngshè 【动】radiate：～光芒 send forth rays ～出万道金光 emit a thousand golden rays

放射线 fàngshèxiàn 【名】radioactive rays

放射性 fàngshèxìng 【名】radiation

放手 fàng = shǒu ❶ let go；release：他一～，鸽子就飞了。As soon as he released his hold, the dove flew away. ❷ have a free hand；go all out to：～去干 have a free hand in doing the work

放肆 fàngsì 【形】unbridled；take liberties with

放松 fàngsōng 【动】relax；slacken；loosen：～警惕 relax one's vigilance ～要求 slacken one's efforts

放下包袱 fàng xià bāofu cast off mental burdens

放心 fàng = xīn feel safe；set one's mind at rest；be at ease：放得下心 be able to set one's mind at rest 放不下心 be unable to set one's mind at rest 这件事交给他去办，我很～。With him in charge of this matter, I'm quite at ease.

放行 fàngxíng 【动】(customs-officer or sentry) let sb. pass

放学 fàng = xué off school (for lunch, for the day, etc.)；school has been dismissed

放映 fàngyìng 【动】show (a film)

放映机 fàngyìngjī 【名】〔架 jià、台 tái〕(film) projector

放债 fàng = zhài lend money for interest

放之四海而皆准 fàng zhī sì hǎi ér jiē zhǔn (of truth) universally applicable；valid everywhere

放逐 fàngzhú 【动】exile；banish

放纵 fàngzòng 【动】let sb. have his own way；give a free rein to

fēi

飞(飛) fēi 【动】❶ fly：大雁南～。The wild geese flew south. 每天有班机～广州。There is a scheduled flight to Guangzhou every day. ❷ hover of flutter in the air：～雪花了。Snowflakes danced in the air. ❸ swiftly：～跑 dash；run fast ❹ come unexpectedly：～来横祸。An unexpected disaster descended on him.

飞驰 fēichí 【动】(of vehicle or horse) move very fast

飞船 fēichuán 【名】spaceship

飞黄腾达 fēihuáng téngdá make a rapid advance in one's career; experience a meteoric rise

飞机 fēijī 【名】〔架 jià〕aeroplane

飞机场 fēijīchǎng 【名】airport

飞快 fēikuài 【形】❶ extremely sharp; razor-sharp: 这把刀子～。This knife is razor-sharp. ❷ very fast; at lightning speed: 摩托车～地从街上驶过。The motorcycle raced along the street at lightning speed.

飞轮 fēilún 【名】fly-wheel

飞速 fēisù 【副】at full speed: ～前进 advance at full speed 工农业～发展。Agriculture and industry are developing at great speed.

飞舞 fēiwǔ 【动】dance in the air; flutter: 雪花～。Snowflakes are dancing in the air. 柳絮在空中～。Willow catkins are fluttering in the air.

飞翔 fēixiáng 【动】circle in the air; hover

飞行 fēixíng 【动】(of aeroplane) fly

飞行器 fēixíngqì 【名】aircraft

飞行员 fēixíngyuán 【名】pilot; air-man

飞扬 fēiyáng 【动】fly upward; rise: 歌声～。The sound of singing rang out. 尘土～。Clouds of dust flew up.

飞扬跋扈 fēiyáng báhù arrogant and unruly

飞跃 fēiyuè 【动】❶ leap; by leaps and bounds: 形势～发展。The situation is developing rapidly. ❷ leap (e. g. from perceptual to rational knowledge)

非 fēi 【名】◇ wrong (as opp. to 是): 是～不辨 confuse right and wrong 【形】un-, non-, in-: ～正义战争 unjust war ～正式 informal ～金属 non-metal ～工作人员 non-staff member 【副】insist on: 他～要去，就让他去吧! He insists on going. Please let him go.

非…不… fēi...bù... means 如果不…就不…: 这批建筑材料非经批准不得动用。These building materials cannot be used without official approval. 非仔细校对几遍不能消灭差错。Errors cannot be eliminated without carefully reading the proofs several times.

非…不可 fēi...bùkě an emphatic expression ❶ indicates certainty or necessity: 天气又闷又热，一会儿非下雨不可。It is swelteringly hot. I'm sure it's going to rain soon. ❷ indicates resoluteness: 我们非把这个技术难关攻下来不可。We are determined to solve this difficult technical problem. Note: …不行 or …不成 can also be used instead of …不可

非…才… fēi...cái... means 一定要…才…: 他知道非天天练口语才能说流利的外语。He understands that he has to practise every day to speak a foreign language fluently. 这种害虫不一定非用 666 粉才能杀死，用别的农药也可以。666 is not the only insecticide which will kill these pests; other insecticides will do as well.

非常 fēicháng 【形】unusual; abnormal; extraordinary: ～时期 an extraordinary period ～事件 an unusual incident 【副】very; extraordinarily: 他跑得～快。He was running extremely fast. 他今天～不高兴，不知道为什么。He is very unhappy today. I wonder why.

非但 fēidàn 【连】同"不但" bùdàn (usu. in written language)

非得 fēiděi 【助动】must; have to;

insist on *can be used in conjunction with* 不可,不行,*etc*.;这个角色～你演(不行)。You, and only you, can play this role. 我不让他穿大衣,他～穿(不可)。I told him not to wear his overcoat, but he insisted on wearing it.

非法 fēifǎ 【形】illegal; unlawful;～活动 illegal activities ～占有 illegally occupy; illegally take possession of

非凡 fēifán 【形】outstanding; extraordinary; uncommon;～的成就 extraordinary achievement ～的才能 uncommon ability 市场上热闹～。The market is unusually busy.

非礼 fēilǐ 【动】not conform to etiquette

非驴非马 fēi lǘ fēi mǎ   neither fish, nor fowl

非卖品 fēimàipǐn 【名】not for sale

非难 fēinàn 【动】blame; censure; reproach (*usu. in the negative*):他的做法全然正确,无可～。He has acted quite correctly and in a manner above reproach.

非人待遇 fēi rén dàiyù   inhuman treatment

非同小可 fēi tóng xiǎo kě   no trivial matter used to describe the importance and seriousness of a matter or situation

非洲 Fēizhōu 【名】Africa

扉 fēi

扉页 fēiyè 【名】(of a book) flyleaf

féi

肥 féi 【形】❶ fat; loose; wide; large (*as opp. to* 瘦 *usu. not used of human beings*):～肉 fat meat ～鸭 fat duck 裤腿太～了。The trousers are too wide in the leg. ❷ fertile; rich:这块地真～。This piece of land is very fertile. 【名】fertilizer; manure:追～ additional applications of manure 运～ transport fertilizer 菜地还缺～。The vegetable field lacks fertilizer.

肥料 féiliào 【名】fertilizer

肥瘦 féishòu 【名】(of clothes) girth:这件衣服你穿着～正合适。The size of this coat is just right for you.

肥沃 féiwò 【形】fertile; rich

肥皂 féizào 【名】〔块 kuài〕soap

肥壮 féizhuàng 【形】(cattle, etc.) strong and fat

fěi

匪 fěi 【名】bandit

匪帮 fěibāng 【名】bandit gang

匪巢 fěicháo 【名】bandits' hide-out

匪徒 fěitú 【名】bandit

诽(誹) fěi

诽谤 fěibàng 【动】vilify; slander

fèi

废(廢) fèi 【形】waste; useless; disused:～纸 waste paper ～钢铁 scrap iron and steel 【动】waste:你去看球赛吧,不然票就要～了。You'd better go to the ball game; otherwise the ticket will be wasted.

废除 fèichú 【动】(of law, treaty, rule, etc.) abrogate; abolish:～不平等条约 abrogate unequal treaties ～不合理的规章制度 do away with unreasonable rules and regulations

废黜 fèichù 【动】dethrone; depose

废话 fèihuà 【名】remarks which are too obvious to need saying

废料 fèiliào 【名】waste material (in the process of production)

废品 fèipǐn 【名】❶ reject ❷ scrap

废气 fèiqì 【名】waste gas or steam

废弃 fèiqì 【动】cast aside; abandon; neglect; scrap

废寝忘食 fèi qǐn wàng shí (be so absorbed and occupied as to) forget to eat and sleep 也作"废寝忘餐"。

废水 fèishuǐ 【名】waste water

废物 fèiwù 【名】waste material; trash; ~利用 make use of waste materials

废物 fèiwu 【形】good-for-nothing; 真~,连这点儿事都不会干。What a good-for-nothing you are! You cannot even take care of such a trivial matter!

废墟 fèixū 【名】ruins

废止 fèizhǐ 【动】abolish; annul; rescind; revoke (a law, regulation, etc.)

沸 fèi

沸点 fèidiǎn 【名】boiling point

沸腾 fèiténg 【动】❶ (of liquid) boil ❷ (fig.) seethe with excitement; 热血~ one's blood boils ~的工地 a bustling work-site

肺 fèi 【名】lung

肺病 fèibìng 【名】tuberculosis; TB

肺腑 fèifǔ 【名】(fig.) heart; deepest part of one's nature; 感人~ tear at one's heart strings ~之言 words spoken from the bottom of one's heart

肺结核 fèijiéhé 【名】同"肺病"

肺炎 fèiyán 【名】pneumonia

费（費） fèi 【动】cost; spend; expend; consume too much; expend too quickly; ~时间 time-consuming 不~力气 without much effort 这种汽车既跑得快,又不~油。This make of car is fast and doesn't consume much oil. 【名】fee; charge; dues; expenses; 办公~ administrative expenses 【形】(use or spend) too much; too many; 电用得太~了。Too much electricity was used.

费工 fèi=gōng take a lot of work; labour-demanding; demanding on time

费话 fèi=huà nonsense

费解 fèijiě 【形】hard to understand; abstruse; 这首古诗的文字很艰深,十分~。The language of this classical poem is abstruse and hard to understand.

费尽心机 fèi jìn xīnjī rack one's brains (in scheming and plotting, often derog.)

费力 fèi=lì require or use great effort; be strenuous; 他的腿才治好,走路还有一点儿~。It is not long since his leg healed, and he still walks with difficulty. 那位老工人一点儿也不~就把机器的故障排除了。It did not take much effort on the part of that veteran worker to fix the machine.

费钱 fèi=qián cost a lot; be costly

费事 fèi=shì take a lot of effort; give a lot of trouble; troublesome; 别看小小的一个景泰蓝花瓶,制作起来很~呢！It's only a small cloisonné vase, but it took a lot of work to make. 把记录稿整理一下,费不了多少事。It won't take much work to straighten out the minutes of the meeting.

费心 fèi=xīn take the trouble; 这篇发言稿请你~帮我润色一下。Would you be so kind as to touch up the draft of my speech? 为了帮助我们搞好工厂实习,老师们费了不少心。The teachers have put a lot of effort into helping us do our practical course in the factory.

费用 fèiyòng 【名】〔笔 bǐ〕expenses; expenditure

fēn

分　fēn　【动】❶ divide；separate；part；一年级共～五个班。The first grade is divided into five classes. 这个数学定理～两点来讲。This mathematical law is to be explained in two steps. ❷ distribute；allot；assign：～口粮 distribute food grain（provisions, rations）老王～到了一套新房子。Lao Wang was assigned a new flat. 小张～到化工厂工作。Xiao Zhang has been assigned to work in a chemical plant. ❸ tell one from another；differentiate；distinguish：～清是非 distinguish right from wrong 不～青红皂白 make no distinction between black and white（right and wrong）❹（of an organization）branch：铁路～局 railway ministry branch office 中国人民银行北京～行（háng）Beijing branch of the Chinese People's Bank 第四～册 Book Four 【名】（～儿）point；mark：这场球赛双方只差几～。The scores of the two teams in the match were within a few points of each other. 【量】❶ Chinese measure of length, weight and area；equivalent to 1/100 chi, 1/100 jin and 1/10 mu respectively ❷ unit of Chinese currency 1/100 of a yuan ❸ minute；1/60 of an hour：五十～钟一节课。A class lasts fifty minutes. ❹ interest-rate

另见 fèn

分贝　fēnbèi　decibel

分崩离析　fēn bēng lí xī（of a state or clique）disintegrate；fall to pieces

分辨　fēnbiàn　【动】tell one from another；distinguish；differentiate；～字迹 identify sb.'s handwriting

分辩　fēnbiàn　【动】defend oneself（against a charge）；offer an explanation：～清楚 offer a clear explanation 不要再～了,有错误就承认嘛！Don't try to explain away the situation. If you have made mistakes, just admit them.

分别　fēnbié　【动】❶ part；be separated from each other：～了十多年的老朋友,又碰到一起了。After a separation of more than ten years, the old friends met again. ❷ distinguish；differentiate：～好坏 tell good from bad ～轻重缓急 in order of relative importance and urgency 【副】❶ differently：～对待 treat differently ❷ respectively；separately：～执行各项任务 separate and perform different tasks

分布　fēnbù　【动】distribute；spread；scatter

分餐　fēncān　【动】eat one's own portion；eat separately

分寸　fēncùn　【名】proper limits for speech or action；sense of propriety：掌握～ observe the proprieties 在辩论当中,他的原则性很强,而说话又很有～。He stuck to his principled position, but was also careful in his choice of words.

分担　fēndān　【动】share（responsibility or sorrow, etc.）：～责任 share the responsibility ～任务 share a task

分道扬镳　fēn dào yáng biāo　separate and go different ways；part company, each going his own way

分封制　fēnfēngzhì　【名】feudal system of land-holding

分割　fēngē　【动】cut；sever：台湾是中国领土不可～的一部分。Taiwan is an inalienable part of Chinese territory.

分隔　fēngé　【动】separate；part：剧毒农药和其他农药要严格～开。Highly poisonous insecticides

should be kept strictly separate from ordinary insecticides.

分工 fēn=gōng division of labour

分号 fēnhào 【名】semicolon

分化 fēnhuà 【动】❶ become divided；split up：两极～ polarization 那个班的同学后来逐渐～，有的喜欢文学，有的迷上数学，还有的要当运动员。A division was gradually apparent among the students of the class，some loved literature，others took to maths，and still others wanted to be in sports. ❷ cause to split up：～瓦解敌人 cause splits among the enemy and bring on its collapse

分机 fēnjī 【名】extension

分解 fēnjiě 【动】❶ resolve；decompose；break down into elements or constituents：力的～（phys.）resolution of forces 水可以～为氧和氢。Water can be resolved into oxygen and hydrogen. ❷ be explained；be disclosed（*used in classical serial novels*）：且听下回～。As to what happened thereafter，that will be disclosed in the next chapter.

分界 fēn=jiè be demarcated by；have as a boundary

分界线 fēnjièxiàn 【名】demarcation line

分句 fēnjù 【名】clause

分开 fēn//kāi ❶ separate；part：在中国的几年里，我俩从来没有～过。During our years in China，the two of us were never separated. 这座水电站的提前建成是与群众的努力分不开的。The completion of the hydro-electric power-station ahead of schedule would have been impossible but for the hard work of the masses. ❷ cause to separate；separate：把英文报和法文报～。The English papers and the French papers must be separated.

分类 fēn=lèi classify

分离 fēnlí 【动】❶ separate；resolve：理论与实践不可～。Theory shouldn't be separated from practice. ❷ part；separate：我见到了～多年的战友。I met an old army comrade from whom I had been parted for many years.

分裂 fēnliè 【动】❶（of a thing）split；divide；splinter：细胞～ cell division；cell fission 内部～ internal split；dissension ❷ cause to split；create division

分门别类 fēn mén bié lèi classify into different categories：阅览室里的图书～陈列得整整齐齐。The books in the reading-room are classified into different categories and arranged in order.

分泌 fēnmì 【动】secrete

分娩 fēnmiǎn 【动】give birth to a child

分秒必争 fēn miǎo bì zhēng seize every minute and second；every second counts；not a second is to be lost：目前正是插秧季节，村民们都在～，日夜奋战。It is the season when rice seedlings are transplanted. The villagers aren't losing a minute，but working day and night.

分明 fēnmíng 【形】clearly demarcated；distinct：黑白～ as distinct as black from white 界线～ clear demarcation 【副】同"明明"míngmíng：～是他错了，你为什么怪我？It's obvious that he is wrong. Why should you blame me? 我～看见他进来了，怎么现在又找不到他了？I'm certain that I saw him come in，but I can't find him now!

分母 fēnmǔ 【名】（maths.）denominator of a fraction

分蘖 fēnniè （agr.）tillering

分配 fēnpèi 【动】❶ distribute；allot：～粮食 distribute grain ～任务 allot tasks ❷ assign：服从组织～ accept the work that is assigned

分批　fēn＝pī　in groups；in batches

分期　fēn＝qī　❶at designated intervals；by stages；～付款 pay in installments；hire purchase ❷ divide into different periods；历史～ the division of history into historical periods

分歧　fēnqí　【名】dispute；difference；divergence；原则上的～ difference on matters of principle 大家对这个问题的看法还存在～。People are still divided over this question.【形】different；divergent；意见很～ sharp divergence of views；sharp difference of opinion

分散　fēnsàn　【动】disperse；scatter；decentralize；～精力 disperse one's energies ～注意力 distract one's attention【形】scattered；dispersed；把～的人力集中起来 concentrate scattered personnel 兵力很～。The forces are very much dispersed.

分数　fēnshù　【名】❶ fraction ❷ marks in a test or examination

分水岭　fēnshuǐlǐng　【名】❶ watershed ❷ demarcation line

分摊　fēntān　【动】share

分庭抗礼　fēn tíng kàng lǐ　stand up to sb. as an equal；act independently and defiantly

分析　fēnxī　【动】analyse；～问题 analyse a problem【名】analysis；这种～很有说服力。That analysis is very convincing.

分享　fēnxiǎng　【动】share（joy, rights, etc.）；～劳动果实 share the fruits of one's labour ～胜利的欢乐 share the joy of victory

分心　fēn＝xīn　divert one's attention；干活儿时要精力集中，不要～。When working, one should concentrate and not allow oneself to be distracted.

分忧　fēn＝yōu　share sb.'s care and burdens

分赃　fēn＝zāng　share the spoils

…分之…　… fēn zhī …　*the way a fraction is read*，*e.g.* 2/3：三～二，4/5：五～四，75/100：百～七十五

分子　fēnzǐ　【名】❶（maths.）numerator of a fraction ❷（chem.）molecule

另见 fènzǐ

芬　fēn

芬芳　fēnfāng　【形】fragrant

吩　fēn

吩咐　fēnfù　【动】（of a superior to an inferior）instruct or give orders

纷（紛）　fēn

纷繁　fēnfán　【形】numerous and complicated；～的事务 complicated daily routine 头绪～ have too many things to take care of；too many loose ends

纷飞　fēnfēi　【动】flutter about；大雪～。The snow is falling thick and fast. 战火～。The war is raging.

纷纷　fēnfēn　【形】❶ numerous and confused；你一言，我一语，议论～。One spoke after another, in heated discussion. ❷ unceasingly；continuously；in batches or groups；领导人～深入生产第一线。Many leaders are going down to grassroots to take part in production. 工人们～表示要鼓起更大干劲，创造新的生产纪录。The workers all pledged that they would work harder to achieve a new production record.

纷乱　fēnluàn　【形】numerous and disorderly；helter-skelter；～的脚步声 a clatter of footsteps 心绪～ disturbed state of mind

fén

坟（墳）　fén　【名】〔座 zuò〕grave

坟墓　fénmù　【名】〔座 zuò〕grave; tomb

焚　fén　【动】〈书〉burn

焚毁　fénhuǐ　【动】destroy by fire; burn down

焚烧　fénshāo　【动】burn

fěn

粉　fěn　【名】❶ powder: 药～ medicine in the form of a powder 花～ the pollen of flowers ❷ face-powder: 扑点儿～ powder one's face 香～ face-powder 【形】pink: ～色 pink colour ～纸 pink paper

粉笔　fěnbǐ　【名】〔根儿 gēnr〕chalk

粉红　fěnhóng　【形】pink; rosy

粉末　fěnmò　【名】powder

粉墨登场　fěn mò dēng chǎng　(of actors) make oneself up and go on stage; (fig.) pose as a big shot and enter upon the political scene

粉身碎骨　fěn shēn suì gǔ　utterly crushed; ground to dust

粉饰　fěnshì　【动】gloss over; cover up (faults); white-wash: ～太平 present a false picture of peace

粉刷　fěnshuā　【动】white-wash

粉丝　fěnsī　【名】vermicelli made of starch extracted from peas

粉碎　fěnsuì　【动】smash; shatter; crush: 阴谋被～了。The conspiracy was smashed. 【形】break into pieces: 碗摔得～。The bowl fell and broke into pieces.

粉条　fěntiáo　【名】noodles made of starch extracted from soy beans

fèn

分　fèn
另见 fēn

分量　fènliang　【名】weight: 这口袋米 ～可不轻。This bag of rice is quite heavy. 他的话很有～。His words carried great weight.

分内　fènnèi　【名】duty-bound; one's duty: 这是你～的事，为什么不管? It is within your duty, why don't you do it?

分外　fènwài　【名】above and beyond one's duty; additional; extra: 他对 ～的工作也总是抢着干。He was always willing to do extra work. 【副】extremely; extraordinarily; especially: ～有趣 extremely amusing 雨后初晴的天空～明朗。The sky was extraordinarily clear after the rain.

分子　fènzǐ　【名】person of a specific class or with a particular characteristic: 先进～ advanced element
另见 fēnzǐ

份　fèn　【名】(～儿) share; portion: 这次旅行有你们的～。You are all included in this trip. 【量】❶ for things where more than one is referred to: 一～礼物 a collection of gifts 一～饭菜 a serving of food ❷ for papers, etc.: 订一～报 subscribe to a paper

奋(奮)　fèn

奋不顾身　fèn bù gù shēn　dash ahead regardless of one's own safety

奋斗　fèndòu　【动】struggle; fight hard; strive: 艰苦～ work hard and with perseverance; struggle arduously

奋发　fènfā　【动】exert oneself; be spurred on by a high aim

奋发图强　fènfā tú qiáng　work with stamina for the prosperity of the country 也作"发愤图强"。

奋起　fènqǐ　【动】make a vigorous start; rise up with ardour: ～直追 do all one can to catch up ～反抗 rise up in resistance

奋勇　fènyǒng　【副】 summoning one's courage：～杀敌 fight the enemy bravely ～向前 forge ahead bravely

奋勇当先　fènyǒng dāngxiān　muster one's courage and fight in the vanguard：在灭火过程中，解放军战士个个～，抢救人民的生命财产。Every P.L.A. man vied to be the first in saving lives and property from the fire.

奋战　fènzhàn　【动】fight bravely：英勇～ fight bravely ～在炼钢炉旁（steel workers）work hard at the furnaces

愤（憤）　fèn

愤愤　fènfèn　【形】indignant：～不平 be indignant

愤恨　fènhèn　【形】resentful

愤慨　fènkǎi　【形】indignant

愤懑　fènmèn　【形】〈书〉frustrated and depressed

愤怒　fènnù　【形】indignant；angry；wrathful：～声讨 denounce angrily 老太太～地控诉了旧时代的性别歧视。The old lady made an angry denunciation of the gender discrimination of the past.

粪（糞）　fèn　【名】manure；dung；night-soil

粪便　fènbiàn　【名】excrement

粪肥　fènféi　【名】manure

粪土　fèntǔ　【名】dung and dirt；sth. worthless：把功名利禄视如～ consider fame and gain to be utterly without value

fēng

丰（豐）　fēng

丰产　fēngchǎn　【动】high yield

丰产田　fēngchǎntián　【名】high-yield land

丰富　fēngfù　【形】rich；abundant；plentiful：～的知识 rich knowledge 资源～ rich in natural resources 【动】enrich：～文娱生活 provide enriched cultural and recreational activities ～工作经验 enrich one's work experience

丰功伟绩　fēng gōng wěi jì　great contributions and heroic deeds；magnificent contribution

丰满　fēngmǎn　【形】❶ plentiful；full：～的人物形象 well-rounded portrayal of characters 羽毛～ full plumage ❷ full and round；well-developed；plump

丰年　fēngnián　【名】year of good harvest

丰盛　fēngshèng　【形】(of material things) ample and of good quality

丰收　fēngshōu　【动】have a bumper harvest：苹果～了。We've had a good harvest of apples. 【名】bumper harvest：今年的土豆获得了特大～。There was a bumper harvest of potatoes this year.

丰硕　fēngshuò　【形】plentiful and big：～的果实 abundant and excellent results ～的成果 great successes

丰衣足食　fēng yī zú shí　have plenty of food and clothing；amply fed and clothed：自己动手，～。Let's produce ample food and clothing with our own hands.

风（風）　fēng　【名】〔阵 zhèn〕

❶ wind ❷ ◇ style；practice；custom：纠正不正之～ correct unhealthy tendencies 此～不可长（zhǎng）。Such trends must not be encouraged. ❸ ◇（～儿）news；information：千万别走了～。Don't let the cat out of the bag. ❹ term for certain diseases in Chinese traditional medicine：中～ stroke

风暴　fēngbào　【名】windstorm；tempest (*usu. used figuratively*)

风波 fēngbō 【名】〔场 chǎng〕a storm in a teacup

风餐露宿 fēng cān lù sù eat in the wind and sleep in the open；(fig.) endure the hardships of working and sleeping in the open

风潮 fēngcháo 【名】demonstration and agitation for a political end

风车 fēngchē 【名】wind-mill

风尘 fēngchén 【名】hardships of a journey：满面～ look travel-stained

风尘仆仆 fēngchén púpú travel-stained；travel-weary

风驰电掣 fēng chí diàn chè swift as wind and quick as lightning：列车～般向前飞奔。The train rushed on at lightning speed.

风吹草动 fēng chuī cǎo dòng a rustle of leaves in the wind；(fig.) a sign of disturbance or trouble

风度 fēngdù 【名】good manners and an elegant carriage

风格 fēnggé 【名】❶ (of a person) style：～高 honourable style 发扬实事求是的～。Develop a down-to-earth work-style. ❷ (of an artistic school or school of thought) style：每个画家的作品都有自己的～。The work of each painter has a style of its own.

风光 fēngguāng 【名】scenery (with stress on local colour)

风化 fēnghuà 【动】❶ (geol.) weather；wear away ❷ (chem.) efflorescence

风化 fēnghuà 【名】morals and manners

风景 fēngjǐng 【名】scenery

风镜 fēngjìng 【名】goggles

风浪 fēnglàng 【名】❶ wind and waves：海上～很大。The sea is rough. ❷ hardship；difficulties

风雷 fēngléi 【名】strong wind and thunder；(fig.) violent forces

风力 fēnglì 【名】wind-intensity

风凉话 fēngliánghuà 【名】irresponsible and sarcastic remark

风流 fēngliú 【形】❶〈书〉soldierly and accomplished ❷ flirtatious

风马牛不相及 fēng mǎ niú bù xiāng jí have absolutely nothing to do with each other；totally unrelated；mixing oranges and apples

风貌 fēngmào 【名】(of a district, art form, etc.) characteristic features

风靡一时 fēngmǐ yīshí be fashionable for a time (sometimes derog.)

风平浪静 fēng píng làng jìng the wind has subsided and the waves have calmed down；calm and tranquil

风起云涌 fēng qǐ yún yǒng the wind is rising and clouds are gathering；(fig.) a lot of big events take place one after another：民族解放斗争～。Struggles for national liberation are surging forward.

风气 fēngqì 【名】〔种 zhǒng〕common practice；fashion：社会～ common practice in a society 我们要养成勤俭节约的好～。We should cultivate the good habits of diligence and frugality.

风趣 fēngqù 【名】humour；wit：说话很有～ talk wittily 【形】witty；humorous：这个人很～。He is witty and humorous.

风沙 fēngshā 【名】sand blown by the wind

风扇 fēngshàn 【名】〔台 tái〕fan

风尚 fēngshàng 【名】(of behaviour, thought, dress) fashion；trend

风声鹤唳 fēng shēng hè lì be frightened by the sound of the wind and the cry of cranes；(fig.) an extremely nervous state in which one is alarmed by the slightest sound

风霜 fēngshuāng 【名】wind and frost；(fig.) hardships met on a journey or in one's life

风俗 fēngsú 【名】〔种 zhǒng〕social

customs

风调雨顺 fēng tiáo yǔ shùn favourable weather (for agriculture)

风头 fēngtou 【名】❶ trend of events; tendency of a movement ❷ publicity seeking: 他真是～十足。He's really in the limelight!

风土人情 fēngtǔ rénqíng specific customs and practices of a certain place

风味 fēngwèi 【名】(of food, music, etc.) (local) flavour; characteristic of a particular place

风险 fēngxiǎn 【名】〔场 chǎng〕risk; (possible) danger

风向 fēngxiàng 【名】wind direction

风言风语 fēng yán fēng yǔ groundless remark intended to slander; (unfounded) gossip

风雨 fēngyǔ 【名】〔场 chǎng〕wind and rain; storm and stress

风雨飘摇 fēngyǔ piāoyáo buffeted about in the midst of a raging storm; (fig.) precarious; unstable; tottering: 处于～之中 find oneself buffeted about in the midst of a raging storm

风雨同舟 fēng yǔ tóng zhōu stand together through thick and thin: 我们是～的战友。We are old comrades who have stood together through thick and thin.

风雨无阻 fēng yǔ wú zǔ rain or shine

风雨衣 fēngyǔyī 【名】〔件 jiàn〕a rainproof windbreaker

风云 fēngyún 【名】wind and cloud; (fig.) stormy or unstable political situation: ～突变 a sudden change in the political situation 战争～ winds of war

风云人物 fēngyún rénwù man of the hour

风灾 fēngzāi 【名】〔场 chǎng〕disaster caused by typhoon

风筝 fēngzheng 【名】〔只 zhī〕kite

枫（楓）fēng 【名】◇ maple

枫树 fēngshù 【名】〔棵 kē〕maple tree

封 fēng 【动】seal; close: 把信～好 seal the letter 腿上的伤还没～口。His leg wound has not healed yet. 大雪～山。The heavy snow has sealed the mountain passes. 【量】一～信 a letter

封闭 fēngbì 【动】❶ seal up; close up: ～瓶口 seal a bottle ❷ forcibly close (e.g. a newspaper office); order to close down

封存 fēngcún 【动】seal up for storage or safekeeping

封底 fēngdǐ 【名】back cover (of a book)

封顶 fēngdǐng 【动】set the upper limit; impose a ceiling; cease growing any taller; top out

封官许愿 fēng guān xǔ yuàn offer official posts and make lavish promises; promise high posts and other favours (out of ulterior motives)

封面 fēngmiàn 【名】front cover (of a book)

封山育林 fēng shān yù lín prohibit entry to forested hills to prevent the cutting of trees

封锁 fēngsuǒ 【动】blockade; seal off: ～交通要道 seal off the roads ～消息 news blackout 经济～ economic blockade

封锁线 fēngsuǒxiàn 【名】blockade-line

封条 fēngtiáo 【名】strip of paper stuck across a door, cupboard, etc. as a seal to prevent entry or removal of objects

疯（瘋）fēng 【形】insane; mad

疯疯癫癫 fēngfēngdiāndiān 【形】be-

have in a crazy manner

疯狂　fēngkuáng　【形】crazy；wild；frantic

疯子　fēngzi　【名】madman；lunatic

峰　fēng　【名】◇ peak【量】*for camels*

烽　fēng

烽火　fēnghuǒ　【名】beacon-fire used as border-alarm in ancient China；(*fig*.) flames of war

烽火连天　fēnghuǒ lián tiān　the flames of battle rage everywhere；～的战争年代 years of raging war

锋（鋒）　fēng

锋利　fēnglì　【形】(of knives，etc.) sharp

锋芒　fēngmáng　【名】❶ tip of a sword (*usu．fig*.)：批判的～是指向官僚主义的。The sharp edge of criticism is pointed at bureaucratism. ❷ dynamism and abilities displayed by sb.：初露～ display one's energy and abilities for the first time

锋芒毕露　fēngmáng bì lù　prone to show off one's own abilities (sometimes at the expense of others)

锋芒所向　fēngmáng suǒ xiàng　direct the spearhead against；the target of attack

蜂　fēng　【名】〔只 zhī〕bee

蜂蜜　fēngmì　【名】honey

蜂拥　fēngyōng　【动】(of a crowd of people) gather；collect；～ 而上 swarm forward ～ 而来 come swarming

féng

逢　féng　【动】◇ chance upon；

meet；come across；～年过节 on festival days and at the New Year ～山开路，遇水搭桥 break a trail when passing over a mountain and construct a bridge to cross a river

缝（縫）　féng　【动】sew

另见 fèng

缝补　féngbǔ　【动】mend；patch

缝纫　féngrèn　【动】do dress-making，tailoring，etc.

缝纫机　féngrènjī　【名】〔架 jià〕sewing machine

fěng

讽（諷）　fěng

讽刺　fěngcì　【动】satirize【名】sarcasm

fèng

凤（鳳）　fèng　【名】phoenix

凤凰　fènghuáng　【名】同"凤"

奉　fèng　【动】◇ ❶ respectfully present or receive：～ 上级命令 in accordance with instructions from higher authorities ❷ revere；esteem (*usu．ironical*)：～为至宝 revere as a priceless treasure

奉承　fèngcheng　【动】flatter；fawn upon

奉告　fènggào　【动】have the honour to inform

奉公守法　fèng gōng shǒu fǎ　law-abiding

奉令　fèng = lìng　act upon orders

奉命　fèng = mìng　follow orders or instructions；be under orders

奉陪　fèngpéi　【动】(courteous way of volunteering to) keep sb. company

奉劝　fèngquàn　【动】give a piece of

advice

奉若神明 fèng ruò shénmíng revere as sacred；treat with great reverence

奉送 fèngsòng 【动】allow me to present (a gift)

奉献 fèngxiàn 【动】offer as a tribute

奉行 fèngxíng 【动】pursue (a policy, etc.)；～各国一律平等的国际准则 to abide by the international norm that all countries are equal

缝（縫） fèng 【名】❶ seam ❷ crack；slit
另见 féng

缝儿 fèngr 【名】〔条 tiáo〕同"缝" fèng

缝隙 fèngxì 【名】slit；crack

fó

佛 fó 【名】❶ Buddha ❷ Buddhism ❸ statue of the Buddha

佛教 Fójiào 【名】Buddhism

fǒu

否 fǒu 【动】❶ deny；negate；这个意见被～了。The proposal was turned down. ❷〈书〉no *equal to* 不 *in colloquial speech* ❸ 是否，能否，可否，*etc. are equivalent to* 是不是，能不能，可以不可以，*etc.*：能～按时起飞? Can we take off on time or not? 是～派他去? Shall we send him or not?

否定 fǒudìng 【动】negate

否决 fǒujué 【动】vote against；veto

否决权 fǒujuéquán 【名】veto

否认 fǒurèn 【动】deny

否则 fǒuzé 【连】otherwise (*usu. in written language*)：这个零件得赶快配上，～这台机器用起来容易出危险。We must replace this missing part,

otherwise there may be safety problems when the machine is operating.

fū

夫 fū 【名】◇ ❶ husband ❷ man

夫妇 fūfù 【名】husband and wife

夫妻 fūqī 【名】同"夫妇"

夫人 fūrén 【名】❶ wife ❷ Madame (*form of address*)

肤（膚） fū

肤浅 fūqiǎn 【形】superficial；shallow：对问题的理解很～ have a superficial understanding of the problem 我来谈一下自己的～认识。Let me share with you my own limited understanding (of sth.).

肤色 fūsè 【名】❶ complexion ❷ skin-colour (e. g. black, white, yellow, etc.)

敷 fū 【动】apply (powder ointment, etc.)

敷衍 fūyǎn 【动】be perfunctory；do sth. or deal with others in a perfunctory or insincere manner；be half-hearted：～了事 perform a task perfunctorily ～塞责 go through the motions

fú

伏 fú 【动】〈书〉❶ bend over：～案 bend over the desk ❷ subside；go down：波浪一起一～。The waves rise and subside. ❸ hide：～兵 troops in ambush 昼～夜出 hide during the day and come out at night ❹ submit；admit (defeat or guilt)：～罪 plead guilty；admit one's guilt 【名】"dog days"；初～ first ten days of the hot season 中

~ middle ten days of the hot season 末~ last ten days of the hot season 入~已三天了。 It's three days already since the hot season began.

伏击 fújī 【动】ambush 【名】ambush

伏特 fútè 【量】volt

伏天 fútiān 【名】the hottest days of the year — the first, second and third ten day periods after the summer solstice

扶 fú 【动】❶ support with the hand；~着栏杆 with one's hand on the banister 民警~着盲人过马路。 Holding the blind man by the arm, the policeman helped him across the street. ❷ help sb. up； straighten sth. up；~起病人 prop up a patient 把苗~起来 straighten up seedlings

扶持 fúchí 【动】support；help

扶老携幼 fú lǎo xié yòu helping old people and holding children by the hand

扶贫 fú=pín alleviate poverty

扶手 fúshǒu 【名】❶ hand-rail ❷ arm-rest

扶植 fúzhí 【动】support and foster （new emerging forces, etc.）

扶助 fúzhù 【动】help；aid；assist

拂 fú

拂晓 fúxiǎo 【名】dawn

服 fú 【动】❶ take（medicine）； ~药 take medicine ❷ serve；~兵役 serve in the army ❸ be convinced； 心里不~ remain unconvinced in one's heart ❹ ◇ be accustomed to；水土不~ not acclimatized

服从 fúcóng 【动】obey；be subordinate to

服毒 fú=dú take poison

服服帖帖 fúfutiētiē 【形】submissive； resigned；docile and obedient；马

戏团的猴子训练得~的。 Circus monkeys are trained to respond to orders.

服气 fúqì 【动】be convinced；摆事实、讲道理，才能让人~。 Only by presenting facts and reasoning things out can we convince people.

服务 fúwù 【动】serve；render service to

服务行业 fúwù hángyè service trades

服务台 fúwùtái 【名】service desk

服务员 fúwùyuán 【名】service personnel；attendant

服务站 fúwùzhàn 【名】（neighbourhood）centre providing services for residents

服役 fú=yì serve（in army, etc.）

服装 fúzhuāng 【名】costume；garments；dress

服罪 fú=zuì plead guilty

俘 fú 【动】◇ capture

俘获 fúhuò 【动】capture

俘虏 fúlǔ 【动】capture；take sb. prisoner；~了许多敌人 capture a large number of enemy troops 【名】prisoner of war（P. O. W.）；captive；抓了几个~ capture some enemy soldiers as prisoners of war ~政策 prisoner-of-war policy

浮 fú 【动】float；浮萍~在湖面上。 Duck-weed was floating on the lake. 蓝蓝的天空~着几朵白云。 A few white clouds were floating in the blue sky.

浮雕 fúdiāo 【名】bas-relief；relief

浮动 fúdòng 【动】❶ float；drift；冰块在水面上~。 Chunks of ice floated on the water. ❷ be unsteady； fluctuate；汇率~ floating exchange rate 人心~。 The people have a feeling of insecurity.

浮光掠影 fú guāng lüè yǐng skim-

ming over the surface; (fig.) in a hasty and casual manner; cursory; superficial

浮华　fúhuá　【形】showy; flashy

浮夸　fúkuā　【动】exaggerate; boast; 言语～ use boastful words 实事求是,反对～ be practical and realistic, and oppose exaggeration

浮力　fúlì　【名】buoyancy

浮浅　fúqiǎn　【形】同"肤浅" fūqiǎn

浮现　fúxiàn　【动】reappear (in one's mind's eye)

浮云　fúyún　【名】floating clouds

浮躁　fúzào　【形】impetuous

浮肿　fúzhǒng　【动】(med.) oedema; dropsy

符　fú　【动】◇ tally with; accord with; 与事实不～ not tally with the facts

符号　fúhào　【名】mark; sign

符合　fúhé　【动】accord with; tally with; conform to; ～实际 conform to reality ～条件 meet the requirements 这两个数据应该相～。 The two figures should tally.

幅　fú　【量】*for things in long strips, esp. paintings, cloth*; 三～国画 three Chinese paintings 用两～布缝个窗帘儿 sew a curtain using two lengths of cloth 墙上挂着一～地图。 There was a map hanging on the wall.

幅度　fúdù　【名】length of the arc through which sth. swings (e.g. a pendulum)

幅员　fúyuán　【名】size, area of territory

辐（輻）　fú

辐射　fúshè　【动】radiate

福　fú　【名】happiness; good luck; prosperity

福利　fúlì　【名】welfare; well-being

福气　fúqi　【名】good luck blessings

fǔ

抚（撫）　fǔ

抚摩　fǔmó　【动】stroke; fondle

抚恤　fǔxù　【动】(used of an organization or government) condole with and render material assistance to a person injured or disabled in work or the family of a person who has died or been killed while working

抚养　fǔyǎng　【动】bring up

抚育　fǔyù　【动】❶ 同"抚养" ❷ protect (a forest)

斧　fǔ　【名】axe

斧正　fǔzhèng　【动】(please) make corrections

斧子　fǔzi　【名】〔把 bǎ〕axe

俯　fǔ　【动】◇ bend; lower

俯冲　fǔchōng　【动】(aeroplane) dive

俯拾即是　fǔ shí jí shì　can be found everywhere; easily obtainable; be extremely common; 预防脑炎的草药在这一地区～。 Herbs for the prevention of encephalitis can be found everywhere in this area. 用"吧"的句子在口语中几乎是～。 In speech "ba" is extensively used. 也作"俯拾皆是"。

俯首贴耳　fǔ shǒu tiē ěr　be submissive; be docile and obedient; be servile; ～,唯命是从的奴才 a servile and obedient flunkey

釜　fǔ

釜底抽薪　fǔ dǐ chōu xīn　take away the firewood from under the cauldron; (fig.) take drastic measures to strike at the source of a problem

辅(輔) fǔ

辅导 fǔdǎo 【动】tutor；coach 【名】coaching；tutorial

辅导员 fǔdǎoyuán 【名】instructor

辅音 fǔyīn 【名】consonant

辅助 fǔzhù 【动】assist：这项任务由他 ~你去完成。He will assist you to complete the task.

腐 fǔ

腐败 fǔbài 【形】❶ go bad；rot：~ 的食物 rotten food ❷ corrupt；rotten

腐化 fǔhuà 【形】corrupt；depraved：生活 ~ lead a dissolute life 【动】corrupt；deprave

腐烂 fǔlàn 【动】❶ become putrid；decompose；rot ❷ corrupt；depraved：生活~透顶 a life rotten to the core

腐蚀 fǔshí 【动】❶ corrode ❷ deprave；corrupt：拒 ~，永不沾 immune to corruption

腐朽 fǔxiǔ 【形】❶ rotten；decayed：~ 的木头 rotten timber ❷ decadent；degenerate：~ 的生活方式 decadent life-style

fù

讣(訃) fù

讣电 fùdiàn 【名】telegraphed obituary notice

讣告 fùgào 【名】obituary notice

父 fù 【名】◇ father：~子 father and son ~女 father and daughter

父母 fù mǔ father and mother；parents

父亲 fùqin 【名】father

父兄 fùxiōng 【名】father and elder brother；elders

付 fù 【动】❶ pay：~款 pay money ❷ 〈书〉take a certain action：~诸实践 put into practice ~ 之一笑 laugh off sth.（and forget about it)

付出 fùchū 【动】pay out

付印 fùyìn 【动】send to the printer

付账 fù=zhàng　pay a bill

付诸东流 fù zhū dōng liú carried away by the river, that is, lost forever：一场大火，使他的科研成果全部 ~。In the great fire, all his research papers were lost forever. 也说"付之东流"。

付诸实施 fù zhū shíshī be carried out；be put into practice

负(負) fù 【动】◇ ❶ carry on the back or shoulder：~重竞走 a walking race in which weight is carried on the back (etc.)：肩 ~ 重任 shoulder heavy responsibilities 背 ~着人民的希望 the people expect a great deal of sb. ❸ rely on：~险固守 put up a stubborn defence by relying on a naturally advantageous position ❹ owe：他 ~了一笔债。He has got into debt. ❺ lose (a battle, game, etc.)；be defeated：不分胜 ~ end in a draw ~一局 lose a game ❻ suffer：~重伤 be seriously wounded ❼ enjoy；have：久 ~盛名 have long enjoyed a good reputation

负担 fùdān 【动】bear (a burden)；shoulder：~任务 shoulder the task ~ 费用 bear the expenses 【名】(mental or material) burden；load：家庭 ~ the burden of supporting a family 思想 ~ mental burden ~沉重 heavy load 减轻 ~ ease (or lighten) a burden

负电 fùdiàn 【名】negative (electric) charge

负号 fùhào 【名】minus sign；negative sign

负荷 fùhè 【名】(electr.) load；capacity

负伤 fù=shāng be wounded；be injured

负数 fùshù 【名】negative quantity；negative number

负隅顽抗 fùyú wánkàng fight stubbornly with one's back to a precipice；(fig.) (of the enemy) resist stubbornly 也作"负嵎顽抗"。

负约 fù=yuē break one's promise

负责 fùzé 【动】bear responsibility；be responsible for；be in charge of：这期杂志由他～组稿。He is in charge of collecting articles for this issue of the magazine. 【形】conscientious：他工作认真～。He does his work very conscientiously.

负债 fù=zhài owe debts

负重 fùzhòng be loaded with

妇（婦） fù 【名】◇ woman：～幼卫生 maternal and child hygiene

妇产科 fùchǎnkē 【名】obstetrics and gynecology department of a hospital

妇女 fùnǚ 【名】woman

妇女节 Fùnǚjié 【名】International Women's Day

附 fù 【动】❶ add；attach；enclose：在他的信后～上一笔 add a word or two at the end of his letter ～寄照片一张。Enclosed is a photo. ❷〈书〉be near；be close to：～耳交谈 whisper in each other's ears

附带 fùdài 【动】include；(as adverbial adjunct) by the way；incidentally：一台录音机～十盘磁带 a tape-recorder and 10 tapes ～告诉你一个好消息。Incidentally, here's a piece of good news. 你上街么？请～给我捎点儿东西。You're going shopping, aren't you? Could you please get something for me?

附和 fùhè 【动】echo；chime in with (usu. derog.)：随声～ echo others without careful thought

附加 fùjiā 【动】attach as an extra (condition, etc.)

附件 fùjiàn 【名】❶ appendix：正文及～一并发出。The text and its appendix were sent out together. ❷ accessory；attachment：汽车～ car accessories

附近 fùjìn 【名】nearby；close to；in the vicinity：～地区 nearby regions ～工厂 a nearby factory 北京大学就在颐和园～。Beijing University is in the vicinity of the Summer Palace.

附录 fùlù 【名】appendix

附设 fùshè 【动】have...attached to it

附属 fùshǔ 【动】be affiliated with

附庸 fùyōng 【名】dependency (a country)

赴 fù 【动】〈书〉attend；go to

赴汤蹈火 fù tāng dǎo huǒ walk through fire and water

复（復） fù 【动】◇ ❶ turn around；turn back：循环往～ repeat in a cyclical pattern ❷ answer；reply：～信 reply to a letter 电～ answer by telegraph ❸ recover；resume：～工 return to work (after a strike or lay-off) 官～原职 restoration of an official to his original post 【副】◇ again：死而～苏 come to life again 一去不～返 gone, never to come back

复辟 fùbì 【动】stage a comeback；restore

复查 fùchá 【动】check once again

复仇 fù=chóu avenge；revenge

复出 fùchū 【动】resume office；be active again

复发 fùfā 【动】recur；have a relapse

复工 fù=gōng return to work (after a strike)

复古 fù=gǔ restore the ancient ways

复核 fùhé 【动】check；re-examine；double-check

复合句 fùhéjù 【名】compound sentence

复合元音 fùhé yuányīn diphthong

复会 fù=huì resume a session

复婚 fù=hūn (of a divorced couple) remarry each other

复活 fùhuó 【动】revive

复交 fùjiāo 【动】make up；re-establish diplomatic relations

复刊 fù=kān resume publication (of a periodical)

复述 fùshù 【动】retell

复数 fùshù 【名】plural number

复习 fùxí 【动】review

复写 fùxiě 【动】duplicate；make copies of

复兴 fùxīng 【动】revive；rejuvenate；民族～ national revival 文艺～ renaissance

复员 fùyuán 【动】❶ (of military forces, economic, political and cultural departments) return to normal peacetime operations after a war ❷ (of soldiers) be demobilized

复原 fùyuán 【动】❶ recover from an illness ❷ restore；rehabilitate

复杂 fùzá 【形】complicated；complex

复杂化 fùzáhuà 【动】complicate

复职 fù=zhí be reinstated；be rehabilitated

复制 fùzhì 【动】make a reproduction；duplicate

副 fù 【形】deputy；assistant；vice-；subsidiary；～主任 vice-dean；vice-director ～品 substandard goods 【量】❶ pair；set；一～手套 a pair of gloves 几～对联 pairs of couplets 全～武装 fully-armed ❷ *for facial expressions*：一～笑脸 a smiling face 一～严肃的面孔 a stern face

副本 fùběn 【名】a copy or duplicate of a document

副产品 fùchǎnpǐn 【名】by-product

副词 fùcí 【名】adverb

副教授 fùjiàoshòu 【名】associate professor

副刊 fùkān 【名】supplement

副食 fùshí 【名】foods such as meat, fish, vegetables, which are supplementary to staple grains

副研究员 fùyánjiūyuán 【名】associate research-fellow

副业 fùyè 【名】side-line occupation

副总工程师 fùzǒnggōngchéngshī 【名】deputy chief engineer

副作用 fùzuòyòng 【名】side-effect

赋(賦) fù 【名】❶ tax (archaic)：田～ land tax ❷ a form of writing in ancient China, which is a combination of prose and verse 【动】◇ compose (a poem)：～诗一首 compose a poem

赋税 fùshuì 【名】tax；levy

赋予 fùyǔ 【动】bestow；endow (important task, mission, etc.)：这是人民～我们的重任。This is an important task which the people have entrusted to us.

富 fù 【形】❶ rich；wealthy ❷ abundant；rich in；～矿 rich ore；high-quality ore

富贵 fùguì 【形】rich and powerful

富丽 fùlì 【形】gorgeous；magnificent (buildings, furnishings, etc.)

富民 fù=mín 【动】enrich the people；～政策 enrichment policy

富强 fùqiáng 【形】prosperous and strong

富饶　fùráo　【形】rich；bountiful

富庶　fùshù　【形】rich in resources and densely populated

富有　fùyǒu　【形】well-off；wealthy 【动】be rich；be full of：～生命力 be full of vitality　～实践经验 have rich practical experience　这种面～地方风味。Noodles cooked this way have a characteristic local flavour.

富于　fùyú　【动】be rich in；be full of：劳动人民～创造精神。The labouring people are highly creative. 新鲜蔬菜～营养。Fresh vegetables are very nutritious.

富裕　fùyù　【形】wealthy；well-to-do：生活很～。One's living conditions are quite comfortable.

富裕中农　fùyù zhōngnóng　well-to-do middle peasant

富余　fùyu　【动】have more than one needs；have enough to spare：这块布做一套衣服还能～二尺。After a suit has been cut from this piece of cloth, there will be two-thirds of a metre left over.

富足　fùzú　【形】rich；well-off

腹　fù　【名】◇ abdomen：～痛 have a stomachache

腹背受敌　fù bèi shòu dí　be attacked front and rear

覆　fù　【动】◇ ❶ cover ❷ overturn

覆盖　fùgài　【动】cover：白雪～着大地。The land was covered with snow. 用塑料薄膜～秧苗。The rice seedlings were covered with plastic sheeting.

覆灭　fùmiè　【动】同"覆没"❷

覆没　fùmò　【动】❶ capsize；sink：三艘敌舰全部～。All three enemy warships were sunk. ❷ be annihilated：全军～。The troops were annihilated.

覆亡　fùwáng　【动】(of a nation) be subjugated；fall

G

gā

旮 gā

旮旯儿　gālár　【名】〈口〉 corner (e.g. of a room, courtyard)

伽 gā

伽马射线　gāmǎshèxiàn　【名】(phys.) gamma ray

gāi

该(該)　gāi　【助动】同"应该" yīnggāi　*but cannot be used as a predicate in the structure* "是…的" (*often used in colloquial speech*)：大家的事～由大家来管。What concerns everybody ought to be taken care of by everybody. 都七点了,他～回来了。It's already seven. He ought to be back.【动】be one's turn：下一个节目～你了。You're next on the programme. 明天不～我值班,～他。It isn't my turn to be on duty tomorrow, it's his.【代】〈书〉 *indicates the aforementioned person or thing*：老李正为《历史研究》写稿,～杂志已于最近复刊。Lao Li is writing an article for *Historical Studies*, which has recently resumed publication.【副】probably

(*no negative form*)：这回小张～高兴了,考上大学了。Xiao Zhang has passed the entrance exam for university, he is probably very happy. 你老不注意休息,又～犯病了。If you don't get enough rest, you'll probably be sick again. 奶奶要能活到今天,～多好啊! If only granny were alive today!

gǎi

改　gǎi　【动】❶ alter；change：刚离开两年,家乡就～样儿了。It's only two years that I have been away, but my hometown has taken on a new look. 这条河十年里～了两次道。This river has changed its course twice in ten years. ❷ correct；make alterations：这首诗的结尾部分这么一～,好多了。The ending of this poem is much better now that it has been revised. 昨天学生交的作文本子还没有～完。I haven't yet finished correcting the compositions that the children handed in yesterday. 你能把这件上衣～瘦一点吗? Do you think you can take this jacket in a bit? ❸ correct；amend；rectify：家庭作业写错了不要紧,～了就好。If you have made mistakes in your homework, it's all right as long as you correct them. 我知道我

这个字的发音不对，可是很难～。I know my pronunciation of this character is wrong, but it is very difficult for me to correct it.

改编 gǎibiān 【动】❶ adapt；rewrite：这部小说已～成电影剧本了。This novel has been adapted as a screenplay. ❷（of troops）reorganize；regroup

改变 gǎibiàn 【动】change；alter：～面貌 take on a new look ～计划 change a plan 【名】change：山区的卫生条件有了很大的～。The hygienic conditions in the mountain areas have been greatly improved.

改朝换代 gǎi cháo huàn dài change of dynasty

改动 gǎidòng 【动】alter；change；modify

改革 gǎigé 【动】reform；transform：～工艺 improve technology ～旧的管理制度 reform the old administrative system 【名】reform；transformation：这是一项重大的～。This is a major reform measure.

改革开放 gǎigé kāifàng reform and opening up

改观 gǎiguān 【动】have a new look；be quite different from；change in appearance

改过 gǎiguò 【动】correct one's error (misdeed)

改过自新 gǎiguò zìxīn correct one's errors and make a fresh start；mend one's ways；turn over a new leaf

改行 gǎi = háng change one's profession

改换 gǎihuàn 【动】change；replace：～词句 make changes in the wording ～说法 say in another way

改悔 gǎihuǐ 【动】repent；amend

改嫁 gǎijià 【动】(of a woman) remarry

改进 gǎijìn 【动】improve：～操作方法 improve our methods of opera-

tion 【名】improvement：他在服务态度方面有明显的～。His attitude towards the customers has shown obvious improvement.

改良 gǎiliáng 【动】improve；ameliorate；reform：～品种 improve seed strains ～农具 improve farm tools 【名】improvement；amelioration：土壤～ soil improvement

改良主义 gǎiliángzhǔyì 【名】reformism

改判 gǎipàn 【动】amend a judgment

改期 gǎi = qī change the date；change the scheduled time

改日 gǎirì 【动】some other day

改善 gǎishàn 【动】improve；better：～生活 better one's living conditions ～两国关系 improve the relationship between two countries 【名】improvement：井下作业条件有了不少的～。Considerable improvement has been made in the working conditions in the pits.

改天 gǎitiān 【副】〈口〉another day；some other day：～谈吧！Let's talk about it some other day. ～见。See you some other time. 你要的书，～带给你。I'll bring you the book some other time.

改天换地 gǎi tiān huàn dì transform heaven and earth

改头换面 gǎi tóu huàn miàn change the external appearance of sth. only；a change only in form，not in essence (*derog.*)

改弦更张 gǎi xián gēng zhāng make a fresh start；change one's method of doing things

改邪归正 gǎi xié guī zhèng give up evil ways and return to the right path；mend one's ways

改写 gǎixiě 【动】rewrite；adapt

改选 gǎixuǎn 【动】re-elect

改造 gǎizào 【动】transform；remould；reform：～盐碱地 trans-

form alkaline land ～世界观 remould one's world outlook

改正　gǎizhèng　【动】correct

改锥　gǎizhuī　【名】〔把 bǎ〕screwdriver

改组　gǎizǔ　【动】reorganize; reshuffle

gài

盖(蓋)　gài　【名】lid; cover: 锅～ lid of a pan 茶壶～儿 teapot lid 【动】❶ cover: ～上被子 cover up with a quilt ❷ affix (seal): ～图章 affix a seal ❸ overwhelm; drown out: 欢呼声～过了锣鼓声。Cheers drowned out the sounds of gongs and drums. ❹ build: ～房子 build a house

盖戳　gài=chuō　put a stamp on

盖棺论定　gài guān lùn dìng　only after a person is dead can the final judgement on him be passed

盖子　gàizi　【名】cover of a container; lid

概　gài

概况　gàikuàng　【名】general conditions; basic facts

概括　gàikuò　【动】summarize: 把大家的意见～起来主要有两个方面。The general opinion can be summarized in two main points. 【副】briefly; in broad outline: 他把会议的精神～地介绍了一下。He gave a sense of the meeting in a few words.

概略　gàilüè　【名】(brief) outline; summary: 故事的～ outline of a story 【形】brief: ～的情况 brief account of a situation 大家就这个问题～地谈谈。Let's have a brief talk about this matter.

概论　gàilùn　【名】outline; introduction (often used in book titles):

《政治经济学～》An Introduction to Political Economy

概貌　gàimào　【名】a general picture; a broad outline

概念　gàiniàn　【名】concept; notion; idea

概念化　gàiniànhuà　【形】(of sth. written) too abstract

概述　gàishù　【动】give a very general account of; deal with in general outline

概数　gàishù　【名】approximate number *it can either be expressed by using* 几、多、来、左右、上下, *etc.* *e.g.* 十几年 more than 10 years 三斤多油 more than 3 *jin* of oil 十来个人 about 10 people 一百米左右 about 100 metres 五十(岁)上下 about 50 years old *or by juxtaposition of two numerals*, *e.g.* 三四个 3 or 4 两三点钟 between 2 and 3 o'clock 七八十人 70 to 80 people

概要　gàiyào　【名】outline; summary; essentials (often used in book titles):《中国哲学史～》*An Outline of the History of Chinese Philosophy*

gān

干(乾)　gān　【形】❶ dry: ～柴 dry firewood 衣服晾～了。The washing is dry. ❷ dried up: 天旱河～。There was a drought and the river is dry. ❸ relatives by affection (not by blood): ～妈 mother by affection; godmother ～姐妹 sisters by affection; godsisters; sworn sisters 【副】futile; do sth. to no purpose: ～着急 be worried but unable to do anything ～打雷不下雨 all thunder and no rain; (*fig.*) make a lot of noise, but take no action

另见 gàn

干巴巴 gānbābā 【形】❶ dry；completely lack moisture or oil：这种～的点心实在不好吃。This pastry is as dry as a bone and tastes awful. ❷ (of language) dry and dull；insipid：他的报告～的，没人爱听。His report was dry and dull, and nobody was interested.

干巴 gānba 【形】〈口〉❶ shrivelled；dried up；parched：这块面包都放～了。This loaf of bread has been left for so long that it is stale and hard. ❷ wizened；lacking oil or moisture：人老了，皮肤就变得～了。When a person grows old, his skin becomes dry.

干杯 gān = bēi drink a toast；cheers；"Bottoms up!"

干瘪 gānbiě 【形】❶ shrivelled；wizened：这些枣已经晒～了。These dried dates have shrivelled up. ～老头往往活得很长。Wizened old men often live very long. ❷ (of writing) dull；dry；colourless：脱离生活，写出来的文章一定是～的。If you isolate yourself from life, your writing is bound to be dull and dry.

干脆 gāncuì 【形】straightforward；decisive, not hesitant：我们队长办事很～，从不拖泥带水。Our team leader is very decisive and never shilly-shallies. Note: *when used as an adverbial adjunct, it can be reduplicated as* 干干脆脆：你有什么意见就干干脆脆地说吧，别绕弯子。If you have something on your mind, speak out and don't beat about the bush. 【副】*indicates that one takes resolute action*：我虽然学过一点汉语，但为了打好基础，～从头学起。Although I have already learned some Chinese, I might as well start again from the beginning for a solid grounding. 小顾的扁桃腺常发炎，～把它割掉。Xiao Gu has fre-

quent attacks of tonsilitis. He'd better have his tonsils taken out.

干果 gānguǒ 【名】dry fruit；dried fruit

干旱 gānhàn 【形】dry spell；drought

干涸 gānhé 【动】dry up

干净 gānjìng 【形】❶ clean：教室里非常～。The classroom is very clean. 床单洗得干干净净的。The sheets have been washed spotlessly clean. ❷ not a bit is left：地里的萝卜都拔～了。All the turnips in the field have been pulled up.

干枯 gānkū 【形】dried up；withered：～的树叶 withered leaves 小河～了。The stream has dried up.

干粮 gānliang 【名】pre-prepared food made of grain (e. g. to take on a journey)

干扰 gānrǎo 【动】interfere；disturb：别为这点小事去～他们的工作。Don't disturb their work with such trifles.【名】(electr.) interference；jamming

干涉 gānshè 【动】interfere；intervene；meddle：反对～别国内政 oppose interference in the internal affairs of other countries 对影响公共秩序的行为要进行～。One should intervene in acts which are disturbing to the public order.

干爽 gānshuǎng 【形】dry；(of weather) dry and refreshing

干预 gānyù 【动】intervene；meddle in

干燥 gānzào 【形】❶ dry；arid：空气～。The air is dry. 气候～。The climate is arid. ❷ dull；uninteresting：～无味 dry as dust

甘 gān 【形】◇ sweet；pleasant：～泉 sweet spring water 味～色美 sweet taste and beautiful colour 苦尽～来。When the bitterness is gone, then comes the sweet.

(*fig.*) The bitterness of the past is over and prospects for the future are bright. 【副】◇ willingly; of one's own accord：～冒风险 willingly run risks

甘拜下风 gān bài xià fēng willingly accept one's defeat or inferiority (in a skill, etc.)：你的兵乓球打得真好，我～。You are great at table tennis, I'm not your match at all.

甘居中游 gān jū zhōngyóu be content with the mediocre

甘苦 gānkǔ 【名】❶ sweetness and bitterness; weal and woe; pleasure and sorrow：干部与战士同～。Officers and men share joys and hardships. ❷ one's experience of pleasures and hardships (with stress on hardships)：只有亲身参加这项工作，才知道其中的～。Only those who are involved in this work know its pleasures and hardships.

甘甜 gāntián 【形】sweet

甘心 gānxīn 【动】❶ be willing to; be ready to ❷ be satisfied; resign oneself to：不达目的，绝不～。We won't give up until we have accomplished our goal.

甘心情愿 gānxīn qíngyuàn completely willing; willingly and gladly：为了美好的未来，目前吃点苦也～。I'm entirely willing to suffer present hardships so that the future may be bright. 也说"心甘情愿"。

甘休 gānxiū 【动】willing to let sth. go; take sth. lying down

甘于 gānyú 【动】be willing to; be ready to

甘愿 gānyuàn 【助动】willingly：她～到偏僻的农村去当教师。She is willing to go to the remote countryside to be a teacher. (甘愿 *cannot be modified by any negative adverb*)

甘蔗 gānzhe 【名】sugarcane

杆 gān 【名】pole
另见 gǎn
杆子 gānzi 【名】〔根 gēn〕pole

肝 gān 【名】liver
肝火 gānhuǒ 【名】irascibility; irritability; spleen：他这个人～旺。His is a very irascible nature. 冷静点儿，别动～。Keep calm. Don't get worked up.
肝炎 gānyán 【名】hepatitis
肝脏 gānzàng 【名】liver

尴(尷) gān
尴尬 gāngà 【形】awkward; embarrassed; embarrassing

gǎn

杆 gǎn 【名】(～儿) stick; pole：钢笔～ shaft of a fountain pen; pen-holder 枪～ barrel of a rifle 【量】*for sticklike things*：两～枪 two rifles
另见 gān

赶(趕) gǎn 【动】❶ catch up with：学先进，～先进 learn from and catch up with those who are ahead ❷ hurry up; rush for：～时间 race against time 八点以前务必到会场。We must hurry to get to the meeting before 8 o'clock. ❸ drive：～羊上山 drive the sheep up the hill ～大车 drive a cart ❹ (of a situation) happen to (*often followed by* 上)：～上一场雨。It happened to rain at that moment. 我去他家的时候，正～上他下班回来。When I got to his place, he happened to be just back from work.
赶车 gǎn=chē drive a cart
赶集 gǎn=jí go to the village fair
赶紧 gǎnjǐn 【副】同"赶快"

赶快　gǎnkuài　【副】quickly：他们一看天气不好，～把晒在场院的小麦收起来了。As soon as they saw that the weather was turning bad, they quickly gathered in the wheat which was drying on the threshing ground. 时间不早了，我们～走吧！It is quite late；let's go quickly.

赶路　gǎn=lù　hurry on one's way

赶忙　gǎnmáng　【副】同"赶快" but not used in imperative sentences

赶任务　gǎn rènwu　get one's work done quickly

赶时髦　gǎn shímáo　follow the fashion

敢　gǎn　【助动】dare：～想～说～干。Have the courage to think big, speak up and act on it.

敢于　gǎnyú　【动】dare to；have the courage to（often followed by a polysyllabic verb or phrase）：～提出不同意见 have the courage to give a differing opinion

感　gǎn

感触　gǎnchù　【名】thoughts and feelings aroused by what one sees

感到　gǎndào　【动】feel：～光荣 feel honoured ～高兴 feel happy ～遗憾 feel regretful

感动　gǎndòng　【动】move；touch：他的高贵品质深深地～了我们。His noble character moved us deeply. 她～得哭了。She was moved to tears.

感恩戴德　gǎn ēn dài dé　be grateful for favours bestowed on one

感官　gǎnguān　【名】sense organs

感光　gǎn=guāng　affected by light；photo-sensitive

感化　gǎnhuà　【动】reform a misguided or erring person through persuasion and education or by setting an example

感激　gǎnjī　【动】be grateful；feel indebted：得到你们的帮助，我非常～。I am very grateful for your help.

感激涕零　gǎnjī tì líng　shed tears of gratitude

感觉　gǎnjué　【动】❶ feel；sense：我～有点儿冷。I'm feeling a bit cold. ❷ think；perceive；feel：人们都～他很热情。Everyone thinks he is very friendly and warm. 【名】feeling；sense perception；sensation：幸福的～ happy feeling 针灸的时候，你有什么～? What kind of sensations did you experience while you were having the acupuncture treatment?

感慨　gǎnkǎi　【动】be nostalgic or admire and be awed by the change in sth.：他～地说："好像不久前我还是足球中锋，现在都当祖父了。时间多快啊!" He said nostalgically："It seems such a short time ago that I was a centre forward and now here I am a grandfather. How time flies!" 看着一片碧绿的葡萄园，想起原来的沼泽地，老张真是～万分。Looking at the vast green vineyard and thinking of the original swamp, Lao Zhang was extremely moved by the change.

感冒　gǎnmào　【动】catch cold【名】cold；influenza

感情　gǎnqíng　【名】feelings；emotions；sentiments

感情用事　gǎnqíng yòng shì　be motivated by one's emotions；act on impulse：我们要按照政策处理问题，不能～。We should follow policy in dealing with problems and not act on the impulse of the moment.

感染　gǎnrǎn　【动】❶ infect：伤口～了。The wound has become infected. ❷ influence；infect：他的欢乐情绪～了大家。His high spirits were infectious.

感人　gǎnrén　【形】moving；touching

感伤　gǎnshāng　【形】sorrowful；sentimental

感受　gǎnshòu　【名】a deep impression made on one's thinking by sth.：生活～ influence of one's life experiences on one 【动】be affected；feel；experience：～风寒 be affected by the cold ～到家庭的温暖 to experience the warmth of family life

感叹词　gǎntàncí　【名】interjection

感叹号　gǎntànhào　【名】exclamation mark

感叹句　gǎntànjù　【名】exclamatory sentence

感想　gǎnxiǎng　【名】impression；feeling

感谢　gǎnxiè　【动】thank；be grateful：～信 letter of thanks

感性　gǎnxìng　【名】perceptual (e.g. knowledge)

感应　gǎnyìng　【动】(electr.) induction

感召　gǎnzhào　【动】inspire；rally (sb.) to a worthy cause

gàn

干(幹)

gàn　【动】do *words which can be used as the object of* 干 *are rather limited. The most frequently used are* 活儿 (*usu. indicating physical labour*) *and the interrogative pronoun* 什么 (*here,* 干 *is not used in the answer*)：～具体工作 handle the concrete affairs 上午～半天活儿，下午学习。They work in the morning and study in the afternoon. 你毕业以后想～什么？——想当记者。What do you want to do after graduation? — I want to be a reporter. Note：干 *often doesn't take any object*：活儿不多了，一会儿就可以～完。There isn't much work left. It will be

finished in no time. 你们不～，我们～。If you don't do it, we'll do it. 【名】◇ ❶ the main part of sth. ❷ *short for* 干部：～群关系 the relationship between masses and cadres

另见 gān

干部　gànbù　【名】cadre

干活　gàn = huó　(～儿) work；do manual labour

干将　gànjiàng　【名】a capable, daring person

干劲　gànjìn　【名】vigour；energy；drive

干练　gànliàn　【形】capable and experienced

干吗　gànmá　【口】❶同"做什么" zuò shénme：今天下午咱们～? What are we going to do this afternoon? ❷同"为什么" wèi shénme：你～起得这么早? Why do you get up so early?

干事　gànshi　【名】person in charge of a particular kind of work

干线　gànxiàn　【名】trunk line；main line

gāng

刚(剛)

gāng　【形】◇ hard (*as opp. to* 柔)：以柔克～。Toughness succumbs to gentleness. 【副】❶ *indicates the immediate past*：我们～吃完饭。We've just finished our dinner. 他～毕业不久就结婚了。He had no sooner graduated than he got married. 她～到中国的时候，一句汉语也不会说。When she first came to China, she couldn't speak a word of Chinese. ❷ *indicates that sth. happens at the moment when sth. else is about to take place*：汽车～要开他就赶来了。Just as the bus was about to leave, he came running up. 我～想给他写信，他的信就来了。His letter came just

as I was about to write to him. ❸ barely；just：这块布～够做一条裤子。This piece of cloth is barely enough to make a pair of trousers. 这笔钱买一辆卡车～合适。That amount of money is just enough to buy a truck. ❹ *indicates small quantity or low degree*：他进厂～两年。He has been working in the factory for just two years. 咱们从这儿过河吧，这儿水～没(mò)膝盖。Let's wade the river here. The water is barely up to our knees.

刚愎自用　gāngbì zìyòng　opinionated and dogmatic

刚才　gāngcái　【名】just now：～是休息时间，现在是工作时间。Just now, it was time for rest, and now it is time for work. 对于～的争论，我想发表一点儿意见。I'd like to give you a piece of my mind concerning our disagreement just now. ～少年儿童的武术表演非常精彩。The youngsters' *Wushu* performance just now was excellent. 他～讲的我都同意。I agree with everything he said just now.

刚刚　gānggāng　【副】同"刚"【副】

刚劲　gāngjìng　【形】(of calligraphy or writing style) forceful；vigorous

刚强　gāngqiáng　【形】staunch；firm

刚柔相济　gāng róu xiāng jì　make the tough complement the gentle；have toughness and softness complement each other

刚毅　gāngyì　【形】resolute and firm；possessing fortitude

刚直　gāngzhí　【形】upright；upright and tenacious

肛　gāng

肛门　gāngmén　【名】anus

纲（綱）　gāng　【名】❶ main rope of net；key link；guiding principle：～和目要分清。A clear distinction should be made between the principal and secondary aspects of any situation. 这本汉语教科书是以语法为～编写的。The guiding principle in compiling this Chinese reader is that it should illustrate grammatical points. ❷ (biol.) class (e.g. fish, birds, and mammals are all classes within the sub-phylum "vertebrates")

纲纪　gāngjì　【名】law and order

纲举目张　gāng jǔ mù zhāng　once the key link is grasped, everything falls into place

纲领　gānglǐng　【名】programme；platform

纲目　gāngmù　【名】outline and details：调查～ detailed outline for an investigation《本草～》*The Compendium of Materia Medica*

纲要　gāngyào　【名】programme；general outline

钢（鋼）　gāng　【名】steel

钢板　gāngbǎn　【名】〔块 kuài〕❶steel plate；steel sheet ❷ stencil

钢笔　gāngbǐ　【名】〔枝 zhī〕pen；fountain pen

钢材　gāngcái　【名】rolled steel

钢锭　gāngdìng　【名】steel ingot

钢管　gāngguǎn　【名】〔根 gēn〕steel tube

钢筋　gāngjīn　【名】steel bar；steel reinforcement (e.g. for concrete)

钢盔　gāngkuī　【名】〔顶 dǐng〕steel helmet

钢钎　gāngqiān　【名】drill shaft；steel rod

钢琴　gāngqín　【名】〔架 jià〕piano

钢水　gāngshuǐ　【名】molten steel

钢丝　gāngsī　【名】steel wire

钢铁　gāngtiě　【名】iron and steel

缸　gāng　【名】〔口 kǒu〕big crock；jar

gǎng

岗（崗） gǎng 【名】❶ hillock ❷ sentry；sentry post

岗楼 gǎnglóu 【名】watch-tower

岗哨 gǎngshào 【名】❶ guard post；sentry post：边界～ frontier sentry post ❷ sentinel；sentry：部队每到一地,都要首先派出～。Whenever the troops arrived at a place, the first thing they did was to post sentries.

岗位 gǎngwèi 【名】post (e.g. stick to one's post)

港 gǎng 【名】port

港口 gǎngkǒu 【名】port；harbour

港湾 gǎngwān 【名】bay；harbour

gàng

杠 gàng 【名】❶ ◇ (thick) stick；bar ❷ (～儿) thick line drawn when one is reading or correcting a book，document，etc. to mark a place

杠杆 gànggǎn 【名】lever

杠子 gàngzi 【名】❶〔根 gēn〕见"杠"❶ ❷〔道 dào〕见"杠"❷

gāo

高 gāo 【形】❶ high；tall：～山 high mountain ～楼大厦 tall buildings ❷ high；in height：这堵墙有两米～。This wall is two metres high. ❸ advanced；superior：～年级 senior grades (in a school) 级别～ of high rank ❹ above average；above normal：～速度 high speed 质量～ high quality 体温～ have a fever 大家热情很～。Everybody was in high spirits. ❺ brilliant；superior：见解比别人～。One's understanding of a matter is superior to that of others. 【名】(maths.) height

高昂 gāo'áng 【形】❶ (of voice，spirits) high；elated：情绪～ be elated 歌声愈来愈～。The singing is getting more and more spirited. ❷ expensive；costly；dear：价格～。The price is high.

高傲 gāo'ào 【形】arrogant；haughty

高不可攀 gāo bù kě pān too high to climb；(fig.) sth. too difficult to attain

高产 gāochǎn 【名】high yield

高产作物 gāochǎn zuòwù high-yield crops

高层 gāocéng 【名】high rise；high level；top level

高超 gāochāo 【形】superb；exquisite

高潮 gāocháo 【名】❶ high tide ❷ upsurge：掀起生产的新～。Initiate a new movement to promote production. ❸ (of a play，drama，etc.) climax：第五场是全剧的～。The fifth scene was the climax of the play.

高大 gāodà 【形】lofty；high and noble；big and tall

高档 gāodàng 【形】high grade

高等 gāoděng 【形】❶ higher；advanced：～数学 advanced mathematics ❷ of a higher level：～学校 institutions of higher learning ～教育 higher education

高低 gāodī 【名】❶ height：这座山的～你能测出来吗? Can you find out the height of this mountain? ❷ difference in degree：他们俩的汉语水平差不多,分不出～。The level of proficiency in the Chinese language of these two people is more or less the same. One cannot tell

who is better. ❸ (of speaking or doing things) appropriateness：说话不知～ make inappropriate remarks

高低杠 gāodīgàng 【名】〔副 fù〕(gymnastics) uneven bars

高地 gāodì 【名】(mil.) high ground；height

高调 gāodiào 【名】high pitch tone；high-sounding：唱～ mouth high-sounding words

高度 gāodù 【名】altitude；height；飞行的～ flight altitude 这个游泳池跳板的～是三米。This swimming pool has a three-metre diving-board. 【形】highly；to a high degree (*attributive or adverbial adjunct only*)：～的责任感 highly-developed sense of responsibility ～赞扬 speak highly of ～评价 have a high opinion of

高分子 gāofēnzǐ 【名】high polymer；macromolecule

高峰 gāofēng 【名】❶ peak；summit：珠穆朗玛峰是世界第一～。Mount Qomolangma is the world's highest peak. ❷ climax

高高在上 gāo gāo zài shàng hold oneself aloof；stand high above the masses：我们反对～脱离群众的官僚主义作风。We are opposed to the bureaucratic style of standing aloof and being divorced from the masses.

高歌猛进 gāo gē měng jìn stride forward singing loudly；(*fig.*) advance triumphantly and high-spiritedly

高官厚禄 gāo guān hòu lù high position and good salary

高贵 gāoguì 【形】❶ noble；honourable：～品质 noble qualities ❷ (of persons in the past) privileged

高呼 gāohū 【动】shout

高级 gāojí 【形】❶ high-grade；high quality ❷ senior；high-ranking

高价 gāojià 【名】high price

高见 gāojiàn 【名】wise idea

高空作业 gāokōng zuòyè work at high altitudes

高利贷 gāolìdài 【名】usury

高利盘剥 gāolì pánbō exploit by charging high interest

高粱 gāoliang 【名】sorghum

高龄 gāolíng 【名】(polite form) advanced in years

高炉 gāolú 【名】〔座 zuò〕blast-furnace

高明 gāomíng 【形】bright；wise；brilliant；医术～ high degree of medical skill 这个主意真～。This is certainly a brilliant idea. 【名】◇ (of person) better qualified；另请～。Please find someone better qualified than I (for the job).

高尚 gāoshàng 【形】noble；lofty：～的人 noble-minded person 品质～ of noble character

高烧 gāoshāo 【名】high fever

高升 gāoshēng 【动】be promoted

高射炮 gāoshèpào 【名】〔门 mén〕anti-aircraft gun

高深 gāoshēn 【形】profound；advanced

高耸 gāosǒng 【动】lofty；high；towering

高速 gāosù 【形】high-speed；swift；fast

高速公路 gāosù gōnglù 〔条 tiáo〕freeway；expressway

高谈阔论 gāo tán kuò lùn harangue；loud and bombastic talk

高温 gāowēn 【名】high temperature

高屋建瓴 gāo wū jiàn líng like water pouring down from the steep roof of a high house；sweep down irresistibly from a commanding position：军队以～之势，勇往直前。The army swept on irresistibly.

高兴 gāoxìng 【形】glad；pleased；happy；elated

高血压 gāoxuèyā 【名】hypertension

高压 gāoyā 【名】❶（phys.）high degree of pressure ❷ high-voltage ❸ high atmospheric pressure ❹（med.）systolic pressure ❺ high-handed：～政策 high-handed policy ～手段 high-handed measure

高压线 gāoyāxiàn 【名】high-tension wire

高原 gāoyuán 【名】plateau

高瞻远瞩 gāo zhān yuǎn zhǔ look far ahead and aim high；take a long and broad view；be far-sighted

高涨 gāozhǎng 【动】run high；surge ahead；rise high；水位～。The water level has risen. 物价～。Prices have gone up. 情绪～。Enthusiasm was running high.

高枕无忧 gāo zhěn wú yōu rest one's head on thick pillows and sleep free of care；relax one's vigilance；set one's mind at ease

高中 gāozhōng 【名】senior middle school

高姿态 gāozītài lofty stance

膏 gāo 【名】ointment；paste：丸、散、～、丹 pill, powder, ointment, granule（4 kinds of pre-prepared Chinese traditional medicine）

膏药 gāoyao 【名】〔贴 tiē〕ointment；paste（medicine）

gǎo

搞 gǎo 【动】❶ do usu. not referring to concrete work , but to a profession or type of activity：你们是～什么工作的？——我是～音乐的。他是～美术的。What kind of work do you do？—I'm a musician. He's an artist. 小李是个印刷工人，可是业余喜欢～半导体。Xiao Li is a print-er, but he makes transistor radioes as a hobby during his spare time. ❷ takes the place of a concrete action which is difficult to describe or of which a description is unnecessary：工人们正在大～技术革新。The workers are making technical innovations on a large scale. 新老同学都要～好团结。Both old and new students must band together. 先把这个词的意思～清楚再谈用法。You must first have a clear understanding of the meaning of this word and then learn its usage. ❸ try to get hold of：你能不能给我～一张今晚上音乐会的票？Do you think you can get me a ticket for the concert this evening？

搞鬼 gǎo=guǐ play tricks

搞活 gǎo// huó vitalize：～经济 enliven the economy

镐（鎬）gǎo 【名】〔把 bǎ〕pick

稿 gǎo 【名】manuscript

稿件 gǎojiàn 【名】manuscript for publication

稿纸 gǎozhǐ 【名】〔张 zhāng〕squared paper for copying manuscripts

稿子 gǎozi 【名】〔篇 piān〕manuscript；draft；sketch

gào

告 gào 【动】❶ ◇ tell：转～ pass on（a message）电～ convey by telegram ❷ lay a complaint against sb.；sue：到法院去～他 sue him through the courts ❸ ◇ ask for：～假 ask for leave ❹ ◇ announce（the completion of sth.）：工作已一段落。This stage of the work has been completed.

告别 gàobié 【动】❶ leave；part

with：挥手～ wave farewell to ～了
父母，～了家乡 take leave of one's
parents and hometown ❷ bid farewell to；say goodbye to；举行～宴
会 hold a farewell banquet 我明天
要走了，特地来向大家～。I'm leav-
ing tomorrow. I came especially to
say goodbye to you all.

告成 gàochéng 【动】be completed；
be successful

告辞 gàocí 【动】take leave；say
goodbye

告急 gàojí 【动】make an urgent request for help in an emergency

告捷 gàojié 【动】❶ win victory（in
war or game, etc.）：首战～。We
won the first battle. ❷ report a
victory

告诫 gàojiè 【动】warn；enjoin；
counsel

告密 gào=mì give secret information against sb.

告示 gàoshi 【名】〔张 zhāng〕official
notice；bulletin

告诉 gàosu 【动】tell；inform

告知 gàozhī 【动】inform

告终 gàozhōng 【动】conclude；end
up

告状 gào=zhuàng bring a law suit
against sb.；lodge a complaint
（with sb.'s superior）

gē

戈 gē 【名】spear；lance

戈壁 gēbì 【名】the Gobi Desert

疙 gē

疙瘩 gēda 【名】〔个 gè〕❶ pimple；
lump or swelling on the skin；腿上
起了个～ have a swelling on one's
leg ❷ knot；lump：土～ small lump
of earth ❸ a knotty problem
which weighs on one's mind；解除
思想～ dispel a burden from one's
mind

哥 gē 【名】elder brother

哥哥 gēge 【名】elder brother

胳 gē

胳膊 gēbo 【名】〔只 zhī〕arm

搁（擱） gē 【动】❶ place；
lay；put：把篮子～在地上 put the
basket down on the ground 这个书
橱里可以～不少书。This book-case
can hold quite a few books. ❷ put
aside；shelve；这事不急，先～在一边
吧！This is not an urgent matter.
Let's put it aside for the moment.

搁浅 gēqiǎn 【动】run aground；（of
a matter）fail to proceed smooth-
ly：船在河里～了。The ship went
aground. 这件事到这儿～了。At
this point, the matter became
deadlocked.

搁置 gēzhì 【动】shelve；put aside

割 gē 【动】cut：～麦 cut wheat
～草 cut grass

割爱 gē'ài 【动】give away or part
with sth. one loves

割断 gē∥duàn cut off；sever：～绳
索 cut a rope ～联系 sever relations
不能～历史。You cannot separate
one part of history from the con-
tinuum.

割据 gējù 【动】set up a separate regime by force of arms

割裂 gēliè 【动】（usu. of something
abstract）separate；sever：不能把政
治与经济～开来。One can't sepa-
rate politics from economics.

割让 gēràng 【动】cede（territory）

鸽（鴿） gē 【名】◇ dove；pi-
geon

鸽子 gēzi 【名】〔只 zhī〕dove；pigeon

歌 gē 【名】〔个 gè、支 zhī〕song：

唱一个～儿 sing a song【动】◇ sing：高～一曲 sing a song loudly

歌唱 gēchàng 【动】❶ sing：尽情～ sing to one's heart's content ❷ praise (in song)：～祖国 sing in praise of our motherland

歌词 gēcí 【名】〔首 shǒu〕words of a song

歌功颂德 gē gōng sòng dé praise sb.'s virtues and achievements；sing sb.'s praises (*now used ironically*)

歌剧 gējù 【名】〔出 chū〕opera

歌迷 gēmí 【名】a singing fan；a singing fanatic

歌谱 gēpǔ 【名】music of a song

歌曲 gēqǔ 【名】〔支 zhī〕song

歌声 gēshēng 【名】singing

歌手 gēshǒu 【名】singer

歌颂 gēsòng 【动】eulogize；sing in praise of；extol

歌舞 gēwǔ 【名】singing and dancing

歌星 gēxīng 【名】a pop singer

歌谣 gēyáo 【名】〔首 shǒu〕general term for folk-songs, nursery rhymes, ballads, etc.

歌咏 gēyǒng 【名】singing

gé

革 gé 【名】leather；hide：制～ tan hides【动】expel；dismiss

革除 géchú 【动】❶ get rid of；abolish；eliminate：～陋习 get rid of bad habits and practices ❷ dismiss；expel；remove (from office)：～公职 dismiss sb. from official position

革命 gémìng 【名】revolution【形】revolutionary

革命者 gémìngzhě 【名】a revolutionary

革新 géxīn 【动】innovate：～工艺 make an innovation in technique

【名】innovation：这三项技术～很重要，一定要搞好。These three technological innovations are of great importance. We must make a good job of putting them into practice.

革职 gé＝zhí dismiss；remove；discharge from a position

阁（閣） gé 【名】❶ a kind of building；closed pavilion：亭台楼～ pavilion, high platform, building with more than one storey, closed pavilion (decorative buildings of various kinds) ❷ short for 内阁：组 ～ form a cabinet

阁楼 gélóu 【名】attic

阁下 géxià 【名】(Your, His) Excellency

格 gé 【名】❶ square；chequer：把字写在～里 write the characters in the squares ❷ shelf：这种柜子有两个～。This wardrobe has two shelves. ❸ ◇ standard；style；pattern：别具一～ have a special style all one's own

格格不入 gé gé bù rù incompatible；a square peg in a round hole：这个人比较落伍，和年轻人的思想感情有点儿～。His thinking is very out of date and he doesn't get along with young people.

格局 géjú 【名】style；manner；arrangement

格律 gélǜ 【名】set rules giving length of lines, pattern of tones, rhyme scheme, etc. for different kinds of Chinese poetry

格式 géshì 【名】form；pattern

格外 géwài 【副】exceptionally；extraordinarily；especially：久别重逢，～亲切。People feel especially drawn to one another when they have been reunited after long years of separation. 深秋的香山～美丽。The Fragrant Hills are ex-

ceptionally beautiful in late autumn.

格言 géyán 【名】maxim

格子 gézi 【名】checkered pattern

隔 gé 【动】❶ separate；partition：两个村庄就～着一条河。The two villages are separated by a river. ❷ at a distance from；at an interval of：他～几天来一次。He comes every few days. 我家和剧场相～不远。My home is not far away from the theatre.

隔壁 gébì 【名】next door

隔断 gé∥duàn cut off；separate：千山万水也不能～我们两国人民之间的友谊。No mountains or seas can stand in the way of the friendship between our two peoples.

隔断 géduàn 【名】separate

隔阂 géhé 【名】estrangement；alienation；lack of understanding

隔绝 géjué 【动】be completely cut off；be isolated：音信～ never hear from (him) 彼此～ be isolated one from the other

隔离 gélí 【动】isolate：传染病患者必须～。Patients who have contagious diseases must be isolated.

隔膜 gémó 【名】estrangement；lack of understanding：消除～ end an estrangement 产生～。An estrangement occurred.

隔音 gé＝yīn give sound insulation

隔音符号 géyīn fúhào syllable-dividing mark

gè

个（個） gè 【量】❶ *the measure word which is most extensively used*：一～人 a person 两～句子 two sentences 几～苹果 a few apples 这～想法不对。This opinion is wrong. ❷ *can sometimes replace another measure word*：一～（or 顶）帽子 a hat 那～（or 张）桌子 that table ❸ *used between a verb or adjective and an approximate number to indicate that one is making an estimate*：这项工作有～三四十人就够了。Between 30 and 40 people will be enough to do the work. 这个基本动作要练～一二十遍才能学会。About 20 repetitions will be required before you can master this basic skill. 他比我也就大～两、三岁。He is only 2 or 3 years older than I. ❹ *inserted between a verb and its object to indicate that something is being illustrated. The noun which is the object may not take* 个 *as its usual measure word*：他兴趣很广泛，唱～歌，演～戏，踢～球样样都喜欢。He has very wide interests：singing, acting, football—they all appeal to him. 理～发，二十分钟还不够吗? Isn't 20 minutes long enough for a hair-cut? ❺ *inserted between a verb and its complement when the latter indicates a very high degree*：雨下～不停。It's been raining without any let-up. 我们今天玩了～痛快。We did have a most wonderful time today. 把敌人打得～落花流水。The enemy was completely defeated.

个别 gèbié 【形】❶ individual；separately：～谈话 talk to sb. privately ～辅导 tutor a student individually ❷ a few；rare：只差～人没来。Only a few haven't come yet. 有这种想法的人不是～的。Those who hold such views are more than a handful.

个人 gèrén 【名】❶ individual；personal (*as opp. to* 集体)：～的力量总是有限的。An individual's ability is always limited. ❷ oneself (*often in apposition to* 我 *on formal occasions*)：我～认为，这个意见是非常正

确的。Personally I think this view is quite correct.

个人主义 gèrénzhǔyì individualism

个体 gètǐ 【名】individual；individuality

个体经济 gètǐ jīngjì economy based on individual production

个体劳动者 gètǐ láodòngzhě individual labourer

个性 gèxìng 【名】individuality；one's individual character

个子 gèzi 【名】size (stature)

各 gè 【代】each；every：世界~国 every country in the world "~位朋友" "Friends …"【副】respectively；variously：~有所长。Each has his strong points. 几种产品~有特点。Each of these varieties has its particular characteristics.

各奔前程 gè bèn qiánchéng each goes his own way

各别 gèbié 【形】❶ in different ways：不同性质的问题，应该~解决，不能一律对待。Different problems should be tackled differently. ❷ peculiar；odd (derog.)：他的脾气有点儿~。His temperament is a bit odd.

各持己见 gè chí jǐ jiàn each persists in his own opinion

各得其所 gè dé qí suǒ each is appropriately dealt with according to his particular talents and characteristics

各个 gègè each；every；one by one：~工厂都接到了通知。Every factory has received the notice. ~方面都要考虑到。Every aspect should be considered.

各个击破 gègè jī pò crush the enemy unit by unit；solve problems one by one

各就各位 gè jiù gè wèi （of sports）On your marks!

各式各样 gè shì gè yàng all kinds of；in various ways；of every description：~的花布 all kinds of cotton prints ~的玩具 all kinds of toys

各抒己见 gè shū jǐ jiàn each expressing his own views

各行其是 gè xíng qí shì act as one pleases；each goes his own way：工作要有统一的领导，不能~。All the work should be put under unified leadership. Nobody should go his own way.

各有千秋 gè yǒu qiān qiū each has its merits：这两个杂技团的表演都很精彩，又~。The performances by both acrobatic troupes were excellent, each having its own particular strengths.

各自 gèzì 【代】by oneself：~为战 each fights his own battle ~坚守岗位。Each holds fast to his own position.

各自为政 gè zì wéi zhèng Each manages his affairs in his own way, with little co-ordination among them.

gěi

给（給）gěi 【动】give：把青春献~祖国 dedicate one's youth to one's motherland 他~我一张照片。He gave me a photo of himself. 连长交~他一项任务。The company commander assigned him a task. 小林一连写了三封信~我。Xiao Lin wrote me three letters one after another.【介】❶ introduces the object of one's service, equivalent to 为：张老师~我们上课。Teacher Zhang lectures to us. 钢琴家~孩子们演出。The pianist gave a recital for the children. If the object of 给 is quite obvious from the context, it can be understood：孩子们

一到，钢琴家就～演出。As soon as the children arrived, the pianist gave a performance for them. ❷ *introduces the recipient of sth.*：他～我们送来了一本《人民画报》。He sent us a copy of *China Pictorial*. 你把这盒烟～他递过去。Would you please hand him this pack of cigarettes? ❸ *equivalent to* 让 *or* 叫：我～你看一本新书。I'll show you a new book. 你做个示范动作～大家看看。Will you teach us how to do it by giving us a demonstration? ❹ *introduces the recipient of an action, equivalent to* 向 *or* 对：小学生～老师鞠了个躬。The child bowed to the teacher. ❺ *introduces the agent of an action, equivalent to* 被：我的钢笔～别人借走了。My pen was borrowed by somebody. 窗户～大风吹开了。The window was blown open by the wind. 【助】 *when used before the main verb of a sentence in the passive voice or when it is used to emphasize the disposal of sth., 给 can be omitted without affecting the meaning*：我把这件事～忘了。I've forgotten this matter. 这一大片麦子，一个小时就让收割机～收完了。This vast expanse of wheat was cut by a combine in an hour. 另见 jǐ

给以 gěiyǐ 【动】give; grant (*its object is usually a dissyllabic verb*)：对于取得优异成绩的同志，要～奖励。Praise should be given to those individuals who have made outstanding achievements. 凡是正义的事业，我们都～支持。We give support to all just causes.

给…以… gěi…yǐ… *the indirect object is placed after* 给 *and the direct object, usu. an abstract noun, after* 以：给生活不幸的人以关怀 show care and concern for the disadvantaged 给侵略者以应得的惩罚 give the aggressors the punishment they deserve 我们应该给学习困难的学生以具体的帮助。We ought to help those students who have difficulties with their studies.

gēn

根 gēn 【名】❶ root：树～ the roots of a tree 稻～儿 the roots of rice plants ～深叶茂 deep roots and lush leaves ❷ foot; root：城～儿 the foot of the city wall 墙～儿 the foot of a wall 舌～ the root of the tongue ❸ cause; origin; root：刨～儿问底儿 get to the root of a matter 我们是老同学，彼此知～知底。Since we are old classmates, we know each other inside out. ❹ base; foundation：扎～于群众 have one's roots among the masses 【量】(～儿) *for long, thin things*：一～火柴 a match 两～绳子 two ropes 几～木头 several logs

根本 gēnběn 【名】foundation; base：抓住～ grasp what is of fundamental importance 从～上解决 achieve a fundamental solution (of a problem) 【形】basic; fundamental; radical：～原因 root cause ～利益 fundamental interests 宪法是国家的～大法。The basic laws of the country are embodied in the constitution. 【副】❶ entirely; totally; at all (*usu. in the negative*)：～不知道 have no idea at all ～不了解 do not understand at all ❷ thoroughly：～推翻 completely overthrow

根本法 gēnběnfǎ 【名】fundamental law

根除 gēnchú 【动】uproot; exterminate; eradicate

根底 gēndǐ 【名】❶ foundation：他

的文言文～很好。He has a very good grounding in classical Chinese. ❷ cause；root：追问～ get to the root of（a matter）知～ know the ins and outs（of a situation）也作"根柢（dǐ）"。

根基 gēnjī　【名】foundation；basis

根据 gēnjù　【动】be based on；according to：～大家的建议把计划修改了一下。The plan was revised according to the suggestions of the collective.【名】basis；grounds：说话要有～。Statements should be made on the basis of facts.

根据地 gēnjùdì　【名】base area（during the civil war）

根绝 gēnjué　【动】exterminate；wipe out；eliminate

根深蒂固 gēn shēn dì gù　deep-rooted；inveterate；ingrained（usu. derog.）也作"根深柢（dǐ）固"。

根源 gēnyuán　【名】source；origin；root：社会～ social roots 历史～ historical roots

根治 gēnzhì　【动】（of disease，calamity）radical cure；cure once and for all；permanent control：海河 bring the Haihe River under permanent control ～疾病 effect a radical cure of a disease

根子 gēnzi　【名】root；root cause

跟 gēn　【动】follow：快点～上队伍 hurry up and follow the troops 代表们一个～一个地把选票投入票箱。The delegates placed their ballots in the ballot box one after another.【介】同"和"hé【介】，usu. in colloquial speech：他～领导上请了两星期的假。He has asked the leadership for two weeks' leave. 快把你的经验～大家介绍介绍。Please tell us about your experiences.【连】同"和"【连】，usu. in colloquial speech：车上装的是农药～化肥。The truck is loaded with insecticide

and chemical fertilizer. 我的书～你的书放在一起了。My books were put together with yours.

跟前 gēnqián　【名】in front of；nearby

跟随 gēnsuí　【动】follow

跟头 gēntou　【名】❶ fall ❷ somersault

跟着 gēnzhe　【动】follow：你在前边走，我～。You go first，and I'll follow.【连】in the wake of；right after（usu. in conjunction with 就）：听完报告，～就讨论。The speech was followed by a discussion. 刮了一阵风，～大雨就下来了。There was a gust of wind and then it began to pour.

跟踪 gēnzōng　【动】tail；shadow sb.；follow sb.'s trail：～追击 trace and pursue（a spy）

gēng

更 gēng
另见 gèng

更迭 gēngdié　【动】alternate；change

更动 gēngdòng　【动】modify；change；alter　【名】alteration；change

更改 gēnggǎi　【动】alter；change：～计划 change a plan ～航线 change the（air or sea）route ～日期 change the date

更换 gēnghuàn　【动】replace；change：～位置 change the position（of sth.）车间里新～的这套设备性能良好。The new equipment which has replaced the old in the workshop works very well.

更替 gēngtì　【动】substitute

更新 gēngxīn　【动】renew

更衣室 gēngyīshì　【名】dressing-room

更正 gēngzhèng　【动】make a cor-

rection (of an error in a statement or a newspaper article)【名】correction (in a newspaper)

耕 gēng 【动】plough；cultivate

耕畜　gēngchù　【名】draught animal

耕地　gēngdì　【名】farmland；cultivated fields

耕具　gēngjù　【名】farming tools

耕种　gēngzhòng　【动】plough and sow；do farm work

gěng

耿 gěng

耿耿于怀　gěnggěng yú huái　take sth. to heart：朋友之间有些小矛盾，过去就算了，不要老是～。Forget about trivial disagreements among friends, and don't take them to heart.

耿直　gěngzhí　【形】frank and upright

哽 gěng

哽咽　gěngyè　【动】〈书〉sob

梗 gěng 【名】the stem of a flower or leaf

梗概　gěnggài　【名】outline

梗塞　gěngsè　【动】obstruct

梗阻　gěngzǔ　【动】impede；hinder；obstruct

gèng

更 gèng 【副】❶ even (*used when making comparisons*)：今年我们县的水利工程规模～大了。Our county's water conservation projects are on an even larger scale this year than last year. 这件事我都办得了 (liǎo)，～不用说他了。If I can handle the matter, then cer-

tainly he can. 看一个人不但要看他的言论，～要看他的行动。Judge a person not just by his words, but, more importantly, by his actions. ❷ in particular：我喜欢诗，～喜欢唐诗。I like poetry, and *Tang* poetry in particular.

另见 gēng

更加　gèngjiā　【副】同"更"，*but usu. in written language, followed by polysyllabic words*：公家的书，应该～爱护。Books belonging to the public must be especially well taken care of. 他这篇作品比前两篇写得～深刻，～感人。This article of his has even more depth and is more affecting than his last two.

更上一层楼　gèng shàng yī céng lóu　climb yet one storey higher；attain a still higher goal：我们要使产品质量～。We should make the quality of our products even better.

gōng

工 gōng 【名】❶ ◇ *short for* 工人：青～ young worker ❷ work；labour：省～省料 save materials and labour ❸ ◇ industry：～商界 industrial and commercial circles ❹ man-day (the amount of work done by one man in one day)：修这个扬水站需要多少个～？How many man-days will it take to build this pumping station?

工本　gōngběn　【名】production costs

工厂　gōngchǎng　【名】factory；plant；mill；works

工程　gōngchéng　【名】〔项 xiàng〕construction work；project

工程兵　gōngchéngbīng　【名】engineering corps

工程师　gōngchéngshī　【名】engineer

工地　gōngdì　【名】work-site；construction site

工段 gōngduàn 【名】section of a workshop；area of a construction site

工夫 gōngfu 【名】❶ the time it takes to do sth.：他半天～就学会骑自行车了。It only took him half a day to learn to ride a bicycle. 他出去不大～就回来了。He was away for a short while and soon came back. ❷ free time；leisure；以后有～再来吧！Please come round again when you have some free time. ❸ effort；labour：只要肯下～，没有什么学不会的。There is nothing you can't master as long as you work at it. ❹ skill；ability：练～ practise a skill 他的小提琴拉得真有～。He plays the violin superbly. ❸、❹也作"功夫"。

工会 gōnghuì 【名】trade union

工具 gōngjù 【名】tool；instrument；means

工具书 gōngjùshū 【名】〔本 běn、部 bù〕reference book

工龄 gōnglíng 【名】length of service；standing

工人 gōngrén 【名】worker

工伤 gōngshāng 【名】injury incurred while working

工时 gōngshí 【名】man-hour

工事 gōngshì 【名】(mil.) defence works

工效 gōngxiào 【名】work efficiency

工薪阶层 gōngxīn jiēcéng salaried workers；wage-earning group

工序 gōngxù 【名】work process

工业 gōngyè 【名】industry

工业化 gōngyèhuà 【动】industrialize

工艺 gōngyì 【名】technology

工艺美术 gōngyì měishù arts and crafts

工艺品 gōngyìpǐn 【名】craft products；handicrafts

工整 gōngzhěng 【形】neat and orderly：他的字写得很～。He writes a neat hand.

工种 gōngzhǒng 【名】the various kinds of work in a factory，e. g. grinding，casting，etc.

工资 gōngzī 【名】wages；salary

工作 gōngzuò 【名】❶ work：组织～ organizational work 工会～ trade-union work 科学研究～ scientific research ❷ occupation；job：找～ look for a job 【动】work：开始～ begin to work 他在县里～。He works at the county seat.

工作服 gōngzuòfú 【名】〔件 jiàn、套 tào〕work-clothes

工作面 gōngzuòmiàn 【名】face (of a mine)

工作母机 gōngzuò mǔjī machine-tool

工作日 gōngzuòrì 【名】working day

工作证 gōngzuòzhèng 【名】〔个 gè、张 zhāng〕personnel I. D. card；staff I.D. card

弓 gōng 【名】bow

公 gōng 【名】❶ father of one's husband：～婆 father-in-law and mother-in-law ❷ official business：因～出差 take a trip on business 请你今天下午等我一下，我办完～去找你。Please wait for me this afternoon. I'll come to look for you after I finish work. 【形】❶ public or collective：～营 publicly owned ～私不分可不行。It is wrong to confuse public with private property. ❷ fair；just：～买～卖 fair in buying and selling 办事不～ unjust in one's manner of doing things ❸ universally acknowledged：～休 public holiday ～议 public or collective evaluation ～制 metric system ❹ (of animal) male (as opp. to 母)：～鸡 cock ～牛 bull 【动】◇ publicize：～之于世 make known to the whole world

公安　gōng'ān　【名】public security

公安部队　gōng'ān bùduì　public security forces

公报　gōngbào　【名】communiqué；bulletin

公倍数　gōngbèishù　【名】（maths.）common multiple

公布　gōngbù　【动】publish；announce

公尺　gōngchǐ　【量】metre

公道　gōngdao　【形】fair；just：说话～ speak fairly；speak impartially 办事～ handle matters justly 价钱～ a reasonable price

公敌　gōngdí　【名】public enemy；common enemy

公费　gōngfèi　【形】at public expense

公费医疗　gōngfèi yīliáo　free medical service

公分　gōngfēn　【量】centimetre

公愤　gōngfèn　【名】public indignation

公告　gōnggào　【名】public announcement；bulletin；communiqué

公共　gōnggòng　【形】public

公共汽车　gōnggòng qìchē〔辆 liàng〕bus

公公　gōnggong　【名】❶ father-in-law（husband's father）❷ a respectful form of address for an old man：老～ grandpa；grand-dad

公关　gōngguān　【名】public relations

公海　gōnghǎi　【名】high seas

公害　gōnghài　【名】environmental pollution；(fig.) public nuisance

公函　gōnghán　【名】official letter

公积金　gōngjījīn　【名】accumulation fund (of a commune or factory)

公祭　gōngjì　【动】(of an organization) pay respect to a deceased person by holding a memorial service

公斤　gōngjīn　【量】kilogram

公开　gōngkāi　【形】open；public；overt：～活动 act openly ～露面 show one's face in public 【动】make public；make known：这件事不能～。This matter cannot be made known to the public.

公款　gōngkuǎn　【名】public funds

公里　gōnglǐ　【量】kilometre

公理　gōnglǐ　【名】❶ axiom ❷ universally accepted truth

公历　gōnglì　【名】the Gregorian calendar

公粮　gōngliáng　【名】agricultural tax paid in grain

公路　gōnglù　【名】〔条 tiáo〕highway

公论　gōnglùn　【名】the verdict of public opinion

公民　gōngmín　【名】citizen

公民权　gōngmínquán　【名】civil rights

公墓　gōngmù　【名】（public）cemetery

公平　gōngpíng　【形】just；fair

公顷　gōngqǐng　【量】hectare

公然　gōngrán　【副】openly；brazenly：～践踏国际法 a flagrant breach of international law ～侵占别国领土 brazenly occupy another country's territory ～违抗命令 openly defy an order

公认　gōngrèn　【动】universally acknowledge；generally recognize：工人们～老王是个好厂长。All the workers acknowledge that Lao Wang is a good director.

公审　gōngshěn　【动】public trial

公使　gōngshǐ　【名】minister（diplomat）

公式　gōngshì　【名】formula

公式化　gōngshìhuà　【动】(of novels，films，etc.) written according to a formula；formulism

公事　gōngshì　【名】public affairs；official business

公司　gōngsī　【名】company

公私合营　gōngsī héyíng　joint state-private ownership (of enterprises)

公文　gōngwén　【名】official docu-

ment

公物 gōngwù 【名】public property；public assets

公务员 gōngwùyuán 【名】civil servant

公演 gōngyǎn 【动】perform in public

公益金 gōngyìjīn 【名】public welfare fund

公用 gōngyòng public use

公有 gōngyǒu publicly owned

公有制 gōngyǒuzhì 【名】public ownership

公寓 gōngyù 【名】❶（in the past）lodging house leased and paid for by the month ❷ apartment house；block of flats

公元 gōngyuán 【名】A.D.；the Christian era

公园 gōngyuán 【名】park

公约 gōngyuē 【名】❶ pact ❷ collectively agreed-upon regulations within a work-unit；joint pledge：服务 ～ collectively agreed-upon regulations regarding service 卫生 ～ collectively agreed-upon regulations regarding hygiene

公约数 gōngyuēshù 【名】（maths.）common divisor

公允 gōngyǔn 【形】fair and just

公债 gōngzhài 【名】government bonds

公正 gōngzhèng 【形】just；impartial

公证 gōngzhèng 【名】notarization

公职 gōngzhí 【名】public service

公众 gōngzhòng 【名】the public

公主 gōngzhǔ 【名】princess

公转 gōngzhuàn 【动】revolve（e.g. around the sun）

功 gōng 【名】❶ meritorious deeds；merit：立了一次三等 ～ win a third class order of merit ❷ skill：芭蕾舞演员每天练 ～。Ballet dancers practise every day. ❸（phys.）work

功夫 gōngfu 【名】Kung fu

功夫片 gōngfupiàn 【名】Kung fu films；Chinese martial art films

功绩 gōngjì 【名】merits；feats；achievements

功课 gōngkè 【名】〔门 mén〕school lesson；homework

功劳 gōngláo 【名】meritorious deed

功利主义 gōnglìzhǔyì 【名】utilitarianism

功能 gōngnéng 【名】function

功效 gōngxiào 【名】effect；efficacy

功勋 gōngxūn 【名】outstanding meritorious deed

功用 gōngyòng 【名】function；use

攻 gōng 【动】❶ attack（as opp. to 守）：～城 attack a city 能～能守 be equally good at offense and defense ❷ study；delve into：她是专～气象学的。She specializes in meteorology.

攻打 gōngdǎ 【动】（mil.）attack

攻读 gōngdú 【动】study hard

攻击 gōngjī 【动】❶ attack；launch an assault；launch an offensive：发动总 ～ launch a general offensive ❷ slander；vilify：不要进行人身～。Don't engage in personal abuse.

攻坚战 gōngjiānzhàn 【名】battle in which fortified positions are stormed

攻克 gōngkè 【动】attack and capture；capture

攻其不备 gōng qí bù bèi take the enemy by stealth

攻势 gōngshì 【名】offensive

攻无不克 gōng wú bù kè succeed in all attacks

攻心 gōng = xīn attempt to demoralize（sb.）：～ 战 psychological warfare

供 gōng 【动】❶ supply；provide：～电 supply electricity ～暖 supply heating ❷ provide for：这几

点意见～你参考。These opinions are for your reference. 这是～旅客休息的地方。This is a lounge for passengers.

另见 gòng

供不应求 gōng bù yìng qiú supply falls short of demand

供给 gōngjǐ 【动】supply；provide；furnish

供求 gōngqiú 【动】supply and demand

供销 gōngxiāo supply to and sell for

供需 gōngxū 【动】supply and demand

供养 gōngyǎng 【动】provide for the needs (of one's parents or elders)

供应 gōngyìng 【动】supply；provide：～点 supply centre ～线 supply line

宫 gōng 【名】❶ palace ❷ a place for cultural activities or recreation：民族～ the Nationalities Palace 劳动人民文化～ the Workers' Cultural Palace

宫灯 gōngdēng 【名】〔盏 zhǎn〕decorative palace lantern

宫殿 gōngdiàn 【名】〔座 zuò〕palace

宫廷 gōngtíng 【名】❶ court ❷ the monarch and his officials

宫廷政变 gōngtíng zhèngbiàn "palace" coup；coup d'état from within the ruling clique

恭 gōng

恭敬 gōngjìng 【形】respectful

恭惟 gōngwei 【动】flatter

gǒng

巩（鞏） gǒng

巩固 gǒnggù 【形】firm；solid；stable：政权～ stable political power

基础～。The foundation is firm. 【动】consolidate；solidify；strengthen：～和发展中国人民和世界各国人民的友谊 strengthen and develop the friendship between the Chinese people and the peoples of the world

拱 gǒng 【名】arch：水泥～ a cement arch ～门 an arched doorway；arch 【动】❶ clasp and raise (one's hands)：～手（pay respect by）clasping and raising one's hands ❷ arch；curve：～肩缩背 hunch one's shoulders and arch one's back 小猫～一～腰。The kitten arched its back. ❸ push up or forward with one's body：用肩膀拱开了门 push open a door with one's shoulder 蚯蚓从地下～出许多土来。The earthworm pushed up little piles of earth. ❹（of plant）sprout up：竹笋～出土来。The bamboo shoots are sprouting through the earth.

拱桥 gǒngqiáo 【名】〔座 zuò〕arch bridge

gòng

共 gòng 【动】share：同甘苦～患难（nàn）share joys and sorrows 【副】❶ together：～进午餐 have lunch together ～饮一江水 draw water from the same river ❷ in total；in all；altogether：出席大会的代表～五千人。A total of five thousand delegates attended the conference.

共产党 gòngchǎndǎng 【名】communist party

共产党员 gòngchǎndǎngyuán 【名】member of the communist party

共产国际 Gòngchǎn Guójì the Com-

munist International

共产主义 gòngchǎnzhǔyì 【名】communism

共产主义青年团 gòngchǎn zhǔyì qīngniántuán the Communist Youth League

共存 gòngcún 【动】coexist

共和国 gònghéguó 【名】republic

共鸣 gòngmíng 【名】❶ resonance ❷ a sympathetic chord：这首诗激起了读者的～。This poem has struck a responsive chord in the hearts of its readers.

共识 gòngshí 【名】consensus；common understanding

共事 gòngshì 【动】work together

共同 gòngtóng 【形】in common：～的目标 common goal ～的语言 common language 五一国际劳动节是全世界劳动人民的～节日。International Labour Day is a festival celebrated by working people all over the world.

共同市场 gòngtóng shìchǎng the Common Market

共性 gòngxìng 【名】common characteristic

贡（貢）gòng

贡献 gòngxiàn 【动】contribute；dedicate；devote：我要把自己毕生的精力～给医学。I will devote my entire life to medical science.【名】contribution：在天文学方面他有一定的～。He has made some contributions in astronomy.

供 gòng 【动】confess；own up

另见 gōng

供词 gòngcí 【名】confession；a statement made under examination

供品 gòngpǐn 【名】offerings

供认 gòngrèn 【动】confess

gōu

勾 gōu 【动】❶ strike out；cancel；remove：节目单上把女声小合唱～掉了。The women's chorus was struck from the programme. 这句话～掉两个字显得更精炼。With these two words struck out, the sentence is more concise. ❷ tick off：把文章中的重要段落用红笔～出来 use red ink to highlight the important paragraphs in the article ❸ delineate；draw (an outline)：～出轮廓 draw the outline of sth. 他几笔就～出一株竹子来。With just a few strokes he drew a bamboo. ❹ evoke；arouse；remind：你这一句话，倒～起了他的一通议论。Your remark gave rise to a long recital of his views.

另见 gòu

勾搭 gōuda 【动】engage jointly (in wrong-doing)

勾画 gōuhuà 【动】roughly sketch out

勾结 gōujié 【动】conspire with

勾销 gōuxiāo 【动】cancel；write off

勾心斗角 gōu xīn dòu jiǎo scheme against each other

勾引 gōuyǐn 【动】tempt；entice；lure

沟（溝）gōu 【名】〔条 tiáo〕❶ ditch；trench；channel：挖一道～ dig a ditch 暗～ sewer ❷ groove；rut：车～ rut ❸ brook；stream：小河～ brook

沟壑 gōuhè 【名】gully；ravine

沟渠 gōuqú 【名】ditch；irrigation channel

沟通 gōutōng 【动】connect；link-up

钩（鉤）gōu 【名】❶ （～儿）

hook；钓鱼～ fishhook　铁～ iron hook ❷（of Chinese characters）hook stroke，e. g. "亅一" ❸（～儿）check mark；tick，e. g. "√"【动】catch hold of with a hook；hook；把掉在井里的水桶～上来 use a hooked pole to pull out the pail which has dropped into the well

钩子　gōuzi　【名】hook

篝　gōu

篝火　gōuhuǒ　【名】campfire

gǒu

苟　gǒu

苟安　gǒu'ān　【动】〈书〉seek comfort and ease when one should take action

苟且　gǒuqiě　【形】❶ muddle along；drift along；～偷生 live an unprincipled life of ease and comfort ❷ muddle through；do perfunctorily；决不能～从事 never just muddle through your work

苟且偷安　gǒuqiě tōu'ān　同"苟安"

苟延残喘　gǒu yán cán chuǎn　eke out a meagre existence

狗　gǒu　【名】〔只 zhǐ〕dog

狗急跳墙　gǒu jí tiào qiáng　a cornered dog will leap over a wall in desperation；be driven to extremes

狗拿耗子　gǒu ná hàozi　a dog meddling with mouse-catching—being a busy body；being a meddler

狗血喷头　gǒuxuè pēn tóu　curse sb.；pour out a torrent of abuse

狗仗人势　gǒu zhàng rén shì　a dog threatening others on the strength of its master's power；play the bully because one has the backing of a powerful person

gòu

勾　gòu

另见 gōu

勾当　gòudàng　【名】fraudulent deal

构（構）　gòu

构成　gòu // chéng　constitute；make up；form

构词法　gòucífǎ　【名】rules for the formation of words；word-formation

构架　gòujià　【动】structural frame

构件　gòujiàn　【名】（architecture）structural member；（mech.）component

构思　gòusī　【动】（of literature or artistic creation）work out the plot of a story or the composition of a picture.

构图　gòu = tú　composition（of a picture）

构想　gòuxiǎng　【名】conception；conceptualization

构造　gòuzào　【名】structure

构筑　gòuzhù　【动】build；construct

购（購）　gòu　【动】buy

购买　gòumǎi　【动】buy；purchase

购买力　gòumǎilì　【名】purchasing power

购销　gòuxiāo　【动】buying and selling

购置　gòuzhì　【动】buy（large durable items）

够　gòu　【动】❶ reach for sth. with one's hand or a tool；书架最上层的书我～不着，请你给我拿下来。I can't reach the books on the top of the bookshelf. Would you please get them down for me? 擦边的玻璃窗，你～得着～不着? Do you think you could reach up and wipe

the window panes at the top? ❷ reach certain standard：这些产品都～出口的标准。These products are all up to the standard for export. 他已经满六十岁，～退休的年龄了。He is already 60, and has reached the age for retirement. 这根绳子～长不～长? Is this piece of rope long enough? 【形】❶ enough：你带的路费～不～? Have you got enough money with you for the trip? 这些木料盖三间房满～了。These logs are quite enough to build a three-room house. 我才睡了五个小时，没睡～。I've only slept five hours and haven't had enough sleep. 麦田里的水浇得～不～? Have the wheat-fields received enough water? ❷ be fed up with：我坐了两天两夜的火车，真坐～了! I've been travelling by train for two days and two nights, and am certainly fed up with it.

够本 gòu = běn （～儿）（make) enough to pay one's expenses

够呛 gòuqiàng 〈口〉同"够受的"

够受的 gòushòude hard to bear (*usu. as a complement*)：疼得～ terribly painful 累得～ dog-tired 忙得～ busy as a bee 寒流来了，这几天冷得真～。This cold front has brought frigid weather.

够味儿 gòu = wèir perfect；superb：你的上海话真～。Your Shanghai accent is true to the teeth.

媾 gòu

媾和 gòuhé 【动】negotiate for peace

gū

估 gū

估计 gūjì 【动】estimate；reckon；appraise；size up：从这儿骑车到颐和园～得半小时。I guess it will take half an hour to get to the Summer Palace from here by bicycle. 一个人要有自信，但也不要把自己～得过高。One must have self-confidence but mustn't overestimate one's ability. 【名】calculation；appraisal：这只是一个大概的～。This is only a rough estimate. 这种粗略的～显然是靠不住的。Rough calculations like these are obviously unreliable.

估价 gūjià evaluate；appraise

估量 gūliang 【动】estimate；appraise；figure；assess：不可～的损失 inestimable loss 我～着他下午会到北京。I guess that he will arrive in Beijing this afternoon.

估算 gūsuàn 【动】estimate；assess：～产值 evaluate the output value

沽 gū

沽名钓誉 gūmíng diàoyù employ any means to seek fame and reputation (*derog.*)

姑 gū 【名】aunt (father's sister)

姑父 gūfu 【名】uncle (husband of father's sister)

姑姑 gūgu 【名】〈口〉同"姑母"

姑母 gūmǔ 【名】aunt (father's sister)

姑娘 gūniang 【名】girl

姑且 gūqiě 【副】for the time being；might as well：这块手表不太好，～将就着用吧! This watch is not very good, but you might as well use it for the time being. 这个办法～试试看。Give this method a try at least.

姑息 gūxī 【动】indulge；appease

姑息养奸 gūxī yǎng jiān to tolerate evil is to abet it；purposely tolerate evil-doers and evil things

孤 gū 【形】◇lonely；solitary；

isolated：～岛 an isolated island ～雁 a lone wild goose 【名】◇orphan；～寡 widows and orphans

孤傲　gū'ào　【形】aloof and arrogant

孤本　gūběn　【名】(～儿) the sole copy

孤单　gūdān　【形】lonely；all by oneself

孤独　gūdú　【形】solitary；lone

孤儿　gū'ér　【名】orphan

孤儿院　gū'éryuàn　【名】orphanage

孤芳自赏　gū fāng zì shǎng　narcissistic

孤家寡人　gūjiā guǎrén　used by feudal kings and emperors to refer to themselves；a person isolated from the masses；a loner (without friends or supporters)

孤军　gūjūn　【名】an isolated army

孤苦伶仃　gūkǔ língdīng　orphaned and helpless；friendless and wretched

孤立　gūlì　【动】isolate：～敌人 isolate the enemy 【形】isolated：处境～ find oneself in an isolated position

孤立无援　gūlì wú yuán　isolated and helpless；isolated and cut off from help

孤零零　gūlínglíng　【形】alone；all by oneself

孤陋寡闻　gū lòu guǎ wén　with very limited knowledge and scanty information

孤僻　gūpì　【形】aloof and eccentric

孤掌难鸣　gū zhǎng nán míng　one cannot clap with one hand；it is difficult to accomplish anything without support

孤注一掷　gū zhù yī zhì　put all one's eggs in one basket

辜　gū

辜负　gūfù　【动】fail to live up to；disappoint；let down；be unworthy of：我们绝不～父母的培养。We mustn't fail to live up to the education given us by our parents.

gǔ

古　gǔ　【形】ancient 【名】◇ancient times

古板　gǔbǎn　【形】old-fashioned：作风～ a rigid way of work

古代　gǔdài　【名】ancient times

古典　gǔdiǎn　【形】classical；classic

古典文学　gǔdiǎn wénxué　classical literature

古董　gǔdǒng　【名】antique；curio；old fogey

古怪　gǔguài　【形】strange；peculiar

古籍　gǔjí　【名】ancient books

古迹　gǔjì　【名】historical site；place of historical interest

古今中外　gǔ jīn zhōng wài　at all times and in all countries

古兰经　Gǔlánjīng　【名】the Koran

古老　gǔlǎo　【形】old；ancient

古朴　gǔpǔ　【形】with a classical simplicity of style

古人　gǔrén　【名】the ancients；the people of ancient times

古色古香　gǔ sè gǔ xiāng　antique

古诗　gǔshī　【名】〔首 shǒu〕❶ ancient poetry ❷ a form of poem having considerable freedom in the use of tones and rhyme scheme, with 4, 5, or 7 characters in each line and an unlimited number of lines

古往今来　gǔ wǎng jīn lái　from ancient times to the present

古为今用　gǔ wéi jīn yòng　make the past serve the present

古文　gǔwén　【名】classical Chinese

古物　gǔwù　【名】historical relic；antique

古语　gǔyǔ　【名】❶ archaism ❷ old saying

古装　gǔzhuāng　【名】ancient costume

谷 gǔ 【名】❶ valley ❷(穀)grain
谷类 gǔlèi 【名】cereals
谷物 gǔwù 【名】cereals
谷子 gǔzi 【名】(粒 lì)millet

股 gǔ 【名】❶thigh ❷ (of an organization) section 【量】❶ *for strand-like things*：一～泉水 a trickle of spring water 这种毛线是三～的。This is 3-ply wool. 山上有两~小道。There are two trails on the mountain. ❷ *for smell*, *gas*, *etc.*(*the numeral is usu.*"一")：一～香味儿 a whiff of fragrance 一~烟 a whiff of smoke 有一~干劲儿 with a burst of energy ❸ *for groups of people* (*usu. derog.*)：两~土匪 two bandit gangs
股东 gǔdōng 【名】shareholder
股份 gǔfèn 【名】share；stock
股金 gǔjīn 【名】money paid for shares
股票 gǔpiào 【名】(张 zhāng)share；stock
股市 gǔshì 【名】stock market
股息 gǔxī 【名】dividend

骨 gǔ 【名】bone
骨干 gǔgàn 【名】mainstay
骨骼 gǔgé 【名】skeleton
骨灰 gǔhuī 【名】ashes of the dead
骨科 gǔkē 【名】orthopaedics department
骨膜 gǔmó 【名】periosteum
骨气 gǔqì 【名】moral integrity；spunk
骨肉 gǔròu 【名】flesh and blood；parents and children, sisters and brothers
骨瘦如柴 gǔ shòu rú chái thin as a scarecrow
骨髓 gǔsuǐ 【名】marrow
骨头 gǔtou 【名】❶ bone；猪 ～ the bone of a pig 牛～ the bone of a cow ❷ backbone；integrity；硬～ an iron-willed person 软～ a weak-kneed person 没 ～ without backbone；spineless
骨折 gǔzhé 【动】(of a bone) fracture；break
骨子里 gǔzilǐ 【名】in one's bones；in one's heart (*usu. derog.*)

蛊(蠱) gǔ
蛊惑人心 gǔhuò rénxīn confuse and poison people's minds；resort to demagogy；～的言辞 inflammatory speeches ～的宣传 inflammatory propaganda

鼓 gǔ 【名】(面 miàn)drum；打～ beat a drum 【动】❶ rouse；urge；agitate；～ 起勇气 pluck up one's courage ～ 干劲 bring one's energies into full play；go all out ❷ pout；thrust out；～着嘴 pout 船帆～起来了。The sail bellies out (in the wind). 【形】swelling；bulging；衣袋～～的 bulging pockets 书包装得挺～的。The satchel is filled to the bursting point.
鼓吹 gǔchuī 【动】advocate；preach (*usu. derog.*)：～ 种族优劣论 preach racism Note：*in some very rare cases there is no derog. sense*；五四时期一些知识分子～新文化, 取得很大成绩。Around the time of the May 4th Movement, some intellectuals successfully propagated a new culture.
鼓动 gǔdòng 【动】agitate；instigate；urge
鼓风机 gǔfēngjī 【名】(台 tái)blower (e.g. of a furnace)
鼓励 gǔlì 【动】encourage；inspire；urge；加以 ～ give encouragement 以资 ～ serve as an encouragement ～大家勇于创新 encourage everybody to create sth. new 【名】encouragement；spur：校长充分肯定了科研的成绩, 这对我们是个～。The

chancellor's strong approval of our achievements in scientific research is a great source of encouragement to us.

鼓手 gǔshǒu 【名】drummer

鼓舞 gǔwǔ 【动】❶ inspire；hearten；encourage；arouse the enthusiasm of：～人心（sth.）inspiring；kindle enthusiasm in the hearts of the people ～士气 boost the morale of the troops ❷ feel encouraged；feel inspired；令人～ be elated and inspired 【名】inspiration；encouragement：受到～ be encouraged 巨大的～变成了巨大的力量。Great inspiration turns into great strength.

鼓掌 gǔ＝zhǎng applaud

鼓足干劲 gǔ zú gànjìn go all out；put forth one's greatest effort

gù

固 gù

固步自封 gù bù zì fēng stop in one's tracks and refuse to make progress 也作"故步自封"。

固定 gùdìng 【动】fix；regularize：把学习时间～下来 fix the time for study 【形】fixed；static：～的位置 fixed position ～基金 fixed funds ～职业 a permanent job（profession）

固然 gùrán 【副】*used to acknowledge a fact in order to make a contrary statement which is the speaker's real purpose*：这个建议从理论上～讲得通，但是实行起来还有问题。This suggestion is feasible in theory but difficult to put into practice. 数学～重要，别的功课也不能忽视。Mathematics is certainly important，but other courses mustn't be neglected.

固态 gùtài 【名】(phys.) solid state

固体 gùtǐ 【名】solid：～饮料 solid drinks

固有 gùyǒu 【动】inherent；intrinsic；innate：～的体系 intrinsic system ～的文化 inherent culture

固执 gùzhí 【形】stubborn；obstinate：性情～ of a stubborn temperament

固执己见 gùzhí jǐ jiàn stick stubbornly to one's own opinion

故 gù 【名】◇❶ cause；reason：不知何～ not know why ❷ friend：沾亲带～ ties of relationship or friendship 【形】◇❶ old；former；previous：黄河～道 the old course of the Huanghe River 依然如～ the same as before ❷ purposely：～作镇静 purposely assume an air of composure（in order to deceive）【连】〈书〉therefore：途中遇事耽搁，～未能如期到达。I was held up by something on the way and so I was late.

故步自封 gù bù zì fēng 同"固步自封" gù bù zì fēng

故都 gùdū 【名】ancient capital

故宫 gùgōng 【名】the Imperial Palace

故伎重演 gù jì chóng yǎn up to one's old tricks

故居 gùjū 【名】former residence

故弄玄虚 gù nòng xuánxū deliberately complicate a simple issue

故去 gùqù 【动】die；pass away

故人 gùrén 【名】old friend；a dead person

故事 gùshi 【名】〔个 gè〕story：讲～ tell a story 民间～ folk-tale 这篇小说～性很强。This novel has an intricate plot.

故事片 gùshipiàn 【名】〔部 bù〕feature film

故土 gùtǔ 【名】native land

故乡 gùxiāng 【名】hometown；native place；birthplace

故意 gùyì 【形】purposely；inten-

tionally;deliberately:～刁难 deliberately put obstacles in sb.'s way; make difficulties for sb. ～开玩笑 deliberately make fun of（sb.）你别怪他了，他又不是～的。Don't blame him. He didn't do it on purpose.

故障　gùzhàng　【名】sth. wrong（with a machine）

顾（顧）

gù　【动】❶ ◇turn around and look at; look around ❷ attend to; care for:～大局 take the whole situation into consideration; for the sake of the larger interest ～面子 be intent on face-saving; save one's face 时间太紧，～不得给她打电话了。I was in such a hurry that I couldn't phone her.

顾不得　gù bu de　forgetting; without thinking of:一忙乱起来就什么也～了。Once he is busy he will forget everything else.

顾此失彼　gù cǐ shī bǐ　be unable to attend to everything at once; take care of one matter while forgetting another:既要好好学习，又要意身体，不能～。One must both study hard and take good care of one's health, neither must be neglected.

顾及　gùjí　【动】attend to; give consideration to

顾忌　gùjì　【动】have scruples; have qualms; hesitate

顾客　gùkè　【名】customer; client; shopper

顾虑　gùlǜ　【名】worries; apprehensions; misgivings:～重重 be full of misgivings 打消～ get rid of one's misgivings【动】worry:有话就说吧，你～什么? Say what's on your mind; you needn't have qualms.

顾名思义　gù míng sī yì　by the name of a thing, one is reminded of its function; as its name suggests: 这

种伞叫阳伞，～，它是遮阳光用的，而不是遮雨用的。This is called a "parasol". You can tell by its name that it is used to keep off the sun and not the rain.

顾全大局　gùquán dàjú　take the interests of the whole into account

顾问　gùwèn　【名】advisor

雇

gù　【动】hire

雇工　gùgōng　【名】hired labourer

雇农　gùnóng　【名】hired farm labourer

雇佣　gùyōng　【动】hire

雇佣军　gùyōngjūn　【名】mercenaries

雇佣劳动　gùyōng láodòng　wage labour

雇员　gùyuán　【名】employee

雇主　gùzhǔ　【名】employer

guā

瓜

guā　【名】❶ melon; gourd:我们这儿～的品种可多啦，西瓜、南瓜、黄瓜都有。We have all kinds of melons and gourds here — watermelons, pumpkins, cucumbers, etc. ❷ sth. which has the shape of a melon:脑袋～儿 "pumpkin"; "gourd"（meaning the human head）傻～ pumpkin head

瓜分　guāfēn　【动】cut up（territory）into parts and annex them

瓜葛　guāgé　【名】inter-relationship; entanglement

瓜熟蒂落　guā shú dì luò　when a melon is mature, it will fall by itself;（fig.）problems can easily be solved when the conditions are ripe.

瓜子儿　guāzǐr　【名】melon seed

刮（颳）

guā　【动】❶ scrape ❷ blow

刮风　guā = fēng　be windy;（the

wind) blow

刮脸　guā=liǎn　shave

刮脸刀　guāliǎndāo　【名】razor

刮目相看　guāmù xiāng kàn　look at afresh；look at in a different light

呱　guā　【象声】quack；croak

呱呱　guāguā　【象声】quack；croak

guǎ

寡　guǎ　【形】◇❶ few；be lacking：索然～味（of a piece of writing）dull and monotonous　～言少语 taciturn；in the habit of saying very little　众～悬殊 one side greatly outnumbers the other ❷ be widowed：～居 be left a widow

寡不敌众　guǎ bù dí zhòng　be vastly outnumbered

寡妇　guǎfu　【名】widow

寡头　guǎtóu　【名】oligarchy

guà

挂　guà　【动】❶ hang；put up；suspend：墙上～着一幅地图。A map is hanging on the wall. 五一节公园里～了很多彩灯。On May Day, there are many coloured lanterns hanging in the parks. ❷ make（a phone call）：我给他～个电话。I'll call him up. ❸ ring off：～上电话 hang up（the receiver）❹ get caught；catch：钉子把衣服～住了。My dress got caught on a nail. ❺ be concerned about：你要安心工作，不要把家中的事情老～在心上。You should keep your mind on your work. Don't think about your family affairs all the time.

挂彩　guà=cǎi　be wounded (in battle)

挂钩　guà=gōu　❶ couple (cars of a train) ❷ link with；establish contact with：产销～ direct link between producer and seller

挂号　guà=hào　register

挂号信　guàhàoxìn　【名】〔封 fēng〕registered letter

挂历　guàlì　【名】hanging calendar；wall calendar

挂名　guà=míng　titular；nominal；only in name

挂念　guàniàn　【动】worry over (sb.)；miss (sb.)

挂失　guà=shī　report the loss of (checks etc.)

挂帅　guà=shuài　put... in command；take command；be in a leading position：这项实验由王教授～。This experiment is under the personal supervision of Professor Wang.

挂毯　guàtǎn　【名】〔幅 fú〕tapestry

挂图　guàtú　【名】〔幅 fú〕map or chart that can be hung on the wall

挂羊头卖狗肉　guà yángtóu mài gǒuròu　hang out a sheep's head but actually sell dog's meat；palm sth. off on sb.

挂一漏万　guà yī lòu wàn　make mention of one item while leaving out ten thousand；incomplete and full of omissions：近几年有很多考古新发现，介绍起来，难免～。There have been so many new archaeological finds in recent years that my account will probably be far from exhaustive.

guāi

乖　guāi　【形】❶ (of a child) obedient；well-behaved ❷ clever

乖巧　guāiqiǎo　【形】good；ingratiating；smart

guǎi

拐　guǎi　【动】❶ turn：车子向左～了个弯儿。The car turned to the left. ❷ limp：他走路一～一～的。He walks with a limp.

拐棍　guǎigùn　【名】〔根 gēn〕walking stick

拐卖　guǎimài　【动】kidnap and sell

拐骗　guǎipiàn　【动】swindle；abduct

拐弯　guǎi = wān　make a turn；turn

拐弯抹角　guǎi wān mò jiǎo　(fig.) in a roundabout way；beat about the bush：老陈性格直爽，说话从不～。Lao Chen is a straightforward man. He never beats about the bush.

guài

怪　guài　【形】strange；peculiar；unusual；abnormal：～事 a strange thing 这个人脾气有点儿～。This person's temperament is a little bit peculiar. 我的英语说得不好，有点～腔～调的。My English is not very good. It sounds peculiar. 【动】blame；rebuke：这不能～他，都～我。He is not to blame, I am. 他没来开会～不得他，忘了通知他了。We can't blame him for not attending the meeting since we forgot to notify him. 这事本来就很难办，不能～他没办法。It was really a knotty problem；he can't be blamed for being unable to find a way out. 【副】very qualifying a descriptive word or phrase and usu. in conjunction with 的：❶ indicating appreciation or fondness：这幅刺绣 ～ 好看的。This piece of embroidery is very attractive. 这孩子～叫人疼的。This child is very lovable. ❷ indicating

slight irritation：这箱子提起来～费劲儿的。This suitcase is really too heavy to carry. 他怎么还不来，～让人着急的。Why hasn't he come yet? We're getting rather worried.

怪不得　guàibude　【副】indicates a sudden understanding of the cause of something which one didn't understand previously：他是在广州长大的，～会讲广东话。So he grew up in Guangzhou! No wonder he can speak the Guangdong dialect! ～这几天没看见他，原来他出国了。So he's gone abroad! No wonder I haven't seen him recently!

怪诞　guàidàn　【形】grotesque

怪话　guàihuà　【名】destructive criticism

怪模怪样　guài mú guài yàng　strange-looking：这种猴子长得～的。This kind of monkey is strange-looking.

怪僻　guàipì　【形】(of a person) eccentric；odd；queer

怪物　guàiwu　【名】monster

怪罪　guàizuì　【动】blame；put the blame on sb.

guān

关（關）　guān　【动】❶ close；shut：把窗户～上 shut the window ❷ turn off：～电灯 turn off the light 请把电视机～了。Please turn off the TV. ❸ shut in ❹ ◇have sth. to do with；have a bearing on：事～大局 sth. which can affect the whole situation 【名】❶ pass (e. g. mountain pass) ❷ turning point；critical juncture：攻克技术～ make a technical break through 只要突破这一～，就好办了。All will be well if we succeed in overcoming this difficulty.

关闭　guānbì　【动】❶ close；shut：～

门窗 shut the doors and windows ～闸门 close the sluice-gate ❷ stop using or not be allowed to use：～工厂 close a factory ～机场 close an airport

关怀 guānhuái 【动】be concerned about；show loving care for；show solicitude：～儿童的健康成长 devote great care to the sound and healthy development of children 新生受到学校无微不至的～。The new students were well taken care of by the school.

关键 guānjiàn 【名】key；crux：～时刻 critical moment 问题的～ the crux of the matter 这是～的一仗，一定要打好。This is the decisive battle, we must fight well.

关节 guānjié 【名】joint

关节炎 guānjiéyán 【名】arthritis

关口 guānkǒu 【名】❶ strategic pass ❷ juncture

关联 guānlián 【动】be related or interconnected：工农业生产的发展，是互相～，不可分割的。Industrial and agricultural production are interrelated and the development of one depends on the development of the other.

关门 guān = mén ❶ fold up；close down ❷ slam the door in sb.'s face

关门主义 guānménzhǔyì 【名】closed-door sectarianism

关卡 guānqiǎ 【名】an outpost of a tax office

关切 guānqiè 【动】be deeply concerned about；care for：对事态的发展十分～ be concerned about the way the situation is developing 老师～地询问学生学习是否有困难。The teacher asked with concern whether the students were having any difficulties with their studies.

关税 guānshuì 【名】(customs) duty；tariff

关头 guāntóu 【名】critical moment or important juncture：生死～ life-and-death crisis 紧要～ important juncture

关系 guānxi 【名】❶ relation；relationship：政治与经济的～ the relationship between politics and economics 上层建筑与经济基础的～ the relationship between superstructure and economic base ❷ ties；connection：师生～ teacher-student relationship 社会～ one's social connections ❸ bearing；impact；significance (*often used with* 有 *or* 没有)：我这点小病没什么～。This indisposition of mine is nothing at all. 土质对作物的生长很有～。The quality of the soil has a lot to do with the growth of crops. ❹ *indicates the cause or condition*：由于时间～，报告到此结束。Since time is limited, I will end my report here. 【动】affect；concern；involve：处理好废水、废气，直接～着大众的健康。The proper disposal of waste water and waste gas directly affects the health of the public.

关系户 guānxìhù 【名】parties of connection

关心 guānxīn 【动】show concern for；be concerned about

关押 guānyā 【动】put into prison；take into custody

关于 guānyú 【介】❶ *forms a P-O construction which is used as a modifier to indicate the scope of what is modified*：我们看了一个～科学种田的电影。We've just seen a film on scientific farming. ～语音的研究叫语音学。The study of speech-sounds is called phonetics. ❷ *forms a P-O construction used as the predicate in the structure* 是…的：我看了一本书，是～淡水养鱼的。I've just read a book about freshwater fish-farming. ❸ *forms a P-O construction which is used as*

an adverbial adjunct indicating the scope of an action. This P-O construction is placed at the beginning of the sentence：～历史人物的评价，我们下一次还要讨论。We need to go over the appraisal of these historical figures again next time. ～目前形势，他作了详细分析。He has made a detailed analysis of the current situation. ❹ 关于… *sometimes is used in the title of a piece of writing*：《～市场经济问题》On the Market Economy

关照 guānzhào 【动】❶ look after; keep an eye on：我不在家，孩子们请您多多～。Please keep an eye on the children while I am away. ❷ give sb. a verbal message：请～传达室一声，如有客人来，就给我打个电话。Please tell the porter to phone me if anyone comes visiting me.

关注 guānzhù 【动】pay close attention to; follow with interest：地震灾区的群众受到了政府的特别～。The people of the earthquake-stricken areas received particular care from the government.

观（觀）guān 【动】look at; watch; observe

观测 guāncè 【动】❶ observe and survey（e.g. astronomy, geography, weather, direction, etc.）❷ observe and analyze：～敌情 observe and analyze the enemy's situation

观察 guānchá 【动】observe; view; examine

观察家 guānchájiā 【名】observer

观察员 guāncháyuán 【名】observer

观潮派 guāncháopài 【名】one who adopts a wait-and-see attitude; an onlooker

观点 guāndiǎn 【名】point of view

观感 guāngǎn 【名】impression; view

观光 guānguāng 【动】be on a sight-seeing trip; tour：归国华侨代表团到祖国各地～。The Overseas-Chinese Delegation is on a sight-seeing trip around the country.

观看 guānkàn 【动】watch

观礼 guānlǐ = 忭 review（a grand celebration or ceremony）：国庆～ attend the National Day celebrations ～代表 a representative attending the celebrations

观礼台 guānlǐtái 【名】reviewing stand

观摩 guānmó 【动】watch and learn from sb.; watch and emulate：互相～ watch and learn from each other ～教学 demonstration teaching

观念 guānniàn 【名】idea; notion; concept

观赏 guānshǎng 【动】watch and enjoy

观望 guānwàng 【动】❶ look on hesitating to interfere; wait and see：持～态度 adopt a wait-and-see attitude 他到现在还在～。He is still an onlooker. ❷ look around：四下～ take a look around

观象台 guānxiàngtái 【名】observatory

观众 guānzhòng 【名】audience

官 guān 【名】❶ government official ❷ government cadre or military officer：外交～ diplomat ～兵一致 unity between officers and men

官邸 guāndǐ 【名】official residence

官方 guānfāng 【名】official;（said or done）with authority

官架子 guānjiàzi 【名】pompous air assumed by officials

官吏 guānlì 【名】government official（in the past）

官僚 guānliáo 【名】bureaucrat

官僚主义 guānliáozhǔyì 【名】bureaucracy

官僚资本　guānliáo zīběn　bureaucrat-capital

官气　guānqì　【名】pompous air assumed by officials

官腔　guānqiāng　【名】official jargon

官商作风　guānshāng zuòfēng　bureaucratic business style

官司　guānsi　【名】lawsuit；case

官衔　guānxián　【名】official title

官样文章　guānyàng wénzhāng　mere formalities；bureaucratic jargon

官员　guānyuán　【名】government official；official

冠

冠　guān　【名】❶ hat ❷ corona；crown
另见 guàn

冠冕堂皇　guānmiǎn tánghuáng　righteous and honourable（irony）；high-sounding

冠心病　guānxīnbìng　【名】coronary heart disease

棺

棺　guān

棺材　guāncai　【名】coffin

鳏（鰥）

鳏（鰥）　guān

鳏夫　guānfū　【名】widower or bachelor

鳏寡孤独　guān guǎ gū dú　widowers, widows, orphans, the elderly and childless

guǎn

管

管　guǎn　【动】❶ be in charge of；run：这个果园由五个人～。Five people run this orchard. 他在工厂里～技术工作。He is in charge of technical work in the factory. ❷ administer：本市的中学都归市教育局～。All the high schools in the city are administered by the Municipal Education Bureau. ❸ control；take care of：少年儿童，学校要～，家长也要～。Schools and parents must both take care of children. ❹ interfere：浪费国家财产的事人人都应该～。Everybody ought to interfere in cases where state property is being misused. 我们不能看着他犯错误不～。We cannot just stand by and watch him commit errors. ❺ mind；attend to：不要～我，抢救国家财产要紧。Never mind me. Go and try to save the state's property. 只是碰破点皮，不用～它，一会儿就好了。It's just a scrape. It will be all right in no time and doesn't need looking after. 【名】（～儿）pipe：钢～ steel tube 水～ water pipe 玻璃～ glass pipe 【介】（in conjunction with 叫）name sb. or sth.：因为他年龄小，大家都～他叫小张。As he is rather young, everybody calls him Xiao Zhang. 我们～每月出版一次的刊物叫月刊。A magazine published every month is called a "monthly".

管保　guǎnbǎo　【动】guarantee；assure：如果肯刻苦练习，～能把毛笔字写好。You will certainly be able to write well with a brush if you practise hard. 这个西瓜不甜，我可不～。I cannot guarantee that this watermelon is sweet.

管道　guǎndào　【名】pipeline

管教　guǎnjiào　【动】admonish；discipline；instruct（youngsters）

管教所　guǎnjiàosuǒ　【名】reformatory；reform school

管界　guǎnjiè　【名】administered area；boundary

管理　guǎnlǐ　【动】❶ manage；administer；run：～企业 run an enterprise 劳动人民～国家大事 The working people have a say in the affairs of the nation. ❷ take care of（things）：～图书资料 take care of publications and materials 体育用品要～好。Athletic equipment

must be properly maintained.

管事 guǎn·shì （～儿）effective;
useful; efficacious: 针灸很～, 我扎
了两针，头就不痛了。 Acupuncture is
quite effective. My headache was
gone after the insertion of two
needles.

管束 guǎnshù 【动】keep under control; restrain

管辖 guǎnxiá 【动】exercise control
over

管闲事 guǎn xiánshì poke one's
nose into

管弦乐 guǎnxiányuè 【名】orchestral
music

管用 guǎn = yòng be effective;
function: 这部发电机虽然旧了，但还
～。 This generator is old, but it
still functions. 这种咳嗽药水不管什
么用。 This mixture doesn't do
anything for a cough.

管制 guǎnzhì 【动】❶ control: ～灯
火 (during war-time) blackout 军事
～ be under martial law ❷ (of
criminals or bad elements) put under surveillance

管子 guǎnzi 【名】〔根 gēn〕pipe;
tube

guàn

贯（貫）guàn 【动】❶ pierce;
penetrate ❷ link up; be joined

贯彻 guànchè 【动】carry out; implement: ～大会决议 put the decisions of the meeting into effect ～
到底 carry through to completion
～执行 put into practice

贯彻始终 guànchè shǐzhōng carry
through to the end; thorough im-
plementation

贯穿 guànchuān 【动】❶ run
through; pass through: 这条输油管
道～好几个省。 This pipeline passes

through several provinces. ❷ per-
meate; be permeated with: 勤俭节
约的精神要～在整个生产过程中。
The spirit of industry and thrift
must pervade the entire process of
production.

贯通 guàntōng 【动】❶ have a thorough understanding of; be well
versed in: 豁然～ have a sudden insight ❷ connect; link up; 这条铁路
已全线～。 The whole railway line
has been linked up and completed.

贯注 guànzhù 【动】concentrate on:
把全部精力～在工作上 concentrate
all one's energy on work

冠 guàn
另见 guān

冠军 guànjūn 【名】champion (in
games and sports)

惯（慣）guàn 【形】be accus-
tomed to; be used to; be in the
habit of: 劳动～了的人总是闲不住。
Those who are used to physical labour cannot bear to remain idle.
中国的饭菜你吃得～吗? Are you
used to Chinese food? 这是他～用的
手法。 He's up to his usual tricks.
你不吃早点饿不饿? ——不饿,已经～
了。 Don't you get hungry if you
skip breakfast? —No, I'm used to
it. 【动】spoil; indulge: 这孩子被大
人～坏了。 This child has been
spoiled by the adults around him.

惯犯 guànfàn 【名】habitual offender

惯匪 guànfěi 【名】incorrigible bandits

惯技 guànjì 【名】old trick

惯例 guànlì 【名】established practice; convention

惯性 guànxìng 【名】(phys.) inertia

惯用 guànyòng 【动】habitually use;
consistantly practise: ～手法 habit-

ual practice (*derog.*)

惯于　guànyú　【动】be used to; be in the habit of (*used before a verb or a verb phrase*): ～拨弄是非 habitually sow discord 他～使用偷梁换柱的手法。He is addicted to practising tricks and fraud. 他已～晚上工作。He is used to working at night.

盥　guàn

盥洗　guànxǐ　【动】wash one's hands and face

盥洗室　guànxǐshì　【名】toilet; washroom; lavatory

灌　guàn　【动】❶ water: 引水～田 channel water to irrigate the fields ❷ pour into: ～一瓶开水 fill the bottle with boiled water ❸ penetrate: 从门缝往里直～风。The wind penetrates through the cracks in the door. 嘈杂的声音直往耳朵里～。My ears are filled with noise.

灌唱片　guàn chàngpiàn　make a gramophone record

灌溉　guàngài　【动】irrigate

灌木　guànmù　【名】shrub; bush

灌区　guànqū　【名】irrigated area

灌渠　guànqú　【名】irrigation channel

灌输　guànshū　【动】(of knowledge, idea, etc.) instil in; inculcate: ～科学知识 impart scientific knowledge

灌注　guànzhù　【动】pour into; fill

罐　guàn　【名】jug; jar; pot

罐头　guàntou　【名】tinned food; tin; can

罐装　guànzhuāng　【动】to can: ～食品 tinned food

罐子　guànzi　【名】〔个 gè〕pot; jar

guāng

光　guāng　【名】light; brilliance: 有一分热发一分～。As long as there is heat, there is light. (*fig.*) However slight one's resources, one should make the best of them. 这种灯的～比较柔和。The light from this kind of lamp is rather soft. 【动】(of the body or part of the body) bare: ～着脚 barefoot ～着头 bare-headed 【形】❶ *indicates finality*: 钱花～了。The money is used up. 把院子里的草拔得～～的。All the weeds in the courtyard were pulled up. ❷ bare (*usu. reduplicated*): 墙上～～的,一张画儿也没有。The wall was completely bare, without a single picture. 原来～～的山头,现在都栽满了果树。The mountains, which used to be bare, are now completely covered with apple trees. ❸ smooth: 这种纸太～,不好写字。This kind of paper is too smooth. It is hard to write on. 建筑工人把地面抹得～～的。The floor was polished by the builder to a high sheen. 【副】only ❶ *What is modified by* 光 *is contrasted with sth. else*: ～说不干 all words and no action 咱们不能～看眼前利益,还要考虑远大目标。We mustn't just focus on immediate gains, but must keep in mind the long-term goals as well. 屋里的人都走了,～剩他一个了。Everyone else in the room had gone, and he was left alone. ❷ *sth. must be said about what is modified by* 光: 这么多的工作,～靠你们两个人干得过来吗? That's a lot of work! Do you think just two of you can cope with it all? 这两间屋子～打扫不行,还得粉刷。You can't simply clean

these two rooms; they must also be white-washed. ❸ *can be used immediately before a noun or pronoun*：今年这个村子丰收，～麦子就产了五十多万斤。This village had an excellent harvest this year. They harvested 500,000 catties of wheat alone. ～我们一个组去就够了，不用派别的组去了。Our group alone can cope. There is no need for any other group to go.

光彩 guāngcǎi【名】splendour; brilliance【形】glorious; (feel) honoured

光彩夺目 guāngcǎi duómù dazzling and colourful：红绿宝石～。The brilliant jewels shone with dazzling beauty.

光辐射 guāngfúshè【名】the radiation of light; ray radiation

光复 guāngfù【动】recover; restore：～河山 recover territory ～旧物 restore the nation

光顾 guānggù【动】patronize

光合作用 guānghé zuòyòng photosynthesis

光滑 guānghuá【形】smooth; sleek

光辉 guānghuī【名】splendour; radiance; glory：太阳的～ the radiance of the sun【形】glorious; brilliant; magnificent：～的榜样 magnificent example

光景 guāngjǐng【名】❶ circumstances; living; life：美好的～ happy life ❷ scenes：童年时代的～还历历在目。Scenes from our childhood still appear vividly before us. ❸ *indicates an approximation, having to do with time*：这事距现在有一、二年～。The event took place about two years ago. 这个老汉也就六十岁～。This old man is only about 60.

光缆 guānglǎn【名】optical fibre cable：～通讯 communications by optical fibre

光临 guānglín【动】(of a guest) be present (*polite term used in extending an invitation to sb.*)：请您～指导。We would welcome your presence, along with any advice you might care to give. 敬请～。Your presence is cordially requested.

光溜溜 guāngliūliū【形】❶ shiny and slippery; smooth：～的冰场 gleaming and slippery skating rink 地板～的 highly polished floor ❷ naked; bare：楼前空地上种点花草，就不那么～的了。Plant some flowers and grass in front of the building so that it will not look so bare.

光芒 guāngmáng【名】radiant light; ray

光明 guāngmíng【形】bright; brilliant

光明磊落 guāngmíng lěiluò frank and forthright; open and honourable：这位老工人一贯～，公而忘私。This veteran worker is always upright and above-the-board in the service of the people.

光明正大 guāngmíng zhèngdà open and above-board; frank and upright; just and honourable：为人处事要～。One must be open and above-board in going about the business of life.

光年 guāngnián【量】light year

光谱 guāngpǔ【名】spectrum

光圈 guāngquān【名】diaphragm

光荣 guāngróng【名】glory; honour【形】glorious; (feel) honoured

光荣榜 guāngróngbǎng【名】honour roll

光速 guāngsù【名】the speed of light

光天化日 guāng tiān huà rì broad daylight：把他的阴谋诡计暴露在～之下。Expose his machinations to the light of day.

光头 guāngtóu【名】❶ bareheaded

❷ shaven head

光秃秃　guāngtūtū　【形】barren；
bald；bare

光线　guāngxiàn　【名】light ray

光学　guāngxué　【名】optics

光焰　guāngyàn　【名】brilliance

光阴　guāngyīn　【名】time（in the
abstract sense）

光源　guāngyuán　【名】light source

光泽　guāngzé　【名】lustre；shine

光柱　guāngzhù　【名】light beam；
beam

guǎng

广（廣）　guǎng　【形】❶
broad；extensive；vast：地～人稀 a
vast and thinly-populated area 消
息流传很～。The news has spread
far and wide. ❷ extensive（usu. of
knowledge）：知识～ have extensive
knowledge 见识～ possess wide experience and extensive knowledge
【动】◇ broaden：以～见闻 extend
one's knowledge

广播　guǎngbō　【动】broadcast

广播电台　guǎngbō diàntái　broadcasting station

广播剧　guǎngbōjù　radio-play

广播体操　guǎngbō tǐcāo　setting-up
exercises done to broadcast music

广博　guǎngbó　【形】（of knowledge）
wide-ranging；extensive

广场　guǎngchǎng　【名】square

广大　guǎngdà　【形】❶ wide；exten-
sive；vast：～地区 vast areas ❷（of
people）numerous：～群众 the
broad masses of the people ～科技
人员 the great majority of scientific and technical personnel

广度　guǎngdù　【名】scope；range

广泛　guǎngfàn　【形】extensive；
widespread；wide-ranging：内容～
wide-ranging topics ～地征求意见
solicit opinions from all sides 给予

～的同情和支持 provide with wide
sympathy and support.

广告　guǎnggào　【名】advertisement

广开言路　guǎng kāi yán lù　encourage the free airing of opinions

广阔　guǎngkuò　【形】broad；wide

广阔天地　guǎngkuò tiāndì　wide
prospect；vast areas

广义　guǎngyì　【名】（in the）broad
sense（of）

guàng

逛　guàng　【动】stroll；visit（a
park，etc.）

guī

归（歸）　guī　【动】❶ ◇ re-
turn；get back：～国 return to
one's own country 胜利而～ return
in victory ❷ ◇ return sth. to：get
back to：物～原主。The object has
been returned to its owner. ❸
converge；come together：众望所～
enjoy high prestige among the
people 条条江河～大海。Rivers lead
to the sea. ❹ lump together；
group together：把这些东西～在一
起 group these things together 把问
题～～类 categorize these problems
❺ put under sb.'s care；turn over
to：这些书全～你。All these books
are now turned over to you. 这件
事～他办。He will be responsible
for handling this affair.

归案　guī＝àn　bring to justice

归队　guī＝duì　❶（mil.）rejoin one's
unit ❷ return to one's original pro-
fession：我原来就是搞炼钢的，现在又
～了。I used to be a steel worker，
and now I'm back at my old job
again.

归根结底　guī gēn jié dǐ　in the final

analysis 也作"归根结柢（dǐ）、归根结蒂（dì）"。

归公 guīgōng 【动】be made public property

归功 guīgōng 【动】(*usu. used with* 于) give the credit to；attribute one's success to：我今天能取得一些成绩应～于老师的教导。I owe what I have achieved today to the instructions of my teachers.

归还 guīhuán 【动】return (sth. borrowed)

归结 guījié 【动】sum up：车间主任把大家的意见～为三点。The head of the workshop summed up the various views in three points.

归咎 guījiù 【动】lay the blame on；blame

归拢 guīlǒng 【动】put together

归纳 guīnà 【动】❶ induce ❷ sum up；conclude：～大家的意见 sum up everybody's opinions ～出几个问题 sum up in several questions

归侨 guīqiáo 【名】returned overseas Chinese

归属 guīshǔ 【动】belong to

归宿 guīsù 【名】end-result；one's home and final refuge

归心似箭 guī xīn sì jiàn one's mind is bent like a flying arrow on returning home

归于 guīyú 【动】❶ belong to：光荣～祖国和人民。All the glory belongs to the motherland and the people. ❷ result in；end in：经过讨论，大家的意见逐渐～一致。Our discussion gradually ended in agreement.

归总 guīzǒng 【动】Sum up；summarize：把各方面的意见～一下。Sum up the opinions from all quarters.

归罪 guīzuì 【动】lay the blame on

龟（龜） guī 【名】〔只 zhī〕tortoise

龟甲 guījiǎ 【名】shell of a tortoise

龟缩 guīsuō 【动】retreat into one's shell like a tortoise

规（規） guī

规程 guīchéng 【名】rules and regulations

规定 guīdìng 【动】❶ define；stipulate；provide for：～计划指标 set a quota ～了参加会议的人数。The number of persons to take part in the meeting has been set. ❷ fix；set；decide：我们学校～下午四点半以后是体育活动时间。Our school has made a rule that after 4：30 p.m. every weekday is reserved for sports activities. 【名】stipulation：按照中国宪法的～，保卫祖国，抵抗侵略，是每一个公民的崇高职责。As stipulated by the Chinese Constitution, it is the solemn obligation of every citizen to safeguard the country and resist aggression.

规范 guīfàn 【名】standard；norm：语法～ grammatical correctness 技术～ technical standard 【形】standard：他的普通话说得不太～。His *putonghua* is not quite up to standard.

规范化 guīfànhuà 【动】standardization：语言～ standardization of the language

规格 guīgé 【名】specifications

规划 guīhuà 【名】long-standing plan：订～ draw up a plan 城市建设～ the city's construction plan 【动】把今后五年的科学研究工作～一下 make a plan for scientific research for the coming five years

规矩 guīju 【名】rule；established practice：守～ keep to the rules 不能什么事都按老～办。Not everything can be done according to the old ways. 【形】well-behaved

规律 guīlǜ 【名】law

规律性 guīlǜxìng 【名】regularity

规模 guīmó 【名】scale；extent

规劝 guīquàn 【动】admonish；persuade；offer advice to

规则 guīzé 【名】rule；regulation：交通～ traffic regulations 游泳～ a swimming pool's regulations 【形】regular；orderly：这一片建筑物的布局十分～。The buildings in this area are laid out in an orderly fashion.

规章 guīzhāng 【名】rules and regulations

闺（閨） guī

闺女 guīnü 【名】❶ an unmarried woman ❷ daughter

硅 guī 【名】silicon (Si)

瑰 guī

瑰宝 guībǎo 【名】treasure；rarity

瑰丽 guīlì 【形】extremely beautiful；very pretty：～的景色 beautiful scenery ～的花朵 pretty flowers

guǐ

轨（軌） guǐ 【名】❶ rail；track：这条铁路开始铺～。The laying of the rails for this railway line is started. ❷ ◇ order；regularity：这是一种越～行动。This is an action which oversteps the bounds of propriety.

轨道 guǐdào 【名】❶ (of railway) track ❷ orbit：卫星运行的～ the orbit of a satellite ❸ order；course：工作已走上～。The work has got itself into a proper routine.

轨迹 guǐjì 【名】❶ locus ❷ orbit

诡（詭） guǐ

诡辩 guǐbiàn 【动】resort to sophistry

诡计 guǐjì 【名】trick；scheme

诡计多端 guǐjì duō duān crafty；full of tricks：这个坏家伙～，我们可得小心点儿。This fellow is very crafty；we'd better be on guard.

诡秘 guǐmì 【形】secret

诡诈 guǐzhà 【形】crafty

鬼 guǐ 【名】❶ ghost；spirit；apparition ❷ *added to another word to form a term of abuse*：吸血～ leech 胆小～ coward ❸ dirty trick；sinister design：心里有～ harbour some guilty secret 【形】❶ stealthy；surreptitious；underhanded；～头～脑 stealthy；sneaky ❷ damnable：～天气 damnable weather ～地方 cursed place ❸ (usu. of children) smart；clever：这孩子真～。This boy is very clever.

鬼把戏 guǐbǎxì dirty trick；underhanded trick：玩弄～ play a dirty trick 识破～ see through a trick

鬼点子 guǐdiǎnzi 【名】sinister idea；wicked idea

鬼鬼祟祟 guǐ guǐ suì suì 【形】stealthy；sneaky；furtive

鬼话 guǐhuà 【名】deceptive remark；lie

鬼魂 guǐhún 【名】ghost；spirit

鬼混 guǐhùn 【动】lead an aimless or irregular existence：别总跟那些不务正业的人～。Don't fool around with those loafers.

鬼迷心窍 guǐ mí xīn qiào be possessed by evil thoughts

鬼蜮 guǐyù 【名】demon

鬼子 guǐzi 【名】devil (*a term of abuse for foreign invaders*)

guì

柜（櫃） guì 【名】◇ cupboard；cabinet：书～ bookcase 衣～ wardrobe 食品～ kitchen cupboard

柜台 guìtái 【名】sales-counter

柜子　guìzi　【名】〔个 gè〕cupboard; wardrobe

剑（劍）guì

剑子手　guìzishǒu　【名】executioner; hangman

贵（貴）guì　【形】❶ expensive; dear; 这个地方橘子比香蕉～。Oranges are more expensive here than bananas. ❷ ◇ precious; valuable; 春雨～如油。Rain in spring is as precious as oil. ❸ ◇ (of a certain state of affairs, situation) admirable; to be valued; 人～有自知之明。It is of inestimable value to know oneself. 兵～神速。Speed is crucial in military affairs.

贵宾　guìbīn　【名】honoured guest; distinguished guest

贵客　guìkè　【名】honoured guest

贵姓　guì xìng　May I ask your name?

贵重　guìzhòng　【形】valuable; precious

贵族　guìzú　【名】aristocrat; nobleman

桂 guì

桂冠　guìguān　【名】laurel

桂花　guìhuā　【名】sweet osmanthus

跪 guì　【动】kneel

gǔn

滚 gǔn　【动】❶ roll; 球～出场外。The ball rolled out of the playground. ❷ (abusive language) get away; beat it; ～开! Beat it! ～出去! Get out! 【名】(～儿) roll over; 打～ roll over 打了两个～ roll over a couple of times

滚蛋　gǔn=dàn　get out; beat it

滚动　gǔndòng　【动】roll

滚瓜烂熟　gǔnguā lànshú　(of reading aloud or recitation from memory) fluent

滚滚　gǔngǔn　【形】rushing; rolling; surging; 浪涛～ rolling waves 历史的车轮～向前。The wheel of history rolls on.

滚热　gǔnrè　【形】(usu. of drinks or temperature of the human body) boiling hot; ～的浓茶 a cup of strong steaming hot tea 孩子身上～，一定是发烧了。The child is burning hot. He must be having a fever.

滚雪球　gǔn xuěqiú　snowball; snowballing

滚珠　gǔnzhū　【名】〔粒 lì〕ball (of a ball bearing)

滚珠轴承　gǔnzhū zhóuchéng　ball bearing

gùn

棍 gùn　【名】(～儿)〔根 gēn〕stick; cudgel

棍棒　gùnbàng　【名】❶ rod; stick; club; staff ❷ stick or staff used in gymnastics

棍子　gùnzi　【名】〔根 gēn〕stick; club

guō

锅（鍋）guō　【名】〔口 kǒu〕cooking-pot

锅炉　guōlú　【名】boiler

guó

国（國）guó　【名】country; nation; state

国宝　guóbǎo　【名】national treasure

国宾　guóbīn　【名】state guest

国策　guócè　【名】state policy

国产　guó chǎn　domestic product

国耻 guóchǐ 【名】national shame; national humiliation; 不忘～。Never forget the national humiliation.

国粹 guócuì 【名】the quintessence of Chinese culture

国都 guódū 【名】the capital of a country

国度 guódù 【名】country; nation

国法 guófǎ 【名】the laws of a country

国防 guófáng 【名】national defense

国歌 guógē 【名】national anthem

国格 guógé 【名】national prestige

国画 guóhuà 〔幅 fú〕traditional Chinese painting

国徽 guóhuī 【名】national emblem

国会 guóhuì 【名】parliament; congress; the highest organ of legislature in some countries

国货 guóhuò 【名】China-made goods; Chinese goods

国籍 guójí 【名】nationality

国计民生 guó jì mín shēng national economy and the people's livelihood; 发展农业是有关～的大事。To develop agriculture is all important to the national economy and the people's livelihood.

国际 guójì 【名】international

国际法 guójìfǎ 【名】international law

国际歌 Guójìgē 【名】The Internationale (song)

国际惯例 guójì guànlì international practice

国际社会 guójì shèhuì international society; international community

国际音标 guójì yīnbiāo the International Phonetic Alphabet

国际主义 guójì zhǔyì 【名】internationalism

国家 guójiā 【名】country; state; nation

国界 guójiè 【名】national boundaries

国境 guójìng 【名】extent of territory

国库 guókù 【名】national treasury

国库券 guókùquàn 【名】treasury bill (T.B.)

国民 guómín 【名】a national (of a country)

国民党 guómíndǎng 【名】the Kuomintang

国民经济 guómín jīngjì the national economy

国民收入 guómín shōurù national income

国内 guónèi 【名】domestic; internal

国旗 guóqí 【名】〔面 miàn〕national flag

国情 guóqíng 【名】the condition of a country

国庆节 Guóqìngjié 【名】national day

国事 guóshì 【名】state affairs; 进行～访问 be on a state visit 为～操劳 work hard on behalf of the state

国书 guóshū 【名】(diplomatic) credentials

国体 guótǐ 【名】political nature of a state

国土 guótǔ 【名】territory of a nation

国外 guówài 【名】abroad

国王 guówáng 【名】king

国威 guówēi 【名】national prestige

国务委员 guówù wěiyuán State Council member; State Councillor

国务院 guówùyuàn 【名】the State Council

国宴 guóyàn 【名】a state banquet

国营 guóyíng state-owned

国营经济 guóyíng jīngjì state-owned economy

国有 guóyǒu state-owned; nationalized

国有化 guóyǒuhuà 【动】nationalize; nationalization

国语 guóyǔ 【名】standard Chinese language

国葬　guózàng　【动】state funeral
国债　guózhài　【名】national debt

guǒ

果　guǒ　【名】❶◇ fruit：开花结～ blossom and bear fruit ❷ result；outcome；consequence（ *as opp. to* 因）：事情的前因后～ causes and effects of a matter

果断　guǒduàn　【形】resolute；decisive：机动灵活，指挥～ both flexible and decisive in taking command 采取～措施 take decisive measures

果脯　guǒfǔ　【名】preserved fruits

果敢　guǒgǎn　【形】courageous and resolute：～的行动 take resolute and daring action

果酱　guǒjiàng　【名】jam

果然　guǒrán　【副】just as expected or stated：昨天预报有小雨，今天～下起来了 Yesterday the radio forecast a drizzle, and today it is indeed raining. 都说庐（Lú）山风景好，这次去一看，～名不虚传。Everybody says that Lushan Mountain is beautiful. Now that I see it, I must agree that its reputation is, indeed, justified.

果实　guǒshí　【名】❶ fruit ❷ gain

果树　guǒshù　【名】〔棵 kē〕fruit-tree

果园　guǒyuán　【名】orchard

果真　guǒzhēn　【副】❶ 同"果然"❷ really *used in interrogative sentences*：这个消息～可靠吗？Is the news really reliable? ❸ if it is true that...：听说这里要修一条公路，～修起来，那可太方便了。It is said that a highway will be built here. If completed, it will be a great convenience.

果汁　guǒzhī　【名】fruit juice

裹　guǒ　【动】wrap；bind

裹足不前　guǒ zú bù qián　hesitate to move forward：一个人在困难面前决不能畏缩动摇，～。In the face of difficulties, one must not drag one's feet, but should go forward without hesitation.

guò

过（過）　guò　【动】❶（ *of space or time*）pass；cross：～马路 cross the road ～长江 cross the Changjiang River 我的生日已经～了一个星期了。A week has passed since my birthday. 你～两天再来吧。You'd better come in two days. ❷ *indicates a specific way of dealing with things*：～一～ 数 count it ～筛子 sift it ～秤 weigh it ❸ over：～半数 more than half (of sth.) ❹ celebrate：～生日 celebrate one's birthday ～节 celebrate the festival 新年你们准备怎么～? How are you going to celebrate the New Year? ❺ live one's life：日子越～越幸福。Life is getting better with each passing day. 老太太说，她愿意跟女儿一起～。The old woman said that she'd like to make her home with her daughter. Note：*used after a verb as a complement*：① finished；done with：桃花开～了，等着看梨花吧。The peach blossoms are over；let's wait and enjoy the pear blossoms. 我吃～饭就去看你。I'll come and see you after supper（ or lunch）. 上课铃响～了吗？Has the bell rung for class? ② over：她跳～一米七〇了。She's jumped 1.70m. 跨～这条线就算出界。If you cross this line, you are out of bounds. ③ pass by：小河流～他家门口。The stream passes by the door of his house. 每天上班我都走～动物园。I pass the zoo every day going to work. ④ defeat；do better than：

他的乒乓球打得很好，我打不～他。He is very good at ping-pong and I can't beat him. 小李赛～了所有的对手，取得第一名。Xiao Li defeated all his opponents and won the championship. ⑤ *indicates a movement involving an object not right at hand*：他抓～一把铁锨就干起活儿来。He grabbed a spade and began to work. 老张扔～损坏的零件让小李看。Lao Zhang tossed over a damaged part for Xiao Li to look at. ⑥ *turn round*：他转～身对后面的人说了一句什么，又转～身向前走。He turned round, said something to the person behind him, then turned back to continue on his way. 你翻～这一页，看下一页。Please turn this page over and look at the next page. ⑦ *indicates passing over a certain distance*：一道闪电划～天空。Lightning flashed across the sky. 你穿～树林，就可以看见海了。If you walk through the wood, you'll see the sea. 飞机飞～祖国大地。The plane flew over the breadth of the country. (⑤、⑥、⑦ *are the same as* ①、②、③ *of* 过来 *or* 过去, *except that direction is not indicated. An object is necessary.*) ⑧ *indicates the passing away of a period of time*：晃～了一辈子 while away one's whole life 等我忙～了这一阵以后，再谈咱们写剧本的事。We'll talk over the play we are going to write together after I finish the work at hand. ⑨ *indicates avoiding sth.*：咱们躲～这一阵大雨再走吧！Let's take shelter somewhere until the heavy rain is over. 岁数终归是瞒不～人的。The marks of age are bound to show; no use lying. 必须面对现实，不要绕～困难。One must face reality and not take the easy way out. (⑧ *and* ⑨ *are the same as* 过去 *as a complement* ④ *and* ⑤, *but in this case it usu. takes an object*)【名】◇ error; mistake：知～必改 amend one's ways as soon as one sees the light 功大于～。One's merits outweigh one's shortcomings.

另见 guo

过不去 guòbu qù ❶ find fault with：面子上～ feel ashamed or disgraced 同志们批评你，是为了帮助你，绝不是跟你～。Your comrades criticized you because they wanted to help you, not to make things hard for you. ❷ feel apologetic：让大家等了这么半天，我心里～。I'm awfully sorry to have kept you waiting for such a long time.

过场 guòchǎng 【名】❶ (of Chinese operas) cross the stage ❷ (of drama) interlude ❸ (*often used with* 走) make a mere formality out of sth.：总结工作要认真，不要走～。We must take a serious attitude in summing up our work, and not just make it a mere formality.

过程 guòchéng 【名】process; course

过错 guòcuò 【名】error; fault

过道 guòdào 【名】corridor

过得去 guòde qù ❶ just fulfil the lowest requirement：四十多岁的人，长跑有这样的成绩，也算～了。His record for the long distance race was pretty good, considering that he is over forty. 总的说来，小刘的木工活还～。On the whole, Xiao Liu's carpentry is not too bad. ❷ *used in a rhetorical question to mean* 过意不去：为我的事这么麻烦你，叫我心里怎么～呢？How can I help feeling bad about having caused you such a lot of trouble!

过度 guòdù 【形】excessive; over：～疲劳 be over-tired 磨损～ (of a thing) totally worn-out

过渡 guòdù 【动】pass over; transition

过渡时期 guòdù shíqī transition period

过分 guòfèn 【形】excessive；over-；undue：~讲究 unduly luxurious ~夸大 over-exaggerate 未免太~了 have gone too far 说老张是咱们的好管家，一点也不~。It is by no means an exaggeration to say that Lao Zhang is a superb caretaker.

过关 guò = guān go through a mountain pass；pass a test；reach a standard：蒙混~ slide through (a test) 这种产品质量~了。This product has reached the standard.

过河拆桥 guò hé chāi qiáo remove the plank after crossing the bridge；bite the hand which has fed one

过户 guò = hù transfer ownership

过活 guòhuó 【动】make a living：以前我们全家就靠父亲一人做工~。In the past, our whole family was dependent on my father, who worked as a labourer for a living.

过火 guòhuǒ 【形】(of talking or action) overdo；carry things too far；overstep the limits；excessive：~的行动 behaviour which oversteps the limits 玩笑开得~了。That is carrying the joke too far.

过激 guòjī 【形】radical

过街天桥 guò jiē tiānqiáo pedestrian overpass

过来 guò//lái indicates movement from far away towards the speaker：你~，我跟你说一件事。Please come here. I want to talk to you. 我刚从商店那边~，商店还没有开门呢！I've just passed the store. It isn't open yet. 路太窄了，车过不来。The road is too narrow for the car to get through. Note：过来 is used after a verb as a complement ① indicates movement from far away towards the speaker：路太窄，车开不~。The road is too narrow；the car can't get through. 他也是从困苦中熬~的人。He is a person who has seen bitter days. 请你把香烟递~。Please toss over the cigarettes. ② indicates turning (from the wrong side to the right side or towards the speaker)：他转过身来对我说：“快点走哇!” He turned round and said to me：“Please walk faster.” 把前一页翻~，看看前面是怎么说的。Turn back to the previous page and see what was said there. ③ indicates crossing an area moving towards the speaker：等后面的队伍翻过山来再休息。Let's wait till the troops behind have climbed the mountain, and then take a break. 汽车从桥上开~了。The car drove over the bridge towards us. (①、②、③ are the same as 过 as a complement ⑤、⑥、⑦, but the use of an object is optional) ④ indicates dealing with a number of things one by one, usu. with 得 or 不 to form the potential form：树上的苹果多得数不~。There are so many apples on the trees, they are beyond counting. 最近报刊上的好文章很多，简直看不~。There are so many good articles in the papers and periodicals recently that one can't read them all. 这么多事情，你一个人忙得~忙不~? There are so many things to be done；do you think you can cope? ⑤ indicates return to a normal state：他从昏迷中醒~了。He's regained consciousness. 你一说，我就明白~了。After your explanation, I understand everything. 这孩子的坏毛病都改~了。This child's bad habits have all been corrected.

过路 guò = lù 【动】pass by：~人 a passer-by ~车 a passing car or vehicle

过虑 guòlǜ 【动】be over-anxious；

worry too much; worry needlessly

过滤　guòlǜ　【动】filter

过滤嘴　guòlǜzuǐ　【名】(～儿) filter tip (of cigarettes)

过敏　guòmǐn　【形】allergic; oversensitive

过目　guò = mù　look or read over sth. (often for checking or approval): 计划已订好，请～。The plan has been drafted. Please look it over. 这篇报告请你过一下目。Here's the report for you to look over.

过年　guò = nián　❶ celebrate the New Year ❷ after New Year's Day or Spring Festival: 过了年弟弟就十八岁了。My younger brother will be 18 after the New Year.

过期　guò = qī　overdue

过去　guòqù　【名】the past

过去　guò // qù　*indicates movement from far away in a direction away from the speaker*: 你在那儿等我，我马上就～。Please wait for me there. I'll be with you in a moment. 邮递员刚从门口～，报纸一定送来了。The postman has just passed our door, so the paper must have come. 路太窄，车过不去。The road is too narrow; the car can't get through. Note: 过去 *is used after a verb as a complement* ① *indicates movement from far away in a direction away from the speaker*: 他递～一捆信。He tossed over a package of mail. 老张把损坏的零件扔～，让小李看。Lao Zhang threw over a damaged part for Xiao Li to see. 一转眼小林已经跑～了。In the twinkling of an eye, Xiao Lin ran past. ② *indicates turning (from the right side to the wrong side or in a direction away from the speaker)*: 他跟后面的人说完话，又转过身去向前走。After having talked to the person behind him, he turned and walked on. 你翻过这页去，看下面怎么说。Please turn the page and see what is said further on. ③ *indicates crossing an area in a direction away from the speaker*: 你穿过树林去，就可以看见海了。If you walk through the wood, you'll see the sea. 这条河相当宽，你游得～游不～? This river is quite wide; do you think you can swim across? (①，②，③ *are the same as* 过 *as a complement* ⑤，⑥，⑦, *but the use of an object is optional*) ④ *indicates the passing of a period of time*: 把这一段困难时期熬～，以后就好了。If we can tide over this difficult period, we'll be all right. 我忙过这一个月去，就能来帮助你了。After I've finished this month's work, I'll be able to come and help you. 不要把时间白白浪费～。Don't just fritter away your time. ⑤ *indicates an attempt to avoid sth.*: 你做什么是瞒不过我去的。Whatever you are up to, they can never fool me. 必须面对现实，困难想绕也绕不～。One must face reality. There's no easy way out. (④ *and* ⑤ *are the same as* 过 *as a complement* ⑧ *and* ⑨, *but the use of an object is optional*) ⑥ *indicates loss of consciousness*: 他昏～了。He's fainted.

过日子　guò rìzi　run a household: 老奶奶真会～，处处精打细算。Grandma is an excellent housekeeper and budgets carefully.

过甚其词　guò shèn qí cí　overstate sth.: 他说的情况完全符合实际，一点儿也不～。What he says is true and not at all exaggerated. 他的意见提得很中肯，没有～的地方。His criticism is pertinent. There is no overstatement whatsoever.

过剩　guòshèng　【形】exceeding what is the necessary; surplus

过失 guòshī 【名】error

过失犯罪 guòshī fànzuì crimes of negligence

过时 guò=shí ❶ out-of-date；obsolete；out-moded：这种汽车早已～。This kind of car is obsolete. ❷ pass a fixed time：～作废 null and void after the deadline ～不候。We won't wait past the appointed time.

过头 guò=tóu （～儿）go beyond the limit；overdo

过往 guòwǎng 【动】❶ to and fro：路上～的车辆很多。Traffic is very heavy in the street. ❷ association：他和小王～密切。He is very close to Xiao Wang.

过问 guòwèn 【动】take an interest in；concern oneself with；intervene：集体的事,大家都要～。Everybody should take an interest in the affairs of the collective.

过细 guòxì 【形】careful；meticulous：这种～的工作,她做最合适。She is cut out for this kind of meticulous work.

过夜 guò=yè ❶ put up for the night：今天我在姐姐家～。I'll put up for the night at my sister's. ❷ overnight：～的饭菜 food overnight；leftover food

过意不去 guò yì bù qù feel sorry；feel apologetic：你这样照顾我,我真～。I'm very sorry to have caused you so much trouble.

过瘾 guò=yǐn be greatly satisfied：今天晚上的音乐会非常好,可惜太短,还过不了瘾。The concert tonight was excellent, but it was just a bit too short. I was not quite satisfied. 这次旅行玩儿得可真～。This was an extremely successful trip. It couldn't have been better.

过硬 guòyìng become truly proficient in sth.；have a perfect mastery of sth.：～的本领 be perfect at a skill 技术～。His technique is perfect.

过于 guòyú 【副】too；over-；excessively；unduly（used before disyllabic words）：～谨慎 overly scrupulous ～紧张 too nervous

guo

过（過） guo 【助】used after a verb or an adjective to indicate a past experience or some action or state of affairs that has taken place at least once before：你去～他家吗？Have you ever been to his house？这本小说我看～,他没看～。I've read this novel, but he hasn't. 他当～教师,也当～编辑。He once worked as a teacher, and also as an editor. 前几天冷～一阵,这两天又暖和了。It was pretty cold for a few days, but has become warm recently. 这孩子从来没病～。This child has never been ill. Note：the negative of a sentence with 过【助】can only be indicated by 没有, never by 不.
另见 guò

H

hā

哈 hā 【动】❶ exhale；breathe out；blow：～了一口气 exhale ❷ bow：点头～腰 nod and bow slightly in greeting 【叹】 *expressing satisfaction*（*usu. reduplicated*）：～～, 这回可找着你了! Aha! I've found you at last! 【象声】 *the sound of laughter*（*usu. reduplicated*）

哈哈大笑 hāhā dàxiào laugh heartily

哈欠 hāqian 【名】yawn

hāi

咳 hāi 【叹】 *a term of exclamation to express surprise，self-depreciation，etc.*：～, 我真是老得不中用了! Oh, my goodness! I'm really getting old and losing my brains.

另见 ké

嗨 hāi

嗨哟 hāiyō 【叹】 heave ho；yo-heave-ho；yo-ho

hái

还（還） hái 【副】❶ still：直到深夜大雪～没停。Heavy snow kept falling deep into the night. 明天咱们～去找他。We are still going to call on him tomorrow. ❷ *used before a word or phrase of time to indicate a long time ago，usu. followed by* 是 *or* 在：～在公元前二世纪, 中国就发明了造纸法。Paper-making was invented in China as early as the 2nd century B.C. 我～是一大早看见他的, 谁知他现在哪儿去了。It was early this morning that I saw him；who knows where he is now! ❸ in addition to：要勇敢, ～要机智。One must be courageous and also quick-witted. 煤除了做燃料, ～有很多用途。Besides being a fuel, coal has many other uses. ❹ *indicates future repetition of an action*：稿子先别拿走, 一会儿～看一遍。Please don't take away the manuscript；I'll read it over again later on. 这个戏明天晚上～演。This play will be performed again tomorrow evening. ❺ *used in a rhetorical question to emphasize certainty*：我和他同班, ～能不认识? How can I not know him since we are classmates? 这么大的字～看不清楚? Surely such big characters can be seen clearly? ❻ *often in conjunction with* 比 even：你的天文知识似乎比我～少。You seem to know even less about the stars than I do. 他比我～喜欢下棋。He is even fonder of playing chess than I am. ❼ *indicates sth. of passable quality*：

这个剧本写的～可以。This drama is tolerable. 他说法语说得～不错。His French is not bad. ❽ *indicates slight surprise*：你～真有两下子。Good for you!（I didn't expect you to make it.）这种病～真难治。This disease is hard to cure, to be sure. ❾ *even*：你们俩～搬不动，我一个人怎么行呢? Even the two of you can't move it, so how can I move it by myself? 五千米我～跑不下来呢，更不用说一万米了。I can't run 5,000 metres, let alone 10,000 metres. 另见 huán

还是 háishi 【副】❶ 同"还"【副】❶❷ ❷ *after all*（*introduces a comment after a comparison*）：吃来吃去，～中国菜好吃。I've tried all sorts of food but Chinese food is after all the best. ～郊外空气新鲜。The air in the suburbs certainly is fresher. ❸ *had better*（*used in making a suggestion*）：那个地方不好找，～请他带你去吧! That place is difficult to find. You'd better ask him to take you there. 天气凉了，～多穿点儿好! It is getting cold. You'd better put on more clothes. 【连】*used in alternative questions*：是泰山高，～华山高? Which is higher, Mt. Tai or Mt. Hua? 你喜欢喝绿茶，～喜欢喝红茶? Which do you prefer, green tea or black tea?

孩 hái

孩子 háizi 【名】child
孩子气 háiziqì 【名】childish

hǎi

海 hǎi 【名】sea

海岸 hǎi'àn 【名】coast；shore
海岸线 hǎi'ànxiàn 【名】coast-line
海拔 hǎibá 【名】altitude；height above sea-level

海报 hǎibào 【名】poster
海滨 hǎibīn 【名】sea-shore
海产 hǎichǎn 【名】marine products
海潮 hǎicháo 【名】tide
海带 hǎidài 【名】kelp（edible sea-weed）
海岛 hǎidǎo 【名】island（in the sea）
海盗 hǎidào 【名】pirate
海底 hǎidǐ 【名】bottom of the sea
海底捞月 hǎi dǐ lāo yuè dredge for the moon in the sea；have nothing to show for one's efforts：～一场空。It all ended in complete failure. 也说"水中捞月"。
海防 hǎifáng 【名】coastal defences
海港 hǎigǎng 【名】harbour；seaport
海关 hǎiguān 【名】customs-house
海军 hǎijūn 【名】navy
海口 hǎikǒu 【名】seaport
海枯石烂 hǎi kū shí làn until the seas dry up and the rocks decay（expressing one's eternal determination or loyalty, usu. used in an oath or pledge）
海阔天空 hǎi kuò tiān kōng （of talk, imagination）as broad as sea and sky；without restriction or limit：他们俩碰到一起，总是～地聊起来没个完。When the two of them get together talking, there are no holds barred, and they can go on for hours.
海蓝 hǎilán 【形】sea green；sea blue
海里 hǎilǐ 【量】nautical mile；sea mile
海轮 hǎilún 【名】seagoing vessel
海洛因 hǎiluòyīn 【名】heroin
海米 hǎimǐ 【名】dried shrimps
海绵 hǎimián 【名】sponge（a plant-like sea animal）
海面 hǎimiàn 【名】the surface of the sea
海难 hǎinàn 【名】perils of the sea
海鸥 hǎi'ōu 【名】〔只 zhī〕seagull

海参 hǎishēn 【名】 sea cucumber；sea slug

海市蜃楼 hǎi shì shèn lóu castles in the air；illusions or hopes that cannot be realized

海滩 hǎitān 【名】 beach

海外 hǎiwài 【名】 overseas；abroad

海湾 hǎiwān 【名】 gulf；bay

海味 hǎiwèi 【名】 sea food

海峡 hǎixiá 【名】 straits；channel

海鲜 hǎixiān 【名】 seafood

海啸 hǎixiào 【名】 tidal wave

海燕 hǎiyàn 【名】〔只 zhī〕petrel

海洋 hǎiyáng 【名】 ocean

海洋权 hǎiyángquán 【名】 maritime rights

海洋性气候 hǎiyángxìng qìhòu maritime climate

海域 hǎiyù 【名】 waters（the part of the sea adjacent to a specified country，land mass，etc.）

海员 hǎiyuán 【名】 seaman

海运 hǎiyùn 【名】 sea transport

hài

骇（駭） hài

骇人听闻 hài rén tīng wén shocking；terrifying；horrifying：这是～的地震消息。The news of earthquake is horrifying.

害 hài 【动】 ❶ injure；harm：～人不浅 do sb. a great deal of harm 损人～己 in hurting someone else，harm oneself as well ❷ ◇（unjustly）kill；murder：不幸遇～ be unfortunately murdered ❸ contract a disease：～眼 have eye trouble ～病 fall ill 【名】 ❶ a bane；an evil；a harm：为民除～ rid the people of a deadly harm 吸烟有～。Smoking is harmful. ❷ disaster；pest：消灭虫～ exterminate（insect）pests

害虫 hàichóng 【名】 destructive in-sect

害处 hàichu 【名】 harm

害鸟 hàiniǎo 【名】 harmful bird

害怕 hàipà 【动】 fear；be afraid of；be scared

害人虫 hàirénchóng 【名】 vermin，an epithet applied to people engaging in violently anti-social behaviour

害羞 hàixiū 【形】 shy；bashful

嗐 hài 【叹】 expresses regret，sorrow，disgust，etc.：～，我真糊涂！Damn it! How stupid I am! ～，别提那件事了! Oh，don't bring that up any more. ～，真讨厌! Blast it! What a nuisance!

hān

酣 hān 【形】 to one's heart's content

酣睡 hānshuì 【动】 sleep soundly

酣战 hānzhàn 【动】 fight fiercely；fight a fierce battle：～三昼夜 three days and nights of bitter fighting 两军～。The opposing armies fought a fierce battle.

憨 hān

憨厚 hānhòu 【形】 simple and honest

憨直 hānzhí 【形】 honest and straightforward

鼾 hān 【名】 snore：～声 sound of snoring

hán

含 hán 【动】 ❶ keep；hold（sth. in the mouth）：～一口水 keep a mouthful of water in one's mouth ～着一块糖 suck a piece of candy ❷ contain；hold back：～着热泪 with

tears in one's eyes 胡萝卜～有大量维生素 C。Carrots contain a considerable amount of vitamin C. ❸ (of sentiment, feelings) imply rather than reveal outright：～怒 contain one's anger ～羞 be bashful; be overcome by shyness ～笑不语 smile without speaking

含糊 hánhu 【形】❶ vague; unclear; ambiguous：～其辞 make sth. very vague 关于开会的事,他讲得很～,还得再问他一下。He spoke very vaguely about the meeting. We'd better go and ask him again. ❷ (used in the negative or in a rhetorical question) perfunctory; careless; sloppy：这项任务很重要,可不能～。This task is very important; we must not be careless about it. ❸ be shown up by：他们白班干得很出色,我们夜班也决不～! They've done pretty well on the day shift; we on the night shift are certainly not going to be outdone by them. ❹ 不含糊 outstanding (expresses commendation)：她的针线活儿真不～。She does beautiful needlework.

含混 hánhùn 【形】 ambiguous; equivocal

含量 hánliàng 【名】content

含沙射影 hán shā shè yǐng insinuate; insinuation; attack by innuendo：进行～的攻击 make insinuations about sb. ～地谩骂 make veiled insinuations about sb. while openly criticising someone else

含辛菇苦 hán xīn rú kǔ endure all kinds of hardships

含蓄 hánxù 【形】 (of speech or writing) restrained; understated; suggestive rather than explicit：他的话很～,我得好好琢磨。His remarks were full of implications; I'll have to think them over carefully. 这篇寓言写得很～。This fable is written in a restrained but evoc-

ative style.

含义 hányì 【名】meaning (of word, phrase, etc.)

函 hán 【名】〈书〉letter：来～敬悉。I acknowledge with pleasure the receipt of your letter.

函购 hángòu 【动】purchase by mail; mail order

函授 hánshòu 【名】correspondence course; lessons by correspondence

函数 hánshù 【名】(maths.) functions

涵 hán

涵洞 hándòng 【名】culvert

涵养 hányǎng 【名】 self-control; forbearance usual collocations are 有涵养,没有涵养：这位经理很有～,能听取各种不同的意见。The manager, tolerant and broad-minded, is open to all kinds of opinions.

寒 hán 【形】◇❶ cold：～风刺骨 a bitterly cold wind ❷ be afraid; tremble：心惊胆～ tremble with fright

寒潮 háncháo 【名】cold wave

寒带 hándài 【名】(geog.) frigid zone

寒假 hánjià 【名】winter vacation

寒噤 hánjìn 【名】shiver：他打了个～ a shiver ran through him

寒冷 hánlěng 【形】cold

寒流 hánliú 【名】cold current

寒毛 hánmáo 【名】〔根 gēn〕fine hair on the human body 也作"汗毛"。

寒暑表 hánshǔbiǎo 【名】thermometer

寒酸 hánsuān 【形】shabby

寒心 hánxīn 【形】be entirely disillusioned when one's hard work or enthusiasm is not appreciated or reciprocated or when one sees someone else suffer such a fate

寒暄 hánxuān 【动】make formal re-

marks when one meets sb.

寒意　hányì　【名】chill；a tinge of cold

寒战　hánzhàn　【名】shiver

hǎn

罕　hǎn

罕见　hǎnjiàn　【形】rare；unusual；uncommon

喊　hǎn　【动】❶ shout；yell；～口号 shout slogans ❷ call；好像有人～我．It seems that somebody is calling me.

喊话　hǎn=huà　shout，using a loud-speaker（*esp. at the battle-front, calling on enemy soldiers to surrender*）

喊叫　hǎnjiào　【动】shout；yell

hàn

汉（漢）　hàn

汉白玉　hànbáiyù　【名】white marble

汉堡包　hànbǎobāo　【名】hamburger

汉奸　hànjiān　【名】traitor（to China）

汉学家　Hànxuéjiā　【名】sinologist

汉语　Hànyǔ　【名】Chinese（language）

汉语拼音方案　Hànyǔ Pīnyīn Fāng'àn the Scheme of the Chinese Phonetic Alphabet

汉字　Hànzì　【名】Chinese character

汉子　hànzi　【名】man；fellow

汗　hàn　【名】〔滴 dī〕sweat；perspiration

汗流浃背　hàn liú jiā bèi　soaked with sweat

汗马功劳　hàn mǎ gōngláo　achievement in war；merit laboriously achieved

汗衫　hànshān　【名】〔件 jiàn〕under-shirt；T-shirt

汗水　hànshuǐ　【名】sweat；perspiration

汗渍　hànzì　【名】❶ sweat stain ❷ be soaked with sweat

旱　hàn　【名】drought；防～drought prevention 抗～斗争 struggle to combat drought 【动】suffer from drought；～死了一些小苗．Some of the seedlings have been killed by drought.【形】dry；～季dry season 庄稼有点儿～．The crops are suffering from a slight drought.

旱冰场　hànbīngchǎng　【名】roller-skating rink

旱冰鞋　hànbīngxié　【名】roller skates

旱涝保收　hàn lào bǎo shōu　give high yields irrespective of drought or waterlogging

旱情　hànqíng　【名】damage to crops by drought

旱灾　hànzāi　【名】disastrous drought

捍　hàn

捍卫　hànwèi　【动】defend；safe-guard

悍　hàn

悍然　hànrán　【副】arbitrarily；defi-antly；～不顾 rudely brush aside ～拒绝 flatly reject

焊　hàn　【动】weld

焊工　hàngōng　【名】❶ welding；soldering ❷ welder；solderer

焊接　hànjiē　【动】join by welding

háng

行　háng　【名】❶ line；row；马路两旁，绿树成～．Trees lined both sides of the avenue. ❷ a branch of

a trade：各～各业 all trades and occupations ～～出状元．Every profession produces its own specialists．【量】row；column；line：一～字 a line or column of words 两～热泪 streams of tears

另见 xíng

行当 hángdang 【名】trade；profession；line of business

行家 hángjiā 【名】expert；a person who is skilled in a certain field

行列 hánglie 【名】rank；line of persons

行情 hángqíng 【名】market price

行市 ·hángshi 【名】quotations（on the market）；prices

行业 hángyè 【名】a branch of a trade；profession

航 háng

航班 hángbān 【名】scheduled flight；flight number

航标 hángbiāo 【名】buoy

航程 hángchéng 【名】distance travelled by plane or ship；voyage

航道 hángdào 【名】channel；waterway

航海 hánghǎi 【名】navigation

航空 hángkōng 【名】aviation：～信 air mail ～事业 the aviation industry

航空港 hángkōnggǎng 【名】airport

航空母舰 hángkōngmǔjiàn 【名】〔艘 sōu〕aircraft carrier

航模 hángmó 【名】model of a plane or a ship

航天 hángtiān 【名】space flight：～飞机 space shuttle

航线 hángxiàn 【名】air or navigation route

航向 hángxiàng 【名】（of ship or aeroplane）heading

航行 hángxíng 【动】sail；navigate

航运 hángyùn 【名】transportation by water；shipping

hāo

薅 hāo 【动】weed；pull out（weeds）

háo

号（號）háo 【动】howl；wail

另见 hào

号啕大哭 háotáo dà kū wail loudly；cry loudly

蚝（蠔）háo 【名】oyster

蚝油 háoyóu 【名】oyster sauce

毫 háo

毫不 háo bù not the least bit；without the slightest：～掩饰 totally undisguised ～犹豫 without the least hesitation ～畏惧 without a trace of fear

毫毛 háomáo 【名】〔根 gēn〕hair（on the body）

毫升 háoshēng 【量】millilitre

毫无 háo wú by no means；without the least；devoid of：～准备 utterly unprepared ～惧色 without the least sign of fear ～感觉 completely numb（usu. physical）～自私自利之心 absolutely selfless

毫无二致 háo wú èr zhì identical；exactly alike

豪 háo

豪放 háofàng 【形】（of a person）generous；not petty；uninhibited

豪华 háohuá 【形】luxurious；sumptuous

豪杰 háojié 【名】hero；heroine

豪迈 háomài 【形】（of persons，causes）great；valiant；not petty

豪门 háomén 【名】a rich and influential family：～子弟 children of a

rich and powerful family

豪情 háoqíng 【名】 lofty sentiments

豪情壮志 háoqíng zhuàngzhì lofty sentiments and high ambition

豪绅 háoshēn 【名】 despotic gentry

豪爽 háoshuǎng 【形】 noble-minded and forthright

豪言壮语 háo yán zhuàng yǔ remarks which reveal a noble mind; resounding statements

豪壮 háozhuàng 【形】 heroic; daring; bold: ~的誓言 bold pledge ~的事业 heroic cause

壕

壕 háo 【名】◇ ❶ moat: 护城~ city moat ❷ trench: 防坦克~ anti-tank trench 防空~ air raid shelter

壕沟 háogōu 【名】〔条 tiáo〕 trench dug for protection in time of war; dugout

hǎo

好 hǎo 【形】❶ good; well; having the desired quality: ~传统 good tradition 服务态度~ satisfactory service ❷ friendly: ~邻居 good neighbours 两国关系~。The two countries are on good terms. ❸ of a high level: 技术~ highly skilled 他的诗写得~。He writes beautiful poetry. 这孩子算术比语文~。This child's arithmetic is better than his Chinese. ❹ beneficial; useful; efficient: ~药 good medicine 长跑对身体很~。Long-distance running is good for one's health. 煤是~东西。Coal is something which is very useful. ❺ healthy; sound: 他最近身体挺~。He's been very well lately. 这些苹果都是~的，没有烂的。These are all good apples; there are no rotten ones. 这么冷不穿棉袄，~人都受不了，何况你有病呢! A healthy person can't get

along without a warm jacket in such cold weather, let alone a sick person like you. ❻ used as a resultative complement: ① indicates that sth. is ready to be used: 会场布置~了。The room for the conference is ready. 你的发言稿什么时候可以写~? When will your speech be available in written form? ② in proper order: 书架上的书太乱,你把它摆~! The books on the shelves are in a mess. Please put them in order. 请大家坐~,我们开会了。Please sit down and we'll begin our meeting. ❼ indicates approval or agreement: ~(吧),就照你说的办。All right, do just as you suggested. ❽ 好了 that's enough; stop: ~了,你不用再说了,我已经懂了。That's enough. Please don't explain any more. I understand. 【副】❶ used with an exclamatory sense before an adjective to indicate high degree: 这水库~大呀! What a huge reservoir! 春节过得~热闹! What a pleasant Spring Festival we've had! ~危险哪! How dangerous! ❷ quite (used before 几,多,一会儿,一阵,半天, etc.): 有~几天没见到他了。We haven't seen him for quite a few days. 小王病了,~多人都去看他。When Xiao Wang was ill, quite a few people went to see him. 我们等了~半天他才来。We had waited for quite a while before he came. ❸ used before certain verbs to indicate that sth. is easy: 这个问题~回答。This question is easy to answer. 这首歌不~唱。This song isn't easy to sing. ❹ used before the predicate of the second clause of a compound sentence to introduce the purpose for which one does sth.: 带上点干粮,路上~吃。Please take along some food for the trip. 我们要努力学习,

将来～为人民服务。We must study hard so that we can serve the people in the future.

另见 hào

好比 hǎobǐ 【动】❶ be like; just like：学习～逆水行舟，不进则退。Learning is just like sailing against a current; unless one makes constant progress, one falls behind. ❷ for example; by way of example (*usu. used with* 说)：汉语不少名词各有特殊的量词，～说，"帽子"的量词是"顶"，"灯"的量词是"盏"。Many Chinese nouns have specific measure words; for example, the measure word for 帽子 (hat) is 顶 and for 灯 (lamp) is 盏。

好吃 hǎochī 【形】good to eat; delicious; tasty

好处 hǎochu 【名】benefit; advantage：没有什么～ doesn't do any good 体育锻炼的～很多。Physical training has many benefits.

好处费 hǎochùfèi 【名】kickback

好歹 hǎodǎi 【名】❶ good and bad：不知～ does not know good from bad ❷ danger (a possible future danger to one's life)：他的病不轻，万一有个～可怎么办呢？He's pretty sick; what will we do if he gets worse? 【副】❶ make do with：老王也不是外人，～吃点儿就行了。Lao Wang is like one of the family. Let's just make do with what's available. ❷ in some fashion; after a fashion：小张要是在这儿，～也能帮你把车修好。If Xiao Zhang were here, he could help you fix up your bike after a fashion.

好感 hǎogǎn 【名】favour; liking

好过 hǎoguò 【形】❶ living an easy life; having an easy time ❷ feeling good or comfortable

好汉 hǎohàn 【名】a determined and brave man

好好儿 hǎohǎor 【形】(～的) be in good condition; be in good shape：你看，我不是～的吗？怎么会病呢！Look at me! Don't I look healthy? How could I be sick? ～的一张画儿给弄脏了。A fine painting has been spoiled. 【副】properly; thoroughly：他提的这个问题，你得～考虑考虑。Do consider carefully the issue he raised. 有时间咱们～地聊聊。When you have time, let's have a good chat.

好话 hǎohuà 【名】❶ good words ❷ fine words

好久 hǎojiǔ 【名】a long time：我～没回家乡了。It's been a long time since I went back home. 我等了他～。I've been waiting for him for a long time.

好看 hǎokàn 【形】❶ good-looking; handsome：这个台灯很～。That is a very handsome desk lamp. ❷ do credit to：儿子立了功，妈妈脸上也～。The merits of the son reflect credit on the mother. ❸ 要人的好看 deliberately embarrass sb.：明知我不会唱歌，还硬要我唱，简直是要我的～。You all know I'm no singer, but you persist in asking me to sing. Is it because you want to embarrass me?

好评 hǎopíng 【名】favourable comment：受到～ be favourably commented 博得～ be well received

好人 hǎorén 【名】❶ good person ❷ a person who tries to get along with everyone

好人好事 hǎo rén hǎo shì good persons and their good deeds

好容易 hǎoróngyì 【副】with great difficulty *applies to a past event, often used with* 才 *and can also be said as* 好不容易：这些资料～才找到。It was only with considerable difficulty that we finally found this information. 我～才把他说服了。It was with great difficulty that I fi-

nally managed to convince him.

好手 hǎoshǒu 【名】 past master; capable person

好受 hǎoshòu 【形】 feel better; feel comfortable

好似 hǎosì 【动】 look like; seem

好听 hǎotīng 【形】 ❶ pleasing to the ear; pleasant to listen to: 这支曲子 ~。 This melody is very pleasant to listen to. 你唱得真 ~。 You do sing very well! ❷ (of language, words) high-sounding: 光说 ~ 的不行，还要看 行 动。 High-sounding words aren't any good; only deeds count.

好玩儿 hǎowánr 【形】 interesting

好闻 hǎowén 【形】 smell good

好像 hǎoxiàng 【动】 ❶ be like (*used in a simile*): 小伙子们干起活儿来 ~ 小老虎一样。 When these youngsters pitch into a job, they are like a bunch of tiger cubs. 今天真暖和，~ 春天了。 It's warm today; just like spring. ❷ seem: 我 ~ 在哪儿见过你。 I seem to have met you somewhere before. 他 ~ 有点不高兴。 He seems a bit depressed. Note: 好像 *can take 是 after it without affecting the meaning*: ① *can be used in conjunction with* 一样 *or* 似的, ② *with* 似的 *without affecting the meaning*

好笑 hǎoxiào 【形】 funny

好些 hǎoxiē 【形】 a good many

好心 hǎoxīn 【名】 good intentions

好样儿的 hǎoyàngrde 【名】 a good sort (person)

好意 hǎoyì 【名】 good will

好在 hǎozài 【副】 fortunately; luckily *used to point out an advantageous condition in disadvantageous circumstances*: 这事我们下星期再商量吧，~ 不是很急。 Let's talk about this next week, shall we? It's not that urgent anyway. 我有空再来看你，~ 我的宿舍离这儿不远。 I'll come and see you again when I have

time. Fortunately, I live close by. (It won't hurt me to come for a second time.)

好转 hǎozhuǎn 【动】 take a turn for the better

hào

号（號） hào 【名】 ❶ bugle ❷ *indicates order*: 挂个 ~ register (e.g. at a hospital) 编个 ~ put serial numbers on things 五 ~ 儿铅字 (printing) 5 point type 大 ~ 儿皮鞋 large size shoes 六 ~ 房间 Room No. 6 ❸ day of the month: 十月一 ~ October 1st.

另见 hǎo。

号称 hàochēng 【动】 ❶ be known as; be by reputation: 中国四川省 ~ 天府之国。 Sichuan is by reputation a province of fertile land and abundant natural resources. ❷ claim to be: 敌军 ~ 有五个师的兵力，实际上还不足两个师。 The enemy claimed to be five divisions strong, but in fact numbered less than two divisions.

号角 hàojiǎo 【名】 ❶ bugle; horn ❷ clarion call; bugle call

号令 hàolìng 【名】 order; command

号码 hàomǎ 【名】 number (No.)

号手 hàoshǒu 【名】 trumpeter; bugler

号外 hàowài 【名】 extra (of a newspaper)

号召 hàozhào 【动】 call; call upon; exhort: 厂长 ~ 青年工人钻研科学技术。 The factory director appeals to the young workers to study the natural sciences and technology. 【名】 call; appeal; exhortation: 发出 ~ issue an appeal 响应 ~ respond to an appeal

好 hào 【动】 ❶ be fond of; like;

他～放风筝。He likes flying kites.
❷ be liable to; be likely to; be apt
to：～哭 be apt to cry ～发火 be apt
to lose one's temper easily
另见 hǎo

好大喜功 hào dà xǐ gōng seek after
vainglory

好高务远 hào gāo wù yuǎn crave
something which is out of reach;
vainly attempt to do sth. beyond
one's abilities 也作"好高骛远"。

好客 hàokè 【形】hospitable

好奇 hàoqí 【形】curious

好强 hàoqiáng 【形】aspiring; eager
to do well in whatever one does

好胜 hàoshèng 【形】having a desire
to excel

好恶 hàowù 【名】likes and dislikes

好逸恶劳 hào yì wù láo love ease,
dislike work

好战 hàozhàn 【形】bellicose

耗 hào 【动】❶ consume：～油
consume a lot of oil ～电 use a lot
of electricity ❷ stay idle：你别～着
了,快干吧！Don't sit there doing
nothing. Get moving!

耗费 hàofèi 【动】consume 【名】con-
sumption

耗损 hàosǔn 【动】consume; waste
【名】wastage

耗资 hàozī 【动】spend; cost：～近亿
元 cost nearly a hundred million
yuan

浩 hào

浩大 hàodà 【形】very large; gigan-
tic：工程～ a gigantic engineering
project

浩荡 hàodàng 【形】(of rivers,
lakes, etc.) mighty; majestic：～的
长江 the mighty Changjiang
(Yangtze)River 浩浩荡荡的游行队
伍 a majestic parading procession

浩瀚 hàohàn 【形】〈书〉vast; limit-
less：～的沙漠 a vast desert

浩劫 hàojié 【名】great calamity

浩如烟海 hào rú yān hǎi as vast as
the infinite ocean; astronomical
amount of：文献古籍～ an enor-
mous number of documents and
ancient books

hē

呵 hē 【动】exhale; blow;
breathe on：～了一口气 breathe on
(e.g. one's glasses to clean them)
～一～手 blow on one's hands 【叹】
expressing surprise：～,这小伙子真
棒！Well, I'll be damned! That
young fellow's really bright!

呵斥 hēchì 【动】scold

呵呵 hēhē 【象声】happily; be hap-
py：～地笑着 laugh happily 他整天
乐～的。He goes through life in a
happy-go-lucky fashion.

喝 hē 【动】❶ drink ❷ drink
(alcoholic beverages)
另见 hè

嗬 hē 【叹】ah; oh：～,这座楼真
高！Oh, this is certainly a tall
building!

hé

禾 hé

禾苗 hémiáo 【名】seedling of any
kind of grain

合 hé 【动】❶ close; shut：～上
眼 close one's eyes 把书～上 close a
book ❷ combine; unite; join：～办
co-operate in doing sth.; run sth.
jointly 同心～力 make a concerted
effort ❸ coincide with; be in
keeping with; conform to：正～心
意 be in conformance with one's

desires ❹ be the equivalent of; add up to：这件大衣连料子带手工算在一起～多少钱? How much did your overcoat cost, for both the material and tailoring? 一英镑～多少人民币? How much is the British pound worth in *renminbi*?

合并 hébìng 【动】merge; amalgamate

合不来 hé bu lái be unable to get along with sb.：他们两人有点儿～。Those two seem unable to get along with each other.

合唱 héchàng 【动】chorus【名】chorus

合成 héchéng 【动】❶ be composed of; combine parts to form a whole：三年级的两个班～一个班了。The two grade 3 classes have now been combined into one. ❷ synthesize：～染料 synthetic dye

合成词 héchéngcí 【名】compound (word)

合成纤维 héchéng xiānwéi synthetic fibre

合成橡胶 héchéng xiàngjiāo synthetic rubber

合得来 hé de lái get along with sb.：他跟小何还算～。He and Xiao He get along all right.

合法 héfǎ 【形】legal; legitimate; lawful：～斗争 legal struggle

合法化 héfǎhuà 【动】be legalized

合格 hégé 【形】qualified; up to the standard

合股 hé = gǔ (of several people) pool their capital (to run a business)

合乎 héhū 【动】conform with; correspond to：～情理 reasonable ～要求 conform with the request

合伙 hé = huǒ pool (money, capital)

合计 héjì 【动】amount to; add up to：两个月～收入三千元。The income of two months amounts to 3,000 yuan.

合计 héji 【动】❶ consult：咱们～一下，怎么办更好。Let us put our heads together to work out a better solution. ❷ think over; figure out：我～了半天，怎么做都不好。I've been weighing the pros and cons for a long time but still can't make a decision.

合金 héjīn 【名】alloy

合金钢 héjīngāng 【名】alloy steel

合理 hélǐ 【形】reasonable; rational

合理化 hélǐhuà 【动】rationalize

合流 héliú 【动】❶ (of rivers) become one; flow together; converge ❷ (of actions, opinions) share the same (mistaken) views and actions

合龙 hélóng 【动】complete the construction of a dam or bridge by joining its two ends together in the middle

合拢 hé // lǒng close; join

合情合理 hé qíng hé lǐ reasonable

合身 héshēn 【形】(of clothes) fit

合适 héshì 【形】be suitable; fit：这顶皮帽我戴着正～。This fur cap fits me perfectly. 这个词用在这里不～，有点儿词不达意。That word is not appropriate in this context. It is not expressive enough.

合算 hésuàn 【形】spending less while getting more; reasonable in price; worthwhile：这段路坐船比坐火车～。It's to our advantage to make this part of the journey by boat rather than by train. 【动】figure out; calculate：办任何事情都要好好～一下,怎样才能又快、又好、又省钱。Before starting anything, we should always figure out how to achieve good results in a quick and economical way.

合同 hétong 【名】contract

合同工 hétonggōng 【名】contract workers

合意 hé=yì to one's satisfaction；in conformance with one's desire

合营 héyíng 【动】jointly-own（enterprises）

合影 héyǐng 【名】group photo

合影 hé=yǐng take a group photo

合资 hézī 【动】(joint venture) pool money

合奏 hézòu 【动】perform on several different musical instruments 【名】instrumental ensemble

合作 hézuò 【动】cooperate；collaborate

合作医疗 hézuò yīliáo cooperative medical service

何 hé

何必 hébì 【副】needless；unnecessary（used in a rhetorical question）：用不着的东西，～买它? Why buy unnecessary things? 都是自己人，这么客气，～呢? We are all close friends；why stand on ceremony?

何尝 hécháng 【副】used in a rhetorical question to make a denial：我～说过这样的话呢，他大概记错了。Did I ever say anything like that? He probably remembered wrongly. 我～不想去香山玩呢，只是没有时间。It isn't that I don't want to go to the Fragrant Hills. I simply don't have time to go.

何等 héděng 【副】how（used in an exclamatory sentence）：儿童是～幸福啊! How fortunate the children are!

何妨 héfáng 【副】might as well（used in a rhetorical question）：这件事你～跟大家商量商量呢? Why not discuss this matter with someone else?

何苦 hékǔ 【副】used in a rhetorical question to indicate that sth. is not worthwhile：你～老是计较这些小事呢? Why on earth do you concern yourself with such trifles? 这

么大风，为一点儿小事进一趟城，～呢? Why go to town in such a strong wind for something so trivial?

何况 hékuàng 【连】let alone；to say nothing of（used in a rhetorical question）：这个消息你告诉他吧! 免得他着急，～早晚也得告诉他。Since we are going to tell him the news sooner or later anyway，why not let him know right now and relieve his anxiety? 上海都这么冷，～北京呢! It is cold enough in Shanghai，let alone in Beijing.

何其毒也 hé qí dú yě How vicious!

何其相似乃尔 hé qí xiāngsì nǎi ěr What a striking likeness!

何去何从 hé qù hé cóng which course should be followed and which course should be rejected（referring to making a decision in a serious matter）

何如 hé rú 〈书〉... how about it?

何谓 héwèi 【动】What is meant by...?

何以 hé yǐ Why...?

何在 hé zài Where is...?：理由～? Where is the argument? 原因～? Wherein lies the cause?

何止 hé zhǐ far more than：要看的书～这几本? There are far more books to read than these.

和 hé 【名】(maths.) sum：二加三的～是五。The sum of 3 and 2 is 5. 【形】◇ ❶ calm；gentle：风～日暖。The breeze is gentle and the sun is warm. ❷ on good terms；friendly：～衷共济 work together in complete accord（in difficult times）姐弟二人不～。The brother and sister can't get along with each other. 【连】and；connects nouns，pronouns or nominal phrases：工人～农民 workers and farmers 母亲～我都很同情她。Both my mother and I feel great sympathy

for her. 他寄来的书～汇来的钱都收到了。The money and books he sent have arrived. Note：① *sometimes* 和 *can connect verbs or adjectives*：我们必须及时发现～纠正错误。We must discover and correct mistakes in time. 大家都要学习他那种无私～无畏的精神。Everyone must learn from his selfless and fearless spirit. ② 和 *cannot connect clauses* 【介】to；with：你～他好好说说，他不会不同意的。If you talk to him nicely, he won't disagree. 我们厂～他们厂比，差距还很大。Compared to their factory, ours is way behind. 另见 huó；huò

和蔼 hé'ǎi 【形】amiable；kindly

和风细雨 hé fēng xì yǔ gentle breeze and fine rain；gentle；not rough：你跟他～地谈一谈，不要发脾气。Go and have a friendly talk with him；don't lose your temper.

和好 héhǎo 【动】become reconciled with sb.；iron out a dispute：～如初 be reconciled with sb. and be as close as before 他们～了。They are reconciled with each other.

和缓 héhuǎn 【形】conciliatory；mild；moderate：态度～ a conciliatory attitude 这种药的药性～。This medicine is rather mild. 局势逐渐～下来。The situation has become more relaxed.

和解 héjiě 【动】become reconciled

和局 héjú 【名】draw；tie

和美 héměi 【形】in harmony；harmonious

和睦 hémù 【形】friendly；harmonious

和平 hépíng 【名】peace

和平共处 hépíng gòng chǔ peaceful coexistence

和平共处五项原则 hépíng gòng chǔ wǔ xiàng yuánzé The Five Principles of Peaceful Coexistence；mutual respect for territorial integrity and sovereignty，mutual non-aggression，non-interference in each other's internal affairs，equality and mutual benefit，and peaceful coexistence

和平演变 hépíng yǎnbiàn peaceful evolution (i. e. the peaceful evolution of a socialist state back into a capitalist one)

和气 héqi 【形】❶ kindly；gentle；placid：说话～ soft-spoken ❷ friendly；amiable：相处得很～ be on friendly terms with each other 【名】friendliness；friendship：别为小事伤了～。Don't let trivial differences interfere with our friendship.

和善 héshàn 【形】kind and gentle；genial

和尚 héshang 【名】Buddhist monk

和顺 héshùn 【形】amiable and submissive；easygoing

和谈 hétán 【名】peace talks 【动】hold peace talks

和谐 héxié 【形】harmonious

和颜悦色 hé yán yuè sè amiable and endearing manner；friendly and accessible

和约 héyuē 【名】peace treaty

河

hé 【名】〔条 tiáo〕river

河床 héchuáng 【名】river-bed

河道 hédào 【名】river course

河堤 hédī 【名】river embankment；dike

河谷 hégǔ 【名】river valley

河流 héliú 【名】〔条 tiáo〕rivers

河山 héshān 【名】rivers and mountains (territory of a country)

河水 héshuǐ 【名】river water

荷

hé

荷花 héhuā 【名】〔朵 duǒ〕lotus flower

核

hé 【名】❶ kernel ❷ nucleus

核保护伞 hé bǎohùsǎn nuclear umbrella

核查 héchá 【动】examine and verify

核弹头 hé dàntóu nuclear warhead

核电站 hédiànzhàn 【名】nuclear power station

核定 hédìng 【动】check and ratify

核对 héduì 【动】check up；verify：～账目 check accounts ～数字 verify figures

核讹诈 hé ézhà nuclear blackmail

核垄断 hé lǒngduàn nuclear monopoly

核潜艇 héqiántǐng 【名】nuclear-powered submarine

核燃料 héránliào 【名】nuclear fuel

核实 héshí 【动】verify；confirm：～情况 verify the facts of a situation 材料需要～一下。This data requires verification.

核算 hésuàn 【动】calculate；reckon

核桃 hétao 【名】walnut

核武器 hé wǔqì nuclear weapon

核心 héxīn 【名】nucleus；core

核装置 hé zhuāngzhì nuclear device

核准 hézhǔn 【动】examine and approve

核子 hézǐ 【名】nucleon

盒

盒 hé 【名】box；case

盒饭 héfàn 【名】boxed meals

盒式磁带 héshì cídài cassette tape

盒子 hézi 【名】box；case

hè

贺（賀）

贺（賀）hè 【动】congratulate

贺词 hècí 【名】speech of congratulation

贺电 hèdiàn 【名】message of congratulation

贺卡 hèkǎ 【名】〔张 zhāng〕greeting card

贺礼 hèlǐ 【名】congratulatory present

贺年 hè = nián wish sb. a happy New Year

贺喜 hè = xǐ congratulate on a happy occasion

贺信 hèxìn 【名】〔封 fēng〕letter of greeting

喝

喝 hè 【动】shout
另见 hē

喝彩 hè = cǎi give shouts of approval；cheer（at a performance or game）

赫

赫 hè

赫赫有名 hèhè yǒumíng be of great renown

褐

褐 hè 【形】◇brown

褐色 hèsè 【名】brown colour

hēi

黑

黑 hēi 【形】❶ black ❷ dark：天～了。It's getting dark. 走廊里很～。It's very dark in the corridor. ❸ bad；wicked：～心肠 evil in nature；evil-hearted

黑暗 hēi'àn 【形】❶ dim；dark：～的角落 a dark corner ❷（fig.）reactionary；decadent：～的社会 a decadent society ～的势力 sinister forces；evil influence

黑白片 hēibáipiàn 【名】black-and-white film

黑板 hēibǎn 【名】〔块 kuài〕blackboard

黑板报 hēibǎnbào 【名】blackboard newspaper

黑道 hēidào 【名】（～儿）❶ dark road ❷ illegal acts ❸ sinister gangs：～上的人 a member of an illegal gang

黑洞洞 hēidōngdōng 【形】pitch

dark；very dark：～的坑道 a pitch dark tunnel ～的夜晚 a very dark night

黑话 hēihuà 【名】❶ gangsters' slang ❷ malicious words

黑货 hēihuò 【名】❶ contraband ❷ sinister stuff

黑名单 hēimíngdān 【名】blacklist

黑色 hēisè 【名】black colour

黑社会 hēishèhuì 【名】underworld；gangland

黑市 hēishì 【名】black market

黑手 hēishǒu 【名】"black hand"

黑体字 hēitǐzì 【名】boldface type

黑匣子 hēixiázi 【名】black box

黑压压 hēiyāyā 【形】a dark mass of

黑夜 hēiyè 【名】night

黑油油 hēiyóuyōu 【形】black and shiny：～的土地 rich black earth 她的头发～的发亮。Her hair is black and glossy.

嘿

嘿 hēi 【叹】hey! ❶ *used to address sb. or to catch sb.'s attention*：～，老李，看电视吗？Hey, Lao Li! Aren't you going to watch T.V.? ❷ *used to express satisfaction*：～，你看，咱们的扬水站建成啦! Hey! Look! Our pumping station is finished! ❸ *used to express surprise*，*praise*：～，这球扣得真漂亮! Hey, what a beautiful smash!

hén

痕

痕 hén

痕迹 hénjì 【名】mark；trace；track

hěn

狠

狠 hěn 【形】❶ ferocious；cruel；merciless：心肠太～ too hard-hearted ❷ resolute；firm：～～打击 strike relentlessly

狠毒 hěndú 【形】malicious

狠心 hěnxīn 【形】hard-hearted

很

很 hěn 【副】very；quite：我～了解这个厂的情况。I am quite well acquainted with the situation in this factory. 这个人～会办事。This man is very capable at managing things. 我～不喜欢夸夸其谈的人。I very much dislike people who brag. 他是一个～好的同志。He is a very good comrade. 今天天气～好。The weather today is very pleasant. Note：*when it is used before an adjective which is the predicate*，很 *no longer indicates high degree*. 得很 *is a complement of degree*，*indicating high degree*：近来他忙得～。He has been very busy recently.

hèn

恨

恨 hèn 【动】hate

恨不得 hènbude 【副】wish one could *usu. followed by an exaggerated statement which expresses a very strong or urgent desire*：这些花太好看了，我～都买回去。These flowers are so gorgeous；I wish I could buy them all and take them home. 听说老同学来了，我～马上见到他。When I heard that an old schoolmate has arrived, I wish I could see him immediately.

恨铁不成钢 hèn tiě bù chéng gāng be disappointed in sb. who failed to live up to one's high expectations

hēng

哼

哼 hēng 【动】❶ groan；moan：他virtue坚强，伤这么重都没～过一声。How brave he was! He didn't let

out so much as a groan, though he was seriously wounded. ❷ hum：他一面走，一面～着歌儿。He hummed a tune as he strolled along.

另见 hng

héng

恒 héng

恒温　héngwēn　【名】constant temperature

恒心　héngxīn　【名】perseverance

恒星　héngxīng　【名】〔颗 kē〕fixed star

横 héng　【形】❶ horizontal：一根～梁 a horizontal beam ～排本 a horizontally (as opp. to vertically) printed book 人行～道 a pedestrian crossing ❷ criss-cross；in all directions：血肉～飞 splattered with blood and strewn with bodies ～七竖八 be scattered in all directions ❸ unreasonable；irrational：～加阻拦 obstruct unreasonably ～加指责 censure unreasonably 【动】set across or athwart：～下一条心 be determined to do sth. whatever the cost 把竹竿～过来 hold the bamboo pole cross-wise 眼前～着一条大河。Ahead of us, across our path, there is a river. 【名】(of Chinese characters) horizontal stroke："一"

另见 hèng

横冲直撞　héng chōng zhí zhuàng reckless action；colliding with (vehicles, etc.) in every direction

横渡　héngdù　【动】sail；be ferried or swim across

横幅　héngfú　【名】streamer

横贯　héngguàn　【动】(of a railway, mountain range, etc.) cross；traverse

横加　héngjiā　【动】wantonly：～指责 wantonly accuse

横扫　héngsǎo　【动】sweep away；completely annihilate

横竖　héngshù　【副】〈口〉同"反正" fǎnzhèng

横向　héngxiàng　【名】horizontal；crosswise：～联合 horizontal linkage

横行　héngxíng　【动】play the tyrant

横行霸道　héngxíng bàdào　ride roughshod over；play the bully

横征暴敛　héng zhēng bào liǎn extort exorbitant taxes and levies；levy excessive taxes

衡 héng

衡量　héngliáng　【动】weigh；judge；consider

hèng

横 hèng　【形】unreasonable；savage

另见 héng

横暴　hèngbào　【形】brutal；tyrannical；high-handed

横财　hèngcái　【名】fortune made by taking dishonest advantage of circumstances

横祸　hènghuò　【名】unexpected misfortune；disaster；calamity

hng

哼 hng　【叹】expressing dissatisfaction or disbelief：～，真不像话！Humph, that is really ridiculous!

另见 hēng

hōng

轰（轟）hōng　【动】❶ bombard：万炮齐～ bombard with thousands of guns ❷ scare away；

shoo away：～麻雀 shoo away sparrows 把鸡～出去 shoo chickens out 【象声】(of thunder, an explosion, etc.) crash；roar：～的一声 a crashing sound

轰动 hōngdòng 【动】cause a sensation；create a stir：～一时 a nine days' wonder 全场～。The play created a sensation among the audience. 也作"哄动"。

轰轰烈烈 hōnghōnglièliè 【形】stormy and heroic；stirring and seething

轰击 hōngjī 【动】bombard

轰隆 hōnglōng 【象声】crash；roar (sound of thunder, explosion, etc.)

轰鸣 hōngmíng 【动】roar (of a machine, etc.)

轰炸 hōngzhà 【动】bomb

轰炸机 hōngzhàjī 【名】〔架 jià〕bomber

哄 hōng

另见 hǒng；hòng

哄动 hōngdòng 【动】cause a sensation；stir

哄抢 hōngqiǎng 【动】looting

哄堂大笑 hōngtáng dàxiào set the room rocking with laughter

烘 hōng 【动】❶ get warm at a fire：～～手 warm one's hands at a fire ❷ dry by a fire：～衣服 dry laundry by a fire ～干木料 dry lumber in a kiln

烘托 hōngtuō 【动】set off against a background in a way that makes an object more prominent

hóng

弘 hóng

弘扬 hóngyáng 【动】carry forward；develop

红（紅）hóng 【形】❶ red：～花 a red flower ～铅笔 a red pencil ❷ lucky；eminent；successful；specially favoured；popular：～人 one's blue-eyed boy

红包 hóngbāo 【名】a red paper envelope containing money as a gift, tip, or bonus

红宝石 hóngbǎoshí 【名】ruby

红茶 hóngchá 【名】black tea

红灯 hóngdēng 【名】〔盏 zhǎn〕red traffic light

红光满面 hóng guāng mǎn miàn (of one's face) glowing with health

红火 hónghuo 【形】flourishing；prosperous

红军 Hóngjūn 【名】❶ the Red Army；short for 中国工农红军 ❷ the Soviet Army prior to 1946

红利 hónglì 【名】dividend；bonus

红领巾 hónglǐngjīn 【名】red scarf；the badge of the Young Pioneers

红绿灯 hónglǜdēng 【名】traffic lights

红娘 hóngniáng 【名】match-maker

红牌 hóngpái 【名】(～儿) red card

红扑扑 hóngpūpū 【形】ruddy

红旗 hóngqí 【名】〔面 miàn〕red flag；red banner

红润 hóngrùn 【形】rosy (e.g. cheeks)

红色 hóngsè 【名】❶ red colour ❷ revolutionary

红十字会 Hóngshízìhuì 【名】the Red Cross

红糖 hóngtáng 【名】brown sugar

红通通 hóngtōngtōng 【形】bright red 也作"红彤彤"。

红外线 hóngwàixiàn 【名】infrared ray

红星 hóngxīng 【名】〔颗 kē〕red star

红血球 hóngxuèqiú 【名】red corpuscle；erythrocyte

红眼病 hóngyǎnbìng 【名】❶ conjunctiva ❷ envy；jealousy

红药水　hóngyàoshuǐ　【名】mercuro-
chrome

红缨枪　hóngyīngqiāng　【名】〔枝 zhī〕
red-tasselled spear

宏 hóng

宏大　hóngdà　【形】great；grand（in
scale)

宏观　hóngguān　【名】macroscopic：
～世界 macrocosm

宏图　hóngtú　【名】far-reaching
plan；great plan

宏伟　hóngwěi　【形】(of scale, plan,
etc.) magnificent；grand

虹 hóng 【名】rainbow

洪 hóng

洪峰　hóngfēng　【名】flood peak

洪亮　hóngliàng　【形】(of voice) loud
and clear

洪流　hóngliú　【名】powerful cur-
rent；tide (of history, etc.)

洪炉　hónglú　【名】crucible：时代的～
the whirlwind of an era

洪水　hóngshuǐ　【名】flood；inunda-
tion

鸿（鴻）hóng

鸿沟　hónggōu　【名】〔道 dào〕gap；
chasm

鸿毛　hóngmáo　【名】the down of a
wild goose

hǒng

哄 hǒng 【动】❶ perpetrate a
hoax；mislead with fine words：他
编了一套瞎话来～别人,谁信哪！He is
trying to mislead people with a
false story. Who is going to believe him？❷ coax (a child)
另见 hōng；hòng

哄骗　hǒngpiàn　【动】coax

hòng

哄 hòng 【动】uproar；horseplay
另见 hōng；hǒng

哄闹　hòngnào　【动】boo；make cat-
calls

hóu

喉 hóu 【名】throat

喉咙　hóulóng　【名】throat

喉舌　hóushé　【名】(fig.) spokes-
man；voice：人民的～ the voice of
the people

猴 hóu 【名】monkey

猴子　hóuzi　【名】〔只 zhī〕monkey

hǒu

吼 hǒu 【动】❶ roar；bellow；
howl：大～一声 a howling cry 狮子
～ the roar of a lion ❷ (of wind,
siren, artillery, etc.) howl；whis-
tle；thunder：汽笛长～了一声。The
siren gave a long blast.

吼叫　hǒujiào　【动】roar；bellow

hòu

后（後）hòu 【名】❶ (as opp.
to 前 or 先) back；behind；rear；
afterwards：村前村～ in front of
and behind the village 先来的有座
儿,～来的没座儿。Those who ar-
rived early got seats, but many
late-comers couldn't find seats. ❷
towards the end；back：～排 the
back rows ～十名 the last ten (persons)

后半天　hòubàntiān　【名】after noon

后半夜 hòubànyè 【名】midnight till dawn; small hours of the morning

后备 hòubèi 【名】reserves

后备军 hòubèijūn 【名】(mil.) reserves

后辈 hòubèi 【名】❶ younger generation ❷ posterity

后边 hòubiān 【名】rear; back

后代 hòudài 【名】❶ succeeding era ❷ descendant; offspring

后盾 hòudùn 【名】backing; support

后发制人 hòu fā zhì rén gain advantage by striking only after one's opponent has struck

后方 hòufāng 【名】(mil.) rear

后跟 hòugēn 【名】heel

后顾之忧 hòugù zhī yōu fear of attack from the rear; a worry which distracts one from one's main concern: 没有～ without any fear of attack from behind 孩子长大了，她没有～，可以一心搞科研。With her children grown up, she is free of care and can put all her heart into her scientific research.

后果 hòuguǒ 【名】consequence

后患 hòuhuàn 【名】disastrous consequences; aftermath

后悔 hòuhuǐ 【动】regret; repent; feel remorseful: 我真～当初没有好好帮助他。I regret not having helped him enough at that time! 他没去报考音乐学院，感到～极了。He very much regretted not having applied for admission to the conservatory.

后悔莫及 hòuhuǐ mò jí regret sth. too late

后记 hòujì 【名】(of a book or article) postscript

后继有人 hòu jì yǒu rén have qualified successors

后进 hòujìn 【形】lagging behind; less advanced

后来 hòulái 【名】later on; afterwards: 十年前我去过一次上海，～再没有去过。I went to Shanghai once ten years ago, but since then I have never been back.

后来居上 hòu lái jū shàng new-comers overtake the old hands; present feats surpass previous ones

后浪推前浪 hòu làng tuī qián làng waves surge on one after the other; one thing pushes another forward; the continuous march of events: 建设的高潮像长江之水，～，一浪高一浪。The high tide of construction, like the Changjiang River, surges forward wave upon wave.

后路 hòulù 【名】〔条 tiáo〕escape route; room for manoeuvre or retreat

后门 hòumén 【名】(～儿) ❶ back door ❷ backdoor influence: 走～ go in for back-door deals

后面 hòumiàn 【名】❶ back ❷ later

后年 hòunián 【名】the year after next

后期 hòuqī 【名】later stage

后起之秀 hòu qǐ zhī xiù outstanding members of the new generation: 体育战线涌现出不少～。In the area of sports, many promising youngsters of the new generation are coming forward. 他是美术界的～。He is one of the up-and-coming youngsters in the field of fine arts.

后勤 hòuqín 【名】logistics; service staff

后人 hòurén 【名】❶ people of future generations ❷ descendants

后台 hòutái 【名】❶ backstage: 演员在～准备出场。The performers are backstage getting ready for the show. ❷ behind-the-scenes boss: ～老板 behind-the-scenes boss 谁是他的～? Who is his boss behind the scenes?

后天 hòutiān 【名】❶ day after tomorrow ❷ acquired (as opp. to 先

天)

后头 hòutou 【名】同"后面"

后退 hòutuì 【动】retreat

后卫 hòuwèi 【名】❶（mil.）rear-guard ❷（football）fullback ❸（basketball）guard

后效 hòuxiào 【名】later effect；later improvement

后遗症 hòuyízhèng 【名】（med.）sequela

后裔 hòuyì 【名】descendants；posterity

后者 hòuzhě 【名】the latter

后缀 hòuzhuì 【名】suffix

厚

厚 hòu 【形】thick：五公分～的木板 a plank 5 cm. thick 这床棉被太～了。This quilt is too thick. 大雪下了一尺～。Snow fell a foot deep.

厚爱 hòu'ài 【动】fondness；kindness：承蒙～ thank you for the kindness

厚此薄彼 hòu cǐ bó bǐ discriminate against one and favour another

厚道 hòudao 【形】sincere and tolerant

厚度 hòudù 【名】thickness

厚古薄今 hòu gǔ bó jīn stress the past rather than the present

厚今薄古 hòu jīn bó gǔ stress the present rather than the past

厚实 hòushi 【形】thick and solid

厚望 hòuwàng 【名】great expectations：寄～ place high hopes on

厚颜无耻 hòuyán wúchǐ have no sense of shame

候

候 hòu 【动】wait

候补 hòubǔ 【动】alternate（member）

候车室 hòuchēshì 【名】（of railway station, etc.）waiting room

候选人 hòuxuǎnrén 【名】candidate

候诊 hòuzhěn 【动】wait to see the doctor：～室 waiting room （in a hospital）

hū

呼

呼 hū 【动】❶ exhale：～出一口气 exhale；breathe out ❷ shout：～口号 shout slogans ❸ ◇call：一～百应 ready to respond in their hundreds to one's orders 【象声】（of wind）whistle：北风～～地吹。The north wind whistles as it blows.

呼喊 hūhǎn 【动】cry；call；shout

呼号 hūháo 【动】wail

呼号 hūhào 【名】❶（radio）call sign；call letters ❷ catchword（of an organization）

呼唤 hūhuàn 【动】summon；call up

呼叫 hūjiào 【动】shout loudly；call；page

呼喇喇 hūlālā 【象声】*sound of fluttering of flags, sound of flapping, etc.* 也作"呼啦啦"

呼声 hūshēng 【名】expressed opinion, will, judgement or wish（of the people or of a number of persons）

呼吸 hūxī 【动】breathe；respire

呼吸道 hūxīdào 【名】respiratory tract

呼啸 hūxiào 【动】（of wind）howl

呼应 hūyìng 【动】work in concert with；be used in conjunction with

呼吁 hūyù 【动】appeal to

忽

忽而 hū'ér 【副】❶ 同"忽然"，*but less frequently used*：～他的表情严肃起来。Suddenly his face wore a serious expression. ❷ *two or more* 忽而 *modifying different adjectives, verbs or verbal phrases indicate alternation*：声音～高，～低。The sound was loud one moment and soft the next. 这个战士抱起炸药包冲了出去，～向左，～向右，迅速接近敌

人的碉堡。The soldier dashed out carrying sticks of dynamite and, dodging now to the left, now to the right, swiftly approached the enemy's fortifications.

忽…忽…　hū…hū…　now…now…; now…then… (usu. *used with two contrasting adjectives, etc. to express change*): 天气忽冷忽热。The weather is cold one minute, warm the next. 灯光忽明忽暗。The light shone first brightly, then dimly. 风忽大忽小。The wind blew now strongly now gently.

忽略　hūlüè　【动】fail to see or notice; overlook: 一个螺丝钉松动, 如果～了, 有时也会造成事故。Sometimes a single loose screw, if overlooked, can lead to a disastrous accident. 数值虽小, 但不可～。Although the amount involved is nominal, nonetheless, it shouldn't be overlooked.

忽然　hūrán　【副】suddenly; all of a sudden: 窗外～传来一阵笑声。We suddenly heard a burst of laughter outside the window. ～一只小鸟从我眼前飞过。A little bird suddenly flew past me.

忽视　hūshì　【动】give no or not enough care to; neglect: 学外语不能～发音的练习。In learning a foreign language, one should never neglect pronunciation practice. 感冒虽不是大病, 但容易引起并发症, 不能～。A cold is not a serious illness, but it can, if neglected, give rise to complications.

hú

囫 hú

囫囵吞枣　húlún tūn zǎo　swallow a date whole without chewing or tasting it; uncritical acceptance without real comprehension: 学习一定要结合实际, 独立思考, ～是决然收不到效果的。It is essential to combine book-learning with practice and independent thinking. An uncritical acceptance of what one reads will not yield desirable results.

狐 hú　【名】fox

狐假虎威　hú jiǎ hǔ wēi　the fox borrows the tiger's ferocity; assume someone else's authority to browbeat others

狐狸　húli　【名】〔只 zhī〕fox

狐群狗党　hú qún gǒu dǎng　a gang of scoundrels

狐疑　húyí　【动】be suspicious (in Chinese legend, the fox is said to have a suspicious nature): ～不决 suspicious and hence indecisive 满腹～ filled with suspicion

弧 hú　【名】arc

弧度　húdù　【名】(maths.) radian

弧光　húguāng　【名】(electr.) arc; arc light

弧形　húxíng　【名】arc-shaped

胡 hú　【副】meaninglessly; foolishly; not in the proper way

胡扯　húchě　【动】talk nonsense; tell a lie

胡椒粉　hújiāofěn　【名】ground pepper

胡萝卜　húluóbo　【名】carrot

胡闹　húnào　【动】behave foolishly or unreasonably

胡琴　húqin　【名】〔把 bǎ〕two-stringed Chinese fiddle

胡说　húshuō　【动】talk nonsense

胡说八道　hú shuō bā dào　talk nonsense or rubbish

胡思乱想　hú sī luàn xiǎng　indulge in wild fancies; let one's imagination

run away with one

胡同　hútòng　【名】〔条 tiáo〕lane

胡言　húyán　【名】nonsense；rubbish：一派～ utter nonsense

胡言乱语　hú yán luàn yǔ　talk nonsense

胡子　húzi　【名】beard；moustache；whiskers

胡作非为　hú zuò fēi wéi　run wild；behave unlawfully

壶（壺）　hú　【名】〔把 bǎ〕kettle；pot

馄　hú　【名】◇ porridge

馄口　húkǒu　【动】keep body and soul together

湖　hú　【名】lake

湖泊　húpō　【名】lakes

湖色　húsè　【名】light green

湖泽　húzé　【名】lakes and marshes

蝴　hú

蝴蝶　húdié　【名】〔只 zhī〕butterfly

蝴蝶结　húdiéjié　【名】bowknot；bow

糊　hú　【动】❶ be burned；be singed ❷ paste

糊里糊涂　hú li hútū　muddled

糊涂　hútú　【形】❶ confused；muddle-headed：碰到大事不～ not get muddle-headed when faced with major issues 你不讲我还清楚，你越讲我越～。If you had said less, it would have made sense. The more you explained, the more confused I was. ❷ in a mess：一本～账 accounts which are in a mess；a messy business

hǔ

虎　hǔ　【名】〔只 zhī〕tiger

虎口　hǔkǒu　【名】❶ (fig.) the lion's mouth ❷ area between thumb and index finger

虎视眈眈　hǔ shì dāndān　look with covetous eyes at sth.

虎头蛇尾　hǔtóushéwěi　a brave beginning, but a weak ending：我们做任何事情都要善始善终，不能～。Whatever we do, we must persevere right to the end.

虎穴　hǔxué　【名】❶ tiger's den ❷ dangerous spot：深入～ put one's head in the lion's mouth

hù

互　hù

互不侵犯条约　hù bù qīnfàn tiáoyuē mutual non-aggression treaty

互惠　hù huì　reciprocal（between countries）

互利　hù lì　mutual benefit

互通有无　hù tōng yǒu wú help supply each other's wants

互相　hùxiāng　【副】mutual：～关心 mutual concern ～支持 mutual support

互助　hùzhù　【动】help each other

户　hù　【名】◇household【量】for households

户口　hùkǒu　【名】one's registered place of residence

户头　hùtóu　【名】(bank) account：开～ open an account

护（護）　hù　【动】❶ protect；guard：～航 escort；convoy ～路 guard a road or railway ❷ be partial to one side：～短 attempt to justify one's mistakes

护理　hùlǐ　【动】look after；nurse：～病人 nurse patients ～幼苗 look after seedlings

护员　hùlǐyuán　【名】nursing assistant；medical orderly

护林员　hùlínyuán　【名】forest ranger

护身符　hùshēnfú　【名】amulet; charm; shield

护士　hùshi　【名】nurse

护士长　hùshizhǎng　【名】head nurse

护送　hùsòng　【动】escort

护照　hùzhào　【名】passport

怙　hù

怙恶不悛　hù è bù quān　unrepentantly persist in evil

huā

花　huā　【名】〔朵 duǒ〕❶ flower: 一朵～（儿）a flower ～开了没有? Has the flower opened? ❷ anything which is flower-like: 钢～四溅 sparks of molten steel flashed about ❸ fireworks: 国庆节晚上放～ There is a display of fireworks on the evening of National Day. ❹ 挂～ be wounded in battle 【动】consume; spend: ～时间 spend time ～力气 consume energy ～钱 spend money 【形】❶ flowered; of many colours: 小～猫 a spotted kitten 这块布太～。This cotton print has too many colours in it. ❷ deterioration of vision due to old age; presbyopic: 我的眼睛～了。My vision is dim.

花白　huābái　【形】(of hair, beard, etc.) grizzled

花瓣　huābàn　【名】flower petal

花苞　huābāo　【名】bud

花边　huābiān　【名】lace

花布　huābù　【名】printed calico

花茶　huāchá　【名】perfumed tea; jasmine tea

花朵　huāduǒ　【名】flowers; blossoms

花房　huāfáng　【名】greenhouse

花费　huāfèi　【动】spend; use up

花岗岩　huāgāngyán　【名】granite

花花绿绿　huāhuālǜlǜ　【形】multi-coloured; colourful

花花世界　huā huā shìjiè　a world full of temptations

花环　huāhuán　【名】garland

花甲　huājiǎ　【名】a cycle of sixty years: ～之年 sixty (years of age)

花镜　huājìng　【名】〔副 fù〕eyeglasses for people who are far-sighted due to old age

花卷儿　huājuǎnr　【名】steamed roll shaped like a flower

花篮　huālán　【名】a basket of flowers

花蕾　huālěi　【名】(flower) bud

花炮　huāpào　【名】fireworks; fire-crackers

花盆儿　huāpénr　【名】〔个 gè〕flower pot

花瓶　huāpíng　【名】〔个 gè〕flower vase

花圈　huāquān　【名】wreath

花色品种　huāsè pǐnzhǒng　(of merchandise) variety

花生　huāshēng　【名】peanut

花生米　huāshēngmǐ　【名】〔粒 lì〕shelled peanut

花束　huāshù　【名】bouquet

花纹　huāwén　【名】ornamental design; pattern

花絮　huāxù　【名】interesting side-lights

花言巧语　huā yán qiǎo yǔ　honeyed and deceiving words

花样　huāyàng　【名】❶ pattern; design: 这种～很新颖。This pattern is rather unique. ❷ variety: 食堂的主食～很多。The food served in the dining hall has a considerable variety. ❸ trick: 鬼～ dirty trick

花园　huāyuán　【名】garden

花招　huāzhāo　【名】trick

花枝招展　huā zhī zhāo zhǎn　be showily dressed

哗（嘩）　huā　【象声】rattling

sound made by sth. metal
另见 huá
哗哗 huāhuā 【象声】 *the sound of rain or flowing water*

huá

划 huá 【动】❶ （劃）draw；cut；scratch：～火柴 strike a match 玻璃上～了一道印儿。A line was cut on the glass. ❷ paddle：一个人～一只小船。Paddle a small boat by oneself.
另见 huà
划不来 huá bu lái not worthwhile；(sth.) doesn't pay：坐船去上海很费时间，太～了! It takes a lot of time to travel to Shanghai by boat. It's not worth it.
划船 huá = chuán paddle a boat；row
划得来 huá de lái it will pay to…；it's worth it to…：投资不多，当年受益，真～。This undertaking requires only a small investment and yields benefits in the same year, so it is a worthwhile thing to do. 这块地还是种麦子～。It will pay to grow wheat on this plot after all.
划算 huásuàn 【动】plan；calculate；该怎么干得好好～一下。We need to plan ahead carefully for what to do next. 【形】profitable；pay：买布自己做衣服很～。It pays to buy the material and sew your own dress.

华（華） huá
华表 huábiǎo 【名】carved marble pillar
华而不实 huá ér bù shí flower that doesn't bear fruit, that is, (of style of work, behaviour) flashy without substance
华丽 huálì 【形】gorgeous
华侨 huáqiáo 【名】overseas Chinese

华裔 huáyì 【名】foreign citizen of Chinese origin
华语 Huáyǔ 【名】the Chinese lauguage

哗（嘩） huá
另见 huā
哗然 huárán 【形】(of protest, complaint, etc.) clamourous
哗众取宠 huá zhòng qǔ chǒng impress people or attempt to win favour with high-sounding phrases

滑 huá 【形】❶ (of a surface) smooth；slippery：路～ a slippery road 冰面很～。The ice is very slippery. ❷ (of persons) dishonest；sly；cunning：这人很～。This man is very sly. 【动】slip；slide：他～了一跤。He slipped and fell. 孩子们从滑梯上～下来。The children are going down the slide.
滑冰 huá = bīng skate
滑稽 huájī 【形】funny
滑轮 huálún 【名】pulley
滑坡 huápō 【动】landslide；landslip；decrease；drop
滑梯 huátī 【名】slide for children
滑头 huátóu 【形】(of persons) smooth；slippery 【名】sly person
滑翔 huáxiáng 【动】(of a glider) glide
滑翔机 huáxiángjī 【名】〔架 jià〕glider (plane)
滑雪 huá = xuě ski
滑雪板 huáxuěbǎn 【名】〔副 fù〕skis

huà

化 huà 【动】❶ melt；thaw：雪～了。The snow has melted. 铁烧～了。The iron has been melted. ❷ ◇ change；become：～消极因素为积极因素 turn negative factors into positive ones 大事～小，小事～了

(liǎo)。Turn a serious matter into a trifle, and a trifle into nothing at all;deflect a contention by playing down the issue. 【尾】*used after certain nouns and adjectives to form verbs*：绿～荒山 plant the barren hills with trees 美～校园 make the campus beautiful（by planting trees and flowers）简～汉字 simplify some Chinese characters 机械～ mechanize 现代～ modernize Note：*with the exception of a few verbs which are formed by adding* 化 *to monosyllabic adjectives，all other verbs with* 化 *cannot take any object*.

化肥 huàféi 【名】fertilizer

化工 huàgōng 【名】*short for* 化学工业

化公为私 huà gōng wéi sī embezzle public property

化合 huàhé 【动】(chem.) combine

化合反应 huàhé fǎnyìng （chem.）combination reaction

化合物 huàhéwù 【名】(chem.) compound

化疗 huàliáo 【动】*short for* 化学疗法

化身 huàshēn 【名】❶（Budd.）incarnation of the Buddha ❷ embodiment；incarnation（of sth. abstract）：理想的～ the embodiment of an ideal 真理的～ embodiment of the truth（*sarcasm*）

化石 huàshí 【名】fossil

化纤 huàxiān 【名】chemical fibre

化险为夷 huà xiǎn wéi yí emerge safely from danger

化学 huàxué 【名】chemistry

化学变化 huàxué biànhuà chemical change

化学反应 huàxué fǎnyìng chemical reaction

化学方程式 huàxué fāngchéngshì chemical equation

化学工业 huàxué gōngyè chemical industry

化学疗法 huàxué liáofǎ chemotherapy

化学武器 huàxué wǔqì chemical weapon；weapon of chemical warfare

化学纤维 huàxué xiānwéi chemical fibre

化学元素 huàxué yuánsù chemical element

化验 huàyàn 【动】(chem.) analyze；test（e.g. blood）

化整为零 huà zhěng wéi líng break the whole up into parts

化妆 huà zhuāng put on make-up

化妆品 huàzhuāngpǐn 【名】cosmetics

化装 huàzhuāng 【动】❶（of actors）make up ❷ disguise

划（劃） huà 【动】❶ draw；classify：～界 delineate a boundary line ❷ transfer（funds）；allocate；～账 transfer funds to another account；credit to another account ～款 allocate funds（for a particular purpose）

另见 huá

划分 huàfēn 【动】divide；classify：～地段 temporarily divide land into sections（for the purpose of some project）～势力范围 carve out spheres of influence

划清 huàqīng 【动】draw a clear line between；make a distinction between

划时代 huà shídài epoch-making

画（畫） huà 【动】paint；draw：～画儿 paint a picture 这幅画儿～得不错。This painting is not badly done. 【名】❶（～儿）〔张 zhāng、幅 fú〕painting；drawing：我喜欢这张山水～。I like this landscape very much. ❷（of a Chinese character）stroke：“上”字有三～。The character "上" has three strokes.

画板 huàbǎn 【名】drawing board

画报 huàbào 【名】〔本 běn〕pictorial magazine

画饼充饥 huà bǐng chōng jī draw a cake to satisfy one's hunger；make an ineffectual attempt

画册 huàcè 【名】〔本 běn〕picture album

画家 huàjiā 【名】painter

画卷 huàjuàn 【名】〔幅 fú〕picture scroll

画刊 huàkān 【名】pictorial section of a newspaper

画廊 huàláng 【名】art gallery

画龙点睛 huà lóng diǎn jīng draw the eyes when painting a dragon；(fig.) a crucial touch which drives home a point otherwise difficult to explain：话虽然简短，但是抓住了问题的本质，起到了～的作用。He spoke briefly but grasped the essence of the problem, and brought out the crucial point.

画面 huàmiàn 【名】(of painting) a picture

画皮 huàpí 【名】(fig.) a painted disguise (which transforms a monster into a beauty)

画片 huàpiàn 【名】〔张 zhāng〕small reproductions of paintings

画蛇添足 huà shé tiān zú draw a snake and add claws；(fig.) spoil the effect by adding sth. superfluous：这个词的意思已经解释清楚了，再多说，岂不是～? The meaning of the word is already clear；further explanation would be superfluous.

画像 huàxiàng 【名】〔张 zhāng〕portrait

画像 huà＝xiàng draw a portrait

画展 huàzhǎn 【名】exhibition of paintings

话（話）huà 【名】〔句 jù〕speech；talk；words

话别 huàbié 【动】say good-bye；make one's farewells

话柄 huàbǐng 【名】person or affair often gossiped about

话剧 huàjù 【名】play；drama (as opp. to 歌剧)

话题 huàtí 【名】topic (for discussion or conversation)

话筒 huàtǒng 【名】microphone

话务员 huàwùyuán 【名】(telephone) operator

话语 huàyǔ 【名】spoken words；discourse：他平时～不多。Generally, he is a man of few words.

huái

怀（懷）huái 【名】bosom：把小孩抱在～里 hug the child to one's bosom 【动】◇ cherish；harbour：不～好意 harbour evil intentions

怀抱 huáibào 【动】embrace；(clutch to) one's bosom：母亲的～ one's mother's arms 回到祖国的～ return to the bosom of one's motherland 【动】❶ embrace；hold in one's arms：～着婴儿 hold a baby in one's arms ❷ cherish：～着远大理想 cherish great ideals

怀表 huáibiǎo 【名】pocket watch

怀恨 huáihèn 【动】harbour resentment against

怀念 huáiniàn 【动】cherish the memory of

怀疑 huáiyí 【动】❶ have doubts about；doubt：我～你的结论。I have doubts about your conclusion. 我丝毫不～这份材料的真实性。I don't have the slightest doubt as to the veracity of this data. ❷ suspect：我～他今天不来了。I suspect that he will not turn up today.【名】doubt：对这个说法难道还有什么～吗? Is there still room for doubt about this account of the situation? 这种～是多余的。Such doubts

are unwarranted.

怀孕　huái＝yùn　be pregnant

怀着　huáizhe　【动】(often of ideals, wishes, sentiments) cherish; harbour; be filled with: ～崇高的理想 cherish a lofty ideal ～良好愿望 be full of good wishes ～无比激动的心情 be filled with agitated feelings

槐　huái　【名】◇ locust; acacia

槐树　huáishù　【名】〔棵 kē〕locust tree; acacia tree

huài

坏（壞）　huài　【形】❶ (as opp. to 好) bad; evil: 跟～人～事作斗争 combat evil-doers and evil deeds ❷ break down; rot: 这辆车～了. This car has broken down. 西红柿～了. These tomatoes are rotten. ❸ used after some verbs to indicate high degree: 气～了 livid with rage 忙～了 frantically busy 乐～了 overjoyed 【动】cause to be ill; spoil: 吃这样的东西容易～肚子. Eating such things is likely to give you stomach trouble. 工作方法简单往往～事. Using a method which is too simple can sometimes mess up things.

坏处　huàichu　【名】harm

坏蛋　huàidàn　【名】"bad egg"; villain; blackguard; rascal; scoundrel

坏分子　huàifènzǐ　【名】bad element

坏话　huàihuà　【名】❶ talk about another person in a negative way: 别在背后说人家的～. Don't badmouth other people. ❷ unpleasant words: 好话～都要听. You should listen to criticism as well as praise.

坏人　huàirén　【名】❶ bad person ❷ evildoer

坏死　huàisǐ　【动】necrosis

huān

欢（歡）　huān　【形】❶ ◇ joyful; happy: ～度国庆 celebrate National Day joyfully ❷ vigorous; lively: 孩子们玩儿得正～呢! The children are playing very happily.

欢畅　huānchàng　【形】happy and buoyant

欢呼　huānhū　【动】cheer; acclaim

欢聚一堂　huānjù yī táng　a happy gathering (used of formal occasions): 朋友们～,畅叙友情. Friends gather together and exchange expressions of friendship.

欢乐　huānlè　【形】happy; delighted; elated

欢声雷动　huān shēng léi dòng　a thunderous ovation; cheers and applause

欢送　huānsòng　【动】send off (usu. with a farewell party)

欢腾　huānténg　【动】be overjoyed; rejoice; be elated

欢天喜地　huān tiān xǐ dì　greatly delighted: 一家人～给爷爷过生日. The whole family celebrated grandpa's birthday with great cheer.

欢喜　huānxǐ　【形】happy; joyous: 满心～ extremely happy 欢欢喜喜过新年 joyously celebrate New Year's Day

欢笑　huānxiào　【动】laugh happily

欢心　huānxīn　【名】favour; friendly regard

欢欣鼓舞　huānxīn gǔwǔ　be exultant; jump for joy: 在讨论学校的远景规划时,教员们无不～,精神振奋. The teachers were elated as they discussed the school's long-term plans.

欢迎　huānyíng　【动】❶ welcome; greet ❷ be glad to have (sb.)

huán

还(還) huán 【动】❶ ◇ return：～乡 return to one's hometown 公物～家 return public property to where it belongs ❷ give back：～书 return a book ～钱 repay money ❸ reciprocate；give in return：～手 hit back 血债定要血来～。A blood-debt must be paid in blood.
另见 hái

还击 huánjī 【动】fight back；counter-attack

还价 huán＝jià （～儿）counter-bid

还礼 huán＝lǐ ❶ return a greeting：战士小李给师长敬了个礼，师长～后，亲切地让他坐下。Xiao Li saluted the division commander, who returned his greeting, then warmly invited him to sit down. ❷ give a gift in return

还手 huán＝shǒu fight or hit back

还原 huán＝yuán ❶（chem.）reduce ❷ restore；return to original shape or condition

还债 huán＝zhài pay one's debt

还账 huán＝zhàng pay bills；settle account on credit sales

环(環) huán 【名】❶ ring ❷ link：重要的一～ the key link；the crucial step ❸ unit used for scoring in target practice：九发子弹，他打了八十八～。He scored 88 points with only 9 shots.

环抱 huánbào 【动】encircle；embrace：群山～ encircled by mountains

环顾 huángù 【动】look round

环节 huánjié 【名】（fig.）link：中心～ key link 薄弱～ weak link

环境 huánjìng 【名】❶ environment ❷ circumstances

环境保护 huánjìng bǎohù environmental protection

环境卫生 huánjìng wèishēng environmental sanitation；general sanitation

环球 huánqiú 【名】❶ the earth；the world ❷ round the world

环绕 huánrào 【动】go round；centre on

环视 huánshì 【动】look round

环行 huánxíng 【动】go round；make a circuit of；circular（route）

huǎn

缓(緩) huǎn 【动】❶ postpone；put aside and deal with later：～办 put（some matter）aside to be dealt with later ～一～再说吧！Let's wait before we decide what to do. ❷（often of plants）revive：这棵晒蔫了的小树苗浇水以后又～过来了。The drooping sapling has revived after being watered. 【形】slow：～～而行 walk slowly；walk at a relaxed pace

缓兵之计 huǎn bīng zhī jì measures to stave off an attack；stalling tactics

缓冲 huǎnchōng 【动】❶（chem.）buffer ❷ mediate（a conflict）

缓和 huǎnhé 【动】allay；relax；ease：～紧张气氛 ease a strained atmosphere 紧张的心情慢慢～下来了。His tension was gradually eased. 【形】❶ moderate：他说话的语气比较～。His tone was quite moderate. ❷ détente

缓解 huǎnjiě 【动】relieve；alleviate；ease

缓慢 huǎnmàn 【形】slow

缓期 huǎn＝qī postpone

缓刑 huǎnxíng 【动】probation；suspension of sentence

huàn

`

幻 huàn

幻灯 huàndēng 【名】slide projector

幻觉 huànjué 【名】hallucination

幻灭 huànmiè 【动】disappear like an illusion

幻想 huànxiǎng 【动】fantasize 【名】illusion

幻影 huànyǐng 【名】illusory appearance；mirage

换 huàn 【动】❶ change；exchange：以物～物 exchange one commodity for another ～货支付协定 agreement on the exchange of and payment for commodities ❷ change：～车 change buses or trains ～衣服 change clothes ～了人间。The world has changed.

换班 huàn=bān change shifts；relieve sb. on duty

换代 huàn=dài produce a new crop of sth.；replace the old by the new：～产品 a new generation of products

换工 huàn=gōng exchange labour （between farmers or agricultural units）

换算 huànsuàn 【动】convert （from one unit of measurement to another）

换汤不换药 huàn tāng bù huàn yào old wine in new bottles

换文 huànwén 【名】（diplomatic）notes（in an exchange of diplomatic notes）

换文 huàn=wén exchange（diplomatic）notes

唤 huàn 【动】call

唤起 huàn=qǐ 【动】❶ arouse：～民众 arouse the masses ❷ give rise to；recall：～了对童年生活的回忆 recall memories of childhood

唤醒 huànxǐng 【动】awaken

涣 huàn

涣散 huànsàn 【形】demoralized：士气～ low morale 纪律～ lax discipline 精神～ in low spirits 【动】sap；dissipate：～人心 cause people to lose heart ～斗志 sap the people's will to fight

患 huàn 【动】contract；suffer from：～肺炎 suffer from pneumonia 【名】◇ trouble；disaster：水～ flood 防～于未然 nip disaster in the bud

患病 huàn=bìng be afflicted with a disease；fall ill；suffer from an illness

患得患失 huàn dé huàn shī worry about personal gains and losses；be overanxious about one's own interests：～是个人主义的一种表现。To think and act in terms of one's personal profit and loss is a manifestation of individualism.

患难 huànnàn 【名】adversity；hardship

患难与共 huànnàn yǔ gòng share weal and woe；stick together through thick and thin：他们始终～，并肩战斗。They always fought shoulder to shoulder and stuck together through thick and thin.

患者 huànzhě 【名】person who suffers（from a certain disease）

焕 huàn

焕发 huànfā 【动】❶ sparkle；brim over with：青春～ brim over with youthful vigour ❷ rally；gain renewed vigour：～精神，努力工作 rally one's flagging spirits and work with renewed vigour

焕然一新 huànrán yī xīn take on an entirely new aspect

豢 huàn

豢养 huànyǎng 【动】make sb. eat out of one's hand

huāng

荒 huāng 【形】waste；desolate：一座～岛 a desert island 地～了。The land has gone wild.【名】◇ ❶ wasteland；uncultivated land ❷ famine；crop failure；lean year；储粮备～ store grain against a famine 节约度～ survive a famine period by practising economy ❸ shortage；scarcity：煤～ coal shortage 房～ housing shortage【动】neglect；abandon：别～了功课。Don't neglect your lessons.

荒诞 huāngdàn 【形】fantastic；ludicrous；absurd

荒诞无稽 huāngdàn wújī absurd

荒地 huāngdì 【名】wasteland

荒废 huāngfèi 【动】❶ lie fallow；be left uncultivated：土地不能～。No farmland should be left uncultivated. ❷ waste：～时间 waste time ❸ neglect：～学业 neglect one's studies

荒凉 huāngliáng 【形】desolate

荒谬 huāngmiù 【形】absurd；ridiculous：～的论调 an absurd view 论点太～ a ridiculous argument

荒谬绝伦 huāngmiù juélún absolutely ridiculous；utterly absurd

荒漠 huāngmò 【名】bleak desert or vast empty plain 【形】desolate；bleak：～的草原 desolate grassland

荒年 huāngnián 【名】crop failure；famine year

荒山 huāngshān 【名】barren hill

荒疏 huāngshū 【形】rusty；out of practice

荒唐 huāngtáng 【形】absurd；fantastic：这种说法太～，谁信哪！That's an absurd explanation. How could anybody believe it!

荒芜 huāngwú 【形】(of land) grown over with underbrush

荒野 huāngyě 【名】wilderness

荒淫无耻 huāngyín wúchǐ given to debauchery

慌 huāng 【形】nervous；flustered：～手～脚 in a nervous and flurried manner 要镇静，不要～。Keep calm! Don't get flustered!【动】◇ be scared：～了神儿 be scared out of one's wits ～了手脚 be scared and not know what to do

慌乱 huāngluàn 【形】flurried；nervous and confused

慌忙 huāngmáng 【形】hurried；in a great rush

慌张 huāngzhāng 【形】flustered

huáng

皇 huáng

皇帝 huángdì 【名】emperor

皇宫 huánggōng 【名】(imperial) palace

皇后 huánghòu 【名】empress

皇室 huángshì 【名】imperial family

黄 huáng 【形】yellow

黄豆 huángdòu 【名】〔粒 lì〕soybean

黄瓜 huángguā 【名】〔根 gēn、条 tiáo〕cucumber

黄昏 huánghūn 【名】dusk

黄金 huángjīn 【名】gold

黄金时代 huángjīn shídài golden age

黄牌 huángpái 【名】(～儿) yellow card

黄色 huángsè 【名】❶ yellow (colour) ❷ decadent；obscene；pornographic：～小说 a pornographic novel ～歌曲 a vulgar song

黄土 huángtǔ 【名】loess

黄油 huángyóu 【名】❶ grease；lu-

bricating grease ❷ butter

惶 huáng

惶惶 huánghuáng 【形】be in a state of anxious suspense

惶惶不可终日 huánghuáng bù kě zhōng rì be so worried that you don't feel able to survive another day

惶惑 huánghuò 【形】perplexed and anxious

惶恐 huángkǒng 【形】anxious and frightened

蝗 huáng 【名】◇ locust (insect)

蝗虫 huángchóng 【名】locust (insect)

蝗灾 huángzāi 【名】plague of locusts

磺 huáng

磺胺 huáng'àn 【名】sulpha (sulphanilamide)

huǎng

恍 huǎng

恍惚 huǎnghū 【形】❶ in a trance：精神 ～ be in a trance ❷ dimly；faintly：～听见 hear faintly ～记得 faintly recall

恍然大悟 huǎngrán dà wù suddenly realize

晃 huǎng 【动】❶ dazzle：亮得～眼 be dazzlingly bright ❷ flash past：人影一～就不见了。The shadow of a person flashed past and disappeared.

谎（謊） huǎng 【名】lie；falsehood

谎报 huǎngbào 【动】lie about sth.；make a false report

谎话 huǎnghuà 【名】lie

谎言 huǎngyán 【名】lie（usu. in written language）

幌 huǎng

幌子 huǎngzi 【名】signboard；sign on a shop；(fig.) (under the) guise (of)；pretext

huàng

晃 huàng 【动】sway

晃荡 huàngdang 【动】❶ rock；shake；sway：小船～得很厉害。The small boat is being badly tossed about. ❷ roam about；ramble

晃动 huàngdòng 【动】shake；sway

晃晃悠悠 huànghuàngyōuyōu 【形】sway from side to side；wobble；stagger：身子～地要倒 stagger along and almost fall

晃悠 huàngyou 【动】swing：风吹得树枝来回～。The branches of the trees are swaying in the wind.

huī

灰 huī 【名】❶ ashes：炉～ ashes from a stove 烧成～ reduce sth. to ashes ❷ dust：桌子上落了一层～。A layer of dust has settled on the table. 看你那一脸～，快去洗洗吧。Your face is all covered with dirt. Go and wash it at once! ❸ lime：墙上抹（mò）一层～。The wall has been coated with lime. 【形】grey：～布 grey cloth

灰暗 huī'àn 【形】dingy

灰白 huībái 【形】greyish white

灰尘 huīchén 【名】dust

灰烬 huījìn 【名】〈书〉ashes

灰溜溜 huīliūliū 【形】disheartened；dejected：犯了错误改了就好，别总是～的，抬不起头来。As long as you correct your mistakes, it's all right. Don't go around looking de-

jected and hanging your head.

灰蒙蒙 huīmēngmēng 【形】dusky; dim

灰色 huīsè 【名】grey；gloomy：～制服 grey uniforms ～的人生观 pessimistic outlook on life

灰心 huīxīn 【形】disheartened；discouraged

灰心丧气 huīxīn sàng qì downhearted；downcast

诙（詼） huī

诙谐 huīxié 【形】humorous

挥（揮） huī

huī 【动】❶ wave；wield：～刀 wield a sword ～笔 use a pen or writing brush 把手一～ wave one's hand ❷ ◇ wipe off；wipe away：～泪 wipe away tears ～汗如雨 wipe away streams of sweat

挥动 huīdòng 【动】wave

挥发 huīfā 【动】be volatile

挥霍 huīhuò 【动】spend extravagantly；spend freely

挥金如土 huī jīn rú tǔ spend money like water

挥手 huī=shǒu wave one's hand

挥舞 huīwǔ 【动】wave；brandish

恢 huī

恢复 huīfù 【动】restore；regain；recover：～健康 regain one's health 交通～了。The traffic has returned to normal.

恢弘 huīhóng 【形】vast；extensive

辉（輝） huī

辉煌 huīhuáng 【形】brilliant；splendid；glorious：灯火～ brilliantly illuminated；ablaze with lights 金碧～ magnificent ～的战果 brilliant military victories

辉映 huīyìng 【动】〈书〉shine and reflect one thing on another

徽 huī

徽章 huīzhāng 【名】〔枚 méi〕badge

huí

回 huí 【动】❶ return to；go or come back：～国 return to one's country ～原单位工作 return to one's original organization to work ❷ turn back：～手把门关上（when one goes out）put one's hand behind one and close the door ❸ write an answer；reply：～他一封信 answer his letter 给我～一个电话。Please ring me back. Note：回 *is used after a verb as a complement to indicate that sth. or sb. is put in or returns to the original place*：工具用完一定要放～原来的地方。After use, the tools must be put back where they were before. 昨天我们看完戏是走～家的。We walked home from the theatre yesterday.（*same as* 回来 *or* 回去 *as a complement, except that no direction is implied and an object is necessary*）【名】the original place：往～走 walk back 往～看 look back 【量】❶ time（e. g. once, twice, etc.）我去过一～长城。I've been to the Great Wall once. 我是第二～来中国了。This is the second time I have come to China. ❷ a chapter of a classical Chinese novel：《红楼梦》总共一百二十～。*The Dream of the Red Chamber* has 120 chapters altogether.

回拜 huíbài 【动】return sb.'s visit

回报 huíbào 【动】repay

回避 huíbì 【动】evade；bypass

回潮 huícháo 【动】reverse；stage a come-back 【名】come-back

回答 huídá 【动】answer；reply 【名】answer；reply

回荡　huídàng　【动】resound；reverberate：悦耳的钢琴声在耳边～。The pleasant notes of the piano are still resounding.

回电　huídiàn　【动】reply by telegram【名】a reply by telegram

回访　huífǎng　【动】return a visit

回复　huífù　【动】❶ answer；reply（by letter）❷ restore：～原状 restore to its original shape

回顾　huígù　【动】look back

回归　huíguī　【动】go back；return

回归线　huíguīxiàn　【名】Tropic（of Cancer, of Capricorn）

回合　huíhé　【名】round（e.g. in boxing）

回话　huíhuà　【名】reply；answer

回击　huíjī　【动】counter-attack；fight back

回家　huí = jiā　go home

回敬　huíjìng　【动】❶ repay；requite；reciprocate：请允许我～你一杯。Allow me to reciprocate by proposing a toast to your health. ❷ retort（sarcasm）

回绝　huíjué　【动】turn down；reject

回扣　huíkòu　【名】sales commission

回来　huí // lái　return to the original place（*towards the speaker*）：我很快～。I'll be right back. 他下个月才回我们学校来呢！He won't come back to our school until next month. Note：回来 *is used after a verb as a complement to indicate that sb. or sth. returns to the original place（towards the speaker）*：他把借的书送～了。He has sent back the borrowed book. 你去农村参观的时候，带点儿稻种～。When you go to visit the village, please bring back some rice seeds. 张先生调回北京来了。Mr. Zhang has been transferred back to Beijing. (*same as* 回 *as a complement but the use of an object is optional*)

回礼　huí = lǐ　❶ return a salute ❷ send a present in return

回落　huíluò　【动】fall again（after a rise）

回民　Huímín　【名】the Hui people（one of China's national minorities）

回请　huíqǐng　【动】give a return banquet

回去　huí // qù　return to the original place（*any direction not towards the speaker*）：昨天她回家去了。She went back home yesterday. 今天晚上他加班，不～了。He's going to take an extra shift tonight, and so is not going back. Note：回去 *is used after a verb as a complement to indicate that sb. or sth. returns or is sent back to his or its original place（any direction not towards the speaker）*：把借的东西送～。Please send back the things you borrowed. 班机飞回上海去了。The regularly scheduled return flight has left for Shanghai. 下班的时候，你带两本书～。When you finish work, please take back the two books. (*same as* 回 *as a complement but the use of an object is optional*)

回升　huíshēng　【动】rise again

回声　huíshēng　【名】echo

回收　huíshōu　【动】reclaim；collect（cast-off things）

回条　huítiáo　【名】receipt

回头　huítóu　【副】〈口〉in a moment；by and by：～见。See you later. ～再谈。Let's talk about it again later. 请等一会儿，我～就来。Wait a minute. I'll be with you in no time.

回头　huí = tóu　❶turn one's head：请你回过头来。Please turn back around this way. ❷ mend one's ways：浪子～。The prodigal son has turned over a new leaf. ～是

岸。One has redeemed oneself as soon as one returns to the right course.

回头路　huítóulù　【名】path which will lead back to the old state of things without any improvement

回味　huíwèi　【动】❶ aftertaste ❷ realize through recollection

回响　huíxiǎng　【动】echo；resound；reverberate：火车的汽笛声在山谷中～。The sound of the train whistle echoed in the valley.

回想　huíxiǎng　【动】recall

回心转意　huí xīn zhuǎn yì　（of one's husband, wife, or beloved）re-establish old bonds after a period of estrangement

回信　huíxìn　【名】❶ a reply（letter）：写封～ write a reply；write back ❷（～儿）a verbal reply：明天上午等你的～。We will be waiting for your answer tomorrow morning.

回信　huí=xìn　make a reply：我给他回了一封信。I wrote to him in reply.

回旋　huíxuán　【动】❶ circle：雄鹰在天空～。The eagle is circling in the sky. ❷ manoeuvre：～的余地 room for manoeuvre

回忆　huíyì　【动】recollect

回忆录　huíyìlù　【名】memoirs

回音　huíyīn　【名】❶ echo：这间房子有～。This room has an echo. ❷ letter of reply：盼望～。We look forward to your reply.

回执　huízhí　【名】receipt

huǐ

悔 huǐ

悔改　huǐgǎi　【动】mend one's ways

悔过　huǐguò　【动】feel self-reproachful

悔过自新　huǐguò zìxīn　feel contrite and start anew

悔恨　huǐhèn　【动】regret

悔悟　huǐwù　【动】realize and regret one's errors

悔之不及　huǐ zhī bù jí　too late for regret

毁 huǐ

【动】destroy；spoil；damage；ruin：不能让虫子～了庄稼。We must not let insects damage the crops. 好好儿的一本书叫他给～了。It's a pity that this handsome book is ruined by him.

毁坏　huǐhuài　【动】damage；destroy

毁灭　huǐmiè　【动】wipe out；exterminate

毁誉　huǐyù　【动】praise and censure；commendation and condemnation：～参半 praise mingled with as much censure

huì

汇（匯） huì

【动】❶ flow into；gather together；converge：小小溪流～成河。Small streams converge to become a river. ❷ transmit；remit（money）：电～ cable money 给表弟一一笔款 remit a sum of money to a cousin

汇报　huìbào　【动】report；give an account of：～生产情况 report（to sb.）on production 【名】account；report：听取～（of a superior）listen to a report（by an inferior）

汇编　huìbiān　【动】assemble；collect and edit：～成书 compile a book 把现有的材料～一下 compile all available materials 【名】compilation；collection：资料～ a compilation of data

汇兑　huìduì　【动】remit（money）

汇费　huìfèi　【名】remittance fee

汇合　huìhé　【动】flow together

汇集　huìjí　【动】come together；gather together

汇款　huìkuǎn　【名】remittance
汇款　huì＝kuǎn　remit money
汇率　huìlǜ　【名】rate of exchange
汇票　huìpiào　【名】money order
汇总　huìzǒng　【动】gather together

会（會）huì　【名】meeting；rally：群众大～ a mass rally 联欢～ a get-together 开一个碰头～ put (our) heads together；meet and discuss【动】❶ assemble：下午在老王家～齐。Let's assemble at Lao Wang's in the afternoon. ❷ meet with；see：前天你～着他没有？Did you meet with him the day before yesterday? ❸ (of a language, song, etc.) know：我～英文，不～中文。I know some English, but I don't know any Chinese.【助动】❶ be able to do sth.；be proficient at sth.；be good at sth.：他既～种田，又～做工。He knows how to do both farm and factory work. 我不太～讲话。I am not very good at talking. ❷ indicates probability：他不～不同意。He won't disagree. 今天不～下雨的。It won't rain today.
另见 kuài

会餐　huìcān　【动】dine together
会场　huìchǎng　【名】place of meeting
会费　huìfèi　【名】(of a union, association, etc.) membership dues
会合　huìhé　【动】meet；join
会话　huìhuà　【动】converse；engage in dialogue【名】dialogue；conversation
会集　huìjí　【动】assemble
会见　huìjiàn　【动】meet with
会考　huìkǎo　【动】general examinations
会客　huì＝kè　receive visitors
会客室　huìkèshì　【名】reception room
会面　huì＝miàn　meet each other
会商　huìshāng　【动】hold a consulta-tion

会师　huìshī　【动】join forces
会谈　huìtán　【动】confer with；hold talks
会同　huìtóng　【动】join；be together with：这件事由总务科～有关单位办理。This matter is to be jointly managed by the General Affairs Section and other units concerned.
会晤　huìwù　【动】meet
会心　huìxīn　【形】understanding
会演　huìyǎn　【动】different artistic troupes come together to perform and learn from each other
会议　huìyì　【名】meeting
会意　huìyì　【动】show silent under-standing【名】one of the six catego-ries of Chinese characters（见“六书”）
会员　huìyuán　【名】member of an association, union, etc.
会战　huìzhàn　【动】(the main forces of the opposing armies) fight a de-cisive battle【名】decisive battle between the main forces of the opposing armies
会账　huì＝zhàng　pay a bill
会诊　huìzhěn　【动】(med.) have a consultation

讳（諱）huì
讳疾忌医　huì jí jì yī　keep one's ill-ness to oneself rather than see a doctor；conceal one's shortcom-ings or mistakes and be reluctant to admit them
讳莫如深　huì mò rú shēn　take great pains to avoid mentioning (sth.)

诲（誨）huì
诲人不倦　huì rén bù juàn　show great patience in helping others to learn

绘（繪）huì　【动】draw；paint
绘画　huìhuà　【名】drawing；painting
绘声绘色　huì shēng huì sè　vividly

portray or depict

绘图　huì = tú　make a chart of; make a map of

绘制　huìzhì　【动】draw (plan, blueprint, etc.)

贿 (賄) huì

贿赂　huìlù　【动】bribe【名】bribe

烩 (燴) huì

【动】(cooking) braise: ~豆腐 braised bean-curd ~鲜蘑 braised mushrooms

彗 (篲) huì

彗星　huìxīng　【名】〔颗 kē〕comet

晦 huì

晦气　huìqì　【名】bad luck; ghastly looks: 满脸～ ghastly looks on the face【形】unlucky: 真～，一出门就把钱包丢了。I've lost my wallet as soon as I left home. Rotten luck!

晦涩　huìsè　【形】obscure in meaning

惠 huì

惠存　huìcún　【动】be so kind as to keep

惠顾　huìgù　【动】favour; patronize: 欢迎～。Your patronage is welcome.

hūn

昏 hūn 【动】faint: 病人～过去了。The patient has fainted.【形】❶ muddled; mentally confused: 头～脑胀 be in a confused state of mind ❷ gloomy; dim

昏暗　hūn'àn　【形】dark; dim

昏沉　hūnchén　【形】❶ dim: 暮色～ the dimness of twilight ❷ dazed: 头脑～ be dazed 我昨晚没睡好觉，今天有点儿昏昏沉沉的。I didn't sleep well last night, so I feel in a bit of

a daze today.

昏花　hūnhuā　【形】(of one's vision) becoming dim

昏迷　hūnmí　【动】faint

昏天黑地　hūn tiān hēi dì　❶ pitch-dark: 这么晚了，～的，你还上哪儿去? Where are you off to? It's late and pitch-dark outside. ❷ (of society) dark: ～的生活 an immoral, dissipated life

昏庸　hūnyōng　【形】stupid and muddle-headed

荤 (葷) hūn 【形】(of a dish) made of meat, fish, poultry or eggs

荤菜　hūncài　【名】dish made of meat, fish, poultry or eggs

婚 hūn 【名】◇ marriage

婚礼　hūnlǐ　【名】wedding ceremony

婚姻　hūnyīn　【名】marriage

婚姻法　hūnyīnfǎ　【名】the Marriage Law

婚约　hūnyuē　【名】engagement

hún

浑 (渾) hún 【形】❶ muddy; turbid: ～水 muddy water ❷ muddled; confused: ～头～脑 muddle-headed; be confused

浑厚　húnhòu　【形】❶ simple and honest: 为人～ be straightforward and honest by nature ～的性格 simple and honest in character ❷ (of poetry, calligraphy, painting) natural and forceful: 笔力～ powerful brush strokes 色调～ (of painting) subdued harmonious colours

浑身　húnshēn　【名】the whole body

浑水摸鱼　hún shuǐ mō yú　fish in troubled waters 也作"混（hún）水摸

鱼"。

馄（餛） hún

馄饨 húntun 【名】stuffed dumpling

魂 hún 【名】❶ soul ❷ spirit；mood：～不守舍 distracted；preoccupied

魂不附体 hún bù fù tǐ be scared out of one's wits

hùn

混 hùn 【动】❶ mix：这两种药你千万别～在一块儿。You must not mix these two drugs together. ❷ palm off ❸ muddle along：～日子 drift through the day

混纺 hùnfǎng 【名】(of fabric) a blend of natural and synthetic fibres

混合 hùnhé 【动】❶ mix；blend：男女～双打 mixed doubles ～编队 team or military unit of mixed composition ❷ (chem.) mix

混乱 hùnluàn 【形】chaotic；disorderly

混凝土 hùnníngtǔ 【名】cement

混同 hùntóng 【动】confuse sth. with sth. else

混为一谈 hùn wéi yī tán equate sth. with sth. else；fail to differentiate

混淆 hùnxiáo 【动】mix up；confuse：真伪～ confuse true with false ～不清 blur the distinction between 是非界限，不容～。The distinction between right and wrong should never be obscured.

混血儿 hùnxuè'ér 【名】children of mixed parentage；half-breed

混杂 hùnzá 【动】mix

混战 hùnzhàn 【动】tangled warfare

混浊 hùnzhuó 【形】(of air，water，etc.) thick；turbid

huō

豁 huō 【动】tear；rip (enlargement of an already existing hole)
另见 huò

豁出去 huō chū qù stop at nothing；be ready to risk everything：～喝几口水，也要把游泳学会。I'll learn to swim even if I have to swallow many mouthfuls of water in the process.

豁口 huōkǒu 【名】opening (in a wall，city wall，etc.)

huó

和 huó 【动】mix (powder with liquid)
另见 hé；huò

活 huó 【动】live；be alive：新栽的苹果树都～了。The newly-planted apple trees are all doing well. ～到老，学到老。As long as one is alive，one should be learning. or One's never too old to learn. 【形】❶ lively；vivid；life-like：这条鱼画得真～。The fish in this painting looks very real. ❷ flexible：他学习的方法很～。His study method allows for great flexibility. 【名】❶ (～儿) job；work (usu. manual labour)：庄稼～ farm work ❷ product：这批（e.g. of shirts) 做得真精细。This batch (e.g. of shirts) is very nicely finished.

活动 huódòng 【动】❶ move about；exercise：出去～～。Go out and stretch your legs. ❷ loose：这个螺丝钉～了。This screw is loose. ❸ movable；mobile；not fixed：～模型 animated scale model ～房屋 mobile home 【名】activity：文娱～

recreational activities 体育~ physical training activities 政治~ political activities

活动家　huódòngjiā　【名】a person who takes an active part and is influential in political and social life

活该　huógāi　【动】〈口〉it serves (you) right：~如此。It's what you deserve. 屡教不改，落得这样的下场，~! Despite all the help and good advice we gave him, he didn't change his ways. Now he's failed. It serves him right!

活力　huólì　【名】vitality

活灵活现　huó líng huó xiàn　vividly (portray)：故事讲得~。The story was vividly told. 也说"活龙活现"。

活路　huólù　【名】〔条 tiáo〕way out

活命　huómìng　【名】life (as opp. to death)

活命　huó=mìng　make a bare living

活泼　huópo　【形】lively；vivacious：性格~ a vivacious temperament 这篇通讯的文字很~。This report is written in a very lively style.

活期　huóqī　【形】current (deposit)

活塞　huósāi　【名】piston

活生生　huóshēngshēng　【形】❶ real；live；living：~的事实 an actual fact ~的例子 a living example；a real instance ❷ be very much alive (used only in the context of inflicting suffering, torture)：~打死 beat to death ~累死 die from overwork

活像　huóxiàng　【动】be remarkably like；be just like

活页　huóyè　【名】loose-leaf

活跃　huóyuè　【动】be active；lively；enliven；make dynamic：~文化生活 enliven (the people's) cultural life ~气氛 liven up the atmosphere 【形】lively：那个班的同学都很~。The students of that class are very lively.

活字印刷　huózì yìnshuā　printing using movable-type

huǒ

火　huǒ　【名】❶ fire：玩~者，必自焚。He who plays with fire will surely get burned. ❷ (of traditional Chinese medicine) internal heat：上~了 suffer from internal heat 这种草药败~。This medicinal herb has a cooling effect. ❸ surge of anger；rage：~冒三丈 fly into a rage 【动】(～儿) lose one's temper：你有意见只可提，别~呀! You can voice your opinions all right, but don't lose your temper. 他一听这话就~啦! As soon as he heard that, he flared up.

火把　huǒbǎ　【名】torch

火并　huǒbìng　【动】open fight between factions

火柴　huǒchái　【名】match

火车　huǒchē　【名】〔列 liè〕train

火车头　huǒchētóu　【名】locomotive

火锅　huǒguō　【名】chafing dish；hot pot

火海　huǒhǎi　【名】a sea of flames

火海刀山　huǒhǎi dāoshān　an extremely dangerous situation：即使是~也敢闯 dare to brave any danger 也作"刀山火海"。

火红　huǒhóng　【形】fiery

火候　huǒhou　【名】❶ duration and intensity of heat for cooking, smelting, etc.：炒菜做饭要掌握~。Temperature control and timing matter a lot in cooking. ❷ crucial moment

火花　huǒhuā　【名】spark

火化　huǒhuà　【动】cremate

火箭　huǒjiàn　【名】rocket

火警　huǒjǐng　【名】❶ fire-alarm ❷ an outbreak of fire

火炬　huǒjù　【名】torch

火坑　huǒkēng　【名】fiery pit；ex-

tremely miserable situation

火辣辣 huǒlālā 【形】❶ fiery；scorching：夏天的太阳～的。In summer the sun is scorching. ❷ searing（pain）：手烫伤了,～地疼。He scalded his hand and is suffering searing pain. ❸ burning with shame or troubled by anxiety：试验又失败了,急得他心里～的。The experiment has failed again, and he is suffering great anxiety. 小王脸上～的,很不好意思。Xiao Wang was very embarrassed, and felt his cheeks burning.

火力 huǒlì 【名】fire-power

火力点 huǒlìdiǎn 【名】firing position

火力发电 huǒlì fā diàn thermo-electric generation

火炉 huǒlú 【名】stove；furnace

火苗 huǒmiáo 【名】flame

火气 huǒqì 【名】❶ heat（cause of inflammation, swelling or irritability according to traditional Chinese medicine）❷ anger；bad temper：哪儿来这么大～? Why such rage?

火热 huǒrè 【形】burning；very hot：～的太阳 a blazing sun ～的心 an ardent heart ～的斗争 fierce struggle

火山 huǒshān 【名】volcano

火上浇油 huǒ shàng jiāo yóu pour oil on the flames；make an already difficult situation worse 也说"火上加油"。

火烧 huǒshao 【名】a kind of baked bread

火烧眉毛 huǒ shāo méimao fire is singing one's eyebrows；extremely urgent：这是～的事儿,得赶快解决。This is an extremely urgent matter demanding an immediate solution.

火舌 huǒshé 【名】tongues of fire

火石 huǒshí 【名】flint

火势 huǒshì 【名】state of a fire as in a house blaze

火速 huǒsù 【副】at top speed；posthaste：～前进 proceed with the utmost speed ～完成 complete in the shortest possible time ～追击 in hot pursuit of

火腿 huǒtuǐ 【名】ham

火线 huǒxiàn 【名】❶ the front；the front-line in battle ❷ live wire

火星 huǒxīng 【名】❶ Mars ❷〔颗 kē〕(～儿) spark

火焰 huǒyàn 【名】flame

火药 huǒyào 【名】gun-powder

火药味 huǒyàowèi 【名】(～儿) the smell of gunpowder（fig.）

火灾 huǒzāi 【名】fire；conflagration

火葬 huǒzàng 【动】cremate

火中取栗 huǒ zhōng qǔ lì be a cat's paw

火种 huǒzhǒng 【名】tinder

伙

伙 huǒ 【名】❶（夥）group；band：散～ disband；part company 结～ band together；gang up in a work unit（derog.）❷ daily meals in a work unit：入～ take one's daily meals in a work unit【量】(夥) band；group：一～人 a group of people 三个一群,五个一～ in threes and fours

伙伴 huǒbàn 【名】companion；partner

伙房 huǒfáng 【名】kitchen

伙计 huǒji 【名】shop assistant or farmhand

伙食 huǒshí 【名】(in a unit or institution) meals

伙同 huǒtóng 【动】get together (with others to do sth.)

huò

或

或 huò 【连】or【副】perhaps

或许 huòxǔ 【副】perhaps

或者 huòzhě 【连】❶ or；either...

or…；neither…nor…：他全家明天～后天动身。His whole family will leave tomorrow or the day after. ～我们去，～他们来，都行。Either we go or they come；it makes little difference. 你们叫我的名字～老张都可以。It is all the same to me whether you call me by name or Lao Zhang. ❷ *equivalent to* "有时候…，有时候…"：星期日我们常去公园，～划船，～爬山。We often go to the park on Sundays to go boating or climbing the hill. 【副】perhaps 同"或许"，"也许"yěxǔ：你休息几天～就好了。Take a rest for a few days and you'll probably get better.

和 huò 【动】mix
另见 hé；huó

和稀泥 huò xīní mix mud；(*fig.*)(in mediating a dispute between two people) compromise at the expense of one's principles：他们两个人之间的争论是原则问题，可不能～。Since the dispute is over a matter of principle, we must not make compromises.

货（貨）huò 【名】goods；commodities：送～上门 door-to-door-selling of goods (for the convenience of the customers)

货币 huòbì 【名】currency
货舱 huòcāng 【名】cargo hold of a ship
货车 huòchē 【名】freight train
货架子 huòjiàzi 【名】shelf for displaying goods
货轮 huòlún 【名】〔艘 sōu〕cargo vessel
货色 huòsè 【名】❶ (the variety and quality of) goods：～齐全 a large assortment of goods 上等～ goods of high quality ❷ (of persons, things, ideas) scum；junk；rubbish：他的作品中贩卖的是什么～。He is preaching such rubbish in his works!

货物 huòwù 【名】goods
货源 huòyuán 【名】(factory, etc. which is) the source of supply for commodities
货运 huòyùn 【名】transport of freight
货栈 huòzhàn 【名】warehouse
货真价实 huò zhēn jià shí quality goods at reasonable prices

获（獲）huò 【动】receive；obtain：～奖 receive an award 一无所～ gain nothing

获得 huòdé 【动】get；gain；obtain；acquire：～好评 win praise；be acclaimed ～优异成绩 make outstanding achievements ～一定的效果 achieve a certain effect
获救 huòjiù 【动】be rescued；be saved
获取 huòqǔ 【动】win；obtain
获胜 huò = shèng win victory
获悉 huòxī 【动】〈书〉learn (news, etc.)
获准 huòzhǔn 【动】obtain permission

祸（禍）huò 【名】misfortune

祸根 huògēn 【名】source of trouble；root of evil
祸国殃民 huò guó yāng mín wreck the country and ruin the people
祸害 huòhai 【名】misfortune；disaster；cause of disaster：曾经给沿岸人民带来不少～的淮河终于被驯服了。The Huaihe River, which used to bring untold disaster to the people along its banks, has now finally been brought under control. 猎人打死凶恶的狼为村里人除了～。With the ferocious wolf killed, a scourge to the villagers has been removed. 【动】destroy；harm：蝗虫～农作物。Locusts destroy crops.

祸首　huòshǒu　【名】arch-criminal

霍　huò

霍乱　huòluàn　【名】cholera

霍然　huòrán　【副】suddenly

豁　huò

另见 huō

豁达　huòdá　【形】broad-minded

豁亮　huòliang　【形】❶ spacious and bright ❷ (of mind) enlightened

豁免　huòmiǎn　【动】exempt

豁免权　huòmiǎnquán　【名】immunity (from taxation)

豁然　huòrán　【副】suddenly (see the light); be enlightened: ～贯通 suddenly understand everything 经过老师指点，他心里～一亮，找到了问题的症结。After the teacher gave him a hint, he suddenly saw the light and could lay his finger on the problem.

豁然开朗　huòrán kāilǎng　suddenly see a broad expanse before one

J

几(幾) jī

另见 jǐ

几乎 jīhū 【副】❶ 同"差不多" chà bu duō：参加今天庆祝大会的～有两万人。Nearly 20,000 people attended today's celebration. 他们俩跑得～一样快。The two of them ran at more or less the same speed. ❷ 同"差(一)点儿" usu. referring to undesirable events；我们俩十几年没见，～不认识了。We hadn't seen each other for more than ten years and barely recognized each other.

讥(譏) jī

讥讽 jīfěng 【动】satirize

讥笑 jīxiào 【动】ridicule；jeer；make fun of

击(擊) jī 【动】〈书〉❶ hit；strike；beat：～鼓 beat a drum ～球有力 hit the ball hard ❷ attack；assault：～中要害 touch sb. to the quick；hit the nail on the head

击败 jībài 【动】defeat

击毙 jībì 【动】kill (in fighting)

击毁 jīhuǐ 【动】destroy

击剑 jījiàn 【名】fencing

击溃 jīkuì 【动】defeat utterly；crush；put to rout

击落 jīluò 【动】shoot down

击破 jīpò 【动】crush；put to rout；break up

击伤 jīshāng 【动】wound；injure

击退 jītuì 【动】repulse；beat back；repel

饥(饑) jī 【形】hungry

饥不择食 jī bù zé shí a hungry person is not particular about what he eats；(fig.) when one is badly in need of sth., he can't afford to pick and choose

饥饿 jī'è 【形】hungry

饥寒 jīhán 【名】hunger and cold

饥寒交迫 jī hán jiāo pò suffer from hunger and cold

饥荒 jīhuang 【名】famine

机(機) jī

机场 jīchǎng 【名】airport

机车 jīchē 【名】locomotive

机床 jīchuáng 【名】〔台 tái〕machine tool

机动 jīdòng 【形】❶ motorized；power-driven ❷ manoeuvrable；flexible：～粮 emergency grain reserve ～人员 reserve personnel 灵活～ highly flexible

机动车 jīdòngchē 【名】motor-driven vehicle

机帆船 jīfānchuán 【名】motor sailboat

机房 jīfáng 【名】❶ generator or motor room ❷ engine room (of a ship)

机耕 jīgēng 【名】tractor-ploughing

机构 jīgòu【名】❶ mechanism：传动～ transmission ❷ organisation；institution：精简～ simplify the (administrative) structure 这个～是新成立的。This is a newly-established organization.

机关 jīguān【名】❶ organ；office；institute：国家～ state organ 公安～ office of public security ❷ plot；intrigue；scheme：识破～ see through (sb.'s) scheme

机关枪 jīguānqiāng【名】〔挺 tǐng〕machine gun

机会 jīhuì【名】opportunity；chance

机会主义 jīhuìzhǔyì【名】opportunism

机件 jījiàn【名】parts；works：钟表的～ the works of a clock or watch

机井 jījǐng【名】〔眼 yǎn〕well which uses an electric pump

机警 jījǐng【形】alert；sharp-witted；vigilant：～的侦察兵 a vigilant scout

机灵 jīling【形】intelligent；clever；smart：这孩子真够～的。This child is really clever.

机密 jīmì【形】confidential；secret；classified：～文件 classified documents【名】secret：军事～ military secrets 保守国家～ do not reveal state secrets

机敏 jīmǐn【形】alert and keen

机能 jīnéng【名】function

机器 jīqì【名】〔台 tái、架 jià〕machine

机器人 jīqìrén【名】robot

机枪 jīqiāng【名】同"机关枪"

机体 jītǐ【名】organism

机械 jīxiè【名】machine；machinery；mechanism【形】inflexible：你这种作法太～了。Your way of doing things is too inflexible.

机械化 jīxièhuà【动】mechanize

机械能 jīxiènéng【名】(phys.) mechanical energy

机械唯物主义 jīxiè wéiwùzhǔyì mechanical materialism

机械运动 jīxiè yùndòng mechanical motion

机要 jīyào【形】confidential

机油 jīyóu【名】lubricant；machine oil

机遇 jīyù【名】opportunity；favourable circumstances

机制 jīzhì【名】mechanism

机智 jīzhì【形】quick-witted；resourceful

机组 jīzǔ【名】❶ unit；set ❷ aircrew

肌 jī

肌肉 jīròu【名】muscle

肌体 jītǐ【名】human body；organism

鸡（鷄） jī【名】〔只 zhī〕hen or cock；fowl；chicken

鸡蛋 jīdàn【名】〔个 gè〕hen's egg

鸡毛蒜皮 jīmáo suànpí chicken feathers and garlic skin；trifles；trivialities：不要为一些～的小事争论不休。Don't argue over trifles.

鸡犬不宁 jī quǎn bù níng general turmoil

鸡尾酒 jīwěijiǔ【名】cocktail

奇 jī

另见 qí

奇数 jīshù【名】odd number

积（積） jī【动】◇ accumulate；store up：～小胜为大胜 accumulate small victories until they become large ones【名】(maths.) short for 乘积

积存 jīcún【动】store up；lay up

积肥 jī＝féi store up manure

积极 jījí【形】❶ positive；constructive (usu. used of abstract things)：～因素 positive factors 起～作用 play a positive role ❷ active；enthusiastic；energetic：态度～ enthusiastic attitude 工作～

work energetically ～肯干 enthusiastic and hard-working

积极分子 jījí fènzǐ activist

积极性 jījíxìng 【名】initiative；enthusiasm

积聚 jījù 【动】accumulate

积累 jīlěi 【动】accumulate

积少成多 jī shǎo chéng duō take care of the pennies, and the pounds will take care of themselves

积习 jīxí 【名】old habit；long-standing practice

积蓄 jīxù 【动】accumulate；save：～力量 save one's strength ～财富 accumulate wealth 【名】savings：他每月都有～。He saves some money every month.

积压 jīyā 【动】overstock

积攒 jīzǎn 【动】save bit by bit

积重难返 jī zhòng nán fǎn deeply ingrained bad habits are hard to root out

基 jī

基本 jīběn 【形】❶ basic；fundamental；essential：～群众 the most reliable elements among the masses ～要求 fundamental demands ❷ rudimentary；basic (usu. as adverbial adjunct)：他在工厂实习了几个月，已经～掌握了这种新技术。He has been taking a practical course at a factory for several months, and already has a basic grasp of the new technique.

基本词汇 jīběn cíhuì basic vocabulary

基本功 jīběngōng 【名】(of dancers, athletes, etc.) basic training；(of workers) essential skill

基本建设 jīběn jiànshè capital construction

基本粒子 jīběn lìzǐ (phys.) elementary particle

基本路线 jīběn lùxiàn basic line

基本矛盾 jīběn máodùn basic contradiction；fundamental contradiction

基本上 jīběnshang 【副】❶ basically；primarily；mainly：这项任务～靠你们两个组来完成。Your two teams will be primarily responsible for the completion of this task. ❷ generally；in the main：我来北京一年了，～适应了这里的气候。I've been in Beijing for a year now, and I've got used to the weather here for the most part. 他只学了一年汉语，就～能看中文报了。He has only studied Chinese for a year, but he can read Chinese newspapers after a fashion.

基层 jīcéng 【名】basic unit or level；grassroots：深入～ be in close contact with basic units ～干部 basic level cadres ～单位 basic level units

基础 jīchǔ 【名】❶ foundation of a building ❷ foundation；basis：～知识 fundamental knowledge ～理论 basic theory 农业是国民经济的～。Agriculture is the foundation of the national economy.

基础教育 jīchǔ jiàoyù elementary education

基础科学 jīchǔ kēxué basic science

基地 jīdì 【名】base；base area：工业～ industrial base 海军～ naval base

基点 jīdiǎn 【名】starting point；basic point

基调 jīdiào 【名】❶ (of music) key ❷ keynote；prevailing tone or idea：这部小说虽然有缺点，但它的～是健康的。The basic idea of this novel is sound, although it has some weak points.

基督教 Jīdūjiào 【名】Christianity

基金 jījīn 【名】fund

基石 jīshí 【名】foundation stone

基数 jīshù 【名】cardinal number

基因 jīyīn 【名】gene

缉 jī

缉捕 jībǔ 【动】arrest；seize

缉拿 jīná 【动】arrest；apprehend

缉私 jīsī 【动】seize smugglers or smuggled goods；suppress smuggling

畸 jī

畸形 jīxíng 【名】deformity

激 jī

jī 【动】❶（of water）be dashed：～起了一片浪花。The waves were dashed into a spray. ❷ goad；spur：～将（jiàng）goad a warrior（to take up arms）用话～他 make goading remarks to someone

激昂 jī'áng 【形】emotionally wrought up

激荡 jīdàng 【动】surge；rage

激动 jīdòng 【动】stir；work up；agitate：～人心 soul-stirring 【形】be emotionally aroused：情绪～ be in the grip of strong emotions

激发 jīfā 【动】arouse；stimulate；evoke：～学习科学的热情 stimulate the enthusiasm for science

激愤 jīfèn 【形】aroused and indignant

激光 jīguāng 【名】laser

激化 jīhuà 【动】intensify；become acute

激进 jījìn 【形】radical

激励 jīlì 【动】inspire；encourage；urge：～士气 boost the morale of the fighters

激烈 jīliè 【形】violent；drastic；intense

激流 jīliú 【名】torrent

激怒 jīnù 【动】irritate；enrage

激情 jīqíng 【名】strong emotion

激素 jīsù 【名】hormone

激增 jīzēng 【动】increase rapidly

激战 jīzhàn 【名】fierce battle 【动】fight a fierce battle

jí

及 jí 【动】◇ reach；attain：力所能～ within reach，considering one's abilities 【连】similar to 和，usu. in written language：参加国庆招待会的有工人、农民、解放军～知识分子的代表。Those who attended the National Day reception included representatives of the workers, farmers, P. L. A. men and intellectuals. Note：① to indicate priority in an enumeration，what is to be given priority should be put before 及：书店里陈列着政治、经济、科技、文学～其他各类书籍。On display in the bookstore are books on political science, economics, science and technology, literature etc. ② 及 is often used with 其 to mean "and"：介绍作家的生平～其作品 give an account of the writer's life and his works

及格 jí=gé pass（an examination）；be up to the standard

及时 jíshí 【形】in good time；promptly；timely：这场雨下得真～呀！This is a timely rain！有病要～治疗。Get prompt treatment when you are ill.

及物动词 jíwùdòngcí 【名】transitive verb

及早 jízǎo 【副】while there is still time；lose no time；make haste：～准备 make preparations while there is still time ～解决 lose no time solving（the problem）

吉 jí

吉 jí 【形】◇ lucky

吉利 jílì 【形】lucky；auspicious

吉普车 jípǔchē 【名】〔辆 liàng〕jeep

吉庆 jíqìng 【形】auspicious；celebratory

吉他 jítā 【名】〔把 bǎ〕guitar

吉祥 jíxiáng 【形】lucky；auspicious

吉祥物 jíxiángwù 【名】mascot

炭 jí

炭炭可危 jíjí kě wēi in imminent danger

级（級） jí 【量】rank；grade；step；rung

级别 jíbié 【名】rank；grade；class

级数 jíshù 【名】(maths.) progression

极（極） jí 【名】extreme；farthest point 【副】very；utmost；extremely；extraordinarily：～大的鼓舞 extremely great encouragement ～好的教训 a very good lesson ～少数 a very few ～不理想 far from ideal *usu. used with*"了"*as a complement of degree*：好～了 extremely good 干净～了 extraordinarily clean 没意思～了 decidedly uninteresting；boring

极点 jídiǎn 【名】farthest point；highest point；limit：达到～ reach the limit 发展到了～ develop to the furthest limit 可恨到了～ extremely hateful

极度 jídù 【副】extremely；excessively

极端 jíduān 【名】extreme：别走～ don't go to extremes 好（hào）走～ be apt to go to extremes 【形】extreme；out-and-out：他对工作～负责。He displays a great sense of responsibility in his work.

极力 jílì 【副】by every means possible；do one's utmost：～避免 avoid by every means possible ～鼓吹 speak up for or advocate for the best of one's ability ～否认 deny by every means possible 我～劝他参加冬泳,他不干。I urged him to go in for winter swimming, but he refused.

极其 jíqí 【副】同"极" *used before some disyllabic adjectives or verbs, or phrases*：～重要 extremely important ～深刻 extremely profound ～恶劣 extraordinarily vicious ～不容易 extremely difficult ～厌恶 dislike profoundly

极为 jíwéi 【副】同"极其"(*usu. in written language*)

极限 jíxiàn 【名】limit

极刑 jíxíng 【名】capital punishment；death penalty

即 jí 【动】❶ ◇ approach；be close to：不～不离 neither too intimate nor too distant ❷ (*usu. in written language*) that is；namely：非此～彼 either this or that 鲁迅～周树人。Lu Xun's real name was Zhou Shuren.

即便 jíbiàn 【连】同"即使" *but less frequently used*：这种梨～熟了也不甜。This kind of pear is not sweet, even when ripe.

即或 jíhuò 【连】同"即使"(*usu. in written language*)

即将 jíjiāng 【副】soon；in no time；be about to：节日～来临。The festival is approaching. 访问～结束。The visit is about to end.

即刻 jíkè 【副】at once；immediately：～执行 carry out at once ～停止 stop immediately

即日 jírì 【名】〈书〉❶ the very day；that day；this day：～生效 come into effect beginning this very day 美展从～起售票。Tickets for the art exhibit will be on sale starting today. ❷ within the coming few days：歌剧《白毛女》～在首都剧场公演。The opera *The White-haired Girl* will be on at the Capital Theatre in the next few days.

即使 jíshǐ 【连】*used as an intensive serving to indicate an extreme or hypothetical case；usu. used in*

conjunction with 也、还 etc. even if; even though; even：～剩下一个人，也要坚守阵地。Even should there be only one man left, he is expected to stick to his post. ～人再多一倍，今天也摘不完这些苹果。Even if there were twice as many people, it would be impossible to pick all the apples today. ～是年老的、体弱的，也参加了这次庆祝胜利的游行。Even the aged and the weak joined in the parade in celebration of the victory.

即席 jíxí 【形】〈书〉(at a banquet or gathering)；impromptu (speech, etc.)

即兴 jíxìng 【动】impromptu; extemporaneous：～发言 make an extemporaneous speech; speak (or talk) off the cuff

急 jí 【形】❶ impatient; impetuous：～脾气 quick-tempered ❷ hasty; rapid：汽车来了个～转弯。The car made a quick turn. 水流很～。The water flows swiftly. ❸ urgent：～事 an urgent matter ～件 a document containing urgent information; urgent dispatch 这批建筑材料要得很～。These construction materials are urgently needed. 【动】❶ ◇ be eager or anxious to do something：～人之难 (nàn) be eager to help those in need ～灾民之所急 be eager to do what the victims (of a natural calamity) want done ❷ be anxious; be worried：～着赶火车 be anxious to catch the train 你怎么才来？真～死人了。Why did you come so late? You had me worried to death!

急促 jícù 【形】❶ short and quick (e.g. breaths)；rapid：呼吸～ take rapid, shallow breaths ～的敲门声 short, quick knocks at the door ❷

(of time) pressing：时间～，快决定吧! Time is pressing. Make up your mind quickly!

急电 jídiàn 【名】a high priority telegram; an urgent telegram

急风暴雨 jí fēng bào yǔ violent storm (usu. referring to class struggle)：经受过～的考验 have weathered violent storms; stand up to the test of fierce struggles

急件 jíjiàn 【名】urgent dispatch

急救 jíjiù 【动】give first aid treatment

急剧 jíjù 【形】abrupt; drastic：血压～下降 drastic drop in sb.'s blood pressure 局势变化～ a drastic change in the situation

急流 jíliú 【名】rapids

急忙 jímáng 【形】hasty; hurried：他拿起冰鞋～奔向冰场。He picked up his skates and hurried to the rink. 他急急忙忙地跑来了。He came running over in a great hurry.

急迫 jípò 【形】urgent; pressing：任务～ urgent task 形势～ critical situation

急起直追 jí qǐ zhí zhuī hurry and catch up with

急切 jíqiè 【形】pressing; imperative; urgent：～需要 urgent need ～盼望 look forward expectantly

急速 jísù 【副】swiftly

急先锋 jíxiānfēng 【名】fearless vanguard：充当～ serve as the vanguard

急性 jíxìng 【形】❶ acute：～肠炎 acute enteritis ～痢疾 acute dysentery ❷ hot-headed：小王是个～人。Xiao Wang is often hot-headed.

急性病 jíxìngbìng 【名】❶ acute disease ❷ impetuosity

急需 jíxū 【动】be badly in need of

急于 jíyú 【动】eager to; anxious to：～下结论 anxious to reach a conclu-

sion ~求成 overly anxious to make achievements; be impatient for success

急躁 jízào 【形】impetuous; ~情绪 impetuous mood 性情~ impetuous nature

急诊 jízhěn 【名】(med.) emergency; emergency treatment

急中生智 jí zhōng shēng zhì be quick-witted in an emergency; find a way out in an emergency

急转直下 jí zhuǎn zhí xià (of a situation) rapid change in a situation (usu. from bad to worse)

疾 jí

疾病 jíbìng 【名】disease; illness

疾驰 jíchí 【动】gallop at full speed

疾风劲草 jí fēng jìng cǎo The strong wind reveals the strength of the grass; (fig.) Only severe trials can test one's strength of character. 也作"疾风知劲草"。

疾苦 jíkǔ 【名】misery; suffering

棘 jí

棘手 jíshǒu 【形】thorny; knotty; difficult

集 jí 【动】◇assemble; gather together 【名】country fair

集成电路 jí chéng diàn lù integrated circuit

集合 jíhé 【动】assemble; rally; muster; ~队伍 muster the troops 看演出的同学在校门口~。All students going to the performance are to assemble at the school gate.

集会 jíhuì 【动】hold a mass rally

集结 jíjié 【动】concentrate; assemble; ~待命 assemble and await orders

集聚 jíjù 【动】assemble in one place

集权 jí = quán centralization of state power

集市 jíshì 【名】country fair

集市贸易 jíshì màoyì country fair trade; open market

集思广益 jí sī guǎng yì increase one's wisdom by collecting opinions from others

集体 jítǐ 【名】collective

集体化 jítǐhuà 【动】collectivize

集体经济 jítǐ jīngjì collective economy

集体所有制 jítǐ suǒyǒuzhì collective ownership

集体舞 jítǐwǔ 【名】a dance in which many people take part

集体主义 jítǐzhǔyì 【名】collectivism

集团 jítuán 【名】group; clique; bloc

集训 jíxùn 【动】bring people together for training

集邮 jí = yóu stamp collecting; philately

集镇 jízhèn 【名】town

集中 jízhōng 【动】concentrate; centralize; ~优势兵力，各个歼灭敌人 concentrate a superior force to destroy the enemy armies one by one ~大家的智慧，才能把这件事情办好。Only by pooling everybody's wisdom can we do this well. 【形】concentrate fully on; 思想不~ be distracted 这些意见~地反映了民众的要求。These opinions reflect the demands of the public as a whole.

集中营 jízhōngyíng 【名】concentration camp

集装箱 jízhuāngxiāng 【名】container

集资 jízī 【动】raise funds; collect money; ~办学 raise fund to run a school

集子 jízi 【名】collection of (essays, poems etc.); anthology

籍 jí

籍贯 jíguàn 【名】(item on a form)

place where one's family is from; place of one's birth

jǐ

几（幾） jǐ 【数】 *stands for an indefinite number less than ten; can be used by itself, or before（or after）a round number* ❶ how many: 你到中国~天了? How many days have you been in China? 孩子~岁啦? How old is your child? 这个学校有一~百学生? How many hundreds of students are there in this school? ❷ some; a few: 十~个人 more than ten persons 三十~年 over thirty years ~十斤鱼 several dozen catties of fish（literally, "tens of"）~千里路 several thousand *li* away 所剩无~ barely any left

另见 jǐ

几何 jǐhé 【名】geometry

几何级数 jǐhé jíshù geometric progression

几时 jǐshí 【代】when; what time: 你~来的? When did you come? 你们~有空就来玩儿吧! Drop by when you have time.

挤（擠） jǐ 【动】 ❶ crowd; squeeze: 他一侧身就~进去了。He turned sideways, and squeezed his way in. ❷ squeeze: ~牛奶 milk the cow ~牙膏 squeeze out the toothpaste 【形】crowded: 今天公共汽车上一点儿也不~。The bus is not crowded at all today.

给（給） jǐ

另见 gěi

给养 jǐyǎng 【名】(mil.) provisions

给予 jǐyǔ 【动】offer; render; give（*usu. in written language, followed by dissyllabic verbs*）: ~帮助 offer help ~支持 render support

脊 jǐ 【名】spine; ridge

脊背 jǐbèi 【名】back

脊梁 jǐliáng 【名】the back

脊髓 jǐsuǐ 【名】spinal cord

脊柱 jǐzhù 【名】backbones; spine

脊椎动物 jǐzhuī dòngwù vertebrate

脊椎骨 jǐzhuīgǔ 【名】vertebra

jì

计（計） jì 【名】◇ ❶ stratagem: 调虎离山~ a plan to lure the tiger out of the mountains 眉头一皱，~上心来。Rack your brains and you will hit upon a stratagem. ❷ plan; scheme; project: 长远之~ long-range plan 一年之~在于春。The year's plan should be made in spring. 【动】◇ estimate; calculate; reckon: 数以万~ in tens of thousands 今天参加义务劳动的共~五十人。A total of fifty people took part in voluntary labour today.

计策 jìcè 【名】stratagem; device

计程车 jìchéngchē 【名】taxicab; taxi

计划 jìhuà 【名】plan; project; programme: 五年~ five-year plan 国家~ state plan 【动】make a plan; map out a plan: 先初步~一下，大约需要多少工作日 make a preliminary plan and see how many work-days are required

计划经济 jìhuà jīngjì planned economy

计划生育 jìhuà shēngyù family planning

计划性 jìhuàxìng 【名】planning

计较 jìjiào 【动】 ❶ be concerned about; calculate: 不~个人得失 give no thought to personal gain ❷ find fault with; take to heart: 他在气头上说错了话,你们别和他~。He said something he shouldn't say in the heat of the moment. Don't take it

to heart.

计量 jìliàng 【动】 measure

计谋 jìmóu 【名】 scheme；plot；stratagem

计算 jìsuàn 【动】 calculate；reckon

计算尺 jìsuànchǐ 【名】 slide rule

计算机 jìsuànjī 【名】〔台 tái〕computer

计算机病毒 jìsuànjī bìngdú computer virus

计算机程序 jìsuànjī chéngxù computer program

计算器 jìsuànqì 【名】 electronic calculator

记（記）jì 【动】❶ remember；keep in mind；memorize：事隔多年，我已经～不清了。It's been a long time now and I don't remember it. ❷ take notes；write down；record：～下报告的大意 take rough notes on the report ～事 record an event ～一大功（mil.）record a meritorious action

记得 jìde 【动】 remember

记分 jì＝fēn keep score

记工 jì＝gōng keep an account of workpoints

记功 jì＝gōng record a merit

记过 jì＝guò record a demerit

记号 jìhao 【名】 sign；mark

记录 jìlù 【动】 take notes；record；take minutes：他的发言我都～下来了。I've taken notes on what he said. 【名】❶ minutes；memorandum：会议～ the minutes of the meeting ❷ minute-taker；secretary：请你当～。Will you please take the minutes（for the meeting）? ❸ record：打破世界～ break the world record 创造新～ set a new record

记录片 jìlùpiàn 【名】〔部 bù〕documentary film

记取 jìqǔ 【动】 remember（advice）；bear in mind；learn（e.g. a lesson）

记述 jìshù 【动】 narrate

记性 jìxing 【名】 memory

记叙 jìxù 【动】 narrate（in writing）

记忆 jìyì 【动】 remember；recall：童年时代的情景我还～得十分清楚。I can still clearly recall my childhood. 【名】 memory：难忘的～ an unforgettable memory

记忆力 jìyìlì 【名】 memory；faculty of memory

记忆犹新 jìyì yóu xīn remain fresh in one's mind；小时候，在家乡过年的情景至今～。Childhood memories of Spring Festival celebrations in his hometown are still fresh in his mind.

记载 jìzǎi 【动】 put down in writing 【名】 record

记者 jìzhě 【名】 newspaper reporter；journalist；correspondent

记住 jì∥zhù bear in mind；remember

伎 jì

伎俩 jìliǎng 【名】 ruse；trick

纪（紀）jì

纪检 jìjiǎn 【动】 *short for* 纪律检查

纪律 jìlǜ 【名】 discipline

纪律检查 jìlǜ jiǎnchá inspect discipline

纪律性 jìlǜxìng 【名】 sense of discipline

纪念 jìniàn 【动】 commemorate；celebrate：～革命先烈 commemorate the deeds of the revolutionary martyrs ～三八妇女节 celebrate Women's Day on March the 8th 【名】 souvenir：这支钢笔送给你留做～。Please accept this fountain pen as a souvenir.

纪念碑 jìniànbēi 【名】 monument；memorial tablet

纪念册 jìniàncè 【名】〔本 běn〕souvenir album

纪念品 jìniànpǐn 【名】 souvenir

纪念日 jìniànrì 【名】anniversary

纪念邮票 jìniàn yóupiào commemorative stamp

纪念章 jìniànzhāng 【名】〔枚 méi〕badge

纪要 jìyào 【名】summary；minutes (of a meeting)

纪元 jìyuán 【名】the beginning of a reign or an era

技 jì

技工 jìgōng 【名】*short for* 技术工人

技能 jìnéng 【名】skill

技巧 jìqiǎo 【名】skill

技师 jìshī 【名】senior technician

技术 jìshù 【名】technique；skill

技术革新 jìshù géxīn technical innovation

技术工人 jìshù gōngrén skilled worker

技术员 jìshùyuán 【名】technician

技艺 jìyì 【名】feat；skill

系（繫） jì 【动】tie；fasten：
～鞋带儿 tie one's shoelaces ～着围裙 wearing an apron
另见 xì

忌 jì 【动】❶ avoid；be taboo：～嘴 avoid eating certain foods (because of illness) ～生冷 avoid cold and uncooked food ❷ abstain from；give up：～烟 give up smoking ～酒 give up drinking；abstain from alcohol

忌妒 jìdu 【动】be jealous of

忌讳 jìhuì 【动】❶ be taboo；prohibit as taboo：他～别人叫他的绰号。He hates people calling him by his nickname. ❷ avoid doing something：气管炎患者～抽烟。People suffering from bronchitis should avoid smoking.

忌日 jìrì 【名】day of sb.'s death

妓 jì 【名】prostitute

妓女 jìnǚ 【名】prostitute

季 jì 【名】season

季度 jìdù 【名】(of a year) quarter：第四～ the fourth quarter ～预算 a quarterly budget

季节 jìjié 【名】season：农忙～ busy farming season 游泳～ swimming season

季刊 jìkān 【名】quarterly publication

迹 jì 【名】◇ trace；mark

迹象 jìxiàng 【名】situation；fact；indication from which one deduces sth.

既 jì 【连】同"既然"（*usu. in written language*），*can never be put before the subject*：～来之，则安之。Since you find yourself in this situation, you might as well deal with it. ～要游泳，就不要怕喝几口水。Now that you have decided to learn swimming, why be bothered by a few mouthfuls of water? 【副】◇ already：～成事实 an already established fact；status quo

既得利益 jì dé lìyì vested interest；advantage already secured

既定 jì dìng alread committed；already decided；fixed

既然 jìrán 【连】*used in conjunction with* 就，也，还，*etc.* since：～你也去剧场，那我们就一块儿走吧！Since you are going to the theatre too, let's go together. 他～不同意，你们也不必勉强了。Since he doesn't agree, just leave him alone.

既往不咎 jì wǎng bù jiù let bygones be bygones 也说"不咎既往"

既…也… jì… yě…，同"既…又…"，*but can connect phrases only，not words*：我们既要坚持原则，也要讲究策略。We must uphold our principles and at the same time be flexi-

ble.

既…又… jì...yòu... both...and... *used to connect two words (adjectives or verbs) or phrases*：既整齐，又干净 both neat and tidy 这个人既大胆，又细心。This man is both courageous and cautious. 既要认真读书，又要努力实践。One must acquire both book learning and practical experience.

觊（覬） jì

觊觎 jìyú 【动】〈书〉covet (sth. that one should not have)

继（繼） jì

继承 jìchéng 【动】inherit；succeed to：～遗产 inherit property ～遗志 carry out sb.'s unrealized goal ～优良传统 be a successor to the good tradition

继承权 jìchéngquán 【名】right of inheritance

继而 jì'ér 【副】after this；following which；then：他先去了上海，～又去了西安。He went first to Shanghai, and then to Xi'an.

继父 jìfù 【名】step-father

继母 jìmǔ 【名】step-mother

继任 jìrèn 【动】succeed (sb.) as...；succeed (sb.) in office

继往开来 jì wǎng kāi lái carry forward one's predecessors' projects and break new ground

继续 jìxù 【动】continue；carry on；go on；keep on：～努力 make efforts continuously 文艺演出～了三个晚上。The performance was on for three successive evenings.

祭 jì 【动】hold a memorial ceremony for

祭祀 jìsì 【动】offer a sacrifice to gods or ancestors

祭文 jìwén 【名】funeral oration

寄 jì 【动】❶ post；mail：～信 mail a letter ～包裹 mail a parcel ❷ entrust；consign；place (hopes) on：～放行李 entrust the luggage for safe-keeping ～希望于各国人民 place (one's) hopes on the peoples of all countries

寄存 jìcún 【动】put somewhere for safe-keeping

寄居 jìjū 【动】live in another person's house or at a place which is not one's native town

寄人篱下 jì rén lí xià depend on sb. for a living

寄生 jìshēng 【动】❶ (biol.) live on or in another organism，usu. causing harm ❷ be a parasite：不劳而获的～生活是可耻的。A parasitic existence is despicable.

寄生虫 jìshēngchóng 【名】❶ parasite ❷ (*fig.*) parasite

寄售 jìshòu 【动】consign for sale；put up for sale

寄宿 jìsù 【动】❶ stay (at sb.'s house for some time)：那次到广东，我～在一个老朋友家里。I stayed at the house of an old friend when I went to Guangdong. ❷ (of students) live in residence at school (*as opp. to* 走读)：我上中学的时候，在学校～。I was a boarder when I went to middle school.

寄托 jìtuō 【动】❶ entrust to the care of：我把小孩～在张大妈家里。I leave my child with Auntie Zhang's family. ❷ place (one's hope) in：～着希望 place one's hope in 这个作曲家把他对祖国的热爱～在乐曲中。This composer's patriotism was expressed in his music.

寄养 jìyǎng 【动】entrust one's child to the care of sb.

寄予 jìyǔ 【动】❶ place (hope or confidence) in：祖国人民对青年一代

～极大的希望。The people of our country place great hope in the younger generation. ❷ offer; give; render; show (sympathy, concern, etc.): ～深切的同情 express deep sympathy for

寂 jì

寂静　jìjìng　【形】silent; quiet

寂寞　jìmò　【形】lonely

加 jiā

加　jiā　【动】❶ add; plus: 三～四等于七。Three plus four equals seven. ❷ increase; add: 大坝～高五米 increase the height of the dam by five metres ～一个符号 make a mark (on sth.) ～注释 add explanatory notes 好上～好 make what is good even better ❸ ◇ give...to; deal: 不～考虑 refuse to give further consideration to 严～惩罚 mete out harsh punishment

加班　jiā=bān　work overtime

加倍　jiābèi　【动】double: 药量～ double the dose 【副】redouble: ～努力 redouble one's efforts

加餐　jiā=cān　to add a snack

加法　jiāfǎ　【名】(maths.) addition

加工　jiāgōng　【动】process (into a finished product)

加号　jiāhào　【名】plus sign

加紧　jiājǐn　【动】accelerate; intensify; step up: 排练节目要～ step up (the pace of) rehearsals for the performance ～收割 speed up the harvesting ～施工 speed up the construction work

加剧　jiājù　【动】intensify; heighten

加快　jiākuài　【动】speed up

加盟　jiāméng　【动】join; be a member of: ～足球队 join a football team ～影业公司 join a film company

加强　jiāqiáng　【动】strengthen; consolidate: ～团结 strengthen unity 领导力量～了。The leadership has been consolidated.

加热　jiā=rè　heat up

加入　jiārù　【动】join; enter; take part in: ～工会 join a trade union

加深　jiāshēn　【动】deepen; intensify

加数　jiāshù　【名】(maths.) addend; a number or quantity to be added to another

加速　jiāsù　【动】accelerate; speed up

加速度　jiāsùdù　【名】(phys.) acceleration

加速器　jiāsùqì　【名】accelerator

加速运动　jiāsù yùndòng　(phys.) accelerated motion

加以　jiāyǐ　【动】*used before a dissyllabic verb, adds nothing to the meaning of the verb; the object of the verb must appear somewhere preceding it, (usu. in written language)*: 对他取得的点滴进步，要～肯定。We must acknowledge every indication of progress he makes however slight it may be. 我们对前一阶段的工作不～总结，就不能改进今后的工作。If we don't evaluate our work so far, we won't be able to improve on our future work. 学生提出的问题，老师应及时～解决。The teacher must promptly answer all the questions raised by the students. *The negative form is* 不加.【连】*introduces an additional clause or condition, (usu. in written language)*: 那个村子土地肥沃,～村民们深耕细作,所以连年增产。Given the fertile soil of the fields, plus the villagers' efforts at deep ploughing and meticulous cultivation, this village has achieved yearly increases in yield.

加油　jiā=yóu　cheer on (game player)

加重 jiāzhòng 【动】make heavier; (of illness) become more serious; make more emphatic

夹（夾）jiā 【动】❶ clip (e.g. papers together); pick up with tweezers; 用筷子～菜 pick up food with chopsticks 用老虎钳～住零件 hold the spare part with a pair of pliers 两山～一水。A river flows between the two mountains. ❷ hold sth. between two fingers or carry sth. under one's arm; 他～着书包走进了教室 He walked into the classroom carrying his schoolbag under his arm. ❸ fill the space between two things with sth.; squeeze into the midst of . . .; ～馅的糖 stuffed sweets 他～在人群里。He is in the thick of the crowd. 歌声～着笑声。Singing mingled with laughter.
另见 jiá

夹道欢迎 jiā dào huānyíng line the streets to welcome sb.

夹攻 jiāgōng 【动】(mil.) catch in a pincer movement

夹角 jiājiǎo 【名】(geom.) included angle

夹克 jiākè 【名】〔件 jiàn〕jacket

夹生饭 jiāshēngfàn 【名】half-cooked rice; work not properly done

夹杂 jiāzá 【动】mix up; blend

夹子 jiāzi 【名】clips; tongs

佳 jiā

佳话 jiāhuà 【名】〈书〉matter of great interest; charming story

佳节 jiājié 【名】〈书〉joyful festival

佳人 jiārén 【名】〈书〉beauty; beautiful woman

佳音 jiāyīn 【名】〈书〉good news

佳作 jiāzuò 【名】fine piece of writing or art

枷 jiā

枷锁 jiāsuǒ 【名】fetters; shackles

痂 jiā 【名】scab

家 jiā 【名】❶ family; 我～有五口人。There are five people in my family. 我的东邻是张～。My neighbours to the east are the Zhangs. 工农是一～人。The workers and farmers are like members of one family. ❷ home; 他的～在上海。His home is in Shanghai. 我～住在学院路 100 号。My home is at No.100 Xue Yuan Rd. 【量】for households or enterprises; 一～人家 a household 一～银行 a bank 【尾】-ist; -er; etc.; 革命～ revolutionary 社会活动～ social worker 科学～ scientist 艺术～ artist 作～ author 哲学～ philosopher 历史学～ historian 数学～ mathematician

家产 jiāchǎn 【名】family property

家常 jiācháng 【名】❶ domestic affairs ❷ commonplace

家常便饭 jiācháng biànfàn ordinary meal; family meal; 没有什么好东西招待你们，吃点儿～吧。I don't have any special delicacies to offer you. We'll just have a simple meal together. 隆冬腊月洗冷水浴，这对他来说,已经是～了。Taking a cold bath in severe winter weather is not at all unusual for him.

家畜 jiāchù 【名】domestic animal

家当 jiādang 【名】family property; family possessions

家电 jiādiàn 【名】abbreviation of 家用电器

家伙 jiāhuo 【名】❶ tool; utensil; weapon; 抄起一～干起来 pick up a tool and start working ❷ (of person or animal showing scorn or for fun) fellow; guy; creature

家家户户 jiā jiā hù hù each and every family

家教 jiājiào 【名】❶ family educa-

tion；upbringing ❷ tutor；private teacher

家具 jiājù 【名】furniture

家眷 jiājuàn 【名】a man's family (wife and children)

家破人亡 jiā pò rén wáng with one's family broken up and reduced in number

家禽 jiāqín 【名】fowl；poultry

家史 jiāshǐ 【名】family history

家属 jiāshǔ 【名】one's dependents；family

家庭 jiātíng 【名】family；home

家庭妇女 jiātíng fùnǚ housewife

家徒四壁 jiā tú sì bì be utterly destitute

家务 jiāwù 【名】housework

家乡 jiāxiāng 【名】native place；hometown

家信 jiāxìn 【名】〔封 fēng〕letter between child and parent or between husband and wife

家业 jiāyè 【名】family property

家用 jiāyòng 【形】family expenses

家用电器 jiāyòng diànqì household appliances

家喻户晓 jiā yù hù xiǎo make known to every family；要使各项政策～，人人皆知。The policies must be made known to every family and to each individual.

家园 jiāyuán 【名】native place；home

家长 jiāzhǎng 【名】❶ head of a family ❷ parent or guardian of a child：学校要开个～座谈会。The school is going to call a meeting of the children's parents.

家长制 jiāzhǎngzhì 【名】patriarchal system

家族 jiāzú 【名】clan

嘉 jiā

嘉宾 jiābīn 【名】honoured guest

嘉奖 jiājiǎng 【动】(of institution)

bestow praise, honour or reward on sb.

jiá

夹（夾） jiá 【形】lined；这衣服是～的。This is a lined jacket.
另见 jiā

jiǎ

甲 jiǎ 【名】❶ used to represent "first" according to old Chinese tradition：～级 first grade ～等 first class ❷ shell (e.g. of a tortoise) ❸ armour

甲板 jiǎbǎn 【名】deck of a ship

甲虫 jiǎchóng 【名】beetle

甲骨文 jiǎgǔwén 【名】inscriptions on oracle bones

甲状腺 jiǎzhuàngxiàn 【名】the thyroid gland

钾（鉀） jiǎ 【名】potassium

钾肥 jiǎféi 【名】fertilizer containing potassium；potash

假 jiǎ 【形】❶ artificial；false：～牙 false tooth；denture ～发 wig ～山 rockery ❷ false；unreal；sham；feint：～动作 make a feint ❸ hypocritical；lying：～话 a lie ～正经 pretend to be serious
另见 jià

假充 jiǎchōng 【动】pass oneself off as；pose as

假定 jiǎdìng 【动】suppose；assume；presume：～一天学五个汉字，一年就能学两千来字呢! Suppose we were to learn five Chinese characters a day, in a year we would have learned about two thousand characters. 【名】hypothesis；assumption

假公济私 jiǎ gōng jì sī promote one's private interests under the guise of serving the public

假借 jiǎjiè 【动】use as a pretext；do sth. under the guise of；use or act in（the name of）：～出差的名义到处游山玩水。Under the pretext of making business trips one travels around sightseeing. 【名】*one of the six categories of Chinese characters*（见 "六书" liùshū）

假冒 jiǎmào 【动】palm off（a fake as genuine）pass oneself off as

假面具 jiǎmiànjù 【名】❶ mask ❷ hypocrisy

假如 jiǎrú 【连】if 同 "如果" rúguǒ：～不兴修这些水利工程，就不会有今年的大丰收。If it had not been for our irrigation project, we wouldn't have had this year's excellent harvest.

假若 jiǎruò 【连】if 同 "如果" rúguǒ：～这样不行,我们再另想办法。If this won't do, we'll try another approach.

假山 jiǎshān 【名】rockery

假设 jiǎshè 【动】suppose；grant；assume 【名】hypothesis

假使 jiǎshǐ 【连】if 同 "如果" rúguǒ：～不是他拦住惊马，就会出一场事故。If he had not stopped the runaway horse, there might have been an accident.

假释 jiǎshì 【动】release on parole

假想 jiǎxiǎng 【名】imagination

假象 jiǎxiàng 【名】feint；false appearance；false impression

假惺惺 jiǎxīngxīng 【形】hypocritical；狐狸～地对乌鸦说："您唱得真好听。" The fox said hypocritically to the crow：" Your singing is very sweet."

假造 jiǎzào 【动】❶ forge；counterfeit ❷ fabricate

假装 jiǎzhuāng 【动】pretend

jià

价（價）jià 【名】price：涨～ raise the price 落～ lower the price

价格 jiàgé 【名】price

价廉物美 jià lián wù měi（of a commodity）low-priced but of superior quality

价目 jiàmù 【名】marked price

价钱 jiàqián 【名】price

价值 jiàzhí 【名】value

价值规律 jiàzhí guīlǜ the law of value

驾（駕）jià 【动】❶ drive（a draught animal）：～着牲口耕地 use a draught animal for ploughing ❷ ◇ drive；pilot；sail：～车离去 drive away ～机返航 pilot the plane on a homeward flight

驾驶 jiàshǐ 【动】drive；pilot

驾驶员 jiàshǐyuán 【名】driver；pilot

驾驭 jiàyù 【动】❶ hold the reins of（a draught animal）：这匹烈马不易～。This spirited horse is difficult to control. ❷ master；control：～全局 control the whole situation ～自然 prevail over nature 也作 "驾御"。

架 jià 【名】◇（～儿）shelf；framework：房～ framework of a building 衣～ clothes rack 【动】❶ put up；prop up；erect：～桥 erect a bridge ～电线 put up power lines 梯子～起来了。A ladder was put up. ❷ support；hold up：～拐 go about on crutches 他受伤了,同学～着他走。He had been injured, and a classmate supported him as he walked. 【量】*for machines*，*aeroplanes*，*etc.*：买一～缝纫机 buy a sewing machine 几百～飞机 several hundred aeroplanes

架次 jiàcì 【量】sortie

架空 jiàkōng 【动】❶ be without foundation；end in nothing：计划必须要有相应的措施，才不会～。All plans must involve concrete measures；otherwise they will come to nothing. ❷ isolate (sb.) so that he is powerless

架设 jiàshè 【动】put up；erect

架式 jiàshi 【名】posture；pose 也作"架势"。

架子 jiàzi 【名】❶ framework；shelf；rack：脸盆～ wash-stand 木～ wooden shelf 货～ shelf for goods (e.g. in a store) ❷ structure；outline：这篇文章刚搭了个～。I've just made an outline for the article. ❸ arrogance；airs；haughtiness；pretentiousness：官～ official airs 这位著名作家一点儿～都没有。This famous writer has not the slightest touch of arrogance about him.

假

假 jià 【名】leave；holiday
另见 jiǎ

假期 jiàqī 【名】holidays；vacation

假日 jiàrì 【名】holiday

假条 jiàtiáo 【名】leave certificate (e.g. sick leave certificate)

嫁

嫁 jià 【动】❶ (of a girl) marry ❷ shift；transfer (of loss, burden, responsibility for a crime, etc.)

嫁祸于人 jià huò yú rén shift one's misfortune to someone else

嫁接 jiàjiē 【动】graft

嫁妆 jiàzhuang 【名】dowry

jiān

尖

尖 jiān 【名】(～儿) sharp point；tip：针～ the point of a needle 刀～ the point of a knife 塔～ top of a tower 【形】❶ pointed；sharp：铅笔削得很～。The pencil has been sharpened to a fine point. ❷ shrill；sharp：～叫 shrill outcry ❸ keenly sensitive；sharp：眼～ sharp-eyed 耳朵～ acute sense of hearing

尖兵 jiānbīng 【名】❶ vanguard：～班 vanguard squad ～排 vanguard platoon ❷ pioneer；trail-blazer：我们是环境保护的～。We are trail-blazers in environmental protection.

尖刀 jiāndāo 【名】〔把 bǎ〕dagger；sharp knife

尖端 jiānduān 【名】the highest point；pinnacle；peak 【形】(of science or technology) the most advanced：～科学 most advanced branches of science ～技术 the most advanced technology ～产品 most technologically advanced product

尖端放电 jiānduān fàng diàn (electr.) point discharge

尖刻 jiānkè 【形】(of words, remarks) sharp；acrimonious

尖利 jiānlì 【形】sharp；keen

尖锐 jiānruì 【形】❶ sharp：～的长矛 a sharp lance ❷ acute；sharp：他看问题很～。His perceptions are very acute. 大家提的意见非常～。The opinions expressed by all of you are very pointed. ❸ acute；fierce：～的斗争 acute struggle ❹ sharp；shrill：飞驰的消防车发出～的叫声 The sirens of the speeding fire trucks resounded shrilly as they sped on.

尖子 jiānzi 【名】the best of its kind；the pick of the bunch；the cream of the crop

奸

奸 jiān 【形】evil；wicked；treacherous；crafty：耍～使坏 play dirty tricks 【名】◇ traitor；treacherous person：为国除～ do away with the traitor for the good of

the country

奸商　jiānshāng　【名】profiteer；unscrupulous merchant

奸细　jiānxi　【名】spy；enemy agent

奸险　jiānxiǎn　【形】crafty and dangerous

奸笑　jiānxiào　【动】smile sinisterly　【名】sinister smile

奸诈　jiānzhà　【形】crafty

歼（殲）　jiān　【动】wipe out；annihilate；exterminate

歼击机　jiānjījī　【名】〔架 jià〕fighter（aeroplane）

歼灭　jiānmiè　【动】annihilate；destroy

歼灭战　jiānmièzhàn　【名】battle of annihilation

坚（堅）　jiān　【形】◇ solid；firm；hard：～不可摧 indestructible

坚壁清野　jiān bì qīng yě　strengthen one's defences and hide the crop，leaving nothing in the fields for the enemy

坚持　jiānchí　【动】persist in；adhere to；insist on；uphold：～原则 adhere to principle ～锻炼身体 persevere in physical training 学校坚持农忙时派学生参加麦收的制度。The school upholds the system of sending students to the countryside to help with wheat cutting during harvest time.

坚持不懈　jiānchí bù xiè　persist；persevere

坚定　jiāndìng　【形】firm；resolute；steady；determined：意志～ firm-willed ～地执行改革开放政策 firmly carry out the policy of reform and opening to the world 【动】make firm；strengthen：～必胜的信念 strengthen our confidence in eventual victory ～自己的立场 be firm in one's stand

坚定不移　jiāndìng bù yí　firm and

unshakable；unswerving

坚固　jiāngù　【形】solid；firm；hard

坚决　jiānjué　【形】resolute；determined；firm：态度～ determined attitude ～服从命令 resolutely obey orders

坚苦卓绝　jiānkǔ zhuōjué　（of struggle）extremely hard and bitter

坚强　jiānqiáng　【形】strong；staunch；firm：性格～ strong character ～的核心 firm core

坚忍不拔　jiānrěn bù bá　firm and unyielding

坚韧　jiānrèn　【形】tough and firm

坚如磐石　jiān rú pánshí　firm as a rock

坚实　jiānshí　【形】solid；strong

坚守　jiānshǒu　【动】guard securely；stick to（one's post）；hold fast to（one's position）

坚挺　jiāntǐng　【形】(finance) strong

坚信　jiānxìn　【动】firmly believe；have strong faith in：中国人民～一定能把自己的国家建设好。The Chinese people firmly believe that they will be able to build their country into a prosperous one.

坚毅　jiānyì　【形】strong-willed

坚硬　jiānyìng　【形】hard；strong and hard

坚贞　jiānzhēn　【形】faithful and firm

坚贞不屈　jiānzhēn bùqū　faithful and unyielding

间（間）　jiān　【名】◇ room：洗澡～ bathroom【量】for room：一～屋子 a room 一～会客室 a reception room
另见 jiàn

肩　jiān　【名】shoulder

肩膀　jiānbǎng　【名】shoulder

肩负　jiānfù　【动】(of responsibility or burden) bear；shoulder：～重任 be charged with important tasks ～

着伟大的历史使命 bear the responsibility of the great historic mission

肩章 jiānzhāng 【名】epaulet

艰(艱) jiān

艰巨 jiānjù 【形】extremely difficult and heavy：～的任务 difficult and heavy task 工作～。The work is very difficult.

艰苦 jiānkǔ 【形】hard and arduous; hard and bitter：～的年代 hard and bitter years ～的生活 hard and arduous life ～奋斗，勤俭建国 struggle hard and practise economy in developing our country

艰难 jiānnán 【形】difficult；hard；arduous

艰难险阻 jiānnán xiǎnzǔ difficulties and dangers

艰深 jiānshēn 【形】difficult to understand

艰险 jiānxiǎn 【形】difficult and dangerous；perilous

艰辛 jiānxīn 【形】arduous

监(監) jiān

监测 jiāncè 【动】monitor

监察 jiānchá 【动】supervise；control

监督 jiāndū 【动】supervise

监护 jiānhù 【动】serve as a guardian (for a child)

监护人 jiānhùrén 【名】guardian

监禁 jiānjìn 【动】take into custody

监考 jiānkǎo 【动】supervise a test

监牢 jiānláo 【名】prison

监视 jiānshì 【动】watch；keep an eye on

监狱 jiānyù 【名】jail；prison

监制 jiānzhì 【动】supervise the manufacture of

兼 jiān 【动】do things concurrently；身～数职 hold several posts concurrently 住在这一带，安静、方便两种优点～而有之。Living in this neighbourhood, one finds it both very quiet and within reach of all sorts of facilities. 他是这个大学的副校长，～历史系主任。He is one of the vice-presidents of this university and also head of the history department.

兼备 jiānbèi 【动】have both (qualities)

兼并 jiānbìng 【动】annex (territory, etc.)

兼顾 jiāngù 【动】consider both... and...；pay attention to both... and...

兼课 jiān = kè teach as well as do one's own work；hold two or more teaching jobs concurrently

兼任 jiānrèn 【动】hold concurrent posts

兼收并蓄 jiān shōu bìng xù accept anything and everything, usually referring to theories and systems of thought

兼听则明，偏信则暗 jiān tīng zé míng, piān xìn zé àn listen to both sides and you will be enlightened；listen to only one side and you will remain ignorant

兼语句 jiānyǔjù 【名】pivotal sentence

兼职 jiānzhí 【名】concurrent job

兼职 jiān = zhí hold concurrent jobs

缄(緘) jiān

缄默 jiānmò 【动】keep silent and say nothing

煎 jiān 【动】❶ fry ❷ decoct

煎熬 jiān'áo 【动】❶ decoct ❷ suffer；be afflicted

jiǎn

拣(揀) jiǎn 【动】❶ select；

pick；choose：农民～最好的粮食交公粮。The farmers select their best grain to pay the state grain tax. 小李对工作从不挑～～。Xiao Li does not pick and choose as far as work is concerned. ❷ 同"捡"

茧（繭）jiǎn 【名】cocoon of the silkworm

俭（儉）jiǎn

俭朴 jiǎnpǔ 【形】frugal and simple
俭省 jiǎnshěng 【形】frugal；economical

捡（撿）jiǎn 【动】pick up：～柴火 gather firewood 小红～到一个钱包交给了警察叔叔。Xiao Hong found a purse and turned it over to the policeman.

检（檢）jiǎn 【动】◇ ❶ check；examine：～疫 quarantine ❷ keep within the bounds of；confine；restrain：行为失～ improper conduct

检查 jiǎnchá 【动】inspect；examine；check：～工作 check the work ～身体 have a physical examination；have a general check-up ～质量 inspect the quality（of sth.）【名】self-criticism；inspection：写～ make a written self-criticism 质量～是必要的。Quality inspection is indispensable.
检察 jiǎnchá 【动】to investigate（legal）
检察院 jiǎncháyuàn 【名】procuratorate
检点 jiǎndiǎn 【动】❶ examine；check：～书籍 check the books（e.g. in a library）～行李 check the number of pieces of luggage ❷（of words or behaviour）be careful about：言行要多加～。We must be careful about our words and acts.

检举 jiǎnjǔ 【动】to expose，to report（an offense）
检索 jiǎnsuǒ 【动】retrieve；refer to；look up
检讨 jiǎntǎo 【动】examine one's own mistakes 【名】self-criticism
检修 jiǎnxiū 【动】（of machine）overhaul
检验 jiǎnyàn 【动】check；examine；test 【名】test
检疫 jiǎnyì 【动】quarantine
检阅 jiǎnyuè 【动】review；inspect（troops，parade，etc.）
检字法 jiǎnzìfǎ 【名】the way in which Chinese characters are arranged and the system for finding them in a dictionary

减 jiǎn 【动】❶ deduct；subtract；minus：三～二等于一。Three minus two is one. ❷ reduce：～价 reduce the price ～员 reduce the number of personnel ～刑 mitigate a penalty ❸ lessen；weaken：他的干劲不～当年。His enthusiasm for work has not diminished with advancing years.

减产 jiǎn = chǎn decrease in output；drop in yield
减低 jiǎndī 【动】lessen；reduce：～速度 reduce in speed；slow down
减法 jiǎnfǎ 【名】subtraction
减号 jiǎnhào 【名】minus sign
减缓 jiǎnhuǎn 【动】retard；slow down
减慢 jiǎnmàn 【动】slow down
减免 jiǎnmiǎn 【动】exempt from；mitigate（punishment）
减轻 jiǎnqīng 【动】lighten；extenuate；mitigate：～负担 lighten a burden ～工作 cut down on work
减弱 jiǎnruò 【动】weaken；abate；wane：风力～ the wind has abated 火势～了。The fire is dying down.
减色 jiǎn = sè become less attractive；become less perfect

减少　jiǎnshǎo　【动】diminish；lessen；reduce；cut down

减数　jiǎnshù　【名】(maths.) number or quantity to be subtracted from another；subtrahend

减速运动　jiǎnsù yùndòng　(phys.) retarded motion

减缩　jiǎnsuō　【动】reduce and compress；cut down：～开支 cut down on expenses ～经费 reduce budget allocation

减退　jiǎntuì　【动】(of temperature) drop；abate；subside

减员　jiǎn = yuán　depletion of numbers（in the armed forces）

减租减息　jiǎn zū jiǎn xī　reduction of rent and interest

剪

剪　jiǎn　【动】cut with scissors

剪裁　jiǎncái　【动】❶ cut out（a dress or a suit）❷（of writing）cut away unwanted material；prune

剪彩　jiǎn = cǎi　cut the ribbon（e. g. for an exhibition）

剪刀　jiǎndāo　【名】〔把 bǎ〕scissors

剪辑　jiǎnjí　【名】❶（of motion picture）editing ❷ editing and rearrangement：电影（或话剧）录音～ an edited version of a film（or play）for broadcast 【动】cut out，mount and caption（pictures，etc. to illustrate an idea or event）：～图片 cut out and caption pictures

剪接　jiǎnjiē　【动】montage；film editing

剪贴　jiǎntiē　【名】make paper cutouts and paste them on white paper 【动】cut out and paste up（materials from newspapers，magazines，etc.）：～画报 cut out pictures from magazines and mount them

剪影　jiǎnyǐng　【名】paper-cut；silhouette

剪纸　jiǎnzhǐ　【名】paper-cut

剪子　jiǎnzi　【名】〔把 bǎ〕scissors

简（簡）

简（簡）　jiǎn　【形】simple；brief

简报　jiǎnbào　【名】bulletin

简便　jiǎnbiàn　【形】simple and convenient

简称　jiǎnchēng　【动】be called...for short：北京大学～北大。北京大学 is called 北大 for short. 【名】abbreviated form of a name；abbreviation："化肥"是"化学肥料"的～。化肥 is the abbreviation for 化学肥料.

简单　jiǎndān　【形】simple；uncomplicated；*sometimes* 不简单 *means* "outstanding"：她只上了一年大学就考取了研究生，真不～! She was an undergraduate for only one year and then became a graduate student. Isn't that marvellous!

简单化　jiǎndānhuà　【动】oversimplify

简单句　jiǎndānjù　【名】simple sentence

简短　jiǎnduǎn　【形】short and brief

简化　jiǎnhuà　【动】simplify

简化汉字　jiǎnhuà Hànzì　simplified Chinese characters

简洁　jiǎnjié　【形】concise

简捷　jiǎnjié　【形】simple and direct

简介　jiǎnjiè　【名】brief introduction；synopsis；summary

简历　jiǎnlì　【名】biographical notes

简练　jiǎnliàn　【形】succinct；concise

简陋　jiǎnlòu　【形】rough（e. g. accommodation）；simple

简略　jiǎnlüè　【形】simple；brief

简明　jiǎnmíng　【形】concise；simple and clear

简明扼要　jiǎnmíng èyào　brief and concise

简明新闻　jiǎnmíng xīnwén　news summary

简朴　jiǎnpǔ　【形】simple and unadorned

简谱　jiǎnpǔ　【名】numbered musical notation

简体字 jiǎntǐzì 【名】simplified Chinese characters

简写 jiǎnxiě 【动】write a Chinese character in simplified form 【名】simplified character

简写本 jiǎnxiěběn 【名】simplified edition

简讯 jiǎnxùn 【名】news summary

简要 jiǎnyào 【形】concise; brief and to the point

简易 jiǎnyì 【形】simple and easy

简直 jiǎnzhí 【副】*emphasizes the exaggerated way in which some situation or state of affairs is described*: 这位英国朋友汉语说得很好，～跟中国人一样。This Englishman speaks Chinese like a native. 屋子里热得～呆不住！The room is so hot, it is simply unbearable.

简装 jiǎnzhuāng 【形】simple packing

碱 jiǎn 【名】alkali

碱性 jiǎnxìng 【名】alkalinity; basicity

jiàn

见（見）jiàn 【动】❶ see; catch sight of: 那是我亲眼～的，没错。There's no mistake. I saw it with my own eyes. 我刚才还～着他了。I saw him only a moment ago. ❷ be exposed to; be in contact with: 这种材料怕～火。This material must not be placed near an open flame. 我的眼睛发炎了，～风就流泪。My eyes are inflamed; they well up in tears against the wind. ❸ ◇ appear; show: 施肥之后，菜很～长。The vegetables have grown perceptibly since the fertilizer was applied. ❹ refer to; see: 注释～108页 explanation, see page 108 ❺ interview; meet; see: 他说要亲自来～

你。He said that he was coming in person to see you. 【名】◇ understanding; view; insight: 真知灼～ real knowledge and deep insight

见报 jiàn = bào appear in a newspaper

见地 jiàndì 【名】insight; judgment

见缝插针 jiàn fèng chā zhēn stick a pin wherever there is room; (*fig.*) seize any time or space available (to get some thing done)

见怪 jiànguài 【动】take offence; be offended

见鬼 jiàn = guǐ ❶ unbelievable; absurd ❷ go to hell

见机行事 jiàn jī xíng shì let one's actions be governed by the circumstances

见解 jiànjiě 【名】understanding; view

见面 jiàn = miàn meet face to face with; meet: 他们俩一～，就亲切地交谈起来。As soon as they met, they began to talk animatedly. 我们这个方案，应该跟大家见见面。Our plan should be made known to the others.

见面礼 jiànmiànlǐ 【名】a present given to sb. at a first meeting

见识 jiànshi 【名】insight; experience; general knowledge: 长～ enrich (one's) knowledge 【动】increase one's knowledge by seeing with one's own eyes: 听说你的武术很有功夫，让我们～～。We understand that you are pretty good at *Wushu*. Please let us see you perform.

见外 jiànwài 【动】estrange; alienate

见闻 jiànwén 【名】what one sees and hears; general knowledge; information

见习 jiànxí 【动】learn through practice

见笑 jiànxiào 【动】laugh at（me；

us）；lay oneself open to ridicule

见效 jiànxiào 【动】obtain the desired result；be effective

见义勇为 jiàn yì yǒng wéi ready to take up the cudgels on behalf of（a person or a cause）

见异思迁 jiàn yì sī qiān wish to change one's mind the moment one sees something different；对工作不应～，挑挑拣拣。In work, one mustn't pick and choose, or change one's mind the moment one sees something different.

见证 jiànzhèng 【名】❶ evidence ❷ witness

件 jiàn 【量】piece；article；item：一～衣服 a piece of clothing 两～事 two things

间（間）jiàn 【动】◇ separate；divide：黑白相～ alternately black and white 晴～多云（of sky）clear and occasionally cloudy 另见 jiān

间谍 jiàndié 【名】spy；espionage；agent

间断 jiànduàn 【动】stop；discontinue

间隔 jiàngé 【动】leave a space or interval 【名】interval

间隔号 jiàngéhào 【名】dots which separate day and month or groups of characters in the transliteration of a foreign name

间或 jiànhuò 【副】occasionally；now and then（usu. in written language）：宁静的夏夜里，～传来几声蛙鸣。The stillness of the summer night was occasionally broken by the croaking of frogs. 大家都聚精会神地听着，～有人咳嗽一两声。Everybody listened attentively；the only sound was an occasional cough.

间接 jiànjiē 【形】indirect

间接宾语 jiànjiēbīnyǔ 【名】indirect object

间苗 jiàn＝miáo thin out seedlings

间隙 jiànxì 【名】interval；gap

间歇 jiànxiē 【名】intermission

间作 jiànzuò 【动】intercrop

饯（餞）jiàn

饯别 jiànbié 【动】同"饯行"

饯行 jiànxíng 【动】give a farewell dinner

建 jiàn 【动】❶ build；erect；construct；put up：新～了两栋楼。Two buildings have just been constructed. ❷ set up；found；establish：～党 found a party

建材 jiàncái 【名】building materials

建都 jiàn＝dū found a capital

建国 jiàn＝guó found a state

建交 jiàn＝jiāo establish diplomatic relations

建军 jiàn＝jūn found an army

建立 jiànlì 【动】establish；set up；build：～外交关系 establish diplomatic relations ～友谊 develop friendship ～一个独立的比较完整的工业体系 set up an independent and comprehensive industrial system

建设 jiànshè 【动】build；construct：～边疆 build up the areas along the borders ～国家 build a country ～新农村 give a new face to the countryside 【名】construction：农田基本～ capital construction of farm land 经济～ the building-up of the economy

建设性 jiànshèxìng 【名】constructive

建树 jiànshù 【动】made achievements

建议 jiànyì 【动】suggest；propose 【名】suggestion；proposal：合理化～ proposal for improvements 他们的这个～很值得重视。Their proposal is worth considering.

建造 jiànzào 【动】construct；build

建制 jiànzhì 【名】organizational and administrative system

建筑 jiànzhù 【名】building：古代～ ancient building 高大的～ gigantic building 【动】build；construct； erect：～桥梁 build bridges ～地下铁道 build a subway

建筑物 jiànzhùwù 【名】〔座 zuò〕building；edifice

建筑学 jiànzhùxué 【名】architectonics；architecture

贱（賤）jiàn 【形】❶（of price）cheap（*opp. to* 贵）：这里的西红柿～极了。The tomatoes here are extremely cheap. ❷ cheap；base

剑（劍）jiàn 【名】〔把 bǎ〕double-edged sword

剑拔弩张 jiàn bá nǔ zhāng（*fig.*）the situation is very tense and hostilities may break out at any moment：两军对峙，处于～的状态。The two armies are confronting each other and are ready for a battle.

健 jiàn

健步 jiànbù 【名】walk with firm strides：～如飞 walk with quick and firm strides

健将 jiànjiàng 【名】master；expert 运动～ master sportsman

健康 jiànkāng 【名】health 【形】healthy；sound

健美 jiànměi 【形】strong and handsome

健全 jiànquán 【形】(of one's body) sound and strong；(of sth.) sound：体魄～ sound in mind and body 组织～ organizationally perfect 【动】regulate；make perfect：～规章制度 perfect the rules and regulations ～各种学生组织 regulate the various student organizations

健身房 jiànshēnfáng 【名】gymnasium；fitness room

健谈 jiàntán 【形】be fond of talking and able to talk well

健忘 jiànwàng 【形】forgetful；oblivious

健在 jiànzài 【动】still alive and in good health（referring to elderly people）；still going strong

健壮 jiànzhuàng 【形】vigorous and healthy；hale and hearty

舰（艦）jiàn 【名】〔艘 sōu〕naval vessel

舰队 jiànduì 【名】fleet

舰艇 jiàntǐng 【名】〔艘 sōu〕vessels

渐（漸）jiàn 【副】gradually；step by step；little by little

渐变 jiànbiàn 【名】gradual change

渐渐 jiànjiàn 【副】gradually；slowly：风～停了。The wind is gradually subsiding. 我到这个工厂快一个月了，跟同事们～地熟悉了。It's now almost a month since I came to this factory, and I have gradually become acquainted with my colleagues.

渐进 jiànjìn 【动】develop gradually；advance step by step

践（踐）jiàn

践踏 jiàntà 【动】❶ trample underfoot：行军的时候不要～庄稼。We mustn't trample the crops underfoot while marching. ❷ ravage；devastate：中国的领土决不允许侵略者任意～。The Chinese people will never allow China's territory to be ravaged by aggressors.

溅（濺）jiàn 【动】spatter；splash：～了一身泥（I）was spattered all over with mud

鉴（鑒）jiàn

鉴别　jiànbié　【动】discern；judge

鉴定　jiàndìng　【动】appraise；judge；authenticate；identify；～真假 judge which is false and which is genuine ～产品合格不合格 judge whether or not the products are up to standard【名】evaluation；appraisal；assessment：工作～ an evaluation of one's work

鉴戒　jiànjiè　【名】(take) warning (from)

鉴赏　jiànshǎng　【动】appreciate (paintings, antiques etc.)

鉴于　jiànyú　【介】in view of；considering that；seeing that... (usu. in written language)：～形势发展的需要,我们必须改变原来的计划。In view of developments in the situation, we must change the original plan. ～以上种种原因,这次会议延期了。Owing to the reasons stated above, the meeting has been postponed.

箭　jiàn　【名】〔枝 zhī〕arrow

箭步　jiànbù　【名】quick stride

箭头　jiàntóu　【名】❶ arrowhead ❷ arrow-shaped mark

箭在弦上　jiàn zài xián shàng　the arrow is already on the bow-string；(fig.) it must happen；a point of no return (often used in conjunction with 势在必发 or 不得不发)

jiāng

江　jiāng　【名】〔条 tiáo〕large river

江河日下　jiāng hé rì xià　deteriorating fast；going from bad to worse；be on the decline

江湖　jiānghú　【名】◇ used as an epithet referring to a wandering life in the old society：走～ wander about doing odd jobs 流落～ be-come homeless and drift about ～艺人 wandering performer (e.g. acrobat, singer, etc.)

江米　jiāngmǐ　【名】glutinous rice

江南　jiāngnán　【名】❶ south of the Changjiang (Yangtse) River (area south of the lower reaches of the Changjiang River—the southern part of Jiangsu and Anhui Provinces and the northern part of Zhejiang Province) ❷ all regions south of the Changjiang River

江山　jiāngshān　【名】land；country

将(將)　jiāng　【介】❶ ◇ with；use：～功折罪 make amends for one's wrong doing by meritorious service ❷ 同"把" bǎ【介】(usu. in written language)：～房间打扫干净 give the room a thorough cleaning【副】同"将要"(usu. in written language)：气象预报明晨～有霜冻。According to the weather forecast, frost is expected tomorrow morning.

另见 jiàng

将功赎罪　jiāng gōng shú zuì　make amends for one's crime by good deeds

将计就计　jiāng jì jiù jì　turn a person's scheme against himself

将近　jiāngjìn　【动】near；be close to；nearly；almost (usu. referring to quantity or time)：～三年 nearly three years ～黄昏 dusk is approaching 观众～一万人 an audience of nearly ten thousand people

将就　jiāngjiu　【动】have to make do with；在质量方面,不能～,要精益求精。As far as quality is concerned, we should not make do with the second-rate but must constantly strive for excellence. 这枝毛笔不太好,先～着用吧。This writing brush is not very good, but just make do with it for the time being.

将军　jiāngjūn　【名】（mil.）general

将来　jiānglái　【名】in the future：现在办不到，～总会办到的。What cannot be done now will be achieved in the future. 我们今天的劳动是为了创造更加美好的～。Our work today is for the purpose of creating a better future.

将信将疑　jiāng xìn jiāng yí　（of attitude）dubious；doubtful

将要　jiāngyào　【副】will；be going to：他们～去天津学习专业。They are going to Tianjin to take a professional course. 冰上运动会～在这里举行。The winter sports meet will soon be held here.

姜（薑）　jiāng　【名】〔块 kuài〕ginger

浆（漿）　jiāng　【名】thick liquid：泥～ mud【动】starch：～衣服 starch clothes

浆果　jiāngguǒ　【名】berry

浆洗　jiāngxǐ　【动】wash and starch

僵　jiāng　【形】❶ stiff；numb；rigid：手冻～了 hands stiff with cold 百足之虫，死而不～。A centipede, though dead, doesn't become stiff immediately. (fig.) Though an individual, or a group, is in decline, his(its) influence is still felt. ❷ be dead-locked；have reached a stalemate：别把事情搞～了，那样问题就更不好解决了。Do not allow the matter to reach a stalemate or it will be more difficult to solve.

僵持　jiāngchí　【动】reach a deadlock

僵化　jiānghuà　【动】become rigid；be inflexible

僵局　jiāngjú　【名】deadlock；impasse

僵尸　jiāngshī　【名】corpse

僵死　jiāngsǐ　【动】become stiff and dead

僵硬　jiāngyìng　【形】❶（of limbs and joints）inflexible；numb；rigid：关节～ stiff joints ❷ inflexible；rigid：态度～ stiff manner

疆　jiāng

疆场　jiāngchǎng　【名】battlefield

疆界　jiāngjiè　【名】〔条 tiáo〕boundary；border

疆土　jiāngtǔ　【名】a country's territory

疆域　jiāngyù　【名】territory of a nation-state

jiǎng

讲（講）　jiǎng　【动】❶ tell；say；speak；relate：～故事 tell a story ～家史 relate one's family history ❷ lecture；explain：～一堂课 give a lecture ～力学的书 a book on mechanics ❸ consult；discuss；negotiate：～条件 negotiate terms ～价钱 bargain over price ❹ stress；be particular about；pay great attention to；lay stress on：～卫生 be particular about hygiene ～实际 stress the practical side of sth.

讲稿　jiǎnggǎo　【名】〔篇 piān〕draft for a speech；lecture notes；a speech

讲和　jiǎng=hé　make peace

讲话　jiǎnghuà　【名】talk；speech

讲话　jiǎng=huà　speak；talk

讲解　jiǎngjiě　【动】explain【名】explanation

讲究　jiǎngjiu　【动】stress；be particular about；pay great attention to：我们一贯～实事求是，反对夸夸其谈。We always stress seeking truth from facts and oppose bragging. 不要过于～吃穿。Don't pay undue attention to food and clothing.【形】costly；luxurious：会客室布置

得很～。The reception room is very luxuriously furnished.

讲课　jiǎng=kè　give a lecture；give a lesson

讲理　jiǎng=lǐ　❶ be reasonable ❷ argue things out

讲排场　jiǎng páichang　love ostentation：婚、丧、嫁、娶，不～ to do away with ostentatious display on occasions such as weddings and funerals

讲评　jiǎngpíng　【动】comment on and appraise

讲求　jiǎngqiú　【动】pay attention to and attempt to achieve：工作要～效果。One must look for results in one's work.

讲师　jiǎngshī　【名】lecturer

讲授　jiǎngshòu　【动】teach；lecture

讲述　jiǎngshù　【动】recount；relate

讲台　jiǎngtái　【名】lecture platform

讲坛　jiǎngtán　【名】rostrum；dais；a place for public speech or discussion

讲学　jiǎng=xué　give lectures（on an academic subject）

讲演　jiǎngyǎn　【动】give a lecture【名】lecture：他的～博得了热烈的掌声。His lecture was received with enthusiastic applause.

讲义　jiǎngyì　【名】lecture notes；teaching material

讲桌　jiǎngzhuō　【名】〔张 zhāng〕lectern

讲座　jiǎngzuò · 【名】series of lectures；course of lectures

奖（獎）　jiǎng　【名】prize；reward；commendation：发～ award a prize 得～ win a prize【动】praise；commend：立功者～。Anyone who performs meritoriously will be praised and rewarded.

奖杯　jiǎngbēi　【名】cup（as a prize）

奖惩　jiǎngchéng　【名】reward and punishment

奖金　jiǎngjīn　【名】bonus；prize

奖励　jiǎnglì　【动】encourage by giving a reward or prize【名】encouragement；commendation

奖品　jiǎngpǐn　【名】award；prize

奖券　jiǎngquàn　【名】〔张 zhāng〕lottery ticket

奖赏　jiǎngshǎng　【动】award

奖学金　jiǎngxuéjīn　【名】scholarship

奖章　jiǎngzhāng　【名】〔枚 méi〕medal

奖状　jiǎngzhuàng　【名】〔张 zhāng〕citation of merit；certificate of merit

桨（槳）　jiǎng　【名】oar；paddle

jiàng

降　jiàng　【动】fall；drop；descend
另见 xiáng

降半旗　jiàng bàn qí　fly a flag at half-mast

降低　jiàngdī　【动】lower；debase

降级　jiàng=jí　reduce in rank；demote

降价　jiàng=jià　cut the price；reduce the price

降临　jiànglín　【动】〈书〉fall；come down：夜色～。Darkness falls.

降落　jiàngluò　【动】alight；descend；（of airplanes）land

降落伞　jiàngluòsǎn　【名】parachute

降旗　jiàng=qí　lower a flag

降生　jiàngshēng　【动】〈书〉be born

降温　jiàng=wēn　❶ lower the temperature：～设备 cooling system 采取～措施 take steps to lower the temperature（in a place）❷ a drop in temperature：大风～警报 a warning of a gale accompanied by a drop in temperature

将（將）　jiàng　【名】com-

mander
另见 jiāng

将领　jiànglǐng　【名】generals

将士　jiàngshì　【名】commanders and fighters

酱（醬）　jiàng　【名】thick sauce as a condiment：黄～ thick sauce made of soybeans 甜～ sweet brown sauce

酱油　jiàngyóu　【名】soya sauce

糨　jiàng　【形】thick

糨糊　jiànghu　【名】paste

jiāo

交　jiāo　【动】❶ hand in；turn over；pay：～税 pay a tax ～公粮 pay the grain tax（to the state）❷ intersect；cross：两线～于一点。The two lines intersect. ❸ make friends with：两个人很快就～上了朋友。They two very quickly made friends with each other. ❹ reach（a certain time or season）：农历才～九月，就呼呼地刮起了西北风。It is barely September by the lunar calendar, but a north-west wind is already howling.

交班　jiāo＝bān　pass work over to the next shift

交叉　jiāochā　【动】❶ intersect；cross：铁轨～ the two railway lines crossing each other ～路口 an intersection ❷ overlap；intersect：～作业 overlapping jobs

交差　jiāo＝chāi　report on what one has done while on duty

交错　jiāocuò　【动】interlace；crisscross

交代　jiāodài　【动】❶ hand over；transfer：～一下工作。Let me hand over my work（to you）. ❷ explain and make arrangements for；give

an account of：领导已经把任务～清楚了。The leadership has already given a clear explanation of the task（to be done）. ❸ explain；explicate：～政策 explain the policy ❹ own up；confess：～罪行 confess one's crime ～问题 confess what one has done（one's mistake, fault, etc.）也作"交待"。

交底　jiāo＝dǐ　put one's cards on the table；confide to（sb.）what one has in mind

交点　jiāodiǎn　【名】point of intersection

交锋　jiāo＝fēng　cross swords with；engage each other（in battle or a game）

交付　jiāofù　【动】❶ pay（money）❷ turn over；hand over

交工　jiāo＝gōng　hand over a completed construction（building, dam, etc.）

交还　jiāohuán　【动】return；give back

交换　jiāohuàn　【动】exchange

交火　jiāo＝huǒ　fight

交际　jiāojì　【名】social activities；social intercourse；communication：～广 has a very wide circle of acquaintances 【动】communicate；make friends：善于～ be very good at making friends

交加　jiāojiā　【动】two things occur simultaneously：风雨～ endure both wind and rain 贫病～ suffer from poverty and illness simultaneously 悲喜～ with mixed feelings of both joy and sorrow

交接　jiāojiē　【动】❶ join；be linked with ❷ hand over and accept；transfer：～工作 hand over and accept a job ～班 hand over to a new shift

交界　jiāojiè　【动】border on each other

交卷　jiāo＝juàn　❶ hand in an ex-

amination paper ❷ (of written assignment) finish；complete

交流 jiāoliú 【动】exchange：文化～ cultural exchange ～经验 exchange experiences

交流电 jiāoliúdiàn 【名】(electr.) alternating current

交纳 jiāonà 【动】pay；hand in (e.g. fees, membership dues)

交情 jiāoqíng 【名】friendship；mutual affection

交融 jiāoróng 【动】blend；mingle：情景～ with the setting and sentiments well matched, highlighting each other

交涉 jiāoshè 【动】negotiate：已经和农机站～好了，拖拉机明天来我们组耕地。Arrangements have already been made with the farm machinery station for tractors to do our team's ploughing tomorrow.

交谈 jiāotán 【动】talk with each other；converse

交替 jiāotì 【动】❶ replace：新旧～ the new takes the place of the old ❷ alternate：两项工作～进行。The two different kinds of work should be carried on alternately.

交通 jiāotōng 【名】❶ communications ❷ traffic：～要道 traffic artery ～很便利 have easy access to transportation facilities

交通工具 jiāotōng gōngjù means of transport

交头接耳 jiāo tóu jiē ěr whisper to each other：小玲和小刚～，不知道在说些什么。Xiao Ling and Xiao Gang kept whispering to each other；who knows what they were talking about.

交往 jiāowǎng 【动】associate with；have dealings with；make contact with：互相～ make contact with each other 中国人民和世界各国人民之间～日益频繁。The Chinese people are having increasingly greater

contact with the peoples of the world.

交响乐 jiāoxiǎngyuè 【名】symphony

交心 jiāo ＝ xīn open one's heart

交易 jiāoyì 【名】transaction；business deal；trade

交易所 jiāoyìsuǒ 【名】exchange (the building)

交谊舞 jiāoyìwǔ 【名】ballroom dancing

交游 jiāoyóu 【动】make friends

交战 jiāozhàn 【动】be at war；fight

交织 jiāozhī 【动】interlace；be interwoven

郊 jiāo

郊区 jiāoqū 【名】suburban areas

郊外 jiāowài 【名】outskirts；suburbs

郊游 jiāoyóu 【动】go for an outing；go on an excursion

浇（澆） jiāo 【动】water；sprinkle water；irrigate：～花 water the flowers 用井水～地 irrigate the land with well water 他没带伞，挨～了。He didn't take an umbrella, so he was wet through.

浇灌 jiāoguàn 【动】❶ pour：～混凝土 pour concrete ❷ irrigate；water：～菜地 irrigate the vegetable plot

浇注 jiāozhù 【动】to pour into a mould

骄（驕） jiāo 【形】arrogant；conceited

骄傲 jiāo'ào 【形】❶ arrogant；proud；conceited ❷ (laudatory) proud：我们为伟大的祖国而感到～。We feel proud of our great country. 【名】pride：灿烂的古代文化遗产是我们的～。The glorious legacy of ancient culture is our pride.

骄横 jiāohèng 【形】insufferably arrogant；extremely overbearing

骄气 jiāoqì 【名】arrogance；conceit

骄阳 jiāoyáng 【名】blazing sun

骄纵 jiāozòng 【动】arrogant and wild；proud and uncontrollable

娇（嬌）jiāo 【形】❶ ◇ beautiful；lovely：江山如此多～。The land is so beautiful. ❷ spoil；indulge：对孩子别太～了。Don't spoil your child. ❸ soft；spoiled：走了这么一点儿路就说累，未免太～了。You've walked only a short distance and you're already complaining of being tired. How soft you are!

娇惯 jiāoguàn 【动】pamper；coddle；spoil；dote on

娇嫩 jiāonen 【形】delicate；frail

娇气 jiāoqì 【名】liking comfort；being unable to endure hardship 【形】soft；unable to endure hardship

娇生惯养 jiāo shēng guàn yǎng brought up in comfort and doted upon；be pampered

胶（膠）jiāo 【名】glue

胶布 jiāobù 【名】adhesive plaster；bandage

胶合 jiāohé 【动】cement（sth.）；glue（sth.）

胶卷 jiāojuǎn 【名】〔卷 juǎn〕photographic film

胶皮 jiāopí 【名】（vulcanized）rubber

胶片 jiāopiàn 【名】film

胶水 jiāoshuǐ 【名】liquid glue；mucilage

胶鞋 jiāoxié 【名】〔只 zhī，双 shuāng〕rubber boots；canvas shoes with rubber soles；running shoes

教 jiāo 【动】teach
另见 jiào

教书 jiāo＝shū teach

教学 jiāo＝xué teaching（as a profession)

焦 jiāo 【形】burnt；scorched；charred：烧～了 scorched by fire 【名】coke

焦点 jiāodiǎn 【名】❶（phys.）focus；focal point ❷（maths.）focus ❸（of an argument etc.）focus：争论的～ the focus of an argument

焦耳 jiāo'ěr 【量】（phys.）joule

焦黄 jiāohuáng 【形】dry and yellowish

焦急 jiāojí 【形】anxious and restless；worried

焦距 jiāojù 【名】focal distance

焦虑 jiāolù 【形】very worried；extremely anxious

焦炭 jiāotàn 【名】coke

焦头烂额 jiāo tóu làn é with a scorched head and bruised forehead；in a very awkward situation

焦土 jiāotǔ 【名】scorched earth

焦躁 jiāozào 【形】anxious and fretful

礁 jiāo 【名】reef

礁石 jiāoshí 【名】〔块 kuài〕reef

jiáo

嚼 jiáo 【动】chew

jiǎo

角 jiǎo 【名】❶ horn：牛～ horn of a cow 羊～ horn of a sheep ❷（gèom.）angle ❸（～儿）corner；angle：屋子的一～ one corner of the room 东北～ northeast corner 【量】one-tenth of yuan — Chinese currency：一～等于十分。One jiao is worth ten fen.
另见 jué

角度 jiǎodù 【名】❶ the degree of

an angle：～太大 the angle is too great 调整～ re-adjust the angle ❷ angle；aspect；point of view；从个人～看问题，往往是片面的。Looking at a question from a personal point of view often results in one-sidedness.

角楼　jiǎolóu　【名】watchtower at a corner of a city wall；a corner tower

角落　jiǎoluò　【名】❶ corner；nook；院子的每一个～都打扫得很干净。Every corner of the courtyard has been thoroughly cleaned. ❷ remote or secluded place；阴暗的～ a dark corner

侥（僥）jiǎo

侥幸　jiǎoxìng　【形】luck；chance；～心理 take a chance ～取胜 win by good luck

狡 jiǎo

狡辩　jiǎobiàn　【动】quibble；resort to sophistry

狡猾　jiǎohuá　【形】sly；cunning

狡赖　jiǎolài　【动】deny（by resorting to sophistry）

狡诈　jiǎozhà　【形】deceitful；cunning

饺（餃）jiǎo

饺子　jiǎozi　【名】stuffed dumpling

绞（絞）jiǎo　【动】❶ twist；wind；两条绳子～在一起了。Two ropes twisted together. ❷ execute；put to death by hanging；～死 put to death by hanging

绞尽脑汁　jiǎo jìn nǎozhī　rack one's brains；我一也没想出个好注意。I racked my brains，but I wasn't able to come up with a good idea.

绞肉机　jiǎoròujī　【名】meat grinder

绞索　jiǎosuǒ　【名】〔条 tiáo〕noose

绞痛　jiǎotòng　【动】（med.）angina

矫（矯）jiǎo

矫健　jiǎojiàn　【形】robust；vigorous；～的步伐 walk with vigorous strides ～的身影 robust physique

矫捷　jiǎojié　【形】agile；nimble

矫揉造作　jiǎo róu zào zuò　（of manner，behaviour，etc.）extremely unnatural and affected

矫枉过正　jiǎo wǎng guò zhèng　straighten sth. crooked past the point where it is straight；（fig.）exceed the proper limits in righting a wrong

矫正　jiǎozhèng　【动】make corrections；set right；straighten out；adjust；～发音 correct（sb.'s）pronunciation ～误差 correct an error

皎 jiǎo

皎洁　jiǎojié　【形】（of moon）bright and pure

脚 jiǎo　【名】〔只 zhī〕foot

脚本　jiǎoběn　【名】script；scenario

脚步　jiǎobù　【名】pace；step；footstep；放轻～ walk lightly ～重 tread heavily

脚跟　jiǎogēn　【名】❶ heel ❷ footing；站稳～ stand firmly

脚镣　jiǎoliào　【名】shackles

脚手架　jiǎoshǒujià　【名】scaffolding

脚踏两只船　jiǎo tà liǎng zhī chuán　❶ unwilling to give up either alternative when a choice is required ❷ sit on the fence；在大是大非面前决不能～。One cannot be a fence-sitter on questions of principle.

脚踏实地　jiǎo tà shídì　do solid work；be down-to-earth

脚印　jiǎoyìn　【名】footprint

脚指头　jiǎozhǐtou　【名】toe

脚注　jiǎozhù　【名】footnote

搅（攪）jiǎo　【动】❶ stir；mix；泥浆～得很匀。The mortar

has been thoroughly mixed. 不要把缸里的水～浑了。Don't stir up the sediment in the crock. ❷ annoy; disturb: 他们在图书馆大声说话, ～得别人无法看书。They chatted in the library creating a disturbance, so that no one else could read.

搅拌 jiǎobàn 【动】mix; stir

搅动 jiǎodòng 【动】stir

搅乱 jiǎoluàn 【动】confuse; throw into disorder

搅扰 jiǎorǎo 【动】disturb; harass

剿 jiǎo 【动】annihilate; wipe out (bandits)

缴（繳）jiǎo 【动】❶ pay; hand over: ～学费 pay school fees ～房租 pay house rent ❷ surrender (e.g. weapons); be forced to hand over: ～枪 surrender weapons

缴获 jiǎohuò 【动】capture (during battle) 【名】booty; things captured

缴纳 jiǎonà 【动】pay (tax, fee, etc.)

缴械 jiǎo = xiè disarm: 缴了敌军的械 disarm the enemy ～投降 hand over one's arms and surrender

jiào

叫 jiào 【动】❶ yell; cry: 拍手好～ clap one's hands and cheer 大～一声 give a loud cry 狗～。The dog is barking. 鸟儿喳喳～。The birds are chirping. ❷ call; be called: 你～什么名字？What's your name? 这种花～牡丹。This flower is called a peony. 孩子们～他王叔叔。The children call him Uncle Wang. ❸ call: 外边有人～你。Somebody is out there calling you. 把他们～进来。Please call them in. ❹ make; order (usu. in a pivotal sentence): ～荒山献宝。Let's make the

barren hills contribute their precious ores. 我刚才～人找他去了。I sent somebody to look for him just now. ❺ hire; order: 打电话～辆汽车 order a taxi by telephone 我～了三个菜, 够吃了吧？I've ordered three dishes, I guess that's enough. 【介】同“被”bèi【介】(usu. in colloquial speech, the agent cannot be omitted): 羊群～小勇赶回来了。The flocks of sheep were brought back by Xiao Yong.

叫喊 jiàohǎn 【动】cry; shout; call out; yell

叫唤 jiàohuan 【动】❶ scream: 痛得他直～。He couldn't help screaming with pain. ❷ (of animal) utter a cry: 小狗不停地～。The puppy kept yipping all the time.

叫苦连天 jiào kǔ lián tiān constantly complain

叫卖 jiàomài 【动】hawk

叫门 jiào = mén knock at the door

叫嚷 jiàorǎng 【动】bluster; clamour; yell

叫嚣 jiàoxiāo 【动】clamour; bluster (usu. in written language): 狂妄～ clamour madly

叫做 jiàozuò 【动】be named; be called; be known as: 这种松树～白皮松。This pine tree is called a "lacebark pine". 以各种鸟类、花卉为题材的中国画, ～花鸟画。Chinese paintings depicting various sorts of birds and flowers are known as flower-and-bird paintings.

觉（覺）jiào 【名】sleep
另见 jué

校 jiào 【动】correct; proof-read
另见 xiào

校订 jiàodìng 【动】check against the authoritative text

校对 jiàoduì 【动】proof-read

校勘 jiàokān 【动】collate

校正 jiàozhèng 【动】proofread and correct

轿（轎）jiào 【名】sedan chair

轿车 jiàochē 【名】〔辆 liàng〕sedan；limousine

较（較）jiào 【介】同"比"bǐ【介】(usu. in written language)：这种药～那种药效果更好。This medicine is more effective than that. 他工作～前更加努力了。He works harder than before. 【副】同"比较"【副】(usu. in written language)：赵村是县城附近～大的村子。Zhaocun Village is a comparatively big village near the county seat. 我们要用～少的钱，办～多的事。We must make a relatively small amount of money go somewhat further.

较量 jiàoliàng 【动】match strength with；compete；contest：进行～ compete with each other 反复～ repeatedly match strength with each other ～一番 have a contest

教 jiào 【名】❶ education；teaching ❷ religion
另见 jiāo

教案 jiào'àn 【名】teaching plan

教材 jiàocái 【名】teaching materials (textbooks, etc.)；text

教程 jiàochéng 【名】course (on a particular subject)

教导 jiàodǎo 【动】teach；instruct 【名】teaching；instruction

教导员 jiàodǎoyuán 【名】(mil.) political instructor

教改 jiàogǎi 【名】short for 教学改革 educational reform

教皇 jiàohuáng 【名】Pope

教会 jiàohuì 【名】church (organization)

教诲 jiàohuì 【动】teach；instruct

教具 jiàojù 【名】teaching aid

教科书 jiàokēshū 【名】〔本 běn〕textbook

教练 jiàoliàn 【名】❶ coaching ❷ instructor；coach：他是排球～。He is a volleyball coach.

教师 jiàoshī 【名】teacher

教室 jiàoshì 【名】classroom

教授 jiàoshòu 【名】professor 【动】teach；lecture on：～地理 teach geography ～化学 teach chemistry

教唆 jiàosuō 【动】incite；instigate；abet

教唆犯 jiàosuōfàn 【名】abettor；instigator

教堂 jiàotáng 【名】church；chapel；cathedral

教条 jiàotiáo 【名】dogma；creed；doctrine

教条主义 jiàotiáozhǔyì 【名】dogmatism

教徒 jiàotú 【名】(of religion) believer；follower

教务 jiàowù 【名】educational administration

教学 jiàoxué 【名】teaching；process of teaching

教学大纲 jiàoxué dàgāng teaching programme；syllabus

教学相长 jiào xué xiāng zhǎng teaching benefits teachers as well as students

教训 jiàoxun 【动】teach；educate；reprimand 【名】lesson；lecture：总结经验 ～ learn from experience 吸取～ draw a lesson from

教研室 jiàoyánshì 【名】teaching and research section

教养 jiàoyǎng 【动】bring up 【名】(of a person) breeding：有 ～ cultured；well-bred 缺乏 ～ uncultured；uncouth

教益 jiàoyì 【名】benefit from advice

教育 jiàoyù 【动】educate 【名】education

教育家 jiàoyùjiā 【名】educator

教育学 jiàoyùxué 【名】pedagogy；education

教员 jiàoyuán 【名】teacher（profession）

酵 jiào 【动】◇ ferment

酵母 jiàomǔ 【名】yeast

jiē

阶（階）jiē

阶层 jiēcéng 【名】❶ social stratum ❷ groupings in society which cut across class lines：知识分子 ～ the intelligentsia

阶段 jiēduàn 【名】stage；phase

阶级 jiējí 【名】class

阶级观点 jiējí guāndiǎn class viewpoint

阶级觉悟 jiējí juéwù class consciousness

阶级立场 jiējí lìchǎng class stand

阶级矛盾 jiējí máodùn class contradiction

阶级性 jiējíxìng 【名】class nature；class character

阶梯 jiētī 【名】steps；ladder

皆 jiē 【副】all；each and every；all and sundry：人人 ～ 知。It is known to all and sundry.

结（結）jiē 【动】bear（fruit）另见 jié

结巴 jiēba 【形】stutter；stammer：他说话有点儿 ～。He has a slight stutter.【名】stutter；stuttering；stammerer

结实 jiēshi 【形】sturdy；strongly built；durable：身体挺 ～ be strongly built ～ 的房子 a solidly built house 这双袜子真 ～。This pair of socks is very durable.

接 jiē 【动】❶ join；link；con-nect：～ 纱头（of weaving）piece together broken ends of yarn 你看看内容，这一页是不是 ～ 着那一页的？Please look and see if this page follows the previous one. ❷ receive；accept：～ 球（of ball games）catch the ball ～ 电话 answer a phone call ～ 到一封信 receive a letter ❸ ◇ be close to；be in contact with：两山相 ～。The mountains are linked up with each other. ❹ take over：他调到上海去了，我 ～ 他的工作。He is transferred to Shanghai, and I'm supposed to take over his work. ❺ meet：我去机场 ～ 一个朋友。I'm going to the airport to meet a friend.

接班 jiē=bān take over sb.'s shift

接班人 jiēbānrén 【名】（fig.）successor

接触 jiēchù 【动】❶ touch；bring in-to contact with：一般的橡胶制品都不能 ～ 酸。Most things made of rubber must not come into contact with acid. 这盏台灯有点儿 ～ 不良。This table lamp seems to have a loose contact. ❷ link up with；be in contact with；be associated with：～ 实际 be confronted with reality 我从来没有 ～ 过这门科学。I've never had any contact with this branch of science. 老师要多 ～ 学生。Teachers must be in close contact with their students. ❸（mil.）come into conflict with；engage：先头部队已经跟敌人的前哨 ～ 了。The vanguard forces have already engaged the enemy's forward units.

接待 jiēdài 【动】act as host to

接待室 jiēdàishì 【名】reception room

接到 jiē//dào receive：他一 ～ 通知，马上就出发了。He set out as soon as he received the notice. 我寄去的包裹你 ～ 没有？Have you received the

parcel I sent by post?

接二连三 jiē èr lián sān　one after the other; successive: 喜讯～传来。 Good tidings kept pouring in. ～收到朋友来信。 I've been receiving letters from my friends one after another.

接管 jiēguǎn 【动】take over and be in charge of

接济 jiējì 【动】give material or financial help to

接见 jiējiàn 【动】grant an interview to

接交 jiējiāo 【动】hand over and accept (a job); transfer

接近 jiējìn 【动】come close to; approach; draw near: ～预定目标 close to the pre-determined target 上半年的指标已～完成。 The first half year's quota is nearly fulfilled. 这几位先生的意见非常～。 These gentlemen have similar opinions.

接力 jiēlì 【名】relay (e.g. relay race)

接力赛 jiēlìsài 【名】relay

接连 jiēlián 【副】one after another; consecutively; in succession: 这个作家～发表了几篇散文。 This author has published several essays in succession. 这篇重要社论～广播了三次。 This important editorial has been broadcast three times in succession.

接纳 jiēnà 【动】accept; admit

接洽 jiēqià 【动】contact and negotiate about

接壤 jiērǎng 【动】border on each other

接生 jiēshēng 【动】act as midwife

接收 jiēshōu 【动】❶ accept; receive: 电台正～前线发来的电报。 The radio station is now receiving messages from the battle-front. ❷ lawfully take over: ～官僚资产阶级的企业 take over the enterprises of the bureaucrat-capitalist class ❸

take in; accept; admit: ～新会员 admit new members

接手 jiēshǒu 【动】take over (duties etc.)

接受 jiēshòu 【动】accept (criticism, task, etc.)

接替 jiētì 【动】take someone's place; replace sb.

接头 jiē = tóu ❶ join two ends ❷ contact; get in touch with: 这件事上级派我去～。 The leadership sent me to make contact with the person concerned in this matter. 今天你先去跟他接个头。 Today you will first go and get in touch with him.

接吻 jiē = wěn　kiss each other

接应 jiēyìng 【动】❶ (mil.) act in coordination with; come to sb.'s aid: 一排打先锋，二排随后～。 The first platoon will spearhead the offensive, while the second platoon will provide back-up and reinforcements. ❷ supply: 由于运输中断,物资一时～不上。 The flow of supplies cannot be kept up just now because the transportation lines have been cut.

接着 jiēzhe 【副】continue; carry on: 你讲得好极了，请～往下讲。 You talk very well; please continue. 这本书，你看完了我～看。 I'll read this book after you have finished it. 【连】immediately after; following: 下了一夜大雪，～又刮起了刺骨的寒风。 It snowed heavily all night, followed immediately by a biting wind. 她唱了一个歌，～又跳了一个舞。 She sang a song, and then danced.

接种 jiēzhòng 【动】inoculate

揭 jiē 【动】❶ uncover; take off; lift up: ～锅盖 take the lid off the pot ～下墙上的地图 take down the map from the wall ❷ expose; lay bare; disclose: ～老底 expose

(sb.'s) past ～矛盾 bring to light a hidden conflict

揭穿 jiēchuān 【动】expose；lay bare：～阴谋 expose a plot 假面目被～了 unmask sb.

揭发 jiēfā 【动】bring to light；expose；lay bare

揭盖子 jiē gàizi take the lid off；bring things into the open：只有彻底～，才能解决问题。Only by bringing everything out into the open can we solve the problem.

揭竿而起 jiē gān ér qǐ rise in rebellion；start an uprising：公元前209年，陈胜、吴广领导贫苦农民～，反抗秦二世的残暴统治。In 209 B.C., Chen Sheng and Wu Guang led a peasant uprising against the tyrannical rule of the Second Emperor of the Qin dynasty.

揭开 jiē//kāi uncover；reveal

揭露 jiēlù 【动】expose；unmask

揭幕 jiē = mù unveil；inaugurate

揭破 jiēpò 【动】unmask；disclose

揭示 jiēshì 【动】reveal；bring to light：这篇论文～了一条重要的数学定理。The thesis brings to light an important mathematical theorem.

揭晓 jiēxiǎo 【动】announce the results

街 jiē 【名】〔条 tiáo〕street

街道 jiēdào 【名】〔条 tiáo〕❶ street ❷ neighbourhood：～工作 neighbourhood service work ～托儿所 neighbourhood-run nursery

街坊 jiēfang 【名】neighbour

街谈巷议 jiē tán xiàng yì casual conversation；street gossip

街头巷尾 jiē tóu xiàng wěi on the streets and in the lanes；in all parts of the city：节日的首都，～都挤满了欢乐的人群。The streets of the capital were swarming with merry-making crowds on the day of the festival.

街心 jiēxīn 【名】centre of a street：～公园 a street park

jié

节（節）jié 【名】❶ joint；knot；node：竹～ the joint of a bamboo pole 骨～（anat.）joint ❷ festival：三八妇女～ Women's Day, March Eighth 过～ celebrate a festival 【动】◇ economize；save：～油 save oil ～粮 economize on grain 【量】length，period，paragraph，etc.：一～甘蔗 one length of sugar cane 九～车厢 nine railway cars 第三～课 the third period

节俭 jiéjiǎn 【形】economical；frugal

节节败退 jié jié bài tuì （of troops in battle）keep on retreating

节节胜利 jié jié shènglì （of troops in battle）win one victory after another

节流 jiéliú 【动】reduce expenditure

节录 jiélù 【动】extract 【名】excerpt

节目 jiémù 【名】〔个 gè〕performance；item in a performance

节能 jié = néng conserve energy；economize on energy

节拍 jiépāi 【名】metre

节气 jiéqi 【名】❶ one of the traditional 24 divisions of the year based on changes in weather ❷ season：都什么～啦，你还穿棉衣呀！Don't you know what season it is now? Imagine still wearing warm clothes!

节日 jiérì 【名】festival

节省 jiéshěng 【动】economize；save；use sth. sparingly：～人力 economize on manpower ～原材料 use raw materials sparingly ～资金 use capital wisely

节外生枝 jié wài shēng zhī purposely cause complication

节衣缩食　jié yī suō shí　live frugally
也说"缩衣节食"。

节余　jiéyú　【动】save as a result of economizing：修游泳池，～了不少材料。We saved a lot of material when we built the swimming pool.【名】surplus：伙食～ surplus left over from boarding fees 年终～ the surplus in an account at the end of a year

节育　jié = yù　short for 节制生育 birth control

节约　jiéyuē　【动】practise economy；economize

节支　jiézhī　【动】economize on expenditure

节制　jiézhì　【动】regulate；control；check；be moderate：～生育 practise birth control ～饮食 be moderate in one's eating and drinking

节奏　jiézòu　【名】❶ rhythm ❷ evenness；regularity：安排工作要有～。Work must be planned so that there is an even flow to it.

劫　jié　【动】plunder；rob；hold up：～狱 execute a jail break ～道 highway robbery 打家～舍 rob sb.'s house

劫持　jiéchí　【动】hijack；kidnap

劫掠　jiélüè　【动】plunder；rob

杰（傑）　jié

杰出　jiéchū　【形】excellent；outstanding；distinguished

杰作　jiézuò　【名】masterpiece

洁（潔）　jié

洁白　jiébái　【形】pure white

洁净　jiéjìng　【形】clean；spotless

结（結）　jié　【动】❶ ◇ tie；fasten；join or tie sth. together：绳 knot string or cord ～网 knot string to make a net ❷ ◇ gather together：成群～队 form into groups 集会～社 form an organization or society ❸ congeal；freeze；cement：伤口已经～了痂。A scab has formed over the wound.【名】knot：打个～ tie a knot 活～ slipknot

另见 jiē

结案　jié = àn　finalize or finish with a case

结伴　jié = bàn　（～儿）be a companion；go together：～走 go together

结冰　jié = bīng　freeze

结成　jié // chéng　come together and form：～兄弟般的友谊 strike up friendship ～夫妻 become husband and wife ～一帮 form a clique

结构　jiégòu　【名】composition；structure：经济～ economic structure 原子～ atomic structure ～严密（of organization，piece of writing etc.）a tightly-knit structure 钢筋混凝土～ a reinforced concrete structure

结果　jiéguǒ　【名】result：对谈判的～双方都非常满意。Both sides are extremely satisfied with the results of the talk.【连】as a result；in the end：经过热烈的讨论，～大家的意见一致了。After a heated debate, they reached an agreement. 他本来答应给我们杂志写两篇文章，～只写了一篇。He had promised to write two articles for our magazine, but in the end, he only wrote one.

结合　jiéhé　【动】combine；integrate：提高与普及相～ combine raising the level of sth. with popularizing it

结核　jiéhé　【名】tuberculosis；T.B.

结婚　jié = hūn　get married

结交　jiéjiāo　【动】make friends with

结晶　jiéjīng　【名】❶ crystal ❷ valuable results：劳动的～ the valuable fruits of labour 群众智慧的～ the distillation of the wisdom of the masses【动】crystalize

结局　jiéjú　【名】end；result；out-come

结论　jiélùn　【名】conclusion

结盟　jié＝méng　form an alliance

结社　jiéshè　【动】form a society or association

结识　jiéshí　【动】become acquainted with

结束　jiéshù　【动】finish；terminate；end；～了参观访问 wind up a visit 大学生活就要～了。His life as a university student will end soon.

结束语　jiéshùyǔ　【名】concluding remarks

结算　jiésuàn　【动】balance accounts

结尾　jiéwěi　【名】ending；winding-up of sth.

结业　jié＝yè　finish school

结余　jiéyú　【名】surplus

结扎　jiézā　【动】（med.）ligature

结账　jié＝zhàng　settle one's accounts

捷　jié ◇【形】fast；speedy【动】win victory

捷报　jiébào　【名】news of victory

捷径　jiéjìng　【名】shortcut

捷足先登　jié zú xiān dēng　the race goes to the quick

睫　jié

睫毛　jiémáo　【名】eyelash

截　jié　【动】❶ cut；sever：把绳子～成两段 cut the string in two ❷ intercept；stop：这儿水流得太急，～不住。The current runs too fast here and we can't dam the flow.【量】（～儿）portion；part：半～粉笔 half a piece of chalk 一～木头 a section of a log

截断　jié//duàn　cut off；block：～火源 isolate the fire at its source 把钢筋～ cut the steel bars

截获　jiéhuò　【动】intercept and capture

截击　jiéjī　【动】intercept

截面　jiémiàn　【名】cross-section

截然　jiérán　【副】abruptly；entirely：～相反 diametrically opposite 这两个问题不能～分开。No hard and fast line can be drawn these two problems.

截瘫　jiétān　【动】paraplegia

截肢　jié＝zhī　amputate

截止　jiézhǐ　【动】close；end：考生报名到八月十日～。The registration of examinees for the entrance examination will end on August 10th.

截至　jiézhì　【介】up to (e. g. a certain time)；by：～昨天已有三百多名留学生报名参加旅行。By yesterday, more than 300 foreign students had put down their names for the trip.

竭　jié　【动】exhaust

竭力　jiélì　【副】do one's utmost；do one's best

jiě

姐　jiě　【名】elder sister

姐夫　jiěfu　【名】brother-in-law (husband of one's elder sister)

姐姐　jiějie　【名】elder sister

姐妹　jiěmèi　【名】sisters

解　jiě　【动】❶ ◇ separate；divide：难分难～ difficult to separate from each other ❷ untie：～扣儿 untie a knot ～绳子 untie a string (on the package) ～背包 undo a knapsack ❸ relieve sb. of sth.；counteract：～毒 counteract the effects of poison ～恨 find an outlet for one's hatred ～职 relieve (sb.) of his post ❹ explain：～字 explain the meaning of a Chinese character ～词 explain the meaning of a word ❺ ◇ understand；com-

prehend：百思不～ still fail to understand after thinking hard 【名】(maths.) solution

解除 jiěchú 【动】relieve（pain, worries）；remove（doubts, obligations, etc.）；deprive of（weapons）

解答 jiědá 【动】answer

解冻 jiě＝dòng ❶（of ice）thaw ❷（of frozen assets）thaw

解饿 jiě＝è satisfy hunger

解乏 jiě＝fá alleviate fatigue

解放 jiěfàng 【动】liberate；emancipate；～思想 emancipate one's thinking；emancipate ideologically 【名】liberation；emancipation；民族的～ the liberation of a nation 妇女的～ the emancipation of women

解放军 jiěfàngjūn 【名】army of liberation

解放区 jiěfàngqū 【名】liberated area

解放战争 jiěfàng zhànzhēng war of liberation

解雇 jiěgù 【动】dismiss；fire

解禁 jiě＝jìn lift a ban

解救 jiějiù 【动】rescue；save

解决 jiějué 【动】❶ settle；solve；～纠纷 settle a dispute 这个问题我去～，I will solve this problem. ❷ wipe out；finish；把这股敌人全部～ wipe out the enemy completely

解渴 jiě＝kě slake one's thirst；quench one's thirst

解闷 jiě＝mèn kill time；seek distraction

解难 jiě＝nán remove doubt；释疑～ clear up doubts and remove problems

解难 jiě＝nàn relieve from difficulty；排忧～ help sb. out of worries and problems

解聘 jiě＝pìn dismiss；fire

解剖 jiěpōu 【动】dissect；analyse

解剖学 jiěpōuxué 【名】anatomy

解劝 jiěquàn 【动】soothe；mollify

解散 jiěsàn 【动】❶ scatter；break up；disperse：队伍～了。The troops have been dispersed. ❷ dissolve；dismiss；disband：～议会 dissolve a parliament 这个临时小组等任务完成后就～。This temporary group will disband as soon as it has finished its task.

解释 jiěshì 【动】explain；expound 【名】explanation

解说 jiěshuō 【动】explain

解体 jiětǐ 【动】disintegrate；fall into pieces

解脱 jiětuō 【动】free from；extricate from：～危机 extricate sb. from a critical situation 无法～ unable to extricate oneself

解围 jiě＝wéi ❶ raise a siege ❷ save sb. from embarrassment；help sb. out of a tight spot

解析几何 jiěxī jǐhé analitical geometry

解严 jiě＝yán lift a curfew

jiè

介 jiè

介词 jiècí 【名】preposition

介入 jièrù 【动】take sides in；intervene；involve oneself in：你们双方之间的这种争论我不～。I won't have anything to do with the argument between you two.

介绍 jièshào 【动】❶ introduce；make（persons）known to one another：我给你～一下，这位是唐先生。Let me introduce you to Mr. Tang. ❷ acquaint（sb.）with（e.g. a situation, circumstances）：～情况 describe the situation ～经验 pass on one's experience 给大家～故事的梗概 give a general idea of the story ❸ bring in for the first time：把进化论～到中国来 introduce the theory of evolution into China 【名】introduction

介意　jièyì　【动】care；mind；take sth. seriously（*usu. in the neg.*）：对于这件事，我并不～。I really don't take this matter very seriously. 他提意见比较直率，要是有不恰当的地方，你可别～呀! He is very honest in stating his opinions. If there is anything inappropriate, please don't take it to heart.

戒　jiè　【动】◇ ❶ guard against；be on the alert against：力～骄傲 be on guard against self-conceit ❷ get rid of（e.g. bad habits）；put a stop to（酒 give up drinking ～烟 stop smoking

戒备　jièbèi　【动】guard against；be on the alert against

戒骄戒躁　jiè jiāo jiè zào　be on guard against arrogance and impetuosity

戒心　jièxīn　【名】alertness；vigilance

戒严　jiè＝yán　proclaim martial law

戒指　jièzhi　【名】ring（jewellery）

届　jiè　【量】*similar to* 次 cì，a session of a conference；year of graduation：第二十九～联合国大会 the 29th session of the General Assembly of the United Nations 第五～全国人民代表大会代表 a deputy of the Fifth Session of the National People's Congress 上～毕业生 last year's graduate

届时　jièshí　【副】〈书〉when the time comes

界　jiè　【名】❶ boundary：划～ draw a boundary line 这两个省以黄河为～。The Huanghe River forms the boundary between these two provinces. ❷ limits；confines：发球出～ an out-of-bounds serve ❸ circle：科教～ scientific and educational circles 体育～ sports circles 全国各～（people from）all walks of life throughout the country ❹ one of the divisions of the natural world：无机～ inorganic world 有机～ organic world 动物～ animal kingdom 植物～ plant kingdom

界碑　jièbēi　【名】boundary tablet

界河　jièhé　【名】〔条 tiáo〕boundary river

界石　jièshí　【名】boundary stone

界限　jièxiàn　【名】demarcation line：划清～ draw a distinction 动物和植物的～ the distinction between animal and plant

界线　jièxiàn　【名】❶ boundary line ❷ demarcation line

界桩　jièzhuāng　【名】boundary post

借　jiè　【动】❶ borrow；lend：我从图书馆～（来）了一本画报。I borrowed an illustrated magazine from the library. 他从我这儿～（去）几本语言学资料。He borrowed some linguistic materials from me. 我的词典～给他了。I lent him my dictionary. 老方，把自行车～（给）我骑两天。Lao Fang, will you please lend me your bicycle for a couple of days? ❷（藉）use...as a means；make use of：外国留学生～看电影的机会，练习听中国话。Foreign students use Chinese films as a means of practising aural comprehension.

借贷　jièdài　【动】borrow money

借刀杀人　jiè dāo shā rén　kill or do harm to sb. through the agency of another

借古讽今　jiè gǔ fěng jīn　use the past to disparage the present

借故　jiègù　【副】use sth. as an excuse；on the pretext of

借光　jiè＝guāng　*polite way of asking sb. to make room for one*

借鉴　jièjiàn　【动】benefit by another person's experience, that is, imitate his good points and avoid his mistakes 【名】an experience, mod-

el, from which one can benefit

借据　jièjù　【名】receipt for a loan (IOU)

借口　jièkǒu　【动】use sth. as an excuse or pretext *often followed by a S-P or V-O construction*：～没时间而放松学习是不对的。Lack of time is no excuse for being slack in your studies. 不能～提高速度而忽视质量。Increased speed is no excuse for neglecting quality. 【名】excuse：不能把条件的变化当作自己犯错误的～。We must not use a change in conditions as an excuse for our own mistakes.

借款　jièkuǎn　【名】loan

借款　jiè = kuǎn　borrow or lend money

借题发挥　jiè tí fāhuī　seize on a topic as an opportunity to express one's own views

借条　jiètiáo　【名】〔张 zhāng〕receipt；IOU

借以　jièyǐ　【动】by means of；for the purpose of；so as to：宣传他们的成绩，～教育青年一代 publicize their achievements so as to educate the young

借用　jièyòng　【动】❶ borrow ❷ use sth. for another purpose

借债　jiè = zhài　borrow money

借助　jièzhù　【动】with the help of

jīn

斤　jīn　【量】catty；*Chinese unit of weight* (= 1/2Kg.)

斤斤计较　jīnjīn jìjiào　square accounts to the smallest detail (where the matter is trivial)：对于个人利益，不应～。Don't be petty where one's own interests are concerned.

今　jīn　【名】◇ ❶ present-day；modern (*as opp*. to 古) ❷ the present：～冬明春 this winter and next spring ❸ today：～晚 this evening

今后　jīnhòu　【名】from now on；future

今年　jīnnián　【名】this year

今天　jīntiān　【名】❶ today ❷ the present time or period：～的中国已经不是 30 年前的中国了。China today is not the same country it was 30 years ago.

今昔　jīnxī　【名】the present and the past

今朝　jīnzhāo　【名】〈书〉today；at present

金　jīn　【名】❶ gold ❷ ◇ money：抚恤～ compensation 拾～不昧 refuse to keep the money one finds ❸ ◇ an ancient percussion instrument made of metal：鸣 ～ 击鼓 clang the cymbals and beat the drums ～鼓齐鸣 beat the gongs and drums

金笔　jīnbǐ　【名】〔枝 zhī〕fountain pen with a gold nib

金碧辉煌　jīn bì huīhuáng　magnificent；splendid

金额　jīn'é　【名】amount of money

金刚石　jīngāngshí　【名】diamond (jewel)

金黄　jīnhuáng　【形】golden yellow

金奖　jīnjiǎng　【名】gold medal award

金科玉律　jīn kē yù lǜ　inalterable law

金牌　jīnpái　【名】gold medal：获得两块～ win two gold medals

金钱　jīnqián　【名】money

金融　jīnróng　【名】finance

金色　jīnsè　【名】gold colour

金属　jīnshǔ　【名】metal

金文　jīnwén　【名】inscriptions on ancient bronze vessels

金星　jīnxīng　【名】❶ Venus (the planet) ❷ spots which appear be-

fore one's eyes when one is dizzy：眼睛直冒～。Stars dance before my eyes.

金鱼 jīnyú 【名】〔条 tiáo〕goldfish

金字塔 jīnzìtǎ 【名】pyramid

金子 jīnzi 【名】gold

津 jīn

津津有味 jīnjīn yǒu wèi　with zest or relish；with enormous gusto

津贴 jīntiē 【名】allowance；subsidy 【动】subsidize：每月～他一些钱 give him a monthly allowance

矜 jīn

矜持 jīnchí 【形】reserved；restrained

筋 jīn 【名】❶ sinew ❷ vein

筋斗 jīndǒu 【名】同"跟头"gēntou

筋骨 jīngǔ 【名】muscles and bones；physique

禁 jīn 【动】be able to withstand or endure：～冻 endure cold ～磨 capable of withstanding wear and tear ～穿（of clothes）durable
另见 jìn

禁不起 jīn bu qǐ 同"禁不住❶"：有的文学作品初看还可以，但～时间的考验。Some works of literature are all right on first reading but cannot stand the test of time.

禁不住 jīn bu zhù ❶ cannot withstand：这座小木桥～大卡车。This little wooden bridge cannot bear the weight of a lorry. 不在大风大浪中锻炼，就～风吹浪打。If one is not tempered in storms, one cannot withstand a tempest. ❷ cannot help (doing sth.)：听了他的话，大家都～笑了起来。Hearing what he said, we couldn't help laughing. 看到这种激动人心的场面，我～流下了热泪。Looking at such a soul-stirring scene, I couldn't hold back my

tears.

禁得起 jīn de qǐ 同"禁得住"：好文章～推敲。Good writing can be subjected to any amount of critical analysis.

禁得住 jīn de zhù　can bear；can stand：这么重的东西，这根绳子～吗？Do you think this rope can stand the strain of such a heavy load? 青年要～艰苦环境的考验。Young people ought to be able to stand the test of hardship.

禁受 jīnshòu 【动】undergo；go through

襟 jīn 【名】front part of a Chinese jacket or gown

襟怀坦白 jīnhuái tǎnbái　open and frank

jǐn

仅（僅） jǐn 【副】only；merely；同"只"zhǐ（usu. in written language）：～供参考 for reference only 他们俩～说了几句话就分手了。The two of them separated after having spoken only a few words.

仅仅 jǐnjǐn 【副】only

尽（儘） jǐn 【动】❶ be at the furthest end of：村子的～西头，有一棵老槐树。There is an ancient locust tree at the west end of the village. ❷ be within a certain limit *often used with* 着：这件事～着在两天内解决。This matter must be solved within two days. ❸ give priority to a certain person or thing *often used with* 着：车上的座位先～着老人坐。Elderly people should be given priority as far as seats on buses are concerned.
另见 jìn

尽管 jǐnguǎn 【副】*used to urge sb. to do sth. boldly*：有什么困难你～

说，我们一定帮助你解决。Do tell us any difficulties you might have and we'll certainly help solve them. 【连】同"虽然" suīrán, *but more emphatic*：～他们的说法不同，但基本意思是一致的。They mean the same thing, though they put it in different words. 雨～很大，他们还是出发了。They set out despite the pouring rain.

尽快 jǐnkuài 【副】as quickly as possible：～作好准备 get prepared as quickly as possible ～改变山区面貌 change the face of the mountainous area as quickly as possible

尽量 jǐnliàng 【副】to the greatest extent：～帮忙 do one's best to help ～抽出时间 try (our) best to find time (to do sth.)

尽先 jǐnxiān 【副】give priority to：这批缝纫机～供应农村。The countryside will be given priority where this batch of sewing machines is concerned. 这次参观的票不多，要～照顾新来的同事。There are not many tickets for this visit, so the newly arrived colleagues will be given priority.

尽早 jǐnzǎo 【副】as early as possible；as soon as possible：～回信 write back as soon as possible

紧（緊）jǐn 【形】❶ tight；taut：～～握住他的手 hold his hand tight 一定要把绳子系～。The rope must be tied tight. 这个盒盖儿～不～? Is the lid of the box tight? ❷ close；with little space in between：这双鞋我穿太～。This pair of shoes is too tight for me. 星期三这天的课程安排得很～。Wednesday is tightly scheduled with classes the whole day. 枪声～。The firing is very heavy. 我们两家～挨着。Our two families are next door neighbours. 会后，～接着放映电影。A film was

shown immediately after the meeting. ❸ urgent；tense：任务很～。The task is urgent. 父母管得不～。His parents are not strict (with him). ❹ short of money；hard up：手头儿有点儿～。I am a little short of money. 【动】tighten：～一～弦 tighten the (violin) string a bit 螺丝都～了吗? Have all the screws been tightened?

紧凑 jǐncòu 【形】(of language, structure) concise；tightly knit

紧急 jǐnjí 【形】urgent；pressing：～命令 an urgent order ～刹车 apply the emergency brake 采取～措施 take emergency measures 情况～ critical situation

紧急状态 jǐnjí zhuàngtài state of emergency

紧密 jǐnmì 【形】❶ close；intimate：～联系 close contact ～合作 close cooperation ❷ coming closely one after the other：～的鞭炮声 quick, successive bangs of firecrackers

紧迫 jǐnpò 【形】urgent；pressing

紧俏 jǐnqiào 【形】popular but in short supply：～商品 goods in great demand but in short supply

紧缺 jǐnquē 【形】in short supply；badly needed

紧缩 jǐnsuō 【动】decrease in quantity；cut (expenses)；retrench；tighten (encirclement)

紧要 jǐnyào 【形】important；critical

紧张 jǐnzhāng 【形】❶ nervous：他发言的时候有点儿～。He was a bit nervous when he spoke at the meeting. 考试的时候千万别～。When sitting for an examination, one mustn't get nervous. ❷ tense；strained；intense：～而愉快的劳动 intense but pleasant work 象棋比赛进入～阶段。The chess match has entered a tense phase. 故事情节～。The plot of the story is full of tension. 他们俩的关系有点儿～。Their

relationship is a bit tense. ❸ insufficient; inadequate: 人力~ inadequate manpower 供应~ inadequate supply (of foods)

锦(錦) jǐn 【名】brocade

锦标 jǐnbiāo 【名】championship

锦标赛 jǐnbiāosài 【名】championship match

锦缎 jǐnduàn 【名】brocade

锦纶 jǐnlún 【名】polyamide fibre

锦旗 jǐnqí 【名】〔面 miàn〕embroidered flag

锦上添花 jǐn shàng tiān huā add more flowers to the brocade; embellish what is already beautiful

锦绣 jǐnxiù 【名】(fig.) as beautiful as embroidered silk

锦绣山河 jǐnxiù shānhé beautiful land

谨(謹) jǐn

谨慎 jǐnshèn 【形】careful; cautious

谨小慎微 jǐn xiǎo shèn wēi over-cautious

谨严 jǐnyán 【形】careful; cautious: 文章结构~。The writing is compact and tightly organized.

jìn

尽(盡) jìn 【动】❶ exhaust: 想~办法 exhaust every possible means 用~力气 exhaust one's strength 数不~的星星 countless stars ❷ exert oneself to do: ~到做父母的责任 do all one can as a parent 为国~忠 do all one can do to serve one's country ❸ use to the fullest extent: ~一切可能抢救 try every possible means of rescue 人~其才,物~其用。Give everyone's abilities full play and use everything properly.

另见 jǐn

尽力 jìn = lì to the best of one's ability; do one's utmost: 你有什么困难,我们一定~帮助你。We will certainly help you to the best of our ability. 我们要~把工作做好。We will try our best to do our work well.

尽情 jìnqíng 【副】to one's heart's content

尽人皆知 jìn rén jiē zhī known to all

尽善尽美 jìn shàn jìn měi perfect

尽心 jìn=xīn with all one's heart

尽兴 jìnxìng 【动】be fully satisfied; (enjoy oneself) heartily

尽职 jìn = zhí faithfully carry out one's duties

进(進) jìn 【动】❶ enter (as opp. to 出): 她一~门,就忙起来了。As soon as she entered the house, she was immediately busy. 请~屋来坐。Please come in and take a seat. Note: 进 is used after a verb as a complement to indicate entering from outside: 他急急忙忙跑~屋子拿了一本书,又出去了。He ran into the room, snatched up a book and went out again. 那笔款子已经存~银行了。That sum of money has been deposited in the bank. (same as 进来 or 进去 as a complement, except that it does not indicate direction, but an object is necessary) ❷ move forward (as opp. to 退): 秧歌舞步一般是~两步,退一步。The steps of the Yangge Dance are two steps forward and one step back.

进步 jìnbù 【形】progressive: ~力量 progressive forces ~人士 progressive personages 思想~ progressive thinking 【动】progress; improve; advance: 世界在~。The world is advancing. 【名】progress; advance: 你的~很快,我很高兴。I'm glad that you are making such pro-

gress.

进程　jìnchéng　【名】development；progress；course

进度　jìndù　【名】rate of progress

进而　jìn'ér　【连】*indicates that a further step is taken or a further result gained as a result of a previously mentioned condition*：大家深入进行了调查研究，～做出了正确的判断。They made an in-depth study of the case and then gave a correct judgement. 把历史背景弄清楚以后，就能～理解这篇文章的深层含义。If you know the historical background, you will have a better idea of the underlying implications of this paper.

进犯　jìnfàn　【动】invade

进攻　jìngōng　【动】attack；assault；offensive

进化　jìnhuà　【动】evolve；evolution

进化论　jìnhuàlùn　【名】theory of evolution

进货　jìn = huò　lay in a stock of goods

进军　jìnjūn　【动】march on；advance；push on (to an area)

进口　jìnkǒu　【动】import

进来　jìn // lái　enter from outside (*towards the speaker*)：我看见～一个陌生人。I saw a stranger come in. 进来吧，外边太晒。Please come in. The sun is scorching hot outside. Note：进来 *is used after a verb as a complement to indicate a movement from outside (towards the speaker)*：他急急忙忙地从外面跑～。He rushed in from outside. 你把晒的衣服收～。Please gather up the washing and bring it in. (*same as 进 as a complement, but the use of an object is optional*)

进取　jìnqǔ　【动】strive for self-improvement

进去　jìn // qù　enter from outside (*not towards the speaker*)：你先～吧，我在外面等他。Please go in first. I'll wait for him outside. 要下雨了，咱们都进屋去吧！It's going to rain. Let's go in. Note：进去 *is used after a verb as a complement to indicate a movement from outside (not towards the speaker)*：咱们把这张桌子搬～吧！Let's move the table inside. 他跑进教室去了。He ran into the classroom. 你给我照相的时候，把这棵松树也照～。When you take my photo, please see that you include this pine tree as well. 他的总结发言把大家的意见都包括～了。His summing-up included everybody's opinions. (*same as 进 as a complement, but the use of an object is optional*)

进入　jìnrù　【动】make way into；enter

进退两难　jìn tuì liǎng nán　be in a dilemma

进退维谷　jìn tuì wéi gǔ　同"进退两难"

进行　jìnxíng　【动】❶ be engaged in (some formal or serious action which lasts for some time) *usu. followed by a dissyllabic word or a phrase*：～讨论 hold discussions ～耐心的说服 carry out patient persuasion ❷ be in progress；last：大会正在～。The meeting is in progress. 羽毛球表演～了两个小时。The badminton match lasted for two hours.

进行曲　jìnxíngqǔ　【名】march (music)

进修　jìnxiū　【动】take an advanced course

进一步　jìnyíbù　【形】further：～实现农业机械化 take further steps in the mechanization of agriculture 事业有了～发展。Further progress has been made in his career.

进展　jìnzhǎn　【动】advance；progress；make headway：～神速 make rapid progress ～缓慢 progress

slowly 工作~得很快。The work is making headway.

进驻 jìnzhù 【动】(of troops) march to (a place) and be stationed there

近 jìn 【形】❶ near; close (*as opp. to* 远):~路 short cut ~几天 the last few days ~百年 the last hundred years 现在离暑假很~了。Now the summer vacation is drawing near. ❷ intimate; close ❸ nearly (*often followed by a numeral*):~五百万人口 a population of nearly 5 million

近代 jìndài 【名】❶ the term used by most historians to designate the period of capitalism ❷ in Chinese history, between 1840 (the Opium War) and 1919 (the May Fourth Movement) ❸ modern times

近郊 jìnjiāo 【名】suburbs; outskirts

近况 jìnkuàng 【名】current situation; present condition:朋友来信询问我~如何。My friend wrote asking after my present situation.

近来 jìnlái 【名】recently; of late:~我们工作很顺利。Our work has recently been going smoothly.

近邻 jìnlín 【名】near neighbour

近亲 jìnqīn 【名】close relative

近日 jìnrì 【名】in recent days; recently

近视 jìnshì 【名】myopia 【形】near-sighted

近水楼台先得月 jìn shuǐ lóu tái xiān dé yuè a waterfront pavilion gets the moonlight first; (*fig.*) a person in a favourable position has the advantage

近似 jìnsì 【动】be similar; approximate

近似值 jìnsìzhí 【名】(maths.) approximate value

近义词 jìnyìcí 【名】words whose meaning is similar; synonyms

近因 jìnyīn 【名】immediate cause

劲(勁) jìn 【名】❶ strength; energy:手~(儿) strength of (one's) hand ❷ (~儿) spirit; vigour; drive:冲 (chōng)~(full of) vigour 鼓~ boost sb.'s morale ❸ interest; gusto:干得挺有~(儿)的 do sth. with great gusto 看这个戏没~。This play's not interesting at all. ❹ ◇ (~儿) manner; airs:看他那神气~! Just look at his self-important airs!
另见 jìng

劲头 jìntóu 【名】(~儿) ❶ strength:他~真大。How strong he is! ❷ zeal; vigour; drive:提起建排灌站来,农民们~十足。The peasants talk animatedly about the building of drainage and irrigation stations.

晋 jìn

晋升 jìnshēng 【动】promote (to a higher office)

浸 jìn 【动】soak; immerse:把麦种放在水里~一~ soak the wheat seeds in water 汗水~湿了衣裳。His clothes are soaked through with sweat.

浸泡 jìnpào 【动】soak; immerse

浸透 jìntòu 【动】be saturated

浸种 jìn=zhǒng soak seeds

禁 jìn 【动】prohibit; forbid; ban:~酒。Drinking is prohibited. ~(鸦片)烟。Opium is banned.
另见 jīn

禁闭 jìnbì 【名】detain; hold in detention

禁锢 jìngù 【动】〈书〉❶ ban; prohibit; debar (the feudal ruling clique prohibited those who held opposing views from taking part in political activity) ❷ put in jail; imprison ❸ seal up

禁忌 jìnjì 【动】❶ taboo ❷ (of

med.) be forbidden to eat (certain foods)

禁绝　jìnjué　【动】absolutely prohibit

禁令　jìnlìng　【名】prohibition；ban

禁区　jìnqū　【名】❶ preserve；a protected area for animals，birds，etc. ❷ out-of-bounds area

禁书　jìnshū　【名】banned book

禁运　jìnyùn　【动】embargo

禁止　jìnzhǐ　【动】forbid；prohibit；ban

jīng

茎（莖）　jīng　【名】stem；stalk

京　jīng　【名】◇ ❶ capital (of a country)；metropolis ❷ short for 北京

京剧　jīngjù　【名】Beijing (Peking) opera 也作"京戏"。

经（經）　jīng　【名】❶ (of textile) warp (as opp. to 纬)：～纱 warp ～线 warp threads ❷ longitude：东～四十度 40 degrees E longitude ❸ canon；scripture；classics：《诗～》the Book of Odes 佛～ Buddhist scriptures 念～ read scriptures【动】❶ go or pass through；experience：这件事没～我的手，我不知道。This matter didn't pass through my hands so I know nothing about it. ～他一说，我才明白。After his explanation I begin to understand it. ❷ ◇ manage；run：～商 do business；be in trade

经办　jīngbàn　【动】handle；deal with

经不起　jīng bu qǐ　同"禁不起"jīn bu qǐ

经常　jīngcháng　【形】constant；frequent (indicates that sth. is regularly repeated)：爱国卫生运动是一项～的工作。The public health cam-paign is a matter of routine. 他晚上 12 点回家是～的。It is not uncommon for him to get back home at midnight. 他会吸烟，但不～吸。He smokes，but not regularly.

经得起　jīng de qǐ　同"禁得起"jīn de qǐ

经典　jīngdiǎn　【名】classics；classical

经度　jīngdù　【名】longitude

经费　jīngfèi　【名】〔笔 b①〕(of an institution) funds allocated for operating expenses

经风雨，见世面　jīng fēngyǔ，jiàn shìmiàn　face the world and brave the storm

经管　jīngguǎn　【动】manage；be in charge of

经过　jīngguò　【动】pass through：从北京到广州要～武汉。Going from Beijing to Guangzhou，you have to pass through Wuhan. 机器～检修好用多了。The machine works much better since it was overhauled.【名】process；things that have happened：我把这件事的～简单地介绍一下。Let me tell you briefly what has happened.

经纪人　jīngjìrén　【名】broker；agent

经济　jīngjì　【名】❶ economics ❷ economy：工业～ industrial economy 农业～ agricultural economy ❸ financial circumstance：他们家的～比较宽裕。Their family is well off.【形】economical；thrifty：食堂的饭菜～可口。The food in the dining hall is tasty and inexpensive.

经济核算　jīngjì hésuàn　economic accounting

经济基础　jīngjì jīchǔ　economic base

经济特区　jīngjì tèqū　a special economic zone

经济危机　jīngjì wēijī　economic crisis

经济学　jīngjìxué　【名】economics

经济制裁　jīngjì zhìcái　economic sanctions

经济作物　jīngjì zuòwù　industrial

crop；cash crop；agricultrual crop used as raw material for industry

经久不息 jīngjiǔ bù xī prolonged (applause，ovation，etc.)

经理 jīnglǐ 【名】manager 【动】manage；run

经历 jīnglì 【动】experience；undergo；go through：他～过解放战争。He took part in the Liberation War. 【名】career；one's progress through life：生活～ the experiences of one's life 复杂的～ a varied career

经商 jīng = shāng engage in trade；be in business

经手 jīng = shǒu transact business；arrange a matter

经受 jīngshòu 【动】sustain；undergo；suffer；go through：～锻炼 be steeled and tempered ～考验 undergo a test

经销 jīngxiāo 【动】sell on commission

经心 jīngxīn 【形】careful；with care

经验 jīngyàn 【名】experience

经验主义 jīngyànzhǔyì 【名】empiricism

经营 jīngyíng 【动】（of business，etc.）manage；run；be in charge of：～商业 be in trade 合理～ carry out rational management

荆 jīng

荆棘 jīngjí 【名】brambles

惊（驚）jīng 【动】❶ be frightened；be startled：忽然飞来一只马蜂，他一～，手里的书也掉了。Suddenly a wasp landed on him. He was startled and let the book fall from his hand. 这段山路真是危险，坐在车上一直担～受怕。The last part of the mountain road was really dangerous, my heart was in my throat all the way. ❷ startle：有人放了一枪，～起一大群野鸭子。Somebody fired a gun and startled a flock of wild ducks. ❸（of horses，mules，etc.）shy：马～了。The horse shied.

惊动 jīngdòng 【动】a polite way of saying disturb：这一点小事，就别～大家了。This is only a minor matter, and we mustn't let it inconvenience a lot of people.

惊弓之鸟 jīng gōng zhī niǎo the mere twang of the bowstring frightens the bird；a person who had a fright before，trembles at the slightest sound：他做了坏事，心里害怕，犹如～。After his evil deed, he was as nervous as a frightened bird.

惊慌 jīnghuāng 【形】alarmed；startled

惊慌失措 jīnghuāng shīcuò be in such a panic that one is helpless

惊恐 jīngkǒng 【形】scared；frightened

惊恐万状 jīngkǒng wànzhuàng panic-stricken

惊奇 jīngqí 【形】surprised；astonished

惊扰 jīngrǎo 【动】scare；alarm；frighten

惊人 jīngrén 【形】astonishing；surprising

惊叹 jīngtàn 【动】make a laudatory exclamation

惊叹号 jīngtànhào 【名】exclamation mark

惊涛骇浪 jīng tāo hài làng tempestuous storm；fierce and frightening storm

惊天动地 jīng tiān dòng dì earth-shaking

惊喜 jīngxǐ 【形】surprised and delighted

惊吓 jīngxià 【动】frighten；alarm；scare：受了～ be frightened；be scared

惊险 jīngxiǎn 【形】thrilling

惊心动魄　jīng xīn dòng pò　soul-stirring；profoundly affecting

惊醒　jīngxǐng　【动】be startled out of a sound sleep

惊讶　jīngyà　【形】surprised；alarmed

惊疑　jīngyí　【动】surprised and bewildered

惊异　jīngyì　【形】astonished

旌　jīng

旌旗　jīngqí　【名】〈书〉banners；flags

晶　jīng

晶体　jīngtǐ　【名】crystal

晶体管　jīngtǐguǎn　【名】transistor

晶莹　jīngyíng　【形】crystalline；crystal clear

兢　jīng

兢兢业业　jīngjīngyèyè　【形】in a conscientious and down-to-earth manner

精　jīng　【形】❶ refined；fine；careful：～选 carefully select ～盐 fine salt ❷ choice；fine：兵要～，武器要好。An army must be made up of picked men and good weapons. ❸ smart；bright；sharp：这小伙子真～。That young man is really bright.

精兵简政　jīng bīng jiǎn zhèng　fewer and better troops and simplified administration

精彩　jīngcǎi　【形】excellent (e.g. performance)

精粹　jīngcuì　【形】concise；pithy

精打细算　jīng dǎ xì suàn　calculate very carefully (in order to economize)

精雕细刻　jīng diāo xì kè　work with meticulous care (on a work of art or piece of writing)

精读　jīngdú　【动】do intensive reading

精干　jīnggàn　【形】同"精明强干"

精耕细作　jīng gēng xì zuò　intensive cultivation；intensive and meticulous working of the fields

精悍　jīnghàn　【形】❶ (of person) capable and smart ❷ (of writing style) terse and vigorous：文笔～ vigorous writing style

精华　jīnghuá　【名】essence；quintessence

精简　jīngjiǎn　【动】cut down by eliminating the unnecessary

精简机构　jīngjiǎn jīgòu　slim down the administrative structure

精力　jīnglì　【名】(physical and mental) energy

精练　jīngliàn　【形】terse；succinct

精良　jīngliáng　【形】of very fine quality；meticulously made

精美　jīngměi　【形】exquisite

精密　jīngmì　【形】(of instrument) precise

精密度　jīngmìdù　【名】degree of precision；precision

精明　jīngmíng　【形】smart；bright；quick

精明强干　jīngmíng qiáng gàn　clever and efficient

精疲力竭　jīng pí lì jié　completely exhausted；tired out

精辟　jīngpì　【形】incisive and penetrating

精品　jīngpǐn　【名】quality goods；an exquisite article

精巧　jīngqiǎo　【形】skilful；delicate；fine (workmenship)

精确　jīngquè　【形】accurate；precise

精锐　jīngruì　【形】crack (troops，etc.)

精神　jīngshén　【名】❶ spirit；mental state：大无畏 ～ dauntless spirit ～面貌大改变 a great change in mental outlook ～负担 a spiritual (or mental) burden ❷ vitality；vigour：焕发～ brimming over with vitality 这两天我感冒了，～不太好。I've had

a cold for the last couple of days and feel in rather low spirits. ❸ gist; essence: 讲话～ the essence of the speech 文件的主要～ the gist of the document

精神　jīngshén　【形】spirited; vigorous: 他目光炯炯, 显得很～。His eyes are sparkling and he looks alive.

精神病　jīngshénbìng　【名】mental disease

精神贵族　jīngshén guìzú　intellectual elite

精神面貌　jīngshén miànmào　mental outlook; mental attitude

精神食粮　jīngshén shíliáng　spiritual food; food for thought

精神文明　jīngshén wénmíng　spiritual civilization

精髓　jīngsuǐ　【名】quintessence

精通　jīngtōng　【动】be proficient in; be versed in; master

精细　jīngxì　【形】fine; delicate

精心　jīngxīn　【形】meticulous; elaborate; with special care: ～治疗和护理 treat and look after with special care ～培育 painstakingly cultivate 这是他～之作。This is a piece of work he devoted special care to.

精益求精　jīng yì qiú jīng　constantly perfect one's skill; keep improving

精英　jīngyīng　【名】elite; flower

精湛　jīngzhàn　【形】(of skill, art) approaching perfection; consummate

精制　jīngzhì　【动】manufacture, or create with extra care

精致　jīngzhì　【形】of fine workmanship

精装　jīngzhuāng　【名】de luxe edition; hard-cover edition

鲸(鯨)　jīng　【名】whale

鲸吞　jīngtūn　【动】annex (land)

鲸鱼　jīngyú　【名】whale

jǐng

井　jǐng　【名】〔眼 yǎn、口 kǒu〕well

井底之蛙　jǐng dǐ zhī wā　a frog at the bottom of a well; a person with a very limited outlook

井架　jǐngjià　【名】derrick

井井有条　jǐng jǐng yǒu tiáo　(of work, life, a great variety of things) in perfect order

井然　jǐngrán　【形】well arranged; in good order

井田制　jǐngtiánzhì　【名】the nine-square system of dividing the land in China's ancient slave society

颈(頸)　jǐng

颈项　jǐngxiàng　【名】〈书〉neck

景　jǐng　【名】❶ ◇ view; scenery; scene: 雪～ snowy scene 西湖十～ the 10 scenic spots of the West Lake ❷ a set or shooting location for a play or motion picture: 内～ (motion picture) studio sets 外～ (motion picture) shooting location

景点　jǐngdiǎn　【名】a scenic spot; a place of interest

景观　jǐngguān　【名】landscape

景况　jǐngkuàng　【名】state of affairs; condition

景气　jǐngqì　【形】prosperous; flourishing

景色　jǐngsè　【名】landscape; scenery

景泰蓝　jǐngtàilán　【名】cloisonné (one of the famous handicraft specialities of Beijing)

景物　jǐngwù　【名】scenery and places of interest

景象　jǐngxiàng　【名】prospect; view

景仰　jǐngyǎng　【动】admire; respect

景致　jǐngzhì　【名】scenery

警　jǐng　【名】◇ ❶ alarm ❷ police

警报　jǐngbào　【名】alarm; alert

警察　jǐngchá　【名】police; policeman

警笛　jǐngdí　【名】siren

警告　jǐnggào　【动】caution; warn 【名】caution; warning

警戒　jǐngjiè　【动】be on guard against; keep a watchful eye on; 担任 ~ be on sentry duty 部队在国境线上严密 ~。The troops keep a close watch on the boundary line.

警句　jǐngjù　【名】epigram; aphorism

警觉　jǐngjué　【名】alertness

警犬　jǐngquǎn　【名】police dog

警惕　jǐngtì　【动】maintain vigilance against; be on the look out for; ~ 有人从中破坏 watch out for possible sabotage from within 【名】vigilance; 提高 ~，保卫祖国 heighten our vigilance and defend our country

警卫　jǐngwèi　【动】post guards around 【名】guard

警钟　jǐngzhōng　【名】alarm bell; alarm

jìng

劲（勁）　jìng
另见 jìn

劲敌　jìngdí　【名】formidable enemy

劲旅　jìnglǚ　【名】crack troops

劲松　jìngsōng　【名】a sturdy pine

径（徑）　jìng

径直　jìngzhí　【副】(go) straight to; directly; 客机 ~ 飞往成都。The plane flew directly to Chengdu. 汽车 ~ 朝城北方向驶去。The car headed directly toward the northern part of the city.

径自　jìngzì　【副】do sth. of one's own accord; do sth. without consulting anyone; 他没等散会，就 ~ 离去。He left without consulting anyone before the meeting was finished.

净（淨）　jìng　【形】❶ clean; ~ 水 clean water 把手洗 ~ wash (one's) hands clean ❷ indicates exhaustiveness; 把地里的麦穗拾 ~ pick up all the ears of wheat in the field 将碗里的饭吃 ~ finish the rice in one's bowl 【副】〈口〉nothing but; 这一带 ~ 是楼房。There is nothing but high buildings in this area. 这几天 ~ 下雨。In the last few days it has done nothing but rain.

净化　jìnghuà　【动】purify

净重　jìngzhòng　【名】net weight

痉（痙）　jìng

痉挛　jìngluán　【动】be seized with a cramp

竞（競）　jìng

竞技　jìngjì　【动】contest; sport; ~ 状态良好 in top form

竞赛　jìngsài　【动】compete; contest; competition

竞选　jìngxuǎn　【动】take part in an election campaign

竞争　jìngzhēng　【动】compete; vie for

竞走　jìngzǒu　【动】heel-and-toe walking race

竟　jìng　【副】同"居然"jūrán; 道理这么简单，他 ~ 不懂。The reasoning is so simple but, believe it or not, he doesn't understand it. 他怎么敢擅自离开工作岗位？How dare he leave work without having applied for leave!

竟然　jìngrán　【副】同"居然"jūrán but rarely used

敬 jìng 【动】◇ ❶ respect；esteem；～请光临。Please honour us with your presence. ❷ offer sth. politely；present sth. with respect：～茶 offer (the guest) a cup of tea ～他一杯酒 propose a toast to him

敬爱 jìng'ài 【动】love and respect；esteem

敬辞 jìngcí 【名】term of respect；polite expression

敬而远之 jìng ér yuǎn zhī stay at a respectful distance from

敬老院 jìnglǎoyuàn 【名】home for the aged

敬礼 jìng＝lǐ salute

敬佩 jìngpèi 【动】admire and respect

敬畏 jìngwèi 【动】hold in awe and veneration

敬献 jìngxiàn 【动】present；offer with respect

敬仰 jìngyǎng 【动】have the highest admiration for

敬业 jìngyè 【形】dedicated to (work, profession, etc.)：～精神 dedication to work；devotion to work

敬意 jìngyì 【名】regards；respects；esteem

敬祝 jìngzhù 【动】wishing (you)

静 jìng 【形】quiet：阅览室里很～。The reading room is very quiet.

静电 jìngdiàn 【名】static electricity

静电感应 jìngdiàn gǎnyìng electrostatic induction

静脉 jìngmài 【名】vein

静默 jìngmò 【动】❶ become silent ❷ mourn in silence

静悄悄 jìngqiāoqiāo 【形】very quiet；silent

静养 jìngyǎng 【动】rest quietly to recuperate

静止 jìngzhǐ 【动】static；stationary；motionless

境 jìng 【名】◇ ❶ border；boundary；frontier：出～ leave a country ❷ area；place：如入无人之～ such fearless behavior as if one's enemies didn't exist

境地 jìngdì 【名】situation；circumstances

境界 jìngjiè 【名】❶ boundary ❷ state extent reached：理想～ ideal state of things 思想～ mental state

境况 jìngkuàng 【名】(a person's) financial situation

境内 jìngnèi 【名】within the boundaries

境遇 jìngyù 【名】(a person's) present circumstances and past life

镜（鏡） jìng 【名】◇ mirror：水平如～。The lake is as calm as a mirror.

镜框 jìngkuàng 【名】picture frame

镜头 jìngtóu 【名】❶ camera lens ❷ (phot.) shot：这张照片～选得好。This is a well framed shot. ❸ (of movie) shot：特写～ a close-up

镜子 jìngzi 【名】〔面 miàn〕looking glass；mirror

jiǒng

迥 jiǒng

迥然 jiǒngrán 【副】utterly (different)

炯 jiǒng

炯炯 jiǒngjiǒng 【形】(of eyes) sparkling

窘 jiǒng 【形】embarrassed；awkward：搞得他很～ put him in an awkward position ～得他手足无措 so embarrassed that he hardly knows what to do

窘况　jiǒngkuàng　【名】dilemma; predicament

窘迫　jiǒngpò　【形】❶ wretched; poor; poverty-stricken：生活 ~ a poor and wretched life ❷ trying; embarrassing：处境 ~ be in a predicament

窘态　jiǒngtài　【名】embarrassed; embarrassment

jiū

纠(糾)　jiū　【动】rectify

纠察　jiūchá　【名】(of strike) picket; (of demonstration) monitor

纠缠　jiūchán　【动】❶ be entangled; ~不清 (of a situation) hard to unravel ❷ nag; pester：别来 ~ 我。Don't keep nagging at me.

纠纷　jiūfēn　【名】dispute

纠葛　jiūgé　【名】quarrel; complication

纠合　jiūhé　【动】muster (derog.)

纠集　jiūjí　【动】gather; muster; gang up (derog.)

纠正　jiūzhèng　【动】correct (a mistake); rectify

究　jiū

究竟　jiūjìng　【名】the whys and wherefores; the ins and outs of sth.：这到底是怎么回事，大家都想知道个 ~。What, after all, is it all about? People want to know the facts. 【副】❶ used in an interrogative sentence to indicate an attempt to get to the bottom of things, must not be used in the answer：这两个词的意思 ~ 有什么不同? But what, after all, is the difference between these two terms? 这工作 ~ 怎么搞，咱们大家先讨论一下。Just how do we start this work? That's what we must discuss first. ❷ used in a declarative sentence to empha-

size the key point：~ 是老师傅有经验，一眼就看出毛病来了。He was, after all, a veteran worker with experience and could see at a glance what was wrong. ~ 是春天了，雪花一落地就化了。It is spring, after all, the snow flakes melt as soon as they touch the ground.

揪　jiū　【动】hold fast and pull; grasp; clutch：~ 住绳子往上爬 climb up by grasping a rope 不小心把扣子 ~ 下来了。He accidently pulled off a button. 人家说错了一句话，不要老 ~ 着不放。Though he said something he shouldn't have, you mustn't keep picking at him.

揪心　jiū＝xīn　be anxious about; be worried about

jiǔ

九　jiǔ　【数】nine

九牛二虎之力　jiǔ niú èr hǔ zhī lì　the strength of two tigers and nine oxen; (fig.) great strength; tremendous effort：我费了 ~，也没能说服他。I made great efforts, but was unable to convince him.

九牛一毛　jiǔ niú yī máo　a hair from nine cows; (fig.) a drop in the ocean

九死一生　jiǔ sǐ yī shēng　nine chances to die and one chance to live; (fig.) a narrow escape; a close shave

九霄云外　jiǔ xiāo yún wài　the farthest limits of the sky; (fling to) the four winds (often used after 到 or 在)：他早把这件事抛到 ~ 了。He has long since forgotten about this matter.

九一八事变　Jiǔ Yī Bā Shìbiàn　the September 18th Incident (1931), in which the Japanese army opened

fire on the city of Shenyang and mounted attacks in the provinces of Jilin and Heilongjiang

九月　jiǔyuè　【名】September

久

jiǔ　【形】for a long time; long: ～别重逢 meet again after a long separation 天长日～ a very long time 我想了很～,也没想起来。I thought for a long time, but could not remember. 你们谈了多～了? How long have you people been talking?

久经　jiǔjīng　【动】have gone through for a long time: ～风霜 weathered; showing the traces of a hard life ～考验 long-tested; steeled

久违　jiǔwéi　【动】be absent for a long time; not to have seen sb. for ages

久仰　jiǔyǎng　【动】long admire; to have long desired to know sb.

久远　jiǔyuǎn　【形】a long time

玖

jiǔ　【数】nine (the complicated form of 九) 见 "捌" bā

酒

jiǔ　【名】alcoholic beverage

酒吧　jiǔbā　【名】bar; pub

酒杯　jiǔbēi　【名】〔个 gè〕wine cup or glass

酒会　jiǔhuì　【名】cocktail party

酒家　jiǔjiā　【名】a wine bar; a pub

酒精　jiǔjīng　【名】alcohol; spirits

酒量　jiǔliàng　【名】one's drinking capacity

酒席　jiǔxí　【名】formal banquet

jiù

旧(舊)

jiù　【形】(as opp. to 新) ❶ old; old-fashioned; outdated: ～社会 old society ～脑筋 old idea; old way of thinking ～习惯

old habit ❷ old; having been in use for a long time: 一件～大衣 an old overcoat 买了几本～书 buy a few second-hand books

旧居　jiùjū　【名】former dwelling place; former residence

旧历　jiùlì　【名】lunar calendar

旧式　jiùshì　【形】of an old type; old-style

旧俗　jiùsú　【名】institutionalized customs

旧账　jiùzhàng　【名】old grievance; old score; grudge

救

jiù　【动】save; rescue; free (sb.) from danger: 把孩子从水里～上来了。The drowning child has been rescued.

救兵　jiùbīng　【名】relief troops

救国　jiù=guó　save the nation

救护　jiùhù　【动】give first aid to

救荒　jiù=huāng　provide famine relief

救火　jiù=huǒ　put out a fire (e.g. a burning building)

救急　jiù=jí　help meet an urgent need

救济　jiùjì　【动】give emergency assistance to

救命　jiù=mìng　save a person's life; life-saving

救生圈　jiùshēngquān　【名】life buoy

救生艇　jiùshēngtǐng　【名】lifeboat

救生衣　jiùshēngyī　【名】〔件 jiàn、套 tào〕life jacket

救世主　jiùshìzhǔ　【名】the Saviour; Christ

救死扶伤　jiù sǐ fú shāng　look after the wounded, save the dying

救亡　jiùwáng　【动】save the nation from subjugation

救星　jiùxīng　【名】liberator; saviour

救援　jiùyuán　【动】rescue; come to sb.'s help

救灾　jiù=zāi　give disaster relief

救助　jiùzhù　【动】rescue; come to

the aid of; save and help

就 jiù 【动】❶ get near to: 避难
~易 shirk the hard and choose the
easy ~着灯看书 get close to the
light so as to be able to read better
❷ eat with staple food or wine: 他
光喝酒，不~什么菜。He is only
drinking and has nothing to go
with his wine. 【介】 *indicates the
scope of one's consideration, analysis or statement, and is often used
in conjunction with* 说,说来 (*or* 来
说),看,看来 (*or* 来看): 大家~怎样发
展副业的问题进行了热烈的讨论。
They animatedly discussed the best
ways of developing side-line occupations. 这本书~内容来说，很值得一
读。This book is worth reading so
far as its content goes. ~他的身体
状况看来，再工作十年八年肯定不成问
题。So far as his health is concerned, he can definitely work another 8 or 10 years. 【副】❶ *preceded by a word or phrase of time,
indicates earliness or that the time
is short*: 从这儿到他家一刻钟~到。
It only takes a quarter of an hour
to get to his house from here. 丁香
花早~开过了。The lilacs bloomed
long ago. 这种杂志很快~卖光了。
These magazines were quickly sold
out. ❷ *indicates short distance*: 幼
儿园~在工厂附近，送孩子很方便。
The kindergarten is just around
the corner from the factory, and
so it's very convenient for parents. ❸ *preceded by a numeral
plus a measure word, indicates
that a small amount is sufficient*:
我要写的信不长，一张纸~够。I
won't write a long letter, a single
sheet of paper is quite enough. 要
做的事不多，两个人~能完成。There
is not much to do, two people are
quite enough to get it over with.

❹ only: 以前这里~产苹果，现在还产
葡萄。They used to only grow apples here, but now they also grow
grapes. 他们~一个女儿。They've
only got a daughter. ❺ all along;
from the start: 屋子本来~不大，人
多更显得小了。This room was never
very spacious and now with so
many people in it, it seems even
smaller. 我~知道他会来看画展的，你
看，他来了吧! I knew he would
come to see this painting exhibition, and look, here he is! ❻ *indicates immediate future, usu. with*
了 *at the end of the sentence*, 就
must be stressed: 老李~回来，你等
一会儿吧! Lao Li will be back
straight away; please wait. 商店~
要关门了，现在去来不及了。The
shops are going to close immediately. It's too late to go now. ❼
*indicates further verification or ex-
planation of sth. mentioned before*: 老张~住在这个楼里。This is
the very building in which Lao
Zhang lives. 他说的那个电影~是这
本小说改编的。The movie he men-
tioned was adapted from this novel. ❽ *indicates obstinacy*, 就
must be stressed: 不合理的事，我们
~得管。We must put our foot
down when things are going too
far. 我~不信说不服他。I simply
don't believe that we can't win
him over. ❾ *inserted in the reduplication of a word or phrase, indicates that one is conceding sth.*:
衣服大点儿~大点儿吧，不必换了。
The jacket may be a bit too loose,
but that's all right. I won't change
it for another. 老林走了~走了吧，
我以后再找他。If Lao Lin is gone,
never mind, I'll look him up later.
❿ *indicates that sth. immediately
follows sth. else*: 坐下~吃 eat
straight away after sitting at the

table 进屋～嚷 start shouting as soon as he stepped into the room Note: *if used in conjunction with* 刚, *the immediacy is intensified*: 我昨天累极了，（刚）躺下～睡着了。Yesterday I was exhausted, and had no sooner thrown myself in bed than I fell asleep. ⓫ *connecting two clauses to indicate that the first clause is the premise of the second*: 要是不努力，～学不好。If one doesn't work hard, one will never learn anything. 你看怎么办好，～怎么办吧。Do whatever you think is best. 只要你在这儿，我心里～踏实了。So long as you are here, I feel reassured. 听说来劳动的人不少，他～赶快去准备工具了。Having heard that a lot of people were coming to work, he went at once to get the tools ready. ⓬ *contrasts two things and indicates that the latter is different from the former*: 这个作家的短篇小说不错，长篇～差一些。This writer's short stories are excellent, but his novels are not so impressive.

就便 jiùbiàn 【副】at sb.'s convenience: 我去寄信的时候，～买了几张明信片。When I went to post a letter, I also picked up a few postcards.

就餐 jiùcān 【动】eat; dine

就地 jiùdì 【副】on the spot; locally

就地取材 jiùdì qǔ cái obtain raw materials locally; use local materials

就读 jiùdú 【动】attend school

就近 jiùjìn 【副】(do sth.) at a nearby place; in the neighbourhood

就势 jiùshì 【副】making use of momentum: 我推了他一把，他～倒地。I gave him a shove, and sent him sprawling to the ground.

就事论事 jiù shì lùn shì deal with the superficial aspects of a matter rather than with its cause; consider sth. as it stands

就是 jiùshì 【连】同"即使"jíshǐ：这块表～修好了，也用不了多久了。Even if I get this watch repaired, it won't last long. 为了保卫祖国，～牺牲生命，也在所不惜。I wouldn't hesitate to die in defence of my country. ～很热的天气，这房间也很凉快。Even on very hot days, this room is very cool.

就是说 jiù shì shuō that is to say; in other words："不经一事，不长一智"，～实践会使人聪明起来。"No down-to-earth work, no gain in your wit", that is to say, practice makes you wise.

就算 jiùsuàn 【连】*used in a conditional clause to indicate that an assumption has been made*：～你有理吧，你也应该注意态度。Let's assume that you are right; still, you might modify your attitude.

就绪 jiùxù 【动】(of preparations) be completed

就业 jiù＝yè be given a job

就义 jiù＝yì lay down one's life for a just cause; die a martyr

就职 jiù＝zhí assume office; take up one's duties

舅 jiù 【名】◇ uncle (mother's brother)

舅舅 jiùjiu 【名】uncle (mother's brother)

舅母 jiùmu 【名】aunt (wife of mother's brother)

jū

拘 jū 【动】◇ restrain; curb; inhibit; limit：无～无束 free and easy; unrestrained 多少不～。Any amount will do.

拘捕 jūbǔ 【动】arrest

拘谨 jūjǐn 【形】prim；stiff

拘留 jūliú 【动】detain；hold in custody

拘泥 jūnì 【形】formal；overscrupulous：过分～ too stiff and formal in one's behavior ～于形式 too formal

拘束 jūshù 【形】restrained；inhibited；ill at ease：她第一次在大家面前讲话，显得有点儿～。She seems a little ill at ease because this is her first time to speak in public. 大家随便坐吧，不要～。Make yourselves at home, please don't stand on ceremony.

居 jū 【动】◇ ❶ occupy；be at：～于首位 occupy first place ❷ style oneself as；claim；appoint：不以功臣自～ not pat oneself on the back for one's contributions ❸ live；reside；dwell：分～两地（man and wife）live in different places 久～农村 live in the countryside for a long time 【名】◇ dwelling；residence：新～ new home

居高临下 jū gāo lín xià take up a commanding position

居功 jūgōng 【动】claim the credit for sth.

居留 jūliú 【动】reside；stay

居留权 jūliúquán 【名】right of residence

居民 jūmín 【名】resident；inhabitant

居民点 jūmíndiǎn 【名】residential area

居民委员会 jūmín wěiyuánhuì residents committee

居然 jūrán 【副】*indicates that sth. which the speaker thought was impossible or should not have happened actually took place*：这么简单的问题他～没回答上来。The question was so simple, and yet he couldn't answer it. 这么一个小厂，这样旧的设备，～生产出这么精密的仪器。It was surprising that such a small factory with such outdated equipment was able to produce such fine precision equipments.

居心 jū = xīn harbour；be bent on；be up to：～险恶 harbour evil intentions ～不良 be up to no good 是何～? What are you up to?

居心叵测 jū xīn pǒcè have an ulterior motive

居住 jūzhù 【动】live；reside；inhabit

鞠 jū

鞠躬 jū = gōng bow

鞠躬尽瘁，死而后已 jū gōng jìn cuì, sǐ ér hòu yǐ bend one's back to the task till one's dying day；spare no effort in the performance of one's duty

jú

局 jú 【名】bureau；department；office：教育～ department of education 卫生～ Bureau of Public Health 【量】*for chess*, *tabletennis*, *etc.*：第三～比赛 the third game of a match

局部 júbù 【名】part（in contrast to the whole）；local

局促 júcù 【形】ill at ease；restrained：～不安 feel awkward and ill at ease

局面 júmiàn 【名】situation；condition：打开～ make a start by getting over initial difficulties 崭新的～ a completely new situation

局势 júshì 【名】（political or military）situation at a certain period

局外人 jú wài rén a person who has no involvement in a matter

局限 júxiàn 【动】be limited；confine：不要受旧框框的～ not bound by old conventions 不要把自己～在

狭小的天地里。Do not restrict yourself to a limited sphere.

局限性　júxiànxìng　【名】limitation (*in an abstract sense*)

菊　jú　【名】◇ chrysanthemum
菊花　júhuā　【名】〔朵 duǒ〕chrysanthemum

橘　jú　【名】◇ tangerine
橘子　júzi　【名】tangerine

jǔ

咀　jǔ
咀嚼　jǔjué　【动】chew；munch；(*fig.*) ponder

沮　jǔ
沮丧　jǔsàng　【形】dispirited；depressed；dejected

矩　jǔ
矩形　jǔxíng　【名】rectangle

举（舉）　jǔ　【动】❶ hold up；lift；raise：～手 raise one's hand ～起铁锤 raise the hammer ❷ enumerate；name；cite：～例说明 explain things by citing an example ～出事实 give facts

举办　jǔbàn　【动】hold；conduct：～学习班 hold a study class ～时事讲座 give a lecture on current affairs ～展览会 hold an exhibition

举报　jǔbào　【动】report：向检察机关 ～ report to the procuratorial organ

举措　jǔcuò　【名】move；act

举动　jǔdòng　【名】conduct

举国　jǔguó　【名】the whole country

举例　jǔ=lì　give example；cite an instance

举目　jǔ=mù　〈书〉lift one's eyes：～远眺 look into the distance ～四望 look around ～无亲 have no relatives to turn to

举棋不定　jǔ qí bù dìng　hesitate in making a move at chess；indecisive；hesitant；wavering

举世　jǔshì　【名】the whole world

举世闻名　jǔshì wénmíng　be known to all the world；world renowned；world famous

举行　jǔxíng　【动】(of meeting, etc.) hold；stage：～奠基仪式 hold a ceremony to lay a foundation stone ～宴会 give a banquet 工艺美术展览在中国美术馆～。An arts and crafts exhibition is being held at the Art Gallery of China.

举一反三　jǔ yī fǎn sān　make inferences by analogy

举止　jǔzhǐ　【名】behaviour；manner

举重　jǔzhòng　【名】weight-lifting

举足轻重　jǔ zú qīng zhòng　hold the balance

jù

巨　jù　【形】great；huge；gigantic
巨变　jùbiàn　【名】great changes

巨大　jùdà　【形】huge；immense

巨额　jù'é　【名】a huge sum (of money)

巨幅　jùfú　【名】very large (portrait, painting, etc.)

巨型　jùxíng　【形】large (scale)；gigantic；mammoth

巨著　jùzhù　【名】monumental work；magnum opus

句　jù　【名】sentence 【量】*for sentence；line*：几～台词 a few lines of an actor's part in a play 三～话不离本行（háng）never open one's mouth without talking shop

句法　jùfǎ　【名】syntax

句号　jùhào　【名】full stop；period

句型　jùxíng　【名】sentence pattern

句子 jùzi 【名】sentence

拒

jù 【动】◇ ❶ resist；struggle against：～敌 resist the enemy ❷ reject；refuse；decline：～不执行 refuse to carry out 来者不～。Those who come won't be turned away.

拒绝 jùjué 【动】reject；refuse；turn down

具

jù 【量】*for corpse*

具备 jùbèi 【动】possess；be provided with：～领导才能 possess leadership ability 条件不～。The necessary conditions are lacking.

具体 jùtǐ 【形】concrete；specific；actual

具体化 jùtǐhuà 【动】the concrete application (of a principle)

具有 jùyǒu 【动】have；possess (*the object of* 具有 *is usually an abstract noun*)：～强大的生命力 have great potential 这段话～讽刺意味。This paragraph is very satirical.

俱

jù 【副】〈书〉all

俱乐部 jùlèbù 【名】club

剧（劇）

jù 【名】drama

剧变 jùbiàn 【名】a violent (or drastic) change

剧本 jùběn 【名】play (script)

剧场 jùchǎng 【名】theatre

剧烈 jùliè 【形】violent；acute；drastic

剧目 jùmù 【名】a list of plays or operas

剧评 jùpíng 【名】dramatic criticism

剧情 jùqíng 【名】plot of a play

剧团 jùtuán 【名】theatrical troupe

剧院 jùyuàn 【名】theatre

剧增 jùzēng 【动】sharp increase；explosion

剧种 jùzhǒng 【名】types of drama

据（據）

jù 【动】◇ take possession of；occupy 【介】❶ by means of；with the help of；by virtue of：～险固守 rely on favourable terrain to protect one's position ～理力争 have strong grounds to argue ❷ according to：～调查,这种新产品很受欢迎。According to our investigation, the new product is being well received. ～老师说,他这次考得不错。According to the teacher, he did pretty well in the examination.

据点 jùdiǎn 【名】strong-hold

据说 jùshuō 【副】it is said；allegedly：他～就要回国了。It is said that he is going back to his country. ～,旅行社要组织大家去庐山游览。It is said that the tourist agency will organize a trip to Lushan.

据为己有 jù wéi jǐ yǒu seize and take possession of

惧（懼）

jù

惧怕 jùpà 【动】fear；be afraid

惧色 jùsè 【名】frightened expression

距

jù 【介】from (certain time or place)

距离 jùlí 【名】distance；discrepancy：两地的～很近。The distance between the two places is very small. 两种看法有很大～。There is a great difference between the two points of view. 【介】from：天津 ～ 北京约有 240 里。Tianjin is 240 *li* from Beijing. 现在～春秋战国时代已经有两千多年了。It is more than 2,000 years since the Spring and Autumn Period Warring States Period. 我们的工作虽然有了一些成绩,但是～要求还差得很远。Although we have made some achievements, we are still a long way from expectations.

飓（颶） jù

飓风　jùfēng　【名】hurricane

锯（鋸） jù

【名】〔把 bǎ〕saw （tool）【动】saw：～ 树 saw down a tree 把木头～断 saw a log in two

锯齿　jùchǐ　【名】teeth of a saw

聚 jù

【动】gather together；assemble；herd...together

聚餐　jùcān　【动】dine together

聚会　jùhuì　【动】gather together；meet

聚集　jùjí　【动】gather together；assemble

聚精会神　jù jīng huì shén　concentrate fully；with complete concentration

聚居　jùjū　【动】live closely together；live in a tightly-knit community

聚拢　jùlǒng　【动】gather together

juān

捐 juān

【动】contribute；donate：～钱 contribute money 【名】tax；duty：上～ pay duty

捐款　juānkuǎn　【名】donation

捐款　juān＝kuǎn　contribute money

捐躯　juānqū　【动】lay down one's life（for a just cause）：为国～ lay down one's life for one's country

捐税　juānshuì　【名】taxes

捐献　juānxiàn　【动】contribute

捐赠　juānzèng　【动】donate；contribute

捐助　juānzhù　【动】donate；contribute

捐资　juān＝zī　donate money；raise money

镌（鐫） juān

镌刻　juānkè　【动】〈书〉engrave

juǎn

卷（捲） juǎn

【动】❶ roll up：～袖子 roll up（one's）sleeves 他把那幅画儿～起来了。He rolled up the picture. ❷ churn up；drag into：风～黄沙。The wind churned up the sand. 他不愿意～进这场无原则的纠纷。He doesn't want to be dragged into such a meaningless dispute. 【名】（～儿）roll：纸～ paper cylinder 行李～ bedding roll 【量】for anything rolled up：一～报纸 a roll of newspapers 一～传单 a bundle of leaflets

另见 juàn

卷入　juǎnrù　【动】be drawn into；be involved in

卷舌元音　juǎn shé yuányīn　retroflex vowel

卷土重来　juǎn tǔ chóng lái　stage a comeback

卷扬机　juǎnyángjī　【名】hoist

juàn

卷 juàn

【名】◇ examination paper 【量】volume：藏书万～ a book collection numbering thousands of volumes 第一～ volume one 这部书分上下两～。This book consists of two volumes.

另见 juǎn

卷子　juànzi　【名】examination paper

卷宗　juànzōng　【名】❶ folder ❷ file

绢（絹） juàn

【名】plain unpatterned silk（e.g. for painting）

圈 juàn

【名】pen（for cattle, sheep, etc.）

另见 quān

眷 juàn

眷恋 juànliàn 【动】feel emotionally attached to

眷属 juànshǔ 【名】family（wife and children，etc.）

juē

撅 juē 【动】❶ stick up；pout ❷ break off（e.g. a branch）

jué

决 jué 【动】❶ breach；crack：大堤~了个口子。There is a breach in the dyke. ❷ ◇ decide；determine：犹豫不~ be unable to make up one's mind ~一胜负 battle it out（with sb.）【副】definitely；surely（*used before a negative word*）：这样做~没有好结果。Such doings will lead to no good end.

决不 jué bù under no circumstances；in no way；by no means；never：~退缩 will never give in ~妥协 will not compromise under any circumstances 不获全胜，~收兵。We will never give up until we have won complete victory.

决策 juécè 【动】make a strategic decision：运筹~ formulate and decide on strategic plans 【名】policy of strategic importance：英明~ decision displaying great wisdom

决定 juédìng 【动】determine；decide；resolve：存在~意识。Man's social being determines his consciousness. 旅行日程由大家讨论~。The travel schedule will be discussed and decided on by us together. 上级~让他执行这项任务。The leadership has decided to have him undertake this task. 【名】decision；resolution：我们要把大会做出

的~及时地向大家传达。We must communicate the resolution agreed upon at the meeting to the others without delay.

决定性 juédìngxìng 【名】decisive；crucial

决断 juéduàn 【动】make a decision

决口 jué = kǒu （of embankment；dike，etc.）be breached

决裂 juéliè 【动】break with；split from

决然 juérán 【副】❶ decidedly：东张西望，道听途说，~得不到什么像样的知识。Picking up bits of gossip here and there certainly won't add up to wholesome knowledge. ❷ resolutely：为了寻找真理，鲁迅~地离开了自己的家乡。Lu Xun was determined to leave home in order to seek the truth.

决赛 juésài 【动】play the final（match）；play in the finals 【名】finals；final match

决胜 juéshèng 【动】〈书〉take the decisive action in a battle

决算 juésuàn 【动】draw up the final accounts 【名】final accounting of revenue and expenditures

决心 juéxīn 【名】determination 【副】be determined to

决议 juéyì 【名】（of a meeting，conference）resolution

决战 juézhàn 【动】fight a decisive battle 【名】decisive battle

诀（訣） jué

诀别 juébié 【动】bid farewell；part for good

诀窍 juéqiào 【名】secret of success；key to success

抉 jué

抉择 juézé 【动】choose；select

角 jué 【名】◇ role（in a play，film，etc.）

另见 jiǎo

角色 juésè 【名】role（in a play or movie）

角逐 juézhú 【动】contend for；fight for mastery

觉（覺） jué 【动】feel；be aware，*usu. takes* 着 *or* 出 *after it*：我～着有点儿冷。I'm feeling a bit cold. 他最近工作特别出色，大家都～出这一点了。He has been doing excellent work recently. Everybody is aware of it.

另见 jiào

觉察 juéchá 【动】sense；discern；discover

觉得 juéde 【动】❶ feel；be aware；sense：一点儿也不～累。I don't feel the slightest bit tired. 我～屋里很暖和。I feel pretty warm in this room. ❷ think；be of the opinion：我～这件事很重要。I think this matter is very important. 大家都～应该这样做。Everybody thinks it should be done this way.

觉悟 juéwù 【动】become aware；come to understand：他已经～了。He has come to his senses. 【名】consciousness：～提高了。Political consciousness has increased.

觉醒 juéxǐng 【动】awake（*fig.*）

绝（絶） jué 【动】◇ end；break off；cut off；sever：弹尽粮～ completely run out of ammunition and food ～了后路。The line of retreat has been cut off. 【副】◇ ❶ most；extremely：～大部分 the biggest part ～大多数 the overwhelming majority ❷ very definitely；absolutely：～无此意 have absolutely no such intentions ～不可信 absolutely unbelievable 【形】exhausted；final：办法都想～了 exhaust one's methods（of solving the problem）不要把话说～了。Do not say that

this is final，always leave a way out.

绝笔 juébǐ 【名】❶ last words written before one's death ❷ last work of a writer or painter

绝唱 juéchàng 【名】the peak of poetic perfection

绝顶 juédǐng 【名】summit 【副】extremely：～聪明 extremely intelligent

绝对 juéduì 【形】❶ absolute；definite；sure：～没错儿 absolutely no mistake 我们有～胜利的把握。We have absolute confidence in victory. ❷ absolute；pure；sheer：反对～平均主义 oppose absolute egalitarianism 物质世界的存在是～的。The existence of the material world is an absolute.

绝对化 juéduìhuà 【动】go to extremes

绝对真理 juéduì zhēnlǐ absolute truth

绝对值 juéduìzhí 【名】（maths.）absolute value

绝技 juéjì 【名】unique skill；exceptional skill

绝迹 jué＝jì completely disappear

绝交 jué＝jiāo break off relations with；sever relations with

绝境 juéjìng 【名】hopeless straits；impasse

绝句 juéjù 【名】a classical poem which has four lines. If it has 5 characters to the line, it is called "五言绝句"；if 7 characters，"七言绝句".

绝路 juélù 【名】dead end；blind alley；road to ruin

绝密 juémì 【形】top secret；strictly confidential

绝妙 juémiào 【形】absolutely marvellous

绝食 jué＝shí go on a hunger strike

绝望 jué＝wàng have no hope；despair；lose all hope

绝无仅有 jué wú jǐn yǒu extremely rare；the only one of its kind；unique

绝育 jué＝yù sterilization；be sterilized

绝缘 juéyuán 【动】insulate

绝缘体 juéyuántǐ 【名】(electr.) insulator

绝症 juézhèng 【名】incurable disease

绝种 jué＝zhǒng become extinct

倔 jué

另见 jué

倔强 juéjiàng 【形】obstinate；stubborn

掘 jué 【动】dig：～井 dig a well ～土 dig in the earth

掘进 juéjìn 【动】drive（a mine shaft）；tunnel

掘墓人 juémùrén 【名】grave-digger

掘土机 juétǔjī 【名】excavator

崛 jué

崛起 juéqǐ 【动】(of a mountain) rise up abruptly

攫 jué

攫取 juéqǔ 【动】seize；grab

juè

倔 juè 【形】gruff；headstrong：他脾气～。He has a surly temper.

另见 jué

jūn

军（軍）jūn 【名】❶ ◇ army；armed forces；troops ❷ army（unit above a division）：第三～ the 3rd army 一个～的兵力 a force one army strong 【量】army：调来了一～

人。One army was transferred here.

军备 jūnbèi 【名】armaments

军队 jūnduì 【名】forces；troops；army

军阀 jūnfá 【名】warlord

军法 jūnfǎ 【名】military law

军费 jūnfèi 【名】military expenditure

军港 jūngǎng 【名】naval port

军工 jūngōng 【名】❶ war industry ❷ military project

军官 jūnguān 【名】officer

军国主义 jūnguózhǔyì 【名】militarism

军徽 jūnhuī 【名】army emblem

军火 jūnhuǒ 【名】munitions

军火商 jūnhuǒshāng 【名】munitions dealer

军纪 jūnjì 【名】military discipline

军舰 jūnjiàn 【名】〔艘 sōu〕warship

军礼 jūnlǐ 【名】military salute

军民 jūn mín the army and the people；soldiers and civilians

军旗 jūnqí 【名】〔面 miàn〕army flag

军区 jūnqū 【名】military area

军人 jūnrén 【名】serviceman；military personnel

军士 jūnshì 【名】noncommissioned officer

军事 jūnshì 【名】military affairs

军事管制 jūnshì guǎnzhì military control

军事基地 jūnshì jīdì military base

军事家 jūnshìjiā 【名】person versed in military science；strategist

军属 jūnshǔ 【名】armyman's family

军衔 jūnxián 【名】military rank

军心 jūnxīn 【名】morale of the troops

军训 jūnxùn 【名】military training

军医 jūnyī 【名】medical officer；military surgeon

军营 jūnyíng 【名】military camp；barracks

军用 jūnyòng 【形】for military use

军乐　jūnyuè　【名】military music

军长　jūnzhǎng　【名】army commander

军种　jūnzhǒng　【名】services（army, navy, air force）

军装　jūnzhuāng　【名】〔套 tào〕military uniform

均　jūn　【形】◇ equal；even；balanced【副】〈书〉all；without exception

均等　jūnděng　【动】on an equal footing；impartial

均衡　jūnhéng　【动】keep ... in balance；equilibrium

均势　jūnshì　【名】balance of power

均匀　jūnyún　【形】even

君　jūn　【代】〈书〉you【名】◇ sovereign；monarch

君子　jūnzǐ　【名】a gentleman；a man of virtue

jùn

俊　jùn　【形】good-looking

俊杰　jùnjié　【名】person of outstanding ability

郡　jùn　【名】an administrative district in ancient times

峻　jùn

峻岭　jùnlǐng　【名】steep mountain

峻峭　jùnqiào　【形】（of mountain, cliff）precipitous

骏（駿）　jùn

骏马　jùnmǎ　【名】〔匹 pǐ〕a fine horse；steed

竣　jùn　【动】finish；complete；end

竣工　jùn＝gōng　complete construction

K

kā

咖 kā
咖啡 kāfēi 【名】coffee
咖啡馆 kāfēiguǎn 【名】a coffee shop

kǎ

卡 kǎ 【动】(of people, materials, funds, etc.) withhold; refuse to give or allocate; hold or keep back 【量】short for "卡路里"
另见 qiǎ
卡车 kǎchē 【名】〔辆 liàng〕lorry; truck
卡尺 kǎchǐ 【名】sliding callipers
卡路里 kǎlùlǐ 【量】calorie
卡片 kǎpiàn 【名】〔张 zhāng〕card

咔 kǎ
咔叽 kǎjī 【名】khaki drill

kāi

开(開) kāi 【动】❶ open：~窗户 open the window 扣儿~了。A button was undone. 梅花~了。The plum trees are blooming. ❷ open up：~运河 dig a canal 这条路是新~出来的。This is a newly opened road. ~三十亩水田。They've created 30 *mu* of flooded paddy fields. ❸ drive; run; operate：~汽车 drive a car ~机器 operate a machine ❹ turn on：~电灯 turn on the light ~电视机 turn on the TV set ~水龙头 turn on the tap ❺ hold (meeting, party, etc.)：~座谈会 hold a forum ~运动会 hold an athletic meet 联欢会~了两小时。The party lasted two hours. ❻ write out：~药方 write out a prescription ~名单 make a list of names ~介绍信 write a letter of introduction ❼ boil：水~了。The water is boiling. Note：开 *is used after a verb as a complement*：① open：开~窗户 throw open the window 推~门 push open the door ② disperse：消息传~了。The news has spread. 队伍散~了。The troops have spread out. ③ away from the original position：吃饭了，把桌子上的东西拿~。Dinner will be ready soon. Let's move these things off the table. 汽车来了，咱们躲~吧！There's a car coming. Let's get out of the way. ④ be big enough to hold：这间屋子坐不~五十人。This room is not big enough to hold 50 people. 这个大厅很宽敞，三十张桌子能摆~。This hall is very large. It can hold 30 tables. ⑤ *indicates*

some action which begins and continues：他一唱，大家都跟着唱～了。He started to sing, and everybody else joined in.

开拔 kāibá 【动】move; set out (of troops)

开办 kāibàn 【动】(of factory, school, hospital, etc.) set up; start; open

开采 kāicǎi 【动】extract (coal, petroleum, etc.)

开场 kāi = chǎng (of a performance) begin

开场白 kāichǎngbái 【名】❶ prologue of a play ❷ opening or introductory remarks

开车 kāi = chē drive a vehicle

开诚布公 kāi chéng bù gōng (when exchanging or airing views) come straight to the point and speak frankly and sincerely：我想～地和你谈一谈。I would like to have a frank and sincere talk with you.

开初 kāichū 【名】at first; at the outset

开除 kāichú 【动】discharge; expel; dismiss; sack (as a punishment)

开创 kāichuàng 【动】found; initiate; start; usher in：～事业 start a career ～新时代 usher in a new era

开刀 kāi = dāo perform a surgical operation：拿…～ punish (sb.) first; make sb. or sth. the first target of attack

开导 kāidǎo 【动】help sb. to see what is sensible or right; bring sb. to his senses

开倒车 kāi dàochē (*fig.*) turn back the clock; turn back the wheel of history

开动 kāidòng 【动】(of cars, ships, machines, etc.) start; operate：～机器 operate a machine ～脑筋 use one's brains

开端 kāiduān 【名】beginning; start

开发 kāifā 【动】open up; tap：～油田 open up an oil field 把地下宝藏～出来 tap underground resources

开饭 kāi = fàn (of canteen or public dining hall) serve a meal

开方 kāi = fāng ❶ (maths.) find the root ❷ make out a prescription

开放 kāifàng 【动】❶ (of flowers) be out; open：鲜花～。The flowers are blooming; The flowers are out. ❷ (of park, exhibition, garden, etc.) be open to the public：港口～ open a port to trade (with foreign countries) ～政策 open policy 机场～。The airport is now open to the public. 节日公园免费～。On festival days, parks are open to the public free of charge.

开赴 kāifù 【动】set out for; be on the way to; be bound for：～战场 set out for the battle-front ～边疆 head for the border

开工 kāi = gōng start construction; (of production) go into operation; begin to work

开关 kāiguān 【名】switch

开国 kāi = guó found a state (*usu. used as an attributive*)：～大典 founding ceremony of a state

开航 kāiháng 【动】❶ open up a sea route or airline ❷ (of ship) set sail; cast off

开后门 kāi hòumén (～儿) give the go-ahead for backdoor business

开户 kāi = hù open an account

开花 kāi = huā ❶ be in bloom ❷ (of a bomb, shell, etc.) burst; explode：手榴弹在敌人头上开了花。The handgrenade exploded right on top of the enemy. 心里乐开了花。My heart is bursting with joy. ❸ (of work, undertaking) be prosperous; flourishing：各项工作全面～。Work in all fields is in full swing.

开化 kāihuà 【动】become civilized

开荒　kāi＝huāng　reclaim land

开会　kāi＝huì　hold a meeting；attend a meeting

开火　kāi＝huǒ　open fire

开卷考试　kāi juàn kǎoshì　an "open book" examination

开掘　kāijué　【动】dig；excavate

开垦　kāikěn　【动】reclaim (wasteland)

开口　kāi＝kǒu　open one's mouth to speak

开矿　kāi＝kuàng　open up a mine

开阔　kāikuò　【形】❶ wide；broad；open：～的原野 broad fields 一片～地 a vast expanse of land ❷ open；generous；optimistic：思想～ a wider perspective；a broader view 心胸～ of an optimistic disposition 【动】widen；broaden：～一下眼界 broaden one's horizons；broaden (increase) one's knowledge

开朗　kāilǎng　【形】(of character, mind) open；frank；cheerful：性格～ open and frank disposition 思想～ openminded；broad-minded

开例　kāi＝lì　create a precedent

开路　kāi＝lù　❶ open a new road ❷ lead the way

开绿灯　kāi lǜdēng　give the green light；give the go-ahead

开门　kāi＝mén　❶ (of a shop) open；start business ❷ give an opportunity to (sb.)

开门红　kāi mén hóng　make a good beginning；get off to a good start：这个煤矿在新年的第一天就夺得了～。The coal mine made a good start on the day's work on New Year's Day.

开门见山　kāi mén jiàn shān　put sth. bluntly without beating about the bush；come straight to the point：有什么要求就～地提吧！If you have any requests, please be straightforward about raising them.

开明　kāimíng　【形】enlightened：～

绅士 enlightened gentry ～人士 enlightened personages

开幕　kāi＝mù　❶ the curtain rises (at the beginning of a performance) ❷ inaugurate

开幕式　kāimùshì　【名】opening ceremony

开炮　kāi＝pào　❶ fire a cannon ❷ unleash one's criticisms of sb. (usu. in a meeting)

开辟　kāipì　【动】open up；usher in；break (new ground)；pave the way for：～航线 open up an air or sea route ～新天地 carve out a new world for ～了一条新路 open up a new road

开启　kāiqǐ　【动】open

开腔　kāi＝qiāng　同"开口"

开窍　kāi＝qiào　❶ straighten out (one's thinking)：思想开了窍。One's thinking has been straightened out. ❷ become more receptive (to new ideas)：脑筋没～ be completely unreceptive to new ideas

开山　kāi＝shān　blast away part of a mountain

开设　kāishè　【动】establish；found；start；set up；open：～两门课程 offer two courses (of study)

开始　kāishǐ　【动】❶ begin；start：新学年～了。The new academic year has begun. 今天我们从第三章～讲。Today, let's begin from the third chapter. ❷ start；set out on；set about：～一项新的工作 begin a new job ～播种 start sowing 【名】(at the) beginning；at first：～他不赞成，后来赞成了。At first he didn't agree, but later he did.

开市　kāi＝shì　❶ reopen after a cessation of business ❷ the first transaction of a day's business

开水　kāishuǐ　【名】boiling water；boiled water

开天辟地　kāi tiān pì dì　since the be-

ginning of history：～的壮举 an un-precedented heroic event in human history

开庭 kāi = tíng open a court session

开通 kāitong 【形】 enlightened；liberal；open-minded：思想～ hold liberal views 她婆婆可～啦! Her mother-in-law is very liberal-minded indeed.

开头 kāitóu 【名】 beginning；start：万事～难。The first step is always difficult whatever you do. 故事刚讲了个～。The part of the story which has just been told is only the beginning.

开头 kāi = tóu begin；make a start：这出戏一～就很吸引人。From its very first moment, the play had a strong appeal. 现在讨论, 我先开个头。Now let's begin our discussion. I'll start off.

开脱 kāituō 【动】 absolve；exonerate：～责任 shirk one's responsibility ～罪责 absolve sb. from guilt

开拓 kāituò 【动】 carve out；open up；expand（farmland, etc.）：把荒原～成良田 turn the wilderness into fertile farmland 他们办工厂的经验为农村发展工业～了广阔的道路。Their experience in running factories comes in handy for the development of industry in the countryside.

开外 kāiwài 【助】（of age or distance）over；more than：五十岁～ more than fifty years of age 三十里～ over 30 li

开玩笑 kāi wánxiào joke；make a joke

开销 kāixiāo 【动】 pay（expenses）【名】（of a person or family) expenses

开小差 kāi xiǎochāi（of a soldier）desert：工作的时候, 思想不能～。Don't let your mind wander while working.

开心 kāixīn 【形】 happy；joyous；pleasant：玩儿得真～。We've had a splendid time! 【动】 make fun of sb.：别拿人～了, 我哪儿会演戏呀! Don't make fun of me；I really don't know a thing about acting.

开学 kāi = xué begin a school term

开眼 kāi = yǎn open one's eyes；widen one's view

开演 kāiyǎn 【动】（of play, film）start

开业 kāi = yè ❶ start business ❷ open a private practice

开夜车 kāi yèchē work late into the night；burn the midnight oil：注意劳逸结合, 今天别再～了。Be sure to have enough rest and don't work too late again tonight. 开两个夜车这个剧本就可以改完。If we put in two late nights, we can finish the revisions on the play.

开源节流 kāi yuán jié liú develop resources and reduce expenditures

开凿 kāizáo 【动】 cut；dig（a canal, etc.）；tunnel：～运河 dig a canal ～隧道 dig a tunnel

开斋节 kāizhāijié 【名】 come to the end of Ramadan

开展 kāizhǎn 【动】 develop；launch；promote；carry on；unfold：～计划生育的宣传 launch a campaign to promote family planning ～劳动竞赛 carry on emulation drive 【形】（of mind or mental outlook) open；optimistic：他思想很不～。He is rather narrow-minded.

开战 kāi = zhàn make war

开张 kāi = zhāng（of shops) open for business

开支 kāizhī 【动】 pay（expenses）【名】（of an institution) expenses

kǎi

凯（凯）kǎi

凯歌　kǎigē　【名】song of triumph

凯旋　kǎixuán　【动】return in triumph

楷　kǎi

楷模　kǎimó　【名】model；pattern

楷书　kǎishū　【名】style of Chinese calligraphy which is in common use, and in which the characters are very regular in form

楷体　kǎitǐ　【名】❶ regular script ❷ block letter

kān

刊　kān　【动】publish【名】◇ periodical

刊登　kāndēng　【动】publish（in a newspaper or magazine）

刊物　kānwù　【名】journals；periodicals；publications

刊印　kānyìn　【动】print

刊载　kānzǎi　【动】同"刊登"

看　kān　【动】❶ watch；look after：～门 watch the gate ～孩子 look after the child 一个人～两台机器。One person is in charge of two machines. ❷ guard（prisoners）：把那个犯罪分子～起来。Put the criminal under guard.
另见 kàn

看管　kānguǎn　【动】❶ guard：～俘虏 guard the captives ❷ take care of；look after；attend to：～仓库 look after the storehouse ～抽水机 look after the pump

看护　kānhù　【动】nurse

看守　kānshǒu　【动】❶ keep watch ❷ guard（prisoner）

看守所　kānshǒusuǒ　【名】lock up for prisoners awaiting trial

看押　kānyā　【动】take into custody；detain

勘　kān

勘测　kāncè　【动】*short for* 勘察和测量 prospect and survey

勘察　kānchá　【动】prospect

勘探　kāntàn　【动】prospect（for minerals）

勘误　kānwù　【动】correct printing errors：～表 errata

kǎn

坎　kǎn　【名】bank；ridge

坎坷　kǎnkě　【形】full of ups and downs（*usu. fig.*）

砍　kǎn　【动】hew；chop；hack

砍伐　kǎnfá　【动】fell（trees）

kàn

看　kàn　【动】❶ look；watch；see：～电影 see a film ～冰球表演 watch an ice-hockey game ❷ read：～书 read a book；do some reading ～报 read a newspaper ❸ observe and judge：要全面地～问题。One should look at a matter from every angle. 我～他确实是真心实意，你～呢？I think that he was very sincere. What do you think? 这件事得你去～情况办。You must be on the spot and deal with the matter according to the circumstances. ❹ depend on：一个人的品质如何，不是～他说什么，而是～他做什么。A person's character must be judged by how he acts and not by what he says. 明天能不能去野餐，就～天气了。Whether or not we have a picnic tomorrow depends on the weather. ❺ regard as：不要把别人对你的看法～得那么重。Don't take others' opinions of you too much to

heart. 我一直把这项工作～作我的终身事业。I've always looked on this work as my life's career. ❻ visit; call on：～朋友 call on a friend ～病人 visit a patient ❼ (of a doctor) treat：王大夫说他今天要～的病人不多。Dr. Wang said that he did not expect to have many patients today. ❽ see or consult (a doctor)：你发烧了，赶快去～医生吧！You have a fever. Go and see a doctor. ❾ *used at the beginning of a sentence to indicate admiration, concern, dissatisfaction, etc.*：～这个鬼天气！What abominable weather! ～你累的，快歇会儿吧！Look, you must be exhausted. Do take a break. ～这些风景照片多漂亮啊！How beautiful these scenic shots are! ❿ *used after a reduplicated verb or a verbal phrase to indicate that one is trying sth.*：这双鞋你穿穿～。You'd better try on this pair of shoes. 让我想想～。Let me think. 咱们先观察几天～。Let's observe things for a few days first. 另见 kān

看病 kàn=bìng ❶ (of a doctor) see a patient; examine a patient; treat a sick person：大夫到病人家～了。The doctor is on a home visit. ❷ (of a sick person) see or consult a doctor：老王上医院去～了。Lao Wang has gone to see a doctor.

看不起 kàn bu qǐ look down upon; despise

看穿 kàn//chuān see through

看待 kàndài 【动】regard; look on; treat

看得起 kàn de qǐ think highly of

看跌 kàndiē 【动】dip; drop; decrease; fall：股票行情～。The stock market quotations are expected to fall.

看法 kànfǎ 【名】view; approach：对同一个问题，立场不同，～就不同。People with different outlooks have different views on the same question.

看风使舵 kàn fēng shǐ duò trim one's sails to the wind; change one's opinion or viewpoint opportunistically

看好 kànhǎo 【动】predict a good sale：对那种家电的销售，一致～。They unanimously predicted a good sale for that kind of household appliance.

看见 kàn//jiàn see; catch sight of

看开 kàn//kāi take one's mind off sth. bad, unfortunate, etc.; not take sth. to heart：遇到烦恼的事要～一些。Try and hope for the best when you are in trouble.

看来 kàn lái 【连】it seems (*used either at the beginning of a sentence or inserted parenthetically*)：人口的增长～非控制不可。Population increase, it seems, has to be controlled. ～这项工程再有十天就完工了。It seems that this construction project will be finished in ten more days.

看破 kàn//pò be disillusioned with：～红尘 be disillusioned with the mortal world

看齐 kànqí 【动】❶ (mil.) dress：向右～! Dress right! ❷ follow the example of; measure up to; keep up with：向先进人物～ emulate those who are advanced

看轻 kànqīng 【动】look down upon; underestimate

看台 kàntái 【名】(of a sports-ground) stand

看望 kànwàng 【动】visit; call on：～多年不见的老朋友 call on an old friend whom one has not seen for a long time

看涨 kànzhǎng 【动】be likely to go up; be expected to rise：黄金价格～。The price of gold is likely to

rise.

看中 kànzhòng 【动】see and take a fancy to：他～了这种式样的手表。He looked around and this brand of watch has caught his fancy.

看重 kànzhòng 【动】think highly of；value

kāng

康 kāng

康复 kāngfù 【动】restore to health；recover

康庄大道 kāngzhuāng dàdào broad and well-paved road

慷 kāng

慷慨 kāngkǎi 【形】❶ generous；liberal；magnanimous：～援助 generous assistance ～大方 be generous ❷ filled with a noble spirit：～就义 be executed and die a hero's death ～高歌 sing energetically and spiritedly

慷慨激昂 kāngkǎi jī'áng impassioned and inspired：歌声～。The singing was impassioned and inspired.

糠 kāng 【名】husk；chaff

káng

扛 káng 【动】carry sth. on one's shoulder；shoulder：～枪 shoulder a gun ～着滑雪板 carry skis on one's shoulder

扛活 káng = huó work as a farmhand in the old society

kàng

抗 kàng 【动】◇ ❶ resist；combat；fight against：～灾 fight natu-ral disasters ～涝 fight against water-logging of the fields ❷ resist；oppose；defy；refuse：～命 defy an order ～捐～税 refuse to pay levies and taxes

抗暴 kàng = bào resist tyranny；fight against violent repression：～斗争 the struggle against tyranny

抗旱 kàng = hàn fight against drought

抗衡 kànghéng 【动】contend with；match

抗击 kàngjī 【动】resist

抗拒 kàngjù 【动】resist；defy

抗美援朝战争 Kàng Měi Yuán Cháo Zhànzhēng the War to Resist U.S. Aggression and Aid Korea (1950.10 – 1953.7)

抗日救亡运动 Kàng Rì Jiù Wáng Yùndòng the Movement to Resist Japanese Aggression and Save the Nation led by the Chinese Communist Party（prior to the Anti-Japanese War）

抗日军政大学 Kàng Rì Jūn Zhèng Dàxué The Chinese People's Anti-Japanese Military and Political College—founded at Yan'an in June, 1936

抗日战争 Kàng Rì Zhànzhēng the War of Resistance Against Japanese Aggression (1937.7.7 – 1945.8.15)

抗生素 kàngshēngsù 【名】antibiotic

抗诉 kàngsù 【动】protest：～书 written protest

抗体 kàngtǐ 【名】antibody

抗议 kàngyì 【动】protest：强烈～侵略者的暴行 protest strongly against the atrocities of the aggressors 【名】protest：提出最强烈的～ lodge the strongest protest 表示～ make clear one's protest

抗战 kàng = zhàn ❶ war of resistance against aggression ❷ short for 抗日战争

抗震　kàng=zhèn　anti-seismic

抗争　kàngzhēng　【动】make a stand against；resist

炕　kàng　【名】a heatable brick bed（in north China）

kǎo

考　kǎo　【动】test；examine：～物理 hold a physics examination 我出个题～～你。I'll ask you a question to quiz you.

考查　kǎochá　【动】test；examine

考察　kǎochá　【动】investigate；test；inspect；observe and study：～地下水的分布 make an investigation of the flow of underground water【名】investigation；study：进行科学～ undertake scientific investigation

考场　kǎochǎng　【名】examination hall

考古　kǎogǔ　【动】do archaeological work【名】同"考古学"

考古学　kǎogǔxué　【名】archaeology

考核　kǎohé　【动】check；test；examine；look over：～成绩 assess one's achievements in work or study 定期～ give regular examinations；routine check

考究　kǎojiu　【动】study；investigate：如何管理好企业，很值得～。The management of enterprises is a subject worth studying.【形】sumptuous；陈设～ sumptuous furnishings 京剧的服装很～。The costumes for Beijing Opera are lavish.

考据　kǎojù　【动】textual research

考卷　kǎojuàn　【名】examination paper

考虑　kǎolǜ　【动】consider；think over；ponder

考评　kǎopíng　【动】evaluate（one's professional work）

考勤　kǎoqín　【动】（of work，study）check attendance

考取　kǎo//qǔ　be admitted to school or college after an examination

考生　kǎoshēng　【名】candidate for an examination；examinee

考试　kǎoshì　【动】sit for an examination【名】examination；test

考验　kǎoyàn　【动】test：条件越艰苦，越能～人。The harder the conditions, the better one can be tested.【名】ordeal；test；trial：经受了一场严峻的～。He was subjected to a severe test.

考证　kǎozhèng　【动】engage in textual research

拷　kǎo

拷贝　kǎobèi　【名】（of film）copy；print

拷打　kǎodǎ　【动】beat（as a torture）

拷问　kǎowèn　【动】interrogate with torture

烤　kǎo　【动】roast；bake

烤电　kǎo=diàn　diathermy；have a diathermic treatment

烤箱　kǎoxiāng　【名】oven

烤鸭　kǎoyā　【名】roast duck

kào

靠　kào　【动】❶ lean：把梯子～在墙上 lean the ladder against the wall ❷ be near：这个村子～山近水。The village is situated at the foot of a mountain, and a river flows beside it. ～东墙种了一行（háng）向日葵。A row of sunflowers was planted along the east wall. ❸ rely on；depend on：～集体的力量 rely on the strength of the collective 会议的筹备工作全～你们了。The preparatory work for the meeting will be entirely on your shoulders.

靠岸　kào＝àn　steer ... to shore

靠背　kàobèi　【名】back (of a chair)

靠边　kào＝biān　(～儿) to the side：大家～点儿，让出一条路来。Please keep to the side, clear a path (through the crowd). 这个座位太～了. This seat is too far to the side. 东西～放. Please keep your things out of the way.

靠不住　kào bu zhù　not dependable；unreliable：这话～. What has been said can't be relied on. 这个消息～. This information is unreliable.

靠得住　kào de zhù　reliable；dependable；trustworthy：这是第一手材料，～. This is first-hand material, and can be relied on. 你把任务交给小李吧，这人～. You can give this job to Xiao Li; he is very reliable.

靠垫　kàodiàn　【名】(backrest) cushion

靠近　kàojìn　【动】get close to；approach：渔船渐渐向小岛～. The fishing-boat is nearing the small island. ～湖边新建了一所学校. A new school has just been built near the lake.

靠拢　kàolǒng　【动】come close to；draw close；close ranks：向左边～keep to the left 两翼部队向主力部队～. The left and right flanks closed ranks with the main force.

靠山　kàoshān　【名】powerful person or group of people whose support one can rely on；backing

kē

苛　kē　【形】exacting

苛捐杂税　kē juān zá shuì　exorbitant taxes and levies

苛刻　kēkè　【形】exacting；harsh

苛求　kēqiú　【动】ask too much；be too exacting

科　kē　【名】❶ branch or subject of academic or vocational study：理～ the natural sciences 工～ branches of engineering ❷ division or subdivision of an administrative unit；department；section：总务～ services department (administers dining-hall, lights, heat, etc.) 检验～ quality-control department

科幻　kēhuàn　【形】science fiction：～影片 science fiction film

科技　kējì　【名】science and technology

科教片　kējiàopiàn　【名】〔部 bù〕short for 科学教育影片 popular science film

科目　kēmù　【名】branch of study；subject

科学　kēxué　【名】science【形】scientific：这个方法很～. This method is very scientific.

科学家　kēxuéjiā　【名】scientist

科学试验　kēxué shìyàn　scientific experiment

科学性　kēxuéxìng　【名】in accord with scientific principles

科学院　kēxuéyuàn　【名】Academy of Sciences

科学种田　kēxué zhòng tián　scientific farming

科研　kēyán　【名】short for 科学研究 scientific research

棵　kē　【量】for trees, etc.

颗（顆）　kē　【量】grain

颗粒　kēlì　【名】grain (of sand, etc.)

磕　kē　【动】knock

磕碰　kēpèng　【动】knock against；collide with

磕头　kē＝tóu　kowtow

瞌　kē

瞌睡　kēshuì　【形】sleepy：除夕一直玩

儿到天亮，大家一点儿也不～。On New Year's Eve, we celebrated until daybreak, and nobody was the least bit sleepy.

ké

壳（殼） ké 【名】shell（of nuts etc.）
另见 qiào

咳 ké 【动】cough
另见 hāi

咳嗽 késou 【动】cough

kě

可 kě 【助动】❶ 同"可以"【助动】(*usu. in written language*)：本阅览室的工具书不～携出室外。The dictionaries in this reading room are not to be removed. 这里地势险要，～攻～守。This is a strategic vantage point, both offensively and defensively. ❷ worthy：我没有什么经验～介绍的。I haven't got any experience worth talking about. 中国现代和古典文学作品中都有很多～借鉴的东西。There are a lot of things worthy of our attention in modern as well as in classical Chinese literature.【连】but；yet，可 *is pronounced in the neutral tone and may be placed either before or after the subject of the second clause*：别看他年纪小，志气～不小。He is young, but quite ambitious. 水果店新到了一批桃子，～我没买。The greengrocer had a new shipment of peaches, but I didn't buy any.【副】❶ *used to emphasize the truth of sth.*（*usu. in the negative*），可 *is pronounced in the neutral tone*：那本书我～没借。I certainly didn't take out that book. 他～不知道这件事。I'm sure he knows nothing about this matter. ❷ *used to form an interrogative sentence*，可 *is pronounced in the neutral tone*：朋友，你～听过长征的故事? My friend, have you ever heard the story of the Long March? ❸ *used to express high degree*：参观的人～多了。There were such a lot of visitors! 这个电影～动人了。This film is moving indeed! ❹ *used to indicate that sth. has been long awaited*：我们等了你好久，你～回来了。We've waited for you for such a long time, and here you are finally! 他的伤～好了。His wound has healed at long last! ❺ *used together with* 得（děi）*or* 不要，*indicating prohibition, to form an emphatic expression*：路上都是雪，骑车～得小心啊! There is snow on the road. You must really be careful on bicycle. 你～不要再这样了。You must never act like that again! Note：*in* ❸❹❺ 可 *may be pronounced with stress*，*in* ❸ *and* ❹ *there must be a* 了 *at the end of the sentence*.

可爱 kě'ài 【形】lovable；lovely；charming

可悲 kěbēi 【形】deplorable；lamentable

可不是 kěbushì 【动】*in a conversation，indicates agreement with what the other party says*：这里商品真齐全啊! ——～，什么都有。They certainly have a wide selection here. — Yes, they do. They seem to have everything!

可乘之机 kě chéng zhī jī loophole that can be exploited to one's advantage：不让他有～。Don't give him a handle to use against us.

可耻 kěchǐ 【形】ignominious；shameful

可歌可泣 kě gē kě qì heroic and

moving；～的英雄事迹 moving and heroic deeds

可观　kěguān　【形】considerable；quite：一笔～的收入 a sizable income 这个化工厂的规模是相当～的。The size and scale of operations of this chemical factory is really considerable.

可贵　kěguì　【形】valuable；precious

可恨　kěhèn　【形】hateful

可见　kějiàn　【连】*introduces a conclusion drawn from the fact which precedes it*：玻璃窗上结了一层冰，～天气非常冷。The window panes are covered with ice, so it must be very cold. 这段铁路一百公里，就有十几个隧道，～工程是非常艰巨的。This railway is only 100 km. long, yet there are more than ten tunnels, so you can tell the difficulties in its construction.

可见度　kějiàndù　【名】visibility

可靠　kěkào　【形】reliable；trustworthy；dependable：～的同盟军 a dependable alliance ～的后方 a secure rear area 这个数据很～。This data is very reliable.

可可　kěkě　【名】cocoa

可控硅　kěkòngguī　【名】(electr.) silicon controlled rectifier

可口　kěkǒu　【形】tasty；delicious

可怜　kělián　【形】❶ pitiable；pitiful；poor ❷ *used with "得" as a complement following* 少、穷、矮、瘦，*etc. to indicate superlative degree*：少得～ far from adequate；far too little 内容贫乏得～。It is shamefully lacking in content. 【动】pity；have pity on：我们不～那些自己不努力的人。We do not pity people who don't help themselves.

可怜虫　kěliánchóng　【名】pitiful creature

可能　kěnéng　【名】possibility；potentiality：事情的发展有两种～。The situation may develop in two possible directions. 【动】❶ maybe；may：他～去参观。He may go to visit. ❷ possible：团结一切～团结的人。Unite with all the people with whom it is possible to unite. ❸ possible；likely；probable：实践证明，在西藏高原种小麦是完全～的。Practice has shown that it is possible to grow wheat on the Tibetan Plateau.

可能性　kěnéngxìng　【名】possibility；potentiality

可怕　kěpà　【形】horrible；terrible

可巧　kěqiǎo　【副】as it happens；by chance；coincidentally：我正要找你，～你就来了。I was just going to look for you when you turned up. 小苗正缺水，～下了一场透雨。The young seedlings were urgently in need of water when, by luck, it rained heavily.

可取　kěqǔ　【形】worth having；worth learning：这意见很～。This proposal is worth consideration. 这个办法有几分～之处。This method has several worthwhile points.

可是　kěshì　【连】but (*can be placed either before or after the subject of the clause*)：这条胡同住户不少，～小孩儿不多。There are many households in this lane, but very few children. 岛虽不大，地理位置～很重要。The island is not big, but its geographical position makes it very important.

可塑性　kěsùxìng　【名】plasticity

可望而不可即　kě wàng ér bù kě jí　within sight but beyond reach；unattainable：科学高峰并不是～的。The heights of science aren't beyond our reach. 也作"可望而不可及"。

可恶　kěwù　【形】hateful；wicked；disgusting

可惜　kěxī　【形】it is a pity；it is a shame：这些木料还能用，烧掉太～了。

This wood is still useful. It's a shame to burn it. 听说这场球赛很精彩，～我没去看。 I heard that the ball game was wonderful. It's too bad I didn't go to watch it.

可喜 kěxǐ 【形】 encouraging; gratifying

可笑 kěxiào 【形】 laughable; ridiculous

可心 kěxīn 【形】 pleasing; to one's liking

可行 kěxíng 【形】 feasible practicable; 这个办法是否～? Is this method workable?

可疑 kěyí 【形】 suspicious; questionable; dubious

可以 kěyǐ 【助动】 ❶ may; can; 去参加宴会，你完全～穿那套深蓝衣服嘛! You can certainly wear that dark blue suit of yours to the banquet. 许多野生植物，既～当菜吃，也～做药材。 There are many wild plants which can both be eaten as vegetables and used as medical herbs. 这条沟不宽，我～跳过去。 The ditch is not very wide. I can jump across it. Note: *the negative of* 可以 *in* ❶ *is* 不能, *not* 不可以 ❷ permissible; 这里～抽烟吗? ——不～。 Is smoking allowed here? —No. 明天的会提前开好不好? ——～。 The meeting is scheduled for tomorrow. How about holding it sooner? —All right. 你刚才读的那首诗很好，～不～把它写下来给我? The poem you've just recited is very good. Could you write it down for me? 【形】 neither very good nor very bad (*usu. used with* 还 (hái); 你看这张画儿画得怎么样? ——还～。 What do you think of this painting? —Not bad.

渴 kě 【形】 thirsty

渴求 kěqiú 【动】 long for; yearn for

渴望 kěwàng 【动】 yearn; hope eagerly for; long for

kè

克 kè 【动】 ◇ conquer; defeat; subdue; capture; 战必胜，攻必～。 There is no battle that we cannot win, and no fortress that we cannot storm. 【量】 gram

克敌制胜 kè dí zhì shèng defeat the enemy and win victory

克分子 kèfēnzǐ 【名】 (chem.) gram molecule; mole

克服 kèfú 【动】 overcome; surmount (difficulties, obstacles, etc.); conquer; ～缺点 overcome one's shortcomings 困难被～了。 The difficulties have been surmounted.

克己奉公 kè jǐ fèng gōng work selflessly in the public interest; 他埋头苦干～的精神，值得学习。 His hard work and devotion to the public interest are examples worth our emulation.

克朗 kèlǎng 【名】 krona; krone (currency)

克制 kèzhì 【动】 restrain; restrict; control (oneself)

刻 kè 【动】 engrave; carve; ～图章 engrave a seal 【量】 a quarter (of an hour); 15 minutes; 现在是两点一～。 It's 2:15. 骑车三～钟就可以到学校。 It takes us three quarters of an hour to get to school by bike.

刻板 kèbǎn 【形】 mechanical; inflexible

刻薄 kèbó 【形】 acrimonious; harsh; unkind

刻不容缓 kè bù róng huǎn brook no delay; very urgent; pressing

刻度 kèdù 【名】 graduation

刻骨仇恨 kègǔ chóuhèn bitter hatred

刻骨铭心　kè gǔ míng xīn　be carved in one's bones and engraved in one's heart

刻画　kèhuà　【动】portray；depict

刻苦　kèkǔ　【形】❶ painstaking；hardworking ❷ frugal and simple

客　kè　【名】guest；visitor

客车　kèchē　【名】〔列 liè〕passenger train

客店　kèdiàn　【名】inn

客队　kèduì　【名】visiting team

客饭　kèfàn　【名】guest meal

客房　kèfáng　【名】guest room

客观　kèguān　【名】objectivity；～事物 objective reality ～规律 objective law【形】objective：～地分析情况 analyze the situation objectively 他看问题很～。He takes an objective view of things.

客观唯心主义　kèguān wéixīnzhǔyì　objective idealism

客观主义　kèguānzhǔyì　【名】objectivism

客机　kèjī　【名】〔架 jià〕passenger plane；airliner

客轮　kèlún　【名】〔艘 sōu〕passenger ship

客满　kèmǎn　【形】(of theatre) full house；(of hotel) no vacancies

客气　kèqi　【形】❶ polite；courteous：昨天来的客人，彼此都不很熟，所以都是客客气气的。The guests who came yesterday didn't know each other very well, so their manner was very formal. ❷ modest：你这么说，就太～了。When you talk like that, you are being too modest.【动】stand on ceremony；be modest：他～了半天，最后答应来给我们讲讲汉语的词类问题。He demurred politely for a long time, but finally agreed to talk to us about the parts of speech of the Chinese language.

客人　kèren　【名】guest；visitor

客套　kètào　【名】polite formula；civilities【动】exchange greetings

客厅　kètīng　【名】sitting-room；parlour

客运　kèyùn　【动】passenger transport

客栈　kèzhàn　【名】inn

课（課）　kè　【名】❶ class：上午有三节～。There are three classes in the morning. ❷ course；subject：这个学期有四门～。There are four courses this term. ❸ lesson：这本教科书有三十～。There are 30 lessons in this textbook.【量】for lesson：这～书比那～书难。This lesson is more difficult than that one.

课本　kèběn　【名】text-book

课表　kèbiǎo　【名】school timetable

课程　kèchéng　【名】curriculum；course

课堂　kètáng　【名】classroom

课题　kètí　【名】main topic；subject

课外　kèwài　【名】extracurricular：～读物 supplementary reading material ～辅导 after-class tutoring

课文　kèwén　【名】〔篇 piān〕text

课余　kèyú　【形】extracurricular：～时间 extracurricular time；after class

kěn

肯　kěn　【助动】indicates willingness followed by actual action：世上无难事，只要～登攀。There is nothing one cannot do, so long as one dares to scale the heights. 他在学习上～下功夫。He really and truly works hard at his studies. 他原来不～去，我劝了半天，他才去了。He refused to go at first, but I finally talked him into it.

肯定　kěndìng　【动】❶ affirm；confirm；approve：～成绩 confirm

that sb. has made an achievement
～事实 confirm a fact 对他的进步加
以 ～ affirm the progress he has
made ❷ regard as positive；be
sure；be definite：去不去还不能～。
We are not sure whether we'll go
or not.【形】affirmative；positive：
～的答复 an affirmative answer 他
说话的语气非常～。He sounds very
positive.

肯干　kěngàn　【形】hard-working

垦（墾）　kěn　【动】reclaim
(land)

垦荒　kěn=huāng　reclaim wasteland

恳（懇）　kěn

恳切　kěnqiè　【形】earnest；sincere

恳求　kěnqiú　【动】implore；entreat

啃　kěn　【动】❶ gnaw：～骨头
gnaw a bone ❷〈口〉take great
pains with one's studies：～书本
pore over books 他～了两年外语，很
有成绩。He has worked hard on
language study for two years and
has made visible progress.

kēng

坑　kēng　【名】pit

坑道　kēngdào　【名】❶ tunnel ❷ gallery (in a mine)

坑害　kēnghài　【动】entrap；frame；
do harm to (sb.)

吭　kēng　【动】talk (usu. in the
negative)

吭气　kēng＝qì　speak；open one's
mouth (to speak) (usu. in the
negative)：我问了他半天，他也不～。
I kept on asking him about it, but
he didn't say a word.

吭声　kēng＝shēng　同"吭气" (the
usage is sometimes different)：别人

都在热烈争论，他却一声不吭。Every-
body was arguing heatedly. He
kept his mouth shut.

铿（鏗）　kēng

铿锵　kēngqiāng　【形】ring；clang
(e.g. the rhythmic beat of a powerful poem)

kōng

空　kōng　【形】empty；hollow；
void：～箱子 an empty trunk 车厢里
还有几个～位子。There are still
some empty seats in this car of the
train. 这篇作文写得比较～。There
isn't much content in this composition.【名】◇ the air；sky：对～射击
anti-aircraft barrage ～降部队 airborne troops【副】fruitlessly；in
vain；for nothing：～跑一趟 make a
trip for nothing ～忙一阵 time
spent in fruitless effort
另见 kòng

空洞　kōngdòng　【形】(of speech,
etc.) devoid of content

空洞无物　kōngdòng wú wù　同"空洞"

空话　kōnghuà　【名】empty or meaningless talk

空间　kōngjiān　【名】space

空降　kōngjiàng　【动】airborne：～兵
airborne force；paratroops

空军　kōngjūn　【名】air-force

空口无凭　kōng kǒu wú píng　a verbal
statement without proof or guarantee

空旷　kōngkuàng　【形】open；wide；
spacious

空难　kōngnàn　【名】air crash；air
calamity

空气　kōngqì　【名】❶ air：～新鲜
The air is fresh. ❷ atmosphere：学
术～很浓 a strongly academic atmosphere

空前　kōngqián　【形】unprecedented；

盛况～ a grand occasion such as has never before been seen 近年来世界上的科学技术以～的速度向前发展。Science and technology have developed with unprecedented speed in recent years. 生产力～发展。The productive forces are flourishing as never before.

空前绝后 kōng qián jué hòu without parallel before or since

空前未有 kōng qián wèi yǒu unprecedented

空谈 kōngtán 【动】talk idly：别总是～，要实际去干。Don't just talk；do something! 【名】empty talk：脱离实际的计划，只能是纸上～。Unrealistic plans are no more than empty words on paper.

空调 kōngtiáo 【名】air-conditioner

空头 kōngtóu 【形】phony（writer，politician, etc.）

空头支票 kōngtóu zhīpiào ❶ bad cheque ❷ empty promise：说话要算数，不能开～。One should stick to one's words；don't just make empty promises.

空投 kōngtóu 【动】air-drop

空袭 kōngxí 【动】air-raid

空想 kōngxiǎng 【动】indulge in fantasies【名】fantasy；fancy

空心 kōng = xīn become hollow：～砖 hollow brick 这棵树太老了，空了心儿了。The tree is too old；it has become hollow.

空虚 kōngxū 【形】（of spiritual life）void of content

空运 kōngyùn 【动】air transport

空中 kōngzhōng 【名】in the air

空中楼阁 kōngzhōng lóugé castle in the air

kǒng

孔　kǒng 【名】opening；hole；aperture：通气～ ventilator 钻个～ drill a hole 这座桥有十七个～。This bridge has 17 arches.

孔雀 kǒngquè 【名】〔只 zhī〕peacock

孔穴 kǒngxué 【名】hole；cavity

恐　kǒng

恐怖 kǒngbù 【形】horrible；terrifying

恐吓 kǒnghè 【动】terrify；frighten；intimidate

恐慌 kǒnghuāng 【形】panic-stricken；desperately afraid：吓得敌人～万状。The enemy was thrown into a desperate panic.

恐惧 kǒngjù 【动】fear；dread

恐龙 kǒnglóng 【名】dinosaur

恐怕 kǒngpà 【副】indicates one's estimate of probability, sometimes implying anxiety：他来中国～有半年多了。He's probably been in China six months by now. 你们现在才去，～赶不上火车了。There's no point in your going now. I'm afraid you won't be able to catch the train. ～夜里要刮风，把窗户关上吧！It looks as if it might be windy during the night. We'd better close the windows.

kòng

空　kòng 【动】vacate：～出一排房子 vacate a row of houses ～两行（háng）再写 leave two lines blank and then write 【形】vacant；blank：～地 vacant lot 这个办公室比较～。This office is fairly empty. 【名】（～儿）empty space；leisure time：仓库放满了东西，一点儿～都没有。The warehouse is full of goods, and there is no space left. 有～请来一趟。Please come when you are free.

另见 kōng

空白 kòngbái 【名】blank；space；gap：在～的地方加了几句批语 put comments in the space provided 这项技术革新搞成功了，将填补中国冶金工业的一项～。If this technological innovation works, it will fill a gap in Chinese metallurgical industry.

空白点 kòngbáidiǎn 【名】blank spot；gap

空额 kòng'é 【名】(of personnel) vacancy

空缺 kòngquē 【名】vacancy

空隙 kòngxì 【名】unfilled space；gap

空闲 kòngxián 【名】leisure；spare time 【动】be unoccupied；be free

空心 kòngxīn 【形】with empty stomach：喝～酒容易醉。If you drink on an empty stomach, you are likely to get drunk.

空余 kòngyú 【名】(of room, time, etc.) unoccupied：这几天工作排得满满的，没有一点儿～。These next few days will be completely taken up with work. We won't have any free time.

空子 kòngzi 【名】❶ unoccupied space ❷ opportunity to take advantage of；loophole

控 kòng

控告 kònggào 【动】accuse；charge with

控诉 kòngsù 【动】accuse；bring an accusation against；complain；denounce：开～大会 hold an accusation meeting

控制 kòngzhì 【动】control；dominate；command：～人数 control the number of people attending 自动～ automatically controlled ～不住激动的心情 be in a state of uncontrollable emotion

kōu

抠（掻） kōu 【动】❶ dig or dig out with a finger or sth. pointed；pick ❷〈口〉adhere rigidly to (what one finds in books)：～字眼 get hung up over the meaning of a word 他就爱死～书本儿。He is apt to adhere rigidly to what is put down in books.

kǒu

口 kǒu 【名】❶ ◇ mouth ❷ ◇ opening；outlet；mouth：枪～ the muzzle of a gun 胡同～ entrance to a lane 瓶～ mouth of a bottle ❸ ◇ edge：刀～ edge of a knife ❹（～儿）rip；tear；chip；cut：衣服撕了个～。The jacket was torn. 花盆碰了个～。The flower-pot was chipped. ❺ ◇ department；section：文教～ organizations supervising culture and education 工交～ organizations supervising industry and transportation 【量】for wells, family members, pigs, etc.：打一～井 sink a well 他家里四～人。His family has four members.

口岸 kǒu'àn 【名】port；seaport

口才 kǒucái 【名】eloquence；the ability to talk well

口吃 kǒuchī 【形】stammering；stammer

口齿 kǒuchǐ 【名】speaking ability：～清楚 clear enunciation ～伶俐 speak fluently；speak glibly

口袋 kǒudài 【名】❶（～儿）pocket ❷ bag；sack：面～ flour sack 纸～ paper bag 塑料～ plastic bag

口服 kǒufú 【动】(of medicine) take orally

口感 kǒugǎn 【名】texture：这种饼干

~不错。These biscuits have a fine texture.

口供 kǒugòng 【名】 confession; statement made by the accused under examination

口号 kǒuhào 【名】 slogan; catchword

口技 kǒujì 【名】 vocal imitations

口径 kǒujìng 【名】 ❶ the diameter of an opening; bore; calibre; gauge: 小~步枪 small-bore rifle ❷ requirements; specifications: ~不合 not meet the requirements 统一~ agree on a story; have the same version of an event

口诀 kǒujué 【名】 mnemonics

口角 kǒujué 【名】 quarrel

口口声声 kǒu kǒu shēng shēng keep on saying; say repeatedly (usu. say sth. one doesn't mean): 他~说要锻炼身体,怎么不见行动? He talks time and time again about exercise, but why don't we see action?

口粮 kǒuliáng 【名】 ration of grain

口令 kǒulìng 【名】 ❶ pass-word ❷ word of command

口蜜腹剑 kǒu mì fù jiàn honey on one's lips and murder in one's heart; sing someone's praises while plotting his ruin: 要警惕那种~的假朋友。Be on guard against false friends who sing your praises while plotting your ruin.

口气 kǒuqì 【名】 ❶ one's manner of speaking; tone: ~很硬 in an uncompromising tone; in a manner of speaking which admits no discussion 抱怨的~ in a grumbling tone ❷ what is actually meant; implication: 听~, 他明天是不准备来了。Judging by the way he spoke, it's clear that he's not coming tomorrow.

口腔 kǒuqiāng 【名】 oral cavity

口琴 kǒuqín 【名】 harmonica

口若悬河 kǒu ruò xuán hé be eloquent

口哨儿 kǒushàor 【名】 whistling

口舌 kǒushé 【名】 words used in persuading, arguing etc.; persuasion; argument: 我费了许多~才说服了他。It was only after a lot of arguing that I talked him round. 不要白费~了,他不会同意的。Don't waste your breath; he won't agree.

口实 kǒushí 【名】 (give people) sth. to gossip about

口试 kǒushì 【名】 oral examination 【动】 take an oral examination

口是心非 kǒu shì xīn fēi say yes and mean no; say one thing and mean another: ~,阳奉阴违,这就是两面派的特点。Saying yes and meaning no, complying in public but opposing in private, this is the characteristic of double-dealers.

口述 kǒushù 【动】 give an oral account

口算 kǒusuàn 【动】 calculate orally

口头 kǒutóu 【形】 verbal; oral: ~传达 transmit sth. verbally ~汇报 verbal report 四个现代化~上说说是不行的,必须脚踏实地去干。The four modernizations cannot be accomplished by mere words. What we need is action.

口头语 kǒutóuyǔ 【名】 pet phrase

口味 kǒuwèi 【名】 a person's taste: 这个菜不合他的~。This dish is not to his liking. 一部作品,不可能合乎所有人的~。It is impossible that a literary work suits the tastes of everybody.

口吻 kǒuwěn 【名】 (of one's voice) tone

口香糖 kǒuxiāngtáng 【名】〔块 kuài〕 chewing gum

口信 kǒuxìn 【名】 verbal message

口形 kǒuxíng 【名】 (phonetics) de-

gree of lip-rounding

口译 kǒuyì 【名】oral interpretation 【动】interpret

口音 kǒuyīn 【名】❶（of a locality or a country）accent ❷ a person's voice（as a distinguishing characteristic）

口语 kǒuyǔ 【名】❶ colloquialism ❷ spoken language

口罩 kǒuzhào 【名】（～儿）surgical mask；flu mask

口诛笔伐 kǒu zhū bǐ fá condemn both in speech and in writing

口子 kǒuzi 【名】❶（in bank, canal, sewer system, etc.）opening；渠道跑水了，快把～堵上。There is a breach in the canal wall. Hurry and stop it up. ❷ tear；rip；chip；cut；窗帘撕了个～。There is a tear in the curtain.

kòu

扣 kòu 【动】❶ button；～扣子 button the buttons ❷ place a cup, bowl, etc. upside down；cover with an inverted cup, bowl, etc.；把杯子～在茶盘里。Place the cup upside down on the tray. ❸ detain；take sb. into custody；arrest；把罪犯～起来 keep the criminal in custody ❹ deduct；take off；每月的房租从工资中～。One's monthly rent is deducted from one's monthly wages. 【名】（～儿）button

扣除 kòuchú 【动】deduct

扣留 kòuliú 【动】detain by force

扣帽子 kòu màozi put a label on；label；批评要实事求是，不要乱～。Criticism should be based on facts. Don't brand others with unwarranted labels.

扣押 kòuyā 【动】❶ detain（person）❷（legal）distrain

扣子 kòuzi 【名】〔个 gè〕❶ knot ❷ button

kū

枯 kū 【形】❶（of plants, etc.）dried up；withered；这棵树～了。This tree has withered. ❷（of well, river, etc.）dry；一口～井 a dry well

枯槁 kūgǎo 【形】dried and withered

枯黄 kūhuáng 【形】withered and yellow

枯竭 kūjié 【动】dry up；exhaust；水源～。The source of the water has dried up. 资金～。The capital has been exhausted. 他因劳累过度而精力～。He is exhausted from overwork.

枯木逢春 kū mù féng chūn spring comes to a withered tree；get a new lease on life

枯涩 kūsè 【形】dull and heavy going；文字～ a dull and heavy style of writing 双眼～难受。My eyes are smarting and painful.

枯萎 kūwěi 【动】dry up；wither

枯燥 kūzào 【形】dull and boring；uninteresting；～无味 dry as dust 他说话很有风趣，和他在一起不会感到～。His conversation is full of humour and wit. One never feels bored in his company.

哭 kū 【动】weep；cry

哭哭啼啼 kūkūtítí 【形】wail and whine；keep on weeping

哭泣 kūqì 【动】weep；sob

窟 kū

窟窿 kūlong 【名】❶ hole；cavity；冰～ a hole in the ice ❷ deficit；debt；补～ make up a deficit

骷 kū

骷髅 kūlóu 【名】skeleton

kǔ

苦 kǔ 【形】❶ bitter：～药 bitter medicine 味道很～. It tastes bitter. ❷ hard；painful：为了解决这个难题,想得我好～! It's been sheer agony trying to find a solution to this problem. 【名】 hardship；bitterness；suffering：他很能吃～. He is a stoic who can bear up against hardship. 【副】 energetically；painstakingly：～练基本功 work hard to master the basic skill ～干加巧干 work hard and intelligently

苦处 kǔchu 【名】suffering；distress

苦功 kǔgōng 【名】painstaking effort；hard work：下一番～ make a painstaking effort 语言这东西,不是随便可以学好的,非下～不可。The mastery of a language is not easy；it requires painstaking effort.

苦果 kǔguǒ 【名】a bitter pill (to swallow)

苦口婆心 kǔ kǒu pó xīn speak earnestly and patiently, and with the best intentions：对犯错误的人,要～地进行帮助,不能操之过急。We should earnestly and kindly help those who have made a slip.

苦闷 kǔmèn 【形】(of state of mind) gloomy；depressed

苦难 kǔnàn 【名】suffering；misery；distress：～岁月 hard times ～家史 a family history filled with sufferings 她很年轻,没经受过什么～。She's very young, and has never suffered any hardship.

苦恼 kǔnǎo 【形】worried；anxious；distressed

苦涩 kǔsè 【形】bitter and astringent

苦水 kǔshuǐ 【名】❶ water which tastes bitter ❷ gastric secretion, etc. vomited when ill ❸ untold suffering；bitterness：老张跟我倒(dào)了一晚上～. The other day, I listened for a whole evening to Lao Zhang pouring out his grievances.

苦痛 kǔtòng 【形】painful

苦头 kǔtou 【名】bitterness；suffering

苦笑 kǔxiào 【动】smile bitterly 【名】bitter smile

苦心 kǔxīn 【名】trouble taken；pains：费了一番～ take great pains 一片～ with patience and good intentions ～钻研 study painstakingly

苦心孤诣 kǔ xīn gū yì make extraordinarily painstaking efforts

苦战 kǔzhàn 【动】engage in bitter fighting

苦衷 kǔzhōng 【名】suffering due to troubles one finds it difficult to give voice to；诉说～ confide one's troubles 难言的～ troubles that one finds it difficult to voice to

kù

库 (庫) kù 【名】warehouse；storehouse；冷藏～ storage locker for frozen food 军火～ armoury 夏粮已入～。The summer's grain has been stored in the granary.

库藏 kùcáng 【动】have in storage

库存 kùcún 【名】goods in stock 【动】keep in stock

库房 kùfáng 【名】storehouse

库仑 kùlún 【量】(electr.) coulomb

裤 (褲) kù 【名】◇ trousers

裤衩 kùchǎ 【名】(～儿)〔条 tiáo〕panties

裤腿 kùtuǐ 【名】(～儿) trouser leg

裤子 kùzi 【名】〔条 tiáo〕trousers；slacks

酷 kù

酷爱　kù'ài　【动】have an ardent love for（not of persons）

酷热　kùrè　【形】exceedingly hot

酷暑　kùshǔ　【名】scorching summer heat

酷刑　kùxíng　【名】torture

kuā

夸（誇）　kuā　【动】❶ exaggerate；overstate；boast：什么事情一到他嘴里，就～得神乎其神。No matter what he talks about, he exaggerates wildly. ❷ praise：好人好事人人～。Praise for good deeds are on everyone's lips. 大家都～她心灵手巧。Everyone praised her for her quick mind and clever hands.

夸大　kuādà　【动】exaggerate

夸奖　kuājiǎng　【动】praise

夸口　kuā=kǒu　boast；brag

夸夸其谈　kuā kuā qí tán　indulge in exaggerated rhetoric：说话或写文章要实事求是，切不可～，华而不实。Speeches and writing should be simple and stick to the facts and not be full of bombast.

夸耀　kuāyào　【动】show off；brag about

夸张　kuāzhāng　【动】exaggerated；overstated：～的描写 exaggerated description 说得太～了。He exaggerates too much. 一点儿也不～。It's not overstated at all.

kuǎ

垮　kuǎ　【动】collapse；break down；fall：堤坝冲～了。The river bank collapsed. 我的身体～不了。My health won't break down.

垮台　kuǎ=tái　break down；collapse

kuà

挎　kuà　【动】carry over the arm；carry sth. over one's shoulder or at one's side：胳膊上～着篮子 carry a basket on one's arm 骑马～枪 ride a horse with a gun slung over one's shoulder 腰里～着刀 wear a sword dangling from one's waist

挎包　kuàbāo　【名】〔个 gè〕shoulder-bag

跨　kuà　【动】❶ step；stride：向前～一步 take a step forward ～进大门 step in through the gate ～过千山万水 pass over countless mountains and rivers ❷ straddle；bestride：～上骏马 straddle a fine horse 彩虹横～蓝天。The rainbow arches across the blue sky. ❸ cut across：～年度 over the year-end ～地区 transregional ～行（háng）业的大协作 large scale cooperation among different professions

跨度　kuàdù　【名】span

跨国公司　kuà guó gōngsī　transnational corporation

跨越　kuàyuè　【动】cross（of district or period of time）；pass

kuài

会（會）　kuài
　另见 huì

会计　kuàijì　【名】accountant

会计师　kuàijìshī　【名】certified accountant

块（塊）　kuài　【名】〔～儿〕piece；lump；chunk：石～ stones；blocks of stone 把土豆切成～ cut

the potatoes into cubes 【量】❶ a piece of; a lump of: 两～巧克力 two bars of chocolate 五～蛋糕 five cakes 这～地种玉米。This plot of land is to be planted with maize. ❷ colloq. for yuan: 五～钱 five kuai (i.e. 5 yuan)

快 kuài 【形】❶ quick; fast; swift; rapid: 跑得很～ run very fast 工农业发展很～。Industry and agriculture are developing quickly. ❷ quick-witted; clever: 他脑子～。 He is very quick-witted. ❸ sharp: 这把刀真～。This knife is really sharp. ❹ ◇ pleased; gratified: 人心大～ to the immense satisfaction of the masses 【副】❶ quickly; hurriedly; at once: ～来呀! Come at once! ❷ be about to; soon; before long (usu. takes 了 at the end of the sentence): ～放暑假了。Summer vacation is about to begin. 稿子～写完了。The manuscript will soon be finished.

快板儿 kuàibǎnr 【名】verses or rhythmic talk accompanied by bamboo clapper

快报 kuàibào 【名】short news bulletin; news flash

快餐 kuàicān 【名】quick meal; fast food

快车 kuàichē 【名】express train or bus

快感 kuàigǎn 【名】pleasant feeling

快活 kuàihuo 【形】joyful; happy

快乐 kuàilè 【形】happy

快马加鞭 kuài mǎ jiā biān spur the flying horse to full speed; at top speed

快慢 kuàimàn 【名】speed

快门 kuàimén 【名】(camera) shutter

快速 kuàisù 【形】fast; speedy

快慰 kuàiwèi 【形】happy and relieved

脍(膾) kuài

脍炙人口 kuài zhì rén kǒu (of a piece of good writing, etc.) win universal praise; enjoy great popularity

筷 kuài 【名】◇ chopstick

筷子 kuàizi 【名】〔根 gēn、双 shuāng〕 chopstick

kuān

宽(寬) kuān 【形】❶ wide; broad: 这条公路很～。This highway is very wide. ❷ lenient; generous: 坦白从～，抗拒从严 leniency towards those who confess their crimes, and severe punishment for those who refuse 【名】width: 这个游泳池的长是五十米，～是二十五米。 This swimming-pool is 50 metres long and 25 metres wide.

宽敞 kuānchang 【形】spacious

宽绰 kuānchuo 【形】❶ spacious; commodious: 这间屋子住两个人很～。Having only two people in a room of this size gives each a lot of space. 这个院子很～。This courtyard is very spacious. ❷ well-off; comfortably off: 经济～ be well-off

宽打窄用 kuān dǎ zhǎi yòng budget liberally and spend sparingly

宽大 kuāndà 【形】spacious; roomy; commodious: ～的厂房 spacious workshop 【动】be lenient; magnanimous (in the punishment of criminals)

宽度 kuāndù 【名】width

宽广 kuānguǎng 【形】broad and extensive (e.g. wilderness)

宽宏大量 kuānhóng dàliàng broad-minded

宽厚 kuānhòu 【形】lenient

宽阔　kuānkuò　【形】broad

宽容　kuānróng　【动】be forbearing

宽恕　kuānshù　【动】forgive; tolerate

宽慰　kuānwèi　【形】relieved

宽心　kuān=xīn　be at ease

宽银幕电影　kuānyínmù diànyǐng　wide-screen film; cinemascope

宽裕　kuānyù　【形】well-off; well-to-do; ample: 生活～ be comfortably off 时间～ ample time; plenty of time

宽窄　kuānzhǎi　【名】width

kuǎn

款　kuǎn　【名】❶〔笔 bǐ〕sum of money; fund: 取～ draw money 拨一笔～给幼儿园 allocate a sum of money for the kindergarten ❷ section of an article in a document, etc.: 第二条第三～ Article II, Section 3 ❸ the name of painter or calligrapher or of recipient inscribed on a painting or a piece of calligraphy presented as a gift: 上～ the name of recipient 下～ the name of painter or calligrapher

款待　kuǎndài　【动】entertain

款式　kuǎnshì　【名】style; pattern

款项　kuǎnxiàng　【名】sum of money (esp. of an institution)

款子　kuǎnzi　【名】sum of money

kuāng

筐　kuāng　【名】basket

筐子　kuāngzi　【名】〔个 gè〕basket

kuáng

狂　kuáng　【形】❶ mad; insane; crazy: 发～ become insane ❷ wild; unrestrained: ～笑 laugh wildly ～

叫 scream aloud ❸ violent: ～奔 run madly ❹ arrogant; overbearing: 这人说话太～了。This man's remarks are very arrogant.

狂吠　kuángfèi　【动】bark

狂风　kuángfēng　【名】gale

狂欢　kuánghuān　【动】go merrymaking; public merrymaking

狂澜　kuánglán　【名】(usu. fig.) pounding waves

狂热　kuángrè　【形】frantic; feverish; frenzied

狂人　kuángrén　【名】(usu. fig.) madman; maniac

狂妄　kuángwàng　【形】arrogant

狂妄自大　kuángwàng zìdà　arrogant and conceited

狂笑　kuángxiào　【动】laugh wildly 【名】roars of langhter

狂言　kuángyán　【名】arrogant remarks

kuàng

旷（曠）　kuàng　【动】desert; skip【形】spacious; wide; open

旷工　kuàng=gōng　skip work

旷课　kuàng=kè　skip school; play hookey

旷日持久　kuàng rì chí jiǔ　long-drawn-out; protracted; prolonged: ～的战争 a long-drawn-out war

旷野　kuàngyě　【名】wilderness

况　kuàng

况且　kuàngqiě　【连】besides (usu. in written language, introduces an additional reason): 他说话很快,～又带南方口音,我只听懂了一半。He spoke rapidly and in a southern accent, so I only understood about half of what he said. 我水性很好,让我去吧,～我又熟悉沿江的情况。I'm a very good swimmer, so you should let me go. Besides, I'm fa-

miliar with the conditions along the river.

矿（礦）kuàng 【名】❶ deposit ❷ mine ❸ ore

矿藏　kuàngcáng　【名】mineral deposit

矿产　kuàngchǎn　【名】mineral products

矿工　kuànggōng　【名】miner

矿井　kuàngjǐng　【名】mine shaft

矿泉水　kuàngquánshuǐ　【名】mineral water

矿山　kuàngshān　【名】a mountain beneath which there is a mine; mine

矿石　kuàngshí　【名】❶ ore ❷ pyrites (of a cryster receiver)

矿物　kuàngwù　【名】mineral

框　kuàng　【名】frame

框框　kuàngkuang　【名】❶ frame: 用红笔画了个～ frame with a red pencil ❷ restriction; conventions; set pattern: 打破旧～ break through set conventions

框子　kuàngzi　【名】frame

kuī

亏（虧）kuī　【动】◇ ❶ (of business) lose: ～本 lose one's capital ❷ be short of; lack: ～理 lack justification 身大力不～ a big-sized person will not be lacking in strength【连】❶ 同"幸亏" xìngkuī: ～他把汽车停住,要不孩子就受伤了。Fortunately he was able to stop the car in time. Otherwise, the child would have been injured. ❷ indicates that one has succeeded in doing sth. difficult: 这么多书,～他一个人都拿来了。Such a lot of books! It's amazing that he was able to bring them here all by him-

self. Note: 亏 is used as a sarcastic remark: 这么不合理的要求,～他提得出来! What an unreasonable request! It's shocking that he should make it! 天热成这样,～你还穿得住毛衣! It's so hot! How on earth can you still be wearing a sweater! ❸ indicates that it is a pity one didn't make use of a good opportunity: ～你还是海边长大的,连游泳都不会。Just imagine: you grew up near the sea and don't know how to swim! ～他去了一趟北京,怎么没去看长城! Can you imagine? He was in Beijing and didn't go to the Great Wall!

亏得　kuīde　【连】同"亏"【连】❶

亏空　kuīkong　【名】debt【动】suffer a financial loss: ～4000 元 be £4,000 in the red

亏欠　kuīqiàn　【动】have a deficit

亏损　kuīsǔn　【动】lose money (in business)【名】loss; deficit

岿（巋）kuī

岿然　kuīrán　【副】towering

窥（窺）kuī

窥测　kuīcè　【动】secretly watch and make conjectures

窥伺　kuīsì　【动】secretly watch and wait for (an opportunity)

窥探　kuītàn　【动】spy on; pry about: ～情况 snoop about to find out the state of affairs 暗中～ secretly spy on

kuí

葵　kuí

葵花　kuíhuā　【名】〔朵 duǒ〕sunflower

魁　kuí

魁伟　kuíwěi　【形】tall and physically

strong

魁梧　kuíwú　【形】同"魁伟"

kuǐ

傀　kuǐ

傀儡　kuǐlěi　【名】puppet：～政府 puppet government

kuì

溃（潰）　kuì　【动】◇ ❶ be routed：～逃 in pell-mell flight ～不成军 be utterly routed ❷ (of a dam or dike) burst：～堤 burst the dike

溃败　kuìbài　【动】suffer utter defeat and retreat in disorder

溃烂　kuìlàn　【动】fester；ulcerate

溃散　kuìsàn　【动】scatter after being defeated

溃疡　kuìyáng　【名】ulcer

愧　kuì

愧色　kuìsè　【名】a shame-faced look

kūn

昆　kūn

昆虫　kūnchóng　【名】insect

kǔn

捆　kǔn　【动】tie up；bundle up：～行李 tie up the luggage 把这些木棍～好 tie up these wooden sticks 【量】bundle；bunch：一小～葱 a small bunch of spring onions 两～稻草 two bales of hay

捆绑　kǔnbǎng　【动】truss up；tie up；bind

kùn

困　kùn　【动】❶ ◇ be hard-pressed；be in difficulty：为疾病所～ suffer the ravages of an illness ❷ surround；pin down：把敌人～在山里 pin down the enemy in the mountains 【形】（睏）tired；sleepy：走了一天一夜山路，又累又～。We are exhausted and sleepy after a day and night walking in the mountains.

困惑　kùnhuò　【形】perplexed；bewildered；puzzled：令人～ puzzling ～不解 feel bewildered

困境　kùnjìng　【名】difficult position；difficult straits；predicament：陷入～ find oneself in a tight corner 摆脱～ extricate oneself from a difficult position

困倦　kùnjuàn　【形】sleepy

困苦　kùnkǔ　【形】poverty-stricken

困难　kùnnan　【形】difficult；hard：～的条件 difficult conditions 处于～的境地 be in a difficult situation 生活～ live in straitened circumstances 【名】difficulty：不怕～ fear no hardships 克服～ surmount difficulties 迎着～上 face difficulties and make headway

困守　kùnshǒu　【动】defend against a siege

困兽犹斗　kùn shòu yóu dòu　cornered animals fight desperately

kuò

扩（擴）　kuò　【动】expand；enlarge；extend

扩充　kuòchōng　【动】expand and make substantial；extend；enlarge：～力量 increase in strength ～队伍 enlarge the number of our troops

~军备 arms expansion

扩大 kuòdà 【动】enlarge；expand；extend：~范围 extend the limits ~眼界 enlarge one's field of vision 这个村的机耕面积~了。The machine-ploughed area of the village has been increased. 影响不断~。The impact is expanding steadily.

扩大化 kuòdàhuà 【动】broaden the scope，usually in a negative sense

扩建 kuòjiàn 【动】enlarge；expand (a building)：~体育场 enlarge the stadium 这个工厂又~了一批厂房。This factory has expanded by the addition of several buildings.

扩军 kuò=jūn increase armaments；escalation of the arms race

扩军备战 kuò jūn bèi zhàn arms expansion and preparations for war

扩散 kuòsàn 【动】❶ spread ❷ diffuse ❸ proliferate

扩音机 kuòyīnjī 【名】amplifier

扩音器 kuòyīnqì megaphone；amplifier；loud-speaker

扩展 kuòzhǎn 【动】expand；extend；develop

扩张 kuòzhāng 【动】expand (territory)

扩张主义 kuòzhāngzhǔyì 【名】expansionism

括 kuò 【动】put... in brackets；bracket：把那两个字~起来 put those two characters in brackets

括号 kuòhào 【名】brackets；parentheses

括弧 kuòhú 【名】brackets

阔（闊）kuò 【形】❶ wide；broad；vast ❷ ostentatiously wealthy：摆~ ostentatious display of wealth

阔别 kuòbié 【动】be parted for a long time

阔步 kuòbù 【副】stride；long steps

阔绰 kuòchuò 【形】in a rich and extravagant manner

阔气 kuòqi 【形】同"阔绰"

L

lā

拉 lā 【动】❶ pull; drag; tug; draw：～上窗帘 draw the curtains 这个火车头能～多少节车厢? How many coaches can this engine pull? ❷ transport（by vehicle）：～货 haul goods ～化肥 haul chemical fertilizer ❸ play（some kinds of musical instruments）：～小提琴 play the violin ～手风琴 play the accordion ❹ help：～他一把 give him a helping hand ❺ make（a connection or an acquaintance which is to one's advantage）：有人特别喜欢～关系。Some people are very fond of forming connections which may be to their advantage. 注意不要被坏人～下水。One must be careful not to be dragged into trouble by bad people. ❻ prolong; drag out：～长声 drawl ～开距离 leave a long distance between ❼ defecate：～屎 have a bowel movement
另见 lá

拉丁美洲 Lādīngměizhōu 【名】Latin America

拉丁字母 Lādīng zìmǔ Roman letter

拉肚子 lā dùzi have loose bowels; suffer from diarrhoea

拉后腿 lā hòutuǐ selfishly hold sb. back from acting in the common interest 也说"扯后腿"。

拉拉扯扯 lā lā chě chě tug; exchange flattery and favours

拉拉队 lālāduì 【名】cheering squad

拉力 lālì 【名】tensile strength

拉链儿 lāliànr 【名】zipper; zip fastener

拉拢 lālong 【动】form a friendship with a self-serving motive

拉锁 lāsuǒ 【名】zip fastener

拉杂 lāzá 【形】（of writing or speech）rambling; disorganized：他拉拉杂杂说了半天,也没把问题说清楚。He rambled on and didn't get to the point.

lā

垃 lā

垃圾 lājī 【名】garbage; rubbish; refuse

lá

拉 lá 【动】cut; gash：～玻璃 cut glass 手上～了个口子 have a cut on one's hand
另见 lā

lǎ

喇 lǎ

喇叭 lǎba 【名】❶ trumpet; horn ❷ loudspeaker

喇嘛 lǎma 【名】lama; Buddhist

priest in Tibet and some other places

là

落 là 【动】❶ miss; leave out: 这个句子~了个字。A word is missing from this sentence. 开会的时间都通知到了吗? 可别~下人。Has everyone been informed of the meeting? Make sure no one is left out. ❷ forget and leave (a thing) behind: 我把词典~在教室了。I left the dictionary behind in the classroom. ❸ lag behind; fall behind: 老李自行车骑得飞快, 一会儿我就被~下一大截。Lao Li cycled very fast, and I was soon left far behind. 在工作中大家你追我赶, 谁都不甘~在后边。Everyone was engaged in friendly competition at work, and no one wanted to fall behind.
另见 luò; lào

腊(臘) là
腊肠 làcháng 【名】sausage
腊月 làyuè 【名】the 12th lunar month

蜡(蠟) là 【名】❶ wax ❷ candle
蜡版 làbǎn 【名】mimeograph stencil
蜡笔 làbǐ 【名】〔枝 zhī〕wax crayon
蜡黄 làhuáng 【形】sallow
蜡纸 làzhǐ 【名】〔张 zhāng〕❶ waxpaper ❷ mimeograph stencil
蜡烛 làzhú 【名】〔枝 zhī〕candle

辣 là 【形】❶ peppery; hot ❷ cruel
辣椒 làjiāo 【名】red pepper
辣手 làshǒu 【形】thorny; difficult to solve

la

啦 la 【助】 *the combination of the modal particle* 了 *and the modal particle* 啊 *in sound as well as in meaning*: 客人来~! Here comes our guest! 水位又上涨~! The water level has gone up! 我们明天要走~! We are leaving tomorrow! 人都到齐~! Everybody's here!

lái

来(來) lái 【动】❶ come; cause to come: 客人~了。The guests have come. 老张~了个电话。Lao Zhang telephoned. 新的一年又~了。Another year has come round. 请他~办公室一下儿。Please ask him to come to the office. 明天~一个会计支援你们。Tomorrow an accountant will be sent here to help you. ❷ *replaces another verb*: 你搬不动, 我~吧! It's too heavy for you to move. Let me do it. 咱俩~一盘(棋)! Let's play a game of chess. 她刚唱完, 观众热烈鼓掌并高喊:"再~一个!" No sooner had she finished singing than the audience applauded and shouted: "Encore!" ❸ arise; appear: 问题~了。A problem has arisen. 工农业发展的新高潮就要~了。A rising tide in agricultural and industrial development is approaching. ❹ *used in an imperative sentence before a verb to indicate that one is about to do sth. then and there*: 我~说两句。Let me put in a few words. 咱们~研究研究。Let's look into this. ❺ *preceded by a verb or verbal construction to indicate the purpose of coming to a place*: 你干什么~

了？——我看你～了。Why are you here? — I've come to see you. 儿子回家探亲～了。The son has come home to see his parents. ❻ *inserted between a verbal construction or prepositional construction and a verb or a verbal construction to indicate that what goes before is the way, means or agent and what follows is the purpose or action*：今天由王老师～讲课。Today Teacher Wang is to lecture to you. 用实际行动～表明决心。Let our action demonstrate our resolution. 我们想开个座谈会～交流经验。We are thinking of holding an informal discussion to exchange experiences. Note：来 *is used after a verb as a complement to indicate that the direction of the action is towards the speaker*：厨师给我们送～了热汤。The cook has served us some hot soup. 各地传～振奋人心的消息。Inspiring news of all sorts is pouring in from everywhere. 路太远，他今晚回不～了。It's very far away, he won't be able to get back tonight. 【助】❶ *used after the numerals* 十，百，千，*etc. or any numeral from 1 to 10 plus measure word to indicate approximate number*：十～个 about 10 五百～斤 around 500 *jin* 两个～月 about 2 months 七尺～长 about 7 *chi* long ❷ *used after a word or phrase referring to a period of time to indicate that period of time up to this moment*：十多天～ in the last fortnight or so 两千年～ in the past 2000 years 近几年～本地区电子工业发展较快。In the last few years, the local electronics industry has developed rapidly.

来宾 láibīn 【名】visitor；guest

来不及 lái bu jí there is not enough time (to do sth.)：赶头班汽车恐怕～了。I'm afraid it's too late to catch the first bus. 快上班了，～跟你细说了。We are about to begin work. There isn't time to tell you about it in detail.

来得及 lái de jí there is still time (to do sth.)；be able to do sth. in time：晚会七点钟开始，你现在去还～。The party begins at seven o'clock. You can still make it if you go now. 大坝赶在雨季以前修好，肯定～。There is certainly enough time to repair the dam before the rainy season starts.

来电 láidiàn 【名】incoming telegram

来电 lái = diàn ❶ inform by telegram ❷ power is on again

来访 láifǎng 【动】come to visit；come to call

来函 láihán 【名】〈书〉the letter which you wrote

来回 láihuí 【名】back and forth：他在游泳池里游了五个～。He swam back and forth five times in the swimming pool. 【副】to and fro：边防战士在国境线上～巡逻。The frontier guards patrolled to and fro along the frontier. 工地上车辆～奔驰，正在紧张施工。Lorries ran back and forth on the construction site, which was bustling with activity. 通讯员小李到团部～跑了两趟。Xiao Li, the messenger, has run to the regimental headquarters and back again twice.

来客 láikè 【名】visitor；guest

来历 láilì 【名】source；origin；past history：～不明 of unknown origin 查明～ trace sth. to its source 说起这幅画，可有一段不平凡的～。Talking about this painting, there is a remarkable story behind it.

来临 láilín 【动】come；arrive

来龙去脉 lái lóng qù mài origin and subsequent development (of a

matter)：事情的～ the whole story of an event 要弄清这个问题的～，必须进行调查研究。To get to the ins and outs of this matter, it is necessary to hold an investigation.

来年 láinián 【名】next year; the coming year

…来…去 … lái … qù ❶ back and forth (*used with a verb expressing some concrete action*)：他在院子里走来走去，像在思考什么问题。He walked back and forth in the courtyard as if he was immersed in a problem. 海鸥在天空中飞来飞去。Seagulls were flying back and forth in the sky. ❷ over and over again (*used in the subordinate clause of a compound sentence to show how sth. mentioned previously was dealt with repeatedly*)：这个问题大家讨论来讨论去，好容易才找到了解决的办法。We had wrestled with this question over and over again until at last we found a way out. 这篇发言稿改来改去，又改回原来的样子。The draft of the speech had been revised many times, and was finally restored to its original form.

来日方长 láirì fāng cháng there will be time for that; there is ample time (for doing sth.)

来势 láishì 【名】oncoming force; momentum：～凶猛 descend upon with shocking impact

来头 láitou 【名】❶ backing; connection：此人～不小。This person had powerful backing. 这篇文章看来大有～。You can tell that this article must have some backing. ❷ (of a speech or piece of writing) motive behind：他的话是有～的，是讽刺我的。He didn't say all that for nothing. He was being ironic at my expense.

来往 láiwǎng 【动】❶ come and go；

～的车太多，过马路不容易。There is a lot of traffic, it's not easy to cross the road. ❷ mix socially：我们俩不大～。We two don't mix much. 【名】social intercourse：这两家邻居之间～很多。These two neighbours are very close friends.

来信 láixìn 【名】同"来函"

来意 láiyì 【名】the purpose of one's visit; one's purpose in coming

来由 láiyóu 【名】cause

来源 láiyuán 【名】source; cause：原料的～ a source of raw materials 经济～ source of income 【动】have its source in; originate from：一种理论认为，理性认识～于感性认识。One school of theory holds that rational knowledge arises from perceptual knowledge. 一种理论认为，文艺创作～于生活。One school of theory holds that literary and artistic creation has life as its source.

来自 láizì 【动】come from (a place)：老黄～基层，有丰富的实践经验。Lao Huang is from the rank and file, and has practical experience. 在北京学习的外国留学生～世界各地。The foreign students studying in Beijing come from all parts of the world.

lài

赖（賴） lài 【动】❶ rely on; depend on ❷ deny (one's error, etc.)：～账 refuse to honour a debt 耍～ behave ignobly ❸ stay on (in a place)：许多小孩儿到了动物园总喜欢～在猴山前不走。Many children plant themselves in front of the monkey hill in the Zoo and refuse to move. ❹ blame：这事是我做的，不要～他。I did it. Don't blame him. 【形】not good; bad：白菜长得真不～。The cabbages are growing

well.

赖以 làiyǐ 【动】rely on；depend：那时他家只有一条破船，父女二人～为生。At that time, the only thing they had was a dilapidated boat on which father and daughter relied for a living. 空气、阳光和水是植物～生存的条件。Air, sunlight and water are necessary conditions for the existence of plants.

lán

兰(蘭) lán
兰花 lánhuā 【名】orchid

拦(攔) lán 【动】stop；block：他把汽车～住了。He waved the car to a halt. 山再高，也～不住我们。No mountains can stop us, however high they may be. 他刚说了半句话，就被别人～回去了。He had uttered barely half a sentence when he was cut off.
拦洪坝 lánhóngbà 【名】regulating dam
拦截 lánjié 【动】intercept
拦路 lán=lù block the way
拦路虎 lánlùhǔ 【名】(fig.) obstacle；stumbling block：煤层里的石头是采煤时的～。Rock in the coal seams is one of the problems in coal-mining.
拦阻 lánzǔ 【动】block；obstruct；hinder

栏(欄) lán 【名】❶ fence；railing：木～ wooden fence 高～ (sports) high hurdles ❷ pen；shed (for cattle)：牛～ corral for cattle 羊～ sheep pen ❸ column：新闻～ news column 广告～ classified ads 备注～ space for additional information (on a form)
栏杆 lángān 【名】railing；balus-

trade；banisters

阑(闌) lán
阑尾炎 lánwěiyán 【名】appendicitis

蓝(藍) lán 【形】blue
蓝本 lánběn 【名】piece of writing upon which later work is based
蓝色 lánsè 【名】blue
蓝图 lántú 【名】❶ blueprint：晒～ make a blueprint (by exposure to light) ❷ (fig.) plan for construction；revolutionary ideals：建设～ blueprint for the construction work 远景规划的～ a long-range plan

谰(讕) lán
谰言 lányán 【名】slander：无耻～ a shameless slander

褴(襤) lán
褴褛 lánlǚ 【形】〈书〉ragged：衣衫～ be in rags

篮(籃) lán 【名】❶ basket ❷ (of basketball) basket：投～ shoot a basket
篮球 lánqiú 【名】❶ basketball game ❷〔个 gè〕basketball
篮子 lánzi 【名】〔个 gè〕basket

lǎn

缆 lǎn
缆车 lǎnchē 【名】cable car

懒(懶) lǎn 【形】❶ lazy；indolent ❷ enervated
懒得 lǎnde 【副】not be in the mood (to do sth.)；be disinclined (to do sth.)：～动 not incline to move ～去 not feel like going 那篇文章又长又没意思，真～看！That article is

long and tedious, and I don't feel like reading it.

懒惰　lǎnduò　【形】lazy

懒汉　lǎnhàn　【名】lazy-bones; idler

懒散　lǎnsǎn　【形】slack; lazy; careless: 作风～ negligent work-style 懒懒散散的, 干不好工作。If you slack off, you can't do a job well.

懒洋洋　lǎnyángyāng　【形】languid

làn

烂（爛）　làn　【动】rot; become rotten; go bad: 这筐葡萄～了。This basket of grapes has gone bad.【形】❶ soft; tender: ～泥 mud 肉煮～了。The meat is boiled very well. ❷ worn-out; scrap: 破铜～铁 copper and iron scrap ❸ messy: ～摊子 an awful mess 一本～账 The accounts are in a mess.

烂漫　lànmàn　【形】❶ bright-coloured: 山坡上开满了～的野花。The slopes of the hills were covered with brightly coloured flowers. ❷ natural: 天真～ naive and innocent

烂熟　lànshú　【形】❶ thoroughly cooked; thoroughly ripe ❷ (learn) thoroughly: 这首诗他背得～。He can recite this poem very fluently.

滥（濫）　làn　【形】lavish; excessive: 这个词用得太～了。This word is used excessively.

滥用　lànyòng　【动】abuse; misuse

滥竽充数　làn yú chōng shù　refers to a Chinese story about a man who was unable to play the *Yu* (an ancient musical instrument), but got into an orchestra anyway to make up the required number of players; (*fig.*) be unable to do sth., but was present to fill in the numbers

láng

狼　láng　【名】〔只 zhǐ〕wolf

狼狈　lángbèi　【形】in an awkward predicament; in a difficult position: ～相 awkward look ～不堪 be in an extremely awkward position ～逃窜 be badly beaten and flee panic-stricken

狼狈为奸　láng bèi wéi jiān　refers to a legend in which the "狈" and the wolf often joined forces to prey on cattle; (*fig.*) collude in doing evil; work hand-in-glove with each other: 那些家伙～, 干尽坏事。They are thick as thieves and stop at nothing on their path of evil-doing.

狼藉　lángjí　【形】◇ ❶ in a mess: 杯盘～ wine cups and plates lying about in a mess ❷ notorious

狼吞虎咽　láng tūn hǔ yàn　wolf down; devour ravenously

狼心狗肺　láng xīn gǒu fèi　❶ cruel and unscrupulous ❷ ungrateful

狼子野心　lángzǐ yěxīn　the devouring ambition of a careerist

榔　láng

榔头　lángtou　【名】〔把 bǎ〕hammer

lǎng

朗　lǎng

朗读　lǎngdú　【动】read aloud

朗诵　lǎngsòng　【动】recite

làng

浪　làng　【名】❶ wave: 海～ wave of the sea ❷ wave-like thing: 声～ sound-wave 气～ blast

of air

浪潮 làngcháo 【名】tide；wave

浪费 làngfèi 【动】waste；be extravagant；squander

浪花 lànghuā 【名】❶ spray ❷ (fig.) an unusual event (in one's life)：在他平静的一生里，爱情曾激起过一朵～，不久又消失了。In his whole uneventful life，love had once stirred up a ripple which soon calmed down.

浪漫 làngmàn 【形】romantic

浪漫主义 làngmànzhǔyì 【名】romanticism

浪头 làngtou 【名】❶ wave ❷ trend；赶～ follow the fashion

lāo

捞（撈）lāo 【动】❶ scoop up (from water or other liquid)：～鱼 net fish ❷ garner by evil means：～政治资本 build up one's political capital ❸〈口〉have the chance to do sth. which is to one's advantage：昨天的精彩表演我没～着看。I didn't have a chance to see yesterday's splendid performance.

捞稻草 lāo dàocǎo grasp at a straw：谁想在这个问题上～，那是枉费心机。Anyone who tries to use this issue to his advantage will be like a drowning man grasping at a straw.

捞取 lāoqǔ 【动】fish for

捞一把 lāo yī bǎ rake in profits

láo

劳（勞）láo

劳保 láobǎo 【动】short for "劳动保险"

劳动 láodòng 【动】work；do physical or manual labour

劳动保护 láodòng bǎohù labour protection

劳动保险 láodòng bǎoxiǎn labour insurance

劳动改造 láodòng gǎizào short for "劳改"（of criminals）reform through labour

劳动教养 láodòng jiàoyǎng short for "劳教" rehabilitation through education and labour

劳动节 Láodòngjié 【名】May Day

劳动竞赛 láodòng jìngsài labour emulation；emulation drive

劳动力 láodònglì 【名】❶ capacity for work ❷ labour force ❸ able-bodied person

劳动模范 láodòng mófàn model-worker

劳动日 láodòngrì 【名】work-day

劳动者 láodòngzhě 【名】worker；labourer

劳改 láogǎi 【动】reform through labour

劳工 láogōng 【名】labourer (a term used in the old society)

劳驾 láo = jià may I trouble you；would you mind：劳您驾，帮我拿一下这个箱子。Would you mind helping me carry this case? ～告诉他一声，老李已经到了。May I trouble you to pass on a message that Lao Li has arrived?

劳苦 láokǔ 【形】toil-worn

劳累 láolèi 【形】tired；exhausted；fatigued

劳力 láolì 【名】〈口〉❶ labour force ❷ able-bodied person：节约～ use man-power sparingly 合理安排～ allocate man-power wisely

劳碌 láolù 【形】filled with toil

劳民伤财 láo mín shāng cái waste man-power and material resources

劳模 láomó 【名】short for "劳动模范"

劳神 láo = shén ❶ exert (oneself) ❷ (could I) trouble (you)

劳务 láowù 【名】services

劳役 láoyì 【名】forced labour；penal servitude

劳逸结合 láo yì jiéhé alternate work with rest and recreation

劳资 láo zī labour and capital：～双方 labour and management；the two parties of labour and capital

牢 láo 【名】prison；jail 【形】firm；secure；fast：这个钉子没钉～，再钉两下。The nail hasn't been driven home. You'd better hit it again. 马跳过小河，他仍然～～骑在马背上。He was still firmly in the saddle after his horse had jumped the stream.

牢不可破 láo bù kě pò indissoluble；indestructible：～的团结 indivisible unity ～的友谊 indestructible friendship

牢房 láofáng 【名】prison cell

牢固 láogù 【形】firm；strong：～的地基 solid foundation 工事～ strong fortifications

牢记 láojì 【动】remember well；keep firmly in mind：～过去的教训 remember well the lessons of the past

牢靠 láokào 【形】❶ solid；firm：这个架子搭得很～。This scaffolding is solidly put up. ❷ reliable；dependable：办事～ reliable in handling affairs 他这个人比较～。He is quite a reliable person.

牢骚 láosāo 【名】complaint：发～ grumble 他一肚子～。He is full of complaints.

唠（嘮） láo

唠叨 láodao 【动】chatter：算了，别～了。That's enough. Stop chattering. 【形】garrulous；loquacious：你这个人真～。You really do talk a lot. 他唠唠叨叨地说了些什么？What was he going on about?

lǎo

老 lǎo 【形】❶ old；aged ❷ veteran；experienced：～工人 a veteran worker ～干部 a veteran cadre ❸ former；original：～同学 a former classmate 我在成都时候的～邻居 my former neighbour when I lived in Chengdu 他还是～样子。He still looks like his former self. ❹ old；outdated：～机器 outdated machine ～式样 old fashion ❺ having been in existence for a long time：～朋友 old friend ～牌子 old brand ～习惯 old habit ❻ (of food) tough；hard (as opp. to 嫩)：这牛肉可真～，嚼不动。The beef is too tough. I can't chew it. 豆角～了。The beans were picked too late. 【副】❶ very：～远 very far 他～早就起来了。He got up very early. ❷ used before a negative completed action to mean "for a long time"：最近怎么～没见你呀？Why has it been such a long time since I have seen you? 他～没来。He hasn't been here for a long time. ❸ always：他～爱开玩笑。He is always fond of a joke. 他～是乐呵呵的。He is always cheerful. ～不运动可不行。It's not good for you never to have any exercise. 【头】before the surname of a person or a numeral indicating the order of birth of the children in a family to indicate affection or familiarity：～张 Lao Chang ～李 Lao Li ～大 the eldest child ～二 the second child

老百姓 lǎobǎixìng 【名】common people

老板 lǎobǎn 【名】shopkeeper；boss

老伴儿 lǎobànr 【名】(of an old couple) husband or wife

老本 lǎoběn 【名】(～儿) ❶ found-

ing capital for a business ❷ past experience, glory, merit, etc.；吃～ live off one's past laurels 没什么～ be without any laurels to rest on

老成 lǎochéng 【形】experienced and steady

老大难 lǎodànán 【名】problem of long-standing difficulty；这个～问题终于解决了。This long-standing problem was eventually solved.

老大娘 lǎodàniáng 【名】*respectful form of address for an old woman*

老大爷 lǎodàye 【名】*respectful form of address for an old man*

老当益壮 lǎo dāng yì zhuàng：这位地质学家六十多岁还长年搞野外考察，真是～。That geologist is over sixty, but he still does fieldwork all year round. That's a good example of "the older one gets the more vigorous one becomes".

老底 lǎodǐ 【名】(～儿) sb.'s unsavory past

老调 lǎodiào 【名】the same old story；～重弹 harp on the same old story

老好人 lǎohǎorén 【名】one who tries never to offend anybody

老虎 lǎohǔ 【名】〔只 zhī〕tiger

老化 lǎohuà 【动】(of rubber or plastic) perish；deteriorate

老家 lǎojiā 【名】native place

老奸巨猾 lǎo jiān jù huá old and crafty

老茧 lǎojiǎn 【名】callous

老练 lǎoliàn 【形】experienced

老马识途 lǎo mǎ shí tú an old horse knows the way；(fig.) an experienced person knows the ropes

老年 lǎonián 【名】old age

老农 lǎonóng 【名】old farmer；veteran farmer

老牌 lǎopái 【名】(～儿) time-honoured；old brand

老婆 lǎopo 【名】〈口〉wife

老气横秋 lǎo qì héng qiū old and lifeless；lacking youthful vigour

老前辈 lǎoqiánbèi 【名】senior

老人 lǎorén 【名】aged parents or grandparents

老人家 lǎorenjia 【名】*a respectful form of address for old people*：您～是老高的母亲吗? Are you Lao Gao's mother?

老弱残兵 lǎo ruò cán bīng a remaining handful of troops who are too old or too weak to fight；old and weak persons

老少 lǎoshào 【名】◇ the old and the young：他们全家～都喜欢老刘。His whole family, old and young alike, is fond of Lao Liu.

老生常谈 lǎo shēng cháng tán platitude；truism

老师 lǎoshī 【名】❶ teacher ❷ *form of address for a teacher*

老式 lǎoshì 【形】old-fashioned；～家具 period furniture；antique furniture

老实 lǎoshi 【形】❶ simple and honest：忠诚～ loyal and honest 当～人，说～话，做～事 be an honest person；speak the truth and behave honestly ❷ behave oneself (*as opp. to* 调皮 *or* 滑头, *no negative form*)：这孩子今天怎么这么～? I wonder why this child is behaving so well today? ❸ frank；factual (*often used with* 说)：～说, 对这个问题, 我们是早有觉察的。To be frank, we were aware of this problem long ago.

老手 lǎoshǒu 【名】old hand；veteran；experienced person

老鼠 lǎoshǔ 【名】〔只 zhī〕mouse；rat

老鼠过街, 人人喊打 lǎoshǔ guò jiē, rénrén hǎn dǎ a rat running across the street with everyone yelling "kill it"；(fig.) sb. or sth. universally hated

老太太 lǎotàitai 【名】*form of ad-*

dress or term denoting respect for an old woman

老头儿 lǎotóur 【名】an old man; old chap

老乡 lǎoxiāng 【名】❶ fellow-townsman; fellow-villager ❷ *a term of address applied to a farmer whose name one doesn't know*

老小 lǎoxiǎo 【名】◇ grown-ups and children (in a family)：他一家一六七口人，负担不轻。He has a family of six or seven to support and that is quite a burden.

老羞成怒 lǎo xiū chéng nù resort to angry outburst when one is exposed 也作"恼羞成怒"。

老爷 lǎoye 【名】*a respectful form of address used in the past for a man from the upper classes, especially an official; now used ironically of those who keep aloof from the masses*：～作风 bureaucratic style of work 干部是普通劳动者，而不是骑在人民头上的～。The cadres are ordinary workers, not overlords of the people.

老一套 lǎoyītào 【名】（of habits, working methods）the same old way（*derog.*）：～行不通了。Using the same old methods will get you nowhere.

老者 lǎozhě 【名】old man

老子 lǎozi 【名】❶ father ❷ *referring to oneself, showing contempt for the person spoken to or used jokingly*：～不买你的账! I don't give a damn about what you do!

lào

涝（澇）lào 【动】be water-logged：地都～了。The fields are waterlogged. 防～ prevent waterlogging 旱～保收 stable harvest despite drought or waterlogging 排～ drain waterlogged fields

烙 lào 【动】❶ bake：～馅儿饼 bake pies ❷ iron：～衣服 iron clothes

烙饼 làobǐng 【名】〔张 zhāng〕flat baked cake

烙铁 làotie 【名】❶ iron (for pressing clothes) ❷ soldering iron

烙印 làoyìn 【名】❶ brand or mark burned on cattle or stamped on utensils, etc. ❷ ideological influence：他的头脑中有不少封建思想的～。His thinking bears the stamp of feudal ideology.

落 lào 【动】❶ fall; drop：你来晚了，玫瑰花全～了。You've come too late. The roses are all faded. 有些东西涨价，有些东西～价了。The prices of certain commodities have gone up, while those of others have gone down. ❷ get：～埋怨 get the blame
另见 là; luò

lè

乐（樂）lè 【动】❶ be happy; be delighted：孙子参加了工作，送奶奶一件礼物，把奶奶一坏了。When her grandson began to earn a living and presented her with a gift, she was overcome with joy. ❷ laugh：把大家都逗～了 make everybody laugh
另见 yuè

乐得 lèdé 【动】be only too glad to：他们不让我去，我～休息。They wouldn't let me go, and I was only too glad to take a break.

乐观 lèguān 【形】optimistic; hopeful

乐观主义 lèguānzhǔyì 【名】optimism

乐趣 lèqù 【名】delight；pleasure；joy

乐意 lèyì 【助动】❶ be willing to；be ready to；～去 be willing to go ～帮助 be glad to help 你要让他去，他准～。If you ask him to go, he will be sure to do so. ❷ pleased；我知道他会不～的，可是还得批评他。I knew that he would be displeased, but I still had to give him a piece of my mind.

乐于 lèyú 【动】be glad to；be happy to ～助人 be ready to help people ～承担 be happy to undertake (a task) ～接受 be glad to accept (sth.)

乐园 lèyuán 【名】paradise

勒 lè

另见 lēi

勒令 lèlìng 【动】order sb. to do one's bidding

勒索 lèsuǒ 【动】extort；～钱财 extort money 敲诈～ practise blackmail and extortion

le

了 le 【助】❶ aspect particle, used after the verb to indicate completion：① actual completion：他买～一台电视机。He's just bought a television set. 这个工厂提前完成～全年的生产任务。This factory fulfilled its year's production quota ahead of time. 我看～那本小说。I have read that novel. ② future or subjunctive completion：你先走，我下～班就去。You go first, and I'll join you straight after work. 等这棵树结～果，你一定来尝尝。When this tree begins to bear fruit, you must come and taste it. 只要解决～主要问题，其他问题也就好办了。If the main problem is solved, the remaining ones will take care of themselves. ❷ modal particle, placed at the end of a sentence：① indicates that there has been a change：我明白他的意思～。Now I understand what he meant. 他们现在是大学生～。They are university students now. 天气暖和～。It has become warm. 还有问题没有？——没有～。Do you have any more questions? — No, no more questions. 原来他说去，现在不去～。He said that he was going, but now he isn't going after all. ② indicates a past event：星期日上午我去看朋友～。I went to call on a friend on Sunday morning. 他滑冰去～。He's gone skating. ③ indicates future certainty：明天又是星期六～。It's Saturday again tomorrow. 要过新年～，人们都很高兴。New Year is coming and everybody is very happy. 下一个节目该是独唱～。The next piece is a solo. 我们出海～，两天以后回来。We are going out to sea, and will be back in two days. 你记在本子上，就不会忘～。If you write it down in your notebook, you won't forget it. ④ used at the end of an imperative sentence to indicate the speeding up or stopping of some action in progress：现在开会，别说话～! The meeting will begin now. Please stop talking. 走～，走～! Hurry up and let's go! ⑤ used at the end of a sentence to indicate superlative degree：这个建议太好～! This suggestion is excellent! 这首诗好极～! This poem is wonderful! 那个地方的天气坏透～! The weather in that place was horrible! 这本小说可有意思～! This novel is extremely interesting. ⑥ When a sentence is ended by a verb with 了，了 is both an aspect particle and a modal particle：水开～。

The water is boiling. 这屋子我打扫
~。I've cleaned up this room.
另见 liǎo；liào

lēi

勒　lēi 【动】strap tight；rein in；
strangle：~紧 strap (sth.) tight ~
得慌 feel that (a belt, strap, etc.)
is too tight 这绳子太滑，~不住。The
rope is too slippery, and I can't
fasten it.
另见 lè

léi

雷　léi 【名】❶ thunder ❷ (mil.)
mine
雷达　léidá 【名】radar
雷厉风行　léi lì fēng xíng　act speedily
and vigorously：~的作风 quick and
vigorous working style
雷鸣　léimíng 【名】❶ thunder clap
❷ loud sound like a clap of thunder
雷霆万钧　léitíng wàn jūn　as powerful as a thunderbolt
雷同　léitóng 【形】(of writing or
speech) similar；the same
(derog.)：两篇文章内容~。The
content of the two articles is more
or less the same.
雷雨　léiyǔ 【名】thunderstorm

lěi

垒（壘）　lěi 【动】build out of
bricks, stones, etc.：~墙 build a
wall ~猪圈 build a pigsty 【名】◇
bastion；rampart：两军对~ two
opposing armies encamped face to
face 深沟高~ deep ditches and
high bastions
垒球　lěiqiú 【名】❶ baseball game

❷〔个 gè〕baseball

累（纍）　lěi
另见 lèi
累积　lěijī 【动】accumulate
累计　lěijì 【动】add up
累进　lěijìn 【动】progress；increase
by arithmetic or geometric pro-
gression：~率 graduated rates ~税
progressive tax
累累　lěilěi 【形】in clusters；innu-
merable；果实~ heavily laden with
fruit 血债~ blood-debts without
number；have murder on his hands

磊　lěi
磊落　lěiluò 【形】open and forth-
right：~的胸怀 open and above-
board 为人~ having an open and
forthright nature

lèi

肋　lèi 【名】◇❶ rib ❷ costal region
肋骨　lèigǔ 【名】rib
肋膜炎　lèimóyán 【名】pleurisy

泪　lèi 【名】tears
泪痕　lèihén 【名】tear stains；tear-
stained
泪花　lèihuā 【名】tears in one's eyes
泪水　lèishuǐ 【名】tear
泪珠　lèizhū 【名】(~儿) teardrop

类（類）　lèi 【名】kind；class；
category；sort 【量】kind；sort (for
people, things, matters)：两~矛盾
two kinds of contradictions
类比　lèibǐ 【动】analogy
类别　lèibié 【名】classification；cat-
egory
类似　lèisì 【形】similar；analogous：
~的现象 a similar phenomenon ~
的条件 similar conditions 他们两个

人的处境相～。The two of them are in a similar position.

类推 lèituī 【动】reason by analogy; draw an analogy：以此～ draw an analogy on this basis 其余～。The rest can be deduced by analogy.

类型 lèixíng 【名】type; class

累 lèi 【动】❶ be tired：今天我～极了。I'm extremely tired today. ❷ tire; fatigue：别把他～着。Don't tire him. 这么棒的小伙子，这点儿活儿～不着他。He is young and strong. A bit of work like this won't tire him. ❸ work hard; exhaust：～了半天，歇一会儿吧！Please take a rest. You've been working hard for a long time.

另见 lěi

léng

棱 léng 【名】❶ arris; edge：见～见角 with sharp edges and corners ❷ corrugation; ridge：瓦～ ridges on a tiled roof

棱角 léngjiǎo 【名】❶ edges and corners ❷ sharp and outspoken：这个人很有～。This person has quite a sharp mind, and is not afraid to speak up.

棱镜 léngjìng 【名】prism

lěng

冷 lěng 【形】❶ cold：天很～。The weather is very cold. ❷ (of manner) cold：他～～地点了一下头。He nodded coldly.

冷冰冰 lěngbīngbīng 【形】❶ cold; icy ❷ (of manner) cold; unenthusiastic：～的面孔 poker face ～的样子 icy manner 对人～ cold towards others

冷不防 lěngbufáng 【副】unawares; off-guard; by surprise：我正在散步，～一个小皮球打在头上，吓我一跳。I was taking a walk when a ball hit me on the head and gave me a start.

冷藏 lěngcáng 【动】keep in cold storage; refrigerate

冷场 lěng = chǎng （of meetings）embarrassing pause; awkward silence：会上，大家发言很热烈，没有～。Everybody spoke enthusiastically at the meeting; there were no awkward silences.

冷嘲热讽 lěng cháo rè fěng biting satire; cutting remarks：对别人的缺点要耐心地帮助，不要～。If someone has shortcomings, we should help him, and not make sarcastic remarks.

冷淡 lěngdàn 【形】indifferent; cold：态度～ indifferent attitude 【动】be indifferent; be apathetic：不要～了客人。Don't treat guests with indifference.

冷冻 lěngdòng 【动】freeze (food)

冷汗 lěnghàn 【名】cold sweat

冷箭 lěngjiàn 【名】an arrow shot from ambush; a stab in the back：放～ shoot an arrow from a place of concealment 防～ be on guard against an under-handed attack

冷静 lěngjìng 【形】calm; sober：遇事～ keep calm when problems crop up 保持～ keep calm 情况愈是紧急，头脑愈要～。The more critical the situation, the more you must keep a level head.

冷库 lěngkù 【名】cold storage

冷酷 lěngkù 【形】grim; hard-hearted; unfeeling：～无情 merciless

冷落 lěngluò 【形】desolate; deserted：城北过去很～，现在成了文化区。The northern part of the city used to be quite run down, but has now become a cultural centre. 【动】

treat sb. coldly; slight sb.; 他注意和在座的每一个人谈话,惟恐～了谁。He made a point of speaking to each person at the gathering lest somebody might feel slighted.

冷门 lěngmén 【名】(～儿) non-preferable occupation or profession; a profession or branch of learning that receives little attention

冷漠 lěngmò 【形】cold and detached; unconcerned

冷气 lěngqì 【名】cool air; air-conditioning

冷清 lěngqing 【形】quiet and desolate; cheerless and cold; 下雨天,公园里显得很～。When it rains, the park is quiet and desolate. 春节前他们家热闹了一阵,春节反而过得冷冷清清。They had quite a jolly time during the weeks before Spring Festival, but the holiday itself was rather cheerless.

冷却 lěngquè 【动】cool down

冷食 lěngshí 【名】cold drinks, icecream, etc.

冷水 lěngshuǐ 【名】❶ unboiled water ❷ 见"泼冷水" pōlěngshuǐ

冷飕飕 lěngsōusōu 【形】chilly; ～的北风 chilly north wind 天冷了,风吹在身上～的。It's getting cold, and one feels chilly when the wind blows.

冷笑 lěngxiào 【动】sneer; laugh scornfully

冷眼 lěngyǎn 【名】❶ cool and objective attitude; ～观察 cool-headed and objective observation ❷ cold and indifferent; ～相待 treat coolly

冷眼旁观 lěngyǎn pángguān look on coldly; 他～了几天,觉得这些人的行动还是对的。He watched on the side for a few days and found that these people were doing the right thing.

冷饮 lěngyǐn 【名】cold drinks

冷遇 lěngyù 【名】cold-shoulder; 受到～ be given the cold-shoulder 遭到～ be left out in the cold

冷战 lěngzhàn 【名】the Cold War

冷战 lěngzhan 【名】〈口〉shiver; 打了个～ (sb.) shivered with cold

lèng

愣 lèng 【动】be stunned; 吓得我一～。I was paralysed with fear. 一推门,没想到一屋子的人,他～住了。He was stunned when he pushed open the door and found the room packed with people. 【形】rash; foolhardy; reckless; ～小伙子 a rash young man ～干 act recklessly

愣头愣脑 lèng tóu lèng nǎo foolhardy; bumbling

lí

厘 lí 【量】❶ one thousandth of a *chi* 尺 ❷ one thousandth of a *liang* 两

厘米 límǐ 【量】centimetre

离(離) lí 【动】❶ leave; be away from; 去年她到北京来上大学是她第一次～家。When she came to Beijing last year to go to university, it was the first time she had left home. 他定于星期四～日赴美。He is scheduled to leave Japan for the U. S. A. on Thursday. ❷ do without; ～了水,就没法种菜了。One can't grow vegetables without water. 鱼～不了水。A fish can't live without water. 【介】from; away; ～她的生日只有三天了。Her birthday is only three days away. 我家

～博物馆很近。My home is very close to the museum.

离别 líbié 【动】part；leave

离婚 lí=hūn get a divorce

离间 líjiàn 【动】sow discord between；drive a wedge between；alienate（persons）from each other

离开 lí//kāi leave；depart from：他已经～北京了。He has already left Beijing. 五点以前，你不要～办公室。Please don't leave your office before five.

离奇 líqí 【形】fantastic；odd；strange；extraordinary

离任 lírèn 【动】leave one's post

离散 lísàn 【动】be separated from one another；be scattered（by war, natural disaster, etc.）

离乡背井 lí xiāng bèi jǐng leave one's native place（often against one's will）也作"背井离乡"。

离心离德 lí xīn lí dé discord；disunity（as opp. to 同心同德 or 一心一德）

离心力 líxīnlì 【名】centrifugal force

离休 líxiū 【动】（of veteran cadres）retire：～干部 retired veteran cadre

离职 lí=zhí leave one's post

离子 lízǐ 【名】ion

梨 lí 【名】❶ pear ❷ pear tree

犁 lí 【名】〔张 zhāng〕plough 【动】plough

黎 lí

黎明 límíng 【名】dawn；daybreak

罹 lí

罹难 línàn 【动】die in a disaster or an accident

篱（籬）lí

篱笆 líba 【名】fence；hedge

lǐ

礼（禮）lǐ 【名】❶ rites ❷ ceremony：婚～ wedding ceremony 丧～ funeral service ❸ salute：行了个～ salute ❹ courtesy：彬彬有～ have very good manners；be impeccably polite ❺ gift；present：送～ give a gift

礼拜 lǐbài 【名】❶（religious）service；church service：做～ attend a service；go to church ❷ week：上～ last week 下～ next week 他在上海呆了两个～。He stayed in Shanghai for two weeks. ❸ weekday（used with 天 or 日，or 一，二，三，四，五，六）：今天～六，明天～天。Today is Saturday and tomorrow is Sunday. ❹ short for "礼拜天"：明天～，我休息。Tomorrow is Sunday, and it's my day off.

礼拜堂 lǐbàitáng 【名】church

礼服 lǐfú 【名】〔套 tào〕formal dress

礼花 lǐhuā 【名】fireworks display at a celebration

礼教 lǐjiào 【名】feudal code of ethics：吃人的～ the life-destroying feudal code of ethics

礼节 lǐjié 【名】etiquette；formality；courtesy；protocol

礼帽 lǐmào 【名】〔顶 dǐng〕a hat that matches formal dress；top hat

礼貌 lǐmào 【名】politeness；manners；courtesy

礼炮 lǐpào 【名】gun salute；salvo

礼品 lǐpǐn 【名】present；gift

礼让 lǐràng 【动】give precedence to sb. out of courtesy or thoughtfulness

礼尚往来 lǐ shàng wǎng lái ❶ courtesy demands reciprocity ❷ treat sb. in the same way as he treats you

礼堂 lǐtáng 【名】auditorium；as-

sembly hall; hall

礼物 lǐwù 【名】present; gift

礼仪 lǐyí 【名】etiquette

礼遇 lǐyù 【名】polite reception; courteous reception：受到很高的～ be received with great courtesy 隆重的～ grand reception

里 lǐ 【名】(裏) ❶ lining ❷ inside 【量】equals 500 metres

里边 lǐbiān 【名】inside; in; within：他在～呢! He is inside. 屋子～很热。It is very hot in the room. 工作～出些漏洞也难免。Slips in work are hard to avoid. 这～有问题。There is something wrong here.

里程 lǐchéng 【名】❶ mileage ❷ course of development

里程碑 lǐchéngbēi 【名】milestone

里拉 lǐlā 【名】lira

里面 lǐmiàn 【名】同"里边"

里通外国 lǐ tōng wàiguó have treasonous relations with a foreign country

里头 lǐtou 【名】同"里边"

里亚尔 lǐyà'ěr 【名】rial (currency)

里应外合 lǐ yìng wài hé in attacking from the outside, coordinate with forces on the inside

里子 lǐzi 【名】lining

俚 lǐ

俚语 lǐyǔ 【名】slang

理 lǐ 【名】❶ reason ❷ ◇ natural science (sometimes refers specifically to physics)：～科 natural sciences 数～化 mathematics, physics and chemistry 【动】❶ put in order; tidy up：她用手～一～头发。She smoothed her hair with her hand. ❷〈口〉pay attention to; take notice of (often used in the negative)：他是跟你开玩笑，你别～他。He was only joking with you. Never mind him. 叫你半天，你怎么

不～? I have been calling out to you; why don't you answer?

理睬 lǐcǎi 【动】take notice of; heed

理发 lǐ // fà have a haircut; have one's hair done

理发馆 lǐfàguǎn 【名】barber shop; hairdresser's

理发员 lǐfàyuán 【名】barber; hairdresser

理会 lǐhuì 【动】❶ understand; comprehend ❷ pay attention to (usu. in the negative) ❸ talk to (sb.) (usu. in the negative)

理解 lǐjiě 【动】understand; apprehend; comprehend

理亏 lǐkuī 【形】unjustifiable; in the wrong：感到～ feel that one is in the wrong ～气不壮 falter because one is in the wrong

理疗 lǐliáo 【动】physiotherapy

理论 lǐlùn 【名】theory

理论家 lǐlùnjiā 【名】theorist

理屈词穷 lǐ qū cí qióng be unable to advance any more arguments in one's defense because one is in the wrong

理事 lǐshì 【名】member of a council

理所当然 lǐ suǒ dāngrán only right and natural; a matter of course

理想 lǐxiǎng 【名】ideal; aspiration：崇高的～ lofty ideal 他实现了当医生的～。He has realized his ideal of becoming a doctor. 【形】ideal; satisfactory; perfect：你不可能找到比这个更～的工作了。You can't find a job more ideal than this. 这个问题这么解决不大～。Solving the problem this way is not entirely satisfactory.

理性 lǐxìng 【名】❶ rational (as opp. to 感性) ❷ reason; rationality

理由 lǐyóu 【名】reason; ground; argument

理直气壮 lǐ zhí qì zhuàng be bold and self-confident because one feels justified；说话～ speak with great confidence ～地回答 reply confidently

理智 lǐzhì 【名】sense；reason；intellect：丧失～ lose one's senses 【形】sensible；reasonable：不～ unreasonable 别感情用事，～一点儿! Don't be carried away by your feelings；be sensible.

lì

力 lì 【名】❶（phys.）force ❷◇ power；strength；ability：～所能及 within one's ability 理解～ ability to comprehend；comprehension 你这些理由的说服～不强。Your reasons aren't very convincing.

力不从心 lì bù cóng xīn one's abilities fall short of one's desires

力度 lìdù 【名】dynamics：加大～ do sth. with renewed efforts or with added force

力量 lìliang 【名】❶ physical strength ❷ mental ability ❸ effect

力气 lìqi 【名】strength；effort

力求 lìqiú 【动】do one's best；make every effort；strive：～准确 try one's best to be precise（in doing sth.）～完善 strive for perfection

力图 lìtú 【动】try hard；strive：～压倒对方 strive to overpower one's opponent

力挽狂澜 lì wǎn kuáng lán spare no efforts to turn the tide

力学 lìxué 【名】mechanics

力争 lìzhēng 【动】❶ struggle hard；make every effort；～主动 do all one can to gain the initiative ～提前完成任务 work hard to complete the job ahead of schedule ❷ argue heatedly：据理～ argue strongly on just grounds

力争上游 lìzhēng shàngyóu strive to be among the front ranks

历（歷、曆）lì

历程 lìchéng 【名】course；progress

历次 lìcì 【名】various occasions，events，etc. in the past：～会议 previous meetings ～比赛 previous contests

历代 lìdài 【名】past dynasties；eras

历法 lìfǎ 【名】calendar（system for arranging year into days, weeks, months）

历届 lìjiè 【名】all previous sessions（of meetings）or past graduating classes

历来 lìlái 【名】from the past down to the present：～的主张 consistent proposition ～的作法 usual way of doing sth. 这项工作～受到重视。Great importance has always been attached to this work.

历历在目 lìlì zài mù come clearly into view；leap up before the eyes：童年时代的情景～。My childhood scenes came clearly into view.

历年 lìnián 【名】over the years；in past years

历时 lìshí 【动】last（a period of time）：这次海洋生物考察～三个月。This field trip to investigate marine organisms lasted three months.

历史 lìshǐ 【名】❶ history：中国的～很长。China has a long history. ❷ history（book）：他计划写一本给孩子们看的中国～。He is planning to write a book on Chinese history for children. ❸ history（discipline）：他大概是一位～教员。He is probably a teacher of history.

历史剧 lìshǐjù 【名】historical drama

历史唯物主义 lìshǐ wéiwùzhǔyì historical materialism

历史唯心主义 lìshǐ wéixīnzhǔyì historical idealism

历史学 lìshǐxué 【名】history（discipline）; historiography

厉（厲） lì

厉害 lìhai 【形】同"利害" lìhai【形】

厉行 lìxíng 【动】strictly carry out; ～节约 practise strict economy

立 lì 【动】❶ ◇ stand: 他的腰坏了，坐～都有困难。He's hurt his back, and has problems sitting and standing. ❷ erect; set upright: ～着放 stand sth. upright 把井架一起来 erect a derrick ❸ found; set up; establish: ～新功 make new contributions 树雄心，～大志 foster lofty ideals, set high goals 旧的管理制度不行了，要另～一套制度。The old management system doesn't work any more. Let's set up a new system. 【副】◇ immediately: ～等回信 wait for an immediate answer

立场 lìchǎng 【名】（class）stand; standpoint

立法 lì＝fǎ legislate; legislation; legislative

立方 lìfāng 【名】（maths.）cube

立方根 lìfānggēn 【名】（maths.）cube root

立方米 lìfāngmǐ 【量】cubic metre

立竿见影 lì gān jiàn yǐng set up a pole and see its shadow instantly; （fig.）get instant results

立功 lì＝gōng perform deeds of merit; render meritorious service

立功赎罪 lì gōng shú zuì perform meritorious service to atone for one's misdeeds

立即 lìjí 【副】at once; immediately; promptly: ～出发 start off at once ～开始 begin immediately ～行动 take immediate action

立交桥 lìjiāoqiáo 【名】〔座 zuò〕❶ overpass; flyover ❷ motorway interchange

立刻 lìkè 【副】immediately; at once; instantly

立体 lìtǐ 【名】（geom.）solid; three-dimensional

立体几何 lìtǐ jǐhé solid geometry

立体声 lìtǐshēng 【名】stereophony; stereo: ～收录机 stereo radio-tape recorder

立正 lìzhèng 【动】stand at attention

立志 lì＝zhì set one's heart on sth. （an ambition）

立锥之地 lì zhuī zhī dì a place just big enough to stick an awl（usu. used in the negative）: 家无～。The family has no land of its own at all.

立足 lìzú 【动】gain a foothold

立足点 lìzúdiǎn 【名】❶ foothold ❷ standpoint 也说"立脚点"。

利 lì 【名】❶ profit ❷ interest

利弊 lìbì 【名】advantages and disadvantages

利害 lìhài 【名】gains and losses

利害 lìhai 【形】fierce; severe; terrible; formidable: 豹子这种野兽可～了。The leopard is a very fierce animal. 这是一种很～的手段。This is a formidable move. 真正的好老师对学生并不～。A really good teacher is never severe with his students. Note: 利害 is used with 得 to form a complement of degree indicating very high degree: 路不平，车颠得～。The road was bad and the car jolted terribly. 她晕船,吐得～。She was seasick and threw up a lot. 也作"厉害"。

利己主义 lìjǐzhǔyì 【名】egoism

利令智昏 lì lìng zhì hūn be blinded by one's desire for gain

利落 lìluo 【形】❶ nimble; agile; deft: 讲话～ speak with facility 干活～ do things deftly ❷ tidy; orderly: 大娘把院子收拾得很～。The old woman has put the courtyard in very good order. ❸ finished;

settled：病好～了 completely recovered from illness 手续都办～了吗? Have you gone through all the formalities?

利率 lìlǜ 【名】interest rate

利润 lìrùn 【名】profit

利索 lìsuo 【形】同"利落"

利息 lìxī 【名】interest

利益 lìyì 【名】interest；benefit；gain；profit

利用 lìyòng 【动】use；make use of；utilize

利诱 lìyòu 【动】lure by the promise of gain

利欲熏心 lì yù xūn xīn be blinded by avarice；be obsessed with the desire for gain

沥（瀝）lì

沥青 lìqīng 【名】pitch；asphalt

丽（麗）lì 【形】◇ beautiful：

景色奇～ a uniquely beautiful sight 风和日～ a lovely sunny day with a warm breeze

例 lì 【名】◇ ❶ example；instance ❷ example；person or thing to be followed ❸ case

例会 lìhuì 【名】regular meeting

例假 lìjià 【名】❶ official holidays ❷ menstrual period

例句 lìjù 【名】sentence used as an example；model sentence

例如 lìrú 【动】for instance；for example；such as：有节奏、韵律的文体叫韵文，～诗、歌、赋等。Literary compositions with rhythm（and rhyme）are called verse, e. g. poetry, songs, poetic prose, etc.

例题 lìtí 【名】〔道 dào〕(of maths., chem., etc.) example

例外 lìwài 【动】be an exception：全体公民都要遵守国家法律，谁也不能～。All citizens with no exception must abide by the laws. 【名】exception：我每天晚上都自学一个半小时，星期六是～。I study for an hour and a half every evening with the exception of Saturdays. 产品在出厂前都毫无～地经过质量检查。All products, without exception, are subject to quality inspection before they leave the factory.

例行公事 lì xíng gōngshì routine；routine business

例证 lìzhèng 【名】illustration, example to prove sth.

例子 lìzi 【名】〔个 gè〕example；instance

隶（隸）lì

隶书 lìshū 【名】one of the ancient styles of Chinese calligraphy prevalent in the Han Dynasty

隶属 lìshǔ 【动】(of district, institution, etc.) be under the administration of；be subordinate to

荔 lì

荔枝 lìzhī 【名】❶ lichee（fruit）❷ lichee tree

栗 lì

栗子 lìzi 【名】❶ chestnut ❷ chestnut tree

粒 lì 【量】for pearls, rice, etc.

粒子 lìzǐ 【名】(phys.) particle

痢 lì

痢疾 lìji 【名】dysentery

li

哩 li 【助】modal particle

liǎ

俩（倆）liǎ 〈口〉equivalent

to 两个, *but cannot replace* 两 *plus any other measure word*：~ 扣子 two buttons 姐妹 ~ two sisters Note：*just like* 两个, 俩 *can replace* 几个 *to show a small indefinite number*. 俩 *must be pronounced in the neutral tone in this case*；只要能有~帮忙的,二十人来吃午饭不成问题。As long as I can have a few helpers, it will be no trouble at all to prepare a lunch for 20 people.

lián

连（連） lián 【名】（mil.） company 【动】connect；join：把这两段水渠~起来。Link up these two stretches of canal. 【量】company：两 ~ 兵力 two companies strong 【副】in succession：~ 喊几声 call several times in succession 老赵~任了五年队长。Lao Zhao has been elected team leader five years in succession. 【介】❶ even *often used in conjunction with* 也、都、还, *etc*.：天上没有月亮,~ 星星也没有。There is no moon in the sky, nor even stars. 他们搞起科研来,有时~时间都忘了。Once they are into a research project, they even lose all sense of time. 他今天不舒服,~饭都不想吃。He's sick today, and doesn't even want to eat. 那种鱼,过去我一听说都没听说过。I've never even heard of that sort of fish. ❷ including：~ 你一共多少人？How many are there including you? ~ 皮重五十斤（This parcel）weighs 50 *jin*, packaging included.

连词 liáncí 【名】（gram.）conjunction

连带 liándài 【动】go along with；be related to：他责备我的时候,把小赵也~上了。When he criticized me, he lumped Xiao Zhao together with me as well. 在很多情况下,作者的文风和他的生活经验是有~关系的。In many cases, the style of an author's writing is closely related to his life experiences. 他们扫除的时候,~把书架也整理了。When they cleaned the room, they also tidied up the bookshelves.

连…带… lián...dài... *This structure is often used as an adverbial adjunct* ❶ *used with two nouns or nominal phrases, it means "include"*：我们学校连中国学生带外国学生一共一千二百多人。There are altogether 1200 students in our institute, including both Chinese and foreign students. 昨天她连吃的带用的买了不少东西。Yesterday, she bought a lot of things, including food and other daily necessities. ❷ *used with two verbs or verbal constructions, it shows two concomitant actions*：孩子们连蹦带跳地跑出去了。The children ran out jumping and skipping.

连动句 liándòngjù 【名】sentence with verbal constructions in series

连队 liánduì 【名】（mil.）company

连贯 liánguàn 【动】❶ link up；connect：这条铁路是~中国东西交通的干线之一。This railway is one of the main lines which link up the east and the west of China. ❷ cohere：这一段话怎么不大~,是不是有的地方抄落（là）了？ This passage isn't very coherent; is it possible that some part has been left out?

连环 liánhuán 【名】a few large connected links, sometimes used as a toy

连环画 liánhuánhuà 【名】serial pictorial

连接 liánjiē 【动】link；join：~ 不断的山岭 a long chain of mountains ~起来 join together 互相~ link up with each other 也作"联接"。

连接号 liánjiēhào 【名】hyphen

连累 liánlěi 【动】incriminate；implicate：怕～别人 be afraid of incriminating others 受到～ be implicated

连忙 liánmáng 【副】同 "赶快" gǎnkuài，*but cannot be used in an imperative sentence*

连绵 liánmián 【动】（of mountain range, river, rain, snow, etc.）continue；go on uninterrupted：～千里 stretch for a thousand *li* 山峦～起伏 undulating mountains 这几天雨雪～。In the last few days, there has been nothing but rain and snow. 也作"联绵"。

连年 liánnián 【名】successive years；consecutive years；year after year：～扩大造林面积 expand the afforested areas with each successive year ～超产 overfulfil the production quotas year after year

连篇累牍 lián piān lěi dú at great length；go on writing for pages and pages（*derog.*）

连任 liánrèn 【动】re-elect；re-appoint：～学生会主席 be re-elected as president of the student union

连日 liánrì 【名】for days on end；day after day：～大雨。It rained hard for days on end. ～来，汽车队运输繁忙。For the last few days, the fleet of trucks has been very busy.

连声 liánshēng 【副】say repeatedly：～说好 express approval repeatedly

连锁店 liánsuǒdiàn 【名】chain store

连锁反应 liánsuǒ fǎnyìng chain reaction

连同 liántóng 【连】plus；and（*usu. in written language, sometimes in conjunction with* 在内）：这个县今年的基建工程已经施工的，～即将施工的（在内）共十一项。This year's plan for capital construction in the county, including those projects already started as well as those to be started, amounts to eleven projects.

连写 liánxiě 【动】（of a polysyllabic word）write in the Chinese phonetic alphabet without a gap between syllables

连续 liánxù 【动】keep on；continue：～不断 keep on without stopping ～发生了几件事。Several things happened one after another. 这个车间～几年都被评为先进集体。This workshop has been appraised as an advanced unit for several years running.

连续剧 liánxùjù 【名】serial

连夜 liányè 【副】before the night is out；that very night：把病人～送往医院。The patient was sent to the hospital before the night was out. 接到紧急通知后，他～赶来了。After receiving the urgent message, he rushed here that same night.

连衣裙 liányīqún 【名】dress；gown

连载 liánzǎi 【动】publish in serial form

连长 liánzhǎng 【名】company commander

连着 liánzhe 【副】in succession；continuously：老师～讲了两遍。The teacher explained（the problem）twice in succession. 他～干了三天。He worked continuously for three days.

怜（憐）lián

怜悯 liánmǐn 【动】pity；have mercy on

怜惜 liánxī 【动】sympathize with and cherish

帘（簾）lián 【名】◇ curtain

帘子 liánzi 【名】curtain

莲（蓮）lián 【名】◇ lotus

莲花 liánhuā 【名】〔朵 duǒ〕lotus

flower

莲蓬 liánpeng 【名】seedpod of the lotus

莲子 liánzǐ 【名】lotus seed

联（聯）lián 【动】unite；join；ally oneself with

联邦 liánbāng 【名】federation；union

联播 liánbō 【动】(of several broadcasting stations) broadcast the same program simultaneously

联合 liánhé 【动】unite；ally oneself with：全世界无产者，～起来。Workers of all countries, unite!

联合公报 liánhé gōngbào joint communiqué

联合国 Liánhéguó 【名】the United Nations

联合声明 liánhé shēngmíng joint statement

联合收割机 liánhé shōugējī combine-harvester

联欢 liánhuān 【动】(of an institution) hold a party

联结 liánjié 【动】tie；bind；join

联络 liánluò 【动】establish contact；establish liaison

联盟 liánméng 【名】alliance；coalition；league

联绵 liánmián 【动】同“连绵”liánmián

联名 lián=míng sign jointly

联席会议 liánxí huìyì joint conference

联系 liánxì 【动】contact；get in touch with；have ties with：理论～实际 integrate theory with practice；通过书信～ keep in touch by correspondence 【名】contact；tie；connection：失掉～ be out of touch with 三年前这两个研究所就建立了～。The two research institutes have established ties with each other for three years.

联想 liánxiǎng 【动】associate sth. with：一说到埃及，人们总～到金字塔。One always associates Egypt with the pyramids. 美丽的风景往往使人～起旅游业。Beautiful scenery often makes people think of tourism. 【名】association of ideas：这个故事引起人们不少的～。This story started a train of ideas in people's minds.

联谊会 liányìhuì 【名】get-together；party

联运 liányùn 【动】through transport；through traffic

廉 lián 【形】❶ honest ❷ cheap

廉价 liánjià 【名】cheap；low-priced；inexpensive

廉洁 liánjié 【形】honest；not morally corrupt

廉正 liánzhèng 【形】honest and upright

廉政 liánzhèng 【名】be honest in performing one's official duty

镰（鐮）lián 【名】◇ sickle：开～收割 begin harvesting

镰刀 liándāo 【名】〔把 bǎ〕sickle

liǎn

脸（臉）liǎn 【名】❶ face ❷ face (credit, reputation, dignity, etc.)：不要～ shameless；lose all sense of shame ❸ countenance；expression；look：笑～相迎 greet with a smiling face 一听这个消息，他的～就变了。When he heard the news, his jaw dropped.

脸盆 liǎnpén 【名】〔个 gè〕washbasin

脸皮 liǎnpí 【名】❶ face；face-saving：撕不破～ be unable to rise above considerations of face ❷ sense of shame：～薄 be self-effacing；shy；hesitate to trouble others ～厚 be thick-skinned

脸色 liǎnsè 【名】❶ complexion；你～不好，是病了吗？ You look ghastly. Are you ill？ ❷ expression；look：不能看人～行事。One mustn't let one's behaviour be dictated by the expression on somebody's face.

liàn

练（練）liàn 【动】practise；train；drill：～字 practise calligraphy ～本领 practise a skill ～枪法 practise marksmanship

练兵 liàn＝bīng　train troops；training of troops

练功 liàn＝gōng　do exercises in gymnastics，*wushu*，acrobatics，martial arts，etc.；practise one's skill

练习 liànxí 【动】practise 【名】exercise

练习本 liànxíběn 【名】〔本 běn〕exercise book

炼（煉）liàn 【动】❶ smelt ❷ refine

炼钢 liàn＝gāng　make steel

炼焦 liàn＝jiāo　turn coal into coke

炼乳 liànrǔ 【名】condensed milk

炼铁 liàn＝tiě　smelt iron

炼油 liàn＝yóu　❶ refine petroleum ❷ render fat to get oil

恋（戀）liàn

恋爱 liàn'ài 【动】be in love 【名】见"谈恋爱"tán liàn'ài

恋恋不舍 liàn liàn bù shě　be reluctant to part：两国运动员分手的时候，真有点儿～。The athletes of the two countries were reluctant to part at the end of the meet.

链（鏈）liàn 【名】chain

链条 liàntiáo 【名】chain

链子 liànzi 【名】〔条 tiáo〕chain；(of bicycle) chain

liáng

良 liáng 【形】good

良好 liánghǎo 【形】(*used with abstract nouns*) good；fine

良田 liángtián 【名】fertile farmland

良心 liángxīn 【名】conscience

良性 liángxìng 【形】benign：～循环 virtuous circle

良种 liángzhǒng 【名】improved variety of seed

凉 liáng 【形】❶ cool；cold ❷ disappointed；discouraged
另见 liàng

凉菜 liángcài 【名】cold dish

凉快 liángkuai 【形】nice and cool；delightfully cool

凉爽 liángshuǎng 【形】同"凉快"

凉水 liángshuǐ 【名】unboiled water

凉台 liángtái 【名】balcony；veranda

凉鞋 liángxié 【名】〔只 zhī、双 shuāng〕sandal

梁 liáng 【名】〔根 gēn〕❶ beam ❷ cross-beam

量 liáng 【动】measure：用尺～一～桌布的长短 measure the length of the table-cloth with a ruler ～体温 take one's temperature ～血压 have one's blood-pressure taken
另见 liàng

量具 liángjù 【名】measuring tool

粮（糧）liáng 【名】grain

粮仓 liángcāng 【名】granary；barn

粮草 liángcǎo 【名】food and provisions (for an army)：兵马未动，～先行。Provisions must be sent in advance of the troops.

粮食　liángshi　【名】〔粒 l〕grain; cereal

粮食作物　liángshi zuòwù　grain crops

liǎng

两（兩）　liǎng　【数】❶ two ① *when "two" comes before a measure word or a noun which does not need a measure word it must be expressed by* 两. *When "two" occurs in a two or more digit number, this does not apply*：～个人 two people ～本书 two books ～封信 two letters ～天 two days ～年 two years ～公斤 two kilos ② *"two" before* 百，千，万，亿 *can be expressed either by* 两 *or* 二 ③ *"two" before traditional Chinese units of measurement or weight can be expressed by either* 两 *or* 二：～（或"二"）尺 two *chi* ～（或"二"）里 two *li* ～（或"二"）斤 two *jin*（Note：二两 *two liang cannot be* ～两）❷ ◇ both parties：～便。Each will do as he pleases. ～相情愿。Both are willing. ❸ a few; several; some：过～天就动工。Construction will start in a few days. 我来说～句。Let me say a few words. 【量】*Chinese traditional unit of weight, equivalent to 0.05 kilo*：二～茶叶 two *liang* of tea 这条鱼重一斤三～。This fish weighs one *jin* three *liang*.

两败俱伤　liǎng bài jù shāng　neither of the two gains anything, and both suffer losses

两重性　liǎngchóngxìng　【名】dual nature

两点论　liǎngdiǎnlùn　【名】the theory of two aspects—dialectical materialist doctrine that everything has two contradictory aspects

两极　liǎngjí　【名】❶ the two poles of the earth：～分化 polarization ❷（phys.）the two poles of a magnet or an electric battery

两口子　liǎngkǒuzi　【名】husband and wife; couple; man and wife

两面派　liǎngmiànpài　【名】double-dealer

两面三刀　liǎng miàn sān dāo　double-dealing; double-faced

两难　liǎngnán　【形】be in a dilemma：进退～ be unable to either advance or retreat 这样做不合适,那样做也不合适,真让人～。It can't be done either way. We have certainly a dilemma.

两栖动物　liǎngqī dòngwù　amphibian

两全其美　liǎngquán qí měi　to the satisfaction of both aspects：这个办法真是～。This method can really work to the satisfaction of both aspects.

两条腿走路　liǎng tiáo tuǐ zǒu lù　walk on two legs（referring to a series of policies for balancing the relationships between big and small enterprises, central and local industries, etc.）

两翼　liǎngyì　【名】❶ both wings of a bird or a plane ❷ the two flanks of an army：～部队（of troops）flank units

liàng

亮　liàng　【形】❶ bright; shiny：屋里很～。It is very bright in the room. 自行车擦得真～。The bicycle has been polished until it is shiny. ❷ clear; enlightened：打开天窗说～话 to put it bluntly 你这一说,我心里就～了。Now that you have said it, I see where the problem is. 【动】❶ light：天～了。Day is breaking. ～灯了。The light is on. ❷ reveal; declare：～思想 reveal one's thoughts ～观点 declare one's

views

亮度 liàngdù 【名】 brightness；brilliance

亮光 liàngguāng 【名】 light

亮晶晶 liàngjīngjīng 【形】 sparkling；glistening

亮堂 liàngtang 【形】❶ bright；light ❷ (of mental state) clear；enlightened

亮相 liàng = xiàng ❶ (of Beijing opera) strike a pose ❷ declare one's views

凉 liàng 【动】 cool
另见 liáng

谅(諒) liàng 【动】 presume；suppose：～你不会见怪. I presume you won't take offense. ～他不能来. I suppose he can't come.

谅解 liàngjiě 【动】 understand；be clearly aware of sb.'s views, feelings, etc.：互相～ understand one another 得到～ get an understanding

辆(輛) liàng 【量】 *for vehicles*

量 liàng 【名】❶ measuring instrument ❷ capacity ❸ quantity；amount【动】estimate
另见 liáng

量变 liàngbiàn 【名】 quantitative change

量词 liàngcí 【名】 measure word

量力 liànglì 【动】 in accordance with one's ability or strength：～而行 act in accordance with one's ability 不自～ over-rate (one's abilities)

量体裁衣 liàng tǐ cái yī cut the cloth to fit the figure；(*fig*.) deal with problems according to circumstances

量刑 liàngxíng 【动】 measurement of penalty

晾 liàng 【动】❶ dry in the air ❷ dry in the sun

liāo

撩 liāo 【动】❶ raise；lift up (sth. drooping or hanging) ❷ sprinkle (water)

liáo

辽(遼) liáo

辽阔 liáokuò 【形】 vast；boundless：～的草原 boundless grasslands 幅员～ vast territory

辽远 liáoyuǎn 【形】 far away；remote：～的地方 remote place

疗(療) liáo

疗程 liáochéng 【名】 course of treatment

疗法 liáofǎ 【名】 therapy；medical treatment

疗效 liáoxiào 【名】 healing effect

疗养 liáoyǎng 【动】 recuperate；convalesce

疗养院 liáoyǎngyuàn 【名】 sanatorium

聊 liáo 【动】 chat；have an casual conversation：闲～ have a chat 这件事他有不同看法,我再和他～一会儿. He has different views on this matter. I'd better talk with him some more. 对工作我还有些想法,想找你～～. I have some more ideas about our work, and I'd like to have a chat with you.

聊天 liáo = tiān chat：有空咱俩聊聊天. Let's have a chat when you have time.

寥 liáo

寥廓 liáokuò 【形】high，vast and unending（e.g. sky）

寥寥无几 liáoliáo wújǐ very few；scanty

嘹 liáo

嘹亮 liáoliàng 【形】resonant and clear：军号～ a clear bugle call 歌声～ resounding song

潦 liáo

潦草 liáocǎo 【形】❶（of handwriting）careless and illegible：字迹～ sloppy handwriting ❷ sloppy；careless（in doing things）：这活儿干得真～。This is really a sloppy piece of work.

缭（繚） liáo

缭乱 liáoluàn 【形】confused

缭绕 liáorào 【动】linger and drift in the air：炊烟～ smoke from cooking fires drifts in the air 云雾～。Cloud and mist linger and drift in the air.

燎 liáo 【动】blaze up；set fire to

燎原 liáo = yuán start a prairie fire：～烈火 prairie fire 革命已成～之势。The revolution has developed like a prairie fire.

liǎo

了 liǎo 【动】❶ end，solve：没完没～ endless ～了一件心事 be relieved of some burden on one's mind ❷ used after a verb as a complement with 得 or 不 to indicate possibility or finality：今天晚上开会，你来得～来不～？There is a meeting this evening. Can you

come or not？这么多煤一个冬天烧不～。One can't burn such a lot of coal in one winter.

另见 le；liào

了不得 liǎobude 【形】❶ unusual；outstanding；exceptional：这可是一件～的大事。This is an exceptionally important matter！就算他会写诗又有什么～的！这么骄傲！So he writes poetry. What's so great about that？Why is he so conceited？❷ Good lord（indicates that sth. serious has happened）：可～，他昏过去了。Good lord！He has fainted！❸ used after 得 to form a complement of degree showing very high degree：大家都高兴得～。All of us are really delighted. 因为儿子不用功，他气得～。He is greatly upset that his son doesn't work hard.

了不起 liǎobuqǐ 【形】同"了不得"❶（but more frequently used）：自以为～ be conceited

了结 liǎojié 【动】finish；get over with；settle

了解 liǎojiě 【动】❶ know；understand：～情况 understand the situation 他很～这事的来龙去脉。He knows the long and short of the whole matter. ❷ enquire；probe：这究竟是怎么回事，请你去～一下。What is it all about？Please go and find out.

了却 liǎoquè 【动】solve；settle；

了如指掌 liǎo rú zhǐ zhǎng know sth. like the palm of one's hand；have sth. at one's finger-tips：周老师对她学生的学习、性格等等都～。Teacher Zhou knows thoroughly the temperament and study habits of each of her students.

了事 liǎo = shì make an end of；settle；conclude a matter（usu. used in cases where things are done perfunctorily）：敷衍～ wind up in a

perfunctory manner 草草～ finish up in a slipshod way

liào

料 liào 【动】predict；expect；guess；conjecture：～不到 fail to anticipate 不出所～ just as expected 我～定他必然失败。I can predict his eventual failure. 【名】❶ material；raw material：～已备齐。All the raw materials are at hand. ❷ grain (for animals)：草～ grain and fodder 给牲口加点儿～ give the livestock a bit more grain

料定 liàodìng 【动】expect；predict；foresee

料理 liàolǐ 【动】look after；arrange：～家务 do housework ～后事 make arrangements for a funeral

料想 liàoxiǎng 【动】expect；imagine；predict：他们的科研项目完成得这么快，真是～不到。It was quite unexpected that their research project should be finished so quickly. 你这样勤奋，我～你会取得很好的成绩的。You are so diligent. I can predict that your achievements will be great.

料子 liàozi 【名】any comparatively expensive dress material，especially wool

瞭 liào

瞭望 liàowàng 【动】watch；look into the distance from a high vantage point：海防战士正聚精会神地～着海面。The guards along the coast watch over the seas vigilantly.

镣（鐐） liào 【名】shackles

镣铐 liàokào 【名】shackles；leg irons and handcuffs

liè

列 liè 【动】❶ line up；queue up ❷ arrange or put sth. in the category of：～入计划 include (sth.) in a plan ～在清单上 include in an inventory 【代】◇❶ kind；sort；category：不在此～ not included in the list just mentioned 这两个人不在今晚邀请之～。The two of them are not among those invited this evening. ❷ various：～国 various countries 【量】rank：一～火车 a train

列车 lièchē 【名】train

列车员 lièchēyuán 【名】attendant；train crew

列车长 lièchēzhǎng 【名】head of a train crew

列岛 lièdǎo 【名】archipelago；a chain of islands

列队 liè＝duì line up

列举 lièjǔ 【动】list；enumerate：～事实 enumerate facts one by one

列强 lièqiáng 【名】imperialist powers

列席 lièxí 【动】be a non-voting delegate (at a conference)：他～了这次会议。He attended the conference as a non-voting delegate.

列传 lièzhuàn 【名】biographies (in ancient Chinese history books)

劣 liè 【形】bad；inferior

劣等 lièděng 【形】inferior

劣根性 liègēnxìng 【名】deeply-rooted evil nature or bad characteristic (of a nationality or a class of people)

劣迹 lièjì 【名】misdeed；evil doing

劣势 lièshì 【名】inferior in strength or position；unfavourable situation

劣质 lièzhì 【形】of poor (or low) quality：～商品 merchandise of poor quality；shoddy goods

烈 liè 【形】❶ fierce; furious; raging ❷ upright ❸ ◇ sacrificing oneself for a just cause

烈火 lièhuǒ 【名】raging flames

烈日 lièrì 【名】scorching sun

烈士 lièshì 【名】martyr; one who died for a just cause

烈属 lièshǔ 【名】family member of one who died for a just cause; family of a martyr

烈性 lièxìng ❶ of fierce, violent temper ❷ strong; potent: ～酒 strong spirits (alcohol) ～炸药 high explosive

猎（獵） liè

猎狗 liègǒu 【名】〔只 zhī〕hunting dog

猎奇 lièqí 【动】seek novelty (usu. derog.)

猎枪 lièqiāng 【名】〔枝 zhī〕hunting gun

猎取 lièqǔ 【动】❶ hunt: ～野兽 hunt wild animals ❷ (of fame or fortune) seize; pursue (derog.): ～暴利 garner steep profits

猎人 lièrén 【名】hunter

猎手 lièshǒu 【名】hunter (usu. a skilled hunter)

裂 liè 【动】crack; break; split: 墙上～了道缝。There is a crack in the wall. 木板～开了。The plank cracked. 山崩地～。Mountains cracked and the earth split. (e. g. in an earthquake) 脚冻～了。His heels were chapped by the cold.

裂缝 lièfèng 【名】fissure; cleft

裂痕 lièhén 【名】slight crack; rift: 这个古瓷瓶十分完好，没发现一点～。This antique porcelain vase is still intact. Not a trace of a crack has been found. 两个人感情上产生了～。There is a emotional rift between the two of them.

裂口 lièkǒu 【名】cleft; breach

裂纹 lièwén 【名】slight crack

lín

邻（鄰） lín

邻邦 línbāng 【名】同“邻国”

邻国 línguó 【名】neighbouring country

邻近 línjìn 【名】vicinity: 学校～是公园。There is a park in the vicinity of the school. 【动】be near; be close to: ～长城的地方，新修了一条公路。A new road has been built near the Great Wall.

邻居 línjū 【名】neighbour

林 lín 【名】◇ ❶ wood; forest; grove: 松～ pine wood 竹～ bamboo grove 防风～ windbreak ❷ forestry: 农～牧副渔 farming, forestry, animal-husbandry, side-line occupations and fishing

林场 línchǎng 【名】tree farm; lumber yard; nursery for tree saplings

林带 líndài 【名】forest belt

林立 línlì 【动】stand in great numbers like trees in a forest: 烟囱～ a forest of chimneys 井架～ a forest of derricks

林网 línwǎng 【名】crisscross forest belts

林业 línyè 【名】forestry

林荫道 línyīndào 【名】〔条 tiáo〕boulevard

临（臨） lín 【动】❶ ◇ arrive; befall: 双喜～门。Two happy occasions occurred in the family. 大祸～头。A calamity struck him. ❷ look out on; overlook: 居高～下 occupy a commanding position 这间屋子窗户～街。The window of this room looks out on the street. 他家的后门～河。The back door of

his house opens on the river. ❸ copy (as a way of practising painting or calligraphy)：～画 make a copy of a picture 他每天都～帖练毛笔字。He copies calligraphy models every day. ❹ on the point of (*always used with another verb as an attributive or adverbial adjunct*)：～终遗言 a will spoken just prior to one's death ～别纪念 parting souvenir 这种药是～睡的时候吃的。This medicine is to be taken before going to bed. 他～走送给我一张照片。He gave me a photo of himself before he left.

临床 línchuáng 【形】clinical (e. g. experience)

临近 línjìn 【动】(of time or space) approach；be close by：已经～考试了,学习更得加紧。Now that our examinations are approaching, we must work even harder.

临渴掘井 lín kě jué jǐng begin to dig a well when feeling thirsty；(*fig.*) do sth. at the last minute and too late

临摹 línmó 【动】copy；imitate

临时 línshí 【形】❶ shortly before sth. happens：我接到一个～通知,说会议改期了。I heard at very short notice that the conference was postponed. 平时不努力学习,～搞突击,这怎么行呢? You don't work hard ordinarily but try to cram at the last minute. That won't work. ❷ temporary；provisional；makeshift：～措施 makeshift measure ～政府 provisional government ～负责 take charge of temporarily

临时代办 línshí dàibàn *chargé d'affaires ad interim*

临危不惧 lín wēi bù jù be undaunted in the face of peril

临阵磨枪 lín zhèn mó qiāng start sharpening one's spear just before going into battle；(*fig.*) begin to prepare only at the last minute

淋 lín 【动】get wet (in the rain)：～了一身水 be soaked through 风吹雨～ be exposed to wind and rain 衣服～湿了。My clothes got wet in the rain.

淋巴 línbā 【名】lymph

淋漓 línlí 【形】❶ dripping wet：大汗～ dripping with sweat ❷ uninhibited：他的这番评论真是痛快～。His comments were uninhibited and very thorough.

淋漓尽致 línlí jìn zhì (of writing or speech) incisive and thorough：把他们的嘴脸揭露得～ to thoroughly expose them for what they are

淋浴 línyù 【名】shower (bath)

琳 lín

琳琅满目 línláng mǎn mù a collection of fine and exquisite things which is a feast for the eyes：美术馆画廊里～的名画,使人流连忘返。The various beautiful masterpieces in the Art Museum are such a feast for the eyes that one cannot bear to leave.

磷 lín 【名】phosphorus

磷肥 línféi 【名】phosphate fertilizer

lǐn

凛 lín

凛冽 lǐnliè 【形】biting cold；bitter cold：北风～ biting north wind

凛凛 lǐnlǐn 【形】❶ awe-inspiring ❷ biting cold

凛然 lǐnrán 【形】awe-inspiring：正气～ overwhelming and awe-inspiring spirit ～不可侵犯 awe-inspiring and inviolable

lìn

吝 lìn

吝啬 lìnsè 【形】miserly；stingy

吝惜 lìnxī 【动】spare；stint：小王为了工作从不～时间。Xiao Wang never stints time on his work.

líng

伶 líng

伶俐 línglì 【形】clever；smart：口齿～ speak sensibly and well 聪明～ quick and sharp

灵（靈）líng 【形】❶ agile；nimble：小孩儿身子比大人～。A child is more agile than an adult. ❷ sensitive：狗的鼻子特别～。The nose of the dog is especially sensitive. ❸ efficacious；effective：～药 efficacious medicine 制动器失～。The brakes are not functioning. 【名】remains（or ashes）of a deceased person：守～ stand guard beside the remains, keeping awake ～前摆满了花圈 Wreaths were laid in front of the remains.

灵便 língbiàn 【形】❶（of limbs）nimble：手脚～ light of hand and nimble of foot ❷ easy to handle；handy：这种钳子用起来很～。This kind of pliers is very handy.

灵车 língchē 【名】〔辆 liàng〕hearse

灵感 línggǎn 【名】inspiration

灵魂 línghún 【名】❶ soul；spirit；thought：～深处 one's inner-most being 纯洁的～ a pure and simple soul ❷ vital core（of sth.）

灵活 línghuó 【形】flexible；agile：脑筋～ quick-witted 他的学习方法很～。His method of study is quite flexible. 学生不但懂得这些词的意思，而且还能～运用。The students not only know the meanings of these words, but can also use them readily. 战略战术要机动～。Strategy and tactics should be flexible.

灵活性 línghuóxìng 【名】flexibility

灵机一动 língjī yī dòng have a sudden inspiration；hit upon a bright idea：事关大局，要深思熟虑，不要～就干起来。This is something bearing on the overall situation, so think it over. Don't act on the spur of the moment.

灵柩 língjiù 【名】coffin containing a corpse

灵敏 língmǐn 【形】keen；sensitive：嗅觉～ have a sensitive nose 仪器～。The instruments are sensitive.

灵敏度 língmǐndù 【名】sensitivity

灵巧 língqiǎo 【形】nimble；dexterous：动作～ nimble movements ～的双手 a dexterous pair of hands

灵堂 língtáng 【名】mourning hall；funeral hall

灵通 língtōng 【形】have quick and easy access to information：消息～ be well-informed

灵验 língyàn 【形】efficacious；effective

玲 líng

玲珑 línglóng 【形】❶（of things）small and exquisite ❷（of person）clever and dainty：八面～ smooth and able to win favour on all sides

铃（鈴）líng 【名】bell

凌 líng

凌晨 língchén 【名】time just before dawn

凌驾 língjià 【动】override（other matters）：～一切 lord it over everybody

凌空 língkōng 【动】soar；fly high：高阁～ tower soaring to the sky 飞

机～而起。The airplane soared into the sky. 雄鹰～而过。The eagle soared high in the sky.

凌厉 línglì 【形】quick and forceful：攻势～ a quick and powerful attack

凌乱 língluàn 【形】untidy; disorderly; messy：～的脚步声 the sound of disorderly footsteps 室内～不堪。The room is a complete mess. 东西放得很～。Things were strewn about in great disorder.

凌辱 língrǔ 【动】humiliate

凌云 língyún 【动】soaring into the skies：壮志～ soaring aspirations

陵 líng

陵墓 língmù 【名】mausoleum; tomb

陵园 língyuán 【名】cemetery

菱 líng 【名】water-chestnut

菱形 língxíng 【名】rhombus

零 líng 【数】❶ zero："108" is read 一百～八 or 一一八 "1005" is read 一千～五 or 一～～五 "120" is read 一百二十 or 一二～ "1200" is read 一千二百 or 一二～～ "5.05 jin" is read 五斤～五钱 or 五点～五斤 "8.03 yuan" is read 八块～三分 or 八点～三元 "the year 1970" is read 一九七～年 ❷ indicates that a larger and a smaller unit are being used together：两年～三个月 two years and three months 一小时～五分 one hour and five minutes 【形】opp. to 整：～存整取（of banking）deposit in small sums and withdraw the whole amount 酒可以买整瓶的，也可以～打。Liquor can be bought by the bottle or by any unit of weight.

零点 língdiǎn 【名】zero point; zero hour

零度 língdù 【名】zero：～以下 below zero; sub-zero

零花 línghuā 【名】〈口〉(～儿) pocket money 【动】use for pocket money：这几块钱留着～吧！Keep these few yuan for your pocket money.

零活儿 línghuór 【名】odd jobs; chores

零件 língjiàn 【名】spare part

零乱 língluàn 【形】同"凌乱" língluàn

零七八碎 língqībāsuì 【形】disorderly; odds and ends：～的事儿 all sorts of chores 【名】(～儿) messy odds and ends：把屋里的～都收拾起来。Clear up the mess in the room.

零钱 língqián 【名】❶ (of money) small change：没有～找 have no change ❷ pocket money：一个星期花不了多少～ won't spend a lot of pocket money in a week

零敲碎打 líng qiāo suì dǎ do things piecemeal; do sth. bit by bit 也说 "零打碎敲"。

零散 língsǎn 【形】scattered：把～的木材集中起来 gather up the scattered timber 孩子们把玩具～地扔在草地上。The children left their toys lying about on the lawn.

零食 língshí 【名】between-meal snack

零售 língshòu 【动】retail

零碎 língsuì 【形】odds and ends：～活儿 odd jobs 这些零零碎碎的东西很占地方。These odds and ends take up a lot of space. 【名】(～儿) scraps; bits and pieces：把这些～收拾一下。Clear away these bits and pieces.

零星 língxīng 【形】sporadic：今天有～小雨。There will be scattered rain today. 远处不时响起零零星星的枪声。From time to time, there were sounds of sporadic shots in the distance.

零用 língyòng 【名】同"零花"【名】【动】spend on minor purchases：二十块钱全～掉了。Twenty yuan

were all spent on minor purchases.

lǐng

领（領）lǐng 【动】❶ get (sth. from an institution)：～工作服 go to get one's work clothes ～工资 draw one's wages ～奖 receive an award ❷ lead；take：～学生参观博物馆 take the students to a museum ❸ accept：～情 appreciate sb.'s kindness 【名】◇ collar；neck (e.g. of a sweater)：大衣～ coat collar 尖～ V-neck 圆～ round neck

领班 lǐngbān 【名】foreman

领带 lǐngdài 【名】〔条 tiáo〕necktie

领导 lǐngdǎo 【动】lead 【名】leader；leadership：～要深入基层。Leaders should go mix with the rank and file. 他是我们的～。He is our leader.

领导班子 lǐngdǎo bānzi leading group；leading body

领导权 lǐngdǎoquán 【名】leadership

领地 lǐngdì 【名】❶ manor ❷ territory

领队 lǐngduì 【名】leader of a group, sports team etc.

领海 lǐnghǎi 【名】territorial waters

领航 lǐngháng 【动】pilot；navigate

领会 lǐnghuì 【动】understand；comprehend；grasp：深刻～文件的精神 have a thorough grasp of the gist of the document

领教 lǐngjiào 【动】❶ *polite way of asking for advice*：有点儿事向您～。There's something I'd like to ask you to explain to me. ❷ have experience of（some scheme or trick）：他们这种作法我们早就～了。We have experienced their tricks long before.

领空 lǐngkōng 【名】air space

领略 lǐnglüè 【动】have a taste of

领取 lǐngqǔ 【动】go and get：～奖学金 get one's scholarship money ～退休金 draw one's pension

领事 lǐngshì 【名】consul

领事馆 lǐngshìguǎn 【名】consulate

领属 lǐngshǔ 【动】subject；subordinate；put under the control of

领头 lǐngtóu=tóu 〈口〉（～儿）take the lead；be the first to do sth.

领土 lǐngtǔ 【名】territory

领悟 lǐngwù 【动】comprehend

领先 lǐngxiān 【动】take the lead；be in the lead（usu. in sports）：暂时～ hold a temporary lead 一度～ hold the lead for a while 在三千米赛跑中，小赵一直遥遥～。Xiao Zhao held a safe lead throughout the three thousand metre race.

领衔 lǐngxián 【动】head the list of signers（of a document）

领袖 lǐngxiù 【名】leader

领养 lǐngyǎng 【动】adopt（a child）

领域 lǐngyù 【名】❶（a nation's）territory ❷ sphere；realm；field：人文～ sphere of the arts and humanities 自然科学～ the realm of natural sciences

领章 lǐngzhāng 【名】collar flash；collar badge

领子 lǐngzi 【名】collar

lìng

另 lìng 【形】*used before the numeral or a monosyllabic verb to stand for* 另外：～一个人 another person ～一回事 another matter ～想办法 think of another method ～有任务 have another task 【副】同"另外"【副】：那几笔账算在一起，这笔～算。Those accounts are to be taken together；this one, separately.

另起炉灶 lìng qǐ lúzào make a fresh start

另外　lìngwài　【形】other；another：这块地种花生，～两块地种棉花。This plot is to be sown with peanuts, the other two with cotton. 你说的是～一个问题，和我们谈的不是一回事。You are raising a different matter; it isn't what we are talking about. 【连】besides：你把这个文件送给他，～让他下午来找我一趟。Please give him this document, and ask him to come and see me in the afternoon. 【副】separately；alone：我没和他们住在一起，我～住。I am not living with them; I live by myself. 我今天有事，咱们～找时间谈吧！I've other things to do today. We'll have to find some other time to talk it over.

另眼看待　lìng yǎn kàndài　regard sb. with special favour

令　lìng　【动】make；cause；order：～人兴奋 make one feel elated ～人肃然起敬 fill one with respect ～你舰立即返航。Your vessel is to return to base at once. 【名】order：～行禁止。Orders and prohibitions are both acted on immediately.

令人发指　lìng rén fàzhǐ　make one's hair stand on end (in horror)

令人作呕　lìng rén zuò'ǒu　nauseating；make one sick

liū

溜　liū　【动】❶ slide：从滑梯上～下来 slide down the slide ❷ slip away；slink away：他悄悄地从后门～走了。He slunk away through the back door. 我要赶火车，只好从会场～掉。I had to catch a train, so I slipped away from the rally.

溜冰　liū=bīng　skate；ice-skating

溜达　liūda　【动】go for a walk；stroll：来回～ stroll back and forth

liú

浏（瀏）　liú

浏览　liúlǎn　【动】go over；browse through；glance over：这些报刊我只～了一下。I only glanced through the papers and magazines.

留　liú　【动】❶ stay；remain；keep (sb.)：如果你非要走，我也不～你了。I won't keep you any longer if you are determined to go. ❷ keep (sth.) for；leave (sth.) for：～做纪念 keep sth. as a souvenir 这是古人给我们～下的文化遗产。This is an example of the rich cultural heritage left us by our ancestors. 把困难～给自己，把方便让给别人。Tackle what is difficult yourself, while leaving the easy tasks for others.

留步　liúbù　【动】(a departing guest's polite word to the host) Don't bother to see me out.

留后路　liú hòulù　leave (oneself) a way out

留级　liú＝jí　remain in the same grade (through failure to be promoted)

留恋　liúliàn　【动】be reluctant to part with；be nostalgic about：那一段海上生活，真值得～。That period of our life on board ship will always linger in our memory. 我非常～第一次参加工作的那个地方。I often think nostalgically of the place where I held my first job.

留念　liúniàn　【动】keep (this) as a memento (inscription on a photograph or other souvenir)

留情　liú＝qíng　show consideration or mercy：手下～ have mercy on those who are at your mercy 他批评起人来可毫不～。When he gives

people a piece of his mind, he doesn't mince words.

留神 liú = shén take care; be careful: 抄数目字得(děi)特别～。One must be especially careful when copying figures. 你带个西瓜骑车，要多留点儿神。If you carry a watermelon on the back of your bicycle, you must be really careful.

留声机 liúshēngjī 【名】gramophone; record player

留守 liúshǒu 【动】stay behind to take care of things for an institution

留宿 liúsù 【动】put sb. up for the night

留心 liú = xīn pay attention; be attentive: 要想提高自己的篮球技术，必须～看别人打球。If you want to improve your basketball skill, you should watch the other players closely. 考试的时候留点儿心，别慌慌张张的。You must sit for examinations carefully and not get flustered.

留学 liúxué 【动】study abroad

留学生 liúxuéshēng 【名】student studying abroad

留言 liúyán 【名】words or message written at departure: ～簿 visitors' book

留意 liú = yì keep one's eyes open; be attentive: 算账得(děi)专心，一不～就要出错。You must pay careful attention when doing accounts. You're likely to make errors if you're not careful. 他什么时候进屋来的，我没～。I didn't notice when he came in. 你去买东西的时候替我留点儿意，看有没有这种活页本。When you go shopping, please look and see if there are any loose-leaf notebooks like this.

留影 liúyǐng 【名】a photo taken for souvenir

留影 liú = yǐng have a picture taken as a souvenir

留有余地 liú yǒu yúdì leave some leeway: 订计划要～。When making a plan, leave some leeway.

流

流 liú 【动】flow; drift: ～血(xiě)～汗 bleeding and sweating 水～得很急。The water is flowing rapidly.

流弊 liúbì 【名】prevalent abuses

流产 liú = chǎn ❶ miscarriage ❷ abortive attempt

流畅 liúchàng 【形】fluent: 文笔～ flowing writing-style 语言～ in fluent language

流程 liúchéng 【名】technological process

流传 liúchuán 【动】spread; get about; hand down: 消息～得很快。The news got about very fast. 许多古代传说一直～到今天。Many ancient legends have been handed down right to the present.

流窜 liúcuàn 【动】flee in confusion; flee in disorder: 被打败的残匪到处～。The remaining bandit troops fled in all directions.

流弹 liúdàn 【名】stray bullet

流动 liúdòng 【动】flow; circulate: 空气～。The air is circulating. 河水缓缓地～。The river is flowing slowly. 【形】fluid; mobile: ～哨 soldiers on patrol

流动资产 liúdòng zīchǎn floating assets

流动资金 liúdòng zījīn operating fund

流感 liúgǎn 【名】influenza

流寇 liúkòu 【名】❶ roving bandits ❷ roving rebel bands

流寇主义 liúkòuzhǔyì 【名】the view that one should not establish revolutionary bases, but simply engage in roving attacks

流浪 liúlàng 【动】roam; wander

流离 liúlí 【动】become homeless and wander about because of some

disaster

流离失所 liú lí shī suǒ　become destitute and homeless

流利 liúlì 【形】fluid；smooth；fluent：文章写得很～。The article is written in a flowing style. 汉语说得很～。He speaks fluent Chinese.

流连忘返 liúlián wàng fǎn　enjoys oneself so much that one forgets to leave 也作"留连忘返"。

流量 liú liàng 【名】rate of flow

流露 liúlù 【动】reveal；show (feelings, sentiments, etc.)：～出喜悦的心情 show delight 真情～ reveal one's true feelings

流落 liúluò 【动】become destitute and wander：～他乡 be destitute and far from home

流氓 liúmáng 【名】hoodlum

流派 liúpài 【名】school (of thought, e. g. in philosophy, the arts, or sciences)

流失 liúshī 【动】(soil or minerals, etc.)be washed away or shifted by wind or water：防止水土～ prevent loss of water and soil erosion

流食 liúshí 【名】liquid food

流逝 liúshì 【动】pass；elapse

流水 liúshuǐ 【名】❶ flowing water ❷ anything which is like flowing water：～线 assembly line

流水不腐，户枢不蠹 liúshuǐ bù fǔ, hùshū bù dù　running water is always fresh, and a door hinge is never worm-eaten；(fig.) moving things are unlikely to go bad

流水线 liúshuǐxiàn 【名】assembly-line

流水作业 liúshuǐ zuòyè　assembly-line method of production

流速 liúsù 【名】velocity of flow

流通 liútōng 【动】circulate：货币～ currency circulation 商品～ commodity circulation ～手段 medium (or means) of circulation 开开窗户，让空气～一下。Open the window to ventilate the room.

流亡 liúwáng 【动】exile；live in exile abroad

流线型 liúxiànxíng 【名】streamlining

流星 liúxīng 【名】〔颗 kē〕meteor

流行 liúxíng 【动】be prevalent；be popular：这种样式的鞋～了一阵子。Shoes like this were popular for a time. 【形】popular：这几首歌很～。These songs are quite popular.

流行病 liúxíngbìng 【名】epidemic disease

流血 liúxuè 【动】shed blood (attrib. only)

流言 liúyán 【名】rumour；gossip

流言蜚语 liúyán fēiyǔ　rumour and gossip

流域 liúyù 【名】river basin

硫 liú 【名】sulphur

硫磺 liúhuáng 【名】sulphur

硫酸 liúsuān 【名】sulphuric acid

瘤 liú 【名】tumour

瘤子 liúzi 【名】〔个 gè〕tumour

liǔ

柳 liǔ 【名】willow

柳树 liǔshù 【名】〔棵 kē〕willow

liù

六 liù 【数】six

六书 liùshū 【名】the six principles of formation of Chinese characters：1.象形 pictograph (马、山) 2.指事 form indicates action or state (上、下) 3.会意 form suggests meaning (尘、信) 4.形声 one part suggests meaning, the other sound

（洋、枫）5.转注 synonymous character（考、老）6.假借 use of one character to stand for another（谷、后）

六一国际儿童节　Liù Yī Guójì Értóngjié　June lst, International Children's Day

六月　liùyuè　【名】June

陆（陸）liù　【数】six（*the complicated form of* 六）见"捌"bā
另见 lù

lóng

龙（龍）lóng　【名】dragon

龙飞凤舞　lóng fēi 'fèng wǔ　(of calligraphy) flamboyant and vigorous

龙井茶　lóngjǐngchá　【名】Longjing tea

龙腾虎跃　lóng téng hǔ yuè　dragons rise and tigers leap；(*fig.*) a scene of bustling activity

龙头　lóngtóu　【名】water tap

聋（聾）lóng　【动】become deaf【形】deaf

聋哑　lóngyǎ　【形】deaf and dumb

聋子　lóngzi　【名】deaf person

笼（籠）lóng　【名】◇cage；coop
另见 lǒng

笼子　lóngzi　【名】cage；coop

隆　lóng

隆冬　lóngdōng　【名】the depths of winter；midwinter

隆隆　lónglóng　【象声】rumbling；booming：炮 声 ～ the thunder of guns 马达～ the roar of a motor

隆重　lóngzhòng　【形】solemn；grand；ceremonious：婚礼很～。The wedding ceremony was very grand. 大会～开幕。The conference was opened with great ceremony.

lǒng

垄（壟）lǒng　【名】ridge along a furrow

垄断　lǒngduàn　【动】monopolize

垄断资本　lǒngduàn zīběn　monopoly capital

垄断资产阶级　lǒngduàn zīchǎnjiējí　monopoly capitalist class

笼（籠）lǒng
另见 lóng

笼络　lǒngluò　【动】use any means to win people over（*derog.*）：他很会～人。He is very good at winning people over.

笼统　lǒngtǒng　【形】vague；in general terms：你讲得太～了，请具体点儿。You are speaking too generally. Please be more specific.

笼罩　lǒngzhào　【动】envelop；blanket：晨 雾 ～ 着原野。The morning fog blanketed the open fields.

lóu

喽（嘍）lóu

喽罗　lóuluo　【名】hanger-on；pawn

楼（樓）lóu　【名】〔座 zuò〕❶ building with more than one storey ❷ storey；floor

楼房　lóufáng　【名】〔座 zuò〕building with more than one storey

楼梯　lóutī　【名】staircase

lǒu

搂（摟）lǒu　【动】embrace；hug

篓（簍）lǒu　【名】basket

篓子　lǒuzi　【名】〔个 gè〕round deep

basket with a small opening at the top

lòu

陌 lòu
陌俗 lòusú 【名】undesirable customs

陌习 lòuxí 【名】vulgar habit

漏 lòu 【动】❶ leak；水管～水。
The pipe is leaking. 锅～了。The pot leaks. 房子～了。The roof leaks. ❷ leave out：这行（háng）～了两个字。Two words have been left out in this line. 统计人数时，把他给～了。He was overlooked in a head count. ❸（of news, secret）become known：～了风声。The news has leaked.

漏洞 lòudòng 【名】❶ leak ❷ inconsistency；loophole：堵塞工作中的～ fix up the weak spots in the work 他说话严密，没有～。He was consistent in what he said, and there was no loophole in his argument.

漏洞百出 lòudòng bǎi chū （of speech, writing and actions）flawed；full of flaws

漏斗 lòudǒu 【名】funnel

漏税 lòu = shuì tax evasion；evade taxation

漏网 lòu = wǎng escape from the net：～之鱼 a fish which slipped out of the net 决不让一个犯罪分子～。Don't let a single criminal slip through.

露 lòu 【动】expose；reveal；show
另见 lù

露马脚 lòu mǎjiǎo give oneself away；show one's true colours：不管诈骗犯伪装得多么巧妙，总是要～的。No matter how well disguised, swindlers will eventually show themselves in their true colours.

露面 lòu = miàn show up；show one's face；appear on public occasions

露头 lòu = tóu emerge；appear：太阳还没～，街上就有了车辆声。The sun had not yet appeared when sounds of traffic began to be heard in the streets. 旱象刚一～就马上采取措施。Prompt measures were taken as soon as signs of drought appeared.

lú

卢（盧）lú
卢比 lúbǐ 【名】rupee (currency)

卢布 lúbù 【名】rouble (currency)

芦（蘆）lú
芦苇 lúwěi 【名】reed

炉（爐）lú 【名】stove；furnace
炉火纯青 lú huǒ chún qīng high degree of proficiency；complete mastery：这位演员艺术造诣很深，他的表演可以说是～了。This actor has attained such a high degree of proficiency that his performance was perfect.

炉灶 lúzào 【名】kitchen stove

炉子 lúzi 【名】〔个 gè〕stove

lǔ

卤（鹵、滷）lǔ 【名】halogen

掳（擄）lǔ
掳掠 lǔlüè 【动】（of person or things）carry away by force；loot

鲁（魯）lǔ
鲁莽 lǔmǎng 【形】reckless；rash；

hotheaded 也作"卤莽"。

lù

陆（陸） lù 【名】◇land：这种动物水～两栖。This animal is an amphibian.

另见 liù

陆地 lùdì 【名】land

陆军 lùjūn 【名】army；land force

陆路 lùlù 【名】road；by land

陆陆续续 lùlùxùxù 【副】one after another；in succession：他～给我寄来过五、六本杂志。He mailed me five or six magazines in succession.

陆续 lùxù 【副】one after another：～出发 set out one after another ～发表 publish in succession 新生～到校了。The new students have come to the college one after another.

录（録） lù 【动】record (e.g. notetaking, sound-recording)

录取 lùqǔ 【动】select (from among examinees)

录像 lù = xiàng to videotape；to video

录像带 lùxiàngdài 【名】videotape

录像机 lùxiàngjī 【名】video-recorder

录音 lù = yīn sound-recording

录音带 lùyīndài 【名】magnetic tape；tape

录音机 lùyīnjī 【名】tape-recorder

录用 lùyòng 【动】employ；take sb. on the staff

录制 lùzhì 【动】to make audio tapes or videotapes

鹿 lù 【名】〔只 zhī〕deer

鹿茸 lùróng 【名】newly-sprouted deer antler (used as Chinese medicine)

路 lù 【名】❶〔条 tiáo〕road；highway ❷ journey；distance：～很远 a long way ❸ route；line：坐五号公共汽车去 go there on a No. 5 bus 三～进军。The army marched by three different routes. ❹ sort；kind：一～货色 the same sort of stuff (derog.) ❺ way out；way to follow

路标 lùbiāo 【名】road sign

路程 lùchéng 【名】distance travelled；journey

路灯 lùdēng 【名】street lamp

路费 lùfèi 【名】travelling expenses

路过 lùguò 【动】pass by

路考 lùkǎo 【动】road test

路口 lùkǒu 【名】the intersection of streets or roads

路况 lùkuàng 【名】road condition；traffic condition

路牌 lùpái 【名】street name plate or road signs

路上 lùshang 【名】on the way

路途 lùtú 【名】❶ road；way ❷ distance travelled

路线 lùxiàn 【名】❶ route；itinerary：按照规定的～进行越野比赛 run the cross-country race over a set course ❷ (ideological, political) line

路遥知马力 lù yáo zhī mǎ lì a long journey tests a horse's strength：～，日久见人心。As a long journey tests a horse's strength, so time shows a person's heart.

路子 lùzi 【名】means or method (of achieving one's aim)

露 lù 【名】◇❶ dew：阳光雨～ sunshine, rain and dew ❷ syrup：果子～ fruit syrup 【动】show；reveal；appear：脸上～出了笑容。A smile appeared on (his) face.

另见 lòu

露骨 lùgǔ 【形】barefaced；undis-

guised

露水 lùshuǐ 【名】dew

露宿 lùsù 【动】pass the night in the open

露天 lùtiān 【名】open-air

露营 lùyíng 【动】camp in the open

lǘ

驴(驢) lǘ 【名】〔头 tóu〕donkey

lǚ

捋 lǚ 【动】stroke；smooth：～胡子 stroke one's beard 把这些绳子～一～ straighten out these threads 另见 luō

旅 lǚ 【名】brigade 【量】brigade：一～骑兵 a brigade of cavalry

旅程 lǚchéng 【名】journey

旅费 lǚfèi 【名】travelling expenses

旅馆 lǚguǎn 【名】hotel

旅居 lǚjū 【动】live (at a place other than one's native town, esp. abroad)

旅客 lǚkè 【名】traveller

旅社 lǚshè 【名】hotel

旅途 lǚtú 【名】journey；while travelling

旅行 lǚxíng 【动】travel；make a trip 【名】travel；trip

旅行袋 lǚxíngdài 【名】〔个 gè〕travelling bag

旅行社 lǚxíngshè 【名】travel agency

旅游 lǚyóu 【动】tour：～业 tourism

旅长 lǚzhǎng 【名】brigadier

屡(屢) lǚ 【副】◇repeatedly：～战～胜 fight many battles and win them all

屡次 lǚcì 【副】repeatedly；time and again：～发生 happen time and again 在生产上他～创造新记录。He has set one new production record after another.

屡次三番 lǚcì sān fān again and again；time and again：～地嘱咐 enjoin time and again

屡见不鲜 lǚ jiàn bù xiān a thing loses its novelty when it takes place again and again：狮子在动物园繁殖，早已～了。More and more lions are given birth to in the zoos and they are nothing new now.

屡教不改 lǚ jiào bù gǎi refuse to mend one's ways despite repeated exhortations

履 lǚ

履历 lǚlì 【名】personal record

履行 lǚxíng 【动】carry out；perform；fulfil：～诺言 keep a promise ～合同 fulfil a contract ～手续 go through the procedures

lǜ

律 lǜ

律师 lǜshī 【名】lawyer

律诗 lǜshī 【名】〔首 shǒu〕a classical poem of eight lines with a strict tone pattern and rhyme scheme：五言～ a poem of this kind which has 5 characters to the line 七言～ a poem of this kind which has 7 characters to the line

率 lǜ 【名】◇rate；proportion；ratio：人口增长～ the rate of population increase 另见 shuài

绿(綠) lǜ 【形】green

绿茶 lǜchá 【名】green tea

绿灯 lǜdēng 【名】❶ green (traffic) light ❷ 开绿灯 make way for；facilitate

绿豆 lǜdòu【名】lentil

绿化 lǜhuà【动】afforest；植树造林，~祖国。Plant trees and cover the whole country with vegetation.

绿色 lǜsè【名】green colour

绿油油 lǜyōuyōu【形】dark green and lustrous

绿洲 lǜzhōu【名】oasis

luán

孪（孿）luán

孪生 luánshēng【形】twin

luǎn

卵 luǎn【名】egg

卵翼 luǎnyì【动】〈书〉be under the protection of the wings of a nesting bird；be under the protection of (derog.)：~之下 be shielded by (sb.)

luàn

乱（亂）luàn【形】❶ disordered；untidy：人很多，但秩序不~。Though there were many people, they were very orderly. 箱子里太~了，得（děi）整理一下。The box is too badly packed. It needs rearranging. 他写得太~，看不清楚。His handwriting is so sloppy, I can't make it out. ❷ chaotic；disturbing：~世 troubled days ❸ at will；random：穿过森林的时候不要~跑，免得迷路。When passing through the forest, don't wander about, or you might get lost. 机器是~动不得的。The machinery is not to be tampered with. ❹ (of mind) be troubled；be in a turmoil：这几天工作不顺心，我心里很~。

My work has not been going well recently, and I'm worried.【动】◇confuse：以假~真 confuse the genuine with the false

乱窜 luàncuàn【动】run helter-skelter

乱哄哄 luànhōnghōng【形】noisy；tumultuous

乱七八糟 luànqībāzāo【形】at sixes and sevens；topsy-turvy：宿舍要整洁，不要搞得~的。Keep the dormitory tidy. Don't mess it up. 看你把抽屉翻得~的。Look, you've made a mess of the drawer.

乱弹琴 luàntánqín mess-up；cockup；sheer nonsense

乱子 luànzi【名】disturbance；trouble：出~ disturbances that erupted 闹~ create trouble

lüè

掠 lüè【动】❶ plunder：贪天之功，~为己有 appropriate to oneself the merits of others 土匪~走了村里的粮食。The bandits made off with the grain from the village. ❷ flit；skim：蜻蜓~过水面。The dragonfly skimmed over the surface of the water.

掠夺 lüèduó【动】plunder；rob；pillage

掠取 lüèqǔ【动】seize；grab

略 lüè【名】◇ strategy；tactics：雄才大~（of a statesman, etc.）outstanding ability and farsightedness【动】❶ omit；leave out：~去细节 leave out the details ❷ ◇ seize；capture：攻城~地 attack and occupy cities and territory【形】sketchy；slightly；a little：~知一二 know just a little about it ~有所闻 have heard sth. about it 这样~~几行叙述不能说明问题。Such a sketchy

account doesn't tell you much.

略微 lüèwēi 【副】同"稍微"shāowēi but less frequently used

略语 lüèyǔ 【名】abbreviation

lūn

抡（掄）lūn 【动】wield：～刀 wield a chopper ～铁锤 swing a sledgehammer ～起斧子 swing an axe

lún

伦（倫）lún

伦理 lúnlǐ 【名】ethics

沦（淪）lún

沦落 lúnluò 【动】fall low；be reduced to poverty

沦丧 lúnsàng 【动】be lost or ruined

沦亡 lúnwáng 【动】(of a country) be subjugated

沦陷 lúnxiàn 【动】(of territory) fall (into the enemy's hands)

轮（輪）lún 【名】◇wheel：十～卡车 ten wheel truck 【动】take turns：每人～一天。Everybody takes his turn for a day. 今天～到我值班。It's my turn to be on duty today. 【量】❶ for sun, moon：一～红日 a red sun 一～明月 a bright full moon ❷（～儿）round（for something rotating）：第一～比赛结束了。The first round of the tournament has ended.

轮班 lún=bān (work) in shifts

轮船 lúnchuán 【名】〔艘 sōu〕ship；steamer；steamship

轮渡 lúndù 【名】ferry

轮换 lúnhuàn 【动】take turns；rotate：定期～ take turns by a fixed period 这个车间的工人上白班和上夜

班每周～一次。The workers in this workshop do day and night shifts in weekly rotation.

轮廓 lúnkuò 【名】❶ contour ❷ outline（of a situation）

轮流 lúnliú 【动】take turns：～值日 be on duty in turn 医疗们～参加巡回医疗队。The doctors take turns participating in the mobile medical team.

轮胎 lúntāi 【名】tire

轮休 lúnxiū 【动】❶ have holidays in turn ❷（of land）lie fallow in rotation

轮训 lúnxùn 【动】receive training in rotation

轮椅 lúnyǐ 【名】wheelchair

轮子 lúnzi 【名】〔个 gè〕wheel

轮作 lúnzuò 【名】crop rotation

lùn

论（論）lùn 【名】❶ treatise；theoretical work：《矛盾论》On Contradiction ❷ theory：相对～ the theory of relativity 【动】❶ discuss；discourse：我们不能就事～事。We must not deal with matters in an isolated fashion. ❷ treat；regard：迟到超过一定时数，以旷工～。If one is late for work by a certain number of hours, it will be treated as an absence from work. ❸ decide on：按质～价 determine the price according to the quality ❹ by；in terms of：这里买布～尺，买呢子～公尺。Cotton cloth is sold here by the chi and woolen cloth by the metre. ～天气，昆明是最理想的了，冬暖夏凉。As far as weather goes, Kunming is ideal：mild in winter and cool in summer.

论处 lùnchǔ 【动】judge；decide (punishment)：按贪污罪～ be found guilty of corruption；bring in a

verdict of guilty of corruption 依法～ decide the punishment according to law

论点 lùndiǎn 【名】thesis; argument

论调 lùndiào 【名】view; argument (*usu*. *derog*.):错误～ wrong view 荒谬的～ absurd argument

论断 lùnduàn 【名】judgement; inference

论据 lùnjù 【名】basis of an argument

论述 lùnshù 【动】expound; elaborate

论说 lùnshuō 【动】talk about

论坛 lùntán 【名】forum; tribune (usu. magazine title)

论文 lùnwén 【名】〔篇 piān〕thesis; treatise

论战 lùnzhàn 【名】polemics; debate:展开～ launch a debate 这是一场唯物主义与唯心主义的大～。This is a heated debate which involves materialism as opposed to idealist views. 【动】argue; debate:继续～ continue to argue ～到底 debate to the end

论争 lùnzhēng 【名】argument 【动】debate; argue

论证 lùnzhèng 【动】expound and prove

论著 lùnzhù 【名】written research report

论罪 lùn = zuì decide according to the nature of the guilt

luō

捋 luō 【动】rub one's hand over or along sth.:～树叶 strip off tree leaves (by running one's hand along a branch) ～起袖子 roll up one's sleeves
另见 lǚ

啰（囉）luō

啰唆 luōsuo 〈口〉【形】❶ (of speech) verbose; wordy:他说话太～。He is always long-winded. ❷ (of matters) troublesome:这真是件～事儿! This is really a troublesome matter! 【动】be verbose; be long-winded:写文章和说话一样,千万别～。Writing is the same as speaking; one mustn't be long-winded. 他刚才来～了半天,也没把问题说清楚。He came over and rambled on for a long time, but I couldn't make out what he's driving at.

luó

罗（羅）luó 【名】❶ net ❷ fine sieve ❸ gauze
另见 luó

罗列 luóliè 【动】list; cite:～事实 enumerate facts ～现象 list the phenomena one by one

罗盘 luópán 【名】compass

罗网 luówǎng 【名】snare; trap

萝（蘿）luó

萝卜 luóbo 【名】turnip; radish

逻（邏）luó

逻辑 luóji 【名】logic

逻辑学 luójíxué 【名】logic (discipline)

锣（鑼）luó 【名】gong

锣鼓 luógǔ 【名】drums and gongs

锣鼓喧天 luógǔ xuān tiān beating of drums and gongs (in celebration)

骡（騾）luó 【名】mule

骡子 luózi 【名】〔头 tóu〕mule

螺 luó

螺母 luómǔ 【名】nut (for a screw)

螺丝钉 luósīdīng 【名】〔颗 kē〕screw

螺蛳 luósī 【名】spiral shell; snail

螺旋 luóxuán 【名】spiral

螺旋桨 luóxuánjiǎng 【名】propeller

luǒ

裸 luǒ 【动】bare

裸露 luǒlù 【动】lay bare; be exposed

裸体 luǒtǐ 【名】nude

luò

骆(駱) luò

骆驼 luòtuo 【名】〔峰 fēng〕camel

络(絡) luò

络绎不绝 luòyì bù jué （of people, vehicles, etc.） in an endless stream; 长安大街车辆行人～。There is an endless stream of traffic on Chang'an Street.

落 luò 【动】❶ go down; set; 潮水～了。The tide is going out. 太阳～了。The sun has set. ❷ drop; fall; ～泪 shed tears 树叶～了。The leaves have fallen. ❸ stay; stop over; 小鸟～在树枝上。Little birds perched on the tree branch. ❹ be placed on; 这项任务～在我们肩上了。This task was put on our shoulders.

另见 là; lào

落成 luòchéng 【动】（of building) be completed; 大厦～。The construction of that big building is completed. 大桥胜利～。The big bridge has been successfully completed.

落地窗 luòdìchuāng 【名】French window

落地灯 luòdìdēng 【名】floor lamp; standard lamp

落后 luòhòu 【形】backward 【动】fall behind; lag behind; 别人走在前面,我们～了。The others are walking ahead of us, while we are lagging behind. 在学习上他从来不肯～。He is never willing to fall behind in his studies.

落户 luò＝hù settle down in a place; 他是十年前在这里～的。He settled down here ten years ago.

落花流水 luò huā liú shuǐ irretrievable as fallen flowers carried away by the stream; utterly routed

落脚 luò＝jiǎo stay at or stop temporarily; ～谋生 stay at a place and find a way to make one's living ～之地 a place where one can stop for a rest or live temporarily

落井下石 luò jǐng xià shí drop stones on sb. who has fallen into a well; (fig.) take advantage of someone's difficulties to victimize him

落空 luò＝kōng come to nothing; end up with nothing; 两头～ fall between two stools 他的希望～。His hopes were dashed to the ground. 打算落了空。The plan fell through.

落款 luòkuǎn 【名】signature of the artist on a painting or piece of calligraphy, or of the sender on a gift; name of the recipient written on a gift

落款 luò＝kuǎn （of an artist) sign a painting or piece of calligraphy and dedicate it to a recipient; write the name of the sender and recipient on a gift

落落大方 luòluò dàfāng （of demeanour, manner） natural and self-confident; natural and graceful

落实 luòshí 【动】carry out to the full; implement; ～措施 take concrete measures to ensure ～政策 implement a policy 层层～ implement at every level

落水狗　luòshuǐgǒu　【名】drowning dog；(*fig.*) bad person who has lost favour or power：对贩毒分子，我们要像打～那样严加惩处。We should deal with drug-traffickers most severely, like thrashing drowning dogs.

落汤鸡　luòtāngjī　【名】like a drenched chicken；soaked through

落体　luòtǐ　【名】(phys.) falling body

落网　luò = wǎng　(of criminal) be caught

落伍　luò = wǔ　lag behind；fall behind the ranks；behind the times

落选　luò = xuǎn　fail to be elected

M

mā

妈（媽） mā 【名】mother

妈妈 māma 【名】mama

抹 mā 【动】wipe：～桌子 wipe the table clean ～玻璃 wipe the panes clean
另见 mǒ；mò

抹布 mābù 【名】cloth for wiping

má

麻 má 【名】❶ hemp；flax；jute ❷ hemp；flax；jute fibres：这块料子是～的。This material is linen. 【形】❶ rough；coarse：有一种墙面是～的，据说可以吸音。There's a kind of rough wall surface，which is said to be sound-absorbing. ❷ become numb；have pins and needles；tingle：腿压～了。Something has been pressing on my leg and it tingles. 舌头发～。My tongue is tingling.

麻痹 mábì 【动】❶（med.）paralysis：小儿～ infantile paralysis ❷ be numbed；lull：～对手 lull the suspicions of the opponent 【形】lacking in vigilance：你太～了。You've slackened your vigilance too much.

麻痹大意 mábì dàyi be caught off guard；lack of vigilance

麻布 mábù 【名】linen

麻袋 mádài 【名】hempen sack；gunnysack

麻烦 máfan 【形】troublesome；inconvenient：～事 a troublesome business 老师总是耐心解答问题，从不嫌～。The teachers always answer questions with great patience and nothing is too much trouble for them. 【动】*polite way of asking sb. to do sth.*；*bother sb.*：～你把这本书交给李先生。Please pass this book on to Mr. Li if it's not too much trouble. 他挺忙的，不要老去～他。He's very busy. We shouldn't be bothering him all the time.

麻利 máli 【形】quick and neat；dexterous；deft：手脚～ be quick and neat 做事～ work dexterously

麻木 mámù 【形】numb

麻木不仁 mámù bùrén apathetic；insensitive

麻雀 máquè 【名】〔只 zhī〕sparrow

麻绳 máshéng 【名】〔条 tiáo〕hempen cord；rope made of hemp，flax，etc.

麻药 máyào 【名】anaesthetic

麻疹 mázhěn 【名】measles

麻醉 mázuì 【动】❶ anaesthetize：药物～ chemical anaesthesia 全身～ general anaesthesia ❷ drug

麻醉剂　mázuìjì　【名】anaesthetic

mǎ

马（馬）　mǎ　【名】〔匹 pǐ〕horse

马鞍　mǎ'ān　【名】saddle

马车　mǎchē　【名】〔辆 liàng〕horse-drawn carriage；cart

马达　mǎdá　【名】motor

马到成功　mǎ dào chénggōng　win success immediately on arrival；gain an immediate victory：旗开得胜，～win victory as soon as one's banner is displayed

马灯　mǎdēng　【名】〔盏 zhǎn〕hurricane lantern

马蜂　mǎfēng　【名】wasp；hornet

马后炮　mǎhòupào　【名】belated effort；action taken after the event：你有什么好办法就及时提出来，不要放～。If you have any good ideas, let's have them in time. Don't come up with wisdom in hindsight.

马虎　mǎhu　【形】careless；sloppy；casual：刺绣要求很高，一针也不能～。Embroidery calls for great care. There must not be a single stitch out of place.粗枝大叶，马马虎虎，一定会把事情搞坏。Carelessness and sloppiness will certainly spoil things.

马克　mǎkè　【名】mark（currency）

马克思主义　Mǎkèsīzhǔyì　【名】Marxism

马拉松　mǎlāsōng　【名】marathon race

马力　mǎlì　【量】horse-power

马铃薯　mǎlíngshǔ　【名】potato

马路　mǎlù　【名】〔条 tiáo〕avenue；road

马前卒　mǎqiánzú　【名】pawn；cat's paw

马上　mǎshàng　【副】at once；instantly；immediately；straight away：～出发 set off at once 我～就来。I'll be there immediately.飞机～就要起飞了。The airplane will take off immediately.

马桶　mǎtǒng　【名】nightstool

马戏　mǎxì　【名】circus

吗

吗　mǎ
另见 ma

吗啡　mǎfēi　【名】morphine

玛（瑪）　mǎ

玛瑙　mǎnǎo　【名】agate

码（碼）　mǎ　【动】pile up【量】yard（unit of length）

码头　mǎtou　【名】dock；wharf

蚂（螞）　mǎ

蚂蜂　mǎfēng　【名】〔只 zhī〕同“马蜂”mǎfēng

蚂蚁　mǎyǐ　【名】〔只 zhī〕ant

蚂蚁啃骨头　mǎyǐ kěn gútou　ants gnawing at a bone；(fig.) a concentration of small machines on a big job：几个小厂用～的办法造出了大型机件。A few small factories, using small and simple machines, have been able to turn out parts for large machinery.

mà

骂（罵）　mà　【动】scold；curse

ma

吗（嗎）　ma　【助】used at the end of a declarative sentence to transform it into a question：你到过北京～? Have you ever been in Beijing? 这种汽车是你们厂出的～? Is it your factory that produces cars of

this make?

另见 mǎ

嘛 ma 【助】❶ *used at the end of a sentence to show that what precedes it is very obvious*：这样做就是对~! Of course it is right to act this way! ❷ *used within a sentence creating a pause which draws attention to what follows*：这个道理~,是不难明白的。As to this argument it is not difficult to follow. 意见~,当然要提,但也要注意方式方法。As to a differing opinion, of course you should raise it, but you should do it discreetly.

mái

埋 mái 【动】bury

另见 mán

埋藏 máicáng 【动】❶ bury; lie hidden in the earth：这里~着丰富的铁矿。There is rich iron ore here. ❷ hide away：把粮食~起来 hide away grain ~着危机 hidden crisis

埋伏 máifu 【动】ambush; lie in wait：~了一部分兵力 have part of the troops wait in ambush 【名】ambush：中 (zhòng) ~ fall into an ambush 打~ lie in ambush

埋没 máimò 【动】stifle; fail to bring out：~人才 stifle talents

埋头 mái = tóu immerse (oneself) in; be engrossed in：~学习 bury oneself in one's books ~工作 be engrossed in one's work

埋头苦干 mái tóu kǔ gàn quietly immerse oneself in hard work：~的精神是非常可贵的。Quietly burying oneself in hard work is a rare and highly commendable quality.

埋葬 máizàng 【动】bury

mǎi

买（買） mǎi 【动】buy; purchase

买办 mǎibàn 【名】comprador

买办资产阶级 mǎibàn zīchǎnjiējí comprador bourgeoisie

买方 mǎifāng 【名】the buying party

买卖 mǎimai 【名】trade

买账 mǎi = zhàng acknowledge the superiority or seniority of; show respect for (*usu. used in the negative*)：不~ not give a damn for 谁买你的账! Who cares what you do! 你越摆官架子,人们就越不买你的账。The more pompous airs you put on, the less respect the others will show you!

买主 mǎizhǔ 【名】the buyer (*as opp. to* 卖主)

mài

迈（邁） mài 【动】step forward; stride：~(过)门坎 cross the threshold ~入新的一年 enter upon a new year

迈步 mài = bù take a step

迈进 màijìn 【动】move forward with large strides

麦（麥） mài 【名】wheat

麦克风 màikèfēng 【名】microphone

麦浪 màilàng 【名】rippling wheat fields

麦苗 màimiáo 【名】wheat seedling

麦片 màipiàn 【名】oatmeal

麦收 màishōu 【动】wheat harvest

麦芽糖 màiyátáng 【名】malt sugar

麦种 màizhǒng 【名】wheat seed

麦子 màizi 【名】〔粒 lì〕wheat

卖（賣） mài 【名】❶ sell：~东

西 sell things 把余粮～给国家 sell surplus grain to the state 这件玉器～多少钱？How much does this piece of jadeware sell for？❷ betray：～友求荣 betray one's friend in the pursuit of high position ❸ make an effort：～力气 exert oneself

卖唱　mài = chàng　roam the streets singing for a living（in the past）

卖方　màifāng　【名】the selling party

卖国　mài = guó　betray one's country；sell out one's country

卖国贼　màiguózéi　【名】traitor

卖国主义　màiguózhǔyì　【名】policies which lead to national betrayal

卖劲　mài = jìn　do one's utmost；spare no effort

卖力　mài = lì　exert all one's strength；spare no effort；do all one can：他工作很～。He spared no effort in his work.

卖命　mài = mìng　work oneself to death（for sb. against one's will or for an ignoble cause）：为法西斯～，没有好下场。There is no good end for anyone who works himself to death for Fascism.

卖弄　màinong　【动】show off

卖身契　màishēnqì　【名】bond of indenture by which one is sold as a slave

卖身投靠　mài shēn tóukào　sell one's soul for personal gain

卖艺　mài = yì　wander from town to town performing acrobatics，etc. to make a living（in the past）

卖主　màizhǔ　【名】the seller（as opp. to 买主）

卖座　mài = zuò　attract large numbers of audience or customers

脉　mài　【名】pulse：诊～ feel sb.'s pulse 你的～跳得太快。Your pulse is too fast.

脉搏　màibó　【名】pulse

脉络　màiluò　【名】❶ general term for veins and arteries used in traditional Chinese medicine ❷ one's train of thought；sequence of ideas：～分明（of writing）ideas presented in a clear and logical way

mán

埋　mán
另见 mái

埋怨　mányuàn　【动】grumble；complain；blame（sb. for sth.）：受到～ be blamed ～别人 blame others

蛮（蠻）　mán

蛮不讲理　mán bù jiǎng lǐ　refuse to listen to reason；unreasonable

蛮干　mángàn　【动】act rashly；be foolhardy

蛮横　mánhèng　【形】arrogant and unreasonable

馒（饅）　mán

馒头　mántou　【名】〔个 gè〕steamed bread；steamed bun

瞒（瞞）　mán　【动】hide the truth from：你们好像有什么事～着我。You seem to be keeping something from me.

瞒上欺下　mán shàng qī xià　hoodwink those above and bully those below

瞒天过海　mán tiān guò hǎi　practise an audacious piece of deception：～的伎俩 deceptive manoeuvre

mǎn

满（滿）　mǎn　【形】full；packed：～～的一杯茶 a full cup of tea 水库里的水很～。The reservoir is full of water. 瓶子里装～了油。

The bottle was filled with oil.
Note：满 *is often used with a noun in which case the two together function as a subject，a modifier or an adverbial adjunct*：～天都是星星。The whole sky is dotted with stars. 他刚劳动完，～脸的汗。He's just done manual labour, and his face is streaming with sweat. 这孩子已经能～地(dì)跑了。The child can run about quite freely now. 你怎么把土弄得～身都是？How did you get yourself completely covered with dust?【动】expire；reach a certain limit：假期还没～。Vacation isn't over yet. 这班学生不～十个。There are fewer than ten students in the class. 他的女儿～一岁了吗？Is his daughter one year old yet?【副】completely；entirely：～不在乎 not care in the least 这屋子这么一收拾，～可以住人了。Once this room has been tidied up, it's perfectly comfortable to live in. 他～以为我能帮忙，没想到那天我病了。He was counting on my helping him, but I was suddenly taken ill that day. 听人说那里风景不错，他到那儿一看，～不是那么一回事。He was told that it was a scenic spot, but when he got there, he found the place not at all beautiful.

满城风雨 mǎn chéng fēng yǔ (some event has) become the gossip of the town；scandalous

满额 mǎn é = é to have reached the amount or quota

满怀 mǎnhuái【动】have one's heart filled with；be full of：～信心 filled with confidence ～着胜利的喜悦 filled with the joy of success【名】◇bosom；chest：他出来我进去，两个人撞了个～。He came out just as I went in, and we bumped into each other.

满面春风 mǎn miàn chūnfēng beam with satisfaction；be all smiles：张大娘～地站在大门口，等待着从城里来的儿媳妇。Aunt Zhang, her face radiating happiness, stood at the door waiting for her daugther-in-law who was coming from town. 也作"春风满面"。

满腔 mǎnqiāng【名】have one's breast filled with：～悲愤 be filled with grief and indignation ～怒火 be filled with rage

满堂红 mǎn táng hóng all-round victory；success in all fields：我们连这次打靶得了个～。Our company got excellent over-all results in this target practice.

满意 mǎnyì【形】satisfied；content

满员 mǎnyuán【动】❶ (mil.) keep at full strength ❷ be filled to capacity (of passengers on a train, etc.)

满载 mǎnzài【动】loaded to capacity

满载而归 mǎnzài ér guī return from a rewarding journey；come back with fruitful results：我们到别的单位学习，收获很大，可以说是～。We have been to other units to learn from their experience and we can say with confidence that the result has been satisfactory.

满足 mǎnzú【动】❶ feel content；feel satisfied：他从不～于已有的成绩。He is never satisfied with what he has achieved. ❷ satisfy；meet (a demand)：～要求 meet the demands of ～需要 meet the needs of ～愿望 satisfy one's desire

满座 mǎnzuò【动】have a capacity audience；have a full house

màn

谩(謾) màn

谩骂 mànmà【动】abuse；vilify

蔓 màn

蔓延 mànyán 【动】draw out; spread; extend:阻止火势～ stop the fire from spreading 疾病～。The disease is spreading.

慢 màn 【形】❶ slow:跑～ jog ～手～脚 be slow in one's movements 你走得太～了。You are walking too slowly. ❷ postpone; defer:～点儿决定，了解了解再说。Let's put off making a decision till we have more data.

慢车 mànchē 【名】slow train; train which stops frequently

慢待 màndài 【动】snub; slight; cold shoulder

慢慢腾腾 mànmantēngtēng 【形】at a snail's pace; sluggish

慢条斯理 màn tiáo sī lǐ unhurried and unperturbed

慢性 mànxìng 【形】❶ chronic:～中毒 slow poisoning ～肝炎 chronic hepatitis ❷【名】(～儿)(of persons) of phlegmantic temperament; slow to respond:这个人真是～，干什么事也不着急。This man is really a slowpoke; he never hurries in anything.

慢性病 mànxìngbìng 【名】chronic disease

漫 màn 【动】❶overflow; brim-over:酒从杯子里～出来了。The cup was brimming over with wine. ❷ flood:河水～过桥面。The river flooded the bridge. ❸ all over the place; everywhere:～山都是红叶。The whole mountain was covered with red foliage.

漫笔 mànbǐ 【名】a short piece of casual writing; sketch

漫不经心 màn bù jīngxīn careless; casual; negligent

漫步 mànbù 【动】stroll; ramble; roam:～在林荫道上 stroll along the boulevard 在湖边～ stroll by the lake

漫长 màncháng 【形】very long; endless:～的道路 an endless road ～的岁月 long years

漫画 mànhuà 【名】cartoon

漫骂 mànmà 【动】hurl carses at

漫漫 mànmàn 【形】(of time) endless; (of space) boundless:～长夜 long nights ～黄沙 boundless desert

漫山遍野 màn shān biàn yě over hill and dale; all over the mountains and plains:绚丽的山花～。Beautiful wild flowers blanketed hill and dale.

漫谈 màntán 【动】informal discussion:～国际形势 a casual talk about the international situation 小组～ casual group discussion

漫天 màntiān 【形】❶ filling the whole sky:～飞雪 whirling snow ～大雾 a dense fog obscuring the whole sky ❷ boundless; limitless:～大谎 a monstrous lie

漫游 mànyóu 【动】travel leisurely with no definite purpose; roam

máng

忙 máng 【形】busy 【动】be occupied

忙碌 mánglù 【形】busily occupied

忙乱 mángluàn 【形】be in a rush with everything in a mess

忙音 mángyīn 【名】engaged signal; engaged tone; busy signal

盲 máng

盲从 mángcóng 【动】follow blindly

盲动 mángdòng 【动】act blindly

盲动主义 mángdòngzhǔyì 【名】putschism

盲目 mángmù 【形】blind; without clear understanding

盲目性　mángmùxìng　【名】(*fig.*) blindness

盲人　mángrén　【名】blind person

盲文　mángwén　【名】braille

茫 máng

茫茫　mángmáng　【形】❶ boundless and blurred；vast：～大海 vast sea ～草原 boundless grasslands ❷ (of future) vague；uncertain：前途～ bleak prospects

茫然　mángrán　【形】ignorant；in the dark；at sea：～无知 be utterly ignorant 这件事使我感到～。I feel completely in the dark on this question.

茫无头绪　máng wú tóuxù confused and without a clue；not know where to begin：我刚接触这项工作，还觉得～。I've just started on this job, and I feel completely at sea.

mǎng

莽 mǎng

莽撞　mǎngzhuàng　【形】reckless；impetuous；rash

蟒 mǎng　【名】〔条 tiáo〕boa-constrictor；python

māo

猫 māo　【名】〔只 zhī〕cat

猫头鹰　māotóuyīng　【名】〔只 zhī〕owl

máo

毛 máo　【名】❶ hair；feather；down：叶片上有细～。There is fine down on the leaves. 小鸡在脱～。The chicks are just beginning to moult. ❷ mildew 【形】panicky；

scared；flurried：心里发～ feel scared；be panic-stricken 【量】*mao*, one-tenth of a *yuan*：一～钱 one *mao*

毛笔　máobǐ　【名】〔枝 zhī〕writing brush

毛病　máobìng　【名】❶ trouble；breakdown：收音机出～了。Something has gone wrong with the radio. 汽车没～，你开吧! There is nothing wrong with the car. Go ahead and drive it. ❷ defect；shortcoming；flaw：她一发现自己的发音有～，就坚决改正。As soon as she realized she had a particular problem with her accent, she resolutely overcame it. 这个杯子很好看，可惜有点儿小～。This is a pretty cup; it's a pity there's a flaw in it. 我们工作中的～还不少，欢迎大家提意见。There are still some defects in our work. Comments are welcome. ❸ illness：我身体很好，什么～也没有。I'm in perfectly good health；there's nothing wrong with me.

毛玻璃　máobōli　【名】frosted glass

毛糙　máocao　【形】coarse；careless；(of workmanship) crude

毛发　máofà　【名】hair

毛骨悚然　máo gǔ sǒngrán one's hair stands on end and one's spine tingles；absolutely horrified：听了那种惨无人道的事情，真令人～。One is simply horrified to hear of such cold-blooded cruelties.

毛巾　máojīn　【名】〔条 tiáo〕towel

毛孔　máokǒng　【名】pore

毛裤　máokù　【名】〔条 tiáo〕knitted pants of wool

毛利　máolì　【名】gross profit

毛料　máoliào　【名】woolen fabric

毛毛雨　máomaoyǔ　【名】drizzle

毛茸茸　máorōngrōng　【形】hairy；downy：～的小鸭子 downy little ducks

毛手毛脚　máo shǒu máo jiǎo awk-

ward (in handling things)

毛遂自荐 Máo Suì zì jiàn put oneself forward as Mao Sui (of the Warring States Period) did; volunteer one's services:你如果到苏州来玩,我可以～给你导游。If you come to Suzhou on a tour, I'll volunteer to be your guide.

毛细管 máoxìguǎn 【名】capillary

毛线 máoxiàn 【名】wool for knitting

毛衣 máoyī 【名】〔件 jiàn〕woolen jacket; woolen sweater

毛泽东思想 Máo Zédōng Sīxiǎng Mao Zedong Thought

毛织品 máozhīpǐn 【名】wool fabric

毛值 máozhí 【名】gross value

矛 máo 【名】spear

矛盾 máodùn 【名】❶ contradiction;～百出 full of contradictions 分析～ analyse a contradiction 解决～ resolve a contradiction ❷ disunity;他俩闹～了。The two had a falling out.【动】contradict;自相～ be inconsistent; contradict oneself 互相～ contradict each other ～着的双方 the two opposing sides【形】hesitating between (doing and not doing sth.):他心情很～,去不去一时定不下来。He is hesitating, and cannot make up his mind whether to go or not.

矛头 máotóu 【名】spearhead:这张漫画讽刺的～指向了文牍主义。This cartoon is targetting red tape.

茅 máo

茅草 máocǎo 【名】couch grass; straw

茅塞顿开 máo sè dùn kāi suddenly see the light 也作"顿开茅塞"。

茅台酒 máotáijiǔ 【名】Maotai spirit

茅屋 máowū 【名】〔间 jiān〕thatched cottage

锚(錨) máo 【名】anchor

蟊 máo

蟊贼 máozéi 【名】pernicious enemy of the people

mǎo

铆(鉚) mǎo 【动】rivet

铆钉 mǎodīng 【名】rivet

铆接 mǎojiē 【动】riveting

mào

茂 mào 【形】◇❶ luxuriant; lush:枝繁叶～ crowded branches and lush foliage ❷ rich and splendid:图文并～。Both the paintings and the texts are excellent.

茂密 màomì 【形】luxuriant and thick

茂盛 màoshèng 【形】(of vegetation) luxuriant; thriving

冒 mào 【动】❶ send (up, forth); give off; emit:浑身～汗 sweat all over 烟囱正在～烟。The chimney is belching smoke. 开水～着热气。The boiling water is giving off steam. 怕困难的想法又～出来了。The tendency to evade problems has cropped up again. ❷ risk; brave (*often used with* 风,雨,危险, *etc. to form a V-O construction used as an adverbial adjunct*):～雨抢种 brave the rain to do the rush planting ～着生命危险抢救国家财产 risk one's life to save state property【副】falsely (claim):～领物资 fraudulently obtain materials (from an institution)

冒充 màochōng 【动】pretend to be; pass oneself off as:～好人 pass

oneself off as a good man 次品～正品 pass shoddy products off as quality ones

冒犯 màofàn【动】give offence; affront; 刚才～了你, 请原谅。Please excuse me for having offended you just now.

冒号 màohào【名】colon

冒火 mào = huǒ be enraged; flare up; get angry

冒尖 mào = jiān（～儿）stand out; be conspicuous

冒进 màojìn【动】premature advance; advance rashly

冒昧 màomèi【形】make bold; venture; take the liberty of（*used as an apology*）: 我提这个问题, 太～了吧! Am I being presumptuous in asking this question? 我～地写信给你。I am taking the liberty of writing to you.

冒名 mào = míng assume another's name

冒牌 mào = pái counterfeit of a well-known trade mark; imitation; fake; ～货 imitation; fake ～专家 fake expert

冒失 màoshi【形】rash; abrupt; 别太～了, 看好图纸再干。Don't be too rash. You'd better not start before you have studied the blue print. 这小伙子总是冒冒失失的。This young man is always reckless.

冒天下之大不韪 mào tiānxià zhī dà bù wěi risk universal condemnation

冒险 mào = xiǎn run a risk; lay oneself open to danger

冒险主义 màoxiǎnzhǔyì【名】adventurism

贸（貿） mào

贸然 màorán【副】rashly; hastily; without careful consideration; 不要～行事。Do not act rashly. 这个问题还需进一步研究, 不要～做结论。The matter needs further study. Don't

jump to a conclusion.

贸易 màoyì【名】trade

帽 mào【名】◇ cap; hat; headgear; 脱～ take off one's cap ～店 hat shop 衣～整洁 be neatly dressed

帽徽 màohuī【名】insignia on a cap

帽檐 màoyán【名】（～儿）brim of a hat

帽子 màozi【名】〔顶 dǐng〕❶ headgear; hat; cap ❷（*fig.*）label; tag; brand; 这是乱扣～, 不是批评。This is just irresponsibly labelling people; it's not criticism.

貌 mào【名】◇ appearance

貌合神离 mào hé shén lí（of two people）seemingly in agreement, but actually at odds

貌似 màosì【动】appear to be; seem; 这种论调～有理, 实际上是错误的。This argument sounds reasonable, but actually untenable.

méi

没 méi【副】❶ *used to negate* 有（*in colloquial speech*, 有 *after* 没 *can be omitted except at the end of the sentence or when it stands by itself as the answer to a question*）: 壶里～（有）水。There isn't any water in the kettle. 我的帽子怎么～（有）了? How is it that my cap has disappeared? 我～（有）他高。I'm not as tall as he is. ～有共产党就～有新中国。There wouldn't have been a new China without the Chinese Communist Party. ❷ *short for* "没有": 他～来。He hasn't turned up. 昨天我～进城。I didn't go to town yesterday.

另见 mò

没关系 méi guānxi does not matter;

it's nothing; that's all right; never mind; 对不起，让你久等了。——～。Sorry to have kept you waiting. — It's all right. ～你们尽管谈话，不会影响我。Never mind. You just go on with your talk. It won't bother me.

没劲 méijìn 【形】dull; boring; 这电影真～。This film is really boring.

没精打采 méi jīng dǎ cǎi listless; in low spirits; 怪不得他今天～的，原来是病了。No wonder he was so listless today. It turned out he was ill. 也说"无精打采"。

没趣 méiqù 【形】(～儿) feel rejected; feel snubbed; 自讨～ be asking to be snubbed 给他一个～ snub him 他感到十分～，悄悄走开了。He felt very much snubbed, so he left quietly.

没什么 méi shénme ❶nothing serious; never mind; that's all right; 摔疼了吧? ——～。Did the fall hurt you? — It's nothing. ❷ don't mention it; it's a pleasure; you're welcome; 谢谢你的帮助。——～，这是应该的。Thank you for your help.—Don't mention it. It's something I should do.

没事 méi=shì ❶ be free; 今天我～，出去玩玩。Since I am at a loose end today, I'll go out to enjoy myself. ❷be out of work; be unemployed; 他现在～，在家闲着。Being out of job, he is at home doing nothing. ❸ it doesn't matter; it's all right; no big deal; 有点儿感冒，～，吃点药就好了。It's just a slight cold, no big deal. Take some medicine and it'll be all right. ❹never mind; don't worry; ～，他不会生气的。Don't worry, He won't get cross.

没说的 méi shuō de ❶unimpeachable; really good; 小王既肯干又肯学，真是～。Xiao Wang studies hard and works hard. His behaviour leaves nothing to be desired. ❷ there's no need to say any more about it; it goes without saying; ～，这事儿交给我们吧! There's no need to say any more about it. Leave the matter to us.

没有 méiyǒu 【副】❶ used to form the negation of a completed action; 商店还～关门。The stores haven't closed yet. 昨天我哪儿也～去。I didn't go anywhere yesterday. ❷ used to form the negation of a past experience; 我～上过大学。I have never attended a university or college. 你见过这个人～? ——～。Have you ever seen this man before? — No. Note: 没有 can be shortened into 没 except at the end of a sentence or when it stands by itself as the answer to a question.

没准儿 méi = zhǔnr might not; may not; 他～不来了。He might not come after all.

玫 méi

玫瑰 méigui 【名】rose

枚 méi 【量】for small objects; 一～纪念章 a badge 两～硬币 two coins

眉 méi 【名】◇ eyebrow

眉飞色舞 méi fēi sè wǔ animated; lively (usu. of person speaking); 你看小李那～的样子，一定又在讲他那次有趣的旅行了。Look at Xiao Li's animated expression! I'm sure he's talking again about the interesting trip he had.

眉开眼笑 méi kāi yǎn xiào beam with joy; be all smiles; 李大爷看到小孙子的奖状，乐得～的。Grandpa Li was all smiles when he saw his grandson's citation.

眉毛 méimao 【名】eyebrow

眉目 méimù 【名】❶ features；looks：~清秀 have delicate features ❷ （of writing）logic；sequence of ideas：~不清 neither clear nor logical

眉目 méimu 【名】prospect for a solution；sign of a positive outcome：调工作的事有没有~？Have you got anywhere with your plan to change jobs?

眉头 méitóu 【名】brow

梅 méi 【名】◇plum

梅花 méihuā 【名】〔朵 duǒ〕plum blossom

媒 méi

媒介 méijiè 【名】medium；vehicle

媒人 méiren 【名】matchmaker

媒体 méitǐ 【名】medium：新闻~ news media

煤 méi 【名】coal

煤矿 méikuàng 【名】coal mine

煤气 méiqì 【名】❶ coal gas；gas ❷ carbon monoxide from burning coal

煤气灶 méiqìzào 【名】gas range；gas cooker

煤炭 méitàn 【名】coal

煤田 méitián 【名】coalfield

煤油 méiyóu 【名】kerosene

霉 méi 【名】mildew；mould

霉菌 méijūn 【名】mould

霉烂 méilàn 【动】become mildewed and decay

měi

每 měi 【代】every；each（usu. followed by a measure word or a numeral plus measure word）：~张桌子 every table ~件衣服 each dress ~间屋子有一个电话。There is a telephone in each room. 这种药~四小时吃一次。This medicine is to be taken every four hours. Note：① 每 can be followed directly by a noun which does not take a measure word：~天 everyday ~星期 every week ② 每 is often used in conjunction with 都：他~天都坚持跑步。He persists in running everyday for exercise. 尽管~个人的业务不同，但是都应当学点哲学。Everyone has his own speciality, but everyone should learn a little philosophy. 【副】used before a verb to mean "every time"：我们~做完一项工作都要认真总结经验。Every time we have finished a project, we must sum up our experience. 他~看一本书都要写些心得体会。Every time he finishes a book, he puts down his thoughts on it.

每到 měi dào ❶ whenever；every time：~农忙的时候他们都到农村参加劳动。Every busy farming season, they go to the countryside to participate in manual labour. ~冬季他都参加长跑。Every winter, he does long-distance running. ❷ wherever；every place：~一个地方，他都要去看看当地的名胜古迹。Wherever he goes, he always goes to visit the local scenic spots.

每逢 měi féng on every occasion；when：~大雨，那边山谷里就形成一条小河。Whenever there is a heavy rain, a torrent runs through that valley over there. ~我们在学习上遇到困难，老师总是耐心辅导。Whenever we have trouble with our studies, our teachers help us patiently.

每况愈下 měi kuàng yù xià go from bad to worse；steadily deteriorate：大病缠身，~，他的身体被折磨得不像样子了。His health had gone steadily from bad to worse and he was in

an awful shape. 本作 "每下愈况"。

每每　měiměi　【副】同 " 往 往 " wǎngwǎng（usu. in written language）：他最近很忙，～工作到深夜。He has been busy recently, and often works late into the night.

每日每时　měi rì měi shí　daily and hourly

美　měi　【形】❶ pretty；beautiful：这姑娘真～。This girl is really pretty. 景色很～。The view is very beautiful. ❷ ◇ good：物～价廉（of commodities）good and inexpensive

美不胜收　měi bù shèng shōu　so many fine things that one simply can't take them all in：这里展出的大量工艺美术品，琳琅满目，～。There are so many beautiful handicrafts on display that one can hardly take them all in.

美德　měidé　【名】virtue

美感　měigǎn　【名】sense of beauty, aesthetic taste

美工　měigōng　【名】❶ art designing ❷ art designer

美观　měiguān　【形】（of man-made things）pleasing to the eye：这套家具既～又实用。This furniture is beautiful and practical as well.

美好　měihǎo　【形】（of abstract things）happy；fine：～的生活 happy life ～的理想 fine ideals 我们的前途无限～。Our future is extremely bright.

美化　měihuà　【动】prettify；beautify；whitewash

美景　měijǐng　【名】beautiful scenery

美丽　měilì　【形】beautiful

美满　měimǎn　【形】happy；perfectly satisfactory：～的家庭 a happy family 生活～ a contented and happy life

美妙　měimiào　【形】wonderful；excellent；beautiful；splendid：～的诗篇 excellent poetry ～的歌声 beau-

tiful singing ～的青春 the lovely days of one's youth

美名　měimíng　【名】good name；good reputation

美容　měiróng　【动】❶ improve（a woman's）looks ❷ cosmetology

美术　měishù　【名】fine arts

美术字　měishùzì　【名】characters （e.g. on a sign）written in an artistic way

美味　měiwèi　【名】delicious or tasty food；delicacy

美学　měixué　【名】aesthetics

美意　měiyì　【名】good intention

美元　měiyuán　【名】U.S. dollar

美中不足　měi zhōng bù zú　a blemish in an otherwise perfect thing；a fly in the ointment：昨晚的音乐会非常成功，～的是小林咳嗽，没有独唱。The concert last night was perfect except that Xiao Lin was unable to sing the solo because of a cough.

mèi

妹　mèi　【名】◇ younger sister

妹夫　mèifu　【名】brother-in-law （younger sister's husband）

妹妹　mèimei　【名】younger sister

媚　mèi　【动】◇ flatter；fawn；toady；curry favour with

媚外　mèiwài　【动】fawn on foreigners or foreign countries

魅　mèi

魅力　mèilì　【名】charm；attractiveness；charisma

mēn

闷（悶）　mēn　【形】stuffy；close：屋子又低又小，真～。The

room is very low and small, and it's really stuffy. 【动】❶ cover tightly：茶沏上了，～一会儿再喝。The tea is made, but let it draw for a while. ❷ shut oneself or sb. indoors：他在图书馆里～了一天。He shut himself in the library for a whole day.

另见 mèn

闷热 mēnrè 【形】hot and stuffy

闷头儿 mēn = tóur quiet and absorbed (in work)：他只顾～看书，一句话不说。He is quiet and absorbed in his reading.

mén

门（門） mén 【名】〔扇 shàn〕❶door；gate ❷ ◇ house；home：送货上～ sell goods near people's home (for their convenience) 登～拜访 call on sb. at home ❸ (～儿) method of solving problem or doing sth.：这件事有～了。The matter is beginning to look hopeful. 对新工作，我还不摸～。I don't yet know the ropes in my new job.【量】❶ for cannon：一～炮 one cannon ❷ for techniques，etc.：两～技术 two techniques 三～功课 three courses (or subjects)

门第 méndì 【名】family status

门户 ménhù 【名】❶ door；gate：～大开 with all the doors and gates widely open 夜间要留神～。Be sure the doors are locked during the night. ❷ gateway；passageway：广州是中国南方的重要～。Guangzhou is an important gateway to South China. ❸ sect；faction：～之见 sectarian bias 另立～ establish one's own faction

门镜 ménjìng 【名】door lens peep-hole lens

门槛 ménkǎn 【名】threshold 也作"门坎"。

门口 ménkǒu 【名】doorway

门类 ménlèi 【名】class；kind；category

门帘 ménlián 【名】door curtain

门路 ménlu 【名】❶ social connections that can be made use of：找～ try to find some connection that will help ❷ method of solving a problem：要解决这个技术问题，就得广开～。If you want to solve this technical problem, you must tap all sorts of new sources.

门面 ménmiàn 【名】❶ facade of a shop；shop front ❷ appearance；facade：装点～ keep up appearances

门牌 ménpái 【名】house number；number plate (on a house)

门市部 ménshìbù 【名】sales department

门庭若市 mén tíng ruò shì the courtyard is as crowded as a market；(fig.) swarming with visitors

门徒 méntú 【名】disciple；follower

门外汉 ménwàihàn 【名】layman：对医学我可是个～。As far as medical science is concerned, I'm simply a layman.

门卫 ménwèi 【名】entrance guard；doorman；janitor

门诊 ménzhěn 【名】out-patient department of a hospital

扪（捫） mén 【动】lay one's hand on

扪心自问 mén xīn zì wèn examine one's conscience

mèn

闷（悶） mèn 【形】depressed；bored；in low spirits：他心里～得慌。He felt very depressed.

另见 mēn

闷闷不乐 mèn mèn bù lè　depressed；unhappy

闷气 mènqì　【名】suppressed indignation or anger；the sulks

焖（燜） mèn　【动】braise

men

们（們） men　【尾】*used after a personal pronoun or a noun which indicates a person to show plural number*：我～ we 你～ you 他～ they 朋友～ friends 孩子～ children Note：*if there is a numeral or any other word in front of the noun which indicates that the noun is in the plural number，*们 *must not be added，e. g. it is ungrammatical to say* 三个同志～ *or* 很多朋友～，*etc. If the context makes it clear that the noun is in the plural number，*们 *is optional，e. g.* 火车忽然停下来，旅客（～）都问："怎么了？怎么了？" The train stopped unexpectedly，and all the passengers asked each other："What's happening? What's happening?"

mēng

蒙 mēng　【动】〈口〉❶（矇）deceive；cheat：别～人。Don't deceive others. ❷（矇）make a wild guess：你～着（zháo）了。You've guessed it! ❸ confused：～头转向 be wildered

另见 méng；měng

蒙蒙亮 mēngmēngliàng　【形】at break of dawn

蒙骗 mēngpiàn　【动】deceive

méng

萌 méng

萌发 méngfā　【动】sprout；germinate

萌芽 méng ＝ yá　❶ germinate；sprout；bud：～状态 in the bud ❷ rudiment；shoot：中外合资的～ the prototype of Sino-foreign partnership in investment

蒙 méng　【动】❶ cover：～上一层布 cover with a cloth ～头大睡 tuck oneself in and sleep like a log ❷ receive（*polite expression*）：～您热情帮助，十分感谢。Thank you very much for your kind help.

另见 mēng；měng

蒙蔽 méngbì　【动】hoodwink；deceive；pull the wool over sb.'s eyes：不受～ not be taken in 谎言不能长期～人。Lies cannot fool people for long.

蒙混 ménghùn　【动】deceive people into believing in one's innocence：～不过去 cannot get off the hook by lying ～过关 get by under false pretences

蒙眬 ménglóng　【形】drowsy；half asleep：睡眼～ eyes heavy with sleep 也作"矇眬"。

蒙昧 méngmèi　【形】❶ barbaric；uncivilized；uncultured ❷ ignorant：～无知 childishly ignorant

蒙蒙 méngméng　【形】drizzly；misty：～细雨 fine drizzle

蒙难 méng ＝ nàn　suffer disaster；be in great distress

蒙受 méngshòu　【动】suffer；sustain：～耻辱 suffer humiliation ～损失 sustain a loss ～恩惠 be favoured with a special kindness or gift

蒙冤 méng ＝ yuān　be wronged

盟 méng 【名】❶ ◇ alliance ❷ an administrative division（corresponding to a prefecture）in the Inner Mongolia Autonomous Region

盟国 méngguó 【名】ally（country）

盟友 méngyǒu 【名】ally

盟约 méngyuē 【名】treaty of alliance

朦 méng

朦胧 ménglóng 【形】dim；hazy：月色～ dim moonlight ～的夜空 dim night sky 远处景物～不清 hazy view in the distance

měng

猛 měng 【形】❶ fierce；violent：炮火很～。The gunfire was very heavy. 发球时用力过～，球出界了。He served the ball too vigorously, and it went out. ❷ suddenly；abruptly：～一回头 turned one's head suddenly ～地一跳 jump suddenly

猛不防 měngbufáng 【副】all of a sudden；unexpectedly：他正在走着，～有人撞了他一下。While he was walking along, someone suddenly bumped into him.

猛烈 měngliè 【形】fierce；furious；violent

猛禽 měngqín 【名】bird of prey

猛然 měngrán 【副】suddenly；abruptly：～一惊 a sudden shock ～刹车 put on the brakes suddenly 他～想起一件事。Something suddenly crossed his mind.

猛兽 měngshòu 【名】beast of prey

猛醒 měngxǐng 【动】realize suddenly

蒙 měng

另见 mēng；méng

蒙古包 měnggǔbāo 【名】yurt

锰（錳）měng 【名】manganese

锰钢 měnggāng 【名】manganese steel

mèng

孟 mèng

孟什维克 Mèngshíwéikè 【名】Menshevik

梦（夢）mèng 【名】dream

梦话 mènghuà 【名】❶ words spoken in one's sleep ❷ nonsense；raving

梦见 mèng∥jiàn dream：我昨天晚上做了一个梦，～我飞起来了。I had a dream last night. I dreamt that I was flying.

梦境 mèngjìng 【名】the land of one's dreams

梦寐以求 mèngmèi yǐ qiú crave sth. even in one's dreams；long for sth. day and night；dream of sth.：～的愿望实现了。His long-cherished dream came true.

梦乡 mèngxiāng 【名】sound sleep：进入～ fall asleep；be in dreamland

梦想 mèngxiǎng 【动】hope in vain 【名】daydream

梦呓 mèngyì 【名】同"梦话"

mī

眯 mī 【动】narrow（one's）eyes

mí

弥（彌、瀰）mí

弥补 míbǔ 【动】make up；remedy；

make good：~缺陷 remedy a defect (of fault)～不足 make up for a weakness 不可～的损失 irreparable loss

弥留 míliú 【动】be in one's deathbed；be dying

弥漫 mímàn 【动】fill（the air）with：硝烟～ pervasive fumes of gunpowder 云雾～ a sky filled with clouds and fog

弥天大谎 mí tiān dà huǎng big lie；outrageous lie

迷 mí 【动】❶ be confused；be lost：~了方向 lose one's bearings ❷ be fascinated by：景色～人 fascinating scenery 他被这部小说～住了。He can't tear himself away from that novel. ❸ be absorbed in（often used as the object of 入 or 着）：看书看得入了～ be absorbed in one's reading 他学绘画着了～。He learned to paint and was completely taken up with it.

迷航 mí＝háng（of plane of ship）stray from one's course

迷糊 míhu 【形】❶ muddle-headed ❷（of vision）dim

迷惑 míhuò 【动】❶ be puzzled；be perplexed：~不解 feel puzzled ❷ puzzle；confuse；bewilder：花言巧语～不了人。Fine words cannot delude people.

迷恋 míliàn 【动】be enamoured with；indulge in

迷路 mí＝lù lose one's way

迷漫 mímàn 【形】vast and hazy：云雾～misty with cloud and fog

迷茫 mímáng 【形】vast and hazy：连日阴雨，海面上一片～。It's been raining for days and haze stretches everywhere over the sea.

迷梦 mímèng 【名】fond dream

迷人 mírén 【形】enrapture；intoxicate：~的景色 enchanting scenery

迷失 míshī 【动】lose（one's bearings,etc.）：~道路 lose one's way ~方向 lose one's bearings

迷途 mítú 【名】wrong path

迷雾 míwù 【名】❶ dense fog：漫天～heavy mist ❷ things which mislead people：拨开～ sweep away the obscurities 驱散～ dispel confusions

迷信 míxìn 【动】have blind faith in；blindly worship：不～鬼神 do not believe in ghosts and spirits 不要～核武器。Don't have blind faith in nuclear weapons. 【名】superstition：破除～，解放思想 do away with superstition and emancipate the mind

谜（謎）mí 【名】❶ riddle ❷ enigma；puzzle

谜语 míyǔ 【名】〔个 gè〕riddle

糜 mí

糜烂 mílàn 【形】❶ fester ❷ debauched

mǐ

米 mǐ 【名】〔粒 lì〕rice 【量】metre

米饭 mǐfàn 【名】(cooked) rice

米黄 mǐhuáng 【形】cream-coloured

米粒 mǐlì 【名】（~儿）grain of rice

米色 mǐsè 【名】同"米黄"

米汤 mǐtāng 【名】water in which rice was boiled

靡 mǐ

靡靡之音 mǐmǐ zhī yīn decadent music

mì

觅（覓）mì 【动】look for；hunt for；seek：~食 look for food ~路 look for the road

泌 mì

泌尿科　mìniàokē　【名】urology department

秘 mì

秘方　mìfāng　【名】secret recipe

秘诀　mìjué　【名】key to success

秘密　mìmì　【形】secret；confidential：～工作 confidential work ～文件 secret papers；confidential document 【名】secret：保守 ～ keep (sth.) secret 泄露～ divulge a secret

秘书　mìshū　【名】secretary

秘书长　mìshūzhǎng　【名】secretary general

密 mì

密　mì　【形】❶ dense；thick；close：～不透风 airtight 马路边的树种得太～了。The trees along the street are planted too closely together. ❷ ◇ close；intimate：～友 close friend ❸ ◇ secret：～电 telegram in code ～约 secret agreement

密闭　mìbì　【动】airtight；hermetic

密布　mìbù　【动】be thick with；be densely covered with：阴云 ～ overcast

密度　mìdù　【名】density

密封　mìfēng　【动】seal up；seal airtight

密集　mìjí　【形】dense；thick；concentrated：人口 ～ densely populated 村外响起～的枪声。There was heavy gun fire outside the village.

密件　mìjiàn　【名】confidential paper

密码　mìmǎ　【名】secret code

密密层层　mìmìcéngcéng　【形】dense；thick；packed closely layer upon layer：～的人群 a dense crowd ～的树丛 rows of trees planted close together

密密麻麻　mìmimámá　【形】〈口〉thickly dotted；close together and in great numbers：～的星星 thickly studded with stars 纸上写满了～的小字。The paper was filled with small, closely written characters.

密谋　mìmóu　【动】conspire

密切　mìqiè　【形】❶ close；intimate：关系 ～ close relationship 来往 ～ frequent contact ～ 配合 act in close cooperation ❷ closely；intently：～注意 pay close attention to 【动】establish closer（links with）：～两国之间的关系 establish closer relations between the two countries

密实　mìshi　【形】❶ tightly woven ❷ with fine, close stitches

密探　mìtàn　【名】spy；secret agent

密植　mìzhí　【动】plant closely together

幂 mì 　【名】(maths.) power

蜜 mì 　【名】honey

蜜蜂　mìfēng　【名】〔只 zhī〕honey bee

蜜饯　mìjiàn　【名】candied fruit

蜜月　mìyuè　【名】honeymoon

mián

绵(綿) mián

绵绸　miánchóu　【名】cloth made from odds and ends of silk

绵亘　miángèn　【动】(of mountains, etc.) stretch in an unbroken chain：群山 ～ 在两国交界线上。Mountains extend in an unbroken chain along the border between the two countries.

绵绵　miánmián　【形】continuous；unbroken：秋雨～。A fine autumn rain falls unceasingly.

绵软　miánruǎn　【形】soft：～的羊毛 soft wool

绵延　miányán　【动】continue or extend in a meandering way over

some distance（e. g. a mountain range）

绵羊　miányáng　【名】〔只 zhī〕sheep

棉　mián　【名】cotton

棉袄　mián'ǎo　【名】〔件 jiàn〕cotton-padded jacket

棉被　miánbèi　【名】〔床 chuáng〕cotton-padded quilt

棉布　miánbù　【名】cotton cloth

棉纺　miánfǎng　【名】cotton textiles

棉花　miánhua　【名】❶ cotton ❷ cotton-wool

棉裤　miánkù　【名】〔条 tiáo〕cotton-padded trousers

棉毛裤　miánmáokù　【名】〔条 tiáo〕long underwear of knitted cotton

棉毛衫　miánmáoshān　【名】〔件 jiàn〕knitted cotton vest with long sleeves

棉纱　miánshā　【名】cotton yarn

棉线　miánxiàn　【名】cotton thread

棉絮　miánxù　【名】cotton wadding

棉衣　miányī　【名】〔件 jiàn〕cotton-padded clothes

棉织品　miánzhīpǐn　【名】cotton goods

miǎn

免　miǎn　【动】❶ free sb. from sth.；exempt：～税 exempt from taxation, duty free ～职 remove sb. from a position 这层手续可以～掉。This part of the formalities can be dispensed with. ❷ avoid；avert；escape：～受其害 avoid being harmed ～遭毒手 escape with one's life ❸ ◇ not allowed；prohibited：闲人～进。No admittance except on business；or No admittance, staff only.

免不得　miǎn bu de　be bound to；be unavoidable *usu. used as an adverbial adjunct*

免不了　miǎn bu liǎo　be unavoidable；be bound to：要学会游泳，就～喝几口水。If you want to learn to swim, you can't avoid drinking a few mouthfuls of water. 做任何值得做的事，困难是～的。In doing anything worthwhile, difficulties are unavoidable.

免除　miǎnchú　【动】avoid；be freed from；be excused from：这座水库修成后，附近几个村子就能～旱涝灾害。When this reservoir is completed, the villages nearby will be freed from droughts and floods. 他身体不好，可以～体力劳动。He is in poor health, and should be excused from manual labour.

免得　miǎnde　【连】同"以免"yǐmiǎn，*but more colloquial*：学过的东西要常复习，～忘了。You should often review what you have learned, lest you should forget it. 我带你去吧，～你走错路。I'd better take you there or else you will lose your way.

免费　miǎn = fèi　free of charge；free；gratis：～医疗 free medical care ～参观 a free visit（e. g. to an exhibition）

免验　miǎnyàn　【动】exempt from customs examination

免疫力　miǎnyìlì　【名】immunity（from disease）

勉　miǎn

勉励　miǎnlì　【动】encourage；urge：互相～ encourage each other 教练～运动员苦练基本功。The coach urged the athletes to do a lot of drill on basic skills.

勉强　miǎnqiǎng　【形】❶ do with difficulty；manage with an effort：你不舒服就去休息吧，不要～支持了。Take a break since you are not feeling well. Don't overtax your strength. ❷ unconvincing；far-fetched：你的理由很～，不能说服人。

The reason you gave was rather far-fetched and not at all convincing.这个形容词用在这里有些～。This adjective is a bit out of place in this context. ❸ unwillingly；reluctantly；grudgingly：～答应 make a promise unwillingly ～同意 agree reluctantly ❹ barely：这些木料～够做一个方桌。This will be just enough wood to make a square table.他说的是上海话，我～能听懂。He spoke Shanghai dialect，and I could only just understand him. 【动】force sb. to do sth.；他不愿意去就不要～他了。Don't force him to go if he doesn't want to.

勉为其难 miǎn wéi qí nán manage to do what seemed beyond one's power

缅(緬) miǎn

缅怀 miǎnhuái 【动】cherish a fond memory of；recall

腼 miǎn

腼腆 miǎntiǎn 【形】shy；bashful：这孩子太～了。This child is too shy.

miàn

面 miàn 【名】❶ face：他～朝里躺着。He was lying there with his back to us.两个人～对～坐着。The two of them sat there face to face. ❷ ◇ personally；directly：～谈 face-to-face talk ～交 personally hand sth. to sb. ❸ surface；top；face：水～ the surface of the water 桥～ bridge floor 这张桌子～很光。This table-top is very smooth. ❹ (麺) wheat flour：一袋～a bag of wheat flour ❺ (麺) noodles：肉丝～ noodles with shreded meat 今天中午吃～。We'll have noodles for

lunch. ❻ (geom.) surface ❼ an entire area；the whole：做好～上的工作 deal with the overall aspects of the work well ❽ used to form a noun of locality：上～ above；on top of 下～ under；below 里～ inside 外～ outside 前～ in front 后～ at the back of；behind 这～ this side 那～ that side 哪～ which side 左～ on the left 右～ on the right 东～ east side 西～ west side 南～ south side 北～ north side 【量】for flat objects：一～红旗 a flag 两～镜子 two mirrors

面包 miànbāo 【名】bread

面包车 miànbāochē 【名】〔辆 liàng〕minibus；van

面的 miàndī 【名】〔辆 liàng〕minibus as taxi

面对 miànduì 【动】face：～现实 face reality；face fact

面红耳赤 miàn hóng ěr chì be red in the face：争得～ argue until everyone is red in the face 羞得～ blush with embarrassment

面积 miànjī 【名】area

面具 miànjù 【名】mask

面孔 miànkǒng 【名】(a person's) face

面临 miànlín 【动】be faced with；be up against：～毕业考试 be faced with the graduation examination 我们～着一场考验。A severe test lies ahead of us.

面貌 miànmào 【名】❶ face ❷ (of things) look；appearance；aspect：改变落后～ change the backward state of things 山村出现新～。The mountain village has taken on a new look.

面面俱到 miàn miàn jù dào attend to all aspects of a matter；cover everything superficially but deal with nothing in depth：写总结不必～，要重点突出。When you write a summary, you needn't cover every-

thing, just highlight the important points.

面面相觑 miàn miàn xiāng qù look at each other in blank dismay; look at each other helplessly

面目 miànmù 【名】❶ face; features; ～ 狰狞 vicious appearance ～ 可憎 repulsive appearance ❷ 同 "面貌" ❷; 把本来～掩盖起来 cover up the true colours of sth.

面目全非 miànmù quán fēi changed beyond recognition (*derog.*); 好好的一篇文章, 让你给改得～了。 What was a good article has been changed beyond recognition by your alterations.

面目一新 miànmù yī xīn take on an entirely new look; assume a completely new appearance; 改进了经营管理以后, 这个工厂～。 After improving management and administration this factory has taken on a completely new look.

面前 miànqián 【名】in front of; in the face of; before; 我把茶送到客人～。 I placed cups of tea before the guests. 胜利～不骄傲。 Don't be arrogant in the face of victory. 现在摆在他～的有好几种选择, 他感到为难起来。 Now he is faced with quite a few choices, and he finds it difficult to make up his mind.

面色 miànsè 【名】complexion

面生 miànshēng 【形】look unfamiliar; 这位先生～得很, 是新来的吧! This gentleman looks unfamiliar to me; you must be a new-comer.

面食 miànshí 【名】cooked wheaten food

面试 miànshì 【动】interview

面熟 miànshú 【形】look familiar; 这个女孩子很～, 是小李的妹妹吧! That girl looks very familiar. Isn't she Xiao Li's sister?

面谈 miàntán 【动】speak to sb. face to face; take up a matter with

sb. personally

面条 miàntiáo 【名】(～儿) noodles

面值 miànzhí 【名】face value

面子 miànzi 【名】❶ outer part; outside; 棉袄～ the outside of a cotton-padded jacket ❷ face; self-respect; 爱～ be keen on face-saving 怕丢～ be afraid to lose face ❸ consideration for someone's feelings; 坚持原则, 不讲～。 Stick to your principles and don't spare anybody's sensibilities.

miáo

苗 miáo 【名】〔棵 kē〕sprout; seedling

苗床 miáochuáng 【名】seedbed

苗圃 miáopǔ 【名】nursery (for plants or trees)

苗条 miáotiao 【形】(of figure) slender; slim

苗头 miáotou 【名】symptom of a trend; indication of a new development; 出现了不团结的～。 Some symptoms of disunity appeared. ～不对。 Things are not going the right way.

描 miáo 【动】❶ trace; copy; ～花 trace a flower pattern ～图样 trace a design ❷ touch up; retouch; ～眉 pencil one's eyebrows 这几个字写得太淡了, 还得～～。 The ink in which these characters were written is too pale. They need to be retouched.

描画 miáohuà 【动】draw; paint; describe; depict; 这幅木刻～了边疆的美丽景色。 This woodcut portrays the beautiful scenery of one of the border areas. 这篇特写生动地～了钢铁工人的生活。 This feature article portrays very vividly the life of steel workers.

描绘 miáohuì【动】同"描画"

描摹 miáomó【动】depict；portray；delineate

描写 miáoxiě【动】describe；portray；depict

瞄 miáo【动】aim

瞄准 miáozhǔn【动】take aim

miǎo

秒 miǎo【量】second (1/60 of a minute)

秒针 miǎozhēn【名】(of clock or watch) second hand

渺 miǎo

渺茫 miǎománg【形】❶ remote and indistinct：音信～。Nothing has been heard from him. ❷ uncertain：前途～ uncertain prospects

渺小 miǎoxiǎo【形】negligible；paltry

藐 miǎo

藐视 miǎoshì【动】despise；look down upon；belittle：～困难 make light of difficulties 他很～那些专为个人名利奋斗的人。He despises those who work only for personal fame and gain.

miào

妙 miào【形】❶ wonderful；excellent；fine：这个主意～极了。This is an excellent idea. ❷ ◇ ingenious；clever；subtle：神机～算 rare wisdom and clever calculation

妙计 miàojì【名】an excellent plan；a brilliant scheme

庙（廟）miào【名】〔座 zuò〕temple

庙宇 miàoyǔ【名】temple

miè

灭（滅）miè【动】❶ (of fire, light, etc.) put out；go out：～火 put out a fire 炉子～了。The fire in the stove went out. 电灯～了。The lights went out. ❷ destroy；exterminate；wipe out：～蚊蝇 kill mosquitoes and flies 不要长他人志气，～自己威风。We should not always praise others while constantly belittling ourselves.

灭顶之灾 miè dǐng zhī zāi complete annihilation：面临～ be confronted with the threat of complete annihilation

灭火机 mièhuǒjī【名】fire extinguisher

灭火器 mièhuǒqì【名】fire extinguisher

灭迹 miè＝jì obliterate traces

灭绝 mièjué【动】❶ become extinct：有许多珍奇的动物现在有～的危险。Some rare animals are in danger of becoming extinct. ❷ lose completely：～人性的法西斯暴行 inhuman fascist atrocities

灭口 miè＝kǒu silence a witness (e.g. of a crime)

灭亡 mièwáng【动】(of nation, race, etc.) perish；go to one's doom；die out

蔑（衊）miè

蔑视 mièshì【动】show contempt for；despise；scorn

mín

民 mín【名】◇ people：～富国强 the people are well-off and the country is strong 军～团结 unity of

the army and the people

民办 mín bàn run by the local people：～小学 a primary school run by the local people ～托儿所 a nursery run by the local people

民兵 mínbīng 【名】militia

民不聊生 mín bù liáo shēng the people are deprived of their means of survival

民法 mínfǎ 【名】civil law

民愤 mínfèn 【名】the indignation of the people

民歌 míngē 【名】〔首 shǒu〕folk song

民工 míngōng 【名】commune member who takes part as a temporary worker in a public project

民航 mínháng 【名】civil aviation

民间 mínjiān 【名】of the common people；folk（as attrib. only）

民间文学 mínjiān wénxué folk literature

民间艺术 mínjiān yìshù folk arts

民警 mínjǐng 【名】people's police

民俗 mínsú 【名】folk custom

民谣 mínyáo 【名】〔首 shǒu〕little rhymes with political content popular among the people

民意 mínyì 【名】the will of the people；popular will：～测验 public opinion poll

民用 mínyòng 【形】civilian；civil

民乐 mínyuè 【名】music for traditional Chinese instruments

民政 mínzhèng 【名】civil administration

民众 mínzhòng 【名】masses；the common people

民主 mínzhǔ 【名】democracy 【形】democratic

民主党派 mínzhǔ dǎngpài democratic parties（bourgeois and petty-bourgeois political parties that have accepted the leadership of the Chinese Communist Party and joined the united front）

民主集中制 mínzhǔ jízhōngzhì democratic centralism

民主人士 mínzhǔ rénshì democratic personages

民族 mínzú 【名】nationality；national（attrib. only）

民族败类 mínzú bàilèi dregs or degenerate members of a nationality

民族解放运动 mínzú jiěfàng yùndòng national liberation movement

民族统一战线 mínzú tǒngyī zhànxiàn national united front

民族形式 mínzú xíngshì national form（architecture，style of dress，etc.）

民族英雄 mínzú yīngxióng national hero

民族主义 mínzúzhǔyì 【名】nationalism

民族资产阶级 mínzú zīchǎnjiējí national bourgeoisie

民族自决 mínzú zìjué national self-determination

民族自治 mínzú zìzhì national autonomy

mǐn

抿 mǐn 【动】❶ close：～着嘴笑 smile with lips closed ❷ sip：～了点儿酒 sip a little wine ❸ brush（hair）with a small wet brush：～一～头发 give the hair a brush

敏 mǐn

敏感 mǐngǎn 【形】sensitive；susceptible：有关节炎的人对天气的变化非常～。Arthritis sufferers are very sensitive to changes in weather. 他在语言上很～，适合学外语。He is very sensitive to nuances in language and is suited to study foreign languages.

敏捷 mǐnjié 【形】agile；nimble：动作～ agile movements

敏锐 mǐnruì 【形】sharp；acute；

keen: 感觉～ have quick and sensitive reactions 眼光 ～ have sharp eyes

míng

名 míng 【名】◇ ❶ name: 书～ the title of a book 街～ the name of a street 给小孩儿起个～儿 name a baby ❷ in the name of: 有些干部以出差为～,游山玩水,给国家造成浪费。Under the pretext of travelling on business, some cadres go holidaying and waste public money. ❸ fame; reputation; renown: 不为～,不为利 seek neither fame nor gain 【形】famous; well-known; celebrated; noted (*as attributive only*): ～画家 a well-known painter ～山大川 famous mountains and rivers 【动】◇ (his or her) given name is: 她姓李～惠民。Her surname is Li, and her given name is Hui-min. 【量】*for persons*: 一百多～工人 more than a hundred workers 竞赛中他得了第一～。He won first place in the competition.

名不副实 míng bù fù shí the title does not correspond to the reality 也作"名不符(fú)实"。

名不虚传 míng bù xū chuán have a well-deserved reputation; deserve the reputation one enjoys: 景德镇的瓷器～。Jingdezhen porcelain has a well-deserved reputation.

名册 míngcè 【名】personnel roster

名产 míngchǎn 【名】famous product

名称 míngchēng 【名】name (of a thing or organization)

名词 míngcí 【名】❶ noun ❷ term

名次 míngcì 【名】position of a name or names in a list

名存实亡 míng cún shí wáng exist in name only; cease to exist except in name

名单 míngdān 【名】〔张 zhāng〕list of names

名额 míng'é 【名】stipulated number of people (e. g. of enrollment)

名副其实 míng fù qí shí worthy of the name; in reality as well as in name: 他真是～的"活字典"。He really lives up to his reputation as "a walking dictionary". 也作"名符(fú)其实"。

名利 mínglì 【名】fame and gain; fame and wealth: 不求～ not seek fame and gain ～思想 desire for fame and gain

名列前茅 míng liè qiánmáo be among the best of the successful candidates: 在演讲比赛中谢力同学～。Xie Li was one of the best students in the public speaking contest.

名目 míngmù 【名】name; item: 巧立～ invent all kinds of items (as pretexts for) 他们那个科研小组～倒搞了不少,不一定都能搞成。Their research group has made plans for quite a few experiments, but I wonder whether all will prove successful.

名牌 míngpái 【名】famous brand; name brand

名片 míngpiàn 【名】〔张 zhāng〕visiting card

名气 míngqi 【名】reputation; fame; name: 他的书法有点儿～。His calligraphy enjoys a measure of fame. 在医学界这位老中医～不小。In medical circles, this old Chinese traditional doctor has a considerable reputation.

名人 míngrén 【名】famous person

名声 míngshēng 【名】reputation; repute; renown: 好～ of good repute ～很坏 be notorious ～在外 quite well-known ～远扬 known

far and wide

名胜 míngshèng 【名】well-known scenic spot

名堂 míngtang 【名】❶ a variety of：鬼～ dirty trick 他们在搞什么～? What are they up to? 游园活动～真多,歌舞游戏样样俱全. At the gala party in the park there were all sorts of activities—songs, dances and games, everything! ❷ result；achievement：这次试验一定要搞出点儿～来. This time our experiment must have something to show. ❸ thing worth learning；learning：种菜也大有～. There is also a lot worth learning in the cultivation of vegetables.

名望 míngwàng 【名】reputation

名言 míngyán 【名】famous saying

名义 míngyì 【名】❶（in the）name of；（in the）capacity（of）：以个人～ in the name of an individual 以小组～ in the name of the group ❷ nominal；in name only（usu. followed by 上）：她～上是我们班的班长,实际上什么都不管. She is our monitor in name only；actually she does nothing for us.

名优产品 míngyōu chǎnpǐn famous quality products

名誉 míngyù 【名】❶ reputation：珍惜～ value（one's）reputation highly 恢复～ rehabilitate sb.；restore to sb. his former reputation ❷ honorary：～主席 honorary chairman ～会员 honorary member

名著 míngzhù 【名】famous book or treatise

名字 míngzi 【名】name

明 míng 【形】◇ ❶ bright；brilliant：一轮～月 a bright moon 灯火通～ be brightly lit ❷ clear；distinct：问～情况 clarify the situation 去向不～ whereabouts unknown 来路不～ of unknown origin ❸ open；

overt；explicit：～沟 open sewer 有话就～说吧. Whatever's on your mind, out with it! ～枪易躲,暗箭难防. It is easy to dodge an open attack, but hard to guard against sniping. ❹ clearsighted；sharp-eyed：耳聪目～ have sharp eyes and ears

明白 míngbai 【形】❶ clear；obvious：这篇文章写得很～,一看就懂. This article is clearly written and very easy to understand. ❷ reasonable；sensible：他是个～人. He is a sensible man. 【动】understand；realize；know：我不～,请你再讲一遍. I'm still in the dark. Will you please explain it once more?

明摆着 míng bǎizhe plain；clear；obvious：～的道理 an evident logic ～的问题 an obvious problem 这办法～行不通,你就不要再坚持了. It's as clear as day that this method doesn't work. You'd better not insist any more（on using it）.

明辨是非 míngbiàn shìfēi distinguish right from wrong

明察秋毫 míng chá qiū háo have eyes sharp enough to perceive a single hair of an animal's autumn coat；be perceptive to the minutest detail

明澈 míngchè 【形】bright and limpid；crystal clear：溪水～. The brook is crystal clear.

明灯 míngdēng 【名】beacon（fig.）

明晃晃 mínghuǎnghuǎng 【形】shining；gleaming

明火执仗 míng huǒ zhí zhàng carry torches and weapons（while committing a robbery）；（fig.）do evil openly

明快 míngkuài 【形】❶ lucid and lively；sprightly：文字～ lucid writing 语言～ clear language ～的节奏 sprightly rhythm ❷ straight-forward；forthright

明朗 mínglǎng 【形】❶ bright and clear；~的天空 clear sky ❷ clear；obvious：态度~ take a clear-cut stand 经过争论，问题更加~了。The matter has become even clearer after discussion. ❸ forthright；bright and cheerful：~的风格 forthright style

明亮 míngliàng 【形】❶ bright；well-lit：~的教室 bright classroom 窗户擦得很~。The panes were very clear. ❷ shining；bright：灯光~ bright lights ~的眼睛 bright eyes 今晚的星星异常~。The stars are specially bright tonight. ❸ clear：听你一解释，我心里~多了。After your explanation, I'm much clearer on the matter.

明了 míngliǎo 【动】understand；be clear about：通过学习，我~了很多道理。I got to know the whys and wherefores of many things through study. 【形】clear；plain：他的发言简单~。His speech was simple and clear.

明媚 míngmèi 【形】❶ bright and beautiful；radiant and enchanting：春光~ the freshness and beauty of spring ~的阳光 bright and beautiful sunshine ❷（of eyes）bright and charming

明明 míngmíng 【副】obviously（*when there is an event which seemingly proves the contrary*, 明明 *is used to affirm the truth of one's original belief*）：我~看见他跑过来了，怎么找不到他了？I swear I saw him running in this direction, why's he nowhere to be found? 他是色盲，~是红的，他说是绿的。He is colour-blind, so what is clearly red to us appears green to him.

明目张胆 míng mù zhāng dǎn blatant；flagrant

明年 míngnián 【名】next year

明枪暗箭 míngqiāng ànjiàn attack by overt and covert means

明确 míngquè 【形】explicit；definite；clear-cut：分工~ clear division of labour ~地表态 be definite in one's attitude ~指出 point out unequivocally 【动】make clear；make definite；understand clearly：~方向 clearly understand the trend of development of sth. ~每个人的职责 make clear the responsibility of each person

明日 míngrì 【名】tomorrow

明天 míngtiān 【名】tomorrow；future

明晰 míngxī 【形】distinct；clear：轮廓~ clearly defined contour 一件件往事~地浮现在我的脑海里。Things of the past flashed across my mind one after another.

明显 míngxiǎn 【形】clear；obvious；evident；distinct：~的变化 obvious changes 很~，他是不同意你们的观点的。It was obvious that he didn't agree with your point of view.

明信片 míngxìnpiàn 【名】〔张 zhāng〕postcard

明星 míngxīng 【名】a star；a star performer or athlete；an outstanding person

明眼人 míngyǎnrén 【名】a shrewd-minded person：~一看就明白。A shrewd-minded person can see through it at a glance.

明哲保身 míng zhé bǎo shēn be worldly wise and play it safe (often referring to people who refuse to take a stand even on matters of principle in order to play it safe)

明知故犯 míng zhī gù fàn commit an error deliberately

明智 míngzhì 【形】wise；sensible；sagacious

鸣（鳴） míng 【动】◇ ❶ (of birds, animals or insects) cry；utter a cry：鸡~ the crow of a cock

蝉～ the chirp of a cicada ❷ sound；ring：以～枪为号 fire a gun as a signal 汽笛长～ the long blast of a steam-whistle 礼炮齐～。A salvo was fired. ❸ (of feeling, opinion) express；voice：～冤 cry out against injustice ～不平 complain of unfairness

鸣锣开道 míng luó kāi dào beat the gongs to clear the way (for officials in feudal times)；(*fig.*) prepare public for the advent of sth. (*derog.*)

冥 míng

冥思苦想 míng sī kǔ xiǎng rack one's brains：不深入实际，光靠～是搞不好设计的。One cannot make a good plan simply by thinking hard with no understanding of the actual situation.

冥想 míngxiǎng 【动】contemplate；be in deep thought

铭(銘) míng

铭记 míngjì 【动】always remember；be engraved on one's mind：～在心 keep in mind 时刻～ bear in mind all the time

铭刻 míngkè 【动】be engraved (in one's mind)；always remember：～心头 be engraved in one's heart

瞑 míng

瞑目 míngmù 【动】close the eyes, i.e. die with an easy mind

mìng

命 mìng 【名】❶ life：医生救了他的～。The doctor saved his life. ❷ ◇ order；command：奉上级之～，部队继续前进。Following orders from above, the troops continued to advance. ❸ a person's fortune

or destiny：～苦 hard lot 【动】◇ order：速～渔船返航。Order the immediate return of the fishing boats.

命根子 mìnggēnzi 【名】life-blood；one's very life

命令 mìnglìng 【动】order；command：连长～全连立即投入战斗。The company commander ordered the whole company to go into action immediately. 【名】order；command：下了一道～ give an order 发布～ issue orders 服从～ obey orders

命令主义 mìnglìngzhǔyì 【名】commandism

命脉 mìngmài 【名】life-blood；life-line：国家的～ the life-blood of a nation 工业的～ the life-blood of industry

命名 mìng = míng give a name to (e.g. a building)

命题 mìngtí 【名】proposition (logic)

命题 mìng = tí assign an essay topic

命运 mìngyùn 【名】destiny；fate；lot：中国人民已经掌握了自己的～。The Chinese people have taken their destiny into their own hands.

命中 mìngzhòng 【动】hit the target

miù

谬(謬) miù

谬论 miùlùn 【名】fallacy

谬误 miùwù 【名】falsehood

谬种流传 miùzhǒng liúchuán erroneous ideology keeps spreading

mō

摸 mō 【动】❶ feel；stroke；touch ❷ grope for；fumble for：～鱼 catch fish with one's hands 他从口

袋里～出来一张电影票。He fished out a film ticket from his pocket. ❸ try to find out; feel out; sound out: ～情况 try to find out about the situation ～不着头脑 be unable to make head or tail of sth. 他们～出了一套淡水养鱼的经验。They have gradually accumulated a great deal of experience in raising fresh-water fish. ❹ grope in the dark; do sth. in the dark: 起早～黑儿地干 work hard morning and night

摸底　mō＝dǐ　find out the real situation; feel out; sound out: 他刚来, 对这里情况还不～。He's just come, and doesn't yet fully know the state of affairs here. 不忙下结论, 摸摸底再说。We should be in no hurry to draw conclusions. Let's first find out the real situation.

摸索　mōsuo　【动】❶ grope; feel about; fumble: 战士们在漆黑的夜晚～前进。The soldiers groped their way forward in the pitch-dark night. ❷ try to find out: 他们～出一套工作方法。By trial and error, they worked out the steps in the work method.

mó

模 mó
另见 mú

模范　mófàn　【名】model (e. g. model worker); example

模仿　mófǎng　【动】imitate; mimic; pattern after: ～他的动作 imitate his gestures ～得很像 be a very clever mimic 你是在～谁的样子? Whom are you aping?

模糊　móhu　【形】dim; vague; indistinct; blurred: 字迹～ faded handwriting 神志～ semi-conscious 认识～ have a confused understanding

of sth. 【动】confuse; mix up; obscure: 不要～了是非界限 don't blur the distinction between right and wrong

模棱两可　móléng liǎngkě　in an equivocal way; ambiguous

模拟　mónǐ　【动】simulate; imitate

模式　móshì　【名】pattern; model

模特儿　mótèr　【名】model; person who poses for sculptors and painters

模型　móxíng　【名】model; pattern

摩 mó

摩擦　mócā　【名】❶ (phys.) friction: ～生电。Friction generates static electricity. ❷ clash (between two parties); friction: ～一定会发生。Frictions are bound to occur. 相互之间闹～。There's been a clash between the two of them. 【动】rub (only as a technical term)

摩擦力　mócālì　【名】friction

摩拳擦掌　mó quán cā zhǎng　prepare to do battle; get ready to have a try

摩托车　mótuōchē　【名】〔辆 liàng〕motorcycle

磨 mó　【动】❶ rub: 手上～了一个泡。The palm of (his) hand was blistered from the rubbing. ❷ grind; sharpen; polish: ～刀 sharpen a knife ～剪子 sharpen a pair of scissors ❸ dawdle; while away (time): ～时间 kill time ❹ wear down; torment; trouble; pester; worry: 这种慢性病真～人。This sort of chronic disease is really a torment.
另见 mò

磨蹭　móceng　【动】move slowly; dawdle: 快干, 别～了! Work faster! Stop dawdling! 【形】slow-moving; dawdling: 他总是磨磨蹭蹭的, 真急人。He's always dawdling; it's re-

ally irritating.

磨床 móchuáng 【名】grinder

磨练 móliàn 【动】steel oneself；temper oneself；～意志 steel one's will 她经受过艰苦岁月的～。She has been tempered through years of hardship.

磨灭 mómiè 【动】obliterate；wear away；blunt (*usu. used in the neg.*)：不可～的功绩 glorious never-to-be-forgotten deeds 这件事给我留下了难以～的印象。This matter has left an indelible impression on me.

磨损 mósǔn 【动】wear；wear out

蘑 mó

蘑菇 mógu 【名】mushroom 【动】〈口〉❶ worry；pester；keep on at：你再～也没用，反正我不同意让你去。There's no point in nagging at me. I won't let you go anyway. ❷ dawdle：音乐会都快开始了，你还在这儿～什么！The concert will begin very soon. Why are you still dawdling around here!

蘑菇云 móguyún 【名】mushroom cloud

魔 mó 【名】◇ monster；evil spirit；devil；demon；(*fig.*) reactionary forces 【形】◇ magical

魔鬼 móguǐ 【名】devil

魔力 mólì 【名】magic；magic power

魔术 móshù 【名】magic；conjurer's tricks

魔爪 mózhǎo 【名】evil clutches

mǒ

抹 mǒ 【动】❶ smear；apply：在伤口上～点儿药 apply a little ointment to a sore 饼干上～点儿蜂蜜 spread some honey on a biscuit ❷ wipe：把脸上的汗～掉 wipe the sweat from one's face ❸ strike

out；erase：～零儿 make it a round number by cancelling the odd amount 刚才录的音千万别～了！Please take care not to erase the recording just made.

另见 mā；mò

抹杀 mǒshā 【动】blot out；obliterate；negate：～成绩 negate the achievements of 一笔～ obliterate at one stroke 想～事实是～不了的。It is impossible to deny facts, however hard one may try.

mò

末 mò 【名】❶ end；tip ❷ non-essentials；minor details (*as opp. to* 本)：本～不能颠倒。One must not put the cart before the horse. ❸ end；last stage：周～ weekend ❹ (～儿) powder；dust：肉～ minced meat 茶叶～ powdered tea leaves (from the bottom of the box) 把药研成～ grind the medicinal herbs into powder

末班车 mòbānchē 【名】last train or bus；the last chance

末代 mòdài 【名】last reign：～皇帝 the last emperor

末了 mòliǎo 【名】at the end

末路 mòlù 【名】doom；the end

末年 mònián 【名】the last years (e.g. of a dynasty)

末日 mòrì 【名】doomsday

末梢 mòshāo 【名】tip；end

末尾 mòwěi 【名】end (of a book, lecture, queue, etc.)

末叶 mòyè 【名】last part of a century or dynasty

没 mò 【动】❶ sink；submerge：～入水中 sink into the water ❷ rise beyond：大水～过了屋顶。The flood waters rose above the roofs of the houses.

另见 méi

没落 mòluò 【动】decline

没收 mòshōu 【动】confiscate

抹 mò 【动】smooth with a trowel；trowel：～墙 plaster a wall 地面～得很光。The（cement）floor was trowelled very smooth.

另见 mā；mǒ

茉 mò

茉莉 mòli 【名】jasmine

沫 mò 【名】froth；foam

陌 mò

陌生 mòshēng 【形】strange；unfamiliar

莫 mò 【副】not

莫不 mòbù 【副】no...not...：这条铁路通车了，沿线各族人民～欢欣鼓舞。The new railway has come into operation. The people of all nationalities living along the line are overjoyed at the news. 听到这个消息，大家～感到惊奇。None of us who had heard the news was not surprised.

莫大 mòdà 【形】greatest（attrib. only）

莫非 mòfēi 【副】could it be possible（not frequently used）：灯还亮着，～他还在看书？The light is still on, is it possible that he is still reading? 他怎么还没来，～他忘了今天的活动？How come that he hasn't shown up yet? Could he possibly forget about today's activities?

莫名其妙 mò míng qí miào unable to make head or tail of sth.；be baffled：他一进门就发这么大的火儿，人们都～。We were baffled by his flaring up as soon as he entered the room. 也作"莫明其妙"。

莫如 mòrú 【连】it would be better：这种文章不认真读～不读。Unless you read this kind of essay with great care, you might as well not read it at all.

莫若 mòruò 【连】同"莫如"

莫须有 mòxūyǒu 【形】fabricated：～的罪名 a fabricated charge

莫衷一是 mò zhōng yī shì opinions are so diverse that one is unable to draw a conclusion or decide which is right

漠 mò

漠不关心 mò bù guānxīn indifferent；unconcerned：他对世界大事不应该～。He shouldn't be indifferent to important matters happening in the world.

漠漠 mòmò 【形】❶ misty；foggy ❷ vast and lonely：～荒原 a vast expanse of wasteland

漠然 mòrán 【形】indifferent；apathetic；unconcerned：～置之 look on indifferently 处之～ treat apathetically

漠视 mòshì 【动】ignore；regard as unimportant；look at apathetically

墨 mò 【名】❶ ink stick：一块～ an ink stick 研～ rub an ink stick（against the inkstone）❷ liquid ink made by rubbing the ink stick in water on an inkstone ❸ black；dark：～菊 black（dark purple）chrysanthemums

墨盒 mòhé 【名】〔个 gè〕box containing an ink-pad

墨迹未干 mòjī wèi gān scarcely had the ink dried

墨镜 mòjìng 【名】〔副 fù〕sun glasses

墨绿 mòlǜ 【形】dark green

墨守成规 mòshǒu chéngguī stick to the established practice；remain in

a rut：要勇于创新，不能～。We should dare to be creative instead of remaining in a rut. 也说"墨守陈规"。

墨水 mòshuǐ 【名】(～儿) ink；红～ red ink 蓝～ blue ink

墨汁 mòzhī 【名】prepared liquid Chinese ink

默 mò

默哀 mò'āi 【动】observe a moment's silence in memory of sb.

默不作声 mò bù zuò shēng keep silent

默默无闻 mòmò wú wén unknown to the public；without attracting public attention

默契 mòqì 【形】by tacit agreement；配合～ coordinate actions in unspoken agreement 【名】secret agreement；双方早有～。The two parties reached secret agreement long ago.

默然 mòrán 【形】in silence

默认 mòrèn 【动】acquiesce

默写 mòxiě 【动】write on dictation

默许 mòxǔ 【动】tacitly approve

磨 mò 【名】〔盘 pán〕mill；millstone；推～ use a hand-mill 【动】mill；grind；～麦子 grind wheat ～豆腐 grind soya beans to make bean curd
另见 mó

磨房 mòfáng 【名】mill（building）

磨盘 mòpán 【名】❶ round tray beneath the grindstone which receives the flour ❷ millstone

móu

牟 móu

牟利 móulì 【动】make a profit

牟取 móuqǔ 【动】try to gain；seek；obtain（derog.）；～暴利 seek exorbitant profits

谋（謀） móu 【动】◇ ❶ plan；work for；seek；另～出路 try to find another way out 为人民～幸福 work for the welfare of the people ❷ consult；各不相～。Each acts without consulting the other. 【名】◇ cleverness；足智多～ clever and full of stratagems；resourceful

谋害 móuhài 【动】plot to murder or ruin sb.

谋划 móuhuà 【动】plan and contrive

谋求 móuqiú 【动】plan to achieve

谋杀 móushā 【动】plan to murder；attempt to murder

谋生 móushēng 【动】(in old society) strive to make a living

mǒu

某 mǒu 【代】certain；some；～人 a certain man ～地 a certain place 张～ a certain person called Zhang ～年～月 in a certain month of a certain year ～种情况 certain conditions；a certain situation

mú

模 mú 【名】◇ model
另见 mó

模具 mújù 【名】mould for use in casting metals

模样 múyàng 【名】❶ look；appearance；这兄弟两个～长得差不多。The two brothers look very much alike. ❷ approximately；about；around；来的人有三十岁～。The

man who has just arrived, looks around thirty.

模子 múzi 【名】mould

mǔ

母 mǔ 【名】❶ ◇ mother：～女二人 the two of them, mother and daughter ❷ (of birds and animals) female：～兔 female rabbit 这头牛是～的。It's a cow. ❸ ◇ (*fig.*) origin：失败是成功之～。Failure is the mother of success.

母爱 mǔ'ài 【名】maternal love
母亲 mǔqin 【名】mother
母乳 mǔrǔ 【名】breast milk
母体 mǔtǐ 【名】the female parent
母校 mǔxiào 【名】alma mater
母音 mǔyīn 【名】vowel
母语 mǔyǔ 【名】mother tongue
母子 mǔzǐ 【名】mother and son

牡 mǔ

牡丹 mǔdan 【名】tree peony

亩(畝) mǔ 【量】*unit of area* (0.0667 hectares)

亩产 mǔchǎn 【动】per *mu* yield

mù

木 mù 【名】❶ ◇ tree：草～茂盛 lush undergrowth and trees ❷ wooden；made of wood：～床 wooden bed ～桥 wooden bridge 【形】numb；insensitive；wooden：舌头～了。My tongue has lost all sensation. 脑袋发～。One's thinking processes slow down. 两只脚都冻～了。Both feet were numb with cold.

木板 mùbǎn 【名】〔块 kuài〕board
木本 mùběn 【名】xylogen：～植物 woody plant

木材 mùcái 【名】timber
木柴 mùchái 【名】firewood
木耳 mù'ěr 【名】an edible fungus
木筏 mùfá 【名】raft
木工 mùgōng 【名】❶ carpentry；wood-work ❷ carpenter
木匠 mùjiang 【名】同"木工"❷
木刻 mùkè 【名】wood carving
木料 mùliào 【名】lumber；roughly prepared wood
木偶 mù'ǒu 【名】wooden figure；puppet
木偶戏 mù'ǒuxì 【名】puppet show
木排 mùpái 【名】同"木筏"
木器 mùqì 【名】wooden furniture
木然 mùrán 【形】unresponsive；expressionless
木炭 mùtàn 【名】charcoal
木头 mùtou 【名】wood
木头人儿 mùtourénr 【名】wooden figure
木星 mùxīng 【名】Jupiter
木已成舟 mù yǐ chéng zhōu the wood is already made into a boat；(*fig.*) what's done cannot be undone

目 mù 【名】◇ ❶ eye：双～失明 lose one's sight；be blind 一切历历在～。Everything is very distinct in one's mind's eye. ❷ item；detail：摆正纲和～的关系 put the relationship between the main aspect and secondary details in right perspective

目标 mùbiāo 【名】target；objective：暴露～(mil.) reveal one's position；give away one's position 奋斗的～ the goal of struggle
目不转睛 mù bù zhuǎn jīng (look) with fixed gaze；(watch) with utmost concentration：雷达兵～地注视着荧光屏。The soldier from the radar unit watched the radar screen with fixed attention.
目瞪口呆 mù dèng kǒu dāi dumb-

founded; stunned

目的　mùdì　【名】aim; objective; goal; purpose: ～明确 have a definite purpose 达到～。The objective was attained.

目睹　mùdǔ　【动】witness

目光　mùguāng　【名】❶ sight; vision ❷ brightness of the eye

目击　mùjī　【动】同"目睹"

目空一切　mù kōng yīqiè　look down upon everything

目录　mùlù　【名】table of contents (of book); catalogue

目前　mùqián　【名】at present; at the moment: ～形势 the present situation 到～为止 up to the present; up till now ～正是春暖花开的季节。It's spring now, and flowers are in bloom.

目无法纪　mù wú fǎjì　disregard law and discipline

目中无人　mù zhōng wú rén　look down on everyone

沐 mù

沐浴　mùyù　【动】bathe; be bathed in (fig.)

牧 mù 【动】(of sheep, cattle, etc.) graze

牧草　mùcǎo　【名】graze; pasturage for grazing

牧场　mùchǎng　【名】live-stock farm; pasture

牧歌　mùgē　【名】〔首 shǒu〕pastoral song

牧民　mùmín　【名】herdsman

牧区　mùqū　【名】pastoral area

牧师　mùshī　【名】minister; clergyman

牧童　mùtóng　【名】cow-herd; shepherd

牧畜　mùxù　【名】livestock breeding; cattle breeding

牧业　mùyè　【名】animal husbundary; stock raising

牧主　mùzhǔ　【名】owner of land and lifestock

募 mù 【动】enlist (e. g. soldiers)

募捐　mùjuān　【动】raise funds

墓 mù 【名】grave; tomb

墓碑　mùbēi　【名】tombstone

墓地　mùdì　【名】graveyard; cemetery

幕 mù 【名】(cinema) screen; (theatre) curtain 【量】act: 三～七场话剧 a play in three acts and seven scenes 回忆起一～～的童年生活 recall scene after scene from his childhood 惊险的一～ a thrilling scene

幕布　mùbù　【名】curtain; screen

幕后　mùhòu　【名】backstage; behind the scenes: ～指挥 direct from behind the scenes ～策划 backstage manoeuvring ～操纵 pull strings behind the scenes

睦 mù

睦邻　mù lín　neighbourliness

暮 mù

暮年　mùnián　【名】old age

暮气　mùqì　【名】lethargy; apathy: ～太重 weighed down by lethargy ～沉沉 lifeless; lethargic; apathetic

暮色　mùsè　【名】dusk; twilight: ～苍茫 deepening dusk; spreading shades of dusk ～笼罩着大地。Dusk enveloped the vast land.

N

ná

拿 ná 【动】❶ take hold of; take; hold; ~笔 take up one's pen ~着镰刀 with a sickle in one's hand 把面包~来。Bring me the loaf of bread. ❷ grasp; decide; be sure of: 这件事我~不稳。I am not quite sure about this matter. ❸ seize; capture; take by force (*usu. used with* 下):一连~下了几个据点 capture several strongholds one after another ~下大油田 develop a big oilfield ❹ make things difficult for sb. on purpose; put (sb.) in a difficult position: ~一手 make things difficult for sb. by withholding certain skills or information ~他一把 put him in a difficult position 【介】❶ with: ~水冲洗 rinse sth. with water ~这笔钱买拖拉机 use the money to buy tractors ❷ *equivalent to* 把:不~困难当回事 make light of difficulties 老范~我当亲兄弟看待。Lao Fan treats me as his own brother.

拿大头 ná dàtóu take the lion's share

拿架子 ná jiàzi put on airs

拿…来说 ná…láishuō for example; for instance: 要学会任何东西都得实践,拿游泳来说吧,不下水是学不会的。If you want to learn a skill, you must learn it through practice, for example, you can't learn to swim without actually going into the water.

拿手 náshǒu 【形】excel at; (be) expert in; (be) adept at: 糖醋鱼是她的~菜。Sweet and sour fish is her speciality. 他写毛笔字很~。He excels at writing Chinese characters with a writing brush.

拿手好戏 náshǒu hǎo xì forte; strong point

拿主意 ná zhǔyi decide; make a decision; make up one's mind: 暑假回不回家,你自己~。It is up to you to to go home or not during the summer vacation.

nǎ

哪 nǎ 【代】which ❶ *used before a measure word or a numeral plus measure word or before a noun which does not take a measure word*: 你要借~本书? Which book do you want to borrow? 你要~种颜色的毛线? What colour wool would you like for your knitting? 这本论文集里~几篇是你写的? What articles in this anthology did you write? 你~一天有时间? Which day are you free? ❷ *together with a measure word, a numeral plus measure word or a noun which*

doesn't take a measure word, *placed before* 都 *or* 也 *to mean* "*any*"：你上～节课都行。You can teach any class you like. 我要借книга《中国文学史》，～年的版本都没关系。I want to borrow a copy of the *History of Chinese Literature*, any edition will do. 拖鞋只有这两种吗? ～种我都（或"也"）不喜欢。Do you just have these two kinds of slippers? I don't like either. ❸ *one phrase with* 哪 *precedes another*, *in which case the latter refers to the former*：你看～朵花好就摘～朵吧! Pick any flower you like. 不能他要～样的，你就给他～样的。I don't think you should give him any kind he wants.

另见 na

哪个 nǎge 【代】❶ which：他是～单位的? Which unit is he from? ❷ who：～叫我? Who is calling me?

哪里 nǎli 【代】❶ where：你的工作单位在～? Where is your place of work? ～能找到这种大理石? Where can this kind of marble be found? ❷ *used before* 都 *or* 也 *to mean* "*anywhere*"：在～工作都一样。It doesn't make any difference to me where I work. 他这个人到～都能发挥作用。He always turns out to be useful wherever he goes. 我们问了好几个旅馆，～都（或"也"）没有空房间。We've called a number of hotels but there was no vacancy in any of them. ❸ *one phrase with* 哪里 *precedes another*, *in which case the latter refers to the former*：祖国需要我们到～，我们就到～。We'll go anywhere our country needs us most. ❹ *used before an affirmative verb*, *auxiliary verb or adjective to form a rhetorical question expressing refutation of some statement*：昨天我～出门了! 我病了一天。How could I have gone out yester-

day! I was ill the whole day. 这件事他～能不知道! It is impossible for him not to have known about the matter. 老唐～会说日语! 他是学越南语的。Lao Tang certainly can't speak Japanese. He studied Vietnamese. 老黄做事～慢! 我看比你还快呢! Who said Lao Huang was slow! I think he's faster than you! ❺ 哪里知道（*sometimes means* "*unexpectedly*"）：我是跟他开玩笑，～知道他认真了，生起气来。I was only joking with him, but to my surprise he took it seriously and was offended.

哪怕 nǎpà 【连】〈口〉同"即使" jíshǐ：～你本领再大，脱离实际也不行。Even if you have the know-how, you must stay in touch with reality to get anything done. ～一个钉子也不要浪费。Not even a single nail is to be wasted. Note：*The clause with* 哪怕 *can be the second clause in a sentence*. 即使 *cannot be used in this way*：我们都想听你讲讲你的有趣经历，～就讲一件呢! We all want to hear about your interesting experiences. Please tell one episode at least.

哪儿 nǎr 【代】同"哪里"，*but more colloquial*. *In written language*, 哪 *can take the place of* 哪儿。

哪些 nǎxiē 【代】which ❶ *used before nouns in the plural number*（*no measure word is necessary*）：你订了～报纸杂志? What newspapers and magazines have you subscribed to? 你们都解决了～问题? Which of the problems have you solved? ～地方发展旅游事业最好? What places are most suitable for opening up for tourism? ❷ *used before* 都 *or* 也 *to mean* "*any*"：你们讨论～问题都行。You can discuss any questions you like. 这些树，～都（或"也"）不是今年种的。None of these trees was

planted this year. ❸ *A phrase with* 哪些 *precedes another*, *in which case the latter refers to the former*：～房子该修理，就修理～。We'll repair whichever buildings need repair.

哪样　nǎyàng 【代】what kind

nà

那　nà 【代】❶ that；those：～棵树 that tree ～两个人 those two people ～时候 at that time ～地区 that area ～有什么! It's nothing! ～很容易理解。That's very easy to understand. ❷ *used together with* 这 *to mean "all sorts of things"*：他想想这，想想～，考虑再三。He turned the matter over in his mind, giving it very careful consideration. 临走的时候，她看看这，看看～，十分留恋。At the moment of departure, she looked at everything and felt very reluctant to leave. 【连】then；in that case：如果有时间，～就去一趟吧! If you have time, then you had better go. 你把票都给大家了，～你自己呢? You have given us all the tickets. What about yourself then?

那个　nàge 【代】❶ that (one)：这个西瓜比～甜多了。This watermelon is much sweeter than that one. ❷ that matter；that thing：您就别为～操心啦! You don't have to worry about that. 你买～干吗? What did you buy that for? ❸ 〈口〉*used before a verb or an adjective in an exclamatory tone to indicate exaggeration*：几个老朋友谈得～高兴呀! How delighted these old friends were to be talking with each other! 你看他～得意劲儿。Look how complacent he is! ❹ 〈口〉*take the place of some expression one prefers to avoid using*：老张的性子也太～了。Lao Zhang's temperament is really a bit too..., you know what I mean! 你舅舅的作法可真有点儿～。Your uncle has really gone too far!

那里　nàli 【代】there；that place (*as opp. to* 这里)：～盛产橡胶。That area is rich in rubber. 他刚从哥哥～回来。He has just come back from his elder brother's. 你们～风沙大不大? Is it very windy and dusty out your way?

那么　nàme 【代】❶ *stand for a state*, *degree*, *way*, *etc.*, *applying to things at some distance in time or space*, *used as an attributive or adverbial adjunct only*：他仍然保持着年轻时一种朝气蓬勃的精神。He still has that vigorous spirit of his younger days. 老石就是～一个心直口快的人。Lao Shi is just that straight-forward kind of person. 就照他说的～干吧! Let's do it the way he said. ❷ *used before an approximate number to stress uncertainty*：他走了有～十五六天了。He's been away for about two weeks already. 【连】in that case：你既然很着急，～咱们就赶快走吧! Since you are very anxious, let's go at once. 如果大家对这个问题都没有意见，～我们就讨论下一个问题。If nobody has any objections, we'll go on to the next question. 也作"那末"。

那么点儿　nàmediǎnr 【代】such a little bit (*can only be used as an attributive*)：你放心，喝～酒醉不了。Don't worry, a little bit of wine like that won't make you drunk.

那么些　nàmexiē 【代】that many；that much (*can only be used as an attributive*)：～论文，会上不可能都念。That many papers can't all be read at the conference.

那么着　nàmezhe 【代】do that

(takes the place of a predicate)：我看你～比这么着省劲儿。I think it will take less energy if you do it that way rather than this way.

那儿 nàr 【代】同"那里"

那些 nàxiē 【代】those

那样 nàyàng 【代】(～儿)(denoting nature, state, manner, degree, etc.) such; so; that way (can be used as an attributive, adverbial adjunct, subject or complement)：妹妹不像姐姐～稳重。The younger sister is not as reserved as the elder sister. 你要是再看见～的毛巾,替我买一条。If you see towels like that on sale again, please buy me one. 他下回再～,大家都会反对的。If he doesn't change his ways, everybody will oppose him! ～并不能使他接受教训。What happened didn't teach him a lesson as might have been expected. 这么点儿事就把你急得～! Why does such a trivial matter worry you so?

呐 nà

呐喊 nàhǎn 【动】〈书〉shout loudly; cry out：～助威 shout one's support

纳(納) nà

【动】❶ ◇ receive; accept; admit：闭门不～ refuse to receive a visitor; shut sb. out ❷ ◇ make payments (of any kind)：～捐 pay levies; pay taxes ❸ stitch closely：～鞋底 stitch the soles of cloth shoes

纳粹 nàcuì 【名】Nazi

纳福 nàfú 【动】enjoy an easy and comfortable life; sit back and enjoy

纳闷儿 nà = mènr be perplexed; feel puzzled：突然有个陌生人来找我,我心里很～。I was puzzled by the call of a stranger.

纳入 nàrù 【动】bring into; incorporate in：～正轨 bring sth. within the orbit of; direct sth. onto a normal course 这个项目应该～今年计划。This item should be incorporated into this year's plan.

纳税 nà = shuì pay a tax

捺 nà 【名】(～儿)(of Chinese characters) a diagonal stroke downward to the right"乀"

na

哪 na 【助】modification of sound of 啊,见"啊"ɑ
另见 nǎ

nǎi

乃 nǎi 〈书〉【动】be：粮食～宝中之宝。Grain is the treasure of treasures. 【副】then; only then：为围歼敌人,我军～兵分两路,迂回出击。In order to surround and wipe out the enemy, our troops divided into two parts and outflanked them.

乃至 nǎizhì 【连】(usu. in written)：他是历史学家,但在文学、语言学～自然科学各方面都有丰富的知识。He is a historian, but his knowledge of literature, linguistics and even natural sciences is very extensive. 也作"乃至于"。

奶 nǎi 【名】❶ (woman's) breasts ❷ milk

奶粉 nǎifěn 【名】powdered milk

奶酪 nǎilào 【名】cheese

奶妈 nǎimā 【名】wet nurse

奶奶 nǎinai 【名】❶ grandmother ❷ respectful term of address used by young people to a woman of about their grandmothers' age

奶牛 nǎiniú 【名】milk cow

奶瓶 nǎipíng 【名】❶ feeding bottle ❷ milk bottle

奶糖 nǎitáng 【名】toffee

奶油 nǎiyóu 【名】cream

nài

耐 nài 【动】◇ be resistant to; endure; be able to bear; last; 吃大苦，～大劳 endure extreme hardship and perform difficult tasks

耐烦 nàifán 【形】patient; tolerant (*usu. used in the neg.*): 不～的样子 signs of impatience 他不～地摇了摇头。He shook his head impatiently.

耐火材料 nài huǒ cáiliào heat-resistant material; refractory material

耐火砖 nàihuǒzhuān 【名】refractory brick

耐久 nàijiǔ 【形】durable

耐劳 nài = láo can endure hardship; have stamina

耐人寻味 nài rén xún wèi thought provoking: 这句话～。These words afford much food for thought.

耐心 nàixīn 【形】patient: ～等待 wait patiently ～帮助 help sb. patiently 张老师对学生很～。Teacher Zhang is very patient with her students. 【名】patience: 缺乏～ be lacking in patience 没有～ have no patience with

耐性 nàixìng 【名】patience

耐用 nàiyòng 【形】capable of standing wear and tear; durable

nán

男 nán 【名】◇ ❶ male; man (*used before 的 or before a noun which indicates a person, can also be used by itself in certain set phrases*): ～演员 actor 刚才有人找你。——～的，女的? Someone asked to see you just now. — A man or a woman? ～～女女 men and women 一～一女 a man and a woman ～女青年 young men and young women ～女学生 male and female students ～女平等 equality between man and women ～厕所 men's lavatory ❷ son (*usu. in written language*): 长(zhǎng)～ the eldest son 次～ the second son

男低音 nándīyīn 【名】❶ bass ❷ singer with a bass voice

男方 nánfāng 【名】the bridegroom's or husband's side

男高音 nángāoyīn 【名】❶ tenor ❷ singer with a tenor voice

男孩儿 nánháir 【名】boy

男家 nánjiā 【名】the bridegroom's or husband's family

男女 nánnǚ 【名】men and women: 青年～ young men and women ～老幼 men and women, old and young

男朋友 nánpéngyou 【名】boyfriend

男人 nánrén 【名】*a term for men in general. Does not apply to a particular man, or a particular group of men.*

男生 nánshēng 【名】male student; schoolboy

男声 nánshēng 【名】(music) male voice

男士 nánshì 【名】man; gentleman

男性 nánxìng 【名】the male sex

男中音 nánzhōngyīn 【名】❶ baritone ❷ singer with a baritone voice

男子 nánzǐ 【名】men: ～排球队 men's volleyball team

男子汉 nánzǐhàn 【名】man

南 nán 【名】south: 印度在亚洲的～部。India is in the south of Asia. 美国在加拿大的～面。U. S. A. is to the south of Canada.

南半球 nánbànqiú 【名】the Southern Hemisphere

南边 nánbiān 【名】❶ (～儿) the south: 房子～有一个小花园。There

is a little garden to the south of the house. ❷ the southern area，见"南方"❷, *but less frequently used*

南方 nánfāng 【名】❶ the south ❷ the southern part of any country (in China, 南方 refers to the Changjiang River valley and the area south of the Changjiang River)：中国～盛产大米。South China produces abundant rice. 他是～人。He is a southerner.

南瓜 nánguā 【名】〔个 gè〕pumpkin

南回归线 nánhuíguīxiàn 【名】Tropic of Capricorn

南极 nánjí 【名】South Pole

南极圈 nánjíquān 【名】Antactic Circle

南极洲 Nánjízhōu 【名】Antarctic

南美洲 Nánměizhōu 【名】South America

南面 nánmiàn 【名】south side

南南合作 nán－nán hézuò the economic cooperation between developing countries

南腔北调 nán qiāng běi diào (speak with a) mixed accent

南亚 Nán Yà South Asia

南洋 Nányáng 【名】Southeast Asia in general

南辕北辙 nán yuán běi zhé try to go south by driving north；(*fig.*) head in the wrong direction；act in a way that defeats one's purpose

南征北战 nán zhēng běi zhàn fight in the north and in the south：这支英雄部队～，屡建战功。This heroic detachment fought all over the country, and performed one outstanding military feat after another.

难（難）nán 【形】❶ hard；difficult：这几道数学题真～。These mathematics questions are really very difficult. 这个汉字比较～写。

This character is a bit hard to write. ❷ bad；unpleasant：～吃 taste bad ❸ hardly possible：底稿这么乱，抄的时候很～不出错。The manuscript is in such a mess that one can hardly avoid making mistakes in copying it.【动】put sb. in a difficult position：困难～不倒英雄汉。A hero is never put off by difficulties. 这回可把我～住了。This puts me in a difficult position!

另见 nàn

难产 nánchǎn 【动】❶ (of childbirth) difficult labour ❷ difficult to bring to fruition

难处 nánchu 【名】difficulty

难道 nándào 【副】❶ *makes a rhetorical question more emphatic*：河水～会倒流吗? Could a river reverse its flow? 这些古老的建筑,～不说明劳动人民的智慧吗? Don't these ancient buildings show the wisdom of the labouring people? ❷ *questions the truth of sth. one was certain about*：～我听错了? Could I possibly have heard wrong? 到处都找不到他,～他走了吗? He can't be found anywhere. Could he possibly have left?

难得 nándé 【形】❶ hard or difficult to get；rare；hard to come by：机会～ rare opportunity 这种人材真～。Talented people like that are rare indeed. ❷ seldom；infrequently；rarely：你～来一次,多住几天吧! You don't come here very often. Do stay a few more days!

难点 nándiǎn 【名】difficulty；difficult point："把"字句是汉语的一～。"把"sentence is a difficult point of the Chinese language.

难度 nándù 【名】degree of difficulty (of gymnastic events, etc.)

难分难解 nán fēn nán jiě ❶ neither would give in：他们争吵得～。They kept on qurrelling and neither

could get the upper hand. ❷ reluctant to part with each other：同学们依依惜别，～。The classmates are reluctant to part with one another.

难怪 nánguài 【动】can't be blamed：他是南方人，说不好普通话也～。He is a southerner, and can hardly be blamed for not speaking *Putonghua* very well. 这也～他，一个徒工哪能干这么复杂的活儿? We can hardly blame him since an apprentice is not expected to handle such a complicated job.【连】no wonder：～你最近胖了，天天喝这么多啤酒。No wonder you've put on weight! You've been drinking so much beer. 窗户都打开了，～这么冷呢! All the windows are open. No wonder it's so cold here!

难关 nánguān 【名】predicament；obstacle；difficulty：遇到～ be confronted with a problem 冲破～ overcome obstacles 攻克～ surmount difficulties

难过 nánguò 【动】have a hard time；lead a miserable life：他的日子～。He has a hard life.【形】❶ dejected；saddened；grieved：听到祖母去世的消息，他心里非常～。He was very much grieved to hear of the death of his grandmother. ❷ physically uncomfortable；not feel well：他感到肚子～。He had an upset stomach.

难堪 nánkān 【形】❶ unbearable；hard to endure；intolerable：他说了一些使人～的话。His words were intolerable. ❷ embarrassed；embarrassing：给人～ embarrass sb. 我感到很～。I feel very much embarrassed. 几个人谈僵了，会上出现了～的沉默。Their discussion had reached a stalemate and an embarrassed silence settled over the meeting.

难看 nánkàn 【形】❶ ugly：这本书的封面很～。The cover of this book is ugly. ❷ (of appearance；complexion) unhealthy；pale：他病刚好，脸色还很～。He has just recovered from an illness and still looks very pale. ❸ disgraceful；shameful：考试不及格，多～哪! It's a shame to fail in the examination!

难免 nánmiǎn 【形】unavoidable；hard to avoid：同学之间～有些小磨擦。It is hard to avoid slight frictions among the students. 他工作头绪多，有些考虑不周也是～的。He has so many things to attend to that he can hardly avoid overlooking something.

难能可贵 nán néng kě guì (of behaviour, deeds, etc.) difficult to achieve and deserving much praise：这个机车组三十年来安全行车三百万公里，真是～。Over the past 30 years, this locomotive has gone 3 million km. in complete safety, a rare achievement by the crew.

难色 nánsè 【名】facial expression conveying reluctance or embarrassment

难舍难分 nán shě nán fēn 同"难分难解"❷

难受 nánshòu 【形】❶ physically uncomfortable：胃里～。My stomach is upset. 这件毛衣太小了，穿着～。This sweater is too tight for me. ❷ dejected；feel bad：工作完成得不好，他心里挺～。He felt badly because he didn't do his job well.

难说 nánshuō 【动】it is hard to say；no one can tell：这两种香烟各有各的特点，很～哪种更好些。These two brands of cigarettes each has its good points. It's hard to say which is better. 他什么时候出差还很～。It's hard to say when he'll go away on business.

难题 nántí 【名】baffling problem

难听 nántīng 【形】❶ (of sound, music, etc.) unpleasant to hear；这个歌倒不～。The song is not bad. ❷ (of speech, remark) rude；offensive；coarse；他说话粗野，实在～! He is rough-spoken and his remarks are offensive. ❸ (of deed, behaviour) scandalous；这种事亏你做得出来，说出去多～! How could you have done such a thing! It will create a scandal once it gets out.

难忘 nánwàng 【形】unforgettable；memorable

难为 nánwei 【动】❶ embarrass sb.；press：她不会跳舞，别让～她了。She doesn't know how to dance, so don't press her. ❷ do difficult job；commiserate with sb. who has done sth. difficult：一个人夜里走了这么远的路，真～她。It must have been hard on her to walk such a long way all alone at night. ❸ polite way of thanking sb. who has rendered one a service：～你了，帮我买了菜。It was very kind of you to get groceries for me.

难为情 nánwéiqíng 【形】❶ shy；embarrassed；有什么困难你就说吧，不要～。If you have any difficulty, don't be embarrassed about letting us know. ❷ embarrassing；拒绝他的邀请，真有点儿～。It would really be a shame to decline his invitation.

难闻 nánwén 【形】bad smelling；stinking

难言之隐 nán yán zhī yǐn secrets one is reluctant to reveal

难以 nányǐ 【副】difficult to；hard to (usu. in written language used before disyllabic verb or V-C construction)：～想像 unimaginable～理解 beyond comprehension ～实现 hard to realize ～形容 indescribable ～做到 barely achievable

难字 nánzì 【名】difficult word

nàn

难 (難) nàn 【名】◇ disaster；calamity

另见 nán

难民 nànmín 【名】refugee

难兄难弟 nàn xiōng nàn dì two of a kind；fellow-sufferers

难友 nànyǒu 【名】fellow sufferer

náng

囊 náng 【名】bag；sack；pocket (usu. in written language)

囊空如洗 náng kōng rú xǐ with empty pockets；penniless；broke

囊括 nángkuò 【动】〈书〉embrace；include

囊肿 nángzhǒng 【名】benign tumour；cyst

náo

挠 (撓) náo 【动】scratch：～痒痒 scratch an itch

挠头 náotóu 【形】difficult to tackle

nǎo

恼 (惱) nǎo 【动】be angry；be enraged：我说的话可能不太好听，你可别～我。What I'm going to say may not be pleasant, but please don't be angry with me. 把他惹～了。Somebody infuriated him.

恼恨 nǎohèn 【动】be resentful

恼火 nǎohuǒ 【形】be enraged

恼怒 nǎonù 【形】be angry

恼人 nǎorén 【形】irritating；annoying

恼羞成怒 nǎo xiū chéng nù be

shamed into anger

脑(腦) nǎo 【名】brain

脑充血 nǎochōngxuè 【名】encephalemia

脑袋 nǎodai 【名】the head

脑电波 nǎodiànbō 【名】brain wave

脑电图 nǎodiàntú 【名】electro-encephalogram（EEG）

脑海 nǎohǎi 【名】brain；mind：深深地印入 ～ be engraved on one's mind

脑浆 nǎojiāng 【名】brains；mass of soft grey matter in the head

脑筋 nǎojīn 【名】❶ mental ability；brains；mind：动 ～ use one's brains 费 ～ rack one's brains ❷ ideas；way of thinking：旧 ～ old-fashioned ideas

脑力 nǎolì 【名】mentality；mind；intelligence

脑力劳动 nǎolì láodòng mental labour

脑满肠肥 nǎo mǎn cháng féi the idle who glut themselves

脑膜 nǎomó 【名】meninx

脑膜炎 nǎomóyán 【名】meningitis

脑炎 nǎoyán 【名】encephalitis

脑溢血 nǎoyìxuè 【名】cerebral haemorrhage

脑子 nǎozi 【名】❶ the brain ❷ mental ability；brains；head

nào

闹(鬧) nào 【动】❶ make a loud noise；create a disturbance：又哭又 ～ make a scene 大 ～ 一场 create a tremendous uproar；raise a rumpus 他俩 ～ 翻了。The two of them have had a falling out. ❷ get；make：～ 明白了 get sth. clear in one's mind ❸（of movements）do；make；undertake：～ 风潮 stage a strike ❹（of misfortune）take

place：～ 误会了 create misunderstandings ～ 水灾。There was a flood. ～ 了个大笑话。He made a fool of himself. ❺ give vent to（one's anger，resentment，etc.）：～ 意气 sulk ❻ contend for；strive for：～ 名誉 angling for fame ～ 待遇 contend for higher wages and improved living conditions 【形】noisy；clamorous：屋子里 ～ 得很。The room is very noisy. 这孩子太 ～ 了。This child is making too much noise.

闹别扭 nào bièniu be at odds

闹病 nào＝bìng be ill

闹肚子 nào dùzi suffer from diarrhoea

闹哄哄 nàohōnghōng 【形】noisy；boisterous

闹脾气 nào píqi show ill temper；lose one's temper

闹气 nàoqì 【动】get angry with；be at adds with

闹情绪 nào qíngxù be moody；be dejected；be depressed：小张因为恋爱不顺利正 ～ 呢! Xiao Zhang is in low spirits becuase his romance didn't work out.

闹嚷嚷 nàorāngrāng 【形】noisy；clamorous

闹市 nàoshì 【名】downtown area；busy streets

闹事 nào＝shì make trouble；create disturbances

闹腾 nàoteng 【动】❶ make a loud noise；create a disturbance：别在这儿 ～，有人休息呢! Please don't make so much noise! Someone is sleeping. ❷ make merry；make a joke：俱乐部里大家说说笑笑 ～ 得挺欢。There was a great deal of merry-making going on at the club.

闹笑话 nào xiàohua make a fool of oneself；make a stupid mistake

闹意见 nào yìjiàn quarrel；be on bad terms

闹灾 nào zāi be hit by natural disasters

闹着玩儿 nàozhe wánr ❶ (of a child) be engaged in aimless play ❷ make a joke; joke

闹钟 nàozhōng 【名】alarm clock

ne

呢 ne 【助】❶ *except for questions ended in* "吗", *all other interrogative sentences can take* 呢 *at the end to modify the tone*: 怎么办～? What shall we do? 是你来～, 还是我去～? Will you come to my place, or shall I go to yours? 他吸烟不吸烟～? Does he smoke? ❷ *used after a noun, pronoun, or nominal phrase to form a question*: ① *what the question inquires about depends on the contest*: 这本小说是反映农村生活的, 那本～? This novel depicts life in the countryside. What about the other one? 我们骑车去, 你～? We are going by bike. What about you? ② *without any context, it is a question asking the whereabouts of sb. or sth. when the person or thing is missing*: 你哥哥～? Where is your brother? 我的书～? Where is my book? ❸ *indicates that the action is in progress*: 他们(正在)开讨论会～! They are holding a discussion. 外边下(着)雪～。 It's snowing. 夜班的人睡觉～! The night shift are sleeping. ❹ *gives a reassuring tone*: 离开车的时间还早～。 There is plenty of time before the train leaves. 我也要去～, 你等我一会儿。 I'm going too; please wait for me. ❺ *used at the end of a sentence with a numeral to indicate a large quantity*: 今天有七、八十人来参加义务劳动～。 There are as many as 70 or 80 people coming to do voluntary labour today. 我家离这儿有一百多里～。 My home is as much as 100 *li* from here. ❻ *used to make a pause within a sentence, usu. to emphasize a contrast*: 过去这里是一片荒地, 现在～, 已经开成稻田了。 This used to be a vast wasteland, but now it has been turned into paddy fields. 他要来～, 你就把这篇稿子给他; 他要不来～, 你就给他送去。 If he turns up, give him the manuscript; if he doesn't, have it sent to him.

另见 ní

nèi

内 nèi 【名】◇ (*as opp. to* 外) inside; within: 校～ inside the school 年～ within a year 我们小组连我在～, 共十人。 There are ten people in our group, including me.

内部 nèibù 【名】internal; inside; within: ～矛盾 internal contradictions 国家～事务 the domestic affairs of a country

内地 nèidì 【名】infand; hinterland

内服 nèifú 【动】to be taken orally

内阁 nèigé 【名】cabinet

内海 nèihǎi 【名】inland sea

内行 nèiháng 【形】expert; adept: 她对种棉花很～。 She is very expert at growing cotton. 【名】one with know how; old hand: 在搞无线电方面, 他可是个～。 He is really an expert in radio engineering.

内耗 nèihào 【动】❶ energy consumed by a machine without doing any useful work ❷ losses caused by internal strife

内河 nèihé 【名】inland waterway

内讧 nèihòng 【名】internal dissension; internal conflicts

内奸 nèijiān 【名】hidden traitor;

whistle blower

内角 nèijiǎo 【名】(maths.) interior angle

内疚 nèijiù 【形】prickings of conscience; self-reproach

内科 nèikē 【名】department of internal medicine

内乱 nèiluàn 【名】civil strife; internal disorder

内幕 nèimù 【名】inside story (usu. derog.); what goes on behind the scenes: 了解～ know the inside story 揭穿～ disclose the inside story

内切 nèiqiē 【动】(maths.) inscribed

内勤 nèiqín 【名】❶ office staff (as opp. to those whose work is outside the office) ❷ office work

内情 nèiqíng 【名】the ins and outs of a matter not known to the outside world

内燃机 nèiránjī 【名】diesel engine

内燃机车 nèiránjīchē 【名】diesel locomotive

内人 nèiren 【名】(one's) wife

内容 nèiróng 【名】content (of a book, etc.)

内伤 nèishāng 【名】internal injury

内外交困 nèi wài jiāo kùn beset with difficulties both at home and abroad; beset by problems in private and in the public domain at home and in the workplace

内务 nèiwù 【名】internal affairs

内线 nèixiàn 【名】❶ planted agent; planted informer; undercover agent ❷ (of a telephone) inside connections

内向 nèixiàng 【形】introverted; withdrawn: 性格～ introverted by temperament

内项 nèixiàng 【名】(maths.) inner term

内销 nèixiāo 【动】(of domestically produced goods) sell on the home market

内心 nèixīn 【名】in one's heart of hearts; inner heart; 发自深处 from the bottom of one's heart ～世界 a person's inner world

内衣 nèiyī 【名】〔件 jiàn〕underwear

内因 nèiyīn 【名】intrinsic cause: 外因通过～起作用。 The external causes become operative through the internal causes.

内应 nèiyìng 【名】a planted agent

内在 nèizài 【形】(as opp. to 外在) intrinsic; inherent: ～规律 inherent laws ～因素 internal factors ～联系 internal relations

内脏 nèizàng 【名】internal organs of the body

内债 nèizhài 【名】〔笔 bǐ〕domestic debt

内战 nèizhàn 【名】civil war

内政 nèizhèng 【名】internal affairs

nèn

嫩 nèn 【形】❶ tender; delicate: ～芽 tender shoot 小孩儿皮肤很～。 Young children have very delicate skin. ❷ (of cooking) tender: 肉片炒得很～。 The stir-fried meat slices are very tender. 鸡蛋要煮～点儿。 I want my eggs soft-boiled.

néng

能 néng 【名】❶ ◇ ability; skill: 一专多～ be good at many things and expert in one ～者多劳 a capable person has to do more work ❷ (phys.) energy: 电～ electrical energy 【助动】can; be able to: 星期日他不～参加球赛。 He can't play in the basketball game on Sunday. 明天你们～不～去参观? Can you go visiting the exhibition

tomorrow? 他病好了，～下床了了。He's recovered from his illness, and is able to be up and about. 你不～不来啊! You simply have to come.

能动 néngdòng【形】full of initiative

能干 nénggàn【形】able；capable

能够 nénggòu【助动】同"能"【助动】，*but less colloquial*

能耗 nénghào【名】energy consumption

能见度 néngjiàndù【名】visibility

能力 nénglì【名】ability；capability

能量 néngliàng【名】(phys.) energy

能耐 néngnai【名】skill；ability

能人 néngrén【名】capable person

能手 néngshǒu【名】expert；a good hand

能说会道 néng shuō huì dào have a glib tongue：小王～善于交际。Xiao Wang has the gift of the gab and is a good mixer.

能文能武 néng wén néng wǔ equally good in either civilian or military positions；able to do both mental and manual labour：他～，既会干活儿，又会写文章。He's an all-round person；a good worker, and a good writer too.

能源 néngyuán【名】energy source

能愿动词 néngyuàn dòngcí modal verb

ní

尼 ní

尼龙 nílóng【名】nylon

呢 ní【名】kinds of woolen fabric

另见 ne

呢绒 níróng【名】general term for fabrics

呢子 nízi【名】同"呢" ní

泥 ní【名】mud

泥巴 níba【名】mud

泥浆 níjiāng【名】slush；soft mud

泥坑 níkēng【名】❶ quagmire；mire；morass ❷ (*fig.*) morass；quagmire

泥泞 nínìng【形】muddy：雨后道路～。The roads became very muddy after the rain.

泥沙 níshā【名】silt

泥石流 níshíliú【名】mud-rock flow

泥塑 nísù【名】clay modelling

泥潭 nítán【名】swamp；quagmire

泥塘 nítáng【名】mire

泥土 nítǔ【名】soil；earth

泥瓦匠 níwǎjiàng【名】bricklayer

泥沼 nízhǎo【名】quagmire；marsh；swamp

霓 ní

霓虹灯 níhóngdēng【名】neon light

nǐ

拟（擬） nǐ【动】❶ draw up；draft：～了个发言提纲 draft the outline for a speech ❷〈书〉intend；plan (*usu. in written language*)：我～于月底返京。I plan to return to Beijing by the end of this month.

拟订 nǐdìng【动】draw up；work out；map out：～计划 draw up a plan ～方案 map out a program

拟定 nǐdìng【动】draft：～城市规划草案 draw up a draft of city planning

拟稿 nǐ＝gǎo make a draft：我先拟个稿儿，然后大家补充。I'll draw up a draft first, and then you all can fill it out.

你 nǐ【代】❶ you (*second person, singular*) when used before a monosyllabic collective noun, it

stands for 你们 and usu. occurs in written language：～校 your school ～院 your college ～最好不要一个人去。You'd better not go there all by yourself. ❷ one；anyone：这件事真叫～哭笑不得。This is most awkward. One doesn't know whether to laugh or cry. ～不能不佩服他的洞察力。One can't fail to admire his insight.

你们 nǐmen 【代】you（pl.）

你死我活 nǐ sǐ wǒ huó life-and-death：～的搏斗 life-and-death struggle

nì

逆 nì 【动】◇ ❶ counter；go against（as opp. to 顺）：～历史潮流 go against the tide of history ❷ jar on；have a harsh, irritating effect（on one）

逆差 nìchā 【名】deficit；unfavorable balance；adverse balance

逆定理 nìdìnglǐ 【名】converse theorem

逆耳 nì'ěr 【形】unpleasant to hear

逆反 nìfǎn 【形】rebellious；defiant：～心理 defiance；rebellion defiant complex

逆风 nìfēng 【名】contrary wind；head wind

逆风 nì＝fēng against the wind

逆光 nìguāng 【名】against the light

逆境 nìjìng 【名】adversity unfavourable situation

逆流 nìliú 【名】adverse current；counter-current；（fig.）一股～ an adverse current

逆时针方向 nì shízhēn fāngxiàng counter clockwise

逆水行舟 nì shuǐ xíng zhōu sail against the current usu. used in conjunction with 不进则退；（fig.）

unless one continues to advance, one will certainly fall behind

逆行 nìxíng 【动】go in the wrong direction

逆运算 nìyùnsuàn 【名】inverse operation

逆转 nìzhuǎn 【动】reverse；become worse：形势～ situation took a turn for the worse

匿 nì 【动】◇ hide；conceal：～影藏形 conceal one's identity；lie low

匿名 nìmíng 【形】anonymous

匿名信 nìmíngxìn 【名】〔封 fēng〕anonymous letter

腻（膩） nì 【形】❶（of food, meat, etc.）rich；oily；greasy：这盘肉太～了。This pork dish is too rich. ❷ bored；tired of；sick of：听～了 be sick of hearing；be tired of listening to 这类电影内容都差不多，真看～了。This sort of films are so repetitive, you get tired of seeing them.

腻烦 nìfan 〈口〉【形】bored；tiresome；tired of；sick of：芝麻大的事来回讲，也不嫌～! She keeps bringing up this niggling matter. It seems as if she will never get tired of it. 【动】be bored with；be tired of；hate；be disgusted with：那个女人就爱拨弄是非，大家都～她。That woman likes to gossip and stir up trouble. Everybody is disgusted with her.

腻人 nì＝rén greasy：肥肉～。The fat meat is too greasy.

腻味 nìwei 【动】be fed up：我真～他没完没了地说。I'm really fed up with his endless talk. 【形】sick of；tired of：老吃这一种菜，我都吃～了。We've been eating the same dish for ages and I'm quite fed up with

it.

溺 nì

溺爱　nì'ài　【动】spoil (e.g. a child)

溺水　nìshuǐ　【动】drown

niān

拈 niān　【动】pick up with fingers

拈轻怕重　niān qīng pà zhòng　pick light jobs and avoid heavy ones：对待工作，要勇挑重担，不要～。The proper attitude towards work is to be willing to take on heavy tasks, not to avoid them.

nián

年 nián　【名】❶ year：三～以前 three years ago 他在研究所工作过两～半。He worked in a research institute for two and a half years. ❷ ◇ period；years：近～ the last few years；recent years ❸ ◇ New Year's Day；New Year；Spring Festival：过了～就开学。The new term begins after Spring Festival. ❹◇person's age：～满十八岁 reach the age of eighteen ～过半百 over fifty ～老 be advanced in years

年表　niánbiǎo　【名】chronological table

年成　niáncheng　【名】a year's harvest：今年～不坏。This year's harvest was pretty good.

年初　niánchū　【名】the beginning of a year

年代　niándài　【名】❶ epoch；period；years；time：战争～ in time of war；during the war years ❷ decade：二十世纪七十～ the 70's of the 20th century；the 1970s

年底　niándǐ　【名】the end of a year

年度　niándù　【名】(fiscal) year

年份　niánfèn　【名】❶ a specific year ❷ age (of a thing)

年富力强　nián fù lì qiáng　in the prime of life：他～，工作干劲大。He is in his prime and very energetic in his work.

年糕　niángāo　【名】〔块 kuài〕New Year cake made of glutinous rice flour

年号　niánhào　【名】the title of an emperor's reign

年华　niánhuá　【名】time；years：虚度～ idle away one's time

年画　niánhuà　【名】〔张 zhāng〕New Year picture

年级　niánjí　【名】grade in a school

年纪　niánjì　【名】a person's age：～轻 young 上～了 be advanced in years 您多大～了？(asked of an old person) How old are you?

年景　niánjǐng　【名】a year's harvest

年龄　niánlíng　【名】age (of a person, animal, plant)

年轮　niánlún　【名】annual ring

年迈　niánmài　【形】advanced in age；aged

年轻　niánqīng　【形】young

年轻化　niánqīnghuà　【动】let more younger people replace older people(on different posts)

年少　niánshào　【形】young；youthful

年岁　niánsuì　【名】age

年头　niántóu　【名】(～儿) ❶ year：我参加友协已经三个～了。It's been three years since I joined the Friendship Association. ❷ for a long time；for many years：他这把雨伞可有～了。This umbrella has lasted him for many years. ❸ a year's harvest

年息　niánxī　【名】yearly interest

年限　niánxiàn　【名】period of time (years)；fixed number of years

年薪　niánxīn　【名】annual salary

年月　niányuè　【名】❶ times；era ❷ time（in terms of years）

年终　niánzhōng　【名】the end of a year

粘　nián　【形】同"黏" glutinous；sticky

另见 zhān

黏　nián　【形】sticky

黏度　niándù　【名】viscosity

黏糕　niángāo　【名】〔块 kuài〕cake made of glutinuous rice or flour

黏膜　niánmó　【名】mucous membrane

黏土　niántǔ　【名】clay

黏液　niányè　【名】mucus

黏着语　niánzhuóyǔ　【名】agglutinative language

niǎn

捻　niǎn　【动】twist sth. with one's fingers：～线 twist thread ～麻绳 twist hemp fibres into rope

撵（攆）　niǎn　【动】❶ drive away；expel；oust：把侵略者～出去 drive out the invaders ❷ catch up with：他快要～上你了。He'll soon catch up with you.

碾　niǎn　【动】grind；husk；crush：～米 husk rice 被历史车轮～得粉碎 crushed by the wheel of history

碾子　niǎnzi　【名】mill for husking grain or rice

niàn

念　niàn　【动】❶〈动〉think of；miss：多日不见，甚～。I haven't seen you for a long time, and I miss you very much. ❷ be a student of （a school or particular descipline）：～中学 go to middle school 他是～法律的。He is a law student. ❸ read aloud：～信 read a letter 【名】◇ idea；thought；notion：克服私心杂～ overcome selfish considerations

念叨　niàndao　【动】〈口〉❶ harp on sth.；mutter about：你嘴里～什么呢? What are you muttering about? 这件事我还得跟大家～～。I must talk over this matter with all of you. ❷ talk nostalgically about （sb.）：老王虽然调走了，可是大家还时常～他。Lao Wang has been transferred, but we often talk about him.

念经　niàn = jīng　recite scriptures

念旧　niànjiù　【动】treasure old friendships；nostalgia

念念不忘　niàn niàn bù wàng　bear in mind constantly；cling to

念书　niàn = shū　study or read；study in school；receive an education

念头　niàntou　【名】idea；thought

niáng

娘　niáng　【名】mother

娘家　niángjia　【名】married woman's parents' home

娘子军　niángzǐjūn　【名】women's detachment

niàng

酿（釀）　niàng　【动】❶ make by fermentation ❷ make （honey）：蜜蜂～蜜。Bees make honey. ❸

lead to (sth. disastrous)：～成一场灾祸。A catastrophe is brewing.

酿酒 niàng＝jiǔ make wine

酿造 niàngzào【动】make by fermentation

niǎo

鸟（鳥）niǎo 【名】〔只 zhī〕bird

鸟瞰 niǎokàn〈书〉【动】look down from above；have a bird's-eye view：登山～全城 have a bird's-eye view of the whole city from the top of the mountain【名】a bird's-eye view：世界大势～ a bird's-eye view of the world situation 西湖～ a bird's-eye view of West Lake

鸟枪 niǎoqiāng【名】〔枝 zhī〕gun used for hunting birds；air-rifle；shot-gun

鸟枪换炮 niǎoqiāng huàn pào change from a fowling piece to a cannon — a dramatic change for the better

鸟语花香 niǎo yǔ huā xiāng birds sing and flowers give forth their fragrance

袅（裊）niǎo

袅袅 niǎoniǎo【形】〈书〉❶（of smoke）spiralling upward：炊烟～ Smoke is spiralling upward from kitchen chimneys. ❷（of sound, voice, etc.）linger：余音～。The sound of singing seemed to linger on after the performance was over.

niào

尿 niào【名】urine【动】urinate

尿道 niàodào【名】urethra

尿素 niàosù【名】urea

niē

捏 niē【动】❶ pinch；hold between the thumb and forefinger or fingers：手里～着一枝笔 hold a pen ～住，别掉了! Hold it firmly, don't let it drop! ❷ mould with thumb and fingers：～泥人儿 mould clay figures ～饺子 make dumplings

捏合 niēhé【动】bring together

捏一把汗 niē yī bǎ hàn be seized with great fear or anxiety

捏造 niēzào【动】fabricate

nín

您 nín【代】（polite form of address）you（second person singular）

níng

宁（寧）níng

另见 nìng

宁静 níngjìng【形】（of mind, environment）calm；tranquil；quiet；peaceful：～的夜晚 tranquil evening ～的湖面 the calm surface of the lake 最近，他心里很不～。He has been rather upset recently.

拧（擰）níng【动】wring；twist：～干毛巾 wring out a towel ～耳朵 twist sb.'s ear ～了他一把 give him a pinch 把线～成绳 twist string into rope 大家～成一股绳，力量就大了。If we pool our strength together, we'll be stronger.

另见 nǐng

狞（獰）níng

狞笑 níngxiào【动】smile hideously and hypocitically

柠(檸) níng

柠檬 níngméng 【名】lemon

柠檬酸 níngméngsuān 【名】citric acid

凝 níng 【动】coagulate；congeal；condense

凝成 níng//chéng congeal into；solidify；cement：水蒸气～了小水滴。Steam condenses into drops of water. 肉汤～冻了。The broth has congealed.

凝固 nínggù 【动】coagulate；solidify

凝固点 nínggùdiǎn 【名】(phys.) solidifying point

凝结 níngjié 【动】condense；congeal；coagulate：晨雾～成露珠。The early morning fog has condensed into dew.

凝聚 níngjù 【动】condense：这部名著～着他毕生的心血。In this masterpiece is embodied his lifetime of painstaking work.

凝聚力 níngjùlì 【名】cohesion；cohesive force

凝神 níngshén 【形】(of mind, thought) concentrating fully；with fixed attention：～思索 deep in thought；be absorbed in thought～注视 stare with fixed gaze

凝视 níngshì 【动】stare at；look intently at

凝思 níngsī 【动】meditate；ponder over：对窗～ stand by the window meditating 他陷入了～。He is buried in thought.

凝滞 níngzhì 【动】not flow freely；stagnate

nǐng

拧(擰) nǐng 【动】❶ twist；

screw：～螺丝 tighten a screw 别把瓶盖～得太紧。Don't screw the lid of the jar on too tight. ❷ twist；wrench (meaning, facts, etc.)：你把我的意思搞～了。You have twisted my meaning. ❸ be at cross-purposes：他的想法老跟别人～着。His way of thinking is always at cross-purposes with that of others.

另见 níng

nìng

宁(寧) nìng 【连】同"宁可"

(usu. in written language)：～为玉碎，不为瓦全 prefer to be a broken piece of jadeware rather than an unbroken piece of pottery

另见 níng

宁可 nìngkě 【连】 ... rather than ... (often used in conjunction with 也)：她～不睡觉，也要护理好病人。She would watch over the patient all night long instead of going to bed herself. 为了照顾别人，他～自己麻烦点儿。He would rather take on a burden himself to make things easier for others.

宁肯 nìngkěn 【副】would rather：今晚～不睡觉，也要把这篇稿子写完。I would rather not go to bed tonight than not finish writing this article.

宁缺毋滥 nìng quē wù làn prefer to do without rather than make do with sth. not up to standard

宁死不屈 nìng sǐ bù qū prefer to die rather than surrender

宁愿 nìngyuàn 【连】同"宁可"

niú

牛 niú 【名】〔头 tóu〕ox；cow

牛痘 niúdòu 【名】vaccine：种～ give or get smallpox vaccination

牛犊　niúdú　【名】calf

牛角尖　niújiǎojiān　【名】(～儿) tip of a horn; an insignificant or insoluble problem; 钻～ split hairs

牛劲　niújìn　【名】❶ the strength of an ox; great strength; 把这箱子书搬上楼, 可费了～了。It took great strength to carry this box of books upstairs. ❷ (～儿) stubbornness; obstinacy; 他那股～上来了, 一时不容易说服。When he's in his stubborn mood, he isn't easily talked round.

牛郎织女　niúláng zhīnǚ　long separated man and wife

牛马　niúmǎ　【名】ox and horse; beasts of burden; slave labour

牛奶　niúnǎi　【名】cow's milk

牛排　niúpái　【名】beefsteak

牛皮　niúpí　【名】❶ ox-hide; cow hide ❷ boasting; bragging; 吹～ boast; brag 〜大王 braggart

牛脾气　niúpíqi　【名】the temperament of an stubborn ox

牛皮纸　niúpízhǐ　【名】kraft paper

牛气　niúqì　【形】arrogant; overbearing

牛肉　niúròu　【名】beef

牛仔裤　niúzǎikù　【名】〔条 tiáo〕也作 "牛崽裤" jeans

niǔ

扭　niǔ　【动】❶ turn (round); 〜过头去 turn one's head away (from sb.); look back over one's shoulder 〜过脸来 turn one's face round (toward sb.) ❷ twist; wrench; 〜断铁丝 twist and break a piece of wire ❸ sprain; 〜了胳臂 sprain one's arm 把腰～了 sprain one's back ❹ (of bodily movement) sway from side to side; swing; 她走路～来～去的。She walks with a swaying gait. ❺ grapple with;

wrestle with; 两人～在一起。The two are wrestling with each other.

扭亏为盈　niǔ kuī wéi yíng　make up deficits and make profits

扭捏　niǔnie　【形】be affectedly bashful; 〜作态 assume an affected manner 别扭扭捏捏啦, 痛痛快快地唱一个吧! Don't be bashful! Please sing us a song!

扭送　niǔsòng　【动】seize and turn over

扭秧歌　niǔ yāngge　do the *yangge* (dance)

扭转　niǔzhuǎn　【动】❶ turn round; 〜身子 (of a person) turn round ❷ reverse; turn back; 〜局面 reverse a critical situation

忸　niǔ

忸怩　niǔní　【形】coy

纽（鈕）　niǔ

纽带　niǔdài　【名】tie; link; bond; 团结的～ ties of unity 友谊的～ ties of friendship

纽扣　niǔkòu　【名】〔个 gè〕button

niù

拗　niù　【动】be contrary to; 他怎么老跟你～着? Why does he always disagree with you? 【形】stubborn; obstinate; self-willed; 他脾气很～。He is very obstinate.

拗不过　niù bu guò　be unable to dissuade sb. from sth. or persuade sb. to do sth.; fail to talk sb. out of doing sth.; 你～他, 随他去吧! You won't be able to change his mind. Let him do what he likes! 医生～小兰, 只好同意她带病参加考试。The doctor couldn't convince Xiao Lan, and had to let her sit the exam, sick as she was.

nóng

农（農） nóng 【名】◇ ❶
farming; agriculture：～副产品 agricultural products and products of sideline occupations ❷ peasant; farmer：工、～、兵 workers, farmers and soldiers

农产品 nóngchǎnpǐn 【名】farm produce

农场 nóngchǎng 【名】farm

农村 nóngcūn 【名】countryside; rural area

农会 nónghuì 【名】peasants' association

农活 nónghuó 【名】farm work

农具 nóngjù 【名】farm implement

农历 nónglì 【名】the lunar calendar

农忙 nóng máng busy farming season

农贸市场 nóngmào shìchǎng a market of farm produce (in urban areas)

农民 nóngmín 【名】peasants; farmers

农民起义 nóngmín qǐyì peasant uprising

农奴 nóngnú 【名】serf

农奴主 nóngnúzhǔ 【名】serf owner

农时 nóngshí 【名】farming season

农事 nóngshì 【名】farm work

农田 nóngtián 【名】farm land

农田基本建设 nóngtián jīběn jiànshè capital construction of land

农田水利 nóngtián shuǐlì water conservation

农闲 nóng xián slack farming season

农谚 nóngyàn 【名】proverb relating to farming

农药 nóngyào 【名】general term for insecticide, fungicide, etc.

农业 nóngyè 【名】agriculture; farming

农业国 nóngyèguó 【名】agricultural country

农业税 nóngyèshuì 【名】agricultural tax

农作物 nóngzuòwù 【名】crops

浓（濃） nóng 【形】❶ thick; dense：～雾 dense fog ～茶 strong tea ❷ (of degree or extent) high; great：兴趣很～ take a keen interest in 生活气息～ be imbued with a rich flavour of life

浓度 nóngdù 【名】concentration; density

浓厚 nónghòu 【形】❶ (of fog) thick; (of clouds) dense：～的黑烟 dense black smoke ❷ (of atmosphere, colour, etc.) strong：～的乡土气息 with a strong local flavour ～的民族色彩 (be infused with) rich flavour of a specific nationality 兴趣～ taking a keen interest in sth.

浓眉 nóngméi 【名】heavy eyebrows

浓密 nóngmì 【形】dense; thick

浓缩 nóngsuō 【动】concentrate; enrich

浓郁 nóngyù 【形】(of fragrance) strong

浓重 nóngzhòng 【形】dense; strong; rich：雾气～ dense fog 色彩～ rich colour ～的香味 strong fragrance

脓（膿） nóng 【名】pus

脓包 nóngbāo 【名】boil; pustule; a good-for-nothing

脓肿 nóngzhǒng 【名】abscess

nòng

弄 nòng 【动】❶ do; make (usu. do sth. with one's hands)：这个台灯开关有点毛病，我～不好，你替我～～。There is something

wrong with this table lamp. I can't fix it. Could you please fix it for me? ❷ *used to express an action which can't be concretely described or which it is not necessary to decribe, usu. stressing the outcome of the action*：别把书～脏了。Please take care not to get the book soiled. 哲学上有些概念很不容易～懂。It isn't easy to have a clear understanding of certain terms in philosophy. ❸ get；fetch：你去～点水来。Will you please get some water for me? 村民们～了几条船来，送他们过河。The villagers succeeded in finding a few boats to take them across the river.

弄假成真 nòng jiǎ chéng zhēn what was intended as make-believe has become reality

弄巧成拙 nòng qiǎo chéng zhuō try to be clever but make a blunder

弄虚作假 nòng xū zuò jiǎ resort to deception

nú

奴 nú 【名】◇ slave
奴才 núcai 【名】stooge；flunkey
奴化 núhuà 【动】(in old society) cultivate servility
奴隶 núlì 【名】slave
奴隶社会 núlì shèhuì slave society
奴隶主 núlìzhǔ 【名】slave-owner
奴隶主义 núlìzhǔyì 【名】slavishness；servility
奴仆 núpú 【名】servant
奴颜婢膝 nú yán bì xī servility；subservience
奴颜媚骨 nú yán mèi gǔ servility；sycophancy
奴役 núyì 【动】enslave；keep in bondage

nǔ

努 nǔ
努力 nǔ = lì make great efforts；strive；exert oneself：你只要再努一把力，功课就能赶上。If you make an even greater effort, I'm sure you'll catch up with your studies. 我一定～把工作做好。I'll do my best at my work. 小杨学习不很～。Xiao Yang doesn't work very hard at his studies.
努嘴 nǔ = zuǐ signal with a pont

nù

怒 nù 【形】◇ ❶ angry；furious：～容满面 look very angry 大～ fly into a rage ❷ raging；vigorous：鲜花～放。The flowers are all in full bloom.
怒不可遏 nù bù kě è be unable to restrain one's anger
怒潮 nùcháo 【名】raging tide
怒冲冲 nùchōngchōng 【形】in a great rage
怒发冲冠 nù fà chōng guān be so angry that one's hackles rise；bristle with anger
怒放 nùfàng 【动】put forth in vigor
怒号 nùháo 【动】howl
怒吼 nùhǒu 【动】roar；howl；bellow：雄狮～。A lion is roaring. 狂风～。The wind is howling angrily. 大海在～。The sea is roaring.
怒火 nùhuǒ 【名】anger；fury；rage：满腔～ be filled with anger 胸中～在燃烧 burning with anger ～高万丈 be in a towering rage
怒目而视 nùmù ér shì glare angrily at
怒气 nùqì 【名】anger；fury；wrath
怒视 nùshì 【动】look at with angry

eyes

怒涛 nùtāo 【名】angry waves

nǔ

女 nǔ 【名】◇❶ female; woman（*used before* 的 *or a noun which indicates a person, can also be used by itself in some set phrases*, 见"男" nán）:～学生 woman student; girl student ～浴室 woman's shower room ❷ daughter（*usu. in written language*）:长（zhǎng）～eldest daughter

女低音 nǔdīyīn 【名】❶ alto ❷ singer with an alto voice

女儿 nǔ'ér 【名】daughter

女方 nǔfāng 【名】the bride's or wife's side

女高音 nǔgāoyīn 【名】❶ soprano ❷ singer with a soprano voice

女工 nǔgōng 【名】woman worker

女孩儿 nǔháir 【名】girl（child）

女将 nǔjiàng 【名】woman general

女朋友 nǔpéngyou 【名】girl friend

女人 nǔrén 【名】❶ *a term for women in general*, 见"男人" nánrén ❷ *denotes a specific woman, implying dislike or scorn*:这种～整天议论人长短,少和她来往。That woman does nothing but gossip all day long. Don't have anything to do with her.

女神 nǔshén 【名】goddess

女生 nǔshēng 【名】woman student; girl student; schoolgirl

女声 nǔshēng 【名】（music）female voice

女士 nǔshì 【名】*polite form of address for woman*:"～们,先生们…""Ladies and gentlemen…"

女王 nǔwáng 【名】queen

女性 nǔxìng 【名】the female sex

女婿 nǔxu 【名】son-in-law

女主人 nǔzhǔrén 【名】hostess

女子 nǔzǐ 【名】girl or woman

nuǎn

暖 nuǎn 【形】warm;天～了,暖气都停了。It's getting warm so the central heating was shut off. 【动】warm up:来,喝口酒～～身子。Come and have a little wine to warm you up.

暖房 nuǎnfáng 【名】greenhouse

暖烘烘 nuǎnhōnghōng 【形】comfortably warm

暖壶 nuǎnhú 【名】〔个 gè〕thermos bottle

暖和 nuǎnhuo 【形】warm

暖流 nuǎnliú 【名】warm current

暖瓶 nuǎnpíng 【名】〔个 gè〕thermos bottle 也作"暖水瓶"。

暖气 nuǎnqì 【名】central heating

暖洋洋 nuǎnyángyáng 【形】nice and warm

nüè

疟（瘧） nüè

疟疾 nüèji 【名】malaria

虐 nüè

虐待 nüèdài 【动】ill-treat; maltreatment

虐杀 nüèshā 【动】kill sb. with maltreatment

nuó

挪 nuó 【动】move:把柜子～一下儿 move the wardrobe 我们由南屋～到北屋。We have moved from a room facing north to one facing south.

挪动 nuódòng 【动】move; remove

挪用 nuóyòng 【动】❶ divert

(funds) to some other purpose：专款专用,不得～。A special fund, for a specific purpose, must not be diverted to any other use. ❷ embezzle：～公款 embezzle public funds

nuò

诺(諾) nuò

诺言 nuòyán 【名】promise

懦 nuò

懦夫 nuòfū 【名】coward

懦弱 nuòruò 【形】cowardly；weak

糯 nuò

糯米 nuòmǐ 【名】glutinous rice

糯米纸 nuòmǐzhǐ 【名】glutinous rice film

o

ó

哦 ó 【叹】 *indicates suspicion* oh；what：～，他会说出这种话来？ Oh..., could he really have said such a thing?

另见 ò

ò

哦 ò 【叹】 *indicates realization, understanding, etc.* oh；ah：～，我明白了。Oh, I see. ～，我想起来了。 Ah, yes now I remember it.

另见 ó

ōu

欧（歐） ōu

欧共体 Ōugòngtǐ 【名】 *short for* 欧洲经济共同体

欧姆 ōumǔ 【量】 ohm

欧洲 Ōuzhōu 【名】 Europe

欧洲经济共同体 Ōuzhōu Jīngjì Gòngtóngtǐ European Economic Community

殴（毆） ōu

殴打 ōudǎ 【动】 beat up；fight with one's fists

ǒu

呕（嘔） ǒu

呕吐 ǒutù 【动】 vomit

呕心沥血 ǒu xīn lì xuè shed one's heart's blood；throw oneself into one's work heart and soul；take great pains（over sth.）

呕血 ǒu=xuè spit blood

偶 ǒu

偶尔 ǒu'ěr 【副】 occasionally；once in a while：我最喜欢踢足球，～也打打乒乓球。I like playing football best，but occasionally I play table tennis.

偶发 ǒufā 【动】 accidental；happen by chance

偶合 ǒuhé 【动】 coincidence

偶然 ǒurán 【形】 accidental；fortuitous；contingent；by chance：～事件 accident；a chance event ～发生 accidental occurrence 出现这种问题绝不是～的。The occurrence of such problems is by no means fortuitous.

偶然性 ǒuránxìng 【名】 chance；fortuity

偶数 ǒushù 【名】 even number

偶像 ǒuxiàng 【名】 idol

藕 ǒu 【名】 lotus root

藕断丝连 ǒu duàn sī lián the lotus

root breaks but its fibres remain joined; (*fig.*) two lovers may be forced to part but their love remains

藕粉 ǒufěn 【名】 starch made from lotus root

P

pā

趴 pā【动】❶ lie on one's face；lie prone：猎人～在草丛中。The hunter lay crouching in the bush. ❷ bend over：～在桌子上写字 write bending over the desk

啪 pā【象声】bang

pá

扒 pá【动】scratch；rake（together）；gather up
另见 bā

扒窃 páqiè【动】pick people's pockets

扒手 páshǒu【名】pick-pocket

爬 pá【动】❶ crawl；creep ❷ climb：～山 climb a mountain

爬虫 páchóng【名】reptile

爬山虎 páshānhǔ【名】Boston ivy

爬行 páxíng【动】crawl；creep

爬行动物 páxíng dòngwù reptile

耙 pá【名】rake；harrow【动】rake

耙子 pázi【名】〔把 bǎ〕rake
另见 bà

pà

怕 pà【动】❶ fear；be afraid of：野兔胆小～人。Hares are timid and are afraid of human beings. ～困难就不能搞革新。One cannot make innovations if one is afraid of difficulties. ❷ worry；for fear that；be afraid (*its object is often a S-P construction，V-O construction，V-C construction，etc*.)：～你不认识路，特地来接你。In case you get lost, I came especially to meet you. 我～听错了，又问了一遍。I asked again for fear that I had heard it wrong. ❸ not care to；not like to：我～坐船。I don't like to travel by boat. 他不～冷。He doesn't mind the cold.【副】perhaps；I'm afraid：事情～不那么简单。I'm afraid the matter is not all that simple. 他～又犯病了吧！I'm afraid that he is having another bout of illness.

怕人 pàrén【形】frightening：这种野兽，样子怪得～。This wild beast looks horrible.

怕生 pà=shēng（of a child）be shy with strangers

怕事 pà=shì be afraid of getting involved

怕羞 pà=xiū bashful；shy

pāi

拍 pāi 【动】❶ clap；pat；beat：
~球 bounce a ball ❷ (of picture or
film) take；shoot：~电影 shoot a
film ~照片 take a photo ❸ send (a
telegram, letter, etc.)：~电报
send a telegram ❹ flatter；toady：
吹吹~~ engage in boasting and
flattery【名】(of music) ❶ time：合
~ keep time 四四~ four-four time
❷ beat

拍板 pāi＝bǎn bang auctioneer's
gavel；(fig.) make a final decision

拍板成交 pāi bǎn chéngjiāo strike a
bargain；clinch a deal

拍打 pāidǎ 【动】pat；beat

拍马屁 pāi mǎpì〈口〉flatter；fawn
on

拍卖 pāimài 【动】auction

拍摄 pāishè 【动】take photo；pho-
tograph

拍手 pāi＝shǒu clap hands

拍手称快 pāi shǒu chēng kuài clap
one's hands with delight and satisfaction (at some misdeed being
punished)

拍照 pāizhào 【动】have photograph
taken；take photograph

拍子 pāizi 【名】❶〔个 gè、副 fù〕bat
or racket：乒乓球~ table tennis bat
❷ (of music) time；beat

pái

排 pái 【动】❶ line up；arrange
in order：~好队 queue up；stand in
line 把椅子~成一圈 arrange the
chairs in a circle ❷ drain；get rid
of：~水 drain the water away ❸
rehearse：~戏 rehearse a play ~节
目 rehearse items of a perform-
ance【名】❶ (mil.) platoon ❷

row：前~ front row 后~ back row
【量】❶ row：两~椅子 two rows of
chairs 一~~杨柳 row upon row of
willows ❷ platoon

排版 pái＝bǎn set type

排比 páibǐ 【名】rhetorical use of
parallel constructions

排场 páichang 【名】extravagant
and ostentatious display：讲~ indulge in extravagant and ostentatious display【形】extravagant

排斥 páichì 【动】shut out；exclude；
discriminate against

排除 páichú 【动】dispel；remove；
exclude；surmount：~地雷 remove
a mine ~困难 eliminate difficulties
故障被~了。The obstacles were removed.

排队 pái＝duì ❶ line up；queue up
❷ classify and list

排放 páifàng 【动】❶ arrange：把这
些书报~整齐。Please put these
books and papers in order. ❷
emit：~污水 emit waste water

排风扇 páifēngshàn 【名】ventilating
fan

排骨 páigǔ 【名】spareribs

排灌 páiguàn 【动】drain and irrigate

排行 páiháng 【动】seniority among
brothers and sisters

排挤 páijǐ 【动】crowd out or oust
sb. (to one's own advantage)

排解 páijiě 【动】mediate

排涝 pái＝lào drain waterlogged
farmland

排练 páiliàn 【动】rehearse

排列 páiliè 【动】arrange in order；
rank

排名 pái＝míng arrange names (according to rank, seniority, performance, etc.)

排球 páiqiú 【名】❶〔个 gè〕volley-
ball ❷ volleyball game

排山倒海 pái shān dǎo hǎi topple
mountains and drain seas；(fig.)

irresistible, avalanche-like（force）：以～之势改造大自然 transform nature with irresistible momentum

排水量 páishuǐliàng 【名】（of ship）displacement

排他性 páitāxìng 【名】exclusivity；exclusiveness

排头 páitóu 【名】the first person in a row

排外 pái＝wài ❶ anti-foreign ❷ sectarian tendencies leading to exclusiveness

排尾 páiwěi 【名】the last person in a row

排险 pái＝xiǎn remove danger

排泄 páixiè 【动】❶ excrete ❷ drain

排演 páiyǎn 【动】rehearse

排印 páiyìn 【动】set type and print

排忧解难 pái yōu jiě nàn remove hardships and solve problems

排长 páizhǎng 【名】platoon leader

排字 pái＝zì set type

徘 pái

徘徊 páihuái 【动】❶ pace up and down：他最近好像有什么心事，经常在院子里～。It seems that he has something on his mind as he often paces up and down the courtyard. ❷ waver；hesitate：快拿主意吧，不要再～了。You'd better make up your mind at once；don't hesitate any more. ❸ stagnate：这个厂前几年的产量总是～不前。In the past few years the output of this factory had not increased.

牌 pái

pái 【名】❶（～儿）trademark；brand：这辆汽车是什么～的？What make is this car？ ❷ playing cards：打～ play cards

牌坊 páifāng 【名】memorial archway

牌价 páijià 【名】❶ list price ❷ market quotation

牌楼 páilou 【名】decorated archway

牌照 páizhào 【名】license

牌子 páizi 【名】❶ sign post：在交叉路口立了个"车辆慢行"的。At the crossroads, there is a "Go Slow" sign. ❷同"牌"❶："大前门"香烟是老～了。"Da Qian Men" is an old and established brand of cigarettes.

pài

派 pài

pài 【动】send；dispatch：～人去联系 send sb. to make contact with 【名】clique；school（of thought）；faction：反对～ opposition party 【量】❶ for factions：在讨论当中，形成两～意见。During the discussion, there were two sets of contending views. ❷ for 景象，形势 etc.；the numeral preceding it can only be "一"：一～兴旺景象 a prosperous scene 形势一～大好。The situation is excellent.

派别 pàibié 【名】（of thought）clique；school；（of religion）sect

派出所 pàichūsuǒ 【名】local police station

派遣 pàiqiǎn 【动】send someone on a mission；dispatch

派生 pàishēng 【动】derive from；derivative

派生词 pàishēngcí 【名】derivative

派头 pàitóu 【名】（～儿）（of person）air；style；manner

派系 pàixì 【名】clique；faction

派驻 pàizhù 【动】station；accredit

pān

攀 pān

pān 【动】climb up；scale by gripping sth.：～山越岭 climb up hills and mountains 咱们可以～着这根野藤爬上山顶。We can climb hand over hand up to the top of

the peak by grasping this vine.

攀比 pānbǐ 【动】 vie in rivalry：互相 ~ vie in rivalry with each other；keep up with the Joneses

攀登 pāndēng 【动】 climb up；scale

攀高枝 pān gāozhī be associated with people in a better social or economical position

攀亲 pān＝qīn claim kinship

攀谈 pāntán 【动】 chatter idly；indulge in small talk

攀折 pānzhé 【动】 break (branches)

pán

盘（盤） pán 【名】 plate；tray；dish 【动】 ❶ circle around；wind：辫子~在头上 coil the braid round one's head 汽车~山而上。The car wound its way up the hill. ❷ lay (bricks)：~炕 build a *kang* (brick bed) ~灶 build a brick cooking range ❸ take (inventory)：~库 take stock 【量】 *for things wound flat or things that have sth. to do with a plate or board*：两~磁带 two spools of tape 咱们下一~棋。Let's have a game of chess.

盘剥 pánbō 【动】 exploit by means of usury：重利~ exploit by lending money at an exorbitant rate of interest

盘查 pánchá 【动】 examine thoroughly；cross-examine；interrogate

盘秤 pánchèng 【名】 a steelyard with a pan

盘点 pándiǎn 【动】 make an inventory；take (stock)：售货员正在~存货。The shop assistants are taking stock.

盘费 pánfèi 【名】 travelling expenses

盘根错节 pán gēn cuò jié (of trees) criss-crossing roots and inter-twining branches；(*fig.*) complicated

situation difficult to deal with：~的关系 very complicated network of relationships 大殿前面是一排枝桠 (zhīyā) 纵横，~的古松。In front of the hall is a line of ancient pines with gnarled branches and inter-twining roots.

盘桓 pánhuán 【动】〈书〉 stay；linger

盘货 pán＝huò take inventory：商店今天晚上~。They are taking inventory at the shop tonight.

盘踞 pánjù 【动】 illegally or forcibly occupy：一群土匪~在山里。A gang of bandits have entrenched themselves in a mountain hideout.

盘绕 pánrào 【动】 coil on top of something；twine around

盘儿菜 pánrcài 【名】 a dish of ready-to-cook food

盘山 pánshān 【形】 winding up a mountain：~公路 a highway winding up a mountain

盘算 pánsuàn 【动】 calculate；plan：张大娘~着秋天去看看女儿。Auntie Zhang is planning to go and see her daughter in the autumn.

盘问 pánwèn 【动】 interrogate；crossexamine

盘旋 pánxuán 【动】 circle；wind：顺着山路~而上 wind one's way up the mountain path 山鹰在天空~。The eagle is wheeling in the sky.

盘账 pán＝zhàng check accounts；do an audit

盘子 pánzi 【名】〔个 gè〕plate；dish

磐 pán

磐石 pánshí 【名】 huge rock：稳如~ as firm as a rock

pàn

判 pàn 【名】 ❶ appraise；evaluate；assess：~卷子 mark (examination) papers ❷ judge；decide；ar-

rive at a verdict；～徒刑 sentence to imprisonment

判案 pàn = àn decide a case

判别 pànbié 【动】differentiate；distinguish

判处 pànchǔ 【动】sentence；condemn

判定 pàndìng 【动】judge；decide

判断 pànduàn 【动】judge；decide；determine；～是非 judge what is right and what is wrong 【名】judgement；assertion；你的前提不可靠,怎么能得出正确的～呢? If your premise is not sound, how can you make a correct judgement?

判罚 pànfá 【动】penalize；～点球 be penalized with a penalty kick

判决 pànjué 【动】bring in a verdict

判决书 pànjuéshū 【名】verdict (of a court)

判刑 pàn = xíng pass sentence on

判罪 pàn = zuì declare guilty

盼 pàn 【动】expect；long for；look forward to；hope；盼你早日归来。I look forward to your early return.

盼头 pàntou 【名】good prospects；hope；实现农业机械化以后,我们就更有～啦! Our prospects will be even brighter when the mechanization of agriculture is achieved.

盼望 pànwàng 【动】hope；yearn for；long for

叛 pàn 【动】◇ betray

叛变 pànbiàn 【动】betray；turn traitor

叛国 pàn = guó betray one's country

叛乱 pànluàn 【动】revolt；rebel；mutiny

叛卖 pànmài 【动】commit an act of treachery；betray

叛逆 pànnì 【名】rebel

叛徒 pàntú 【名】traitor；renegade

畔 pàn 【名】side；bank (of a river, lake, etc.)；河～ river bank

pāng

滂 pāng

滂沱 pāngtuó 【形】(of rain) pouring；torrential；大雨～ torrential rain

páng

彷 páng

彷徨 pánghuáng 【动】walk up and down, not knowing which road to take；～不定 be unable to make up one's mind ～歧途 hesitate at the crossroads

庞(龐) páng

庞大 pángdà 【形】colossal；huge；massive；机构～ huge organization ～的开支 massive expenditure

庞然大物 pángrán dà wù colossus；formidable giant；大象虽然是个～,但并不可怕。The elephant is certainly a huge creature, yet one doesn't find it terrifying.

庞杂 pángzá 【形】heterogeneous and disorderly；人员～ staffed with people of every description 这本书内容～。The content of this book is a mishmash.

旁 páng 【名】side；大路两～ both sides of the road

旁边 pángbiān 【名】side

旁的 pángde 【代】other；(sth.) else；～事情 something else ～话

other remarks

旁观 pángguān 【动】look on（instead of taking part in）

旁观者清 páng guān zhě qīng the onlooker sees more clearly

旁及 pángjí 【动】involve additionally

旁门 pángmén 【名】side door

旁敲侧击 páng qiāo cè jī beat about the bush；attack by innuendo

旁人 pángrén 【代】others；other people

旁若无人 páng ruò wú rén act with disregard to others present；(*fig.*) supercilious；very self-confident

旁听 pángtīng 【动】❶ audit a class ❷ be a guest at a meeting

旁证 pángzhèng 【名】circumstantial evidence

膀 páng

膀胱 pángguāng 【名】bladder

磅 páng

另见 bàng

磅礴 pángbó 【形】〈书〉overwhelming；majestic

螃 páng

螃蟹 pángxiè 【名】〔只 zhī〕crab

pàng

胖 pàng 【形】fat；plump

胖乎乎 pànghūhū 【形】plump；chubby：这孩子小脸儿～的真可爱。This child with a chubby little face is so cute.

胖子 pàngzi 【名】a fat person

pāo

抛 pāo 【动】❶ throw；cast；

fling ❷ leave（behind）：赶上去，不要被～在后边。Catch up. Don't be left behind.

抛锚 pāo = máo cast anchor；(of cars) get stuck

抛弃 pāoqì 【动】throw away；abandon；discard

抛售 pāoshòu 【动】sell at a discount in large quantities

抛头露面 pāo tóu lù miàn show one's face blatanly in public

抛物线 pāowùxiàn 【名】parabola

抛砖引玉 pāo zhuān yǐn yù cast away a brick to attract jade；(*fig.*) a polite expression which means that one will give one's (humble) opinions to elicit others' valuable ones；我先说几句，作为～吧！I'll say a few words first, in the hope that you'll give us very valuable opinions.

páo

刨 páo 【动】❶ dig with a pick：～土 dig the earth ～坑 dig a pit ❷ deduct；take off；minus：～去出差的，我们组还有七个人。There are still seven of us in the group, not counting those away on business.

另见 bào

刨根问底 páo gēn wèn dǐ get to the bottom of things

páo

咆 páo

咆哮 páoxiào 【动】roar：～如雷 roar like thunder 大海在～。The sea is roaring.

炮 páo

另见 pào

炮制 páozhì 【动】❶ the process of making Chinese medicine ❷ concoct；cook up (*derog*.)

pǎo

跑 pǎo 【动】❶ run：看谁～得快！ Let's see who can run faster. 汽车在公路上飞～. The car is speeding along the highway. ❷ run away；flee：关好圈门，别让羊～了. Close the pen gate and don't let the sheep get out. ❸ walk：今天我～了好多路. I've walked miles today. ❹ rush around on some business：～建筑材料 go to various places, looking for building materials ～了好几家印刷厂，才找到这种铅字. Only after I'd been to several printing houses did I find this kind of type. ❺ leak：～电 leakage of electricity 水管子～水. The water pipe is leaking. ❻ (of liquid) lose by evaporation：汽油～了半瓶. Half the bottle of gasoline has evaporated. ❼ away (*used as the complement of a verb*)：把几只鸡吓～了 frighten away a few chickens 报纸让风刮～了. The newspaper was blown away by the wind.

跑步 pǎo = bù ❶ double march ❷ run as an exercise

跑车 pǎochē 【名】〔辆 liàng〕a racing bike；a racing car

跑道 pǎodào 【名】〔条 tiáo〕❶ runway ❷ (sports) track

跑电 pǎo = diàn leakage of electricity

跑买卖 pǎo mǎimai be a commercial traveller

跑腿儿 pǎo = tuǐr 〈口〉 run an errand

跑外 pǎowài 【动】travelling agent

跑鞋 pǎoxié 【名】track shoes

pào

泡 pào 【动】soak；steep：～茶 make tea 这些种子在温水里～过了. These seeds have been soaked in lukewarm water. 【名】❶ bubble：冒～儿 bubble up ❷ blister：脚上打了个～. He's got a blister on his foot.

泡病号 pào bìnghào feign to be ill：小李常常不上班，～. Xiao Li often doesn't go to work under the pretext of being ill.

泡菜 pàocài 【名】pickles

泡沫 pàomò 【名】foam；froth

泡沫塑料 pàomò sùliào foamed plastics

泡泡糖 pàopaotáng 【名】bubble gum

泡汤 pào = tāng fall flat；fall through；burst like a bubble；be of no avail

泡影 pàoyǐng 【名】bubble；visionary plan, hope, etc.：化为～ vanish like a bubble；fall through

炮 pào 【名】❶ firecrackers ❷ artillery

另见 páo

炮兵 pàobīng 【名】artilleryman；artillery

炮弹 pàodàn 【名】〔发 fā〕shell

炮灰 pàohuī 【名】cannon fodder

炮火 pàohuǒ 【名】gunfire

炮舰 pàojiàn 【名】gunboat

炮舰外交 pàojiàn wàijiāo gunboat diplomacy

炮楼 pàolóu 【名】〔座 zuò〕blockhouse

炮声 pàoshēng 【名】report of a gun

炮艇 pàotǐng 【名】gunboat

炮筒子 pàotǒngzi 【名】a blunt person a forthright person

pēi

胚 pēi

胚胎　pēitāi　【名】embryo

péi

陪 péi　【动】accompany；keep company：～客人 accompany a visitor 我～你去。I'll accompany you.

陪伴　péibàn　【动】keep sb. company；accompany

陪衬　péichèn　【动】serve as a contrast；set off：蓝蓝的天空把红旗～得更加庄严、美丽。The background of the blue sky makes the red flag, by contrast, even more magnificent and beautiful.【名】foil；set-off：当～ serve as a foil

陪床　péichuáng　【名】(of a relative) staying with an in-patient day and night to offer necessary care

陪嫁　péijià　【名】dowry

陪客　péike　【名】guest invited to help entertain the guest of honor

陪审　péishěn　【动】serve on a jury

陪审员　péishěnyuán　【名】juror

陪同　péitóng　【动】accompany；keep company with：～前往 accompany sb. (to a place) 外宾们在车间主任～下参观了轧钢车间。Accompanied by the workshop director, the foreign visitors went to see the steel-rolling workshop.

陪葬　péizàng　【动】be buried alive with the dead【名】(of objects) be buried with the dead

培 péi　【动】bank up (with earth)：给小树苗～点儿土 bank up the roots of the saplings

培训　péixùn　【动】train；cultivate：～业务骨干 train a core of professionals ～技术工人 train technical workers

培养　péiyǎng　【动】❶ bring up；foster；cultivate：～建设人材 train qualified personnel for construction ❷ culture：～疫苗 culture vaccine

培养基　péiyǎngjī　【名】culture medium

培育　péiyù　【动】grow；breed；bring up：～幼苗 grow seedlings ～良种 cultivate good strains ～新的一代 bring up a new generation

培植　péizhí　【动】❶ (of plants) cultivate：这种植物需要较高的温度，在寒带不易～。This kind of plant needs fairly high temperatures；it is not easy to grow it in cold climates. ❷ (of person) cultivate (derog.)：～亲信 cultivate one's own coterie

赔(賠)　péi　【动】❶ compensate：损坏公物要～。Compensation must be paid for the damage done to public property. ❷ lose (in business)：～钱 lose money (in business)

赔本　péi＝běn　lose one's capital

赔不是　péi búshi　apologize

赔偿　péicháng　【动】compensate；pay for

赔款　péikuǎn　【名】indemnity

赔款　péi＝kuǎn　pay an indemnity

赔礼　péi＝lǐ　apologize：～道歉 make an apology 我错了，向你赔个礼。I was wrong. I apologize to you.

赔钱　péi＝qián　❶ sustain losses in business：做生意赔了钱 ran a business at a loss ❷ compensate：打破玻璃要～。One must compensate for the broken plate.

赔笑　péi＝xiào　smile apologetically or obsequiously

赔账　péi＝zhàng　❶ pay for the loss

of cash or goods entrusted to one ❷ lose money in business

赔罪 péi＝zuì　make an apology to sb. (for sth. one has done)

pèi

佩 pèi

佩带 pèidài 【动】(of a badge, epaulet, pistol, sword, etc.) wear (on the breast, arm, shoulder, or around the waist)

佩服 pèifu 【动】admire；have a high opinion of sb.：我打心眼儿里～他。I admire him from the bottom of my heart.

配 pèi 【动】❶ (of animals) mate：～马 mate horses ❷ compound；mix：～颜色 mix colours ～药 make up a prescription ❸ replace：～零件 replace spare parts ～钥匙 have a key duplicated；make a key to fit a lock ❹ match；accompany：给这首歌词～曲 set the words of this song to music 白花～上蓝底。The white floral pattern against a blue background. 只送一个瓷盘礼太薄，再～上一个花瓶吧! A single porcelain plate is too meagre a gift. Let's add a vase. ❺ suit；deserve (its object is a verb or V-O construction)：我工作做得差，不～当先进工作者。I haven't done my job well. I don't deserve the title of "advanced worker".

配备 pèibèi 【动】❶ allocate；equip；furnish with；provide：～干部 allocate cadres to... 给这个工地～两台起重机 allocate two cranes to the construction site ❷ deploy；furnish：～兵力 deploy troops 火力～很强 concentration of firepower

配餐 pèicān 【名】table-d'hôte；set meal

配搭 pèidā 【动】arrange in pairs or groups，同"搭配" dāpèi。

配电 pèi＝diàn　distribution of power supply

配方 pèi＝fāng　make up a prescription

配合 pèihé 【动】coordinate；cooperate with：在比赛中，他们～得很默契。They coordinated in perfect harmony in the match. 他们俩在工作中能密切～。Those two cooperate closely in their work.

配给 pèijǐ 【动】be rationed

配件 pèijiàn 【名】accessory；part

配角儿 pèijuér 【名】(of theatre) minor role；supporting role

配偶 pèi'ǒu 【名】spouse

配色 pèisè 【动】match colours

配售 pèishòu 【动】ration

配套 pèi＝tào　form a complete set；serialize：设备～ put together a complete equipment 成龙～ link up the parts to form a whole

配音 pèi＝yīn　(of a film) dub

配乐 pèi＝yuè　select passages to serve as background music

配制 pèizhì 【动】compound；make up

配种 pèi＝zhǒng　breeding；mate male and female animals or practise artificial insemination

pēn

喷（噴） pēn 【动】spray；sprinkle；spurt

喷薄 pēnbó 【形】〈书〉(of sun) burst forth；emerge：红日～欲出。The sun is blazing through the morning mist.

喷发 pēnfā 【动】erupt；throw out

喷灌 pēnguàn 【动】sprinkling irri-

gation

喷壶　pēnhú　【名】〔把 bǎ〕sprinkler (for flowers)

喷漆　pēn = qī　spray-paint

喷气发动机　pēnqì fādòngjī〔台 tái〕jet engine

喷气式飞机　pēnqìshì fēijī　〔架 jià〕jet plane

喷泉　pēnquán　【名】fountain

喷洒　pēnsǎ　【动】spray；sprinkle

喷射　pēnshè　【动】jet

喷水池　pēnshuǐchí　【名】fountain

喷嚏　pēntì　【名】sneeze 也作"嚏喷"。

喷头　pēntóu　【名】sprayer；sprinkler

喷雾器　pēnwùqì　【名】sprayer

喷嘴儿　pēnzuǐr　【名】spray nozzle

pén

盆　pén　【名】basin

盆地　péndì　【名】(geog.) basin

盆景　pénjǐng　【名】miniature landscape

盆浴　pényù　【名】bath in a tub

盆子　pénzi　【名】basin

pēng

抨　pēng

抨击　pēngjī　【动】denounce；attack (in speech or writing)

烹　pēng　【动】cook

烹饪　pēngrèn　【名】cooking；the culinary arts

烹调　pēngtiáo　【名】cuisine【动】cook (as a trade or art)

péng

朋　péng　【名】◇ friend

朋友　péngyou　【名】friend

棚　péng　【名】◇ shed

棚子　péngzi　【名】shed

蓬　péng

蓬勃　péngbó　【形】flourishing；vigorous：～发展 develop vigorously

蓬松　péngsōng　【形】(of hair) fluffy

蓬头垢面　péng tóu gòu miàn　with dishevelled hair and a dirty face

鹏（鵬）　péng　【名】◇ roc

鹏程万里　péng chéng wàn lǐ　have a bright future

澎　péng

澎湃　péngpài　【形】❶ surge：江潮～。The river was rising high. ❷ (fig.) surge

膨　péng

膨化食品　pénghuà shípǐn　puff pastry

膨体纱　péngtǐshā　【名】bulk yarn

膨胀　péngzhàng　【动】(phys.) expand；inflate；swell

膨胀系数　péngzhàng xìshù　(phys.) coefficient of expansion

pěng

捧　pěng　【动】❶ hold with both hands：～着碗 hold a bowl with both hands ～着糖果 hold sweets with both hands ❷ flatter；toady to：把他～得太高，没有好处。It doesn't do him any good to praise him too highly.

捧场　pěng = chǎng　flatter

捧腹大笑　pěngfù dàxiào　laugh until one's sides ache：观众看到那个演员的滑稽表演，无不～。Everyone in the audience burst out laughing as they watched the antics of the actor.

pèng

碰 pèng 【动】❶ collide；knock against：别～坏了仪器。Be careful not to bump against and damage the instrument. ❷ meet；encounter：～面 meet each other ～到一个朋友 run into a friend ～到难题了 meet with a difficult problem ❸ try one's luck；take one's chance（*usu. reduplicated or followed by* 一下）：去～～看，他可能有这种花子儿。You can go and try your luck；he may have seeds for this kind of flower. ❹ meet to discuss（*usu. reduplicated or followed by* 一下）：咱们～一下各组讨论的情况。Let's meet and review each group's discussion.

碰杯 pèng=bēi　clink glasses

碰壁 pèng=bì　run one's head against a wall；(*fig.*) be rebuffed；meet with a setback：到处～ get snubbed everywhere

碰钉子 pèng dīngzi 同"碰壁"（*but more colloquial*）：不老实的人非～不可。A dishonest person is bound to meet with setback sooner or later.

碰见 pèng // jiàn　run into；chance upon；meet

碰碰车 pèngpengchē 【名】bumper car

碰巧 pèngqiǎo 【副】coincidentally；by chance：我走到他家门口，他～出来了。As I approached his door, he was just coming out.

碰头 pèng=tóu ❶ meet：他们俩经常～。Those two often meet. ❷ meet（briefly）to exchange information：咱们碰个头，研究一下明天的工作。Let's meet briefly to discuss tomorrow's work.

碰一鼻子灰 pèng yìbízi huī　get snubbed；get thwarted

碰运气 pèng yùnqi　try one's luck；take a chance

碰撞 pèngzhuàng 【动】collide：互相～ collide with each other

pī

批 pī 【动】❶ make notes or comments（often on the original document or report, etc.）：～文件 make instructive notes on a document 报告～下来了。The report has been sent back with comments. 在文章后面～了几句话。He wrote some comments at the end of the article. ❷ criticize；repudiate：挨～ be criticized 【量】batch；group；lot：卸了一～～货。One lot of goods has been unloaded. 到国外去的留学生分三～～走。The students going abroad will leave in three groups.

批驳 pībó 【动】refute；rebut；criticize：～错误观点 refute incorrect viewpoints 遭到～ be refuted

批发 pīfā 【动】wholesale

批复 pīfù 【动】make a written reply to subordinates with comments on their report

批改 pīgǎi 【动】（of composition, etc.）correct and comment on

批量 pīliàng 【形】❶ batch：～生产 batch process ❷ batch：大～输出石油 export petroleum in big batches

批判 pīpàn 【动】repudiate；criticize：～错误思想 repudiate incorrect thinking 【名】criticism；repudiation：遭到严厉的～ be seriously criticised

批评 pīpíng 【动】criticize 【名】criticism

批示 pīshì 【动】write instructions or comments（on a report, etc. submitted by a subordinate）【名】instructions or comments（written on a report, etc.）

批语 pīyǔ 【名】comments

批阅 pīyuè 【动】read and make comments on（official papers, composition, etc.）

批注 pīzhù 【动】annotate 【名】notes; annotations

批准 pīzhǔn 【动】sanction; endorse; approve

拢 pī 【动】❶ throw on（clothes）; drape over one's shoulders; ～着大衣 throw one's overcoat around one's shoulders 广阔的田野～上了银装。The vast fields were mantled in silver. ❷（of bamboo, wood, etc.）split; crack; 竹竿～了。The bamboo pole cracked.

拢肝沥胆 pī gān lì dǎn open and sincere; open one's heart; loyal and steadfast

拢肩 pījiān 【名】shawl

拢荆斩棘 pī jīng zhǎn jí〈书〉hack one's way through brambles and thistles;（fig.）clear obstacles from one's path

拢露 pīlù 【动】❶ publish; announce ❷ reveal; disclose

拢头散发 pī tóu sàn fà shaggy-haired

拢星戴月 pī xīng dài yuè（of work or travel）start very early in the morning and go on until late at night; 巡道工人～地执行任务。The trackmen work very hard from morning till dusk.

砒 pī

砒霜 pīshuāng 【名】arsenic

劈 pī 【动】❶ cleave; split; chop; ～木头 chop wood ❷（of lightning）strike; 雷把那个亭子～了个角儿。Lightning split off a corner of that pavilion.

另见 pǐ

劈波斩浪 pī bō zhǎn làng brave the waves and torrents

劈里啪啦 pī li pā lā 【象声】pit-a-pat; pitter-patter

劈山造田 pī shān zào tián level hills to make fields

劈头盖脸 pī tóu gài liǎn right in the face; 狂风卷着沙石～打来。Sand and stones propelled by the hurricane drove right into our faces.

霹 pī

霹雷 pīléi 【名】thunderclap

霹雳 pīlì 【名】thunderbolt;（fig.）unexpected, sudden event; 晴天～ a bolt from the blue

pí

皮 pí 【名】❶ skin; hide; fur; leather; 羊～ sheep-skin 树～（of trees）bark 植～ skin-grafting ❷ wrapper; cover; 这书得（děi）包个～儿。This book needs a jacket. 饺子～太厚了。The dumpling wrappers are too thick. 【形】❶（of food）no longer crisp; soggy; 这些花生～了。These peanuts aren't crisp any more. ❷ naughty; 小弟弟真～。The little boy is very naughty. ❸ thick-skinned; impervious（to criticism）; 老说这孩子,他都有点儿～了。This child has been scolded so often that he has become indifferent.

皮袄 pí'ǎo 【名】〔件 jiàn〕fur-lined jacket

皮包 píbāo 【名】〔个 gè〕leather case; briefcase

皮包公司 píbāo gōngsī a briefcase company

皮包骨 pí bāo gǔ skinny; all skin and bone

皮鞭 píbiān 【名】〔条 tiáo〕leather whip

皮带 pídài 【名】〔条 tiáo〕leather belt

皮带轮 pídàilún 【名】pulley

皮肤 pífū 【名】skin

皮革 pígé 【名】hide；leather

皮货 píhuò 【名】fur；pelt

皮筋儿 píjīnr 【名】rubber band

皮科 píkē 【名】dermatological department；dermatology

皮毛 pímáo 【名】❶ fur：贵重的～有貂（diāo）皮、豹皮、狐皮等。Among the more expensive furs are marten, leopard, fox, etc. ❷ superficial knowledge：关于这门学问我只知道些～，哪里谈得上研究。My knowledge of this discipline is superficial, so doing research is quite out of the question.

皮棉 pímián 【名】ginned cotton

皮球 píqiú 【名】〔个 gè〕rubber ball；ball

皮实 píshi 【形】❶ sturdy：这孩子很～。This child is very sturdy. ❷ strong：这块表真～，没摔坏。This watch is really strong; the fall didn't harm it at all.

皮箱 píxiāng 【名】leather suitcase；leather trunk

皮鞋 píxié 【名】〔只 zhī、双 shuāng〕leather shoes

皮衣 píyī 【名】〔件 jiàn〕fur clothes；leather clothing

皮重 pízhòng 【名】tare；the weight of wrapping material

皮子 pízi 【名】❶ hide；leather ❷ fur

毗 pí

毗连 pílián 【动】〈书〉adjoin；be adjacent to：山西省南部同河南省～。The southern part of Shanxi Province borders on Henan Province.

毗邻 pílín 【动】同"毗连"

疲 pí 【形】◇tired

疲惫 píbèi 【形】very tired；exhausted：～不堪 very tired 万分～ extremely tired

疲乏 pífá 【形】worn-out；fatigued：走了一天的山路，倒不觉得～。I have walked the mountain road for a whole day, yet I don't feel tired.

疲倦 píjuàn 【形】tired and sleepy：他连坐两天火车，显得很～。He had travelled by train for two days, and he looked worn-out.

疲劳 píláo 【形】fatigued；tired；weary：～过度 be over-tired 不怕～ not mind being fatigued

疲软 píruǎn 【形】❶ fatigued and weak ❷ weaken；slump：市场～ slumping market

疲塌 píta 【形】sluggish；slack：他改变了过去～的作风。He has changed his former indolent style of work. 干活儿不要疲疲塌塌的。Don't slack off when you work. 也作"疲沓"。

疲于奔命 pí yú bēn mìng be kept constantly on the run：工作繁杂，～ be weighed down with a multitude of work

啤 pí

啤酒 píjiǔ 【名】beer

琵 pí

琵琶 pípa 【名】〔把 bǎ〕Chinese lute：他会弹（tán）～。He knows how to play the Chinese lute.

脾 pí 【名】spleen

脾气 píqi 【名】❶ temperament；disposition：急～ quick-tempered 他～很好。He has a good temper. ❷ bad temper：～大 hot-tempered 对儿童应该循循善诱，不要发～。One should teach and guide children patiently step by step and not be short-tempered with them.

pǐ

匹 pǐ 【量】❶ *for horses, etc.*：两～马 two horses ❷ *for cloth*：一～布 a bolt of cloth 三～绸子 three bolts of silk

匹敌 pǐdí 【动】〈书〉match；be equal to；无与～ without equal

匹夫之勇 pǐfū zhī yǒng be foolhardy；foolhardiness

痞 pǐ

痞子 pǐzi 【名】riff-raff

劈 pǐ 【动】❶ split；divide：把丝线～成两股 split the silk thread into two strands ❷ peel off：～白菜帮 peel off the outer leaves of the cabbage ❸ get one's legs or fingers injured by spreading them far apart

另见 pī

劈柴 pǐchái 【名】firewood

癖 pǐ

癖好 pǐhào 【名】fondness for；weakness for；partiality：饮酒这种～对身体有害。Too great a fondness for alcohol is harmful to the health.

癖性 pǐxìng 【名】eccentricity

pì

屁 pì 【名】wind (from bowels)；fart

屁股 pìgu 【名】buttocks

屁滚尿流 pì gǔn niào liú be panic-stricken；be scared out of one's wits

辟（闢） pì 【动】❶ open up；create；pave：在教室后边～块园地种花 dig a plot behind the classroom for growing flowers 黑板报上～个诗歌专栏 start a poetry column in the blackboard newspaper ❷（of rumour）refute；deny

辟谣 pì=yáo deny a rumour

媲 pì

媲美 pìměi 【动】be on a par with；match (in excellence or beauty)；compare favourably with：无锡的太湖可以与杭州的西湖～。Lake Tai in Wuxi rivals Hangzhou's West Lake in beauty.

僻 pì

僻静 pìjìng 【形】quiet and out of the way；secluded：那个疗养所倒挺～。That sanatorium is quite secluded.

僻壤 pìrǎng 【名】remote area；an out-of-the-way place：穷乡～ poor and remote places

譬 pì

譬如 pìrú 【动】take for example

piān

片 piān

另见 piàn

片子 piānzi 【名】❶ film；movie ❷ photograph record

偏 piān 【形】inclined to one side：他一刀下去，切～了，西瓜半个大半个小。His stroke with the knife was off-centre, so the water melon was not evenly divided. 这孩子的脸有点儿～。The baby's face is a little bit lopsided. 【动】move to one side：正要拍照的时候，他把脸一～，照了个侧面像。Just as I was going to snap the picture, he suddenly turned his head and I got his face

in profile. 太阳～西了。The sun is moving to the west. 桌子没摆正,再往左～一点儿。The table isn't quite in the centre; it must be moved a bit to the left. 指标～高,不易达到。The quota is too high; it is difficult to meet. 【副】deliberately (do things contrary to the norm): 大夫劝他不要喝酒,他～喝,结果病又犯了。He deliberately disobeyed the doctor's instructions and continued drinking. As a result, he had a relapse. 庄稼正需要水的时候,天～不下雨。Just when the crops needed water, it didn't rain at all!

偏爱 piān'ài 【动】be partial to sb. or sth.; favour: 老师对学生一样看待,对谁也不～。The teacher treated the students alike and showed no favouritism to any of them.

偏差 piānchā 【名】❶ deviation ❷ error in work made by deviating from principles or policies

偏方 piānfāng 【名】(of Chinese traditional medicine) folk prescription

偏废 piānfèi 【动】attach too much importance to one thing to the neglect of others: 要兼顾积累和消费,二者不可～。Accumulation and consumption should be equally considered; neither should be emphasized to the detriment of the other.

偏激 piānjī 【形】extreme; radical: 思想～ be extreme in one's thinking ～情绪 radical sentiments 这个意见很～。This is a radical opinion.

偏见 piānjiàn 【名】prejudice; bias

偏离 piānlí 【动】deviate; diverge

偏旁 piānpáng 【名】(of Chinese characters) component, e.g. "氵" and "可" in "河".

偏僻 piānpì 【形】remote; out-of-the-way: ～的山村 remote mountain village

偏偏 piānpiān 【副】❶ indicates that sth. turns out just the opposite of what one expected or what is normal. Sometimes it implies bad luck: 正在我要出去的时候,天～下起雨来了。Just as I was going out, it started to rain. 他们兄弟几个,老二一直身体不好,可是～他活得年纪最大。Of all the brothers, it was the second one whose health was poorest, yet he was the one who lived the longest. 明天要赛足球了,我们的主力队员小李～把脚扭伤了。We have a football game tomorrow, and one of our top players, Xiao Li, had to go and sprain his ankle! ❷ singles out an exception, usu. with an element of dissatisfaction, surprise, praise, etc.: 他在学校里门门功课都好,～体育不行。He is good at every subject in school, with the sole exception of physical education. 老江什么都吃,不知道为什么～不吃鸡蛋。Lao Jiang isn't particular about food at all, so it surprises me that he doesn't eat eggs of all things!

偏瘫 piāntān 【动】hemiplegia

偏袒 piāntǎn 【动】be partial to; take sides on: 我不会～哪一个的,他们俩谁错我就批评谁。I won't take sides. I'll criticize whichever of the two is wrong.

偏听偏信 piān tīng piān xìn be partial to; hear and believe a one-sided story

偏向 piānxiàng 【动】同"偏袒", be biased towards: 裁判员要公正,不能～某一方。A referee should be impartial and not biased towards either side. 【名】erroneous tendency; deviation: 纠正不关心业务的～ reverse the erroneous tendency of neglecting professional training

偏心 piānxīn 【形】partial: 母亲对大女儿有点儿～。The mother was

partial to her eldest daughter.

偏远 piānyuǎn 【形】faraway；remote：～地区 remote area

偏重 piānzhòng 【动】lay special stress on one to the detriment of the other：这几门功课都要学好，不能只～某一门。We should study all these subjects equally well and not stress one to the detriment of the rest.

篇 piān 【量】for article, etc.：一～论文 a thesis 两～手稿 two manuscripts

篇幅 piānfu 【名】❶ the length of an article：这篇社论～不长。This editorial is not long. ❷ total number of pages in a book, newspaper or periodical：这本杂志～很大，共有二百多页。This magazine has many pages, more than two hundred in all.

篇目 piānmù 【名】table of contents

篇章 piānzhāng 【名】sections and chapters；a piece of writing：～结构 structure of a piece of writing 历史的新～（fig.）a new chapter in history 光辉的～ a brilliant chapter

翩 piān

翩翩 piānpiān 【形】❶ (of dancing or the flying of birds, etc.) graceful and light：～起舞 dance gracefully ❷ (of one's bearing) graceful and elegant：风度～ with graceful and elegant bearing

翩跹 piānxiān 【形】elegantly and swiftly

pián

便 pián
另见 biàn

便宜 piányi 【形】cheap；inexpensive 【名】small unjustified advantage：占～ gain unfair advantage 不要贪～。Don't covet small gains. 【动】let off lightly：这一回可～你了。We let you off lightly this time.

piàn

片 piàn 【名】❶ (～儿) slice：把馒头切成～ cut the steamed bun into slices ❷ subdivision of a larger area：分～管理 divide into small areas to be administered 【动】slice (into thin slices)：把肉皮～下来 slice off the skin from the meat 【量】❶ tablet, slice, etc.：两～面包 two slices of bread 一～药 one tablet ❷ for 景象，气象，心意，etc. the only numeral which can be used is "一"：一～欢乐景象 a joyful scene 一～好心 with pure good will
另见

片段 piànduàn 【名】(of writing, novel, life, etc.) passage；section；part；fragment 也作"片断"。

片警 piànjǐng 【名】policeman of a beat

片刻 piànkè 【名】a moment；a little while：休息～ have a short rest 停留～ stop for a minute

片面 piànmiàn 【形】❶ unilateral：～之词 version given by one party only ～撕毁协议 tear up an agreement unilaterally ❷ one-sided：看问题～ one-sided way of thinking

片面性 piànmiànxìng 【名】one-sidedness

片纸只字 piàn zhǐ zhī zì fragments of writing

骗（騙） piàn 【动】❶ deceive；fool：他真来了吗？你可别～人。Is it not true that he has come? You're not pulling my leg, are you? 我不知道他们在跟我开玩笑，所

以受了～。I was fooled because I didn't know that they were just joking. ❷ cheat；swindle：～钱 cheat sb. out of his money

骗局 piànjú 【名】fraud；swindle；double-dealing；trickery

骗取 piànqǔ 【动】get sth. by cheating：～钱财 cheat sb. out of money and property ～信任 worm one's way into sb.'s confidence

骗人 piàn＝rén deceive people

骗术 piànshù 【名】trick；fraud

骗子 piànzi 【名】deceiver；swindler

piāo

劏 piāo

劏悍 piāohàn 【形】brave and agile；quick and fierce：勇敢～的牧民 courageous and fierce herdsmen

劏窃 piāoqiè 【动】plagiarize：～别人的成果是可耻的。Taking credits for other people's achievements is a shameful thing to do.

漂 piāo 【动】drift；float
另见 piǎo；piào

漂泊 piāobó 【动】drift aimlessly；wander from place to place；lead a wandering life 也作"飘泊"。

漂浮 piāofú 【动】float：湖面上～着一朵朵的睡莲。Water-lilies are floating on the lake. 【形】(fig.) (of a person or his style of work) superficial；slipshod：工作作风～ a slipshod work-style 也作"飘浮"。

漂流 piāoliú 【动】❶ drift about ❷ lead a wandering life；drift：他在外地～。He is roaming over the interior of the country. 也作"飘流"。

漂游 piāoyóu 【动】wander；drift；roam

缥（縹） piāo

缥缈 piāomiǎo 【形】misty；elusive；

intangible：烟雾～ misty 虚无～ visionary；illusory

飘（飄） piāo 【动】float (in the air)；flutter：窗外～着雪花。Outside the window, snowflakes were floating in the air. 田野里～来菜花香。The fragrance of the rape flowers wafted over from the fields.

飘带 piāodài 【名】ribbon；streamer

飘荡 piāodàng 【动】flutter；drift about；float：气球在空中～。A balloon floated in the air. 小船顺水～。The small boat drifted down the river.

飘浮 piāofú 【动】同"漂浮"piāofú

飘渺 piāomiǎo 【形】同"缥缈"piāomiǎo

飘飘然 piāopiāorán 【形】self-satisfied；smug；be carried away with one's own importance (derog.)：不要一听到表扬就～。Don't let a little praise make you smug.

飘扬 piāoyáng 【动】flutter；fly in the wind：五星红旗迎风～。The Five-Starred Red Flag of China fluttered in the wind.

飘摇 piāoyáo 【动】flutter in the wind

piáo

瓢 piáo 【名】half of a dried gourd which serves as a dipper

瓢泼大雨 piáopō dàyǔ torrential rain；downpour

piǎo

漂 piǎo 【动】❶ 同"漂白" ❷ rinse；wash out (stains, dirt, etc.)：～丝 rinse silk ～麻 rinse flax 用清水把洗过的衣服～干净 rinse the

washing in clean water
另见 piāo；piào

漂白　piǎobái　【动】bleach

漂白粉　piǎobáifěn　【名】powdered
bleach

漂洗　piǎoxǐ　【动】rinse

瞟　piǎo　【动】take a glance at；
look askance at：～了他一眼 take a
glance at him

piào

票　piào　【名】〔张 zhāng〕ticket

票房　piàofáng　【名】box office；
ticket window

票价　piàojià　【名】price of a ticket

票据　piàojù　【名】❶ bill；note ❷
voucher；receipt

票面　piàomiàn　【名】face value

票子　piàozi　【名】banknote；bill

漂　piào
另见 piāo；piǎo

漂亮　piàoliang　【形】❶ handsome；
good-looking：这人长得～。This
man is very handsome. 演员的服装
很～。The costumes of the actors
were beautiful. ❷ brilliant；excel-
lent：他的汉语说得很～。He speaks
excellent Chinese.

漂亮话　piàolianghuà　【名】fine
words；high-sounding words：别光
说～，要脚踏实地（dì）去做。Don't
just mouth high-sounding words；
get down to work!

piē

撇　piē　【动】❶ skim：～油 skim
off the oil ❷ cast aside：他把自己的
家事～在一边，照顾别人去了。He put
his own domestic affairs to one
side, and went to look after others.

另见 piě

撇开　piē // kāi　put aside；by-pass：
咱们～这个问题，先谈其他的事吧!
Let's put this question aside and
talk about other matters.

piě

撇　piě　【动】throw；skip；put
aside：～砖头 throw away a piece
of brick 我早就把那件事～到脑后
了。I put this matter out of my
mind long ago. 【名】（～儿）（of
Chinese characters) a down stroke
to the left "丿"【量】for sth. in the
shape of the stroke "丿" of a Chinese character：两～胡子 two small
tufts of moustache
另见 piē

撇嘴　piě = zuǐ　curl one's lip（in disdain)：她看了小摊上的食品之后，直
～。She kept on curling her lips
when she looked at the food on
the stall.

pīn

拼　pīn　【动】❶ put together；
piece together；knock together：两
个音素连在一起，～成一个音。Two
morphemes are linked to form a
sound. 用几块木板～了一个小方凳
Several bits of wood were pieced
together to make a stool. ❷ no
matter what the risk；do sth. regardless of the danger；do sth.
desperately：～刺刀 bayonet charge
我跟你～了。I'll fight it out with
you.

拼搏　pīnbó　【动】struggle；wrestle
with：顽强～ struggle, obstinately 学
习他的～精神 learn from his fighting spirit

拼凑　pīncòu　【动】piece together；
patch：～雇佣军 put together a

band of mercenaries 这个手提包是用碎皮子～起来的。This handbag was pieced together out of bits of leather.

拼接 pīnjiē【动】piece together

拼命 pīn=mìng　risk one's life for; fight tooth and nail; (fig.) do one's utmost: ～学习 throw oneself wholeheartedly into study 拼着命干 work with all one's might

拼盘儿 pīnpánr【名】a cold plate (of assorted meats, eggs, vegetables, etc.)

拼死 pīnsǐ【副】(struggle) desperately: ～地斗争 fight to the death ～拼活地干 work flat out; work with all one's might

拼死拼活 pīnsǐ-pīnhuó put up a life-and-death struggle; struggle desperately

拼写 pīnxiě【动】❶ spell ❷ transliterate

拼音 pīn=yīn　transcribe into a phonetic alphabet; phoneticize

拼音文字 pīnyīn wénzì　alphabetic (system of) writing

拼音字母 pīnyīn zìmǔ　phonetic alphabet

pín

贫（貧） pín【形】❶ ◇ poor; poverty-stricken: 一～如洗 be destitute ❷ ◇ lack; be short of ❸〈口〉garrulous; verbose: 这个人真～,老说些无聊的话。This person is really a chatterbox. He always talks nonsense.

贫乏 pínfá【形】meagre; needy: 生活经验～ lack experience of life 知识～ be lacking in knowledge

贫寒 pínhán【形】poor; needy: 家境～ a poor family; a family living in poverty

贫瘠 pínjí【形】(of land) poor; arid

贫苦 pínkǔ【形】poor; poverty-stricken

贫困 pínkùn【形】poor; hard up; impoverished

贫民 pínmín【名】poor people

贫民窟 pínmínkū【名】slum

贫穷 pínqióng【形】poor; poverty-stricken

贫血 pínxuè【名】anaemia

贫嘴 pínzuǐ【名】garrulous; voluble: 耍～ be garrulous

频（頻）pín

频传 pínchuán【动】keep pouring in; keep spreading: 捷报～。Good news kept flooding in.

频道 píndào【名】frequency channel

频繁 pínfán【形】frequent: 来往很～ have frequent contacts with 活动很～ frequent activities

频率 pínlǜ【名】frequency

频谱 pínpǔ【名】frequency spectrum

pǐn

品 pǐn【名】◇ goods; articles 【动】evaluate; savour: ～茶 taste and evaluate tea ～～味儿 savour the flavour of sth.

品尝 pǐncháng【动】taste; savor: 这是她的拿手菜,请大家～～。This is her best dish, please try it.

品德 pǐndé【名】(of person) moral character

品格 pǐngé【名】(of person) character: ～高尚 noble character

品牌 pǐnpái【名】brand

品头论足 pǐn tóu lùn zú ❶ make frivolous remarks on a woman's appearance ❷ comment on and find fault with (sb. or sth.) 也说

"评头论足"、"评头品足"。

品位 pǐnwèi 【名】grade

品行 pǐnxíng 【名】(personal) conduct; behaviour (which shows one's character)

品性 pǐnxìng 【名】moral character

品质 pǐnzhì 【名】❶ (of person) character; character trait; quality; 舍己为人的高贵～ the noble quality of making sacrifices or others' sake ❷ (of goods, articles) quality; 这种绸子～优良。This is fine quality silk.

品种 pǐnzhǒng 【名】variety

pìn

聘　pìn

聘金 pìnjīn 【名】money paid to sb for his service; betrothal money

聘礼 pìnlǐ 【名】betrothal gifts; gifts offered for soliciting sb.'s service

聘请 pìnqǐng 【动】invite; engage; employ; ～专家 engage an expert ～一位老运动员担任教练。An old athlete was engaged as a coach.

聘任 pìnrèn 【动】appoint; engage; ～汉语教师 engage a Chinese language teacher

聘书 pìnshū 【名】〔份儿 fènr〕letter of appointment

聘用 pìnyòng 【动】employ; engage; appoint to a position

pīng

乒　pīng

乒乓 pīngpāng 【象声】rattling 【名】table tennis

乒乓球 pīngpāngqiú 【名】❶〔个 gè〕ping-pong ball ❷ table tennis; pingpong

píng

平　píng 【形】❶ flat; smooth; level; 把坑填～ fill in a pit until it is level 玻璃板很～。The plate glass is flawless. ❷ on a level with; 在足球比赛中，我们两队踢～了。The match between our two teams ended in a draw. 【动】❶ level; ～了这块地，好种蓖麻 level this piece of land so that castor beans can be grown on it 把路～一～ level the road ❷ suppress; put down; ～叛 suppress a rebellion ～乱 put down a riot ❸ pacify; appease; ～民愤 appease the anger of the masses

平安 píng'ān 【形】safe; peaceful; ～到达 arrive safely 一路～ Bon voyage!

平白无故 píngbái wúgù without any reason; groundless; 你～地发什么火？Why are you getting angry for no reason at all?

平步青云 píng bù qīng yún rise to the top of one's career over night; meteoric rise to a high social position

平常 píngcháng 【形】ordinary; common; 一个～的人 an ordinary person 不～的一年 an unusual year 在班里他的学习成绩很～。He is just a run of the mill student academically. 别看他平平常常的样子，他是我们厂的总工程师。Don't judge people by appearances only — he is the chief engineer of our factory. 【名】ordinary times; usually; ～他不喝酒，到过年过节才喝两杯。He doesn't drink as a rule, and drinks only a little at festival times.

平川 píngchuān 【名】vast plains

平淡 píngdàn 【形】insipid; uninteresting; dull; ～无奇 pedestrian ～无味 insipid 这个故事本来很精彩，可惜

他讲得太~了。This is a marvellous story. Unfortunately, he told it in such a way that it fell flat.

平等 píngděng 【形】equal：~待人 treat people equally 国家无论大小，应该一律~。Countries, whether big or small, should be equal. 【名】equality：中国实现了各民族间的~。In China, equality has been achieved among the various nationalities.

平等互利 píngděng hùlì equality and mutual benefit；reciprocity based on equality

平地 píngdì 【名】flat ground；level ground

平定 píngdìng 【动】put down；quell；suppress：~叛乱 suppress a riot 愤怒的情绪久久不能~。For a long time, he could not suppress his feelings of anger.

平凡 píngfán 【形】ordinary；common；undistinguished：在~的岗位上，可以做出不~的贡献。One can still make extraordinary contributions in an ordinary job.

平反 píng＝fǎn redress (a mishandled case)；rehabilitate

平方 píngfāng 【名】(maths.) square

平方根 píngfānggēn 【名】(maths.) square-root

平方公里 píngfānggōnglǐ 【量】square kilometre

平方米 píngfāngmǐ 【量】square metre

平房 píngfáng 【名】〔间 jiān〕one-storey house

平分 píngfēn 【动】divide equally

平分秋色 píngfēn qiūsè share equally (honour, power, glory, etc.)：从这次游泳比赛得奖情况看，两队~，不相上下。Judging from the results of this swim-meet, the two teams are equally good.

平衡 pínghéng 【形】❶ (phys.) balanced ❷ balance；equilibrium：收支~ balance between income and expenditure 【动】balance：把两个组的强弱劳力~一下。Balance the two groups so that they are equal in man-power.

平衡木 pínghéngmù 【名】❶ balance beam ❷ (gym.) balance beam

平滑 pínghuá 【形】level and smooth

平价 píngjià 【名】❶ normal price；fixed price ❷ par；parity

平静 píngjìng 【形】quiet；tranquil

平均 píngjūn 【动】average：把两个数~一下 take the average of the two numbers 【形】equal；average：分得很~ equally divided ~分配 fair division 这班学生~年龄十六岁。The average age of the students in this class is sixteen.

平均主义 píngjūnzhǔyì 【名】equalitarianism；egalitarianism

平炉 pínglú 【名】open hearth furnace

平面 píngmiàn 【名】(maths.) plane

平面几何 píngmiàn jǐhé plane geometry

平面图 píngmiàntú 【名】plane figure

平民 píngmín 【名】the common people；the public

平铺直叙 píng pū zhí xù (of writing or speech) tell in a straightforward, matter-of-fact way：这篇文章的缺点是~，不生动。This article's weakness is that the writing is too flat.

平起平坐 píng qǐ píng zuò sit as equals at the same table；be on an equal footing

平日 píngrì 【名】ordinary days

平生 píngshēng 【名】during one's lifetime：他~没犯过什么严重错误，但也没有什么作为。He didn't commit any serious errors during his lifetime, but nor did he accomplish anything.

平时 píngshí 【名】in normal times；

ordinarily

平素　píngsù　【名】ordinarily；always；usually：他～好(hào)学。He has always been fond of learning. 老郑～乐于助人。Lao Zheng is always ready to help others.

平坦　píngtǎn　【形】(of land) flat；even：～宽阔的公路 a broad and level road 前进的道路是不～的。The road of progress is never smooth.

平稳　píngwěn　【形】steady；even；stable：汽车开得很～。The car ran very smoothly. 局势～。The situation was stable.

平息　píngxī　【动】put down；subside；stamp out：一场风波终于逐渐～下去了。The controversy eventually subsided.

平心静气　píng xīn jìng qì　dispassionately；calmly：别激动，咱们～地谈谈。Don't get touchy. Let's talk about it calmly.

平信　píngxìn　【名】〔封 fēng〕ordinary mail

平行　píngxíng　【形】❶ on an equal footing；of equal rank：～单位 units at the same level ❷ simultaneous：～作业 parallel operations ❸ (math.) parallel：两条～的直线 two parallel lines

平行四边形　píngxíng sìbiānxíng　parallelogram

平行线　píngxíngxiàn　【名】〔条 tiáo〕parallel lines

平抑　píngyì　【动】keep under control；stabilize：～物价 stabilize prices

平易近人　píngyì jìn rén　amiable and approachable

平原　píngyuán　【名】plain

平整　píngzhěng　【动】(of land) level：～土地 level the land 把这个足球场～一下。Level the football field. 【形】level：菜园里的地全都是平平整整的。The plots in the vegetable garden are all very level.

平正　píngzheng　【形】neat and smooth：洗干净的枕套和床单叠得很～。The clean sheets and pillow slips are neatly and smoothly folded.

平装　píngzhuāng　【名】paperback

评（評）

评　píng　【动】judge；evaluate：～分数 give marks ～上了一等功 awarded the First Class Order of Merit 谁是谁非请大家来～～。Let everyone concerned judge between us.

评比　píngbǐ　【动】compare and appraise：年终～ make annual appraisal ～产品质量 compare and appraise the quality of the products

评定　píngdìng　【动】judge；evaluate；assess：～考试成绩 evaluate the results of the examination ～优劣 judge on the quality

评分　píng = fēn　mark (papers, etc.)

评功　píng = gōng　appraise one's merits

评估　pínggū　【动】appraise；evaluate

评级　píng = jí　grade

评价　píngjià　【动】appraise：～历史人物 appraise historical figures ～文学作品 appraise a literary work 【名】appraisal；evaluation：学术界对这位数学家的研究成果给予高度的～。This mathematician's research is highly valued in academic circles.

评奖　píng = jiǎng　select recipients for awards

评理　píng = lǐ　decide who is right；judge right and wrong：你们两个人不要争吵，让大家来评评理。Don't quarrel, you two. Let others judge between you.

评论　pínglùn　【动】comment on 【名】commentary

评论家　pínglùnjiā　【名】critic；re-

viewer

评论员 pínglùnyuán 【名】 commentator

评判 píngpàn 【动】 pass judgement; decide

评述 píngshù 【动】 comment on

评说 píngshuō 【动】 appraise; comment

评头论足 píng tóu lùn zú 同"品头论足" pǐn tóu lùn zú

评选 píngxuǎn 【动】 choose through public appraisal: ～先进工作者 choose advanced workers ～积极分子 select activists

评议 píngyì 【动】 appraise through discussion: 经过大家～,他再次担任队长。After discussion, he was re-elected the team leader.

评语 píngyǔ 【名】 comment

评注 píngzhù 【动】 make comments and annotations (on a book or article): ～《红楼梦》 make comments and annotations on *The Dream of the Red Chamber* 【名】 notes and commentary

苹(蘋) píng

苹果 píngguǒ 【名】 ❶ apple ❷ apple tree

凭(憑) píng 【名】 ◇ evidence; proof: 不足为～ can't serve as evidence 【动】 rely on; be based on: ～票入场 admission by ticket only 作战不能光～勇敢,还要机智灵活。In war, one can't rely on courage only, one must be quick-witted and resourceful. 【连】 no matter: ～你跑多快,我也能追上。No matter how fast you run, I can catch up with you. 这么多粮食,～你怎么吃也吃不完。You can't exhaust such a large reserve of grain no matter how much you eat.

凭单 píngdān 【名】 voucher

凭借 píngjiè 【动】 resort to; rely

on; by means of: 人类思想的交流是～语言进行的。Language is the medium for communication of thought among human beings.

凭据 píngjù 【名】 proof; evidence

凭空 píngkōng 【副】 without basis; groundless; out of thin air: ～设想 figment of the imagination ～捏造 fabricate

凭信 píngxìn 【动】 trust; believe: 一面之词不可～。A one-sided view is not reliable.

凭证 píngzhèng 【名】 proof; certificate

屏 píng

屏风 píngfēng 【名】〔扇 shàn〕screen

屏幕 píngmù 【名】 screen

屏障 píngzhàng 【名】 protective screen: 这些大山是平原的天然～。These mountains form a natural screen on one side of the plain.

瓶 píng 【名】◇ bottle

瓶装 píngzhuāng 【形】 bottled

瓶子 píngzi 【名】〔个 gè〕bottle

pō

坡 pō 【名】 slope

坡地 pōdì 【名】 sloping fields; fields on hillside

坡度 pōdù 【名】 slope; gradient

泼(潑) pō 【动】 pour out; splash: ～水 sprinkle water; splash water

泼辣 pōlà 【形】 ❶ bold and vigorous; not afraid of difficulties and very energetic: 工作～ be bold and vigorous in one's work 他办事很～。He does things vigorously and smartly. ❷ shrewish

泼冷水 pō lěngshuǐ pour cold water

on; dampen sb.'s spirits: 让他继续学小提琴吧，不要给他～。Let him go on learning to play the violin and don't pour cold water on his efforts.

颇（頗）pō 【副】〈书〉rather; quite; fairly; considerable: ～不容易 rather difficult ～有感触 deeply touched

颇为 pōwéi 【副】quite; rather: ～满意 quite satisfactory

pó

婆 pó 【名】◇old woman

婆家 pójiā 【名】husband's family

婆婆 pópo 【名】❶ husband's mother ❷ old woman ❸ grandmother (*used in some parts of China*)

婆婆妈妈 pópomāmā 【形】❶ mawkish ❷ slow in action and longwinded in speech

婆娑 pósuō 【形】〈书〉whirling; dancing

婆媳 póxí 【名】mother-in-law and daughter-in-law: ～关系 relationship between the mother-in-law and the daughter-in-law

pò

迫 pò 【动】◇ force; compel: ～于压力 under duress

迫不得已 pò bù dé yǐ be forced to; have no alternative: ～才这样做 be forced to do it this way

迫不及待 pò bù jí dài hurriedly; impatiently; in haste: 一听说那本新小说出版了，他就～地跑到书店去买。On hearing that the new novel was out, he rushed at once to the bookshop for a copy.

迫害 pòhài 【动】persecute

迫近 pòjìn 【动】〈书〉get close to; draw near: 新年～。New Year is approaching. ～胜利 close to victory 完工的日期已经～。The deadline for completion of the work is drawing near.

迫切 pòqiè 【形】urgent; pressing; imperative: ～需要 crying need 小王要求进步很～。Xiao Wang is anxious to make progress. 办好基层图书馆，满足了广大群众的～要求。Running libraries at the grass-roots level had met the need of the masses.

迫使 pòshǐ 【动】compel; force; oblige: ～他让步 force him to give in 家庭困难～他辍学。He was forced to drop out of school by the straitened circumstances of his family.

迫在眉睫 pò zài méi jié urgent; imminent: 抗旱保苗～。To combat drought and protect the seedlings is a matter of great urgency.

破 pò 【动】❶ be broken; be damaged; be torn: 手～了。His hand was cut. 衣服磨～了。The clothes were worn out. ❷ cleave; split: 把整块的木头～开 split the log 一～两半 break (sth.) into two ❸ get rid of; free oneself from (conventions, habits, old ideology, etc.): ～记录 break a record ～常规 free oneself from old conventions ❹ defeat (the enemy) or capture (the enemy's stronghold): 大～敌军 smash the enemy ❺ change (money): 把这张五块钱的票子～开 change this five-*yuan* note 【形】❶ worn-out; ragged: ～皮鞋 worn-out shoes ～被子 tattered quilt ❷〈口〉of poor quality; poor; bad: 我这～嗓子，唱不了歌。I've got a poor voice, and can't sing.

破案 pò = àn solve a case; solve a

criminal case

破冰船 pòbīngchuán 【名】icebreaker

破产 pò=chǎn go bankrupt

破除 pòchú 【动】do away with; abolish：～迷信 do away with superstitions ～不合理的规章制度 abolish unreasonable rules and regulations

破费 pòfèi 【动】spend lots of money；go to some expense

破釜沉舟 pò fǔ chén zhōu burn one's boats；cut off retreat in order to show one's determination

破格 pò=gé make an exception of conventions or rules；make an exception：～提拔 break the rules in order to promote (sb.)～接待 give an honoured reception beyond protocol

破坏 pòhuài 【动】destroy；undermine；wreck；sabotage

破获 pòhuò 【动】solve a criminal case and arrest the criminal

破旧立新 pò jiù lì xīn destroy the old and establish the new

破口大骂 pò kǒu dà mà hurl abuse；abuse roundly

破烂 pòlàn 【形】ragged；worn-out；tattered：～的轮胎 a worn-out tyre ～的车子 a broken-down car 【名】(～儿) rags；odds and ends：一堆～ a heap of odds and ends

破例 pò=lì make an exception；break a rule：展览馆本来星期一不开放，这次是～接待我们。The Exhibition Hall is not open on Mondays. They have made an exception for us this time.

破裂 pòliè 【动】split；break

破落 pòluò 【动】decline (in wealth and position)：家道～ the family suffered a decline in wealth and position

破灭 pòmiè 【动】(of hopes, illu-sions) vanish；be dashed：幻想～ one's illusions shattered 希望～ one's hopes dashed

破伤风 pòshāngfēng 【名】tetanus

破碎 pòsuì 【动】break into pieces：～的玻璃片 bits of broken glass 这堆石块太大，不合规格，还得再～一次。The stones in this pile are too big and do not meet the standard. They must be broken up again.

破损 pòsǔn 【动】damaged；broken；worn

破天荒 pòtiānhuāng 【形】(fig.) for the first time；unprecedented：苗寨通了火车，还是～第一次呢! For the first time in its history, train service has been extended to the Miao village.

破土 pòtǔ 【动】break ground (for construction)

破绽 pòzhàn 【名】(of clothes) a burst seam；(fig.)(of speech, action) flaw；loophole：～百出 numerous flaws 他的讲话～很多。His speech is full of flaws.

破折号 pòzhéhào 【名】dash "——"

魄 pò

魄力 pòlì 【名】boldness and resolution：这个人工作很有～。This person does his work boldly and resolutely.

pōu

剖 pōu 【动】◇cut；dissect：～开 cut open

剖腹 pōufù 【动】make an abdominal incision：～产 Caesarean birth

剖面 pōumiàn 【名】section

剖析 pōuxī 【动】dissect；analyze：～思想 analyze one's thinking ～问题 analyze a problem ～事理 analyze the whys and wherefores

pū

扑（撲） pū 【动】❶ flap：海鸥～着翅膀落在海面。The seagull flapped its wings slowly as it settled on to the surface of the water. ❷ pounce：猫一～上去，把老鼠捉住了。The cat pounced and caught the rat. 孩子～到妈妈怀里。The child rushed into his mother's arms. ❸ rush at：香气～鼻。A fragrant scent assails one's nostrils. ❹ slap at；strike downwards：～蜻蜓 slap at a dragonfly 直～匪巢 swoop down upon the bandits' den

扑哧 pūchī 【象声】titter；snigger

扑救 pūjiù 【动】put out a fire and avoid damage

扑克牌 pūkèpái 【名】playing cards

扑空 pū=kōng　fail to meet (sb.) as expected；fail to achieve (sth.)：你要去看他，最好先联系，免得～。If you want to see him, try to get an appointment so you won't make a trip for nothing. 昨天我去找老李，扑了个空。Yesterday I went to see Lao Li, but he was out.

扑灭 pūmiè 【动】stamp out；extinguish：～蚊蝇 wipe out mosquitoes and flies 火被～了。The fire was extinguished.

扑腾 pūteng 【动】throb；flop：她心里直～。Her heart was throbbing.

扑通 pūtōng 【象声】thud；thump；splash：他～一声，跳进水里。He jumped into the water with a splash.

铺（鋪） pū 【动】spread；pave：～席子 spread a mat 把床单～上 spread the sheet (on the bed) ～轨 lay a railway track ～平道路 pave the road
另见 pù

铺床 pū=chuáng　make the bed

铺盖 pūgai 【名】bedroll；bedding

铺路 pū=lù　build a road；pave the way for

铺设 pūshè 【动】lay：～输油管 lay an oil pipeline ～海底电缆 lay a submarine cable

铺天盖地 pū tiān gài dì　sweep；overwhelm

铺张 pūzhāng 【形】extravagant：反对～浪费 oppose extravagance and waste

pú

仆（僕） pú 【名】◇ servant

仆从 púcóng 【名】servant

仆人 púrén 【名】servant

匍 pú

匍匐 púfú 【动】〈书〉❶ crawl：～前进 advance on all fours ❷ lie on one's face；lie prone：白薯蔓在地面上～生长。Sweet potato vines crept over the ground.

葡 pú

葡萄 pútao 【名】grape

葡萄酒 pútaojiǔ 【名】(grape)wine

葡萄糖 pútaotáng 【名】glucose

pǔ

朴（樸） pǔ

朴实 pǔshí 【形】simple；honest：为人～ act in a direct and honest way 作风～ simple and honest style

朴素 pǔsù 【形】❶ simple；plain：穿着（zhuó）～ be simply dressed 文章～ written in a simple style with no flowery language ❷ (of living) simple：～的生活 plain living

朴质 pǔzhì 【形】simple and unadorned

普 pǔ

普遍 pǔbiàn 【形】universal；general：～现象 universal phenomenon ～真理 universal truth 生活水平～提高。The standard of living has been raised.

普遍性 pǔbiànxìng 【名】universality

普查 pǔchá 【动】make an overall survey

普法 pǔfǎ 【动】disseminate knowledge of the law

普及 pǔjí 【动】❶ widely diffused；spread widely：这本小册子已经～全国。This booklet has been distributed all over the country. ❷ popularize；become universal：～中学教育 make secondary education compulsory ～卫生常识 raise general consciousness of hygiene 【形】popular：太极拳在这个地区很～。T'ai chi ch'uan (Chinese shadow boxing) is very popular in this area.

普及本 pǔjíběn 【名】popular edition

普通 pǔtōng 【形】common；ordinary：～劳动者 ordinary worker 她穿着一件普普通通的蓝衣服。She's wearing an ordinary blue jacket.

普通话 pǔtōnghuà 【名】common speech (spoken Chinese language) — a standard modern Chinese language, based on the sounds of Beijing speech as the standard pronunciation, the Northern dialect as the basic dialect, and modern classics written in colloquial language as grammatical models

普选 pǔxuǎn 【名】general election 【动】hold a general election

普照 pǔzhào 【动】illuminate；shine everywhere：太阳的光辉～人间。The sun shines over the whole world.

谱（譜） pǔ

【动】compose；set to music：～一个曲子 set (a poem or song) to music 为祖国～新篇 write a new song for the motherland 【名】❶ musical score：识～ be able to read a musical score ❷ (～儿) sth. that can be counted：心里有～ know what one is about 做事没～ has no clue as to what one is up to

谱写 pǔxiě 【动】compose (music)：～电影歌曲 compose songs and music for film 青年英雄们用他们短短的一生～了一曲保卫祖国的凯歌。The lives of the young heroes, sacrificed in safeguarding their country, were a beautiful song of triumph.

谱子 pǔzi 【名】musical score

pù

铺（鋪） pù

【名】❶ ◇ shop；store：小～儿 small shop 杂货～ grocery store ❷ plank bed
另见 pū

铺板 pùbǎn 【名】bed board

铺面 pùmiàn 【名】shop front

铺面房 pùmiànfáng 【名】houses by the street suitable for use as shops

铺位 pùwèi 【名】berth

铺子 pùzi 【名】shop

瀑 pù

瀑布 pùbù 【名】waterfall

Q

qī

七 qī 【数】seven

七…八… qī...bā... *inserted with two nouns, two verbs or two morphemes of a noun or verb, indicates a disorderly state of things, or some kind of distortion*：七扭八歪 very crooked 七拼八凑 piece together odds and ends 七嘴八舌 all talking simultaneously producing great confusion 心中七上八下，非常不安 be greatly perturbed 风把牡丹刮得七零八落，十分可惜。It's such a pity that the peonies were so damaged by the wind. 大伙儿七手八脚地把零件装上汽车。With everybody lending a hand, we managed to load the spare parts on to the truck.

七手八脚 qī shǒu bā jiǎo with everyone lending a hand

七月 qīyuè 【名】July

妻 qī 【名】◇wife

妻离子散 qī lí zǐ sàn the breaking up of a family (by war, disaster, etc.)

妻子 qīzi 【名】wife

柒 qī 【数】seven (*the complicated form of* 七) 见"捌"bā

栖 qī

栖身 qīshēn 【动】〈书〉stay；obtain shelter；live (usu. under another man's roof)：～国外 make one's home abroad ～虎穴 take shelter in a place of danger

栖息 qīxī 【动】〈书〉(of birds) roost；perch：喜鹊～在枝头。A magpie is perching on a branch.

凄 qī

凄惨 qīcǎn 【形】(of scene, situation, feeling) sad and miserable

凄风苦雨 qī fēng kǔ yǔ wailing wind and mournful rain；(*fig.*) wretched circumstances

凄厉 qīlì 【形】(of voice, sound) shrill and mournful

凄凉 qīliáng 【形】(of scene, environment, etc.) miserable；dreary：～的景象 a desolate scene 生活～ a miserable and dreary life

期 qī 【名】◇appointed time：按～前往 go at the appointed time 从图书馆借的书已经到～。The library book is due.【量】*for term；class；course；issue*：外语训练班刚办了一～。The foreign language training course has just completed its first session. 第二～《科学》杂志已经出版。The second issue of the magazine "Science" is already out.

期待 qīdài【动】look forward to; wait in hope; expect：～着渔船满载而归 look forward to the fishing boats returning with a big catch ～着胜利的消息 be eagerly awaiting news of a victory

期货 qīhuò【名】futures

期间 qījiān【名】(during) a certain period of time：寒假～ during the winter vacation

期刊 qīkān【名】periodical

期考 qīkǎo【名】end-of-term examination; final examination

期求 qīqiú【动】crave; expect：～帮助 count on others' help; expect others' support ～支援 expect support

期望 qīwàng【动】hope; expect; look forward to; count on：人们都～着能看到更多更好的文艺作品。People look forward to more and better literary and artistic works.【名】expectation：决不辜负人民对我们的殷切～。We must never fail to live up to the people's expectations.

期限 qīxiàn【名】time limit：十天的～ a ten-day time limit ～已到 the time is up 超过～ exceed the time limit

欺 qī【动】◇❶ cheat; deceive; hoodwink：～上瞒下 deceive one's superiors and hide the truth from one's subordinates ❷ bully：仗势～人 abuse one's power and play the bully

欺负 qīfu【动】bully; ride roughshod over (sb.); browbeat：哥哥不要～弟弟。An elder brother should never bully a younger one. 决不容许大国～小国，强国～弱国。Big nations must not be allowed to intimidate small ones, nor strong nations weak ones.

欺行霸市 qī háng bà shì be a bully in the market

欺凌 qīlíng【动】browbeat; humiliate：受尽～ suffer bullying and humiliation

欺瞒 qīmán【动】hide sth. from sb.; cheat; deceive

欺骗 qīpiàn【动】deceive; swindle

欺人太甚 qī rén tài shèn bully others to an extreme degree; be a terrible bully：警告你，你不能～! I'm warning you, stop being such a bully!

欺人之谈 qī rén zhī tán deceitful talk; lie

欺软怕硬 qī ruǎn pà yìng browbeat the weak and fear the strong

欺侮 qīwǔ【动】bully; humiliate：从此之后，他再也不敢～人了。After that he no longer dared to bully others.

欺压 qīyā【动】bully and oppress

欺诈 qīzhà【动】cheat; deceive

漆 qī【名】paint; lacquer; varnish【动】varnish; paint

漆包线 qībāoxiàn【名】enamel-insulated wire

漆黑 qīhēi【形】pitch dark

漆黑一团 qīhēi yī tuán ❶ totally dark without a glimmer of light：问题是存在的，但不能说是～。You can't paint such a dark picture of the situation though there are problems. ❷ be completely ignorant; be completely in the dark about：对这个问题我心目中还是～。I am still completely in the dark on this question.

漆器 qīqì【名】lacquerware

qí

齐（齊）qí【形】❶ neat; tidy; even; in good order：队列很～ neat ranks 秧苗插得很～。The rice seedlings are planted in neat rows.

❷ ◇ alike；be of one：人心～，泰山移。When people are of one mind, they can move Mt. Tai. ❸ simultaneously；together：放声～歌唱 sing in unison 大家～动手。Everyone lends a hand. ❹ ready；complete：人都到～了。Everyone is here. 材料还没有备～。The materials are not yet complete. 【动】reach the height of：河水～腰深。The river is waist-deep. 蓖麻都～了房檐了。The castor beans have grown to the height of the eaves.

齐备 qíbèi 【动】(usu. of articles, etc.) ready；complete：货物～。All the goods are ready. 万事～。Everything is ready.

齐唱 qíchàng 【动】sing in unison；chorus

齐名 qímíng 【动】be equally well-known

齐全 qíquán 【形】(of stock, etc.) complete：这个百货店商品十分～。This department store has a complete range of goods.

齐头并进 qí tóu bìng jìn move abreast；advance side by side

齐心 qíxīn 【形】be of one mind

齐心协力 qíxīn xiélì work together as one man；be of one mind

齐奏 qízòu 【动】play (musical instruments) in unison

其 qí 【代】〈书〉❶ he；she；it；they (usu. not used at the beginning of a sentence，but within the sentence referring to sb. or sth. just mentioned)：这个计划很好，应促～早日实现。This plan is good, and we ought to put it into effect as soon as possible. ❷ his；her；its；their：各显～能 let each display his ability 物尽～用 let everything be properly and fully used ❸ that：确有～事 that was certainly a fact

其次 qícì 【名】❶ next；secondly：

首先由他讲话，～是我发言。He was the first to speak, and I came next. ❷ secondary：内容是主要的，形式还在～。The content is of the first importance；the form is secondary.

其间 qíjiān 【名】between；during；within (a period of time)

其实 qíshí 【副】as a matter of fact；actually；in truth：别看今天风很大，～一点也不冷。It is very windy today, but not the least bit cold. ～，你用不着去接他，他没带什么重东西。As a matter of fact you don't need to go to meet him；because he doesn't have much to carry.

其它 qítā 【代】other；else

其他 qítā 【代】others；the other：第一组收稻子，～组干什么? Group 1 is to gather the rice；what should the other groups do? 这个地区先后办起了钢铁、电力和～一些小型工业。This district has set up an iron and steel plant，an electric-power plant and other similar small-scale industrial plants one after another.

其余 qíyú 【代】the remainder；the rest：除这家外，～都是本地人。Except for this family, all the rest are local people. 除了这几本，～都是英文杂志。All the rest are English magazines except these few copies.

其中 qízhōng 【名】among which；among whom：这里有很多新建筑，～百货大楼最引人注目。Among the many new buildings in this part of the city, the department store is the most striking. 北京有不少著名的公园，北海公园就是～之一。Beijing has many well-known parks, one of which is the Beihai Park.

奇 qí 【形】◇ ❶ rare；unusual；odd；strange；remarkable：～事 an

unusual thing ～景 strange and wonderful sight ❷ unexpected; surprising: ～计 an ingenious stratagem ～兵 an army which appears unexpectedly from nowhere 另见 jī

奇才 qícái 【名】rare talent; great genius

奇耻大辱 qí chǐ dà rǔ a most extreme humiliation

奇怪 qíguài 【形】❶ unusual; strange: ～的现象 a strange phenomenon 这个建筑物的形状很～. This building has a very unusual shape. ❷ unexpected; hard to understand: ～,他怎么能讲这样的话! How could he say such a thing!

奇观 qíguān 【名】miraculous sight; remarkable spectacle

奇货可居 qí huò kě jū rare commodity worth hoarding against a later higher price

奇迹 qíjì 【名】miracle; wonder: 创造～ create a miracle 历史上的～ a miracle in history

奇妙 qímiào 【形】wonderful; marvellous: ～的魔术表演 a wonderful magic performance

奇谈 qítán 【名】strange tale

奇谈怪论 qítán guàilùn absurd argument; fantastic theories

奇特 qítè 【形】peculiar; unusual: ～的景象 unique scene 山石～ peculiar rock formations

奇闻 qíwén 【名】strange story (usu. derog.)

奇袭 qíxí 【动】launch a surprise attack on: ～敌人运输队 make a raid on the enemy's transport troops

奇效 qíxiào 【名】extraordinary efficacy

奇形怪状 qí xíng guài zhuàng (of shape) queer; grotesque; bizarre: ～的钟乳石 grotesque stalactites 海底生物～. The animals and plants at the bottom of the sea have all sorts of strange shapes.

奇异 qíyì 【形】❶ queer; fantastic: ～的海底世界 fantastic world at the bottom of the sea ～的花草 exotic flowers and plants ～的鸟兽 rare birds and animals ❷ amazing; amazed: 第一次来到沙漠地带,大家都用～的目光注视着一切. On our first visit to the desert, we looked at everything in amazement.

奇遇 qíyù 【名】❶ fortuitous meeting ❷ adventure

奇装异服 qí zhuāng yì fú strange fashions; outlandish clothes; peculiar dress

歧 qí

歧路 qílù 【名】a fork in a road

歧视 qíshì 【动】discriminate against: 如今妇女不再受～. Women are no longer discriminated against nowadays. 反对种族～ protest against racial discrimination

歧途 qítú 【名】(fig.) wrong road: 误入～ stray into a wrong path 走上～ go astray

歧义 qíyì 【名】two or more different meanings; different interpretations

祈 qí

祈祷 qídǎo 【动】pray

祈求 qíqiú 【动】entreat earnestly: 不能～大自然的恩赐,而要努力创造我们所需要的一切. We must never entreat nature to bestow favours, but must work hard to produce everything we need.

祈使句 qíshǐjù 【名】imperative sentence

畦 qí 【名】a small, usu. rectangular, plot of land, esp. for vegetables

崎 qí

崎岖　qíqū　【形】（of mountain paths) rugged；rough；～小路 a rough trail 人生的道路是～不平的。The road of life is full of twists and turns.

骑（騎）　qí　【动】ride（especially on horseback，bicycle，etc.）

骑兵　qíbīng　【名】cavalry

骑虎难下　qí hǔ nán xià　he who rides a tiger finds it difficult to get off；（fig.) find oneself in a situation from which it is difficult to back out

骑墙　qí=qiáng　sit on the fence；～派 fence-sitters ～观望 sit on the fence and take a wait-and-see attitude

骑士　qíshì　【名】knight

棋　qí　【名】game of chess

棋逢对手　qí féng duìshǒu　be equally matched in a game of chess；（fig.) be equally matched

棋迷　qímí　【名】chess fan

棋盘　qípán　【名】chess board

棋子　qízǐ　【名】(～儿)〔个 gè〕chess-man

旗　qí　【名】〔面 miàn〕flag；banner

旗杆　qígān　【名】〔根 gēn〕flagpole

旗鼓相当　qí gǔ xiāngdāng　well-matched in strength；两个球队～，一定会有一番激烈的争夺。Since the two teams are evenly matched, there is bound to be a fierce contest.

旗号　qíhào　【名】banner；standard（now usu. fig. and derog.）；打着培养青年干部的～培植自己的亲信 flaunt the banner of fostering young cadres，while building up one's own clique

旗开得胜　qí kāi dé shèng　win a victory as soon as one's standard is unfurled；（fig.) win a quick victory；make a successful beginning

旗袍　qípáo　【名】Chinese-style woman's dress；cheongsam

旗手　qíshǒu　【名】standard bearer；鲁迅先生是中国新文化运动的伟大～。Lu Xun was the great standard-bearer of China's New Culture Movement.

旗帜　qízhì　【名】❶ flag；banner ❷ good example；model；pace-setter；这个煤矿是煤炭工业的一面～。That coal mine is setting an example in the coal industry. ❸ thought；theory，or political power which provides a rallying point；丰产的～ the banner of high yield

旗帜鲜明　qízhì xiānmíng　have a clearcut stand；他～地主张改革。He categorically stood up for the reform programme.

旗子　qízi　【名】〔面 miàn〕flag；banner

qǐ

乞　qǐ

乞丐　qǐgài　【名】beggar

乞怜　qǐlián　【动】beg for mercy

乞灵　qǐlíng　【动】〈书〉resort to；seek help from；turn to sth. for help（to no avail）

乞求　qǐqiú　【动】beg；go down on one's knees（to sb.）（derog.）

乞讨　qǐtǎo　【动】go begging

岂（豈）　qǐ　【副】about the same as 难道，usu. used in written language，often before a negative word to form a rhetorical question；～能容忍 how could one tolerate it ～非咄咄怪事！Isn't that absurd! 你这样做～不使亲者痛，仇者快吗？If you act in this way, you will only grieve those dear to you and please

your enemies. 荒山造林，既能生产木材，又能保持水土，～不是一举两得吗？Afforestation can both increase timber production and aid water and soil conservation. Isn't that killing two birds with one stone?

岂但 qǐdàn 【连】not only

岂有此理 qǐ yǒu cǐ lǐ how could such a thing be possible；outrageous (expressing indignation at injustice)：只许州官放火，不许百姓点灯，真是～! The priviliged can set fire to a house and get away with it, while the common people are not allowed even to burn a candle. What blatant injustice!

企 qǐ

企求 qǐqiú 【动】同"期求" qīqiú

企图 qǐtú 【动】attempt；try；contrive：我们～把工具改进一下，但是没有成功。We made an attempt to improve the tools, but to no avail. ～撬门的小偷被捉住了。The thief was caught as he was attempting to pry open a door lock. 【名】attempt；scheme：他的～明眼人一看就知道。Anyone with a discerning eye could easily see through his game.

企业 qǐyè 【名】enterprise；undertaking

企业化 qǐyèhuà 【动】❶ turn a government-run enterprise into a separate accounting unit ❷ turn a non-profit enterprise into an accounting one with regular income

企业家 qǐyèjiā 【名】entrepreneur；big businessman；industrialist

杞 qǐ

杞人忧天 Qǐ rén yōu tiān the man of Qi worried lest the sky should fall；(fig.) have groundless fears

启（啓）qǐ

启程 qǐchéng 【动】.set out；start on a journey

启迪 qǐdí 【动】enlighten：从这个理论中得到～ be enlightened by this theory

启动 qǐdòng 【动】start (a machine)：电冰箱～了。The refrigerator is switched on.

启发 qǐfā 【动】enlighten；arouse；inspire：～他们的觉悟 awaken their consciousness 【名】inspiration；enlightenment：这个防风治沙的经验对我们改造沙地很有～。Their experience in wind-prevention and sand-control served as a great source of inspiration to us in transforming our own sandy soil.

启发式 qǐfāshì 【名】elicitation (method of teaching)

启蒙 qǐméng 【动】enlighten

启示 qǐshì 【动】enlighten；inspire：他的话～我们，使我们深思了许多问题。Inspired by his remarks, we began to think deeply about a lot of questions. 【名】enlightenment；inspiration：这位杰出人物的事迹给了我们很多～。We derived great inspiration from the exploits of this outstanding personage.

启事 qǐshì 【名】notice；announcement

启用 qǐyòng 【动】start using；start operating

起 qǐ 【动】❶ get up：早睡早～ go to bed early and get up early 他每天天刚亮就～。He gets up at dawn every day. ❷ ◇ begin：成昆铁路北～成都南至昆明，全长 1085 公里。The Chengkun Railway starts from Chengdu in the north and ends at Kunming in the south covering a total length of 1085 km. ❸ rise；grow：～风了。The wind is rising. 大规模的植树造林使这里的气候～了很大的变化。Afforestation

on a large scale has brought about a great change in the climate here. 这一仗在整个战役中一了很大的作用。This battle had a great effect on the whole campaign. ❹ extract; pull: ~地雷 clear away mines 把墙上的图钉~下来 take out all the thumbtacks from the wall. ❺ ◇ appear: ~水泡 break out in small blisters 头上~了个包。A lump came up on（his）head. Note: 起 *is used as a complement after a verb*: ① up: 他提~箱子就走了。He picked up his suitcase and left. 她撩~窗帘一看，原来下雪了。She lifted up the curtain and found that it was snowing. ② *indicates gathering together or closing*: 组织~坚强的拳击队伍 organize a strong boxing team 收集了大量材料之后，他现在关~门写论文了。After having collected large quantities of data, he locked himself in his room and began to write his paper. ③ *indicates concealment*: 隐瞒~过去的一段历史 hold back a period of one's past history 收~暂时不用的东西 put away things which one does not need for the time being ④ *indicates appearance（of abstract things）*: 提~精神 brace oneself 想~他那天说的话 remembered what he said the other day 昨天谈话的时候，老张还问~你呢! When we talked yesterday, Lao Zhang asked about you.（①②③④ *are the same as* 起来 *as the complement* ①②③④, *except that an object is necessary*.）❺ *together with* 得 *or* 不 *to mean* "*can afford*" *or* "*cannot afford*": 买得~ can afford（to buy）买不~ cannot afford（to buy）【量】❶ case: 几~民事案件 several civil cases ❷ batch; group: 今天来过好几~人参观。There have been several groups of visitors today.

起笔　qǐbǐ　【名】❶ the first stroke of a Chinese character ❷ the beginning of each stroke in writing a Chinese character

起步　qǐbù　【动】❶ begin to walk（run）❷ make a start

起草　qǐ＝cǎo　draft; draw up: ~文件 draft a document 这个布告怎么写，你先起个草。Please first make a draft of how this notice should be written.

起程　qǐchéng　【动】start on a journey

起初　qǐchū　【名】at first; in the beginning

起床　qǐ＝chuáng　get up; get out of bed

起点　qǐdiǎn　【名】starting point

起飞　qǐfēi　【动】（of aeroplane）take off

起伏　qǐfú　【动】rise and fall: 连绵~的群山 mountains extending in an unbroken rise and fall 心潮~ one's emotion goes up and down

起航　qǐháng　【动】（of ship）weigh anchor; set sail

起哄　qǐhòng　【动】a lot of people create an uproar（often making fun of sb.）小赵不会唱歌，大家~，非让他唱一个不可。Xiao Zhao was no singer, but we all set up a great uproar, and would settle for nothing but his singing us a song.

起获　qǐhuò　【动】track down and seize

起家　qǐ＝jiā　build up a fortune; start an enterprise; start off: 白手~ start from scratch

起劲　qǐjìn　【形】enthusiastic; in high spirits; energetic: 你看，他们唱得多~! See how enthusiastically they are singing! 工地上，大家你追我赶，干得非常~。Everybody worked enthusiastically at the worksite, each trying to outdo the others.

起居 qǐjū 【名】daily life

起来 qǐ // lái get up; sit up; stand up: 我刚～，还没洗脸呢! I've just got up, and have not washed my face yet. 他看见老年人上车,就～让座。When he saw an old woman get on the bus, he stood up and gave her his seat. 他昨天睡得太晚了,今天早上起不来了。He went to bed too late last night and had trouble getting up this morning. Note: 起来 *is used after a verb as a complement*: ① *up*: 把红旗举～ raise the red flag 中国人民站～了。The Chinese people have stood up. 他提起箱子来就走了。He picked up his suitcase and left. ② *indicates gathering together or closing*: 捆～ tie into a bundle 组织～ form into an organization 团结～ unite together 关起门来 shut the door 把这些衣服包～ wrap up these clothes ③ *indicates concealment*: 收～ put aside 藏～ conceal 躲～ hide (oneself) 把这些垃圾埋～。Get the rubbish buried! ④ *indicates appearance* (of abstract things): 我想～了,那本书是小李借去了。Now I've got it! That book was borrowed by Xiao Li. 这次争论是谁挑～的? Who was it that started this argument? (① ② ③ ④ *are the same as* 起 *as a complement* ① ② ③ ④, *but an object is optional*.) *used after a verb or an adjective as a complement*) ⑤ *indicates beginning and continuation of an action*: 他和对面的乘客说起话来。He struck up a conversation with the passenger seated opposite him. 大家立刻行动～。Everybody began to act at once. 全场顿时沸腾～。The whole audience was immediately animated. 天气渐渐热～。It's getting hot. ⑥ *indicates the time when an action actually takes place* (*usu. in the subordinate clause of a compound sentence or as an adverbial adjunct*.): 天气真冷～,你穿这点衣服就不够了。When it gets really cold, what you are wearing won't be enough to keep you warm. 这辆自行车骑～很轻。This bicycle rides smoothly.

起立 qǐlì 【动】stand up

起码 qǐmǎ 【形】minimum; rudimentary; at least: ～的常识 basic common sense ～的条件 minimum conditions 五月份以前,我们～应完成全年任务的一半。We should fulfil at least half of the annual quota by May. 徐教授这次出国,～要一个半月才能回来。Prof. Xu's present mission abroad will take at least a month and a half.

起色 qǐsè 【名】a change for the better; improvement: 健康状况有了～。There is a change for the better in his health. 工作很有～。The work has improved greatly.

起身 qǐ = shēn ❶ start a journey ❷ get up in the morning

起诉 qǐsù 【动】bring a suit against sb.

起诉书 qǐsùshū 【名】indictment

起头 qǐtóu 【名】(～儿) ❶ at first; to start with: 他～不懂这种技术,是后来学的。At first he knew little about this technique; it was only afterwards that he acquired it. ❷ beginning; starting-point: 这故事的～是怎么回事? What is the beginning of the story like?

起头 qǐ = tóu (～儿) take the lead; start; make a start: 现在大家唱歌,我来～。Now everybody sing! I'll lead. 我不会织毛衣,你给我起个头儿吧! I'm not very good at knitting sweaters. Please start it for me.

起先 qǐxiān 【名】at first; in the beginning: ～我住在南方,后来才搬到北京的。At first I lived in the

South. It was only later that I moved to Beijing. 我~不知道无锡是座古城,后来才听说它已有三千多年的历史了。I didn't know that Wuxi is an ancient city. Later I heard that it has a history of over three thousand years.

起义 qǐyì 【动】❶ stage an uprising ❷ (mil.) revolt and join the enemy army in the belief that their cause is just 【名】uprising; insurrection

起因 qǐyīn 【名】cause

起用 qǐyòng 【动】reinstate (a person in an official post); appoint (somebody to a position)

起源 qǐyuán 【动】originate in; arise from: 根据一派学说,音乐、诗歌、舞蹈等都~于劳动。According to one school of thought, music, poetry, dance and so on all have their origin in labour. 【名】origin; beginning; source: 人类的~ the origin of mankind 生物的~ the origin of living things

起早贪黑 qǐ zǎo tān hēi start work early and knock off late; work hard from morning till night

起重机 qǐzhòngjī 【名】〔台 tái〕crane (used in construction)

起…作用 qǐ…zuòyòng play a part in; serve as: 起决定性作用 play a decisive role 汉语拼音方案对推广普通话起了很大作用。The Chinese Phonetic Alphabet plays an important role in popularizing *Putonghua*.

qì

气(氣) qì 【名】❶ air; gas; fresh air: 给自行车打点儿~ pump up the bike tyres 这个煤气灶是不是漏~? Is the gas stove leaking? 快打开窗户透透~吧! Open the window at once and let in some fresh air. ❷ breath: 天闷得人喘不过~来。The weather is so stifling that nobody can breathe. 跑得上~不接下~ be out of breath from running ❸ ◇ bullying; insult; maltreatment: 她常受丈夫的~。She was often bullied by her husband. ❹ smell; odour; flavour: 一股香~ a whiff of fragrance 【动】get angry; fly into a rage: 他~得连饭都没有吃。He was so angry that he skipped a meal. 他是开玩笑,不是真~你。He meant no offence; he was merely joking.

气昂昂 qì'áng'áng 【形】in high spirits; with high morale

气冲冲 qìchōngchōng 【形】enraged; angry

气喘 qìchuǎn 【动】asthma

气度 qìdù 【名】breadth of vision and magnanimity

气氛 qìfēn 【名】atmosphere; air

气愤 qìfèn 【形】angry; indignant; enraging; causing indignation 令人~ 我们对这种损坏公物的现象非常~。We were indignant at the damage done to public property.

气概 qìgài 【名】heroic spirit: 大无畏的英雄~ fearless heroic spirit

气管 qìguǎn 【名】windpipe; trachea

气管炎 qìguǎnyán 【名】tracheitis

气焊 qìhàn 【动】gas-welding

气候 qìhòu 【名】climate

气呼呼 qìhūhū 【形】spluttering with rage; panting with rage

气急败坏 qì jí bài huài wrought-up; flustered and exasperated

气节 qìjié 【名】integrity; moral courage: 民族~ patriotic moral courage 英雄~ heroic integrity

气孔 qìkǒng 【名】❶ (bot.) stoma ❷ (zool.) spiracle ❸ (met.) gas hole ❹ (arch.) air hole

气力 qìlì 【名】physical strength;

effort

气量 qìliàng 【名】one's breadth of mind：气量大 broad-minded 气量小 narrow-minded

气流 qìliú 【名】❶ air current ❷ (ling.) breath

气馁 qìněi 【形】down-hearted；become dejected：碰到困难不要～。Don't be discouraged by difficulties.

气派 qìpài 【名】(of person or certain things) bearing；manner；style：这座建筑物很有～。How imposing this building is!

气魄 qìpò 【名】❶ daring；boldness which comes from foresight：伟大政治家的～ the courage and foresight of a great statesman ❷ imposing manner：雄伟的～ magnificent spirit 这组交响乐雄壮有力，～很大。This symphony is spirited and powerful.

气球 qìqiú 【名】〔个 gè〕balloon

气色 qìsè 【名】complexion (as an indication of one's state of health)

气势 qìshì 【名】(of events or things) grandeur；majesty：喜马拉雅山～逼人。The Himalayas are awe-inspiring.

气势磅礴 qìshì pángbó imposing；impressive：长城绵延万里，～。The Great Wall stretches impressively for thousands of miles.

气势汹汹 qìshì xiōngxiōng ferocious；overbearing

气态 qìtài 【名】(phys.) gaseous state

气体 qìtǐ 【名】(phys.) gas

气筒 qìtǒng 【名】bicycle pump

气味 qìwèi 【名】❶ scent；smell：～芬芳 fragrant scent ❷ taste；likes and dislikes (derog.)

气味相投 qìwèi xiāngtóu congenial；sharing the same views and preferences (derog.)

气温 qìwēn 【名】air temperature；atmospheric temperature

气息 qìxī 【名】❶ breath ❷ (of abstract things) flavour；odour：生活～ the flavour of life 这个节目富有时代～。The performance certainly had a contemporary flavour.

气息奄奄 qìxī yǎnyǎn dying；at one's last gasp

气象 qìxiàng 【名】❶ meteorological phenomena：～预报 weather forecast ❷ (fig.) atmosphere：新～ a new atmosphere

气象台 qìxiàngtái 【名】meteorological observatory

气象万千 qìxiàng wànqiān magnificent and varied sights：我们伟大的祖国，山河壮丽，～。Our great country presents vast panoramas of mountains and rivers.

气象卫星 qìxiàng wèixīng meteorological satellite

气象学 qìxiàngxué 【名】meteorology

气象站 qìxiàngzhàn 【名】weather station

气压 qìyā 【名】barometric pressure

气焰 qìyàn 【名】arrogance；bluster：～嚣张 be swollen with arrogance ～万丈 extreme arrogance

气质 qìzhì 【名】❶ temperament；disposition ❷ (of a person) qualities；makings

气壮如牛 qì zhuàng rú niú appear to be as strong as an ox (usu. in conjunction with 胆小如鼠 as timid as a mouse)

气壮山河 qì zhuàng shān hé sublime and heroic：这是一部～的史诗。This is a heroic epic.

迄 qì

迄今 qì = jīn 〈书〉to this day；to date：人类～已有几十万年的历史了。Up to now mankind has had a history of several hundred thousands years.

弃 qì 【动】〈书〉abandon；forsake：～城而逃 abandon the city and flee 食之无味，～之可惜。It's lacking in flavour, but a pity to throw away.

弃暗投明 qì àn tóu míng abandon darkness for light；(*fig.*) quit the reactionary camp and come over to the side of progress

弃权 qì = quán abstain from voting；abstention

汽 qì 【名】steam；vapour

汽车 qìchē 【名】〔辆 liàng〕automobile

汽船 qìchuán 【名】〔艘 sōu〕steamship

汽笛 qìdí 【名】siren of a ship or locomotive

汽化 qìhuà 【动】vaporize

汽酒 qìjiǔ 【名】fizzy wine；sparkling wine

汽轮机 qìlúnjī 【名】steam turbine

汽水 qìshuǐ 【名】(～儿) carbonated drink；pop

汽艇 qìtǐng 【名】〔艘 sōu〕motorboat

汽油 qìyóu 【名】gasoline；petrol

泣 qì 【动】◇sob

泣不成声 qì bù chéng shēng be choked with tears：一谈到过去的遭遇，她就～。When she began describing her miserable life in the past, she was so choked with tears she could hardly go on.

契 qì 【名】contract；agreement

契机 qìjī 【名】moment；turning point；juncture

契约 qìyuē 【名】〔张 zhāng〕contract；agreement；deed

器 qì 【名】◇utensil；ware

器材 qìcái 【名】equipment；materials and equipment

器官 qìguān 【名】(physiol.) organ

器具 qìjù 【名】utensil；appliance

器皿 qìmǐn 【名】kitchenware；household utensils；container

器物 qìwù 【名】utensils；implements

器械 qìxiè 【名】❶ apparatus ❷ military weapons

器乐 qìyuè 【名】instrumental music

器重 qìzhòng 【动】think highly of (someone at a higher level towards someone at a lower level)

qiā

揢 qiā 【动】❶ squeeze between thumb and finger ❷ pinch

揢算 qiāsuàn 【动】count on the fingers

qiǎ

卡 qiǎ 【动】〈口〉be wedged；get stuck：鱼刺～在嗓子里 have a fishbone stuck in one's throat
另见 kǎ

卡脖子 qiǎ bózi throttle；strangle

qià

恰 qià 【副】◇ just；exactly：～到好处 just right ～合时宜 exactly appropriate to the occasion；exactly in keeping with the times

恰当 qiàdàng 【形】fitting and proper：这个词用在这儿不～。This is not the appropriate word in this context. 这个问题处理得十分～。This problem has been properly settled. 找不到～的词来表达我的激动心情。I couldn't find adequate words to express the intensity of my feelings.

恰好　qiàhǎo　【副】同"正好" zhènghǎo【副】❶

恰恰　qiàqià　【副】同"正好" zhènghǎo【副】❷ (*but more emphatic and not as colloquial*)：～相反 exactly the opposite 这工作～符合他的专长。This job is exactly suited to his expertise. 他一箭～射中了靶心。With the first shot, his arrow hit the very centre of the target.

恰巧　qiàqiǎo　【副】同"正好" zhènghǎo【副】❶

恰如　qiàrú　【动】exactly resemble；just like

恰如其分　qià rú qí fèn　just right；appropriate：做出～的结论 draw an appropriate conclusion 对历史人物的评价要～。Historical figures should be appraised from a proper perspective.

洽　qià

洽商　qiàshāng　【动】negotiate；arrange by discussion

洽谈　qiàtán　【动】同"洽商"

qiān

千　qiān　【数】thousand

千百万　qiānbǎiwàn　【数】millions

千变万化　qiān biàn wàn huà　kaleidoscopic change；ever-changing：节日的焰火～，绚丽多彩。The fireworks display on the festival evening made the scene a riot of colour.

千差万别　qiān chā wàn bié　differ in a thousand ways：世界上的事物是～的。Things in the world differ from each other in a thousand ways.

千疮百孔　qiān chuāng bǎi kǒng　同"百孔千疮"

千锤百炼　qiān chuí bǎi liàn　❶ thoroughly steeled and tempered：经过艰苦生活的～，他夺取成功的决心更坚定了。Having been tempered by the hardships of life, he was more determined than ever to succeed. ❷ (of literary or artistic works) be revised and polished over and over again

千方百计　qiān fāng bǎi jì　leave no stone unturned；do all in one's power：我们应当～地完成任务。We must use every possible means to fulfill our task. 炊事员～办好伙食。The kitchen staff do everything in their power to ensure that the meals are satisfactory.

千金　qiānjīn　【名】large amount of money；(a polite term referring to other people's) daughter

千军万马　qiān jūn wàn mǎ　a powerful army with thousands of horses：大河一出峡谷就以～之势向东奔腾而去。The river flows out of the gorge and thunders toward the east like thousands of galloping horses.

千钧一发　qiān jūn yī fà　(*lit.*) a hundred weight hanging by a hair；(*fig.*) extremely delicate and dangerous situation；very critical situation 也作"一发千钧"。

千卡　qiānkǎ　【量】kilocalorie

千克　qiānkè　【量】kilogram

千里送鹅毛　qiān lǐ sòng émáo　a goose feather sent from a thousand *li* away；(*fig.*) the gift may be small, but it's the thought that counts

千里迢迢　qiān lǐ tiáotiáo　from afar；over a great distance：青年们为了建设边疆，～来到西藏。These young people have come all the way to Tibet to help build up the border regions of our country.

千难万险　qiān nán wàn xiǎn　untold hardships and risks：他们历尽了～，才取得今天的胜利。They went through untold hardships and risks

before today's victory could finally be owned.

千篇一律 qiān piān yīlù （of writings）repetitious；stereotyped；following the same pattern

千奇百怪 qiān qí bǎi guài all sorts of strange（things）：～的现象 all sorts of bizarre phenomena ～的形状 all sorts of strange shapes

千秋万代 qiān qiū wàn dài forever；through the ages；for many generations to come

千丝万缕 qiān sī wàn lǚ a thousand and one links or ties：有～的联系 bound together by countless ties

千头万绪 qiān tóu wàn xù many loose ends；a thousand things to attend to：工作～，必须逐项解决。Even if we have a thousand things to attend to, we must still tackle them one by one.

千瓦 qiānwǎ 【量】kilowatt

千万 qiānwàn 【数】ten million 【副】同"务必"wùbì, *can be reduplicated*：～不要忘记这个教训。Be sure never to forget this lesson. 你这次出车走那条山路，～～可得小心。You'll be driving along that mountainous road, be sure to drive carefully.

千辛万苦 qiān xīn wàn kǔ untold hardships；all kinds of hardships：历尽～ undergo untold hardships 不畏～ brave all kinds of hardships

千言万语 qiān yán wàn yǔ torrent of words；thousands of words：～也表达不尽我的感激心情。No words can fully express my gratitude.

千载难逢 qiān zǎi nán féng an opportunity which comes once in a thousand years；an extremely rare opportunity：～的好机会 a once-in-a-lifetime opportunity

千真万确 qiān zhēn wàn què absolutely true；indisputable：～的事实 absolute fact 他的话～。What he said was absolutely true.

千周 qiānzhōu 【量】kilocycle

千姿百态 qiān zī bǎi tài infinite variety of beauty and charm

仟 qiān 【数】thousand（*the complicated form of* 千）见"捌"bā

阡 qiān

阡陌 qiānmò 【名】criss-cross paths in the field

迁（遷） qiān 【动】move（to another place）：那个商店～到新楼里去了。That store has moved into the new building.

迁就 qiānjiù 【动】accommodate oneself to；give in to：对他的错误不能～。We mustn't pass over his mistakes.

迁居 qiānjū 【动】move house

迁徙 qiānxǐ 【动】migrate；move

迁移 qiānyí 【动】remove；move；migrate

牵（牽） qiān 【动】（of persons, cattle）lead；pull；drag：手～着手 hand in hand 把马～到树林里去 lead the horse into the woods

牵扯 qiānchě 【动】drag；involve：请你集中谈这件事，不要～其他问题。Please stick to the business at hand and don't drag in irrelevant issues.

牵动 qiāndòng 【动】（change in one part）affect（other parts）

牵挂 qiānguà 【动】be concerned about；worry over：我这里一切都好,不用～。Everything is fine with me；don't worry.

牵累 qiānlěi 【动】❶ be tied down by：家务～ be tied down by housework ❷ involve in；implicate：别～他人。Don't involve others.

牵连 qiānlián 【动】implicate；involve：这个案件～了一些人。Several persons were implicated in this lawsuit.

牵强　qiānqiǎng　【形】far-fetched：你这个解释有些～。Your explanation sounds far-fetched.

牵强附会　qiānqiǎng fùhuì　make a far-fetched comparison；make a strained interpretation：举这个例子来说明你的论点，太～了。Using that kind of example to illustrate your argument is really far-fetched.

牵涉　qiānshè　【动】involve；be linked up with：这个方案～到许多复杂的技术问题。This project involves a lot of complex technical problems.

牵引　qiānyǐn　【动】pull；draw；haul

牵引力　qiānyǐnlì　【名】(phys.) traction；traction force

牵制　qiānzhì　【动】(mil.) contain；pin down：他们团的任务是～对方的侧翼。The task of their regiment was to pin down the flanks of the enemy.

铅（鉛）　qiān　【名】lead

铅版　qiānbǎn　【名】〔块 kuài〕stereotype；printing plate

铅笔　qiānbǐ　【名】〔枝 zhī〕pencil

铅球　qiānqiú　【名】〔个 gè〕❶ shot (used in shot-put) ❷ shot-put

铅印　qiānyìn　【动】print by the use of stereotypes

铅字　qiānzì　【名】(printing) type

谦（謙）　qiān

谦辞　qiāncí　【名】polite words；courteous expressions【动】decline；turn down politely

谦让　qiānràng　【动】modestly decline

谦虚　qiānxū　【形】modest：取得一些成绩，更要～。The fact that you have made some achievements should make you more modest.

谦逊　qiānxùn　【形】modest；unassuming

签（簽）　qiān　【动】sign (one's name)：～上你的名字 please sign your name

签到　qiān = dào　sign in on arrival

签订　qiāndìng　【动】conclude and sign (an agreement, etc.)：两国～了文化协定。The two countries signed a cultural agreement.

签发　qiānfā　【动】sign and issue (documents, etc.)：～文件 sign and dispatch a document ～护照 issue a passport

签名　qiānmíng　【名】signature

签名　qiān = míng　sign one's name

签收　qiānshōu　【动】sign to acknowledge the receipt of

签署　qiānshǔ　【动】sign (an official document)

签约　qiān = yuē　sign a treaty or an agreement

签证　qiānzhèng　【名】visa

签字　qiānzì　【名】同"签名"【名】

签字　qiān = zì　同"签名"

qián

前　qián　【名】❶ ◇ in front；before：门～停着一辆小汽车。There was a car parked in front of the door. 汉字在～，拼音在后。The Chinese character came first；the phonetic transcription followed. ❷ ago：三年～，这里还是一片荒地呢！Three years ago, this place was a waste land. ❸ ◇ forward；ahead；the future：往～看，美好的远景展现在眼前。Look ahead, and a bright prospect unfolding before you. 【形】(attrib. only) ❶ first；front：～五名 the first five persons ～几排 the first few rows ❷ former；previous：～总统 the former president ～部长 the previous minister

前辈　qiánbèi　【名】older genera-

tion；predecessor

前边　qiánbiān　【名】❶ in front；before：个子矮的孩子坐在～。The shorter children are to sit at the front. 名单上你的名字在我的名字～。Your name comes before mine on the list. ❷ above；preceding：～一页是这本书的序言。The preface to this book is on the preceding page. 问题～已经摆出来了，咱们研究一下吧！Now that the problems have already been raised as stated above, let's look into them.

前车之鉴　qián chē zhī jiàn　the overturned cart in front serves as a warning to the carts behind；(fig.) learn from sb. else's mistakes

前程　qiánchéng　【名】(of a person) prospects；future career：～万里 bright prospects ～远大 brilliant prospects

前导　qiándǎo　【名】the person or thing that leads the way：游行队伍以仪仗队为～。The procession was led by a guard of honour.

前额　qián'é　【名】forehead

前方　qiánfāng　【名】❶ (mil.) the front；the front lines ❷ place ahead

前锋　qiánfēng　【名】vanguard；forward

前赴后继　qián fù hòu jì　no sooner had one stepped forward than others followed

前功尽弃　qián gōng jìn qì　all previous work has been wasted：雨季前大坝必须建成，不然，洪水一来就～。The dam must be completed before the rainy season sets in; otherwise, all our work so far will have been wasted.

前后　qiánhòu　【名】❶ (of time) around：估计他在五一节～能回北京。According to my calculations, he will be back in Beijing around May Day. ❷ (of time) from beginning to end：这篇小说从动笔到定稿，～用了一年时间。The novel took a year to write, from start to finish. ❸ in front and behind：房子～都是果树。There are fruit trees in front and at the back of the house.

前进　qiánjìn　【动】advance；go forward

前景　qiánjǐng　【名】visions of the future

前科　qiánkē　【名】criminal record；previous crime

前列　qiánliè　【名】foremost；forefront

前列腺　qiánlièxiàn　【名】prostate gland

前面　qiánmiàn　【名】同"前边"

前年　qiánnián　【名】the year before last

前怕狼，后怕虎　qián pà láng, hòu pà hǔ　fear the wolf in front and the tiger behind；(fig.) be full of fears and misgivings：放心干吧，不要～的！Go ahead and do it, and don't be hampered by unnecessary scruples! 也作"前怕龙，后怕虎"。

前仆后继　qián pū hòu jì　no sooner had one fallen, than another stepped into the breach

前驱　qiánqū　【名】forerunner；vanguard；precursor

前人　qiánrén　【名】forefather；predecessor

前任　qiánrèn　【名】predecessor (in office or position)

前哨　qiánshào　【名】outpost

前身　qiánshēn　【名】predecessor：这个大学的～是女子师范学校。This university grew out of the Women's Normal School.

前所未有　qián suǒ wèi yǒu　unprecedented

前提　qiántí　【名】❶ prerequisite ❷

premise

前天 qiántiān 【名】the day before yesterday

前头 qiántou 【名】同"前边"

前途 qiántú 【名】prospects；future

前往 qiánwǎng 【动】〈书〉leave for；proceed toward：启程～欧洲 leave for Europe ～机场迎接贵宾 go to the airport to welcome a distinguished guest

前卫 qiánwèi 【名】❶（mil.）vanguard；advance guard ❷（sports）half-back

前无古人 qián wú gǔrén unprecedented；unparalleled in history

前夕 qiánxī 【名】(on the)eve (of)

前线 qiánxiàn 【名】battle front

前言 qiányán 【名】preface；foreword

前沿 qiányán 【名】（mil.）forward position

前夜 qiányè 【名】同"前夕"

前因后果 qiányīn hòuguǒ cause and effect；the whole story

前者 qiánzhě 【代】the former

前缀 qiánzhuì 【名】prefix

前奏 qiánzòu 【名】prelude；(music) prelude

虔 qián

虔诚 qiánchéng 【形】(of religion) pious；devout

钱（錢）qián 【名】money 【量】1/10 liang (equivalent to 5 grams)

钱包 qiánbāo 【名】〔个 gè〕purse；wallet

钱财 qiáncái 【名】〔笔 bǐ〕wealth；money

钳（鉗）qián 【名】◇pincers；pliers

钳工 qiángōng 【名】fitter

钳制 qiánzhì 【动】hold fast；hold tight；pin down

钳子 qiánzi 【名】〔把 bǎ〕pincers；pliers；forceps

掮 qián

掮客 qiánkè 【名】broker

乾 qián

乾坤 qiánkūn 【名】the universe

潜 qián 【动】hide；go under

潜藏 qiáncáng 【动】hide：～在海底 hidden at the bottom of the sea

潜伏 qiánfú 【动】lie low；live in hiding：～下来的特务 a hidden enemy agent

潜伏期 qiánfúqī 【名】incubation period

潜力 qiánlì 【名】potential；latent force

潜入 qiánrù 【动】❶ sneak in；enter secretly ❷ submerge；dive

潜水 qián=shuǐ dive

潜水艇 qiánshuǐtǐng 【名】〔艘 sōu〕submarine

潜台词 qiántáicí 【名】what is implied；the hidden meaning；subtext

潜逃 qiántáo 【动】abscond

潜移默化 qián yí mò huà imperceptibly and gradually influence and change (sb.'s thinking, character, etc.)

潜泳 qiányǒng 【名】underwater swimming

潜在 qiánzài 【形】latent；potential

黔 qián

黔驴技穷 qián lǘ jì qióng 黔 is short for Guizhou Province and the fabled donkey there, after having exhausted its tricks, was eaten up by a tiger；(fig.) at one's wit's end

qiǎn

浅（淺）qiǎn 【形】❶ shal-

low：这口井很～。This well is very shallow. 河水很～。The river is rather shallow. ❷ simple；easy：这套历史小丛书内容比较～。The content of this series of booklets on history is quite simple. ❸（of colour）light：～颜色的衣服 light-coloured clothes ❹ superficial：见识～ superficial knowledge and experience

浅薄 qiǎnbó 【形】superficial；shallow

浅见 qiǎnjiàn 【名】superficial point of view

浅近 qiǎnjìn 【形】simple and easy（to understand）：～的道理 plain and simple reasoning

浅陋 qiǎnlòu 【形】（of knowledge）meagre；shallow：知识～ meagre and superficial knowledge 见识～ scanty and superficial knowledge and experience

浅显 qiǎnxiǎn 【形】plain；easy（to understand）：文字～易懂。The language（in which it is written）is easy to understand.

浅易 qiǎnyì 【形】simple and easy：～读物 easy reading material

遣 qiǎn

遣词 qiǎncí 【动】make a choice of wording：～造句 build up a sentence by the choice of words

遣返 qiǎnfǎn 【动】repatriate：～战俘 repatriate P.O.Ws

遣散 qiǎnsàn 【动】disband；send away

遣送 qiǎnsòng 【动】send sb. away forcibly：～出境 deport

谴（譴）qiǎn

谴责 qiǎnzé 【动】denounce；condemn：～占领者的罪行 condemn atrocities of the occupiers

qiàn

欠 qiàn 【动】❶ owe：～债 owe a debt ～他五块钱 owe him five *yuan* ❷ short of；lacking in：～妥 not very appropriate ～考虑 without due consideration 这样做～斟酌。This matter has been handled with a lack of discretion. ❸ raise slightly：～一～身 raise oneself slightly

欠安 qiàn'ān 【动】be under the weather；be unwell

欠情 qiàn = qíng be indebted to sb.；owe sb. a debt of gratitude：欠他的情 feel indebted to him

欠缺 qiànquē 【动】be short of；be deficient in 【名】deficiency；shortcoming

欠债 qiàn = zhài be in debt：欠了一身债 be heavily indebted

欠账 qiàn = zhàng ❶ owe a debt；run into debt ❷ bills due；outstanding accounts

嵌 qiàn 【动】inlay：桌面上～着象牙雕成的花 a table inlaid with ivory

歉 qiàn

歉收 qiànshōu 【动】have a poor harvest

歉意 qiànyì 【名】apology

qiāng

枪（槍）qiāng 【名】〔枝 zhī〕gun；rifle；pistol

枪毙 qiāngbì 【动】execute by shooting

枪法 qiāngfǎ 【名】marksmanship

枪杆 qiānggǎn 【名】（～儿）the barrel of a gun；gun；arms 也作"枪杆

子"。

枪决 qiāngjué 【动】同"枪毙"

枪林弹雨 qiāng lín dàn yǔ　in the midst of heavy gunfire：战士们冒着～冲上高地。Under heavy fire, the soldiers charged the height.

枪炮 qiāngpào 【名】firearms；arms；guns

枪杀 qiāngshā 【动】kill by shooting

枪支 qiāngzhī 【名】guns

腔 qiāng 【名】❶（of human or animal body）cavity：胸～ chest cavity 腹～ abdominal cavity 一～热血 full of enthusiasm ❷（～儿）（of speech）accent：他一口山东～。He speaks with a heavy Shandong accent. ❸（～儿）（of music）melody；tune：他唱得糟透了，没～没调的！His singing was awful, quite out of tune!

腔调 qiāngdiào 【名】❶ melody；tune ❷（of speech）accent：一听他的～，就知道是四川人。As soon as we heard his accent, we knew he was from Sichuan.

腔骨 qiānggǔ 【名】spinal joints（of pig, sheep etc. for food）

qiáng

强 qiáng 【形】❶ physically strong：身～力壮 strong and healthy 劳动力～（of a person）physically strong；（of a family, etc.）having many able-bodied labourers ❷ of high degree：阳光很～ strong sunshine 风力不～ the wind is not strong ❸ having moral or intellectual strength：纪律性～ be highly disciplined 责任心～ a strong sense of responsibility 理解力～ grasp things quickly；have a quick understanding ❹ better：生活一年比一年～。Life is getting bet-

ter every year. 这块地比那块地土质～。The soil of this plot is richer than that of the other plot. ❺ slightly more than：三分之一～ more than one-third 另见 qiǎng

强暴 qiángbào 【形】violent；brutal：～的行为 violent behaviour 【名】violence；brutality；不畏～ defy brutal force 抗击～ resist brutality

强大 qiángdà 【形】powerful；mighty

强盗 qiángdào 【名】robber；bandit

强调 qiángdiào 【动】lay stress on；emphasize

强度 qiángdù 【名】（phys.）intensity

强攻 qiánggōng 【动】storm；raid with violence

强国 qiángguó 【名】powerful nation

强化 qiánghuà 【动】strengthen；intensify

强加 qiángjiā 【动】force on；impose upon：把莫须有的罪名～在他头上 impose a fabricated charge on him

强加于人 qiángjiā yú rén　impose one's views upon others；force sth. on sb.

强奸 qiángjiān 【动】rape

强健 qiángjiàn 【形】strong and healthy

强劲 qiángjìng 【形】forceful：～的西风 a strong west wind

强烈 qiángliè 【形】strong；violent；intense：～的光线 strong light ～的愿望 an intense desire 表示～不满 express strong discontent ～的战斗气氛 a strong militant atmosphere ～的对比 strong contrast ～的仇恨 intense hatred

强权 qiángquán 【名】might；power：～政治 power politics 正义战胜～。Right triumphs over might.

强人 qiángrén 【名】person of initia-

tive；strongman；go-getter：女～a very capable woman；a queen or mistress of sth.

强盛 qiángshèng 【形】prosperous and powerful

强手 qiángshǒu 【名】expert；dab；man of high calibre

强项 qiángxiàng 【名】a strong point；sth. one is good at

强行 qiángxíng 【动】by force：～通过封锁线 forcibly break through the blockade

强硬 qiángyìng 【形】unyielding；strong

强占 qiángzhàn 【动】occupy by force

强制 qiángzhì 【动】compel；force：～执行 carry out under coercion

强壮 qiángzhuàng 【形】strong；robust；sturdy

墙（墙）qiáng 【名】〔堵 dǔ〕wall

墙报 qiángbào 【名】〔期 qī〕wall-newspaper

墙壁 qiángbì 【名】wall

墙角 qiángjiǎo 【名】corner enclosed by two walls

墙脚 qiángjiǎo 【名】❶ foot of a wall ❷ (fig.) foundation；cornerstone

qiǎng

抢（搶）qiǎng 【动】❶ snatch；take by force；rob；loot：～球 grab the ball 他把我的书～走了。He snatched my book from me. ❷ vie with each other to be the first：～着发表意见 vie with others to be the first to voice one's opinion ❸ rush：～季节 (of agriculture) rush in order to complete on time 争时间，～速度 race against time

抢答 qiǎngdá 【动】vie to answer；compete to answer：～题 competitive questions for instant answers

抢渡 qiǎngdù 【动】cross (a river) with all possible speed

抢夺 qiǎngduó 【动】grab；seize by force

抢购 qiǎnggòu 【动】rush to purchase：～粮食 a buying spree for grain；rush to purchase grain

抢劫 qiǎngjié 【动】loot；rob；plunder

抢救 qiǎngjiù 【动】rush to rescue；rush to save：～车祸中的儿童 rush to rescue children in a traffic accident ～国家财产 rush to save state property

抢收 qiǎngshōu 【动】get the harvest in quickly

抢手 qiǎngshǒu 【形】hot；in demand：～货 goods in great demand；hot goods or items；merchandize which is much sought after

抢先 qiǎng = xiān compete to be the first：～占领制高点 rush to occupy a commanding height 刚一开会小高就～发言。Xiao Gao began to speak before everybody else，just as the meeting started.

抢险 qiǎngxiǎn 【动】make emergency repairs in dangerous circumstances：河堤决口，大家都赶来～。As the dyke was breached, everybody rushed to make emergency repairs.

抢修 qiǎngxiū 【动】rush to repair

抢种 qiǎngzhòng 【动】rush to plant or sow

强 qiǎng
另见 qiáng

强辩 qiǎngbiàn 【动】use lame arguments to justify oneself

强词夺理 qiǎng cí duó lǐ use lame arguments；resort to sophistry：错

了就要承认，不要～。If you are wrong, just admit it, do not resort to lame arguments.

强迫 qiǎngpò 【动】compel；force；～命令 command and compel ～执行 force sb. to do sth. ～他交出赃款 compel him to hand over the stolen money

强求 qiǎngqiú 【动】impose；forcibly demand

强人所难 qiǎng rén suǒ nán try to force sb. to do what is beyond his power or against his will

qiāo

悄 qiāo

悄悄 qiāoqiāo 【副】❶ silently；quietly；stealthily：～说话 speak quietly 他～地走进来。He stole in silently. ❷ (of actions) secretly；quietly：他～地把小高的衣服拿去洗了。Without telling anyone, he did Xiao Gao's laundry.

锹 (鍬) qiāo 【名】〔把 bǎ〕shovel；spade

敲 qiāo 【动】knock；beat (a drum)：～门 knock on the door ～锣打鼓 beat gongs and drums ～警钟 (fig.) sound the alarm

敲边鼓 qiāo biāngǔ play a secondary role；play a supporting role

敲打 qiāodǎ 【动】beat；strike (gong or drum)

敲定 qiāodìng 【动】settle；decide on

敲骨吸髓 qiāo gǔ xī suǐ break the bone and suck the marrow；(fig.) enforce the most relentless oppression and exploitation

敲门砖 qiāoménzhuān 【名】stepping stone to success

敲诈 qiāozhà 【动】blackmail；extort

敲诈勒索 qiāozhà lèsuǒ practise extortion

敲竹杠 qiāo zhúgàng take advantage of a person's weak position to extort money, goods, etc.

qiáo

乔 (喬) qiáo

乔木 qiáomù 【名】(bot.) arbor；tree

乔装打扮 qiáozhuāng dǎbàn disguise oneself：不管他怎样～，迟早总会被识破。No matter how he disguises himself, he will be seen through sooner or later.

侨 (僑) qiáo 【名】◇a person living abroad

侨胞 qiáobāo 【名】one's fellow countryman who lives abroad

侨汇 qiáohuì 【名】remittance from a national residing abroad

侨居 qiáojū 【动】live abroad

侨眷 qiáojuàn 【名】relatives of overseas residents

侨民 qiáomín 【名】person living abroad but retaining his or her original nationality；a national (of a certain country) residing abroad

侨务 qiáowù 【名】affairs concerning nationals living abroad

侨乡 qiáoxiāng 【名】location with many of its natives having relatives living abroad

侨资 qiáozī 【名】investment from overseas residents

桥 (橋) qiáo 【名】〔座 zuò〕bridge

桥洞 qiáodòng 【名】bridge opening

桥墩 qiáodūn 【名】bridge pier

桥梁 qiáoliáng 【名】〔座 zuò〕bridges

桥牌 qiáopái 【名】bridge (card

game)：打～ play bridge

桥头堡　qiáotóubǎo　【名】❶ bridge-head ❷ bridge tower

樵 qiáo

樵悴　qiáocuì　【形】haggard

瞧 qiáo　【动】〈口〉see；look

瞧不起　qiáo bu qǐ　hold in low esteem；look down upon

瞧得起　qiáo de qǐ　have a high regard for；hold sb. in esteem

瞧见　qiáo//jiàn　see

qiǎo

巧 qiǎo　【形】❶（of hand, speech, etc.）clever：他嘴～，学谁像谁。He's got a clever tongue, and can mimic anyone's voice. ❷ skilful；intelligent：苦干加～干 work hard and skilfully 能工～匠 skilled workmen ～媳妇难为（wéi）无米之炊。Even a clever housewife cannot cook a meal without rice. ❸ coincidental；fortuitous；by a happy chance：～极了，我一下火车就碰上了他。What a coincidence! I met him the moment I got off the train. 真不～，我前面的人买走了最后两张票。What bad luck! The man right before me bought the last two tickets.

巧夺天工　qiǎo duó tiān gōng　workmanship which excels nature：刺绣的小猫，栩栩如生，真是～。The embroidered kittens were so lifelike they seem to jump out of the frame.

巧合　qiǎohé　【动】coincide；by chance；by coincidence：在英语和汉语中都用"趁热打铁"表示抓紧时机做一件事，真是～! Both in English and Chinese, "strike while the iron is hot" is used to express the idea of seizing a good opportunity. What a coincidence!

巧克力　qiǎokèlì　【名】chocolate

巧立名目　qiǎo lì míngmù　think up all sorts of pretexts

巧妙　qiǎomiào　【形】（of method, skills, etc.）clever；wonderful；ingenious：～的办法 an ingenious method 伪装得很～ cleverly camouflaged

巧取豪夺　qiǎo qǔ háo duó　obtain by force or deception；rob by force or by trick

qiào

俏 qiào　【形】chic；smart：她打扮得很～。She is smartly dressed.

俏货　qiàohuò　【名】goods in great demand

俏皮　qiàopi　【形】（of manners or speech）humorous；witty

俏皮话　qiàopihuà　【名】witty remarks；witty and sarcastic remarks：小李爱说～。Xiao Li is fond of making witty remarks.

峭 qiào

峭壁　qiàobì　【名】cliff；precipice

窍（竅）qiào

窍门　qiàomén　【名】（～儿）knack；know-how：找～ get the knack of it 任务完成得这么漂亮，一定有不少～吧! You must have a real knack for it since you've done such a splendid job.

翘（翹）qiào　【动】rise on one end；tilt

翘尾巴　qiào wěiba　be cocky：他一有点成绩就爱～。Even the slightest achievement tends to make him cocky.

qiē

切　qiē【动】❶ cut：～菜 chop vegetables 把西瓜～开 cut open a watermelon ❷（maths.）tangent：两圆相～ two circles tangent to each other
另见 qiè

切除 qiēchú【动】cut off；（med.）excise；resection

切磋 qiēcuō【动】同"切磋琢磨"：这个方案经过多次～，更加切实可行了。After the plan had been discussed and amended many times, it became more practical.

切磋琢磨 qiēcuō zhuómó study and learn by mutual discussion

切断 qiē∥duàn cut off；disconnect；sever：～交通 sever communication lines 联系被～了。Contacts were cut off.

切汇 qiēhuì【动】short change sb. in foreign exchange transaction；cheat for profits in foreign exchange transaction

切片 qiēpiàn【名】（med.）section

切线 qiēxiàn【名】（maths.）tangent (line)

切削 qiēxiāo【动】（mech.）cut

qié

茄　qié

茄子 qiézi【名】〔个 gè〕eggplant

qiě

且　qiě【副】❶ for the time being（usu. in written language）：你～别忙下结论，还是先听听大家的意见。Don't jump to any conclusion yet；listen to what others have to say. ❷〈口〉且…呢 for a long time to come（this structure allows no object）：这种花～开呢! These flowers will be blooming for a long time yet. 这种料子～穿不坏呢! This kind of dress material will last for ages.【连】❶ both… and…（used in conjunction with 既 to connect two monosyllabic adjectives）：新疆马既高～大。Xinjiang horses are both tall and big-boned. ❷ 且…且… connecting two monosyllabic verbs, denoting two actions that happen concurrently：我们～走～谈，不一会儿就到目的地了。We kept up a conversation as we walked, and soon arrived.

qiè

切　qiè【动】fit；correspond to：～题 stick to the topic 他的计划不～实际。His plan doesn't fit the realities of the situation.【形】◇ urgent；eager：学习心～ eager to study 他救人心～，根本没考虑个人安危。In his eagerness to save lives, he simply ignored his own safety altogether.【副】make sure；by all means：这种病～不可吃刺激性强的东西。Make sure that patients suffering from this illness never eat anything which might be irritating. ～～不可麻痹大意。Make sure that this is not taken lightly.
另见 qiē

切齿 qièchǐ【形】grind one's teeth (in hatred or anger)：～痛恨 grind one's teeth in hatred

切肤之痛 qiè fū zhī tòng sorrow which cuts to the quick；a piercing sorrow

切合实际 qièhé shíjì accurately reflect actual conditions

切记 qièjì 【动】be sure to remember (*used when giving advice*)

切身 qièshēn 【形】❶ of immediate concern to oneself：～利益 one's vital interests ❷ personal；first-hand：～体验到长跑的好处 first-hand experience of the benefits of long-distance running ～感受 personal impressions and experience

切实 qièshí 【形】❶ practical；realistic：办法～可行。The measures are feasible. ❷ conscientious；earnest：切切实实地进行工作 work conscientiously

切题 qiètí 【形】keep to the point

切中要害 qièzhòng yàohài hit the nail on the head：他提的几点意见都～。The points he raised hit the nail right on the head.

怯 qiè 【形】timid；cowardly；nervous

怯懦 qiènuò 【形】timid；cowardly：他在困难面前毫不～。In the face of difficulties, he was completely unafraid.

怯弱 qièruò 【形】timid and weak

怯阵 qiè=zhèn be battle-shy；have stage fright

窃（竊）qiè 【动】◇ steal 【副】secretly；stealthily：～听 eavesdrop；wiretap；bug ～笑 laugh up one's sleeve

窃据 qièjù 【动】usurp

窃取 qièqǔ 【动】steal；usurp：～荣誉 take credit where none is due ～要职 usurp a key post

窃听器 qiètīngqì 【名】bug device；wire-tapping device

窃贼 qièzéi 【名】thief

惬（愜）qiè

惬意 qièyì 【形】pleased；satisfied

qīn

钦（欽）qīn

钦差大臣 qīnchāi dàchén imperial envoy

钦佩 qīnpèi 【动】admire；esteem；think highly of：大家对他这种苦干实干的精神非常～。We all think highly of his hard-working and down-to-earth work-style.

侵 qīn

侵犯 qīnfàn 【动】encroach upon；intrude；violate：～主权 violate the sovereignty of 祖国的神圣领土不容～。We will not tolerate any encroachment upon the territory of our country.

侵害 qīnhài 【动】violate；infringe upon；injure：田鼠～农作物。Field mice damage crops. 有些化学药品会～人的肌体。Some chemical medicines harm the human body.

侵略 qīnlüè 【动】invade；commit aggression

侵略战争 qīnlüè zhànzhēng aggressive war

侵略者 qīnlüèzhě 【名】aggressor；invader

侵权 qīn=quán tort：～行为 infringement act

侵扰 qīnrǎo 【动】invade and harass

侵入 qīnrù 【动】invade；intrude into

侵蚀 qīnshí 【动】corrode；erode；weather：这所老房子经过多年风雨的～,墙皮已经脱落了。Due to weathering by long years of wind and rain, the covering has peeled off the walls of this old house.

侵吞 qīntūn 【动】❶ embezzle；misappropriate ❷ annex forcibly；swallow up

侵袭 qīnxí 【动】make a sneak at-

tack on

侵占 qīnzhàn 【动】invade and occupy；encroach upon

亲（親） qīn 【形】❶ related by blood；next-of-kin：～姐妹 sisters ❷ intimate；loving；close：～如一家 be like one family【名】◇ relative（by blood or by marriage）：表～ relative on one's mother's side 沾～带故 be either a relative or a friend【动】kiss：妈妈～了孩子一下。The mother kissed her baby.

另见 qìng

亲爱 qīn'ài 【形】dear；beloved

亲笔 qīnbǐ 【名】one's own handwriting：你来看看这几行字是不是他的～。Please come and see if these few lines are in his own handwriting.【副】（written）in one's own hand：这封信是他～写的。This letter was written in his own hand.

亲传 qīnchuán 【动】impart in person；pass on（knowledge，skill）personally

亲近 qīnjìn 【形】intimate；close：他们俩从小就很～。Those two have been very close since childhood.【动】be friends with；seek sb.'s company：赵老师又热情又耐心，同学们都愿意～她。Comrade Zhao is an enthusiastic and patient teacher, and her students all enjoy being with her.

亲口 qīnkǒu 【副】(say sth.) personally；(taste sth.) oneself；in person：～尝一尝 taste it for oneself 这是他～对我说的。He told me this in person.

亲密 qīnmì 【形】very intimate；close：关系～ close relationship ～的伙伴 close pals ～无间 on intimate terms with each other

亲朋 qīnpéng 【名】kith and kin；relatives and friends

亲戚 qīnqi 【名】relative；kin

亲切 qīnqiè 【形】cordial；warm；sincere；～的关怀 kind concern；loving care 我回到久别的家乡，感到格外～。When I returned to my hometown which I had left so long ago, I was especially aware of its warmth and closeness.

亲热 qīnrè 【形】warm；cordial；warm and affectionate：老同学一见面显得特别～。When old classmates meet again, they feel a special closeness.

亲人 qīnrén 【名】relative；kin：他从小就死了父母，没有什么～。He lost his parents as a child, and has no near kin. 边疆人民像迎接～一样迎接北京来的医生。The people in the border region welcomed the medical team from Beijing as if they were their own kin.

亲身 qīnshēn 【形】personal；firsthand：～的体验 personal experience ～的感受 first-hand experience 他要不是～经历过这些事，怎么能讲得这样具体、生动呢！How could he have talked so concretely and vividly without personal experience of these things?

亲生 qīnshēng 【形】(of parents or children) related biologically not by adoption

亲手 qīnshǒu 【副】with one's own hand

亲属 qīnshǔ 【名】relatives

亲王 qīnwáng 【名】prince

亲吻 qīnwěn 【动】kiss；peck on the cheek

亲信 qīnxìn 【名】trusted follower

亲眼 qīnyǎn 【副】with one's own eyes：不是～看到的话，我真不能相信可以用针麻来进行手术。If I had not seen it with my own eyes, I wouldn't have believed that acupuncture anaesthesia could be used in surgical operations.

亲友 qīnyǒu 【名】friends and relatives

亲者痛,仇者快 qīnzhě tòng, chóuzhě kuài grieve those near and dear to you and gladden your enemy

亲自 qīnzì 【副】(do sth.) in person; oneself (out of concern): ～动手 do the job oneself ～过问 look into (the matter) personally 院长请您～来一趟,他想跟您当面谈谈。The president of the institute would like you to come over in person, as he wants to have a face-to-face talk with you.

亲嘴 qīn=zuǐ kiss

qín

琴 qín 【名】a general term for stringed instruments (including piano)

勤 qín 【形】❶ diligent; industrious; hard-working (as opp. to 懒):他这个人手～,屋子总是收拾得干干净净的。He is very handy about the house and always keeps his place neat. ❷ often; constant; frequent: ～换衣服 ～洗澡 bath and change regularly 今年雨下得太～了。It has rained too much this year.

勤奋 qínfèn 【形】hard-working; diligent

勤工俭学 qín gōng jiǎn xué part-work and part-study system

勤俭 qínjiǎn 【形】industrious and frugal: ～持家 frugal management of a household ～办一切事业 run all undertakings with thrift

勤俭建国 qínjiǎn jiàn guó build the country through hard work and thrift

勤俭节约 qínjiǎn jiéyuē be industrious and economical

勤谨 qínjin 【形】dutiful and industrious:他是个～人,整天闲不住。He is conscientious and diligent, and is never idle.

勤恳 qínkěn 【形】diligent and conscientious:学习很～ study earnestly and diligently 勤勤恳恳的工作态度 an earnest and conscientious attitude towards work

勤快 qínkuài 【形】diligent and efficient:老李非常～,总是一大早就起来打扫院子。Lao Li is diligent. He gets up early every morning to sweep the courtyard.

勤劳 qínláo 【形】hard-working; industrious: ～勇敢的民族 a hard-working and valiant people

勤勉 qínmiǎn 【形】earnest and diligent (oft. used as predicate)

勤务员 qínwùyuán 【名】orderly; army or government service personnel:干部不论职位高低,都是人民的～。All cadres, regardless of rank or position, are servants of the people.

勤学苦练 qín xué kǔ liàn study hard and practise painstakingly

勤杂人员 qínzá rényuán odd-job man; supporting staff

qīng

青 qīng 【形】❶ blue; green: ～山绿水 green hills and blue waters ～草 green grass ❷ ◇ black: ～布 black coloured cloth ～线 black thread

青菜 qīngcài 【名】green vegetable; greens

青草 qīngcǎo 【名】〔棵 kē〕green grass

青出于蓝 qīng chū yú lán blue is extracted from the indigo plant, but is bluer than the original; (fig.) the pupil learns from and outshines his teacher

青春 qīngchūn 【名】youth

青春期 qīngchūnqī 【名】puberty

青翠 qīngcuì 【形】green and fresh

青光眼 qīngguāngyǎn 【名】glaucoma

青红皂白 qīng hóng zào bái distinction between black and white, right and wrong：他刚进会议室，也不分～，就支持一方，反对另一方。Hardly had he entered the meeting room when, without sorting out the issues, he began to support one side and oppose the other.

青黄不接 qīng huáng bù jiē when the new crop is still growing and the old stock has been consumed；(fig.) a temporary shortage

青睐 qīnglài 【名】favor：受到～ be favored

青霉素 qīngméisù 【名】penicillin

青梅竹马 qīngméi zhúmǎ affection between opposite sexes developed from playing together innocently in childhood；childhood attachment (of opposite sexes)

青年 qīngnián 【名】young person

青纱帐 qīngshāzhàng 【名】a "green curtain" of tall and thick crops：游击队员利用～作掩护，开展武装斗争。Making use of the tall and thick crops as cover the gurrillas went into battle.

青山绿水 qīngshān lǜshuǐ blue hills and green water (beautiful scenery)

青饲料 qīngsìliào 【名】green fodder

青天 qīngtiān 【名】the blue sky；an uncorrupt and upright official

青铜 qīngtóng 【名】bronze

青铜器时代 qīngtóngqì shídài the Bronze Age

青蛙 qīngwā 【名】〔只 zhī〕frog

青云直上 qīngyún zhí shàng rocket up in the social ladder；rapid rise in career

轻（輕）qīng 【形】❶ light in weight：塑料制品都很～。Plastics is very light. 活儿很～。It's an easy job. ❷ small in number or degree：年纪～ young in age 伤得不～ seriously wounded 处罚太～。The punishment is too light. ❸ light；gentle：手～点儿 do it gently ～拿～放 handle with care ❹ (of voice) low：请你说话声音～点儿。Please keep your voice down. 【动】◇ slight；belittle：重男～女 value boys and belittle girls

轻便 qīngbiàn 【形】easy and convenient；light；handy；portable：～自行车 a light bicycle 这种行军床携带～。This cot is easy to carry.

轻敌 qīng = dí underestimate the enemy

轻而易举 qīng ér yì jǔ easy；effortless

轻浮 qīngfú 【形】frivolous；flighty

轻工业 qīnggōngyè 【名】light industry

轻举妄动 qīng jǔ wàng dòng be imprudent；act rashly；take a reckless action：作战方案尚需慎重考虑，且不要～。Since the battle-plan needs further careful consideration, we must not act rashly.

轻快 qīngkuài 【形】❶ brisk：脚步～ with brisk steps ❷ lively；light-hearted：～的乐曲 a light-hearted melody

轻描淡写 qīng miáo dàn xiě touch lightly on；gloss over (important points)：这是个关键问题，不能～，一笔带过。Since this is a pivotal question, we must not gloss it over.

轻蔑 qīngmiè 【形】contemptuous

轻飘飘 qīngpiāopiāo 【形】❶ light as a feather ❷ (of remarks, behaviour) frivolous

轻巧 qīngqiǎo 【形】❶ light and

portable; delicate and well-made: ~的电子计算机 a compact and handy electronic computer ❷ agile; dexterous: 她的平衡木表演,动作~, 姿势优美。She performed on the balance beam with agility and grace. ❸ light; easy: 你说的倒~, 哪有那么容易的事! When you talk, you make it sound easy, but nothing is that simple. 这活儿看起来很容易,其实并不~。The work is not as easy as it looks.

轻取　qīngqǔ　【动】win hands down; win easily

轻生　qīngshēng　【动】make light of one's own life; take one's own life

轻声　qīngshēng　【名】neutral tone

轻视　qīngshì　【动】make light of; slight; look down upon

轻率　qīngshuài　【形】rash; hasty

轻松　qīngsōng　【形】relaxed; light-hearted; light (work)

轻微　qīngwēi　【形】slight; light

轻信　qīngxìn　【动】be credulous; readily believe

轻易　qīngyì　【形】simple and easy (*usu. in neg.*): 考虑不成熟,他~不会往外说的。He is never in a hurry to make commitments without first thinking the matter over. 这种鸟北方~见不到。This species of bird is rarely seen in the North.

轻于鸿毛　qīng yú hóngmáo　lighter than a feather; extremely insignificant

轻重　qīngzhòng　【名】❶ weight ❷ degree of seriousness; relative importance: 根据病情~来确定治疗方案。A treatment plan will be made based on the patient's condition. ❸ (of speech or action) propriety: 说话不知~ talk without propriety

轻重缓急　qīng zhòng huǎn jí　order of importance and urgency; order of priority: 各项工作要根据~合理安排。All the work should be suit-ably arranged in order of importance and urgency.

轻装　qīngzhuāng　【名】light equipment; light pack

氢(氫)　qīng　【名】hydrogen

氢弹　qīngdàn　【名】〔枚 méi〕hydrogen bomb

倾(傾)　qīng　【动】❶ incline ❷ ◇ pour out; empty: ~囊相助 empty one's pockets to help sb. ~巢出动 turn out in full force (derog.)

倾家荡产　qīng jiā dàng chǎn　be completely ruined financially; go bankrupt

倾盆大雨　qīngpén dàyǔ　pouring rain; down-pour

倾诉　qīngsù　【动】〈书〉make a clean breast of: ~衷情 pour out one's innermost feelings 她心里有许多话要向母亲~。She had such a lot of things to tell her mother.

倾听　qīngtīng　【动】listen attentively to; hear out(used of a person in a higher position toward his subordinates): ~意见 listen attentively to different opinions ~群众的呼声 listen to what the people have to say

倾向　qīngxiàng　【动】be inclined to support one side rather than the other; tend to: 我比较~于老王的意见。I rather tend toward Lao Wang's opinion. 【名】inclination; tendency: 纠正不良~ rectify (correct) undesirable tendencies 我们要注意在防范一种不良~时不要忽视其他不良~的存在。Our vigilance towards one kind of tendency may blind us to the existence of others.

倾向性　qīngxiàngxìng　【名】bias; tendentiousness

倾销　qīngxiāo　【动】dump (e. g. goods)

倾斜 qīngxié 【形】 slanting；inclined

倾泻 qīngxiè 【动】(of large quantities of liquid) pour

倾轧 qīngyà 【动】(of different cliques in a political party) engage in factional strife

倾注 qīngzhù 【动】❶ pour into；empty into ❷ (of force, energy) concentrate on sth.：他把全部心血都～在教育事业上。He devotes all of his energy to educational work.

清 qīng 【形】❶ pure；clean；clear：～～的流水，蓝蓝的天 clear water and blue skies ❷ clear；clarified：道理要讲～ explain the reasons clearly 认～方向 be sure of one's bearings ❸ with nothing left：把借的东西还～了。Everything borrowed has been returned. ❹ simple；pure：～汤 clear soup ～茶 pure green tea (without sugar, etc.) 京剧～唱 sing Beijing opera without make-up or acting 【动】❶ (of accounts) settle：～账 settle the account ❷ take inventory；check up：～仓 take inventory in the warehouse ❸ ◇ clear：她～～嗓子，唱了起来。She cleared her throat, and began singing.

清白 qīngbái 【形】 pure；unsullied；unblemished：历史～ have a clean record 为人～ be open and honest

清查 qīngchá 【动】 investigate；inquire into；examine；check up：～账目 examine the accounts ～库存物资 check the goods in stock ～户口 make a residence-check

清澈 qīngchè 【形】 clear；lucid：～的泉水 clear spring water

清晨 qīngchén 【名】 early morning

清除 qīngchú 【动】 clear out；get rid of：～垃圾 clear away rubbish ～障碍物 clear away obstacles

清楚 qīngchu 【形】❶ (of photograph, print, etc.) distinct；clear：字迹～ clear handwriting 口齿～ speak distinctly 讲得清清楚楚 explain very clearly ❷ lucid：头脑～ a lucid mind 看问题～ a clear-headed approach to problems 【动】 understand；be clear about：他最～这件事。He knows the ins and outs of the matter.

清脆 qīngcuì 【形】(of sounds) clear

清单 qīngdān 【名】 detailed list

清淡 qīngdàn 【形】❶ (of colour, flavour) light；delicate：～的茶水 weak tea ～的花香 the delicate fragrance of flowers ❷ (of food) not greasy；not strongly flavoured：～的饭菜 a light diet

清点 qīngdiǎn 【动】 take inventory；sort and count

清高 qīnggāo 【形】 aloof and above material pursuits and politics：自命～ describe oneself as "pure and aloof" 这个人很～，一般的人不容易接近他。This guy is rather stand-offish and not easily accessible.

清规戒律 qīngguī jièlǜ taboos and prohibitions；outmoded restrictions：打破～ break through taboos and prohibitions

清洁 qīngjié 【形】 clean

清洁工 qīngjiégōng 【名】 sanitation worker

清净 qīngjìng 【形】 free of annoyance

清静 qīngjìng 【形】 quiet；tranquil

清理 qīnglǐ 【动】 clean up；make final disposal of

清廉 qīnglián 【形】 clean；honest and upright

清凉 qīngliáng 【形】 refreshing and cool

清明(节) qīngmíng(jié) 【名】 the fifth of the 24 divisions of the solar year in the traditional Chinese calendar, occurring on April 5th. or 6th., a day for commemoration of the dead

清爽 qīngshuǎng 【形】❶ cool and refreshing：初秋之夜，空气格外～。On early autumn evening, the air is unusually cool and bracing. ❷ relaxed；relieved：精神负担打消了，他心情～多了。With his mental-burden resolved, he found himself very much relieved.

清水衙门 qīngshuǐ yámen a low-budgetted institution

清算 qīngsuàn 【动】❶ settle (accounts)；settle (scores)：～账目 settle accounts ❷ expose and criticize：～贩毒罪行 condemn and expose drug trafficking

清谈 qīngtán 【名】empty talk

清晰 qīngxī 【形】crystal-clear；distinct：声音～ a clear voice 河底石子～可见。You can see very clearly pebbles lying on the river bed.

清洗 qīngxǐ 【动】❶ clean：～零件 clean parts or accessories ❷ (of political party, etc.) purge；get rid of (undesirable elements)

清闲 qīngxián 【形】have plenty of leisure

清香 qīngxiāng 【形】delicate and fresh fragrance

清新 qīngxīn 【形】delightfully fresh；pure and fresh：文笔～ a refreshing style 空气～。The air is delightfully fresh.

清醒 qīngxǐng 【形】sober；sane；clear-headed：神志～ mentally sound 头脑～ clear-headed ～的认识 (have) a sober understanding 【动】return to one's senses；sober up：他从昏迷中～过来。He's come to himself. 在严酷的事实面前，他～了。Faced with harsh reality, he sobered up.

清秀 qīngxiù 【形】delicate-looking

清样 qīngyàng 【名】final proof (prior to printing)

清一色 qīngyīsè 【形】all of the same suit；all of the same colour；homogeneous：这个果园是～的桃树。This orchard is planted with nothing but peach trees.

清音 qīngyīn 【名】voiceless sound

清早 qīngzǎo 【名】同"清晨"

清账 qīng＝zhàng square (or clear) an account

清真 qīngzhēn 【名】Moslem

蜻

qīng

蜻蜓 qīngtíng 【名】〔只 zhī〕dragon-fly

蜻蜓点水 qīngtíng diǎn shuǐ dragon-flies skim over the water；(fig.) touch superficially：这篇文章虽涉及不少问题，但都是～，阐述得不深不透。This article touches on a lot of problems, but only superficially.

qíng

情

qíng 【名】◇ ❶ feelings ❷ condition

情报 qíngbào 【名】information；intelligence

情不自禁 qíng bù zì jīn cannot help：喜讯传来，大家～地欢呼起来。As soon as the good news reached us, we could not help bursting into cheers.

情敌 qíngdí 【名】rival in love

情调 qíngdiào 【名】sentiment；flavour：异国～ exotic flavour

情夫 qíngfū 【名】a (married) woman's lover

情妇 qíngfù 【名】a mistress

情感 qínggǎn 【名】emotion；feelings

情节 qíngjié 【名】❶ (of a story, etc.) plot；details：故事～曲折 a story with a complicated plot ❷ circumstances；details of a legal case：根据～轻重，分别处理 to deal with a case according to its degree of seriousness

情景　qíngjǐng　【名】scene；sight

情况　qíngkuàng　【名】❶ state of affairs；circumstances；condition；situation：生产～ production situation 思想～ mental state ❷（mil.）new developments：密切注意周围～ pay close attention to what's happening around

情理　qínglǐ　【名】sense；reason：合乎～ stand to reason；sensible 不近～ unreasonable

情侣　qínglǚ　【名】lovers

情面　qíngmiàn　【名】face；feelings：打破～ do not attempt to spare anybody's feelings 碍于～ because of facesaving considerations 在原则问题上不能讲～。We must not act out of facesaving considerations where matters of principle are concerned.

情人　qíngrén　【名】lover；sweetheart

情书　qíngshū　【名】〔封 fēng〕a love letter；billet-doux

情投意合　qíng tóu yì hé　（usu. in a romantic relationship）find each other congenial

情形　qíngxing　【名】general condition；situation

情绪　qíngxù　【名】❶ spirit；morale；mood：生产～高涨。Enthusiasm for production is mounting. 产生了急躁～ be impetuous ❷ moodiness；sulkiness：有一点儿～ have a fit of sulks 他正在闹～呢！He is in a bad mood.

情义　qíngyì　【名】ties of friendship

情谊　qíngyì　【名】friendly feelings

情意　qíngyì　【名】cordiality；love and affection

情由　qíngyóu　【名】the hows and whys (of sth.)

情有可原　qíng yǒu kě yuán　excusable

情愿　qíngyuàn　【助动】be willing to；wish to；would rather：我～少休息一会儿，也不愿把工作拖到明天。I would rather have less sleep today than put off the work till tomorrow.

晴

晴　qíng　【形】clear；fine

晴空万里　qíngkōng wàn lǐ　clear open sky

晴朗　qínglǎng　【形】bright and clear (weather)

晴纶　qínglún　【名】Orlon

晴天霹雳　qíngtiān pīlì　a bolt from the blue：祖父不幸去世的消息传来，好像～一样，全家顿时沉浸在深切的悲痛之中。The news of grandfather's death was a bolt from the blue, and plunged the whole family into grief.

晴雨表　qíngyǔbiǎo　【名】barometer

qǐng

顷（頃）　qǐng　【量】unit of area（6.6667 hectares）

顷刻　qǐngkè　【名】〈书〉in an instant：～瓦解 instant collapse ～之间雷雨大作。Within an instant, thunder roared and rain poured down.

请（請）　qǐng　【动】❶ request；ask for：我们想～他再讲一遍。We'd like to ask him to repeat what he has just said. ❷（polite form of request）please：～喝茶。Please have a cup of tea. ～不要客气。Please don't stand on ceremony. ❸ invite；send for：～医生看病 send for a doctor ～老工人作报告 invite a veteran worker to talk to us

请安　qǐng＝ān　ask after sb；go and greet

请便　qǐngbiàn　【动】do what pleases one；please oneself：会不开了，大家

要干什么～吧! The meeting is postponed. Everyone is free to leave.

请功　qǐnggōng　【动】ask the higher authorities to record sb.'s meritorious deeds：为得奖运动员～ ask the higher authorities to record the prize-winning athlete's meritorious deeds

请假　qǐng = jià　ask for leave

请教　qǐngjiào　【动】ask for advice；consult

请客　qǐng = kè　entertain；stand treat

请求　qǐngqiú　【动】request；ask：～任务 request a new assignment【名】request：上级批准了他的～。The higher authorities granted his request.

请示　qǐngshì　【动】ask for instructions

请帖　qǐngtiě　【名】invitation card

请问　qǐngwèn　【动】may I ask...：～,去动物园怎么走? Excuse me, but could you tell me how to get to the zoo? ～,这本书多少钱? Excuse me, can you tell me the price of this book? 你说这样做是事倍功半,那么～,究竟该怎么做才能事半功倍? If you say this is the way to get half the result with twice the effort, may I ask you how to get twice the result with half the effort?

请愿　qǐng = yuàn　present a petition

请罪　qǐng = zuì　admit one's error and ask to be punished

请坐　qǐng zuò　please sit down

qìng

庆（慶）　qìng　【动】◇ celebrate；congratulate

庆典　qìngdiǎn　【名】celebration

庆贺　qìnghè　【动】congratulate；celebrate

庆幸　qìngxìng　【动】rejoice (e.g. over a narrow escape)：虽然发生了事故,但值得～的是发觉较早,损失不大。Although there was an accident, we can be thankful that it was discovered early, with minimum damage.

庆祝　qìngzhù　【动】celebrate；congratulate

亲（親）　qīng

另见 qīn

亲家　qìngjia　【名】❶ families related by marriage：他们两家是～。These two families are related by marriage. ❷ parent of one's son-in-law or daughter-in-law

亲家公　qìngjiagōng　【名】father-in-law (of sons or daughters)

亲家母　qìngjiamǔ　【名】mother-in-law (of sons or daughters)

罄　qìng

罄竹难书　qìng zhú nán shū　(of crimes) too numerous to be recorded；罪恶累累,～。His crimes are too numerous to mention.

qióng

穷（窮）　qióng　【形】❶ poor；impoverished ❷ exhausted；hard pressed；pushed to limit

穷兵黩武　qióngbīng dúwǔ　indulge in aggressive wars to the extreme limit of one's armed strength

穷光蛋　qióngguāngdàn　【名】a poor wretch；a poverty-stricken person

穷尽　qióngjìn　【名】end (of resources)：技术的提高是没有～的。There is no end to the possibilities of technological improvement.

穷苦　qióngkǔ　【形】poverty-stricken

穷困　qióngkùn　【形】impoverished

穷人　qióngrén　【名】poor person；

poor people

穷奢极欲 qióng shē jí yù indulge in luxury and extravagance：以前他家过着～的生活。His family used to live a life of wanton extravagance.

穷途末路 qióngtú mòlù dead end

穷乡僻壤 qióngxiāng pìrǎng the remotest corners of the countryside：过去的～现在建成了繁华的城市。This once remote and backward place has now become a prosperous city.

穷凶极恶 qióng xiōng jí è utterly ferocious；extremely evil：～的匪帮 a ferocious bandit gang

穷则思变 qióng zé sī biàn poverty gives rise to the desire for change

qiū

丘 qiū 【名】mound；hillock

丘陵 qiūlíng 【名】hills；hilly

秋 qiū 【名】◇ ❶ autumn；fall：一九四八年～ autumn，1948 ❷ year：千～永志 be remembered forever ❸ period of time（usu. a period in which bad things happen）：多事之～ troubled times

秋风扫落叶 qiūfēng sǎo luòyè autumn wind sweeping away dead leaves；（fig.）irresistible force：以～之势，消灭了全部残匪。The remaining bandits were completely wiped out，like dead leaves swept away by the autumn wind.

秋高气爽 qiū gāo qì shuǎng with clear autumn sky and crisp air

秋耕 qiūgēng 【动】autumn ploughing

秋毫无犯 qiūháo wú fàn （of highly disciplined troops）not commit the slightest offence against civilians：这支军队纪律严明，所到之处～。A highly disciplined army，it never infringed upon civilian interests wherever it is stationed.

秋后蚂蚱 qiūhòu màzha grasshopper in late autumn；（fig.）one's days are numbered

秋季 qiūjì 【名】autumn

秋千 qiūqiān 【名】swing：打～ have a ride on a swing

秋收 qiūshōu 【动】autumn harvest

秋天 qiūtiān 【名】autumn

秋种 qiūzhòng 【动】autumn sowing

蚯 qiū

蚯蚓 qiūyǐn 【名】earthworm

qiú

囚 qiú

囚犯 qiúfàn 【名】prisoner

囚禁 qiújìn 【动】imprison；put in prison

囚徒 qiútú 【名】prisoner

求 qiú 【动】❶ beg；entreat；request：～教 seek advice ～你帮帮忙，好吗？May I ask for your help？❷ strive for；try to obtain；seek：不～名利 not strive for personal fame or gain ～出未知数（maths.）find the value of x ❸ ◇（econ.）demand：供～关系 relationship between supply and demand

求爱 qiú'ài 【动】pay court to；court；woo

求得 qiúdé 【动】obtain

求和 qiú = hé ❶ sue for peace ❷ try to end a game in a draw

求婚 qiú = hūn propose marriage；ask for a girl's hand

求教 qiújiào 【动】ask sb. for help：向别人～ ask sb. to come to the rescue

求救 qiújiù 【动】cry for help；seek help：遇险的船只发出～信号。The

ship in distress sent out an S.O.S.

求情 qiú = qíng　ask a favour；appeal for mercy；plead with sb.

求全 qiúquán　【动】demand perfection：由于过分～，所以迟迟不能定稿。Because they are too exacting they still can't finalize their manuscript.

求全责备 qiú quán zé bèi　be hypercritical and demand perfection

求实 qiúshí　【动】adopt a down-to-earth attitude；be practical or realistic：～精神 a realistic attitude

求同存异 qiú tóng cún yì　seek common ground while reserving differences：双方～才能解决问题。Only by seeking common ground while reserving differences can the two sides resolve their problems.

求学 qiúxué　【动】go to school or college to study

求医 qiúyī　【动】go to the doctor：登门～ go to the doctor

求援 qiúyuán　【动】ask for help

求证 qiúzhèng　【动】(maths.) prove

求之不得 qiú zhī bù dé　just what one wished for；exceedingly welcome：～的机会 a rare but most welcome opportunity ～的事情 a godsend；a welcome event

求知 qiúzhī　【动】seek knowledge：～欲 thirst (craving) for knowledge

求职 qiúzhí　【动】look for a job

求治 qiúzhì　【动】seek medical treatment

泅 qiú　【动】swim

泅渡 qiúdù　【动】swim across；wade through

泅水 qiú = shuǐ　swim

酋 qiú

酋长 qiúzhǎng　【名】tribal chieftain

球 qiú　【名】❶〔个 gè〕ball ❷

ball game：打了一场～ play in a ball game ❸（～儿）anything in the shape of a ball：棉花～ a ball of cotton-wool ❹ (maths.) sphere

球场 qiúchǎng　【名】ground for any kind of ball game

球门 qiúmén　【名】goal

球迷 qiúmí　【名】(of a ball game) fan

球面 qiúmiàn　【名】(maths.) surface of a sphere

球拍 qiúpāi　【名】〔个 gè、副 fù〕racket；bat

球赛 qiúsài　【名】ball game

球体 qiútǐ　【名】(maths.) spheroid

球鞋 qiúxié　【名】〔只 zhī、双 shuāng〕gym shoes；sneakers

球星 qiúxīng　【名】star ball-player

球艺 qiúyì　【名】ball game skills

qū

区（區） qū　【名】❶ region；area；district：游览～ tourist area 游击～ guerrilla area ❷ administrative unit；region；district：自治～ autonomous region 这个市分几个～? How many districts is this municipality divided into?

区别 qūbié　【动】distinguish between；differentiate among：～对待 treat differently ～好坏 distinguish between good and bad ～真假 distinguish genuine from fake 不同类型的东西必须～开来。One must make distinctions among things which are different in kinds. 【名】difference：这两种意见其实没有什么～，只是强调的重点不同。As a matter of fact, there is virtually no difference between these two views except that they differ in emphasis.

区分 qūfēn　【动】differentiate：这两种小麦很难～。It's hard to tell the

difference between these two kinds of wheat.

区划 qūhuà 【名】division into districts

区间 qūjiān 【名】a section of the transporting route：～车 sectional service bus or train

区域 qūyù 【名】area；region

曲 qū 【形】◇ bent；winding；curving 另见 qǔ

曲别针 qūbiézhēn 【名】paper clip

曲解 qūjiě 【动】distort；twist；misinterpret

曲线 qūxiàn 【名】curve

曲线运动 qūxiàn yùndòng （phys.）curvilinear motion

曲折 qūzhé 【形】❶ winding；curving：～的小路 a winding path ❷ not straightforward or smooth：生活是～的。Life is full of ups and downs. 这个故事很～。The plot of the story is rather complicated.

曲直 qūzhí 【名】just and unjust：是非～ rights and wrongs

驱（驅） qū 【动】◇ ❶ drive：～马前进 drive a horse ～车前往 drive to ❷ expel：～逐出境 deport (sb.) from a country

驱除 qūchú 【动】drive away；get rid of

驱使 qūshǐ 【动】❶ order about ❷ urge；prompt：越来越大的欲望～他走上了犯罪的道路。His insatiable greed drove him to crime.

驱逐 qūzhú 【动】expel；oust

驱逐出境 qūzhú chū jìng deport；expel (sb.) from a country

驱逐舰 qūzhújiàn 【名】〔艘 sōu〕destroyer

屈 qū 【动】◇ ❶ bend：～指一算，来校已有五个月了。Come to think of it, he has been at this in-

stitute for five months. ❷ yield to；surrender to：威武不能～ will not submit to force ❸ suffer wrong, injustice：受～ be accused falsely 鸣冤叫～ complain about the injustice one suffers

屈服 qūfú 【动】submit；bow to；yield to

屈辱 qūrǔ 【名】humiliation；disgrace

屈膝 qūxī 【动】succumb；knuckle under

屈指可数 qū zhǐ kě shǔ can be counted on one's fingers：以前，本市的公共汽车～。In the past, the number buses in this city could be counted on the fingers of one hand.

躯（軀） qū

躯干 qūgàn 【名】(physiol.) trunk

躯体 qūtǐ 【名】human body

曲（麯） qū 【名】yeast used in brewing

趋（趨） qū 【动】〈书〉❶ run quickly：疾～而过 pass by quickly ❷ tend to；lean toward：条件日～成熟。The conditions are maturing with each passing day. 意见逐渐～于一致。Their views are gradually tending toward unanimity.

趋势 qūshì 【名】trend；tendency：世界在前进，前途是光明的，这个历史的总～任何人也改变不了。The world is making progress and the future is bright；this is the general trend of history which is irrevocable.

趋向 qūxiàng 【名】tendency；trend：总～ the general trend 历史发展的～ the tendency of the development of history 【动】tend to；head toward：情况～明朗。The situation is becoming clearer. 问题～

解决。The problem is progressing toward a solution.

趋向动词　qūxiàng dòngcí　directional verb

趋炎附势　qū yán fù shì　curry favour with the powerful

qú

渠　qú　【名】〔条 tiáo〕canal

渠道　qúdào　【名】〔条 tiáo〕❶ irrigation canal：这条~全长 15 华里。This canal is 7.5 km. in length. ❷ channel；medium：通过文化交流的~,加强各国人民之间的友谊。The peoples of different countries strengthen the ties of friendship through the medium of cultural exchange.

qǔ

曲　qǔ　【名】❶ music of a song：这首歌是他作的~。He was the one who set the words of this song to music. ❷（~儿）tune；melody：小~ a ditty【量】*for songs，used only with* "一"：一~悲壮的战歌 a solemn and stirring song of battle 另见 qū

曲调　qǔdiào　melody of a song；tune

曲高和寡　qǔ gāo hè guǎ　highbrow tunes find few singers；(*fig.*) sth. too elitist to be popular

曲艺　qǔyì　【名】general term for different folk art forms, e.g. ballad singing, story telling, crosstalks, comic dialogues, etc.

曲子　qǔzi　【名】〔支 zhī〕tune；song

取　qǔ　【动】❶ take；get；obtain：~款 draw money 到邮局~包裹 collect a parcel from the post office

❷ select：~矿样儿 take a sample of ore or mineral ~慎重态度 take the prudent approach ❸ ◇ obtain；court；invite：~信于人 win the confidence of the people 自~灭亡 court one's own ruin

取材　qǔcái　【动】collect material；obtain raw materials

取长补短　qǔ cháng bǔ duǎn　make up for one's deficiencies by learning from others：各国应加强科学技术的交流,互相~,加快发展速度。Frequent international exchanges would allow scientists to learn from each other, and speed up scientific and technological development.

取代　qǔdài　【动】replace；step into sb.'s shoes；substitute for

取道　qǔdào　【动】by way of；via

取得　qǔdé　【动】obtain；get；gain：~成绩 gain results ~进展 make progress ~信任 win confidence

取缔　qǔdì　【动】ban；outlaw

取而代之　qǔ ér dài zhī　replace sb. or sth.

取经　qǔ = jīng　seek experience

取决　qǔjué　【动】(*usu. followed by* 于) depend on；be decided by：一个人对文学作品的欣赏能力,~于他的艺术修养。One's appreciation of literature depends on one's level of aesthetic knowledge.

取暖　qǔnuǎn　【动】warm oneself (e. g. by a fire)

取其精华,去其糟粕　qǔ qí jīnghuá, qù qí zāopò　select the essence and discard the dross

取巧　qǔqiǎo　【动】resort to clever manipulation；resort to trickery

取舍　qǔshě　【动】decide (what) to adopt and (what) to discard：~得当 adopt or discard material properly 可用的资料很多,就看你如何~了。There are plenty of materials you can choose from；the problem

now is to make your selection.

取胜 qǔshèng 【动】win victory

取消 qǔxiāo 【动】cancel; abolish; do away with: ~代表资格 disqualify sb. as a representative ~原订计划 cancel the original plan

取笑 qǔxiào 【动】make fun of; pull sb.'s leg

取信于民 qǔ xìn yú mín win people's trust

取之不尽, 用之不竭 qǔ zhī bù jìn, yòng zhī bù jié inexhaustible (source): 人民生活是文学艺术~的源泉之一。 The life of the people is one of the inexhaustible sources of literature and art.

娶 qǔ 【动】marry (a wife)

qù

去 qù 【动】❶ go; make sb. go; send sth. (as opp. to 来): ~信 write a letter to sb. ~一个电话 telephone sb. 你~旅行吗? Will you go travelling? 我们昨天~故宫参观了。 We went to the Palace Museum yesterday. ❷ remove; get rid of: ~了皮的土豆 peeled potatoes ~了这个字, 这句话就通顺了。 If you strike out this word, the sentence will read smoothly. ❸ used before a verb to indicate immediate future, implying movement away from the speaker and hence the non-participation of one of the parties: 我~试一试。 Let me go and have a try. 你们~商量商量。 You go along and talk it over. ❹ used after a verb or a verbal phrase to indicate the purpose of leaving the place where the speaker is: 你干什么~了? Why have you been away? 我看他~了。 I went to see him. 下午我买票~。 I'm going to buy some

tickets this afternoon. ❺ used between a verbal phrase (or prepositional construction) and a verb (or verbal phrase) to indicate that what precedes 去 is the way of doing sth. or the person doing it and what follows 去 is the action: 从儿童的角度~检验演出效果 examine the effect of the performance from the point of view of the children 用科学的方法~分析问题 analyze questions in a scientific manner 那个会由他~主持。 We'll let him preside over the meeting. ❻ used after a verb as a complement to indicate that the action is directed away from the speaker: 船向前慢慢开~。 The ship is slowly moving forward. 我们已经把东西给他送~了。 We've already sent his things along.

去粗取精 qù cū qǔ jīng 同 "取其精华, 去其糟粕" qǔ qí jīnghuá, qù qí zāopò

去掉 qù // diào do away with; get rid of; abandon: ~杂质 get rid of foreign matter 这个字是多余的, 可以~。 This word is redundant; it can be deleted.

去路 qùlù 【名】the way to advance; the way leading to a certain place: 切断~ cut off one's route (to a certain place) 挡住了~ block the way

去年 qùnián 【名】last year

去声 qùshēng 【名】the fourth tone

去世 qùshì 【动】pass away; die

去伪存真 qù wěi cún zhēn eliminate the false and retain the true

去向 qùxiàng 【名】direction in which sb. or sth. has gone: 不知~ do not know where (they) have gone ~不明。 (Their) destination is unknown.

去职 qù zhí leave office; resign from office

趣 qù

趣味 qùwèi 【名】interest：研究天文、气象是很有～的。Astronomy and meteorology are very interesting fields of study.

趣闻 qùwén 【名】interesting anecdote

quān

圈 quān

【名】(～儿) circle；ring；hoop：马钻火～的表演，很吸引人。The performances of horses jumping through flaming hoops were simply enchanting. 飞机在空中转了几个～。The airplane circled several times in the sky. 【动】❶ encircle；enclose：把工地～起来 fence off the construction site ❷ mark with a circle：～阅 a circle over one's name on a document to indicate that one has read it 把这段多余的文字～了。Circle this redundant paragraph for deletion.
另见 juàn

圈套 quāntào 【名】trap：上了～ fall into a trap 设下～ set a trap for 识破他的～ see through his trap

圈子 quānzi 【名】❶ 同"圈"【名】❷ circle；range：扩大生活～ enlarge the scope of one's circle in life 要广泛联系群众，不要搞小～。Mix with people. Don't always stay within a clique.

quán

权(權) quán

【名】❶ power；authority：有职有～ exercise the authority that goes with position 有～过问 have the authority to look into the matter ❷ right：优先～ prior right ❸ advantageous situation：掌握主动～ grasp the initiative

权衡 quánhéng 【动】weigh and balance (factors)：～利弊 weigh the advantages and disadvantages 反复～ weigh and balance over and over again ～再三 weigh and balance again and again

权力 quánlì 【名】power；authority：国家～ state power ～机关 organs of power 行使～ exercise the power of

权利 quánlì 【名】right；privilege：民主～ democratic rights 享有公民～ enjoy the rights of a citizen

权势 quánshì 【名】power and influence

权术 quánshù 【名】political trickery：玩弄～ play politics

权威 quánwēi 【名】❶ a person of authority (on some subject) ❷ authority；authoritativeness

权限 quánxiàn 【名】limits of one's authority

权宜之计 quányí zhī jì expedient measure

权益 quányì 【名】rights and interests

全 quán

【形】❶ complete：这个商店日用百货品种很～。The varieties of daily necessities available in this store are quite comprehensive. 这套杂志～不～? ——不很～。Is this set of periodicals complete? — No, not quite. ❷ whole *can only qualify nouns or measure words which are divisible into parts*：～中国人民 the people in the whole China 昨天我们～家都去长城了。Yesterday our whole family went to the Great Wall. 这个电站的～套设备都是上海制造的。All the equipment in this power plant was made in Shanghai. 【副】❶ 同"都" dōu 【副】❶：这里的居民～用上电话了。

All the residents here have installed telephones. 树把阳光～遮住了,屋子里比较暗。The tree is blocking the light and the room is rather dark. 新疆维吾尔自治区不～是维吾尔族,也有别的民族。Not all the people in the Xinjiang Uighur Autonomous Region are of the Uighur nationality. Some are of other nationalities. Note：全 *and* 都 *can be used together to form a more emphatic expression*：人们～都穿上了棉衣。Everybody has put on padded clothes. ❷ *used with certain negative expressions to mean "not at all"*：他一心钻到科研里,～不为家庭生活打算。He throws himself wholeheartedly into his research project and gives no thought to his family life. 他～不顾医生的劝告,坚持要出院。He completely ignored the doctor's advice and insisted on being discharged from hospital.

全部 quánbù 【名】whole；all；complete：～时间 all one's time ～力量 all one's energy 你了解的只是事情的一部分,而不是～。What you know is only part of the matter, not the whole picture. 学过的词汇我～掌握了。I've completely mastered the use of all the words that were taught.

全程 quánchéng 【名】entire journey；the whole journey

全副 quánfù 【形】complete；full：～武装 fully armed ～精力 with all one's energy

全会 quánhuì 【名】*short for* 全体会议：中国共产党十一届三中～ the Third Plenary Session of the 11th Central Committee of the C.P.C.

全集 quánjí 【名】the complete works (of an author)

全局 quánjú 【名】the situation as a whole：统筹～ keep the overall situation in mind and plan accordingly 从～出发 proceed from the situation as a whole 摆正局部与～的关系 maintain a proper relationship between the part and the whole

全力 quánlì 【名】all one's strength：竭尽～ exert all one's strength 集中～支援农业 do everything in our power to support agriculture ～支持 support with all one's strength ～投入 spare no effort when engaged in sth.

全力以赴 quánlì yǐ fù go all out；make every effort to；do one's utmost：～参加抗旱斗争 spare no effort in combating drought 这是他当研究生的最后一年,必须～地写论文了。This is his last year as a graduate student and he must put all his effort into writing his thesis.

全貌 quánmào 【名】complete picture；full view

全面 quánmiàn 【形】overall；all-round；comprehensive：了解～情况 have a grasp of the overall situation 考虑问题很～ view problems in their entirety 学生要德、智、体～发展。Students are expected to develop in an all-round way—ethically, intellectually and physically.

全民 quánmín 【名】the whole people；entire people

全民所有制 quánmín suǒyǒuzhì ownership by the whole people

全能 quánnéng 【名】(of sports) all-round：五项～ pentathlon 男子体操～冠军 all-round champion in men's gymnastics

全盘 quánpán 【名】(of abstract things) overall；comprehensive；whole：从～考虑问题 give a comprehensive assessment of the problem 措施 comprehensive measure ～否定 totally repudiate

全球 quánqiú 【名】the whole world；the entire globe

全权 quánquán 【名】full powers; plenary powers

全权代表 quánquán dàibiǎo plenipotentiary; a representative with full authority

全身 quánshēn 【名】whole body: ～无力 feel weak all over

全神贯注 quán shén guàn zhù be utterly absorbed in; with rapt attention

全体 quántǐ 【名】(of a group of people) entire; whole; all: 他代表～教职员工讲了话。He spoke on behalf of all the members of the faculty and staff. 我们～都参加了会议。We all attended the meeting.

全天候 quántiānhòu 【名】all-weather

全心全意 quán xīn quán yì heart and soul; whole-heartedly: ～为人民服务 serve the people whole-heartedly ～做好本职工作 do one's own job whole-heartedly

全新 quánxīn 【形】brand-new: 面貌～ brand-new appearance

全休 quánxiū 【动】complete rest: ～一周 complete rest for a week

泉 quán 【名】spring

泉水 quánshuǐ 【名】spring; spring water

泉眼 quányǎn 【名】mouth of a spring

泉源 quányuán 【名】❶ spring ❷ source: 智慧的～ the source of wisdom 力量的～ the source of strength 创作的～ the source of literary and artistic creation

拳 quán 【名】❶ fist ❷ the art of boxing: 打～ practise boxing 练一会儿～ practise boxing for a little while

拳击 quánjī 【名】boxing

拳头 quántou 【名】〔个 gè〕fist

拳头产品 quántou chǎnpǐn outstanding product

痊 quán

痊愈 quányù 【动】fully recover from illness

蜷 quán 【动】curled up

蜷伏 quánfú 【动】huddle up

蜷曲 quánqū 【动】curl; coil

蜷缩 quánsuō 【动】roll up; curl up

quǎn

犬 quǎn 【名】dog

犬牙交错 quǎnyá jiāocuò in a jigsaw pattern; interlocking

quàn

劝（勸） quàn 【动】persuade; advise

劝导 quàndǎo 【动】exhort; try to persuade: 经过大家再三～,他终于想通了。After repeated exhortation, he finally thought the problem through.

劝告 quàngào 【动】advise; counsel: 医生多次～他少吸烟。The doctor has urged him many a time not to smoke so heavily. 【名】advice; admonition: 小学生听了老师的～,不再擅自游泳去了。The school children took their teacher's advice and no longer went swimming by themselves.

劝架 quàn = jià try to reconcile parties to a quarrel; try to stop people from fighting each other

劝解 quànjiě 【动】❶ help sb. to get over his worries: 经大家反复～,她的情绪才好了一些。After talking it over with her friends, she became reconciled to the situation. ❷ make peace between; mediate: 他

们之间最近有些矛盾,我们去～一下。Lately there has been some disagreement between them; let's go and help them smooth it out.

劝说 quànshuō 【动】persuade

劝阻 quànzǔ 【动】dissuade sb. from doing sth.; discourage sb. from; advise against

券

券 quàn 【名】◇ ticket; coupon; 入场～ admission ticket 公债～ government bond 国库～ treasury bill (T.B.)

quē

缺

缺 quē 【动】❶ be short of; lack: ～水 be short of water 不～吃,不～穿 not be short of food or clothing 我们踢足球还～两个人。We are still short of two players for the football game. ❷ be missing: 这本书～了两页。There are two pages missing from this book. 这张桌子～了一条腿。The table is missing one leg. 这星期他因病～了四节课。He missed four classes this week due to illness. 【形】lacking (*usu. as a predicate*): 我手头这方面的资料比较～。I still lack adequate data on this point.

缺德 quē=dé wicked, immoral

缺点 quēdiǎn 【名】shortcoming; weak point; defect

缺额 quē'é 【名】vacancy; opening; place

缺乏 quēfá 【动】lack; be short of *usu. followed by an abstract noun; cannot be followed by a noun with a numeral plus measure word*: ～经验 lack experience ～勇气 lack courage ～信心 be wanting confidence ～工具 be short of tools 【形】lacking (*usu. as a predicate*): 人力～ be lacking in man-power

缺斤少两 quē jīn shǎo liǎng short in weight

缺课 quē=kè away from class

缺口 quēkǒu 【名】❶ crack; chip: 杯子上有个～。The cup is chipped. ❷ breach; gap: 打开～ make a breach

缺门 quēmén 【名】gap (in knowledge or study of a subject, esp. scientific)

缺欠 quēqiàn 【名】defect; imperfection; shortcoming: 这个计划有什么～,希望大家提出来。Please let us know of any shortcomings which you see in this plan. 【动】lack; be short of

缺勤 quēqín 【动】be absent from work

缺少 quēshǎo 【动】lack; be short of

缺席 quēxí 【动】be absent from (a meeting, etc.)

缺席审判 quēxí shěnpàn trial by default

缺陷 quēxiàn 【名】defect; drawback; flaw: 他生理上有～。He is physically handicapped. 这条路的～是弯儿太多。The problem with this road is that it has too many turns.

qué

瘸

瘸 qué 【动】lame 【形】lame

瘸子 quézi 【名】cripple

què

却

却 què 【副】yet *can be used in conjunction with* 可是,但是,不过, *etc.*: 这个商店不大,货～不少。This shop is small, yet it is well-stocked with goods. 他的话虽然不多,可是道理～很深刻。He didn't speak much, but there was depth in what he

said.

雀 què 【名】◇ sparrow

雀斑 quèbān 【名】freckle

确(確) què

确保 quèbǎo 【动】make sure; ensure; guarantee

确定 quèdìng 【动】fix; determine

确立 quèlì 【动】firmly establish

确切 quèqiè 【形】❶ precise; exact: 用词很～ exact wording ～的数字 precise figures 请你解释一下这个成语的～含义. Will you please explain exactly what this idiom implies? ❷ true; reliable: ～的保证 a reliable guarantee

确认 quèrèn 【动】acknowledge or accept with great definiteness; affirm

确实 quèshí 【形】true; certain: ～的消息 hard news 这件事是～的. It is certain that this event took place. 【副】indeed; really: 他的按摩技术～不错. He is really quite skilled in doing massage. 天～不早了. It is indeed quite late now.

确信 quèxìn 【动】be sure; be confident

确凿 quèzáo 【形】based on truth; reliable

确诊 quèzhěn 【动】make a definite diagnosis

qún

裙 qún 【名】◇skirt

裙带关系 qúndài guānxi nepotism; petticoat influence

裙子 qúnzi 【名】〔条 tiáo〕skirt

群 qún 【名】crowd; group: 人～ crowds of people ～情激愤 mounting public indignation 马～ a herd of horses 【量】group; herd; flock: 一～孩子 a group of children 一～羊 a flock of sheep

群策群力 qún cè qún lì pool the wisdom and efforts of all the people: 大家～, 绿化美化了厂内环境. Through a collective effort, the surroundings of the factory were covered with trees, lawns and flowers.

群岛 qúndǎo 【名】archipelago

群集 qúnjí 【动】gather; swarm; crowd together

群居 qúnjū 【动】live in groups

群龙无首 qún lóng wú shǒu like a crowd without a leader; a disorganized group

群氓 qúnméng 【名】mob

群起而攻之 qún qǐ ér gōng zhī everybody rallies together to oppose sth.

群体 qúntǐ 【名】colony; group

群英会 qúnyīnghuì 【名】conference of outstanding workers

群众 qúnzhòng 【名】masses

群众性 qúnzhòngxìng 【名】quality of mass-participation; participation by the masses

R

rán

然 rán

然而 rán'ér 【连】but; yet; however; nevertheless

然后 ránhòu 【副】then; afterwards: 先有实践,～有经验。First we do practical work and, through it, we gain experience. 我们到了工厂,首先参观车间,～又和工人座谈。On arriving at the factory, we first visited the workshops and then talked with the workers.

燃 rán 【动】burn; kindle: ～起了熊熊烈火。A blazing fire started to burn.

燃点 rándiǎn 【名】point of ignition

燃放 ránfàng 【动】set off (fireworks)

燃料 ránliào 【名】fuel

燃眉之急 rán méi zhī jí as imminent as fire singeing one's eyebrows

燃烧 ránshāo 【动】burn; be on fire

燃烧弹 ránshāodàn 【名】incendiary bomb

rǎn

染 rǎn 【动】❶ dye: ～布 dye some cloth 晚霞～红了天空。The sunset glow tinted the sky red. ❷ catch (disease); acquire (bad habit): 不要～上坏习惯。Don't acquire a bad habit.

染病 rǎn=bìng fall ill; be infected with a disease

染料 rǎnliào 【名】dye

染色 rǎnsè 【动】dye; dyeing

染色体 rǎnsètǐ 【名】(biol.) chromosome

染指 rǎnzhǐ 【动】〈书〉take a share of sth. one is not entitled to: 保护国家资源,不容他人～。Protect the nation's resources against the depredations of other countries.

rāng

嚷 rāng
另见 rǎng
嚷嚷 rāngrang 【动】❶ shout or call out noisily: 乱～ make an uproar ❷ make known: 这消息先别～出去。Don't blurt out this piece of news.

ráng

瓤 ráng 【名】(～儿) pulp; pith: 丝瓜～ loofah; vegetable sponge 红～西瓜 a watermelon with red pulp

rǎng

嚷　rǎng　【动】shout；yell：大～大叫 shout and yell at the top of one's voice 别～，那边屋里在开会呢! Don't yell! There is a meeting going on in the other room.

另见 rāng

ràng

让（讓）　ràng　【动】❶ give way；yield；give up：把方便～给别人 make things easy for others 弟弟小，你～着他点儿。Your brother is still young；just humour him a little. 咱们可以～给他一台抽水机。We can let him have one of our pumps. ❷ let；ask used in a pivotal sentence：老张～你去给他打个电话。Lao Zhang wants you to phone him. 绝不能～恶劣作风自由泛滥。We mustn't let rude behavior go unchecked. 【介】同 "被" bèi 【介】（usu. in colloquial speech）the agent which follows it can never be omitted：这个谜～他猜着了。He solved the riddle. 水泥别～雨淋湿。Cement must never be allowed to get into the rain.

让步　ràng = bù　make a concession：在原则问题上绝不能～。(We) must never compromise on matters of principle.

让利　ràng = lì　agree to reduce the profit；give a rebate

让路　ràng = lù　make way for：大车过不去了，劳驾，给让路。The cart cannot get past. Please make way for it. 一般工程应该给重点工程～。Minor projects ought to make way for major ones.

让位　ràng = wèi　❶ resign sovereign authority；abdicate ❷ give way to

让座　ràng = zuò　give up one's seat (to sb.)

ráo

饶（饒）　ráo　【动】❶ have mercy on；forgive：～他这一回。Let him off this time. 决不轻～他。On no account should he be let off lightly. ❷ give sth. extra；let sb. have sth. into the bargain：买一个，再～上一个。If you buy one, get one free.

饶命　ráo = mìng　spare sb.'s life

饶恕　ráoshù　【动】forgive；pardon；excuse

rǎo

扰（擾）　rǎo

扰乱　rǎoluàn　【动】harass；disturb：～治安 threaten security；create social unrest ～人心 make people confused 思路被～了。One's train of thought was interrupted.

扰民　rǎo = mín　disturb the life of the inhabitants

rào

绕（繞）　rào　【动】❶ wind：～线 wind thread 把绳子～起来 coil a rope ❷ move round：～场一周 parade around the arena 人造卫星～地球运行。Man-made satellites revolve round the earth. ❸ by pass；make a detour：～过暗礁 go around a submerged reef 车辆～行 detour ～到敌人后方去 detour to the rear of the enemy

绕道　rào = dào　make a detour

绕圈子　rào quānzi　take a round-

about way；beat about the bush；昨天夜里走错了路，绕了一个大圈子。Last night I got lost, and took a roundabout way. 他说话爱～。He likes to beat about the bush when he speaks.

绕远儿 rào = yuǎnr　go the long way round；走大路～，还是抄小路去吧！The main road is the long way round; let's take the shortcut!

绕嘴 ràozuǐ　【形】difficult to pronounce quickly and correctly；a tongue twister

rě

惹 rě　【动】❶ invite；court；～麻烦 invite trouble ～是非 provoke a dispute ❷ attract；cause；～人讨厌 annoy sb. ～人注意 attract attention ❸ provoke；～不得 not to be provoked 一句话把他～翻了。A single word was enough to make him angry. 他可不是好～的。He is not a person to be trifled with.

惹不起 rě bu qǐ　dare not offend

惹得起 rě de qǐ　(*usu. in a rhetorical question*) dare to offend；他可厉害了，谁～他呀！He is very formidable; how could anybody be so brave as to provoke him?

惹祸 rě = huò　court disaster；小心！别惹出祸来。Be careful! Don't get yourself into trouble.

惹气 rě = qì　get angry

惹事 rě = shì　create trouble

惹是生非 rě shì shēng fēi　stir up trouble

rè

热(熱) rè　【形】❶ hot；～茶 hot tea 天～了。The weather is getting hot. ❷ (of feelings, etc.) heated；头脑发～ be carried away (e.g. by one's success)【动】heat；～一～饭 heat up the rice【名】❶ (phys.) heat；摩擦生～。Friction generates heat. 有一分～，发一分光。One's accomplishments should be commensurate with one's abilities. ❷ fever；退～ (of one's temperature) go down

热爱 rè'ài　【动】love ardently；have a deep love for

热潮 rècháo　【名】upsurge；旅游的～ an upsurge in tourism 学习的～ an upsurge in pursuing their studies

热忱 rèchén　【名】zeal；enthusiasm；warmheartedness；极端的～ extraordinary ardour 满腔的～ full of warmth (towards other people)

热带 rèdài　【名】the tropics

热点 rèdiǎn　【名】popular spot or topic；旅游～ popular tourist spot 讨论的～ popular topic for discussion

热电厂 rèdiànchǎng　【名】heat and power plant

热敷 rèfū　【动】(med.) hot compress

热辐射 rèfúshè　【名】(phys.) heat radiation

热核反应 rèhé fǎnyìng　thermonuclear reaction

热烘烘 rèhōnghōng　【形】very warm；暖气很烫，屋子里～的。The radiator is very hot, so the room is quite warm.

热火朝天 rè huǒ cháo tiān　in full swing；bustling with activity；同学们正在操场上～地进行各种体育活动。On the playground, the students' sports activities are in full swing. 工地上，小伙子们正干得～。On the worksite, the young fellows are working in high spirits.

热火 rèhuo　【形】❶ nice and warm；刚出锅的馒头真～。The steamed buns fresh from the steamer were

nice and warm. ❷ showing great enthusiasm：庆祝大会开得真～! The celebration meeting was held with great enthusiasm. ❸ warm and friendly：这两个人谈得很～。Those two people are having an animated talk.

热货 rèhuò 【名】hot item

热泪盈眶 rè lèi yíng kuàng eyes full of tears：感动得～ be moved to the point of tears

热力 rèlì 【名】heating power

热恋 rèliàn 【动】be head over heels in love

热量 rèliàng 【名】quantity of heat

热烈 rèliè 【形】warm；ardent：～欢迎 warmly welcome ～的掌声 warm and hearty applause 发言很～。The discussion was very lively and enthusiastic.

热门 rèmén 【形】(～儿) popular：～话题 popular topic；hot topic

热闹 rènao 【形】(of a scene) bustling and lively：大街上～得很。The street is bustling and full of life. 昨天晚上我们玩儿得挺～! Last night, we had lots of fun. 【名】(～儿) a bustling scene：看～ watch the fun

热能 rènéng 【名】(phys.) thermal energy

热切 rèqiè 【形】earnest：～的愿望 earnest wish ～盼望 very much look forward to

热情 rèqíng 【名】enthusiasm；zeal：爱国～ fervently patriotic spirit 劳动～ enthusiasm towards one's work ～洋溢 full of warmth 【形】warm-hearted：～接待贵客 warmly entertain the distinguished guests 他对穷亲戚很～。He is very warm-hearted towards his poor relations.

热身赛 rèshēnsài 【名】warm-up match

热水袋 rèshuǐdài 【名】〔个 gè〕hot-water bottle

热水瓶 rèshuǐpíng 【名】〔个 gè〕thermos flask

热水器 rèshuǐqì 【名】hot water heater；geyser

热望 rèwàng 【动】we earnestly hope：～得到你们的帮助 earnestly hope to get your help ～收到你的回信 eagerly await your reply (to a letter)

热线 rèxiàn 【名】infrared ray：～电话 hot line

热销 rèxiāo 【动】sell well

热心 rèxīn 【形】warmhearted；enthusiastic：～人 a warm-hearted person 她对残疾人的事很～。She is very enthusiastic in matters concerning the handicapped people.

热心肠 rèxīncháng 【名】warmheartedness：王大娘有一副～。Auntie Wang is very warmhearted. 老李是个～的人。Lao Li is a warmhearted fellow.

热血 rèxuè 【名】(fig.) righteous ardour：满腔～在沸腾。burning with righteous ardour

热饮 rèyǐn 【名】hot drink

热源 rèyuán 【名】(phys.) heat source

热中 rèzhōng 【动】❶ hanker after；crave (derog.)：～名利 crave personal fame and gain ❷ be fond of：～于绘画 be very fond of painting

rén

人 rén 【名】❶ person；human being ❷ a person engaged in a particular activity：庄稼～ peasant 介绍～ one who introduces or recommends sb. 负责～ the person who is responsible for sth 领导～ leader ❸ ◇ other people：先～后己 Put others' interests before one's own 乐于助～ enjoy helping others

❹ ◇ everybody：～手一册。Everyone has a copy.

人才 réncái 【名】a talented person：～出众 with outstanding ability 为国家培养～ train qualified people to meet the needs of the country 建设祖国，需要各方面的～. Building the homeland requires people with different abilities. 也作"人材"。

人才流动 réncái liúdòng qualified personnel moving from place to place so as to make the best possible use of their abilities

人称 rénchēng 【名】(gram.) person

人称代词 rénchēng dàicí personal pronoun

人大 réndà 【名】short for 全国人民代表大会 the National People's Congress

人道主义 réndàozhǔyì 【名】humanitarianism

人定胜天 rén dìng shèng tiān man can conquer nature：发扬～的精神，战胜自然灾害 Foster the spirit of "it is man's will, not heaven, that decides", and overcome natural calamities.

人贩子 rénfànzi 【名】trafficker in human beings

人浮于事 rén fú yú shì be overstaffed

人格 réngé 【名】personality；character：～高尚 sterling qualities；noble in character

人格化 rénghuà 【动】personify；personification

人工 réngōng 【名】❶ artificial；man-made：～呼吸 artificial respiration ～授粉 artificial pollination ❷ man-day；manpower：修这个发电站需要很多～. To build the power station will require a great number of man-days.

人工降雨 réngōng jiàng yǔ artificial rain fall

人工智能 réngōng zhìnéng artificial intelligence

人际关系 rénjì guānxì interpersonal relationships

人家 rénjiā 【名】(～儿)❶ household：这个大院里有二十户～. There are about twenty households in this courtyard. ❷ family：勤俭的～ a hard-working and frugal family 另见 rénjia

人家 rénjia 【代】❶ other person；other people：～能吃苦，我就不能吗？ If other people can endure hardship, why can't I？ 我们应当走自己工业发展的道路，不要只是模仿～. We must pursue our own method of industrialization, rather than imitate others. ❷ takes the place of 他 or 他们：① implying respect：～跑这么远来换稻种，咱们无论如何也得换给～. Since they have come such a long way to trade their rice for an improved variety, we simply must make the exchange whatever happens. ～全组个个都是好样的，咱们得向～学习. Everyone in their group is a good worker. We ought to learn from them. ② implying dissatisfaction or alienation, used sarcastically：我倒是好心好意，可是～不领情. I was full of good intentions but they weren't appreciated. 你比得了～？～多有办法！ How can you hope to be like him？ How resourceful he is！ ❸ a noun denoting a person can be used in apposition to 人家 and has the same implications as in ❷：～老白才是全心全意为人民服务呢！ Look at Lao Bai. That's what we call serving the people wholeheartedly！ ❹ takes the place of 我, implying complaint：～不愿意去，你偏要～去. I'm really unwilling to go, but you keep on nagging at me！ 另见 rénjiā

人间 rénjiān 【名】the world：换了
~。The world of men has under-
gone great changes. ~奇迹 a mar-
vel created on earth by human beings

人均 rénjūn 【动】average per capi-
ta：~收入 average income per ca-
pita

人口 rénkǒu 【名】❶ population：这
是一个有一百万~的城市。This is a
city with a population of one million. ❷ number of people in a
family：他家~不多。His family is
not big.

人类 rénlèi 【名】mankind；human
beings

人类学 rénlèixué 【名】anthropology

人力 rénlì 【名】man power；labour
power：爱惜~物力 use manpower
and materials sparingly 合理安排~
allocate manpower properly

人流 rénliú 【名】① steady flow of
people；stream of people ② artificial abortion；induced abortion

人马 rénmǎ 【名】❶ forces；troops：
全部~渡过了黄河。The whole army
crossed the Yellow River. ❷
staff：这个研究所的~相当整齐。The
staff members of this research institute are well-qualified and all
necessary skills are represented.

人们 rénmen 【名】people；the pub-
lic：建设边疆的~ the people who
are opening up the frontiers ~都在
全神贯注地记笔记。The audience is
all concentrated on taking notes.

人面兽心 rén miàn shòu xīn a beast
in human shape

人民 rénmín 【名】the people

人民币 rénmínbì 【名】Renminbi
(currency of the People's Republic
of China)

人民代表大会 rénmín dàibiǎo dàhuì
the People's Congress

人民法院 rénmín fǎyuàn the people's
court

人民民主专政 rénmín mínzhǔ
zhuānzhèng people's democratic
dictatorship

人民群众 rénmín qúnzhòng the
masses

人品 rénpǐn 【名】character；moral
quality

人情 rénqíng 【名】❶ human feel-
ings；sympathy：不近~ harsh and
unreasonable ❷ favour：托~ ask
sb. to do sth. as a personal favour
❸ gift：不要拿公家的东西做~。One
mustn't make gifts of public property to court sb.'s favour.

人情味 rénqíngwèi 【名】(~儿) hu-
mane；human interest

人权 rénquán 【名】human rights

人群 rénqún 【名】crowd

人山人海 rén shān rén hǎi crowds of
people：节日的夜晚，广场上~。On
festival nights, there are huge
crowds in the square.

人身 rénshēn 【名】person；living
body of a human being：~自由
personal freedom ~攻击 a personal attack ~事故 an accident causing personal injury

人身保险 rénshēn bǎoxiǎn life insurance and insurance against accidents

人参 rénshēn 【名】ginseng

人生 rénshēng 【名】life

人生观 rénshēngguān 【名】outlook
on life；philosophy of life

人士 rénshì 【名】personage；public
figure：爱国~ patriotic personages
(usu. referring to overseas Chi-
nese）无党派~ non-party figures 民
主~ democratic personages 知名~
well-known public figures

人事 rénshì 【名】❶ occurrences in
human life：~变迁 births and
deaths, comings and goings ❷
matters having to do with person-
nel：~工作 personnel work ~安排
assignment of personnel ❸ con-

sciousness of the outside world：他病得不省（xǐng）～。He is so ill that he has lost consciousness.

人手 rénshǒu 【名】hand；manpower：～不足 short of hands

人所共知 rén suǒ gòng zhī it is common knowledge that...；widely known

人体 réntǐ 【名】human body

人头税 réntóushuì 【名】poll tax；capitation

人为 rénwéi 【形】man-made：～的困难 man-made difficulties ～的障碍 man-made obstacles

人文 rénwén 【名】humanities

人物 rénwù 【名】❶ figure；personage：新闻人物 celebrity 赫赫有名的大～ a well-known bigwig 不知名的小～ an unknown；a small fry 历史～ historical figures ❷ character (in a novel, etc.)：～形象 image of a character 刻画～ portray a character

人心 rénxīn 【名】will of the people：振奋～ raise popular morale 大得～ win the support of the people ～丧尽 lose the support of the people completely

人心所向 rénxīn suǒ xiàng accord with the will of the people：摆脱压迫是～，大势所趋。Liberation from oppression is in accordance with the desires of the people and is the general trend in the world today.

人心向背 rénxīn xiàngbèi support or opposition of the people：战争的胜败决定于～。Victory or defeat in war depends on the support or opposition of the people.

人行道 rénxíngdào 【名】〔条 tiáo〕pavement；sidewalk

人行横道 rénxíng héngdào zebra crossing；pedestrian crossing

人性 rénxìng 【名】human nature

人性论 rénxìnglùn 【名】the theory of human nature

人选 rénxuǎn 【名】person selected：决定～ decide who are qualified candidates 合适的～ suitable person (for a job)

人烟 rényān 【名】indications of human habitation：～稠密 densely populated ～稀少 sparsely populated 荒无～的深山老林 uninhabited, remote and thickly forested mountains

人影儿 rényǐngr 【名】❶ a person's shadow ❷ trace of a person's presence：天黑得对面看不见～。It is so dark you can't see the person in front of you. 李大娘成天忙着街道的事儿，家里见不到她的～。Aunt Li is busy with the affairs of the street committee all day long；you can hardly ever find her at home.

人员 rényuán 【名】personnel：工作～ all the staff 值勤～（of armyman, policeman, etc.）personnel on duty ～配备 allocation of staff ～调动 transfer of personnel

人云亦云 rén yún yì yún repeat the views of others：对任何问题都要进行独立思考，不能～。Think through problems on your own；don't parrot the views of others.

人造 rénzào 【形】man-made；artificial：～丝 artificial silk；rayon ～纤维 artificial fibre ～胰岛素 artificial insulin ～地球卫星 man-made earth satellite

人证 rénzhèng 【名】testimony of a witness

人质 rénzhì 【名】hostage

人种 rénzhǒng 【名】race；ethnic group

仁 rén 【形】benevolent 【名】❶ sympathy；benevolence ❷（～儿）kernel：花生～ shelled peanut 核桃～ meat of a walnut

仁慈 réncí 【形】benevolent；kind：～的圣诞老人 the kindhearted San-

ta Claus

仁政　rénzhèng　【名】policy of benevolence：施～ apply a policy of benevolence

仁至义尽　rén zhì yì jìn　be very tolerant and do one's utmost to help sb.

rěn

忍　rěn　【动】❶ bear；endure：～痛 endure pain ～饥受冻 endure hunger and cold ❷ ◇ 同"忍心"：于心不～ not have the heart to

忍不住　rěn bu zhù　cannot help：相声很幽默，谁听了都～要发笑。Crosstalks are very funny；they make you inspite of yourself.

忍得住　rěn de zhù　can bear；can stand

忍耐　rěnnài　【动】exercise patience

忍气吞声　rěn qì tūn shēng　swallow insults in meek submission

忍让　rěnràng　【动】exercise forbearance；be forbearing and conciliatory

忍受　rěnshòu　【动】put up with；stand：无法～ intolerable ～不住 be unable to stand (sth.)

忍无可忍　rěn wú kě rěn　be driven past the limits of endurance；come to the end of one's patience

忍心　rěn = xīn　have the heart to：我们作大夫的难道～看着病人受痛苦吗？As doctors，how can we have the heart to watch patients suffer and do nothing?

rèn

刃　rèn　【名】(～儿) edge (of a knife)：这把菜刀卷(了)～了。The edge of this kitchen knife has been bent.

刃具　rènjù　【名】cutting tool

认(認)　rèn　【动】❶ identify；recognize：～字 learn to read Chinese characters ～清是非 tell right from wrong 几年不见，我都～不出你了。I haven't seen you for years；I wouldn't have recognized you! ❷ admit；acknowledge：～错儿 admit one's mistake

认错　rèn = cuò　acknowledge a mistake；admit one's mistake

认得　rènde　【动】recognize；know：这个字你～吗？Do you recognize this character? 这匹马～路。This horse knows the way.

认定　rèndìng　【动】firmly believe：他已经～医学作为他的终身事业。He firmly believed that medicine would be his life's work.

认罚　rènfá　【动】be ready to pay the penalty

认购　rèngòu　【动】offer to buy；subscribe：～国库券 offer to buy state treasury bond

认可　rènkě　【动】approve；agree：点头～ signify agreement by nodding one's head 这事领导已经～了。The leadership has already approved it.

认领　rènlǐng　【动】claim：～失物 claim a lost object

认生　rènshēng　【形】(of child) be shy with strangers：这孩子～。The child feels shy in front of strangers.

认识　rènshi　【动】know；recognize：我不～他，请你给我们介绍一下。I never met this "gentleman"；please introduce me to him. 我们十年前就～了。We got to know each other ten years ago. 【名】knowledge；cognition：感性～ perceptual knowledge 理性～ rational knowledge

认识论　rènshilùn　【名】theory of knowledge

认输 rèn = shū admit defeat

认同 rèntóng 【动】agree to; identify: 这个方案他已经～。He has agreed to this plan.

认为 rènwéi 【动】think; consider: 辩证唯物主义～, 一切事物都是发展变化的。Dialectical materialism sees everything in the light of change and development.

认贼作父 rèn zéi zuò fù take one's enemy as one's father

认账 rèn = zhàng admit what one has said or done (*usu. in the negative*): 瓷盘是谁摔坏的, 怎么没人～呢? Who broke the porcelain plate? And why didn't anybody admit it?

认真 rènzhēn 【形】conscientious; earnest

认真 rèn = zhēn take sth. seriously: 我只是开玩笑, 你认什么真呢? I was just making a joke. Why did you take it so seriously?

认罪 rèn = zuì acknowledge one's guilt; plead guilty

任 rèn 【动】◇ ❶ appoint: 被～为研究所所长 be appointed head of the research institute ❷ assume; take up a position: ～课 take up the position as teacher 连选连～ to be elected again and serve another term. 【介】let; allow: ～你挑选。You can choose any one you like. ～其自然 let it take its course 【连】*used together with an interrogative pronoun to mean* 不论: ～他怎么说, 我也不信。No matter what he says, I won't believe him.

任何 rènhé 【代】any; whatever: 我们做～工作, 都要认真。Whatever work we do, we must do it conscientiously. 在～情况下, 我们都不应该放弃原则。We must not abandon our principles under any circumstances.

任教 rèn = jiào take up teaching: 在中学～ teach in a middle school

任课 rèn = kè take up teaching: 他在数学系～。He teaches in the mathematics department.

任劳任怨 rèn láo rèn yuàn willing to work hard and not be upset even if your work is not appreciated

任免 rènmiǎn 【动】appoint and dismiss: ～干部 appoint and remove cadres ～名单 a list of appointments and dismissals

任命 rènmìng 【动】appoint; nominate

任凭 rènpíng 【介】at one's discretion: 打电报还是打长途电话, ～你决定。Should we send a telegram or to make a trunk call, make up your mind. 【连】同"凭"píng: ～大家怎么劝解, 他也听不进去。No matter how hard everybody tried to explain things and pacify him, he simply refused to listen.

任期 rènqī 【名】term of office

任人摆布 rèn rén bǎibù allow oneself to be ordered about

任人唯亲 rèn rén wéi qīn appoint people on the basis of favouritism

任人唯贤 rèn rén wéi xián appoint people on their merits

任务 rènwu 【名】assignment; task; job

任性 rènxìng 【形】wilful, self-willed

任意 rènyì 【副】just as one likes; wantonly: ～选购 choose and buy whatever one likes ～夸大 wantonly exaggerate (sth.)

任用 rènyòng 【动】appoint; assign sb. to a post: ～干部 appoint cadres

任职 rèn = zhí hold a post: 从前他在铁路上～。He was previously a railway worker.

任重道远 rèn zhòng dào yuǎn a heavy responsibility and a long

road：我们的事业～。Our task is a heavy responsibility and we must embark on a long journey for its accomplishment.

韧（韌） rèn 【形】tough；flexible but strong

韧带 rèndài 【名】ligament

韧性 rènxìng 【名】tenacity；toughness；富有～ with tenacity ～很强 very tenacious

妊 rèn

妊娠 rènshēn 【动】〈书〉be pregnant

rēng

扔 rēng 【动】throw；toss：～手榴弹 throw hand-grenades 果皮、纸屑不要随地乱～。Don't litter. 这件事他早就～在脑后了。The matter has been put aside for a long time.

扔掉 rēng // diào throw away：把烟头～ throw the cigarette butt away 好传统绝不能～。On no account should we discard our fine traditions.

réng

仍 réng 【副】同"仍然"（*usu. in written language*）：他年已七十，身体～很健康。He is seventy and yet he's still as sound as a bell.

仍旧 réngjiù 【副】still；as before：老张的干劲～不减当年。Lao Zhang is still full of energy just as he was in the old days. 鲁迅故居的摆设～和当年一样。Lu Xun's former residence is kept as it was in his day.

仍然 réngrán 【副】❶ still：他～住在那条街上。He is still living on that street. 老王～保持着艰苦朴素的作风。Lao Wang still maintains his

philosophy of hard work and plain-living. ❷ as before：他看完报，～放回原处。He replaced the paper after reading it.

rì

日 rì 【名】❶ ◇ sun：～出东方红。The sun is rising, and the eastern sky is tinged with red. ～落西山。The sun is setting behind the western hills. ❷ ◇ day time：～夜夜 day and night ❸ ◇ day：一年三百六十五～。There are 365 days in a year. 改～再谈。Let's talk about it some other day. 多～不见。I haven't seen you for days. ❹ a day of the month：五月一～ May 1 ❺ ◇ day by day；daily：～渐炎热。It is getting hotter day by day. 经济～趋繁荣。The economy is becoming more prosperous everyday.

日报 rìbào 【名】daily paper；daily

日薄西山 rì bó xī shān the sun is setting beyond the western hills；（*fig.*）decline rapidly

日常 rìcháng 【形】daily；everyday：～工作 daily work ～用品 daily necessities

日程 rìchéng 【名】programme；schedule：会议～ the agenda for a meeting 把这项工作提到议事～上来。Put this item on our daily work schedule.

日光 rìguāng 【名】sunshine；sunlight

日光灯 rìguāngdēng 【名】fluorescent light

日光浴 rìguāngyù 【名】sun-bath

日积月累 rì jī yuè lěi accumulate over a long period：老教员的宝贵经验，是通过长期教学实践～得来的。The experience of the veteran teachers has been accumulated

through years of teaching.

日记 rìjì 【名】〔篇 piān〕diary

日见 rìjiàn 【副】with each passing day：病情～好转. His condition improves by the day. 他的收入～增加. His income is increasing day by day.

日理万机 rì lǐ wàn jī have a myriad of things to attend to

日历 rìlì 【名】calendar

日暮途穷 rì mù tú qióng the day is nearly over and the road is near its end；(*fig.*) drawing close to the end of one's days

日期 rìqī 【名】date

日食 rìshí 【名】eclipse of the sun；solar eclipse

日新月异 rì xīn yuè yì change for the better day by day and month by month：山区面貌～. The appearance of the mountainous areas has been changing rapidly.

日夜 rìyè 【名】day and night

日以继夜 rì yǐ jì yè night and day

日益 rìyì 【副】more and more；day by day：～提高 rise day by day ～改善 improve daily

日用 rìyòng 【形】of everyday use

日用品 rìyòngpǐn 【名】daily necessities；articles of daily use

日元 rìyuán 【名】*yen* (Japanese currency)

日照 rìzhào 【名】(met.) sunshine

日志 rìzhì 【名】daily record

日子 rìzi 【名】❶ (a special) day：十月一日对中国人民来说是一个有特殊意义的～. October the first is a special day for the Chinese people. 他们夫妇每年到他们结婚的～都要稍微庆祝一下. That couple always holds a little celebration on their wedding anniversary. ❷ date：开会的～定了吗？ Has the date of the meeting been fixed？ 准备工作都做好了，定个～就可以开工.

Since all preparations are completed，we can start the construction any day. ❸ time counted by days：他练长跑已经不少～了. He has kept up long distance running for a long time now. 这些～你忙什么呢？ What have you been doing these days？ ❹ life：他工作上有不少困难，～不好过. His work has been filled with problems and he's having a hard time. 老太太现在和女儿一块儿过～. The old woman is now living with her daughter.

róng

荣（榮）róng 【形】◇ honourable：以艰苦朴素为～ regard enduring hardships and living simply as an honour

荣华 rónghuá 【形】prosperous；glory，honour；well-famed

荣获 rónghuò 【动】have the honor to win：～世界冠军 have the honor to win the world championship

荣幸 róngxìng 【形】honoured：你们来这里参观，我们感到十分～. We are honoured by your visit.

荣耀 róngyào 【形】glorious

荣誉 róngyù 【名】honour；credit：要爱护集体的～. (We) must treasure the honour of the collective.

荣誉军人 róngyù jūnrén disabled soldier (*title of honour*)

绒（絨）róng 【名】❶ down；fine hair：鸭～ eider down ❷ cloth with a soft nap：丝～ velvet 灯芯～ corduroy

绒布 róngbù 【名】flannelette

绒裤 róngkù 【名】〔条 tiáo〕sweat pants

绒衣 róngyī 【名】〔件 jiàn〕sweat shirt

容 róng 【动】❶ hold；contain：这个剧场能～三千人。This theatre can hold 3,000 people. ❷ be tolerant；不能～人 be intolerant of others 情理难～ incompatible with reason and common sense ❸ be allowed to；be permitted to：不～分说 not be allowed to explain 不～侵犯 permit no encroachment（into one's territory）【名】◇ looks；appearance：整～ face-lift 病～ sickly appearance

容光焕发 róngguāng huànfā with a face glowing with health：仪仗队队员个个精神抖擞，～。Everyone in the guard of honour is full of vigour and glowing with health.

容积 róngjī 【名】volume

容量 róngliàng 【名】capacity

容貌 róngmào 【名】（of a person）looks

容纳 róngnà 【动】hold；have a capacity of：这个体育场可以～十万人。This stadium can hold 100,000 people.

容器 róngqì 【名】container

容忍 róngrěn 【动】tolerate；put up with：无法～ intolerable 不能～ be unable to tolerate

容许 róngxǔ 【动】allow；permit：这件事不～再耽搁了。The matter brooks no further delay.

容易 róngyì 【形】❶ easy：不要把这事看得那么～。Don't think it will all be that easy. ❷ be likely to：暴食暴饮～得胃病。Excessive eating and drinking is likely to cause stomach trouble. 汽车超速行驶～出事故。Exceeding the speed limit when driving is prone to accidents.

溶 róng 【动】同"溶化"：食盐能～于水。Salt is soluble in water.

溶化 rónghuà 【动】❶ dissolve：樟脑在酒精中可以～。Camphor is soluble in alcohol. ❷ 同"融化"

溶剂 róngjì 【名】solvent

溶解 róngjiě 【动】同"溶化"

溶液 róngyè 【名】solution

熔 róng 【动】◇ 同"熔化"：～铁 smelt iron

熔点 róngdiǎn 【名】melting point

熔化 rónghuà 【动】smelt；melt：锡是比较容易～的金属。Tin is a comparatively easy metal to smelt.

熔炉 rónglú 【名】❶ smelting furnace ❷ crucible；furnace

融 róng

融合 rónghé 【动】amalgamate；blend；merge together；melt together

融化 rónghuà 【动】melt；thaw：太阳一出来，雪就～了。The snow melted as soon as the sun was out. 也作"溶化"。

融会贯通 rónghuì guàntōng make a comprehensive study and have a thorough mastery of：对任何理论，先得～，才谈得上运用自如。One must have thoroughly mastered a theory before one can put it into practice.

融解 róngjiě 【动】melt；fuse

融洽 róngqià 【形】on friendly terms：感情～ (of two people) very friendly 同学之间相处得很～。The members of the class are getting on very well with one another.

rǒng

冗 rǒng

冗长 rǒngcháng 【形】tedious and lengthy：文字～ tedious and wordy

冗杂 rǒngzá 【形】（of affairs）miscellaneous

róu

柔　róu　【形】◇ ❶ soft；supple：
~枝嫩叶 supple branches and tender leaves ❷ gentle（as opp. to
刚）：刚~相济 combination of firmness and gentleness

柔和　róuhé　【形】soft；gentle：~的
声音 gentle voice 光线~ soft lighting

柔软　róuruǎn　【形】supple；lithe：~
体操 callisthenics 质地~ soft in
texture

揉　róu　【动】knead；rub：~面
knead dough ~一~发麻的腿 rub
one's leg which has gone to sleep
不要~眼睛。Don't rub your eyes.

蹂　róu

蹂躏　róulìn　【动】trample upon；rav-
age；(fig.) crush under one's feet

ròu

肉　ròu　【名】❶ meat；flesh ❷
pulp；flesh：荔枝~ the fleshy part
of a lichee

肉搏　ròubó　【动】fight hand-to-
hand：~战 hand-to-hand combat
战士们与敌人展开了~。The soldiers
were engaged in hand-to-hand
combat with the enemy.

肉丁　ròudīng　【名】diced meat

肉麻　ròumá　【形】disgusting；nause-
ating；sickening

肉排　ròupái　【名】steak

肉食　ròushí　【名】meat（food）

肉松　ròusōng　【名】 stir-fried
mashed meat

肉体　ròutǐ　【名】the human body

肉刑　ròuxíng　【名】corporal punishment

肉眼　ròuyǎn　【名】unaided eye；na-
ked eye：细菌是~看不见的。Germs
are so tiny that they can't be seen
by the naked eye.

rú

如　rú　【动】❶ ◇ according to；
in compliance with：~数还清。Ev-
ery single item has been returned.
~期出版。(The book) was pub-
lished as scheduled. ❷ ◇ just like：
坚强~钢 as firm as steel 几十年~一
日 remain unchanged through decades ❸ e. g.；such as：北京名胜很
多，~长城、故宫、十三陵、颐和园等。
Beijing has quite a lot of scenic
spots, e. g. the Great Wall, the
Palace Museum, the Ming Tombs,
the Summer Palace.【连】同"如果"
（usu. in written language）：~有不
妥，请批评指正。If you find any-
thing inappropriate, please let us
know.

如常　rúcháng　【动】as usual：平静~
as tranquil as usual 一切~。Every-
thing is the same as usual.

如出一辙　rú chū yī zhé　be exactly
the same（derog.）：这两个人所处的
时代虽然不同，而言论却十分相似，~。
The two of them lived through
different times, yet their statements were strangely alike.

如此　rúcǐ　【代】❶ so：想得~周到 so
considerate 理当~ a matter of
course 他一直谦虚谨慎，成名之后仍
然~。He had always been modest
and prudent and remained so after
he became famous. ❷ so-called
(ironical)：~"援助" so-called "aid"
~"英雄" so-called "hero"

如此而已　rúcǐ éryǐ　that's all；that's
all there is to it

如法炮制　rú fǎ páozhì　follow suit
（derog.）

如故　rúgù　【动】the same as before；依然～ remain the same；remain unchanged

如果　rúguǒ　【连】if（*often in conjunction with* 就）：～一个人骄傲自满，就很难进步。If you become conceited, it will be difficult for you to make any progress. 星期天你不用照相机，借我用用。If you aren't using your camera on Sunday, would you mind lending it to me? ～我有你那么高，我就当篮球运动员。If I were as tall as you are, I'd play basketball.

如何　rúhé　【代】how（*usu. in written language*）：近况～? How have you been recently? ～办理，请指示。Please give us instructions as to how to handle this matter.

如虎添翼　rú hǔ tiān yì　just like a tiger that has grown wings；(*fig.*) with might redoubled：这个领导班子加上两位经济学家真是～了。When two economists joined the leading group, its might was redoubled.

如火如荼　rú huǒ rú tú　be like a raging fire：山上的杜鹃花正开得～。The azaleas in bloom have set the mountain on fire.

如获至宝　rú huò zhìbǎo　as if one has found a treasure

如饥似渴　rú jī sì kě　with great eagerness；as urgent as hunger or thirst

如今　rújīn　【名】now；the present：原来的沙滩～变成了米粮川。What was formerly a sandbank has now become fertile paddy fields.

如期　rúqī　【副】as scheduled：～完成 finish on time ～到达 arrive on schedule

如丧考妣　rú sàng kǎo bǐ　grieved as if one had lost one's parents (*derog.*)

如上　rú＝shàng　as above：～所述 as stated above 特将调查结果报告～。

The result of the investigation was reported as stated above.

如实　rúshí　【副】exactly according to the facts：～汇报 report accurately ～反映 truthfully reflect

如释重负　rú shì zhòng fù　as if relieved of a heavy burden：病人抢救过来了，大夫～，十分高兴。When the patient was out of danger, the doctor felt happy and relieved.

如数　rúshù　【副】exactly the number or amount：借去的书报～归还。All the borrowed books and papers were returned.

如同　rútóng　【动】like；as：广场上灯火辉煌，～白昼。The public square is as brightly lit as in daylight.

如下　rú＝xià　as below：列举～ as listed below 理由～ for the following reasons 说明～。The explanation is as follows.

如意　rúyì　【形】as one wishes：称心～ have everything one could wish for ～算盘 wishful thinking

如鱼得水　rú yú dé shuǐ　feel like a fish in water；feel in one's natural element：他学有所用，～。Like fish in water, he can put all he has learned to good use.

如愿以偿　rú yuàn yǐ cháng　have one's wishes fulfilled：小李很早就想当气象员，现在终于～了。Xiao Li had always wanted to be a meteorologist, and now he has his wish fulfilled.

如坐针毡　rú zuò zhēn zhān　be on tenterhooks；on pins and needles

儒　rú　【名】Confucianism；Confucianist

儒家　Rújiā　【名】Confucianists；Confucian school

蠕　rú

蠕动　rúdòng　【动】wriggle

rǔ

乳 rǔ 【名】❶ breast ❷ milk
乳房 rǔfáng 【名】breast
乳牛 rǔniú 【名】〔头 tóu〕milk cow
乳汁 rǔzhī 【名】milk
乳制品 rǔzhìpǐn·【名】dairy products

辱 rǔ
辱骂 rǔmà 【动】vilify；abuse；revile

rù

入 rù 【动】❶ ◇ enter：～冬 Winter has begun. 病从口～。Disease enters through the mouth. ❷ join（an organization）：～党 join the Party ～团 join the（Youth）League
入不敷出 rù bù fū chū cannot make ends meet
入场 rù = chǎng entrance：～仪式 entrance ceremony
入超 rùchāo 【动】import surplus；unfavourable balance of trade
入股 rù = gǔ buy a share；become a shareholder
入境 rù = jìng enter a country；entry
入口 rùkǒu 【名】entrance
入门 rùmén 【名】elementary course：《英语～》"An Introduction to English"《书法～》"An Introduction to Calligraphy"
入门 rù = mén （～儿）learn the rudiments（of an art or science）：他学汉语刚刚～。He has just learned the rudiments of Chinese. ～不难，深造不易。To cross the threshold is not difficult, but mastery is another question.
入迷 rù = mí be fascinated：这孩子做飞机模型都入了迷了。The boy has become fascinated with making model aeroplanes.
入侵 rùqīn 【动】invade
入神 rù = shén ❶ be entranced：听得～ be deeply absorbed in listening to（sth. or sb.）看得入了神 watch sth. spellbound ❷（of art or music）marvellous：这只老虎画得真～。The tiger in the painting is very life-like.
入时 rùshí 【形】fashionable：穿着～ be fashionably dressed
入手 rùshǒu 【动】begin with：不知从何～ not know where to begin 学习外语，先从语音～。One begins a foreign language by learning the speech sounds.
入睡 rùshuì 【动】fall asleep
入伍 rù = wǔ enlist；join the army
入席 rù = xí take one's seat at a banquet
入学 rù = xué ❶ start school：老王的孩子到～年龄了。Lao Wang's child has reached school age. ❷ begin attending a certain school
入座 rùzuò 【动】be seated：请大家～. Please be seated.

褥 rù 【名】◇ mattress
褥子 rùzi 【名】〔条 tiáo〕mattress

ruǎn

软（軟） ruǎn 【形】❶ soft：垫子很～。The cushion is quite soft. ❷ weak：～的欺，硬的怕 bully the weak and give in to the strong 两腿发～。My legs felt weak. ❸ easily moved or influenced：心～ tender-hearted 手～ be indecisive when firmness is needed 耳朵～ be easily swayed by others' opinions
软包装 ruǎnbāozhuāng 【名】foods sold in soft packages
软化 ruǎnhuà 【动】❶ soften：塑料适

当加热就可以～。Plastics will soften when exposed to heat. ❷ soften up；become compliant：态度～。One's attitude has softened.

软和 ruǎnhuo 【形】soft：床上铺得～极了。The bed was extremely soft.

软件 ruǎnjiàn 【名】software

软绵绵 ruǎnmiānmiān 【形】❶ soft；downy：～的羊毛衫 a downy cardigan ～的草坪 a lawn like velvet ❷ feeble；weak：他病刚好，身上～的。He's just recovered from an illness and feels weak. 这支歌～的。It is a languorous melody.

软盘 ruǎnpán 【名】floppy disk；diskette

软弱 ruǎnruò 【形】❶ weak；feeble：身体～无力 physically weak and lacking in energy ❷ weak in character：～无能 weak and incompetent

软弱性 ruǎnruòxìng 【名】weakness；flabbiness

软设备 ruǎnshèbèi 【名】another name for 软件 ruǎnjiàn

软通货 ruǎntōnghuò 【名】soft currency

软卧 ruǎnwò 【名】soft berth

软席 ruǎnxí 【名】soft berth or seat

软硬兼施 ruǎn yìng jiān shī use both hard and soft tactics (*derog.*)：尽管那些家伙～，也动摇不了他的意志。The scoundrels used both harsh and conciliatory tactics, but they had no effect on his determination.

ruì

锐（鋭） ruì

锐减 ruìjiǎn 【动】sharp fall (or decline)；sudden drop

锐角 ruìjiǎo 【名】acute angle

锐利 ruìlì 【形】sharp；keen：～的匕首 a sharp dagger ～的武器 sharp weapons 眼光～ keen vision ～的笔锋 an acerbic style of writing

锐气 ruìqì 【名】drive：一股势不可挡的～ an invincible spirit ～大挫。His drive was greatly blunted.

瑞 ruì

瑞雪 ruìxuě 【名】timely snow

rùn

闰（閏） rùn

闰年 rùnnián 【名】❶ leap year ❷ lunar year with an intercalary month

闰月 rùnyuè 【名】intercalary month

润（潤） rùn 【动】moisten；lubricate：～肠（a substance which）causes the bowels to move ～～嗓子 moisten one's throat 【形】moist and sleek：墨色很～（of the ink of a piece of calligraphy）thick and shining

润滑 rùnhuá 【形】lubricating

润滑油 rùnhuáyóu 【名】lubricating grease；lubricating oil

润色 rùnsè 【动】(of writing) polish：这篇文章还需要～一下。The article still needs polishing.

ruò

若 ruò 【连】〈书〉if；in case：～要人不知，除非己莫为。If you don't want people to know something, the only way is not to do it. 情况～有变化，请及时通知。If there should be any change, please let me know in time.

若非 ruòfēi 【连】〈书〉had it not

若干 ruògān 【数】〈书〉a certain number：～年前，这里还是一个小渔

村。A certain number of years ago, this place was still a little fishing village. 两队人数相差～? What is the difference in number of members between the two teams?

若即若离 ruò jí ruò lí neither friendly nor alienated

若是 ruòshì 【连】if; supposing (*usu. in written language*)：有的诗人说,～离开了沸腾的生活,他们是写不出感人的诗篇的。Some poets claim that if they are shut off from the bustle of life, they can't write inspiring poetry.

若无其事 ruò wú qí shì as if nothing had happened：显得～ look as if nothing had happened 装出～的样子 be very casual, as if nothing had happened

弱 ruò 【形】❶ weak：体～ physically weak ～不禁风 too weak to stand up against the wind ❷ less than：三分之一～ less than one-third

弱点 ruòdiǎn 【名】weakness; weak point

弱国 ruòguó 【名】weak country

弱肉强食 ruò ròu qiáng shí the law of the jungle：～是一切侵略者的强盗逻辑。The law of the jungle is the logic of all aggressors.

弱项 ruòxiàng 【名】weak point; sth. one is weak at

弱小 ruòxiǎo 【形】small and weak

弱者 ruòzhě 【名】the weak

弱智 ruòzhì 【名】mentally retarded

S

sā

撒 sā 【动】❶ let go; cast: ～网 cast a net ～腿就跑 take to one's heels 把鸟～了 release the bird ❷ ◇ throw off all restrain; let oneself go (*derog.*): ～泼 be unreasonable and make a scene ～赖 act shamelessly (to achieve one's shameful end)
另见 sǎ

撒谎 sā=huǎng tell a lie

撒娇 sā=jiāo (of a child) indulge in spoiled behaviour

撒气 sā=qì ❶ leak ❷ vent one's anger: 拿孩子～ vent one's anger on the child

撒手 sā=shǒu take one's hand away; let go

撒野 sā=yě behave unreasonably; act rough and wild

sǎ

洒(灑) sǎ 【动】❶ splash; sprinkle: 扫地前先～点儿水。Sprinkle the ground with water before sweeping it ❷ (of liquid) spill: 牛奶～了。The milk has spilt.

洒泪 sǎ=lèi shed tears: ～惜别 take a tearful leave

撒 sǎ 【动】❶ scatter; spread: ～种(zhǒng) sow seeds ～化肥 spread fertilizer 她～了一把米喂小鸡。She scattered a handful of rice to feed the chicks. ❷ spill; drop: 米饭～了一地。The floor is strewn with spilt rice.
另见 sā

sà

飒(颯) sà

飒爽 sàshuǎng 【形】〈书〉 valiant; bright and brave: ～英姿 a bright and brave look

sāi

腮 sāi 【名】jaw

腮腺 sīxiàn 【名】parotid gland

塞 sāi 【动】❶ stuff; cram; pack: 衣服～满一箱子。The case is stuffed with clothes. 他把手套脱下来，～在口袋里。He took off his gloves and stuffed them in his pocket. ❷ stop up; block up: 把窟窿～住 block up the hole 【名】(～儿) stopper; cork: 瓶～ a bottle cork
另见 sè

塞车 sāi = chē traffic congestion; traffic jam

塞子 sāizi 【名】〔个 gè〕stopper; cork

sài

赛(賽) sài 【动】❶ contest; compete：～了一场篮球 play a basketball game ❷ surpass; excel（in quality）：这些年轻人,干起活来一个～一个。These young people try to outdo one another in their work.

赛场 sàichǎng 【名】racecourse

赛车 sàichē 【名】racing bicycle

赛车 sài = chē motorcycle racing; bicycle racing; car racing

赛程 sàichéng 【名】schedule of contests：～过半 finish half of the contests

赛跑 sài = pǎo race

赛球 sài = qiú play a（football, basketball, etc.）match

sān

三 sān 【数】three

三八国际劳动妇女节 Sān Bā Guójì Láodòng Fùnǚjié March Eighth, International Working Women's Day

三包 sānbāo 【名】a factory's three guarantees when selling its products: a guarantee to either repair, refund or exchange faulty products

三长两短 sān cháng liǎng duǎn unexpected misfortune

三大纪律,八项注意 sān dà jìlǜ, bā xiàng zhùyì（of the Chinese People's Liberation Army）the Three Main Rules of Discipline（1. Obey orders in all your actions. 2. Don't take a single needle or piece of thread from the masses. 3. Turn in everything captured.）and The Eight Points for Attention（1. Speak Politely. 2. Pay fairly for what you buy. 3. Return everything you borrow. 4. Pay for everything you damage. 5. Don't hit or swear at people. 6. Don't damage crops. 7. Don't take liberties with women. 8. Don't ill-treat captives.）

三番五次 sān fān wǔ cì time and again; many a time; repeatedly（*often functions as an adverbial adjunct*）：老赵～地来催他快点动身。Lao Zhao has come repeatedly to persuade him to leave without delay.

三废 sānfèi 【名】waste gas, waste water and waste residue

三伏 sānfú 【名】❶ the three ten-day periods which are the hottest days of the year ❷ the "dog days"—the last of these 10-day periods

三好学生 sān hǎo xuéshēng an honorific title awarded to a student who is good in the following three aspects: work, study and health

三角 sānjiǎo 【名】❶ trigonometry ❷ triangle

三角板 sānjiǎobǎn 【名】set-square

三角函数 sānjiǎo hánshù trigonometric function

三角恋爱 sānjiǎo liàn'ài love triangle

三角形 sānjiǎoxíng 【名】triangle

三角洲 sānjiǎozhōu 【名】river delta

三脚架 sānjiǎojià 【名】tripod

三九 sānjiǔ 【名】the third nine days after the Winter Solstice—the coldest days of winter

三军 sānjūn 【名】❶ the army（in ancient times）❷ the army, navy and air force

三令五申 sān lìng wǔ shēn repeated orders

三轮车　sānlúnchē　【名】〔辆 liàng〕pedicab；child's tricycle

三民主义　sānmínzhǔyì　【名】the Three People's Principles of Sun Yat-sen — Nationalism, Democracy and People's Welfare

三明治　sānmíngzhì　【名】sandwich

三秋　sānqiū　【名】❶ three autumn jobs：harvesting, ploughing and sowing ❷ three years：一日不见，如隔～。A day which goes by without seeing (you) seems as long as three years.

三三两两　sān sān liǎng liǎng　in twos and threes (usu. used as an adverbial adjunct)：晚饭后人们～在路边散步。After supper, people would stroll along the road in twos and threes.

三天打鱼，两天晒网　sān tiān dǎ yú, liǎng tiān shài wǎng　spend two days fishing and three days drying nets；(fig.) do sth. by fits and starts：锻炼身体要长期坚持，～可不行。Physical training requires consistent effort. It cannot be done by fits and starts.

三天两头　sān tiān liǎng tóu　(～儿) at two or three day intervals；often

三夏　sānxià　【名】three summer jobs：harvesting, planting and field management

三心二意　sān xīn èr yì　❶ half-heartedly：为人民服务要全心全意，不能～。We must serve the people with all our energy, not half-heartedly. ❷ undecided；be of two minds about sth.：别～的，要去就快去吧！Don't shilly-shally. If you want to go, go.

三言两语　sān yán liǎng yǔ　in a few words：这件事～说不清楚。It is not something that can be explained in just a few words.

三月　sānyuè　【名】March

三座大山　sān zuò dà shān　the three big mountains—imperialism, feudalism and bureaucratic capitalism, which oppressed the Chinese people before Liberation

叁　sān　【数】three (the complicated form of 三) 见"捌" bā

sǎn

伞（傘）　sǎn　【名】〔把 bǎ〕umbrella；parasol

伞兵　sǎnbīng　【名】paratrooper

伞形花序　sǎnxíng huāxù　umbel

散　sǎn　【动】come loose；come apart：把书捆好，别～了。Tie up the books and see that they don't come apart.【形】loose；scattered：～装 in bulk；not pre-packaged 我们坐得太～了，集中一点吧！We're sitting too far apart. Let's move a bit closer together.

另见 sàn

散工　sǎngōng　【名】same as

散光　sǎnguāng　【名】astigmatism

散漫　sǎnmàn　【形】undisciplined；careless and sloppy：自由～ undisciplined and care-free 必须改变散散漫漫的生活作风。We must change our undisciplined way of life.

散文　sǎnwén　【名】〔篇 piān〕prose

散文诗　sǎnwénshī　【名】prose poem；poetic prose

散装　sǎnzhuāng　【形】bulk；in bulk

sàn

散　sàn　【动】❶ disband；scatter；disperse；break up：乌云被风吹～了。The dark clouds have been dispersed by the wind. 会～了没有？Is the meeting over? ❷ distribute；circulate：～传单 distribute leaflets

另见 sǎn

散布 sànbù 【动】spread；disseminate；scatter；diffuse：～谣言 spread rumours；到处～他的观点。He airs his views everywhere. 草原上～着牧民的羊群。The herdsmen's flocks of sheep are scattered aboat the prairie.

散步 sàn＝bù stroll；take a walk

散场 sàn＝chǎng （of a theatre, cinema, etc.）empty after a performance

散发 sànfā 【动】❶ issue；distribute：～宣传品 distribute propaganda material ❷ give off；exude：花儿～着清香。The flowers exude a delicate fragrance.

散会 sàn＝huì （of a meeting）break up

散开 sànkāi 【动】scatter；disperse

散失 sànshī 【动】❶ scatter and disappear；be lost：这部书的原稿大部分都～了。Most of the original manuscripts of this set of books have been lost. ❷ evaporate；dissipate；be lost：～热量 lose heat 水分～得很快。The water has evaporated quickly.

散摊子 sàn tānzi disintegrate；disband；break up

散心 sàn＝xīn relax；enjoy a diversion

sāng

丧（喪） sāng 【名】◇ funeral：婚、～、嫁、娶 weddings and funerals
另见 sàng

丧事 sāngshì 【名】funeral arrangements

丧钟 sāngzhōng 【名】(death) knell

桑 sāng 【名】mulberry tree

桑蚕 sāngcán 【名】silkworm

桑那浴 sāngnàyù 【名】sauna bath

桑树 sāngshù 【名】〔棵 kē〕mulberry tree

sǎng

嗓 sǎng

嗓门 sǎngmén 【名】(～儿) the pitch of one's voice

嗓音 sǎngyīn 【名】voice

嗓子 sǎngzi 【名】❶ throat ❷ voice

sàng

丧（喪） sàng 【动】◇ lose：良心～尽 have no conscience 他幼年～父。He lost his father when he was a child.
另见 sāng

丧家之犬 sàng jiā zhī quǎn stray dog；(fig.) one who has deservedly lost his supporters and has nowhere to turn (usu. derog.)

丧命 sàng＝mìng be killed

丧气 sàngqì 【形】downcast；dispirited；disheartened：事情没办好，他觉得很～。Because he did not handle the affair satisfactorily, he feels rather disheartened.

丧权辱国 sàng quán rǔ guó relinguish sovereignty and bring humiliation to one's country

丧生 sàng＝shēng lose one's life；be killed

丧失 sàngshī 【动】lose；forfeit；forsake；be deprived of：～劳动能力 lose the ability to do manual labour；become disabled ～信心 lose confidence 千万不要～警惕性。We must never relax our vigilance.

丧心病狂 sàng xīn bìng kuáng frenzied；be in a frenzy

sāo

骚(騷) sāo

骚动 sāodòng 【动】be in a tumult; become disorderly; 引起～ create a disturbance 敌军内部～起来。Dissension has arisen within the ranks of the enemy.

骚乱 sāoluàn 【动】become disorderly and noisy; riot; 会场里～起来。A commotion broke out at the meeting.

骚扰 sāorǎo 【动】harass; disturb

臊 sāo 【形】the smell of urine; smelling of urine
另见 sào

sǎo

扫(掃) sǎo 【动】❶ sweep (with a broom); ～雪 sweep away the snow ❷ remove; dispel; ～障碍 remove the barriers 烦闷、忧愁一～光 completely dispel one's worries ❸ move swiftly from one side to another; 机枪～了一梭子。The machine-gun fired a whole clip sweeping from side to side. 向屋里～了一眼。He scanned the room with a single glance.
另见 sào

扫除 sǎochú 【动】❶ sweep away; clear away; 经常～，保持室内外清洁 sweep regularly to keep the house clean ❷ eradicate; eliminate; sweep away; ～文盲 eliminate illiteracy

扫荡 sǎodàng 【动】(mil.) mop up; wipe out

扫地 sǎo = dì ❶ sweep the floor ❷ (of reputation, credit, etc.) lose totally; 名誉～ be discredited 威信～ with one's prestige totally destroyed

扫黄 sǎo = huáng eliminate pornography

扫雷 sǎo = léi mine-sweeping

扫盲 sǎo = máng eliminate illiteracy

扫描 sǎomiáo 【动】(electr.) scanning

扫墓 sǎo = mù visit a grave — pay respects to a dead person at his grave

扫射 sǎoshè 【动】strafe

扫视 sǎoshì 【动】sweep; glance

扫尾 sǎo = wěi complete the last stages of the work; round off

扫兴 sǎoxìng 【形】feel disappointed; 真～，想约他一起去故宫，他偏不在。We were really disappointed when, hoping he would join us to the Palace Museum, we found he was not at home.

嫂 sǎo 【名】◇ wife of one's elder brother

嫂子 sǎozi 【名】wife of one's elder brother

sào

扫(掃) sào
另见 sǎo

扫帚 sàozhou 【名】〔把 bǎ〕broom

臊 sào 【形】bashful; shy; ～得脸通红 blush scarlet
另见 sāo

sè

色 sè 【名】◇ ❶ colour; 浅绿～ light green colour ❷ facial expression; 面不改～ face remained unchanged (e. g. when confronted

with death) ❸ kind; species; sort; variety: 各～品种 various varieties

色彩 sècǎi 【名】❶ shade of colour; hue: ～鲜艳 a vivid shade ❷ (fig.) colour; flavour: 地方～ local colour 感情～ emotional colouring (e.g. of language)

色拉 sèlā 【名】salad

色厉内荏 sè lì nèi rěn fierce of visage but faint of heart; strong-looking on the outside but weak within

色盲 sèmáng 【名】colour blindness

色情 sèqíng 【名】salacity; pornographic

色素 sèsù 【名】(biol.) pigment

色泽 sèzé 【名】colour and lustre: ～鲜明 brightly coloured and lustrous

涩（澀） sè 【形】❶ astringent: 这些柿子太～，还不能吃。These persimmons make your mouth pucker. You can't eat them yet. ❷ not smooth; rough: 车轴发～，上点儿油吧! The axle is not turning smoothly; let's oil it.

瑟 sè

瑟瑟 sèsè 【象声】(of wind) whispering

塞 sè
另见 sāi

塞擦音 sècāyīn 【名】affricate

塞音 sèyīn 【名】plosive

sēn

森 sēn

森林 sēnlín 【名】forest

森严 sēnyán 【形】severe; stern: 壁垒～ strongly fortified 戒备～ heavily guarded

sēng

僧 sēng

僧侣 sēnglǚ 【名】monks; priests

僧人 sēngrén 【名】Buddhist monk

shā

杀（殺） shā 【动】❶ kill; slay; slaughter: ～虫 kill insects ～敌 kill the enemy ❷ fight: ～出重围 fight one's way out of heavy encirclement ❸ check; curtail: ～住不正之风 curtail unhealthy tendencies ～～他的威风 check his arrogance

杀虫剂 shāchóngjì 【名】insecticide; pesticide

杀风景 shā fēngjǐng spoil the landscape; (fig.) dampen one's enthusiasm; spoil the fun: 划船比赛正进行得紧张激烈，忽然刮起大风，真是大～。The boat race was at its most exciting stage when a strong wind began to blow and spoiled the fun!

杀害 shāhài 【动】kill unjustly

杀鸡取卵 shā jī qǔ luǎn kill the hen for its eggs; (fig.) be concerned with one's short term interests only to the detriment of longer range interests

杀价 shā = jià beat a seller down; beat a price down

杀菌 shā = jūn disinfect

杀戮 shālù 【动】slaughter; massacre: 无辜人民惨遭～。Great numbers of innocent people were massacred.

杀人不见血 shā rén bù jiàn xiě kill a person without spilling blood; kill sb. by subtle means

杀人不眨眼 shā rén bù zhǎ yǎn murder in cold blood; kill without the

slightest qualm：～ 的刽子手 a butcher who kills without the slightest qualm

杀人犯　shārénfàn　【名】homicidal person；murderer or manslayer

杀伤　shāshāng　【动】inflict casualties on

杀手　shāshǒu　【名】murderer

杀一儆百　shā yī jǐng bǎi　execute one man to warn a hundred；（fig.）punish one person as a warning to many others

沙　shā　【名】sand

沙丁鱼　shādīngyú　【名】sardine

沙发　shāfā　【名】sofa

沙龙　shālóng　【名】salon

沙漠　shāmò　【名】desert

沙滩　shātān　【名】sand beach

沙土　shātǔ　【名】sandy soil

沙文主义　Shāwénzhǔyì　【名】chauvinism

沙哑　shāyǎ　【形】hoarse；husky

沙眼　shāyǎn　【名】trachoma

沙子　shāzi　【名】sand

纱（紗）　shā　【名】❶ yarn；纺～ spin yarn ❷ gauze：这窗帘是～做的。This window curtain is made of muslin.

纱布　shābù　【名】gauze

纱窗　shāchuāng　【名】window screen

纱锭　shādìng　【名】spindle

刹　shā　【动】halt；check
另见 chà

刹车　shāchē　【名】brakes 也作 "煞车"。

刹车　shā = chē　apply brakes 也作 "煞车"。

砂　shā　【名】sand；grit

砂轮　shālún　【名】emery wheel；grinding wheel

砂糖　shātáng　【名】granulated sugar

煞　shā　【动】❶ put a stop to；stop：锣鼓一～住，演员就唱起来。As soon as the beating of drums and gongs stopped, the actor began to sing. ❷ tighten；check：～住车 brake the car 把腰带～紧 tighten one's belt
另见 shà

煞尾　shā = wěi　bring to an end；wind up；round off

鲨（鯊）　shā

鲨鱼　shāyú　【名】〔条 tiáo〕shark

shá

啥　shá　【代】what

shǎ

傻　shǎ　【形】❶ foolish；silly：～头～脑 muddle-headed 吓～了 be stupefied ❷ have a one-track mind：别～等了，他不会来了。Don't wait any longer. It's stupid. He won't come.

傻瓜　shǎguā　【名】fool

傻气　shǎqì　【名】stupidity

傻子　shǎzi　【名】fool；idiot

煞　shà
另见 shā

煞白　shàbái　【形】deathly pale

煞费苦心　shà fèi kǔ xīn　（do sth.）painstakingly：这座园林安排得这样精致，建造者可谓～了。This garden is so beautifully laid out! Whoever did it has certainly taken great pains with it.

煞有介事　shà yǒu jiè shì　pretend to be serious：小红～地背上了木枪，雄赳赳地好像真要上战场似的。Xiao Hong slung her toy rifle over her

shoulder with great seriousness and marched off into battle.

霎 shà

霎时间 shàshíjiān 【名】in an instant; in a twinkling

shāi

筛(篩) shāi 【动】sift

筛选法 shāixuǎnfǎ 【名】screening method by which unsuitable elements are systematically removed

筛子 shāizi 【名】〔个 gè〕sieve

shài

晒(曬) shài 【动】❶ (of the sun) shine on; 烈日～得人头昏。The sun glared down and I felt dizzy. ❷ dry (sth.) in the sun; bask in the sun; ～被子 air the quilt in the sun 到外边去～～太阳 go out and bask in the sun

晒台 shàitái 【名】sundeck

晒图 shàitú 【动】make a blueprint

shān

山 shān 【名】〔座 zuò〕❶ mountain ❷ hill

山坳 shān'ào 【名】a small area of level ground among mountains

山城 shānchéng 【名】mountain city

山村 shāncūn 【名】mountain village

山地 shāndì 【名】❶ mountainous area; mountainous region; 这一带全是～,行车很困难。It is very difficult to drive through this mountainous terrain. ❷ fields on a hill; terraced fields; 我们村有～两千多亩。Our village has more than 2000 *mu* of terraced fields.

山洞 shāndòng 【名】cave; cavern

山峰 shānfēng 【名】〔座 zuò〕mountain peak

山冈 shāngāng 【名】hillock

山歌 shāngē 【名】〔支 zhī〕a kind of folk song

山沟 shāngōu 【名】small valley

山谷 shāngǔ 【名】valley

山河 shānhé 【名】mountains and rivers; (*fig.*) a country's land or the land of a part of the country; 祖国一片大好～ our country's beautiful mountains and rivers 也作"河山"。

山洪 shānhóng 【名】mountain torrents

山货 shānhuò 【名】❶ produce of various kinds from a mountain region, e.g. chestnuts, haws, etc. ❷ rustic goods made of earthenware, wood, bamboo, etc.

山涧 shānjiàn 【名】mountain stream

山脚 shānjiǎo 【名】the foot of a mountain

山岭 shānlǐng 【名】mountain ridge

山路 shānlù 【名】〔条 tiáo〕road in the mountain

山麓 shānlù 【名】the foot of a mountain

山峦 shānluán 【名】chain of mountains

山脉 shānmài 【名】mountain range

山明水秀 shān míng shuǐ xiù green hills and clear waters; 中国的江南～,风景优美。South China has green hills and clear waters and is full of beautiful scenery. 也作"山清水秀"。

山南海北 shān nán hǎi běi the remote corners of the country; from all over the country; 这个单位的人员～哪儿来的都有。The personnel in this organization come from all parts of the country. ～,各个岗位上都有这个大学毕业的学生。You can find graduates from this uni-

versity all over the country.

山坡 shānpō 【名】mountain slope; hillside

山清水秀 shān qīng shuǐ xiù green hills and clear waters

山穷水尽 shān qióng shuǐ jìn at the end of one's tether; in desperate straits

山区 shānqū 【名】mountainous area

山水 shānshuǐ 【名】❶ water flowing down from a mountain ❷ natural scenery with hills and streams: 桂林～ the landscape of Guilin 他是专画～的。He specializes in landscape painting.

山头 shāntóu 【名】❶ hill top; the top of a mountain ❷ (～儿) mountain stronghold; (fig.) faction; political clique: 拉～ form a faction

山崖 shānyá 【名】cliff

山羊 shānyáng 【名】〔只 zhī〕goat

山腰 shānyāo 【名】half way up a mountain or a hill

山珍海味 shān zhēn hǎi wèi rare delicacies from mountains and seas

删 shān 【动】delete; strike out

删除 shānchú 【动】delete; cut

删繁就简 shān fán jiù jiǎn simplify by deleting the irrelevant: 这份材料要～。These texts must be simplified.

删改 shāngǎi 【动】make corrections and deletions

删节 shānjié 【动】abridge

删节号 shānjiéhào 【名】ellipsis (mark); suspension points

珊 shān

珊瑚 shānhú 【名】coral

舢 shān

舢板 shānbǎn 【名】〔只 zhī〕sampan (small boat) 也作"舢舨"。

扇 shān 【动】fan: ～扇子 wave a fan 真热! 请你给我一把扇子～～吧! Isn't it hot! Please give me a fan.

另见 shàn

扇动 shāndòng 【动】❶ flap: 大雁～着翅膀向南方飞去。The wild geese flap their wings and fly south. ❷ instigate; incite: ～暴乱 incite a riot 他犯错误是受了坏人的～。It was at the instigation of villains that he committed the error.

扇风点火 shān fēng diǎn huǒ fan up the flames; (fig.) stir up trouble; agitate among people so that they do evil

shǎn

闪(閃) shǎn 【名】lightning: 打～了。Look at the lightning! 【动】❶ dodge; duck: ～开 duck aside ～在一边 step quickly aside ❷ strain; twist: ～了腰 strain the muscles in the small of one's back ❸ flash; shine; sparkle: 金光～～ shine with golden light ～～发亮 glitter 灯光一～。A light flashes.

闪电 shǎndiàn 【名】lightning

闪电战 shǎndiànzhàn 【名】blitzkrieg

闪光 shǎnguāng 【名】flash; gleam

闪光灯 shǎnguāngdēng 【名】flash lamp

闪烁 shǎnshuò 【动】❶ twinkle; glimmer; glisten: 星光～。The stars twinkle. 他的眼中～着刚毅的目光。His eyes flashed with unyielding determination. ❷ dodge; evade; elude: ～其词 talk evasively; be non-committal

闪耀 shǎnyào 【动】flash; glitter; sparkle: 银光～ sparkles with silver light 塔顶～着金光。The top of the pagoda glitters with golden light.

shàn

苫 shàn 【动】cover（with a mat, canvas, etc.）

扇 shàn 【名】◇ fan：檀香～ a sandal-wood fan 【量】for door, window, screen, etc.：两～门 two doors 四～屏风 a four-panelled screen 一～窗户 one frame of a casement window
另见 shān
扇形 shànxíng 【名】fan-shaped；sector
扇子 shànzi 【名】〔把 bǎ〕fan

善 shàn 【形】（usu. in written language）❶（of one's conduct）kind；good and honest（as opp. to 恶）：心怀不～ with evil intent 来者不～。Whoever comes will come with bad intentions. ❷ proper：～自保重 take proper care of yourself ❸ be good at；be skilled in；know-how：英勇～战 brave and skilled in the business of fighting 能歌～舞 be good at both singing and dancing ❹ be apt to；be liable to：～变 be very changeable ～忘 be apt to forget things
善后 shànhòu 【名】necessary arrangements（after an accident）：～问题由他处理。Let him take care of the remaining problems.
善良 shànliáng 【形】good and honest
善始善终 shàn shǐ shàn zhōng start well and end well：工作要～ do well from start to finish
善心 shànxīn 【名】kindness
善意 shànyì 【名】goodwill
善于 shànyú 【动】be good at（usu. followed by a verbal phrase）：要～挤时间学习。We must be good at finding time to study. ～思考问题 be good at reflecting on matters

擅 shàn
擅长 shàncháng 【动】be proficient at；be skilled at（its object is usually a polysyllabic verb or a verbal phrase）：～摄影 be skilled at photography 他～写古体诗。He is good at writing poems in the ancient style.
擅自 shànzì 【副】take the liberty；take it upon oneself to：不能～离开岗位。One must not leave one's post without permission. 禁止～动用公款。No one is allowed to misappropriate public funds.

膳 shàn
膳费 shànfèi 【名】（monthly）fee for meals
膳食 shànshí 【名】meals（in an institution）

赡（贍）shàn
赡养 shànyǎng 【动】support financially（e.g. aged parents）；provide sb. with the means of subsistence：～费 maintainance allowance ～父母 provide for one's parents

shāng

伤（傷）shāng 【名】injury；wound：内～ internal injury 受了重～ be seriously wounded 轻～不下火线。Slight wounds cannot drive us from the battlefield. 【动】❶ injure；impair；hurt：～了筋骨 suffer an injury to bones and tendons ～了感情 damage friendship 有～和气 spoil a harmonious relationship ❷ be fed up with；dislike because of having had too much of it：他吃这种药吃～了。He is fed up with that

medicine.

伤疤 shāngbā 【名】scar

伤风 shāngfēng 【动】catch cold 【名】cold

伤感 shānggǎn 【动】be sentimental

伤害 shānghài 【动】harm；hurt；impair：～自尊心 damage one's self-respect 饮酒过多会～身体。Excessive drinking is injurious to one's health.

伤寒 shānghán 【名】typhoid；typhoid fever

伤痕 shānghén 【名】scar；bruise

伤口 shāngkǒu 【名】wound

伤脑筋 shāng nǎojīn （of a matter）be a headache for sb.；cause sb. trouble：真叫人伤透了脑筋 be extremely difficult to tackle 这件事真～。This matter is really a headache.

伤势 shāngshì 【名】condition of a wound

伤亡 shāngwáng 【动】suffer casualties：敌人～惨重。The enemy suffered heavy casualties.【名】casualty：造成重大～ result in heavy casualties 减少不必要的～ reduce unnecessary casualties

伤心 shāng = xīn grieved；broken-hearted

伤员 shāngyuán 【名】wounded soldier；the wounded

商 shāng 【名】◇ ❶ commerce；trade ❷ businessman；dealer；tradesman：皮货～ a fur dealer 富～ a rich businessman ❸ （maths.）quotient：四被二除，～是二。Four divided by two is two.【动】◇ ❶ consult with （sb.）；confer with （sb.）：有要事相～. I have something important to discuss （with you.）❷ the quotient is...：八除以四～二。Eight divided by four is two.

商标 shāngbiāo 【名】trademark

商标法 shāngbiāofǎ 【名】trademark law

商标权 shāngbiāoquán 【名】trademark rights

商场 shāngchǎng 【名】a building or group of buildings containing different kinds of shops

商店 shāngdiàn 【名】shop；store

商定 shāngdìng 【动】make a decision through consultation or discussion：～日期 discuss and fix the date 旅行日程早已～。The itinerary for the trip was decided long ago through consultation.

商法 shāngfǎ 【名】commercial law

商贩 shāngfàn 【名】pedlar

商量 shāngliang 【动】talk over；discuss；consult：遇事要多和大家～。Always confer with the masses when you come across a problem. 这件事我要跟他～一下。I should like to consult with him about the matter.

商品 shāngpǐn 【名】commodity

商品房 shāngpǐnfáng 【名】commercial housing

商品化 shāngpǐnhuà 【动】be on the market as a commodity

商品经济 shāngpǐn jīngjì commodity economy

商品流通 shāngpǐn liútōng commodity circulation

商品生产 shāngpǐn shēngchǎn commodity production

商洽 shāngqià 【动】take up （a matter）with sb.：这些物资怎样处理要有关单位共同～。The departments concerned will hold a discussion to decide what to do with the goods and materials.

商情 shāngqíng 【名】market conditions

商榷 shāngquè 【动】discuss；deliberate over （on matters where different opinions exist）（usu. in written language）：值得～。It is

open to discussion. 有些不同看法提出来和作者~。 Here are some different approaches which can be raised with the author.

商人 shāngrén 【名】 merchant; tradesman; businessman

商谈 shāngtán 【动】 confer; discuss; exchange opinions; ~贸易协定 negotiate a trade agreement 两国就文化交流问题进行~。 The two countries discussed the question of cultural exchange.

商讨 shāngtǎo 【动】 discuss; confer with; ~对策 confer with sb. about what counter-measures to take ~两国经济合作问题 hold discussions on economic cooperation between the two countries

商务 shāngwù 【名】 commercial affairs

商务参赞 shāngwù cānzàn commercial counsellor

商业 shāngyè 【名】 commerce

商议 shāngyì 【动】 discuss; confer; 会前主席团~并通过了大会议程。 The presidium held a discussion before the meeting and adopted the agenda.

商酌 shāngzhuó 【动】 discuss and consider

墒 shāng 【名】 moisture in the soil

墒情 shāngqíng 【名】 moisture content; moisture content of soil

shǎng

赏（賞） shǎng 【动】 ❶ reward; award; bestow; 立功者~。 Those who have performed meritorious acts are to be rewarded. ❷ ◇ admire; appreciate; enjoy; ~花 enjoy the flowers ~月 admire the full moon

赏赐 shǎngcì 【动】 bestow as a favour (upon one's inferior)

赏罚分明 shǎng fá fēnmíng the practice of giving rewards and punishments in strict accordance with deserts; be strict and fair in meting out rewards and punishments

赏脸 shǎng = liǎn grant sb. an honour; do sb. the honour of

赏钱 shǎngqián 【名】 tips

赏识 shǎngshí 【动】 appreciate; recognize the worth of (one's inferior); 这个研究生的导师很~他的分析能力。 The tutor thinks highly of the graduate student's powers of analysis.

晌 shǎng 【名】 part of a day; 前半~ the early part of the day 后半~ the latter part of the day

晌午 shǎngwu 【名】 noon

shàng

上 shàng 【名】 ❶ up; above; on as opp. to 下; 往~走 go up 朝~看 look upward ❷ used after a noun, pronounced in the neutral tone; ① indicates a higher position; 山~ on the mountain 房~ on top of the house 树~ in the tree ② indicates the surface of sth.; 墙~ on the wall 脸~ on one's face 海~ on the sea 椅子~ on the chair ③ indicates a certain range or a certain aspect; 报纸~登了他的文章。 His article was published in the paper. 会~讨论得很热烈。 The issue was discussed vehemently in the meeting. 信~说他下个月就来。 He says in his letter that he is coming next month. 工作~要认真负责,学习~要刻苦努力。 One must be conscientious at work and hard-working in studies. ❸ used before certain

nouns to indicate precedence：～册 first volume ～次 last time ～星期 last week ～半年 the first half year 【动】❶ move from a lower position to a higher one：～山 go up the mountain ～楼 go upstairs ～车 get on the bus ❷ go to (a place)：～街 go shopping ～商店 go shopping ～哪儿去？Where are you going? ❸ enter the court or field；appear on the stage：教练说："一号～，三号下。" The coach said："Player No.1 for No.3." 女主角什么时候～? When is the female lead to enter? ❹ fill：锅炉～水 fill the boiler with water ～货 put goods on shelves ❺ apply；smear：～油漆 apply the paint ～颜色 apply colour ～药 apply ointment ❻ install；fix：～刺刀 fix bayonets ～玻璃 fix the window pane ～螺丝 tighten a screw ❼ wind：表该～弦了。(My) watch needs winding. ❽ take part in a certain activity as scheduled：～工 begin to work ～操 begin drilling 你～完课就回家吗？Are you going home after class? ❾ publish：～账 enter in the accounts：你的事迹都～报了。An account of your deed was published in the paper. ❿ used before 百，千，万，to indicate approximate numbers：～百人 up to a hundred or over ～千元 up to a thousand yuan or over Note：上 is used as a complement after a verb ❶ indicates moving from a lower position to a higher one：汽车顺着公路开～山了。The car is driving up the mountain road. 把行李搬～车吧! Please put your luggage on the bus. 先端～两盘菜，再端汤。Serve two dishes first and then the soup. (same as 上来 or 上去 as a complement ❶, but no direction is indicated and an object is necessary) ❷ indicates moving from the back to

the front：赶快撵～前边的队伍。Hurry and catch up with the advancing troops. 她还没赶～她们班最好的学生。She hasn't caught up with the best students in her class yet. 他们已经走了一个小时了，咱们追不～了。They left more than an hour ago so we can't catch up with them. ❸ indicates reaching (a level previously considered beyond one's reach)：过～了好日子 lead a comfortable life now 许多农民用～了拖拉机。Many farmers have used tractors now. 山区人民也吃得～大米，穿得～呢子衣服了。The people in the mountain district now eat rice and wear clothes made of woolen cloth. ❹ be in a state of readiness：他沏～一杯茶，点～一支烟，坐下来看报。He made a cup of tea, lit a cigarette and sat down to read the paper. 你可以带～点干粮去钓鱼。You can take along a snack and go fishing. 把西瓜冰～了吗? Have you put the watermelon in the refrigerator? ❺ indicates that sth. is placed in a certain position：把大衣穿～，帽子戴～。Put on your coat and hat. 写～你的名字。Write your name on it. 路边都种～了树。Trees have been planted along the road. ❻ contract；be connected with：爱～了自己的工作 become attached to one's work 注意别传染～流感。Be careful not to catch the flu. 他无论去哪儿，总爱拉～一个伴儿。Wherever he goes, he likes to have somebody keep him company. ❼ indicates achievement of one's goal：他一定会考～大学的。I'm sure he will pass the university entrance exams. 买票的人太多，我恐怕买不～了。There is such a crowd of people queuing for tickets that I'm afraid I won't be able to buy any. 我总算看～那个

戏了。I managed to see that play after all. ❽ *indicates bringing or coming together*：把窗帘拉～。Draw the curtains. 关～门。Close the door. 系（jì）～鞋带。Tie your shoes. 把水果糖包～。Wrap up the candy.

上班 shàng = bān go to work；start work

上边 shàngbiān 【名】*same as* ❶ ❷ ❸ ❹ *of* "上面"

上宾 shàngbīn 【名】distinguished guest

上策 shàngcè 【名】best or wisest way；best solution

上层 shàngcéng 【名】upper stratum

上层建筑 shàngcéng jiànzhù superstructure

上当 shàng = dàng be taken in；be fooled：我已经上过一次当了，这次你可骗不了（liǎo）我了。I've been taken in before. You won't be able to fool me again.

上等 shàngděng 【形】first-grade；first-class：～绸缎 top quality silks ～绿茶 finest quality green tea

上帝 shàngdì 【名】❶ god ❷ God

上吊 shàng = diào commit suicide by hanging

上冻 shàng = dòng (of ground, rivers, etc.) freeze for the winter

上访 shàngfǎng 【动】for common people to make known their problems to higher authorities and appeal for help

上岗 shàng = gǎng go to one's post；perform one's duty

上告 shànggào 【动】❶ complain to the higher authorities or appeal to a higher court ❷ report to one's superior

上钩 shàng = gōu take the bait

上古 shànggǔ 【名】ancient times

上火 shàng = huǒ ❶ (of Chinese traditional medicine) suffer from excessive internal heat ❷ get angry

上级 shàngjí 【名】❶ higher rank；higher level ❷ one's superior

上缴 shàngjiǎo 【动】hand over to a higher organization

上进 shàngjìn 【动】make progress

上课 shàng = kè ❶ give a lesson to a class ❷ attend class

上空 shàngkōng 【名】the sky over a specific place

上口 shàng = kǒu suitable for reading aloud

上来 shàng // lái *indicates moving from a lower position to a higher one (towards the speaker)*：你快～看吧，烟火好看极了。Please come and look. The fireworks are marvellous! 这座山很难爬，有的人上不来了。This mountain is very steep；some people are unable to make it to the top. 这两年粮食产量～了。In the last few years grain output has increased. *used after a verb as a complement* ❶ *indicates moving from a lower position to a higher one*：汽车顺着盘山公路开～了。The car is driving up the road. 你把那些东西拿上楼来吧！Please bring those things upstairs. 主人端～一大盘切好的西瓜。Their host served them slices of watermelon on a tray. (*same as* 上 *as a complement* ❶, *towards the speaker, an object is optional*) ❷ *indicates approaching sb. or sth.* (*towards the speaker*)：我们刚下飞机就有人迎～问是不是参加科学讨论会的。No sooner had we got off the plane than someone came up and asked whether we were coming to attend the scientific conference. 张老师走进教室，孩子们都围～欢迎她。When Teacher Zhang entered the classroom, all the children gathered around to welcome her. 咱们先休息一会儿，等后面的人赶～再一起走吧。Let's stop

and have a rest. When those who are behind catch up with us, we'll go on together. ❸ *indicates giving an answer which complies with a question or request*：这些题目他都答～了，但不一定全对。He has answered all the questions, but he may not have got every one right. 这篇文章的中心思想你说得～说不～？Can you tell us the main idea of this article? 刚才排演的时候，小王的台词背不～了。In the rehearsal just now, Xiao Wang forgot his lines.

上马 shàng=mǎ ❶ mount a horse ❷ (of a project, enterprise, etc.) start; get under way

上面 shàngmiàn 【名】 ❶ above; over; on the surface of; on top of：飞机从云层～飞过去了。The plane flew above the clouds. ❷ foregoing; above-mentioned; aforesaid：～所说的都是我自己的体会。The foregoing has been entirely my own understanding (of the situation). ❸ on the surface of sth.：毛衣～绣了两朵小花。The sweater has two small flowers embroidered on it. ❹ higher authorities：这个文件是～发下来的。The document was issued by the higher authorities. ❺ (in a certain) respect：他在作曲～下了不少工夫。He takes great pains in composing music.

上去 shàng // qù *indicates moving from a lower position to a higher one* (*away from the speaker*)：我先～，在山顶上等你们。I'll go up first and wait for you at the top of the mountain. 他上五层去了。He went up to the fifth floor. 采取一切可能的措施，今年的产量不会上不去。If we do everything within our power, this year's crop yield can't fail to rise. *used after a verb as a complement* ❶ *indicates moving from*

a lower position to a higher one (*away from the speaker*)：汽车已经开上山去了。The car has driven up the mountain. 前方打得很激烈，弹药得及时送～。A fierce battle is being waged at the front and ammunition must be sent up on time. (*same as* 上 *as a complement* ❶ *but away from the speaker; an object is optional*) ❷ *indicates approaching sb. or sth.* (*away from the speaker*)：刚下船的老太太不是你大姨吗，赶快迎～吧。Isn't the old woman who has just got off the ship your aunt? Let's go up to her at once. 那条狗摇着尾巴跑～了，一定是看见了它的主人。The dog ran up wagging its tail. It must have seen its master.

上任 shàng=rèn (for an official) assume office

上身 shàngshēn 【名】 ❶ the upper part of the body：他～穿的是中山装。He is wearing a Chinese style jacket. ❷ (～儿) 〈口〉 jacket：她穿着一件灰～。She is wearing a grey jacket.

上升 shàngshēng 【动】 rise; go up; ascend：气球慢慢～。The balloon is ascending slowly. 气温～。The temperature is rising. 产量稳步～。The production output has been rising steadily.

上声 shàngshēng 【名】 the third tone 又读 shǎngshēng

上市 shàng=shì (of vegetables, fruits, etc.) be in season; be on the market

上述 shàngshù 【名】〈书〉 above-mentioned; aforesaid：经调查，～情况全部属实。An investigation has verified that the facts of the matter are as stated above.

上税 shàng=shuì pay a tax

上诉 shàngsù 【动】 appeal (to a

higher court)

上诉权 shàngsùquán 【名】right of appeal

上诉人 shàngsùrén 【名】appellant

上溯 shàngsù 【动】trace back

上台 shàng = tái ❶ appear on the stage：~表演 appear on stage and perform ~讲话 mount the platform to give a speech ❷ come into power；assume power：在英国，哪个政党~，哪个政党的领袖就是当然的首相。In Britain, the leader of whichever party assumes power automatically becomes the prime minister.

上头 shàngtou 【名】same as ❶ ❸ ❹ ❺ of "上面"

上文 shàngwén 【名】the preceding part of the text

上午 shàngwǔ 【名】before noon；morning

上下 shàngxià 【名】❶ the leadership and the rank-and-file；elders and youngsters：举国~ the whole nation 全军~ the whole army, officers and men alike 全家上上下下 the whole family, young and old alike ❷ up and down；from top to bottom：浑身~ from top to toe 大河~ from the upper to the lower reaches of the river (usu. the Yellow River) ❸ relative superiority or inferiority：不相~。It is hard to tell which is better. 不分~。There is practically no difference. 【助】(used after a numeral or a numeral plus measure word to indicate approximate number) about；or so：三十岁~ about 30 years old 一千斤~ one thousand jin or so 五十~ around fifty

上学 shàng = xué ❶ go to school ❷ be at school

上旬 shàngxún 【名】the first ten days of the month

上演 shàngyǎn 【动】(of a film, play) be showing；perform

上衣 shàngyī 【名】〔件 jiàn〕jacket；coat

上映 shàngyìng 【动】show (a film)

上游 shàngyóu 【名】❶ upper reaches ❷ the best；争~ strive to be among the most advanced 高居~ be in an advanced position

上涨 shàngzhǎng 【动】rise；go up：水位~。The water level has risen. 物价~。Prices have risen.

上肢 shàngzhī 【名】upper limbs

尚 shàng 【副】〈书〉still；yet：现在下结论为时~早。It is still too early to draw any conclusion. 问题~待解决。The problem remains to be solved. 我虽年迈，~能做些工作。I may be old, but I think there is still work I can do.

尚且 shàngqiě 【副】even used as an intensive to indicate an extreme or hypothetical case：生命~不惜，何况流点汗呢！One is willing to give even one's life, so one certainly doesn't squabble over a little hard work. 他对一个初次见面的朋友~如此热情，对老朋友就可想而知了。He was so cordial towards someone he met for the first time. You can imagine how warm he would be towards old friends.

尚未 shàngwèi 【副】〈书〉not yet：~完工。The work is not yet finished. ~实现。It has not yet been realized.

shāo

捎 shāo 【动】bring to sb.；take sth. to sb.：~个信儿 carry a message ~点家乡土产 bring local products from one's home village (to

sb.) ～上几句话 take a short message (to sb.)

捎带 shāodài 【动】do sth. incidentally; do sth. in passing: 你进城～着给我买本词典。Please get me a dictionary if you happen to be going to town. 这件事我～着就办了。I can take care of this matter without going out of my way.

烧（燒）shāo 【动】❶ burn: 火～得真旺。The fire is burning brightly. 柴～完了。The firewood has been completely used up. ❷ cook; heat; bake: ～饭 cook rice ～砖 fire bricks ❸ fry and then stew: ～茄子 braised eggplant ～排骨 braised porkchops ❹ have a fever: 病人这会儿～得厉害。The patient is running a high temperature.

烧杯 shāobēi 【名】〔个 gè〕beaker

烧饼 shāobǐng 【名】sesame seed cake

烧火 shāo = huǒ make a fire (for cooking)

烧酒 shāojiǔ 【名】strong alcoholic drink distilled from grain

烧烤 shāokǎo 【名】barbecue

烧伤 shāo//shāng (med.) burn

稍 shāo 【副】(usu. in written language) slightly; a little; a bit: ～有区别 slightly different ～加改动 make a slight change ～等一下 wait for a while

稍微 shāowēi 【副】a little always followed by 一点儿, 一会儿, etc. indicating small amount, short time, slight movement, etc.: 今天～有点儿冷。It's a bit cold today. ～等一会儿,他就来了。Please wait a moment. He'll come soon. 天真热,～动两下儿就满头汗。It's really hot. If you just move around a bit you're sweating all over.

sháo

勺 sháo 【名】◇ spoon; ladle

勺子 sháozi 【名】〔把 bǎ〕spoon; ladle

芍 sháo

芍药 sháoyao 【名】Chinese herbaceous peony

韶 sháo

韶光 sháoguāng 【名】〈书〉beautiful spring-time

shǎo

少 shǎo 【形】❶ a little; a few (as opp. to 多): 来的人很～。Only a few people have come. ❷ (used in combination with "很" as an adverbial adjunct) seldom; rarely: 这一带很～下暴雨。There are seldom, if ever, torrential rains in this region. 最近他很～抽烟。He hardly ever smokes now. ❸ 〈书〉a short while; a moment: 请～候。Please wait a moment. 【动】❶ be short of; lack: 账目很对,一分钱不～。The accounts were correct. There was not a cent short. 我们学校～两位数学教员。Our school is short two mathematics teachers. ❷ miss; lose: ～了件行李。One piece of luggage is missing. 这个字～了一撇。This character has a stroke missing.
另见 shào

少不了 shǎo bu liǎo indispensable; cannot do without: 对外联系的事～你。We cannot do without you as far as making contact with outside people is concerned. 这次来你家,～给你添麻烦。We are afraid we may

cause you a lot of inconvenience by coming to your home.

少而精 shǎo ér jīng fewer but better

少见多怪 shǎo jiàn duō guài the less seen a thing is, the more strange it appears：这种时而下雨时而下雪的现象，在高原上很常见，你不要～。Don't be surprised if you find that it rains one minute and snows the next. It's not at all unusual in the highlands.

少量 shǎoliàng 【形】 a small amount；a little；a few

少时 shǎoshí 【副】〈书〉after a little while

少数 shǎoshù 【名】❶ minority ❷ a small number

少数民族 shǎoshù mínzú minority nationality

少许 shǎoxǔ 【形】〈书〉a few；a little：寄去红茶～，请收下。Please accept this small amount of black tea we are sending you.

shào

少 shào
另见 shǎo

少年 shàonián 【名】❶ teenage ❷ teenager；youngster

少年犯 shàoniánfàn 【名】 juvenile delinquent

少年犯罪 shàonián fàn zuì juvenile delinquency

少年宫 shàoniángōng 【名】 Children's Palace

少年先锋队 shàonián xiānfēngduì the Young Pioneers

少女 shàonǚ 【名】 young girl

少先队 shàoxiānduì 【名】 short for 少年先锋队

哨 shào 【名】❶ sentry post：～卡 sentry post ❷（～儿）whistle：吹

～ blow a whistle

哨兵 shàobīng 【名】sentinel；sentry

哨所 shàosuǒ 【名】sentry post；sentry box

哨子 shàozi 【名】whistle

shē

奢 shē

奢侈 shēchǐ 【形】luxurious；extravagant：～的生活 a luxurious life 要提倡俭朴，反对～浪费。(We) must encourage frugal living and oppose extravagance and waste.

奢华 shēhuá 【形】luxurious；sumptuous：陈设过于～ be extremely sumptuously furnished

奢望 shēwàng 【名】wild hope；extravagant wish

赊（賒）shē 【动】buy or sell on credit

赊购 shēgòu 【动】buy on credit

赊账 shē = zhàng buy or sell on credit

shé

舌 shé 【名】◇ tongue：唇枪～剑 engage in a fierce battle of words

舌根音 shégēnyīn 【名】velar

舌尖音 shéjiānyīn 【名】apical

舌面音 shémiànyīn 【名】palatal

舌头 shétou 【名】❶ tongue ❷ a prisoner captured from the enemy army for the purpose of getting information：抓来一个～。We've captured a prisoner to get information.

舌战 shézhàn 【动】have a verbal battle；argue vehemently

折 shé 【动】❶ break off；snap off：树枝～了。The branch broke

off. ❷ lose (in business)：～本儿 lose one's capital
另见 zhē；zhé

蛇 shé 【名】〔条 tiáo〕snake

shě

舍（捨） shě 【动】give up；part with；abandon：～命干 work for all one is worth ～命不～财 prefer to forfeit one's life rather than one's money

舍本逐末 shě běn zhú mò pay attention to trifles but neglect essentials：～必定把事情搞糟。Clutching at trifles and neglecting essentials is bound to make a mess of things.

舍不得 shě bu de be loath to part with or leave；be reluctant to give up：快要毕业了，学生们都～离开母校。The students who are about to graduate feel sad at leaving the school. 这么好的日记本，我真有点儿～用。Such a nice diary! I really hate to use it!

舍得 shěde 【动】be willing to give or part with：～花时间 be willing to spare more time 这枝钢笔你～送他吗? Are you willing to part with your pen as a present for him?

舍己为公 shě jǐ wèi gōng sacrifice one's own interests for the sake of the people

舍己为人 shě jǐ wèi rén sacrifice one's own interests for the sake of others：～的事迹 a case of sacrificing oneself for the sake of others

舍近求远 shě jìn qiú yuǎn seek something far and wide when it is within reach：这本书附近书店就有，何必～，跑到城里去买? Why go all the way to town to get the book when you can find it in the book-store just around the corner?

舍弃 shěqì 【动】discard；abandon；give up；delete：这篇稿子里重复的材料必须～。The repetitive parts of this article must be deleted.

舍死忘生 shě sǐ wàng shēng disregard one's own safety；risk one's life：战争年代革命根据地人民常常～支援自己的子弟兵。During the war, the people in the revolutionary base areas often risked their lives to support the army.

shè

设（設） shè 【动】set up；establish；found：～宴 arrange a banquet for sb. 指挥所～在阵地前沿。The command post is set up where the fighting is fiercest.

设备 shèbèi 【名】equipment；facilities；installation：～完善 well-equipped 增加一套～ install another set of equipment

设法 shèfǎ 【动】think of a way；try：多方～筹备资金 try by all possible means to raise funds ～克服 try to overcome (difficulties)

设防 shè＝fáng set up defences：步步～ set up defences at each stage of the fighting 不～的城市 an open city；an undefended city

设计 shèjì 【动】design；plan：精心～ design carefully 【名】design；plan：按总工程师的～施工 do the work according to the plan drawn up by the chief engineer

设计 shè＝jì plot against sb.；set a trap for sb.：～陷害 scheme to frame (an innocent man) 设下了毒计 put a vicious scheme into effect

设立 shèlì 【动】set up；establish；found：～办事机构 set up an office 医疗站就～在这里。The medical station will be set up here.

设身处地 shè shēn chǔ dì put oneself in another person's position; be considerate：～地替他想一想 be considerate towards him 服务人员应该～为大家着想。Service personnel should look at things from the point of view of the public and act accordingly.

设施 shèshī 【名】installation; facilities：军事～ military installation 医疗～ medical facilities

设想 shèxiǎng 【动】assume; imagine; envisage; conceive：难以～! It is inconceivable! 怎么能～一个早晨就把所有的问题都解决了呢! How could you have imagined that the problems could all be solved in one morning! 【名】assumption; tentative idea：这只是个～。This is just a tentative assumption. 请谈谈你的～。Let's hear your view.

设宴 shèyàn 【动】give a banquet：～招待 give a banquet to entertain

设置 shèzhì 【动】❶ set up; place：～专业课程 set up special courses (in a college) ❷ install; fix：会场里～了同声传译设备。Simultaneous translation equipment was installed in the meeting hall.

社 shè 【名】◇ agency; organized body; society：集会结～ hold a meeting and form a society 诗～ a poets' club

社会 shèhuì 【名】society

社会保险 shèhuì bǎoxiǎn social insurance

社会存在 shèhuì cúnzài social being

社会分工 shèhuì fēngōng social division of labour

社会工作 shèhuì gōngzuò duties outside of one's regular work done for the collective

社会关系 shèhuì guānxi personal social relationships (relatives and friends)

社会活动 shèhuì huódòng one's activities in the society

社会科学 shèhuì kēxué social science

社会意识 shèhuì yìshí social consciousness

社会制度 shèhuì zhìdù social system

社会主义 shèhuìzhǔyì 【名】socialism

社交 shèjiāo 【名】social intercourse

社论 shèlùn 【名】〔篇 piān〕editorial

射 shè 【动】❶ shoot; fire：～出三发炮弹 fire three rounds 把球～入球门 score a goal 一箭～中靶心 hit the target with one arrow ❷ discharge; emit：光芒四～ emitting a brilliant light

射程 shèchéng 【名】range (of gunfire)

射击 shèjī 【动】shoot; fire：开枪～ shoot with a gun 对准目标～ take aim and fire 看～表演 watch a display of marksmanship

射箭 shè = jiàn ❶ shoot an arrow; do archery ❷ (sports) archery

射流 shèliú 【名】(phys.) efflux

射线 shèxiàn 【名】(phys.) ray

涉 shè

涉及 shèjí 【动】involve; relate to; touch upon; range over：他在报告中～到几个方面的问题。In his report, he touched on several problems. 调整工资～的面很广。The readjustment of wages involves large numbers of people.

涉猎 shèliè 【动】read in a cursory way：这些书稍加～即可。These books can be skimmed through.

涉外 shèwài 【动】concerning foreign affairs or foreign nationals：～单位 unit concerning foreign affairs ～工作 foreign work

涉嫌 shèxián 【动】be a suspect

赦 shè 【动】◇ pardon; remit：

～罪 absolve sb. from guilt

赦免 shèmiǎn 【动】(law) pardon; remit (punishment)

摄（攝） shè 【动】◇ photograph

摄取 shèqǔ 【动】❶ absorb; take in: ～养料 absorb nourishment ❷ take (a photograph); shoot (a film); ～几个镜头 (of a film) shoot several scenes

摄氏度 shèshìdù 【名】Celsius centigrade

摄氏温度计 shèshì wēndùjì Celsius thermometer

摄像机 shèxiàngjī 【名】pickup camera

摄影 shè=yǐng photograph

摄影师 shèyǐngshī 【名】photographer; cameraman

摄制 shèzhì 【动】produce (a film)

慑（懾） shè

慑服 shèfú 【动】❶ submit out of fear ❷ cow sb. into submission

慑于 shèyú 【动】〈书〉be cowed: 敌人～我军威力, 未敢妄动。Cowed by our might, the enemy dared not make any reckless move.

shēn

申 shēn

申报 shēnbào 【动】report in writing to a higher body; mostly used for legal documents and papers

申辩 shēnbiàn 【动】(law) defend oneself; plead or argue one's case

申斥 shēnchì 【动】rebuke; reproach (one's subordinate)

申明 shēnmíng 【动】state; declare; avow: ～理由 state one's reasons ～立场 state one's position

申请 shēnqǐng 【动】apply for: ～调动工作 apply for a transfer ～入党 apply for party membership 【名】application: 提出～ put in an application 这份～是办公室刚转来的。This application form has just been sent here by the office.

申请书 shēnqǐngshū 【名】application form

申述 shēnshù 【动】state; explain in detail: 向法院～理由 state one's reasons to the court 向对方～来意 explain one's intention in calling on sb.

申诉 shēnsù 【动】(law) appeal

申冤 shēn = yuān redress an injustice

伸 shēn 【动】hold out; stretch; extend: ～出手来 stretch out (one's) hand ～开腿 stretch one's legs 手指受伤, 不能屈～。I've hurt my finger and can't bend or straighten it.

伸懒腰 shēn lǎnyāo stretch oneself

伸手 shēn = shǒu stretch out one's hand; (fig.) ask others for sth. (derog.)

伸缩 shēnsuō 【动】❶ expand and contract; stretch out and draw back; lengthen and shorten: 镜头能够～。The (camera) lens can zoom in and out. ❷ flexible; adjustable: 留有～的余地 allow (sb.) some leeway

伸缩性 shēnsuōxìng 【名】elasticity

伸展 shēnzhǎn 【动】extend; stretch: 这片树林一直～到河边。The wood stretches right to the river bank.

伸张 shēnzhāng 【动】promote; uphold (usu. abstract things): 打击歪风, ～正气 combat unhealthy tendencies and promote healthy ones

身 shēn 【名】◇ ❶ body: ～高一米七 1.7m. in height ❷ main part

of a structure；body：车～ a car body 船～ the hull of a boat ❸ life：舍～抢救人民的生命财产 give one's life to save the lives and property of the people ❹ oneself；in person；personally：教师应该以～作则。Teachers should set a good example.【量】(～儿) suit：一～新衣服 a new suit (of clothes)

身败名裂　shēn bài míng liè　lose all standing and reputation；bring ruin and shame upon oneself；be utterly discredited

身边　shēnbiān　【名】❶ by one's side：他～有两个徒弟。He has two apprentices with him. ❷ (have sth.) on one's person：他眼睛花了，～总带着老花镜。He suffers from presbyopia and always carries a pair of glasses.

身材　shēncái　【名】(human) figure

身长　shēncháng　【名】exact measurement of a person's height

身份　shēnfen　【名】status；identity；capacity：～很高 of high social standing ～不明 of unknown identity 无论什么时候,他总是以普通劳动者的～出现。He always appears in the capacity of an ordinary worker.

身份证　shēnfènzhèng　【名】identity card

身价　shēnjià　【名】social status (derog.)：抬高～ raise (one's) social status ～百倍 increase one's status in society a hundredfold

身教　shēnjiào　【动】teach by personal example

身经百战　shēn jīng bǎi zhàn　have been through many battles；battle-tested：～的老将为人民立下了不朽的功勋。This veteran was tested in many battles and performed immortal feats for the people.

身量　shēnliang　【名】(of a person) stature；height

身临其境　shēn lín qí jìng　be on the scene oneself：这个故事讲得太好了,让人听了好像～一般。The story was so vividly told that the people listening felt as if they had actually witnessed the action.

身躯　shēnqū　【名】body

身上　shēnshang　【名】❶ on one's body：今天他～穿的是灰制服。He has a grey uniform on today. 希望寄托在你们～。We place our hopes on you. ❷ (carry sth.) with one；(have sth.) about one：你～带钱了吗？Do you have any money with you?

身世　shēnshì　【名】life (usu. implying a sequence of misfortunes)

身体　shēntǐ　【名】❶ body ❷ health

身体力行　shēn tǐ lì xíng　earnestly practise what one advocates

身心　shēnxīn　【名】in body and in mind

身子　shēnzi　【名】body：光着～ be naked 这老人～还挺硬朗。The old man is still going strong.

呻　shēn

呻吟　shēnyín　【动】groan；moan

绅(紳)　shēn

绅士　shēnshì　【名】gentry

深　shēn　【形】❶ deep：～井 a deep well 河水两米～。The river is two metres deep. ❷ late；far off in time or long after sth. began：～秋 late autumn 夜～人静 in the dead of night ❸ difficult；profound：这个课本内容太～了。The content of this textbook is too difficult. ❹ penetrating；thoroughgoing；profound：～谈 have a penetrating discussion 影响很～ produce a profound effect ❺ (of feelings) intimate；close：感情～ deep feelings 两人的交情很～。The two

of them have a very close relationship. ❻ (of colour) deep; dark：～红 deep red 颜色太～了。The colour is too dark. 【副】deeply; greatly; very (*usu.* 深深地)：～感不安 feeling very uneasy ～～地怀念自己的一位中学老师 cherish deep memories of a teacher from one's middle school days

深奥 shēn'ào 【形】(of meaning, reason) profound; abstruse：～的道理 profound argument

深长 shēncháng 【形】profound and significant：情意～ profound and lasting friendship

深沉 shēnchén 【形】❶ dark and silent; deep：夜色～ in the dark of night ❷ (of sound or voice) deep; sombre：～的哀乐 sombre dirge ❸ not revealing one's feelings; deep and reserved：性格～ of a deep and reserved disposition

深仇大恨 shēn chóu dà hèn bitter and deep-seated hatred; intense hatred：怀着～ have intense hatred for

深度 shēndù 【名】depth

深更半夜 shēn gēng bàn yè in the dead of night; late at night

深耕 shēngēng 【动】plough deeply

深耕细作 shēn gēng xì zuò deep ploughing and careful cultivation

深厚 shēnhòu 【形】❶ deep; profound：～的友谊 deep friendship ～的基本功 thoroughly trained in basic skills ❷ (of foundation) deep-seated; firm; solid：～的理论基础 a solid theoretical base

深化 shēnhuà 【动】deepen (*used with abstract nouns*)

深交 shēnjiāo 【动】deep friendship

深究 shēnjiū 【动】inquire deeply into

深刻 shēnkè 【形】❶ penetrating; thorough-going; profound：内容～ having content which is profound

❷ strongly felt：～印象 deep impression ～的教训 a profoundly significant lesson

深谋远虑 shēn móu yuǎn lǜ think deeply and see far; be circumspect and farsighted：～是一个指挥员应具备的条件之一。Circumspection and far-sightedness are requirements for being a commander.

深浅 shēnqiǎn 【名】❶ depth：河水的～ the depth of the river ❷ sense of propriety：小孩子说话没个～，您别见怪。The child spoke thoughtlessly. Please don't blame him. ❸ degree of difficulty：这几篇文章～不一。These essays vary in difficulty.

深切 shēnqiè 【形】❶ heartfelt; deeply felt; deep and sincere：～的关怀 heartfelt concern ～的慰问 heartfelt regard and concern for ❷ deep and sincere：～的体会 deep and intimate experience of sth. 对他的为人有～的了解 have a deep and genuine understanding of his character

深情 shēnqíng 【名】deep feeling; profound feeling

深情厚谊 shēn qíng hòu yì deep feelings of friendship：我们两国人民之间的～是源远流长的。The deep friendship between our two countries has a long history.

深入 shēnrù 【动】go deep among; penetrate into；(do sth.) in a thorough-going way：～生活 live life to the full ～的调查研究 conduct investigations in a thorough-going way 工作做得很～ do one's work thoroughly

深入浅出 shēn rù qiǎn chū explain the profound in simple terms; explain sth. difficult simply and clearly

深入人心 shēnrù rénxīn strike deep roots in the hearts of the people：

改革开放～。The reform and open policy has taken root in the hearts of the people.

深山 shēnshān 【名】deep in the mountains

深思 shēnsī 【动】think deeply about; ponder over

深思熟虑 shēn sī shú lǜ careful consideration; weigh and consider thoroughly：他经过～以后，才提出了自己的看法。It was only after careful consideration that he put forward his views.

深恶痛绝 shēn wù tòng jué thoroughly hate and detest：人们对于损公肥私危害集体利益的行为～。The people harbour a bitter hatred for the practice of private gain at the expense of collective interests.

深信 shēnxìn 【动】firmly believe; be thoroughly convinced：～无疑 completely convinced 我们～我们的目的一定能够达到。We are convinced that we shall attain our goal.

深夜 shēnyè 【名】in the dead of night

深渊 shēnyuān 【名】abyss

深远 shēnyuǎn 【形】far-reaching; profound and lasting：～的影响 far-reaching effect 意义～ profound and lasting significance

深造 shēnzào 【动】take a more advanced course of study or training; go on for further study：他大学毕业以后，又进研究院～。He went on for advanced study in a research institute after graduation.

深重 shēnzhòng 【形】very serious; extremely grave：～的危机 grave crisis 灾难～ great catastrophe

shén

什 shén

什么 shénme 【代】❶ what (*indicating interrogation*)：你在想～? What are you thinking about? ～是可控硅? What is a silicon controlled rectifier? 他是～人? What is his profession? ❷ *used before* 都 *or* 也 *to indicate inclusion*：他～书都看。He reads anything. 天黑得～也看不见。It's so dark that one can't see anything. 你不能～电影都看，太浪费时间了。You mustn't see all these films, and it's a waste of time. ❸ *indicates something indefinite*：他好像有～心事。He seems to have something on his mind. 咱们～时候好好谈谈。Let's have a good talk sometime. ❹ *one phrase with* 什么 *precedes another，in which case the latter refers to the former*：你爱～时候去，就～时候去。You can go whenever you like. 他想到～就说～，一点不系统。He said whatever came into his head, without the least attention to logic. ❺ *forms rhetorical questions*：① *used after a verb to indicate disapproval*：你嚷～! 大家还没起呢! Why are you yelling? There are people who are still sleeping. 他急～! 不会赶不上车的! Why is he in such a hurry? There is plenty of time to catch the train. ② *used before a predicative word or phrase to indicate disbelief*：～不会做! 他不愿意做罢了! Not know how to do it? He doesn't want to do it. That's all! ～头疼! 全是借口! A headache? That's just an excuse! ～三天完工! 十天也完不了! Be finished in 3 days? It won't be finished in 10 days! ③ *used before a noun to indicate dissatisfaction or scorn*：你写的～诗呀! 我们都看不懂。That's supposed to be poetry? We can't make head on tail of it! 这干的叫～活儿! 太粗了。What sort of work is

this? So carelessly done! ④ *used by itself to indicate surprise or dissatisfaction*：～！都八点了！今天可睡过头了。What! Already eight o'clock! I certainly have overslept! ～！钱都用没了？你可真能花！What! All the money gone? You certainly are a spendthrift! ～！三本书都看完了！怎么这么快？What! You have finished all three books? How could you have gone through them so fast? ⑤ 有什么（*used before an adjective or any descriptive word or phrase to indicate disapproval*）：这事有～难办的！What is so difficult about this matter? 这种衣柜有～好！质量次，又装不了多少东西。What is so special about this kind of wardrobe? Its quality is poor and there's very little room to hold things. 没（有）什么（*indicates negation*）：不会就承认不会，没（有）～可难为情的。If you don't know how to do it, just admit it. That's nothing to be ashamed of. ❻ *used before parallel words or phrases to indicate enumeration*：他对体育的爱好是多方面的，～游泳啦，溜冰啦，足球啦——全都喜欢。He has a broad interest in sports：swimming, skating, football—he's fond of all of them.

什么的 shénmede 【代】and so on；etc.（*used after a word or phrase or several parallel words or phrases to indicate similarity of persons or things*）：小说、诗歌、剧本～他都爱看。He is fond of reading novels, poetry, plays, etc. 星期日他总喜欢看个球赛～。On Sundays, he likes to go and watch ball games and that sort of thing.

神 shén 【名】❶ god；deity ❷ ◇ spirit；vigour；energy；费～（sth.）takes up one's energy 两眼炯炯有～

with bright penetrating eyes

神采 shéncǎi 【名】（of appearance）radiant health

神采奕奕 shéncǎi yìyì having an appearance which is radiant with health and vigour

神出鬼没 shén chū guǐ mò mysteriously appear and disappear；act swiftly and cleverly；come and go like a shadow：这几个人～，不知道他们在干什么。These few guys here one day and gone the next, there is no knowing what they are up to.

神甫 shénfu 【名】Catholic father；priest 也作"神父"。

神乎其神 shén hū qí shén （of exaggerated remarks）fantastic：这件事让小王一吹，就～了。If Xiao Wang is telling the story, of course it will be filled with fantasy.

神话 shénhuà 【名】 mythology；myth

神经 shénjīng 【名】nerve

神经病 shénjīngbìng 【名】neuropathy

神经科 shénjīngkē 【名】department of neurology

神经衰弱 shénjīng shuāiruò neurasthenia

神经质 shénjīngzhì 【形】neurotic；nervous

神灵 shénlíng 【名】deities；gods

神秘 shénmì 【形】mysterious；mystical

神奇 shénqí 【形】magical；miraculous

神气 shénqì 【形】❶ spirited；vigorous；energetic：这孩子戴上了红领巾，显得很～。The boy looks very impressive when he wears his red scarf. ❷ swagger；be cocky；put on airs：～十足 enormously cocky 没什么可～的。There's nothing to swagger about. 【名】expression；look；air：他说话的～很严肃。He

speaks in a serious and dignified manner. 摆出一副高人一等的～。(He) is striking a pose as if he is superior to others.

神枪手　shénqiāngshǒu　【名】crack shot

神情　shénqíng　【名】facial expression revealing of one's mental state

神色　shénsè　【名】同"神情"

神圣　shénshèng　【形】sacred；holy：～的职责 sacred duty

神速　shénsù　【形】amazingly quick；with lightning speed：收效～ produce incredibly quick results 兵贵～。Speed is precious in military operations.

神态　shéntài　【名】(of a person) look and manner；mien

神通　shéntōng　【名】magical power

神往　shénwǎng　【动】be carried away；be charmed by：黄山景色令人～。The scenery of Huang Shan is enchanting.

神仙　shénxian　【名】supernatural being；fairy

神志　shénzhì　【名】consciousness；mental faculties

神州　shénzhōu　【名】the divine land (a poetic name for China)

shěn

审（審）　shěn　【动】❶ examine；read over；check over：～稿 go over a manuscript to approve it ❷ interrogate；cross-examine；try：～犯人 interrogate a criminal ～案 try a case

审查　shěnchá　【动】examine；check：～计划 check the plan ～干部 investigate a cadre

审定　shěndìng　【动】examine and approve：这个方案由领导～。This plan is to be examined and approved by the leadership.

审核　shěnhé　【动】examine and verify；check and approve：～经费 examine and verify the expenses ～预算 check and approve a budget

审计　shěnjì　【动】audit

审理　shěnlǐ　【动】(law) try；hear

审美　shěnměi　【动】aesthetic appreciation

审判　shěnpàn　【动】put on trial；try：～罪犯 put a criminal on trial

审判员　shěnpànyuán　【名】judge；judicial officer

审判长　shěnpànzhǎng　【名】presiding judge

审批　shěnpī　【动】examine and endorse；check and approve

审慎　shěnshèn　【形】careful；cautious

审问　shěnwèn　【动】interrogate；cross-examine

审讯　shěnxùn　【动】同"审问"

审阅　shěnyuè　【动】check and approve：～稿件 go over a manuscript

婶（嬸）　shěn　【名】◇ aunt；wife of one's father's younger brother

婶母　shěnmǔ　【名】同"婶"

shèn

肾（腎）　shèn　【名】kidney

肾炎　shènyán　【名】nephritis

肾脏　shènzàng　【名】kidney

甚　shèn　【副】〈书〉very；extremely：～佳 very good ～念 miss sb. very much 言之～当 (of an idea) appropriately put 两家关系～为密切。The two families are on very intimate terms.

甚而　shèn'ér　【连】同"甚至"

甚或　shènhuò　【连】even；go so far as to

甚为　shènwéi　【副】very：～高兴 very delighted ～不安 very uneasy

甚嚣尘上　shèn xiāo chén shàng　（of reactionary statements）cause a great clamour：这种谬论一个时期～。At one time, such fallacies created quite an uproar.

甚至　shènzhì　【副】even：他激动得～流下了眼泪。He was moved to tears. 他忙得～连我的信也没回。He was so busy that he didn't even answer my letter. 【连】even（introduces an extreme case）：他为科学献出自己的一切,～生命。He dedicated everything, even his life, to science. 他走得很急,～把车票都忘了。He left in such a hurry that he even forgot his train ticket.

渗（滲）　shèn　【动】seep；permeate；ooze：水～进土里。Water seeps into the earth. 伤口～出血来。Blood oozed from the wound.

渗入　shènrù　【动】❶ permeate；seep into ❷ penetrate；infiltrate：防止～坏人。Be on guard against the infiltration of bad elements.

渗透　shèntòu　【动】❶ osmose；seep：雨水～了土地。The rain water seeps into the earth. ❷ infiltrate；penetrate：经济～ economic penetration 文化～ cultural penetration 这个新产品～着老李几年来的心血。This new product embodies years of painstaking effort on the part of Lao Li.

慎　shèn

慎重　shènzhòng　【形】careful；cautious；prudent：～处理 be prudent in dealing with sth. ～研究 careful study 对这个问题应持～的态度。We must adopt a cautious approach to this problem.

shēng

升　shēng　【动】rise；hoist；ascend：太阳～起来了。The sun is rising. 温度～高。The temperature is rising. 【量】❶ litre：一～啤酒 a litre of beer ❷ *a Chinese unit of dry measure for grain*：十～是一斗。Ten *sheng* equal one *dou*.

升官　shēng = guān　be promoted

升华　shēnghuá　【动】❶ sublimate ❷ raise things to a higher level；distill；sublimate：艺术应是现实生活的～。Art is the sublimation of life.

升级　shēng = jí　❶ be promoted（to a higher grade in school）：今年我们全班的同学都～了。This year all the students in our class have been promoted to the next grade. ❷ escalate：战争～ escalation of a war

升旗　shēng = qí　raise the flag：～仪式 flag-raising ceremony

升学　shēng = xué　go up a level in schooling（e. g. from primary school to middle school）

升值　shēng = zhí　appreciation（of currency）

生　shēng　【动】❶ give birth to；bear：～孩子 give birth to a child 他～在北京,长在南京。He was born in Beijing and brought up in Nanjing. ❷ grow：～根开花 take root and blossom ❸ light（a fire）：～炉子 light a fire in the stove ❹ generate；give rise to：摩擦～热。Friction generates heat. 【形】❶ raw；uncooked；not ripe：～肉 raw meat 香蕉太～,还不能摘。The bananas are not ripe and cannot be picked yet. 这种蔬菜可以～吃。This vegetable can be eaten raw. ❷ unfamiliar：人～地不熟 find oneself in an unfamiliar place and among

strangers【副】very；extremely：~ 疼 very painful【名】◇ ❶ student；pupil：毕业~ a graduate 师~员工 teachers, students, office staff and workers ❷ life：舍~取义 lay down one's life in defense of justice

生搬硬套 shēng bān yìng tào apply mechanically（regardless of actual conditions）：学习别人的经验要结合自己的实际情况，不能~。One must consider the experience of others in the light of one's own particular conditions, not apply it mechanically.

生病 shēng=bìng fall ill；be taken ill

生产 shēngchǎn【动】❶ produce；yield；manufacture；turn out：~粮食 produce grain ❷ give birth to a child【名】production：发展~ develop production

生产方式 shēngchǎn fāngshì mode of production

生产关系 shēngchǎn guānxi relations of production

生产过剩 shēngchǎn guòshèng overproduction

生产基金 shēngchǎn jījīn production fund

生产力 shēngchǎnlì【名】productive forces

生产率 shēngchǎnlǜ【名】productivity

生产手段 shēngchǎn shǒuduàn means of production

生产资料 shēngchǎn zīliào 同"生产手段"

生产总值 shēngchǎn zǒngzhí total output value

生词 shēngcí【名】new word

生存 shēngcún【动】exist

生存权 shēngcúnquán【名】right of existence

生动 shēngdòng【形】vivid；lively：~的事例 a vivid example 语言~ using lively language ~地说明 il-lustrate with a vivid example

生活 shēnghuó【名】❶ life；living conditions：我们的~越来越美好。Our living conditions are getting better and better. ❷ life（business, pleasure, social activities, etc.）：文化~ cultural life 日常~ daily life【动】❶ live；carry on all sorts of activities：我们~在一个集体里。We live a collective life. ❷ live；exist：人类要想~下去，就要进行生产劳动。Man must engage in productive labour in order to survive.

生活费 shēnghuófèi【名】living expenses；cost of living

生活水平 shēnghuó shuǐpíng living standard

生活资料 shēnghuó zīliào means of livelihood

生火 shēng=huǒ make a fire；light a fire

生机 shēngjī【名】❶ chance of living, lease of life ❷ vitality, life, life-force

生理 shēnglǐ【名】physiology

生理学 shēnglǐxué【名】physiology

生力军 shēnglìjūn【名】fresh troops；new force

生龙活虎 shēng lóng huó hǔ extremely energetic and lively；full of vigour：一群~的跳水队员 a group of lively divers

生猛 shēngměng【形】live, active, alive；living：~海鲜 live seafood

生命 shēngmìng【名】life

生命力 shēngmìnglì【名】vitality；life-force

生命线 shēngmìngxiàn【名】lifeline；lifeblood

生怕 shēngpà【动】fear（that sth. may happen）*the object is usu. a verbal phrase or a S－P construction*：他下班后悄悄地走进宿舍，~惊醒了别人。When his shift was over, he walked very quietly into the

dormitory for fear waking the others. 老师～我们听不懂,讲得特别仔细。 Our teacher was afraid that we might not understand what he said, so he explained everything very carefully.

生僻 shēngpì 【形】(of words, etc.) rarely used

生平 shēngpíng 【名】all one's life; lifetime

生气 shēngqì 【名】vigour; life

生气 shēng=qì get angry; anger

生气勃勃 shēngqì bóbó vigorous; full of vigour and vitality

生前 shēngqián 【名】(of a person) while he was alive; during his lifetime

生人 shēngrén 【名】stranger

生日 shēngrì 【名】birthday

生色 shēngsè 【动】add lustre to: 你要背来独唱,一定会使音乐会～不少。 The concert will certainly be more enjoyable if you sing a solo.

生手 shēngshǒu 【名】a person new to a job; novice: 他刚来,干这一行还是个～。 He has just come and still has little experience at doing his job.

生疏 shēngshū 【形】❶ not familiar: 人地～ in an unfamiliar place and among strangers ❷ out of practice; rusty: 技艺～ be rusty at this technique 业务～ be out of practice where one's profession is concerned ❸ not as close as before; estranged: 分别多年,他们俩有些～了。 After many years of separation, the two of them have become estranged from each other.

生死存亡 shēng sǐ cún wáng (a matter of) life and death

生死与共 shēng sǐ yǔ gòng share life and death; through thick and thin: 我们是～的战友。 We've been comrades-in-arms through thick and thin.

生态 shēngtài 【名】the relationship between organisms and their environment

生态平衡 shēngtài pínghéng ecological balance

生态学 shēngtàixué 【名】ecology

生铁 shēngtiě 【名】pig iron

生吞活剥 shēng tūn huó bō swallow sth. raw and whole; (fig.) imitate mechanically: 他改变了～的学习方法,进步很大。 He has corrected his mechanical way of learning things and has made considerable progress.

生物 shēngwù 【名】living thing

生物学 shēngwùxué 【名】biology

生效 shēng=xiào come into force; become effective

生锈 shēng=xiù rust; rusty

生意 shēngyi 【名】trade; business

生硬 shēngyìng 【形】❶ not natural; stiff: 他的西班牙语说得很～。 His spoken Spanish is rather stiff. ❷ rigid; stiff; inflexible; arbitrary: 态度～ have a stiff manner 工作方法～。 His method of working is inflexible.

生育 shēngyù 【动】give birth to (children)

生长 shēngzhǎng 【动】grow; grow up

生殖 shēngzhí 【动】reproduce

生字 shēngzì 【名】〔个 gè〕new character

声（聲） shēng 【名】◇ ❶ voice; sound: 脚步～ the sound of footsteps 高～朗读 read aloud ❷ (of Chinese characters) tone: 第四～ the fourth tone ❸ short for 声母 【量】for sounds: 我喊了几～,他都没听见。 I called him several times, but he didn't hear me.

声波 shēngbō 【名】sound wave

声称 shēngchēng 【动】claim; assert (usu. derog.)

声带　shēngdài　【名】❶ vocal chord
❷ sound track

声调　shēngdiào　【名】(of Chinese
characters) tone

声东击西　shēng dōng jī xī　make a
feint to the east while attacking in
the west：～的战术 the tactic of
making an attack in one direction
to divert attention from the quarter where the real attack is to be
made

声控　shēngkòng　【动】sound-con-
trolled

声泪俱下　shēng lèi jù xià　speak bro-
kenly；speak in a voice filled with
tears：老人～地诉说了自己的苦难家
史。The old man tearfully related
his tragic family history.

声名狼藉　shēngmíng lángjí　be utterly discredited；lose all honour and
reputation

声明　shēngmíng　【动】declare；an-
nounce；state：事先～一下 declare
beforehand 公开～ declare publicly
【名】declaration；statement：发表
一项～ issue a public statement

声母　shēngmǔ　【名】(of a Chinese
syllable) initial

声旁　shēngpáng　【名】sound radical

声色　shēngsè　【名】a person's voice
and countenance：～俱厉 having a
stern voice and countenance 不动
～ remain calm and composed

声势　shēngshì　【名】impetus；mo-
mentum (usu. of a mass movement
or mass organization)

声势浩大　shēngshì hàodà　great
strength and impetus：～的游行 a
grand parade

声嘶力竭　shēng sī lì jié　shout oneself hoarse

声速　shēngsù　【名】the speed of
sound

声讨　shēngtǎo　【动】denounce；cen-
sure；condemn：愤怒～ denounce
indignantly 开～大会 hold a denun-

ciation meeting

声望　shēngwàng　【名】prestige

声响　shēngxiǎng　【名】sound

声学　shēngxué　【名】acoustics

声音　shēngyīn　【名】❶ voice ❷
sound

声誉　shēngyù　【名】prestige；(of
person or thing) fame

声援　shēngyuán　【动】publicly declare oneself in support of：～殖民
地人民的正义斗争 support the colo-
nial peoples in their just struggle

声源　shēngyuán　【名】the source of
a sound

声乐　shēngyuè　【名】vocal music

声张　shēngzhāng　【动】make
known；make public；disclose：事
情还没弄清楚，先别～。The matter
has not been clarified yet，so don't
breathe a word of it to anyone for
the time being.

牲　shēng

牲畜　shēngchù　【名】domestic ani-
mals；livestock

牲口　shēngkou　【名】draught animal

笙　shēng　【名】gourd-shaped
musical instrument with reed pipes

shéng

绳(繩)　shéng　【名】〔条 tiáo〕
rope

绳索　shéngsuǒ　【名】rope

绳子　shéngzi　【名】〔条 tiáo〕rope；
cord；string

shěng

省　shěng　【名】province：～、市、
自治区 the provinces，municipali-
ties，and autonomous regions 湖南
～ Hunan Province 【动】❶ econo-

mise；save：～工夫 save time ～钱 save money ❷ omit；leave out：～一道手续 omit one procedure ～去两个字 cut out two words

省得　shěngde　【连】同"以免" yǐmiǎn but much more colloquial：多穿点儿衣服，～冻着。Put on more clothes, or you'll catch cold. 你到了上海赶快来信，～家里惦记。When you get to Shanghai, write at once, so that we at home won't worry.

省份　shěngfèn　【名】province

省会　shěnghuì　【名】provincial capital

省力　shěng = lì　save labour

省略　shěnglüè　【动】omit；leave out

省事　shěng = shì　save trouble；simplify matters：检验产品要十分仔细，绝不能图～。One must be very conscientious in inspecting products, and not just try to save oneself trouble. 孩子进了托儿所，家长～多了。Sending their children to nursery school saves the parents a lot of trouble.

省心　shěng = xīn　save oneself worry

shèng

圣（聖）　shèng

圣诞节　Shèngdànjié　【名】Christmas

圣诞老人　shèngdàn lǎorén　Father Christmas；Santa Claus

圣诞树　shèngdànshù　【名】Christmas tree

圣地　shèngdì　【名】sacred place

圣经　shèngjīng　【名】Bible

圣人　shèngrén　【名】saint

胜（勝）　shèng　【动】◇ ❶ (as opp. to "负" or "败") win；triumph over：～不骄，败不馁。Don't let victory turn your head, nor defeat break your spirit. ❷ defeat：

战而～之 fight and defeat the enemy 以少～多 use a small force to defeat a large one ❸ be superior to；surpass：一个～似一个 each surpasses the other 事实～于雄辩。Facts are more convincing than argument.

胜地　shèngdì　【名】scenic spot；resort：游览～ beauty spot 疗养～ resort good for rest and convalescence

胜利　shènglì　【名】victory；triumph：取得～ win victory 从～走向～ from victory to victory 【动】succeed；win victory：我们～了。We have won victory.

胜任　shèngrèn　【动】be competent；be equal to：～愉快 be equal to the task 领导一个车间的工作，他是完全能够～的。He would be quite competent as a workshop leader in a factory.

胜诉　shèngsù　【动】win a lawsuit (or court case)

胜仗　shèngzhàng　【名】victory：打～ win a victory；win a battle

盛　shèng　【形】◇ ❶ prosperous；thriving；flourishing：全～时期 the golden age ❷ grand；majestic；stately；ceremonious：～宴 a grand banquet ❸ plentiful；profound；abundant：～意 great kindness ❹ vigorous；energetic：火势很～。The fire is burning vigorously. ❺ widespread；prevalent：～传 (of news) widely known 学习风气很～。A studious atmosphere prevails (e.g. in our unit).

另见 chéng

盛产　shèngchǎn　【动】abound in (cultivated or wild produce)

盛大　shèngdà　【形】grand；ceremonious；magnificent：～的集会 grand assembly ～的欢迎仪式 grand welcoming ceremony

盛典　shèngdiǎn　【名】grand ceremony

盛会　shènghuì　【名】grand occasion；impressive gathering

盛开　shèngkāi　【动】be in full bloom

盛况　shèngkuàng　【名】large festive gathering；spectacular event

盛名　shèngmíng　【名】great fame

盛气凌人　shèng qì líng rén　arrogant；overbearing；domineering：要谦虚谨慎，决不可～。We should be modest and conscientious, and not overbearing.

盛情　shèngqíng　【名】great kindness；very warm hospitality

盛夏　shèngxià　【名】the hottest days of summer

盛行　shèngxíng　【动】be current；be in vogue；be in fashion：～一时 be in vogue for a time

盛装　shèngzhuāng　【名】festive dress；splendid attire

剩　shèng　【动】be left over；leave as a remainder：用了两块钱还～十八块（钱）。He has spent two *yuan* and has eighteen *yuan* left over. 别人都走了，屋子里只～下他一个人。All the others have gone and he was left alone in the room. 花～下的钱我都存在银行里了。I've deposited all the remaining money in the bank.

剩余　shèngyú　【动】be left over；leave as a remainder：～五百斤种子。500 *jin* of seed is left over. 【名】surplus；remainder：口粮年年有～。There is a surplus of food grain every year.

剩余产品　shèngyú chǎnpǐn　surplus products

剩余价值　shèngyú jiàzhí　surplus value

剩余劳动　shèngyú láodòng　surplus labor

shī

尸　shī　【名】corpse

尸骸　shīhái　【名】corpse

尸首　shīshǒu　【名】dead body；corpse

尸体　shītǐ　【名】〔具 jù〕corpse；dead body

失　shī　【动】❶ lose：～血过多 lose too much blood 机不可～。Don't miss the opportunity! ❷ get lost：～群之雁 a wild goose which has strayed from its flock ❸ fail to keep；fail to live up to：他～约了。He did not keep his word. ❹ fail to attain one's end：～意 be thwarted in one's ambition

失败　shībài　【动】fail；be defeated；lose：侵略者注定要～。The aggressors are doomed to fail. 【名】failure；defeat

失策　shī = cè　miscalculate；adopt the wrong strategy

失常　shīcháng　【形】odd；not normal：精神～ not in one's right mind 举动～ behave oddly

失传　shīchuán　【动】be lost；not be handed down from past generations

失当　shīdàng　【形】inappropriate；improper

失盗　shīdào　【动】have things stolen

失道寡助　shī dào guǎ zhù　An unjust cause finds meagre support.

失地　shīdì　【名】lost territory

失掉　shīdiào　【动】❶ lose；be unable to keep：～信心 lose confidence in ～联系 lose contact with ❷ miss；lose；fail to use：～机会 miss a chance

失魂落魄　shī hún luò pò　distraught：～的样子 be in a distraught state ～的神色 driven to distraction

失火　shī = huǒ　(of a building, etc.)

catch fire

失控　shīkòng　【动】get out of control; uncontrolled

失礼　shīlǐ　【动】(of a single occasion) be impolite; commit a breach of etiquette

失利　shīlì　【动】suffer a setback; lose ground

失恋　shī = liàn　be disappointed in love

失灵　shīlíng　【动】(of a machine, etc.) fail to work effectively; be out of order

失落　shīluò　【动】lose; be unable to find

失密　shīmì　【动】let out an official secret due to carelessness

失眠　shīmián　【动】suffer from insomnia

失明　shīmíng　【动】lose one's sight; become blind

失去　shīqù　【动】同"失掉"

失散　shīsàn　【动】❶ be separated from and lose contact with sb.: 他找到了~多年的姐姐。He has found his elder sister with whom he had lost contact for many years. ❷ (of materials) be scattered and lost: 手稿的后一部分已经~了。The last part of the manuscript has been scattered and lost.

失神　shīshén　【动】❶ be inattentive ❷ be in low spirits

失声　shīshēng　【动】❶ cry out involuntarily ❷ be choked with tears

失实　shīshí　【动】inaccurate; untrue

失事　shīshì　【动】have an accident; mishap

失手　shī = shǒu　one's hand slips; drop accidently: 一~把杯子打碎了。A cup slipped from his hand and broke.

失守　shīshǒu　【动】fall (to the enemy)

失算　shīsuàn　【动】miscalculate; make a mistaken move or decision

失调　shītiáo　【动】❶ be out of balance: 供求~ imbalance of supply and demand 经济周转~。The turnover of the economy is dislocated. ❷ lack of proper convalescence: 由于病后~,他至今还未恢复健康。Owing to a lack of proper convalescence after his illness, he has not fully recovered.

失望　shīwàng　【动】be disappointed

失物　shīwù　【名】lost property

失误　shīwù　【动】(of ball games or chess) make a faulty move or a bad play; muff; fumble: 发球~ a faulty serve 判断~ a wrong judgement

失陷　shīxiàn　【动】be occupied by the enemy; fall into enemy hands

失效　shī = xiào　lose efficacy

失信　shī = xìn　break one's promise

失学　shī = xué　be deprived of education; be unable to continue one's studies

失血　shīxuè　【动】lose blood; loss of blood: ~过多 excessive loss of blood

失言　shīyán　【动】make a slip of the tongue

失业　shī = yè　lose one's job; be unemployed

失真　shī = zhēn　❶ lack of fidelity; ❷ distortion

失职　shī = zhí　neglect one's duty

失主　shīzhǔ　【名】owner of lost property

失踪　shī = zōng　(of person) disappear; be missing

失足　shī = zú　❶ slip and fall; lose one's footing: ~落水 slip and fall into the water 一~从山坡上滚了下来。He took a false step and tumbled down the hillside. ❷ (fig.) make a wrong spin in life; go astray

师(師)　shī　【名】❶ ◇ teach-

er；tutor；master；能者为～。Whoever knows the job will be the teacher. 尊～爱生（of students）hold teachers in esteem，（of teachers）show genuine affection for pupils ❷ ◇ example；model；pattern：前事不忘，后事之～。Lessons learned in the past can guide one in one's future work. ❸ ◇ a person skilled in a profession or science：建筑～ architect ❹ ◇ of the master-apprentice relationship：～母 wife of one's teacher or master-worker ～兄 a respectful term for a fellow apprentice who is senior to oneself ❺（mil.）division：～长 ① division commander ②（a respectful term for）teachers ❻ ◇ army：挥～南下 march the army down south【量】（mil.）division

师出无名　shī chū wú míng （mil.）there is no justification for sending troops；（fig.）an action without any justification

师范　shīfàn【名】a school for the training of teachers：～学校 normal school ～学院 normal college ～大学 teachers' university 他是中等～毕业的。He graduated from a normal school.

师傅　shīfu【名】❶ a qualified worker ❷ *respectful form of address for a worker*

师生　shīshēng【名】teachers and students

师长　shīzhǎng【名】❶ divisional commander ❷ *respectful form of address for a teacher*

师资　shīzī【名】❶ teaching staff ❷ qualified teacher

诗（詩）　shī【名】〔首 shǒu〕poetry；poem；verse

诗歌　shīgē【名】〔首 shǒu〕poem
诗集　shījí【名】anthology of poetry
诗句　shījù【名】verse；line

诗篇　shīpiān【名】❶ poem：人们把最美的～献给他们最爱的人。People dedicated their most beautiful poems to their beloved. ❷ vivid and poetic story or essay；epic：英雄的～ heroic epic

诗人　shīrén【名】poet

诗意　shīyì【名】poetic quality or flavour

虱　shī【名】◇ louse

虱子　shīzi【名】louse

施　shī【动】❶ carry out；enforce：无计可～ at a loss as to what to do 己所不欲，勿～于人。Don't do to others what you don't want done to you. ❷ use；apply：一亩地要～多少肥？How much fertilizer should be used on one *mu* of land？

施肥　shī = féi apply fertilizer or manure

施工　shī = gōng be in the process of construction；be under construction

施加　shījiā【动】bring；exert；exercise：～压力 exert pressure on ～影响 exercise one's influence over（sb.）

施事　shīshì【名】the doer of action in a sentence；the agent

施行　shīxíng【动】enforce；carry out；put sth. into practice；implement：～八小时工作制 implement the policy of the eight-hour workday 岗位责任制自今日起～。A system of personal responsibility will be put into effect as of today.

施展　shīzhǎn【动】display；give full play to：～本领 give full scope to one's abilities ～威力 make a show of power 能力～不开 be unable to give full play to one's abilities

狮（獅）　shī【名】◇ lion

狮子　shīzi【名】〔头 tóu〕lion

狮子舞　shīziwǔ　【名】lion dance

湿（濕）　shī　【形】wet；moist

湿度　shīdù　【名】humidity

湿淋淋　shīlīnlīn　【形】dripping wet

湿漉漉　shīlūlū　【形】damp；wet

湿润　shīrùn　【形】moist：土壤～ moist earth 空气～ moist air

湿疹　shīzhěn　【名】eczema

嘘　shī　【叹】hush

shí

十　shí　【数】ten

十冬腊月　shí dōng làyuè　the cold months of the year；the tenth, eleventh and twelfth months of the lunar year

十恶不赦　shí è bù shè　guilty of unpardonable crimes；guilty beyond forgiveness

十二分　shí'èrfēn　【副】more than 100%；extremely

十二月　shí'èryuè　【名】December

十分　shífēn　【副】very；extremely；fully；completely：～满意 fully satisfied ～高兴 very pleased 不～忙 not too busy

十拿九稳　shí ná jiǔ wěn　be quite certain of；a certainty；a sure thing：这件事叫他办，～，准能成功。If you put the matter in his hands, he's sure to do a good job of it.

十全十美　shí quán shí měi　perfect in every respect；leaving nothing to be desired：我们的工作不可能～，但要尽量做好。It is impossible to expect our work to be perfect, but we will try our best.

十万　shíwàn　【数】one hundred thousand

十万八千里　shí wàn bā qiān lǐ　a long distance；poles apart

十万火急　shí wàn huǒ jí　extremely urgent

十·一　Shí·Yī　October 1, National Day of the People's Republic of China

十一月　shíyīyuè　【名】November

十月　shíyuè　【名】October

十月革命　Shíyuè Gémìng　the October Revolution

十字架　shízìjià　【名】cross；crucifix

十字路口　shízì lùkǒu　crossroads

十足　shízú　【形】complete；entire；out-and-out：干劲～ extremely enthusiastic in one's work；very energetic；work all-out ～的理由 (have) every reason (to)

石　shí　【名】stone；rock ·另见 dàn

石板　shíbǎn　【名】slate

石笔　shíbǐ　【名】slate pencil

石沉大海　shí chén dàhǎi　sink like a stone, leaving no trace：他的弟弟三十年前离家出走，从此如～,没有消息。His younger brother left home thirty years ago and has never been heard of since.

石雕　shídiāo　【名】❶ stone carving ❷ carved stone

石方　shífāng　【名】cubic metre of stone

石膏　shígāo　【名】gypsum

石膏像　shígāoxiàng　【名】plaster statue

石灰　shíhuī　【名】lime

石灰石　shíhuīshí　【名】limestone

石匠　shíjiang　【名】mason

石刻　shíkè　【名】❶ carved stone ❷ inscription carved in stone

石窟　shíkū　【名】cave (with stone carvings)

石蜡　shílà　【名】paraffin

石棉　shímián　【名】asbestos

石器时代　shíqì shídài　the Stone Age

石蕊　shíruǐ　【名】litmus

石头　shítou　【名】〔块 kuài〕stone；rock

石英钟 shíyīngzhōng 【名】quartz clock

石油 shíyóu 【名】petroleum

石柱 shízhù 【名】stone pillar

时（時） shí 【名】❶ time; days：古～ ancient times ❷ hour; o'clock：七～半 half past seven ❸ *short for* 时候：下班～，我碰到了老王。After work, I ran into Lao Wang. ❹ ◇ fixed time：按～上班 get to work on time 过～不候。If you don't come on time, we shan't wait for you. ❺ ◇ opportunity; chance：～不再来。The opportunity is gone, never to return. 【副】often; from time to time：～有来往 maintain frequent contact

时差 shíchā 【名】time difference; equation of time

时常 shícháng 【副】同"常"：最近他～去图书馆。Recently he has been going to the liberary very frequently.

Note：时常 *cannot be modified by a negative word*.

时代 shídài 【名】epoch; era; age

时代感 shídàigǎn 【名】a sense of the times; feelings of the times

时而 shí'ér 【副】*usu. in written language* ❶ from time to time：蔚蓝色的海面上，～飞过几只白色的海鸥。Over the dark blue sea, from time to time a few white seagulls sailed across the sky. ❷ 同"忽而" hū'ér：这几天天气不太好，～刮风，～下雨。The weather has been rather depressing recently; one moment it's windy, the next it rains.

时分 shífèn 【名】time（was usu. used during the early period of the vernacular language）：黄昏～ at dusk 掌灯～ the time when lamps are lit

时光 shíguāng 【名】❶ time（abstract）：大好～ splendid time ❷ time; years; days：～过得真快，一晃二十年了。How time flies! In a twinkling, twenty years are gone!

时候 shíhou 【名】❶ a point in time：到～了，该走了。It is time we left. 晚会什么～开始? When will the party start? ❷ duration of time：听录音用了多少～? How long did it take to listen to the recording?

时机 shíjī 【名】occasion; opportunity

时间 shíjiān 【名】time

时间词 shíjiāncí 【名】time word; noun denoting time

时间性 shíjiānxìng 【名】timeliness

时节 shíjié 【名】❶ season：桃花盛开的～ at the time when the peach trees are in bloom 秋收～ the autumn harvest season ❷ time; when：我上学那～，你才五岁。You were only five when I started going to school.

时局 shíjú 【名】the current political situation

时刻 shíkè 【名】❶ time; hour; moment：幸福的～ a moment of happiness 考验我们的～到了。The time has come when we will be put to the test. ❷ at all times; constantly：～准备着 be ready at all times

时令 shílìng 【名】season

时髦 shímáo 【形】fashionable

时期 shíqī 【名】period：战争～ in war time; during the war 非常～ an extraordinary period

时时 shíshí 【副】constantly; all the time：～处处为老百姓着想 always and in all matters keep the interests of the common folk at heart

时…时… shí…shí… now … now …; sometimes … sometimes …（*usu. used with two monosyllabic words opposite in meaning*）：时紧时松 sometimes taut, sometimes slack 时好时坏 sometimes good and

sometimes bad 时快时慢 one minute fast, the next slow 枪声时断时续 intermittent gun fire

时事 shíshì 【名】current affairs

时事述评 shíshì shùpíng comment on current affairs

时速 shísù 【名】hour speed

时兴 shíxīng 【形】fashionable 【动】come into fashion

时宜 shíyí 【名】what is appropriate to the occasion：不合～ inappropriate to the occasion

时针 shízhēn 【名】❶ the hands of a clock or watch ❷ hour-hand

时钟 shízhōng 【名】clock

时装 shízhuāng 【名】❶ latest fashion in dress ❷ modern fashion in dress (as opp. to 古装)

时装模特儿 shízhuāng mótèr fashion model

识（識） shí 【动】◇ know；recognize：有眼不～泰山 He was a VIP, but I didn't recognize him. 【名】◇ knowledge：远见卓～ farsightedness and sagacity 有～之士 a person of insight；a person of keen perception

识别 shíbié 【动】distinguish；discern：善于～真伪 be good at distinguishing truth from falsehood

识破 shípò 【动】see through；penetrate：～诡计 see through the plot

识字 shí = zì able to read；become literate

实（實） shí 【形】◇ ❶ solid：地基要砸～。The foundation must be tamped down solid. ❷ true；honest：真心～意 sincere and honest 【名】◇ ❶ fact；reality：传闻失～ hearsay which turns out not to be true ❷ fruit；results：开花结～ blossom and bear fruit

实词 shící 【名】notional word

实地 shídì 【副】on the spot

实干 shígàn 【动】do solid work：～精神 spirit of working in earnest；down-to-earth attitude

实话 shíhuà 【名】(tell) truth

实惠 shíhuì 【形】substantial；materially beneficial：这个饭馆的饭菜都非常～。They serve substantial meals in this restaurant. 给姥姥带些日用品去，比买个大花瓶～多了。Something that can be used every day is a more practical gift for Granny than a vase.

实际 shíjì 【名】reality；actuality：理论不能脱离～。Theory must not be divorced from practice. 【形】❶ practical；actual：～情况 actual situation ～行动 concrete action ❷ real；actual：举个～的例子来说明 illustrate by citing a real instance ❸ practical；realistic：想法很～ practical way of thinking

实践 shíjiàn 【名】practice：～出真知。True knowledge comes from practice. ～是认识的基础。Practice is the foundation of knowledge. 【动】practise；put into effect；put into practice：～诺言 do what one promised (to do)

实践性 shíjiànxìng 【名】practicality

实况 shíkuàng 【名】what's actually happening

实况转播 shíkuàng zhuānbō live telecast

实力 shílì 【名】actual strength (usu. military or economic)

实情 shíqíng 【名】the actual situation

实权 shíquán 【名】real power；actual power

实施 shíshī 【动】〈书〉implement；enforce；put into effect：～法令 implement a decree 按计划～ carry out according to the plan

实事求是 shí shì qiú shì seek truth from facts；be practical；be realistic：～的态度 a realistic attitude ～

的精神 a down-to-earth spirit 报导要～。A news report must be true to the facts.

实数 shíshù 【名】(maths.) real number

实体 shítǐ 【名】entity：经济～ economic entity

实物 shíwù 【名】❶ (payment) in kind ❷ real object；actual thing：～展览 an exhibition which illustrates something by using actual objects 用～进行教学 use actual objects for illustration when teaching

实习 shíxí 【动】practise；do fieldwork：到工厂～了两个月 do practical training in a factory for two months

实习医师 shíxíyīshī 【名】intern

实现 shíxiàn 【动】realize；achieve；bring into being：～农业机械化 bring about the mechanization of agriculture 他的理想～了。His ideal has been achieved.

实效 shíxiào 【名】actual effect

实心 shíxīn 【形】(～儿) solid；not hollow

实行 shíxíng 【动】carry out；execute；put into practice；put into effect：～夏季作息时间 institute new summer working hours ～民主集中制 practise democratic centralism

实验 shíyàn 【动】test；experiment

实验室 shíyànshì 【名】laboratory

实业 shíyè 【名】industry and commerce：～家 industrialist

实用 shíyòng 【形】practical；useful

实用主义 shíyòngzhǔyì 【名】pragmatism

实在 shízài 【形】❶ real；true：～的本事 real ability 他说话很～。He always speaks truthfully. 他总是实实在在地干。He always works honestly and diligently. ❷ really (usu. used as an adverbial adjunct)：机会～难得。This really is the chance of a lifetime. 情节～感人。The plot of the story is really very moving.

实质 shízhì 【名】essence

拾 shí 【动】pick up；～麦穗 glean wheat 【数】ten (complicated form of 十) 见"捌" bā

拾掇 shíduo 【动】❶ tidy up：他把屋子～得整整齐齐。He has done a very good job of tidying up the room. ❷ repair；mend：收音机坏了，你给～～。The radio isn't working. Please fix it.

拾金不昧 shí jīn bù mèi not pocket the money that one picks up

拾取 shíqǔ 【动】pick up

食 shí 【名】❶ ◇ food：素～ vegetarian dish 消～开胃 good for one's appetite and digestion ❷ feed (for animals)：鱼～ fish food 兔子出来找～了。The rabbits are out looking for food. 【动】〈书〉eat

食道 shídào 【名】esophagus

食粮 shíliáng 【名】foodstuff；grain

食品 shípǐn 【名】foodstuff (as commodity in a shop)

食谱 shípǔ 【名】recipe；cook book

食宿 shísù 【名】board and lodging；room and board：解决～问题 solve the problem of board and lodging

食堂 shítáng 【名】dining room

食糖 shítáng 【名】sugar

食物 shíwù 【名】food；foodstuff

食物中毒 shíwù zhòngdú food poisoning

食言 shí = yán go back on one's words；break one's promise

食盐 shíyán 【名】salt

食用 shíyòng 【动】eat；edible (e.g. edible oil)

食油 shíyóu 【名】edible oil

食欲 shíyù 【名】appetite

食指 shízhǐ 【名】forefinger

shǐ

史 shǐ 【名】history

史册 shǐcè 【名】history book；annals

史料 shǐliào 【名】historical material

史诗 shǐshī 【名】epic

史实 shǐshí 【名】historical fact

史书 shǐshū 【名】historical records

史无前例 shǐ wú qián lì　without parallel in history；unprecedented

史学 shǐxué 【名】historical studies；the science of history

矢 shǐ

矢口否认 shǐ kǒu fǒurèn　flatly deny；他～说过这句话。He flatly denied that he had said it.

使 shǐ 【动】❶ use：把钳子借我～一下。Please lend me your pliers. 无论于什么，他都好像浑身有～不完的劲儿。Whatever he does, he seems to have an inexhaustible supply of energy. ❷ make（*used in pivotal sentences*）：～大家满意 see that everyone is satisfied 虚心～人进步，骄傲～人落后。Modesty makes one go forward，whereas conceit makes one lag behind.

使不得 shǐ bu de　❶ cannot be used ❷ will not do

使得 shǐde 【动】❶ can be used ❷ workable ❸ make；cause

使馆 shǐguǎn 【名】embassy

使节 shǐjié 【名】envoy

使劲 shǐ = jìn　exert strength；make efforts

使命 shǐmìng 【名】mission

使团 shǐtuán 【名】diplomatic corps

使用 shǐyòng 【动】use；apply；employ；exercise

使用价值 shǐyòng jiàzhí　use value

使用权 shǐyòngquán 【名】right of use；right to use a thing

使者 shǐzhě 【名】emissary；messenger；envoy

始 shǐ 【动】◇ begin；start；～于今日 starting from today 不自今日～。It isn't something which started recently.

始末 shǐmò 【名】the whole story

始终 shǐzhōng 【副】from beginning to end；always

始终不渝 shǐzhōng bù yú　unswerving；steadfast：我们～地奉行和平共处五项原则。We are committed to the Five Principles of Peaceful Coexistence.

始祖 shǐzǔ 【名】first ancestor；earliest ancestor

屎 shǐ 【名】excrement；dung

shì

士 shì

士兵 shìbīng 【名】soldier

士气 shìqì 【名】morale；fighting spirit

氏 shì

氏族 shìzú 【名】clan（e.g. clan society）

示 shì

示范 shìfàn 【动】set an example；demonstrate；show：我先给大家～一下。I'll show you how to do it first. 【名】example；demonstration：这节体操，我先做个～。I will demonstrate this set of exercises for a beginning.

示弱 shìruò 【动】give the impression of weakness；take sth. lying down

示威 shìwēi 【动】demonstrate

示意 shìyì 【动】hint; signal; gesture

示意图 shìyìtú 【名】❶ sketch ❷ schematic drawing

示众 shìzhòng 【动】(of a person) put on public display (as a punishment)

世 shì 【名】◇ ❶ lifetime; life: 一生一~ a lifetime ❷ age; era; period: 近~ modern times 当~ nowadays ❸ the world: 公诸于~ make known to the world

世代 shìdài 【名】from generation to generation; for generations: ~相传 pass down from generation to generation ~务农 (a family) which has engaged in farming for generations

世故 shìgù 【名】the ways of the world: 人情~ one's knowledge of people and of the ways of the world

世故 shìgu 【形】sophisticated; worldly-wise

世纪 shìjì 【名】century

世界 shìjiè 【名】❶ the nature and all things created by mankind: ~之大,无奇不有。This great world is full of strange phenomena. ❷ world; the earth: ~人民大团结 the unity of the peoples of the world ❸ world (sphere or domain of a certain activity): 内心~ one's inner world 海底~ undersea world

世界观 shìjièguān 【名】world outlook

世界屋脊 shìjiè wūjǐ the roof of the world

世界语 Shìjièyǔ 【名】Esperanto

世面 shìmiàn 【名】world affairs; the world (e.g. see much of the world)

世上无难事,只怕有心人 shì shàng wú nán shì, zhǐ pà yǒuxīn rén nothing in the world is difficult for someone who sets his mind to it

世态 shìtài 【名】the ways of the world

世外桃源 shì wài táo yuán "Land of Peach Blossoms", an imaginary peaceful place away from the turmoil of the world; heaven of peace; earthly paradise

世袭 shìxí 【动】hereditary; pass on from one generation to another

市 shì 【名】❶ market ❷ city; municipality: 上海 ~ the city of Shanghai ~内交通 city traffic

市场 shìchǎng 【名】market

市场经济 shìchǎng·jīngjì market economy

市价 shìjià 【名】market price

市郊 shìjiāo 【名】suburb

市侩 shìkuài 【名】philistine

市民 shìmín 【名】townsfolk

市区 shìqū 【名】urban area

市容 shìróng 【名】the appearance of a city

市镇 shìzhèn 【名】big market towns; towns

市政 shìzhèng 【名】municipal administration

市制 shìzhì 【名】the Chinese system of weights and measures

式 shì 【名】◇ ❶ type; fashion; style: 老~家具 old-fashioned furniture ❷ ceremony; ritual: 开幕~ opening ceremony

式样 shìyàng 【名】type; style; pattern

式子 shìzi 【名】❶ posture: 他练太极拳,~摆得很好。The positions of his body when he does taijiquan shadow boxing are very precise. ❷ formula: 请你列出这道算术题的~。Please write down the formula for this arithmatical problem.

似 shì

另见 sì

…似的 …shìde 【助】 used after a word or phrase to indicate similarity, often used together with 像, 好像, etc.：孩子们的脸像苹果～，非常可爱。The children were apple-cheeked and very lovely. 他急急忙忙跑出去了,好像有什么事～。He ran out in a hurry as if on urgent business. Note：Sometimes the simile is exaggerated：那匹马飞也～朝远处跑去。The horse raced away like the wind. 粮食堆得像山～。The grain was piled up like a mountain. 也作"…是的"。

势(勢) shì

势必 shìbì 【副】 bound to；certainly will；inevitably：零部件质量差,寿命短,～增加材料消耗。Spare parts which don't last are just a waste of material.

势不可挡 shì bù kě dǎng irresistible；not to be withstood, usually of opposing forces

势不两立 shì bù liǎng lì utterly antagonistic；irreconcilable；implacably hostile："水火不相容"常用来说明一种～的关系。The phrase "be incompatible as fire and water" is often cited to illustrate the irreconcilability between two parties.

势均力敌 shì jūn lì dí balanced forces；match each other in strength：这两个足球队～,今天的比赛一定很激烈。The two football teams are well-matched. Today's match is bound to be close.

势力 shìlì 【名】 power；influence

势力范围 shìlì fànwéi sphere of influence

势利 shìlì 【形】 snobbish

势利眼 shìlìyǎn 【名】 snob；snobbishness

势能 shìnéng 【名】（phys.）potential energy

势如破竹 shì rú pò zhú with the force of a knife splitting bamboo；with irresistible force：军队长驱直入,～,一举占领了杭州市。With irresistible force, the army took over the city of Hangzhou.

势头 shìtou 【名】 tendency；the way things are going；momentum

事 shì 【名】 ❶ affair；matter；business：有～要请假。If you have some business to attend to, ask for leave. 有件～要快办。There is a matter which must be attended to as soon as possible. ❷ accident；trouble：出了什么～? What's happening? 平安无～。All's quiet and peaceful.

事半功倍 shì bàn gōng bèi obtain twice the result with half the effort：技术革新以后,生产效率大大提高,收到了～的效果。With technical innovations which increase efficiency, we are doubling output with half the former man-power.

事倍功半 shì bèi gōng bàn obtain half the result with twice the effort

事变 shìbiàn 【名】 incident (unexpected and significant political or military event)

事不宜迟 shì bù yí chí do sth. without delay：～,马上动手抢修高压线路。Let's repair the high-tension wire right away. It can't wait.

事端 shìduān 【名】 同"事故"。

事故 shìgù 【名】 accident；mishap

事过境迁 shì guò jìng qiān the incident is over and the situation has changed

事后 shìhòu 【名】 after the event；afterwards：～处理 see to things following the event 仓库失火了,～我去看了现场。After the warehouse had burned down, I went to make an on-the-spot investigation.

事迹 shìjī 【名】a creditable deed

事件 shìjiàn 【名】event；incident

事例 shìlì 【名】case；example；instance

事略 shìlüè 【名】biographical sketch

事前 shìqián 【名】prior to the event；in advance；beforehand：～我并不知道他搬家了。I didn't know before I went that he had moved. 你～把工序交代清楚了，就不会乱了。You must make the work process clear beforehand，and then nothing will go wrong.

事情 shìqing 【名】〔件 jiàn〕affair；event；thing；matter

事实 shìshí 【名】fact

事态 shìtài 【名】state of affairs；situation；condition（usu. bad）：～严重。The situation is becoming critical. ～有所缓和。The situation has been somewhat alleviated. 不知～将怎样发展。I have no idea how things are going to develop.

事务 shìwù 【名】❶ affair；work；routine：～繁忙 be tied up with a lot of work ❷ day-to-day work：～工作 routine work

事物 shìwù 【名】thing；object

事先 shìxiān 【名】beforehand；prior to；in advance

事项 shìxiàng 【名】items of business；list of points

事业 shìyè 【名】❶ cause；undertaking：文教～ cultural and educational undertakings ❷ undertakings which produce no revenue and hence are subsidized by the government（e. g. schools）（usu. as an attributive）：各企业～单位 all enterprises and institutions

事业心 shìyèxīn 【名】dedication to one's work：她～很强。Her spirit of dedication is very strong.

事宜 shìyí 【名】arrangements（used in documents）：商谈设立使馆～ discuss matters having to do with the setting up of an embassy 讨论有关招生～ talk over the arrangements for the enrollment of students

事由 shìyóu 【名】❶ particulars of a matter：把～交代明白 explain the particulars of a matter ❷ the subject matter of an official document

事与愿违 shì yǔ yuàn wéi something that does not turn out the way one wishes：做工作如果只凭主观愿望，不顾客观条件，就会～。If we rely on wishful thinking and ignore objective conditions，things will not turn out as planned.

事在人为 shì zài rén wéi achievement depends on human effort：只要你好好干，一定能做出成绩来，～嘛! As long as you work hard，you are bound to achieve，because achievement depends on effort.

事主 shìzhǔ 【名】the victim of a crime（for example，a robbery）

试（試）shì 【动】test；try：～航 make a trial voyage or test flight ～办 run（the enterprise）on a trial basis 这个法子不妨～一～。We might as well try out this method.

试车 shìchē ＝chē（mech.）test run

试点 shìdiǎn 【名】unit where experimentation is done before popularization on a broader level

试管 shìguǎn 【名】test tube

试管婴儿 shìguǎn yīng'ér test-tube baby

试剂 shìjì 【名】（chem.）reagent

试金石 shìjīnshí 【名】touchstone

试卷 shìjuàn 【名】examination paper

试探 shìtàn 【动】feel out；sound out

试题 shìtí 【名】examination question

试图　shìtú　【动】attempt；try

试问　shìwèn　【动】may I ask

试销　shìxiāo　【动】place goods on trial sale to test quality and consumer opinion before full-scale production

试行　shìxíng　【动】try out

试验　shìyàn　【动】test【名】test

试验田　shìyàntián　【名】〔块 kuài〕experimental farm plot；undertaking engaged in on a trial basis

试用　shìyòng　【动】❶ try out ❷ on probation

试纸　shìzhǐ　【名】litmus paper

试制　shìzhì　【动】trial-produce；trial manufacture

视（視）　shì

视察　shìchá　【动】inspect：去外地～工作 be on an inspection tour

视而不见　shì ér bù jiàn　look at something, but fail to see it

视觉　shìjué　【名】visual sense；vision

视力　shìlì　【名】eyesight

视死如归　shì sǐ rú guī　face death calmly；defy death

视线　shìxiàn　【名】line of vision

视野　shìyě　【名】visual field；field of vision

拭　shì

拭目以待　shì mù yǐ dài　wait and see：姑且～。Let's wait and see. 他们的可耻下场，我们～吧！It is to be expected that they will come to no good end.

柿　shì

柿子　shìzi　【名】〔个 gè〕persimmon

柿子椒　shìzijiāo　【名】sweet pepper；bell pepper

是　shì　【动】❶ be：他～工人。He is a worker. 中国～社会主义国家。China is a socialist country. ❷ in-dicates existence（the subject is usu. a word or phrase denoting a place）：山坡上～一片片新修的梯田。On the hillside are newly built terraced fields. ❸ to be sure（with the same word on either side of 是）：工作忙～忙，可是大家很愉快。We are busy to be sure, but everyone is very happy. 我去～去，可是得晚一点儿去。I'm certainly going, but I'll be a little late. ❹ used at the beginning of the sentence to stress the agent：～谁告诉你的? Who was it that told you this? ～哪阵风把您给吹来啦?! What wind blew you here? ❺ pronounced with stress to indicate certainty：我那天～没去。That day I certainly didn't go there. 他的工作效率～高。He certainly is efficient. ❻ used in an alternative question, equivalent to 还是：明天（～）参观工厂～参观农村? Are we going to visit a factory or to see a village? 咱们（～）今天去～明天去? Are we going today or tomorrow? ❼ used to explain away misunderstanding：我不～不想告诉你，～不知道。It isn't that I didn't want to tell you, the truth is that I didn't know. 我～一片好心，你可别误会。I'm only interested in your welfare；I hope you won't misunderstand me.

…是的　…shìde　【助】同"…似的" shìde

是非　shìfēi　【名】❶ right and wrong；truth and falsehood：～要分清。One must differentiate between right and wrong. ❷ dispute；quarrel：招惹～ create discord

是否　shì fǒu　〈书〉同"是不是"：他办事～认真? Does he do his job conscientiously? 这个理论～正确，需要经过实践来检验。Practice will prove whether this theory is right or wrong.

适（適） shì

适当 shìdàng 【形】proper；suitable；appropriate：～的条件 appropriate conditions ～的人选 suitable candidate 这个时机很～。This is an opportune moment.

适得其反 shì dé qí fǎn run counter to one's wishes；accomplish the very opposite of what one desires：假如不注意方式方法,尽管有良好的愿望,结果往往～。Unless one watches one's work-style, one may have good intentions but fail to achieve them.

适度 shìdù 【形】proper degree；moderate degree

适合 shìhé 【动】suit；fit：她～做教师。She is well suited for teaching. 这几种工具书很～我们专业的需要。These reference books are exactly what we need in our special field.

适可而止 shì kě ér zhǐ know when and where to stop；not overdo anything：初练长跑要～,不能过量。A beginner at long-distance running must know how much practice is enough and not overdo it.

适口 shìkǒu 【形】pleasing to the taste；tasty

适量 shìliàng 【形】appropriate amount

适龄 shìlíng 【名】of the right age

适时 shìshí 【形】timely；well-timed；at the right moment：～播种 sow at the right time 这场雪下得很～。That snow we had was very timely.

适销 shìxiāo 【形】(of merchandise) suited to market demands

适宜 shìyí 【形】fit；appropriate

适应 shìyìng 【动】suit；fit；adapt：～需要 meet the needs of ～环境 adjust to circumstances 不～当地气候 be unable to adjust to the climate there

适用 shìyòng 【形】applicable；suitable

适中 shìzhōng 【形】❶ moderate；not extreme ❷ equally distant from different places；well-situated

室 shì 【名】◇ ❶ room：～外 outdoors 休息～ waiting-room；lounge ❷ section；department：资料～ reference room

逝 shì

逝世 shìshì 【动】pass away；die

释（釋） shì 【动】◇ ❶ explain；explicate；elucidate ❷ let go；part with：手不～卷 always have a book in his hand 爱不忍～ be fond of and unwilling to part with (sth.)

释放 shìfàng 【动】set free；release

释义 shì = yì explain the meaning (of sth.)

嗜 shì

嗜好 shìhào 【名】uncontrollable craving for (drug, drink, etc.)；addiction

誓 shì 【动】◇ pledge；swear；vow：不达目的,～不罢休 pledge oneself not to give up an undertaking until it has been accomplished ～为世界和平而奋斗 vow to struggle for world peace 【名】◇ pledge；oath：起～ take an oath

誓词 shìcí 【名】pledge

誓师 shìshī 【动】(of whole army before going to battle) pledge to fight for the cause

誓死 shìsǐ 【副】pledge one's life；vow to；vow to defy death to (do sth.)：～保卫祖国 vow to fight to the death in defense of one's country

誓言　shìyán　【名】oath；vow

shōu

收　shōu　【动】❶ receive；accept：～到一封信 receive a letter 请～下这件礼物。Please accept this gift. ❷ put away；take in：把东西～好了。Put the things away. 把衣服～进衣柜。Put the clothes in the wardrobe. ❸ gather in；harvest：一亩稻子～了八百斤。The rice yield was 800 *jin* per *mu*. ❹ collect (e.g. taxes)：～税 collect taxes

收报机　shōubàojī　【名】〔台 tái〕telegraphic receiver

收兵　shōu＝bīng　withdraw troops

收藏　shōucáng　【动】collect and store

收场　shōu＝chǎng　end up；wind up (*usu*. *derog*.)：这场辩论十分激烈，很不容易～。The argument has become so intense that it is hard to wind down. 他一看情况不妙，赶紧收了场。He saw that things were not turning out as expected and stopped on time.

收成　shōucheng　【名】harvest

收发　shōufā　【名】a person in charge of receiving and dispatching documents and letters 【动】receive and dispatch (documents, letters, etc.)

收费　shōu＝fèi　collect fees；charge：～停车场 paid parking

收复　shōufù　【动】recover；recapture

收割　shōugē　【动】reap；harvest

收割机　shōugējī　【名】harvester

收工　shōu＝gōng　(of manual labour) stop work for the day

收购　shōugòu　【动】buy；purchase

收归国有　shōu guī guó yǒu　nationalize

收回　shōu∥huí　❶ take back；regain；recall：～贷款 call in loans 这个厂子投产后，两年就可以～全部投资。Within its first two years of operation, the factory may be able to recover all its investments. ❷ withdraw；countermand；recant：～原议 revoke a previous decision 我～自己的意见。I withdraw my proposal.

收获　shōuhuò　【动】harvest；reap 【名】results；achievement；gains：学习～ results achieved through study 这次交流经验～不小。We have gained considerably from this exchange of experiences.

收集　shōují　【动】collect；gather together (things)

收据　shōujù　【名】receipt

收看　shōukàn　【动】to watch (television)

收敛　shōuliǎn　【动】❶ restrain oneself：言行有所～ exercise restrain in one's words and deeds ❷ weaken；vanish：～起笑容。The smile vanished from his face.

收留　shōuliú　【动】take in (sb.) and provide (him) with help

收拢　shōulǒng　【动】draw sth. in；gather in

收录机　shōulùjī　【名】〔架 jià〕radio-recorder

收罗　shōuluó　【动】seek and gather up (persons, things)

收买　shōumǎi　【动】❶ purchase ❷ buy off；buy over (*derog*.)：～人心 buy people off

收盘　shōupán　【动】closing quotation

收讫　shōuqì　【动】payment received

收取　shōuqǔ　【动】receive；collect

收容　shōuróng　【动】(of an organization or institution) take in and provide for (people)

收容所　shōuróngsuǒ　【名】collecting

post

收入 shōurù 【动】take in；include：这本词典～不少成语。This dictionary includes quite a few idiomatic expressions. 本月～一百二十元。His income for this month is 120 *yuan*. 【名】income；revenue：一笔不小的～ quite a tidy income 财政～ revenue 增加～ increase one's income

收审 shōushěn 【动】detain for interrogation

收拾 shōushi 【动】❶ tidy up；put in order；clear away：～东西 tidy things up ～残局 clear up the mess ❷ repair；mend：～房子 repair a house 请你把我这件旧衣服～一下。Please mend this old jacket for me. ❸〈口〉punish；settle with；deal with：十几分钟的战斗，我们就把这次登陆的敌人全部～了。In about 10 minutes of fighting, we disposed of the enemy landing party.

收缩 shōusuō 【动】❶ shrink；contract；shorten：木料干燥时会～。Timber shrinks when it is dried. ❷ draw back；concentrate（troops）：～兵力 pull back troops and concentrate them

收条 shōutiáo 【名】(～儿)〔张 zhāng〕receipt

收听 shōutīng 【动】listen to（broadcast）

收尾 shōu = wěi end up；wind up：这篇文章该～了。You ought to conclude your article now. 这项工程已到～阶段。The project is nearing completion.

收效 shōu = xiào produce an effect

收养 shōuyǎng 【动】adopt（a child）

收益 shōuyì 【名】gains；profits

收音机 shōuyīnjī 【名】〔架 jià〕radio

收支 shōuzhī 【名】revenue and expenditure；income and expenses

shǒu

手 shǒu 【名】❶ hand ❷ a person who does or who is good at doing a certain job：拖拉机～ a tractor driver 副～ an assistant 多面～ an all-round person；a generalist 【量】(～儿)❶ *for skill or dexterity*：能写一～好字 write a good hand 这几～是苦练出来的。Such skills are the result of painstaking training. 他真有两～。He really has a thing or two to show. ❷ ways of dealing with matters；move：你这～好，真解决问题。This move of yours is excellent. It will solve the problem. 他组织周末活动有两～。He certainly knows how to organize weekend activities.

手背 shǒubèi 【名】back of the hand

手笔 shǒubǐ 【名】(usu. of a famous person) handwriting：这个题词是一位老书法家的～。This inscription was written by an old calligrapher.

手臂 shǒubì 【名】arm

手表 shǒubiǎo 【名】〔块 kuài〕wristwatch

手册 shǒucè 【名】〔本 běn〕❶ handbook；guide；manual：电工～ an electrician's manual 读报～ a guide to newspaper reading ❷ book in which one's work-record is kept：学生～ student record book

手电筒 shǒudiàntǒng 【名】electric torch；flashlight

手段 shǒuduàn 【名】❶ means；method；measure：～与目的 the means and the end ❷ tricks；manoeuvres；foul means；artifice：要～ play tricks 使～ resort to underhanded manoeuvres

手法 shǒufǎ 【名】❶ (of artistic or literary works) skill；technique：夸

张的 ~ artistic exaggeration; hyperbole ❷ trick; ruse; gimmick; 耍两面派~ resort to double-dealing 卑劣的~ dirty tricks

手风琴 shǒufēngqín 【名】〔架 jià〕accordion

手感 shǒugǎn 【名】feel

手稿 shǒugǎo 【名】manuscript

手工 shǒugōng 【名】❶ work done by hand: 这件衣服的~做得很细。The handwork on this jacket is very nicely done. ❷ by hand (not by machine): ~编织 hand knit ~操作 manually operated

手工业 shǒugōngyè 【名】handicrafts (as an industry)

手工艺 shǒugōngyì 【名】handicrafts (as an art)

手机 shǒujī 【名】mobile phone; hand phone; cellular phone

手迹 shǒujì 【名】handwriting (as opp. to print); calligraphy or painting (of particular calligrapher or painter)

手脚 shǒujiǎo 【名】(of a person) movements (brisk, clumsy, etc.)

手巾 shǒujin 【名】〔条 tiáo〕towel

手绢儿 shǒujuànr 【名】〔块 kuài〕handkerchief

手铐 shǒukào 【名】〔副 fù〕handcuffs

手榴弹 shǒuliúdàn 【名】〔颗 kē〕hand grenade

手忙脚乱 shǒu máng jiǎo luàn in a frantic rush: 事情多,时间紧,搞得他~。There is so much work and so little time that he is frantic.

手帕 shǒupà 【名】〔块 kuài〕handkerchief

手枪 shǒuqiāng 【名】〔枝 zhī〕pistol

手巧 shǒu qiǎo dexterous; skilful with one's hands

手球 shǒuqiú 【名】handball

手软 shǒu ruǎn 【形】❶ too kindhearted to deal a justified blow ❷ so intimidated that one can't display one's skill

手势 shǒushì 【名】gesture

手书 shǒushū 【动】write in one's own hand 【名】personal letter

手术 shǒushù 【名】(med.) operation

手术台 shǒushùtái 【名】operating table

手套 shǒutào 【名】〔只 zhī，副 fù〕glove

手提包 shǒutíbāo 【名】〔个 gè〕handbag

手提电话 shǒutí diànhuà another name for "移动电话" yídòng diànhuà

手头 shǒutóu 【名】(~儿) ❶ on hand: 把~工作先作完 first finish the work on hand 这本书不在~。We don't have the book on hand. ❷ one's financial position at a particular moment: 他~宽裕。He is quite well-off. 我这个月~很紧。I'm a bit short this month.

手腕 shǒuwàn 【名】trick; artifice

手无寸铁 shǒu wú cùn tiě barehanded; defenceless

手舞足蹈 shǒu wǔ zú dǎo dance with joy

手写体 shǒuxiětǐ 【名】printed characters which resemble handwriting

手心 shǒuxīn 【名】❶ the centre of one's palm ❷ (~儿) control: 逃不出他的~。They cannot escape from his clutches.

手续 shǒuxù 【名】procedure; formalities

手续费 shǒuxùfèi 【名】service charges; handling charges; commission

手艺 shǒuyì 【名】workmanship; craftsmanship; skill: ~高 highly skilled workmanship 管理人员也应该学几门~。Administrative personnel should also acquire some technical skills.

手印 shǒuyìn 【名】(~儿) fingerprint

手札 shǒuzhá 【名】letter written with one's own hand

手掌 shǒuzhǎng 【名】palm of the hand

手杖 shǒuzhàng 【名】〔根 gēn〕walking stick

手纸 shǒuzhǐ 【名】toilet paper

手指 shǒuzhǐ 【名】finger

手指头 shǒuzhǐtou 【名】finger

手镯 shǒuzhuó 【名】bracelet

手足 shǒuzú 【名】brothers; sisters

手足无措 shǒu zú wú cuò at a loss as to what to do; helpless and without resources; 事先作好防汛准备，免得事到临头弄得～。We should take flood-prevention measures well in advance so that we will not be caught by surprise when the floods do come.

守 shǒu 【动】❶ guard; defend: ～住阵地 defend one's position ～球门 tend goal (e.g. soccer) ❷ observe; follow; abide by: ～约 keep an appointment ～信用 keep one's word ～纪律 observe discipline ❸ keep watch; look after: ～着病人 attend to the sick ❹ stand by in order to attend to: ～着电话 stand by the telephone to take calls

守财奴 shǒucáinú 【名】miser

守敌 shǒudí 【名】enemy troops on the defensive

守法 shǒu = fǎ abide by the law; law-abiding

守寡 shǒu = guǎ live as a widow; remain a widow

守候 shǒuhòu 【动】同"守"❸

守护 shǒuhù 【动】guard; protect

守旧 shǒujiù 【形】conservative

守口如瓶 shǒu kǒu rú píng tight-lipped; keep a secret: 他～，一点消息也不肯透露。He was very tight-lipped and refused to breathe a single word about it.

守灵 shǒu = líng stand as guard at the bier; keep a wake

守势 shǒushì 【名】state of defence; defensive

守卫 shǒuwèi 【动】guard; defend

守则 shǒuzé 【名】rules; regulations

守株待兔 shǒu zhū dài tù stand by a tree stump waiting for another hare to come and dash itself against it; (fig.) trust to a circumstance that can never materialize

首 shǒu 【名】◇ ❶ head: 昂～ hold one's head high 不堪回～ be painful to look back on one's past ❷ first: ～战告捷 win a victory in the first battle 这是我们～次参加该项展览。This is our first chance to take part in the exhibition. 【量】for songs and poems: 诗二～ two poems 一一～民歌 a folksong

首创 shǒuchuàng 【动】initiate; originate

首创精神 shǒuchuàng jīngshén initiative

首次 shǒu cì the first time: ～参加比赛 to take part in a race for the first time

首当其冲 shǒu dāng qí chōng be the first to be affected; bear the brunt of: 这次战斗，三排～。In this battle, the third platoon bore the brunt of the enemy's attack.

首都 shǒudū 【名】capital

首恶 shǒu'è 【名】chief criminal; ringleader

首府 shǒufǔ 【名】❶ capital of an autonomous region or prefecture in China ❷ capital of a prefecture or colony

首届 shǒu jiè first session

首领 shǒulǐng 【名】chief; head

首脑 shǒunǎo 【名】head; chief; summit (conference)

首屈一指 shǒu qū yī zhǐ be second to none; head the list; the first: 老张的棋艺在我们单位是～的。Lao

Zhang is our unit's champion chess player.

首饰　shǒushi　【名】jewelry

首尾　shǒuwěi　【名】❶ first and last：这部著作的～两章是他执笔的。He wrote the first and last chapters of this book. ～不能相顾。Those in front were cut off from those behind. ❷ from beginning to end：～一贯 be consistent throughout

首位　shǒuwèi　【名】first place：居于～ be in first place 排在～ put in first place

首席　shǒuxí　【名】❶ the seat of honour：他坐～。He sat in the seat of honour. ❷ chief：～代表 chief representative

首先　shǒuxiān　【副】first；in the first place：～报名 be the first to enter one's name ～发言 be the first to speak ～听取介绍，然后参观 first listen to the briefing, then start the visit 我们的困难～是人力，其次是时间，经费倒不成问题。Our primary problem is shortage of man-power, then there's the issue of time, money is no problem at all.

首相　shǒuxiàng　【名】prime minister

首要　shǒuyào　【形】of first importance；primary；cardinal (usu. as an attributive)：～任务 the most important task ～问题 a question of the first importance

首长　shǒuzhǎng　【名】leading cadre

shòu

寿（壽）shòu　【名】◇ ❶ the age of a person；life：高～ longevity ～终正寝 die a natural death at an advanced age ❷ birthday (implying respect)：～礼 birthday gift

寿辰　shòuchén　【名】birthday (of an elderly person)

寿命　shòumìng　【名】span of a human life；life-expectancy；life-span

受　shòu　【动】❶ accept；receive；get：～教育 receive an education ～启发 receive enlightenment ❷ suffer：～损失 suffer losses ～委屈 suffer injustice ❸ bear；stand；endure：～不了 (liǎo) unable to endure；unbearable

受潮　shòu = cháo　be affected by moisture

受宠若惊　shòu chǒng ruò jīng　feel extremely flattered；be overwhelmed by the honour done to one

受害　shòu = hài　suffer injury；suffer damage；be hurt

受害者　shòuhàizhě　【名】victim；sufferer

受贿　shòu = huì　accept a bribe

受惊　shòu = .jīng　be startled

受苦　shòu = kǔ　suffer hardships

受累　shòu = lèi　be caused trouble；put oneself out for sb.：帮我拿了这么多东西,让您～了! Thank you for taking the trouble to help me carry all these things.

受礼　shòu = lǐ　accept another person's gift

受理　shòulǐ　【动】for a court to accept a case and proceed with the hearing

受凉　shòu = liáng　catch cold

受命　shòumìng　【动】be ordered to；receive an order

受难　shòu = nàn　suffer hardship or disaster

受骗　shòu = piàn　be deceived

受聘　shòupìn　【动】be appointed；be hired；be taken on

受气　shòu = qì　be bullied

受权　shòuquán　【动】be authorized

受伤　shòu = shāng　be injured；be wounded

受事　shòushì　【名】object

受暑　shòu = shǔ　suffer from sunstroke

受益　shòu = yì　profit from；benefit by

受援国　shòuyuánguó　【名】recipient country

受灾　shòu = zāi　be hit by a natural calamity

受罪　shòu = zuì　❶ suffer hardship or affliction：过去她在纱厂做工，受够了罪。As a textile worker from the old days, she had gone through every conceivable hardship. ❷ have a rough time：今天遇上了大雪，汽车又抛锚，真～。What a time we've had! We were caught in a snow storm, and then our car broke down.

授　shòu　【动】◇ ❶ award；issue（prize）：～勋 confer an honour；award a medal ～旗 present a flag ❷ teach；instruct：～课 give lessons 面～机宜 give confidential instructions

授奖　shòu = jiǎng　award prize

授课　shòukè　【动】teach（in class）：他每天～两小时。He teaches two hours every day.

授命　shòumìng　【动】authorize sb. to do sth.

授权　shòuquán　【动】authorize；empower

授意　shòuyì　【动】hint；prompt

授予　shòuyǔ　【动】award；confer

售　shòu　【动】◇ sell：～货 sell goods ～票 sell tickets

售货员　shòuhuòyuán　【名】◇ shop assistant

售价　shòujià　【名】selling price；price

售票员　shòupiàoyuán　【名】ticket seller；conductor or conductress

兽（獸）　shòu　【名】◇ animal；beast：驯～ tame an animal

兽行　shòuxíng　【名】brutality

兽性　shòuxìng　【名】brutish nature；brutality

兽医　shòuyī　【名】veterinary surgeon；veterinary

瘦　shòu　【形】❶ thin：他长得很～。He is very thin. ❷ lean：～肉 lean meat ❸ tight：这条裤子太～了。This pair of trousers is too tight.

瘦弱　shòuruò　【形】thin and weak

瘦小　shòuxiǎo　【形】small and thin

shū

书（書）　shū　【名】〔本 běn〕❶ book ❷ letter ❸ documents

书包　shūbāo　【名】〔个 gè〕satchel；schoolbag

书报　shūbào　【名】books and newspapers

书本　shūběn　【名】books；book（knowledge）

书呆子　shūdāizi　【名】bookworm

书店　shūdiàn　【名】bookshop

书法　shūfǎ　【名】calligraphy

书法家　shūfǎjiā　【名】calligrapher

书房　shūfáng　【名】study

书柜　shūguì　【名】〔个 gè〕bookcase

书籍　shūjí　【名】books

书记　shūjì　【名】secretary

书架　shūjià　【名】〔个 gè〕bookshelf

书刊　shūkān　【名】books and magazines

书库　shūkù　【名】stacks（of a library）

书面　shūmiàn　【名】written（as opp. to 口头）

书面语　shūmiànyǔ　【名】written language；literary language

书名号　shūmínghào　【名】a punctuation mark used to indicate the title

of a book：《》

书目　shūmù　【名】 catalogue of books

书皮　shūpí　【名】(～儿) book cover

书评　shūpíng　【名】book review

书签　shūqiān　【名】bookmark

书生气　shūshēngqì　【名】bookish

书市　shūshì　【名】book fair

书写　shūxiě　【动】write

书信　shūxìn　【名】letters；correspondence

书展　shūzhǎn　【名】exhibition of books：举办～ put on an exhibition of books

书桌　shūzhuō　【名】〔张 zhāng〕desk

抒　shū　【动】◇ express；pour out；voice：～ 豪情 express one's noble sentiments

抒发　shūfā　【动】express；pour out (e.g. feelings)

抒情　shū = qíng　give vent to one's emotion

抒情诗　shūqíngshī　【名】〔首 shǒu〕lyric poetry

枢（樞）　shū

枢纽　shūniǔ　【名】pivot；axis；key position

叔　shū　【名】◇ ❶ uncle (father's younger brother) ❷ form of address for any person slightly younger than one's father：大 ～ uncle ❸ one's husband's younger brother：～ 嫂 之间 和睦 相处。The wife and her young brother-in-law get along amicably.

叔父　shūfù　【名】uncle (father's younger brother)

叔叔　shūshu　【名】❶ uncle (father's younger brother) ❷ form of address for any person slightly younger than one's father

殊　shū

殊不知　shū bù zhī　God knows (*usu. in written language, at the beginning of the second clause of a sentence*)：人们都以为上山难，～下山更难。People usually think that it is difficult to climb up a mountain, but God knows it is even more difficult to go down.

殊死　shūsǐ　【形】(*usu. as an attributive*) desperate：～ 的斗争 a life-and-death struggle；fight to the death

殊途同归　shū tú tóng guī　different roads lead to the same goal；all roads lead to Rome

梳　shū　【动】comb：～ 辫子 braid one's hair 把头发～一～ comb one's hair

梳洗　shūxǐ　【动】wash and dress

梳子　shūzi　【名】〔把 bǎ〕comb

舒　shū　【动】◇ loosen；relax：～ 筋活血 relax the tendons and stimulate the circulation

舒畅　shūchàng　【形】(of mental state) free from frustrations, fears and worries：心情 ～ have ease of mind；feel happy and comfortable

舒服　shūfu　【形】comfortable：招待所里又～，又安静。It is comfortable and quiet in the guest house. 老矿工在海滨舒舒服服地度过一个夏天。The old miner spent a summer very comfortably at the seaside.

舒适　shūshì　【形】(of house, environment, life, etc.) comfortable；cosy

舒坦　shūtan　【形】〈口〉(of mental state, life) comfortable

舒心　shūxīn　【形】free from worries

舒展　shūzhǎn　【动】unknit (brow)【形】(of mental state) comfortable

舒张　shūzhāng　【动】diastole

疏　shū

疏导　shūdǎo　【动】dredge；channel；enlighten；remove

疏忽　shūhu　【动】neglect；overlook：～职守 neglect one's duty 我们千万不可～大意。There must not be the slightest error due to carelessness. 统计员一时～会造成大错。A statistician's oversight may easily lead to a serious error.

疏浚　shūjùn　【动】dredge

疏漏　shūlòu　【动】slip；careless omission

疏散　shūsàn　【动】evacuate；disperse

疏通　shūtōng　【动】❶ dredge：～河道 dredge a river bed ❷ mediate：～双方的感情 smooth over the injured feelings of the two parties

疏远　shūyuǎn　【形】be estranged from；be alienated from：关系～ estranged relationship 感情～ estranged feelings【动】keep at arm's length；alienate；drift apart；become estranged：不要～了朋友。Don't become estranged from your friends.

输（輸）
shū　【动】❶ transport；send；deliver：～油 (of a pipeline) carry oil ～电 transmit electricity ❷ lose；be defeated：～了一局 lose one game

输出　shūchū　【动】❶ export：～商品 export goods 资本～ export capital ❷ send out from inside：血液从心脏～。Blood is pumped by the heart. ❸ (of energy, signal, etc.) output

输电　shūdiàn　【动】transmit electricity

输入　shūrù　【动】❶ import：～产品 import products ～新技术 import new techniques ❷ (of energy, signal, etc.) input

输送　shūsòng　【动】transport；convey

输血　shū＝xuè　transfuse blood

输液　shū＝yè　infusion

输油管　shūyóuguǎn　【名】〔条 tiáo〕oil pipe-line

蔬
shū

蔬菜　shūcài　【名】vegetable

shú

赎（贖）
shú　【动】❶ ransom；redeem：把抵押品～回 redeem one's pledge ❷ atone for (wrong doing)

赎买　shúmǎi　【动】redeem；buy out

赎罪　shú＝zuì　atone for one's misdeed：立功～ perform meritorious services to atone for one's crime

熟
shú　【形】❶ ripe (as opp. to 生)：西瓜～了。The watermelons are ripe. ❷ (of food) cooked：～食 pre-cooked food 饼烙～了。The pancakes are done. ❸ be familiar with；be well acquainted with：这条路他最～。He knows this road best. 我跟他很～。I know him quite well. ❹ practised；proficient：背得很～ recite fluently from memory 这个曲子他弹得很～。He plays this piece very proficiently. ❺ (of sleep) deep；sound：睡得正～。be sound asleep

熟练　shúliàn　【形】skilled；proficient

熟路　shúlù　【名】familiar route

熟能生巧　shú néng shēng qiǎo　practice makes perfect

熟人　shúrén　【名】acquaintance；a person one knows quite well

熟视无睹　shú shì wú dǔ　turn a blind eye to sth. because one is very familiar with it

熟识　shúshi　【动】be familiar with；be well acquainted

熟手　shúshǒu　【名】old hand

熟睡 shúshuì 【动】be fast asleep

熟铁 shútiě 【名】wrought iron

熟悉 shúxī 【动】know well；be familiar with：～情况 be familiar with the situation 彼此很～ know each other quite well

熟习 shúxí 【动】be skillful at；be well versed in

熟语 shúyǔ 【名】idiom

熟字 shúzì 【名】familiar character

shǔ

暑 shǔ 【名】◇ heat；hot weather（as opp. to 寒）：寒来～往 hot and cold seasons alternate with one another

暑假 shǔjià 【名】summer vacation

暑期 shǔqī 【名】the time of summer vacation

暑天 shǔtiān 【名】hot summer days

属（屬）shǔ 【动】❶ be under；be subordinate to：这所医学院～北京市。This medical college is under the Beijing municipality. ❷ belong：鲸鱼～哺乳类。The whale belongs to the category of mammals. ❸ be born in the year（of one of the twelve animals）：他～马。He was born in the year of the horse. 【名】(biol.) genus

属地 shǔdì 【名】dependency；colony

属实 shǔ＝shí turn out to be true；be verified

属性 shǔxìng 【名】attribute；property

属于 shǔyú 【动】belong to；pertain to：这块地是～我们学校的。This plot of land belongs to our school. 胜利永远～人民。Victory always belongs to the people.

署 shǔ 【动】sign；affix（one's signature）：请在信后～上你的名字。Please sign this letter.

署名 shǔ＝míng sign one's name

鼠 shǔ 【名】rat；mouse

鼠目寸光 shǔ mù cùn guāng the eyes of a mouse can see only an inch ahead；(fig.) be short-sighted；see only what is under one's nose：～的人心胸必定狭隘。People who see only what is under their noses are without exception narrow-minded.

鼠疫 shǔyì 【名】plague

数（數）shǔ 【动】❶ count：～了好几遍 count it several times over ❷ be considered as（exceptionally）：全班～他力气大。He is considered the strongest member of the class.
另见 shù

数不着 shǔ bu zháo not considered（outstanding）：论射击技术，在我们排还～我。As far as marksmanship is concerned, I don't count in my platoon.

数得着 shǔ de zháo be considered（outstanding）：他是我们这里～的革新能手。He is reckoned to be the outstanding reformer among us.

数伏 shǔ＝fú hot summer days have begun

数九 shǔ＝jiǔ the nine periods（of nine days each）following the Winter Solstice：～寒天 the coldest days of the year

数数儿 shǔ＝shùr count；reckon

数一数二 shǔ yī shǔ èr count as one of the best；outstanding：这个钢铁厂是全国～的大工厂。This steel mill ranks as one of the biggest, if not the biggest, in the whole country.

曙 shǔ

曙光 shǔguāng 【名】the first light of day；dawn

shù

术（術） shù 【名】❶ art；skill；technique ❷ method；tactics

术语 shùyǔ 【名】technical term；terminology

束 shù 【动】tie；bind：腰~皮带 fasten a leather belt around one's waist 【量】〈书〉bunch（for flowers, etc.）：一~鲜花 a bouquet

束缚 shùfù 【动】bind；fetter

束手待毙 shù shǒu dài bì resign oneself to dying；helplessly await death：要千方百计挽救这个企业，不能~。We must do our best to save this business and not give up without a fight.

束手无策 shù shǒu wú cè be at one's wits' end；be at a loss as to what to do

束之高阁 shù zhī gāo gé shelve a matter；put sth. aside：要充分发挥这份资料的作用，不要~。Don't file away this data；we must make good use of it.

述 shù 【动】◇ narrate；relate：简~如下。I'll give a brief account as follows.

述评 shùpíng 【名】commentary

述说 shùshuō 【动】give an account of；narrate

述职 shù＝zhí （of an ambassador）report on one's work

树（樹） shù 【名】〔棵 kē〕tree 【动】set up；foster；hold up：~标兵 hold sb. up as a model 在自力更生方面~起了一面旗帜 hold up as an example of self-reliance

树碑立传 shù bēi lì zhuàn glorify sb. by erecting a monument and writing his biography；build up some-body's image（derog.）：这本所谓回忆录实际上是为他自己~的。These memoirs are, in fact, an attempt on his part to build up his own image.

树丛 shùcóng 【名】grove；thicket

树倒猢狲散 shù dǎo húsūn sàn all the monkeys scatter when the tree falls；rats leave a sinking ship（derog.）

树敌 shù＝dí make an enemy

树干 shùgàn 【名】tree trunk

树立 shùlì 【动】（of abstract things）set up；foster；hold up：~典型 set an example ~艰苦朴素的风尚 foster a habit of working hard and living frugally

树林 shùlín 【名】woods

树苗 shùmiáo 【名】〔棵 kē〕sapling

树木 shùmù 【名】trees in general

树皮 shùpí 【名】bark

树梢 shùshāo 【名】tree top

树荫 shùyīn 【名】shade of a tree

树枝 shùzhī 【名】branch；twig

竖（豎） shù 【形】vertical；upright 【动】erect sth.；set sth. upright：~一根柱子 erect a pillar ~起大拇指 hold up one's thumb（in approval）【名】（of Chinese characters）a vertical stroke "丨"

竖立 shùlì 【动】set upright；stand

竖琴 shùqín 【名】harp

数（數） shù 【名】❶ number；figure：人~ the number of persons 数（shǔ）~ count the number（of sth.）❷ figure；number：两位~ a two digit number ❸（grammar）number 【数】several；a few：~小时 several hours ~百种 several hundred kinds
另见 shǔ

数词 shùcí 【名】numeral

数额 shù'é 【名】number；amount

数据 shùjù 【名】data

数控　shùkòng　【名】numerical control

数量　shùliàng　【名】quantity

数目　shùmù　【名】number

数学　shùxué　【名】mathematics

数值　shùzhí　【名】(maths.) numerical value

数字　shùzì　【名】❶ numeral：汉字的～有大写小写两种。Chinese numerals can be written either in complicated form or in ordinary form. ❷ figures：阿拉伯～ Arabic numerals ❸ quantity；quota；amount：黑板上记录着本周的生产～。The production quota was written on the blackboard.

漱　shù　【动】rinse out (one's mouth)

漱口　shù = kǒu　rinse out one's mouth

shuā

刷　shuā　【动】❶ brush；clean；scrub：～牙 brush one's teeth ～墙 whitewash the wall ❷ eliminate；knock out：他在比赛的第一轮就被～下来了。He was eliminated in the first round of the competition.【名】(～儿) brush：鞋～ a shoebrush【象声】whistling sound：风刮得树叶～～地响。The leaves rustle in the wind. 雨～～地下起来了。The rain came in a downpour.

刷洗　shuāxǐ　【动】scrub

刷新　shuāxīn　【动】break；better (a record)：～记录 break the record ～成绩 better one's record

刷子　shuāzi　【名】〔把 bǎ〕brush

shuǎ

耍　shuǎ　【动】❶ play：～猴儿 put on a circus show using monkeys 男孩子就爱～刀弄枪。Little boys often like to play with toy swords and guns. ❷ play (a trick)：～小聪明 play a petty trick ～态度 be in a huff ～脾气 fly into a rage

耍花招　shuǎ huāzhāo　(～儿) ❶ play tricks ❷ resort to trickery

耍赖　shuǎlài　【动】act shamelessly；be perverse

耍流氓　shuǎ liúmáng　behave like a hoodlum；take liberties with women；act indecently

耍弄　shuǎnòng　【动】make a fool of

耍手腕　shuǎ shǒuwàn　play tricks：要光明磊落，不要～。Be open and above board. Never resort to tricks.

耍嘴皮子　shuǎ zuǐpízi　❶ talk glibly；pay lip service only ❷ mere empty talk；lip service；quibble

shuāi

衰　shuāi　【形】◇ declining；waning：年老力～ old and weak

衰败　shuāibài　【动】decline；be on the wane

衰竭　shuāijié　【动】(med.) exhaustion：心力～ heart failure

衰老　shuāilǎo　【形】old and weak

衰落　shuāiluò　【动】同"衰败"

衰弱　shuāiruò　【形】weak；lack strength

衰退　shuāituì　【动】fail；decline

衰亡　shuāiwáng　【动】die out；wither away

摔　shuāi　【动】❶ fall；stumble；lose one's balance：～跟头 trip and fall ❷ drop and break：碗～了。The bowl fell and broke. 小心，别～下来! Be careful! Don't fall and hurt yourself. ❸ cause to fall and break：一失手～了一个盘子。The

plate slipped out of my hand and broke on the floor. ❹ throw; fling; cast: 他把笔一～,说什么也不写了。He threw down his pen and refused to write any more.

摔打 shuāidǎ 【动】❶ beat; knock: 把鞋上的泥～～ knock the mud off one's shoes ❷ (*fig.*) temper oneself (under difficult circumstances): 青年人应该到艰苦的环境中去～～。Young people should temper themselves in difficult circumstances.

摔跟头 shuāi gēndou ❶ tumble; trip and fall ❷ trip up; come a cropper; make a blunder

摔交 shuāi = jiāo ❶ trip and fall: 他不小心摔了一交。He wasn't being careful and so tripped and fell. ❷ (sports) wrestling: 今晚有～比赛。There is a wrestling match tonight.

shuǎi

甩 shuǎi 【动】❶ fling; move backward and forward with force; flick: ～袖子 (from Chinese opera) flick one's sleeve ～鞭子 crack the whip ～开膀子抢铁锤 swing one's arms to strike with a sledgehammer ❷ throw; hurl; toss: ～手榴弹 throw hand-grenades ❸ cast away; shake off; leave (sb. behind): 那匹白马跑得真快,其他的马被远远地～在后面。The white horse ran very fast, leaving all the others far behind.

甩卖 shuǎimài 【动】clearance sale; sell at a reduced price

shuài

率 shuài 【动】◇ lead (e. g. an

army): ～队入场 lead the team into the arena

另见 lǜ

率领 shuàilǐng 【动】lead (e. g. an army)

率先 shuàixiān 【副】take the lead (in doing sth.): ～报名参加比赛 take the lead in entering for the contest ～到达终点 be the first to reach the terminal point

shuān

闩 (閂) shuān 【动】bolt 【名】door bolt

拴 shuān 【动】tie; fasten: 把马～在树上 tie the horse to a tree

shuàn

涮 shuàn 【动】❶ rinse: ～瓶子 rinse the bottle 洗洗～～ do a lot of washing ❷ cook thin slices of meat by dipping them in boiling water: ～羊肉 dip-boiled mutton slices

涮锅子 shuàn guōzi instant-boil slices of meat and vegetables in a chafing dish

shuāng

双 (雙) shuāng 【形】❶ two; twin; dual (*as opp. to* 单): ～手 both hands ～职工 both man and wife working; double income couple 成～成对 in pairs ❷ double: ～料 of reinforced material; of extra good quality ～份 double portion ❸ even: ～号由南门入场。Those with even numbered tickets are to enter by the south door. 【量】pair;

一～筷子 a pair of chopsticks 买两～袜子 buy two pairs of socks

双胞胎 shuāngbāotāi 【名】twins

双边 shuāngbiān 【名】bilateral：～会谈 bilateral talks ～条约 bilateral treaty

双重 shuāngchóng 【形】double；twofold

双重国籍 shuāngchóng guójí dual nationality

双唇音 shuāngchúnyīn 【名】bilabial

双打 shuāngdǎ 【动】(sports) doubles

双方 shuāngfāng 【名】the two parties；both sides

双杠 shuānggàng 【名】❶ parallel bars ❷ (sports) parallel bars

双关 shuāngguān 【动】having a double meaning

双关语 shuāngguānyǔ 【名】pun

双管齐下 shuāng guǎn qí xià paint a picture with two brushes at the same time；(fig.) work along two fronts, thus making success doubly sure：一方面简化笔划，一方面精简字数，～来简化汉字。By reducing the number of strokes in a character, and at the same time, reducing the number of characters, we are working along two lines to achieve the simplification of Chinese characters.

双轨 shuāngguǐ 【名】double track (railway)

双亲 shuāngqīn 【名】(both) parents

双数 shuāngshù 【名】even number

双语 shuāngyǔ 【名】bilingual：～词典 bilingual dictionary

双职工 shuāngzhígōng 【名】man and wife both at work

霜 shuāng 【名】frost

霜冻 shuāngdòng 【名】frost damage done to plants；frost

shuǎng

爽 shuǎng 【形】◇ ❶ clear and bright；crisp：神清目～ clear-headed and bright-eyed 秋高气～ the clear and crisp air of autumn ❷ feel well：身体不～。I don't feel well.

爽快 shuǎngkuai 【形】❶ cool and refreshing：退烧以后，身上觉得～多了。I felt light and clear-headed after my temperature had gone down. ❷ outspoken；frank and straightforward：老张说话很～。Lao Zhang is very frank and outspoken.

爽朗 shuǎnglǎng 【形】❶ bright and clear：北京的秋天天气非常～。Autumn in Beijing is clear and invigorating. ❷ open and cheerful；hearty；candid：～的笑声 hearty laughter 他很～，整天有说有笑的。He is open and frank and always cheerful.

爽身粉 shuǎngshēnfěn 【名】talcum powder

shuí

谁（誰） shuí 【代】❶ who；whom：你找～? Who are you looking for? ～送你的这把伞? Who gave you this umbrella as a gift? ❷ used before 都 or 也 to mean "anyone"：～也不能违反交通规则。Nobody is permitted to break the traffic regulations. 你要有问题，我们几个人～都可以问。If you have any questions, you can ask any of us. ❸ indicates an indefinite person or persons：我想找～和我一起去买东西。I want to find someone to go shopping with me. 你替我问问下月

有～去武汉没有。Will you please find out for me whether there is anyone going to Wuhan next month? ❹ *one phrase with 谁 precedes another in which case the latter refers to the former*：～买的，～付钱。Whoever bought it had to pay for it. 明天是你的生日，你喜欢请～就请～。Tomorrow is your birthday. You can invite whomever you like to the party. ❺ *used in a rhetorical question to mean "nobody"*：～愿意干这种费力不讨好的傻事！Who is willing to do such a senseless and thankless job? ～知道他干吗发脾气！Who knows why he flew into such a rage? Note：谁知道 *sometimes means "unexpectedly"*：我以为他只是随便说说，～知道他真走了。I had thought that he was just talking, but much to my surprise, he actually left. ❻ 谁 *is used both as the subject and the object to mean "each other", usu. in the negative*：他们俩争了半天，～也说不服～。The two of them argued for a long time but neither could convince the other. 我们这些人原来～也不认识～。We did not know one another before.

shuǐ

水 shuǐ 【名】water

水坝 shuǐbà 【名】dam

水泵 shuǐbèng 【名】〔台 tái〕water pump

水兵 shuǐbīng 【名】sailor；seaman

水彩 shuǐcǎi 【名】water colours

水彩画 shuǐcǎihuà 【名】watercolour (painting)

水产 shuǐchǎn 【名】aquatic product

水产业 shuǐchǎnyè 【名】aquatic products industry

水车 shuǐchē 【名】water wheel

水到渠成 shuǐ dào qú chéng a canal is formed when water comes；(*fig.*) something will materialize when the conditions are ripe

水稻 shuǐdào 【名】paddy (rice)

水滴石穿 shuǐ dī shí chuān dripping water wears through rock；(*fig.*) an action, however imperceptible, if persisted in, will bring results：～的现象启示我们学习要持之以恒。The saying "dripping water will wear through rock" tells us the importance of perseverance in our pursuit of knowledge.

水电站 shuǐdiànzhàn 【名】〔座 zuò〕hydro-electric power station

水分 shuǐfèn 【名】❶ moisture；humidity：吸收～ absorb moisture ❷ exaggeration；something more than is due：这个报导有些～，需要核实。This report seems somewhat exaggerated, and should be verified.

水沟 shuǐgōu 【名】〔条 tiáo〕ditch；gutter

水管子 shuǐguǎnzi 【名】water pipe

水果 shuǐguǒ 【名】fruit

水壶 shuǐhú 【名】〔把 bǎ〕kettle

水货 shuǐhuò 【名】smuggled goods

水浇地 shuǐjiāodì 【名】irrigated land

水井 shuǐjǐng 【名】well

水库 shuǐkù 【名】reservoir

水力 shuǐlì 【名】water-power；hydraulic power

水力发电 shuǐlì fā diàn hydraulic electrogenerating

水利 shuǐlì 【名】water conservancy

水利工程 shuǐlì gōngchéng water conservancy project

水利化 shuǐlìhuà 【动】bring all farmland under irrigation

水龙头 shuǐlóngtóu 【名】water tap

水路 shuǐlù 【名】waterway；water route

水落石出 shuǐ luò shí chū the rock

emerges as the water subsides; (*fig.*) the truth will prevail: 经过反复调查研究，问题终于～了。After repeated investigation and analysis the matter was cleared up at last.

水面 shuǐmiàn 【名】surface of the water

水墨画 shuǐmòhuà 【名】ink and wash drawing

水泥 shuǐní 【名】cement

水牛 shuǐniú 【名】〔头 tóu〕buffalo

水泡 shuǐpào 【名】❶ bubble ❷ blister

水平 shuǐpíng 【名】❶ level ❷ standard; level: 生产～ level of production 思想～ ideological level 文化～高 high cultural level

水平面 shuǐpíngmiàn 【名】horizontal plane

水平线 shuǐpíngxiàn 【名】horizontal line

水球 shuǐqiú 【名】water polo

水渠 shuǐqú 【名】〔条 tiáo〕canal; ditch

水乳交融 shuǐ rǔ jiāo róng mix as well as milk and water; get along well with each other: 他们的关系达到了～的程度。They get along so well that the relationship between them is like milk mingling with water.

水深火热 shuǐ shēn huǒ rè (*fig.*) intense suffering: 旧社会，劳动人民生活在～之中。In the old society, the lives of the working people were filled with untold suffering.

水手 shuǐshǒu 【名】sailor; seaman

水塔 shuǐtǎ 【名】〔座 zuò〕water tower

水田 shuǐtián 【名】wet field; paddy field

水土 shuǐtǔ 【名】❶ water and soil; 植树可以保持～。Tree-planting helps to conserve water and prevent soil erosion. ❷ general term for natural environment or climate: ～不服 not acclimatized

水土保持 shuǐtǔ bǎochí water and soil conservation

水土流失 shuǐtǔ liúshī water loss and soil erosion

水位 shuǐwèi 【名】water level

水文 shuǐwén 【名】hydrology

水仙 shuǐxiān 【名】narcissus

水泄不通 shuǐ xiè bù tōng be watertight; be heavily beseiged and unable to get out; be congested and impassable: 挤得～ crowded so tightly that you can't move 包围得～ so closely surrounded that it is impossible to break out

水星 shuǐxīng 【名】(planet) Mercury

水银 shuǐyín 【名】mercury

水域 shuǐyù 【名】body of water; waters

水源 shuǐyuán 【名】❶ source of a river ❷ source of water

水灾 shuǐzāi 【名】flood

水闸 shuǐzhá 【名】flood-gate

水涨船高 shuǐ zhǎng chuán gāo as the river rises higher, the boat floats higher; (*fig.*) things improve with an improvement in the general situation

水蒸气 shuǐzhēngqì 【名】steam

水质 shuǐzhì 【名】water quality

水中捞月 shuǐ zhōng lāo yuè catch the moon in the water; (*fig.*) a fruitless attempt: ～一场空 as fruitless as to try to catch the moon in the water

水准 shuǐzhǔn 【名】standard; level

水族 shuǐzú 【名】aquatic animals

shuì

税 shuì 【名】tax; duty

税款 shuìkuǎn 【名】tax payment

税率 shuìlǜ 【名】tax rate

税收 shuìshōu 【名】revenue from

tax；taxation

税务 shuìwù 【名】tax；taxation

税制 shuìzhì 【名】tax system

睡 shuì 【动】go to bed；sleep：他～得早起得也早. He goes to bed early and gets up early. 昨天我～了八个小时. I slept for eight hours last night. 他躺了一会儿，但是没～着. He lay there for a while, but didn't fall asleep.

睡觉 shuì=jiào go to bed；fall asleep；sleep：都十一点了，快去～吧. It's already eleven, please go to bed at once. 他～很轻，有点儿声音他就醒. He is a light sleeper and will wake up at the slightest noise. 你还在工作啊，我可已经睡了一觉了. So you are still working! I've already had some sleep.

睡眠 shuìmián 【名】sleep

睡衣 shuìyī 【名】〔件 jiàn〕pyjamas

shùn

顺（順）shùn 【形】(of writings) readable；clear and well-written：文从字～ the language (of the article) is fluent and readable 这篇作文写得挺～. This composition is very lucidly written. 【动】❶ be in the same direction as：～时针方向 clockwise ～潮流 go with the tide ❷ arrange；put in order：把船～过来 bring the boat round 把文字～一～ polish the language 【介】along；in the direction of：～河边走 walk along the river

顺便 shùnbiàn 【副】(do sth.) in passing；if convenient；without extra effort：你去商店，～给我买盒儿烟. When you go to the shop, please get me a packet of cigarettes if it's no trouble.

顺差 shùnchā 【名】favourable balance；surplus

顺从 shùncóng 【动】obey；submit to

顺当 shùndang 【形】smooth；unhindered；plain sailing

顺耳 shùn'ěr 【形】pleasing to the ear

顺风 shùnfēng 【名】favourable wind

顺风 shùn=fēng have a favourable wind；with the wind

顺口 shùnkǒu 【形】❶ fluent；smooth：这段对白改得很～. This dialogue sounds more fluent after revision. ❷ (say) off-handedly：～答应了一声 answer off-handedly

顺口溜 shùnkǒuliū 【名】doggerel

顺理成章 shùn lǐ chéng zhāng logical；matter-of-course；as a matter of course

顺利 shùnlì 【形】plain sailing；smooth going；without a hitch：工作～ work smoothly ～地完成了任务 fulfil the task without a hitch 手术进行得很～. The operation was plain sailing.

顺流而下 shùn liú ér xià go with the current

顺路 shùnlù 【形】❶ on one's way ❷ by a more direct way

顺手 shùnshǒu 【形】❶ with ease；without extra trouble；smoothly：工作～ work smoothly 事办得真～. The work is proceeding without a hitch. ❷ (do sth. involving a thing which is) within easy reach：～从书架上拿起一本书来 take out a book from a shelf within easy reach ❸ in passing：你出去时～把门带上. As you leave, please close the door behind you.

顺手牵羊 shùn shǒu qiān yáng make off with a sheep in passing；(fig.) take sth. on the sly；spirit sth. away

顺水　shùn＝shuǐ　downstream

顺水人情　shùn shuǐ rénqíng　do sb. a favour at little cost

顺水推舟　shùn shuǐ tuī zhōu　push the boat along with the current；follow the line of least resistance；be guided by the prevailing opinion

顺我者昌，逆我者亡　shùn wǒ zhě chāng, nì wǒ zhě wáng　those who bow before me shall survive and those who resist shall perish

顺心　shùnxīn　【形】as one wishes：一切～. Everything is as one would like. 他碰到了不～的事. Things run counter to his wishes.

顺序　shùnxù　【名】sequence

顺延　shùnyán　【动】postpone

顺眼　shùnyǎn　【形】pleasant to the eye：这块花布看着很～. This cotton print is pretty.

顺着　shùnzhe　【动】❶同"顺"【动】❶ ❷ yield to：对孩子不能老～. You can't always let children have their own way.【介】同"顺"【介】

瞬　shùn

瞬息　shùnxī　【名】(in) the twinkling of an eye

瞬息万变　shùnxī wàn biàn　great changes have taken place in a short time：高原的气候～. The weather on the plateau can change in the twinkling of an eye.

shuō

说（说）　shuō　【动】❶ say；speak；talk：～笑话 crack a joke 他会～法语. He speaks French. ❷ explain；elucidate：这个道理一～就懂. The argument became clear as soon as it was explained. ❸ scold；criticize；reprimand：他这样做不对，你应该～～他. He isn't doing the right thing. You should talk to him.

说不定　shuōbudìng　【副】probably：～要下大雨. It looks like rain. 他～早回家了. He probably went home long ago.

说不过去　shuō bu guòqù　cannot be justified；unjustifiable：条件这么好，如果还不满意，可真～. With conditions that good, if you are still not satisfied, you're simply being unreasonable.

说不来　shuō bu lái　cannot get along with each other

说不上　shuōbushàng　【动】❶ cannot tell：我刚到这里，邮局在哪儿我也～. I'm a new comer and don't know where the post office is. 现在电视机的品种很多，我也～哪种最好. There are many models of TV sets, I can hardly tell which is the best. ❷ cannot be said (to have a certain value)：这本书～有什么参考价值. This book cannot be said to have any value as a reference book. 他们俩～是什么好朋友，只是认识. The two of them cannot be said to be good friends. They are just acquaintances.

说穿　shuōchuān　【动】expose；disclose；put it bluntly：什么没工夫～了，你是不想和我们一起去. No time? To put it bluntly, you simply don't want to come with us.

说得来　shuō de lái　get along very well

说法　shuōfa　【名】❶ way of putting things；version：委婉的～ put it in a round-about way 一个意思可以有几种～. There is more than one way of spelling out this point. ❷ statement；opinion：这种～比较中肯. This statement is relatively pertinent.

说服　shuō∥fú　persuade；convince；bring round

说话 shuō=huà ❶ talk；speak；say
❷（～儿）talk；gossip；chat：我们正
说着话，他进来了。We were just
talking when he came in.

说谎 shuō=huǎng tell a lie

说教 shuōjiào 【动】preach

说理 shuō=lǐ ❶ talk reason；rea-
son ❷ be reasonable

说明 shuōmíng 【动】❶ explain；
show；illustrate：～原因 explain the
cause ～情况 give an account of the
circumstances ❷ show；prove：他
不表态，～他有保留意见。His reti-
cence meant that he had reserva-
tions（about this matter）.【名】di-
rections；caption：装仪器的盒子里
有一张～。There is a manual in the
instrument box.

说明书 shuōmíngshū 【名】❶ synop-
sis ❷ directions；manual

说破 shuōpò 【动】同"说穿"

说情 shuō=qíng put in a good
word（for sb.）；plead mercy for

说说笑笑 shuō shuō xiào xiào have a
pleasant talk together；chat and
laugh

说闲话 shuō xiánhuà ❶ gossip：不要
在背后～ don't gossip behind people's backs 他总爱说别人的闲话。He
always likes to gossip about other
people. ❷（～儿）chatter；idle
talk：晚饭后老人坐在一起～。The
old people would sit together chat-
ting after supper.

说一不二 shuō yī bù èr ❶ play the
tyrant：他父亲在家里～，没人敢反对。
He has a tyrant of a father，who
would brook no opposition at
home. ❷ mean what one says；be
true to one's word：工人们说按期完
成任务就按期完成任务，真是～。The
workers said that they would complete the task on schedule，and
they did. They certainly kept their
word.

shuò

硕（碩） shuò

硕果 shuòguǒ 【名】fruit；great
achievement

硕士 shuòshì 【名】Master

sī

司 sī 【名】department in a min-
istry

司法 sīfǎ 【名】jurisdiction

司法机关 sīfǎ jīguān judicial organ

司法权 sīfǎquán 【名】judicial powers

司机 sījī 【名】driver

司空见惯 sīkōng jiàn guàn a common occurrence；something to be
expected：夏天早晚穿棉衣，在我们山
区是～的事。In our mountainous re-
gion，it is not unusual to wear cotton-padded jackets in the mornings
and evenings even in summer.

司令 sīlìng 【名】commander

司令部 sīlìngbù 【名】headquarters

司令员 sīlìngyuán 【名】commanding
officer

司仪 sīyí 【名】master of ceremo-
nies

丝（絲） sī 【名】❶ silk ❷（～
儿）thread-like thing：血～ thread
of blood 把土豆切成细～ cut potatoes into fine shreds ❸ a tiny bit：
天气闷热，一～风也没有。The
weather is stuffy. There isn't the
slightest breath of air.

丝绸 sīchóu 【名】silks

丝绸之路 sīchóu zhī lù the Silk
Road

丝毫 sīháo 【名】slightest bit；a
shred；slightest amount：～不差
not the slightest difference 不能有
～改变。There must never be the

slightest change.

丝绵 sīmián 【名】silk floss; silk wadding

丝织品 sīzhīpǐn 【名】silks; silk fabrics

私 sī 【名】❶ self; private; personal: ~信 personal letter ❷ illicit; illegal: ~卖违禁品 illicit sale of contraband goods ~相授受 illicit exchange

私产 sīchǎn 【名】private property

私愤 sīfèn 【名】personal grudge

私货 sīhuò 【名】contraband goods; smuggled goods

私交 sījiāo 【名】personal friendship

私立 sī lì privately run; private

私利 sīlì 【名】personal gain; private interests

私了 sīliǎo 【动】settle privately

私人 sīrén 【名】personal

私生活 sīshēnghuó 【名】private life

私事 sīshì 【名】private affair

私下 sīxià 【副】❶ in private; in secret: ~议论 discuss in secret ~商量 talk things over privately ❷ (do sth.) between individuals, not officially: ~调解 settle (a matter) privately ~处理 deal with matters on one's own

私心 sīxīn 【名】personal consideration; selfish motive

私营 sī yíng privately-owned (factory, etc.)

私有 sī yǒu private ownership

私有财产 sī yǒu cáichǎn private property

私有化 sīyǒuhuà 【动】privatization; denationalization

私有制 sīyǒuzhì 【名】system of private ownership; private ownership

私自 sīzì 【副】privately; without permission; secretly (do sth. against rules and regulations): ~买卖 take it upon oneself to make

a deal ~决定 make a decision on one's own

思 sī 【动】◇ ❶ think; ponder; consider: 前~后想 weigh and consider 百~不得其解 ponder deeply over the matter, but can't understand it ❷ long for; think of: ~乡 be homesick ~亲 think of one's loved ones

思潮 sīcháo 【名】❶ trend of thought; ideological trend: 文艺~ trends of thought in the fields of art and literature 社会~ ideological trends in society ❷ ideas; thoughts: ~起伏 the ebb and flow of one's thoughts ~澎湃 a multitude thoughts surging in one's mind

思考 sīkǎo 【动】think carefully; meditate; ponder over

思量 sīliang 【动】weigh and consider

思路 sīlù 【名】train of thought

思念 sīniàn 【动】think fondly of; miss

思索 sīsuǒ 【动】ponder; think deeply: ~问题 ponder over questions 用心~ think hard about something

思维 sīwéi 【名】thought; process of thinking

思想 sīxiǎng 【名】thought; thinking

思想斗争 sīxiǎng dòuzhēng ideological struggle; mental struggle

思想家 sīxiǎngjiā 【名】thinker

思想评论 sīxiǎng pínglùn ideological review (usu. as title for newspaper column)

思想性 sīxiǎngxìng 【名】ideological level; ideological content

思绪 sīxù 【名】❶ train of thought: ~纷乱 confused thinking ~万端 have innumerable ideas ❷ feeling; mood: ~不宁 feel uneasy

斯 sī

斯文　sīwen　【形】（looks or manners）refined；gentle

厮 sī

厮杀　sīshā　【动】fight

撕 sī　【动】tear

撕毁　sīhuǐ　【动】tear to pieces；tear up

嘶 sī

嘶哑　sīyǎ　【形】hoarse

sǐ

死 sǐ　【动】die【形】❶ to the death：决一～战 fight to the death ❷ fixed；inflexible；stiff：把螺丝钉拧～ turn the screw until it's tight 脑筋太～ have an inflexible mind ～读书 be pedantic ❸ extremely；exceedingly（usu. as a complement）：笑～人 side-splitting 真把人急～了。We are really worried to death. ❹ stop up：把洞堵～ stop up the hole ～路一条 end up in a blind alley

死板　sǐbǎn　【形】❶ rigid；stiff；inflexible：动作～ stiff movements 这笔字写得太～。His handwriting is too stiff. ❷（of way of doing things）inflexible；mechanical：处理问题不能太～。We should avoid inflexibility in the management of affairs.

死不改悔　sǐ bù gǎihuǐ　would rather die than repent one's wrongs；flatly refuse to mend one's ways

死不瞑目　sǐ bù míngmù　unable to die in peace；die with a grievance unresolved or with everlasting regret over sth.

死党　sǐdǎng　【名】sworn follower；die-hard follower

死得其所　sǐ dé qí suǒ　die a worthy death：为人民的利益而死，就是～。To die for the people is a worthy death.

死敌　sǐdí　【名】deadly enemy

死对头　sǐduìtou　【名】deadly enemy；irreconcilable opponent

死胡同　sǐhútòng　【名】blind alley；impasse

死缓　sǐhuǎn　【名】death sentence with a reprieve and forced labour；stay of execution

死灰复燃　sǐ huī fù rán　dying embers flaring up again；fresh outbreak of an evil which was previously put down（derog.）

死活　sǐhuó　【名】fate；life and death：不顾别人～ not care whether others live or die【副】simply；flatly（usu. used with 不）：～不答应 would rather die than consent ～不肯去 flatly refuse to go

死记硬背　sǐ jì yìng bèi　memorize mechanically

死角　sǐjiǎo　【名】❶ blind angle ❷ a place where a political movement has had no impact

死里逃生　sǐ lǐ táo shēng　have a narrow escape；close call；escape death by a hair's breadth

死路　sǐlù　【名】blind alley；road to destruction

死难　sǐnàn　【动】die a tragic death；die for a cause

死气沉沉　sǐqì chénchén　lifeless；spiritless；dull and dreary：要搞好文娱活动，不要～的。Make a good job of recreational activities and don't let life become dull and dreary.

死去活来　sǐ qù huó lái　half dead；hovering between life and death：被打得～ be beaten within an inch of one's life 哭得～ cry as if one's heart would break

死尸 sǐshī 【名】〔具 jù〕corpse; dead body

死守 sǐshǒu 【动】hold on to the last; defend at all costs

死水 sǐshuǐ 【名】stagnant water

死亡 sǐwáng 【动】die; breathe one's last; death

死亡率 sǐwánglǜ 【名】death rate; mortality

死心 sǐ = xīn give up hope

死心塌地 sǐ xīn tā dì be dead set on; be hell-bent on (usu. used to describe die-hard reactionaries)

死心眼儿 sǐxīnyǎnr 【形】have a one-track mind

死刑 sǐxíng 【名】death penalty; capital punishment

死硬 sǐyìng 【形】very obstinate; diehard

死硬派 sǐyìngpài 【名】diehards

死有余辜 sǐ yǒu yú gū even one's death would not atone for the crime one has committed

死于非命 sǐ yú fēi mìng die a violent death

死罪 sǐzuì 【名】capital crime

SÌ

四 sì 【数】four

四边形 sìbiānxíng 【名】quadrilateral

四方 sìfāng 【名】the four directions — north, south, east, and west; all sides: 胜利歌声传～。Triumphant songs were heard everywhere. 【形】square: ～的石板 a square slate 四四方方的盒子 a square box

四分五裂 sì fēn wǔ liè be scattered and disunited; badly split

四化 sìhuà 【名】the four modernizations (of industry, agriculture, national defence, science and technology)

四季 sìjì 【名】the four seasons

四面 sìmiàn 【名】four sides; (on) all sides: ～受敌 be surrounded on all sides by the enemy 村子的～都是山。The village is surrounded by hills on all sides. 不要～出击。Don't launch simultaneous attacks on all fronts.

四面八方 sì miàn bā fāng in all directions; far and near; everywhere: 欢乐的人群从～涌向天安门广场。Huge crowds of happy people converged from all sides on Tian'anmen Square.

四面楚歌 sìmiàn Chǔ gē be hemmed in (on all sides) by enemy troops; be in dire straits; be completely isolated

四平八稳 sì píng bā wěn steady and sure; over-cautious and loath to take the smallest risk

四舍五入 sì shě wǔ rù (maths.) round (off); to the nearest whole number

四声 sìshēng 【名】the four tones of standard pronunciation of modern Chinese

四体不勤，五谷不分 sì tǐ bù qín, wǔ gǔ bù fēn can neither use one's four limbs nor tell the five grains apart

四通八达 sì tōng bā dá (of communication) extend in all directions; communication lines reaching far and wide: ～的铁路网 a rail network radiating in all directions

四月 sìyuè 【名】April

四肢 sìzhī 【名】limbs; arms and legs

四周 sìzhōu 【名】all around; round

寺 sì 【名】temple; mosque

寺庙 sìmiào 【名】a general term for temples

寺院 sìyuàn 【名】(Buddhist) temples

似 sì 【动】◇ seem；look like：～笑非笑 a faint smile 另见 shì

似乎 sìhū 【副】seemingly；as if；seems as if：我～在哪儿见过他。It seems as if I have met him somewhere. 他～没听懂我的意思。He didn't seem to have understood me.

似是而非 sì shì ér fēi specious；apparently right but actually wrong：～的论断 specious conclusions

伺 sì

伺机 sìjī 【副】await an opportunity

饲（飼）sì

饲料 sìliào 【名】animal feed；fodder

饲养 sìyǎng 【动】raise；rear

肆 sì 【数】four (the complicated form of 四) 见"捌" bā

肆无忌惮 sì wú jì dàn brazen；unscrupulous；unbridled

肆意 sìyì 【副】wantonly；wilfully：～攻击 make wanton attacks on somebody ～妄为 act recklessly ～歪曲 wilfully distort sth.

sōng

松 sōng 【名】◇ pine：～柏常青 the eternally green pine and cypress 【形】（鬆）loose (as opp. to 紧)：捆得太～ loosely tied 土质～ loose friable soil 管得太～ slack discipline 【动】（鬆）loosen；relax；slacken：～～腰带 loosen one's belt ～开手 let go one's grip (on sth. or sb.)

松弛 sōngchí 【形】❶ flabby；slack：肌肉～ relaxed muscles ❷ lax：纪律～ lax discipline

松动 sōngdòng 【动】less crowded；loose；flexible

松紧带 sōngjǐndài 【名】elastic

松劲 sōngjìn（～儿）slacken one's efforts；slack：产生～情绪 be in a sluggish mood 我们可不能～。We must not relax our efforts.

松快 sōngkuai 【形】❶ relieved ❷ relaxed

松气 sōng = qì become less tense or rigid；relax

松软 sōngruǎn 【形】soft；spongy；fluffy：刚出炉的蛋糕～可口。The freshly baked cakes are very light. 这种毛线质地～。This kind of knitting wool is of a very soft quality.

松散 sōngsǎn 【形】loose；not tight：精神～ inattentive 这篇文章结构过于～。This article is loosely organized.

松手 sōng = shǒu let go；loosen grip (on)

松鼠 sōngshǔ 【名】〔只 zhǐ〕squirrel

松树 sōngshù 【名】〔棵 kē〕pine tree

松懈 sōngxiè 【形】slack；relaxed；inattentive；desultory：纪律～ lax in discipline 工作～ work desultorily 【动】slacken；relax：决不能～斗志。We must never let our morale slacken.

松心 sōng = xīn be relieved；feel relaxed

sǒng

怂（慫）sǒng

怂恿 sǒngyǒng 【动】incite；instigate；egg sb. on (to do sth. bad)

耸（聳）sǒng 【动】◇ rise；tower：高山～入云霄。The tall peak pierced the sky.

耸立 sǒnglì 【动】rise straight up；tower

耸人听闻 sǒng rén tīng wén deliber-

ately exaggerate to cause a sensation

sòng

送　sòng　【动】❶ give away as a present; offer: ～礼品 give a gift ～朋友一本书 give a friend a book as a present ❷ send; deliver; carry: ～信 send a letter ～货 deliver goods ❸ see sb. off: ～朋友上火车 see a friend off at the railway station 把客人～出门外 see a visitor to the door

送别　sòngbié　【动】同"送行"

送货　sòng＝huò　deliver goods

送交　sòngjiāo　【动】deliver to; hand over to

送礼　sòng＝lǐ　send a gift; give a present

送命　sòng＝mìng　lose one's life; be killed

送气　sòng＝qì　aspirate

送气音　sòngqìyīn　【名】aspirated sound

送人情　sòng rénqíng　do sb. a favour to please

送审　sòngshěn　【动】send (manuscripts, report, etc.) for approval

送行　sòngxíng　【动】see sb. off

送信儿　sòng＝xìnr　deliver a message; send a word

送葬　sòng＝zàng　take part in a funeral procession

颂（頌）　sòng　【动】◇ praise; laud; extol 【名】◇ song in praise: 祖国～ song in praise of one's country

颂词　sòngcí　【名】eulogy; panegyric

颂歌　sònggē　【名】song of praise

颂古非今　sòng gǔ fēi jīn　praise the past at the expense of the present

颂扬　sòngyáng　【动】sing the praises of

sōu

搜　sōu　【动】search; ransack: ～身 frisk; make a body search 什么 也没～着。Nothing was found in the search.

搜捕　sōubǔ　【动】search and arrest

搜查　sōuchá　【动】search (by police)

搜刮　sōuguā　【动】seek out and loot (people's assets)

搜集　sōují　【动】seek out and collect (things)

搜罗　sōuluó　【动】seek out and gather up (persons or things)

搜索　sōusuǒ　【动】search; hunt for

搜寻　sōuxún　【动】search for; look for

嗖　sōu　【象声】whistle; whine: ～～ 的风声 the soughing of the wind 子弹～的一声飞过去了。A bullet whined past.

馊（餿）　sōu　【形】(of cooked food) become bad; spoiled

艘　sōu　【量】 *for ship*: 一～船 a ship 军舰两～ two warships

sū

苏（蘇）　sū

苏打　sūdá　【名】soda

苏区　Sūqū　【名】(Chinese) Soviet Area (苏 stands for 苏维埃 Soviet), the Revolutionary base areas during the second Revolutionary Civil War (1927—1937)

苏维埃　Sūwéi'āi　【名】Soviet

苏醒　sūxǐng　【动】regain consciousness; come round; revive: 伤员从昏迷中～过来了。The wounded sol-

dier has regained consciousness.

酥 sū 【形】(of the texture of cake) crumbly; melting in one's mouth

酥脆 sūcuì 【形】crisp

酥油 sūyóu 【名】butter

sú

俗 sú 【名】◇ social custom; habit; convention：陈规旧～ old habits and customs 入境问～ when one first arrives in a place, one ought to ask about local customs and ways of life 【形】❶ popular; commonly; colloquially：玉蜀黍～称棒子。Corn is commonly called *bangzi*. ❷ vulgar：～不可耐 unbearably vulgar 这只花瓶的颜色、图案都很大方，一点儿也不～。The colour and design of this vase are in very good taste and not at all vulgar.

俗话 súhuà 【名】common saying; proverb

俗名 súmíng 【名】popular name for sth.; colloquial term

俗气 súqi 【形】vulgar

俗套 sútào 【名】social conventions：不落～ not get into a rut

俗语 súyǔ 【名】同"俗话"

俗字 súzì 【名】popular written form of a character (*not accepted by academic authorities*)

sù

诉(訴) sù 【动】◇ ❶ tell; inform; relate：～委屈 pour out one's grievances ～衷情 say what is on one's mind ❷ accuse; complain：有冤无处～ have nowhere to air one's grievances

诉苦 sù = kǔ pour out grievances

诉述 sùshù 【动】relate; tell

诉说 sùshuō 【动】narrate with feeling

诉讼 sùsòng 【名】lawsuit

诉讼法 sùsòngfǎ 【名】procedural law

诉讼权利 sùsòng quánlì procedural rights

诉讼条例 sùsòng tiáolì rules of procedure

诉诸武力 sù zhū wǔlì have recourse to force; resort to force

肃(肅) sù 【动】◇ mop up; eliminate

肃静 sùjìng 【形】solemn and silent

肃立 sùlì 【动】stand solemnly; stand at attention

肃清 sùqīng 【动】mop up; eliminate

肃然 sùrán 【形】respectful：～起敬 be filled with deep respect (for sb.)

素 sù 【形】❶ white：～服 be dressed in white ❷ (of colour and design) subdued and simple：这块布太～了。The colour of this piece of cloth is too subdued. ❸ vegetable (*as opp. to* 荤)：吃～ eat vegetarian food 二荤一～一汤 two meat dishes, one vegetable dish, and one soup 【副】usually; always (*usu. in the negative*)：～不相识 be unknown to each other ～不来往 never have anything to do with each other

素材 sùcái 【名】source material

素菜 sùcài 【名】vegetarian dish

素常 sùcháng 【名】normally; usually：小张今天说话比～痛快多了。Xiao Zhang is unusually outspoken today.

素来 sùlái 【副】always：老李在同事之中～威信很高。Lao Li has always

enjoyed very high prestige among his colleagues.

素昧平生 sù mèi píngshēng be a complete stranger to; have never had a chance to meet

素描 sùmiáo 【名】❶ (painting) sketch ❷ literary sketch

素食 sùshí 【名】❶ vegetarian food; vegetarian diet ❷ be a vegetarian

素雅 sùyǎ 【形】tasteful and unadorned

素养 sùyǎng 【名】accomplishment; attainment

素质 sùzhì 【名】innate quality

速 sù

速成 sùchéng 【动】speeded-up (educational program)

速冻 sùdòng 【动】quick-freeze

速度 sùdù 【名】speed; pace

速记 sùjì 【动】take sth. down in shorthand 【名】shorthand; stenography

速溶 sùróng 【动】instant：～咖啡 instant coffee

速效 sùxiào 【形】quick results

速写 sùxiě 【名】(painting) sketch

速战速决 sù zhàn sù jué fight a quick battle to force a quick decision：这场战斗真是～，打得痛快。The battle was swiftly fought and won and gave one great satisfaction.

宿 sù

宿疾 sùjí 【名】chronic illness

宿命论 sùmìnglùn 【名】fatalism

宿舍 sùshè 【名】dormitory

宿营 sùyíng 【动】camp; encamp：今夜我们就在村外～。Tonight we will camp outside the village.

宿营地 sùyíngdì 【名】camp site

宿愿 sùyuàn 【名】long-cherished wish 也作"夙愿"。

塑 sù 【动】mould

塑料 sùliào 【名】plastics

塑料袋 sùliàodài 【名】plastic bag

塑像 sùxiàng 【名】statue

塑造 sùzào 【动】mould；(fig.) create; portray; depict：～英雄形象 depict heroic images

簌 sù

簌簌 sùsù 【象声】❶ rustling or whistling of wind：风～地响着。Leaves rustled in the wind. ❷ (of tears) trickle：眼泪～往下掉 with tears streaming down (one's face)

suān

酸 suān 【名】acid 【形】❶ sour; tart：这杏儿～极了。This apricot tastes very sour. ❷ ◇ distressed; grieved; sick at heart：心～ feel sick at heart ❸ stiff and sore; ache：腰～腿疼 have a pain in one's back and legs

酸牛奶 suānniúnǎi 【名】sour milk; yogurt

酸甜苦辣 suān tián kǔ là bittersweet experience of life; joys and sorrows of life

酸痛 suāntòng 【形】ache (usu. from fatigue)

酸味 suānwèi 【名】(～儿) acidity; tart flavour

酸性 suānxìng 【名】(chem.) acidity

suàn

蒜 suàn 【名】〔头 tóu、瓣 bànr〕garlic

蒜苗 suànmiáo 【名】tender garlic bolt

算 suàn 【动】❶ calculate; do sums：能写会～ able to read and write and good at sums 注意，你别

把账～错了。Please be careful and don't get your accounts wrong. ～一～，一共多少钱? Please add the amounts and see how much they total. ❷ include: 明天下午的义务劳动～我一个。Please include me in the voluntary labour tomorrow afternoon. 要是把这笔钱也～上，就可以买一辆汽车。If we take this sum of money into account as well, we can buy a car. ❸ 同"算数": 重大问题不能一个人说了～，要集体讨论决定。Anything important cannot be decided by one person alone, but must be decided by the collective. ❹ be considered as: 他～我们班上最好的学生。He is considered the best student in our class. 就～你说得有道理，目前也做不到。Even if what you said is right, putting it into practice is not feasible at present. 天气不～热。It can't really be called hot. 学校能办这样一个印刷厂～不错了。For a school to run a printing press like this should be considered quite an achievement. 【副】 *indicates the realization of sth. after a lengthy hard work or a long time*: 为了这本书，我跑了好几个书店，这回～买到了。In order to get hold of this book, I had to go to several bookstores, and finally managed to buy a copy. 下了半个多月的雨，这回～晴了。It rained continuously for over a fortnight and now it has cleared up at last.

算计 suànji 【动】❶ calculate; work out: ～～买这么多东西要多少钱。You should work out how much all these things will cost. ❷ consider; plan: 王大妈～着下月买一台电视机。Aunt Wang is planning to buy a TV set next month. ❸ calculate; expect: 我～他今天要来找我。I expect he will be coming to see me today. ❹ plot; scheme: 不要靠～人

过日子。Don't be scheming against others all the time.

算了 suànle 【动】forget it; drop it; leave it at that: 他不同意就～吧，不要勉强。Just drop the matter if he doesn't agree to it. Don't force him. ～，别说了，该休息了。Oh, forget it! Don't say any more about it. It's time for a break.

算命 suàn = mìng fortune-telling

算盘 suànpan 【名】abacus

算是 suànshì 【动】同"算"【动】❹: 这个商店～附近最大的了。This store is the biggest in the vicinity. 【副】同"算"【副】: 这个词的用法我～弄明白了。I have finally figured out the usage of this word.

算术 suànshù 【名】arithmetic

算术级数 suànshù jíshù arithmetic progression

算数 suàn = shù count; hold true; be taken seriously: 我们说话是～的。We mean what we say.

算账 suàn = zhàng ❶ reckon up a bill; settle accounts ❷ (*fig.*) settle accounts with; get even with: 小心，明天跟你～! Look out! I'll get even with you tomorrow.

suī

虽(雖) suī 【连】though; although

虽然 suīrán 【连】although; though (*usu. used together with* 但是 *or* 可是): 这篇杂文～很短，但是很有锐气。This essay is short but to the point. 他～在北京住了二十年了，可是家乡口音一点没变。Though he has lived in Beijing for 20 years now, he still speaks his native dialect.

虽说 suīshuō 【连】同"虽然"，*but more colloquial*: ～小王来厂的时间不长，可是技术已经很熟练了。Xiao Wang is quite skillful and experi-

enced by now though he's been in the factory for only a short time.

suí

绥（綏）suí

绥靖主义 suíjìngzhǔyì 【名】appeasement policy

随（隨）suí 【动】❶ follow；go with；accompany：～军南下 go with the army as it marched south 他曾经～文化代表团到中国来过一次。He had been in China once on a cultural delegation. ❷ do as one wants to；please oneself：去不去由你。You may go or not, as you wish.

随笔 suíbǐ 【名】short informal essay；casual literary notes

随便 suíbiàn 【形】❶ informal；random；casual：～谈谈 have a chat 跟他在一起很～，一点儿也不拘束。We feel quite free and easy with him, not in the least constrained. ❷ as one wishes；please oneself；in a slipshod way：说话很～ speak freely 对工作不能随随便便，要认真负责。Don't do your work in a slipshod manner. You should be conscientious and have a sense of responsibility. 【连】no matter；anyway (used in conjunction with an interrogative pronoun)：芭蕾舞也好，民族舞也好，～什么舞蹈她都喜欢看。She enjoys watching dancing, whether ballet, or national minority dancing or any other sort of dancing. 这种花～你种在哪儿都能活。This flowering plant will thrive and bloom wherever you plant it.

随波逐流 suí bō zhú liú be carried along by the tide；drift with the current：遇事要有主见，决不能～。One must have one's own opinions and not drift with the current.

随处 suíchù 【副】everywhere：～都有 be found everywhere. 在北京，这种杨树～可见。This kind of poplar can be seen everywhere in Beijing.

随从 suícóng 【动】accompany：～首长执行任务 accompany a leading cadre on a mission 【名】member of the entourage

随大溜 suí dàliù do as others do；follow the trend

随地 suídì 【副】anywhere；everywhere：不要～乱扔果皮纸屑。Don't scatter garbage all over the place.

随份子 suí fènzi present a gift of money on a special occasion (such as wedding, funeral, birthday)

随风倒 suí fēng dǎo be easily swayed (by whichever side has more power)

随行就市 suí háng jiù shì fluctuate with market conditions

随和 suíhe 【形】amiable；easy to get along with

随后 suíhòu 【副】(usu. used in conjunction with 就) later on；soon after：你先去，我～就到。You go first. I'll be along in a minute.

随机应变 suí jī yìng biàn do as the circumstances dictate；adjust to changed conditions：这位侦察英雄机智勇敢，善于～。This scout is brave and resourceful, able to cope with unexpected conditions as they arise.

随即 suíjí 【副】immediately；presently (usu. in written language)：那个伤员睁了一下眼睛～又昏了过去。The wounded soldier opened his eyes once, but lost consciousness again immediately. 化工厂提出增产节约的倡议，其他工厂～响应。The chemical plant proposed to increase production and practise

economy and other factories presently responded.

随叫随到 suí jiào suí dào available at all times; on call at all times：方医生不论什么时候～。Doctor Fang is on call at all times.

随口 suíkǒu 【副】 speak without thinking：刚才我～说了句开玩笑的话，你千万别介意。I just made a joke without thinking. Please don't take it to heart.

随身 suíshēn 【形】 carry on one's person：～的物品 the things which one has with one 这次出去旅行我～带的东西不多。I'm not carrying much with me on this trip.

随声附和 suí shēng fùhè parrot the opinions of others; be a yes-man：对他们的意见要加以分析，不要～。We should analyse what they said and not just agree with everything.

随时 suíshí 【副】❶ any time（when it is necessary）：你有问题，～可以来问我。If you have any questions, come and ask me at any time. 他们总是～总结经验，所以工作质量提高很快。They sum up their work experience from time to time, and are making rapid improvements. ❷ any time（referring to the timing of an action or event）：连下几天大雨，～有暴发山洪的危险，要做好准备。It has been raining heavily in the last few days and mountain torrents may become a danger at any moment. We must be prepared. 机器应该～注意维护。Machinery ought to be well maintained all the time.

随时随地 suíshí suídì at all times and all places; anytime and anywhere：在参观访问过程中，我们～都能学到很多东西。In the course of our trip, we have learned a great deal in all the places we visited.

随手 suíshǒu 【副】 handy; convenient：出门时请～关灯。Please switch off the lights when you leave.

随俗 suísú 【动】 go native; follow the local customs：入乡～ do as the local people do

随同 suítóng 【动】 accompany：小王～代表团出国访问去了。Xiao Wang has gone to accompany a delegation on a visit abroad.

随心所欲 suí xīn suǒ yù do as one pleases; do as one's heart desires

随行人员 suíxíng rényuán entourage

随意 suíyì 【副】 as one pleases; at one's convenience; at will（usu. as adverbial adjunct）：～挑选商品 choose freely from among the goods

随员 suíyuán 【名】❶ entourage; suite ❷（diplomatic）attaché

随着 suízhe 【介】 in the wake of; along with：～科学技术的发展，人们征服自然的能力也越来越强了。In the wake of developments in science and technology, man has become more capable of conquering nature. 根据一种学说，语言是～社会的产生而产生，～社会的发展而发展的。According to a certain theory, language emerges and develops with the emergence and development of society.【副】 accordingly：经济发展了，人们的生活也一改善了。As economy developed, the living conditions of the people improved accordingly.

suì

岁（歲） suì 【名】◇ year：～末 the end of the year 辞旧～，迎新春 bid farewell to the old year and usher in the new 【量】 for age：孩子几～了? ——三～了。How old is the child? — Three years old.

岁数　suìshu　【名】〈口〉age；years (*usu. applies to old people*)：～不小了 getting on in years 您多大～了？How old are you？

岁月　suìyuè　【名】years；time and seasons：艰苦～ hard times 漫长的～ a long time

遂　suì　【动】◇ fulfil；satisfy

遂心　suì = xīn　be as one wishes；satisfy one's desire；after one's own heart：～如意 be highly satisfied 这几件事办得太不遂他的心了。He was far from being satisfied with the way the things were handled.

遂愿　suì = yuàn　have one's wish fulfilled

碎　suì　【形】❶ broken；smashed to pieces：玻璃～了。The glass was smashed to pieces. ❷ fragmentary：～布 small scraps of cloth ～石子儿 crushed gravel

隧　suì

隧道　suìdào　【名】〔条 tiáo〕tunnel；underground passage

穗　suì　【名】(～儿) ears of grain：谷～ ears of millet 稻～ ears of rice

sūn

孙(孫)　sūn　【名】grandson；son of one's son

孙女　sūnnǚ　【名】grand-daughter (daughter of one's son)

孙子　sūnzi　【名】grandson (son of one's son)

sǔn

损(損)　sǔn　【动】damage；harm；impair：这种行为有～于集体的荣誉。This sort of activity damages the reputation of the collective.

损公肥私　sǔn gōng féi sī　seek private gain at public expense；feather one's nest at public expense

损害　sǔnhài　【动】harm；injure；damage；impair：～别人利益的事绝对不干 never do anything to harm the interests of others 在汽车上看书容易～眼睛。Reading while riding in a car is injurious to one's eyes.

损耗　sǔnhào　【动】wear out；lose：～燃料 use up fuel 【名】loss；wastage；spoilage：～不大 small wastage 减少～ reduce the wastage

损坏　sǔnhuài　【动】damage；injure；break

损人利己　sǔn rén lì jǐ　seek one's own advantage at the expense of others；harm others to benefit oneself

损伤　sǔnshāng　【动】❶ hurt；injure；damage：不要～大家的积极性。Don't dampen the enthusiasm of the masses. 这场大病～了他的体力。This severe bout of illness has done serious damage to his health. ❷ cause loss to：～兵力 reduce military strength

损失　sǔnshī　【动】lose；suffer loss：～了三架飞机。Three planes were lost. 【名】loss：巨大的～ great losses 挽回～ retrieve a loss

笋　sǔn　【名】bamboo shoot

suō

唆　suō

唆使　suōshǐ　【动】incite；instigate；egg sb. on (to do sth.)

缩(縮)

缩(縮) suō 【动】❶ shrink; contract：热胀冷～ expand with heat and contract with cold 这件衣服洗过以后～了一点。This jacket shrunk a bit after washing. ❷ draw back：刚一露头又～了回去。He put in an appearance and then withdrew again.

缩短 suōduǎn 【动】shorten; cut down; curtail：～篇幅 cut down the number of pages ～距离 narrow the distance ～时间 shorten the time

缩减 suōjiǎn 【动】reduce; cut：～开支 reduce spending ～机构 trim inefficient units and get rid of unnecessary ones

缩手缩脚 suō shǒu suō jiǎo be overcautious：工作你尽管大胆去干，别～的。Be bold in doing your work and don't be overcautious.

缩水 suō = shuǐ （of cloth) shrink through wetting

缩微 suōwēi 【形】microform

缩微技术 suōwēi jìshù microphotography

缩微照片 suōwēi zhàopiàn microfilm; microphotograph

缩小 suōxiǎo 【动】reduce; narrow：～范围 reduce the scope ～差别 reduce the differences

缩写 suōxiě 【名】abbreviation 【动】(of literary work) abridge; shorten

缩影 suōyǐng 【名】miniature; a microcosm：这部历史小说是走向崩溃的封建社会的～。This historical novel illustrates the breaking up of feudal society in a nutshell.

suǒ

所 suǒ 【名】institute：他在物理研究～工作。He works in a physics research institute. 他们～做出了很大成绩。Their institute has made considerable achievements. 【量】 for buildings：一～房子 a house 两～学校 two schools 一～医院 a hospital 【助】❶ used before a verb or a V-C construction together with 被 or 为 (wéi) to indicate the passive voice：为广大群众～欢迎 be welcomed by the masses 不要被表面现象～迷惑。Don't be misled by superficial phenomena. ❷ used before a verb plus 的 to form a nominal phrase：你～看到的是一些片面的情况。What you've seen is just one aspect of things. 他～考虑的我们都没想到。We've never thought of what he has been considering.

所得税 suǒdéshuì 【名】income tax

所属 suǒshǔ 【形】❶ subordinate to one or under one's command：～部队 army units under one's command 国务院～各部委 the ministries and commissions under the State Council 命令～立即行动 order the subordinate (troops) to act immediately ❷ subordinate to or is affiliated with：向～领导机关汇报工作 report to the organization one belongs to

所谓 suǒwèi 【形】so-called ❶ introduces the word or phrase the speaker wants to explain：所谓"公仆"，是指干部要全心全意为人民服务。By "public servant" we mean cadre who serves the people wholeheartedly. ❷ indicates that the speaker disapproves of the idea expressed by the word modified by 所谓：他的那种～批评，实际上就是给人扣帽子。His so-called criticism is in fact just putting labels on people.

所向披靡 suǒ xiàng pīmǐ overcome all obstacles

所向无敌 suǒ·xiàng wú dí all-conquering; be invincible

所以　suǒyǐ　【连】so；therefore ❶ *used at the beginning of the second clause*：由于忙，～我一直没给他回信。I was busy so I didn't answer his letter. 因为他干活儿很仔细，～连续六年不出废品。Because he works very carefully, he has not produced a reject in the last six years. 他年纪大了，～眼睛有点儿花。He is old so his vision is dim. ❷ *used in the first clause of a sentence to stress the reason；must be placed after the subject*：我们～能够取得胜利，主要是因为有正确理论的指导。The reason for our success was that we were guided by a correct theory. ❸ *the structure* "…是…所以…的原因" *is another way of stressing the reason*：正确理论的指导，是我们～取得胜利的主要原因。The fact that we were guided by a correct theory was the main reason for our success.

所以然　suǒyǐrán　【名】the whys and wherefores：知其然而不知其～ know what happened, but not the whys and wherefores .

所有　suǒyǒu　【动】possess；own：全民～ owned by the whole people 集体～ owned by the collective 【形】all；whole：～的材料备齐了。All the materials have been prepared. ～的问题都解决了。All the problems have been solved.

所有权　suǒyǒuquán　【名】ownership

所有制　suǒyǒuzhì　【名】ownership

所在　suǒzài　【动】❶ belong：～地区 the place where one belongs 由～单位开证明。Have your organisation issue you an identifying paper. ❷ the place concerned；症结～ the crux of the problem 问题～ the crux of the problem

所在地　suǒzàidì　【名】seat；location；site：北京是中华人民共和国政府～。Beijing is the seat of the national government of the People's Republic of China.

所作所为　suǒ zuò suǒ wéi　all one's actions；one's deeds；what one does；从他的～，可以看出他比较自私。He is rather selfish, judging by his actions.

索　suǒ

索贿　suǒ＝huì　demand a bribe

索价　suǒ＝jià　ask（or demand）a price；charge

索赔　suǒpéi　【动】demand compensation

索取　suǒqǔ　【动】ask for；demand；extort（*usu. in written language*）：～资料 ask for materials ～财物 extort money and goods

索性　suǒxìng　【副】同"干脆" gāncuì【副】

索引　suǒyǐn　【名】index

琐（瑣）　suǒ

琐事　suǒshì　【名】trifles；trivial matters：生活～ the trivialities of daily life 身边～ chores requiring attention

琐碎　suǒsuì　【形】trifling；trivial；对某些男人来说，家务事很～。To some men, housework is trivial and bothersome.

琐细　suǒxì　【形】trifling；trivial；这工作很～，要做好并不容易。This work involves a mass of detail and is not easy to do well.

锁（鎖）　suǒ　【名】〔把 bǎ〕lock：门上挂着一把～。The door is fastened with a lock. 【动】❶ lock：～门 lock the door 把箱子～上 lock up the chest ❷ do a lock-stitch；～边 lock-stitch a border ～眼儿 lock-stitch a buttonhole

锁链　suǒliàn　【名】〔条 tiáo〕chains；fetters；shackles：砸碎铁～ smash one's fetters

T

tā

他 tā【代】❶ he（*when the sex of the person is unknown or not important*，"他"*may mean either "he" or "she"*）❷◇ other；anothér：留作～用. It is reserved for other purpose.

他们 tāmen【代】they

他人 tārén【代】〈书〉another；other persons；others：关心～比关心自己为重 be more concerned for others than for oneself 在场的只有我们两个,没有～。There was no one else there but the two of us.

他杀 tāshā【动】homicide

他乡 tāxiāng【名】places other than one's native place

它 tā【代】it

它们 tāmen【代】they（neuter）

她 tā【代】she

她们 tāmen【代】they

塌 tā【动】❶ cave in；fall in；collapse：房～了. The house caved in. 桥～了。The bridge collapsed. ❷ sink；subside：～鼻子 a flat nose 路基～下去一段。One section of the road has subsided.

塌方 tā=fāng　landslide

塌陷 tāxiàn【动】cave in；fall in；give way（under pressure）

踏 tā
另见 tà

踏实 tāshi【形】❶ steady and sure；on a firm footing；not perfunctory：学习～ be very thorough in one's studies 他工作总是踏踏实实（tātashīshī）的。He is a steady and thorough worker. ❷（of mood, state of mind, etc.）at ease；free from worry：心里～ feel at ease

tǎ

塔 tǎ【名】〔座 zuò〕pagoda

塔吊 tǎdiào【名】tower crane

塔楼 tǎlóu【名】❶ tower ❷ turret

tà

拓 tà【动】make rubbings from inscriptions, pictures, etc. on bronze or stone
另见 tuò

踏 tà【动】step on；set one's foot on；tread：脚～两只船 straddle two boats；（*fig.*）sit on the fence 一～上辽阔的草原,就看到成群的牛羊。As soon as you set foot on the grassland, you begin to see large herds of cattle and flocks of

sheep.

另见 tā

踏步 tàbù 【动】mark time

tāi

胎 tāi 【名】❶ embryo; foetus ❷ wadding: 棉～ cotton padding 【量】birth: 她生过两～。She has given birth twice before. 母猪一～生了十二只小猪。The pig gave birth to twelve piglets in one litter.

胎儿 tāi'ér 【名】embryo

胎生 tāishēng 【名】viviparity

tái

台 tái 【名】❶（檯）◇ table: 球～ billiard-table; ping-pong table ❷（臺）stage; platform: 上～表演 give a performance on stage 【量】（臺）for machines, etc.: 一～机器 a machine 两～拖拉机 two tractors

台笔 táibǐ 【名】〔枝 zhī〕desk pen

台布 táibù 【名】tablecloth

台词 táicí 【名】actor's lines

台灯 táidēng 【名】〔盏 zhǎn〕table lamp

台风 táifēng 【名】typhoon

台阶 táijiē 【名】❶ steps; flight of stairs ❷ an opportunity (to extricate oneself from a predicament): 看他那狼狈样儿,给他个～下吧! How embarrassed he looks! Let's give him a chance to get himself out of this fix!

台历 táilì 【名】desk calendar

台球 táiqiú 【名】❶ billiards ❷ billiard ball

台子 táizi 【名】table

抬 tái 【动】❶ lift up; raise: ～头 raise one's head ～高物价 raise the price 别把他～得那么高。Don't

praise him so highly. ❷（of several persons）carry: ～担架 carry a stretcher

抬高 táigāo 【动】raise; heighten; enhance

抬价 tái=jià raise the price

抬举 táiju 【动】praise or promote sb. to show favour towards him: 不识～ fail to appreciate someone's favour (in offering a promotion)

tài

太 tài 【副】❶ too; excessively: 天～热了。It's too hot. 这件衣服～瘦了,我不能穿。This jacket is too small. It doesn't fit me. ❷ extremely: 这个电影～好了! The film was excellent! 这种说法～成问题了。This view doesn't hold at all. ❸ very（used after 不）:这座山不～高,我们都能爬上去。This mountain is not very high. We can all climb to the top. 去年冬天不～冷,我一直没穿大衣。It wasn't very cold last winter; I didn't wear my winter coat at all. Note: 太 may indicate a partly concealed disapproval: 小刘的病刚好,就去干这么重的活儿,我看不～合适。Xiao Liu has just recovered from an illness. I don't think it a good idea for him to do such heavy work. 他设计了一种插秧机,但是不～满意,还要改进。He designed a rice transplanter, but it isn't very satisfactory and needs to be improved.

太古 tàigǔ 【名】remote antiquity; very distant past

太后 tàihòu 【名】mother of an emperor

太极拳 tàijíquán 【名】t'ai chi ch'uan (a kind of Chinese shadow boxing)

太监 tàijiàn 【名】eunuch

太空　tàikōng　【名】outer space

太平　tàipíng　【形】having good social order and without war

太平间　tàipíngjiān　【名】mortuary

太平门　tàipíngmén　【名】emergency exit; exit

太平天国运动　Tàipíng Tiānguó Yùndòng　the Taiping Revolutionary Movement (1851-1864) — the biggest peasants' revolutionary movement against imperialism and feudalism in Chinese history

太平洋　Tàipíngyáng　【名】Pacific Ocean

太太　tàitai　【名】madame; Mrs.; madam

太阳　tàiyáng　【名】the sun

太阳能　tàiyángnéng　【名】solar energy

太阳系　tàiyángxì　【名】solar system

太阳穴　tàiyángxué　【名】the temples

态(態)　tài

态度　tàidu　【名】❶ manner; behaviour: ~自然 behave naturally ❷ attitude; approach: ~坚决 have a firm attitude towards sth. 端正学习~ improve one's attitude towards one's studies

态势　tàishì　【名】state; situation

泰　tài

泰然　tàirán　【形】calm; composed; poised: ~自若 be calm; be poised 处之~ take sth. calmly

tān

坍　tān　【动】collapse

坍塌　tāntā　【动】collapse; crumble; fall down

贪(貪)　tān　【动】❶ be greedy for; covet: ~便宜 seek petty advantage ❷ be insatiably greedy; covet: ~睡 like to sleep; hate to get up ~多嚼不烂 bite off more than one can chew

贪财　tān = cái　be greedy for money; be a money-grabber

贪得无厌　tān dé wú yàn　avaricious; insatiably greedy

贪官污吏　tān guān wū lì　corrupt officials

贪婪　tānlán　【形】〈书〉voracious; rapacious; covetous

贪生怕死　tān shēng pà sǐ　display cowardice when faced with death

贪天之功　tān tiān zhī gōng　take credit oneself for the meritorious actions of others

贪图　tāntú　【动】desire; long for: ~方便 choose the easy way ~享受 seek pleasure and comfort 青年不能~安逸, 应当刻苦学习。Young people should not seek a life of ease but should study hard.

贪玩　tānwánr　【动】indulge in playing

贪污　tānwū　【动】embezzle

贪心　tānxīn　【名】greed; avarice 【形】greedy; avaricious

摊(攤)　tān　【动】❶ spread out; display; unfold: 把粮食~开晒晒。Spread out the grain and let it dry in the sun. 书本~了一桌子。The desk was strewn with books. ❷ a method of cooking: ~鸡蛋 make an omelet ❸ share out (cost; expenses, etc.); distribute: 每人~三元钱。Each person's share is 3 yuan.【名】(~儿)booth; stall; 杂货~儿 stall selling odds and ends【量】for water, blood, etc. pool: 一~血 a pool of blood

摊贩　tānfàn　【名】stall keeper

摊牌　tān = pái　put one's cards on the table; show one's hand; have a showdown

摊派　tānpài　【动】apportion

摊子　tānzi　【名】booth; stall

瘫（癱）

tān　【动】paralyze；偏～ partially paralyzed　吓～了 be paralyzed with fear

瘫痪　tānhuàn　【动】paralyze；四肢～ suffer paralysis of all four limbs　机构～。The organ has become paralyzed.　交通～。Transportation is paralyzed.

tán

坛

tán　【名】◇ ❶（壇）altar; platform ❷（罎）earthenware jar

坛坛罐罐　tán tán guàn guàn　pots and pans; household utensils

坛子　tánzi　【名】〔个 gè〕earthenware jar

昙（曇）

tán

昙花一现　tánhuā yī xiàn　vanish as soon as it appears; a flash in the pan；～的人物 a transient figure

谈（談）

tán　【动】talk

谈话　tán = huà　talk; converse

谈恋爱　tán liàn'ài　be in love; court

谈论　tánlùn　【动】discuss; talk about

谈判　tánpàn　【动】negotiate【名】negotiation

谈天　tán = tiān　（～儿）have a chat

谈笑风生　tán xiào fēng shēng　talk wittily and cheerfully

谈心　tán = xīn　have a heart-to-heart talk

弹（彈）

tán　【动】❶ bounce; rebound; spring；篮球从篮板上～回来。The basketball rebounded from the backboard. ❷ fluff：～棉花 fluff cotton ❸ flick：～烟灰 flick the ashes from one's cigarette ❹（of stringed instruments）pluck; play：～钢琴 play the piano　～竖琴 play the harp

另见 dàn

弹劾　tánhé　【动】impeach

弹簧　tánhuáng　【名】spring

弹力　tánlì　【名】elasticity

弹性　tánxìng　【名】elasticity

弹性限度　tánxìng xiàndù　limit of elasticity

痰

tán　【名】phlegm; sputum

痰盂　tányú　【名】〔个 gè〕spittoon

潭

tán　【名】pool; pond

檀

tán

檀香　tánxiāng　【名】sandal wood

tǎn

忐

tǎn

忐忑　tǎntè　【形】perturbed; mentally disturbed：～不安 feel ill at ease

坦

tǎn

坦白　tǎnbái　【形】frank; outspoken; open-minded and straightforward；心地～ be frank and straightforward【动】（of crimes, mistakes, etc.）make a clean breast of; confess：～认罪 make a clean breast of one's guilt

坦克　tǎnkè　【名】〔辆 liàng〕(mil.) tank

坦然　tǎnrán　【形】calm; at ease (because one has nothing to hide)

坦率　tǎnshuài　【形】open and straightforward; frank; outspoken

祖

tǎn

祖护　tǎnhù　【动】be partial to; protect sb. from blame：～一方 be partial to one side　对他的错误不能～。We must not attempt to justify his misdeed.

毯　tǎn　【名】◇ blanket；rug：线～ cotton blanket 毛～ woolen blanket

毯子　tǎnzi　【名】blanket；rug

tàn

叹（嘆）　tàn　【动】sigh：～一口气 heave a sigh 长吁短～ sighs and groans

叹词　tàncí　【名】(gram.) interjection

叹气　tàn=qì　sigh

叹息　tànxī　【动】sigh

炭　tàn　【名】charcoal

探　tàn　【动】❶ look for；explore；probe：～矿 prospect for a mine ～～他的口气 sound him out on a question ～河水的深浅 take sounding of the river ❷ ◇（of friends, relatives, etc.）visit；pay a call ❸ lean forward：～头～脑 poke one's head to take a look 把头～出窗外 lean out of the window

探测　tàncè　【动】explore；prospect；survey：高空～ the exploration of upper air ～森林分布情况 survey the distribution of wooded areas

探亲　tàn=qīn　make a journey to visit one's immediate relatives

探视　tànshì　【动】visit（person）：～病人 visit a sick person

探索　tànsuǒ　【动】seek for；probe：～真理 seek for truth 自古以来，人们就～着天体的起源和变化。Since ancient times, people have sought to understand the origin and change of the celestial bodies.

探讨　tàntǎo　【动】probe into；investigate：这个问题值得～。This problem is worth investigating.

探听　tàntīng　【动】try to find out；make inquiries；pry

探望　tànwàng　【动】❶ look around：他走到门口向外～。He went to the door and looked out. ❷ visit；pay a call；see：～老朋友 visit an old friend

探问　tànwèn　【动】inquire about

探险　tàn=xiǎn　explore

探询　tànxún　【动】make inquiries about

探照灯　tànzhàodēng　【名】searchlight

碳　tàn　【名】carbon

碳水化合物　tànshuǐhuàhéwù　carbonhydrate

碳酸　tànsuān　【名】carbonic acid

tāng

汤（湯）　tāng　【名】❶ soup；broth：白菜～ cabbage soup 清～ clear soup ❷ water in which sth. has been boiled：米～ water in which rice has been boiled 饺子～ water in which damplings have been boiled

汤匙　tāngchí　【名】soup spoon

汤药　tāngyào　【名】medicinal broth

汤圆　tāngyuán　【名】(usu. stuffed) dumplings made of glutinous rice flour served in soup

蹚　tāng　【动】wade：～水过河 wade through a river

táng

堂　táng　【名】◇ ❶ hall；main hall of a building；main room：大会～ large meeting hall 纪念～ a memorial hall ❷ the relationship of being cousins on the father's side：～妹 female cousin（on the

father's side) 【量】 *for classes*：一～课 one class

堂皇 tánghuáng 【形】 majestic；magnificent；stately：富丽～ grand and majestic

堂堂 tángtáng 【形】 dignified；impressive；仪表～ handsome and dignified ～男子 a manly man

搪 táng 【动】❶ ward off；keep out（wind，rain，cold，etc.）：皮袄～寒。A fur coat can keep out the cold. ❷ spread；apply（clay，paint，etc.）：～炉子 line a stove with clay

搪瓷 tángcí 【名】enamel

搪塞 tángsè 【动】do sth. perfunctorily；be evasive with sb.；stall：他无言回答,只得支支吾吾～过去。He found himself without anything to say and had to stall.

糖 táng 【名】❶ sugar ❷ sweets；candy

糖果 tángguǒ 【名】sweets；candy
糖精 tángjīng 【名】saccharin
糖尿病 tángniàobìng 【名】diabetes
糖衣炮弹 tángyī pàodàn "sugar-coated bullets"；(*fig.*) covert attempts at corrupting

螳 táng

螳臂当车 táng bì dāng chē a mantis tries to stop a carriage with its legs；(*fig.*) overestimate one's strength；overreach oneself

螳螂 tángláng 【名】〔只 zhǐ〕mantis

tǎng

倘 tǎng 【连】〈书〉同"如果" rúguǒ

倘若 tǎngruò 【连】同"如果" rúguǒ （ *usu. in written language* ）
倘使 tǎngshǐ 【连】同"倘若"

躺 tǎng 【动】lie；recline
躺椅 tǎngyǐ 【名】〔把 bǎ〕deck chair

tàng

烫（燙） tàng 【动】❶ scald：小心～手! Watch out and don't scald your hands! ❷ apply heat：～衣服 iron clothes ～头发 have a permanent wave 【形】hot；scalding：水太～了,凉凉（liàngliàng）再喝。The water is too hot to drink. Let's wait until it is cooler.

烫发 tàng＝fà have a perm
烫伤 tàngshāng 【名】（med.）scald

趟 tàng 【量】 *for trip*：我今年到兰州去了两～。I have made two trips to Lanzhou this year. 我们俩坐的是同一～车。We both took the same train.

tāo

掏 tāo 【动】❶ take out；draw out；fish out：从衣袋里～出一支钢笔 take a pen out of one's pocket ❷ dig；pick：在墙上～个洞 make a hole in the wall

掏腰包 tāo yāobāo ❶ pay out of one's own pocket；foot a bill ❷ pick sb.'s pocket

滔 tāo

滔滔 tāotāo 【形】❶（of river）rolling；surging：江水～向东流。The river rushes eastward. ❷（of talk，speech，etc.）keep up a constant flow of words：他～不绝地讲了两个小时。He spoke for two hours without stopping.

滔天 tāotiān 【形】❶（of waves）rolling；billowing：白浪～ white-

crested waves surging and billowing sky-high ❷ (of crimes) towering；heinous；monstrous：罪恶～ towering crimes ～大罪 monstrous crimes

táo

逃 táo 【动】❶ flee；escape；run away：～出敌占区 flee the area occupied by the enemy ❷ escape；evade；shirk：～学 play truant

逃避 táobì 【动】evade；shirk（duty）；avoid：～困难 avoid difficulties ～现实 escape reality；escapism

逃兵 táobīng 【名】deserter

逃窜 táocuàn 【动】flee；run away：敌舰仓皇～。The enemy fleet dispersed in utter disorder.

逃犯 táofàn 【名】escaped convict

逃荒 táo＝huāng flee from a famine-stricken area

逃命 táo＝mìng run for one's life

逃难 táo＝nàn flee from any disaster（esp. war）

逃跑 táopǎo 【动】❶ run away；flee ❷ desert

逃生 táoshēng 【动】escape with one's life；flee for one's life

逃税 táo＝shuì evade（or dodge）a tax

逃脱 táotuō 【动】escape；run away；extricate oneself from：～虎口 escape from the tiger's mouth；have a narrow escape ～罪责 evade responsibility for some crime

逃亡 táowáng 【动】seek safety in flight；flee from one's home or country

逃学 táo＝xué run away from school；play truant

逃之夭夭 táo zhī yāo yāo make a get-away；escape；get off scot-free

逃走 táozǒu 【动】flee；run away

桃 táo 【名】◇ peach

桃花 táohuā 【名】〔朵 duǒ〕peach blossom

桃子 táozi 【名】〔个 gè〕peach

陶 táo

陶瓷 táocí 【名】pottery and porcelain

陶器 táoqì 【名】pottery；earthenware

陶冶 táoyě 【动】gradually exert a good influence（over sb.）；mould（usu. in written language）：～性格 mould one's character 他从小就受到文学艺术的～。He has been brought up under the influence of literature and arts.

陶俑 táoyǒng 【名】pottery figurine

陶醉 táozuì 【动】become intoxicated by（success, etc.）：自我～ be infatuated with oneself

淘 táo 【动】❶ rinse out；wash；clean with water：～米 wash rice．～金 pan for gold 大浪～沙。Great waves wash away gravel. ❷ clean out（well）；dredge：～井 clean out a well 把缸里的水～干 empty water from a crock

淘气 táoqì 【形】naughty；mischievous

淘汰 táotài 【动】eliminate through selection；sift out

tǎo

讨（討） tǎo 【动】❶ take punitive action against；launch a punitive campaign against ❷ demand；ask for；try to get：～债 demand payment of a debt ❸ incur；invite：自～苦吃 ask for trouble ～了个没趣 ask for a rebuff 这孩子挺～人喜欢。She is a child whom eve-

rybody likes.

讨伐 tǎofá 【动】(in old China) send troops to suppress (e.g. a local prince)

讨饭 tǎo=fàn　go begging

讨好 tǎohǎo 【动】❶ curry favour with; ingratiate oneself with: ～别人 curry favour with somebody ❷ get or obtain good results (usu. in the negative): 费力不～ do a thankless job

讨价还价 tǎo jià huán jià haggle; bargain

讨教 tǎojiào 【动】seek advice from; consult

讨论 tǎolùn 【动】discuss; talk over

讨嫌 tǎo=xián disgusting; detestable: 令人～ disgusting 太～! What a nuisance! 也说"讨人嫌"。

讨厌 tǎoyàn 【动】loathe; be sick of: 我们～虚伪的人。We loathe hypocrites. 夸夸其谈的作风叫人～。We are sick of empty talk. 【形】annoying; disgusting; loathsome: 苍蝇这种东西～极了。Flies are disgusting.

讨债 tǎo=zhài demand the payment of a debt

tào

套 tào 【名】❶ (～儿) cover: 给皮箱做个～ make a cover for the suitcase ❷ harness: 给牛带上～ harness an ox 【动】❶ cover: 他在棉袄外面～了件制服。He wears a jacket over his cotton-padded coat. ❷ harness; hitch: ～牲口 harness an animal ～车 hitch an animal to a cart ❸ apply; use: ～公式 apply a formula ❹ trick (into talking); draw out (the truth): 想法儿～他的话 try to draw him out and get the truth ❺ put sth. inside sth. bigger; envelop: 大盒子～小盒子 put the small box inside the bigger one 【量】(for furniture, rooms) set; suite: 一～家具 a suite of furniture 一～房间 a suite of rooms 一～办法 a set of methods 一～餐具 a dinner service

套餐 tàocān 【名】table d'hote; set meal

套购 tàogòu 【动】buy up illegally

套汇 tào=huì ❶ buy foreign exchange by illegal means ❷ engage in arbitrage; arbitrage

套语 tàoyǔ 【名】polite formula

套种 tàozhòng 【动】intercrop

套子 tàozi 【名】case; cover; sheath

tè

特 tè 【形】◇ special; exceptional: ～价出售 sell at a special (i.e. low) price ～号工作服 extra-large size overalls 【副】〈口〉specially; especially; particularly: 他的工作能力～强。He is an exceptionally capable man. 护士对病人照顾得～周到。The nurse takes especially good care of her patients. 【名】◇ secret agents; enemy agents; spies: 反～ combat enemy agents 防～ guard against secret agents

特别 tèbié 【形】special; exceptional; extraordinary: ～的景色 an extraordinary sight ～的风味 an unusual flavour 【副】❶ extraordinarily; extremely; particularly: 他跑得～快。He runs extremely fast. ❷ specially; deliberately; on purpose: 临上车时,我～嘱咐了他几句。Just before getting on the train, I made a point of giving him some last minute advice. ❸ especially; particularly; in particular: 在抢险中,大家都很勇敢,～是小王表现更为突出。Everybody was very brave in the dangerous emergency rescue

work, Xiao Wang in particular.

特产 tèchǎn 【名】produce peculiar to a particular place or country

特长 tècháng 【名】speciality; special aptitude; strong point

特出 tèchū 【形】outstanding; prominent

特等 tèděng 【形】special class; top class (*attrib. only*)

特地 tèdì 【副】especially; purposely; on purpose: 怕你不知道,～来告诉你一声。I was afraid that you might not know, so I've come especially to tell you.

特点 tèdiǎn 【名】distinguishing characteristic; special feature

特定 tèdìng 【形】❶ particularly assigned; specially designated: ～的人选 persons specially assigned to a particular job ～的符号 sign or mark which has a particular designation ❷ specified: ～的语言环境 a given context ～的历史条件 given historical conditions

特级 tèjí 【形】special grade; superfine (*attrib. only*)

特技 tèjì 【名】❶ stunt; trick ❷ (movie) special effects

特价 tèjià 【形】special offer; bargain price

特刊 tèkān 【名】(of paper or periodical) special issue

特命全权大使 tèmìng quánquán dàshǐ ambassador extraordinary and plenipotentiary

特派员 tèpàiyuán 【名】specially appointed envoy

特区 tèqū 【名】special zone: 经济～ special economic zone

特权 tèquán 【名】privilege; special right

特色 tèsè 【名】distinctive feature

特赦 tèshè 【动】pardon by special decree; amnesty

特使 tèshǐ 【名】special envoy

特殊 tèshū 【形】special; particular;

out of ordinary: ～情况 special case; special circumstances ～任务 special task 人人都要遵守交通规则,谁也不能～。Everyone must observe traffic regulations. There are no exceptions.

特殊化 tèshūhuà 【动】be different from others by appropriating special privileges to oneself (*derog.*)

特殊性 tèshūxìng 【名】particularity; specific characteristic

特务 tèwù 【名】secret agent; spy

特效 tèxiào 【名】curative effect for a particular disease

特写 tèxiě 【名】❶〔篇 piān〕feature article; feature ❷ (movie) close-up

特性 tèxìng 【名】special characteristic

特邀 tèyāo 【动】specially invite

特意 tèyì 【副】specially; for a special purpose

特约 tèyuē 【动】specially invite or appoint; by special invitation or appointment

特征 tèzhēng 【名】specific feature; distinguishing characteristic

特种 tèzhǒng 【形】special type (*attrib. only*): ～邮票 special stamp

téng

疼 téng 【动】❶ be painful; ache: 头～ have a headache ❷ love dearly; love ardently: 张大娘最～小儿子。Aunt Zhang loves her youngest son best.

疼爱 téng'ài 【动】love (of a grown-up for a child)

疼痛 téngtòng 【形】painful

腾（騰） téng 【动】make room; vacate; clear out: ～地方 make room ～出时间 find time ～不出手来 be unable to finish the work

on hand (so one can't do sth. else)

腾飞　téngfēi　【动】rise; soar

腾空　téngkōng　【动】soar to the skies

腾腾　téngténg　【形】steaming; seething: 热气～ steaming hot 烟雾～ hazy with smoke 杀气～ murderous look

誊（謄）téng　【动】make a fair copy; copy

誊清　téngqīng　【动】make a fair copy; copy out

誊写　téngxiě　【动】copy out

tī

剔　tī　【动】❶ cut meat off a bone ❷ pick: ～牙 pick one's teeth ❸ sort out; pick out and discard: 把子粒不饱满的玉米～出去 pick out and discard the undeveloped grains of maize

剔除　tīchú　【动】reject

梯　tī　【名】◇ ladder: 绳～ rope ladder

梯田　tītián　【名】terraced fields

梯形　tīxíng　【名】trapezoid; trapezium

梯子　tīzi　【名】ladder

踢　tī　【动】kick: ～足球 play football ～了他一脚 kick him

踢皮球　tī píqiú　kick the ball; pass the buck

tí

提　tí　【动】❶ carry (with the arm down): ～手提包 carry a handbag ～着水壶 carry a kettle ❷ raise; lift up: 从井里～水 draw water from a well ❸ refresh oneself;

stimulate (one's mind): 喝咖啡可以～神。Coffee is a stimulant. ❹ promote (in rank or position); advance to a higher position: 他被～到领导岗位。He has been promoted to a leading position. ❺ propose; put forward; suggest; recommend: 我～老王当组长。I propose that Lao Wang be group leader. ❻ do sth. ahead of schedule; advance to an earlier date: 下午的课～到上午上。The classes were moved forward from the afternoon to the morning. ❼ put forward: ～意见 put forward one's views ～问题 raise some questions ❽ take out; extract; withdraw (money): ～款 withdraw money ～货 take delivery of goods ❾ mention; refer to; talk about: 旧事重～ bring up an old matter again ～起老田，人人称赞。Whenever Lao Tian is mentioned, everyone has a few words of praise for him. 【名】(of Chinese characters) starting stroke upward "㇀" 也叫"挑" tiāo。

另见 dī

提案　tí'àn　【名】motion; proposal

提拔　tíbá　【动】promote

提包　tíbāo　【名】handbag; shopping bag

提倡　tíchàng　【动】promote; advocate; encourage: 大力～增产节约 go all out to increase production and practise economy ～民主作风 promote the democratic style of work

提成　tí＝chéng　deduct a percentage (from a sum of money)

提干　tígàn　【动】promote

提纲　tígāng　【名】outline

提纲挈领　tí gāng qiè lǐng　bring out the essentials

提高　tí // gāo　raise; heighten; enhance; increase: ～警惕 heighten one's vigilance ～生活水平 improve living conditions 认识～了 raise

one's level of understanding

提供 tígōng 【动】supply；furnish：
～援助 render assistance 农业为轻工
业～原料和市场。Agriculture pro-
vides light industry with raw materials and markets.

提货 tí = huò pick up goods using a
receipt or money

提价 tí = jià raise the price of
goods

提交 tíjiāo 【动】submit；put forward for discussion

提款 tí = kuǎn draw money (from a
bank)；withdraw money

提炼 tíliàn 【动】extract；separate
from

提名 tí = míng nominate

提前 tíqián 【动】do sth. ahead of
schedule；advance in date：出发的
时间～了。The time of departure
was advanced. 任务～完成。The job
was completed ahead of schedule.

提琴 tíqín 【名】[把 bǎ] general term
for violin, viola, cello, double-
bass

提取 tíqǔ 【动】❶ take delivery；
withdraw：～经费 withdraw money
(from a bank) for an expenditure
～定货 take delivery of goods previously ordered ❷ extract；obtain：
从废气中～有用的物质 extract useful
material from waste gases

提审 tíshěn 【动】bring to trial；
bring (a criminal) before the court

提升 tíshēng 【动】promote (in rank
or position)

提示 tíshì 【动】point out；draw
(sb.'s) attention (to sth.)；prompt

提问 tíwèn 【动】ask question

提箱 tíxiāng 【名】trunk；suitcase

提心吊胆 tí xīn diào dǎn have one's
heart in one's mouth

提醒 tíxǐng 【动】remind；warn：～
大家注意 draw everybody's attention to 亏了你～我，不然真把这事忘
了。If you hadn't reminded me of
this matter, I would certainly have
forgotten it.

提要 tíyào 【名】summary；abstract

提议 tíyì 【动】suggest；propose；
put forward：我们～成立个业余学习
小组。We propose the organization
of a spare time study group. 【名】
proposal；suggestion：同意他的～
agree to his proposal

提早 tízǎo 【动】shift to an earlier
time

啼

啼 tí 【动】〈书〉❶ cry；weep；sob
❷ (of birds or animals) crow；
twitter；howl：鸡～狗吠 cocks crow
and dogs bark 虎啸猿～ tigers roar
and monkeys wail

啼哭 tíkū 【动】cry；weep

啼笑皆非 tí xiào jiē fēi not know
whether to laugh or cry

题(題)

题(題) tí 【名】subject；top-
ic；question：出五道～ set five (examination) questions 作文～ title
of a composition 【动】write (an inscription)；inscribe：亲笔～了一首
诗 write a poem in one's own hand
(on a painting, etc.)

题材 tícái 【名】subject matter

题词 tící 【名】inscription

题词 tí = cí inscribe

题解 tíjiě 【名】❶ explanatory notes
on the title or background of a
book ❷ key to exercises or problems

题名 tímíng 【名】inscription of a
name

题名 tí = míng write down one's
name

题目 tímù 【名】title；topic；subject；
(examination) questions

题字 tízì 【名】inscription

题字 tí = zì inscribe

蹄

蹄 tí 【名】◇ hoof：马～得得 the
clattering of horses' hoofs

蹄子 tízi 【名】〔只 zhī〕hoof

tǐ

体（體） tǐ 【名】❶ ◇ body；part of body：引～向上（gymnastics）chin oneself ❷ (geom.) solid ❸ style of calligraphy；(printing) style of typeface：这字是什么～? What style is this piece of calligraphy? ❹ ◇ form or style：古～诗 poetry in the classical style

体裁 tǐcái 【名】literary form

体操 tǐcāo 【名】gymnastics

体词 tǐcí 【名】nouns, pronouns etc. which can't be modified by adverbs in the Chinese language

体格 tǐgé 【名】physique；build

体会 tǐhuì 【动】experience；appreciate；comprehend：二十年的教学生活使老张深深～到做教员的甘苦。20 years' experience as a teacher has given Lao Zhang a deep understanding of the pleasures as well as the hardships of a teacher. 多看几遍才能～这首诗的含义。You must read this poem over and over again before you can appreciate it. 【名】experience；understanding；appreciation：学习～ what one has learned from studying (sth.) 个人～ one's personal experiences and understanding

体积 tǐjī 【名】volume；bulk

体检 tǐjiǎn 【动】physical examination

体力 tǐlì 【名】physical strength

体力劳动 tǐlì láodòng physical labour；manual work

体例 tǐlì 【名】conventions having to do with style and layout

体谅 tǐliàng 【动】make allowances for；excuse

体面 tǐmiàn 【名】dignity；face：有失～ be beneath one's dignity 【形】❶ honourable；dignified：遇到困难开小差，太不～了! How disgraceful to skulk away the moment one runs up against a challenge! ❷ good-looking；fine-looking：打扮得挺～ be handsomely dressed

体魄 tǐpò 【名】physique

体坛 tǐtán 【名】sports circles

体贴 tǐtiē 【动】be considerate of；be thoughtful towards：对同事～入微 be extremely kind to one's colleagues 他很能～人。He shows great consideration towards others.

体统 tǐtǒng 【名】propriety；decorum：不成～ most improper 有失～ a breach of propriety

体温 tǐwēn 【名】(body) temperature

体温表 tǐwēnbiǎo 【名】clinical thermometer

体无完肤 tǐ wú wán fū with cuts and bruises all over the body (also fig.)：那种形而上学的谬论已经被批得～了。The absurdities of metaphysics have been strongly criticised and repudiated.

体系 tǐxì 【名】system

体现 tǐxiàn 【动】embody；reflect；manifest；show：这座庙宇的结构～了唐代的建筑风格。The structure of this temple reflect the architectural style of the Tang dynasty.

体型 tǐxíng 【名】figure；type of build

体验 tǐyàn 【动】learn through practice；learn through personal experience：他到工厂去～生活。He went to a factory to experience life there.

体育 tǐyù 【名】physical culture；physical education

体育场 tǐyùchǎng 【名】stadium

体育馆 tǐyùguǎn 【名】gymnasium

体制 tǐzhì 【名】system of organization：国家～ state system 管理～

administrative system

体质 tǐzhì 【名】constitution; physique

体重 tǐzhòng 【名】weight (of a person)

tì

剃 tì 【动】shave

剃刀 tìdāo 【名】razor

替 tì 【动】take the place of; replace; substitute for：比赛场上，队长要求换人：五号～三号。The captain asked for a change of players. Number 3 is to be replaced by Number 5. 张老师病了,李老师～他上课。Teacher Zhang is ill so Teacher Li is to teach in his place. 【介】for：你不用～他着急。You needn't be anxious for him. 你如果去天津,请～我捎点儿东西。If you should go to Tianjin, would you please take something there for me?

替补 tìbǔ 【动】substitute for：～队员 substitute

替代 tìdài 【动】replace; take the place of; substitute for

替换 tìhuàn 【动】replace

替身 tìshēn 【名】stand-in; stuntman; stuntwoman; scapegoat

替罪羊 tìzuìyáng 【名】scapegoat

tiān

天 tiān 【名】❶ sky：～上飘着朵朵白云。The sky is fleeced with white clouds. ❷ a day, a period of twenty four hours：这个月是三十一～。This month contains 31 days. 他～～都从这儿路过。He passes by here everyday. 我们去香山玩儿了一～。We went to Xiangshan Park and spent the day there. ❸ time：五更～ at early dawn; at daybreak ～不早了,该动身了。It is getting late. We must be going now. ❹ season：蛇在冷～不出来。Snakes won't come out of their holes in the cold season. ❺ weather：～晴了,太阳出来了。It is clear now, and the sun is coming out. ❻ nature：这里大兴水利以后,改变了靠～吃饭的状况。The development of water conservation has freed this area of its past dependence on the vagaries of nature.

天安门 Tiān'ānmén 【名】Tian'anmen (The Gate of Heavenly Peace)

天才 tiāncái 【名】genius

天车 tiānchē 【名】overhead travelling crane

天窗 tiānchuāng 【名】skylight

天敌 tiāndí 【名】natural enemy

天地 tiāndì 【名】scope of activities：广阔的～ a wide scope (for one's activities) 走出个人生活的小～ break out of the shell of one's personal concerns

天翻地覆 tiān fān dì fù heaven and earth turning upside down; (fig.) earth-shaking (changes)：最近几年这里发生了～的变化。In the last few years there have been earthshaking changes here.

天赋 tiānfù 【名】gift; talent

天花 tiānhuā 【名】smallpox

天花板 tiānhuābǎn 【名】ceiling

天花乱坠 tiān huā luàn zhuì an exaggerated, colourful account; praise to the skies：别听他说得～,其实不是那么回事。Don't listen to his extravagant talk; what he says is not true at all.

天昏地暗 tiān hūn dì àn a murky sky over a dark earth; (fig.) a state of darkness and chaos

天经地义 tiān jīng dì yì universally

accepted principles；absolutely correct and unalterable principles；人类要生存就要生产劳动，这是～的事。It goes without saying that mankind's survival depends on productive labour.

天空 tiānkōng 【名】the sky

天蓝 tiānlán 【形】azure

天罗地网 tiān luó dì wǎng nets above and snares below；(*fig.*) measures which make it impossible for a criminal to elude capture；公安人员早已布下了～。The public security men have already taken foolproof measures.

天幕 tiānmù 【名】(of a stage) backdrop

天南地北 tiān nán dì běi ❶ far away；far apart；他们俩原是老同学，现在～，几十年没见过面。The two of them were schoolmates, but being tossed apart to different parts of the country, they haven't seen each other for several decades. ❷ various distant places；这次代表大会的代表真是～，哪儿的都有。The representatives at this convention are from all over. You can see people from every corner of the country.

天平 tiānpíng 【名】(weighing) scales

天气 tiānqì 【名】weather

天气预报 tiānqì yùbào weather forecast

天堑 tiānqiàn 【名】natural barrier

天桥 tiānqiáo 【名】flyover

天然 tiānrán 【形】natural (not artificial)

天然气 tiānránqì 【名】natural gas

天色 tiānsè 【名】time of day or the weather as judged by the colour of the sky

天生 tiānshēng 【形】inherent；inborn：一个人的本领不是～就有的，而是在实践中学到的。People are not born with abilities；their abilities are developed through practice.

天堂 tiāntáng 【名】paradise；heaven

天体 tiāntǐ 【名】heavenly body；celestial body

天文 tiānwén 【名】astronomy

天文馆 tiānwénguǎn 【名】planetarium

天文数字 tiānwén shùzì astronomical figures

天文台 tiānwéntái 【名】observatory

天文学 tiānwénxué 【名】astronomy

天下 tiānxià 【名】❶ a country；the whole world：有理走遍～。If you are in the right, you'll win sympathy throughout the world. ❷ state power；ruling power：这里是我们的～。This place is our turf.

天险 tiānxiǎn 【名】natural fortification or barrier

天线 tiānxiàn 【名】antenna；aerial

天涯海角 tiānyá hǎijiǎo the edges of the sky and the corners of the sea；(*fig.*) the most remote places 也作"海角天涯"。

天灾 tiānzāi 【名】natural calamity；natural disaster

天灾人祸 tiānzāi rénhuò natural and man-made calamities

天真 tiānzhēn 【形】❶ naive；innocent (*usu. referring to children*)：～活泼 innocent and lively ❷ naive；simple-minded；childish：你的想法太～了。Your ideas are rather naive.

天诛地灭 tiān zhū dì miè condemned by God and men

天主教 tiānzhǔjiào 【名】Catholicism

天资 tiānzī 【名】talent；natural endowment

添 tiān 【动】add；increase：～了许多设备。Additional equipment

has been installed. 对不起，给您～了不少麻烦。I'm sorry to have given you a lot of trouble. 再～一点儿饭吧！Please have some more rice.

添补 tiānbǔ 【动】fill up；replenish：～了一些家具 get a few additional pieces of furniture ～几件衣服 replenish one's wardrobe

添加剂 tiānjiājì 【名】additive

添油加醋 tiān yóu jiā cù add colour and emphasis to（a narration）

添枝加叶 tiān zhī jiā yè embellish （the facts）：要如实反映情况，不要～。Don't embellish the facts；just lay down the facts.

添置 tiānzhì 【动】add to one's possessions

tián

田 tián 【名】field

田地 tiándì 【名】❶ farm land；fields ❷ wretched situation；plight：由于管理不善，这个工厂已经到了产品半数不合格的～。Because of bad management, this factory has deteriorated to such an extent that half of what it produces is not up to standard.

田埂 tiángěng 【名】ridge in a furrowed field

田间管理 tiánjiān guǎnlǐ field management

田径 tiánjìng 【名】track and field

田径赛 tiánjìngsài 【名】field events

田野 tiányě 【名】open country；field

田园 tiányuán 【名】fields and gardens；countryside：～诗人 pastoral poet

恬 tián

恬不知耻 tián bù zhī chǐ past all sense of shame；shameless

恬静 tiánjìng 【形】tranquil；calm

甜 tián 【形】❶ sweet：～面包 bun 这种梨很～。This kind of pear is very sweet. 这孩子嘴真～。This child can really sweet talk. ❷（of sleep）sound：睡得很 ～ sound asleep

甜菜 tiáncài 【名】sugar beet

甜美 tiánměi 【形】❶ sweet and delicious：菠萝味道～。Pineapples are sweet and delicious. ❷（of dreams etc.）sweet；delightful：做了一个～的梦 have a delightful dream

甜蜜 tiánmì 【形】happy；sweet；pleasant；delightful：～的回忆 a happy memory ～的微笑 a sweet smile

甜头 tiántou 【名】（～儿）benefit；advantage：他们尝到了打太极拳的～。They have tasted the benefit of doing *t'ai chi ch'uan*.

甜言蜜语 tián yán mì yǔ sweet words and honeyed phrases（spoken to curry favour）；sweet talk

填 tián 【动】❶ fill up；even up：把坑～平了 fill in the hole ❷ fill out（a form）；fill in（the blanks）：～履历表 fill out a form giving autobiographical data 老师叫学生在空格里～上动词。The teacher asked the students to fill in the blanks with verbs.

填表 tián = biǎo fill in a form

填补 tiánbǔ 【动】fill（a vacancy）

填充 tiánchōng 【动】fill up

填空 tián = kòng fill a gap；fill in the blanks

填写 tiánxiě 【动】fill in（a form）

填鸭式 tiányāshì 【名】cramming （way of teaching）

tiǎn

舔 tiǎn 【动】lick

tiāo

挑　tiāo　【动】❶ carry（with a shoulder-pole）：～水 carry water 勇～重担 be ready to shoulder a heavy task ❷ choose；select；pick out：你喜欢什么样的手提包，自己～吧！Please choose whichever handbag you like. ❸ try to find（fault with sb.）；carp at：～毛病 point out sb.'s faults；carp at sb. ～错儿 find fault with sb. 【量】*for things that can be carried on a shoulder-pole*：一～水 two buckets of water（carried on a shoulder pole）一～土 two baskets of earth（carried on a shoulder pole）

另见 tiǎo

挑拣 tiāojiǎn 【动】pick；pick and choose

挑食 tiāoshí 【动】be particular about food；be picky（or choosy）about what one eats

挑剔 tiāoti 【动】carp at；be critical of；find fault with；be overly fastidious：我看他写得够清楚了，不要过分～。I think what he has written is clear enough. Don't be finicky.

挑选 tiāoxuǎn 【动】choose；select

挑子 tiāozi 【名】carrying pole and its two loads

tiáo

条（條）　tiáo　【名】（～儿）（of paper，cloth，etc.）strip；slip；piece：布～ a strip of cloth 把纸裁成～ cut the paper into strips 他托人带来个～。He asked somebody to bring us a short note. 【量】*for long，thin things*：一～线 a line 五～鱼 five fish 一～板凳 a bench 三～新闻 three news items 两～意见 a couple of opinions

条件 tiáojiàn 【名】condition；term

条件反射 tiáojiàn fǎnshè conditioned reflex

条款 tiáokuǎn 【名】clause（in an agreement）

条理 tiáolǐ 【名】orderliness；proper presentation

条例 tiáolì 【名】regulation；statute

条目 tiáomù 【名】clauses（in a treaty，etc.）

条条框框 tiáotiáo kuàngkuàng regulations and restrictions；do's and dont's

条文 tiáowén 【名】article；clause

条形码 tiáoxíngmǎ 【名】bar code；Universal Product Code

条约 tiáoyuē 【名】treaty；pact

条子 tiáozi 【名】a slip of paper；a short note

调（調）　tiáo　【动】mix：拌菜时放点味精～一～ season a cold dish with gourmet powder

另见 diào

调和 tiáohé 【形】be harmoniously proportioned：雨水～ right amount of rainfall 色彩～。The colours match well. 【动】reconcile；compromise：在这个问题上没有～的余地。There is no room for compromise on this question.

调剂 tiáojì 【动】exchange what is surplus for what is lacking；break monotony：增加文娱活动，～～生活。Let's have more recreational activities to break the monotony of our life. 这两个果园常常互相～水果的品种。These two orchards often exchange fruit varieties.

调价 tiáo＝jià readjust（or modify）prices

调节 tiáojié 【动】regulate；adjust：～温度 regulate the temperature ～空气 adjust the air-conditioning ～水量 regulate the volume of water-

flow

调解 tiáojiě 【动】mediate；conciliate：~纠纷 mediate in a dispute ~争端 settle a dispute by mediation

调控 tiáokòng 【动】adjust and control

调理 tiáolǐ 【动】❶ recuperate：你身体太弱,最好吃中药~一下。You are awfully weak. You had better take some Chinese medicine and try to regain your health. ❷ look after；take good care of：王大爷把牲口~得个个膘肥体壮。Grandpa Wang takes such good care of the livestock that every animal is fat and sturdy.

调料 tiáoliào 【名】seasoning；condiment

调皮 tiáopí 【形】naughty；mischievous

调试 tiáoshì 【动】adjust；debug；regulate

调停 tiáotíng 【动】mediate；conciliate：~两国争端 act as mediator in the dispute between two countries ~军事冲突 mediate in an armed conflict

调味 tiáo = wèi season；add seasoning

调养 tiáoyǎng 【动】recuperate

调整 tiáozhěng 【动】adjust；readjust；reorganise；regulate：~人力 readjust (the allocation of) manpower ~工农业的关系 readjust the relationship between industry and agriculture

笤 tiáo

笤帚 tiáozhou 【名】〔把 bǎ〕broom

tiāo

挑 tiāo 【动】❶ lift up；raise (with a stick, etc.)：把帘子~起来 lift up the curtain ❷ poke；pick

out (with e.g. a needle)：~刺 pick out a thorn (from one's finger) ❸ provoke；stir up；incite；instigate 【名】(of Chinese characters) a slanting stroke upward "╱" 也叫"提" tí。

另见 tiāo

挑拨 tiǎobō 【动】sow discord；stir up (disunity and dissension)：~关系 try to undermine the relationship between 有人从中进行~。Someone is provoking dissension.

挑拨离间 tiǎobō líjiàn sow discord；stir up dissension；incite one against the other：他对大家从来光明正大,不给人以~的机会。He is always open with everyone and provides no opportunity for the sowing of discord.

挑大梁 tiǎo dàliáng function as a pillar of；be a leading actor or actress

挑动 tiǎodòng 【动】provoke；instigate；incite：~战争 provoke a war

挑花 tiāo = huā do cross-stitch work

挑起 tiǎo // qǐ instigate；stir up；provoke

挑唆 tiǎosuō 【动】instigate；incite

挑衅 tiǎoxìn 【动】provoke：敌人胆敢~,我们就坚决给以沉重的打击。If the enemy should dare to attempt an act of provocation, we will certainly retaliate very vigorously. 【名】challenge；provocation：敌人的军事~被粉碎了。The attempt at armed provocation launched by the enemy was smashed.

挑战 tiǎo = zhàn issue a challenge

tiào

眺 tiào 【动】◇ look into the distance：登高远~ go up to a higher place to look into the distance

眺望　tiàowàng　【动】look far away into the distance from a high place

跳　tiào　【动】❶ jump；skip：打篮球既要～得高，又要跑得快。A basketball player has to be able to jump high and run fast. 孩子们又蹦又～，玩得可欢啦! The children were having a marvellous time, jumping and running about! ❷ (of pulse, heart, etc.) beat：心～得厉害。My heart is pounding. ❸ (of a page, a chapter, a grade, etc.) jump over；skip：～班 (of a pupil) skip a grade 这课书～过去不讲了。We skipped this lesson.

跳板　tiàobǎn　【名】❶ gangplank ❷ springboard；diving board

跳槽　tiào = cáo　❶ (of a horse, etc.) leave its own manger to eat at another ❷ throw up one job and take on another

跳动　tiàodòng　【动】(of heart, pulse) beat

跳高　tiào = gāo　high jump

跳伞　tiào = sǎn　parachute；bale out

跳水　tiào = shuǐ　dive

跳台　tiàotái　【名】diving platform；diving tower

跳舞　tiào = wǔ　dance

跳远　tiào = yuǎn　long jump

跳跃　tiàoyuè　【动】jump；hop

跳蚤市场　tiàozao shìchǎng　flea market

tiē

贴（貼）　tiē　【动】❶ paste；stick：～邮票 stick a stamp (on a letter) ～标语 paste up slogans ❷ come close to；be near：～身衣服 underwear 燕子～着水面飞。The swallows were skimming over the surface of the water. ❸ subsidize；give financial help to：姐姐每月～我五十块钱。Every month, my elder sister gives me fifty yuan pocket money. 【量】 for medicated plaster, etc.：一～膏药 a medicated plaster

贴金　tiē = jīn　cover with gold leaf；(fig.) beautify；embellish

贴面　tiēmiàn　【名】veneer

贴切　tiēqiè　【形】(of use of words or phrases) exact and proper；apt；apposite："掩耳盗铃"用来比喻自欺欺人的做法十分～。"Plug one's ears while stealing a bell" is a very apt aphorism to describe self-deception.

贴现　tiēxiàn　【动】discount (on a promissory note)

贴心　tiēxīn　【形】very intimate (e.g. friend or talk)

tiě

铁（鐵）　tiě　【名】❶ iron ❷ (fig.) strong；hard as iron；determined：～的纪律 iron discipline ～的事实 hard facts；ironclad evidence 【动】◇ resolve；determine：～了心了 be unmovable in one's determination

铁板　tiěbǎn　【名】〔块 kuài〕iron plate

铁板一块　tiěbǎn yī kuài　(a group) as united as an iron plate

铁饼　tiěbǐng　【名】(sports) discus

铁道兵　tiědàobīng　【名】railway engineering corps

铁饭碗　tiěfànwǎn　【名】"iron rice bowl"；job security

铁轨　tiěguǐ　【名】(of railway) rail

铁匠　tiějiang　【名】blacksmith

铁路　tiělù　【名】〔条 tiáo〕railway

铁面无私　tiě miàn wú sī　(of a person) impartial and incorruptible

铁器时代　tiěqì shídài　the Iron Age

铁锹　tiěqiāo　【名】〔把 bǎ〕shovel；spade

铁拳 tiěquán 【名】iron fist；(fig.) might

铁石心肠 tiě shí xīncháng be hard-hearted

铁树开花 tiěshù kāi huā an iron tree in blossom；(fig.) extremely rare；once in a blue moon

铁水 tiěshuǐ 【名】molten iron

铁丝 tiěsī 【名】iron wire

铁丝网 tiěsīwǎng 【名】wire netting

铁蹄 tiětí 【名】iron heel；(fig.) atrocities

铁锨 tiěxiān 【名】〔把 bǎ〕spade；shovel

铁证 tiězhèng 【名】ironclad evidence

铁证如山 tiězhèng rú shān ironclad evidence；irrefutable evidence

tīng

厅（廳）tīng 【名】❶ hall ❷ a department in a big organisation (e.g. in a ministry) ❸ a department or bureau under a provincial government

听（聽）tīng 【动】❶ hear；listen to：～音乐 listen to music 我～不清楚。I did not hear clearly. ❷ obey；listen to；follow or take advice：谁说得对，我就～谁的。I will take the advice of whoever I consider best. ❸ resign oneself to；submit to：～天由命 submit to the will of Heaven；resign oneself to one's fate

听从 tīngcóng 【动】obey：～指挥 obey orders ～分配 accept an assignment

听而不闻 tīng ér bù wén hear but pay no attention to；turn a deaf ear to

听候 tīnghòu 【动】wait for (instruction or order from above)

听话 tīnghuà 【形】obedient；docile：这孩子很～。This child is very obedient.

听见 tīng∥jiàn hear

听讲 tīngjiǎng 【动】attend a lecture

听觉 tīngjué 【名】sense of hearing

听课 tīng = kè ❶ observe (or sit in on) a class ❷ attend a lecture

听力 tīnglì 【名】❶ hearing ❷ aural comprehension

听凭 tīngpíng 【动】resign oneself to；submit to：这事怎么办，～你决定。It is up to you to decide what to do.

听其自然 tīng qí zìrán (let) sth. take its natural course；let things drift

听取 tīngqǔ 【动】listen to；take (sb.'s advice)：～你们的意见 listen to your opinions ～汇报 hear reports (from a lower level) 代表大会～了关于妇女工作的报告。The congress heard reports on women's work.

听任 tīngrèn 【动】let things take their course；allow sth. to continue unchecked

听说 tīng = shuō it is said that；(I) hear that：～那座山上有座古庙。It is said that there is an ancient temple at the top of that mountain. 听人说明天我们去天坛。I hear that we are going to the Temple of Heaven tomorrow.

听讼 tīngsòng 【动】try a case

听写 tīngxiě 【动】dictate；be given a dictation 【名】dictation

听信 tīngxìn 【动】listen to and believe (usu. referring to rumours, incorrect views)：～谣言 believe rumours 不能～一面之词。We must not be taken in by one-sided statements.

听诊器 tīngzhěnqì 【名】stethoscope

听之任之 tīng zhī rèn zhī (of bad things) let matters drift；let things

slide：对于无政府主义行为，不能～。We must not allow instances of anarchist behavior to go unchecked.

听众　tīngzhòng　【名】audience

tíng

亭　tíng　【名】◇ pavilion：凉～ wayside pavilion　书～ bookstall

亭子　tíngzi　【名】〔个 gè〕pavilion

庭　tíng

庭院　tíngyuàn　【名】courtyard

停　tíng　【动】❶ stop；halt；cease：手表～了。My watch has stopped. 在成绩面前不能～步。One must not rest on one's laurels after having made an achievement. ❷ stop over；stay：我在上海～了三天。I made a three-day stopover in Shanghai. ❸ park（a car, etc.）；anchor；moor：汽车～在门口。The car is parked at the gate. 码头上～着大小船只。There are many boats of various sizes moored at the wharf.

停泊　tíngbó　【动】（of ship）lie at anchor

停产　tíng＝chǎn　stop production

停车　tíng＝chē　❶ stop a car or vehicle：～十分钟。He stopped the car for ten minutes. ❷ stop（operating a machine）：这台铣床坏了，要～修理。The milling machine is not working properly. It must be shut down and overhauled.

停当　tíngdang　【形】all set；all ready

停顿　tíngdùn　【动】❶ （of things）be at a standstill；stop temporarily：这项工程决不能～下来。The project must be continued without interruption. ❷ pause（in speaking）：念到这个地方要～一下。You should

pause at this point and then go on reading.

停工　tíng＝gōng　stop work

停火　tíng＝huǒ　（mil.）cease fire

停靠　tíngkào　【动】（of a ship）dock；（of a train）stop at a station

停课　tíng＝kè　suspend classes

停留　tíngliú　【动】❶ stop over（e.g. during a journey）❷ remain at a standstill

停学　tíng＝xué　drop out of school

停业　tíng＝yè　stop doing business；close down

停战　tíng＝zhàn　armistice；truce；cessation of hostilities

停职　tíng＝zhí　suspend sb. from his duties

停止　tíngzhǐ　【动】stop；halt

停滞　tíngzhì　【动】come to a standstill；stagnate：经济～。The economy remains stagnant. 生产处于～状态。Production has come to a standstill.

停滞不前　tíngzhì bù qián　be at a standstill；remain stagnant；cease to make progress：世界在发展，人类在进步，永远不会～。The world is developing, mankind is advancing and nothing will remain at a standstill.

tǐng

挺　tǐng　【动】❶ straighten up；erect：～起胸膛 throw out one's chest ～起腰 sit or stand erect ❷ endure；hold out：你不舒服，就别硬～着干了。You're not feeling well, don't try to stick it out. 【副】rather；quite：～好 quite good ～有意思 quite interesting ～勇敢 very brave 【量】for guns：三～机枪 three machine-guns

挺拔　tǐngbá　【形】❶ straight and towering：苍松～。The sturdy pines

are tall and straight. ❷ (of handwriting) firm and powerful: 老吴的毛笔字苍劲～。Lao Wu's calligraphy is firm and powerful.

挺进 tǐngjìn 【动】push forward; advance: 部队正在向大别山～。The troops are advancing toward Dabie Mountain.

挺立 tǐnglì 【动】stand erect

挺身而出 tǐng shēn ér chū step forward boldly; come forward bravely (to undertake a difficult or dangerous task)

铤(鋌) tǐng

铤而走险 tǐng ér zǒu xiǎn risk danger when in a desperate situation

tōng

通 tōng 【动】❶ be passable; be unimpeded: 两个地道～着。These two tunnels are connected. 电话～了。The telephone call has been put through. 此路不～。No Thoroughfare. ❷ dredge: 把下水道～一下 clean the sewer ❸ understand; know; straighten out: 粗～法语 have a passable knowledge of French 思想～了,他终于同意离婚。He thought the matter through and finally agreed to divorce. ❹ inform; communicate (e.g. information): ～个电话 ring sb. up ～消息 inform sb. of the news 【形】(of writings) logical; coherent: 句子不～。This sentence is ungrammatical.

通报 tōngbào 【动】(from a leading organ to a lower unit) circulate a notice: ～批评 circulate a notice criticizing sb. or sth. ～全校,给予表扬 circulate a notice of commendation throughout the whole school 【名】circular: 发一个～ issue a circular

通病 tōngbìng 【名】common failing

通常 tōngcháng 【形】general; usual (*never used as the predicate or complement*): ～的情况 normal conditions ～的做法 usual way of doing things ～的现象 a not unusual phenomenon 星期六下午～没有课。There are usually no classes on Saturday afternoons. 他～晚上不出去,总在家看书。He doesn't go out in the evenings as a rule but reads at home instead. Note: 通常 *cannot be modified by a negative word*.

通畅 tōngchàng 【形】❶ unimpeded; through: 线路～ unobstructed lines of communication ❷ (of writings) fluent; flowing; smooth: 文字～ smooth writing style 语言～ fluent language

通车 tōng = chē ❶ (of railway or road) open to traffic ❷ regular transportation is available (between two fairly distant places)

通称 tōngchēng 【动】be commonly known as: 氯化钠～食盐。Sodium chloride is commonly known as salt. 【名】the common name for sth.: 土豆是马铃薯的～。 *Tudou* is the common name for potato.

通道 tōngdào 【名】〔条 tiáo〕thoroughfare

通敌 tōng = dí conspire with the enemy

通电 tōngdiàn 【动】issue an open telegram; issue a public statement by telegram: ～全国 issue an open telegram to the whole country 【名】circular telegram; open telegram: 发出～ issue an open telegram 大会～ an open telegram issued by the conference

通电 tōng = diàn set up an electric circuit

通风 tōng = fēng ❶ ventilate：～设备 ventilation equipment 菜窖该通通风了。It is high time to air out the root cellar. ❷ divulge information；disclose information，etc.：～报信 divulge information

通告 tōnggào 【动】give public notice；make generally known：这项决定要～全厂。The resolution is to be announced to the whole factory. 【名】public notice；announcement：布告栏里贴着一张～。A notice has been put on the bulletin board.

通观全局 tōngguān quánjú take an overall view of the situation：看问题要～，不能只从局部出发。In considering a problem, we must look at the whole situation, and not just a part.

通过 tōngguò 【动】be approved by：调动工作必须～组织。Job transfers must be approved by the organization. 【介】through；by；from；via：大家～讨论取得了一致的认识。They have arrived at a unanimous view through discussion. ～电影普及科学知识，效果很好。Popularizing scientific knowledge through films has proven to be very effective.

通过 tōng // guò ❶ pass through；go through：～敌人封锁线 pass through the enemy's blockade 这里正在修路，汽车不能～。The road is under repair and not open to traffic. ❷ pass (a resolution)：这个提案一定通得过。This proposal will certainly be passed.

通航 tōngháng 【动】(of a navigation or aviation route) be open

通红 tōnghóng 【形】burning red；glowing red

通话 tōng = huà ❶ converse ❷ communicate by telephone

通婚 tōng = hūn intermarry

通货 tōnghuò 【名】currency

通货膨胀 tōnghuò péngzhàng （econ.） inflation

通缉 tōngjī 【动】issue a wanted circular (by the police)

通令 tōnglìng 【动】issue an order (to different places at the same time) 【名】an order issued to different places at the same time

通明 tōngmíng 【形】brightly lit；ablaze with lights：灯火～ be ablaze with lights

通盘 tōngpán 【副】all-round；overall：～规划 overall plan ～安排 all-round arrangements ～考虑 overall consideration

通气 tōng = qì ventilate；keep each other informed；keep in touch

通情达理 tōng qíng dá lǐ be reasonable and sensible；show common sense

通融 tōngróng 【动】circumvent regulations to accommodate sb.：这些书不能外借，但有特殊情况可以～。These books cannot normally be borrowed, but an exception can be made in special circumstances.

通商 tōng = shāng trade with (e.g. another country)

通史 tōngshǐ 【名】general history；comprehensive history

通顺 tōngshùn 【形】(writing) fluent；flowing

通俗 tōngsú 【形】(of language) popular；simple

通俗化 tōngsúhuà 【动】popularize；【名】popularization

通通 tōngtōng 【副】all；entirely；altogether：书报～搬走了。All the books and newspapers have been moved away. 我们今年收麦子，～用联合收割机。This year we did all of the wheat harvesting with combine-harvesters.

通统 tōngtǒng 【副】同"通通"

通宵 tōngxiāo 【名】all night；through the night

通晓 tōngxiǎo 【动】 be well versed in；understand thoroughly

通信 tōng＝xìn correspond

通信兵 tōngxìnbīng 【名】signalman

通信卫星 tōngxìn wèixīng communications satellite

通信员 tōngxìnyuán 【名】messenger；orderly

通行 tōngxíng 【动】❶ be open to traffic；go through：前面施工，禁止～。Construction ahead. Road closed to traffic. ❷ current；in common use：由邮局送报纸是全中国～的办法。It is current practice in China for all newspapers to be delivered by the post office.

通行证 tōngxíngzhèng 【名】pass；permit

通讯 tōngxùn 【名】❶ communications ❷ news dispatch；correspondence：这篇～写得不错。This news report is well written.

通讯处 tōngxùnchù 【名】address

通讯社 tōngxùnshè 【名】news agency

通讯员 tōngxùnyuán 【名】correspondent

通用 tōngyòng 【动】be in common use；be current；apply or be used universally：标准化零件可以～。The standardized fittings can be employed universally. 这种课本全省～。This textbook is in common use throughout the province.

通邮 tōngyóu 【动】accessible by postal communication

通知 tōngzhī 【动】notify；inform；notice 【名】notice

tóng

同 tóng 【形】same；alike；similar（with the exception of 不同，used only as an attributive）：～年级 of the same grade ～名～姓 have the same full name 【动】◇ be the same as：～上 ditto ～前 ditto 【副】◇ together：～吃～住～劳动 eat together, live together and work together 【介】同"和" hé 【介】（usu. in written language）：～有关人员协商 consult the people concerned 有事要～大家商量。We must put our heads together when problems arise. 【连】同"和"【连】（usu. in written language）：今天我～他都是夜班。Both he and I are on the night shift today.

同案犯 tóng'ànfàn 【名】criminals involved in the same case

同班 tóng＝bān be in the same class in school or university

同伴 tóngbàn 【名】companion；pal

同胞 tóngbāo 【名】compatriot；fellow-countryman

同病相怜 tóng bìng xiāng lián fellow sufferers of a similar complaint sympathize with each other

同步 tóngbù 【动】synchronize【名】synchronism：～卫星 synchronous satellite

同仇敌忾 tóng chóu díkài share hatred for the common enemy：全国人民～，为打败侵略者而战斗。The whole nation felt common hatred for the invaders, and fought to defeat them.

同床异梦 tóng chuáng yì mèng sleep in the same bed but dream different dreams（fig.）seemingly cooperate with each other but each has his own agenda

同等 tóngděng 【形】of the same level or grade

同等学历 tóngděng xuélì the same educational level

同甘共苦 tóng gān gòng kǔ share joys and sorrows；through thick and thin：干部要和群众～。Cadres should share happiness and hardships with the masses.

同感 tónggǎn 【名】common feeling; same feeling

同工同酬 tóng gōng tóng chóu equal pay for equal work

同归于尽 tóng guī yú jìn perish together with: 宁可和敌人～,也决不投降 prefer to die together with the enemy rather than surrender

同行 tóngháng 【名】person of the same walk of life

同化 tónghuà 【动】assimilate

同伙 tónghuǒ 【名】partner

同居 tóngjū 【动】live together; cohabit

同流合污 tóng liú hé wū join in evildoings; associate with an evil person

同盟 tóngméng 【名】alliance; ally

同盟军 tóngméngjūn 【名】allied forces

同情 tóngqíng 【动】sympathize; have sympathy for: 我十分～你的遭遇。I have great sympathy with you in your difficulties.

同声传译 tóngshēng chuányì simultaneous interpretation

同时 tóngshí 【名】at the same time; simultaneously; concurrently: 在努力学习的～,也要注意锻炼身体。On the one hand we must work hard; on the other, we must pay due attention to physical training. 两辆汽车～到达。The two cars arrived at the same time. 【连】moreover; besides; furthermore; meanwhile: 这套茶具不仅实用,～也是很好的艺术品。This tea set is not only useful, it is also a work of art.

同事 tóngshì 【名】colleague

同事 tóng = shì work in the same place

同位素 tóngwèisù 【名】isotope

同位语 tóngwèiyǔ 【名】(gram.) appositive

同乡 tóngxiāng 【名】person of the same village, county or province; fellow-townsman

同心同德 tóng xīn tóng dé (work) with a single heart and mind

同心协力 tóng xīn xié lì unite in a concerted effort; make a concerted effort: 全厂工人～搞好生产。All the workers in the factory are making a concerted effort to promote production.

同心圆 tóngxīnyuán 【名】(maths.) concentric circles

同性 tóngxìng 【名】❶ of the same sex ❷ of the same nature or character

同学 tóngxué 【名】schoolmate

同学 tóng = xué study in the same school

同样 tóngyàng 【形】same; of the same kind; alike: 几次化验,都得到～的结果。We ran the test several times, and got the same results each time. ～一篇散文,他朗诵起来就比我感情充沛。The same essay sounded more moving when he read it than when I did. Note: 同样 is usually placed before, or sometimes in the middle of the second clause to indicate that the circumstances to which the two clauses refer are similar: 对中国古代的文化,我们要吸收其中有益的东西,～,对外国的也应如此。We should assimilate whatever is beneficial in ancient Chinese culture, and deal likewise with foreign culture.

同一性 tóngyīxìng 【名】(phil.) identity

同义词 tóngyìcí 【名】synonym

同意 tóngyì 【动】agree; approve

同音词 tóngyīncí 【名】homonym

同音字 tóngyīnzì 【名】character of the same sound

同志 tóngzhì 【名】comrade

同舟共济 tóng zhōu gòng jì be in the same boat and help each other;

(*fig*.) stick together through thick and thin

铜(銅) tóng 【名】copper

铜匠 tóngjiang 【名】coppersmith

铜牌 tóngpái 【名】bronze medal; bronze

铜器时代 tóngqì shídài the Bronze Age

铜钱 tóngqián 【名】copper cash; copper coin

铜墙铁壁 tóng qiáng tiě bì wall of bronze; bastion of iron; (*fig*.) invincible strength; 人民是真正的～, 是任何力量也打不破的。It is the people who are the invincible strength and no force on earth can defeat them.

铜像 tóngxiàng 【名】bronze statue

童 tóng

童工 tónggōng 【名】child labourer

童话 tónghuà 【名】fairy tale; children's story

童年 tóngnián 【名】childhood

tǒng

统(統) tǒng

统舱 tǒngcāng 【名】steerage

统称 tǒngchēng 【动】be generally named or called; 绘画、雕塑、建筑等～为造型艺术。Painting, sculpture, architecture, etc. are collectively called the "fine arts" or "plastic arts".

统筹 tǒngchóu 【动】plan as a whole

统筹兼顾 tǒngchóu jiāngù overall planning and all-round considerations; 作计划、办事情都要～, 全面安排。In planning or making arrangements, we should take all parties and factors into consideration.

统共 tǒnggòng 【副】altogether; all counted

统计 tǒngjì 【动】add up; count; compile statistics; ～人数 count the number of people; compile statistics on the number of people 【名】 ❶ statistics ❷ statistician; 他是工厂的～。He is the factory statistician.

统计学 tǒngjìxué 【名】statistics

统考 tǒngkǎo 【动】general examination

统帅 tǒngshuài 【名】commander-in-chief; 军队的最高～ the commander-in-chief of the army 【动】command; ～全军 command the whole army

统率 tǒngshuài 【动】command; ～所属部队前往增援 lead the troops and march forward as reinforcements

统统 tǒngtǒng 【副】同 "通通" tōngtōng

统销 tǒngxiāo 【动】state monopoly for marketing (of certain important goods)

统一 tǒngyī 【动】unify; unite; 把意见～起来 reach a common position; ～认识, ～行动 reach a common understanding and adopt unified action 【形】unified; united; 认识很不～。Their views are quite different.

统一体 tǒngyītǐ 【名】entity

统一战线 tǒngyī zhànxiàn united front

统战 tǒngzhàn 【名】*short for* "统一战线"

统治 tǒngzhì 【动】rule; dominate

统治阶级 tǒngzhì jiējí ruling class

捅 tǒng 【动】❶ poke; stab; stir up (trouble, etc.); ～了一刀 stab with a sword; ～马蜂窝 stir up a hornets' nest; 有谁～了我一下。Someone nudged me. ❷〈口〉expose; disclose; reveal; lay open; 他

把看到的事儿都～出来了。He disclosed all that he had seen.

捅娄子　tǒng lóuzi　make a mess of things; cause trouble

桶　tǒng　【名】〔只 zhī〕pail; bucket

筒　tǒng　【名】◇ thick tube-shaped object

筒裤　tǒngkù　【名】〔条 tiáo〕tube trousers

筒裙　tǒngqún　【名】〔条 tiáo〕tube skirt

筒子　tǒngzi　【名】〔个 gè〕tube-shaped object

筒子楼　tǒngzilóu　【名】dormitory-type building

tòng

痛　tòng　【动】同"疼" téng ❶【副】bitterly; thoroughly; severely; ～骂一顿 give sb. a severe scolding ～饮 drink one's fill

痛斥　tòngchì　【动】sharply denounce; ～卖国贼自我辩解的谬论 sharply denounce the outrageous theories of the traitors in their self-justification

痛处　tòngchù　【名】❶ sore spot ❷ (fig.) tender spot; sensitive subject; 这个发言击中了他的～。This speech touched him on his most sensitive spot.

痛改前非　tòng gǎi qián fēi　thoroughly mend one's ways; sincerely rectify one's error

痛感　tònggǎn　【动】feel keenly that

痛恨　tònghèn　【动】hate bitterly

痛哭　tòngkū　【动】cry bitterly

痛哭流涕　tòngkū liú tì　cry and shed bitter tears

痛苦　tòngkǔ　【形】painful; bitter

痛快　tòngkuài　【形】❶ happy; de-

lighted; with great pleasure; to one's heart's content; 心里很～ feel very happy and relieved of a burden 今天遇到了一件不～的事。I had an unpleasant experience today. 我们玩儿得很～。We had an extremely good time. ❷ outspoken; frank and straightforward; 他说话很～。He is outspoken. 他～地答应了我的要求。He readily and without any hesitation acceded to my request. 有什么要求痛痛快快地提出来吧！Please speak up if you have any requests to make.

痛心　tòngxīn　【形】heart-rending

痛心疾首　tòng xīn jí shǒu　feel self-hatred due to one's own error; 她～地说："由于我的溺爱,害了我的孩子！" She said with intense bitterness; "I ruined my child by spoiling him!"

痛痒　tòngyǎng　【名】❶ pain and itch; (fig.) sufferings; 关心群众的～ show concern for the well-being of the masses ❷ (fig.) importance; consequence (used in neg.); 无关～的事 a matter of no consequence

tōu

偷　tōu　【动】❶ steal ❷ ◇ secretly; stealthily; ～看 steal a glance at ～跑 escape; run away ❸ ◇ manage to make (time); find (a spare moment); ～空儿 try to make some free time ❹ ◇ drift along; ～生 live out an ignoble existence

偷盗　tōudào　【动】steal; rob

偷工减料　tōu gōng jiǎn liào　jerry-build

偷懒　tōu = lǎn　loaf on the job

偷梁换柱　tōu liáng huàn zhù　steal the beams and pillars and replace them with rotten timbers; (fig.)

commit an act of fraud

偷窃 tōuqiè 【动】steal；rob

偷税 tōu=shuì evade taxes

偷听 tōutīng 【动】eavesdrop；bug

偷偷 tōutōu 【副】stealthily；secretly；furtively：他趁人不注意，～地溜走了。When he saw that no one was paying attention to him, he slipped away. 几个小学生～地把李爷爷的院子扫干净了。Several school children quietly cleaned the courtyard for Grandpa Li.

偷偷摸摸 tōutōumōmō 【形】covert；furtive（*derog.*）

偷袭 tōuxí 【动】make a surprise attack

tóu

头（頭） tóu 【名】❶ head ❷ ◇ hair：洗～ wash one's hair 梳～ comb one's hair ❸（～儿）top；end：这座大桥真长，一眼望不到～。This bridge is certainly long. You can't see the end of it. 村子西～有棵大槐树。There is a big locust tree at the west end of the village. ❹（～儿）remnant；end：布～ scraps of cloth 线～ pieces of thread 铅笔～ a pencil stub 烟～ a cigarette butt ❺ first（*used before a numeral*）：开学以后～一个星期，同学们就互相熟悉了。The students got to know one another in a week after school started. 把～三排位子留给新来的同学。Let's keep the first three rows of seats for the new students. 这篇文章的～两句最好改一改。You had better revise the first two sentences of that article. 这次运动会他跑了个百米～一名。He came first in the 100m dash in the sports meet.【量】❶ *for some animals*：一～ 牛 a cow 三～驴 three donkeys ❷ *for anything which grows from a bulb*：两～蒜 two bulbs of garlic 买了好几～水仙 buy several narcissus bulbs

头等 tóuděng 【形】first-class；paramount；prime

头顶 tóudǐng 【名】top of the head

头发 tóufa 【名】〔根 gēn〕hair on human head

头号 tóuhào 【名】the first（in order）；number one：～铅字 the largest typeface ～战犯 chief war criminal

头巾 tóujīn 【名】〔块 kuài〕kerchief

头颅 tóulú 【名】〈书〉skull：多少先烈为人民抛～，洒热血。Many revolutionary martyrs shed blood and laid down their lives for the people.

头面人物 tóumiàn rénwù celebrity；bigwig

头目 tóumù 【名】head；boss；chieftain；chief

头脑 tóunǎo 【名】❶ head；brains；mind：～清楚 clear-headed 这个人很有～。This man is pretty brainy. 不要被胜利冲昏～。Don't let success turn your head! ❷ main strands；clue：摸不着～ unable to make heads or tails（of sth.）

头破血流 tóu pò xuè liú suffer a severe head wound；（*fig.*）be badly battered；be bitterly defeated：碰得～ suffer a grave defeat

头痛 tóu tòng ❶ have a headache ❷（*fig.*）headache；troublesome problem：这件事真令人～。This matter is a real headache.

头头是道 tóu tóu shì dào clear and logical；systematic and methodical：他说得～。What he said was clear and logical.

头衔 tóuxián 【名】title

头绪 tóuxù 【名】main threads（of a complicated affair）

头油　tóuyóu　【名】hair oil

头子　tóuzi　【名】chief; boss; head (*derog.*)

投　tóu　【动】❶ throw; hurl; cast: ~手榴弹 throw a grenade 把信~进邮筒 put a letter into a mailbox 我~了他一票。I voted for him. ❷ ◇ throw oneself into (a river, etc. to commit suicide): ~河 throw oneself into a river ~井 drown oneself in a well ❸ deliver (a letter, etc.); send in; submit (a manuscript, etc.): 给报纸~了篇稿子 submit an article to a newspaper ❹ ◇ cater to (tastes, needs, etc.); suit: ~其所好(hào) cater to sb.'s tastes ❺ go and seek refuge with: ~亲靠友 go and seek refuge with one's relatives or friends

投案　tóu＝àn　give oneself up to the police

投保　tóubǎo　【动】insure

投奔　tóubèn　【动】go to (sb.) for help

投标　tóu＝biāo　enter a bid

投产　tóuchǎn　【动】put into production; begin production

投诚　tóuchéng　【动】cross over to the side one believes to be just

投弹　tóu＝dàn　throw a grenade

投敌　tóu＝dí　go over to the enemy

投递　tóudì　【动】deliver (mail)

投稿　tóu＝gǎo　submit a manuscript (for publication)

投合　tóuhé　【动】❶ (of two persons) get along; hit it off together: 两个人脾气挺~。Those two hit it off very well together. ❷ cater to sb.'s tastes; fawn upon: ~对方所好(hào) cater to the tastes of the other party ~南方人的口味 cater to a southerner's tastes in food

投机　tóujī　【形】agreeable; harmonious: 他们谈得很~。They are having a very congenial talk. 话不~半句多。If two people have nothing in common, even exchanging a few words can be difficult. 【动】speculate: ~买卖 speculate (in sth.); be engaged in speculation

投机倒把　tóujī dǎobǎ　engage in speculation and profiteering: 坚决打击~活动。We must crack down on speculation and profiteering.

投机取巧　tóujī qǔqiǎo　gain sth. by fraud or trickery; seize every chance to gain personal advantage by trickery

投机商　tóujīshāng　【名】speculator; profiteer

投靠　tóukào　【动】❶ go and seek refuge with: ~父亲的一个朋友 go and seek refuge with a friend of one's father ❷ give oneself up to; surrender to: ~敌人 surrender to the enemy

投票　tóu＝piào　cast a vote

投入　tóurù　【动】plunge into; throw oneself into: ~祖国的怀抱 return to one's own country ~战斗 join the battle 设备已安装完毕，很快就可~生产。With all the equipment installed, the factory is ready to go into production.

投身　tóushēn　【动】throw oneself into; plunge into; participate in: ~到农业现代化的事业中去 plunge into the cause of the modernization of agriculture ~于服装设计工作 devote oneself to dress designing

投鼠忌器　tóu shǔ jì qì　hesitate to strike the rat for fear of smashing the dishes beside it; (*fig.*) hesitate to take action against an evildoer for fear of involving innocent people

投诉　tóusù　【动】appeal; complain

投宿　tóusù　【动】put up (at a place); find food and lodging

投降 tóuxiáng 【动】surrender; capitulate

投医 tóu = yī go to a doctor; seek medical help

投影 tóuyǐng 【名】(optics) projection

投掷 tóuzhì 【动】throw; cast

投资 tóuzī 【动】invest 【名】investment; 智力 ～ intellectual investment

tòu

透 tòu 【动】❶ (of liquid, light, etc.) pass through; penetrate; 要～过现象看本质 see through superficialities to perceive the essence 雨水～不进帐篷来。Rain cannot leak into the tent. 阳光～过松枝照射下来。The rays of the sun are shining through the pine trees. 半路上忽然下起雨来, 他们的衣服都湿～了。It rained suddenly while they were on their way and they were soaked to the skin. ❷ leak (news); reveal or disclose (a secret; news; information, etc.); ～个信儿 let sb. in on the news ～不出一点儿消息来。Not a word of the news has been revealed. ❸ (of air, etc.) pass through; 打开窗户～～空气。Open the window and let in some fresh air. ❹ show through; 黑里～红 tanned and rosy-cheeked 【形】❶ thorough; complete; to the utmost extent (used only as a complement); 先把文件的精神吃～ have a thorough understanding of the meaning of the document first 道理要讲～。You ought to drive the point home. 他已经摸～了小李的脾气。He has got to know Xiao Li inside out. ❷ complete; sufficient; 下了一场～雨。That was a saturating rain. 苹果熟～了。The apples are completely ripe. Note: 透 used after certain adjectives and verbs to indicate superlative degree; 烦～了 extremely annoyed 糟～了 terrible 我恨～它了! I couldn't detest it more!

透彻 tòuchè 【形】thorough; penetrating; incisive; 把情况了解得很～ have a thorough knowledge of the circumstances 对形势作了～的分析 give an in-depth analysis of the situation

透顶 tòudǐng 【形】extremely; thoroughly (derog.) (usu. as a complement); 反动～ extremely reactionary 腐败～ rotten to the core 顽固～ extremely stubborn

透风 tòu = fēng not airtight; let in air

透镜 tòujìng 【名】lens

透亮 tòu = liàng (～儿) allow light to pass through

透亮 tòuliàng 【形】❶ clear; bright; 玻璃窗擦得真～。How bright and clean the window panes are! ❷ (of understanding) clear; 听了他的解释以后, 我心里～多了。Having heard his explanation, I now have a much clearer understanding of the matter.

透露 tòulù 【动】(of news, information, etc.) reveal; disclose; divulge; ～消息 leak news ～风声 leak information 我对他～过这种打算。I let him in on my plan.

透明 tòumíng 【形】transparent

透辟 tòupì 【形】penetrating; incisive; ～的论述 a penetrating exposition

透气 tòu = qì (～儿) ❶ ventilate; to air ❷ breathe fresh air ❸ give word to; tip off

透视 tòushì 【动】have an X-ray examination; be X-rayed

透支 tòuzhī 【动】overdraw; make an overdraft

tou

头（頭） tou 【尾】 *pronounced in the neutral tone* ❶ *after a noun*：石～ stone 木～ wood 舌～ tongue 馒～ steamed bun ❷ *after a word of locality*：上～ on；over 下～ under 里～ inside 外～ outside 前～ front 后～ back ❸ *after a verb or an adjective to form an abstract noun*：这本小说没什么看～儿。This novel is not worth reading. 他尝到了坚持长跑的甜～儿。He has discovered the benefit of long-distance running.

tū

凸 tū 【形】convex；protruding

秃 tū 【形】❶ bald：头顶～了 be getting bald ～尾巴鸡 a cock with no tail feathers ❷ bare (e.g. hill)；devoid of (leaves, trees, etc.)：～树 a bare tree 荒山～岭 bare hills and mountains ❸ (of sharp point or the sharp end of sth.) worn out；blunt：笔尖磨～了。This pen nib is worn out. ❹ (of article) end abruptly：他那篇文章还没写完呢，怪不得结尾有点儿～。He hasn't written the last part of the article yet and that's why it seems to end rather abruptly.

秃头 tūtóu 【名】bald head；freshly-shaven head

突 tū 【动】rush or dash forward；charge【副】◇ suddenly；abruptly：河水～涨。The river rose suddenly in spate.

突变 tūbiàn 【动】change suddenly；a sudden change takes place

突出 tūchū 【动】❶ stand out；stick out；protrude：那块礁石在落潮时就会～水面。That rock sticks out of the water at low tide. ❷ give prominence to：～重点 emphasize the key point【形】striking；salient；outstanding；prominent：～的特点 prominent characteristic ～的标志 prominent sign

突飞猛进 tū fēi měng jìn (advance) by leaps and bounds；make phenomenal progress；develop quickly：石油工业～地向前发展。The oil industry is developing by leaps and bounds.

突击 tūjī 【动】❶ assault ❷ rush (work)

突击队 tūjīduì 【名】shock brigade；assault force

突破 tūpò 【动】make a breakthrough：～防线 break through the line of defence ～封锁 break through the blockade ～技术难关 break through a technical barrier ～指标 overfulfil a quota 龙教授在数学基础理论研究方面有所～。Professor Long has made a breakthrough in his research on basic mathematical theory.

突破口 tūpòkǒu 【名】breach；gap

突起 tūqǐ 【动】❶ (of forces, events) suddenly arise；emerge or occur suddenly or unexpectedly：异军～. A new force (e. g. a school of thought, etc.) emerged unexpectedly. ❷ tower：山峰～. Mountain peaks tower into the sky.

突然 tūrán 【形】sudden；abrupt；unexpected：这个消息实在太～了。This news is really much too sudden. 下午天气～变冷了。In the afternoon the weather suddenly turned cold.

突如其来 tū rú qí lái sudden；abrupt：大家被这～的喊声惊住了。All

of us were startled at the sudden cry.

突围 tū=wéi break a seige

tú

图（圖） tú 【名】picture; drawing; illustration; chart; 画一张～ make a chart 看～识字 learn words with the aid of pictures【动】seek; pursue: ～方便 choose the easy or more convenient way ～省事 try to do things the easy way 我们干工作不～名，不～利。We work for neither fame nor gain.

图案 tú'àn 【名】design; pattern

图表 túbiǎo 【名】chart; graph; diagram

图钉 túdīng 【名】thumbtack

图画 túhuà 【名】〔张 zhāng〕painting; drawing

图解 tújiě 【动】explain through diagrams

图景 tújǐng 【名】prospects (*fig.*)

图谋 túmóu 【动】plot; scheme; plan (*derog.*): ～私利 seek personal gain

图片 túpiàn 【名】〔张 zhāng〕general term for pictures, photos, graphs, etc. which illustrate a certain topic

图书 túshū 【名】books in general

图书馆 túshūguǎn 【名】library

图像 túxiàng 【名】image

图形 túxíng 【名】pictorial illustration

图样 túyàng 【名】design; plan

图章 túzhāng 【名】〔枚 méi〕seal; stamp

图纸 túzhǐ 【名】〔张 zhāng〕paper on which a design or plan is drawn; blueprint

徒 tú 【名】◇ ❶ apprentice: 他俩是师～关系。They are master and apprentice. ❷ disciple or follower of a religion: 基督教～ a Christian ❸ fellow (*derog.*): 无耻之～ one who has lost all sense of shame【副】◇ ❶ in vain: ～费唇舌 waste one's breath ❷ simply; only; merely: ～有虚名 exist in name only ～具形式 be a mere formality

徒步 túbù 【副】on foot

徒弟 túdi 【名】apprentice; disciple

徒工 túgōng 【名】apprentice

徒劳 túláo 【动】futile effort; fruitless labour: ～无功 work in vain ～往返 go on a fool's errand 要想阻止历史潮流是～的。It is always futile to try to hold back the progress of history.

徒然 túrán 【形】futile; in vain; to no purpose: ～耗费精力 waste one's energy 大家的努力决不是～的。Our endeavour is by no means fruitless.

徒手 túshǒu 【形】bare-handed

徒刑 túxíng 【名】(prison) sentence; imprisonment

徒子徒孙 tú zǐ tú sūn disciples and followers (*derog.*)

途 tú

途径 tújìng 【名】way; channels; ways and means: 通过各种～增进两国人民之间的友谊。The friendship between the peoples of the two countries has been strengthened through various means.

途中 túzhōng 【名】on the way

涂（塗） tú 【动】❶ paint; apply: ～点药膏 apply a bit of ointment ～上一层漆 give it a coat of paint ❷ cross out: ～去两个字 cross out two characters

涂改 túgǎi 【动】cross out and make corrections

涂抹 túmǒ 【动】同"涂" ❶

涂脂抹粉 tú zhī mǒ fěn apply make-

up；(*fig.*) prettify；whitewash；虚伪奸诈的人常为自己～。Liars and hypocrites always make themselves out to be better than they are.

屠 tú

屠刀 túdāo 【名】〔把 bǎ〕butcher's knife

屠夫 túfū 【名】butcher

屠杀 túshā 【动】massacre；slaughter

屠宰 túzǎi 【动】slaughter (esp. for food)

土 tǔ

土 tǔ 【名】❶ earth；soil；dust：松松～ loosen the soil 满身是～ (of a person) be covered all over with dust ❷ ◇ land；territory：寸～不让 fight for every inch of land 【形】local；native：～方法 indigenous methods ～专家 an indigenous expert 他说的是很～的北京话。He speaks pure Beijing dialect.

土崩瓦解 tǔ bēng wǎ jiě disintegrate and collapse；fall apart

土产 tǔchǎn 【名】local product

土地 tǔdì 【名】❶ (farm) land；fields ❷ territory

土地法 tǔdìfǎ 【名】land law；agrarian law

土地改革 tǔdì gǎigé land reform

土豆 tǔdòu 【名】(～儿) potato

土法 tǔfǎ 【名】indigenous method

土方 tǔfāng 【名】cubic metre of earth

土匪 tǔfěi 【名】bandit

土改 tǔgǎi 【名】*short for* "土地改革" land reform

土豪劣绅 tǔháo lièshēn local tyrants and evil gentry

土话 tǔhuà 【名】local dialect

土路 tǔlù 【名】dirt road

土木工程 tǔmù gōngchéng civil engineering

土气 tǔqì 【名】rustic；uncouth；not refined

土壤 tǔrǎng 【名】❶ soil；earth：改良～ soil improvement ❷ hotbed；condition allowing sth. to develop

土生土长 tǔ shēng tǔ zhǎng locally born and brought up

土星 tǔxīng 【名】Saturn

土政策 tǔzhèngcè 【名】indigenous policy；locally cooked-up policy

土质 tǔzhì 【名】quality of the soil

吐 tǔ

吐 tǔ 【动】❶ spit：～痰 spit；spit phlegm 蚕～丝。Silkworms spin silk. ❷ exhale：～了口长气 exhale ❸ ◇ say；enunciate：～字清楚 enunciate words clearly ❹ ear；be in the ear：麦子～穗儿了。The wheat is in the ear.

另见 tù

吐故纳新 tǔ gù nà xīn get rid of the stale and take in the fresh

吐露 tǔlù 【动】speak up and disclose sth.

吐气音 tǔqìyīn 【名】voiced sound

吐 tù

吐 tù 【动】❶ vomit：恶心得要～。I feel very sick and need to throw up. ❷ be compelled to give back (what one has taken illegally)；make restitution

另见 tǔ

吐血 tù = xiě haematemesis；spit blood

兔 tù

兔 tù 【名】◇ hare；rabbit

兔死狐悲 tù sǐ hú bēi the fox mourns the death of the hare；(*fig.*) be compassionate with one's own kind；like grieves for like

兔子 tùzi 【名】〔只 zhī〕hare；rabbit

tuān

湍 tuān

湍急 tuānjí 【形】(of river) flowing rapidly

湍流 tuānliú 【名】a swift flow of water

tuán

团(團) tuán 【名】❶ group; organization：参观～ a group of visitors 旅行～ a tourist group ❷ (mil.) regiment ❸ (～儿) ball：把面揉成一个～ knead dough into a ball 【动】roll (sth.) into a ball：把纸～了 crush a piece of paper into a ball 【量】❶ for sth. in the shape of ball：一～毛线 a ball of wool 心中一～火 with great enthusiasm; warm-hearted; very anxious ❷ regiment

团伙 tuánhuǒ 【名】gang

团结 tuánjié 【动】unite

团聚 tuánjù 【动】have a reunion

团体 tuántǐ 【名】body; group; organization

团体操 tuántǐcāo 【名】group callisthenics

团团转 tuántuánzhuàn 【动】round and round：急得～ be as worried as anything

团员 tuányuán 【名】❶ member of a delegation or organization：他是文工团～。He is a member of the cultural troupe. ❷ League member; a member of the Communist Youth League

团圆 tuányuán 【动】have a family reunion

团长 tuánzhǎng 【名】❶ regimental commander ❷ head of a delegation

tuī

推 tuī 【动】❶ push：～车 push a cart ～门 push open a door ～了他一下 give him a push ❷ push forward; give impetus to; further：这个人物的出场把剧情的发展～向高潮。The appearance of this character brought the play to its climax. ❸ infer; deduce：从已知的前提～出新的判断 draw a further conclusion from a premise ❹ (of invitation, gift) decline; (of duty; responsibility, work) politely refuse; shirk; evade：别～了，这礼物你就收下吧! Please do accept the gift. Don't keep saying no. 不要把重担子～给别人。Don't try to shift the heavy work onto another person. ❺ postpone; delay; put off：动身的日期往后～几天。The departure date has been postponed a few days. ❻ clip; plane：～头 have one's hair clipped 用刨子把木板～光 plane a board

推波助澜 tuī bō zhù lán help intensify the billows and waves; (fig.) fan the fire; add fuel to the fire; incite (derog.)

推测 tuīcè 【动】speculate; guess

推陈出新 tuī chén chū xīn sort and discard some old things to bring forth the new：对于美术、音乐、戏剧等等，都应采取百花齐放，～的方针。In the fields of fine arts, music, and drama, etc. the policy of letting a hundred flowers bloom and discarding some old things to bring forth the new should be adopted.

推迟 tuīchí 【动】postpone

推辞 tuīcí 【动】reject; decline (an invitation, offer, etc.)

推倒 tuī//dǎo overturn

推动 tuīdòng 【动】push forward;

expedite（work）；give impetus to；propel；科学管理～了生产。Scientific management promotes production.

推断 tuīduàn 【动】infer；deduce

推翻 tuī∥fān ❶ overthrow（state power）：～了反动统治。The reactionary rule was overthrown. ❷ （of a proposal）reject；cast aside；（of a judgement）overturn：原来的方案被～了。The previous proposal was rejected.

推广 tuīguǎng 【动】popularize：～新品种 popularize new kinds of products ～普通话 popularize *Putonghua*

推荐 tuījiàn 【动】recommend

推进 tuījìn 【动】push forward；propel；carry forward to a new stage；把工作～一步 push the work forward 部队正在向前～。The troops were advancing.

推举 tuījǔ 【动】elect；choose：大家都～他当代表。We all voted for him as our representative.

推理 tuīlǐ 【名】inference；deduction

推论 tuīlùn 【名】inference；deduction 【动】infer；deduce；conclude：你这个结论是按照形式逻辑的方法～出来的。You arrived at your conclusion through the methods of formal logic.

推敲 tuīqiāo 【动】weigh and consider；deliberate：这个句子要很好地～一下。The wording of this sentence has to be discussed and improved. 这个提法值得～。This formulation of the question must be carefully weighed and considered.

推却 tuīquè 【动】reject；shirk（e.g. responsibility）

推让 tuīràng 【动】decline courteously in favour of another

推算 tuīsuàn 【动】calculate；work out

推土机 tuītǔjī 【名】〔台 tái〕bulldozer

推托 tuītuō 【动】make an excuse；find a pretext for not doing sth.：他～有事，没有参加那天的晚会。He made an excuse and did not come to the party that evening.

推脱 tuītuō 【动】shirk；evade：～责任 shirk one's responsibility

推委 tuīwěi 【动】shift responsibility；evade by giving an excuse

推想 tuīxiǎng 【动】reckon；guess 【名】guess

推销 tuīxiāo 【动】peddle；promote the sale of sth.

推卸 tuīxiè 【动】shift（responsibility）；shirk（duty）：～责任 pass the buck；shirk responsibility

推心置腹 tuī xīn zhì fù deal with others honestly and sincerely；show great confidence in sb.：两人～地谈了一个晚上。The two of them spent the whole evening in a heart-to-heart talk.

推行 tuīxíng 【动】pursue；implement；carry out（a policy）：～承包责任制 implement the contract system of 这种先进操作方法已在各厂～。This advanced method has been introduced in every factory.

推选 tuīxuǎn 【动】choose；elect

推移 tuīyí 【动】（of time）elapse；pass：随着时间的～，农业机械化程度会越来越高。As time passes, the degree of mechanization in agriculture will steadily increase.

推子 tuīzi 【名】〔把 bǎ〕hair clippers

tuí

颓（頽）tuí

颓败 tuíbài 【形】degenerate and corrupt

颓废 tuífèi 【形】decadent

颓丧 tuísàng 【形】downcast and disconsolate

颓唐 tuítáng 【形】dispirited; dejected

tuǐ

腿 tuǐ 【名】〔条 tiáo〕leg

腿脚 tuǐjiǎo 【名】legs and feet：～不灵便 have difficulty in walking 他老人家～很好，走路不成问题。This old man is still vigorous. He can walk a fair distance with no trouble.

tuì

退 tuì 【动】❶ step back; retreat：向后～两步 step back two steps ❷ send back; return（e. g. goods）：～款 refund ～票 return a ticket and get a refund 把稿子～回去 reject a manuscript ❸ withdraw from; resign; leave：～职 resign from office; retire from work ～伙 drop out of a meal-plan ❹ fade; recede：不～色 be colour fast 高烧～了。His fever went down.

退步 tuìbù 【动】backslide; fall behind; retrogress：最近他学习～了。He has lagged behind recently in his studies.【名】leeway; room for manoeuvre

退潮 tuì = cháo ebb tide

退出 tuìchū 【动】withdraw from

退化 tuìhuà 【动】(biol.) become vestigial：鸡的翅膀逐渐～，不会在空中飞行了。The wings of the chicken have become vestigial; it can no longer fly. 土豆种了几年之后就会～。After a few years planting, the quality of the potato crop deteriorates.

退还 tuìhuán 【动】return or send back（a purchase or gift）

退换 tuìhuàn 【动】exchange a purchase

退回 tuìhuí 【动】❶ send back; reject：来信原封～ return unopened letter to the sender ❷ retreat; go back：队伍从原路～。The troops went back by the same route.

退居 tuìjū 【动】❶ withdraw; retreat：～二线 to quit one's original position and keep to the sidelines ❷ retire

退路 tuìlù 【名】route of retreat

退赔 tuìpéi 【动】return what one has unlawfully taken or pay compensation for it

退却 tuìquè 【动】withdraw; retreat; fall back

退让 tuìràng 【动】make concessions to; make a compromise

退色 tuì = sè fade in colour

退烧 tuì = shāo bring down or allay a fever

退缩 tuìsuō 【动】shrink back; cower

退庭 tuìtíng 【动】withdraw from the court

退伍 tuì = wǔ retire or be discharged from active military service

退席 tuìxí 【动】leave meeting or dinner party half way through; walk out

退休 tuìxiū 【动】retire

退休金 tuìxiūjīn 【名】retirement pay; pension

退学 tuì = xué quit school; discontinue one's schooling

蜕

蜕 tuì 【动】❶（of snakes; insects）exuviate ❷（of birds）moult

蜕变 tuìbiàn 【动】(of person or thing) change qualitatively; degenerate

蜕化 tuìhuà 【动】(of insects) exuviate；(fig.) degenerate：思想～ be-

come ideologically corrupt ～为官僚主义者 degenerate and become a bureaucrat

蜕化变质　tuìhuà biàn zhì　degenerate

tūn

吞　tūn　【动】swallow

吞并　tūnbìng　【动】annex

吞没　tūnmò　【动】❶ devour; gobble up; 庄稼被洪水～。The flood engulfed all the crop fields. ❷ embezzle; misappropriate; ～公款 misappropriate public funds

吞噬　tūnshì　【动】gobble up; eat in large mouthfuls

吞吐量　tūntǔliàng　【名】(of a dock) loading and unloading capacity

吞吞吐吐　tūn tūn tǔ tǔ　【形】mince words; speak hesitantly; 别～的,有什么事快说吧! Please don't hesitate; just say what's on your mind.

tún

屯　tún　【动】❶ accumulate; hoard; store up; ～粮 store grain ❷ (of troops) station; ～兵 station troops (at a place)【名】◇ village; hamlet (usu. as part of the name of a village)

屯田　túntián　【名】station soldiers on the border and make them raise their own food (archaic)

囤　tún　【动】hoard; stock up　另见 dùn

囤积　túnjī　【动】hoard (goods for later sale at a higher price)

囤积居奇　túnjī jūqí　hoarding and speculation

臀　tún　【名】buttocks; bottom

tuō

托　tuō　【名】(～儿) sth. used to support sth. else (e.g. tray, saucer, etc.); 花～ (botany) receptacle【动】❶ hold sth. on the palm of one's hand; support sth. with one's hand or hands; ～着茶盘 balance a tray on one's palm ❷ entrust(sth. to sb.); ask (sb. to do sth.); ～人办事 entrust sb. to take care of the matter ～你给他捎点东西 I would like to ask you to take something to him. ❸ give as a pretext or excuse; ～故不来 fail to show up on some pretext

托词　tuōcí　【名】pretext; excuse; 他找了个～谢绝了朋友的邀请。He found some excuse for declining his friend's invitation.

托儿所　tuō'érsuǒ　【名】nursery school

托福　tuō = fú　(polite remark) (my good fortune) rest on yours; 托您的福,一切都还顺利。Everything is going smoothly, thank you.

托福　tuōfú　【名】TOEFL; test of English as a Foreign language

托付　tuōfù　【动】entrust

托管　tuōguǎn　【动】put under trusteeship

托拉斯　tuōlāsī　【名】trust

托人情　tuō rénqíng　get things done through connections

托运　tuōyùn　【动】consign

拖　tuō　【动】❶ tow; pull; haul; 汽艇～着木船。The steamer is taking a boat in tow. ❷ trail; drag; 小松鼠～着长尾巴 a squirrel with a long tail 长裙～到地上。Her skirt is trailing on the floor. ❸ procrastinate; delay; 今天的工作不要～到明天。Don't put off today's work

until tomorrow!

拖把 tuōbǎ 【名】mop

拖车 tuōchē 【名】〔辆 liàng〕trailer

拖后腿 tuō hòutuǐ hold sb. back：那么多家务事拖她的后腿，怎能不影响她的工作？Such a lot of housework holds her back；how could her job not be affected？

拖拉 tuōlā 【形】procrastinating：办事不～ not procrastinate in whatever one does 拖拖拉拉的作风要不得。A procrastinating work-style is something that should be done away with.

拖拉机 tuōlājī 【名】〔台 tái〕tractor

拖累 tuōlèi 【动】be a burden to sb.；encumber

拖泥带水 tuō ní dài shuǐ messy；sloppy；procrastinating：他干什么总是一口气干完，从不～。He gets things done quickly and never procrastinates.

拖欠 tuōqiàn 【动】be behind in payment

拖鞋 tuōxié 【名】〔只 zhī、双 shuāng〕slipper

拖延 tuōyán 【动】procrastinate；delay

脱 tuō 【动】❶ (of skin, hair, paint, leaves) shed；come off：手上～了一层皮。The skin on my hands is flaking. ❷ (of hat, shoes) take off：～帽 take off one's hat ～衣服 take off one's clothes；undress ❸ be divorced from；be separated from：～轨 (of a train) be derailed ～缰之马 a horse that has slipped the bridle ❹ be missing or omitted；be left out：这一版～了几个字。A few words have been left out of this page of proofs. 织毛衣的时候～了几针。I dropped some stitches while I was knitting.

脱产 tuō=chǎn be relieved of one's duty (in order to do administrative

work,study,etc.)

脱稿 tuō=gǎo be completed (a book)：那部新编的词典至今还脱不了稿。That new dictionary is not yet completed.

脱节 tuō=jié come apart；become disconnected：水管子～了，水漏了一地。The water pipes became disconnected and water leaked all over the place. 产销不能～。Production and sales must be properly balanced.

脱口而出 tuō kǒu ér chū speak on impulse or without forethought

脱离 tuōlí 【动】be divorced from；be isolated from：～危险 be out of danger ～接触 (of armed forces) disengage ～群众 divorce oneself from the masses ～关系 break off relations with

脱粒机 tuōlìjī 【名】〔台 tái〕thresher；threshing machine

脱漏 tuōlòu 【动】omit；leave out

脱落 tuōluò 【动】(of hair, leaves, etc.) fall off；drop；fall out：羽毛～ moult 牙齿～了。His tooth came out. 油漆～。The paint is chipping off.

脱毛 tuō=máo moult

脱贫 tuōpín 【动】be lifted out of poverty and backwardness：～致富 shed off poverty and become rich

脱身 tuō=shēn get away (from work, business, etc.)；disengage oneself from；slip away：我今天不能～，改天再去看你吧！I can't get away today, but I'll come to see you some other time. 他正在开会，脱不开身。He is attending a meeting and cannot leave.

脱手 tuō=shǒu get off one's hands：那批货物近期还脱不了手。I can't get that batch of goods off my hands in the near future.

脱胎换骨 tuō tāi huàn gǔ make a thoroughgoing change；completely

remould oneself

脱逃　tuōtáo　【动】run away；flee；畏罪～ abscond to avoid punishment 临阵～ flee from battle

脱险　tuō＝xiǎn　escape from danger

脱销　tuōxiāo　【动】be out of stock；be sold out

脱颖而出　tuō yǐng ér chū　the point of an awl sticking out through a bag—talent revealing itself

脱脂棉　tuōzhīmián　【名】absorbent cotton

tuó

驮（馱）　tuó　【动】(of animals) carry on the back：～粮食 carry a load of grain on its back 马帮～着年货,源源不断地送往山区。Caravans of horses headed toward the mountains one after another, carrying goods for the New Year celebration.

驼（駝）　tuó　【名】◇ camel；～峰 a camel's hump ～绒 camel's hair 【动】hunch：奶奶的背都～了。My grandmother's back has become bent.

驼背　tuóbèi　【名】hunchback

鸵（鴕）　tuó

鸵鸟　tuóniǎo　【名】〔只 zhī〕ostrich

tuǒ

妥　tuǒ　【形】❶ proper；suitable；如有不～之处,望批评指正。If you find anything improper, please make corrections. ❷ ready；settled；货物已经备～。All the goods have been collected and got ready. 出发的日期已经谈～了。The day for departure has been fixed after some consultation.

妥当　tuǒdang　【形】well-thought-out；appropriate；proper

妥善　tuǒshàn　【形】proper；well-arranged：老弱病残得到～安置。Those who are old, weak, ill or disabled are well taken care of.

妥帖　tuǒtiē　【形】proper；appropriate；fitting

妥协　tuǒxié　【动】compromise

椭（橢）　tuǒ

椭圆　tuǒyuán　【名】oval-shaped；ellipse；oval

tuò

拓　tuò　另见 tà

拓荒　tuò＝huāng　reclaim wasteland

唾　tuò　【动】spit

唾骂　tuòmà　【动】abuse；rebuke coarsely

唾沫　tuòmo　【名】spittle

唾弃　tuòqì　【动】cast aside；spurn

唾液　tuòyè　【名】saliva

W

wā

挖　wā 【动】dig：～土 dig earth
～洞 dig a hole ～潜力 tap potential

挖掘　wājué 【动】dig；excavate：～地下宝藏 tap mineral deposits

挖空心思　wā kōng xīnsi　rack one's brains；think hard（derog.）：他～想了半天，也没有想出好办法来。He thought hard for a long while, but wasn't able to think of a good solution.

挖苦　wāku 【动】ridicule；hurt others by sarcastic remarks：学生有缺点要善意帮助，不要～讽刺。We should help our students to overcome their shortcomings, not ridicule them.

挖潜　wāqián 【动】tap the latent power

挖墙脚　wā qiángjiǎo　undermine the foundation；subvert

挖土机　wātǔjī 【名】〔台 tái〕excavator

洼（窪）　wā 【名】（～儿）a hollow place；depression：水～ a small depression（in the earth）filled with water（e.g. after rain）【形】low；hollow；low-lying：～地 low-lying land 这个地方太～了。This place is too low.

蛙　wā 【名】〔只 zhī〕frog
蛙泳　wāyǒng 【名】frog style（in swimming）；breast stroke

wá

娃　wá 【名】◇ baby
娃娃　wáwa 【名】〔个 gè〕❶ baby ❷ doll

wǎ

瓦　wǎ 【名】tile 【量】short for "瓦特"：六十～的电灯泡 a sixty-watt bulb

瓦工　wǎgōng 【名】❶ the work of laying bricks and tiles, whitewashing, etc. ❷ bricklayer

瓦匠　wǎjiang 【名】bricklayer

瓦解　wǎjiě 【动】❶ collapse；break up ❷ demoralize：～敌军 break down the morale of the enemy troops

瓦砾　wǎlì 【名】rubble：一片～（buildings reduced to）nothing but rubble

瓦斯　wǎsī 【名】gas

瓦特　wǎtè 【量】watt

wà

袜（襪）wà 【名】sock; stocking

袜子　wàzi 【名】〔只 zhǐ、双 shuāng〕sock; stocking

wa

哇 wa 【助】a modification of 啊，见"啊" a；你好～? How are you?

wāi

歪 wāi 【形】askew; crooked：～戴着帽子 wear one's cap at an angle 这个字写～了。This character was written crookedly. 【动】incline to one side：他一～头，垒球从他耳边擦过。He ducked his head and the baseball whistled past his ear.

歪风　wāifēng 【名】gust of evil wind; bad tendency：煞住～邪气 check bad tendencies 那是一股～。That's a gust of evil wind.

歪理　wāilǐ 【名】false reasoning; unreasonable excuses

歪门邪道　wāi mén xié dào crooked ways; immoral practice

歪曲　wāiqū 【动】distort; misrepresent; twist：～事实 distort the facts ～原来的意思 twist the original meaning

歪歪扭扭　wāiwāiniǔniǔ 【形】twisted：这些字写得～的，真难看。These characters are written crookedly and look awful.

wài

外 wài 【名】❶ outside (as opp. to 内 or 里, usu. used with a noun)：窗～的丁香花都开了。The lilacs outside the windows are in bloom. 门～有人找你。There is somebody outside asking to see you. 这个陈列室对～开放。This exhibition room is open to the public. ❷ (place) other than where one is (as opp. to 本)：他到～省去了。He's gone to another province. ❸ foreign countries：中～文化交流 cultural exchanges between China and foreign countries

外币　wàibì 【名】foreign currency

外边　wàibiān 【名】❶ outside：墙～有一棵枣树。There is a date tree outside the wall. ❷ exterior; surface：铁桶的～刷了一层油漆。The outside of the iron bucket was given a coat of paint. 这个橘子～还好好的，可是里边烂了。This orange looks all right but it's rotten inside.

外表　wàibiǎo 【名】(of persons or things) outward appearance; surface

外宾　wàibīn 【名】foreign guest

外部　wàibù 【名】❶ outside; external ❷ surface; exterior：这座楼房从～看普普通通，但是里边却很讲究。This building looks quite ordinary on the outside but is very luxurious inside.

外埠　wàibù 【名】city or town other than where one is

外出　wàichū 【动】go out

外地　wàidì 【名】places in a country other than where one is

外电　wàidiàn 【名】dispatches from foreign news agencies

外调　wàidiào 【动】❶ transfer to other localities ❷ go to another work unit to make investigations

外敷　wàifū 【动】(med.) apply (ointment, etc.); external application

外观 wàiguān 【名】(of things) outward appearance

外国 wàiguó 【名】foreign country

外行 wàiháng 【形】not professional；lay：～话 layman's remarks 他开拖拉机是好手，开汽车也不～。He is good at driving a tractor, and not bad at driving a car either. 【名】layman：对生物学我是～。As far as biology goes, I'm a layman.

外号 wàihào 【名】nick-name

外汇 wàihuì 【名】foreign exchange

外籍 wàijí 【名】foreign nationality

外交 wàijiāo 【名】diplomacy

外交部 wàijiāobù 【名】ministry of foreign affairs；foreign ministry

外交关系 wàijiāo guānxì diplomatic relations

外交家 wàijiāojiā 【名】diplomat

外交使团 wàijiāo shǐtuán diplomatic corps

外交特权 wàijiāo tèquán diplomatic privileges

外交政策 wàijiāo zhèngcè foreign policy

外界 wàijiè 【名】outside world；beyond one's own circle：～评论 comment from outside one's own circle 听取～的反应 listen to the response of the outside world 一定要使自己的思想合于客观～的规律性。We must make our thinking conform to the workings of the objective world.

外景 wàijǐng 【名】outdoor scenes a scene shot on location

外科 wàikē 【名】surgery；surgical department

外壳 wàiké 【名】shell；crust

外快 wàikuài 【名】〔笔 bǐ〕extra income：找～ look for extra income 挣～ earn extra income

外来语 wàiláiyǔ 【名】word of foreign origin

外力 wàilì 【名】external force

外流 wàiliú 【动】flow out；outflow

外贸 wàimào 【名】foreign trade

外貌 wàimào 【名】looks；external appearance

外面 wàimiàn 【名】outside；exterior

外婆 wàipó 【名】maternal grandmother

外强中干 wài qiáng zhōng gān strong in appearance but weak in reality；outwardly strong but inwardly weak：你别以为他身强力壮，实际上是～。Though he looks strong, he is actually weak.

外侨 wàiqiáo 【名】foreign national

外勤 wàiqín 【名】❶ work done outside of the office or in the field ❷ someone whose work for an institution involves many errands outside of the office

外人 wàirén 【名】❶ foreigner ❷ outsider；stranger

外伤 wàishāng 【名】trauma

外商 wàishāng 【名】foreign businessman

外省 wàishěng 【名】province other than where one is

外甥 wàisheng 【名】nephew (sister's son)

外甥女 wàishengnǚ 【名】niece (sister's daughter)

外事 wàishì 【名】foreign affairs

外孙女 wàisūnnǚ 【名】granddaughter (daughter's daughter)

外孙子 wàisūnzi 【名】grandson (daughter's son)

外逃 wàitáo 【动】run away；flee

外套 wàitào 【名】〔件 jiàn〕overcoat

外头 wàitou 【名】同"外边"

外围 wàiwéi 【名】outer；periphery：～组织 an above-ground organization which assists an underground party or organization；peripheral organization

外文 wàiwén 【名】foreign language

外项　wàixiàng　【名】（maths.） extreme term

外销　wàixiāo　【动】be for export

外衣　wàiyī　【名】〔件 jiàn〕❶ coat; overcoat ❷ （fig.） camouflage; (under) the cloak of

外因　wàiyīn　【名】external cause

外语　wàiyǔ　【名】foreign language

外援　wàiyuán　【名】foreign aid

外债　wàizhài　【名】foreign debt

外资　wàizī　【名】foreign capital

外祖父　wàizǔfù　【名】 maternal grandfather

外祖母　wàizǔmǔ　【名】 maternal grandmother

wān

弯（彎）　wān　【形】bent; curving：果实累累压～了树枝。The branches were bent under the weight of the heavy fruit. ～～的月牙儿挂在夜空。A crescent moon hung in the night sky.【动】bend：把钢筋～过来 bent the steel bar 他～下腰来查看地上的脚印。He bent down to examine the footprints.【名】（～儿）a bend：拐一个～ make a turn 这根管子有个～。There is a bend in this tube.

弯路　wānlù　【名】❶ crooked road; zigzag path ❷ （fig.）detour; roundabout way：只要善于学习,遇事同别人商量,就可以少走～。If you are good at learning from books and consulting with others, you will avoid making mistakes in your work.

弯曲　wānqū　【形】bent; curving

蜿　wān

蜿蜒　wānyán　【形】winding; meandering

wán

丸　wán　【名】pills：把药制成～剂 make (Chinese) medicine into pills 【量】for pill：每次服一～ take one pill each time

丸药　wányào　【名】（med.）pill

丸子　wánzi　【名】food in the shape of a ball

完　wán　【动】❶ finish; complete：～稿 complete a draft ❷ use up; run out of：墨水用～了。The ink is used up. ❸ end; be closed; conclude：事情办～了。That matter is concluded. 我的话～了,你说吧！I've finished speaking, now you have your say, please!

完备　wánbèi　【形】complete

完毕　wánbì　【动】come to an end; be completed （usu. in written language）：工作～ finish one's work 典礼进行～。The ceremony was over.

完成　wán // chéng　complete; fulfil; accomplish：～定额 fulfil the quota

完蛋　wán = dàn　fall through

完稿　wán = gǎo　finish a piece of writing; complete the manuscript

完工　wán = gōng　finish construction

完好　wánhǎo　【形】in good condition; intact：～如初 restored to its previous perfect condition 这些文物保存得很～。These cultural artifacts have been kept in very good condition. 赵州桥距今虽有一千三百多年了,但仍然～无损。The Zhaozhou Bridge was built more than 1300 years ago, but it is still in perfect condition.

完结　wánjié　【动】end; be over; finish

完竣 wánjùn 【动】(of project, etc.) be completed

完满 wánmǎn 【形】satisfactory; successful

完美 wánměi 【形】satisfactory; perfect：～ 的艺术形式 ideal art form

完美无缺 wánměi wú quē perfect; flawless; leave nothing to be desired：～ 的事物是没有的。Perfection is beyond our grasp.

完全 wánquán 【形】❶ complete; whole; in full：这个词的用法讲得不～。The usages of this word were not given in full. ❷ entirely：我同你的看法～一致。I share your view. 我～同意你的意见。I agree with you entirely.

完人 wánrén 【名】perfect man

完善 wánshàn 【形】perfect; excellent：准备工作做得很～。The preparatory work has been very well done. 这是一所设备～的医院。This is a hospital with excellent facilities.

完事 wán=shì come to an end; be finished

完整 wánzhěng 【形】complete; comprehensive; intact：领土～ territorial integrity ～ 的理论体系 a comprehensive theoretical system

玩 wán 【动】(～儿) ❶ play; amuse oneself; have fun：小方昨天去香山～了一天。Yesterday Xiao Fang went to the Fragrant Hills and spent the day there. 他是说着～的，你别当真。He was only joking. You mustn't take it seriously. ❷ play (a game, etc.)：你喜欢～排球吗? Do you like to play volleyball? ❸ play (tricks); practise (deception)：～ 花招 play tricks

玩忽职守 wánhū zhíshǒu neglect one's duty

玩火自焚 wán huǒ zì fén a person who plays with fire is likely to get burned; (fig.) a person who tries to harm others is likely to harm himself

玩具 wánjù 【名】toy

玩弄 wánnòng 【动】❶ flirt with; trifle with the affections of：小李的女朋友是真爱他，不是在～他。Xiao Li's girlfriend really loves him and is not just leading him on. ❷ toy with：～ 词藻 toy with ornate phrases ❸ play (tricks); practise tricks and deception：～ 权术 engage in the art of political manoeuvering ～ 种种卑劣手法 resort to all sorts of despicable tricks

玩赏 wánshǎng 【动】enjoy; take pleasure in

玩耍 wánshuǎ 【动】play; have fun with; amuse oneself

玩味 wánwèi 【动】meditate; ruminate over (the significance of sth.)

玩笑 wánxiào 【名】joke; jest; fun

玩意儿 wányìr 【名】toy; gadget

顽(頑) wán

顽敌 wándí 【名】die-hard enemy

顽固 wángù 【形】❶ stubborn; pigheaded; opinionated：这个人比较～，不容易接受新鲜事物。This man is rather pig-headed; it's hard for him to accept new things. ❷ diehard：～ 派 die-hards ～ 分子 diehard ❸ (of an illness) stubborn; hard to cure：这种皮肤病很～。This kind of skin disease is very hard to cure.

顽固不化 wángù bù huà incorrigibly obstinate

顽抗 wánkàng 【动】resist stubbornly (derog.)

顽皮 wánpí 【形】naughty; mischievous

顽强 wánqiáng 【形】❶ indomitable; staunch; tenacious：进行～的斗

争 carry out a determined struggle 意志～ indomitable will 这一仗打得很～。This was a stubbornly fought battle. ❷ stubborn (*as an adverbial adjunct*)：一个人如果有封建思想,那么这种思想总是要～地表现出来的。If one has feudal ideas it can't help but express itself.

顽症 wánzhèng 【名】a persistent disease

wǎn

挽 wǎn 【动】❶ draw; pull：手～着手 hand in hand ❷ roll (one's sleeves, etc.)：～袖子 roll up one's sleeves ～起裤腿儿 roll up one's trouserlegs

挽歌 wǎngē 【名】elegy; dirge

挽回 wǎnhuí 【动】retrieve; save：～影响 counteract bad publicity 不可～的损失 an irretrievable loss

挽救 wǎnjiù 【动】save; rescue; redeem：～病人的生命 save a patient's life ～犯错误的人 try to rescue someone who has gone astray

挽联 wǎnlián 【名】elegiac couplet

挽留 wǎnliú 【动】persuade (sb.) to stay：朋友们一再～,他还是走了。He left, though his friends pressed him to stay.

惋 wǎn

惋惜 wǎnxī 【动】feel sorry over a certain loss

婉 wǎn

婉言 wǎnyán 【副】in tactful words：～劝阻 tactfully dissuade sb. from doing sth. ～谢绝 tactfully decline

婉转 wǎnzhuǎn 【形】❶ in a tactful way; mildly and in a roundabout way：措辞～ in tactful terms ～地提出意见 raise one's opinions in an indirect way ❷ (of singing, etc.)

sweet and charming：歌声～ sweet singing 树上的小鸟叫得 ～ 动听。The little birds in the trees sang beautifully.

晚 wǎn 【名】◇ evening; night：从早到～ from morning till night 【形】❶ late：～秋 late autumn ～稻 late rice ❷ late; not on time：来～了 come late ～到了几分钟 arrive a few minutes late

晚安 wǎn'ān 【动】good night

晚报 wǎnbào 【名】evening paper

晚辈 wǎnbèi 【名】the younger generation; one's juniors

晚餐 wǎncān 【名】supper

晚点 wǎn = diǎn behind schedule

晚饭 wǎnfàn 【名】supper; evening meal

晚会 wǎnhuì 【名】evening party

晚婚 wǎnhūn 【名】late marriage

晚间 wǎnjiān 【名】evening

晚节 wǎnjié 【名】a person's integrity in old age：保持～ maintain one's integrity in one's later years

晚年 wǎnnián 【名】old age

晚期 wǎnqī 【名】later period; later stage

晚上 wǎnshang 【名】evening; night

晚霞 wǎnxiá 【名】sunset glow; evening glow

晚宴 wǎnyàn 【名】dinner party

晚育 wǎnyù 【名】give birth at a late age

碗 wǎn 【名】〔个 gè〕bowl

wàn

万 (萬) wàn 【数】ten thousand 【副】under any circumstances (*used for strong emphasis before the negative*)：～没有想到会在这里遇见你。The last thing I expected was to find you here. ～难从命。I

cannot under any circumstances comply with your request.

万变不离其宗 wàn biàn bù lí qí zōng essentialy remain the same in spite of many apparent changes

万恶 wàn'è 【形】thoroughly wicked; diabolical

万分 wànfēn 【形】very; extremely; exceedingly: 惶恐 ～ exceedingly frightened ～ 感动 very much moved

万古长青 wàngǔ cháng qīng flourish forever; be ever-lasting: 祝两国人民的友谊～。May the friendship between the peoples of (our) two countries last forever.

万金油 wànjīnyóu 【名】❶ a kind of cooling ointment ❷ Jack of all trades and master of none

万里长城 Wàn Lǐ Chángchéng the Great Wall

万里长征 Wàn lǐ chángzhēng long march: 今天的胜利不过是～走完了第一步。The present victory is only the first step in a ten thousand *li* long march.

万马奔腾 wàn mǎ bēnténg ten thousand horses gallop forward; (*fig.*) surge ahead: 黄河以～之势滚滚向前。The Yellow River surges onward like ten thousand horses galloping.

万能 wànnéng 【形】❶ all-powerful; omnipotent: 思想教育并不是～的，还需要辅之以必要的制度和措施。Ideological persuasion not all-powerful; it must be supplemented by necessary institutions and measures. ❷ universal; all-purpose: ～铣床 an all-purpose milling machine

万千 wànqiān 【形】innumerable; myriad: 变化～ innumerable changes

万事大吉 wàn shì dà jí everything is fine; all is well; everything goes off without a hitch: 别以为你的病动了手术就～了，其实以后还得继续服药和调养。Don't assume that the surgical operation resolves everything; in fact, you must go on taking medicine and take good care of yourself.

万寿无疆 wàn shòu wú jiāng (wish sb.) a long life

万水千山 wàn shuǐ qiān shān ten thousand mountains and rivers; (*fig.*) long and arduous journey

万岁 wàn suì long live

万万 wànwàn 【数】one hundred million 【副】absolutely (*used before a negative word as an intensive expression*, 同"万"【副】, *but more colloquial*): ～ 不可粗心大意。You simply must not be careless. 他～没有想到那次和她的分别竟是永别了。It certainly never occurred to him when they parted that he would never see her again.

万无一失 wàn wú yī shī not a chance of an error; absolutely certain: 由他掌舵通过这段激流险滩，是～的。With him at the helm, we are a hundred percent safe crossing these treacherous rapids. 他做事小心谨慎，～。He is very prudent and careful and absolutely reliable in whatever he does.

万物 wànwù 【名】all things on earth

万幸 wànxìng 【形】unusually lucky (usu. referring to a narrow escape from disaster): 这样大的暴风雪，牲畜没有伤亡，真是～。We have been unusually lucky in having no loss of livestock despite the severity of the storm.

万一 wànyī 【名】eventuality: 以防～ be prepared for any eventuality 【副】just in case: 要防止情况～发生变化。You must be prepared just in case the situation should

change. 你还是带个手电吧，～回来得晚呢! You'd better take a flashlight with you in case you come back late.

万有引力 wànyǒu yǐnlì （phys.) gravitation

万众一心 wàn zhòng yī xīn all of one heart and one mind; united like one man

万紫千红 wàn zǐ qiān hóng a profusion of colours; a riot of colour; (fig.) rich in variety: 在文艺园地上，～，百花争艳。In the garden of literature and art, a hundred flowers bloom luxuriantly.

腕 wàn

腕子 wànzi 【名】wrist

wāng

汪 wāng

汪洋 wāngyáng 【名】vast expanse of water

汪洋大海 wāngyáng dàhǎi a vast ocean; a boundless ocean: 这片地低洼，下大雨就成～! Whenever it rains, this lowland area becomes a vast ocean!

wáng

亡 wáng 【动】◇ ❶ die; perish ❷ (of a country) destroy; subjugate

亡国 wáng = guó conquer a country; a country is conquered; the fall of a nation

亡国奴 wángguónú 【名】subject of a conquered nation

亡命之徒 wáng mìng zhī tú desperado

亡羊补牢 wáng yáng bǔ láo (often followed by "犹未为晚") it is not too late to mend the fold after one sheep has been lost; (fig.) after an error or failure, it is still worthwhile to take precautions against further problems

王 wáng 【名】❶ king ❷ head; chief ❸ best or strongest of its kind

王八 wángba 【名】❶ popular name for turtle or tortoise ❷ cuckold

王法 wángfǎ 【名】law and order

王国 wángguó 【名】kingdom

王后 wánghòu 【名】queen; wife of a king

王牌 wángpái 【名】trump card

王子 wángzǐ 【名】prince; son of a king

wǎng

网（網） wǎng 【名】net; network: 蜘蛛～ spider's web 交通～ transportation network 雷达～ radar grid

网点 wǎngdiǎn 【名】a network of commercial establishments

网兜 wǎngdōu 【名】〔个 gè〕string bag

网罗 wǎngluó 【动】gather; seek and collect (usu. derog.): ～党羽 seek out and recruit henchmen

网络 wǎngluò 【名】network

网球 wǎngqiú 【名】❶ tennis ❷ tennis ball

枉 wǎng

枉费心机 wǎngfèi xīnjī rack one's brains to no avail; scheme in vain

枉然 wǎngrán 【形】in vain, useless; to no avail: 光有好的条件，主观不努力也是～。Favourable conditions are of no avail without personal effort.

往 wǎng 【动】❶ go：南来北～ coming and going in all directions ❷ go to；leave for：你～东，我～西，咱俩不同路。You're going east, I'm going west. We've chosen different paths. 列车开～北京。This train is bound for Beijing. 【介】to；toward：～前看 look forward ～左边拐 turn to the left

往常 wǎngcháng 【名】what was usual in the past：今天到会的人比～多。There are more people attending the meeting today than usual.

往返 wǎngfǎn 【动】to and fro；back and forth：他经常～于北京上海之间。He often travels back and forth between Beijing and Shanghai. 【名】going and coming back：从我们村到县城，～只要一小时左右。From our village to the town, it takes us only about an hour both ways. 我买的是～票，他买的是单程票。I bought a return-ticket; the one he bought is one-way.

往后 wǎnghòu 【名】from now on；later on；in the future

往来 wǎnglái 【动】come and go；to and fro；back and forth：街上车辆～不断。Buses and cars run back and forth along the streets. 【名】dealings between（countries, etc.）：中国人民同世界各国人民的友好～日益增多。China's friendly contacts with the peoples of other countries are becoming more and more frequent.

往年 wǎngnián 【名】former years；previous years

往日 wǎngrì 【名】former days；the past

往事 wǎngshì 【名】past events

往往 wǎngwǎng 【副】usually（*meaning that this is the case under ordinary conditions or that this is the case under a certain specific condition；can never be modified by a negative word*）：作家写一篇小说，～要修改好几遍。A novelist usually has to revise his manuscript many times. 运动员的成绩每提高一点，～要经过艰苦的努力。Every time an athlete breaks his own record, even if by a fraction, it costs him enormous effort. 星期日他～不在家。He is usually out on Sundays.

wàng

妄 wàng

妄图 wàngtú 【动】try in vain；attempt in vain（*derog.*）

妄想 wàngxiǎng 【动】hope in vain；attempt in vain 【名】vain hope；wishful thinking

妄自菲薄 wàng zì fěibó belittle oneself：我们对自己的估计应该实事求是，不要自高自大，也不要～。Let's be realistic in our self-assessment, don't be conceited, but don't be self-effacing either.

妄自尊大 wàng zì zūn dà have too high an opinion of oneself

忘 wàng 【动】forget

忘本 wàng=běn forget one's bitter past；forget one's class origin

忘掉 wàng//diào forget

忘恩负义 wàng ēn fù yì be ungrateful；lack any sense of gratitude

忘乎所以 wàng hū suǒyǐ forget oneself；be carried away：在胜利面前，不要～。One mustn't be carried away by successes.

忘记 wàngjì 【动】forget

忘却 wàngquè 【动】forget

忘我 wàngwǒ 【形】selfless：～的献身精神 a selfless spirit of dedicating oneself (to a noble cause) ～地劳动 work selflessly

旺 wàng 【形】prosperous；vigorous；flourishing：火 根 ～。The flames are leaping ligh. 麦苗长势很 ～。The wheat seedlings are flourishing.

旺季 wàngjì 【名】season；in season

旺盛 wàngshèng 【形】full of life；vigorous；flourishing：草木 ～ lush vegetation 精力 ～ full of vigour 士 气 ～ with high morale

望 wàng 【动】❶ look into the distance：抬头远 ～ raise one's head and look into the distance ❷〈书〉hope；expect；wish：～你早日恢复 健康。Best wishes for your speedy recovery. ～准时出席。You are expected to be present and on time.

望尘莫及 wàng chén mò jí be so far behind that one can only see the dust raised by the rider ahead；(fig.) be too far behind to catch up：他中国画画得真好，我 ～。He is very good at traditional Chinese painting. He surpasses me by far.

望而生畏 wàng ér shēng wèi be daunted at the sight of sb. or sth.

望风披靡 wàng fēng pīmǐ flee pellmell at the mere sight of the advancing troops

望文生义 wàng wén shēng yì take the words too literally；interpret without real understanding

望眼欲穿 wàng yǎn yù chuān be anxiously expectant：～ 地盼望亲人 归来 be anxiously awaiting the return of one's loved ones

望洋兴叹 wàng yáng xīng tàn be deeply aware of one's own helplessness when faced with a great task

望远镜 wàngyuǎnjìng 【名】telescope；field glasses

望子成龙 wàng zǐ chéng lóng harbour high expectations of one's children

wēi

危 wēi 【形】◇ ❶ dangerous；harmful；risky：～如累卵 as precarious as a pile of eggs ❷ dying：病～ be critically ill

危害 wēihài 【动】harm；endanger：～健康 endanger one's health ～ 集 体 do harm to the collective 【名】harm：无知给这项工作造成了极大的 ～。Ignorance has brought great damage to this project.

危害性 wēihàixìng 【名】harmfulness

危机 wēijī 【名】crisis

危及 wēijí 【动】endanger：～人民的 生命财产 endanger people's lives and property ～群众安全 endanger the safety of the masses

危急 wēijí 【形】critical；in imminent peril；at stake

危惧 wēijù 【动】be in fear

危难 wēinàn 【名】danger and disaster

危亡 wēiwáng 【名】at stake；(of nation) imminent danger of being conquered

危险 wēixiǎn 【形】dangerous

危险性 wēixiǎnxìng 【名】danger；exposure to danger

危言耸听 wēi yán sǒng tīng deliberately create a sensation by making startling statements

危在旦夕 wēi zài dànxī expect death at any moment；in imminent danger

危重 wēizhòng 【形】critically ill

威 wēi

威逼 wēibī 【动】coerce

威风 wēifēng 【名】power and prestige：练兵场上，老英雄～不减当年。Those veteran soldiers were as awe-inspiring on the drill ground

as in the days of their youth.【形】imposing; impressive: 参加检阅的队伍真～。The troops being reviewed are very impressive indeed.

威风凛凛　wēifēng lǐnlǐn　with great dignity; awe-inspiring

威吓　wēihè　【动】threaten; intimidate

威力　wēilì　【名】might; force

威慑　wēishè　【动】threaten with force; deter

威望　wēiwàng　【名】prestige and repute

威武　wēiwǔ　【形】powerful

威武雄壮　wēiwǔ xióngzhuàng　displaying power and grandeur

威胁　wēixié　【动】threaten; menace

威信　wēixìn　【名】prestige

威信扫地　wēixìn sǎo dì　with one's reputation dragged through the mud; be thoroughly discredited

威严　wēiyán　【形】dignified; august

逶 wēi

逶迤　wēiyí　【形】winding; meandering: ～的盘山公路 a road winding through the mountains 河水～东流。The river meanders to the east.

微 wēi　【形】◇ tiny; minute; small: 收效甚～ yield little result

微波　wēibō　【名】microwave

微薄　wēibó　【形】meagre: 力量～ meagre strength ～的礼物 modest gift

微不足道　wēi bù zú dào　so trivial that it is not worth mentioning; insignificant; trivial: 脱离了集体, 个人的力量是～的。Divorced from the collective, the strength of an individual is insignificant.

微风　wēifēng　【名】gentle breeze

微观　wēiguān　【形】microcosmic: ～考察 microcosmic investigation

微乎其微　wēi hū qí wēi　very small;

minute: 地壳一些～的变化, 有的是可以通过仪器测量出来的。Some of the minute changes in the earth's crust can be detected by means of instruments.

微机　wēijī　【名】〔台 tái〕microcomputer

微积分　wēijīfēn　【名】(maths.) infinitesimal calculus

微粒　wēilì　【名】minute particle

微量元素　wēiliàngyuánsù　【名】trace element

微妙　wēimiào　【形】subtle; delicate: ～的道理 complex and subtle argument 关系很～ subtle and delicate relationship

微弱　wēiruò　【形】weak feeble

微生物　wēishēngwù　【名】microbe

微微　wēiwēi　【形】slight; gentle (attributive and adverbial adjunct only): ～的春风 a gentle spring breeze ～一笑 a slight smile ～发颤的手 slightly trembling hands

微细　wēixì　【形】very small; very fine

微小　wēixiǎo　【形】little; tiny

微笑　wēixiào　【动】smile【名】smile

微型　wēixíng　【形】miniature; mini

巍 wēi

巍峨　wēi'é　【形】(of mountains or buildings) towering: ～的高峰 a towering peak

巍然　wēirán　【形】(of mountains or buildings) majestic: ～屹立 stand majestically ～如山 as majestic as a mountain

巍巍　wēiwēi　【形】(of mountains, etc.) towering; lofty

wéi

为(爲)　wéi　【动】❶◇ do; act (usu. in written language): 敢作敢～ bold in action ❷ work as; serve

as：选他～代表 elect him as our representative 拜内行～师，虚心学习科技知识。We should treat everyone with know-how as teachers and learn science and technology from them. 他被评～先进工作者了。He was elected "advanced worker". ❸ be；become：变被动～主动 change from being passive into taking the initiative ❹ be (*usu. in written language*)：长江～中国第一大河。The Changjiang River is the longest in China. 【介】*similar to被*：他们演出了许多～观众欢迎的文艺节目。They have put on many performances which audiences have applauded.

另见 wèi

为非作歹 wéi fēi zuò dǎi　do evils

为难 wéinán 【动】❶ be in a dilemma；be in an awkward position：去也不好，不去也不好，真叫人～。I can neither go nor stay. It certainly is a dilemma！这件事我很～，不知该怎么处理才好。It's very difficult for me to decide how to deal with this matter. ❷ deliberately try to embarrass sb.：他故意提出一个很难回答的问题来～我。He raised a very difficult question just to embarrass me.

为人 wéirén 【名】conduct oneself (in a certain way)：～厚道 be honest and kind ～刻薄 be mean and caustic ～正直 be upright 我很了解他的～。I know very well what kind of person he is.

为首 wéi=shǒu headed by；led by：以你～组成突击队。Form a shock troop with you at the lead.

为…所… wéi...suǒ... (*usu. in written language*) 为 *is similar to 被, and is followed by the agent*；所 *is followed by the verb*，所 *can often be omitted*：我们深深地为他的献身精神所感动。We were deeply moved by his self-sacrificing spirit. 人民的力量是不可战胜的，这条真理已为无数事实所证明。The strength of the people is invincible. This has been repeatedly borne out by the facts.

为所欲为 wéi suǒ yù wéi do whatever one likes；do as one pleases：那个大坏蛋已经被捕了，他再不能～了。That scoundrel was arrested and he cannot lord it over the neighbourhood anymore.

违（違） wéi 【动】disobey；defy；violate：不～农时 always do farm work at the right time 他说这话是～心的。What he said runs counter to his own beliefs.

违背 wéibèi 【动】violate；act contrary to；run counter to

违法 wéi=fǎ break the law

违法乱纪 wéi fǎ luàn jì breach of law and discipline

违反 wéifǎn 【动】go against；infringe；violate

违禁 wéijìn 【形】violate a ban

违抗 wéikàng 【动】defy (order)

违心 wéixīn 【动】against one's will；against one's conscience

违章 wéizhāng 【动】violate rules and regulations：不可～操作 must not operate contrary to instructions ～驾驶受罚 be punished for driving against regulations

围（圍） wéi 【动】surround；encircle：～城打援 beseige a city and strike at troops sent as reinforcements 操场上～了一圈人正在看篮球比赛。The play-ground is surrounded by a crowd of people watching a basketball game. 她头上～了一条花头巾。She wore a flower patterned kerchief.

围脖儿 wéibór 【名】〔条 tiáo〕同 "围巾" (*but more colloquial*)

围攻 wéigōng 【动】encircle and attack

围观 wéiguān 【动】(of a crowd of people) watch; look on

围歼 wéijiān 【动】encircle and wipe out

围剿 wéijiǎo 【动】encircle and suppress; launch a compaign of encirclement and annihilation：～山上的土匪 encircle and annihilate the bandits in the mountains

围巾 wéijīn 【名】〔条 tiáo〕muffler; scarf

围困 wéikùn 【动】besiege; pin down：他们被～在山沟里。They were besieged and pinned down in the valley.

围棋 wéiqí 【名】❶〔盘 pán〕go (a game similar to chess) ❷〔副 fù〕little round pieces used in the game

围墙 wéiqiáng 【名】enclosure; enclosing wall

围裙 wéiqún 【名】apron

围绕 wéirǎo 【动】❶ (walk) around; (revolve) around：仪仗队～着运动场走了一圈儿。The honour-guard marched once around the sports field. ❷ centre around：大家～着这个问题展开了热烈的讨论。A heated discussion broke out over this issue.

桅 wéi

桅杆 wéigān 【名】mast

唯 wéi 【副】◇ 同"惟" wéi ❶
另见 wěi

唯武器论 wéiwǔqìlùn 【名】the theory that weapons alone decide the outcome of war

唯物辩证法 wéiwù biànzhèngfǎ dialectical materialism

唯物论 wéiwùlùn 【名】同"唯物主义"

唯物主义 wéiwùzhǔyì 【名】materialism

唯心论 wéixīnlùn 【名】同"唯心主义"

唯心主义 wéixīnzhǔyì 【名】idealism

惟 wéi 【副】◇ ❶ only ❷ but; except：这种羊毛纤维长，质地柔软，～产量较低。This kind of wool has long fibres and is very soft, the only trouble is that the yield is relatively low.

惟独 wéidú 【副】only：大家都来了，～他没来。Everybody has come except him. 他什么酒都不喝，～喝一点儿黄酒。He doesn't drink any spirits except a little rice wine.

惟恐 wéikǒng 【动】for fear that：大家都专心地听着，～漏掉一个字。Everyone was listening in rapt attention, for fear of missing a single word.

惟利是图 wéi lì shì tú seek profit as one's only aim; engage in unscrupulous profiteering

惟妙惟肖 wéi miào wéi xiào strikingly life-like; be very clever at mimicking：人物形象描绘得～。The characters (in the novel) were very vividly depicted.

惟命是听 wéi mìng shì tīng at sb.'s beck and call; absolutely obedient (*derog.*) 也作"惟命是从"。

惟我独尊 wéi wǒ dú zūn consider oneself above everybody else; be extremely conceited

惟一 wéiyī 【形】only; sole; single：～正确的作法 the only correct method

惟有 wéiyǒu 【连】❶ only：在冰天雪地中，～梅花盛开。In the midst of ice and snow, only plum trees are in bloom. ❷ only when：～双方妥协，才能达成协议。Only when the two sides compromise, can the deal be sealed.

维(維) wéi

维持 wéichí 【动】maintain; preserve：～秩序 keep order ～现状

maintain the status quo ~生命 sustain life 靠劳动所得~生活 support oneself by honest labour

维持和平部队　wéichí hépíng bùduì peace-keeping force

维护　wéihù　【动】safeguard；uphold：~祖国的独立和统一 safeguard the independence and unity of one's country ~国家主权 safeguard national sovereignty

维尼纶　wéinílún　【名】vinylon

维生素　wéishēngsù　【名】vitamin

维修　wéixiū　【动】（of machinery）maintain

wěi

伟（偉）wěi

伟大　wěidà　【形】great

伟绩　wěijì　【名】meritorious service；great feats；great achievements

伟人　wěirén　【名】great personage

伟业　wěiyè　【名】feat；exploit

伪（僞）wěi　【形】◇ ❶

sham；fake：真~难辨 be hard to tell the true from the false ❷ puppet：~军 puppet troops ~政权 puppet regime

伪钞　wěichāo　【名】counterfeit（or forged）bank note

伪君子　wěijūnzǐ　【名】hypocrite

伪劣　wěiliè　【形】fake and inferior：~产品 shoddy goods（products）

伪善　wěishàn　【形】hypocritical；~者 hypocrite ~的面目 hypocrisy

伪造　wěizào　【动】fabricate；counterfeit；forge：~罪 forgery

伪证　wěizhèng　【名】perjury；false witness

伪装　wěizhuāng　【动】disguise；camouflage：把大炮~起来 camouflage the guns ~进步 pretend to be progressive 【名】disguise；camouflage；

mask：假的就是假的，~是骗不了人的。Sham is sham, and in the end, people will see through.

尾　wěi　【名】◇ ❶ tail ❷ end：队

~ the tail of the procession 有头无~ begin well，but fall off towards the end 【量】for fish：一~鱼 one fish

尾巴　wěiba　【名】tail

尾巴主义　wěibāzhǔyì　【名】（of leadership）with no will of one's own but follow the crowd

尾灯　wěidēng　【名】rear lights

尾声　wěishēng　【名】❶ epilogue；finale ❷ last：这场人间喜剧已经接近~了。This human drama is drawing to a close.

尾数　wěishù　【名】odd amount in addition to the round number

尾随　wěisuí　【动】follow；tail after；shadow

纬（緯）wěi　【名】❶（of tex-

tiles）woof（as opp. to 经）❷ latitude：南 ~ south latitude 北 ~ north latitude

纬度　wěidù　【名】degree of latitude

委　wěi

委靡　wěimǐ　【形】feel blue；be in low spirits；be depressed：精神~ depressed 也作"萎靡"。

委靡不振　wěimǐ bù zhèn　dispirited；dejected and apathetic

委派　wěipài　【动】appoint

委曲求全　wěiqū qiú quán　make compromises out of consideration for a greater interest

委屈　wěiqu　【动】❶ feel wronged（because one has been treated unjustly）：姐姐错怪了弟弟，使他感到很~。The elder sister mistakenly blamed her brother and he felt very much wronged. ❷ wrong（sb.）：我错怪了你，~你了。I was

mistaken in blaming you. I'm awfully sorry. 幼儿园的阿姨不会～孩子
的。The kindergarten teachers
won't treat any child unfairly.

委托　wěituō　【动】entrust; put in
charge; consign

委婉　wěiwǎn　【形】(of speech)
mild; tactful

委员　wěiyuán　【名】committee
member

委员会　wěiyuánhuì　【名】committee;
commission; council; 市场管理～
marketing management committee

委员长　wěiyuánzhǎng　【名】chair-
man of a committee

娓　wěi

娓娓动听　wěiwěi dòngtīng　(of way
of talking) vivid and interesting;
他讲故事讲得～，引人入胜。He tells
stories very vividly and holds his
audience spell-bound.

萎　wěi

萎靡　wěimǐ　【形】同"委靡"wěimǐ
萎缩　wěisuō　【动】❶ (med.) atrophy; 肌肉～ muscular atrophy;
amyotrophy ❷ (of economy) suffer a recession

唯　wěi

另见 wéi

唯唯诺诺　wěiwěinuònuò　【形】be a
yes-man; have no will of one's
own

wèi

卫（衛）　wèi　【动】◇ defend;
safeguard; 保家～国 protect our
homes and defend our country

卫兵　wèibīng　【名】guard
卫道士　wèidàoshì　【名】apologist
(for an ideology, system, etc.); 封
建主义制度的～ apologists for feudalism

卫冕　wèimiǎn　【动】defend one's title; ～成功 succeed in defending
one's championship

卫生　wèishēng　【名】hygiene; sanitation; 注意公共～ pay attention to
public health 发展文教～事业 promote culture, education and health
work【形】hygienic; 他不喜欢开窗
户，很不～。He doesn't like to open
his windows and that is unhygien-
ic.

卫生间　wèishēngjiān　【名】toilet
卫生设备　wèishēng shèbèi　sanitary
equipment

卫生所　wèishēngsuǒ　【名】clinic
卫生学　wèishēngxué　【名】hygiene
(discipline)

卫生员　wèishēngyuán　【名】health
worker; orderly

卫生院　wèishēngyuàn　【名】public
health centre

卫生站　wèishēngzhàn　【名】clinic;
health station

卫生纸　wèishēngzhǐ　【名】toilet paper

卫戍　wèishù　【动】garrison
卫星　wèixīng　【名】〔颗 kē〕satellite
卫星城　wèixīngchéng　名〔座 zuò〕
satellite town

为（爲）　wèi　【动】indicates
the object of one's act of service; 他
这样做完全～大家，不是～自己。He
did this for all of us, not for himself.【介】❶ for; ～人民服务 work
for the peole ～这本书写了一篇序
write a preface to the book ❷ in
order to; 我～核对一个数字翻了不少
资料。I've looked through a lot of
data in order to verify this statis-
tic.

另见 wéi

为…而…　wèi...ér...　(usu. in
written language) 为 is followed by
a word or phrase stating the pur-

pose or cause，而 *is followed by a word or phrase stating the means or result*：为建设祖国而钻研科学技术 learn science and technology in order to develop our country 我们都为胜利而欢呼。We all cheered the victory.

为何 wèihé 【副】〈书〉why

为虎作伥 wèi hǔ zuò chāng play the jackal to the tiger；(*fig.*) act as a henchman to an evil-doer

为了 wèile 【动】同"为" wèi【动】：一切～人民的健康。Everything is for the people's health.【介】同"为"【介】❷：大家～追求真理，进行了热烈的讨论。Everybody took part in the heated debate with the purpose of arriving at the truth.

为…起见 wèi…qǐjiàn in order to：为方便顾客起见,这个商店增设了早晚服务部。This shop opened a before-and-after-hours department for the convenience of the customers.

为什么 wèi shénme why

未 wèi 【副】❶〈书〉同"没" méi【副】*as opp. to* 已：天～亮他已起床。He got up before dawn. 现在他们家过着从～有过的幸福生活。Their family is now living comfortably in a way that would never have been possible before. ❷◇ not：～可厚非 can hardly be blamed 他～置可否。He didn't say yes or no.

未必 wèibì 【副】may not：我的意见～对,供你参考。My view may not be right. I simply offer it for your consideration. 这件事他～不知道。I wonder if he really knows nothing at all about this matter.

未曾 wèicéng 【副】never；have not (*as opp. to* 曾经)：～想到 have never thought of ～发生 have never happened ～出现 have never appeared

未尝 wèicháng 【副】〈书〉❶同"未曾"：我～见过他。I have never seen him before. ❷ *used before a negative word e. g.* 不,无,没, *forming a double negative to indicate a probable affirmative*：他～没有时间,恐怕是不愿意来。I wonder whether he really has no time; probably he just doesn't want to come. 这～不是个办法,不妨试一试。This may be a way out; we might as well give it a try.

未婚夫 wèihūnfū 【名】fiancé

未婚妻 wèihūnqī 【名】fiancée

未来 wèilái 【名】future

未免 wèimiǎn 【副】*used in a sentence expressing disagreement or disapproval*；*does not alter the meaning at all*, *only moderates the tone*：你这样说～太客气了。It is too kind of you to say so. 你这种想法～有点儿脱离实际。Your view is a bit unrealistic.

未遂 wèisuì 【动】〈书〉(of a certain goal) not realized：～政变 an attempted coup 行凶 ～ an attempted murder 自杀 ～ an attempted suicide

未知数 wèizhīshù 【名】(maths.) unknown number

位 wèi 【名】◇ ❶ place；position：把这项工作放在第一～ give this job first priority ❷ throne：即～ succeed to the throne 篡～ usurp the throne ❸ digit；place：个～ unit's place 十～ 10's place 百～ 100's place 【量】*for persons* (*polite form*)：三～客人 three guests 各～朋友 friends

位于 wèiyú 【动】be situated：中国～亚洲东部。China is situated in the eastern Asia.

位置 wèizhi 【名】❶ position；

place：这个港口的地理～十分重要。The geographical position of this port is very important. 按指定的～坐好。Please take your assigned seat. ❷ place：这一事件在历史上占有极其重要的～。This event occupies an extremely important place in history.

位子 wèizi 【名】seat

味 wèi 【名】❶ (～儿) taste；flavour；smell：甜～ sweet taste 尝尝～ taste this ❷ interest；fun 【量】 *for Chinese medicine*：这个药方共有九～药。This prescription consists of nine kinds of herbs.

味道 wèidao 【名】❶ (of food) taste；flavour；smell：这个菜～很好。This dish tastes very good. ❷ feeling；trace of (sth.)：心里有一股说不出的～。He was gripped by an indescribable feeling. 他的信有些说教的～。His letter is a little preachy.

味精 wèijīng 【名】monosodium glutamate；gourmet powder

味觉 wèijué 【名】sense of taste

味同嚼蜡 wèi tóng jiáo là it tastes no better than tallow；(*fig.*) dry；as dry as saw dust；insipid

畏 wèi 【动】〈书〉fear；be afraid of：克服～难情绪 overcome one's fear of difficulty 不～艰险 fear no hardships or danger

畏惧 wèijù 【动】fear

畏难 wèinán 【动】fear of difficulty：有～情绪 intimidated by hardship

畏首畏尾 wèi shǒu wèi wěi be filled with misgivings；be overcautious：工作要大胆，不要～。We should be bold in our enterprise and not be overcautious.

畏缩 wèisuō 【动】flinch；recoil in fear：在困难面前怎能～不前呢? How could we hesitate to press forward in the face of difficulties?

畏罪 wèi = zuì fear punishment for one's crime

胃 wèi 【名】stomach

胃病 wèibìng 【名】stomach trouble

胃口 wèikǒu 【名】❶ appetite：～很好 have a good appetite ❷ taste；liking：这种地方戏很对他的～。This sort of local opera is just his cup of tea.

谓(謂) wèi

谓语 wèiyǔ 【名】(gram.) predicate

喂 wèi 【动】❶ feed：～奶 breastfeed (a baby) 护士正给一个重伤员～饭。The nurse is feeding a seriously injured patient. ❷ raise (animals)；feed：～马 feed a horse ～了几只小兔 raise a few rabbits 【叹】hey；hello：～! 停一下车。Hey! Stop the bus for a minute. ～! ～! 你是北京大学吗? Hello! Is that Beijing University?

喂养 wèiyǎng 【动】feed；raise

蔚 wèi

蔚蓝 wèilán 【形】sky-blue；azure：～的天空 an azure sky ～的大海 the blue sea

蔚然成风 wèirán chéng fēng become a common practice (referring to sth. good)：钻研业务已～。To improve one's professional skill has now become a common practice. 也作"蔚成风气"。

慰 wèi

慰劳 wèiláo 【动】同"慰问"

慰问 wèiwèn 【动】visit and extend solicitude to；express regards and concern for

wēn

温 wēn 【形】warm；lukewarm：这水是～的。The water is lukewarm.【动】❶ warm up：～一～酒 warm up the wine ❷ review：～课 review one's lessons

温饱 wēnbǎo 【名】have sufficient food and clothing：边区的农民并不满足～，现在正努力奔小康。Not content with mere survival, the farmers in the borden areas are striving to raise their standard of living.

温差 wēnchā 【名】difference in temperature

温床 wēnchuáng 【名】❶ hotbed：～育苗 breed seedlings in a hotbed ❷ hotbed；advantageous conditions

温带 wēndài 【名】temperate zone

温度 wēndù 【名】temperature

温度计 wēndùjì 【名】thermometer

温故知新 wēn gù zhī xīn gain new insights by reviewing the past

温和 wēnhé 【形】❶ mild；moderate；temperate：气候～ a mild climate ❷ mild；gentle：态度～ a gentle manner 性情～ mild in disposition
另见 wēnhuo

温和 wēnhuo 【形】warm；lukewarm：太阳晒得河水挺～的。The sun had warmed the river.
另见 wēnhé

温暖 wēnnuǎn 【形】warm；pleasantly warm：天气～ warm weather ～的阳光 warm sunshine【动】warm (up)：邻居们的情谊时时～着他的孤独的心。His neighbours' friendliness warmed his lonely heart.

温情 wēnqíng 【名】gentle feeling；tender feeling

温泉 wēnquán 【名】hot spring

温柔 wēnróu 【形】gentle；meek

温室 wēnshì 【名】hot-house；green-house

温习 wēnxí 【动】review（e. g. lessons）

wén

文 wén 【名】◇ ❶ script；writing；written language：藏（Zàng）～ Tibetan script ❷ writing；literary composition：此～尚未发表。This piece of writing has not been published yet. ❸ civilian；mental labour（as opp. to 武）：能～能武 good in both civil and military affairs；good in both mental and manual labour【形】literary：半～半白 half literary, half vernacular（in writing style）这篇文章写得太～了。This article is written in too literary a style.【量】for coins in the old days：一～钱 one penny 一～不值 not worth a farthing

文笔 wénbǐ 【名】style of writing；literary style：～流畅 write in an easy and fluent style

文不对题 wén bù duì tí irrelevant to the subject；beside the point

文采 wéncǎi 【名】❶ gorgeous colours ❷ literary talent：这位作家很有～。He is a very talented writer.

文牍主义 wéndúzhǔyì 【名】red-tapism

文法 wénfǎ 【名】grammar

文风 wénfēng 【名】style of writing

文风不动 wén fēng bù dòng absolutely still

文稿 wéngǎo 【名】manuscript

文工团 wéngōngtuán 【名】art troupe；ensemble

文官 wénguān 【名】civil official

文过饰非 wén guò shì fēi gloss over one's mistakes：要知过必改，不要～。Correct your mistake the moment you realize it and don't try to gloss

it over.

文豪　wénháo　【名】famous writer

文化　wénhuà　【名】culture

文化宫　wénhuàgōng　【名】cultural palace

文化馆　wénhuàguǎn　【名】cultural centre

文化遗产　wénhuà yíchǎn　cultural heritage

文集　wénjí　【名】anthology；collected works

文件　wénjiàn　【名】document

文教　wénjiào　【名】(short for "文化教育") culture and education

文静　wénjìng　【形】gentle and quiet

文具　wénjù　【名】stationery

文科　wénkē　【名】liberal arts

文盲　wénmáng　【名】illiterate；illiteracy

文明　wénmíng　【名】civilization 【形】civilized (as opp. to 野蛮)：～古国 a country with an old civilization 随地吐痰是不～的习惯. Spitting is a very uncivilized habit.

文凭　wénpíng　【名】certificate；diploma

文人　wénrén　【名】man of letters

文人相轻　wénrén xiāng qīng　scholars tend to look down on each other

文山会海　wén shān huì hǎi　a mountain of papers and a sea of meetings—the intricate routine that a leading cadre gets bogged down in

文书　wénshū　【名】❶ documents, papers, letters, etc. ❷ copy clerk

文坛　wéntán　【名】literary circles

文体　wéntǐ　【名】❶ literary form；type of writing ❷ (short for "文娱体育") recreation and sports

文物　wénwù　【名】cultural relic

文献　wénxiàn　【名】literature (of a special subject)

文选　wénxuǎn　【名】selections (of a certain writer)

文学　wénxué　【名】literature

文学家　wénxuéjiā　【名】writer；man of letters

文学史　wénxuéshǐ　【名】history of literature

文雅　wényǎ　【形】refined；elegant

文言　wényán　【名】classical Chinese

文言文　wényánwén　【名】classical Chinese

文艺　wényì　【名】literature and arts

文艺理论　wényì lǐlùn　theory of literature and art

文艺批评　wényì pīpíng　literary and art criticism

文娱　wényú　【名】recreation

文章　wénzhāng　【名】literary composition；essay；article；writing

文职　wénzhí　【名】civilian post：～人员 civilian staff；nonmilitary personnel

文质彬彬　wén zhì bīnbīn　with elegant manners；gentle；refined

文字　wénzì　【名】❶ script；writing；character ❷ written language：这种画报用中文、英文、法文、日文等九种～出版. This pictorial is simultaneously published in nine languages such as Chinese, English, French and Japanese. ❸ a piece of writing；a passage：～通顺 of lucid writing 把这段多余的～删掉. Delete this superfluous passage.

文字处理机　wénzì chǔlǐjī　word processor

文字改革　wénzì gǎigé　reform of a writing system

文字学　wénzìxué　【名】philology

纹(紋)　wén　【名】(～儿)❶ lines；grain：这种木头的～很好看. This kind of wood has a beautiful grain. ❷ crease；wrinkle：这张纸折了几道～. This piece of paper is creased in a few places.

纹丝不动　wén sī bù dòng　completely untouched；absolutely still

闻(聞)　wén　【动】❶ ◇ hear；

耳～不如眼见。One picture is worth a thousand words. ❷ smell：你喜欢～桂花的香味儿吗? Do you like the smell of osmanthus?

闻风而动 wén fēng ér dòng　immediately respond to a call; go into action without delay：命令一下达，战士们～，迅速出发了。As soon as the order came, the soldiers set out without delay.

闻风丧胆 wén fēng sàng dǎn　be panic-stricken at the news

闻名 wénmíng　【动】well-known; famous：全国～ famous throughout the country ～世界 well-known all over the world

闻所未闻 wén suǒ wèi wén　never before heard of; unheard-of：这次旅行，我们见到了许多～的新鲜事物。On our trip, we saw things that we had never heard of before.

闻讯 wénxùn　【动】hear the news：～赶到 rush to the spot on hearing the news

蚊 wén　【名】mosquito

蚊帐 wénzhàng　【名】mosquito net

蚊子 wénzi　【名】〔个 gè〕mosquito

wěn

吻 wěn　【名】◇ kiss【动】kiss

吻合 wěnhé　【动】accord well (with each other); tally with each other

紊 wěn

紊乱 wěnluàn　【形】disorderly; confused：秩序～ chaotic 思路～ confused train of thought

稳（穩） wěn　【形】❶ steady; stable：掌～了舵 be steady with the helm 车停～了再下。Don't get off until the bus has come to a complete stop. ❷ safe; reliable：他办事

很～。He is very reliable in managing affairs. ❸ staid; grave; not flighty

稳步 wěnbù　【副】steadily：～前进 advance steadily 生产～上升。Production is increasing steadily.

稳产高产 wěn chǎn gāo chǎn　stable and high yields

稳当 wěndang　【形】safe and sure

稳定 wěndìng　【动】stabilize：～情绪 reassure sb. ～局势 stabilize the situation【形】stable：物价～。Prices are stable.

稳定性 wěndìngxìng　【名】stability

稳固 wěngù　【形】(of foundation, etc.) solid; stable; firm

稳健 wěnjiàn　【形】solid; steady; firm：～的步伐 a firm stride

稳如泰山 wěn rú Tài Shān　as stable as Mount Tai; stable as a rock

稳妥 wěntuǒ　【形】safe and reliable

稳扎稳打 wěn zhā wěn dǎ　do things steadily and surely

稳重 wěnzhòng　【形】(of persons) staid; grave; not flighty：这位姑娘很～。She is a very sedate young lady.

wèn

问（問） wèn　【动】❶ ask：～问题 ask a question 不懂就～。If you don't understand, please ask. ❷ inquire after：请替我～她好。Please send her my best regards. ❸ cross-examine：～口供 cross-examine sb. ❹ have (sth.) to do with; pay attention to：不～政治 paying no attention to politics

问长问短 wèn cháng wèn duǎn　ask all sorts of questions; bombard (sb.) with questions

问答 wèndá　【名】questions and answers

问寒问暖 wèn hán wèn nuǎn　ask

about one's needs; express concern for

问好　wèn = hǎo　give (one's) regards to

问号　wènhào　【名】question mark

问候　wènhòu　【动】greet; give (one's) regards to

问世　wènshì　【动】be published for the first time; be presented to the public: 这套文集是六十年代～的。This anthology was published in the sixties.

问题　wèntí　【名】❶ question: 我提个～。I have a question to ask. ❷ problem; difficulty: 伦理～ ethical problem 这个办法解决不了什么～。This method cannot solve any problem. ❸ key; crux: 重要的～在善于学习新技术。The most important thing is to be good at learning new techniques. ❹ accident; mishap: 这个汽车司机安全行车五万公里,没出过任何～。This driver has driven fifty thousand kilometres without any accident.

wèng

瓮　wèng　【名】jar

瓮声瓮气　wèng shēng wèng qì　in a low muffled voice

瓮中之鳖　wèng zhōng zhī biē　a turtle in a jar; (fig.) a person or animal which is trapped

wō

窝（窩）　wō　【名】❶ nest; den; lair: 喜鹊搭～。A magpie is building a nest. ❷ hideout（of criminals, etc.）: 土匪～ a bandits' lair 【动】❶ shelter; hide; harbour: ～赃 keep stolen goods ❷ bottle up one's emotions: ～了一肚子火 con-

tain one's anger ❸ bend: 这材料很脆,一～就断。This sort of material is very brittle. It snaps if you try to bend it. 【量】litter; brood: 一～小鸡 a flock of chicks 一～小狗 a litter of puppies

窝藏　wōcáng　【动】conceal（booty）or hide（a fugitive from justice）; harbour

窝点　wōdiǎn　【名】hiding place（of stolen goods or money）

窝工　wō = gōng　work is held up due to poor planning: 快把人力安排好,不然就要～了。Let's allocate manpower properly otherwise work will be held up.

窝火　wō = huǒ　feel annoyed; fill with pent-up anger; smoulder with rage

窝囊　wōnang　【形】cowardly and stupid: 这个人太～了。This guy is a wimp. 再也不受这种～气了! I'll never be subjected to petty tyrannies any longer!

窝棚　wōpeng　【名】mat shed

窝头　wōtóu　【名】〔个 gè〕steamed bread made of cornflour

窝心　wōxīn　【形】feel wronged; nurse a grievance against

窝赃　wō = zāng　harbour stolen goods

蜗（蝸）　wō

蜗牛　wōniú　【名】〔只 zhī〕snail

wǒ

我　wǒ　【代】❶ I; me ❷ ◇ we; our; ourselves: ～国 our country 敌～双方 both the enemy and ourselves ❸ used in conjunction with 你 to mean "everyone": 大家你一言～一语,讨论得可热烈了。We all spoke one after another, discussing the matter heatedly.

我们　wǒmen　【代】we；us

wò

卧　wò　【动】❶ ◇ lie (down)：～床不起 be sick in bed ❷ (of an animal) lie with legs tucked under it：水牛～在树阴下。The buffalo was lying in the shade of the tree.

卧病　wòbìng　【动】be ill in bed

卧倒　wòdǎo　【动】lie down；take a prone position

卧铺　wòpù　【名】berth

卧室　wòshì　【名】bedroom

卧薪尝胆　wò xīn cháng dǎn　sleep on a woodpile and taste gall；(fig.) endure self-imposed hardships and temper oneself (in order to wipe out a humiliation)

握　wò　【动】grasp；hold：～紧拳头 clench one's fist

握手　wò = shǒu　shake hands

斡　wò

斡旋　wòxuán　【动】mediate：从中～ mediate between two parties 多方～ make every effort to mediate

wū

乌 (烏)　wū

乌龟　wūguī　【名】〔只 zhǐ〕turtle

乌合之众　wū hé zhī zhòng　band together like crows；mob；a disorderly rabble：这些土匪是一群～，不堪一击。These bandits are just a disorderly mob and will collapse at the first blow.

乌黑　wūhēi　【形】jet black

乌七八糟　wū qī bā zāo　obscene；filthy

乌纱帽　wūshāmào　【名】the head covering of an official in ancient China；(fig.) official post

乌托邦　wūtuōbāng　【名】Utopia

乌鸦　wūyā　【名】〔只 zhǐ〕crow

乌烟瘴气　wūyān zhàngqì　a foul atmosphere；(fig.) a chaotic state in which corrupt practices prevail

乌云　wūyún　【名】dark cloud

乌贼　wūzéi　【名】inkfish；cuttlefish

污　wū

污点　wūdiǎn　【名】stain；blemish；smirch

污垢　wūgòu　【名】dirt；filth

污秽　wūhuì　【形】filthy

污蔑　wūmiè　【动】slander；vilify

污泥浊水　wū ní zhuó shuǐ　mud and filthy water；(fig.) all backward, corrupt and reactionary things：几千年历史遗留下灿烂的文化，也留下不少～。A long history has left us a splendid culture but also a lot of filth and corruption.

污染　wūrǎn　【动】pollute

污辱　wūrǔ　【动】insult

污水　wūshuǐ　【名】filthy water

污浊　wūzhuó　【形】filthy：～的河水 filthy river water

鸣 (鳴)　wū　【象声】sound of a car horn, train whistle, sobbing, etc.

呜呜咽咽　wūwūyèyè　【形】sobbing

呜咽　wūyè　【动】❶ sob ❷ low sobbing sound of a stream or sad string music

诬 (誣)　wū

诬告　wūgào　【动】make a false charge against

诬赖　wūlài　【动】falsely incriminate

诬蔑　wūmiè　【动】vilify；smear；slander

诬陷　wūxiàn　【动】frame (sb.)

屋　wū　【名】❶ house：半山腰上有间小～。There was a small house

half-way up the mountain. ❷ room：外~ a room with an outside door（where there is an attached inner room）请 ~ 里坐。Please come in and sit down.

屋顶 wūdǐng 【名】roof

屋脊 wūjǐ 【名】ridge of a roof

屋檐 wūyán 【名】eaves

屋子 wūzi 【名】〔间 jiān〕room

wú

无（無）wú 【动】❶同“没有”：从~到有 start from scratch 房~一间，地 ~ 一垄 be without a single room or a single plot of land ~法解决 have no way to solve the problem ❷〈书〉同“不”bù：~须多谈 need not go into detail ❸ regardless of；no matter：事~大小，都应认真对待。All matters, big or small, must be dealt with seriously.

无比 wúbǐ 【形】matchless；incomparable；unparalleled：威力~ unparalleled power ~强大 powerful beyond comparison

无边无际 wú biān wú jì boundless；vast：~的大草原 vast prairie 原始森林~ boundless primeval forests

无产阶级 wúchǎnjiējí 【名】proletariat

无产者 wúchǎnzhě 【名】proletarian

无常 wúcháng 【形】changeable；capricious 反复~ blow hot and cold

无偿 wúcháng 【形】gratis；free of charge

无耻 wúchǐ 【形】shameless

无耻谰言 wúchǐ lányán brazen lie；shameless slander

无从 wúcóng 【副】not know where to begin；not know how（to do sth.）：~说起。I don't know where to start telling you about this. 要写的事情太多，简直~下笔。I have so many things to write about that I don't know where to begin.

无敌 wúdí 【形】matchless；peerless：这支军队~于天下。This army is invincible.

无的放矢 wú dì fàng shǐ shoot at random；shoot without any particular target；（fig.）aimless：写文章、做报告不要~。When you write an article or give a report, don't ramble on and on without a point of focus.

无地自容 wú dì zì róng too ashamed to show one's face：他已感到~了，别再批评他了。He is already too ashamed to show his face, so don't criticize him any more.

无动于衷 wú dòng yú zhōng unmoved；apathetic；aloof and indifferent：我劝了他半天，他却~。I tried for a long time to make him listen to reason, but he remained unmoved.

无恶不作 wú è bù zuò commit all manner of crimes；be as wicked as possible

无法 wúfǎ 【副】no way：~解决的问题 insolvable problem

无法无天 wú fǎ wú tiān lawless；defy laws human and divine

无妨 wúfáng 【形】there is no harm in ...；may as well：这样做也~。We may as well do it this way. 这个办法也~试一试。There's no harm in trying this method too.

无非 wúfēi 【副】nothing but；no more than：他劝说你，~是为了帮助你认清形势。He talked to you for no other purpose than to help you see the real situation. 常到他家来的，~是他的几个老朋友。It is his old friends who frequently visit his home.

无缝钢管 wú fèng gāngguǎn seamless steel tube

无辜 wúgū 【名】innocent person 【形】innocent

无故 wúgù【副】for no reason：～缺席 be absent without reason 不得～迟到或早退。One mustn't be late or leave early without a good reason.

无关 wúguān【动】have nothing to do with：～大局。It does not matter much. ～紧要。It's of little importance. 这事与他～。This has nothing to do with him.

无轨电车 wú guǐ diànchē trolley-bus

无害 wúhài【形】harmless

无机化学 wújī huàxué inorganic chemistry

无机物 wújīwù【名】inorganic matter

无稽之谈 wújī zhī tán a completely unbelievable story；sheer nonsense

无济于事 wú jì yú shì of no use；to no avail：这么冷的天,加一件毛衣也～。Putting on an extra sweater doesn't help at all in such cold weather. 重要的是行动,空谈是～的。What is important is action. Empty talk is no help.

无价之宝 wú jià zhī bǎo priceless treasure

无坚不摧 wú jiān bù cuī smash all fortifications；be all-conquering

无精打采 wú jīng dǎ cǎi in low spirits；crestfallen：看他那～的样子,可能是身体不好吧! How depressed he looks! Maybe he is sick. 也作"没精打采"。

无拘无束 wú jū wú shù free and easy；unrestrained；freely

无可非议 wú kě fēiyì beyond reproach；unimpeachable：他的话合情合理,～。What he said is reasonable and can't be faulted.

无可奉告 wú kě fènggào have nothing to say；no comment

无可奈何 wú kě nàihé helpless；have no way out：眼看人家走最后一本我要买的杂志,真是～。As I watched somebody else buy the last copy of the magazine I wanted

so badly, I felt completely frustrated.

无可争辩 wú kě zhēngbiàn indisputable：～的事实 indisputable fact ～的真理 indisputable truth

无孔不入 wú kǒng bù rù (derog.) lose no chance；seize every opportunity（to do evil）

无愧 wúkuì【动】feel no qualms；have a clear conscience；be worthy of：问心～。Upon introspection, one's conscience is clear. 他样样工作走在前面,～是模范工作者。He takes the lead in every piece of work and is certainly worthy of the title of model worker.

无赖 wúlài【名】❶ rogue；rascal ❷ 见"耍赖"shuǎlài

无理 wúlǐ【形】unreasonable

无理取闹 wú lǐ qǔ nào be deliberately provocative

无聊 wúliáo【形】❶ be bored：他一没事干就觉得～。He feels bored unless he is doing something. ❷（of speech, behaviour, etc.）senseless；silly：为一些生活小事闹意见,太～了。It doesn't make sense to quarrel over trifles.

无论 wúlùn【连】同"不论"bùlùn（usu. in written language）：国～大小,都有它的长处。Whether a country is big or small, it has its good qualities. ～赞成与否,你都应该表明态度。Whether you agree or not, you must let people know. ～天气好还是不好,我都得去。Rain or shine, I will go anyway.

无论如何 wúlùn rúhé at any rate：这件事～明天也要做完。This matter must be finished tomorrow in any event. 也说"无论怎么样"。

无名 wúmíng【形】❶ unnamed：～高地 an unnamed hill ❷ anonymous；nameless：～英雄 an unknown hero ❸ indescribable；indefinable：～的悲哀 an indescribable

sadness

无名小卒 wúmíng xiǎozú a nobody

无奈 wúnài 【形】having no choice：万般～ have absolutely no way out 当年老高出于～，把仅有的二亩地卖了。That year Lao Gao had no alternative but to sell his only two *mu* of land.【连】but；because (things didn't turn out as expected)：原定今天开运动会，～天下大雨，只好改期。Originally，the sports meet was to have taken place today，but it had to be postponed because of rain.

无能 wúnéng 【形】incapable；incompetent

无能为力 wú néng wéi lì unable to do anything about sth.；powerless：对解决地质方面的问题，我实在～。I really can do nothing to help where geological problems are concerned.

无期徒刑 wú qī túxíng life imprisonment

无奇不有 wú qí bù yǒu strange things of every description

无情 wúqíng 【形】❶ unfeeling；hard-hearted ❷ merciless；ruthless：～地揭露 expose ruthlessly 历史是～的。History is ruthless.

无穷 wúqióng 【形】endless；infinite；inexhaustible：～的智慧 inexhaustible wisdom 后患～ endless trouble in the future 榜样的力量是～的。The power of a good example is infinite.

无穷无尽 wú qióng wú jìn inexhaustible；innumerable；infinite：～的宝藏 inexhaustible resources 宇宙是～的。The universe is infinite.

无色 wúsè 【形】colourless

无上 wúshàng 【形】highest；greatest：～光荣 greatest honour

无神论 wúshénlùn 【名】atheism

无声无臭 wú shēng wú xiù (of persons) unknown

无时无刻 wú shí wú kè all the time (*usu. used with* 不)：物质～不在运动。Matter is in constant motion.

无事生非 wú shì shēng fēi make trouble out of nothing；make much ado about nothing

无视 wúshì 【动】disregard；ignore

无数 wúshù 【形】innumerable；countless：～事实 innumerable facts ～志愿者参加山川绿化工作。Many people have volunteered for aforestation work in the mountains and valleys.

无私 wúsī 【形】selfless：～的援助 disinterested assistance 把自己的一生～地贡献给和平事业 devote one's whole life selflessly to the cause of peace ～才能无畏。Only the selfless are without fear.

无所不为 wú suǒ bù wéi stop at nothing (in doing evil deeds)：那伙惯犯，～，必须严惩。That batch of hardened criminals stop at nothing and have to be punished severely.

无所不用其极 wú suǒ bù yòng qí jí (in doing bad things) employ the meanest of tricks；go to any length

无所事事 wú suǒ shì shì be idle；do nothing；loaf：饱食终日～的人是社会上的寄生虫。Those who loaf all day and do nothing are social parasites.

无所适从 wú suǒ shì cóng not know where to turn；be at a loss as to what to do：领导不能朝令夕改，否则群众就会～。The leadership should not make constant changes in policy；if they do, the workers will be at a loss as to what to do.

无所谓 wúsuǒwèi 【动】❶ cannot be taken as；cannot be regarded as：这只是个人的一点体会，～经验。This is only my own understanding of the matter, and cannot be taken as the result of long experience. 这里四季如春；～春夏秋冬。It's like

spring all year round here, and there is no way to define the four seasons. ❷ it does not matter; not care a bit about; be indifferent to: 对待有益的劝告不应该采取～的态度。 We should not take an indifferent attitude towards well-meant advice. 去故宫还是去中山公园,由你决定,我～。It's up to you to decide whether we go to the Palace Museum or Zhongshan Park. It's all the same to me.

无所作为 wú suǒ zuòwéi attempt nothing; lack the ability to make any achievement: 要勇于创新,～的思想是错误的。We should be daring in trying to create new things; it's wrong to feel that one · can't achieve anything.

无条件 wú tiáojiàn unconditional: ～投降 unconditional surrender

无头案 wútóu'àn 【名】unsolved mystery; a case without a clue

无往不胜 wú wǎng bù shèng invincible; all-conquering 也作"无往而不胜"。

无微不至 wú wēi bù zhì meticulously; in every possible way: ～的关怀 be concerned about and take very good care of sb. 那位护士对病人照顾得～。The nurse takes the greatest possible care of her patients.

无味 wúwèi 【形】❶ (of food) tasteless; flat ❷ drab; dull; uninteresting: 枯燥～ as dry as sawdust

无畏 wúwèi 【形】fearless; daring; bold

无谓 wúwèi 【形】meaningless: ～的争吵 a meaningless quarrel ～的牺牲 a meaningless sacrifice

无息 wúxī 【形】interest-free

无隙可乘 wú xì kě chéng no crack to get in by; no loophole to be exploited; leave no opportunity for

无限 wúxiàn 【形】infinite; boundless: ～光明 very bright ～热爱 love

boundlessly 要把有限的生命,投入到～的为残疾人服务之事业中去。One should spend one's limited life in the limitless service of the handicapped.

无限大 wúxiàndà 【名】(maths.) infinitely great 也作"无穷大"。

无限小 wúxiànxiǎo 【名】(maths.) infinitely small 也作"无穷小"。

无线电 wúxiàndiàn 【名】wireless; radio

无线电话 wú xiàn diànhuà radiotelephone; radiophone

无效 wúxiào 【形】invalid; null and void

无懈可击 wú xiè kě jī invulnerable; with no chink in one's armour: 这篇报告观点新颖,材料可靠,可以说是～。With its innovative views and reliable data, this report is almost perfect.

无心 wúxīn 【形】❶ be disinclined to; not feel like: 他急于赶火车,～多谈。He was in a hurry to catch the train and had no desire to talk. ❷ unintentional; not purposely: 我说这话是～的,你可别介意。I didn't mean anything in saying that; I hope you don't mind.

无形 wúxíng 【形】invisible

无形中 wúxíngzhōng 【副】without anybody realizing it: 两人谈得很投机,～一个下午就过去了。The two were having an intimate chat and the whole afternoon slipped away without their realizing it. 晚饭后在湖边散步,～成了他生活中的一条规律。Without his being aware of it, taking a walk by the lake after supper has become a part of his daily routine.

无臭 wúxiù 【形】odourless

无须 wúxū 【副】needlessly; need not; not have to

无烟煤 wúyānméi 【名】anthracite; smokeless coal

无业 wúyè 【形】jobless：～青年 jobless youth

无依无靠 wú yī wú kào have no one to depend upon；be alone in the world

无疑 wúyí 【形】beyond doubt；undoubted；确凿～。It's indisputable. 这个论点～是错误的。This argument is undoubtedly wrong.

无以复加 wú yǐ fù jiā （going to）the extreme；（reach）the limit（usu. referring to bad things）

无意 wúyì 【动】❶ have no wish；have no intention：他～参加这次比赛。He has no wish to take part in the contest. ❷ unintentional：我～之中得罪了他。I unintentionally offended him. 他～中遇见了多年不见的老朋友。Quite by chance, he met an old friend whom he had not seen for many years.

无益 wúyì 【形】no advantage：过度饮酒有害～。Drinking to excess can only injure and has no advantage at all.

无影无踪 wú yǐng wú zōng without a trace；not to be seen anywhere：我出来一看，他早已跑得～了。When I came out to look, he had vanished without a trace.

无用 wúyòng 【形】useless：把～的东西搬走 move away everything which is of no use 他正在气头上，劝也～。He is angry right now, it's useless trying to talk reason to him.

无与伦比 wú yǔ lúnbǐ matchless；beyond compare：在陆地动物中，象的体积之大是～的。Among all the animals on land the bulk of the elephant is beyond compare.

无缘无故 wú yuán wú gù without any reason；without rhyme or reason：很难想象世上有～的爱，或～的恨。It is hard to imagine love without a reason or hatred without a cause love or hatred without reason or cause.

无政府主义 wúzhèngfǔzhǔyì 【名】anarchism

无知 wúzhī 【形】ignorant；lacking knowledge

无中生有 wú zhōng shēng yǒu groundless；sheer fabrication：他的话完全是～，凭空捏造。What he said is groundless and is nothing short of sheer fabrication.

无主句 wúzhǔjù 【名】sentence with no subject

无足轻重 wú zú qīng zhòng insignificant；of little importance：不要把服务工作看得～，它关系到广大人民的切身利益。We must not take service work as something of little importance. It has a lot to do with the vital interests of the people.

无罪 wúzuì 【形】innocent；not guilty

wǔ

五 wǔ 【数】five

五彩 wǔcǎi 【名】multicoloured；colourful

五彩缤纷 wǔcǎi bīnfēn multicoloured；colourful：～的烟火 colourful fireworks

五谷 wǔgǔ 【名】❶ the five cereals：rice, glutinous millet, millet, wheat and beans ❷ grain in general：～丰登 a bumper harvest of grain

五官 wǔguān 【名】general term for facial features

五光十色 wǔ guāng shí sè a great variety；multicoloured：～的宝石 beautiful gems of various colours ～的工艺品 a great variety of handicrafts

五湖四海 wǔ hú sì hǎi all corners of the country

五花八门 wǔ huā bā mén　multifarious；a great variety of

五金 wǔjīn 【名】the five metals （gold，silver，copper，iron and pewter）；metals

五卅运动 Wǔ Sà Yùndòng　the May 30th Movement，1925，a nationwide anti-imperialist movement

五四青年节 Wǔ Sì Qīngniánjié　May 4th Youth Day

五四运动 Wǔ Sì Yùndòng　the May 4th Movement，1919，an anti-imperialist，anti-feudal political and cultural movement

五体投地 wǔ tǐ tóu dì　prostrate oneself before sb. in admiration；have the greatest and most sincere admiration（for sb.）

五线谱 wǔxiànpǔ 【名】(music) staff

五星红旗 wǔ xīng hóngqí　the Five-starred Red Flag (the national flag of the People's Republic of China)

五颜六色 wǔ yán liù sè　colourful；of various colours；百货公司的橱窗里摆着～的纺织品。Colourful textiles are displayed in the show-windows of the department store.

五一国际劳动节 Wǔ Yī Guójì Láodòngjié　May 1, International Labour Day

五月 wǔyuè 【名】May

五脏 wǔzàng 【名】the five internal organs（the heart，liver，spleen，lungs and kidneys）

五洲 wǔzhōu 【名】five continents

午 wǔ

午餐 wǔcān 【名】lunch

午饭 wǔfàn 【名】lunch

午觉 wǔjiào 【名】nap after lunch；睡个～ take a nap after lunch

午睡 wǔshuì 【名】nap after lunch 【动】take a nap

午休 wǔxiū 【动】noon break；mid-day rest

午宴 wǔyàn 【名】luncheon

午夜 wǔyè 【名】midnight

伍 wǔ 【数】five (the complicated form of 五) 见"捌" bā

武 wǔ 【名】(as opp. to 文) military；physical labour；文～双全 be good in both civilian and military work；be good in both mental and manual labour

武打 wǔdǎ 【名】acrobatic fighting in Chinese opera

武断 wǔduàn 【形】arbitrary

武官 wǔguān 【名】❶ military attaché ❷ military officer

武警 wǔjǐng 【名】military police

武力 wǔlì 【名】military force

武器 wǔqì 【名】weapon

武术 wǔshù 【名】Wu Shu (general term for various kinds of Chinese traditional boxing and fencing)

武艺 wǔyì 【名】martial arts；military arts；～超人 excel in military arts

武装 wǔzhuāng 【名】arms；～斗争 armed struggle 全副～ in full battle array；fully armed 【动】arm；用科学文化～头脑 arm one's mind with knowledge of science and culture 民兵都～起来了。The militia-men are all armed.

侮 wǔ

侮辱 wǔrǔ 【动】humiliate；insult 【名】humiliation；insult

捂 wǔ 【动】cover；～着耳朵 cover one's ears（with one's hands）衣服穿得太多，～了一身汗。He was soaked with sweat from wearing too many clothes.

舞 wǔ 【名】dance；唱个歌，跳个～ sing a song and dance a dance 【动】◇ ❶ brandish；wield；～剑 brandish a sword ❷ play；～文弄墨

indulge in rhetoric; use excessive fine-sounding phrases

舞弊 wǔbì 【动】engage in fraudulent practices

舞场 wǔchǎng 【名】dance hall

舞蹈 wǔdǎo 【名】dance

舞会 wǔhuì 【名】dance party

舞剧 wǔjù 【名】dance drama; ballet

舞曲 wǔqǔ 【名】〔支 zhī〕dance music

舞台 wǔtái 【名】stage

舞厅 wǔtīng 【名】ballroom

wù

勿 wù 【副】〈书〉indicates prohibition: 请～吸烟。No Smoking! 请～喧哗。Quiet Please!

戊 wù

戊戌变法 Wùxū Biànfǎ the Bourgeois Reform Movement of 1898

务（務）wù 【动】◇ be engaged in: 不～正业 not be engaged in honest work; not be engaged in carrying out one's proper duties 【副】◇ 同"务必": ～歼入侵之敌。We must annihilate the aggressors. ～请准时到会。Please be on time to attend the meeting.

务必 wùbì 【副】must (used in imperative sentences only): 这封信请你～当面交给他。Please hand him the letter in person. 工具用完～归还。Please return the tools after use without fail.

务农 wù＝nóng take farming as a profession; be engaged in agriculture

务须 wùxū 【副】must; have to: ～出示证件，方可通过。Passage on producing credentials only.

物 wù 【名】◇ ❶ thing; object: 见～不见人 fix one's eyes on material things only, and fail to see the creative power of human beings ❷ content: 言之无～ empty verbiage ❸ outside world; other people: 待人接～ one's way of getting along with people

物产 wùchǎn 【名】produce or manufactured products

物极必反 wù jí bì fǎn when pushed to an extreme, a thing will develop in the opposite direction

物价 wùjià 【名】price

物理 wùlǐ 【名】physics

物理性质 wùlǐ xìngzhì physical property

物理学 wùlǐxué 【名】physics

物力 wùlì 【名】material resources

物美价廉 wù měi jià lián 同"价廉物美" jià lián wù měi

物品 wùpǐn 【名】thing (for daily use)

物色 wùsè 【动】look for; seek out; select: ～演员 recruit potential actors and actresses 我要买件工艺美术品送朋友，你帮我～～。I want to buy a handicraft item as a gift. Would you please help me choose one?

物体 wùtǐ 【名】substance; body; object

物以类聚 wù yǐ lèi jù like attracts like: ～，人以群分。Birds of a feather flock together.

物证 wùzhèng 【名】material evidence

物质 wùzhì 【名】❶ material; matter ❷ material goods, ect. (as opp. to 精神): ～享受 material comforts ～生活 material life ～条件 material conditions

物质不灭定律 wùzhì bù miè dìnglù law of conservation of matter

物主 wùzhǔ 【名】owner: 寻找 ～ look for the owner

物资 wùzī 【名】goods; materials; commodity

误(誤) wù 【形】◇ ❶ mistaken; wrong: ~传 pass on (news, message, etc.) incorrectly　~认为 think mistakenly ❷ unintentional; by accident: ~伤 injure sb. by mistake; accidentally injure 【动】❶ miss; hold up; delay: 不~农时 do farm work at the right time 磨刀不~砍柴工 It's not a waste of time for a wood-cutter to sharpen his axe. ❷ harm: ~人不浅 do people great harm

误差 wùchā 【名】error

误点 wù=diǎn behind schedule

误工 wù=gōng delay one's work

误会 wùhuì 【动】misunderstand: 我根本没有这种想法,你~了。I've never had such an idea; you misunderstood me. 【名】misunderstanding: ~消除了。The misunderstanding has been cleared up.

误解 wùjiě 【动】misunderstand; misinterpret: 你~了这个成语的意思。You got the meaning of this idiom wrong. 【名】misunderstanding: 产生~ give rise to misunderstanding 你应该把话说清楚,免得引起~。You should express yourself clearly so that you will not cause misunderstandings.

误区 wùqū 【名】misconception

误伤 wùshāng 【动】injure accidentally

误事 wù=shì ❶spoil an affair or a thing; bungle a matter ❷ cause delay in work

误诊 wùzhěn 【动】make an erroneous diagnosis: 大夫~,难免致命。The doctor made an erroneous diagnosis and death is unavoidable.

雾(霧) wù 【名】fog

X

xī

夕 xī 【名】◇ evening：～照 sunset glow

夕阳 xīyáng 【名】the setting sun

西 xī 【名】west

西北 xīběi 【名】northwest

西边 xībiān 【名】west side；west

西餐 xīcān 【名】Western-style food（meal）

西方 xīfāng 【名】❶ the west ❷ the West

西服 xīfú 【名】〔件 jiàn、套 tào〕Western-style clothes

西瓜 xīguā 【名】〔个 gè〕watermelon

西红柿 xīhóngshì 【名】〔个 gè〕tomato

西南 xīnán 【名】southwest

西式 xīshì 【形】Western-style：～楼房 a Western-style building ～糕点 Western-style pastries

西药 xīyào 【名】Western medicine

西医 xīyī 【名】❶ doctor trained in Western medicine ❷ Western medicine

西装 xīzhuāng 【名】〔套 tào〕Western style clothes

吸 xī 【动】❶ breathe in：～了一口气 take a breath ❷ absorb：～热 absorb heat ❸ attract；draw：磁能

～铁。Magnets attract iron.

吸尘器 xīchénqì 【名】〔台 tái〕vacuum cleaner

吸毒 xī＝dú take drug

吸取 xīqǔ 【动】absorb；assimilate：～经验教训 learn from experience 从英雄人物身上～精神力量 draw spiritual strength from the example of heroes

吸收 xīshōu 【动】❶ absorb；assimilate：～水分 absorb water ～营养 absorb nourishment ❷ recruit；enrol；admit：工会～新会员。The trade union is taking in new members.

吸铁石 xītiěshí 【名】magnet

吸血鬼 xīxuèguǐ 【名】vampire；bloodsucker

吸烟 xī＝yān smoke（cigarette or pipe）

吸引 xīyǐn 【动】attract：～了很多观众 attract a large audience ～人们的注意力 hold people's attention

吸引力 xīyǐnlì 【名】force of attraction

希 xī 【动】〈书〉hope：～准时到会。We hope you will come to the meeting on time. ～读者指正。We look forward to receiving comments from our readers.

希罕 xīhan 【形】rare；uncommon：～的现象 rare phenomenon ～的东西 rare things 这事儿真～。Such a

thing is rare indeed. 【动】value as a rarity：贝壳我们那儿有的是，谁～它呀！There are plenty of sea shells where we are，nobody cares much for them. 【名】(～儿) rare thing；rarity：看～enjoy looking at sth. because it is unusual 也作"稀罕"。

希奇 xīqí 【形】rare and curious：～古怪 rare and peculiar 北京动物园有许多～的鸟兽。There are lots of rare animals and birds in the Beijing Zoo. 也作"稀奇"。

希望 xīwàng 【动】hope：～你努力学习。I hope you study hard. 【名】❶ hope：你的这个～并不难实现。Your aspiration is not difficult to realize. ❷ person or thing on which hope is based：民族的～the hope of the nation 人类的～the hopes of mankind

昔 xī 【名】◇ the past：抚今追～ reflect on the past in the light of the present

昔日 xīrì 【名】the past；former days：～的奴隶，今天成了国家的栋梁。Those who were serfs in former times have become the pillars of society. ～这里荒无人烟。In the past，this land was barren and unpopulated.

牺(犧) xī

牺牲 xīshēng 【动】❶ sacrifice oneself；die a martyr：流血～lay down one's life for (a just cause) 壮烈～die a heroic death ❷ give up；sacrifice：～个人的一切 sacrifice all that one has ～局部利益 sacrifice the interest of a part (for the sake of the whole) 【名】sacrifice：付出了很大的～make a great sacrifice 避免不必要的～avoid unnecessary sacrifices

牺牲品 xīshēngpǐn 【名】victim：那两

个男女青年成了包办婚姻的～。The young couple were the victims of an arranged marriage.

息 xī 【名】◇ ❶ breath：为祖国独立战斗到生命的最后一～ fight to one's last breath for the independence of one's country ❷ interest 【动】◇ cease；stop：生命不～，战斗不止 keep fighting to one's last breath 请～怒。Don't be angry any more.

息怒 xī=nù calm one's anger；cool down

息事宁人 xī shì níng rén gloss things over

息息相关 xī xī xiāng guān closely related：子弟兵与人民群众～。The people's army have close ties with the people.

奚 xī

奚落 xīluò 【动】taunt；scoff at

惜 xī 【动】◇ cherish；treasure；love and care

惜别 xībié 【动】feel reluctant to leave：依依～part from sb. very reluctantly 怀着～的心情 (leave) with a feeling of reluctance

惜力 xīlì 【动】not do one's best

稀 xī 【形】❶ rare；scarce：物以～为贵。When a thing is rare，it is valued. ❷ with a long distance in between；sparse：地广人～a vast thinly-populated land 月明星～a bright moon with few stars 苗儿出得～。The seedlings have sprouted sparsely. ❸ thin；with a lot of water：粥熬(áo)得太～了。The hot-cereal is too thin.

稀薄 xībó 【形】thin：空气～。The air is thin.

稀饭 xīfàn 【名】porridge

稀客 xīkè 【名】rare visitor

稀少　xīshǎo　【形】few；scarce：人口 ～ sparsely populated 行人～ only a few pedestrians

稀释　xīshì　【动】dilute

稀疏　xīshū　【形】sparse；scanty；few and scattered

稀有　xīyǒu　【形】rare：～动物 a rare animal ～的事情 a rare event

稀有金属　xīyǒu jīnshǔ　rare metal

稀有元素　xīyǒu yuánsù　rare (chemical) element

溪　xī　【名】brook；stream

熙　xī

熙熙攘攘　xīxīrǎngrǎng　【形】bustling with activity：街上行人～，非常热闹。The street is bustling with people coming and going.

熄　xī　【动】put out；go out：～灯 turn the light off 火～了。The fire died out.

熄灭　xīmiè　【动】go out；die out：炉火～了。The fire in the furnace went out. ～了的爱情之火又燃烧起来。The flames of love, which had almost died, have been rekindled.

膝　xī　【名】◇ knee

膝盖　xīgài　【名】knee

嬉　xī

嬉皮笑脸　xī pí xiào liǎn　grinning frivolously

嬉笑　xīxiào　【动】laugh and play

蟋　xī

蟋蟀　xīshuài　【名】〔只 zhī〕cricket

xí

习（習）　xí　【动】◇ be used to：不～水性 be unable to swim 【名】◇ habit；custom：相沿成～（a

practice）which was handed down from the past and has become habit

习惯　xíguàn　【名】habit；custom：养成好～ form good habits 尊重当地的风俗～ respect local customs and practices 【动】be used to：我～早起。I am used to getting up early. 她～于这种紧张生活。She is used to an intense life of this kind. 对于这儿的气候他已经～了。He has become used to the climate here.

习惯势力　xíguàn shìlì　force of habit

习气　xíqì　【名】(bad) habit；(bad) practice：官僚～ bureaucratic habits 坏～ a bad habit 旧～ out-moded behavior

习俗　xísú　【名】custom

习题　xítí　【名】exercises (in school work)

习性　xíxìng　【名】habits and characteristics

习以为常　xí yǐ wéi cháng　be accustomed to：对于隆隆的机器声，小张已～了。Xiao Zhang has become accustomed to the clatter of the machine.

习作　xízuò　【动】practise；do exercise：勤于～ be diligent in practice 【名】exercise：这幅画是我的～，请多指教。This picture is an apprentice work of mine. Please give me your comments.

席　xí　【名】❶〔张 zhāng、领 lǐng〕mat ❷ seat：来宾～ seats for guests ❸ seat；place：在选举中获得六～ (of an election) win six seats 【量】for talks，only with numeral 一：一～话 a talk

席卷　xíjuǎn　【动】roll up everything like a mat：～而逃 make off with everything 暴风雪～草原。The snowstorm is sweeping through the grasslands.

席位　xíwèi　【名】seat (at a confer-

ence or in a legislative assembly)：取得合法～ obtain one's rightful seat 妇女占五个～。Women hold five seats.

席子 xízi 【名】〔张 zhāng、领 lǐng〕mat

袭(襲) xí 【动】◇ raid：夜～ night raid 寒气～人 the penetrating cold

袭击 xíjī 【动】make a surprise attack：～敌人据点 make a surprise attack on the enemy's stronghold 台风～沿海岛屿。A typhoon is hitting the islands along the coast.

袭用 xíyòng 【动】take over；continue to use

媳 xí 【名】◇ daughter-in-law

媳妇 xífù 【名】❶ daughter-in-law ❷ wife；married woman

檄 xí

檄文 xíwén 【名】official denunciation of the enemy

xǐ

洗 xǐ 【动】❶ wash：～脸 wash one's face ～衣服 wash clothes ❷ ◇ kill and loot：血～全城。The whole city was looted and awash in blood. ❸ develop：～相片 develop film ❹ shuffle：～牌 shuffle cards

洗涤 xǐdí 【动】wash；cleanse

洗涤剂 xǐdíjì 【名】detergent

洗礼 xǐlǐ 【名】baptism

洗手间 xǐshǒujiān 【名】toilet

洗刷 xǐshuā 【动】❶ scrub：～地板 scrub the floor ～游泳池 clean the swimming pool ❷ wash off；clear oneself (of a charge)：把自己～得一干二净 (attempt to) completely clear oneself (of a charge)

洗衣粉 xǐyīfěn 【名】washing powder

洗衣机 xǐyījī 【名】〔台 tái〕washing machine

洗澡 xǐ=zǎo take a bath

洗澡间 xǐzǎojiān 【名】bathroom

铣(銑) xǐ 【动】mill

铣床 xǐchuáng 【名】〔台 tái〕miller (machine)

铣工 xǐgōng 【名】❶ miller ❷ milling (work)

喜 xǐ 【动】◇ ❶ be happy：笑在眉梢，～在心头 be all smiles and have great joy in one's heart；be extremely happy ～看一代新人健康成长 be delighted to see a new generation growing up strong and healthy ❷ be fond of；like：～新厌旧 pursue the new and reject the old；be fickle in affection 好 (hào) 大～功 like big undertakings 【名】◇ happy event：双～临门。Two happy events occurred simultaneously.

喜爱 xǐ'ài 【动】like；be fond of

喜报 xǐbào 【名】a bulletin of glad tidings

喜出望外 xǐ chū wàng wài a delightful surprise；be pleasantly surprised；使人～ give sb. a delightful surprise

喜好 xǐhào 【动】be fond of：～木刻 be fond of wood-carving ～下棋 like to play chess

喜欢 xǐhuan 【动】❶ like；be fond of ❷ be delighted

喜酒 xǐjiǔ 【名】celebratory wine (at a wedding)

喜剧 xǐjù 【名】〔出 chū〕comedy

喜气洋洋 xǐqì yángyáng be filled with joy；be very happy：国庆佳节，男女老少～。On National Day, men and women, old and young, are all happy.

喜庆 xǐqìng 【形】joyous；jubilant

喜鹊 xǐquè 【名】〔只 zhī〕magpie

喜人 xǐrén 【形】pleasing；delightful

喜色 xǐsè 【名】happy expression：面带～a happy face 满脸～a face glowing with happiness

喜事 xǐshì 【名】❶ happy event；joyous occasion ❷ wedding

喜糖 xǐtáng 【名】candies（eaten at a wedding）

喜闻乐见 xǐ wén lè jiàn like to listen to and be delighted to see：作家要多创作为（wéi）大众～的作品。Writers should try to make their work appeal to ordinary readers.

喜笑颜开 xǐ xiào yán kāi light up with pleasure；smile radiantly

喜新厌旧 xǐ xīn yàn jiù be fickle in one's affection

喜形于色 xǐ xíng yú sè one's face reveals one's happiness；be visibly pleased

喜讯 xǐxùn 【名】happy news；good news

喜洋洋 xǐyángyáng 【形】radiant；joyful

喜悦 xǐyuè 【形】happy；joyous：～的心情 a happy state of mind 无限～ extremely happy

xì

戏（戲） xì 【名】〔出 chū〕theatrical show；play；drama

戏剧 xìjù 【名】drama；play；opera

戏剧性 xìjùxìng 【名】dramatic

戏迷 xìmí 【名】theatre fan

戏弄 xìnòng 【动】tease；make fun of

戏曲 xìqǔ 【名】Chinese traditional opera

戏院 xìyuàn 【名】theatre

系 xì 【名】a department in a university：哲学～ the philosophy department 他们俩在一个～工作。The two of them work in the same department. 【动】❶（繫）haul up or down with a rope：把几块瓦～到房顶上去 haul a few tiles up to the roof of the house ❷（係）〈书〉be：确～实情。It is an actual fact. ❸（係、繫）〈书〉relate to；bear on：成败～于此举。Success or failure depends on this move.

另见 jì

系列 xìliè 【名】series：～产品 series of production ～工程 systems engineering

系数 xìshù 【名】❶（maths.）coefficient ❷ coefficient：安全～ safety coefficient

系统 xìtǒng 【名】system：工业～ the industrial system 按组织～分配资金 allocate funds according to organizational system 【形】systematic：～地学习 study systematically 内容编排非常～。The content（e. g. of a book）was organized very systematically.

系统性 xìtǒngxìng 【名】systematicness；systematic

细（細） xì 【形】❶ fine；slender：～铁丝 fine wire ～线 fine thread 羊毛又～又长 long delicate fibres of wool ❷ fine；in small particles：～沙 fine sand ～末 fine powder ❸ soft and high-pitched（usu. of a woman's voice）：～嗓子 a soft voice ❹ minute；trifling：事无巨～,他都过问。He always has to have a hand in everything, no matter how unimportant. 故事情节写得很～。The plot of the story was fleshed out with fine descriptive details. ❺ careful；meticulous：～看 look at sth. closely ～说 tell（a story）in detail 队长对工作程序考虑得很～。The team leader pondered over all the details of

the work procedure. ❻ fine；delicate：～瓷 delicate porcelain ～活儿 fine workmanship

细胞　xìbāo　【名】cell

细菜　xìcài　【名】off-season vegetables rare vegetables

细活儿　xìhuó　【名】work demanding skill and care

细节　xìjié　【名】detail

细菌　xìjūn　【名】bacteria；germ

细粮　xìliáng　【名】refined grain (e.g. flour，rice)

细密　xìmì　【形】❶ fine and closely woven：这块头巾织得真～。This kerchief is fine and closely-woven. ❷ detailed：～的分析 a detailed analysis

细嫩　xìnèn　【形】delicate；tender

细腻　xìnì　【形】❶ fine and smooth：皮肤～ delicate skin ❷ exquisite；minute：人物描写得非常～。The characters (in the book) were described in detail.

细软　xìruǎn　【名】valuables：把～收好。Put away the valuables safely.

细水长流　xì shuǐ cháng liú　❶ economize to avoid running short：用钱要有计划，要～ be economical in spending money to avoid running short ❷ do sth. little by little without a break：收集资料要～，日积月累。Data should be accumulated slowly and steadily over time.

细微　xìwēi　【形】fine；slight：声音很～ very weak or soft voice ～的变化 slight change ～的差别 slight difference

细小　xìxiǎo　【形】tiny；trivial；minute；fine

细心　xìxīn　【形】careful；thoughtful：～人 an attentive and thoughtful person ～观察 watch carefully

细则　xìzé　【名】detailed rules and regulations

细致　xìzhì　【形】meticulous；painstaking：工作～ work meticulously

护士耐心～地照顾病人。The nurse looked after the invalid with patience and care.

xiā

虾（蝦）　xiā　【名】〔只 zhī〕prawn；shrimp

虾米　xiāmi　【名】dried shelled shrimp

虾皮　xiāpí　【名】small，dried shrimps

虾仁儿　xiārénr　【名】shelled fresh shrimp

瞎　xiā　【动】lose one's eyesight：眼睛～了 become blind 【副】blindly；aimlessly；foolishly：～说 talk nonsense ～忙 be busy without plan or purpose ～起哄 pointlessly tease and joke with sb.

瞎扯　xiāchě　【动】talk nonsense；tell tall tales

瞎吹　xiāchuī　【动】talk big；boast

瞎话　xiāhuà　【名】lie；fib

瞎说　xiāshuō　【动】talk nonsense

瞎抓　xiāzhuā　【动】go about things without a plan do things at random

瞎子　xiāzi　【名】blind person

xiá

匣　xiá　【名】◇ box

匣子　xiázi　【名】〔个 gè〕box

峡（峽）　xiá　【名】gorge；sharp ravine

峡谷　xiágǔ　【名】gorge；canyon

狭（狹）　xiá　【形】◇ narrow

狭隘　xiá'ài　【形】❶ narrow：～的山路 a narrow mountain path ❷ narrow and limited：心胸～ narrow-

minded ～的民族主义 parochial nationalism

狭路相逢 xiá lù xiāngféng meet on a narrow path; (*fig.*) an unavoidable confrontation

狭小 xiáxiǎo 【形】 narrow and limited: 气量～ be narrow-minded 眼光～ be short-sighted

狭义 xiáyì 【名】 narrow sense

狭窄 xiázhǎi 【形】 ❶ narrow: ～的走廊 a narrow corridor ❷ narrow and limited: 心地～ be narrow-minded 思路～ be limited in one's thinking

霞 xiá 【名】 rosy cloud; roseate cloud

xià

下 xià 【名】 ❶ down; under; below (*as opp. to* 上): 往～走 go down 朝～看 look down ❷ *as opp. to* 上, *used after a noun to indicate a lower position*: 山～ at the foot of the hill 树～ under the tree 台～ off-stage ❸ *as opp. to* 上, *used before a noun or measure word to indicate coming later in time or order*: ～册 vol. II ～次 next time ～星期 next week ～半年 the latter half of the year 【动】 ❶ *as opp. to* 上, *indicates movement from a higher place to a lower place*: ～楼 go downstairs ～山 go down the hill 汽车到站了，让老年人先～。The bus has stopped; we must let the old people get off first. ❷ go to a lower place or to a unit at the grassroots level: ～海 put out to sea ～车间 go to the workshop 师长～连队。The division commander went to live with a company (in order to get to know more about the ordinary soldiers). ❸ fall: ～

雨。It's raining. ～雪。It's snowing. ～霜。There is frost. ～雾。It's foggy. ❹ issue: ～命令 issue an order ～通知 send a notice ❺ put in: ～面条 put noodles in (boiling water to cook) ～网打鱼 cast the net ❻ finish work (at a specific time): ～工 get off work ～操。The drill is over. 你～了第四节课来找我一下。Please come to see me when you get out after the fourth class. ❼ draw; make out: ～结论 draw a conclusion ～定义 give the definition (of a word) ❽ ◇ put into use: 我想自己裁衣服，可是不敢～剪子。I want to cut out a dress myself but I'm afraid to start. 想写的内容很多，不知从哪儿～笔。There are lots of things I'd like to write about but I don't know where to begin. ❾ (of animals) give birth to; lay: 鸡～蛋。The hen laid an egg. 母牛～了头小牛。The cow gave birth to a calf. Note: 下 *is used after a verb as a complement* ① *indicates a movement from a higher place to a lower one*: 跑～山坡 run down the hillside 把货物搬～车 unload the truck 把东西放～ put down your things 传～一道命令 send down an order 播～种子 sow the seeds 埋伏～一连战士 have a company lying in ambush 坐～。Sit down please. (*same as* 下来 *or* 下去 *as a complement, but no direction is indicated*) ② *indicates moving off from a position*: 摘～帽子 take off one's hat 脱～大衣 take off one's coat 拔～一个钉子 pull out a nail ③ capture; take: 打～不少粮食 harvest a lot of grain 这支军队一连攻～几个县城。This army captured several counties one after another. ④ *indicates the keeping of sth. or sb. in one way or another*: 拍～这个难得的镜头 get a pic-

ture of this rare scene 写～你的住址 write down your address 别人都出去了,家里只留下奶奶看家。All the others are out, with grannie left behind to look after the house. (②,③,④ *are the same as* 下来 *as a complement* ②,③,④, *but an object is necessary*) ⑤ *indicates that sth. is to remain in a special state*: 打～坚实的基础 lay a solid foundation 立～丰功伟绩 make an outstanding contribution 闯～大祸 bring about a disaster 材料都准备～了,明天就动工。All the materials are ready and construction will begin tomorrow. ⑥ *indicates that there is enough space to contain sth. or some people*: 这个瓶子二斤油能装～吗? Do you think this bottle will hold 2 *jin* of oil? 这间教室坐得～二百人。This classroom can seat 200 people. 【量】time: 敲了三～门 knock on the door three times 打了他两～ hit him twice

下巴 xiàba 【名】chin

下班 xià = bān go off work; knock off

下笔 xià = bǐ begin to write: 考虑好了就～。When you have made up your mind you can begin to write.

下边 xiàbiān 【名】below; underneath; the following

下不为例 xià bù wéi lì this (behaviour) must not be repeated

下策 xiàcè 【名】ill-advised policy; unwise move

下层 xiàcéng 【名】❶ lower shelf: 柜子的～ the lower shelf of a cupboard ❷ grassroots: 干部深入～。Cadres go down to the grassroots level. ❸ the lower strata: 社会～ the lower strata of society

下场 xiàchǎng 【名】end (*derog.*): 落得个可耻的～ come to a bad end; end up disgraced 与流氓痞子为伍绝没有好～。If you mix with scum and riffraff, you will certainly come to no good end.

下达 xiàdá 【动】convey to a lower level: ～命令 convey an order to lower levels 上级的指示已～到各机关团体。The instructions of the higher level have already been conveyed to all institutions and organizations.

下等 xiàděng 【形】low-grade; inferior

下地 xià = dì ❶ go to the fields: ～劳动 go to work in the fields ～收割 go harvesting in the fields ❷ be up and about: 老大爷的病好了,能～了。The old man has recovered and is up and around.

下跌 xiàdiē 【动】fall: 产品价格～。The price of the product has come down.

下放 xiàfàng 【动】❶ transfer to a lower level: 权力～ pass down administrative power to lower levels ❷ transfer cadres to cadre training schools, to work at lower levels, or to do physical labour in a factory or in the countryside

下风 xiàfēng 【名】disadvantageous position: 处于～ be at a disadvantage

下工夫 xià gōngfu exert effort: 要想在班上拔尖儿,就得～。If you want to be at the top of the class, you must exert great effort. 小周下了一番工夫才学会游泳。After devoting time and effort to it, Xiao Zhou is finally able to swim.

下海 xià = hǎi ❶ go to the sea: ～捕鱼 go to the sea to fish ❷ go into business: 为了另谋生计,他早就～了。To find another means of livelihood, he has long gone into business.

下级 xiàjí 【名】subordinate; lower level

下降 xiàjiàng 【动】descend; go

down

下脚料 xiàjiǎoliào 【名】leftover bits and pieces

下课 xià = kè finish class; the class is over

下款 xiàkuǎn 【名】the signature (of a letter) the name (of a donor)

下来 xià // lái move from a higher position to a lower one (*towards the speaker*): 登山队员是昨天从山顶 ~ 的。The mountaineers descended from the top of the mountain yesterday. 他下楼来了。He's come downstairs. 我昨天发烧，今天体温 ~ 了。I had a high fever yesterday but my temperature has come down today. Note: 下来 *is used after a verb as a complement* ① from a higher position to a lower one: 把货物搬下车来 get the goods off the truck 孩子们跑下山坡来了。The children ran down the hillside. 他们都走了，我一个人留 ~ 了。The others have all gone away, but I continue to stay. 坐 ~ 谈谈。Please sit down and have a chat with me. (*same as* 下 *as a complement* ① *but towards the speaker*) ② *indicates moving sth. from its original position*: 脱下大衣来 take off one's coat 把西瓜摘 ~ pick the watermelon 这个轮胎我卸了半天也卸不 ~。I tried for a long time but failed to get the wheel off. ③ capture; take: 敌人的碉堡攻 ~ 了。The enemy's stronghold was captured. 等收下葡萄来，我教你一个贮存的办法。After we have picked the grapes, I'll tell you how to store them. ④ *indicates keeping or detaining sth. or sb. in one way or another*: 把这个雪景照 ~ take a picture of the snowy scene 他的报告已经录 ~ 了。His speech has been recorded. 剩 ~ 的钱不多了。Very little money is left. (②，③，④ *are the same as* 下

as a complement ②，③，④，*but an object is optional*) ⑤ from some time in the past to some time later or to the present: 这种古代流传 ~ 的纺织技术，到清朝就失传了。Certain textile techniques were passed down from ancient times but got lost in the Qing dynasty. 民间有许多药方是几百年前传 ~ 的。There are many folk prescriptions which have been handed down for hundreds of years. 这些文物保存 ~ 是很不容易的。It has been very difficult to preserve these cultural artefacts. ⑥ *indicates that things have been finally settled*: 他提的意见，我们都接受 ~ 了。We've taken all his suggestions and advice. 我们承担 ~ 的任务保证完成。We guarantee to finish all the jobs that we have committed ourselves to. 代表团的人选还定不 ~。We haven't yet decided who to choose as our delegates. ⑦ *indicates the completion of the whole of a process*: 整篇文章他都念 ~ 了，没错一个字。He's read out loud the whole article without making a single mistake. 五千米你跑得 ~ 跑不 ~? Do you think you can run the whole 5000 metres? ⑧ *used after certain verbs or adjectives to indicate gradual change, usu. from positive to negative*: 一场激烈的争论缓和 ~ 了。It was a heated argument but it has cooled down. 发生了故障机器会自动停 ~ 的。If there is any mishap, the machine will stop automatically. 灯光已经暗 ~，戏就要开演了。The house lights have gone down, and the play will begin right away.

下里巴人 xiàlǐ bārén an ancient popular folk song; (*fig.*) popular literature and art (*as opp. to* 阳春白雪，*high-brow literature and art*)

下列 xiàliè 【形】following; listed

below

下令 xià=lìng issue a decree or order

下流 xiàliú 【名】 lower reaches of a stream 【形】 obscene：～无耻 obscene and shameless ～话 obscene remarks

下落 xiàluò 【名】 whereabouts：～不明 whereabouts unknown 他家走失的老人现在有了～。 The family finally found out the whereabout of the old man who had gone missing. 那本书怎么没有～了? Why does nobody know where that book is?

下马 xià=mǎ （of a project) discontinue：原计划改变了，那项工程～了。 The original plan was changed, so the project was abandoned.

下马看花 xià mǎ kàn huā dismount and look at the flowers；（ fig.) make a comparatively long on-the-spot investigation

下马威 xiàmǎwēi 【名】 a display of his importance（by an official who has just assumed office)：一见面就来个～ deal sb. a head-on blow at the first encounter

下面 xiàmiàn 【名】 ❶ below；under：南京长江大桥有两层，上面是公路桥，～是铁路桥。 The Nanjing Bridge has two levels；the upper being the highway bridge and the lower being the railway bridge. ❷ next；following：刚才介绍了展览的概况，～请大家参观。 I have given you a general introduction to the exhibition；feel free to look around on your own. ❸ lower levels：把这个决定传达到～去 convey this decision to the lower levels

下坡路 xiàpōlù 【名】 decline；downhill path

下棋 xià=qí play chess

下情 xiàqíng 【名】 conditions at the lower level；the feelings and wishes of the masses：不明～ not know the feelings of the common people or the situation at the lower levels 使～得以上达 make the situation at the lower levels known to the higher levels

下去 xià // qù from a higher position to a lower one（ not towards the speaker)：等车停稳你再～。 Wait till the bus has come to a standstill and then get off. 我要下楼去打个电话。 I want to go downstairs to make a phone call. "五一"以后, 我就～。 I'm going down（to the grassroots level) after May Day. Note：下去 is used after a verb as a complement ① downward：滑雪运动员从山上冲～。 The skiers flew downhill. 小桥很窄, 小心别掉～。 The little bridge is very narrow. You must be careful not to fall off. 太阳已经落下山去了。 The sun has already sunk behind the mountains. （ same as 下 as a complement ①, but not towards the speaker) ② indicates continuation：请你说～。 Please go on. 坚持～就是胜利。 If we can persist, we will be successful. 这本书我只看了一半, 后来没有再看～。 I've only read half the book and never finished it. 有了水库, 天再旱～也不怕。 Since we now have a reservoir, it doesn't matter if the drought continues.

下身 xiàshēn 【名】 the lower part of the body：～穿了一条黑裤子 wear a pair of black trousers

下手 xià=shǒu begin；start（doing sth.)：头绪繁杂, 不知从哪儿～。 There are a lot of loose ends, and we don't know where to begin.

下属 xiàshǔ 【名】 subordinate 【动】 subordinate

下水 xià=shuǐ ❶ enter the water：脚上的伤还没好, 不能～。 Since the

wound on your foot has not yet healed, you must not soak it in water. ❷ put in water: 这种布一~就抽。 This kind of cloth shrinks when soaked in water. ❸ take to evil-doing; fall into evil ways: 拖人~ involve sb. in evil-doing; drag sb. into the mire

下水道　xiàshuǐdào　【名】sewer

下榻　xiàtà　【动】〈书〉stay (at a place during a trip)

下台　xià = tái　❶ step down from a stage or platform ❷ lose power; leave office ❸ get out of an awkward position: 这个玩笑开得他下不了台。 The joke put him in an embarrassing situation which he could not easily get out of.

下头　xiàtou　【名】同"下面", but more colloquial

下文　xiàwén　【名】❶ what follows (in an article, passage): 关于这个问题~还要提到。 This question will be discussed again in a later part (of the book). ❷ further development; outcome: 托他办的那件事还没有~。 We haven't heard anything yet about the matter which was entrusted to him.

下午　xiàwǔ　【名】afternoon

下乡　xià = xiāng　go to the countryside to stay (for some time): 他~三个月了。 He has been in the countryside for three months now. 这个剧团星期一就要~演出了。 On Monday, this theatrical troupe is leaving for the countryside to put on performances.

下旬　xiàxún　【名】last ten days of a month

下野　xià = yě　be forced out of office

下游　xiàyóu　【名】❶ lower reaches of a river: 黄河~土地肥沃。 The land along the lower reaches of the Yellow River is fertile. ❷

backward: 不能甘居~ not be willing to lag behind; unwilling to be left behind

下狱　xià = yù　throw into prison; imprison

下肢　xiàzhī　【名】lower limbs; legs

吓（嚇）　xià　【动】frighten; be frightened: 装腔作势, 借以~人 behave in a superior way to intimidate others ~了一跳 get a scare 什么也~不倒我们。 Nothing can intimidate us. ~得他脸色都变了。 He was so frightened that he turned pale.

吓唬　xiàhu　【动】〈口〉frighten: 你别~小孩。 Don't frighten the child.

夏　xià　【名】◇ summer

夏管　xiàguǎn　【名】summer farm-management

夏季　xiàjì　【名】summer

夏历　xiàlì　【名】the lunar calendar

夏粮　xiàliáng　【名】summer grain crops

夏令营　xiàlìngyíng　【名】summer camps

夏收　xiàshōu　【动】harvest in summer 【名】summer harvest

夏天　xiàtiān　【名】summer; summer days

夏种　xiàzhòng　【动】summer planting

夏装　xiàzhuāng　【名】summer clothes

xiān

仙　xiān　【名】◇ celestial being; immortal

仙鹤　xiānhè　【名】〔只 zhī〕crane

仙境　xiānjìng　【名】fairyland

仙女　xiānnǚ　【名】fairy maiden

仙人　xiānrén　【名】immortal; fairy

仙人掌　xiānrénzhǎng　【名】cactus

先 xiān 【名】◇ earlier; first; in advance; before: 有～有后 things must be dealt with in order; first come first serve 有言在～. I've given my word in advance. 【副】first; before: 让他～说. Let him speak first. 没有调查研究，～别下结论. Don't draw conclusions before investigating.

先辈 xiānbèi 【名】the elder generations; forefathers

先导 xiāndǎo 【名】precursor

先睹为快 xiān dǔ wéi kuài enjoy the privilege of being among the first to see or read sth.

先发制人 xiān fā zhì rén gain the initiative by striking first: ～的策略 the tactic of pre-emptive strike 给对方来个～ launch a pre-emptive strike against one's opponent

先锋 xiānfēng 【名】pioneer; vanguard

先锋队 xiānfēngduì 【名】vanguard

先后 xiānhòu 【名】early or late; order: 爱国不分～. As long as one is patriotic, it doesn't matter if one is late showing patriotism. 做事情要有个～次序. Things should be done in an orderly fashion. 【副】in succession; one after another: 同学们～都发了言. The students all spoke at the meeting one after another. 代表团～访问了五个国家. The delegation visited five countries in succession.

先见之明 xiān jiàn zhī míng foresight: 有～ have foresight 缺乏～ lack foresight

先进 xiānjìn 【形】advanced: ～集体 an advanced collective 达到～水平 reach an advanced level

先决条件 xiānjué tiáojiàn precondition; prerequisite

先礼后兵 xiān lǐ hòu bīng try peaceful means before resorting to force

先例 xiānlì 【名】precedent

先烈 xiānliè 【名】martyr

先前 xiānqián 【名】before; previously (as opp. to "后来"): ～我和他是同学. He and I used to be classmates. 他～不这样，现在变了. He was not like that before; he has changed.

先遣 xiānqiǎn 【形】(of units) sent in advance

先遣队 xiānqiǎnduì 【名】advance detachment

先驱 xiānqū 【名】forerunner; harbinger

先人 xiānrén 【名】ancestor; forefather

先入为主 xiān rù wéi zhǔ first impressions are not easily changed

先生 xiānsheng 【名】❶ teacher ❷ *a respectful form of address for teachers* ❸ *a respectful form of address for men*; Mr.

先天 xiāntiān 【名】congenital; inborn; innate

先行者 xiānxíngzhě 【名】forerunner

先验论 xiānyànlùn 【名】apriorism

先斩后奏 xiān zhǎn hòu zòu execute the criminal first and then report to the emperor; (*fig.*) act first and then report: 处理重大问题，一定要先请示上级，不能～. In dealing with important problems, we must get approval from the upper levels in advance; we must not act first and report later.

先知 xiānzhī 【名】a person of foresight; prophet

纤(纖) xiān

纤维 xiānwéi 【名】fibre; filament

纤细 xiānxì 【形】slender; thin; fine

掀 xiān 【动】lift: ～帘子 lift the curtain ～开历史新的一页 write a new page in history

掀起 xiān∥qǐ ❶ surge: 大海～巨浪

The sea was surging high. ❷ cause to surge：～建设高潮 bring about a surge in construction

鲜(鮮) xiān 【形】❶ fresh：～鱼 fresh fish ～黄瓜 newly-picked cucumber ❷ delicious：这汤的味道～极了。The soup is delicious!

鲜红 xiānhóng 【形】bright red；scarlet

鲜花 xiānhuā 【名】〔朵 duǒ、束 shù〕fresh flower；flower

鲜美 xiānměi 【形】delicious；tasty

鲜明 xiānmíng 【形】❶ (of colour) bright：色彩～ brightly coloured ❷ clear-cut；distinct：立场～ a clear-cut (class) stand 两个儿子对待父亲的态度形成～的对比。There is a sharp contrast between the attitudes of the two brothers towards their father.

鲜血 xiānxuè 【名】blood

鲜艳 xiānyàn 【形】gaily coloured：～的花朵 gaily coloured flowers 颜色～ beautiful and gay colours

鲜艳夺目 xiānyàn duómù dazzlingly beautiful：～的民族服装 the bright costumes of the national minorities

xián

闲(閒) xián 【形】❶ unoccupied；idle：她总～不住。She is never idle. 农～时农民可以多搞些家庭副业。In slack farming seasons, farmers have more time to devote to sideline production. 大家都在忙，没有一个人～着。Everybody is busy；there isn't anybody without something to do. ❷ (of things) not in use：充分利用设备能力，别让机器～着。Make full use of the equipment and don't let the machines go idle. 那三间房～着，没人

住。Those three rooms are vacant；there isn't anybody living there. ❸ not to do with business：～谈 talk idly

闲扯 xiánchě 【动】chat；gossip

闲工夫 xiángōngfu 【名】leisure；spare time

闲逛 xiánguàng 【动】take a stroll；saunter；loiter

闲话 xiánhuà 【名】❶ idle chat：我们正说～呢。We are just having a leisurely chat. ❷ gossip；complaint：对这样给自己的亲戚好处有不少～。Giving preference to one's own relatives in this way gave rise to a lot of talk.

闲聊 xiánliáo 【动】talk idly

闲情逸致 xián qíng yì zhì have leisure time and be in the mood for enjoyment

闲人 xiánrén 【名】❶ unoccupied person：家里一个～也没有。There is not a single unoccupied person in the house. ❷ person not concerned：～免进。Staff only.

闲事 xiánshì 【名】other people's business：老太太是个爱管～的人。The old woman is one who likes to poke her nose into other people's business.

弦 xián 【名】❶ bowstring：离～之箭 an arrow which has just left the bow ❷ string (of a musical instrument)：调 (tiáo) ～ tune one's instrument ❸ spring (of a clock or watch)：给闹钟上～ wind an alarm clock ❹ (maths.) chord ❺ (maths.) hypotenuse

弦乐器 xiányuèqì 【名】stringed instruments

咸(鹹) xián 【形】salty；salted

咸菜 xiáncài 【名】salted vegetables；pickles

衔 xián 【动】❶（唧）hold in the mouth：燕子～泥。A swallow carried some clay in its mouth. 嘴里～着烟斗。He had a pipe between his lips. ❷ ◇ harbour (a grudge)：～恨 be filled with hatred ～冤 suffer an injustice 【名】title；rank：公使～ the title of minister 上校～ the rank of colonel

衔接 xiánjiē 【动】connect；link up；join

舷 xián 【名】the side of a ship；board：船～ side of a ship

舷梯 xiántī 【名】gangway ladder

嫌 xián 【动】dislike；mind（*its object is an adjective or S-P construction*）：从不～麻烦。Nothing is too much trouble（for him）. 这次旅行，大家都～时间短。Everybody thought that the trip was far too short.

嫌弃 xiánqì 【动】dislike：自己的孩子再不好，妈妈也不～。A mother never dislikes her own child however naughty he or she may be.

嫌恶 xiánwù 【动】be sick of；detest；loathe

嫌疑 xiányí 【名】suspicion

嫌疑犯 xiányífàn 【名】suspect

xiǎn

显（顯） xiǎn 【动】❶ appear to：她最近～瘦。She appears to have lost weight recently. ❷ display；show：～威风 display one's power ～本领 show off one's skill 【形】obvious；noticeable：效果不～ have no noticeable effect 污点很～。The stain is quite noticeable.

显得 xiǎnde 【动】look；seem；appear（*its object is an adjective*

phrase or S-P construction）：节日的天安门～更加雄伟壮丽。On festival days, Tian'anmen Square appears even grander and more magnificent. 从这个角度拍摄，～树很高大。Taking a picture from this angle makes the trees appear very tall.

显而易见 xiǎn ér yì jiàn obvious：～的道理 an obvious argument

显赫 xiǎnhè 【形】illustrious；celebrated：地位～ an influential social position ～一时 celebrated for a certain period of time

显露 xiǎnlù 【动】become visible；manifest；show：～出高兴的样子 look very happy ～出不满的神色 have a dissatisfied expression on one's face

显然 xiǎnrán 【形】obvious：道理是很～的。The logic is very clear. 大雨过后，天气～冷了。After the heavy rain, it has become noticeably colder. ～，要提高生活水平，必须增加生产。It is obvious that if we want to raise the living standard, we must increase production.

显示 xiǎnshì 【动】display；demonstrate；manifest：～出巨大的威力 reveal a mighty force ～了计件工资的优越性 to demonstrate the advantages of piece rate wages 广大农民在改造自然的战斗中～出无穷的智慧。The peasants demonstrated great ingenuity in the transformation of nature.

显微镜 xiǎnwēijìng 【名】〔架 jià〕microscope

显现 xiǎnxiàn 【动】become visible；show；reveal：放在水里，这些石子的色彩和花纹就～出来了。Immersed in water, the different colours and patterns of these pebbles show up clearly. 幼时的苦难生活至今还时常～在他眼前。The suffering and hardships of his childhood constantly appear in his mind's eye

even to this day.

显像管　xiǎnxiàngguǎn　【名】kine-
scope

显眼　xiǎnyǎn　【形】conspicuous：把
通知贴到～的地方。Put up the no-
tice in a prominent place. 这几件展
品闪烁发光，十分～。These items in
the exhibition shine so brightly
that they are the centre of attention.

显要　xiǎnyào　【形】powerful and in-
fluential：～的地位 an influential
position

显著　xiǎnzhù　【形】remarkable；
striking：～的成绩 a remarkable
achievement 效果～ a remarkable
effect

险(險)　xiǎn　【形】❶ diffi-
cult of access：～路 a dangerous
road 无～可守 be strategically inde-
fensible ❷ dangerous：真～哪! 差一
点儿撞车。What a close shave! We
nearly had a collision! ❸ almost
(meet with a disaster)：～遭不幸
barely escape death

险恶　xiǎn'è　【形】❶ dangerous；per-
ilous：处境～ be in a perilous position ❷ sinister；vicious：～用心 vicious intentions

险峻　xiǎnjùn　【形】dangerously
steep：山势～ high and precipitous
mountains

险情　xiǎnqíng　【名】dangerous state
or situation：出现～ danger emerges

险胜　xiǎnshèng　【动】win by a narrow margin

险滩　xiǎntān　【名】shoal

险些　xiǎnxiē　【副】nearly；by a
hair's breadth：～上了他的当 nearly
fell into his trap 这孩子～掉到江里。
The child nearly fell into the river.

险要　xiǎnyào　【形】difficult of ac-
cess：地势～ strategically situated

terrain which is difficult of access

险阻　xiǎnzǔ　【形】(of roads) dangerous and difficult：山路崎岖～
the winding and dangerous mountain paths 不畏～ not be intimidated by dangers or difficulties

xiàn

县(縣)　xiàn　【名】county

县城　xiànchéng　【名】county seat

现(現)　xiàn　【动】appear；
reveal：～出本来面目 reveal one's
true colours 脸上～出胜利的喜悦。
His face revealed the joy of victory.【副】extempore：～编～演 im-
provise and perform ～学～教 learn
sth. at the same time as one is
teaching 事先不准备，临时～抓，必然
误事。Doing sth. in an impromptu
fashion is likely to make a mess of
things.【形】〈书〉now：～年二十五
岁。I am now 25 years old. ～将这
部词典寄给你。I am now sending
you the dictionary by post.

现场　xiànchǎng　【名】❶ scene (of
an event)：保护～ keep the scene
intact 到～进行调查 make an on-
the-spot investigation ❷ site；spot：
～参观 a visit to the site ～会议 on-
the-spot meeting

现成　xiànchéng　【形】ready-made：
～的设备 facilities ready for use ～
的饭菜 food prepared ahead of
time 吃～的 eat food prepared by
others

现存　xiàncún　【动】in stock；in existence

现代　xiàndài　【名】modern times；
contemporary era

现代化　xiàndàihuà　【动】modernize
【名】modernization

现货　xiànhuò　【名】goods on hand

现金　xiànjīn　【名】❶ cash ❷ cash

reserve in a bank

现款　xiànkuǎn　【名】cash

现钱　xiànqián　【名】cash

现任　xiànrèn　【动】hold at present：张先生～本公司经理。Mr. Zhang at present holds the position of manager of our company.

现身说法　xiàn shēn shuō fǎ　illustrate with one's own experience：老师傅～，对徒工进行安全生产的教育。The old worker used his own experiences to teach the apprentices safety in production.

现实　xiànshí　【名】reality：不能脱离～。We should not be divorced from reality. 要正视～。We must face reality squarely.【形】realistic；practical：你这个办法倒比较～。Your method is fairly practical. 你的想法太不～了。Your ideas are very unrealistic.

现实性　xiànshíxìng　【名】feasibility in present circumstances

现实主义　xiànshízhǔyì　【名】realism

现象　xiànxiàng　【名】〔种 zhǒng〕phenomenon

现行　xiànxíng　【形】❶ in force；currently in effect：～制度 the current system ～条例 rules and regulations in force ❷ (of a criminal) active：～犯 active criminal

现役军人　xiànyì jūnrén　serviceman

现在　xiànzài　【名】nowadays；at present；now

现状　xiànzhuàng　【名】present conditions；existing state；status quo

限　xiàn　【动】set a limit；restrict：形式不～ with no restriction on form ～一个星期完成 finish within a week 每券只～一人。Each ticket will admit one person only. 个人借书证只～本人使用。Each person's library card is restricted to his own use.【名】◇ limit（often used in conjunction with（以）…为）：以一九九九年十二月为～ set December 1999 as the deadline 这次作文一千字为～。This composition should not exceed 1,000 characters.

限定　xiàndìng　【动】set a limit to：～时间 set a time-limit ～人数 set a limit to the number of people 在～范围之内 within the prescribed limit

限度　xiàndù　【名】limit

限额　xiàn'é　【名】quota

限价　xiànjià　【动】set a limit to the price：对某些商品必须～。A limit must be set to the prices of certain commodities.【名】the fixed price：规定商品的最高～ stipulate the highest price limit of the commodity

限量　xiànliàng　【动】❶ limit the quantity of ❷ restriction of purchasable quantity

限期　xiànqī　【动】within a definite period of time：～到达 arrive within a definite period of time ～完成任务 finish the task within the prescribed period of time【名】time limit：无～延长 extend the time indefinitely ～已满。The allotted time is up.

限于　xiànyú　【动】be limited to：今天讨论的内容不～语法问题。The content of our discussion today is not limited just to grammatical questions. ～对情况了解不够，现在还很难下结论。Our understanding of the situation is limited, so it is difficult for us to arrive at any conclusion. ～汉语水平，他还不能翻译小说。His knowledge of Chinese is too limited for him to be able to translate novels.

限制　xiànzhì　【动】restrict：不受条件～ not be constrained by any con-

ditions 他的健康状况～了他的活动。His health sets limits to his activities.

线（綫） xiàn 【名】❶ thread ❷ (maths.) line：两～平行 two parallel lines ❸ route；line：运输～ transportation route 铁路沿～ along a railway line ❹ demarcation line：国境～ border of a country ❺ brink；verge：死亡～ on the verge of death 【量】for abstract things, can only be used with 一：一～希望 a ray of hope 一～光明 a gleam of light

线路 xiànlù 【名】❶ line of communication ❷ circuit (electr.)

线圈 xiànquān 【名】(of radio) coil

线索 xiànsuǒ 【名】clue

线条 xiàntiáo 【名】line in drawing

宪（憲） xiàn

宪兵 xiànbīng 【名】gendarme

宪法 xiànfǎ 【名】〔部 bù〕constitution

宪章 xiànzhāng 【名】charter

陷 xiàn 【动】❶ fall into；get stuck：越～越深 sink deeper and deeper ～于危险境地 find oneself in a dangerous situation ～于被动局面 land oneself in an awkward situation 汽车前轮～进泥里了。The front wheels of the car got stuck in the mud. ❷ sink；cave in：开了两天夜车，他的眼窝都～进去了。After working for two nights in succession, his eyes were sunken. ❸ ◇ (of territory) be captured；fall ❹ ◇ make a false charge against sb.

陷害 xiànhài 【动】frame：～好人 frame an innocent person 遭到～ be framed

陷阱 xiànjǐng 【名】〔个 gè〕trap；pitfall

陷落 xiànluò 【动】❶ subside；cave in：地壳～ the subsidence of the earth's crust ❷ (of territory) be captured

陷入 xiànrù 【动】❶ land oneself in：～包围圈 be besieged ～困境 land oneself in a difficult position ❷ be lost in；be deep in：～沉思 be lost in thought ～痛苦的回忆之中 be lost in painful recollections of the past

陷于 xiànyú 【动】fall into：～孤立 fall into isolation ～僵局 reach an impasse

馅（餡） xiàn

馅儿 xiànr 【名】stuffing (of pastry)

羡 xiàn

羡慕 xiànmù 【动】envy (in the sense of admire)

献（獻） xiàn 【动】offer；dedicate：～旗 present a banner

献策 xiàn = cè present a plan；submit scheme for；suggest a way

献词 xiàncí 【名】congratulatory message (e.g. New Year message)

献词 xiàn = cí make a congratulatory message

献花 xiàn = huā present a bouquet of flowers

献计 xiàn = jì 同"献策"

献礼 xiàn = lǐ present a gift：向"五一"节～ be presented as a gift for May Day

献媚 xiànmèi 【动】lick sb.'s boots；curry favour with：向主子～ curry favour with one's boss

献身 xiànshēn 【动】devote one's life to：消防队员为挽救人民的生命财产而英勇～。The firemen heroically devote their own lives to saving the lives and property of the people.

献殷勤 xiàn yīnqín be eager to please

xiāng

乡（鄉）
xiāng 【名】❶ ◇ countryside（*as opp. to* 城）❷ ◇ (one's) home (in the countryside)：回～探亲 go back to one's native town and visit one's relatives ❸ township (a former rural administrative unit)

乡村　xiāngcūn 【名】village；countryside

乡亲　xiāngqīn 【名】❶ fellow villager：我们俩是～。We two are fellow villagers. ❷ *form of address for villagers*：～们！你们好！How are you, fellow villagers!

乡土　xiāngtǔ 【名】of one's native land；local：～观念 affection, understanding and appreciation of the special flavours of one's own locality ～风味 local flavour ～教材 teaching materials suited to local needs

乡下　xiāngxia 【名】the countryside；village

乡镇　xiāngzhèn 【名】villages and towns：发展～企业 develop township onterprises

相
xiāng 【副】◇ ❶ mutual；each other：～视而笑 look at each other and smile 遥遥～望 look at each other from afar 两地～距数百里 (of two places) be several hundred *li* apart ❷ *indicates how one party behaves towards the other*：好言～劝 try to talk (sb.) around with kind persuasion 以礼～待 treat (sb.) with propriety
另见 xiàng

相爱　xiāng'ài 【动】be in love with each other

相比　xiāngbǐ 【动】compare (of two things)：两者不能～。The two can-not be compared. ～之下，我们还有很大差距。By comparison, we still lag far behind.

相差　xiāngchà 【动】differ

相称　xiāngchèn 【形】match；suit：这张画太小，挂在这么大的一面墙上不～。This picture is too small. It won't look well hanging on such a large expanse of wall. 这件衣服的颜色和他的年龄很～。The colour of his clothing is suitable for his age.

相乘　xiāngchéng 【动】multiply

相持　xiāngchí 【动】be locked in a stalemate：双方意见～不下。Neither party is ready to give way. 这次拔河比赛双方～了两分钟之久。For two minutes during the tug of war neither side could make headway.

相斥　xiāngchì 【动】mutually repel

相处　xiāngchǔ 【动】get along (with each other)：友好～ get along very well together 我们跟老王～得很好，从来不闹别扭。We and Lao Wang are on very good terms with each other and there's never been any unpleasantness between us.

相传　xiāngchuán 【动】❶ pass on from one to another：许多手工艺都是在家族中世代～的。A lot of handicrafts have been passed on from generation to generation in a family. ❷ according to legend：～这棵古松下是明朝的一座坟墓。It's said that under this old pine tree is a tomb of the Ming dynasty.

相待　xiāngdài 【动】treat

相当　xiāngdāng 【动】correspond to；match：两队人数～。The numbers of people of both teams are about the same. 实力～。The actual strength (of both sides) is equal. 他的文化水平～高中程度。His educational level is equivalent to that of a high school graduate. 【形】suitable；proper：我一时找不出～的词句来表达自己的心情。I could not

for the moment think of appropriate words to express my feelings. 他做这个工作很～。 He is a suitable person for this job. 【副】 quite; considerably: ～重视 pay considerable attention to 这个任务～艰巨。 This job is rather difficult. 这出戏演得～不错。 This play is very well done.

相等 xiāngděng 【动】 be equal to each other

相抵 xiāngdǐ 【动】 offset; balance: 收支～ the accounts balance

相对 xiāngduì 【动】 ❶ opposite: 大与小～。 "Big" is the opposite of "small". 美与丑～。 "Beauty" is the opposite of "ugliness". ❷ face to face; face each other: 遥遥～ face each other a long distance apart 隔海～ face each other across the sea 【形】 relative: ～稳定 relatively stable ～而言 comparatively speaking 水平高低是～的,不是绝对的。 When we talk about a high or low level, we are speaking in relative, not in absolute terms.

相对真理 xiāngduì zhēnlǐ relative truth

相反 xiāngfǎn 【形】 opposite; contrary: ～的意见 an opposing opinion ～的方向 the opposite direction 和你想的恰恰～,看电影的人非常多。 Contrary to your expectations, a lot of people went to see the film. 他不但没被困难吓倒,～地,他的意志越来越坚强了。 Far from being intimidated by difficulties, his determination has, on the contrary, become stronger.

相反相成 xiāng fǎn xiāng chéng be both opposite and complementary to each other

相仿 xiāngfǎng 【形】 similar: 年龄～ be about the same age 样子～ be similar in appearance

相逢 xiāngféng 【动】 meet each other; come face to face with each other

相符 xiāngfú 【动】 agree with each other; correspond with each other

相辅相成 xiāng fǔ xiāng chéng complement each other

相干 xiānggān 【动】 have to do with (*usu. used in the negative or in a rhetorical question*): 这事跟我毫不～。 This has nothing to do with me at all. 这和你有什么～? What has it to do with you?

相隔 xiānggé 【动】 be separated by; keep apart

相关 xiāngguān 【动】 be interrelated: 卫生条件和人们的健康水平是密切～的。 The health of the people is closely related to sanitary conditions.

相互 xiānghù 【形】 mutual: ～了解 mutual understanding ～影响 mutual influence 援助是～的。 Aid is usually mutual.

相互作用 xiānghù zuòyòng interaction

相继 xiāngjì 【副】 one after another: ～发言 speak one after another ～诞生 be born one after another

相加 xiāngjiā 【动】 add together

相见 xiāngjiàn 【动】 see each other: 二人很少～。 These two rarely see each other.

相交 xiāngjiāo 【动】 intersect: 有两条铁路在这个城市～。 The two railways intersect in this city.

相接 xiāngjiē 【动】 connect with

相近 xiāngjìn 【形】 ❶ close; near ❷ be similar to

相距 xiāngjù 【动】 apart; away from: 两地～不远,他日内即可到达。 The two places are not far apart, and he will arrive within a day or two.

相连 xiānglián 【动】 be joined: 全县村镇公路～。 The villages and towns of the county are joined by

highways.

相切　xiāngqiē　【动】（maths.）contact

相商　xiāngshāng　【动】consult：有要事～ have important matters to consult sb.

相识　xiāngshí　【动】know each other：彼此～ be acquainted with each other 我们俩早就～。We got to know each other long ago. 【名】acquaintance：他们是老～了。They are old acquaintances.

相似　xiāngsì　【形】similar：观点～ hold a similar point of view 有某些～之处 be similar in some respects

相提并论　xiāng tí bìng lùn　place on a par（usu. in the negative or in a rhetorical question）：卡车和马车的效力当然不能～。The efficiency of a truck and that of a cart can't be mentioned in the same breath. 这两件事性质完全不同，怎么能～呢？These two things are entirely different in nature；how can you place them in the same category?

相同　xiāngtóng　【形】alike；same

相像　xiāngxiàng　【动】be alike：张、王二人年貌～。Zhang and Wang are alike both in age and in appearances.

相信　xiāngxìn　【动】believe；have faith in：不～他的话 disbelieve what he said ～他能完成这项任务。We are confident that he can finish this task. 这种解释无法使人～。This explanation is not convincing.

相形见绌　xiāng xíng jiàn chù　be inferior by comparison：这张画跟那张一比，就～了。If you compare this painting with that one, you will find the other one much better.

相依为命　xiāng yī wéi mìng　be interdependent：母女俩～。The mother and daughter lived together, supporting each other through years of hardship.

相应　xiāngyìng　【形】corresponding；relevant：～的措施 corresponding measures 季节变了，作息时间也要～地改变。Since the season has changed, the time-table must be changed accordingly.

相遇　xiāngyù　【动】run into each other：老朋友～，格外高兴。When old friends run into each other, it is an unexpected pleasure.

香　xiāng　【形】❶ fragrant；smell good：玫瑰花真～！These roses are fragrant indeed! 饭菜很～。The food smells delicious. ❷（of sleep）sound：他睡得正～。He is sleeping soundly. ❸ with relish：我这几天吃东西不～。I have had no appetite these past few days.

香槟酒　xiāngbīnjiǔ　【名】champagne

香波　xiāngbō　【名】shampoo

香肠　xiāngcháng　【名】sausage

香花　xiānghuā　【名】fragrant flower

香蕉　xiāngjiāo　【名】banana

香料　xiāngliào　【名】❶ spice ❷ perfume

香喷喷　xiāngpēnpēn　【形】savoury：～的红烧肉 savoury braised pork

香水　xiāngshuǐ　【名】（～儿）perfume（liquid）

香甜　xiāngtián　【形】❶ sweet and fragrant；delicious ❷（of sleep）sound：昨晚小明睡得格外～。Last night, Xiao Ming slept exceptionally well.

香烟　xiāngyān　【名】〔枝 zhī、盒 hé、包 bāo〕cigarette

香油　xiāngyóu　【名】sesame oil

香皂　xiāngzào　【名】〔块 kuài〕toilet soap

箱　xiāng　【名】◇trunk；box；case

箱子　xiāngzi　【名】〔个 gè〕trunk；box

xiāng

镶（鑲） xiāng 【动】inlay；set；mount：～牙 be fitted for dentures ～花边 edge sth. with lace

镶嵌 xiāngqiàn 【动】inlay；set；mount

xiáng

详（詳） xiáng 【形】〈书〉detailed：～略适当 with appropriate details but not redundant 【动】❶ look for details：内～ see inside (written on an envelope) ～见下文。For further details, please see below. ❷ know clearly：作者生卒年月不～。The author's dates are unknown.

详尽 xiángjìn 【形】detailed；exhaustive：记载～ a detailed record ～地叙述 relate sth. in the minutest detail

详情 xiángqíng 【名】details；all small facts

详细 xiángxì 【形】detailed：～研究 make an exhaustive study 讲～些！Please give us more details. 他问得～极了。He inquired into details.

降 xiáng 【动】❶surrender：宁死不～ prefer to die rather than surrender to the enemy ❷ tame；subdue：他～住了那匹烈马。He succeeded in taming that spirited horse.

另见 jiàng

降服 xiángfú 【动】subdue；overpower

降龙伏虎 xiáng lóng fú hǔ overpower formidable adversaries：～的本领 the ability to subdue powerful opponents ～的英雄 a hero who is able to defeat powerful adversaries

xiǎng

享 xiǎng 【动】◇enjoy

享福 xiǎng = fú live in ease and comfort

享乐 xiǎnglè 【动】enjoy material comforts；seek pleasure；indulge in luxuries

享年 xiǎngnián 【名】die at the age of

享受 xiǎngshòu 【动】enjoy：～助学金 receive a scholarship 【名】enjoyment；comfort；treat：贪图～ seek ease and comfort

享用 xiǎngyòng 【动】enjoy

享有 xiǎngyǒu 【动】enjoy（prestige, fame, etc.）：～盛名 enjoy a high reputation ～威望 enjoy prestige ～平等的权利 enjoy equal rights

响（響） xiǎng 【动】sound；make a sound：全场～起了暴风雨般的掌声。The hall rang with thunderous applause. 炮～了。Cannons roared. 【形】loud：汽笛声真～。The siren is extremely loud.

响彻云霄 xiǎngchè yúnxiāo resound to the sky：～的礼炮声 a salvo which resounded to the sky 欢呼声～。Cheers and applause resounded to the sky.

响动 xiǎngdòng 【名】sound of movement

响亮 xiǎngliàng 【形】loud and clear；resounding

响声 xiǎngshēng 【名】sound

响应 xiǎngyìng 【动】answer；respond：～号召 answer the call 积极～大会倡议 actively respond to the proposals of the conference

想 xiǎng 【动】❶think；ponder：～问题 ponder over the problem ～

出个好主意 think out a good idea ❷ remember with longing; miss: 海外侨胞时刻～着祖国。Overseas Chinese constantly think of their homeland. ❸ suppose; reckon: 我～客人今天会来的。I think that the guests are likely to arrive today. 【助动】want to: 我～考研究生。I want to take the examination for graduate school. 许多外国朋友都～了解中国。A lot of foreigners want to learn about China.

想必 xiǎngbì 【副】probably; presumably: ～她是病了, 要不然怎么没来上班? She is probably ill; if not, why didn't she come to work? 看你笑容满面, ～有什么好消息。I can tell by your delighted expression that you must have good news.

想不到 xiǎng bu dào unexpected: 玻璃杯掉在水泥地上没碎, 真～! A glass dropped on the cement floor but didn't break. Isn't that extraordinary! 他这个从来不写信的人,～给我写了一封信。He never writes to anybody, but much to my surprise, he wrote to me.

想不开 xiǎng bu kāi take sth. too hard; take sth. to heart: 你有什么～的事, 咱们一起谈谈。What do you have on your mind? Let's talk about it. 这个问题很好办, 你有什么～的? This problem is quite simple. Why let it get you down?

想当然 xiǎng dāngrán take for granted; assume as a matter of course: 凭～办事是不行的。Acting on assumptions will never do. 不作调查研究, 根据～下结论, 往往要出错。Drawing conclusions from easy assumptions will invariably lead to error.

想得到 xiǎng de dào it's to be expected (*usu. in a rhetorical question*): 谁～他今天会来! Who would

have expected him to show up today?

想得开 xiǎng de kāi think positive; not take too hard; look on the bright side of things: 对于个人的不幸要～才行。One must not take personal misfortunes too hard.

想法 xiǎngfǎ 【名】idea; way of thinking

想方设法 xiǎng fāng shè fǎ try every means: 大夫～治疗疑难病症。The doctor tried every means possible to cure the incurable.

想见 xiǎngjiàn 【动】infer; gather: 从这首诗里就可以～当年诗人的爱国热情。From this poem you can gather how patriotic the poet was.

想来 xiǎnglái 【副】it may be assumed; presumably: ～他们已经到达目的地了。We may assume that they've already reached their destination. 他的话～很可靠。I suppose his words are reliable.

想念 xiǎngniàn 【动】miss; long to see again

想入非非 xiǎng rù fēi fēi give rein to one's fancy: 要脚踏实地去干, 不要～。Do solid work and don't indulge in fantasy.

想像 xiǎngxiàng 【动】imagine: 不难～ easy to imagine ～不到 unimaginable

想像力 xiǎngxiànglì 【名】imagination

xiàng

向 xiàng 【名】◇ direction: 转 (zhuàn) 了～ lose one's bearings 【动】❶ (篶) face; turn towards: 他住两间～南的屋子。He occupies two rooms facing south. 教员上课要面～学生。When lecturing, teachers must face their students. ❷ to: 指

~东方 point to the east 【介】❶ *indicates direction*：~ 西一直走就到邮局了。If you walk straight west, you'll get to the post office. 这孩子数学很好，应该~这方面发展。This child is very good at mathematics; he ought to develop his proficiency in that direction. ❷ *indicates the object an action is directed towards*：我要~你讲几句心里话。I want to tell you something which has been on my mind. 他~大会提出了一项建议。He made a proposal to the conference. ❸ *indicates the source from which one gets what one wants*：~ 内行学习 learn from experts ~盐碱地要粮 make saline-alkaline soil yield grain

向导 xiàngdǎo 【名】guide; person who shows others the way

向来 xiànglái 【副】all along; always：他工作一贯认真负责。He has always been conscientious in his work. 小张~不会弄虚作假。Xiao Zhang never resorts to deception.

向日葵 xiàngrìkuí 【名】sunflower

向上 xiàng = shàng　make progress：好好学习，天天向上。Study hard and make progress everyday.

向往 xiàngwǎng 【动】yearn for; look forward to：令人~ make people yearn for ~已久 have looked forward to sth. for a long time 中国各地人民都~着北京。People from all over China want very much to visit Beijing.

向心力 xiàngxīnlì 【名】centripetal force

向阳 xiàngyáng 【动】face the sun; face south

向着 xiàngzhe 【动】❶ face; be opposite to：床最好不要~门。The bed should not be facing the door. ❷ be partial to; side with：父母往往~最小的孩子。Parents usually fa-vour their youngest child. 【介】同"向"【介】❶

项（項）
xiàng 【名】〈书〉nape (of the neck) 【量】item：一~重要任务 an important task 几~工作 several items of work 三大纪律，八~注意 the Three Main Rules of Discipline and the Eight Points for Attention (of the Chinese People's Liberation Army)

项链 xiàngliàn 【名】〔条 tiáo〕necklace

项目 xiàngmù 【名】article; clause; item

巷
xiàng 【名】alley; lane

巷战 xiàngzhàn 【名】street fighting; house-to-house fighting

相
xiàng 【名】looks; appearance：可怜~ pitiable appearance 狼狈~ an awkward expression
另见 xiāng

相册 xiàngcè 【名】〔本 běn〕photograph album

相机行事 xiàng jī xíng shì act as dictated by the circumstances; act as one thinks fit

相貌 xiàngmào 【名】appearance; looks

相片儿 xiàngpiānr 【名】〔张 zhāng〕photograph

相声 xiàngsheng 【名】cross talk; comic dialogue

象
xiàng 【名】❶ 〔只 zhī〕elephant ❷ form; appearance; shape：新年伊始，万~更新。Everything has taken on a new look at the beginning of a new year.

象棋 xiàngqí 【名】❶ 〔盘 pán〕(Chinese) chess (game) ❷ 〔副 fù〕chessmen

象声词 xiàngshēngcí 【名】onomato-

poeia

象形文字 xiàngxíng wénzì hiero-glypy；pictograph

象牙 xiàngyá 【名】ivory；elephant tusk

象征 xiàngzhēng 【动】symbolize：火炬～光明。A torch symbolizes brightness（of the future）.【名】symbol：黄河是中华民族的～。The Yellow River is the symbol of the Chinese nation.

像

像 xiàng 【名】portrait：人物～people's portraits 【动】❶ be like；take after：妹妹长得很～姐姐。The younger sister bears a strong resemblance to the elder one. ❷ seem：～要下雨。It looks as if it will rain. ❸such as：～物理、化学这类课程他都能教。He can teach such subjects as physics and chemistry.

像话 xiàng = huà proper；reasonable（usu. in the negative or in a rhetorical question）：人家专程来请你，你不去，～吗? Since they came all the way specially to invite you, wouldn't it be improper for you not to go? 这种官僚主义作风太不～了。These bureaucratic practices are the limit!

像样儿 xiàng = yàngr up to certain standard；presentable；decent：这个学徒工开起机床来很～了。The apprentice can operate a lathe quite smoothly by now. 最后一个发言很不～。The speech of the last speaker was far from what it ought to have been. 也说"像样子"。

橡 xiàng

橡胶 xiàngjiāo 【名】rubber

橡皮 xiàngpí 【名】〔块 kuài〕rubber；eraser

橡皮膏 xiàngpígāo 【名】adhesive plaster

xiāo

削

削 xiāo 【动】❶ peel（with a knife）：～铅笔 sharpen a pencil ～土豆 peel potatoes ❷（of table-tennis）chop：这个球他～得真漂亮。That was a beautiful chop! 另见 xuē

骁（驍）xiāo

骁勇 xiāoyǒng 【形】valiant；brave

逍 xiāo

逍遥 xiāoyáo 【形】leisurely；unhurried；wander about at leisure

逍遥法外 xiāoyáo fǎ wài remain at large

消

消 xiāo 【动】❶disappear：冰～雪化。The ice disappeared and the snow melted. ❷eliminate；dispel：～肿（med.）reduce the swelling

消沉 xiāochén 【形】downhearted

消除 xiāochú 【动】dispel；remove：～顾虑 dispel one's misgivings ～误解 clear up a misunderstanding 隐患～了。The hidden danger was eliminated.

消毒 xiāo = dú disinfect；sterilize

消防 xiāofáng 【动】put out a fire；fight fire

消费 xiāofèi 【动】consume

消费品 xiāofèipǐn 【名】consumer goods

消费者 xiāofèizhě 【名】consumer

消耗 xiāohào 【动】deplete；use up；consume 【名】consumption

消化 xiāohuà 【动】digest

消化不良 xiāohuà bùliáng indigestion；dyspepsia

消火栓 xiāohuǒshuān 【名】fire hydrant

消极 xiāojí 【形】❶negative：～因素 negative factor ～影响 negative in-

fluence ❷ passive；inactive：态度 ～ have an apathetic attitude ～情绪 feel dispirited

消减 xiāojiǎn 【动】decrease；eat down

消灭 xiāomiè 【动】eliminate；exterminate：～蚊蝇 wipe out mosquitoes and flies 把侵略者～光 wipe out all aggressors

消磨 xiāomó 【动】❶ wear down：～ 意志 wear down one's determination ～精力 fritter away one's energy ❷ while away：～岁月 while away months and years ～时光 while away the time

消遣 xiāoqiǎn 【动】amuse oneself

消融 xiāoróng 【动】melt

消散 xiāosàn 【动】disperse：云雾～。 The cloud and fog dispersed. 热气 ～。The heat and humidity was gradually dispelled.

消声器 xiāoshēngqì 【名】muffler

消失 xiāoshī 【动】disappear：晚霞逐 渐地～了。The sunset glow of the sky is gradually fading. 疑虑的神色 ～了。His suspicious look gradually disappeared.

消逝 xiāoshì 【动】die away：时光飞 快地～。Time passes quickly. 飞机 的轰鸣渐渐～在夜空里。The droning of the aeroplane faded away into the night sky.

消瘦 xiāoshòu 【动】emaciate；become thin

消亡 xiāowáng 【动】perish；wither away；die out

消息 xiāoxi 【名】news；information

消炎 xiāo = yán counteract inflammation

萧(蕭) xiāo

萧瑟 xiāosè 【形】❶ rustle in the air：秋风～ the rustling autumn wind ❷ bleak；desolate：一片～的景 象 a bleak scene

萧条 xiāotiáo 【形】bleak；depress-

ing：景象十分～ a depressing scene 市场～ a depressed market

硝 xiāo 【名】saltpeter；nitre

硝酸 xiāosuān 【名】nitric acid

硝烟 xiāoyān 【名】smoke of gunpowder

销(銷) xiāo 【动】❶ cancel；annul；put an end to：～假(jià) report for duty on one's return from leave ❷ sell：一天～了不少货 sell a lot of goods in a single day

销毁 xiāohuǐ 【动】destroy by shredding or incinerating

销量 xiāoliàng 【名】quantity sold；sales made

销路 xiāolù 【名】sale；market

销声匿迹 xiāo shēng nì jì lie low；withdraw from society

销售 xiāoshòu 【动】sell；sale

销赃 xiāo = zāng get rid of stolen goods；dispose of stolen goods：～ 灭迹 dispose of the stolen goods and destroy the evidence

潇(瀟) xiāo

潇洒 xiāosǎ 【形】elegant and unconventional；natural and unrestrained

xiǎo

小 xiǎo 【形】❶ little；small ❷ ◇ for a short time：～坐片刻 sit for a moment ～住数日 stay for a few days ❸ the youngest：～女儿 the youngest daughter ～弟弟 the youngest brother ❹ young：妹妹比 姐姐～两岁。One sister is two years younger than the other. 【头】an endearment，used as a form of address for young people：～马 Xiao Ma ～刘 Xiao Liu

小百货 xiǎobǎihuò 【名】small arti-

cles for daily use

小本经营 xiǎoběn jīngyíng do business with little capital—go in for sth. in a small way

小便 xiǎobiàn 【名】urine 【动】urinate

小吃 xiǎochī 【名】snack

小丑 xiǎochǒu 【名】clown

小聪明 xiǎocōngming 【名】petty trick：耍～ play petty tricks

小道消息 xiǎodào xiāoxi hearsay：～不可信。Hearsay is unreliable.

小动作 xiǎodòngzuò 【名】little tricks：耍（作）～ get up to little tricks 上课时,这孩子的～特别多,影响了学习。In classes this child likes to get up to little tricks which distract him from learning.

小恩小惠 xiǎo ēn xiǎo huì petty favours

小儿科 xiǎo'érkē 【名】paediatrics

小贩 xiǎofàn 【名】pedlar

小费 xiǎofèi 【名】tip；gratuity

小工 xiǎogōng 【名】unskilled labourer

小鬼 xiǎoguǐ 【名】an endearment referring to children, also used as form of address：这～真可爱。This kid is so cute.

小孩儿 xiǎoháir 【名】child

小伙子 xiǎohuǒzi 【名】young fellow；young man

小集团 xiǎojítuán 【名】clique；faction

小节 xiǎojié 【名】trifle；small matter：生活～ matters having to do with one's private life

小结 xiǎojié 【名】brief summing-up 【动】sum up briefly

小姐 xiǎojie 【名】(in the old society) title for an unmarried woman of an upper or middle class family；Miss

小看 xiǎokàn 【动】look down upon；belittle

小康 xiǎokāng 【名】well-to-do：争取家庭生活达到～水平 try to raise the living standards to a well-to-do level

小买卖 xiǎo mǎimai small business

小麦 xiǎomài 【名】wheat

小卖部 xiǎomàibù 【名】a small shop attached to a hotel, a school, etc.

小米 xiǎomǐ 【名】millet

小脑 xiǎonǎo 【名】cerebellum

小农经济 xiǎonóng jīngjì small-scale peasant economy

小朋友 xiǎopéngyǒu 【名】polite form of address for children

小品 xiǎopǐn 【名】short literary or artistic creation；sketch；essay

小品文 xiǎopǐnwén 【名】〔篇 piān〕short essay；sketch

小气 xiǎoqi 【形】❶ stingy ❷ narrow-minded

小巧玲珑 xiǎoqiǎo línglóng small and exquisite：这种半导体收音机～。This make of transistor radio is small and beautifully designed.

小青年 xiǎoqīngnián 【名】young people；boys and girls

小商品 xiǎoshāngpǐn 【名】small commodities

小商品经济 xiǎo shāngpǐn jīngjì small commodity economy

小生产 xiǎoshēngchǎn 【名】small-scale production

小声 xiǎoshēng 【名】low voice；whisper

小时 xiǎoshí 【名】hour

小手工业者 xiǎoshǒugōngyèzhě 【名】petty handicraftsman

小数 xiǎoshù 【名】(maths.) decimal

小数点 xiǎoshùdiǎn 【名】decimal point

小说 xiǎoshuō 【名】〔本 běn〕novel

小私有者 xiǎosīyǒuzhě 【名】petty proprietor

小苏打 xiǎosūdá 【名】sodium bicarbonate；bicarbonate of soda

小提琴 xiǎotíqín 【名】violin

小题大作 xiǎo tí dà zuò　make a fuss about a trifling matter; make a mountain out of a mole hill

小偷 xiǎotōu 【名】(～儿) pilferer; pickpocket

小巫见大巫 xiǎo wū jiàn dà wū　be dwarfed; pale into insignificance by comparison: 我们这个温室，比起你们那个，简直是～。Our greenhouse is nothing, compared to yours.

小写 xiǎoxiě 【名】small letter 【动】write in small letter

小心 xiǎoxīn 【形】careful; cautious: 他为人～谨慎。He is a very careful and prudent man. 【动】be careful: ～火车 watch out for the train。～烫着。Be careful not to scald yourself. 路很滑，你要～点儿。The road is very slippery; you must be careful.

小心翼翼 xiǎoxīn yìyì　with great care and very prudently: 孙子～地搀扶着爷爷。The grandson gave his grandfather his arm and carefully supported him.

小型 xiǎoxíng 【形】small-sized; small scale

小学 xiǎoxué 【名】〔所 suǒ〕primary school; elementary school

小学生 xiǎoxuéshēng 【名】pupils; school children

小篆 xiǎozhuàn 【名】one of the ancient styles of Chinese calligraphy, started in the Qin dynasty (221 – 206 B.C.)

小资产阶级 xiǎozīchǎnjiējí 【名】petty-bourgeoisie

小组 xiǎozǔ 【名】group

晓（曉）

xiǎo 〈书〉【名】morning: ～行夜宿 start one's journey at dawn and seek shelter at night 雄鸡报～。The rooster signals the coming of dawn. 【动】

know: 无人不～。There is no one who does not know.

晓得 xiǎode 【动】know; understand

xiào

孝

xiào ◇ 【形】filial piety 【名】mourning

孝顺 xiàoshùn 【动】show filial obedience to: ～父母 show filial obedience to one's parents 【形】filial

肖

xiào

肖像 xiàoxiàng 【名】〔张 zhāng、幅 fú〕portrait

校

xiào 【名】school; college; university
另见 jiào

校风 xiàofēng 【名】school spirit

校服 xiàofú 【名】〔套 tào〕school uniform

校规 xiàoguī 【名】school regulations

校徽 xiàohuī 【名】〔枚 méi〕school badge

校庆 xiàoqìng 【名】school anniversary

校舍 xiàoshè 【名】school building

校友 xiàoyǒu 【名】alumnus and alumna

校园 xiàoyuán 【名】school campus

校长 xiàozhǎng 【名】head of a school (e.g. president, principal, director)

笑

xiào 【动】❶laugh; smile: 他说着说着就～起来了。He burst into laughter in the middle of the conversation. ❷laugh at: 你应该多帮助指点，不要～他。You should help him and not laugh at him.

笑柄 xiàobǐng 【名】laughing-stock

笑话　xiàohuà　【名】joke：说～ crack a joke 闹了一个大～ make a silly mistake【动】laugh at：我是业余学的小提琴，拉不好，大家别～。I'm just an amateur violinist. Please don't laugh at my performance.

笑里藏刀　xiào lǐ cáng dāo　hide one's murderous intent behind a smile

笑脸　xiàoliǎn　【名】〔张 zhāng〕smiling face

笑眯眯　xiàomīmī　【形】smiling

笑容　xiàoróng　【名】smiling expression

笑嘻嘻　xiàoxīxī　【形】smiling happily

笑星　xiàoxīng　【名】a comedian；a comic star

笑逐颜开　xiào zhú yán kāi　beam with smiles：巡回剧团来到山村，乡亲们～，奔走相告。When the touring theatrical troupe arrived at the mountain village, the villagers all ran to tell one another beaming with delight.

效　xiào　【名】◇ effect：奇～ remarkable effect【动】〈书〉❶ imitate：上行下～ follow the example of their superiors ❷ render：～犬马之劳 work like a dog（in the service of one's master）～命 devote one's life to（a bad cause）

效法　xiàofǎ　【动】follow the example；imitate

效果　xiàoguǒ　【名】effect；result

效劳　xiàoláo　【动】be in the service of；serve the ends of；work for

效力　xiàolì　【名】efficacy；effect

效力　xiào = lì　同"效劳"

效率　xiàolǜ　【名】efficiency

效能　xiàonéng　【名】effectiveness；efficacy

效益　xiàoyì　【名】benefit and effect

效用　xiàoyòng　【名】function and effect

xiē

些　xiē　【量】some：前～时候 some time ago 买了～日用品 buy some everyday necessities 快～走 walk a little bit faster 来了这么～人！Such a lot of people showed up!

歇　xiē　【动】❶ have a rest：～会儿再走吧。Let's rest a while before we continue our walk. ❷ stop：～工 stop working ～班 one's day off

歇工　xiē = gōng　knock off；stop working

歇后语　xiēhòuyǔ　【名】saying in which only the first part is given, the rest being understood, sometimes puns are involved

歇脚　xiē = jiǎo　stop for a break during a walk

歇斯底里　xiēsīdǐlǐ　【名】hysteria

蝎　xiē　【名】◇ scorpion

蝎子　xiēzi　【名】〔只 zhī〕scorpion

xié

协（協）　xié

协定　xiédìng　【名】agreement；convention

协会　xiéhuì　【名】association

协力　xiélì　【动】pull together；cooperate

协商　xiéshāng　【动】consult and discuss with each other

协调　xiétiáo　【动】harmonize；be in tune with；coordinate：～一致 in perfect coordination 色彩～ well-matched colours

协同　xiétóng　【动】work in coordination with

协议　xiéyì　【名】agreement：达成～

reach an agreement 【动】agree on：双方～建立外交关系。Both sides agree on the establishment of diplomatic relations.

协约 xiéyuē　【动】negotiate 【名】agreement；treaty；pact

协助 xiézhù　【动】assist；help；aid

协奏曲 xiézòuqǔ　【名】concerto

协作 xiézuò　【动】cooperate 【名】cooperation

邪 xié　【形】sinister；evil：～说 fallacy；heresy　一股～劲儿 show of strength which exceeds one's normal capacity

邪路 xiélù　【名】〔条 tiáo〕evil ways

邪门歪道 xié mén wāi dào　dishonest practices；crooked ways

邪气 xiéqì　【名】〔股 gǔ〕evil tendency；evil influence

胁(脅) xié

胁从 xiécóng　【动】be coerced to do wrong by another；become an accomplice under duress 【名】accomplice under duress

胁迫 xiépò　【动】coerce；intimidate；compel；force

挟(挾) xié

挟持 xiéchí　【动】force sb. to submit to one's will；place under duress；hijack

偕 xié　【动】(of person) take along

偕同 xiétóng　【动】be in the company of

斜 xié　【形】slanting；inclining；sloping；oblique

斜边 xiébiān　【名】〔条 tiáo〕(maths.) hypotenuse

斜路 xiélù　【名】wrong path

斜面 xiémiàn　【名】inclined plane

斜坡 xiépō　【名】slope

斜射 xiéshè　【动】oblique fire

斜视 xiéshì　【名】strabismus 【动】look sideways；cast a sidelong glance

斜线 xiéxiàn　【名】〔条 tiáo〕(maths.) oblique line

谐(諧) xié

谐和 xiéhé　【形】harmonious；concordant

谐声 xiéshēng　【名】同"形声"

谐音 xiéyīn　【名】homophonic；homonymic

携 xié　【动】〈书〉❶ take with；carry ❷ take sb. by the hand

携带 xiédài　【动】carry；take along；bring

携手 xié＝shǒu　hand in hand

鞋 xié　【名】〔只 zhī、双 shuāng〕shoe

鞋带儿 xiédàir　【名】〔根 gēn、副 fù〕shoe-lace；shoe-string

鞋底 xiédǐ　【名】sole of the shoe

鞋油 xiéyóu　【名】shoe polish

xiě

写(寫) xiě　【动】❶write：～字 write a character；practise calligraphy ❷ compose：～诗 write a poem ❸depict；describe：人物～得很生动。The characters were vividly portrayed.

写生 xiěshēng　【名】sketch 【动】paint from nature；paint from life

写照 xiězhào　【名】portrayal；description

写字台 xiězìtái　【名】writing desk

写作 xiězuò　【动】❶write (as a profession)：从事～ be engaged in writing ❷ write (not necessarily professionally)：埋头～ bury oneself in one's writing

血 xiě 【名】blood
另见 xuè
血淋淋 xiělīnlīn 【形】bleeding

xiè

泄 xiè 【动】❶let out；discharge ❷ give vent to：～私愤 give expression to a personal grudge
泄洪 xiè = hóng release floodwater
泄劲 xiè = jìn lose one's confidence and relax one's efforts
泄漏 xièlòu 【动】betray；leak out；disclose
泄密 xiè = mì betray a secret；disclose a secret
泄气 xiè = qì lose heart；be discouraged：在比赛中不要因失败而～。When playing in competition, don't lose heart when you are defeated.

卸 xiè 【动】❶unload：～船 unload a ship ❷remove：～螺丝钉 remove a screw
卸车 xiè = chē unload (goods, etc.) from a vehicle；unload a truck, car, etc.
卸货 xiè = huò unload (or discharge) a cargo；unload
卸任 xiè = rèn be relieved of one's office

谢（謝）xiè 【动】❶thank；多～。Thank you very much. 不用～。Don't mention it. ❷ ◇ politely decline：闭门～客 close one's door and hold no receptions；retire from society ❸ wither：花 ～ 了。The flowers have withered.
谢绝 xièjué 【动】decline politely
谢幕 xiè = mù answer a curtain call
谢天谢地 xiè tiān xiè dì thank goodness

谢谢 xièxie 【动】thanks
谢意 xièyì 【名】gratitude；thankfulness

懈 xiè
懈怠 xièdài 【形】slack

xīn

心 xīn 【名】❶heart ❷mind：烈士们永远活在我们～中。The martyrs will live forever in our hearts. ❸centre；middle：江 ～ the middle of the river 街 ～ the middle of a street
心爱 xīn'ài 【形】loved；treasured
心安理得 xīn ān lǐ dé feel justified and deserving
心病 xīnbìng 【名】〔块 kuài〕mental anxiety over a personal concern
心不在焉 xīn bù zài yān absentminded：他～，你说什么他都没听见。His thoughts were far away and he didn't hear a word of what you said.
心肠 xīncháng 【名】heart；好 ～ kind-hearted ～狠 hard-hearted
心潮 xīncháo 【名】 motionally changed state of mind
心潮澎湃 xīncháo pēngpài an upsurge of emotion
心得 xīndé 【名】what one learns from one's study or work
心地 xīndì 【名】moral nature；heart
心电图 xīndiàntú 【名】electrocardiogram
心烦 xīnfán 【形】annoyed；vexed
心服口服 xīn fú kǒu fú be utterly convinced
心腹 xīnfù 【名】❶ trusted subordinate (derog.)：他手下有几个～。He has several henchmen under his thumb. ❷ hidden in one's heart；confidential：～ 事 some se-

crete buried in one's heart

心腹之患 xīnfù zhī huàn a serious hidden trouble or danger

心甘情愿 xīngān qíngyuàn perfectly willing

心花怒放 xīn huā nù fàng one's heart is bursting with joy; be extremely happy

心怀鬼胎 xīn huái guǐtāi harbour ulterior motives; have a guilty secret

心慌 xīnhuāng 【形】 flurried; confounded

心慌意乱 xīn huāng yì luàn be flustered; be alarmed and nervous

心机 xīnjī 【名】 scheming: 用尽～ scheme and rack one's brains 枉费～ plot in vain

心急如火 xīn jí rú huǒ burning with anxiety: 听说张大爷犯了心脏病, 唐大夫～, 立即赶去抢救。Hearing of Uncle Zhang's heart attack, Doctor Tang was alarmed and rushed to his bedside.

心绞痛 xīnjiǎotòng 【名】 angina pectoris

心惊胆战 xīn jīng dǎn zhàn be on tenterhooks; be filled with apprehensions

心惊肉跳 xīn jīng ròu tiào extremely nervous; in extreme fear (anticipating disaster)

心坎儿 xīnkǎnr 【名】 the bottom of one's heart: 这些话真说到我们～上了。These remarks really touched the right chord in our hearts.

心理 xīnlǐ 【名】 psychology; mental processes of a person

心理学 xīnlǐxué 【名】 psychology

心里 xīnli 【名】 ❶ in the chest: ～发闷 feel a constriction in one's chest ❷ in mind: 记在～ bear sth. in mind ～怎么想就怎么说 speak out what is on one's mind

心灵 xīnlíng 【名】 mentality; heart; spirit

心灵手巧 xīn líng shǒu qiǎo clever in mind and nimble with fingers

心领神会 xīn lǐng shén huì understand tacitly

心乱如麻 xīn luàn rú má be utterly confused

心满意足 xīn mǎn yì zú perfectly contented

心明眼亮 xīn míng yǎn liàng be sharp-eyed and clear-headed: 一个法官必须～, 公正无私。A judge must be sharp-eyed, clear-headed and just.

心目 xīnmù 【名】 one's mind; one's view: 他在同事们的～中, 不仅是好领导, 而且是知心朋友。In the eyes of his colleagues, he is not only a good leader, but also a close friend.

心平气和 xīn píng qì hé in a goodhumoured and tranquil state of mind: ～地坐下来谈一谈。Let's sit down and have a calm and sensible talk.

心情 xīnqíng 【名】 state of mind; mood

心如刀割 xīn rú dāo gē one's heart is wracked with anguish

心神不定 xīn shén bù dìng be disconcerted: 不知他有什么事, 老是～的样子。I do not know what's on his mind; he is so restless.

心事 xīnshì 【名】 sth. that weighs on one's mind; worries; cares

心思 xīnsi 【名】 ❶ thought; idea: 他的～很不好捉摸。It isn't easy to guess what is on his mind. ❷ thinking: 用～ use one's mind 白费～ rack one's brains in vain 挖空～ rack one's brains in scheming ❸ mood; frame of mind: 没有～玩儿 be in no mood to enjoy oneself

心酸 xīnsuān 【形】 sad: 让人～ make one sad

心算 xīnsuàn 【动】 calculate mentally; mental arithmetic

心态 xīntài 【名】 frame of mind

心疼 xīnténg 【动】❶ love；show concern for：~人 show concern for sb. ❷ be distressed（because sth. is wrecked or wasted）：照相机摔坏了，真让人~。The camera is broken；what a shame!

心跳 xīn tiào palpitate：有点儿~。My heart palpitates.

心头 xīntóu 【名】mind；heart

心心相印 xīn xīn xiāng yìn mutual understanding and attraction；mutual affinity

心胸 xīnxiōng 【名】❶ breadth of mind：~狭窄 narrow-minded ~开阔 broad-minded ❷ aspiration：~远大 a lofty aspiration

心虚 xīnxū 【形】❶ with a guilty conscience：我们没说你，你干吗~？We weren't talking about you；what are you afraid of? ❷ lacking in confidence：我对这项工作没把握，感到有些~。I'm not sure I can do this job well；I am lacking in confidence.

心血 xīnxuè 【名】heart's blood；painstaking care

心血来潮 xīn xuè lái cháo on the spur of the moment；on a sudden impulse：一时~，就改变原来的计划，那么行呢? How can we change our original plan on a sudden impulse?

心眼儿 xīnyǎnr 【名】❶ bottom of one's heart：从~里拥护 support（sb. or sth.）from the bottom of one's heart 打~里高兴 be genuinely delighted ❷ intention：没安好心 have bad intentions ❸ cleverness：长（zhǎng）点儿~ keep one's wits about one 缺~ be not very clever 这个小鬼可~了。This child is really sharp! ❹ unnecessary misgivings：这人~太多。That man thinks too much. ❺ breadth of mind：小~ petty minded

心意 xīnyì 【名】kindly feelings：这点儿礼物是我们的一点儿~，请收下。This gift is just a small token of our regard for you；please accept it.

心愿 xīnyuàn 【名】desire；wish；hope

心悦诚服 xīn yuè chéng fú be sincerely convinced that the other party is in the right：他~地承认对手的优越。He conceded the superiority of his competitor.

心脏 xīnzàng 【名】heart：医生说他的~不太好。His doctor said that the condition of his heart isn't too good. 北京是中国的~。Beijing is the heart of China.

心脏病 xīnzàngbìng 【名】heart trouble；heart disease

心照不宣 xīnzhào bù xuān understand each other without saying a word；have a tacit mutual understanding

心直口快 xīn zhí kǒu kuài be straightforward

心中无数 xīn zhōng wú shù *the opposite of* "心中有数"；not know for certain

心中有数 xīn zhōng yǒu shù have a general understanding of the situation and know what to do

辛 xīn

辛亥革命 Xīnhài Gémìng the Revolution of 1911, the bourgeois democratic revolution, which overthrew the Qing dynasty

辛苦 xīnkǔ 【形】hard working；hard：忙了好几天，你可真~了。These last few days, you have been buried in work! 列车员辛辛苦苦（地）为旅客服务。The crew of the train work hard to serve the passengers. 【动】cause trouble to；go through hardships for：这为难的事还得~你一趟。I'll have to trouble you to go there again about this

sensitive matter. 替我们办了这么多事,真～你了。 We appreciate what you have done for us and are very grateful.

辛劳 xīnláo 【形】painstaking; laborious

辛勤 xīnqín 【形】diligent; industrious

辛酸 xīnsuān 【形】sad; bitter; miserable

欣 xīn

欣然 xīnrán 【副】〈书〉with pleasure; ～接受 accept with pleasure ～同意 gladly agree ～前往 be happy to attend

欣赏 xīnshǎng 【动】appreciate; enjoy

欣慰 xīnwèi 【形】gratified

欣喜若狂 xīnxǐ ruò kuáng be mad with joy; 胜利捷报传来,人人～。 People's joy knew no bounds when news of the victory arrived.

欣欣向荣 xīnxīn xiàng róng flourishing and prosperous; 一派～的景象展现在人们的眼前。 A prosperous scene was spread out before one's eyes.

新 xīn 【形】❶ new; ～经验 a new experience ～旧对比 the contrast between the old and the new ～衣服 new clothes ～房子 a new house ❷newly; recent; ～入学的学生 a new student ～认识的朋友 a newly made friend

新潮 xīncháo 【名】new fashion; new trend; the vogue

新陈代谢 xīn chén dàixiè metabolism

新房 xīnfáng 【名】bridal chamber

新婚 xīnhūn 【动】newly-married

新纪元 xīnjìyuán 【名】new epoch; new era

新近 xīnjìn 【形】recent

新居 xīnjū 【名】new residence

新郎 xīnláng 【名】bridegroom

新民主主义 xīn mínzhǔzhǔyì new-democracy

新民主主义革命 xīn mínzhǔzhǔyì gémìng the New Democratic Revolution, 1919–1949, a revolution aimed against imperialism, feudalism and bureaucratic capitalism

新年 xīnnián 【名】New Year

新娘 xīnniáng 【名】bride

新奇 xīnqí 【形】novel

新生 xīnshēng 【名】❶ new life; 获得～ start a new life 他刑满释放后学了一门技术,获得了～。 After he served his sentence, he learned a craft and started a new life. ❷ new student 【形】newly born; newborn; ～力量 newly emerging forces

新生事物 xīnshēng shìwù newly emerging things; new things

新式 xīnshì 【形】of a new type; of a new fashion

新手 xīnshǒu 【名】a new hand; a raw recruit

新四军 Xīnsìjūn 【名】the New Fourth Army, one of the people's armies under the leadership of the Chinese Communist Party during the War of Resistance against Japan

新闻 xīnwén 【名】news

新闻公报 ·xīnwén gōngbào press communique

新闻记者 xīnwén jìzhě newsman; newspapermen; reporter; journalist

新鲜 xīnxiān 【形】❶ fresh; ～水果 fresh fruit ～蔬菜 fresh vegetables 空气～ fresh air ～经验 fresh experiences ～血液 (fig.) fresh blood ❷ new; novel; strange; ～的式样 new fashion 这可是个～事。 This is really something completely novel!

新兴 xīnxīng 【形】newly emerging;

~的力量 newly emerging forces ~
的城市 a newly developed city

新星　xīnxīng　【名】❶astron nova ❷
new star

新型　xīnxíng　【形】new type；new
pattern；new mould

新秀　xīnxiù　【名】new talent：歌坛
~ new singing talent

新颖　xīnyǐng　【形】novel and original

薪　xīn　【名】❶ ◇ salary ❷〈书〉
firewood

薪金　xīnjīn　【名】salary

薪水　xīnshui　【名】salary；pay

xìn

信　xìn　【名】❶ ◇ trust；faith；
confidence：守 ~ keep one's promise 言而有~ always true to one's
word ❷〔封 fēng〕letter：寄一封 ~
mail a letter 开介绍~ write a letter
of introduction ❸(~儿) a piece of
information：报个 ~ 儿 tell sb. a
piece of news 【动】❶ believe；
trust：这话我不~。I do not believe
what (he) said. 这事可~不可~? Is
the story believable or not? ❷ believe in：不~鬼,不~邪 not intimidated by ghosts or other supersti-
tious nonsense

信不过　xìn bu guò　can't trust：我~
他。I don't trust him.

信贷　xìndài　【名】credit

信得过　xìn de guò　trustworthy：这
是一家~的商店。This is a store
that one can trust.

信封　xìnfēng　【名】〔个 gè〕envelope

信服　xìnfú　【动】be convinced

信号　xìnhào　【名】signal

信号灯　xìnhàodēng　【名】signal lamp

信笺　xìnjiān　【名】letter paper

信件　xìnjiàn　【名】mail；letter

信口开河　xìn kǒu kāi hé　talk freely

and irresponsibly 也作"信口开合"。

信赖　xìnlài　【动】trust；rely on

信念　xìnniàn　【名】faith；belief；
creed

信任　xìnrèn　【动】trust：老王对工作
一丝不苟,大家都很~他。Lao Wang
is very conscientious in his work,
all the others have confidence in
him. 【名】confidence：得到朋友的
~ win his friends' confidence 大家
选你当代表,这是对你的~。We
elected you our representative；
this shows our confidence in you.

信使　xìnshǐ　【名】messenger；courier

信手拈来　xìn shǒu niān lái　have
words, material, etc. at one's fingertips and write with facility：他
~的这首小诗很新颖。The poem
which he dashed off is very original.

信守　xìnshǒu　【名】observe honest-
ly；follow truthfully

信筒　xìntǒng　【名】pillar box

信徒　xìntú　【名】disciple；follower

信托　xìntuō　【动】trust；entrust：~
公司 a trust company

信息　xìnxī　【名】news；message

信箱　xìnxiāng　【名】❶ mail box ❷
post-office box

信心　xìnxīn　【名】confidence

信仰　xìnyǎng　【动】believe in：他死
里逃生以后~了基督教。He em-
braced Christianity after he survived a fatal accident. 【名】faith；
belief：政治~ political belief 宗教
~ religious belief

信义　xìnyì　【名】faith；honesty

信用　xìnyòng　【名】❶ trustworthi-
ness：守~ keep a promise 不讲~
go back on one's word ❷ credit：
~贷款 unsecured loan

信用卡　xìnyòngkǎ　【名】credit card

信誉　xìnyù　【名】credit：买卖应该讲
~。One must stress credit in doing
business.

信纸　xìnzhǐ　【名】〔张 zhāng〕letter

paper

xīng

兴（興） xīng 【动】❶ ◇undertake to do：～利除弊 undertake to do what is beneficial and get rid of what is harmful 百废俱～ undertake to do everything which was previously left undone ❷ ◇ promote：大～调查研究之风 promote study and investigation ❸ become popular：现在不～请客送礼。The practice of entertaining guests lavishly and sending expensive gifts is no longer popular.
另见 xìng

兴办 xīngbàn 【动】establish；set up；found

兴奋 xīngfèn 【形】excited；elated

兴风作浪 xīng fēng zuò làng incite trouble and create confusion

兴建 xīngjiàn 【动】build

兴隆 xīnglóng 【形】prosperous：生意～。Business is brisk.

兴起 xīngqǐ 【动】spring up；come into being

兴盛 xīngshèng 【形】prosperous；flourishing

兴师动众 xīng shī dòng zhòng drag in a lot of people（to take part in some understaking）：这件事几个人就办了，用不着（zháo）～的。This job can be done by a few people；it is unnecessary to mobilise such a crowd.

兴衰 xīngshuāi 【名】rise and decline

兴亡 xīngwáng 【名】rise and fall

兴旺 xīngwàng 【形】prosperous；thriving

兴修 xīngxiū 【动】begin to build；begin to construct

星 xīng 【名】〔颗 kē〕❶ star：满天～ a sky dotted with stars ❷（～儿）bit；particle：火～ a spark

星火 xīnghuǒ 【名】spark

星际 xīngjì 【名】interplanetary；interstellar

星罗棋布 xīng luó qí bù scattered like stars in the sky：～的水利工程 irrigation projects scattered at every turn 中国沿海，岛屿～。Islands are scattered all along China's coastline like stars in the sky.

星期 xīngqī 【名】week

星期二 xīngqī'èr 【名】Tuesday

星期六 xīngqīliù 【名】Saturday

星期日 xīngqīrì 【名】Sunday

星期三 xīngqīsān 【名】Wednesday

星期四 xīngqīsì 【名】Thursday

星期五 xīngqīwǔ 【名】Friday

星期一 xīngqīyī 【名】Monday

星球 xīngqiú 【名】celestial body；heavenly body

星星 xīngxing 【名】star

星星之火，可以燎原 xīngxīng zhī huǒ, kěyǐ liáoyuán a single spark can start a prairie fire

猩 xīng

猩红热 xīnghóngrè 【名】scarlet fever

猩猩 xīngxing 【名】〔只 zhī〕chimpanzee

腥 xīng 【形】of the smell of fish

xíng

刑 xíng 【名】❶ ◇ punishment：～满释放 be released after serving one's sentence ❷ torture：受～ be tortured

刑场 xíngchǎng 【名】execution ground

刑罚 xíngfá 【名】penalty；punishment

刑法 xíngfǎ 【名】penal code；criminal law

刑警 xíngjǐng 【名】 *short for* "刑事警察"

刑律 xínglǜ 【名】criminal law

刑事 xíngshì 【名】criminal（*as opp. to* 民事）

刑事犯 xíngshìfàn 【名】criminal

刑事犯罪 xíngshì fànzuì criminal offence；criminal act

刑事警察 xíngshì jǐngchá criminal police

刑事诉讼 xíngshì sùsòng criminal procedure；criminal suit

刑事责任 xíngshì zérèn criminal responsibility

行 xíng 【动】❶ walk：日～千里 march a thousand *li* a day ❷ do；perform；carry out：～礼 salute 简便易～ simple and practical 这～不通。It won't work. ❸ be all right：这么办～不～？——，就这么办吧！Is it all right to do it like this? — Fine. Go ahead. 【形】capable：他真～，三天就把文章写出来了。He is very capable；he completed the article in three days. 【名】◇ behaviour；action：言～一致 actions matching one's words
另见 háng

行程 xíngchéng 【名】distance of travel

行动 xíngdòng 【动】❶ get about；move：～不便 walk with difficulty ❷ take action：全国人民立即～起来。The people of the whole country went into action at once. 【名】❶ action；operation：军事～ military operation 一切～听指挥。(mil.) Obey orders in everything you do. ❷ behaviour：～异常 unusual behaviour ～可疑 suspicious behaviour 模范～ examplary conduct

行贿 xíng＝huì bribe

行将 xíngjiāng 【副】〈书〉be going to；be about to：代表团～起程。The delegation is about to set out. 这座大桥～完工。The construction of this bridge is to be completed.

行径 xíngjìng 【名】conduct；(bad) behaviour：无耻～ shameless conduct 海盗～ piratical behaviour

行军 xíng＝jūn march

行李 xíngli 【名】baggage；luggage

行骗 xíngpiàn 【动】practise fraud；swindle；cheat

行窃 xíngqiè 【动】steal；thieve

行人 xíngrén 【名】pedestrian

行使 xíngshǐ 【名】exercise (e.g. power, authority)：～职权 exercise the powers of one's office ～主权 exercise one's sovereignty over

行驶 xíngshǐ 【动】(of vehicle, ship) go；travel

行书 xíngshū 【名】a cursive style of Chinese calligraphy

行为 xíngwéi 【名】action；behaviour；conduct；deed

行销 xíngxiāo 【动】be on sale；sell

行星 xíngxīng 【名】planet

行凶 xíng＝xiōng commit assault

行政 xíngzhèng 【名】administration

行之有效 xíng zhī yǒu xiào effective：～的办法 an effective method 这一措施是～的。This measure is effective.

行装 xíngzhuāng 【名】things packed for a journey

行踪 xíngzōng 【名】a person's whereabouts

形 xíng 【名】◇ ❶ shape；form：圆柱～的物体 an object in the form of a cylinder ❷ body；entity

形成 xíngchéng 【动】form；take shape：～习惯 form habits 一百多种化学元素可以～千千万万种化合物。The more than one hundred basic elements can form thousands and millions of chemical compounds.

形而上学 xíng'érshàngxué 【名】metaphysics

形迹可疑 xíngjì kěyí suspicious behaviour

形容 xíngróng 【动】describe：他兴奋的心情是笔墨难以～的。His excitement was impossible to capture in writing. 我来～一下晚会上的情景吧！Let me describe the scene at the party.

形容词 xíngróngcí 【名】adjective

形声 xíngshēng 【名】pictophonetic character

形式 xíngshì 【名】pattern；form

形式主义 xíngshìzhǔyì 【名】formalism

形势 xíngshì 【名】❶（mil.）terrain：～险要 terrain which is strategically important and difficult to access ❷ situation：国际～ the international situation ～喜人。The situation is excellent.

形势逼人 xíngshì bī rén the situation is pressing：其他印刷厂印刷质量都上去了，～，咱们也得迎头赶上。The printing in other printing houses has been greatly improved and it is urgent that we catch up.

形态 xíngtài 【名】❶ form；shape of an organism ❷ manner；form：观念～ ideology ❸ morphology：词的～变化 morphological changes in words

形象 xíngxiàng 【名】image：人物～ the characteristics of a character（in a play，novel，etc.）高大的～ the characteristics of a noble character 通过～进行教学 teach by using pictures and objects 【形】vivid：这个比喻很～。That is a very vivid metaphor.

形象化 xíngxiànghuà 【动】（think，etc.）in terms of images，graphic

形形色色 xíngxíngsèsè 【形】of all shades；of various forms；of all kinds

形影不离 xíng yǐng bù lí （two people）inseparable；follow each other like body and shadow

形状 xíngzhuàng 【名】shape；form

型 xíng 【名】type；pattern；model

型号 xínghào 【名】model（in the sense of style，make）

xǐng

醒 xǐng 【动】❶ wake up：一觉（jiào）～来，天已大亮了。It was already light when（I）woke up. 快～～，都七点钟了。Wake up! Wake up! It is already seven o'clock! 小点儿声，别把他吵～。Be quiet! Don't wake him up. 我想睡一会儿，你三点钟把我叫～。I want to have a nap. Please wake me up at three o'clock. ❷ come to；sober up：酒醉未～ still drunk

醒目 xǐngmù 【形】attractive to the eye；easily seen

醒悟 xǐngwù 【动】come to realize；awaken

xìng

兴（興） xìng

另见 xīng

兴高采烈 xìng gāo cǎi liè with great gusto：青年们～地参加夏令营的活动。The young people took part in the activities of the summer camp in high spirits.

兴趣 xìngqù 【名】interest

兴味 xìngwèi 【名】同“兴趣”（but less frequently used）

兴致 xìngzhì 【名】（state of）being interested in sth.

兴致勃勃 xìngzhì bóbó very much interested and in high spirits：人们

~地去参加节日游园活动。People jubilantly took part in the festival celebrations in the parks.

杏 xìng 【名】〔个 gè〕apricot

杏黄 xìnghuáng 【形】apricot yellow

杏仁 xìngrénr 【名】almond；apricot kernel

幸 xìng

幸存 xìngcún 【动】survive：~者 survivor

幸而 xìng'ér 【副】luckily；fortunately

幸福 xìngfú 【形】happy【名】happiness

幸好 xìnghǎo 【副】同"幸亏"（*usu. in written language*）

幸亏 xìngkuī 【副】fortunately（*used to introduce an advantageous circumstance which made it possible to avoid otherwise unfortunate consequences, often in conjunction with* 不然，要不，否则，*etc.*）：~先给他打了个电话，要不他就出去了。It was fortunate that we telephoned him in advance；otherwise he would have gone out. 张大爷的病~治得及时，不然就耽误了。Fortunately Uncle Zhang's illness was treated in time；otherwise it would have become serious.

幸免 xìngmiǎn 【动】escape a calamity by chance：~于难（nàn）escape death by sheer luck

幸运 xìngyùn 【形】lucky

幸灾乐祸 xìng zāi lè huò gloat over others' misfortune

性 xìng 【名】❶ nature；character ❷ sex（male or female）❸ sexual activity and everything connected with it ❹（gram.）gender【词尾】*placed after a noun, verb or adjective to form a noun indicating a property or characteristic*：碱~basicity；alkalinity 酸~acidity 原则~sense of principle 艺术~artistic quality 复杂~complication 弹（tán）~elasticity 决定~decisiveness 斗争~militancy 思想~ideological content

性别 xìngbié 【名】sex（male or female）

性格 xìnggé 【名】character

性急 xìngjí 【形】quick-tempered；impatient；impetuous

性命 xìngmìng 【名】（of human beings）life

性能 xìngnéng 【名】properties；working capacity

性情 xìngqíng 【名】temperament；disposition

性质 xìngzhì 【名】property；nature；quality

性状 xìngzhuàng 【名】shape and properties

性子 xìngzi 【名】同"性情"

姓 xìng 【名】surname：有名有~（a real person）with a definite name【动】（one's）surname is...：你~什么？——我~方。What is your surname？—My surname is Fang.

姓名 xìngmíng 【名】surname and forename；family name and given name

xiōng

凶 xiōng 【形】❶ ◇ misfortune：~多吉少 most probably an unfortunate rather than a fortunate outcome 吉~难定。It is hard to tell whether it will turn out a misfortune or not. ❷ fierce；ferocious：样子很~（of a man, an animal, etc.）look ferocious 不许逞~！Don't bully people. 此人很~，蛮不讲理。That person is a fierce bully.

❸ terrible；fearful：洪水来势很～。The oncoming force of the flood waters was terrible. 风刮得很～。The wind is blowing fiercely.

凶暴　xiōngbào　【形】cruel；brutal

凶残　xiōngcán　【形】brutal；ruthless；savage

凶恶　xiōng'è　【形】ferocious；vicious

凶犯　xiōngfàn　【名】murderer

凶狠　xiōnghěn　【形】brutal；cruel

凶猛　xiōngměng　【形】fierce；violent：来势～（of storm，wind，etc.）with terrifying force ～的野兽 ferocious beast

凶器　xiōngqì　【名】❶ a tool or weapon for criminal purposes ❷ lethal weapon

凶杀　xiōngshā　【动】homicide；murder

凶手　xiōngshǒu　【名】murderer

凶险　xiōngxiǎn　【形】extremely hazardous；dangerous and terrifying

凶相毕露　xiōng xiàng bì lù　reveal the atrocious features；bare one's fangs

兄　xiōng　【名】◇ elder brother

兄弟　xiōngdì　【名】❶ brothers：～两个 two brothers ❷ fraternal；brotherly：～民族 fraternal nationalities ～关系 brotherly relationship

兄弟　xiōngdi　【名】〈口〉younger brother：他是我～。He is my younger brother.

汹　xiōng

汹涌澎湃　xiōngyǒng péngpài　billowing；rolling waves：大海的波涛～ surging waves at sea

胸　xiōng　【名】❶ chest；breast ❷ mind：～中装着全国人民 have (the interests of) the whole nation in mind

胸部　xiōngbù　【名】thorax；chest

胸怀　xiōnghuái　【名】mind：～狭窄 narrow-minded 宽阔的～ broad-minded 【动】cherish；harbour：～全局 judge the situation as a whole ～远大的目标 cherish a long-range goal ～祖国 have the welfare of one's country in mind

胸襟　xiōngjīn　【名】breadth of mind

胸脯　xiōngpú　【名】chest；breast

胸腔　xiōngqiāng　【名】thoracic cavity

胸膛　xiōngtáng　【名】chest

胸有成竹　xiōng yǒu chéng zhú　have a well-thought-out plan：对设计这个方案,他已～。As far as this project is concerned, he already has a plan in mind.

胸中无数　xiōng zhōng wú shù　同"心中无数"xīn zhōng wú shù

胸中有数　xiōng zhōng yǒu shù　同"心中有数"xīn zhōng yǒu shù

xióng

雄　xióng　【形】❶ male：～鸡 rooster ❷ powerful；mighty：～兵百万 a million mighty warriors

雄辩　xióngbiàn　【名】eloquence 【形】eloquent：最～的莫过于事实。Nothing can be more convincing than facts.

雄厚　xiónghòu　【形】solid：～的物质基础 a solid material base 实力～ solid strength

雄健　xióngjiàn　【形】strong；robust；healthy and mighty

雄赳赳　xióngjiūjiū　【形】strong；strong and valiant

雄师　xióngshī　【名】strong and mighty army

雄伟　xióngwěi　【形】stately；grand；imposing

雄文　xióngwén　【名】impressive and powerful writing

雄心　xióngxīn　【名】lofty ambition

雄心壮志　xióngxīn zhuàngzhì　lofty aspirations and high aims

雄性　xióngxìng　【名】male

雄鹰　xióngyīng　【名】〔只 zhī〕strong and brave eagle

雄壮　xióngzhuàng　【形】full of grandeur; stalwart

雄姿　xióngzī　【名】majestic appearance; awe-inspiring posture

熊

熊　xióng　【名】〔只 zhī〕bear

熊猫　xióngmāo　【名】〔只 zhī〕panda

熊熊　xióngxióng　【形】flaming; raging (e.g. flame): 烈火 ～ raging flames

xiū

休　xiū　【动】◇ ❶ rest: 他因病需要半 ～ 一个星期。Due to health problems, he will work half-time for a week. ❷ stop; cease: 争论不 ～ argue endlessly 【副】〈书〉don't (in imperitive sentences): ～ 走! You are forbidden to go! ～怪我无情。Don't blame me for being harsh with you.

休会　xiū=huì　adjourn

休假　xiū=jià　be on holiday; be on leave

休克　xiūkè　【名】shock 【动】have a shock

休戚相关　xiūqī xiāngguān　go through thick and thin together and be on very intimate terms: 我们两国人民患难与共，～。The peoples of our two countries share joys and sorrows, and are very much concerned for each other.

休戚与共　xiūqī yǔ gòng　share the same fate

休息　xiūxi　【动】rest; relax repose

休闲　xiūxián　【形】lie fallow

休想　xiūxiǎng　【动】don't imagine: ～ 取胜! Don't imagine that you can win! 你要逃走，～! It's hopeless for you to attempt to run away!

休学　xiū = xué　interrupt one's schooling without losing one's status as a student

休养　xiūyǎng　【动】❶ recuperate; convalesce: ～ 胜地 a well-known convalescent resort 他需要 ～一个时期。He needs to recuperate for a time. ❷ (of the people of a country) recuperate: ～生息 recuperate and multiply; rest and build up strength

休战　xiū = zhàn　truce; cease-fire; armistice

休整　xiūzhěng　【动】(mil.) rest and reorganize: 利用战斗间隙进行 ～ make use of the interval between battles to rest and reorganize

休止　xiūzhǐ　【动】cease; pause; rest

修

修　xiū　【动】❶ repair: ～表 repair a watch 这座塔该 ～ 一 ～ 了。The pagoda needs to be repaired. ❷ build: ～地铁 build a subway 新 ～ 了一座桥。A new bridge has been built. ❸ trim; prune: ～ 果树枝 prune fruit trees ～指甲 trim one's finger-nails

修补　xiūbǔ　【动】mend: ～ 旧衣服 mend old clothes

修辞　xiūcí　【名】rhetoric

修辞学　xiūcíxué　【名】rhetoric

修订　xiūdìng　【动】revise; re-edit

修复　xiūfù　【动】renovate; restore

修改　xiūgǎi　【动】modify; revise; correct; amend

修建　xiūjiàn　【动】build

修旧利废　xiū jiù lì fèi　repair old equipment and utilize discarded materials: ～是增产节约的重要措施之一。Making use of old equipment and discarded materials is one of the important measures in cutting costs and increasing production.

修理　xiūlǐ　repair; mend; put right

修配　xiūpèi　repair and replace (the worn out or missing parts of a machine)

修缮　xiūshàn　【动】(of buildings) repair：～完毕。The repairs are completed. 房屋～一新。The houses were completely renovated.

修饰　xiūshì　【动】❶ decorate：～门面 paint and decorate shop front 这所宾馆需要～一下。This guest house needs to be redecorated. ❷ polish；perfect ❸ modify：形容词常用来～名词。Adjectives are usually used to modify nouns.

修养　xiūyǎng　【名】❶ accomplishment；training：文学～ mastery of literature；knowledgeable in the field of literature 理论～ grasp of theory 他在音乐方面很有～。He is very learned musically. ❷ self-cultivation

修业　xiūyè　【动】study in a school (but not necessarily graduate)：～期满 one's period of study (in a particular school) is up ～证书 certificate showing courses attended

修造　xiūzào　【动】repair and manufacture

修整　xiūzhěng　【动】keep in good condition；trim

修正　xiūzhèng　【动】revise：～议案 revise a bill (in parliament)；amend a decision made in a conference 坚持真理，～错误 stick to the truth and correct one's mistakes

修筑　xiūzhù　【动】build

羞　xiū　【动】❶ shy；bashful：～得脸通红 blush for shyness ❷ be ashamed：～与为伍 feel ashamed to be seen in sb.'s company

羞耻　xiūchǐ　【形】ashamed 【名】shame

羞答答　xiūdādā　【形】bashful；shy；coy

羞愧　xiūkuì　【形】ashamed：感到～ feel ashamed ～难言 feel too ashamed to speak；be ashamed beyond words

xiǔ

朽　xiǔ　【形】rot；decay

朽木　xiǔmù　【名】decayed wood；rotten wood

xiù

秀　xiù　【动】(of grain crops) come into ear：高粱刚～穗儿。The sorghum has just come into ear. 【形】beautiful；elegant：山清水～ beautiful mountains and streams 眉清目～ delicate eyebrows and beautiful eyes

秀丽　xiùlì　【形】delicate；graceful；beautiful

秀美　xiùměi　【形】graceful；elegant

秀气　xiùqi　【形】delicate；fine：这个竹篮子编得又精致又～。This bamboo basket is exquisitely made. 他的字写得很～。His handwriting is very fine. 这个小姑娘长得挺～。This little girl has very delicate features.

袖　xiù　【名】sleeve

袖手旁观　xiù shǒu pángguān　look on with folded arms：对有困难的人要尽力帮助，不能～。One ought to help those in difficulty, not just look on with folded arms.

袖章　xiùzhāng　【名】armband；insignia

袖珍　xiùzhēn　【形】pocket (edition)；pocket-sized

袖子　xiùzi　【名】〔只 zhī〕sleeve

绣(綉)　xiù　【动】embroider

绣花　xiù = huā　embroider；do embroidery

锈（鏽）　xiù　【名】rust：擦去刀上的～ scrub the rust off the knife 【动】become rusty：剪子～了。The scissors have become rusty. 铁锁～住了。The lock is rusty and won't open.

嗅　xiù　【动】smell

嗅觉　xiùjué　【名】sense of smell

xū

吁　xū

吁吁　xūxū　【象声】panting：气喘～ puff hard

须　xū　【名】(鬚)◇ beard：～发皆白。Both (his) hair and beard have turned white. 【助动】(须)〈书〉must：务～注意。You must pay attention. 手术前～有周密的计划和准备。Before an operation one must make an all-encompassing plan and careful preparations.

须知　xūzhī　【名】〈书〉points for attention：游览～ tourist guide 会客～ information for visitors 【动】ought to know：～粮食来之不易。We must bear in mind that grain is not easy to come by.

虚　xū　【形】❶◇ void；empty ❷◇ to no avail；waste：弹不～发。Not a shot missed its target. ❸◇ false：～有其名 have an undeserved reputation ～情假意 hypocritical show of friendship ❹ weak：身体很～ in poor health

虚报　xūbào　【动】give a false report

虚词　xūcí　【名】function word；word expressing grammatical relationship

虚构　xūgòu　【动】make up；fictitious：～情节 fictitious plot（of a story, novel）纯属～ sheer fiction

虚假　xūjiǎ　【形】false；sham；unreal

虚惊　xūjīng　【动】false alarm；be alarmed for nothing

虚夸　xūkuā　【动】boast；exaggerate

虚名　xūmíng　【名】undeserved reputation；unwarranted reputation

虚拟　xūnǐ　【动】invent；imagine；suppose：～语气 subjunctive mood 这段故事情节是作者～的。The plot of the story is a product of the author's imagination.

虚荣　xūróng　【形】vanity；vain glory

虚弱　xūruò　【形】❶ physically weak：～的身体 in poor health ❷ weak；feeble：兵力～ militarily weak

虚设　xūshè　【动】nominal；in name only；symbolic；titular

虚实　xūshí　【名】true condition；actual situation

虚数　xūshù　【名】(maths.) imaginary number

虚脱　xūtuō　【名】(med.) collapse；prostration 【动】suffer a collapse

虚伪　xūwěi　【形】hypocritical；false

虚无主义　xūwúzhǔyì　【名】nihilism

虚线　xūxiàn　【名】〔条 tiáo〕dotted line

虚心　xūxīn　【形】modest：～接受意见 be modest and accept others' critical opinions

虚张声势　xū zhāng shēngshì　give the appearance of being powerful；bluff

需　xū　【动】need

需求　xūqiú　【名】requirement；demand

需要　xūyào　【动】need：我们～一支强大的科技队伍。We need a mighty army of technical and scientific workers. 【名】need：我们出版的书，远远不能满足读者的～。The books

we have published are far from adequate to meet the needs of our readers.

xú

徐 xú
徐缓 xúhuǎn 【形】slow and gentle
徐徐 xúxú 【副】〈书〉slowly；gently：幕～落下。The curtain was slowly lowered. 微风～吹来。A breeze is blowing gently.

xǔ

许(許) xǔ 【动】❶ promise (to give sb. sth. or to do sth. for sb.) ❷ allow；be allowed：病房内不～喧哗。One must talk quietly in a hospital ward. 【副】perhaps：这件事他～是不知道吧！Perhaps he did not know about this matter.
许多 xǔduō 【形】a great many；a lot of；numerous；plenty of (*only as attributive*)
许久 xǔjiǔ 【名】a long time
许可 xǔkě 【动】permit；consent；approve
许可证 xǔkězhèng 【名】license；permit
许诺 xǔnuò 【动】promise；give one's word
许愿 xǔ = yuàn make promise；promise sb. a reward

栩 xǔ
栩栩如生 xǔxǔ rú shēng very vivid；lifelike

xù

旭 xù
旭日 xùrì 【名】morning sun；rising sun

旭日东升 xùrì dōng shēng the morning sun rises in the eastern sky

序 xù 【名】❶ ◇ order：井然有～ in good order ❷ preface
序幕 xùmù 【名】prologue；prelude
序曲 xùqǔ 【名】prelude；overture
序数 xùshù 【名】ordinal number
序言 xùyán 【名】introduction；preface；foreword

叙 xù 【动】talk；relate
叙旧 xù = jiù talk about the old days
叙事诗 xùshìshī 【名】〔首 shǒu〕narrative poem
叙述 xùshù 【动】describe；narrate
叙说 xùshuō 【动】narrate；relate；recount (orally)
叙谈 xùtán 【动】chat；chitchat

畜 xù
另见 chù
畜产 xùchǎn 【名】live-stock product
畜牧 xùmù 【动】raise livestock or poultry
畜养 xùyǎng 【动】build up；accumulate

酗 xù
酗酒 xùjiǔ 【动】become drunk and violent；indulge in excessive drinking

绪(緒) xù
绪论 xùlùn 【名】introduction (to a book)

絮 xù 【名】(cotton) wadding；sth. resembling cotton
絮叨 xùdao 【动】keep on talking：老奶奶一讲起年轻时候的事情，就～个没完。Once granny begins talking about her youth, she just keeps on and on. 【形】long-winded：她可真～。She is really long-winded.

絮烦　xùfán　【形】wordy；long-winded

蓄

xù　【动】❶ save up；store up：水库的水已～满。The reservoir is full of water. ❷ ◇ grow：～发（fà）wear one's hair long

蓄电池　xùdiànchí　【名】storage battery

蓄洪　xù＝hóng　store flood；flood storage

蓄谋　xùmóu　【动】conceive a plot in secret；harbour a conspiracy

蓄意　xùyì　【动】premeditate；deliberate（derog.）

xuān

宣

xuān　【动】◇ declare：不～而战 wage an undeclared war

宣布　xuānbù　【动】declare；announce；proclaim

宣称　xuānchēng　【动】make known；declare；announce

宣传　xuānchuán　【动】propagate；publicize：～卫生常识 make knowledge of hygiene widely available ～交通规则 publicize traffic regulations 【名】propaganda

宣传画　xuānchuánhuà　【名】〔张 zhāng〕picture poster

宣传品　xuānchuánpǐn　【名】publicity material

宣读　xuāndú　【动】read out（in public）

宣告　xuāngào　【动】proclaim；declare

宣讲　xuānjiǎng　【动】（of policy, document）explain（in public）

宣判　xuānpàn　【动】pronounce judgment

宣誓　xuān＝shì　swear；take an oath

宣言　xuānyán　【名】declaration；manifesto

宣扬　xuānyáng　【动】advocate；advertise

宣战　xuān＝zhàn　declare war

喧

xuān

喧宾夺主　xuān bīn duó zhǔ　what should be secondary outshines the primary

喧哗　xuānhuá　【动】make a lot of noise

喧闹　xuānnào　【形】noisy；bustling

喧嚣　xuānxiāo　【动】make a clamour；stir up a commotion

xuán

玄

xuán　【形】❶ ◇ black：～色 black colour ❷ fantastic；unbelievable：说得太～了。The way you put it was too fantastic.

玄妙　xuánmiào　【形】mysterious

玄虚　xuánxū　【名】mystery；abstruseness

悬（懸）

xuán　【动】❶ hang：～灯结彩 decorate with lanterns and streamers ❷ suspend；keep in an undecided state：这件事还～着呢！The matter is still pending. 【形】dangerous：真～，树枝差点儿碰着我眼睛。The tree branch almost hit me in the eye. That was a near thing!

悬案　xuán'àn　【名】❶ unresolved legal case ❷ undecided question；unsettled problem

悬而未决　xuán ér wèi jué　pending；outstanding；unresolved：～的问题 outstanding question ～的争端 unsettled dispute

悬挂　xuánguà　【动】hang up；suspend

悬空　xuánkōng　【动】hang in the air；dangle in the air（also fig.）

悬念 xuánniàn 【动】〈书〉be concerned about (sb. elsewhere)：女儿久未来信，父母颇为～。Their daughter hadn't written for a long time, and they were very worried.

悬殊 xuánshū 【形】with a wide gap：双方力量～。The two sides are quite unevenly matched in terms of strength.

悬崖 xuányá 【名】cliff；precipice

悬崖绝壁 xuányá juébì overhanging cliff；precipice

悬崖勒马 xuányá lè mǎ rein in one's horse on the brink of a precipice；(fig.) ward off disaster at the critical moment

旋 xuán

另见 xuàn

旋律 xuánlǜ 【名】melody；cantus

旋涡 xuánwō 【名】whirlpool；eddy；vortex 也作"漩涡"。

旋转 xuánzhuǎn 【动】revolve；spin；rotate

xuǎn

选（選）xuǎn 【动】❶ select；choose：～几篇文章学习 choose a few articles to study ❷ elect：～代表 elect representatives 小李被～进领导班子。Xiao Li was elected to the leading group.【名】◇ selection：短篇小说～ an anthology of short stories 民歌～ a selection of folk songs

选拔 xuǎnbá 【动】select；choose

选拔赛 xuǎnbásài 【名】trial；contest

选编 xuǎnbiān 【动】select and compile 【名】selection；collection of selected material

选材 xuǎn = cái ❶ select material；慎重～ select material with care ❷ selected material：大量～ a large quantity of selected material

选购 xuǎngòu 【动】pick out and buy；choose：任意～。Pick out and buy as you like.

选集 xuǎnjí 【名】selected works；anthology

选辑 xuǎnjí 【动】select and edit

选举 xuǎnjǔ 【动】elect；vote 【名】election

选举权 xuǎnjǔquán 【名】the right to vote (or elect)

选民 xuǎnmín 【名】voter；elector

选派 xuǎnpài 【动】select and appoint；detail

选票 xuǎnpiào 【名】ballot；vote

选手 xuǎnshǒu 【名】selected contestant；(of sports) competitor

选修 xuǎnxiū 【动】take as an elective course

选择 xuǎnzé 【动】pick and choose；make the choice；take one's preference

选种 xuǎn = zhǒng select seed

癣（癬）xuǎn 【名】ringworm；tinea

xuàn

炫 xuàn

炫耀 xuànyào 【动】show off；flaunt：～武力 make a show of force 别总～自己。Don't try to show off.

绚（絢）xuàn

绚烂 xuànlàn 【形】splendid：～夺目的绸缎 gorgeous and dazzling silks and satins ～的山花 wild flowers in myriad colours

绚丽 xuànlì 【形】magnificent：～多彩 brilliant and colourful ～的宝石 magnificent jewels

旋 xuàn 【动】(镟) turn sth. on a lathe; pare; peel: ~铅笔 sharpen a pencil ~一根车轴 shape an axle 【副】at the time; at the last moment: ~吃~买 buy sth. only when you want to eat it（don't buy sth. and store it up）入了冬再~做棉衣，就来不及了 If you wait until winter to start making padded clothing, it will be too late.

另见 xuán

旋床 xuànchuáng 【名】〔台 tái〕lathe; turning-lathe

旋风 xuànfēng 【名】〔阵 zhèn〕whirlwind

渲 xuàn

渲染 xuànrǎn 【动】❶(of traditional Chinese painting) paint with ink diluted with water or paint with any light colour ❷ paly up; exaggerate: 大肆~ greatly exaggerate 故意~ deliberately play up 舞台上秋天的景色~了悲剧的气氛。The autumn scenery on the stage added to the tragic atmosphere.

xuē

削 xuē

另见 xiāo

削价 xuē=jià cut the price: ~百分之十处理 sell at a 10% discount

削减 xuējiǎn 【动】cut down; reduce

削弱 xuēruò 【动】weaken; cripple: ~战斗力 weaken the fighting strength

削足适履 xuē zú shì lǚ trim the feet to fit the shoes;（fig.）act in a Procrustean manner

靴 xuē 【名】◇ boot

靴子 xuēzi 【名】〔只 zhī、双 shuāng〕boot

xué

穴 xué 【名】cave; hole: 蚁~ ants' nest

穴位 xuéwèi 【名】〔个 gè〕acupuncture point

学（學） xué 【动】❶ learn; study: ~理论 study (political) theory 活到老~到老 learn as long as one lives 一切民族、一切国家的长处我们都要~。We must learn from the good qualities of all nationalities and all countries. ❷ imitate; mimic: ~得很像 imitate very cleverly 鹦鹉~舌 parrot; imitate mechanically 【名】◇ ❶ learning; knowledge: 严肃的治~态度 have a rigorous attitude towards doing academic research ❷ school: 上~ go to school

学报 xuébào 【名】academic periodical (e. g. college periodical)

学潮 xuécháo 【名】student strike

学费 xuéfèi 【名】school fees; tuition

学分 xuéfēn 【名】academic credit

学风 xuéfēng 【名】style of study

学会 xuéhuì 【名】society; institute

学籍 xuéjí 【名】one's status as a student of a particular school

学科 xuékē 【名】❶ branch of learning; discipline ❷ course or subject taught in a school

学历 xuélì 【名】summary of one's schooling and degrees

学龄 xuélíng 【名】school age

学龄儿童 xuélíng értóng children of school age

学名 xuémíng 【名】❶ scientific name ❷ (a person's) formal name (usu. given him when he starts to go to school)

学年 xuénián 【名】academic year

学派 xuépài 【名】school of thought

学期 xuéqī 【名】semester; school term

学前教育 xué qián jiàoyù preschool education

学生 xuésheng 【名】student; pupil

学时 xuéshí 【名】teaching period; class hour

学识 xuéshí 【名】knowledge; learning; scholarly attainment

学士 xuéshì 【名】Bachelor of Arts; B.A.

学术 xuéshù 【名】knowledge; learning; science; ～讨论会 academic discussion ～报告 academic lecture ～交流 academic exchange

学说 xuéshuō 【名】theory; teachings; doctrine

学徒 xuétú 【名】apprentice

学徒 xué = tú be an apprentice

学位 xuéwèi 【名】academic degree

学问 xuéwèn 【名】learning; knowledge; scholarship

学习 xuéxí 【动】learn; study 【名】study

学习班 xuéxíbān 【名】study class

学衔 xuéxián 【名】academic rank

学校 xuéxiào 【名】〔所 suǒ〕school

学业 xuéyè 【名】studies; lessons and school assignments

学员 xuéyuán 【名】trainee; participant of training course as different from regular student

学院 xuéyuàn 【名】〔所 suǒ〕academy; institute; college

学者 xuézhě 【名】scholar

学制 xuézhì 【名】educational system; school system

xuě

雪 xuě 【名】snow; 下了一场大～。There was a heavy snowfall. 【动】◇ wipe out (a humiliation, etc.); 报仇～恨 avenge a grievance and settle a score

雪白 xuěbái 【形】snow-white

雪耻 xuě = chǐ wipe out shame

雪糕 xuěgāo 【名】ice cream

雪花 xuěhuā 【名】snow flake

雪茄 xuějiā 【名】〔枝 zhī〕cigar

雪亮 xuěliàng 【形】❶ bright; 把自行车擦得～ polish the bike until it shines ❷ clear (sighted); 群众的眼睛是～的。The masses see very clearly.

雪橇 xuěqiāo 【名】sledge; sleigh

雪球 xuěqiú 【名】snowball

雪人 xuěrén 【名】snow-man

雪山 xuěshān 【名】〔座 zuò〕snow-covered mountain

雪中送炭 xuě zhōng sòng tàn send charcoal in snowy weather; (fig.) give sb. what he needs most; 救灾物资及时送到灾区,真是～。The relief supplies sent to the disaster area were certainly a timely source of help.

xuè

血 xuè 【名】blood
另见 xiě

血癌 xuè'ái 【名】leukemia

血管 xuèguǎn 【名】〔条 tiáo〕blood vessel

血海深仇 xuè hǎi shēn chóu deep-seated hatred caused by blood-debt

血汗 xuèhàn 【名】sweat and blood; hard toil

血红 xuèhóng 【形】blood red

血迹 xuèjì 【名】bloodstain

血口喷人 xuè kǒu pēn rén make unfounded and scurrilous attacks upon sb.

血泪 xuèlèi 【名】blood and tears; hardship and suffering

血泪斑斑 xuèlèi bānbān stained with blood and tears

血泊 xuèpō 【名】pool of blood

血肉　xuèròu　【名】❶ flesh and blood：～模糊 badly injured ❷ as close as flesh and blood：～关系 blood kinship

血肉相连　xuèròu xiānglián　as close to each other as flesh and blood

血栓　xuèshuān　【名】thrombus

血统　xuètǒng　【名】blood lineage

血腥　xuèxīng　【形】bloody；sanguinary

血型　xuèxíng　【名】blood type

血压　xuèyā　【名】blood pressure

血压计　xuèyājì　【名】sphygmomanometer

血液　xuèyè　【名】blood

血缘　xuèyuán　【名】blood relationship

血债　xuèzhài　【名】debt of blood；blood-debt

血战　xuèzhàn　【动】fight to the last drop of one's blood

xūn

勋（勛）　xūn

勋章　xūnzhāng　【名】〔枚 méi〕medal；decoration

熏（燻）　xūn　【动】smoke：～肉 smoked meat ～鱼 smoked fish 香烟把手指～黄了。His fingers are stained brown from smoking.

熏染　xūnrǎn　【动】exercise gradually but deep going influence over sb. (*usu. derog.*)

熏陶　xūntáo　【动】have gradual good influence over sb.

xún

旬　xún　【名】❶ a period of ten days ❷ decade (referring to an old person's age)：八～老人 an old man of eighty 年过七～ over seventy years old

寻（尋）　xún　【动】seek；look for

寻常　xúncháng　【形】ordinary；usual

寻呼　xúnhū　【动】page；beep

寻呼机　xúnhūjī　【名】pager；beeper

寻觅　xúnmì　【动】seek；look for

寻求　xúnqiú　【动】seek；look for and try to get

寻死　xún＝sǐ　attempt suicide；commit suicide

寻衅　xúnxìn　【动】pick a quarrel

寻找　xúnzhǎo　【动】look for；find；search；hunt for

巡　xún　【动】patrol；make one's rounds

巡回　xúnhuí　【动】go on circuit；make rounds：～演出 a performance troupe giving performances at various locations along a certain route ～医疗 mobile medical service

巡逻　xúnluó　【动】patrol

巡视　xúnshì　【动】make an inspection tour

巡洋舰　xúnyángjiàn　【名】〔艘 sōu〕cruiser

询（詢）　xún

询问　xúnwèn　【动】inquire；ask

循　xún

循规蹈矩　xún guī dǎo jǔ　stick rigidly to rules and regulations；toe the line

循环　xúnhuán　【动】move in cycles；circulate 【名】cycle；circulation

循环赛　xúnhuánsài　【名】round robin

循环小数　xúnhuán xiǎoshù　(maths.) recurring decimal

循序渐进　xúnxù jiànjìn　follow in order and advance step by step：学习必须由浅入深，～。Our learning must proceed from the easy to the

difficult and progress step by step.

循循善诱　xún xún shàn yòu　teach with skill and patience

xùn

训（訓）　xùn　【动】lecture；reprove：把他～了一顿 give him a piece of one's mind 【名】◇ standard；model：不足为～ not fit to serve as a model

训斥　xùnchì　【动】scold；rebuke；reprimand

训诂　xùngǔ　【动】exegetical studies

训练　xùnliàn　【动】train；drill

讯（訊）　xùn　【名】◇ news；intelligence：新华社七日～ a Xinhua dispatch of the 7th.

讯问　xùnwèn　【动】❶ make inquiries about：～住址 make inquiries about an address 大夫～病人的症状。The doctor inquired into the details of the patient's symptoms. ❷ interrogate；question：～案件 carry out an interrogation in a legal case

迅　xùn

迅雷不及掩耳　xùn léi bù jí yǎn ěr　as sudden as a thunderbolt

迅猛　xùnměng　【形】swift and violent

迅速　xùnsù　【形】quick；prompt：动作～ quick in one's movements ～前进 advance rapidly

驯（馴）　xùn　【动】tame；subdue

驯服　xùnfú　【动】tame；bring under control：烈马被～了。The spirited horse has been tamed. 我们一定要～黄河。We are determined to control the Yellow River. 【形】docile：马戏班里的熊很～。The bears in the circus were quite tame.

驯化　xùnhuà　【动】domesticate

驯良　xùnliáng　【形】tractable；docile

驯顺　xùnshùn　【形】tame and docile

驯养　xùnyǎng　【动】raise and train；domesticate

逊（遜）　xùn

逊色　xùnsè　【形】inferior：并不～ not inferior by comparison 这幅油画比那幅可～多了。This oil painting is much inferior to that one.

殉　xùn　【动】sacrifice one's life for a cause：以身～国 lay down one's life for one's country

殉难　xùn ＝ nàn　die（for a just cause）：抚恤～烈士家属 comfort and compensate a martyr's family

殉葬　xùnzàng　【动】be buried alive with the dead

殉葬品　xùnzàngpǐn　【名】object buried with the dead

殉职　xùn ＝ zhí　die at one's post：光荣～ die gloriously in the line of duty 他不幸～。It is regrettable that he died at his post.

Y

yā

压(壓)　yā　【动】❶ press；大雪～弯了树枝. The heavy snow weighed the tree branches down. ❷ keep under control；hold down：～不住心头怒火 be unable to control one's anger 这场面只有他才～得住. He was the only one who could keep the situation under control. ❸ bring pressure to bear on；suppress：倚势～人 abuse one's power and bully the people ❹ shelve：这封信在他那儿～了两天. He held this letter up for two days. ～在心底的谜解开了. The mystery, which had preoccupied him for some time was finally dispelled. ❺ ◇ approach；close in on：重兵～境. Huge forces were closing in on the frontier.

压宝　yā＝bǎo　a gambling game，played with dice under a bowl；stake

压倒　yā // dǎo　prevail over；overwhelm；overcome；overpower：～一切的任务 over-riding task 石头滚下来把树苗～了. A rock rolled down and crushed the saplings. 比赛中甲队占～优势. Team A dominated the game.

压服　yā // fú　coerce into submission；suppress；overwhelm

压价　yā＝jià　force prices down

压惊　yājīng　【动】help sb. get over a shock

压力　yālì　【名】pressure；force of pressure

压力锅　yālìguō　【名】〔个 gè〕pressure cooker

压迫　yāpò　【动】❶ constrict：肿瘤～神经. The tumour is pressing on a nerve. ❷ oppress：被～民族 the oppressed peoples

压迫者　yāpòzhě　【名】oppressor

压缩　yāsuō　【动】❶ compress：这种饼干是经过～制成的. These biscuits are made by a process of compression. ❷ (of staff members, expenditures, space, etc.) reduce；cut down；curtail：～开支 cut down expenditures ～机构 streamline the administrative structure 这篇文章需要大大～. This article needs to be shortened considerably.

压抑　yāyì　【动】constrain；inhibit：～不住内心的激动 be unable to contain one's agitation 感情受到～. His feelings were repressed.

压韵　yā＝yùn　rhyme

压榨　yāzhà　【动】❶ press；squeeze：大豆经过～才能出油. Soybeans yield oil when pressed. ❷ oppress and exploit；bleed：不能～雇工. Hired hands are not to be oppressed and exploited.

压制　yāzhì　【动】❶ make sth. by pressing：～塑料板 press plastic in-

to sheets ❷ suppress; clamp down;
～批评 muzzle criticism ～不同意见
suppress differing opinions

呀
yā　【叹】oh; ah; ～，雪下得真
大! Oh! Look how heavily it's
snowing! ～，你怎么这么早就来啦!
Oh you've come so early!
另见 ya

押
yā　【动】❶ detain; keep in
custody; 把犯人～起来 take the
criminal into custody ❷ escort; ～
车 escort goods in transport ～俘虏
escort prisoners-of-war

押金　yājīn【名】cash pledge; deposit

押送　yāsòng【动】send under escort

鸦(鴉)
yā　【名】opium

鸦片　yāpiàn【名】opium

鸦片战争　Yāpiàn Zhànzhēng　the
Opium War (1840 – 1842), a war of
resistance waged by the Chinese
people against British imperialist
aggression

鸦雀无声　yā què wú shēng　dead silence; 手术室里～，医生们在紧张地抢
救病人。There was a dead silence
in the operating room, as the doctors struggled to save the patient.

鸭(鴨)
yā　【名】duck

鸭子　yāzi【名】[只 zhī]duck

yá

牙
yá　【名】tooth

牙齿　yáchǐ【名】tooth

牙床　yáchuáng【名】gum

牙雕　yádiāo【名】ivory carving

牙膏　yágāo【名】toothpaste; dental
cream

牙科　yákē【名】dentistry

牙签儿　yáqiānr【名】tooth pick

牙刷　yáshuā【名】[把 bǎ]toothbrush

芽
yá　【名】sprout; shoot; bud

蚜
yá　【名】◇ aphis

蚜虫　yáchóng【名】aphis

yǎ

哑(啞)
yǎ　【动】dumb;
mute; 又聋又～ be deaf and dumb
【形】hoarse; 他喊得嗓子都～了。He
shouted himself hoarse.

哑巴　yǎba【名】mute; dumb person

哑口无言　yǎ kǒu wú yán　be rendered speechless

雅
yǎ

雅观　yǎguān【形】(of one's clothing, behaviour) presentable (usu.
used in the negative)

雅俗共赏　yǎ sú gòng shǎng　(of literary and artistic works) appeal to
both the masses and the elite

雅致　yǎzhì【形】(of clothing, furnishings of a room) elegant; refined

雅座　yǎzuò【名】a nicely fixed
room (in a restaraunt, etc.)

yà

亚(亞)
yà

亚军　yàjūn【名】runner-up; winner
of second prize

亚热带　yàrèdài【名】subtropics

亚于　yàyú【动】be second to; 这种
酒仅～茅台。This kind of spirit is
second only to Maotai. 小李的棋艺
不～你。Xiao Li's skill at chess is
not inferior to yours.

亚洲　Yàzhōu【名】Asia

ya

呀 ya 【助】 *a sound modification of* 啊，见"啊" a
另见 yǎ

yān

咽 yān 【名】◇ throat
另见 yàn

咽喉 yānhóu 【名】❶ throat：～发炎 an inflammation of the throat ❷ vital passage；key link：马六甲海峡是太平洋与印度洋之间的交通～。The Strait of Malacca forms the vital link between the Pacific and the Indian Oceans.

烟 yān 【名】❶ smoke：一股黑～ a streak of black smoke　冒～ smoke issued forth ❷ tobacco；cigarette：一包～ a pack of cigarettes　种了两亩～。Two *mu* of tobacco were planted.

烟草 yāncǎo 【名】tobacco
烟囱 yāncōng 【名】chimney
烟袋 yāndài 【名】old-fashioned tobacco pipe
烟斗 yāndǒu 【名】tobacco pipe
烟灰 yānhuī 【名】tobacco or cigarette ashes
烟灰缸 yānhuīgāng 【名】ash tray
烟火 yānhuǒ 【名】smoke and fire：库房内严禁～。Smoking and all other uses of fire are strictly prohibited in the warehouse.
烟火 yānhuo 【名】fire-works 也作"焰火" yànhuǒ。
烟煤 yānméi 【名】soft coal；bituminous coal
烟幕 yānmù 【名】❶ smokescreen：施放和平～ put up a peaceful smokescreen ❷ clouds of smoke produced by burning fuel or chemicals to protect crops against frost
烟幕弹 yānmùdàn 【名】smoke-bomb：放～ drop a smoke-bomb
烟丝 yānsī 【名】pipe tobacco
烟筒 yāntong 【名】stove pipe；chimney
烟头儿 yāntóur 【名】〔个 gè〕cigarette end
烟土 yāntǔ 【名】crude opium
烟雾 yānwù 【名】mist；haze
烟消云散 yān xiāo yún sàn vanish like smoke
烟叶 yānyè 【名】tobacco leaf
烟瘾 yānyǐn 【名】a craving for opium；a craving for tobacco；an addiction to tobacco
烟嘴儿 yānzuǐr 【名】cigarette-holder

阉(閹) yān
阉割 yāngē 【动】❶ (of an animal) castrate ❷ emasculate；deprive a theory, etc. of its essence：～精神实质 cut the essentials out of (sth.)

淹 yān 【动】❶ flood；inundate：庄稼被洪水～了。The crops were flooded. ❷ be prickling from sweat
淹没 yānmò 【动】submerge；immerse

腌 yān 【动】pickle；preserve in salt

yán

延 yán 【动】❶ ◇ prolong；lengthen：～年益寿 prolong one's life ❷ postpone；put off：假期向后～了。The holiday has been postponed.
延长 yáncháng 【动】prolong；lengthen

延长线 yáncháng xiàn 【名】extended line；extension

延迟 yánchí 【动】postpone；delay

延搁 yángē 【动】postpone；delay；procrastinate

延缓 yánhuǎn 【动】delay；postpone：手术～几天再做。The operation is postponed for a few days.

延期 yán=qī put off；postpone：学术报告会～举行。The symposium has been postponed.

延伸 yánshēn 【动】extend；stretch

延误 yánwù 【动】incur loss through delay：～期限 incur loss through delay

延续 yánxù 【动】continue

延展性 yánzhǎnxìng 【名】ductility；extensibility

严（嚴） yán 【形】❶ tight：把门关～了。Shut the door tight. ❷ strict：这里作息制度很～。We have a strict work timetable here. ❸ severe；harsh；stern：从～处理 deal with severely

严惩 yánchéng severely punish：罪大恶极者必须按法律～！Those who are guilty of heinous crimes must be severely punished by law.

严冬 yándōng 【名】severe winter

严防 yánfáng 【动】be on sharp guard against；take strict precautions against

严父 yánfù 【名】stern father

严格 yángé 【形】strict；exact：～按规定办事 do things strictly according to the regulations 他对自己的要求很～。He is very strict with himself. 【动】be strict：～产品验收制度 exercise a strict system of quality control

严寒 yánhán 【形】severely cold

严谨 yánjǐn 【形】❶ rigorous；strict：～的态度 rigorous attitude 作风～ in a rigorous style ❷ compact；well-knit：文章结构～。The article is tightly organized.

严紧 yánjǐn 【形】rigid；tight；close：大门关得很～。The door was tightly shut.

严禁 yánjìn 【动】strictly forbid

严峻 yánjùn 【形】severe；stern；rigorous

严酷 yánkù 【形】❶ severe ❷ ruthless；cruel：～的事实 harsh fact ～的压迫 ruthless oppression

严厉 yánlì 【形】severe；stern；austere

严密 yánmì 【形】❶ close；tight：坛子口封得十分～。The jar is tightly sealed. ❷ close-knit：～的组织 tightly-knit organization ～注视敌军行动 keep a close watch on the movements of the enemy

严明 yánmíng 【形】stern and impartial；strict and just

严师 yánshī 【名】strict teacher

严实 yánshi 【形】close；tight：窗户关得挺～，风透不进来。The windows are tightly shut, keeping the wind out.

严守 yánshǒu 【动】strictly observe；strictly abide by；maintain strictly

严肃 yánsù 【形】serious；solemn

严阵以待 yán zhèn yǐ dài stand ready in battle array；remain in combat readiness

严整 yánzhěng 【形】(of troops) orderly；neat；well-disciplined

严正 yánzhèng 【形】(of attitude) solemn；impartial；strict；serious

严重 yánzhòng 【形】serious；grave：～后果 serious consequence ～的任务 serious task 损失～ grave loss ～影响了工程进度 seriously affect the progress of the project

言 yán 【名】◇ ❶ words：有～在先 make the point clear beforehand ❷ Chinese character：五～诗 poem with five characters to the line 全书近二十万～。The whole

book totals 200,000 characters. 【动】〈书〉say；speak：～必信，行必果 true in word and resolute in deed

言不由衷 yán bù yóu zhōng speak insincerely

言传身教 yán chuán shēn jiào teach and also set an example by one's deeds：老师傅～，热情地培养青年工人。The old worker teaches and also sets an example for young workers in order to foster their development.

言辞 yáncí 【名】words：～激烈 in sharp words

言过其实 yán guò qí shí exaggerate；overstate；他的腿是有点儿病，但是说他走不了路，未免～。There is something wrong with his leg, but you're exaggerating when you say he can't walk.

言简意赅 yán jiǎn yì gāi （of speech or writing）concise and comprehensive：这篇演说～，鼓舞人心。The speech was concise and to the point and very inspiring.

言论 yánlùn 【名】speech (e.g. freedom of speech)；expression of opinions；words

言谈 yántán 【名】the way one speaks or what one says

言听计从 yán tīng jì cóng have implicit faith in sb.；take sb.'s advice too readily；have excessive confidence in others

言外之意 yán wài zhī yì insinuation；implication；meaning between lines

言行 yánxíng 【名】words and deeds

言行不一 yánxíng bùyī say one thing and do another；one's words and deeds are at variance

言语 yányǔ 【名】spoken language；speech

言者无罪，闻者足戒 yánzhě wú zuì, wénzhě zú jiè blame not the speaker but be warned by his words

岩 yán 【名】◇ rock；cliff

岩石 yánshí 【名】rock

炎 yán 【形】◇ hot 【名】inflammation

炎热 yánrè 【形】blazing hot；sweltering heat

炎症 yánzhèng 【名】inflammation

沿 yán 【动】◇ follow (old traditions, etc.)：世代相～ be handed down from generation to generation 相～成习 be handed down as a custom 【名】◇ edge；border：前～阵地 a forward position 无边无～的大草原 boundless prairie 【介】along：～河边种了一排柳树。A row of willows was planted along the river. 汽车～公路向前开去。The car drove along the road.

另见 yàn

沿岸 yán'àn 【名】along the bank or coast

沿革 yángé 【名】course of development and changes

沿海 yánhǎi 【名】along the coast；inshore

沿路 yánlù 【名】along the road；on the way

沿途 yántú 【名】along the road

沿袭 yánxí 【动】do sth. according to（old conventions, customs, etc.）：～老办法 do sth. according to the old method 这个做法是～下来的。This way of doing things was handed down from the past.

沿线 yánxiàn 【名】along the line

沿用 yányòng 【动】continue to use（an old method, system, etc.）：中国的夏历～至今已有好几千年。The Chinese lunar calendar has been in use for several thousand years.

沿着 yánzhe 【介】同"沿"【介】，*but the object may be an abstract*

noun：～马路盖了二十座大楼。Twenty big buildings were built along the road. ～着旧观念订的规章不适用于新情况。Rules laid down according to old concepts do not work under new conditions.

研 yán 【动】grind：～墨 grind an ink-stick ～成粉末 grind sth. into powder

研究 yánjiū 【动】research；study

研究生 yánjiūshēng 【名】postgraduate student

研究员 yánjiūyuán 【名】research fellow

研讨 yántǎo 【动】study and discuss

研修 yánxiū 【动】do research：出国～ go abroad to do research

研制 yánzhì 【动】research and produce

盐(鹽) yán 【名】salt

盐碱地 yánjiǎndì 【名】saline and alkaline land

盐酸 yánsuān 【名】hydrochloric acid

阎(閻) yán

阎王 yánwang 【名】❶ the king of Hell ❷ a vicious and cruel person：～债 usurious loan 这个恶霸是个活～。That local bully was a living embodiment of the Devil.

筵 yán

筵席 yánxí 【名】banquet；feast

颜(顔) yán 【名】◇ ❶ facial expression：笑～ smiling face ❷ colour

颜料 yánliào 【名】colour；pigment

颜色 yánsè 【名】❶ colour；pigment ❷ harsh look given sb.（to chastize him）or sth. done to frighten sb.：给他点儿～看看 browbeat him；teach him a lesson

yǎn

奄 yǎn

奄奄一息 yǎnyǎn yī xī at one's last gasp；on the point of dying：病人已经～。The patient was on the point of death. 目前，这个矿处于～的境地。It is obvious that this mine is at its last gasp.

俨(儼) yǎn

俨然 yǎnrán 【形】〈书〉orderly and solemn：屋舍～ houses in neat rows 队伍～有序地行进着。The ranks are marching in good order.【副】just like：看她站在机床边从容不迫的样子，～是个熟练工人了。Standing so relaxed beside the machine, she looks just like a veteran worker.

掩 yǎn 【动】❶ cover up：～人耳目 deceive the public 山洞的出口被乱石～住。The outlet of the cave was concealed by fallen rocks. ❷ ◇ close：虚～着门 the door was closed but not locked

掩蔽 yǎnbì 【动】cover up；shelter

掩蔽部 yǎnbìbù 【名】underground shelter

掩藏 yǎncáng 【动】hide；conceal

掩耳盗铃 yǎn ěr dào líng plug one's ears when stealing a bell；(*fig.*) deceive oneself；bury one's head in the sand

掩盖 yǎngài 【动】❶ cover up：足迹被大雪～了。Footprints were covered by the heavy snow. ❷ conceal；cover up：不要～矛盾。Don't try to cover up contradictions.

掩护 yǎnhù 【动】provide cover；cover；shield：～战友脱险 cover one's comrades while they escape 在老乡们的～下，伤病员安全转移。With the villagers providing cov-

er, the wounded soldiers were safely evacuated.

掩埋　yǎnmái　【动】bury

掩人耳目　yǎn rén ěr mù　deceive the public

掩饰　yǎnshì　【动】cover up; gloss over

掩体　yǎntǐ　【名】pillbox; blindage

眼　yǎn　【名】❶〔只 zhī, 双 shuāng〕eye; 睁～ open one's eyes ❷(～儿) small hole; pinhole; 在木板上打个～ drill a small hole in the board 【量】for well; 生产队打了五～井。The production team has sunk five wells.

眼巴巴　yǎnbābā　【副】eagerly; anxiously (look forward to)

眼馋　yǎnchán　【形】envious; look longingly at

眼福　yǎnfú　【名】good fortune of catching sight of something rare; 大饱～ feast one's eyes on sth.

眼高手低　yǎn gāo shǒu dī　have high aim but no ability; be fastidious but incompetent

眼光　yǎnguāng　【名】❶ eye; 全屋人的～都注视着他。All the people in the room fixed their eyes on him. ❷ insight; judgement; ～短浅 short-sighted (in judgement)～远大 farsighted (in judgement)～别拿老～看他了, 他进步了。Don't judge him from the old perspective. He has changed for the better.

眼红　yǎnhóng　【形】❶ envious or jealous (of other people's reputation, position or possessions) ❷ angry; enraged; 仇人相见, 分外～。When enemies meet, they become even more embittered.

眼花　yǎnhuā　【形】dim-sighted

眼花缭乱　yǎnhuā liáoluàn　be dazzled

眼界　yǎnjiè　【名】field of vision; range of interest; 扩大～ enlarge the range of one's knowledge 这次去敦煌看壁画使我大开～。My recent visit to the murals of Dunhuang was a real eye-opener.

眼睛　yǎnjing　【名】〔只 zhī〕eye

眼镜　yǎnjìng　【名】〔副 fù〕spectacles; glasses

眼看　yǎnkàn　【动】❶ see with one's own eyes (usu. followed by 着, implying verification of the truthfulness of an event); 我～着他从汽车上下来的, 怎么转眼不见了? I saw him getting off the bus with my own eyes. How could he just disappear in the blink of an eye? 这事他忘不了, 我～着他记在本子上了。He won't forget this matter. I saw him jot it down in his notebook. ❷ indicates very evident change; 一场雨过后, 庄稼～长起来了。After the rainfall, the crops seem to have shot up overnight. ～着小李一天天在进步。Anyone can see that Xiao Li is making progress day by day. ❸ look on passively; 我们不能～着洪水冲毁堤坝, 必须采取措施。We can't just stand by and watch while the dam is breached by the flood waters. We must do something. 你怎么能～着这些不合理的现象不管呢? How could you witness such atrocities without doing anything? 【副】soon; presently (usu. in conjunction with 就…了 or 要…了); ～就到"五一"劳动节了。May Day is coming soon. 这条铁路～就要修好了。This railway line will be finished in no time.

眼科　yǎnkē　【名】ophthalmology department

眼泪　yǎnlèi　【名】tears

眼力　yǎnlì　【名】❶ eyesight; 他年纪虽大, 可～还不错。Although he is old, his sight is not too bad. ❷ ability of judgement; power of discrimination; 他真有～, 你看他挑选

的骡子多棒！He certainly is very discerning. He has chosen the best mule!

眼明手快 yǎn míng shǒu kuài quick of eye and deft of hand

眼皮 yǎnpí 【名】 eyelid

眼前 yǎnqián 【名】❶ before one's eyes；right in front of one：～是一片杨树林子。Right in front of us is a forest of poplars. ❷ at present；at this moment：不能只顾～利益而忘了长远利益。One mustn't grasp at immediate interests and forget long-range interests.

眼球 yǎnqiú 【名】 eyeball

眼圈 yǎnquān 【名】(～儿) rim of the eye

眼色 yǎnsè 【名】 meaningful glance；hint given with the eyes

眼神 yǎnshén 【名】❶ the expression in one's eyes：从他的～可以看出他的心情很激动。Judging from the look in his eyes, he was very agitated. ❷ (～儿) eyesight：他～不太好。His sight is not very good.

眼生 yǎnshēng 【形】 look unfamiliar

眼熟 yǎnshú 【形】 look familiar

眼下 yǎnxià 【名】 at present；at this time：～正是播种时节。It is the season for sowing right now.

眼中钉 yǎnzhōngdīng 【名】 a thorn in one's flesh

眼珠 yǎnzhū 【名】 eyeball

演 yǎn 【动】❶ perform：～一个节目 perform one item of a program 她在剧中～主角。She played the leading role in the drama. ❷ show (a film)：今晚～电影。There will be a film tonight.

演变 yǎnbiàn 【动】 evolve；develop；evolution

演唱 yǎnchàng 【动】 sing for an audience

演出 yǎnchū 【动】 perform；put on performance；put on a show 【名】

performance

演化 yǎnhuà 【动】 evolve 【名】 evolution

演技 yǎnjì 【名】 acting skill；acting

演讲 yǎnjiǎng 【动】 make a speech

演练 yǎnliàn 【动】 manoeuvres and training

演示 yǎnshì 【动】 demonstrate；show (using lab. experiment, charts, etc.)：教师通过电影把细菌的生长过程～给学生看。The teacher used a film to demonstrate the process of growth of bacteria.

演说 yǎnshuō 【动】 deliver a speech；make an address to 【名】 speech

演算 yǎnsuàn 【动】 perform mathematical calculations

演习 yǎnxí 【动】 manoeuvre

演义 yǎnyì 【名】 Chinese traditional historical novel：《三国～》 *Romance of the Three Kingdoms*

演绎 yǎnyì 【动】 deduce

演绎法 yǎnyìfǎ 【名】 deduction

演员 yǎnyuán 【名】 actor；performer

演奏 yǎnzòu 【动】 play or perform on a musical instrument 【名】 (instrumental) performance

yàn

厌(厭) yàn 【动】❶ be tired of；be fed up with：吃～了 be sick of eating sth. 听～了 be fed up with listening to sth. 百看不～ (so good that) one can never tire of it no matter how many times one looks at it or reads it ❷ ◇ be satisfied：学而不～ not be satisfied with what one has learned ❸ loathe；detest：令人生～ be loathsome

厌烦 yànfán 【动】 feel annoyed；be tired of：售货员老方接待顾客，从不～。Lao Fang, the shop assistant, never feels annoyed when serving

customers.

厌倦　yànjuàn　【动】be weary of；be tired of：这个工作虽然平凡，但意义重大，我干一辈子也不会～。This job is ordinary but very meaningful. I won't get tired of it even if I do it all my life.

厌弃　yànqì　【动】detest and reject

厌恶　yànwù　【动】detest；loathe；hate；dislike

厌战　yàn=zhàn　be war-weary

沿　yàn　【名】（～儿）water's edge：沟～ edge of a ditch 河～ bank of a river
另见 yán

砚（硯）　yàn　【名】◇ inkstone

砚台　yàntai　【名】inkstone

咽　yàn　【动】swallow
另见 yān

咽气　yàn=qì　breathe one's last；die

艳（艷）　yàn　【形】gorgeous；resplendent

艳丽　yànlì　【形】bright coloured and beautiful；gorgeous

艳阳天　yànyángtiān　【名】bright spring day；bright sunny skies

唁　yàn　【动】〈书〉extend condolences

唁电　yàndiàn　【名】message of condolence

宴　yàn　【名】◇ banquet；feast

宴会　yànhuì　【名】banquet；dinner party

宴请　yànqǐng　【动】invite to dinner；give a dinner in honour of

验（驗）　yàn　【动】test；check：～血 test blood ～货 check goods

验光　yàn=guāng　optometry

验收　yànshōu　【动】check before acceptance

验算　yànsuàn　【动】checking computations

谚（諺）　yàn

谚语　yànyǔ　【名】proverb；saying

雁　yàn　【名】〔只 zhī〕wild goose

燕　yàn　【名】swallow

燕尾服　yànwěifú　【名】swallowtail；swallowtailed coat

燕子　yànzi　【名】〔只 zhī〕swallow

yāng

秧　yāng　【名】❶（～儿）seedling：西红柿～ tomato seedling ❷ rice seedling ❸ vine of certain plants：白薯～ sweet-potato vine ❹ young；fry：鱼～（子）(fish) fry

秧歌　yāngge　【名】yangge dance，a kind of Chinese folk dance：扭～ dance the yangge

秧苗　yāngmiáo　【名】〔棵 kē、株 zhū〕seedling

秧田　yāngtián　【名】〔块 kuài〕rice seedling bed；seedling plot

yáng

扬（揚）　yáng　【动】❶ raise；lift：～帆前进 raise the sail and set out ～一～手 wave one's hand 跃马～鞭 gallop on horseback with whip raised ❷ winnow：把谷子～净 winnow the millet until it's clean ❸ ◇ spread；get about：名～四海 be known throughout the land

扬长避短　yáng cháng bì duǎn　make the best use of one's strength and avoid one's weakness

扬长而去　yáng cháng ér qù　go away

haughtily;stalk off

扬场 yáng＝cháng winnow

扬眉吐气 yáng méi tǔ qì feel proud and elated：过去的穷苦矿工，如今～，成了矿山的主人。Those poor miners have now lifted up their heads and become the proud masters of the mines.

扬弃 yángqì 【动】discard;abandon

扬水站 yángshuǐzhàn 【名】pumping station

扬言 yángyán 【动】publicly threaten

羊 yáng 【名】〔只 zhī〕sheep; goat

羊肠小道 yángcháng xiǎodào small zigzag path

羊羔 yánggāo 【名】〔只 zhī〕lamb; kid

羊倌儿 yángguānr 【名】shepherd

羊毛 yángmáo 【名】sheep's wool

羊肉 yángròu 【名】mutton

阳（陽） yáng 【名】◇ ❶ the sun;sunlight：葵花向～开。Sunflowers turn towards the sun. 骄～似火。The scorching sun is like fire. ❷ open;overt：阴一套，～一套 act in one way in public,another way in private

阳春白雪 yángchūn báixuě "The Spring Snow"—a Chinese song of the 3rd century B.C.;(fig.) highbrow art and literature

阳电 yángdiàn 【名】positive electricity

阳奉阴违 yáng fèng yīn wéi outwardly compliant but inwardly disobedient;overtly agree but covertly oppose

阳光 yángguāng 【名】sunshine

阳极 yángjí 【名】anode

阳历 yánglì 【名】solar calendar

阳面 yángmiàn 【名】the sunny side

阳平 yángpíng 【名】the second of

the four tones of *Putonghua*

阳伞 yángsǎn 【名】〔把 bǎ〕parasol; sunshade

阳台 yángtái 【名】balcony

阳性 yángxìng 【名】❶ masculine gender ❷ (med.) positive

杨（楊） yáng 【名】aspen; poplar

杨树 yángshù 【名】〔棵 kē〕aspen; poplar

洋 yáng 【名】ocean：远隔重(chóng)～ separated by oceans【形】❶ foreign：～货 foreign goods ❷ modern：土～并举 simultaneous employment of modern and indigenous methods

洋白菜 yángbáicài 【名】〔棵 kē〕cabbage

洋葱 yángcōng 【名】onion

洋为中用 yáng wéi zhōng yòng make foreign things serve China

洋洋 yángyáng 【形】◇ ❶ numerous;copious：～万言 run into ten thousand words ❷ complacent：～自得 be complacent;be very pleased with oneself

洋溢 yángyì 【动】(of atmosphere, spirits) be full of;brim with：热情～ be full of enthusiasm 宴会上～着热烈友好的气氛。An warm and friendly atmosphere prevailed at the banquet.

yǎng

仰 yǎng 【动】❶ face upward; look up：～头 raise one's head ❷ ◇ rely on：～人鼻息 be dependent on sb. and at his beck and call

仰慕 yǎngmù 【动】admire and respect

仰望 yǎngwàng 【动】look up; (fig.) admire：～夜空 look up at

the night sky

仰泳 yǎngyǒng 【名】back stroke (in swimming)

仰仗 yǎngzhàng 【动】rely on；look to sb. for backing

养（養）yǎng 【动】❶ give birth to ❷ bring up；support：～儿育女 bring up children 他从小失去父母，是伯父把他～大的。He lost his parents in childhood and was brought up by his uncle. ❸ raise；breed：～鸡 raise chickens ～花 grow flowers ❹ convalesce；recuperate：他的病～了一段时间，已经见好了。He has been convalescing for some time and is much better now. ❺ cultivate；foster；form：儿童从小就要～成劳动的习惯。Children should from childhood form the habit of doing physical labour. ❻ ◇ keep in good repair；maintain：～路 maintain a road

养病 yǎng=bìng convalesce；recuperate from illness through rest and medical treatment

养分 yǎngfèn 【名】nutrient

养护 yǎnghù 【动】maintain

养活 yǎnghuo 【动】〈口〉❶ support (family, etc.)：这老头儿有退休金，不靠儿子～。The old man lives on his pension and doesn't rely on his son for support. ❷ give birth to and bring up：他们夫妇～了一儿一女。That couple had a son and a daughter.

养家 yǎng=jiā support the family：～活口 support one's family

养精蓄锐 yǎng jīng xù ruì conserve strength and store up energy

养料 yǎngliào 【名】nourishment

养路费 yǎnglùfèi 【名】road toll

养伤 yǎng=shāng recuperate from one's wound

养神 yǎng=shén rest to attain tranquility；repose

养育 yǎngyù 【动】bring up；foster

养殖 yǎngzhí 【动】breed (aquatics)

养尊处优 yǎng zūn chǔ yōu enjoy a high position and live in ease and comfort：工厂的领导决不能高高在上，～，要与工人同甘共苦。Leaders of the plant must not hold themselves aloof, and indulge in a luxurious life. They should share the comforts and hardships of the workers.

氧 yǎng 【名】oxygen

氧化 yǎnghuà 【动】oxidize

氧化物 yǎnghuàwù 【名】oxide

氧气 yǎngqì 【名】oxygen

痒（癢）yǎng 【动】itch

yàng

样（樣）yàng 【名】❶ (～儿) shape；pattern；form：他的脾气还是那个～。His temper remains unchanged. 这地方一年一个～。This place changes its appearance with each passing year. 你说的那种树是什么～的? What does the kind of tree you mentioned look like? ❷ model；sample：货 ～ sample (goods) 照着～儿画就行了。Just copy the model.【量】❶ sort；kind：三～水果 three kinds of fruit ❷ *similar to* 件，*for* 东西，工作，*etc.*：两～东西 two things

样板 yàngbǎn 【名】❶ template (for cutting metal, wood, etc.) ❷ model；example：树立～ set an example

样本 yàngběn 【名】sample；sample book

样品 yàngpǐn 【名】sample；specimen

样式 yàngshì 【名】style；form；pattern

样子 yàngzi 【名】❶ shape；form；

appearance：这种～的汽车是什么年代的？What year was this type of car made? 从走路的～就可以认出是小林。You can tell it's Xiao Lin by his walk. ❷ facial expression：露出惊讶的～ show surprise ❸ pattern：衣服～ pattern for clothing 鞋～ pattern for shoes ❹ tendency；likelihood 看～工程可能提前完成。It seems that the project can be finished ahead of schedule.

yāo

夭 yāo
夭折 yāozhé 【动】die young

妖 yāo 【名】evil spirit；demon
妖风 yāofēng 【名】〔股 gǔ〕evil wind；evil trend：要刹住赌博的～。We must stop the evil trend of gambling.
妖精 yāojing 【名】spirit；demon
妖魔鬼怪 yāo mó guǐ guài demons and ghosts；all sorts of evildoers
妖娆 yāoráo 【形】〈书〉charming；fascinating

要 yāo
另见 yào
要求 yāoqiú 【动】demand；request；claim：他～换房。He made a request to change his housing. 【名】requirement；request；demand：合乎～ measure up to requirements 向对方提出一个～ make a request of the other party
要挟 yāoxié 【动】coerce；blackmail

腰 yāo 【名】❶ waist ❷ waist band of a pair of trousers
腰包 yāobāo 【名】purse
腰带 yāodài 【名】belt；girdle

邀 yāo 【动】invite
邀集 yāojí 【动】invite to meet together
邀请 yāoqǐng 【动】invite 【名】invitation
邀请赛 yāoqǐngsài 【名】invitational tournament

yáo

窑 yáo 【名】❶ kiln：砖～ brick kiln ❷ small coal mine：煤～ pit of a coal mine
窑洞 yáodòng 【名】〔孔 kǒng〕cave residence；cave dwelling

谣（謠） yáo 【名】◇ ❶ ballad；nursery rhyme ❷ rumour
谣传 yáochuán 【动】it is rumoured that：外边～着一些关于他的事。There is a rumour circulating about him. 【名】rumour；hearsay：别相信～。Don't believe rumours.
谣言 yáoyán 【名】rumour

摇 yáo 【动】shake；rock；wag：～铃 ring a bell ～船 row a boat 风吹得树梢～来～去。The trees swayed to and fro in the wind.
摇摆 yáobǎi 【动】move to and fro；sway；waver；swing：左右～ swing from side to side 杨柳迎风～。Willows swayed in the wind.
摇动 yáodòng 【动】shake；wave；swing
摇滚乐 yáogǔnyuè 【名】rock and roll；rock music
摇晃 yáohuang 【动】sway；shake；rock
摇篮 yáolán 【名】❶ cradle：婴儿在～里睡得很香。The baby is sleeping soundly in the cradle. ❷ place of origin；home：黄河流域是中国古代文化的～。The Yellow River valley is the cradle of ancient Chinese civilization.

摇旗呐喊　yáo qí nàhǎn　(in ancient times) wave flags and shout to support one's troops in war

摇手　yáo = shǒu　shake one's hand showing disapproval

摇头　yáo = tóu　shake one's head

摇尾乞怜　yáo wěi qǐ lián　be ingratiating;fawn on

摇摇晃晃　yáoyáohuànghuàng　【形】 staggering

摇摇欲坠　yáo yáo yù zhuì　be on the verge of collapse;totter

遥　yáo　【形】 far away;remote

遥感　yáogǎn　【动】 remote sensing

遥控　yáokòng　【动】 remote control

遥相呼应　yáo xiāng hūyìng　respond to and cooperate with each other across a great distance

遥遥　yáoyáo　【形】 ❶ faraway;路途～ a long way off 上半场的比赛客队～领先。The visiting team held a safe lead in the first half. 两座高山～相对。Two high mountains stand apart facing each other. ❷ a long time:～无期 not within the foreseeable future

遥远　yáoyuǎn　【形】 faraway;remote

yǎo

杳　yǎo

杳无音信　yǎo wú yīn xìn　has never been heard of since;no news has been received from sb. for a long time

咬　yǎo　【动】 ❶ bite:～了一口面包 take a bite of bread ❷ (of criminal) drag in (innocent people):乱～好人 make random charges against innocent people 反～一口 (of a guilty person) make a false counter-charge against his accuser

❸ ◇ say sth. with certainty:一口～定 put sth. definitely ❹ ◇ pronounce:他～字清楚。He pronounced the words distinctly.

咬文嚼字　yǎo wén jiáo zì　be excessively particular about wording

咬牙切齿　yǎo yá qiè chǐ　clench one's teeth in bitter hatred

舀　yǎo　【动】 ladle

yào

药(藥)　yào　【名】 medicine:这种～效果不错。This medicine is extremely effective. 【动】 poison:老鼠被～死了。The mice were poisoned.

药材　yàocái　【名】 medical herbs

药店　yàodiàn　【名】 chemist's shop;pharmacy;drugstore

药方　yàofāng　【名】 prescription;medical recipe

药房　yàofáng　【名】 pharmacy;drugstore;dispensary

药费　yàofèi　【名】 charges for medicine

药粉　yàofěn　【名】 (medicinal) powder

药膏　yàogāo　【名】 ointment

药剂　yàojì　【名】 drug

药剂师　yàojìshī　【名】 pharmacist

药棉　yàomián　【名】 antiseptic cotton

药片　yàopiàn　【名】 medicinal tablet

药品　yàopǐn　【名】 medicines and chemical reagents

药水　yàoshuǐ　【名】〔瓶 píng〕liquid medicine

药丸　yàowán　【名】(～儿) pill (medicine)

药物　yàowù　【名】 medicaments;medication

药物学　yàowùxué　【名】 pharmacology;materia medica

药效 yàoxiào 【名】 efficacy of a drug

药性 yàoxìng 【名】 property of a medicine

要 yào 【动】❶ want；need：我借给你的那本词典，你现在还～吗？Do you still need the dictionary I lent you? 庄稼正～水，就下了一场透雨。Just when the crops needed water, it rained. ❷ ask（sb.）for（sth.）：你去跟医生～点儿止痛片。Could you please go and ask the doctor for some painkiller? 我们向大地～石油。We get petroleum from the earth. ❸ used in a pivotal sentence want；let：她～我陪你走一趟。She wants me to go with you. 我们～他介绍一下当地的风俗习惯。We asked him to tell us about local customs. 【助动】❶ must；should：我们～努力学习。We must study hard. 一定～提高警惕。We must heighten our vigilance. 路很滑，大家～小心。The road is slippery, be very careful. ❷ indicates certainty：不按照客观规律办事就～受到惩罚。If one acts contrary to objective laws one will be duly punished. 社会总是～前进的。Society will always make progress. ❸ have a desire for：他～学游泳。He wants to learn to swim. 我们～把中国建设成为现代化的国家。We want to build China into a modernized country. ❹ indicates the immediate future, usu. takes 了 at the end of the sentence：天～下雨了。It's going to rain. 船～靠岸了。The boat is going to dock. 明天他～去疗养院了。He is going to a sanatorium tomorrow. ❺ used in a sentence of comparison as an intensive word（can be omitted）：今天～比昨天热。It's hotter today than yesterday. 这样做比那样做～

快。Doing it this way is faster than doing it that way. 【连】同"要是"：你～不愿意，就算了。If you're unwilling, we'll just forget it.
另见 yāo

要案 yào'àn 【名】 important case

要不 yàobù 【连】 usu. in colloquial speech ❶ otherwise：我得赶快把这份电报给他，～该误事了。I must give him this telegram at once, otherwise the matter will be delayed. ❷ or：今天晚上你来找我吧，～，你在家等我也行。Will you please come to my place this evening, or, will you wait for me at your place? 下雨了，你把雨伞拿去吧，～，就穿我的雨衣。It's raining. You'd better use my umbrella, or wear my raincoat. ❸ use 要不 to negate one's original opinion and make a new suggestion：这篇文章得好好改一改，～干脆重写。This article has to be thoroughly revised, or perhaps we'd better rewrite it.

要不得 yàobude 【形】❶ intolerable；not to be put up with：损人利己的行为～。Such selfish behaviour is simply intolerable! 粗枝大叶的作风～。This haphazard attitude to work is impossible! ❷ used as a complement to indicate high degree：这副手套破得～了。This pair of gloves is completely worn out.

要不然 yàoburán 【连】同"要不"，otherwise；or

要不是 yàobushì 【连】 if not for：～坚持锻炼，他的身体不会这么好。If he did not maintain his to exercises, he would not be in such good health. ～你提醒，我早就忘了。I would have forgotten it long ago if you hadn't reminded me. ～你，我就摔倒了。If it hadn't been for you, I would have tripped and fallen.

要道 yàodào 【名】 strategic pass；

thoroughfare

要地　yàodì　【名】important place; strategic position

要点　yàodiǎn　【名】❶ main point; gist：报告～ the gist of the report 社论～ the main points of the editorial ❷ key stronghold：战略～ strategic point

要犯　yàofàn　【名】important criminal

要饭　yào = fàn　beg for food; go begging

要害　yàohài　【名】❶ vital part of the human body; key point; the crux of a matter：咽喉是人体的～部位之一。The throat is one of the vital parts of the human body. 处理问题要抓住～。In solving a problem, one must grasp the key points. ❷ place of military significance

要紧　yàojǐn　【形】important; serious：目前最～的是搞好运输。At the moment the most important thing of all is to improve the transportation system. 他的病～不～? Is his illness serious?

要领　yàolǐng　【名】main point; essentials

要么　yàome　【连】〈口〉or used in offering two or more choices：天已经晚了，你就住在这儿吧，～就赶快回去。It's already very late. You'd better spend the night here, or else go back at once. 我看你～学文学，～学历史，都可以。If you ask my opinion, I would say you could study either literature or history.

要命　yào = mìng　〈口〉❶ fatal; causing death：去年，他得了一场重病，差点儿要了命。Last year, he was seriously ill and almost died. ❷ extremely (usu. as a complement)：热得～ extremely hot 高兴得～ overjoyed ❸ nuisance：这天气真～，忽冷忽热的。What hellish weath-

er! One minute it's cold, the next minute it's hot.

要强　yàoqiáng　【形】be eager to excel; be anxious to outdo others

要人　yàorén　【名】very important person (V.I.P.)

要塞　yàosài　【名】stronghold; fortress; fort

要是　yàoshi　【连】〈口〉同"如果" rúguǒ, if：～你看见他，替我问好。If you see him, give him my regards.

要素　yàosù　【名】vital factor; essential element

要闻　yàowén　【名】important news

钥(鑰)　yào

钥匙　yàoshi　【名】〔把 bǎ〕key

耀　yào

耀武扬威　yào wǔ yáng wēi　make a big show of one's strength and power

耀眼　yàoyǎn　【形】dazzling

yē

椰　yē coconut

椰油　yēyóu　【名】coconut oil

椰子　yēzi　【名】coconut

噎　yē　【动】choke：吃得太快容易～着。If one eats too fast, one is likely to choke.

yé

爷(爺)　yé　【名】◇❶ grandfather ❷ a respectful form of address for elderly men：高～ Grandpa Gao

爷爷　yéyé　【名】❶ grandfather; grandpa (father's father) ❷ a respectful form of address for elderly men

yě

也　yě【副】❶ also *always precedes a verb, an adjective, a preposition or another adverb*：你去我～去。If you go, I'll go too. 操场上有打球的，～有做操的，～有跑步的。There are people playing ball on the playground, also people doing exercises, and still others running. 他～在这个学校学习。He is also studying in this institute. ❷ 同"都" dōu ❺, *but usu. in a negative sentence* ❸ *used after a word or phrase denoting time followed by a negative expression indicating that a certain state of things remains the same after a long time*：她永远～忘不了奶奶的爱抚。She will never forget her grandmother's loving care. 直到昨天～没争论出个结果。Up to yesterday, they hadn't reached any conclusions in their discussions. 这道算术题半天～没算出来。They've been trying for a long time but haven't yet worked out that mathematical problem.

也罢　yěbà【助】❶ *usu. used at the end of a negative sentence to indicate that there is a good reason for not doing sth.*：不去～，那儿没什么好玩儿的。It's just as well we didn't go, that place isn't much fun anyway. ❷ "…也罢…也罢"，同"…也好…也好"，*but not as colloquial*：你说我老也罢，不老也罢，反正我是个突击队员。Whether or not you think I am too old, I'm still on the shock brigade.

…也好，…也好　… yě hǎo，… yě hǎo *cites two or more examples to show that whatever the circumstances may be, the outcome remains the same*：米饭也好，面食也好，我都能吃。I eat either rice or cooked wheaten food. （无论）写信也好，打电话也好，打电报也好，反正你得通知他。You must let him know somehow, whether by letter, by telephone or by telegram. 你听也好，不听也好，反正这个意见我要提。Whether you listen to me or not, I simply have to give you a piece of my mind!

也许　yěxǔ【副】perhaps；maybe：他今天没来，～有什么要紧事。He hasn't turned up today. He might be kept back by something serious. 他～去划船，～去游泳。Perhaps he'll go boating, or he may go swimming. ～他自己会来取票的。Perhaps he'll come over and fetch the ticket himself.

冶　yě【动】◇ smelt
冶金　yějīn【名】metallurgy
冶炼　yěliàn【动】smelt

野　yě【形】❶ rude；rough：性子～ rude nature ❷ unbridled；unrestrained；unruly：心～了 unable to calm down and concentrate 玩～了 have had too much fun and be unable to keep one's mind on one's work
野菜　yěcài【名】edible wild herbs
野餐　yěcān【名】picnic【动】picnic
野地　yědì【名】open country；wilderness
野蛮　yěmán【形】uncivilized；savage；barbarous
野生　yěshēng【形】wild；uncultivated
野兽　yěshòu【名】beast；wild animal
野外　yěwài【名】open field
野心　yěxīn【名】ambition；careerism
野心家　yěxīnjiā【名】careerist
野营　yěyíng【动】camp

野战军 yězhànjūn 【名】field army

yè

业（業） yè 【名】◇ ❶ line of business；walk of life：各行各～都来支援农业。All trades and professions should support agriculture. ❷ occupation；profession：以经商为～ take trading for a living ❸ cause；enterprise：完成建国大～ complete the great cause of the establishment of the state 守～ safeguard the established business

业绩 yèjī 【名】outstanding accomplishment；great achievement

业务 yèwù 【名】vocational work；professional work

业已 yèyǐ 【副】〈书〉already：情况～调查清楚。The situation has already been cleared up through investigation. 准备工作～完成。Preparations have already been finished.

业余 yèyú 【形】❶ spare-time；off-duty hour；after-hours ❷ amateur

业余教育 yèyú jiàoyù spare-time education

业主 yèzhǔ 【名】owner（of an enterprise）；proprietor

叶（葉） yè 【名】◇ leaf：枝～茂盛 with luxuriant foliage

叶公好龙 Yè Gōng hào lóng legend has it that Lord Yeh claimed to be very fond of dragons；but when a real dragon came，he was frightened and escaped；（*fig.*）profess love of sth. while in reality, one does not

叶绿素 yèlǜsù 【名】chlorophyll

叶子 yèzi 【名】leaf

页（頁） yè 【名】page；leaf：单～ single leaf 双～ double leaf ～码错了。The page number is wrong. 【量】page：这本书共多少～? How many pages does this book have?

页码 yèmǎ 【名】page number

夜 yè 【名】night

夜班 yèbān 【名】night shift

夜长梦多 yè cháng mèng duō a long delay means many hitches；there is many a slip between the cup and the lips

夜间 yèjiān 【名】during the night；at night

夜里 yèli 【名】night

夜市 yèshì 【名】night fair；night market

夜晚 yèwǎn 【名】evening；night

夜宵 yèxiāo 【名】midnight snack

夜校 yèxiào .【名】evening school or class

夜以继日 yè yǐ jì rì day and night

夜总会 yèzǒnghuì 【名】night club

液 yè 【名】◇ liquid；fluid：葡萄糖～ dextrose solution

液化 yèhuà 【动】liquefy；liquefaction

液态 yètài 【名】liquid state

液体 yètǐ 【名】liquid；fluid

液压 yèyā 【名】hydraulic pressure

谒（謁） yè

谒见 yèjiàn 【动】call on（a superior or an older person）

腋 yè 【名】armpit

腋下 yèxià 【名】under the armpit

yī

一 yī 【数】❶ one；a：～张桌子 a table 我以前去过～次。I've been there once. ❷ *used with the reduplication of a monosyllabic verb*

without affecting its meaning：等～ 等 wait for a while 看～看 have a look ❸ whole：坐了～屋子人。The whole room was packed with people. 我打了场球，出了～身汗。I played a game of basketball and was sweating all over. 走了～条街，也没找到个照相馆。I walked the whole length of the street but couldn't find a photography shop. ❹ same：你说的跟他说的不是～回事。What you said is not the same as what he said. 军队和老百姓是～家人。The army and the people are like family. ❺ *used with the name of a part of the body or an instrument as an adverbial adjunct to indicate that sth. is accomplished through a swift action*：他～脚把球踢进了球门。With a kick, he sent the ball into the goal. 他～枪就把那只鸟打下来了。He brought down the bird with his first shot. 【副】❶ *used before a verb which is repeated in the following clause to indicate a swift action*：他～猜就猜中了这个谜语。He got the answer to the riddle on his first guess. 他拿笔～勾，勾掉了文章的最后一段。With a stroke of his pen, he deleted the last paragraph of the article. ❷ *used before verbs such as* 看，听，*etc. to indicate that sth. is discovered through a swift action*：早上起来～看，外边雪下得很厚了。When I got up, I looked out and found a thick layer of snow outside. 我～打听，原来他已经搬家了。I made inquiries and found that he had moved.

一败涂地 yī bài tú dì be completely defeated；suffer a thorough defeat

一般 yībān 【形】❶ alike；just like：飞～地跑过去 run fast across 天下乌鸦～黑。All the crows under the sun are equally black. ❷ usual；

normal：铁在～情况下是固体。Iron is solid under normal conditions. 星期六下午我们～没有课。Usually we don't have any classes on Saturday afternoons. ～地说，上海的冬天不算太冷。Generally speaking, winter in Shanghai is not very cold. ❸ ordinary；not outstanding：这个电影很～。This film is really ordinary. ❹ general；universal：做领导工作要注意～号召和个别指导相结合。Leaders should pay attention to matching general appeals with particular directives.

一半 yībàn 【名】（～儿）half：这片地～种玉米，～种高粱。One half of this field will be planted in corn, the other half in sorghum. 这本书我刚看了～。I have just covered half of this book.

一辈子 yībèizi 【名】lifetime；all one's life

一本正经 yī běn zhèng jīng serious；grave；in dead earnest：他做什么事都是～的。Whatever he does, he does it seriously. 看到他那～的样子，大家都笑了。Seeing him in such dead earnestness, everybody laughed.

一笔勾销 yī bǐ gōuxiāo write off at one stroke

一笔抹杀 yī bǐ mǒshā blot out at one stroke；totally negate

一边 yībiān 【名】（～儿）❶ one side：这张纸～有字。There are some words written on one side of this piece of paper. 马路这～是工人新村，那～是绿油油的庄稼。On this side of the road is the workers' residential area；on the other side are green fields. 在那场辩论中，老师站在学生～。The teacher was on the side of his students throughout the debate. ❷ side；aside：大家都在争论，只有他坐在～思索。Everyone was involved in the debate. Only

he was sitting to one side thinking.

一边倒　yī biān dǎo　lean to one side

一边…一边…　yībiān…yībiān…　*indicates two simultaneous actions*：体育老师一边讲解，一边做示范动作。The physical education teacher lectures and demonstrates at the same time.

一并　yībìng　【副】〈书〉together：今天两个文件～传达。The two documents are going to be read out together today. 这几个问题～解决。These problems will be solved together.

一…不…　yī…bù…　❶ *used before two verbs respectively to show that once an action takes place, it is unalterable*：一病不起 fall ill and die 一去不返 gone never to return 一蹶（jué）不振 unable to recover after a setback ❷ *used before a noun and a verb respectively to form an emphatic expression*：一言不发 not say a word 一钱不值 not worth a penny 一字不漏 not miss a word

一不做，二不休　yī bù zuò, èr bù xiū　carry the undertaking through whatever the consequences

一步登天　yī bù dēng tiān　attain the highest level in one step

一步一个脚印儿　yī bù yī ge jiǎoyìnr　every step leaves one footprint；(*fig.*) do things conscientiously：这位老工人工作踏踏实实，～。This old worker works earnestly and seriously.

一刹那　yīchànà　【名】in an instant

一场空　yī chǎng kōng　come to naught；come to nothing：水中捞月～。Like trying to catch the moon in the water, all efforts are in vain. 无根据的幻想总是幻想，到头来只能落得～。A fantasy is always a fantasy. It will come to nothing in the end.

一尘不染　yī chén bù rǎn　not stained with a speck of dust；spotless

一成不变　yī chéng bù biàn　unchangeable；invariable；unalterable

一筹莫展　yī chóu mò zhǎn　be at one's wits' end；have no way out：正在我～的时候，他替我想了个好办法。When I was at my wits' end, he found a way out for me.

一触即发　yī chù jí fā　be on the verge of breaking out

一次性　yīcìxìng　【形】lump sum：～补助 lump sum subsidy ～削价处理 sell at a reduced price

一带　yīdài　【名】area around a certain place (*usu. following a noun of place or used with* 这 *or* 那)：沿海～ all along the coast 中国东北～冬天非常冷。In the northeast of China it is very cold in winter. 这～是海防第一线。This area is the front lines of coastal defence.

一旦　yīdàn　【副】❶ once (*in a conditional clause*)：这个革新项目～成功，就将提高工效十倍。Once this technological innovation is completed, efficiency will be increased tenfold. ❷ when：我们相处多年，～离别，怎么能不想念呢？We've been together for many years, and now that we must part, we will certainly miss each other.

一刀两断　yī dāo liǎng duàn　break with once for all；make a clean break

一刀切　yī dāo qiē　a set pattern：应从实际出发；不搞～。One ought to act according to the actual situation and not to a set pattern.

一道　yīdào　【副】together：～去～来 come and go together 咱们～走吧！Let's go together.

一得之功　yī dé zhī gōng　occasional and small successes：要谦虚谨慎，不要满足于～。Be modest and prudent. Don't be self-congratulatory

as a result of occasional successes.

一点儿 yī diǎnr ❶ a little; some (*used before an uncountable noun*)：喝～水 drink a little water 这种点心很好,你吃～吧! This sort of cake is very good. You should try some. 这样做可以省～时间。Doing it this way will save some time. ❷ *used in conjunction with* 这么 *or* 那么, *to indicate very small in size or number*：仓库那么～,这些东西装得下吗? The warehouse is so small. Can it hold that much? 这么～纸写不了几条标语。You can't write many slogans with so little paper. ❸ *used after an adjective or verb to indicate low degree*：他睡觉了,你说话轻～。He's asleep, please speak softly. 这几天水位降了～。The water level has gone down a little recently.

一定 yīdìng 【形】❶ certain; fairly：他对教育事业做出了～的贡献。He has made certain contributions to the cause of education. 他的发言在～程度上是反映了客观实际的。His speech reflected realities to a certain extent. ❷ necessary; certain：这两个问题没有～的联系。The two questions are not necessarily related to each other. ❸ fixed; definite：学习、工作都有～的时间。There are fixed times for study and work. 报纸、杂志放在～的地方。Newspapers and magazines are kept in designated places. ❹ certain; particular：人类社会发展到了～的历史阶段,就出现了阶级。Classes emerged when human society reached a certain stage of development. 金属加热到～的温度都会熔化。Metals will melt when heated to a certain temperature. 【副】must; certainly; definitely：你～要把四声念准。You must get the four tones right. 你看,这个～就是他想买的小

钟,二十九块钱。Look, this must be the little clock he wants to buy. The price is 29 yuan. 这次春游我～要参加。I'll definitely go on the spring trip.

一度 yīdù 【副】for a time：他～从事经济工作。He worked in the field of economics for a time.

一…二… yī...èr... 一 *and* 二 *are placed respectively in front of the two morphemes of a disyllabic adjective to give emphasis*：一干二净 with nothing left whatsoever 一清二楚 perfectly clear 一清二白 unimpeachable

一发千钧 yī fà qiān jūn 同"千钧一发" qiān jūn yī fà

一帆风顺 yī fān fēng shùn smooth sailing; very smoothly：创业嘛,当然不会是～的。Pioneering in an enterprise is naturally never smooth sailing.

一反常态 yī fǎn cháng tài behave out of character

一方面…一方面… yī fāngmiàn...yī fāngmiàn... ❶ on one hand,... on the other hand...：青年一方面要有虚心学习的态度,一方面也要有大胆创新的精神。On one hand, young people must be modest and willing to learn; on the other hand, they must be bold in trying new things. ❷ 同"一边…一边…"：县政府书记在我们农场一方面参加劳动,一方面进行调查研究。The secretary of our County government is working at our farm and at the same time carrying on an investigation.

一概 yīgài 【副】all; altogether; without exception：对事物要具体分析,不要～肯定或者～否定。We should make a concrete analysis of each problem, and not regard anything as completely positive or completely negative.

一概而论 yīgài ér lùn lump togeth-

er；treat（different things）as if they were the same（*usu. in the negative*）：问题的性质不同,处理方法也不同,不能～。The problems are different in nature, and should be dealt with differently. Don't lump them together.

一个劲儿　yīgejìnr 【副】persistently；keep on：队伍 ～ 地往前赶。The troops kept on marching. 风～地刮。The wind was blowing ceaselessly.

一共　yīgòng 【副】in all；in total；altogether：你们班 ～ 多少人? How many people are there in your class altogether? 他在国外～呆了三个月。He stayed abroad for three months in all.

一股脑儿　yīgǔnǎor 【副】completely；the whole lot：他把心里话～地说了出来。He poured out everything that was on his mind.

一鼓作气　yī gǔ zuò qì （*fig.*）make a vigorous effort to finish something at one go：他们父子俩～把割的麦子都运了回去。Making a great effort, the father and son carried back all the cut wheat.

一贯　yīguàn 【形】consistent；all along；always；as ever：在提升工作人员的时候,我们～重视人的工作态度。In promoting personnel, we always attach importance to their attitude towards work. 我们～反对这种松松散散的工作作风。We have always opposed such a slack style of work.

一国两制　yī guó liǎng zhì one country with two systems

一哄而散　yī hōng ér sàn disperse in a hubbub

一会儿　yīhuìr 【名】in a while；in a moment

一技之长　yī jì zhī cháng proficiency in a particular line；professional skill

一见如故　yī jiàn rú gù feel like old friends at the first meeting

一箭双雕　yī jiàn shuāng diāo kill two birds with one stone

一经　yījīng 【副】as soon as；once...：问题～澄清,误会就消除了。Once that question had been clarified, the misunderstanding was dispelled. 方案～批准,马上便可行动。As soon as the plan is approved, action will be taken immediately.

一…就…　yī..., jiù... ❶ *indicates close succession of two actions*：我不解释了,大家一看就会明白的。I won't explain any more, since you will all understand as soon as you see it. 我一叫他,他就出来了。As soon as I called him, he came out. ❷ *indicates a condition and its result*：一到春天,映山红就开了。When spring comes, the azaleas burst into bloom. 人一老,腿脚就不灵活了。When one gets old, one's limbs get stiff. ❸ *indicates that when an action takes place, it takes place in a high degree, usu. a numeral plus measure word follows* 就：他们对摄影很感兴趣,一谈就谈了一下午。They were very much interested in photography, and once they got started they talked away the whole afternoon. 没想到我们一别就是三年。When we last parted, I didn't expect that we would not see each other again for three years. 这孩子一玩起来就什么都忘了。Once this child starts to play, he forgets everything else.

一举两得　yī jǔ liǎng dé kill two birds with one stone：深耕土地既松土,又灭虫,真是～。Deep ploughing can loosen the soil and kill insects as well. It is killing two birds with one stone.

一孔之见　yī kǒng zhī jiàn view through a peep-hole；（*fig.*）partial, narrow, parochial view：这仅是

~，谈出来供同志们参考。This is just a partial view. I offer it for your reference.

一口气 yī kǒu qì ❶ one breath；喘~ catch one's breath 只要我还有~，就不能坐着吃闲饭。As long as I'm still breathing, I'll never remain idle. ❷ （of doing things） in one breath；at one go；non-stop：~爬上长城 climb up the Great Wall non-stop ~跑了十几里路 run more than ten *li* at one go

一块儿 yīkuàir 【名】 at the same place：水果糖粘在~了。The sweets have stuck together. 【副】together：咱们~去散散步吧！Let's go for a walk together.

一来…二来… yīlái…èrlái… *used to enumerate causes or purposes*：他学习很好，一来是目的明确，二来是方法对头。He is very good at his studies because, in the first place, he has a very definite goal and secondly, his studying methods are very efficient. 今年秋天我要到南方去一趟，一来看看姐姐，二来休息休息。I am to go to the South this autumn. In the first place, I want to see my sister, and besides, I want to have a rest.

一览 yīlǎn 【名】 general survey

一览表 yīlǎnbiǎo 【名】 table；schedule

一揽子 yīlǎnzi 【形】 package；wholesale

一劳永逸 yī láo yǒng yì get sth. done once and for all；solutions that hold good for all time：想一下子把所有问题都彻底解决，可以~，这是不切实际的。It is impractical to attempt to solve all problems once and for all.

一连 yīlián 【副】 in succession；one after another （*must be followed by a numeral*）：他昨天晚上~看了两个电影。He saw two films, one after another, last night. ~下了三天小雨。It drizzled for three successive days.

一连串 yīliánchuàn 【形】 （of actions, things） a series of；a succession of；a string of：~的喜讯 a series of good news ~的问题 a string of problems

一路 yīlù 【名】 ❶ all the way：这~风景很优美。There are beautiful views all the way. ~上经过好几个城市。We have passed through quite a few cities on our journey. ❷ of the same kind：~人 the same sort of people ~货色 one of a kind ❸ （go） the same way：你也去火车站？正好咱们~走。Are you going to the railway station too? Let's go together.

一路平安 yīlù píng'ān a pleasant journey；bon voyage

一路顺风 yīlù shùn fēng 同"一路平安"

一律 yīlù 【形】 uniform；the same （*usu. not used as an attributive*）：文艺创作应该百花齐放，不能强求~。Creation in literature and art should be like a hundred flowers blooming and should not have a rigid conformity imposed on it. 【副】 without exception；all：中国各民族~平等。In China all nationalities without exception are equal. 参加表演的运动员~穿红上衣蓝短裤。The athletes taking part in the demonstration match were all wearing red shirts and blue shorts.

一落千丈 yī luò qiān zhàng （*lit.*） drop 10,000 feet in one fall；（*fig.*） sudden decline；disastrous drop

一马当先 yī mǎ dāng xiān （*fig.*） （of work or sports） take the lead：小白总是~抢挑重担。Xiao Bai always takes the lead and shoulders the heaviest load.

一脉相承 yī mài xiāng chéng （of

thinking, theory, etc.) come down in a continuous line; able to be traced to the same origin; 这两位哲学家的观点是～的。The views of these two philosophers can be traced to the same origin.

一毛不拔 yī máo bù bá extremely stingy

一面…一面… yīmiàn…, yīmiàn… 同 "一边…一边…"

一面之交 yī miàn zhī jiāo be casually acquainted

一鸣惊人 yī míng jīng rén (fig.) amaze the world with a brilliant feat

一模一样 yī mú yī yàng exactly alike; as like as two peas

一目了然 yī mù liǎorán understand fully at a glance

一年半载 yī nián bàn zǎi about a year; a year or so

一年到头 yī nián dào tóu all the year round

一盘散沙 yī pán sǎn shā a heap of loose sand;(fig.) disunited; 球队不能～,否则很难赢球。A team cannot afford to be like loose sand; or it can never win a game.

一旁 yīpáng 【名】side; by the side of

一片 yī piàn ❶ sheet; a sheet of ❷ a stretch of; a vast expanse; everywhere

一瞥 yīpiē 【名】a glimpse; a quick glance

一齐 yīqí 【副】at the same time; all at once; ～站起来 stand up at the same time 各种情景～涌现在眼前。All sorts of scenes flashed before (his) mind's eye.

一起 yīqǐ 【名】❶ at the same place; 我们几个人住在～。We live at the same place. 把你的东西和我们的放在～吧! Please put your things in the same place as ours. ❷ in company; 那六七个人是～的。

Those six or seven people are from the same group. 我们永远和全世界人民团结在～。We are united with the peoples of the whole world. 这种小麦良种是几个科研单位～研究出来的。This improved strain of wheat was developed through the combined efforts of several research institutes. ❸ at the same time; 几门大炮～发射。Several cannons were fired simultaneously.

一气呵成 yīqì hē chéng complete sth. at a stretch;(of writing) a coherent whole; 这个唱段～,刚劲有力。This aria seems to have been written in one burst of inspiration and sounds very powerful.

一窍不通 yī qiào bù tōng be utterly ignorant; know nothing whatever

一切 yīqiè 【代】all; every; everything; 团结～可能团结的力量 be united with every possible force 这～都很明白。It is all very clear. ～文艺作品都应给人以美的享受。All works of literature and art ought to give people a taste of beauty.

一穷二白 yī qióng èr bái poverty and blankness (referring to the backwardness which was the legacy of old China); 彻底改变国家～的面貌 thoroughly change the backwardness, the poverty and blankness of the country

一丘之貉 yī qiū zhī hé birds of a feather; jackals from the same lair (derog.)

一去不复返 yī qù bù fù fǎn once gone, never to return; be gone for good

一日千里 yī rì qiān lǐ thousand li a day; at a tremendous pace

一如既往 yī rú jì wǎng be just as before

一扫而光 yī sǎo ér guāng make a clean sweep of; sweep away com-

pletely in one go：大风把地上的落叶～。The gale swept away all the falllen leaves from the ground. 喜讯传来，心头的烦恼、忧虑～。The good news came，and all worry was swept away from his mind.

一生 yīshēng【名】all one's life；lifetime；in one's whole life

一声不响 yī shēng bù xiǎng keep silent；say not a word；keep one's mouth shut

一时·yīshí【名】momentary；at a given moment；for the time being；for a while

一事无成 yī shì wú chéng nothing accomplished；have achieved nothing

一视同仁 yī shì tóng rén treat equally；treat without discrimination

一手 yīshǒu【副】by oneself；alone：这是我们的技术员～培育的新稻种。This is a new strain of rice which our agronomist has developed all on his own.

一手包办 yīshǒu bāobàn run the whole show

一手遮天 yī shǒu zhē tiān shut out the heavens with one hand；(fig.) hoodwink the public

一丝不苟 yī sī bù gǒu be scrupulous about every detail

一塌糊涂 yī tā hútú be in a complete mess；in an awful state

一天到晚 yī tiān dào wǎn from morning till night；all day long

一条心 yī tiáo xīn be of one mind：军民～。The army and the people are of one mind. 万众～，黄土变成金。If millions are united as one, the mud will turn into gold.

一同 yītóng【副】together；together with

一团和气 yī tuán héqì stay on good terms with everyone at the expense of principle

一团糟 yītuánzāo【形】in a mess；in a chaotic state

一网打尽 yī wǎng dǎ jìn catch the whole lot in a dragnet

一往无前 yī wǎng wú qián press forward with indomitable spirit

一望无际 yī wàng wú jì endless；extend as far as the eye can see：～的大草原 the vast grassland

一味 yīwèi【副】persistently；without stopping to think：～蛮干 be persistently foolhardy ～推托 persistently make excuses 我们不能～追求产品数量而不顾质量。We shouldn't pursue quantity at the expense of quality.

一无是处 yī wú shì chù having nothing worthy of praise；devoid of any merit：不能把他说得～，他还是有优点的。You can't talk about him as if he had no merit at all. Actually, he does have some strong points.

一无所有 yī wú suǒ yǒu have nothing at all；have not a thing to one's name

一五一十 yī wǔ yī shí in full detail with nothing missing：他把事情的经过～地说了一遍。He gave a full account of the whole matter.

一系列 yīxìliè【形】a series of；a train of（events）：提出～问题 put forward a series of questions 采取了～措施 take a series of measures 发生了～的变化。A number of changes have taken place.

一下 yīxià【副】（～儿）all at once；for the moment：路灯～都亮了。The street lamps went on all at once. 他叫什么名字我～想不起来了。I can't think of his name for the moment. 这次出差，到底去不去上海，～还决定不下来。We can't decide for the moment whether or not we'll go to Shanghai on this business trip.

一下 yī xià *used after a verb, having the same function as the reduplication of the verb, i.e. to indicate that the duration of sth. is short, or that one is trying on or trying out sth.*：请你看～这篇稿子有没有不妥的地方。Could you please glance over this manuscript and see if there are any problems? 你穿～，看这件衣服合适不合适。Please try the jacket on and see if it suits you. 我可以替你打听～他的住址。I can go and find out his address for you.

一下子 yīxiàzi 【副】同"一下"【副】

一向 yīxiàng 【名】*used in conjunction with* 这，那，*etc. to indicate a period of time up to the present or a certain period of time in the past*：你这～身体怎么样？How have you been recently? 前～我到外地去了，最近才回来。I have been away for some time and have only just come back. 【副】consistently; all along：他～住在北京。He has been living in Beijing all along. 我～主张大学生的知识面要宽一些。I've always been of the opinion that university students ought to have a wider range of knowledge.

一些 yīxiē 【量】❶ some; a little; a few：我有～书要送给你。I have a few books which I want to give you. 他给了我～鼓励。He's given me some encouragement. ❷ *used after adjectives and certain verbs to indicate low degree*：他的病好了～。He is a little better now. 他比他哥哥胖～。He is somewhat stouter than his brother.

一心 yīxīn 【形】of one mind：全家～。The whole family is of one mind. 【副】heart and soul; wholeheartedly：那位售票员～为乘客。The bus conductor serves passengers wholeheartedly. 这青年～想当

个科学家。This young man longed with all his heart and soul to become a scientist.

一心为公 yīxīn wèi gōng serve the public interest wholeheartedly：～的人是很难得的。People who serve the public interest wholeheartedly are rare.

一星半点 yī xīng bàn diǎn （～儿）a little; a few; a bit of：我们需要大量农药，～的不够用。We need large quantities of insecticide. A little bit is useless.

一行 yīxíng 【名】a group travelling together; party：参观团～十三人已于昨日离京回国。The visiting delegation, consisting of thirteen people, left Beijing for home yesterday.

一言堂 yīyántáng 【名】(*as opp. to* 群言堂) rule by the voice of one man only：要广泛听取大家的意见，不要搞～。One should listen to the differing views of the others. Do not let one person alone have the say.

一言以蔽之 yī yán yǐ bì zhī in a word; in short; in a nutshell

一眼 yīyǎn 【副】❶ as far as the eye can see：那边是～望不到头的竹林。Over there is a bamboo grove stretching as far as the eye can see. ❷ (see sth.) at a glance：他走进玩具店，～就看中了这个小坦克。He entered the toy shop and at first glance fell in love with the small tank.

一样 yīyàng 【形】same; alike：～的性格 same temperament 火～的热情 blazing enthusiasm 团结像像钢铁～ a bond as firm as steel 水平～高 of equal level 这两种颜色完全不～。These two colours are entirely different.

一一 yīyī 【副】one by one：讲解员把展出的产品向观众～作了介绍。The

guide gave the visitors an explanation of the exhibits one by one.

—…—… yī… yī… ❶ used before two nouns of similar meanings to mean "whole": 一心一意 wholehearted 一生一世 whole life ❷ used before two nouns representing two interrelated things to indicate small amount or short duration: 一针一线 a single needle or a tiny piece of thread 一草一木 a blade of grass or a single tree 一言一行 every word or deed 一朝一夕 one morning or one evening ❸ used before two verbs similar in meaning to indicate simultaneous actions: 他的腿坏了，你看他走路一瘸一拐的样子。He has hurt his leg. Look how he is limping along! ❹ used before two verbs opposite in meaning to indicate actions carried on alternately: 奴才和主子一唱一和（hè）。The lackey echoes his boss' every word. 他回一趟家一往一返得四个小时。It takes him four hours to go home and back. ❺ used before two words of locality to indicate that two things or persons were in opposite positions: 一左一右 one on the left and the other on the right 兄弟两个一前一后走进图书馆去了。The two brothers went into the library one after the other. ❻ used before two adjectives opposite in meaning to indicate contrast: 一大一小 one big and the other small 这两张画没挂好，一高一低。The two paintings weren't properly hung; one is higher than the other. ❼ used before two measure words similar in meaning to indicate a very small amount: 积累起一点一滴的经验 accumulate experience bit by bit 一丝一毫 the minutest particle of sth.

一意孤行 yī yì gū xíng be bent on having one's own way (disregarding other people's opinions)

一语道破 yī yǔ dào pò hit upon the truth with one remark

一月 yīyuè 【名】January

一再 yīzài 【副】over and over again: ～请求 make the request time and again 老师傅～嘱咐徒工注意安全。The veteran worker told the apprentice time and again to pay attention to safety. 我们～留他多住几天，可是他不肯。We tried again and again to keep him for a few more days, but to no avail.

一张一弛 yī zhāng yī chí alternately tighten and relax the bow string; (fig.) (in work or in life) be tense and relaxed in turn; alternately work and rest

一针见血 yī zhēn jiàn xiě hit the nail on the head: ～地指出了问题的实质 go straight to the heart of the matter

一阵 yīzhèn 【名】a burst; a gust; a period of time: 风～大，～小。The wind blew hard for a while, and for a while abated. 我在门外等了～，他还不出来。I waited outside the door for some time, but he still didn't come out. 去年她在南京住了～儿。She lived in Nanjing for some time last year. 也作"一阵子"。

一阵子 yīzhènzi 【名】同"一阵"

一整套 yī zhěng tào a complete set of: ～炼油设备 a complete petrol refining installation ～对外国人进行汉语教学的方法 a series of methods of teaching Chinese to foreigners

一知半解 yī zhī bàn jiě scanty knowledge

一直 yīzhí 【副】❶ straight: 汽车～向北开去了。The car drove straight north. 沿着这条公路～走就到了黄村。If you walk straight along this road, you'll get to village Huangcun. 他是先到济南停一下儿，还是～到北京来？Is he going to stop over

at Jinan, or is he coming straight to Beijing? ❷ all along; keep on: 十年来, 他们俩～没有见面, 但书信从未间断. They have not seen each other for ten years, but have never stopped corresponding. 在病中, 鲁迅还～坚持斗争. All during his illness, Lu Xun continued to fight. 下了一夜雨, ～到今天早晨才停. It rained the whole night and did not stop until this morning.

一纸空文　yī zhǐ kōng wén　empty words on a sheet of paper

一致　yīzhì　【形】unanimous; unified; in agreement: 言行～ one's deeds are in accordance with one's words 步调～ act in unison 经过讨论得出～的结论 come to a unanimous conclusion after discussion ～通过 pass (a resolution) unanimously

伊　yī

伊斯兰教　Yīsīlánjiào　【名】Islam

衣　yī　【名】clothes; dress

衣钵　yībō　【名】(of ideology, technology and learning, etc.) mantle; legacy

衣服　yīfu　【名】〔件 jiàn〕clothes; dress

衣柜　yīguì　【名】〔个 gè〕wardrobe

衣架　yījià　【名】〔个 gè〕hanger; clothes stand

衣料　yīliào　【名】dress material

衣裳　yīshang　【名】〔件 jiàn〕〈口〉同"衣服"

衣食住行　yī shí zhù xíng　clothing, food, lodging, and transportation

衣着　yīzhuó　【名】clothing, headgear and footwear

医(醫)　yī　【名】❶ ◇ doctor of medicine: 牙～ dentist 遵～嘱服药 take medicine according to the doctor's instructions ❷ medical

science: 中西～相结合 combine traditional Chinese and Western medicine 我想学～. I want to study medicine. 【动】cure; heal; give medical treatment: 用偏方～好了他的病. His illness was cured by a folk remedy. 头痛～头, 脚痛～脚, 不是解决问题的办法. Treating isolated symptoms is not the way to solve problems.

医疗　yīliáo　【动】medical care; medical treatment

医疗队　yīliáoduì　【名】medical team

医生　yīshēng　【名】doctor; physician; surgeon

医师　yīshī　【名】qualified doctor; practitioner

医士　yīshì　【名】practitioner with secondary medical school education

医术　yīshù　【名】medical skill; art of healing

医务　yīwù　【名】medical matters

医务所　yīwùsuǒ　【名】clinic

医学　yīxué　【名】medical science

医药　yīyào　【名】medicine

医院　yīyuàn　【名】hospital

医治　yīzhì　【动】cure; treat; give medical treatment; heal

医嘱　yīzhǔ　【名】doctor's advice

依　yī　【动】❶ ◇ rely on; depend on; by: ～山傍水 near the mountain and by the river ～此为生 rely on this (a certain skill, profession) to make one's living ❷ obey; be guided; follow: 你的主意好, 就～(着)你. Yours is a good idea. We'll be guided by it. 【介】according to; in the light of: ～我看, 咱们今天就可以动手. In my opinion, we can start today.

依次　yīcì　【副】in order: ～进场 enter the hall in order ～入座 take their seats in order

依存　yīcún　【动】depend upon (sb.

or sth. for existence)

依法 yīfǎ 【副】according to law：～纳税 pay tax according to law ～惩办 punish according to law

依附 yīfù 【动】become an appendage to；attach to；attach oneself to

依旧 yījiù 【形】as before；still：～如此 still as before 山河～。The mountains and rivers remain the same. 尽管职位高了，他～保持着劳动人民的本色。Though his position is higher than before, he still retains the fine qualities of the working people.

依据 yījù 【动】follow：处理问题要～上述规定。Problems should be dealt with according to the above regulations. 【名】basis；proof：以宪法为～ on the basis of the constitution 你说的话有什么～? What grounds do you have for saying this? 岩芯是认识和了解油层的重要～。The core is an important basis for recognizing and understanding the oil layer.

依靠 yīkào 【动】rest on；rely on；depend on：～群众 rely on the masses ～集体力量 rely on collective strength 【名】reliance；dependency：失去～ lose support 没有～的老人，由国家或集体赡养。Old people without support are maintained by the state or the collective.

依赖 yīlài 【动】be solely dependent on；be entirely dependent on：在学习上不能～别人。One must not be dependent on others in one's studies.

依然 yīrán 【副】still；as before；yet：～如故 just as before 这位老人的身体～很健壮。This old man is still very healthy.

依依不舍 yīyī bù shě unwilling to part with；reluctant to part from

依照 yīzhào 【介】according to；in the light of：～上级的指示办 act according to instructions from one's superior ～图纸加工零件 make the parts according to the blue-print

壹 yī 【数】one (*the complicated form of* "一")见"捌" bā

yí

仪(儀) yí

仪表 yíbiǎo 【名】❶ appearance (usu. good manners, bearing, etc.)：～堂堂 handsome and dignified ～非凡 very distinguished looking ❷ meter

仪器 yíqì 【名】instrument；apparatus

仪容 yíróng 【名】looks；appearance；deportment

仪式 yíshì 【名】ceremony；rite

仪仗队 yízhàngduì 【名】guard of honour

姨 yí 【名】❶ maternal aunt ❷ wife's sister

姨父 yífu 【名】maternal aunt's husband

姨母 yímǔ 【名】maternal aunt

移 yí 【动】❶ move；remove：把柜子～一下 move the cupboard a bit 这株花的盆儿太小了，～到一个大点儿的花盆里去吧。The pot of this plant is too small, so let's transplant it to a bigger pot. ❷ ◇ change：艰苦奋斗志不～ struggle arduously with unwavering determination

移动 yídòng 【动】move；shift

移动电话 yídòng diànhuà cellular telephone

移风易俗 yí fēng yì sú change existing habits and customs；transform established traditions and practices

移交 yíjiāo 【动】❶ turn over；pass

on：这件事～宣传部门处理。This matter should be turned over to the propaganda department. ❷ hand over one's work to one's successor：办～手续 go through a transfer procedure 他临走前把工作～给我了。He had handed over his work to me before he left.

移民　yímín　【名】immigrant；emigrant

移民　yí＝mín　immigrate；emigrate

移山倒海　yí shān dǎo hǎi　remove mountains and drain seas；(*fig.*) transform nature

移植　yízhí　【动】❶ transplant：把苗床里的幼苗～到地里 transplant young seedlings from the seed bed to the fields ❷ graft：表皮～ skin grafting

胰 yí

胰岛素　yídǎosù　【名】insulin

胰腺　yíxiàn　【名】pancreas

遗(遺) yí

遗产　yíchǎn　【名】heritage；inheritance；legacy

遗臭万年　yí chòu wàn nián　leave a bad name for thousands of years；everlasting shame

遗传　yíchuán　【动】be heriditary；inheritance

遗憾　yíhàn　【形】regretful；regrettable：这次没能去南方参观,真～。It is a pity that I was not able to make that visit to the South. 对你方采取的这一行动,我们表示～。We find the action taken by your side regrettable.

遗恨　yíhèn　【名】eternal regret；irremediable regret

遗迹　yíjì　【名】vestige；traces

遗留　yíliú　【动】leave；leave behind；hand down

遗漏　yílòu　【动】miss；leave out

遗弃　yíqì　【动】desert；abandon

遗容　yíróng　【名】❶ portrait of a respectable dead person ❷ remains (of the deceased)

遗失　yíshī　【动】lose

遗书　yíshū　【名】❶ posthumous writings (often used for book titles) ❷ letter written by one immediately before death

遗属　yíshǔ　【名】the bereaved

遗孀　yíshuāng　【名】widow

遗体　yítǐ　【名】remains (of the dead)

遗忘　yíwàng　【动】forget

遗物　yíwù　【名】things left behind by the deceased

遗像　yíxiàng　【名】portrait of deceased

遗言　yíyán　【名】words left by the deceased

遗愿　yíyuàn　【名】unfulfilled wish of the deceased

遗址　yízhǐ　【名】historic site；site

遗志　yízhì　【名】unfulfilled wish

遗嘱　yízhǔ　【名】will；dying words

遗著　yízhù　【名】posthumous work

疑 yí

疑案　yí'àn　【名】disputed case at court；open question

疑惑　yíhuò　【动】have doubts；feel uncertain

疑虑　yílǜ　【名】doubt；misgivings：这件事使我产生了不少～。This matter aroused many misgivings in me.

疑难　yínán　【形】disputed and difficult；knotty

疑团　yítuán　【名】doubts and suspicions

疑问　yíwèn　【名】problem；question；doubt

疑问句　yíwènjù　【名】interrogative sentence

疑心　yíxīn　【动】doubt；suspect：我～他是认错了人。I suspect that he mistook me for someone else. 【名】

doubt；suspicion：起了～ become suspicious

疑义　yíyì　【名】doubt；doubtful point（*usu. in the negative*）

yǐ

乙　yǐ　【名】*used to represent "second" according to old Chinese tradition*：～级 second grade

已　yǐ　【副】already（*usu. in written language*）：中国～和一百多个国家建立了外交关系。China has already established diplomatic relations with more than one hundred countries.

已经　yǐjīng　【副】already：桃花～开了。The peach trees have already blossomed. ～七点多了，该走啦！It's already past seven o'clock. It's time we went.

已知数　yǐzhīshù　【名】known number

以　yǐ　【介】*forms a P-O construction used as an adverbial adjunct*（*usu. in written language*）❶ with：～少胜多 defeat a large force with a small one ～家长的身份参加会议 attend the meeting as his child's guardian 工人们～优质高产的新成绩迎接国庆。The workers greeted National Day by achieving better quality and higher production. ❷ according to：～人口计算 calculate according to population ❸ *indicates the cause of sth.*：不～人废言 not reject a saying because of who the speaker is 我们～生活在新中国而自豪。We are proud of being citizens of new China. 【连】*connects the two parts of a sentence，indicating the purpose of sth.*：使家务劳动社会化～减轻职工的

负担 reduce the burden of wage-earners by socializing housework 青年人应该努力学习，～适应现代化的速度。Young people should study hard to meet the pace of modernization.

以便　yǐbiàn　【连】*indicates the purpose of sth.*（*usu. in written language*）：希望读者多提意见。～我们再版时修改。We hope our readers will let us know their opinions so that we can revise our second edition accordingly. 老干部撰写回忆录，～教育后代。Some veterans are writing their memoirs to educate younger generations.

以点带面　yǐ diǎn dài miàn　use the experience gained from selected units to promote the work in the entire area

以攻为守　yǐ gōng wéi shǒu　use attack as a means of defence；attack in order to defend

以后　yǐhòu　【名】after；later on；afterwards：秦朝～，长城又进行过多次修整。After the Qin dynasty, the Great Wall was repaired many times. ～，希望你常来。In future, I hope you'll drop in often.

以及　yǐjí　【连】and（*usu. in written language*）*does not connect monosyllabic words or clauses；the more important persons or things come before* 以及：出席招待会的有各国代表团团长～部分团员和工作人员。Those present at the reception were the heads of the delegations from various countries and some of the delegates and working personnel. 医院的领导、大夫～其他工作人员都很关心我的病。The leadership, doctors and other staff members in the hospital have all shown great concern over my illness.

…以来　…yǐlái　❶ since *used after a phrase denoting a specific time to*

indicate the time elapsed between that time and the present：开学～ since school started；since the beginning of the term 他到北京～已经交了不少朋友。He's made quite a number of friends since he came to Beijing. ❷ *used to indicate that a period of time is counted back from the present*：三 年 ～ in the past three years 老李长期～因病休养，最近要恢复工作了。Lao Li has been convalescing for a long time but is going back to work soon.

以理服人 yǐ lǐ fú rén　persuade through reasoning；convince people by reasoning

以邻为壑 yǐ lín wéi hè　use one's neighbour's field as a drainage ditch；(*fig.*) shift troubles to others

以卵击石 yǐ luǎn jī shí　(*lit.*) throw an egg against a rock；(*fig.*) court defeat by fighting against overwhelming odds 也作"以卵投石"。

以免 yǐmiǎn　【连】*so that used at the beginning of the main clause to indicate that what follows can be avoided if what goes before is achieved*：改变计划的原因要解释清楚，～引起误解。You must explain clearly why the plan was changed so as to avoid misunderstanding. 仓库附近要严禁烟火，～发生火灾。Smoking or lighting fires is strictly forbidden in the vicinity of the storehouse to prevent fire.

以内 yǐnèi　【名】within；within the limits of；including：方圆百里～都属于这个牧场。The surrounding area for one hundred *li* is all part of this pasture. 这是你权限～的事情，不必请示。This is a matter within your jurisdiction. It's not necessary to ask for instructions. 这种药三年～有效。This medicine is effective if used within three years.

以前 yǐqián　【名】before；ago；previously：两千多年～，中国的丝绸就已运往国外。More than two thousand years ago, Chinese silk began to be transported abroad. ～，我没来过这里。I haven't been here before. 明天下午两点～我给你打电话。I'll phone you tomorrow afternoon before two o'clock.

以上 yǐshàng　【名】❶ above；over：三楼～是办公室。The second floor and above are offices. 小学三年级～的学生可以上计算机课。Pupils in the third year and above can take computer lessons. 这片玉米估计亩产能达到八百斤～。The yield of this corn field is estimated at over eight hundred *jin* per *mu*. ❷ previously；above-mentioned：～讲的是有关工作程序的问题。What I've just said concerns procedures to be followed during the operation.

以身试法 yǐ shēn shì fǎ　defy the law

以身殉职 yǐ shēn xùn zhí　die a martyr at one's post

以身作则 yǐ shēn zuò zé　set an example with one's own conduct：干部处处要～。Cadres should, by their own conduct, set an example in whatever they do.

以外 yǐwài　【名】outside；beyond：八小时～ outside of one's eight (working) hours 篮球场～ outside the basketball court 千里～ beyond one thousand *li* 除此～ except for this

以往 yǐwǎng　【名】past；previously：如今不比～了，不少山区也通了电话了。Quite a few mountainous areas are now equipped with telephones, which is a great change as compared with the past. ～的盐碱滩改造成了稻田。The alkaline soil of the past has been transformed into paddy fields.

以为 yǐwéi　【动】❶ consider；think；

我～这首诗写得很动人。I think that this poem is very moving. ❷ think (wrongly)：我～他还不知道这件事，其实他早知道了。I thought he didn't know about this matter yet. Actually he knew it long ago.

以…为… yǐ...wéi... ❶ consider sth. to be；regard sth. as：以说假话为耻 consider telling lies shameful 我们的医疗卫生工作以预防为主。Our medical work puts prevention first. ❷ used to indicate that sth. is the most outstanding of its kind：北京的公园以颐和园为最大。The Summer Palace is the biggest park in Beijing. 世界上的山峰以珠穆朗玛峰为最高。Mount Quomolangma is the highest peak in the world.

以下 yǐxià 【名】❶ below；underneath；under：这里地面五十米～是岩石。You'll find rocks here fifty metres below the surface of the earth. 我们班同学都在二十岁～。The students in our class are all under 20 years old. ❷ the following：这篇论文的要点可以归纳为～几点。The key points of this thesis can be summarized as follows.

以眼还眼，以牙还牙 yǐ yǎn huán yǎn, yǐ yá huán yá an eye for an eye, a tooth for a tooth

以一当十 yǐ yī dāng shí pit one against ten

以逸待劳 yǐ yì dài láo wait at one's ease for the fatigued enemy

以至 yǐzhì 【连】❶ down to；up to；to such an extent that：我们的经济计划,既要考虑到今年,也要考虑到明年～更远的将来。In our economic planning, we must take into account this year, next year and even the more distant future. 我们参加了种茶、采茶～茶叶加工的全过程。We've taken part in the planting, the picking and even the curing of tea, that is, the whole process of tea production. ❷ used at the beginning of the main clause to indicate a result which illustrates the degree of what has preceded it：他学习非常专心,～有人进来他都不知道。He was so absorbed in his studies that he was not even aware that somebody had come into the room. 他的干劲儿足,～有时连吃饭都忘了。He was so enthusiastic about his work that sometimes he even forgot to eat. 也说"以至于"。

以致 yǐzhì 【连】used at the beginning of the main clause describing a disagreeable result：这场雪太大了,～交通都受到了影响。The snowfall was exceptionally heavy and traffic was held up. 他老躺着看书,～眼睛近视了。Because he always read lying down, he became near-sighted.

迤 yǐ

迤逦 yǐlǐ 【形】winding in a zigzag course；meandering

倚 yǐ 【动】

❶ lean on；lean against：～着门站在那里 stand there leaning against the door ❷ rely on：～势欺人 abuse one's power and bully others

倚靠 yǐkào 【动】depend on；rely on

倚赖 yǐlài 【动】rely on；be dependent on

倚仗 yǐzhàng 【动】rely on；count on

椅 yǐ 【名】◇ chair

椅子 yǐzi 【名】〔把 bǎ〕chair

yì

亿（億） yì 【数】hundred mil-

lion

亿万 yìwàn 【数】hundreds of millions

义（義）yì 【形】◇ just 【名】
◇ ❶ justice：深明大～ have a strong sense of justice ❷ meaning：一词多～ one word which has several meanings

义不容辞 yì bù róng cí be incumbent on；be duty bound：援助灾区人民是我们～的责任。It is incumbent upon us to support victims of a natural calamity.

义愤 yìfèn 【名】righteous indignation

义愤填膺 yìfèn tián yīng be filled with rightful indignation：看到侵略者的残暴行为，战士们个个～。On seeing the atrocities committed by the aggressors, every soldier was filled with rightful indignation.

义务 yìwù 【名】❶ duty；obligation ❷ voluntary service

义务兵役制 yìwù bīngyìzhì compulsory military service

义务教育 yìwù jiàoyù compulsory education

义务劳动 yìwù láodòng voluntary labour

义演 yìyǎn 【动】benefit performance

义诊 yìzhěn 【动】free medical care：大夫为孤寡老人～。The doctor gives the old widows and widowers free medical care.

义正词严 yì zhèng cí yán speak sternly and with justice：～地痛斥了那种谣言 denounce the rumour forcefully

艺（藝）yì
艺人 yìrén 【名】professional player（artist, acrobat, etc.）

艺术 yìshù 【名】❶ art：伟大的～作品 great work of art ❷ skill：领导

～ the art of leadership 斗争～ the art of struggle

艺术标准 yìshù biāozhǔn artistic criteria

艺术家 yìshùjiā 【名】artist

艺术品 yìshùpǐn 【名】work of art

艺术体操 yìshù tǐcāo rhythmic gymnastics

艺术性 yìshùxìng 【名】artistic quality；artistry

忆（憶）yì 【动】◇ recall；think over
忆想 yìxiǎng 【动】think back；recollect

议（議）yì 【动】discuss
议案 yì'àn 【名】bill；proposal

议程 yìchéng 【名】agenda

议定书 yìdìngshū 【名】protocol

议会 yìhuì 【名】parliament

议价 yìjià 【名】negotiated price：大米的价格高于平价大米。The price of rice of a negotiated price is higher than that of rice at par.

议论 yìlùn 【动】talk；comment；discuss：关于植树造林问题，大家～了半天。People talked for a long time about afforestation. 【名】discussion；comment：不负责任地乱发～ make irresponsible comments 他的作法引起了大家不少～。His behavior caused much talk.

议题 yìtí 【名】subject of discussion

议员 yìyuán 【名】member of a legislative assembly

屹 yì
屹立 yìlì 【动】stand rockfirm；stand firmly；stand mighty

亦 yì 【副】〈书〉as well as；also；too：反之～然 and vice versa 这样处理～无不可。It is also quite all right to deal with it in this way.

亦步亦趋 yì bù yì qū blindly follow

suit

异 yì 【形】◇ ❶ different；求大同存小~ seek common ground on major questions while reserving differences on minor ones ❷ extraordinary；exotic；~香扑鼻。An exotic fragrance assailed the nostrils.

异彩 yìcǎi 【名】radiant splendour；大放 ~ exuding extraordinary splendour

异常 yìcháng 【形】unusual；abnormal；extraordinary；表现~ behave abnormally 神色~ an unusual expression ~现象 an extraordinary phenomenon 【副】extremely；particularly；~激动 extremely excited ~复杂 extremely complicated

异乎寻常 yì hū xúncháng extraordinary；unusual

异化 yìhuà 【动】alienate；dissimilate

异己 yìjǐ 【名】not of one's kind；alien

异口同声 yì kǒu tóng shēng cry out in one voice；with one voice

异曲同工 yì qǔ tóng gōng different tunes rendered with equal skill；different approach but equally satisfactory in result 也作"同工异曲"

异体字 yìtǐzì 【名】a variant form of a Chinese character；"仝"是"同"的~。"仝" is a variant of the character "同".

异想天开 yì xiǎng tiān kāi indulge in absurd fantasies；到月球上去，过去认为是~的事，现在已变为现实。Going to the Moon which was once considered fantastic has now become a reality.

异性 yìxìng 【名】opposite sex

异样 yìyàng 【形】unusual；~的感觉 unusual feeling 她神色有些~，不知出了什么事。She looks a little strange. I wonder what happened.

异议 yìyì 【名】disagreement；objection；dissension

抑 yì

抑扬顿挫 yì yáng dùn cuò cadence；rising and falling rhythmically；modulated；他的朗诵~，富有感情。His recitation was cadenced and rich in feeling.

抑止 yìzhǐ 【动】restrain；control

抑制 yìzhì 【动】restrain；repress

呓(囈) yì

呓语 yìyǔ 【名】nonsensical talk；ravings

译(譯) yì 【动】translate；interpret

译本 yìběn 【名】translation

译电员 yìdiànyuán 【名】decoder；code clerk

译文 yìwén 【名】translation

译音 yìyīn 【名】transliteration

译员 yìyuán 【名】interpreter (profession)

译者 yìzhě 【名】translator

译制 yìzhì 【动】dub；这部美国电影是长春电影制片厂~的。This American film was dubbed by the Changchun Film Studio.

易 yì 【形】◇ easy；simple；来之不~ hard-won 简便~行 a simple and practical method 【动】◇ ❶ change；transform；~地疗养 go to another place to convalesce ❷ exchange；以物~物 barter one thing for another

易燃 yìrán 【形】inflammable；combustible

易燃品 yìránpǐn 【名】anything inflammable

易如反掌 yì rú fǎn zhǎng as easy as turning one's palm

易于 yìyú 【动】be easy to；be prone to；be apt to；~识别 be easy to dis-

tinguish (from sth. else) ～掌握 be easy to master

疫 yì

疫苗 yìmiáo 【名】vaccine

疫情 yìqíng 【名】information about a plague; epidemic situation

益 yì 【名】◇ benefit; profit; advantage: 得～不浅 benefit greatly

益虫 yìchóng 【名】beneficial insect

益处 yìchu 【名】benefit; advantage

益鸟 yìniǎo 【名】beneficial bird

意 yì 【名】◇ opinion; idea: 说明来～ explain what one came for 词不达～。The words used did not communicate the idea. 他这样做,不知何～。What did he mean by doing that?

意见 yìjiàn 【名】❶ opinion; view: 这是我个人的～。This is my personal opinion. 对这件事你有什么～? What is your view on this matter? ❷ objection; dissatisfaction: 大家对他的作风都很有～。People around him were dissatisfied with his behavior.

意见簿 yìjiànbù 【名】visitor's book

意见箱 yìjiànxiāng 【名】suggestion box

意境 yìjìng 【名】(of artistic and literary works) conception

意料 yìliào 【动】expect: 这本是～中的事 This is only what is to be expected.

意念 yìniàn 【名】thought; idea; concept

意气 yìqì 【名】❶ spirit; enthusiasm: ～高昂 in high spirits ❷ personal feelings: ～用事 be swayed by personal feelings

意气风发 yìqì fēngfā high-spirited and vigorous: 刚毕业的大学生～地来到各自的工作岗位上。The new university graduates have arrived at their respective posts in high spirits and full of vigor.

意识 yìshí 【名】consciousness; ideology; outlook: 社会存在决定人们的～。Man's social existence determines his consciousness. 【动】be conscious of; be aware of (often used with 到): 他～到问题的严重性 He was aware of the seriousness of the matter.

意识形态 yìshí xíngtài ideology; ideological form

意思 yìsi 【名】❶ meaning; sense: 文章的中心～ the central ideas of an article 请讲讲这个词的～。Please explain the meaning of this word. ❷ opinion: 他的话表达了我们的～。What he said expressed our sentiments. 我的～是坐汽车去。I think that we should take a bus. ❸ touch; hint; sign: 这几天真有点儿秋天的～。We had a touch of autumn weather these last few days. ❹ interest; fun: 这种游戏～不大。This game is not very interesting.

意图 yìtú 【名】intention; purpose

意外 yìwài 【形】beyond expectations; unexpected: 这～的消息使他很惊讶。The unexpected news shocked him. 这件事使我感到～。This matter took me by surprise. 【名】accident: 孩子们去游泳,要进行安全教育,以防发生～。Before children go swimming, they should be taught about safety in order to prevent accidents.

意味 yìwèi 【名】❶ implication; meaning; significance: 他这话可～深长啊! How meaningful his remarks were! ❷ flavour; interest: ～无穷 full of flavour 他的话里含有讽刺。There was a touch of sarcasm in his remark.

意味着 yìwèizhe 【动】imply; signify; mean: 商品销售额的增加～人民

购买力提高了。An increase in the sale of commodities means an increase in people's purchasing power.

意向　yìxiàng　【名】intention

意向书　yìxiàngshū　【名】letter of intent：签订～ sign a letter of intent

意义　yìyì　【名】❶ meaning；sense：这两个词读音相同，但～不同。These two words have the same pronunciation, but different meanings. ❷ significance：教育～ significant in that it is instructive ～深远 far-reaching significance 人固有一死，但死的～有不同。All men must die, but death can vary in its significance.

意译　yìyì　【动】❶ paraphrase；free translation；liberal translation (*as opp. to* 直译) ❷ translation of foreign words based on meaning (*as opp. to* 音译)

意愿　yìyuàn　【名】wish；desire；aspiration

意志　yìzhì　【名】will

肄　yì

肄业　yìyè　【动】study (referring to students studying in school or who have left school before graduation)

溢　yì

溢　yì　【动】◇ overflow：河水～出河堤。The river overflowed its banks.

毅　yì

毅力　yìlì　【名】fortitude；will power

毅然　yìrán　【副】determinedly；resolutely：他不顾重重困难，～接受了那个艰巨的任务。Braving all difficulties, he took on the job with determination.

臆　yì

臆测　yìcè　【动】conjecture；make

baseless assumption

臆断　yìduàn　【动】make arbitrary decision；make groundless conclusion

臆造　yìzào　【动】concoct

翼　yì　【名】❶ (of bird) wing ❷ (of plane or glider) wing

yīn

因　yīn　【名】◇ cause：前～后果 cause and effect 远～ remote cause 近～ immediate cause 事出有～。It must have a cause. 【连】because (*usu. in written language*)：～一事请假 ask for time off to attend to some personal business ～公外出 make a business trip ～故改期。For some reason or other the matter has been postponed.

因材施教　yīn cái shī jiào　teach students in accordance with their aptitude

因此　yīncǐ　【连】so；therefore *usu. not used in conjunction with* 因为：他事先做了许多调查研究，～得出了正确的结论。He made a thorough investigation in advance so he came to the correct conclusion.

因地制宜　yīn dì zhì yí　adapt measures to local conditions；do what local circumstances dictate：农作物的种植要～。The crops planted should be suited to local conditions.

因而　yīn'ér　【连】thus；as a result：我们的事业是正义的，～我们是不可战胜的。Our cause is just, hence we are invincible.

因果　yīnguǒ　【名】the causes and effects

因陋就简　yīn lòu jiù jiǎn　make use of existing conditions and use economical methods：这山村的小水电

站是当地人～用土法建成的。This small hydro-electric power station was built by the local people, using economical and indigenous methods suited to the existing conditions.

因式 yīnshì 【名】(maths.) factor

因式分解 yīnshì fēnjiě factoring; resolution into factors

因势利导 yīn shì lì dǎo adroitly guide sth. in the light of its general tendency; guide sth. along its natural and inevitable course of development; 每个孩子都有各自的长处, 要一发挥他们的才能。Every child has his individual strong points, and we must guide him in such a way as to let him develop his talents.

因素 yīnsù 【名】factor; element

因为 yīnwei 【连】because; on account of; for: ～有了乡村医生, 村民看病一般就不用出村了。Now that there are rural doctors, the villagers don't have to leave the village for medical care. 我得打电报,～写信来不及。I must send a telegram, because there isn't time for a letter. ～他课讲得好, 所以学生爱上他的课。Since he lectures very well, the students like to attend his classes. Note: *if two clauses share a common subject and* 因为 *occurs in the first clause, it can either precede or follow the subject*: ～我刚来北京, 所以对北京的街道还不熟悉。(Since I've just arrived in Beijing and don't know my way around town). or 我～刚来北京, 对北京的街道还不熟悉。

因为…的关系 yīnwei … de guānxì on account of; because of: 因为时间的关系, 他昨天晚上就演奏了一个曲子。Because there wasn't time last night, he played only one piece. 因为天气的关系, 班机推迟起飞一小时。The scheduled flight was postponed for an hour on account of bad weather.

因袭 yīnxí 【动】inherit; follow (the old rules)

因循守旧 yīn xún shǒu jiù follow the beaten track; remain in the old rut

因噎废食 yīn yē fèi shí give up eating for fear of choking; (*fig.*) be put off easily by a slight risk

因由 yīnyóu 【名】cause; reason; origin

阴(陰) yīn 【形】❶ cloudy; overcast: 天～了。It is getting overcast. ❷ hidden secret: ～沟 sewer ❸ insidious; sinister: 这个人～得很。This person is very sinister. 【名】shady place: 山的一面永远不见阳光。The north side of the hill never sees the sun.

阴暗 yīn'àn 【形】dark; gloomy; dim

阴电 yīndiàn 【名】nagative electricity

阴极 yīnjí 【名】cathode; negative pole

阴历 yīnlì 【名】(the Chinese) lunar calendar; lunar year

阴凉 yīnliáng 【形】cool and shady

阴面 yīnmiàn 【名】the shady side; a shady place

阴谋 yīnmóu 【名】conspiracy; plot 【动】conspire; plot; intrigue against: ～夺权 conspire to seize power ～进行破坏 plot to commit an act of sabotage

阴谋家 yīnmóujiā 【名】conspirator; plotter; schemer

阴平 yīnpíng 【名】the even tone or the first tone (of Chinese characters)

阴森 yīnsēn 【形】gruesome; ghastly

阴山背后 xīn shān bèi hòu a remote and desolate place

阴天 yīntiān 【名】overcast sky;

cloudy sky

阴险 yīnxiǎn 【形】insidious；sinister；vicious；malicious

阴性 yīnxìng 【名】❶（med.）negative：～反应 negative reaction ❷（gram.）feminine gender：有的语言名词有～和阳性的区别。In some languages nouns are distinguished by masculine or feminine.

阴影 yīnyǐng 【名】shadow

阴云 yīnyún 【名】dark clouds

荫（蔭）yīn

荫蔽 yīnbì 【动】be shaded by foliage：伐木工的小屋～在森林中。The woodcutters' huts were hidden in the forest.

音 yīn 【名】❶ sound；voice：这个～他没发准。He didn't pronounce this sound correctly. ❷ ◇ news；tidings：佳～ good tidings 望早日回～。An early reply would be highly appreciated.

音标 yīnbiāo 【名】phonetic alphabet；phonetic symbol

音调 yīndiào 【名】tone

音符 yīnfú 【名】note

音节 yīnjié 【名】syllable

音量 yīnliàng 【名】volume of sound

音容 yīnróng 【名】voice and countenance

音色 yīnsè 【名】timbre

音素 yīnsù 【名】allophone；phoneme

音位 yīnwèi 【名】phoneme

音位学 yīnwèixué 【名】〔门 mén〕phonemics

音响 yīnxiǎng 【名】❶ sound ❷ hi-fi

音像 yīnxiàng 【名】audiovisual

音信 yīnxìn 【名】news；tidings

音译 yīnyì 【动】transliterate；transliteration

音域 yīnyù 【名】range（of one's voice）

音乐 yīnyuè 【名】music

音乐会 yīnyuèhuì 【名】concert

音乐家 yīnyuèjiā 【名】musician

音韵学 yīnyùnxué 【名】phonology（science of speech sounds）

音值 yīnzhí 【名】（linguistics）value

殷 yīn

殷切 yīnqiè 【形】earnest；sincere；ardent

殷勤 yīnqín 【形】attentive；solicitous；obliging

yín

银（銀）yín 【名】silver

银白 yínbái 【形】silvery；colour of silver

银行 yínháng 【名】bank

银河 yínhé 【名】the Milky Way

银灰 yínhuī 【形】silvery grey

银幕 yínmù 【名】screen for cinema films

银牌 yínpái 【名】〔枚 méi〕silver medal

银子 yínzi 【名】silver

yǐn

引 yǐn 【动】❶ lead；guide：～路 lead the way ～水上山 draw water up the hill ❷ lure；attract：～蛇出洞 lure the snake out of its hole 一席话～出了他一番议论。The remarks led to his making lots of comments. ❸ quote；cite：～以为荣 consider sth. to be an honour 文章开头～了一段古人的话。The article begins by quoting an ancient saying. ❹ ◇ cause：他这句话～得大家都笑了。His remark made everyone laugh.

引导 yǐndǎo 【动】lead；conduct

引而不发 yǐn ér bù fā draw the bow without shooting; (*fig.*) be good at guiding sb. while allowing him to make his own decisions

引号 yǐnhào 【名】quotation mark

引进 yǐnjìn 【动】introduce (sth. new from outside): ～先进技术 introduce advanced techniques

引经据典 yǐn jīng jù diǎn quote from classical works; quote authoritative works

引狼入室 yǐn láng rù·shì bring a wolf into the house; (*fig.*) invite a dangerous foe into one's house

引力 yǐnlì 【名】同"万有引力" wànyǒu yǐnlì

引路 yǐn=lù lead the way

引起 yǐnqǐ 【动】arouse; give rise to; cause: ～注意 arouse attention ～深思 give rise to deep thought 这次争论是他～的。He had sparked off this argument.

引桥 yǐnqiáo 【名】approach span of a bridge

引人入胜 yǐn rén rù shèng attractive; fascinating; absorbing

引人注目 yǐn rén zhùmù attract one's attention; draw one's attention; conspicuous

引申 yǐnshēn 【动】(of meaning of a word) extend: "纲"的原义是提网的总绳，～义是指事物的主要部分。The literal meaning of "纲" is "the main ropes of a net"; its extended meaning is "the key link of a thing".

引文 yǐnwén 【名】quotation

引言 yǐnyán 【名】introduction; preface

引以为戒 yǐn yǐ wéi jiè take warning; serve as a warning

引用 yǐnyòng 【动】quote; cite

引诱 yǐnyòu 【动】lure; tempt; allure

引证 yǐnzhèng 【动】quote from; cite

引子 yǐnzi 【名】❶ prelude; short introduction to (music, novel, drama, etc.) ❷ introductory remarks ❸ (of Chinese traditional medicine) ancillary medicinal substances such as wine, ginger, etc.

饮(飲) yǐn 【动】〈书〉drink (e.g. water)
另见 yìn

饮料 yǐnliào 【名】beverage

饮食 yǐnshí 【名】food and drink; eating and drinking

饮水思源 yǐn shuǐ sī yuán when drinking water, one thinks of its source; (*fig.*) when happy, one must not forget the source of the happiness

饮鸩止渴 yǐn zhèn zhǐ kě quench one's thirst with poisoned wine; (*fig.*) temporary solution which results in disaster; use an undesirable method to solve a problem, ignoring possible disastrous consequences

隐(隱) yǐn

隐蔽 yǐnbì 【动】hide; take cover

隐藏 yǐncáng 【动】conceal; hide

隐患 yǐnhuàn 【名】hidden danger; latent trouble

隐晦 yǐnhuì 【形】abstruse; obscure

隐瞒 yǐnmán 【动】conceal (sth. from sb.)

隐痛 yǐntòng 【名】untold bitterness

隐约 yǐnyuē 【形】(visibly or audibly) indistinct: 山峦～可见。The mountain ranges can be seen indistinctly in the distance. 悠扬的琴声隐隐约约地从剧场传来。The melodious sound of a piano issued indistinctly from the theatre.

瘾(癮) yǐn 【名】addiction: 烟～ addiction to smoking

yìn

印　yìn　【名】seal：盖上～ affix a seal 【动】print：这本小说第一版～了十万册。100,000 copies of the first edition of that novel were printed. 这种花纹如果～到布上，一定很好看。This pattern would be very beautiful if printed on cloth.

印度洋　Yìndùyáng　【名】Indian Ocean

印发　yìnfā　【动】print and publish; issue

印花税　yìnhuāshuì　【名】stamp duty; stamp tax

印染　yìnrǎn　【动】print and dye

印刷　yìnshuā　【动】print

印刷机　yìnshuājī　【名】printing machine

印刷品　yìnshuāpǐn　【名】printed matter

印刷体　yìnshuātǐ　【名】printed characters

印象　yìnxiàng　【名】impression：不可磨灭的～ indelible impression 留下深刻的～ leave a deep impression 大家对他的～很好。Everybody has a very good impression of him.

印章　yìnzhāng　【名】〔个 gè、枚 méi〕seal; stamp

印证　yìnzhèng　【动】corroborate; verify：这个论点需要在实践中加以～。This argument needs to be verified in practice.

饮（飲）　yìn　【动】give (animals) water to drink：～马 water a horse
另见 yǐn

yīng

应（應）　yīng　【动】❶ answer：我叫了他半天，他才～了一声。I called him for a long time before he finally answered. ❷ promise (to do sth.)：工作你既然～下来了，就要努力去做。Now that you have promised to do the work, you should do it diligently. 【助动】should; must：～有尽有。Everything that should be there is there. 教育好青年是教师～尽的责任。It is the duty of teachers to educate young people well.
另见 yìng

应当　yīngdāng　【助动】should; ought：中国～对于人类有较大的贡献。The Chinese people should make a significant contribution to mankind. 这样做～不～? Is that the way to behave? (imply negative)

应该　yīnggāi　【助动】❶ should; ought to：教师对学生～耐心。Teachers ought to be patient with students. 前一段他很辛苦，现在休息一星期是～的。He has worked very hard recently so he deserves a week's holiday. 我觉得你一点儿也没变，小李不～不认识你呀! I don't think you have changed at all! Xiao Li shouldn't have failed to recognize you. Note：应该 can be placed before the agent of an action to indicate whose obligation it is to do sth.：～谁做的事，谁就～去做。One ought to do that which falls within one's line of duty. ❷ indicates probability：他上星期六就动身了，现在～到了。He set off on his journey last Saturday and ought to have arrived by now. 他的病～好了吧! He ought to have recovered from his illness by now.

应届　yīngjiè　【形】the present graduating year：小王是～毕业生。Xiao Wang is one of this year's graduates.

应有尽有　yīng yǒu jìn yǒu　you can

find everything that you expect

英 yīng

英镑 yīngbàng 【名】 pound sterling

英俊 yīngjùn 【形】❶ brilliant; excellent: ～有为 brilliant and promising ❷ handsome and energetic: 小伙子长得挺～的。The young man is handsome and energetic.

英明 yīngmíng 【形】 wise; brilliant: ～的领袖 wise leader ～的预见 wise prediction

英模 yīngmó 【名】 heroes and exemplary figures

英武 yīngwǔ 【形】 hardsome and powerful

英雄 yīngxióng 【名】 hero 【形】 heroic

英勇 yīngyǒng 【形】 brave; valiant; heroic; courageous

英姿 yīngzī 【名】 bright and valiant look

婴(嬰) yīng

婴儿 yīng'ér 【名】 infant; baby

鹦(鸚) yīng

鹦鹉 yīngwǔ 【名】〔只 zhī〕parrot

鹰(鷹) yīng 【名】〔只 zhī〕eagle; falcon

鹰犬 yīngquǎn 【名】 falcon and hound, that is, obsequious lackeys

yíng

迎 yíng 【动】❶ meet; welcome: ～宾 meet the guests 在凯歌声中～来了新的一年 welcome in a new year amid songs of victory ❷ towards; to-wards: ～风 against the wind ～着朝阳前进 march forward into the morning sunshine

迎风招展 yíng fēng zhāozhǎn flutter in the wind

迎合 yínghé 【动】 cater to; pander to: ～对方心理 anticipate and pander to the wishes of the other party ～别人的需要 cater to the whims of others

迎接 yíngjiē 【动】 meet; welcome; receive

迎面 yíng = miàn in one's face; head-on: 春风～吹来。The spring wind blew directly into our faces. ～开来一辆汽车。A car came head-on towards (him).

迎刃而解 yíng rèn ér jiě bamboo splits all the way down as soon as it touches the knife's edge; (fig.) (of a problem) be readily solved: 主要矛盾解决了,次要矛盾也就～了。Once the principal contradiction is solved, secondary contradictions can be easily solved.

迎头赶上 yíngtóu gǎnshàng try hard to catch up; strive to overtake

迎头痛击 yíng tóu tòng jī deal head-on blows

迎新 yíng = xīn welcome the new comers

荧(熒) yíng

荧光灯 yíngguāngdēng 【名】 fluorescent lamp

荧光屏 yíngguāngpíng 【名】 fluorescent screen

荧屏 yíngpíng 【名】 same as "荧光屏"; television

盈 yíng

盈亏 yíngkuī 【名】❶ (of moon) wax and wane ❷ profit and loss

盈利 yínglì 【动】 make a profit; gain a profit

盈余 yíngyú 【动】 have a surplus: 这个月～五百元。There is a surplus of five hundred yuan this month. 【名】 surplus: 食堂有四千元的～。The dining hall has a surplus of four thousand yuan.

营(營) yíng 【名】battalion 【动】◇ (of business) operate；run 【量】battalion

营地 yíngdì 【名】campsite

营房 yíngfáng 【名】barracks；quarters

营救 yíngjiù 【动】save；rescue；go to the rescue of

营垒 yínglěi 【名】❶ barracks and their surrounding wall ❷ camp

营私 yíngsī 【动】seek private gain

营养 yíngyǎng 【名】 nutrition；nourishment

营业 yíngyè 【动】do business

营业税 yíngyèshuì 【名】sales tax；business tax；turn-over tax

营业员 yíngyèyuán 【名】shop assistant

营长 yíngzhǎng 【名】battalion commander

赢(贏) yíng 【动】win

赢得 yíngdé 【动】win；gain：～时间 gain time ～胜利 win a victory ～大家的好评 win the praise of the masses ～全场的喝彩 bring down the house

yǐng

影 yǐng 【名】❶ (～儿)同"影子" ❶❷❸，❷ ◇ photo：在天安门前留～ have a photo taken in Tian'anmen Square

影集 yǐngjí 【名】photograph album

影片 yǐngpiàn 【名】〔部 bù〕cinema；film

影评 yǐngpíng 【名】movie review；comment on films

影射 yǐngshè 【动】insinuate；use innuendo；hint at sth.：～攻击 attack by innuendo 这个四十年代的电影是～反动政府的。This film of the 40's made insinuations against the reactionary government.

影视 yǐngshì 【名】film and television

影响 yǐngxiǎng 【动】have an effect on；affect；influence：教师要用好的作风去～学生。Teachers should influence students by their own behavior style. 【名】influence；effect；impact：产生～ produce an effect on ～越来越大。The influence is becoming greater and greater.

影星 yǐngxīng 【名】film star；movie star

影印 yǐngyìn 【动】photoprint；photostat

影院 yǐngyuàn 【名】cinema；movie theatre；movie house

影子 yǐngzi 【名】❶ shadow ❷ reflection (in a mirror or on the water)：塔的～倒映在水中。One can see the reflection of the tower in the water. ❸ trace；dim impression：这事经你一提醒，我脑子里才有点儿～。Now that you remind me of this matter, I have a vague memory of it. 脑子里一点儿～也没有。I haven't the dimmest recollection of it.

yìng

应(應) yìng 【动】❶ answer；respond；echo：他～声说："是我。" He answered straight away："It's me." ❷ promise；accept：这位总统是～我国政府的邀请前来进行友好访问的。The president came on a friendly visit at the invitation of our government.

另见 yīng

应承 yìngchéng 【动】promise (to do sth.)

应酬 yìngchou 【动】engage in social activities；have social intercourse

应付 yìngfu【动】❶ deal with；cope with：～局面 deal with the situation 难于～ difficult to cope with 几十年的海上生活锤炼了他～风云突变的能力。Decades of life at sea trained him to cope with sudden changes of weather. ❷ do things perfunctorily；make do with：～差事 do one's job perfunctorily 这双鞋夏天能～过去，就先别买新的了。If you can make do with this pair for the summer, don't buy another pair of shoes yet.

应急 yìngjí【动】meet an urgent need；meet an emergency

应接不暇 yìng jiē bù xiá too much to handle；so many that one can't attend to all of them：一路上湖光山色～。On the way, there were so many beautiful views of lakes and mountains that we couldn't take in everything. 来访的人很多，接待人员～。There were so many visitors that the receptionists couldn't attend to all of them.

应聘 yìngpìn【动】accept an offer of employment：他曾～于中山大学执教。He once accepted a teaching position at Zhongshan University.

应声虫 yìngshēngchóng【名】echo；yes-man

应邀 yìng＝yāo in response to an invitation；answer the invitation of；at the invitation of

应用 yìngyòng【动】use；apply：～知识，解决实际问题 use one's knowledge to solve practical problems 这种药～得很广泛。This medicine is widely used. 学习的目的全在于～。The sole purpose of study is to put one's knowledge into practice.

应用文 yìngyòngwén【名】practical writings（such as business letters, notices, invitations, etc.）

应战 yìng＝zhàn ❶ accept battle；accept combat；meet an enemy attack ❷ accept a challenge

应征 yìng＝zhēng ❶ enlist；join the army ❷ respond to a call for contributions（e.g. to a publication）

硬

yìng【形】❶ hard（as opp. to 软）：这种木头很～。This kind of wood is very hard. ❷ ◇ tough：～汉子 a tough guy ❸ ◇ stiff；strong：他话说得很～，简直没有商量的余地。He expressed himself in very strong terms and there was no room for negotiation. ❹ ◇ good（quality）：领导班子～ a sound group of leaders 牌子～ a well-known, reliable brand 功夫～ superb skill【副】❶ indicates success after perseverance：～把他说服了。We convinced him at long last. 他在战争中失去了右手，～练会了用左手写字。He lost his right hand in the war but finally succeeded in learning to write with his left hand. ❷ resolutely：～不承认错误 obstinately refuse to admit one's error 他～不向敌人投降。He resolutely refused to surrender. 不让他去，他～要去。We didn't want to let him go, but he insisted on going. ❸ manage（to do sth.）but with difficulty：有病别～撑着，要早点儿治。If you are ill, you mustn't force yourself to carry on. You'd better go and see a doctor.

硬币 yìngbì【名】specie；coin

硬度 yìngdù【名】hardness

硬骨头 yìnggǔtou【名】steel-willed person

硬化 yìnghuà【动】harden：血管～ vascular sclerosis 这种塑料遇冷就会～。This kind of plastic hardens when exposed to cold.

硬件 yìngjiàn【名】hardware

硬木 yìngmù【名】hardwood

硬任务 yìngrènwù【名】a tough job；a challenging job；a set task

硬是　yìngshì　【副】同"硬"【副】❶ ❷

硬通货　yìngtōnghuò　【名】hard currency

硬卧　yìngwò　【名】hard sleeper

硬席　yìngxí　【名】hard seat；wooden seat (on a train)

硬仗　yìngzhàng　【名】desperate combat；stiff fight

yō

哟（喲）　yō　【叹】oh! (an expression of surprise)：～,这孩子长这么高了! Oh, the child has grown so tall! ～,是你呀! Oh, it's you!
另见 yo

yo

哟（喲）　yo　【助】❶ *used at the end of a sentence to indicate that a request is being made*：加把劲儿～! Make more of an effort! ❷ *inserted in a line of a song for balance*：太阳一出～,满山红。"When the sun rises, the mountains are suffused with red."
另见 yō

yōng

拥（擁）　yōng　【动】❶ surround：观众～着花样滑冰冠军,要求签名。The spectators surrounded the figure-skating champion, asking for autographs. ❷ crowd；swarm：大家～上前去看热闹。People crowded forward to watch the fun. ❸ ◇ support：军爱民,民～军。The army cherishes the people；the people support the army.

拥抱　yōngbào　【动】embrace；hug；fold in one's arms

拥护　yōnghù　【动】support；stand for；uphold

拥挤　yōngjǐ　【动】crowd；press：大家慢慢走，不要～。Walk slowly, everybody. Don't press forward! 【形】crowded：大街上的人很多,特别～。There were lots of people in the street, and it was extremely crowded.

拥军优属　yōng jūn yōu shǔ　(of the people) support the People's Liberation Army and give preferential treatment to the families of army men.

拥有　yōngyǒu　【动】have；possess (a lot of land, population, wealth, strength, etc.)：～丰富的资源 have rich natural resources ～大面积的原始森林 have large areas of primaeval forests

拥政爱民　yōng zhèng ài mín　(of the army) support the government and cherish the people

庸 yōng

庸俗　yōngsú　【形】vulgar；philistine

庸俗化　yōngsúhuà　【动】vulgarize

臃 yōng

臃肿　yōngzhǒng　【形】obese；corpulent and clumsy；(*fig.*) (of organization) overstaffed：他胖得身体有点儿～了。He is so overweight that he moves awkwardly. 机构～,应该精简。Overstaffed administrative structures should be slimmed down.

yǒng

永　yǒng　【副】◇ forever；for good；permanent：～放光芒 will shine forever ～不掉队 never lag behind

永别　yǒngbié　【动】part forever

永垂不朽　yǒng chuí bù xiǔ　immor-

tal; live forever in the people's hearts

永恒 yǒnghéng 【形】eternal; everlasting

永久 yǒngjiǔ 【形】perpetual; permanent

永久性 yǒngjiǔxìng 【名】eternity; permanence

永生 yǒngshēng 【动】live forever 【名】all one's life; one's whole life: ～难忘 never forget for all one's life

永远 yǒngyuǎn 【副】forever; always; perpetually: 他～是乐观的。He is always optimistic. ～不要忘记这个教训。Never forget this lesson. 胜利～属于人民。Victory always belongs to the people.

甬 yǒng

甬道 yǒngdào 【名】〔条 tiáo〕paved path; passageway; hallway; covered corridor 也说"甬路"。

勇 yǒng 【形】◇brave; valiant; courageous

勇敢 yǒnggǎn 【形】courageous; brave

勇猛 yǒngměng 【形】valiant; militant; fearless

勇气 yǒngqì 【名】courage; dauntless spirit

勇士 yǒngshì 【名】brave man; hero; valiant fighter

勇往直前 yǒng wǎng zhí qián stride bravely forward; advance courageously

勇于 yǒngyú 【动】dare to; have the courage to: ～挑重担 dare to take heavy responsibilities ～创新 dare to create new things ～向权威挑战 dare to challenge authority

涌 yǒng 【动】❶ gush; surge forward: 泪如泉～。One's tears well up like a spring. 潮～浪翻。

The tide surges forward and the waves roll on. ❷ emerge; rise (out of water): 大海中～出一轮红日。A red sun emerged from the sea. ❸ rush; surge: 千头万绪～上心头。Numerous thoughts and feelings welled up in (his) heart. 远处有很多人向这边～来。In the distance a crowd was surging towards us.

涌现 yǒngxiàn 【动】emerge in large quantities: 战争中～出无数英雄人物。Many heroes emerged through the war.

踊(踴) yǒng

踊跃 yǒngyuè 【形】eager; enthusiastic

yòng

用 yòng 【动】❶ use; employ; apply: ～钢笔写字 write with a fountain pen 你会不会～筷子? Do you know how to use chopsticks? ❷ require; need: 这句话还～解释吗? Does this sentence need any explanation?

用不着 yòng bu zháo not need: 活儿不多,～这么多人。There isn't much work. We don't need so many people. 今天不冷,～穿大衣。It isn't cold today. You don't need a coat.

用处 yòngchu 【名】use; function

用得着 yòng de zháo find sth. useful; need: 这些东西先收起来,以后还～。We'd better put these things away for the time being. They'll be useful later. 这儿～你,你先别走。We need you here. Please don't go yet. Note: 用得着 is used before a verb, in a question or a rhetorical question: 这个问题还～讨论吗? ——要讨论。Do we need to discuss this question? ——Yes. 问题这么清楚,还～讨论? The problem is so clear;

why discuss it?

用法　yòngfǎ　【名】usages：虚词的～ usages of function words

用功　yòng＝gōng　study hard；work hard

用户　yònghù　【名】consumer；user

用劲　yòng＝jìn　with one's strength；make great effort

用具　yòngjù　【名】appliance；instrument；tool

用力　yòng＝lì　同"用劲"

用品　yòngpǐn　【名】articles for use

用途　yòngtú　【名】同"用处"

用心　yòngxīn　【名】intention；purpose：～不良 vicious intention 你的～是好的，只是方法不对。You meant well，but your method was wrong.

用心　yòng＝xīn　with great concentration；attentively：他学习很～。He studies with great concentration. 干这个事得用点儿心。Doing this requires concentration.

用以　yòngyǐ　【动】use sth. to achieve an end（*the unstated object of* 以 *can be gathered from the context*）：我们应该学一点儿童心理，～指导我们平时对孩子的管教。We should know something of child psychology which will come useful in child-rearing. 这就是林业工人～运送木材的空中索道。This is the cableway which the lumberjacks use to haul out their timber.

用意　yòngyì　【名】purpose；meaning；intention：他的～是想告诉我们做事要谨慎。His meant to tell us that we should be careful. 他讲这个寓言故事是有～的。He had a message in telling this fable.

用语　yòngyǔ　【名】❶ phraseology ❷ terminology

佣　yòng

佣金　yòngjīn　【名】〔笔 bǐ〕commission

yōu

优（優）　yōu　【形】◇ excellent；superior；fine；outstanding

优待　yōudài　【动】give preferential treatment to

优等　yōuděng　【形】high-grade

优点　yōudiǎn　【名】merit；strong point；advantage；virtue

优抚　yōufǔ　【动】give special care to disabled servicemen or to the families of servicemen or deceased servicemen

优厚　yōuhòu　【形】（of treatment）munificent；generous：待遇～ excellent pay and other benefits

优化　yōuhuà　【动】optimize：～组合 optimization grouping or regrouping

优惠　yōuhuì　【形】favorable：待遇～ preferential treatment ～的条件 favorable conditions

优良　yōuliáng　【形】excellent；good；fine

优美　yōuměi　【形】elegant；beautiful；graceful

优柔寡断　yōu róu guǎ duàn　irresolute and hesitant；indecisive：做事情应该当机立断，～往往误事。In handling matters，one should make prompt decisions. Indecision causes delay and spoils things.

优生学　yōushēngxué　【名】eugenics

优生优育　yōu shēng yōu yù　eugenics and good upbringing

优胜　yōushèng　【形】outstanding；superior

优势　yōushì　【名】（have the）upper hand；dominant position；superiority

优先　yōuxiān　【形】have priority；take precedence：～发展 give priority to the development of ～考虑 give first consideration to ～照顾

give sb. priority in receiving special treatment

优秀　yōuxiù　【形】(of person, work) excellent; outstanding; brilliant; splendid

优选法　yōuxuǎnfǎ　【名】optimization

优雅　yōuyǎ　【形】elegant; graceful; in good taste

优异　yōuyì　【形】(of achievement) excellent; outstanding

优越　yōuyuè　【形】superior; advantageous

优越感　yōuyuègǎn　【名】superiority complex; sense of superiority

优越性　yōuyuèxìng　【名】superiority; advantage; supremacy

优质　yōuzhì　【名】good quality; excellent quality; quality

优质钢　yōuzhìgāng　【名】high-grade steel; quality steel

忧(憂)　yōu

忧愁　yōuchóu　【形】sorrowful; worried; anxious; sad

忧烦　yōufán　【形】worried

忧愤　yōufèn　【形】〈书〉worried and indignant

忧虑　yōulǜ　【动】worry; be anxious; ～不安 be worried ～重重 be extremely concerned over sth.

忧伤　yōushāng　【形】sad; grieved; sorrowful

忧心忡忡　yōuxīn chōngchōng　feeling anxious; worrying; heavy-hearted

忧郁　yōuyù　【形】melancholy; sad; depressed

幽　yōu

幽静　yōujìng　【形】pleasantly tranquil and secluded

幽灵　yōulíng　【名】phantom; apparition

幽默　yōumò　【形】humourous

幽雅　yōuyǎ　【形】quiet and elegant (of environment)

悠　yōu

悠久　yōujiǔ　【形】long; age-old

悠闲　yōuxián　【形】leisurely

悠扬　yōuyáng　【形】(of music, etc.) rising and falling; melodious

yóu

尤　yóu　【副】〈书〉particularly; especially (often used with mono-syllabic words such as 以,为, etc.)：他在学习上进步很快, 近几个月～为显著。He has made rapid progress in his studies, especially in recent months. 此地盛产水果,～以菠萝著称。This area produces abundant fruits, and is especially known for its pineapples.

尤其　yóuqí　【副】(also "尤其是") especially ❶ of the 2 cases mentioned in the sentence, the latter is included in the former：我喜欢游泳, ～喜欢在大海中游泳。I like to swim, especially in the sea. 学习汉语要注意发音,～要注意声调。When you learn Chinese, you must pay attention to pronunciation, especially to the four tones. ❷ the 2 cases are equal：为了做好工作,要提高业务水平,～要提高掌握电脑技术。In order to do one's work well, one must be professionally competent, and, even more important, have a good mastery of computer programs. 他的性格、为人,～是工作态度,给人的印象很深。His disposition, his conduct and especially the way he works leave a very deep impression on other people.

由　yóu　【介】❶ introduces the person who is assigned a task：参观开始以前,～工厂的领导同志介绍了这个厂的历史。Before touring the

factory, the factory leader gave a talk about its history. 各国的事情应当～各国人民自己来管。The affairs of various countries are the concern of the peoples of those countries. ❷ *introduces the constituents of a thing*：南京长江大桥～正桥和引桥组成。The Nanjing Bridge consists of the bridge proper and the approach to the bridge. 水分子～两个氢原子和一个氧原子构成。A water molecule is made up of two atoms of hydrogen and one atom of oxygen. ❸ 同"从" cóng【介】❶ ❷ ❸ ❹ ❺（*usu. in written language*）：这个电影～下星期起在各电影院同时上映。This film will be shown starting next week in all cinemas. 麦穗已经～青变黄了。The ears of wheat have turned from green to gold. 国家足球队员是～各省足球队中选出来的。The members of the national football team were selected from provincial football teams. 大雁～空中飞过。Wild geese flew across the sky.

由表及里 yóu biǎo jí lǐ　from the outside to the inside；proceed from the exterior to the interior；from outward appearance to inner essence

由不得 yóubude【动】(sth.) is not up to (sb.) to decide：旧社会，青年人的婚姻～自己。In the old society, marriage was not up to young people to decide. 这件事～你一个人。This matter can't be decided by you alone.

由此及彼 yóu cǐ jí bǐ　proceed from one to the other；proceed from one point to another

由点到面 yóu diǎn dào miàn　take the experience gained at one unit and popularize it in a whole area

由近及远 yóu jìn jí yuǎn　from close-by examples to those far off

由来 yóulái【名】❶ origin of occurrence ❷ reason；cause

由浅入深 yóu qiǎn rù shēn　from the shallower to the deeper；proceed from the simple to the more complex；from the superficial to the profound

由于 yóuyú【介】owing to；due to：～老师的帮助，他进步很快。Owing to help from his teachers, he has made rapid progress. ～生产不断发展，农民收入逐年增加。Since production has risen steadily, the personal income of the farmers has increased year by year. 这次试验～计算上的错误而失败了。The experiment failed this time owing to some miscalculation.

由衷 yóuzhōng【形】from the heart；from the bottom of one's heart

邮（郵）yóu【动】post

邮包 yóubāo【名】(～儿)〔个 gè〕postal parcel

邮编 yóubiān【名】same as "邮政编码"

邮递员 yóudìyuán【名】postman

邮电局 yóudiànjú【名】post office

邮费 yóufèi【名】postage；postal rates

邮购 yóugòu【动】mail order

邮汇 yóuhuì【动】remit by post

邮寄 yóujì【动】send by post

邮件 yóujiàn【名】letters and parcels；postal matter

邮局 yóujú【名】post office

邮票 yóupiào【名】〔张 zhāng〕postage stamp

邮筒 yóutǒng【名】pillar-box；mailbox

邮箱 yóuxiāng【名】postbox；mailbox

邮政 yóuzhèng【名】postal service

邮政编码 yóuzhèng biānmǎ　postcode；zip code

犹（猶）

yóu 【动】〈书〉as if; like：过～不及。To go too far is as bad as to fall short. 【副】still：话～未了(liǎo)，走进一个人来。A man came in before he had finished talking. 虽死～荣。Although he is dead, his glorious memory lives on.

犹如 yóurú 【动】as if; like：他对待烈士遗孤～亲生儿子一般。He treated the orphan of the martyr like his own son.

犹豫 yóuyù 【形】hesitant; uncertain：毫不～ without the slightest hesitation 他遇事总是犹犹豫豫的，不果断。He is always hesitant rather than decisive when facing a situation.

犹豫不决 yóuyù bù jué indecisive; hesitate to act; be not able to make up one's mind; shilly-shally

油

yóu 【名】oil; petroleum 【动】❶ paint; coat with varnish：这张桌子需要重新～一～。This table needs repainting. ❷ be greased; be smeared with oil：衣服上～了一块 have a grease spot on one's clothes 【形】❶ (of food) oily; rich：这种点心太～，我不想吃。This kind of pastry is too oily. I don't feel like eating it. ❷ (person) cunning; slick：～腔滑调 glib speech and manner

油泵 yóubèng 【名】〔台 tái〕oil pump

油饼 yóubǐng 【名】deep fried dough cake

油画 yóuhuà 【名】〔张 zhāng、幅 fú〕oil painting

油井 yóujǐng 【名】〔口 kǒu〕oil well

油料 yóuliào 【名】oil-bearing seed

油料作物 yóuliào zuòwù oil-bearing crops

油轮 yóulún 【名】oil-tanker

油墨 yóumò 【名】printing ink

油泥 yóuní 【名】greasy filth

油腻 yóunì 【形】greasy; oily (food)

油漆 yóuqī 【名】varnish; paint

油水 yóushui 【名】❶ oil; fat in food ❷ (improper) fringe benefit; profit on the side：想捞点 ～ attempt to pick up some profit on the side

油田 yóutián 【名】oilfield

油汪汪 yóuwāngwāng 【形】shiny; oily

油印 yóuyìn 【动】mimeograph

油毡 yóuzhān 【名】asphalt felt

游

yóu 【动】❶ swim：鱼在水里～来～去。Fish swim to and fro in water. 他蛙泳～得很好。He can swim the breast-stroke very well. ❷ go sightseeing; tour; travel：～长城 go to the Great Wall sightseeing

游船 yóuchuán 【名】〔只 zhī〕pleasure-boat; yacht

游逛 yóuguàng 【动】saunter; stroll about

游击 yóujī 【名】guerrilla：打 ～ wage guerrilla warfare ～战争 guerrilla war

游击队 yóujīduì 【名】guerrillas; partisans

游击战 yóujīzhàn 【名】guerrilla warfare

游记 yóujì 【名】account of one's travels

游客 yóukè 【名】traveller; sightseer

游览 yóulǎn 【动】tour; go sightseeing

游离 yóulí 【动】❶ (chem.) free：～状态 free state ❷ drift away; dissociate oneself from：～在集体之外 sever one's connection with the collective

游历 yóulì 【动】travel for pleasure; tour

游牧 yóumù 【动】roam around as a

nomad

游人 yóurén 【名】sight-seer

游山玩水 yóu shān wán shuǐ go sightseeing

游手好闲 yóu shǒu hào xián loaf; idle

游玩 yóuwán 【动】play; amuse (oneself)

游戏 yóuxì 【名】(play) game

游行 yóuxíng 【动】parade 【名】demonstration

游弋 yóuyì 【动】cruise

游艺 yóuyì 【名】entertainment; amusement

游艺会 yóuyìhuì 【名】amusement gathering

游泳 yóu＝yǒng swim

游泳池 yóuyǒngchí 【名】swimming pool

游园 yóu＝yuán take part in a garden party; gala party

游园会 yóuyuánhuì 【名】garden party; garden carnival

yǒu

友 yǒu 【名】◇ friend：病～ wardmate; fellow-patient 亲～ relatives and friends

友爱 yǒu'ài 【形】brotherly; fraternal 【名】brotherliness; brotherly affection

友邦 yǒubāng 【名】friendly country

友好 yǒuhǎo 【形】friendly; amiable

友情 yǒuqíng 【名】friendship; cordial feelings

友人 yǒurén 【名】friend (usu. in written language)

友谊 yǒuyì 【名】friendship

友谊赛 yǒuyìsài 【名】friendship match

有 yǒu 【动】❶ have; possess the negative is 没有 and not 不有：我～一套《汉语教科书》。I have a

complete set of 《Chinese Readers》. 他～全心全意为人民服务的精神。He has the spirit of serving the people whole-heartedly. ❷ there is; there exists：街中心～个花园。There is a garden at the crossroads. 我们班～五个女同学。There are five female students in our class. 唐朝～个大诗人叫李白。There was a great poet named Li Bai in the Tang Dynasty. 没～水就不能种菜。We can't grow vegetables without water. ❸ indicates an estimate or comparison：他～我这么高了。He is as tall as I. 我看他没～五十岁。I don't think he is fifty yet. ❹ happen; appear：情况～了变化。Some changes have occurred in the situation. 那件事～结果了吗? Has any conclusion been reached in that matter? ❺ 有 in 有一年, 有一次, 有一回, 有一天, etc. means "a certain (time) in the past"：～一年冬天这儿下了一场大雪。One winter there was a very heavy snowfall here. 他～一次给我讲了一个很有趣的故事。Once he told me a very interesting story. 小李～一天把腿伤了。One day Xiao Li hurt his leg. Note：有一天 can also mean "some day (in the future)"：正义的事业总～一天要胜利。A just cause will succeed eventually.

有偿 yǒucháng 【形】with compensation：～服务 paid services

有待 yǒudài 【动】remain (to be done); await (completing)：还遗留下一些小问题～解决。There are some minor problems remaining to be solved.

有的 yǒude 【代】some：这些画，～是专业工作者画的，～是业余爱好者画的。Some of these paintings were painted by professional painters, others by amateur painters. 你说的那些地方，～我没去过。I haven't

been to some of the places you've mentioned. ～树全年都是绿的，叫常绿树。Some trees are green all year round and are known as "evergreens". ～人喜欢爬山，～人喜欢游泳。Some people like to go mountain climbing, while others like to swim. 天气预报～时候准，～时候不准。Sometimes the weather forecast is accurate, sometimes not. Note: 有的人 *and* 有的时候 *can also be said as* 有人 *and* 有时候.

有的是 yǒudeshì 【动】have plenty of; there's no lack of: 他年轻，～力气。He is young and has plenty of energy. 学习的机会～。There is no lack of opportunities for further study.

有的放矢 yǒu dì fàng shǐ shoot the arrow at the target; with a definite object in view

有点儿 yǒudiǎnr 【副】a little; slightly; somewhat (usu. used to modify unpleasant or negative expressions)

有方 yǒufāng 【形】in a proper way; have a way with sb.: 教子～ bring up children in a proper way

有关 yǒuguān 【动】❶ have sth. to do with; in connection with: 这件事和他～。This matter has something to do with him. 老李的身体特别好，这跟他坚持锻炼～。Lao Li is in excellent health. This has something to do with his program of consistent physical exercise. ❷ concerned; relevant: 我喜欢看～地理方面的书籍。I like reading books about geography. 明天讨论新产品的设计方案，请～人员参加。The project for the designing of new products will be discussed tomorrow. All those concerned please attend the meeting.

有过之而无不及 yǒu guò zhī ér wú bù jí go even farther than (*derog.*)

有害 yǒu = hài harmful; detrimental; 强烈的灯光，对眼睛～。Strong light is harmful to the eyes.

有机 yǒujī 【形】❶ organic ❷ related in a system; organic: 这两项工作要～地联系起来。These two jobs should be parts of an organic whole.

有机肥料 yǒujī féiliào organic fertilizer

有机化学 yǒujī huàxué organic chemistry

有机物 yǒujīwù 【名】organic matter

有价证券 yǒujià zhèngquàn securities; negotiable securities

有口皆碑 yǒu kǒu jiē bēi (*fig.*) be praised by all; one's praises are on everybody's lips

有赖 yǒulài 【动】depend on; rely on; rest with (*often used with* "于"): 食品工业的发展～于农业的发展。The development of the food industry depends on that of agriculture.

有理 yǒu = lǐ reasonable; be in the right; with good reason; on just ground

有力 yǒulì 【形】weighty; forceful

有利 yǒulì 【形】favourable; advantageous

有名 yǒu = míng famous; well-known; renowned

有目共睹 yǒu mù gòng dǔ obvious to all; clear to all

有期徒刑 yǒuqī túxíng fixed term imprisonment

有趣 yǒuqù 【形】interesting; amusing

有色金属 yǒusè jīnshǔ nonferrous metal

有神论 yǒushénlùn 【名】theism

有生力量 yǒu shēng lìliàng (*mil.*) effective forces: 消灭敌人的～ wipe out the enemy's effective strength

有时 yǒushí 【副】sometimes; at times; occasionally: 天～晴，～阴。

Sometimes the weather was fine, and sometimes it was overcast. 我～喝点儿茶。Sometimes I drink tea.

有史以来 yǒu shǐ yǐlái since the dawn of history

有始有终 yǒu shǐ yǒu zhōng carry sth. through to a successful end

有数 yǒushù【形】a limited number; not many：这学期只剩下～的几天了。There are only a few days left in this term.

有数 yǒu = shù know what one is doing; know how matters stand and be confident：心里～ know how things stand 观察了几天，我对这事有点数了。After a few days of observation, I have an idea of how things stand concerning this matter.

有条不紊 yǒu tiáo bù wěn systematic; in perfect order; orderly

有头无尾 yǒu tóu wú wěi leave sth. unfinished; stop half-way

有头有尾 yǒu tóu yǒu wěi do sth. from beginning to end

有为 yǒuwéi【形】promising; capable：年轻～ young and promising 小李是个～的青年。Xiao Li is a promising young man.

有…无… yǒu...wú...❶ *indicates a case in which there is only one thing and not the other*：有名无实 in name but not in reality 有气无力 feeble 有利无弊 advantageous, with no drawbacks 有始无终 start off but never finish 有勇无谋 be courageous but not tactically wise ❷ *indicates the fact that the existence of one thing can prevent the existence of the other*：有备无患 where there is no danger 有恃无恐 with strong backing, one is reckless ❸ *indicates a case in which there is only the former and not the latter which*

is the opposite：有增无减 an endless increase (*derog.*) 有加无已 keep on adding (*derog.*)

有隙可乘 yǒu xì kě chéng possibility to take advantage of; there is a crack to wedge oneself into

有限 yǒuxiàn【形】❶ limited; restricted：～授权 invest sb. with limited power ❷ a little; not much：我只认识～的几个汉字。I only know a few Chinese characters. 我的能力～，这项工作恐怕难以胜任。My ability is limited, and I'm afraid I'm not equal to this job.

有限公司 yǒuxiàn gōngsī limited company

有线广播 yǒu xiàn guǎngbō wired broadcasting

有效 yǒuxiào【形】effective; efficient; valid：～措施 effective measure 这张火车票三天之内～。This train ticket is valid for three days. 把人力很好地组织起来，就能更～地战胜自然灾害。If the available man-power is well organized, the natural disaster can be combated more effectively.

有心 yǒuxīn【形】❶ have the intention; intend to：我～去看看他，又怕打扰他。I intended to visit him, but I was afraid I would disturb him. ❷ deliberately; purposely：他可不是～难为你。He didn't purposely make things difficult for you.

有(一)点儿 yǒu(yī)diǎnr【副】a little *usu. used before sth. unpleasant*：今天～热。It's a bit hot today. 我觉得～不舒服。I feel a bit out of sorts. 这事～难办。This matter is a bit difficult. 我～担心他坚持不下来。I'm a bit worried that he may not be able to stick it out.

有(一)些 yǒu(yī)xiē【副】同"有(一)点儿"(*usu. in written language*)

有益 yǒuyì【形】beneficial; useful;

helpful；good for

有意 yǒuyì 【动】❶ want to；have a mind to ❷ intentionally；on purpose；deliberately

有意识 yǒu yìshi consciously；deliberately；on purpose：他～地在克服自己的弱点。He is consciously trying to overcome his weaknesses.

有意思 yǒu yìsi interesting：猴子是很～的动物。Monkeys are very amusing animals. 这种游戏真～。This is really a very interesting game.

有意无意 yǒu yì wú yì intentionally or unintentionally

有用 yǒu = yòng useful；serviceable：这本词典很～。This dictionary is very useful.

有…有… yǒu…yòu… ❶ used with two nouns or verbs having opposite or contrary meanings to mean have both of them：有利有弊 there are advantages and disadvantages 有始有终 start and finish sth. 有张有弛(chí) combine stress wih relaxation 有来有往 reciprocal visits (between friends) ❷ used for emphasis before two nouns or verbs having the same or similar meanings：有声有角 (of performance, etc.) vivid 有条有理 be in perfect order 有血有肉 (of literary works) true to life；lifelike 有凭有据 furnished with proof and evidence 有棱有角 sharp-edged and pointed 有说有笑 talking and laughing

有则改之，无则加勉 yǒu zé gǎi zhī, wú zé jiā miǎn correct mistakes if you have committed them and guard against them if you have not

有朝一日 yǒu zhāo yī rì some day；there will be a day

有着 yǒuzhe 【动】have；possess；there is：他对自己的母校～深厚的感情。He has fond feelings for his Alma Mater.

有志者事竟成 yǒu zhì zhě shì jìng chéng where there is a will, there is a way；strong will leads to success

yòu

又 yòu 【副】❶ indicates repetition which has taken place：她没听懂，我～说了一遍。She didn't understand me and so I repeated the sentence. 我们经过休整～投入了新的战斗。After a break, we took up the battle once again. 我们取得了～一次伟大胜利。We've won another great victory. ❷ indicates the certain recurrence of a regularly occurring event which one expects on the basis of past experience or some natural law. It is followed by 是 or an auxiliary verb and takes 了 at the end of the sentence：春天到了，燕子～该来了。Spring has come, and the swallows will be back again. 明天～是星期日了。Tomorrow is Sunday again. ❸ indicates continuation which has taken place：报告人回答了几个问题以后，～讲了下去。The speaker, after having answered a few questions, went on with his speech. ❹ indicates sth. additional：他上邮局取了包裹，～买了几张邮票。He went to the post office to get his parcel and also bought a few stamps. 路很近，车子～快，一会儿就到了。It was not a long way off, and the car was very fast, so we got there in no time. ❺ indicates the addition of a fraction to a whole sum：三～二分之一 three and a half 一年～三个月 one year and 3 months ❻ indicates contradiction：我～想去、～不想去，一时拿不定主意。I want to go, but I'm not sure, and I can't

make up my mind for the moment. 我想自己裁衣服，～怕裁不好。I'd like to cut out a jacket myself, but I'm afraid I won't be able to do it properly. ❼ *used in a negative sentence to emphasize the negation of a fact in order to show that the consequent action or state is what one would expect*：我～不是外人，何必客气。I'm no stranger, and I don't see why you should stand on ceremony with me. 他～没看过这本书，怎么知道好不好！He hasn't read the book, so how can he know whether it's good or not! ❽ *used with the reduplication of 一 plus a measure word to indicate a sequence or many repetitions*：过了一年～一年 one year after another 艺术团的演出博得了一阵～一阵的掌声。The troupe's performance won one round of applause after another. 最近，出国留学生一批～一批地学成回国工作。Recently group after group of students studying abroad have returned to their homeland after they have finished their studies. ❾ *used with the reduplication of a verb, with the first verb taking a 了, to indicate many repetitions*：他惟恐数据写错了，核对了～核对。He was afraid he might make some mistakes in the figures so he checked them again and again. 我想了～想，就是想不起来他叫什么名字。I thought about it repeatedly but I simply could not think of his name.

又…又…　yòu...yòu...　*indicates that two or more actions, states or qualities coexist*：又说又笑 talk and laugh　又高又大 tall and big　这种灯又亮又不刺眼又省电。This kind of lamp is bright but not dazzling and also electricity-saving. 他又想学语言学，又想学哲学，老定不下来。He

wants to study linguistics but wants to study philosophy too, and so can't make up his mind.

右　yòu　【名】right；right side 【形】rightist（ideas，way of thinking，etc.）

右边　yòubiān　【名】the right side；right hand side

右派　yòupài　【名】rightist

右倾　yòuqīng　【名】right deviation；right opportunist tendencies

右倾机会主义　yòuqīng jīhuìzhǔyì right opportunism

右手　yòushǒu　【名】〔只 zhī〕right hand

右翼　yòuyì　【名】rightwing；right flank

幼　yòu　【形】◇ young：老～皆知 both the old and the young know it

幼儿　yòu'ér　【名】child；baby；infant

幼儿园　yòu'éryuán　【名】kindergarten

幼教　yòujiào　【名】preschool education

幼苗　yòumiáo　【名】sprout；young shoot

幼年　yòunián　【名】childhood

幼小　yòuxiǎo　【形】young；immature

幼稚　yòuzhì　【形】childish；naïve

诱（誘）　yòu　【动】◇ lure；entice：～敌深入 lure the enemy in deep（behind one's own lines）

诱导　yòudǎo　【动】❶ guide and instruct；induce sb. to do sth. ❷（phys.）induction

诱饵　yòu'ěr　【名】bait

诱惑　yòuhuò　【动】❶ lure ❷ fascinate

诱骗　yòupiàn　【动】entice；inveigle（sb. into doing sth.）

诱人　yòurén　【形】attractive：～的景色 attractive scene　～的芳香 alluring fragrance

yū

迂　yū

迂回　yūhuí　【动】❶ be tortuous；meandering：湖边游廊～ winding covered walkway by the lake　～曲折 tortuous and winding ❷（mil.）outflank：向侧面～ outflank（the enemy）～敌后 outflank the enemy and proceed to its rear

淤　yū　【动】silt：河底～的泥沙越来越多。More and more mud and sand are silting up the river.
淤积　yūjī　【动】form sediment
淤泥　yūní　【名】silt；sludge
淤塞　yūsè　【动】silt；be clogged up
淤血　yūxuè　【名】extravasated blood
淤血　yū=xuè　extravasate blood

yú

于　yú　【介】〈书〉❶ similar to 在：中华人民共和国～一九四九年十月一日成立。The People's Republic of China was founded on October 1st, 1949. 老王生～1950 年。Mr. Wang was born in 1950. ❷ similar to 对 or 对于：这种农药的气味～人体有害。The odour of this pesticide is harmful to humans. 文娱活动有益～身心健康。Cultural and recreational activities are beneficial to one's mental as well as physical health. ❸ similar to 给：献身～教育事业 dedicate one's life to educational work 在中国，近年来男士服装有些变化，中山装早已让位～西装了。In recent years, men's wear has seen a change with the Sun Yat-sen suit giving way to the western suit. ❹ similar to 从：出～不得已 have no alternative 认识开始～实践。Knowledge comes from practice. ❺ indicates comparison：人民的利益高～一切。The interests of the people come first of all. 学校演电影每周不少～一次。The institute shows a film at least once a week.

于是　yúshì　【连】thereupon；hence；consequently：看完了电影，时间还早，～我们就到书店去看了看。It was still early when we came out of the cinema, so we went to have a look in the bookstore. 行军途中，突然发现敌机，部队～停止前进，疏散隐蔽。During the march, an enemy plane was suddenly spotted, and the troops scattered and took shelter. 也说“于是乎”。

余（餘）　yú　【动】remain；leave：买完东西，还～十多块钱。I still had more than ten yuan left after finishing shopping.【数】〈书〉more than；odd；over：十～尺 over ten chi 一百～人 one hundred odd people 【名】〈书〉apart from or after（a certain time）：工作之～ after working hours；in one's spare time

余地　yúdì　【名】leeway；margin；room（for a purpose）
余毒　yúdú　【名】pernicious vestige；leftover poison
余额　yú'é　【名】❶ vacancy ❷（in accounting）surplus；balance
余悸　yújì　【名】lingering fear
余粮　yúliáng　【名】grain surplus
余孽　yúniè　【名】leftover evils；remaining evils
余数　yúshù　【名】（maths.）remainder：三十五除以八，商数为四，～为三。When thirty five is divided by eight, the quotient is four and the remainder is three.
余味　yúwèi　【名】remaining taste；

after-taste

余暇 yúxiá 【名】〈书〉leisure；spare time

余下 yúxià 【动】leave；remain 【名】the remaining；the rest

鱼（魚） yú 【名】〔条 tiáo〕fish

鱼肝油 yúgānyóu 【名】cod-liver oil

鱼雷 yúléi 【名】torpedo

鱼雷艇 yúléitǐng 【名】〔艘 sōu〕torpedo boat

鱼米之乡 yú mǐ zhī xiāng region abounding with fish and rice；land of plenty

鱼目混珠 yú mù hùn zhū pass fish eyes for pearls；(fig.) mix the genuine with the fictitious

娱 yú

娱乐 yúlè 【动】amuse；休息时，大家一起唱歌，～～。They sang songs to amuse themselves during the break. 【名】recreation；entertainment：下棋既是一种～，又可以锻炼人的头脑。Chess is recreation as well as mental training.

娱乐场 yúlèchǎng 【名】amusement park

娱乐室 yúlèshì 【名】〔间 jiān〕recreation room

渔（漁） yú 【名】◇ ❶ fishery ❷ fishing for (profit)

渔船 yúchuán 【名】〔只 zhī〕fishing boat

渔利 yúlì 【动】fish for profits at others' expense

渔民 yúmín 【名】fisherman

渔网 yúwǎng 【名】〔张 zhāng〕fishing net

渔业 yúyè 【名】fishery

愉 yú

愉快 yúkuài 【形】happy；merry；pleasant；delightful

逾 yú 【动】exceed；go beyond

逾期 yú = qī go beyond the time fixed；be overdue

逾越 yúyuè 【动】exceed；go beyond；pass；不可～的障碍 insuperable barrier

愚 yú 【形】◇ foolish；dull-witted

愚笨 yúbèn 【形】dull-witted；stupid

愚蠢 yúchǔn 【形】foolish；silly

愚公移山 Yúgōng yí shān "The Foolish Old Man Who Removed the Mountains", an ancient Chinese fable；(fig.) do things with great determination regardless of difficulties

愚昧 yúmèi 【形】ignorant

愚弄 yúnòng 【动】dupe；fool；make fun of

舆（輿） yú

舆论 yúlùn 【名】public opinion

yǔ

与（與） yǔ (usu. in written language) 【介】同"和" hé 【介】：～困难作斗争 struggle with difficulties ～时间赛跑 race against time 【连】同"和" hé 【连】：中央～地方 the central and the local 工业～农业 industry and agriculture 批评～自我批评 criticism and self-criticism 【动】◇ 同"给" gěi：送～ send to 赠～ give as a gift

与其…不如… yǔqí…bùrú… after balancing the pros and cons, one makes one's decision, 与其 is placed before what is rejected and 不如 before what is chosen：与其坐在屋子里争论不休，不如到现场去看看。It would be much better to go to the spot to have a look than to

argue endlessly here. 这屋里的精美陈设，与其说是家具，不如说是工艺品。The exquisite appointments of this room could more correctly be called handicraft items than furniture.

与人为善 yǔ rén wéi shàn　be with the intention of helping others；对同事要采取～的态度。One should deal with one's colleagues with kindness.

与日俱增 yǔ rì jù zēng　increase with each passing day

与世长辞 yǔ shì cháng cí　die；不幸～unfortunately passed away

与世隔绝 yǔ shì géjué　seclude oneself from society

与众不同 yǔ zhòng bù tóng　out of the ordinary；～的想法 an idea out of the ordinary

予 yǔ 【动】〈书〉give；请～指正 please give me your advice 特～奖励 this prize is hereby awarded to...

予以 yǔyǐ 【动】〈书〉give；lend；～协助 render help to ～ 肯定 approve of ～ 照顾 show consideration for

宇 yǔ

宇航 yǔháng 【名】astronavigation；～员 astronaut

宇宙 yǔzhòu 【名】cosmos；universe

宇宙飞船 yǔzhòu fēichuán spaceboat

宇宙观 yǔzhòuguān 【名】同"世界观" shìjièguān

羽 yǔ

羽毛 yǔmáo 【名】feather

羽毛球 yǔmáoqiú 【名】❶ badminton ❷ shuttlecock

羽绒 yǔróng 【名】eider-down

羽绒服 yǔróngfú 【名】〔件 jiàn〕down jacket

雨 yǔ 【名】rain

雨点儿 yǔdiǎnr 【名】raindrop

雨过天晴 yǔ guò tiān qíng　sunny spell after rain；difficult period gives way to bright future

雨后春笋 yǔ hòu chūn sǔn　spring up like bamboo shoots after spring rain；在六一儿童节的竞赛中，小朋友的发明创造像～地涌现出来。During the June 1st Children's Day competition, children's inventions cropped up like bamboo shoots after rain.

雨季 yǔjì 【名】rainy season

雨具 yǔjù 【名】things used as protection against rain（raincoat；umbrella, etc.）

雨量 yǔliàng 【名】rainfall；precipitation

雨露 yǔlù 【名】rain and dew；(fig.) bounty；favour

雨帽 yǔmào 【名】〔顶 dǐng〕rain cap

雨伞 yǔsǎn 【名】〔把 bǎ〕umbrella

雨鞋 yǔxié 【名】〔只 zhī、双 shuāng〕galosh；rubbers

雨衣 yǔyī 【名】〔件 jiàn〕raincoat

语(語) yǔ 【名】◇ ❶ word；片言只～ one or two words ❷ language；外国～ foreign language 用学生的母～进行讲解 explain in the students' mother tongue 【动】◇ speak；默默不～ keep silence 不言不～ remain silent

语病 yǔbìng 【名】mistake in use of words；rhetorical error

语调 yǔdiào 【名】intonation

语法 yǔfǎ 【名】grammar

语感 yǔgǎn 【名】an instinctive feel for the language

语汇 yǔhuì 【名】vocabulary

语句 yǔjù 【名】sentence

语料 yǔliào 【名】linguistic materials

语录 yǔlù 【名】quotation

语气 yǔqì 【名】tone

语气词 yǔqìcí 【名】modal particle

语群 yǔqún 【名】language group

语素 yǔsù 【名】phoneme

语文 yǔwén 【名】❶ Chinese (as a subject in a Chinese school curriculum)：～水平 level of proficiency in Chinese ❷ ◇ short for "语言和文学"

语无伦次 yǔ wú lúncì speak incoherently：这个人说话颠三倒四，～。His speech is totally incoherent.

语系 yǔxì 【名】language family

语言 yǔyán 【名】language

语言规范化 yǔyán guīfànhuà standardization of language

语言学 yǔyánxué 【名】linguistics

语音 yǔyīn 【名】speech sound

语音学 yǔyīnxué 【名】phonetics

语种 yǔzhǒng 【名】different kinds of languages

语重心长 yǔ zhòng xīn cháng sincere and earnest remarks or advice

语助词 yǔzhùcí 【名】(gram.) particle 也作"语气助词"。

语族 yǔzú 【名】(linguistics) branch

yù

玉 yù 【名】〔块 kuài〕jade

玉雕 yùdiāo 【名】jade carving

玉米 yùmǐ 【名】maize；corn

玉蜀黍 yùshǔshǔ 【名】corn；maize

郁(鬱) yù

郁闷 yùmèn 【形】gloomy；depressed

郁郁葱葱 yùyùcōngcōng 【形】luxuriant

育 yù 【动】◇ ❶ give birth to；produce：生儿～女 give birth to children ❷ breed；cultivate：～秧 grow rice seedlings

育林 yùlín 【动】afforestate；nurture a forest：封山～ close hillsides to facilitate afforestation

育苗 yù = miáo cultivate sprout；cultivate seedling

育种 yù = zhǒng breed new varieties

浴 yù

浴场 yùchǎng 【名】outdoor bathing place

浴巾 yùjīn 【名】bath towel

浴室 yùshì 【名】bathroom

浴血奋战 yùxuè fènzhàn fight a bloody battle

预(預) yù 【副】◇ in advance；beforehand：～祝成功 wish sb. success

预报 yùbào 【动】forecast (e.g. weather forecast)

预备 yùbèi 【动】prepare；get ready

预测 yùcè 【动】forecast

预订 yùdìng 【动】subscribe；book (tickets)：邮局开始～下一季度的报纸。The post office is accepting subscriptions to newspapers for the next quarter.

预定 yùdìng 【动】fix in advance；predetermine：按～时间完成 finish sth. on schedule 这本书～今年下半年出版。The book is scheduled to come out in the second half of this year.

预防 yùfáng 【动】prevent；provide against；guard against：～疾病 prevent diseases ～自然灾害 guard against natural disasters

预防为主 yùfáng wéi zhǔ put prevention first

预感 yùgǎn 【动】have a premonition of：～到暴风雪即将来临 have a premonition that a storm is coming 【名】presentiment：不祥的～ ominous presentiment

预告 yùgào 【动】give advance notice of；notify beforehand：星期一的报纸～一周的电视节目。Monday's newspapers advertise the week's

upcoming T. V. programmes.【名】notice or advertisement of a future event：电影 ～ notice of upcoming films 新书 ～ pre-publication notice

预计 yùjì【动】estimate；calculate in advance

预见 yùjiàn【名】foresight；prediction：科学的～ scientific prediction 这个人真有～。This person has great foresight.【动】foresee；predict

预料 yùliào【动】predict；anticipate；expect：难以～ difficult to anticipate ～ 这项任务可以提前完成。It is expected that this task will be finished ahead of schedule.【名】expectation；anticipation：出乎 ～ beyond expectations 同他的～相反，试验进行得非常顺利。Contrary to his expectation, the experiment was carried out smoothly.

预期 yùqī【动】expect；anticipate

预赛 yùsài【动】hold preliminary contest【名】preliminary contest

预示 yùshì【动】presage；betoken；forebode

预算 yùsuàn【名】budget：财政 ～ fiscal budget 这是明年的收支～。This is the budget showing income and expenditure for the coming year.

预习 yùxí【动】(of students) prepare lessons before class

预先 yùxiān【副】beforehand；in advance：这件事我～知道。I knew this in advance. 你到南方去，应该～通知他一声。You should give him warning that you are going to the South.

预想 yùxiǎng【动】expect；think that sth. will happen

预言 yùyán【动】prophesy；predict；foretell【名】prediction；prophecy：他的～已经实现了。His prediction has come true.

预演 yùyǎn【动】(of a performance) preview

预约 yùyuē【动】make an appointment

预展 yùzhǎn【动】(of an exhibition) preview

预兆 yùzhào【名】omen；augury；presage；foreshadow

预支 yùzhī【动】advance：～ 款项 advance a loan

预制 yùzhì【动】prefabricate：～ 板 prefabricated plate

欲 yù【助动】〈书〉wish；want

欲盖弥彰 yù gài mí zhāng the more one tries to hide, the more one is exposed

欲望 yùwàng【名】desire；wish

遇 yù【动】◇ meet

遇到 yù // dào meet；meet with；encounter；run into

遇害 yù = hài be killed unjustly

遇见 yù // jiàn meet；encounter

遇救 yù = jiù be rescued

遇难 yù = nàn be killed in an accident；or be murdered, usu. when engaged in a certain cause

遇险 yù = xiǎn meet with danger

寓 yù

寓所 yùsuǒ【名】lodging

寓言 yùyán【名】fable；parable

寓意 yùyì【名】implied meaning

愈 yù〈书〉【动】recover from an illness：他已病 ～ 出院。He has already recovered from his illness and has been discharged from hospital.【副】more：快到久别的家乡了，他的心 ～ 不能平静。As he approached his hometown after a long absence, he became more and more excited.

愈合 yùhé【动】heal up

愈加 yùjiā【副】同"越发" yuèfā

（*usu. in written language*）

愈来愈 yùláiyù 【副】more and more
（*usu. in written language*）

愈…愈… yù…yù… 同“越…越…”
yuè…yuè…（*usu. in written language*）

yuān

渊（淵） yuān

渊博 yuānbó 【形】broad and profound；erudite

渊深 yuānshēn 【形】profound；deep
（e.g. learning）

冤 yuān 【名】injustice；false accusation；wrong：鸣～叫屈 complain of one's wrongs 【形】not worthwhile：白跑了一趟，真～！I went there to no avail；what a waste of time!

冤仇 yuānchóu 【名】enmity；hatred

冤家 yuānjia 【名】enemy；foe；adversary

冤假错案 yuān jiǎ cuò àn cases wrongly，falsely and unjustly charged

冤屈 yuānqū 【动】wrong；treat unjustly

冤枉 yuānwang 【动】falsely charge；wrong：这不是他的过错，不要～他。It's not his fault；don't blame him.【形】sheer waste：我走了不少～路，才找到那家铺子。After walking in the wrong direction，I finally found that shop.

冤狱 yuānyù 【名】unjust verdict；unjust charge

yuán

元 yuán 【量】*yuan*, unit of Chinese currency，and one *yuan* is equal to ten *jiao* 也作“圆”。

元旦 Yuándàn 【名】New Year's Day

元件 yuánjiàn 【名】parts；accessories（of machine，meter，radio set，etc.）

元老 yuánlǎo 【名】founding member

元首 yuánshǒu 【名】head of state

元帅 yuánshuài 【名】marshal

元素 yuánsù 【名】(chem.) element

元素符号 yuánsù fúhào （chem.）element symbol

元素周期表 yuánsù zhōuqībiǎo the periodic table（of chemical elements）

元宵节 yuánxiāojié 【名】the Lantern Festival

元音 yuányīn 【名】vowel

元月 yuányuè 【名】January（*rarely used*）

园（園） yuán 【名】garden；park

园地 yuándì 【名】❶ a general term for vegetable plot，fruit orchard，flower garden，etc.：这块地是他的实验～。This is his experimental plot. ❷ field；scope（for certain activities）：文艺～ literary column 游艺～ recreation area

园丁 yuándīng 【名】gardener

园林 yuánlín 【名】landscape garden

园田化 yuántiánhuà 【动】gardenize

园艺 yuányì 【名】horticulture

园子 yuánzi 【名】vegetable patch；vegetable garden

员（員） yuán 【名】member of an organization：集体中的一～ a member of the collective 【量】*for generals in the past，now used of any capable person*：他是乒坛上的一～猛将。He is an outstanding table-tennis player.【尾】*used to denote a kind of person*：指战～ com-

manders and soldiers 伤病～ sick and wounded personnel

员工　yuángōng　【名】staff members and workers

原　yuán　【形】❶ primary；original：～作者 original author 物归～主 the lost property was returned to its owner 这些书～是为青年自修编写的。These books were compiled primarily for young people'self-study. ❷ ◇ raw；crude：～煤 raw coal ～粮 unprocessed grain

原材料　yuáncáiliào　【名】raw and processed materials

原地　yuándì　【名】original place；～踏步 make no headway（stamp at the original place）

原封不动　yuán fēng bù dòng　be kept intact；untouched

原稿　yuángǎo　【名】original manuscript；original copy

原告　yuángào　【名】plaintiff

原籍　yuánjí　【名】native home；native place

原件　yuánjiàn　【名】script

原来　yuánlái　【形】同"本来"běnlái【形】：他自己也觉得～的想法不对。He himself also realized that his original idea wouldn't work. 他～是机械厂的工人，现在在大学学习。He was originally a worker in a machinery plant, is now studying in a university.【副】indicates a new discovery regarding something already known：这本书～是你写的。So it was you who wrote this book! 她的孩子～已经那么大了。I didn't know her child was that big!

原理　yuánlǐ　【名】principle；axiom

原谅　yuánliàng　【动】pardon；excuse

原料　yuánliào　【名】raw material

原始　yuánshǐ　【形】❶ primitive；virgin；primeval ❷ original；initial；firsthand

原始社会　yuánshǐ shèhuì　primitive society

原文　yuánwén　【名】original text；the original

原先　yuánxiān　【形】original；former：～的计划不是这样的。The original plan was not like this. 他～是一个工人，现在成长为工厂的领导干部了。He was originally a worker but is now a leader in a factory.

原形毕露　yuánxíng bìlù　reveal one's true nature；show one's true colours（derog.）

原野　yuányě　【名】open country

原因　yuányīn　【名】cause；grounds

原油　yuányóu　【名】crude oil

原原本本　yuányuánběnběn　【副】from beginning to end；in its entirety：把事情的经过～地说一遍 tell the whole story of what has happened 把党的政策～地交给群众 tell the masses exactly what the Party's policy is 也作"源源本本"。

原则　yuánzé　【名】principle；fundamental rule

原则性　yuánzéxìng　【名】sense of principle

原著　yuánzhù　【名】original；original work

原子　yuánzǐ　【名】atom

原子弹　yuánzǐdàn　【名】atom bomb

原子反应堆　yuánzǐ fǎnyìngduī　atomic reactor

原子核　yuánzǐhé　【名】atomic nucleus

原子结构　yuánzǐ jiégòu　atom structure

原子量　yuánzǐliàng　【名】atomic weight

原子能　yuánzǐnéng　【名】atomic energy

原子武器　yuánzǐ wǔqì　atomic weapon

原子序数　yuánzǐ xùshù　atomic number

圆（圓）　yuán　【名】circle

【形】round：今晚的月亮真～。Tonight the moon looks very round. 【动】◇ make plausible：～场 help to effect a compromise；mediate a dispute ～谎 plug the loopholes in a lie 【量】同"元" yuán 【量】

圆白菜　yuánbáicài　【名】〔棵 kē〕cabbage

圆规　yuánguī　【名】compasses

圆滑　yuánhuá　【形】wily；cunning；slippery

圆满　yuánmǎn　【形】satisfactory；complete；perfect

圆圈　yuánquān　【名】(～儿) circle；ring

圆舞曲　yuánwǔqǔ　【名】waltz

圆心　yuánxīn　【名】centre of a circle

圆形　yuánxíng　【名】circular；round

圆周　yuánzhōu　【名】circumference

圆周率　yuánzhōulǜ　【名】the ratio of the circumference of a circle to its diameter (π)

圆珠笔　yuánzhūbǐ　【名】〔枝 zhī〕ballpoint

圆柱　yuánzhù　【名】cylinder；column；pillar

圆锥　yuánzhuī　【名】cone

圆桌　yuánzhuō　【名】〔张 zhāng〕round-table

圆桌会议　yuánzhuō huìyì　round-table conference

援　yuán　【动】◇ ❶ support；help；assist；aid ❷ quote；cite

援救　yuánjiù　【动】rescue；extricate from danger；save

援军　yuánjūn　【名】reinforcement

援外　yuánwài　【动】aid a foreign country：～专家 expert to aid a foreign country ～技术 technique in aid of a foreign country

援引　yuányǐn　【动】quote；cite

援助　yuánzhù　【动】help；support；aid；assist：及时～受害者家属 help the families of victims in a timely fashion 【名】help；support；aid；as-sistance：经济～ financial aid 给予巨大的～ give tremendous support

缘(緣)　yuán

缘分　yuánfèn　【名】luck（by which people are brought together）：她跟他真有～！The two of them were brought together by sheer luck!

缘故　yuángù　【名】reason；cause（used only in the phrases 是什么～ and 因为…的～）：他还不来，不知是什么～。He hasn't turned up yet. I don't know for what reason. 正因为虚心向别人学习的～，所以他进步很快。It is precisely because he learns from others that he makes rapid progress. 也作"原故"。

缘由　yuányóu　【名】reason；cause

猿　yuán　【名】monkey；ape

猿人　yuánrén　【名】ape man

源　yuán　【名】source；fountain

源泉　yuánquán　【名】source spring；fountainhead

源源　yuányuán　【副】continuously；in a steady stream：～而来 come in a steady stream 奔驰在青藏公路上的货车～不断。Trucks run unceasingly on the Qinghai-Xizang Highway.

yuǎn

远(遠)　yuǎn　【形】❶ far；distant：～距离 a long distance 站得高，看得～ stand on a commanding height from which one can see a long distance 我的家离学校很～。My home is quite far from school. ❷ a long time：～在宋朝，中国就有了活字版印刷。As far back as the Song dynasty, China was already using movable type in printing. 现在离国庆节不～了。It is not long

now until National Day. ❸ with big difference：相差很～ there's a big difference（between them）我下象棋～不是他的对手。I'm far from being his equal at playing chess. ❹ ◇ not close；distant：～亲 distant relative

远处 yuǎnchù 【名】faraway place

远大 yuǎndà 【形】（of abstract things）far-reaching；great；broad；long-range

远方 yuǎnfāng 【名】distant place；remote place

远航 yuǎnháng 【动】sail to a far-away place；take a long voyage

远见 yuǎnjiàn 【名】far-sighted view；far-sightedness；foresight

远近 yuǎnjìn 【名】distance（measure of space）

远景 yuǎnjǐng 【名】distant prospect；outlook；long-range prospective

远视 yuǎnshì 【名】farsightedness

远洋 yuǎnyáng 【名】the distant seas；ocean-going

远征 yuǎnzhēng 【动】go on an expedition；make a long march

远走高飞 yuǎn zǒu gāo fēi go away to a distant place

yuàn

怨 yuàn 【名】◇ hatred；resentment：旧～新仇 old grudges and new resentments 【动】blame：这不能～他。You can't blame him for this.

怨不得 yuànbude 【副】no wonder：～她这么黑呢，原来她到海边去了一个月。She has been at the seaside for a month. No wonder she is beautifully tanned.

怨恨 yuànhèn 【动】resent；hate 【名】resentment；hatred：满腔～ full of resentment

怨气 yuànqì 【名】resentment；grudge

怨声载道 yuàn shēng zài dào voices of discontent are heard everywhere

怨天尤人 yuàn tiān yóu rén blame Heaven and man；blame all and sundry

怨言 yuànyán 【名】grumble；repining；complaint

院 yuàn 【名】◇ ❶ courtyard ❷ college；institute：我～教职工将近一千人。Our institute has about one thousand teachers and staff members.

院士 yuànshì 【名】academician

院子 yuànzi 【名】courtyard

愿（願） yuàn 【名】◇ wish；desire：如～ have one's wish fulfilled 【动】wish；hope：～你早日成功！I hope you'll soon meet with success. 【助动】be willing；would like：～去长城的，明天早上七点出发。Those who would like to go to the Great Wall should be ready to leave at seven o'clock tomorrow morning.

愿望 yuànwàng 【名】wish；desire；aspiration；hope；expectation

愿意 yuànyì 【助动】be willing（to do sth.）；be ready（to do sth.）：让你到南方去工作，你～去吗？Are you willing to work in the South if you are asked to? 我～喝白开水，不～喝茶。I prefer plain boiled water to tea. 【动】hope；wish：大家都～你多住几天。We all hope that you can stay for a few more days.

yuē

约（約） yuē 【动】❶ make an appointment：今天到天坛去是我

们上星期～好的。We are going to the Temple of Heaven today. We arranged it last week. ❷ ask; invite: 他～我到他家做客。He invited me to visit him at his home. 【名】◇ appointment: 有～在先 appointment made in advance 失～ fail to keep one's appointment 【副】 about: ～三百人 about three hundred people 我们谈了～有半个钟头。We talked for about half an hour.

约定　yuēdìng　【动】agree on

约定俗成　yuē dìng sú chéng　recognition (of customs or terminology, etc.) as a result of common practice

约分　yuē = fēn　(maths.) reduction of fraction

约会　yuēhuì　【名】appointment; engagement; rendezvous: 今天晚上我有个～。I have an engagement tonight.

约请　yuēqǐng　【动】invite

约束　yuēshù　【动】restrain; control; bind; confine 【名】restraint

约束力　yuēshùlì　【名】binding force

约数　yuēshù　【名】❶ approximate number ❷ (maths.) divisor

yuè

月　yuè　【名】❶◇ the moon ❷ month

月初　yuèchū　【名】the beginning of a month

月底　yuèdǐ　【名】the end of a month

月份　yuèfèn　【名】a specific month

月份牌　yuèfènpái　【名】monthly calendar

月光　yuèguāng　【名】moonlight; moonbeam

月经　yuèjīng　【名】menstruation; menses

月刊　yuèkān　【名】monthly magazine

月亮　yuèliang　【名】moon

月末　yuèmò　【名】end of the month

月票　yuèpiào　【名】〔张 zhāng〕monthly ticket

月球　yuèqiú　【名】moon

月色　yuèsè　【名】moonlight

月食　yuèshí　【名】eclipse of the moon; lunar eclipse

月薪　yuèxīn　【名】monthly pay

月中　yuèzhōng　【名】the middle of a month

月终　yuèzhōng　【名】end of the month

乐（樂）　yuè　【名】◇ music
另见 lè

乐队　yuèduì　【名】orchestra; band

乐理　yuèlǐ　【名】musical theory

乐谱　yuèpǔ　【名】printed music; score

乐器　yuèqì　【名】musical instrument

乐曲　yuèqǔ　【名】music; musical composition

乐团　yuètuán　【名】musical troupe

岳　yuè

岳父　yuèfù　【名】wife's father

岳母　yuèmǔ　【名】wife's mother

悦　yuè

悦耳　yuè'ěr　【形】〈书〉pleasant to listen to; melodious 歌声～ the singing is pleasant ～的音乐 melodious music

悦目　yuèmù　【形】〈书〉pleasing to the eye; easy on the eyes: 鲜艳～ bright and pleasing to the eye

阅（閱）　yuè　【动】〈书〉read: 报刊～后请放回原处。Please replace the newspapers and magazines after you have read them.

阅兵　yuè = bīng　review troops; a military review

阅读　yuèdú　【动】read

阅卷　yuè = juàn　go over examination papers；mark exam papers

阅览　yuèlǎn　【动】read

阅览室　yuèlǎnshì　【名】reading room

跃（躍）　yuè　【动】〈书〉jump：
一～而过 jump over (sth.)

跃进　yuèjìn　【动】make progress by leaps and bounds；make a leap；leap forward

跃跃欲试　yuè yuè yù shì　be anxious to try sth.：看到解放军战士进行射击演习，同学们都～。Watching the P. L. A. soldiers' shooting practice, the students were all eager to have a try.

越　yuè　【动】◇❶ cross：～墙而过 climb over the wall　翻山～岭 travel up hill and down dale ❷ by-pass：～级上诉 appeal bypassing one's immediate leadership

越发　yuèfā　【副】❶ more and more：八月一过，天气～凉爽了。Since the end of August, it has become increasingly cool. ❷ 同"越…越…" when used with "越" or "越是"：发言越多，会场气氛～热烈。The more people spoke, the more heated the meeting became.

越轨　yuè = guǐ　beyond bounds；deviate；departure from (rules, principles, etc.)

越过　yuèguò　【动】surpass；pass over；cross

越境　yuè = jìng　illegally cross over a boundary

越来越　yuèláiyuè　【副】more and more：条件～成熟。The conditions are becoming more and more favourable. 我～喜欢滑冰。I am getting to be more and more fond of skating.

越位　yuè = wèi　offside

越野赛跑　yuèyě sàipǎo　cross-country race

越狱　yuè = yù　escape from prison；break prison

越…越…　yuè…yuè…　the more…the more…：越走越快 walk faster and faster 这本书他越看越爱看。The more he reads the book, the better he likes it. 越想越觉得他说的有道理。The more I think about it, the more I feel that what he said was right.

yūn

晕（暈）　yūn　【动】faint；dizzy
另见 yùn

晕头转向　yūn tóu zhuàn xiàng　confused and disoriented：这几天我忙得～。I have been up to my ears in work these past few days and am feeling quite confused. 那只小鸟被孩子们追得～，不知往哪里飞好。Chased by the children, the little bird was so panic-stricken that it didn't know where to fly.

yún

云（雲）　yún　【名】cloud

云彩　yúncai　【名】cloud

云层　yúncéng　【名】cloud layer

云集　yúnjí　【动】(fig.) (of people in large numbers) gather；get together：全运会期间，各地选手～北京。During the National Games, contestants selected from all parts of the country gathered in Beijing.

云消雾散　yún xiāo wù sàn　clouds disperse；the sky clears up；vanish without a trace

匀　yún　【形】even：颜色很～。The colour is very even. 漆调(tiáo)得不～。The paints are not evenly mixed. 【动】❶ spare：能不能～些树苗给我们？Can you spare us

some tree seedlings? 你～出点时间来帮我改改稿子。Please spare me some time to help with the revision of the manuscript. ❷ even up: 这两束花多少不均,你把它～一～。The two bunches of flowers are not the same size. Please even them up.

匀称　yúnchèn　【形】well-balanced; well-proportioned

匀净　yúnjing　【形】even;uniform:墙刷得很～。The wall is evenly whitewashed.这线纺得多～! How evenly this thread is spun!

匀速运动　yúnsù yùndòng　(phys.) uniform motion

匀速转动　yúnsù zhuàndòng　(phys.) uniform rotation

匀整　yúnzhěng　【形】well-spaced and even

yǔn

允　yǔn　【动】allow; permit; promise;approve;give consent

允许　yǔnxǔ　【动】promise; permit; give permission;allow

yùn

孕　yùn　【名】pregnancy

孕妇　yùnfù　【名】pregnant woman

孕育　yùnyù　【动】be pregnant; breed:黄河～了中华民族的文化。The Yellow River gave birth to the culture of the Chinese nation.

运(運)　yùn　【动】transport: ～东西 transport things 大批水产品～到山区。Large quantities of products from the sea are transported to the mountain areas.

运筹学　yùnchóuxué　【名】operations research;operational research

运动　yùndòng　【动】move:事物总是在不断地～着。Everything is in constant motion.【名】❶ (phys.) motion:天体～ motion of a celestial body ❷ sports;athletics:田径～ track and field events 开展体育～ develop sports activities ❸ movement:增产节约～ the movement to practise economy and increase production 植树～ tree-planting drive

运动场　yùndòngchǎng　【名】sports ground;stadium

运动服　yùndòngfú　【名】〔件 jiàn〕sportswear

运动会　yùndònghuì　【名】sports meet;games

运动员　yùndòngyuán　【名】athlete; sportsman

运动战　yùndòngzhàn　【名】mobile warfare

运费　yùnfèi　【名】freight;carriage

运河　yùnhé　【名】〔条 tiáo〕canal

运气　yùnqi　【名】❶ fate;fortune ❷ luck:你们的～不错,这里正有你们要的那本旧杂志。You're lucky. We just happen to have the back number of the magazine you want. 这种扣子在那个商店也许能配上,去碰碰～吧。You might find this sort of button in that shop. Go and try your luck.

运输　yùnshū　【动】transport 【名】transportation

运输机　yùnshūjī　【名】〔架 jià〕freighter;air-freighter

运送　yùnsòng　【动】send; deliver; transport

运算　yùnsuàn　【动】(maths.) perform operation;operation

运行　yùnxíng　【动】circulate; revolve;move in orbit;(of a train) run

运行图　yùnxíngtú　【名】run chart

运营　yùnyíng　【动】run

运用　yùnyòng　【动】put to use; ap-

ply：～自如 apply skilfully 要把理论～到实践中去。One should put theory into practice. 学习过的知识要能灵活～。One should be able to flexibly apply the knowledge one has acquired.

运载　yùnzài　【动】carry；deliver

运载火箭　yùnzài huǒjiàn　carrier rocket

运转　yùnzhuǎn　【动】operate；revolve；rotate；机器～正常。The machine is operating normally.

运作　yùnzuò　【动】work；operate

晕（暈）　yùn　【动】feel giddy；be dizzy
另见 yūn

晕场　yùn＝chǎng　have stage fright；get dizzy at examinations

晕车　yùn＝chē　car sick

晕船　yùn＝chuán　seasick

酝（醞）　yùn
酝酿　yùnniàng　【动】brew；ferment；(fig.) discuss；deliberate：～候选人名单 discuss and deliberate on the list of candidates 组织机构怎样变动，还需要再～～。The changes in organization and administrative structure require further deliberation and consultation.

韵　yùn　【名】❶ rhyme ❷ short for "韵母"
韵母　yùnmǔ　【名】final of a Chinese syllable

韵文　yùnwén　【名】verse

蕴（蘊）　yùn
蕴藏　yùncáng　【动】contain（mineral deposits）：地下～着丰富的矿藏。There are rich mineral deposits to be found under the ground. 群众中～着极大的积极性。The masses are an inexhaustible source of energy.

熨　yùn　【动】press；iron：～衣服 iron clothes
熨斗　yùndǒu　【名】iron (for pressing clothes)

熨烫　yùntàng　【动】iron；press

熨衣板　yùnyībǎn　【名】ironing board

Z

zā

扎 zā 【动】tie；bind；fasten：把口袋～紧 tie up the sack 辫子上～着蝴蝶结 braids tied with bows
另见 zhā

zá

杂（雜）zá 【形】miscellaneous；mixed；assorted：～色 assorted colours 今天事儿太～，必须安排好。There are a lot of odds and ends of miscellaneous work to do today, so we must organize it carefully. 【动】mix；blend：草丛中～着一些野花 bushes interspersed with wild flowers

杂费 záfèi 【名】miscellaneous expenses；incidental expenses

杂感 zágǎn 【名】〔篇 piān〕a kind of short impressionistic essay

杂货 záhuò 【名】sundry goods；groceries

杂货店 záhuòdiàn 【名】grocery

杂记 zájì 【名】〔篇 piān〕notes；miscellanies（writings）

杂技 zájì 【名】acrobatics

杂交 zájiāo 【动】crossbreed；hybridize

杂粮 záliáng 【名】coarse grain（e.g. maize, millet, etc.）

杂乱 záluàn 【形】disorderly；disarranged

杂乱无章 záluàn wú zhāng in a mess；disorderly

杂牌 zápái 【名】inferior brand：～货 goods of an inferior brand

杂品 zápǐn 【名】sundry goods

杂七杂八 zá qī zá bā odds and ends of things all mixed together

杂事 záshì 【名】miscellaneous affairs

杂文 záwén 【名】〔篇 piān〕essay；the familiar essay

杂务 záwù 【名】odd jobs

杂音 záyīn 【名】❶ atmospherics；noise ❷（med.）murmur

杂志 zázhì 【名】〔本 běn〕magazine；periodical

杂质 zázhì 【名】impurity

砸 zá 【动】❶ pound；tamp：把地基～实 tamp down the earth for the foundation of a building 石头～了脚。His foot was crushed by a rock. ❷ smash；break：碗～了。The bowl was broken.

砸饭碗 zá fànwǎn lose one's job；get the sack

砸锅 zá = guō bungle；ruin the work；end up in failure；get ruined

砸碎 zá // suì ❶ break；smash：玻璃被～了。The pane of glass was smashed to pieces. ❷ smash to

pieces；overthrow：～铁锁链，奴隶得解放。The slaves smashed their chains and freed themselves.

zāi

灾（災） zāi 【名】◇ ❶ disaster；calamity：洪水泛滥成～。The widespread flooding turned into a disaster. ❷ misfortune；adversity：招～惹祸 invite trouble；court disaster

灾害 zāihài 【名】(natural) disaster；calamity

灾荒 zāihuāng 【名】famine

灾祸 zāihuò 【名】disaster；calamity（natural or man-made）

灾民 zāimín 【名】victims of a natural calamity

灾难 zāinàn 【名】〔场 chǎng〕catastrophe：～深重 disaster-ridden

灾情 zāiqíng 【名】actual state of affairs after a natural calamity

灾区 zāiqū 【名】disaster area

灾殃 zāiyāng 【名】同"灾难"

栽 zāi 【动】❶ plant；grow：～花 grow flowers ～树 plant trees ❷ trip；stumble：～了个跟头 tripped and fell 中(zhòng)弹的敌机一头～进大海。The enemy plane was hit and plunged into the sea.

栽培 zāipéi 【动】❶ plant and cultivate：～花木 grow flowers and trees ❷ educate；train；cultivate

栽赃 zāi = zāng　frame sb.；fabricate a charge against sb.

栽种 zāizhòng 【动】plant

zǎi

载（載） zǎi 【名】a year：三年五～ in a few years 【动】put on record；write down：～入史册 go

down in history

另见 zài

宰 zǎi 【动】slaughter；butcher：～了一头牛 slaughter an ox

宰割 zǎigē 【动】trample underfoot；oppress and exploit

宰杀 zǎishā 【动】butcher；slaughter

宰牲节 zǎishēngjié 【名】'Id al-Kurban

zài

再 zài 【副】❶ again indicates regular repetition，expected repetition or repetition which has not taken place：请你～说一遍。Please repeat it once again. 他每天早上听一遍英语广播，晚上～听一遍。He listens to the English broadcast in the morning and again in the evening. 去年接到他一封信以后，没～收到他的信。Since I got a letter from him last year，I've never heard from him again. ❷ indicates regular continuation，expected continuation or continuation which has not taken place：别客气了，～客气大家就不高兴了。Please don't continue to stand on ceremony，or we'll all be uncomfortable. 老张总是下班铃响以后～干一会儿才走。Lao Zhang always continues to work for a while after the bell for knocking off has rung. 他那部文学史出了第一部就没有～写下去。After the first volume of his literary history was published，he didn't keep on writing. ❸ then and only then：活儿不多了，干完了～休息吧！There isn't much work left. We'd better finish it before we take a break. 这个方案先征求征求大家的意见，～决定怎么改。Let's wait for a second opinion before we decide to

change this project. ❹ still; in a higher degree *usu. referring to an expected event or a supposition*: 这件大衣短一点儿,还有～长点儿的吗? This overcoat is a little too short for me. Have you got a longer one? 这座楼～高一点儿就可以看到市中心了。If this building were higher, we would be able to see the centre of town. ❺ 再...也... *is similar to* 无论多么...也... *or* 无论怎么...也...: 天～旱也要夺丰收。No matter how bad the drought, we must strive for a good harvest. 一个人力量～大,也没有集体的力量大。No matter how strong an individual may be, he can't be as strong as a collective. 这种果子～熟也是酸的。Even when it is quite ripe, this fruit remains very sour. 他就是个慢性子人,～催他也没用。He is a slow coach, no matter how hard you try to hurry him up, it won't make a difference. ❻ 再也 *used before a negative word as an intensive expression*: 那种苦日子,～也不会回来了。The hard days will never come back. 这是很多年以前的事了,详细情况我～也想不起来了。That was something which happened ages ago. I simply couldn't recall the details for the life of me. 泰山我十年前去过一次,以后～也没有去过。I went to Mount Tai once ten years ago, and have never been there since. ❼ 再...不过 *indicates the superlative degree*: 今天的试题～容易不过了。The examination questions today couldn't be easier. 这种药～苦不过了。The medicine was awfully bitter.

再版 zàibǎn 【动】reprint; republish; second edition

再度 zàidù 【副】again; once more: ～来中国 come to China for a second time 他～被评为先进生产者。

He has been cited once again as an "advanced worker".

再会 zàihuì 【动】同"再见", *less frequently used*

再婚 zàihūn 【动】remarry

再见 zàijiàn 【动】see you again; good-bye

再接再厉 zài jiē zài lì make sustained and redoubled efforts; make unremitting efforts

再三 zàisān 【副】again and again *referring to some action in the past*: ～嘱咐 enjoin again and again ～劝阻 try again and again to dissuade ～解释 try repeatedly to explain 突击队～要求承担爆破任务。The shock troops repeatedly asked to undertake the blowing-up (of the fortifications).

再生 zàishēng 【动】regenerate

再生产 zàishēngchǎn 【名】(econ.) reproduction

再说 zàishuō 【动】put off to some later time: 事情怎么办,等大家商量以后～。As to what is to be done concerning this matter, we will decide after we have discussed it together. 这个会先不开,过几天～。We'll postpone the meeting for the time being, and see what's to be done after a couple of days.【连】〈口〉moreover: 天晚了,～路又很远,明天去吧! It's pretty late now; moreover, it's a long way away. We'd better go tomorrow.

再现 zàixiàn 【动】reappear; be reproduced

在 zài 【动】❶ at; on *indicates the position of sb. or sth.*: 他不～家。He isn't in. 茶杯～桌上。The tea cup is on the table. ❷ be alive; exist: 人～阵地～ fight to the death in defence of one's position 他的父母都不～了。Both of his parents are dead. 咱们小学毕业时的照片还～吗?

Do you still have our graduation photograph from primary school? 今天他的心好像不～工作上，不知为什么。His mind doesn't seem to be on his work today. I wonder why. ❸ rest with; depend on; 他们俩的婚事成不成，关键在～男方而～女方。Whether they will marry doesn't depend on him as on her. 学习的条件很好，是否能取得成绩，全～你自己了。All the facilities for study are available, whether you use them is up to you. 【介】*indicates time, place or range*: 他～三天前离开了这里。He left here three days ago. 他今天～地里劳动。He is working in the fields today. 这个传说～民间已经流传了几百年了。This legend has spread among the people for hundreds of years. 【副】*indicates action in progress*: 他～干什么呢? What's he doing? 他～写信。He's writing a letter.

在编人员 zàibiān rényuán permanent staff

在场 zàichǎng 【动】be present; be on locality

在朝 zàicháo 【动】hold office at court

在乎 zàihu 【动】be particular about; be mindful of; care about (*usu. used in the negative or in a rhetorical question*: 不在乎 *means* "*do not take to heart*"): 你还～这点儿小事? You are not upset over this trifling matter, are you? 他一心为公，从不～个人得失。He is wholeheartedly devoted to the public interest and does not care about personal gain or loss. 对别人的批评不要满不～。Don't make light of the criticisms of others.

在即 zàijí 【动】will take place soon; be near at hand

在…看来 zài...kànlái judged from sb.'s point of view: 在当时看来，这种做法没有错。By the standard in those days, there was nothing wrong in what was done. 在他看来，解决这个技术问题并不难。As far as he is concerned, this technological problem is not difficult to solve.

在…上 zài...shàng *usu. used together with a dissyllabic abstract noun or a nominal phrase*: ❶ in certain respect: 在这个问题上，我们的观点是一致的。We hold unanimous views on this question. 在原则问题上，不能让步。We do not make concessions on matters of principle. ❷ in certain conditions: 在原有的基础上，继续努力 continue to exert oneself on the basis of one's previous efforts

在世 zàishì 【动】be in this world; (of a person) be alive

在逃犯 zàitáofàn 【名】criminal at large; escaped criminal

在望 zàiwàng 【动】❶ be within sight: 宝塔山遥遥～。Pagoda Hill came into view in the distance. ❷ be within reach; in prospect: 丰收～ a good harvest is in prospect 胜利～ victory within reach

在握 zàiwò 【动】in one's hands; under one's control: 胜券～ victory within grasp

在…下 zài...xià *used with a nominal phrase or expression, dissyllabic at least* under (certain conditions): 在这种复杂的情况下，我们更应该沉着。Under such complex conditions, we ought to be even more cool-headed. 在这种社会制度下，人民的生活是有保障的。Under this social system, the livelihood of the people is secure.

在押 zàiyā 【动】be in prison: ～犯 prisoner

在野 zàiyě 【动】not be in office: ～党 a party not in office

在意 zàiyì 【动】mind; care about (*usu. in the neg*.): 这类小事，他是不大～的。He is not much concerned about such trifling matters. 他是跟您开玩笑，您可别～。He was only joking with you; don't take it to heart.

在于 zàiyú 【动】❶ lie in; rest with: 这种布的优点～耐穿、不退色。The strong points of this kind of cloth are that it wears well and is colour-fast. 那本小说之所以受欢迎，～题材新颖，语言生动。The reason that novel is very popular is its unique theme and vivid language. ❷ be determined by; depend on: 文章的好坏不～长短。Whether a piece of writing is good or not doesn't depend on its length. 农业的根本出路～机械化。The ultimate solution for agriculture is the mechanization of farm work.

在职 zàizhí 【形】being in office; being at one's post (*attrib. only*)

在…中 zài…zhōng ❶ *used with a noun or nominal phrase*, *dissyllabic at least* ① in the process of; in the course of: 在这次球赛中，他打出了风格，打出了水平。He played at the peak of his ability and displayed excellent sportsmanship in the match. 在劳动竞赛中，她表现得很突出。In the labour emulation drive her performance was quite outstanding. ② *indicates the range from which a portion is selected*: 在这些错综复杂的矛盾中，找出主要矛盾 pick out the main contradiction from amongst a complex mass of contradictions 在所有展品中，这几幅油画最吸引人。Of all the items on display, these oil paintings attracted the greatest attention. ❷ *used with a verb or a verbal phrase to indicate that sth. is in progress*: 关于这个新课题，还正在探讨中。As far as this new problem is concerned, it is still in the exploratory stages.

在座 zàizuò 【动】be present at (a banquet, meeting, etc.)

载（載）zài 【动】carry; be loaded with: 卡车～着农物资开往农村。Trucks loaded with goods and material for agricultural production were heading for the rural areas.
另见 zǎi

载歌载舞 zài gē zài wǔ singing and dancing

载体 zàitǐ 【名】carrier

载重 zàizhòng 【动】load; carrying capacity

zán

咱 zán 【代】〈口〉we; us (*including the speaker and the person or persons spoken to*): ～新同学难道组织不起来一个篮球队吗？Can't we new students organize a basketball team?

咱们 zánmen 【代】〈口〉we; us (*including the speaker and the person or persons spoken to*): 你也去看电影？好，～一块儿走吧！Are you going to the movie too? Good, let's go together!

zǎn

攒（攢）zǎn 【动】save; accumulate: ～钱 save money 他～了不少风景画片。He has collected a lot of picture postcards.

zàn

暂（暫）zàn 【形】◇ temporary; of short duration: 时间久～尚

难确定。It's still hard to tell whether it will take a long or a short time.【副】◇ temporarily; for the time being; ～停 (sports) time-out 工作 ～告一段落。The work has been suspended for the time being.

暂缓 zànhuǎn 【动】put off; postpone

暂且 zànqiě 【副】for the time being; for the moment; for the present; 此事 ～ 不谈。Let's drop this matter for the moment. ～就这样吧！Well, let's leave it at that for the time being.

暂时 zànshí 【形】temporary; for the time being; 这只是 ～ 的困难。These are only temporary difficulties. 这个计划～还不能实行。This plan cannot be put into effect for the time being. 运动员说：胜败是～的，友谊是永存的。The athletes say: "Winning or losing is temporary, but friendship is lasting."

暂时性 zànshíxìng 【名】temporariness

赞（贊）zàn 【动】◇ approve; admire; praise

赞不绝口 zàn bù jué kǒu praise unceasingly

赞成 zànchéng 【动】approve; assent; favour; agree

赞歌 zàngē 【名】〔首 shǒu〕song of praise; ode

赞美 zànměi 【动】admire; praise

赞赏 zànshǎng 【动】appreciate; praise

赞叹 zàntàn 【动】praise highly; admire

赞同 zàntóng 【动】assent; agree; favour

赞许 zànxǔ 【动】approve; commend; speak favourably of

赞扬 zànyáng 【动】extol; praise; speak favourably of

赞助 zànzhù 【动】support; aid

zāng

脏（髒）zāng 【形】dirty; filthy

脏话 zānghuà 【名】dirty language; nasty words

脏土 zāngtǔ 【名】rubbish; garbage

赃（贓）zāng 【名】◇ stolen goods; booty

赃款 zāngkuǎn 【名】money stolen; illicit money

赃物 zāngwù 【名】stolen goods; spoils

zàng

葬 zàng 【动】bury

葬礼 zànglǐ 【名】funeral ceremony; funeral

葬送 zàngsòng 【动】bring... to ruin; ruin

zāo

遭 zāo 【动】meet with; suffer; sustain (usu. misfortune); 险 ～ 不幸 have a narrow escape 惨～毒手 be killed in cold blood ～了天灾 be struck by a natural disaster 【量】time; turn; round, etc.; 一～生，两～熟 be strangers at first meeting, but friends thereafter 他最近到南方走了一～。He recently made a tour of the South.

遭到 zāodào 【动】meet with; sustain; ～冷遇 meet with a cold reception ～ 严重破坏 sustain heavy damage

遭受 zāoshòu 【动】suffer; endure; undergo; ～ 歧视 be discriminated

against ～沉重打击 suffer a heavy blow

遭殃　zāo = yāng　suffer a catastrophe; meet with disaster; run into calamity

遭遇　zāoyù　【动】(mil.) meet with; encounter: 侦察小组和敌人巡逻队 ～ 了。Our reconnaissance unit encountered an enemy patrol. 【名】suffering; misfortune: 痛苦的 ～ bitter suffering 不幸的 ～ a misfortune

糟　zāo　【形】❶ decayed; rotten; worn out: ～木头 rotten logs 布 ～ 了。This cloth has disintegrated. ❷ (of things) spoiled; ruined: 这事办得真～。You've made a terrible mess of this problem. ～了, 忘了通知他集合的地点了。Too bad, I've forgotten to inform him about where to assemble.

糟糕　zāogāo　【形】in a terrible mess; too bad; bad luck

糟粕　zāopò　【名】scum; dregs; waste matter; dross

糟蹋　zāota　【动】❶ spoil; waste; misuse: 不要 ～ 粮食。Don't waste grain. ❷ trample on; ravage: 这一带曾被土匪 ～ 得不成样子。This area was once ravaged by bandits and left in a terrible state. 也作"糟踏"。

záo

凿(鑿)　záo　【动】chisel

zǎo

早　zǎo　【名】◇ morning: 从～到晚 from morning till night 一大～儿就有人在小树林里散步。Very early in the morning, there are already people taking a walk in the little

wood. 【形】❶ early: 明天你 ～ 点儿来。Please come earlier tomorrow. 老林来得总是比我～。Lao Lin always comes earlier than I. ❷ long ago: 这件事我～就听说了。I heard about this matter long ago. ❸ Good morning: 老师 ～! Good morning, Teacher!

早班　zǎobān　【名】morning shift

早餐　zǎocān　【名】breakfast

早操　zǎocāo　【名】morning exercise

早晨　zǎochén　【名】同"早上"

早春　zǎochūn　【名】early spring

早点　zǎodiǎn　【名】breakfast

早饭　zǎofàn　【名】〔顿 dùn〕同"早点"

早年　zǎonián　【名】one's early years

早期　zǎoqī　【名】earlier period; early stage

早日　zǎorì　【副】soon; at an early date: 争取 ～ 出成果 strive to achieve some result as early as possible 祝你 ～ 恢复健康。I hope you will recover soon.

早上　zǎoshang　【名】morning

早市　zǎoshì　【名】morning market

早熟　zǎoshú　【形】❶ precocious ❷ premature ❸ early-ripening

早退　zǎotuì　【动】leave early

早晚　zǎowǎn　【名】morning and evening: 他每天 ～ 都要散步。He goes for a walk every morning and evening. 【副】sooner or later: 搞阴谋的人～要垮台。People who are engaged in conspiracy will come to a bad end sooner or later. 别着急, 事情的真相～会水落石出的。Don't you worry; the truth will be known sooner or later.

早先　zǎoxiān　【名】〈口〉previously; in the past: ～我就听说过这位女飞行员的故事。I've heard the story of this woman pilot before. 他的身体比～强多了。He is in much better health now than before.

早已　zǎoyǐ　【副】long ago

枣（棗） zǎo 【名】◇ Chinese date

枣儿 zǎor 【名】〔个 gè〕Chinese date

枣红 zǎohóng 【形】brownish red

zào

灶（竈） zào 【名】kitchen stove

造 zào 【动】❶ make；manufacture：～纸 make paper ～预算 draw up a budget ❷ fabricate：～谣言 fabricate rumours

造成 zào // chéng form；make；manufacture；cause (e. g. difficulties)

造船厂 zàochuánchǎng 【名】shipyard

造船业 zàochuányè 【名】shipbuilding

造反 zào = fǎn rise in rebellion；rebel；launch a revolt：奴隶们造奴隶主的反。The slaves revolted against the slave owners.

造福 zàofú 【动】bring benefit to；benefit：～于人类 benefit mankind 为后代～ benefit future generations

造价 zàojià 【名】construction costs

造就 zàojiù 【动】train；bring up；cultivate：～人才 train qualified personnel ～一支宏大的知识分子队伍 train a great contingent of intellectuals

造句 zào = jù (gram.) make a sentence

造林 zào = lín afforest；afforestation

造型 zàoxíng 【名】modelling；moulding

造型艺术 zàoxíng yìshù plastic；plastic art

造谣 zào = yáo fabricate a rumour

造谣惑众 zào yáo huò zhòng spread rumours to deceive people

造诣 zàoyì 【名】attainments

造影 zàoyǐng 【动】radiography

造作 zàozuo 【形】affected；artificial；laboured

噪 zào

噪音 zàoyīn 【名】noise

zé

则（則） zé 【副】〈书〉❶ 同 "就" jiù：物体热～胀，冷～缩。Objects will expand when heated；will contract when cooled. ❷ 同 "却" què：今年中国乒乓球队捷报频传，而中国足球队～战绩平平。The Chinese National Table-tennis Team has won one victory after another this year，while its National Football Team is rather mediocre in its performance. 南方雨水充沛，北方～比较干燥。There is abundant rainfall in the south，while it's rather dry in the north. 【连】〈书〉同 "那么" nàme：原则既已决定，～具体问题便可着手解决。Now that the principles have been decided upon，we can start to solve specific problems. 【量】item：新闻两～ two items of news 寓言三～ three fables

责（責） zé 【名】◇ duty；responsibility：尽～ do one's duty 保护环境人人有～。Upholding environmental safety standards is everyone's responsibility. 【动】◇ demand；require：严于～己 be strict with oneself

责备 zébèi 【动】reproach；blame；censure

责成 zéchéng 【动】enjoin；entrust

责罚 zéfá 【动】punish

责怪 zéguài 【动】blame

责难 zénàn 【动】find fault with

and rebuke

责任 zérèn 【名】❶ responsibility；obligation；duty：我们的 ～ 是向人民负责。Our duty is to be responsible to the people. 我有～对这项工作提出意见。It is my responsibility to make suggestions about this project. ❷ blame；responsibility for a mistake：追究 ～ ascertain where the responsibility lies

责任编辑 zérèn biānjí executive editor

责任感 zérèngǎn 【名】sense of responsibility

责任事故 zérèn shìgù accident due to negligence

责任心 zérènxīn 【名】sense of responsibility

责任制 zérènzhì 【名】system of job responsibility

责问 zéwèn 【动】ask reprovingly

责无旁贷 zé wú páng dài be duty-bound：培养接班人是我们～的事情。It is our duty to train the young generation.

择(擇) zé 【动】〈书〉choose；select；pick out：两者任 ～ 其一 choose either of the two

择偶 zé = ǒu choose a spouse

择优 zé = yōu select the superior ones：～录取 enroll those who are outstanding

另见 zhái

zéi

贼(賊) zéi 【名】thief

贼喊捉贼 zéi hǎn zhuō zéi a robber cries "stop thief"；(fig.) cover oneself up by shouting with the crowd

贼头贼脑 zéi tóu zéi nǎo be furtive in one's movements；behave like a thief

贼心 zéixīn 【名】a wicked heart：～不死 not give up one's wicked intentions

zěn

怎 zěn 【代】how？why？

怎么 zěnme 【代】how ❶ *inquire about how to do things*：这个字～写？Do you know how to write this character? 你知道到植物园～走吗？Do you know how to get to the Botanical Garden? 这件事你说应该～办？What do you think ought to be done about this matter? ❷ *inquire about the cause of sth., with a touch of surprise or disapproval*：他今天～没上班？Why didn't he go to work? 你不是说明天来吗？～今天来了？Didn't you say that you were coming tomorrow? Why did you come today? ❸ *used before* 都 *or* 也 *to form an intensive expression indicating that no condition will change the result*：这个人很面熟，可是我～也想不起来是谁。That man looks very familiar but I just can't remember who he is for the life of me. 他开始～都不同意，最后才答应了。He simply wouldn't agree at first, but finally he gave in. Note：*A verb may be placed immediately after* 怎么：这个人很面熟，可是我～想也想不起来是谁。That man looks very familiar but I just can't remember who he is for the life of me. 你～问，他也不回答。No matter how you asked him, he simply refused to answer. ❹ *one phrase with* 怎么 *precedes another，in which case the latter refers to the former*：你心里～想，就～说。Say whatever you think. 咱们～决定的，就应该～做。We ought to do whatever we decided on. ❺ *used to*

form rhetorical questions：①同"什么" shénme ❺ ④，*but not as emphatic as* 什么 ② *used before the positive form of an auxiliary verb，the potential form of a complement of result or* 知道 *to stress the negation*：这个字～能这么写！你错了。How could this character be written this way! You're wrong! 又要马儿跑，又要马儿不吃草，这～办得到呢！You want to have your cake and eat it too? Forget it! 他脑子里想什么，我～知道！How was I to know what was in his mind! ③ *used before a negative adjective or verb to show refutation*：这个戏短小精悍，对话俏皮，～不好！This play is pithy and forceful and its dialogue very witty. I don't see why you think it's no good. 我～没写信！写了两封呢！Who said I hadn't written a letter? I've written two! 有这么好的一个儿子，～不让当父母的高兴呢！With such a good son, how could the parents help being proud! 他～不知道！他早知道了！Who said he didn't know? He knew long ago. ❻ 不怎么 *means* 不很：他是不～说话的，可是工作真出色。He is a man of few words, but his work is superb! 小宋刚学开汽车，还不～会呢！Xiao Song has just begun to learn how to drive a car and isn't yet very good at it. 她会弹钢琴，只是弹得不～好。She plays the piano, but not very well. ❼ 怎么了 *means* "what has happened"：你～了? 不舒服吗? What's the matter with you? Are you sick? ～了? 他们为什么笑成那样? What has happened? Why are they laughing so? ❽ 怎么回事 *is used to inquire about the whole story of sth. or the truth of sth.*：昨天他们俩吵了半天，到底是～回事? They had a quarrel yesterday. What was it a-bout? 我还不太清楚所谓认识上的飞跃是～回事。I don't yet understand what a "cognitive leap" means.

怎么办 zěnme bàn　What is to be done?

怎么样 zěnmeyàng　【代】❶ how *usu. used as a predicate or complement*：你身体～? How are you? 他的业务水平～? How good is his professional skill? 你来试试，～? Come and have a try. How about it? ～，这样可以吧? Well，don't you think this will do? ❷ 不怎么样 *means* "not very good"：这张相片儿照得不～。This photograph isn't very good.

怎么着 zěnmezhe　【代】❶ what about *usu. used as the predicate of a sentence*：我们今天都去劳动，你～? We are all going to do physical labour today，what about you? 毕业后他打算～? What are his plans after graduation? 这次旅行我们去桂林，他们去杭州，你到底～? On this trip，we're going to Guilin; they are going to Hangzhou; what about you? ❷ what *usu. used with* 还是 *to inquire about the cause of sth.*：广播喇叭突然不响了，是出故障了还是～? The loudspeaker stopped working suddenly，is there something wrong with it or what? 他今天没来，是病了还是～? He hasn't turned up today; is he ill or what? ❸ *one phrase with* 怎么着 *precedes another，in which case the latter refers to the former*：你想～就～，那哪儿行啊！You want to do whatever you like. I'm afraid it isn't possible. 这匹马驯得真好，叫它～，它就～。This horse is certainly well-trained; it does whatever it is told.

怎样 zěnyàng　【代】（*usu. in written language*）❶ 同"怎么"：这种现象～解释? How do you explain this

phenomenon? ❷ 同"怎么样"：你近来～? How have you been recently? 工程进行得～了? How is the project?

zēng

增　zēng　【动】◇ add；increase：水利化后，小麦产量猛～。With the completion of the water conservation project, the wheat output has risen sharply.

增产　zēng＝chǎn　increase production

增产节约　zēng chǎn jiéyuē　increase production and practise economy

增光　zēng＝guāng　add to the glory

增加　zēngjiā　【动】add；increase：从四十人～到六十人 increase from 40 to 60 people ～品种 add new varieties 在校学生～了一倍。The enrollment of students has doubled.

增进　zēngjìn　【动】promote；improve；enhance：～健康 improve one's health 通过学术交流，～了两国人民之间的友谊。Through the medium of academic exchange, the friendship between the peoples of the two countries has been further strengthened.

增强　zēngqiáng　【动】strengthen；reinforce；intensify：～信心 reinforce confidence ～体质 build up one's physique

增删　zēngshān　【动】augment and delete

增收　zēngshōu　【动】increase income

增添　zēngtiān　【动】add；replenish

增援　zēngyuán　【动】reinforce

增长　zēngzhǎng　【动】rise；increase：～才干 develop one's abilities 产量逐年～。The output has risen year by year.

增值　zēngzhí　rise in value：人民币不断～。Renminbi kept on rising in value.

增值税　zēngzhíshuì　【名】value added tax

憎　zēng

憎恨　zēnghèn　【动】hate；detest

憎恶　zēngwù　【动】detest；dislike strongly

zèng

赠（贈）　zèng　【动】〈书〉present；offer (e.g. gift)

赠送　zèngsòng　【动】give as a present to；present

赠言　zèngyán　【名】parting advice

赠阅　zèngyuè　【动】(of an editor or institute) give publications to others free of charge

zhā

扎　zhā　【动】❶ prick：我不小心～了手指。I carelessly pricked my finger. ❷ plunge into；dive：小王一头～进水里就潜泳到对岸去了。Xiao Wang dove in and swam underwater to the opposite bank. ❸ (mil.) be quartered：～营 pitch camp

另见 zā

扎根　zhā＝gēn　(of plants) take root：～于群众之中 take root among the masses

扎实　zhāshi　【形】❶ sturdy；solid；firm：学过的东西他记得很～。He has a firm grasp of what he has learned. 他的阿拉伯语基础很～。His knowledge of Arabic is solidly based. ❷ solid；reliable；conscientious：他工作一贯扎扎实实。He always does his work in a thoroughly reliable manner.

扎眼　zhāyǎn　【形】❶ dazzling ❷ offensively conspicuous

扎针　zhā = zhēn　give an acupuncture treatment

渣 zhā　【名】❶ dregs；dross ❷ crumbs

渣滓　zhāzǐ　【名】dregs；scum：社会 ~ the dregs of society

zhá

札 zhá

札记　zhájì　【名】〔篇 piān〕notes or comments made while reading

轧（軋）zhá　【动】roll (e.g. steel)

轧钢　zhá = gāng　roll steel；steel-rolling

闸（閘）zhá　【名】❶ floodgate；sluice gate：开 ~ 放水 open the sluice gate ❷ brake ❸〈口〉switch【动】dam (a river)

闸盒　zháhé　【名】fuse box

闸门　zhámén　【名】sluice gate

炸 zhá　【动】fry
另见 zhà

炸糕　zhágāo　【名】deep fried sticky cake

铡（鍘）zhá　【动】cut with a chaff-cutter

铡刀　zhádāo　【名】chaff-cutter

zhǎ

眨 zhǎ　【动】wink；blink

眨眼　zhǎ = yǎn　❶ blink：他不 ~ 地盯着银幕。He stared at the screen without blinking. ❷ in the twinkling of an eye：唉，他怎么一 ~ 工夫就不见了？ Oh, how could he disappear in the twinkling of an eye?

zhà

乍 zhà　【副】first；for the first time；just：我们新来 ~ 到，一切都很生疏。We have just arrived here, and everything is new to us. 他俩久别之后，~ 一见面，都认不出来了。After a long period of separation, at first the two were almost unable to recognize each other.

诈（詐）zhà　【动】❶ cheat；deceive；blackmail；trick sb. into sth.：~ 财 swindle someone out of his money ❷ bluff；deceive；mislead：你想 ~ 他，他才不上你的当呢！So you want to try to bluff him, do you？ Well, he's not a man who can be easily taken in.

诈骗　zhàpiàn　【动】bluff and deceive

炸 zhà　【动】explode；blow up；blast
另见 zhá

炸弹　zhàdàn　【名】〔枚 méi〕bomb

炸药　zhàyào　【名】explosives；dynamite

炸药包　zhàyàobāo　【名】pack (or satchel) of dynamite；explosive package

栅 zhà

栅栏　zhàlan　【名】rails；fence

榨 zhà　【动】squeeze out；extract；press：~ 油 extract oil by pressing ~ 甘蔗 press sugar cane

榨取　zhàqǔ　【动】❶ obtain by press-

ing;extract：～果汁 squeeze fruit to obtain the juice ❷ exploit；extort

zhāi

摘 zhāi 【动】❶ pick；pluck：～棉花 pick cotton ～苹果 pick apples 把帽子～下来 take off one's hat ❷ excerpt：他从这首长诗中～出一节来给大家朗诵。 He excerpted one section from this long poem to recite.

摘抄 zhāichāo 【动】 copy sth. selectively；make extracts

摘除 zhāichú 【动】 excise：～肿瘤 excise a tumor

摘登 zhāidēng 【动】 publish excerpts (or extracts) of sth.

摘录 zhāilù 【动】 make extracts；excerpt 【名】 extracts；excerpts

摘要 zhāiyào 【名】 summary；abstract：社论～ an abstract of the editorial 送上群众来信～三份，请阅。 For your reference, here are three summaries of letters from the people.

摘要 zhāi＝yào summarize；make a summary：～广播 broadcast a (news) summary 关于防汛工作，今天报上～介绍了那个省的先进经验。 Today's paper carries a summary of that province's experience regarding flood prevention.

摘引 zhāiyǐn 【动】 quote

zhái

择（擇） zhái 【动】 select；choose；pick out：～菜 trim vegetables 这团乱毛线，你慢慢～吧！ Take your time untangling the ball of wool.

另见 zé

zhǎi

窄 zhǎi 【形】 narrow

窄小 zhǎixiǎo 【形】 narrow and small

zhài

债（債） zhài 【名】〔笔 bǐ〕 debt

债权 zhàiquán 【名】 creditor's rights：～人 creditor

债券 zhàiquàn 【名】〔张 zhāng〕 bond：发行～ issue bonds

债台高筑 zhài tái gāo zhù run heavily into debt；deep in debt

债务 zhàiwù 【名】 debts

债主 zhàizhǔ 【名】 creditor

寨 zhài 【名】❶ stockade；stronghold ❷ stockaded village：村村～～ various villages

寨子 zhàizi 【名】 village with fence or walled defence

zhān

沾 zhān 【动】❶ wet；moisten：露水把鞋和裤脚都～湿了。 His shoes and trouser-legs are wet with dew. ❷ be spotted with：鞋上～了点儿泥。 His shoes were spotted with mud. ❸ touch：他太累了，头一～枕头就睡着了。 He was so tired that he fell asleep the moment his head touched the pillow. 这件事跟我不～边儿。 This matter has nothing whatever to do with me. ❹ gain (some advantage by being related to sb.)：利益均～。 Everybody grabs his share of the pie.

沾光　zhān=guāng　bask in reflected glory；incidentally enjoy a benefit conferred on another

沾染　zhānrǎn　【动】❶ be contaminated by；be soiled by：伤口别～上脏东西。Be careful not to contaminate your wound. ❷ be tainted with；be affected by：～上坏习气 acquire bad habits

沾沾自喜　zhān zhān zì xǐ　complacent；self-satisfied：不能因为取得了一点成绩就～。One should not become complacent over occasional successes.

粘　zhān　【动】glue；stick
另见 nián

粘连　zhānlián　【动】adhesion：肠～ intestinal adhesion

粘贴　zhāntiē　【动】paste；stick

瞻　zhān

瞻前顾后　zhān qián gù hòu　look forward and backward；(fig.) be full of misgivings and unable to make any decision

瞻望　zhānwàng　【动】look ahead：～未来 look to the future

瞻仰　zhānyǎng　【动】pay one's respects to：～烈士墓 pay one's respects at the martyrs' mausoleum

zhǎn

斩(斬)　zhǎn　【动】cut；chop off；behead

斩草除根　zhǎn cǎo chú gēn　uproot；pull up weeds by the root；exterminate；eradicate

斩钉截铁　zhǎn dīng jié tiě　resolute；determined

盏(盞)　zhǎn　【量】for lamp：一～灯 a lamp

展　zhǎn　【动】◇ spread out；unfold：愁眉不～ knit one's brow in anxiety 雄鹰～翅。The eagle spreads its wings. 【名】◇ exhibition：美～ art exhibition

展播　zhǎnbō　【动】specially transmit programmes on TV or radio

展出　zhǎnchū　【动】exhibit；be on display；put on display

展开　zhǎn // kāi　❶ open up；expand；unroll：～翅膀 spread its wings 把画卷～ unroll a scroll painting ❷ spread out；unfold；develop；launch：对敌军～强大攻势 launch a powerful offensive against the enemy troops 全厂～了生产竞赛。A production emulation drive has spread throughout the whole factory.

展览　zhǎnlǎn　【动】exhibit；be on display 【名】exhibition

展览会　zhǎnlǎnhuì　【名】exhibition

展品　zhǎnpǐn　【名】exhibit

展示　zhǎnshì　【动】spread；display

展望　zhǎnwàng　【动】look forward：～前景 look forward to one's future prospects 【名】forecast；prospect；outlook：二十一世纪的～ prospects for the 21st century

展现　zhǎnxiàn　【动】unfold；be laid out；spread out

展销　zhǎnxiāo　【动】sales exhibition：服装～ fashion exhibition and sale ～会 commodities fair

崭(嶄)　zhǎn

崭新　zhǎnxīn　【形】brand-new

辗(輾)　zhǎn

辗转　zhǎnzhuǎn　【动】❶ toss and turn：～不能入睡 toss and turn all night long ❷ pass through many hands or places：～来到某地 after travelling through many places, arrive at a certain spot 也作"展转"

zhàn

占 zhàn 【动】❶ occupy；seize：
~了有利的地形 seize an advantageous position ~位子 keep a seat
(for sb.) ❷ take and use as one's
own；appropriate：多吃多~ take
more than one is entitled to ❸
constitute；make up；account for：
~优势 occupy a dominant position
~绝大多数 make up the overwhelming majority

占据 zhànjù 【动】occupy；take
over；hold

占理 zhàn=lǐ reasonable；be in the
right

占领 zhànlǐng 【动】occupy；seize
(position，territory)

占便宜 zhàn piányi ❶reap economic gain by foul means：该给多少
(钱)给多少(钱)，咱可不能~。We'll
pay a fair price；we won't try to
take advantage of you. 这个人爱占
小便宜。This fellow's always looking for a chance to grab a little for
himself. ❷ have an advantage；advantageous；favourable over：你个
子高，打篮球可～了。You're tall, so
you have an advantage in playing
basketball.

占上风 zhàn shàngfēng get the upper hand；win an advantage

占线 zhàn=xiàn the line is busy；
the line is engaged

占有 zhànyǒu 【动】❶ possess；own：
~大量的第一手材料 possess a
wealth of first-hand material ❷
hold；constitute：农业在国民经济中
~重要地位。Agriculture occupies
an important position in the national economy.

战（戰） zhàn 【动】◇ wage
war；fight：不宣而~ wage an un-

declared war 不～不和 an uncertain
state between war and peace 为祖
国的独立而 ~ fight for the independence of one's country 【名】◇
war；battle；fight；combat：~ 史
military history 有名的~例 a wellknown battle

战败 zhànbài 【动】❶ be defeated；
lose the battle ❷ defeat；overcome
(the enemy)；overpower

战败国 zhànbàiguó 【名】vanquished
(or defeated) nation

战报 zhànbào 【名】〔份 fèn〕war
communique

战备 zhànbèi 【名】preparation
against war

战场 zhànchǎng 【名】battlefield

战斗 zhàndòu 【动】fight；battle；
struggle：英勇不屈地 ~ fight valiantly ~到最后一个人 fight to the
last man 【名】battle：一场激烈的~
a fierce battle ~打响了。The fighting has begun.

战斗机 zhàndòujī 【名】〔架 jià〕fighter plane

战斗力 zhàndòulì 【名】fighting
strength；fighting capacity

战斗性 zhàndòuxìng 【名】fighting
spirit；militancy

战犯 zhànfàn 【名】war criminal

战俘 zhànfú 【名】prisoner-of-war

战歌 zhàngē 【名】〔首 shǒu〕battle
song

战鼓 zhàngǔ 【名】battle drum

战果 zhànguǒ 【名】results of
battle；success of battle

战壕 zhànháo 【名】〔条 tiáo〕trench

战火 zhànhuǒ 【名】flames of war

战机 zhànjī 【名】(good) opportunity for fighting；the right time to
strike

战绩 zhànjì 【名】success of battle

战局 zhànjú 【名】war situation

战栗 zhànlì 【动】shudder；shiver

战略 zhànlüè 【名】strategy

战旗 zhànqí 【名】〔面 miàn〕the col-

ours; flag of an army

战胜 zhànshèng 【动】❶ defeat; triumph over; ～敌军 defeat the enemy ❷ overcome; bring under control; ～疾病 triumph over one's disease 困难终于被～了。The difficulties were overcome at last.

战士 zhànshì 【名】soldier; fighter

战事 zhànshì 【名】war; hostilities

战术 zhànshù 【名】tactics

战天斗地 zhàn tiān dòu dì fight against heaven and earth; (fig.) combat all forces of nature

战无不胜 zhàn wú bù shèng invincible; ever-victorious ·

战线 zhànxiàn 【名】〔条 tiáo〕(mil.) front

战役 zhànyì 【名】campaign; battle

战友 zhànyǒu 【名】comrade-in-arms

战战兢兢 zhànzhànjīngjīng 【形】trembling with fright; very cautious

战争 zhànzhēng 【名】war; warfare

站 zhàn 【动】❶ stand; ～起来 stand up ～得高,看得远 stand on a high plane and see far ahead ❷ stop; cease; stand still; 红灯亮了, 车全～住了。The traffic stopped for the red light. 【名】❶ (of bus, train, etc.) station; stop; 北京～ Beijing Railway Station 出租汽车～ taxi stand 起点～ starting station ❷ service centre; service station; 保健～ health care centre 观测～ observatory

站队 zhàn = duì fall in; line up; take up one's position; 同学们,集合了,快出来～。Fellow students, come quick and line up! 小学生们站好了队,准备做操。The school children are lined up ready to do exercises.

站岗 zhàn = gǎng keep guard; stand sentry

站立 zhànlì 【动】stand; be on one's feet

站台 zhàntái 【名】platform (usu. of railway)

站住 zhàn // zhù ❶ stop; halt; ～! 不准往前走。Halt! Don't come any further! ❷ stay on one's feet; 他头晕得厉害,站不住。He felt very dizzy and couldn't stay on his feet. ❸ (of reason, explanation, argument) hold water; be tenable; 这个论点站得住吗? Does this argument hold water?

蘸 zhàn 【动】dip

zhāng

张(張) zhāng 【动】❶ open up; unfold; spread out; stretch; ～嘴 open one's mouth ～网捕鱼 cast a net to catch fish ❷ ◇ look; 东～西望 look around 【量】❶ for tables, paper, pictures, etc.; 一～报纸 a newspaper 三～桌子 three tables 五～羊皮 five sheep-skins ❷ for bows; 两～弓 two bows

张冠李戴 Zhāng guān Lǐ dài put Zhang's hat on Li's head; (fig.) mistake the agency; attribute sth. to the wrong person

张皇失措 zhānghuáng shīcuò be scared out of one's wits; be frightened and at a loss what to do

张口结舌 zhāng kǒu jié shé gaping and speechless

张罗 zhāngluo 【动】❶ take care of; be kept busy with; 家里事多,够母亲～的。My mother certainly has a lot of housework to do. 今天客人多,你帮我～～吧! We are expecting many guests today; would you please help me entertain them? ❷ raise (funds); ～一笔钱 try to raise a sum of money

张贴 zhāngtiē 【动】put up (a notice; poster, etc.)

张望 zhāngwàng 【动】look around; look into the distance: 四下～ peer in all directions 他向大道上～着, 好像盼看什么人呢! He was looking up and down the road as if he were expecting someone.

张牙舞爪 zhāng yá wǔ zhǎo bare one's teeth and claws; (fig.) put on a fierce look; be fierce-looking

章 zhāng 【名】❶ seal: 盖个～ affix one's seal ❷ rules and regulations: 照～办事 abide by the rules and regulations 【量】chapter; movement: 小说的第一～ the first chapter of a novel 交响乐通常由四个乐～组成。A symphony is usually made up of 4 movements.

章程 zhāngchéng 【名】rules and regulations; charter

章回体 zhānghuítǐ 【名】a traditional Chinese novel genre with each chapter headed by a couplet giving the gist of its content, similar to the picaresque novel in the west

章节 zhāngjié 【名】chapter; section

樟 zhāng 【名】◇ the camphor tree: ～木箱 camphorwood box

樟脑 zhāngnǎo 【名】camphor

zhǎng

长(長) zhǎng 【动】❶ come into being; begin to grow: 米～虫子了。The rice is infested with worms. 刀～锈了。The knife is getting rusty. 他脸上～了一个疙瘩。There is a pimple on his face. 墙根那儿～出来很多小花。A lot of little flowers are growing out from under the wall. ❷ grow: 孩子～高了。The child has grown taller. 庄稼～

得很好。The crops are growing well. ❸ acquire; increase: ～了一岁 become one year older ～见识 acquire more knowledge and experience 大～了中国人民的志气 greatly strengthen the morale of the Chinese people 【形】elder; older; senior: ～者 elders ～兄 the eldest brother 【尾】head; head of an unit, etc.: 中国科学院院～ President of the Chinese Academy of Sciences 中国外交学会会～ President of the Chinese People's Foreign Affairs Institute
另见 cháng

长辈 zhǎngbèi 【名】the elders; elder member of a family

长官 zhǎngguān 【名】old senior officer or official; commanding officer

长进 zhǎngjìn 【动】make progress 【名】progress

长势 zhǎngshì 【名】the condition of the crops: 晚秋作物～喜人。The late autumn crops are doing well.

长相 zhǎngxiàng 【名】looks: 姐妹俩的～好像双胞胎。These two sisters look like twins.

长者 zhǎngzhě 【名】❶ elder; senior ❷ venerable elder

涨(漲) zhǎng 【动】rise; go up: ～价 prices have gone up 水位又～了。The water level continues to rise.
另见 zhàng

涨潮 zhǎngcháo = cháo tide comes in

涨幅 zhǎngfú 【名】scope of increase; extent of increase

涨价 zhǎngjià = jià raise the price

掌 zhǎng 【动】◇ be in charge of; hold in one's hand: ～印 be in charge of the seal ～财权 have financial control 【名】◇ ❶ (of hand) palm ❷ (of certain animals)

paw：鹅 ～ a goose's foot 熊 ～ a bear's paw ❸（of horse）horse shoe：给马钉～ shoe a horse

掌舵　zhǎng＝duò　helm；be at the helm

掌管　zhǎngguǎn　【动】be in charge of；handle；control

掌权　zhǎng＝quán　come into power

掌声　zhǎngshēng　【名】applause；clapping

掌握　zhǎngwò　【动】❶ grasp；master：～技术 master the technique ～基础理论 have a good command of the basic theory ❷ preside over；exercise：～会场 preside over the meeting ～政权 exercise state power

zhàng

丈　zhàng　【动】measure；survey【量】*measure of length，equal to* 3⅓ *metres*

丈夫　zhàngfu　【名】husband

丈量　zhàngliáng　【动】measure（land）

仗　zhàng　【动】◇ rely on；depend on：狗～人势 bully people on the strength of a powerful patron【名】battle：打了一个大胜～ win a big victory 这一～打得真漂亮。This battle was brilliantly fought.

仗势欺人　zhàng shì qī rén　take advantage of one's or sb. else's power to bully people

仗恃　zhàngshì　【动】rely on（an advantage）

帐（帳）　zhàng　【名】camp；tent

帐篷　zhàngpeng　【名】tent

帐子　zhàngzi　【名】〔顶 dǐng〕mosquito net

账（賬）　zhàng　【名】account

账本　zhàngběn　【名】〔本 běn〕account book

账单　zhàngdān　【名】〔张 zhāng〕bill

账目　zhàngmù　【名】account：结算～ square accounts ～不清 accounts not in order

胀（脹）　zhàng　【动】❶ expand ❷ swell；be bloated：肚子有些发～ feel bloated

涨（漲）　zhàng　【动】❶ become swelled after absorbing water：种子泡了一夜都～起来了。The seeds swelled after being soaked in water overnight. ❷（of one's face）flush；be suffused with blood：他气得脸都～红了。His face flushed with anger.

另见 zhǎng

障　zhàng

障碍　zhàng'ài　【名】obstacle；obstruction；barrier：排除 ～ clear away obstacles 设置～ put obstacles in sb.'s path 【动】obstruct；stand in the way of；hinder：骄傲自满情绪～着我们工作的改进。Complacency is preventing us from improving our work.

zhāo

招　zhāo　【动】❶ beckon；wave：远处有人向我们 ～ 手。Someone beckoned to us from a distance. ❷ attract：马戏团一进镇，就～来一群孩子。The moment the circus entered the country town, it attracted a crowd of children. ❸ inspire love or hatred：～人喜欢 be charming ❹ provoke；incite；incur：把她～哭了 reduce her to tears ❺ con-

fess;admit:不打自～freely confess
【名】(～儿)同"着儿"zháor

招标 zhāo = biāo invite tenders;invite bids

招兵买马 zhāo bīng mǎi mǎ recruit men and buy horses;(*fig.*) enlist followers (*derog.*)

招待 zhāodài 【动】entertain;give a reception to

招待会 zhāodàihuì 【名】reception

招待所 zhāodàisuǒ 【名】hostel

招工 zhāo = gōng recruit workers

招供 zhāogòng 【动】make a confession of one's crime;confess

招呼 zhāohu 【动】❶ call;hail:有人～你。Someone is calling you. ❷ greet:跟客人们一一打～greet the guests one after another ❸〈口〉instruct;tell;inform:～他赶快把总结写出来。Tell him to hurry up with the summary.

招唤 zhāohuàn 【动】summon;call

招架 zhāojià 【动】ward off;resist

招揽 zhāolǎn 【动】solicit (customers)

招领 zhāolǐng 【动】ask owner to claim a lost thing

招募 zhāomù 【动】enlist;recruit

招牌 zhāopai 【名】❶ shop sign ❷ (*fig.*) banner

招聘 zhāopìn 【动】invite applications for a job:公司～职员 the company advertises for staff members

招惹 zhāorě 【动】provoke;incur;arouse

招商 zhāo shāng invite sb. to do business

招生 zhāo = shēng enroll students

招收 zhāoshōu 【动】enrol

招手 zhāo = shǒu beckon;wave to

招贴 zhāotiē 【动】poster;placard;bill

招贴画 zhāotiēhuà 【名】pictorial poster (or placard)

招摇撞骗 zhāoyáo zhuàngpiàn swin-

dle by impersonating sb.

招展 zhāozhǎn 【动】wave;flutter

招致 zhāozhì 【动】❶ enrol;take in ❷ cause;give rise to;result in

招租 zhāozū 【动】let;lease

昭 zhāo

昭然若揭 zhāorán ruò jiē as clear as day

昭雪 zhāoxuě 【动】rehabilitate

着 zhāo

另见 zháo;zhe;zhuó

着儿 zhāor 【名】❶ a move (in chess):这～棋走得好。This was a clever move. ❷ trick;device;move:高～ a master move 没～了 at one's wits' end 没想到他还有这一～。(I) didn't expect him to play such a trick. 也作"招儿"。

朝 zhāo 【名】◇ morning

另见 cháo

朝不虑夕 zhāo bù lǜ xī in the morning one needn't worry about the evening, as danger may happen any moment 也作"朝不谋夕"。

朝令夕改 zhāo lìng xī gǎi issue an order in the morning and rescind it in the evening;be fickle in policy-making

朝气 zhāoqì 【名】vigour;ardour;vitality;animation

朝气蓬勃 zhāoqì péngbó full of vigour and vitality

朝三暮四 zhāo sān mù sì play fast and loose;blow hot and cold;changeable

朝夕 zhāoxī 【名】❶ all day;morning and evening:～相处 be together all day long ❷ a short time:～之间 within a day

朝霞 zhāoxiá 【名】red clouds in the morning

朝阳 zhāoyáng 【名】morning sun;rising sun

zháo

着 zháo 【动】❶ touch：受了伤的脚不能～地。He can't bring his wounded foot down to touch the floor. 储存水泥，很重要的一点是不要～水。When storing cement, the important thing is not to let it get wet. ❷ be lit；start to burn：路灯～了。The street lamps are on. Note：*It is used after a verb as a complement* ① *indicates that one gets what one needs or achieves one's goal*：你需要的那份资料找～了。The data you need have been gathered. 那本书你借～了吗? Have you succeeded in borrowing that book? 打了一枪没打～，让野兔跑了。He shot at the hare but missed it. ② *used after* 睡 *to mean "asleep"*：他睡～了。He's fallen asleep. ③ *indicates that sth. catches fire*：把烟点～了 lit a cigarette
另见 zhǎo；zhe；zhuó

着慌 zháo = huāng be thrown into a panic

着火 zháo = huǒ catch fire

着急 zháo = jí be anxious；be worried

着凉 zháo = liáng catch cold

着魔 zháo = mó be bewitched；be possessed

zhǎo

爪 zhǎo 【名】◇ claw；talon

爪牙 zhǎoyá 【名】underling；minion

找 zhǎo 【动】❶ look for；seek；find：～人 look for someone 丢失的钱包～到了。The lost purse was found. ❷ give (sb. his) change：我付了一元，～回两角。I paid one yuan and got twenty cents change.

找麻烦 zhǎo máfan cause trouble；ask for trouble：对不起，又给您找了不少麻烦! I'm sorry to have caused you so much trouble again.

找钱 zhǎo = qián give (sb. his) change

找寻 zhǎoxún 【动】look for；seek

沼 zhǎo

沼气 zhǎoqì 【名】methane；marsh gas

沼泽 zhǎozé 【名】marsh；swamp；bog；quagmire

zhào

召 zhào 【动】call；beckon；assemble；convene：～之即来 assemble at the first call 奉～来到 report for duty when called

召唤 zhàohuàn 【动】call

召回 zhàohuí 【动】recall；call back

召集 zhàojí 【动】call up；convene；assemble；summon；gather

召集人 zhàojírén 【名】convener

召见 zhàojiàn 【动】summon；send for

召开 zhàokāi 【动】call；summon (meeting)

兆 zhào 【数】million

兆头 zhàotou 【名】sign；omen；portent

兆周 zhàozhōu 【量】megacycle

照 zhào 【动】❶ shine；illuminate：阳光～在窗子上。The sun is shining on the window. 灯光把屋里～得通明。The lights brightly illuminated the room. ❷ mirror；reflect：～镜子 look in a mirror ❸ take (a photograph)：这张相片～得很好。This is a good shot. 【介】❶

to；in the direction of：～直走 go straight ahead ～这个方向前进 march in this direction ❷ according to；in the light of；in accordance with：～你的意见办 act in accordance with your suggestion ～我看,这个电影不错。In my opinion, this film is quite good.

照办 zhàobàn 【动】do as one is told

照本宣科 zhào běn xuān kē read aloud a text mechanically (instead of giving a lively interpretation)

照常 zhàocháng 【形】as usual：节日期间,商店～营业。On holidays, the stores carry on business as usual.

照顾 zhàogu 【动】❶ consider；take notice of：～全局 take the whole into account ～青年的特点 take into consideration the characteristics peculiar to young people ❷ take care of；look after：～伤病员 attend to the sick and wounded 我不在,请你帮忙～一下我的家。While I am away, would you mind helping to look after my family?

照管 zhàoguǎn 【动】take charge of；look after；take care of

照会 zhàohuì 【动】present a note to 【名】(diplomatic) note

照旧 zhàojiù 【形】as before：屋里一切～。Everything in the room remained unchanged. 这件棉衣虽然旧了点儿,但～可以御寒。Though this cotton-padded jacket is a bit worn, it can still keep out the cold.

照看 zhàokàn 【动】look after；attend to：～孩子 take care of the children

照例 zhàolì 【副】as a rule；as usual：不管刮风下雪,他～要跑两千米。Regardless of wind or snow, he still runs his usual 2000 metres.

照料 zhàoliào 【动】take care of

照猫画虎 zhào māo huà hǔ (lit.) draw a tiger after the model of a cat；(fig.) slavishly imitate another

照明 zhàomíng 【动】illuminate；throw light on

照片 zhàopiān 【名】〔张 zhāng〕photograph；photo；picture

照射 zhàoshè 【动】shine；irradiate；(of sunlight) beat down

照说 zhàoshuō 【副】ordinarily；theoretically speaking：～应该你去机场接专家,因为你是系主任。As head of the department, it's your responsibility to go to the airport to meet the new expert. ～这是一个很有特色的剧本,可是演得并不好。This drama is quite an original composition, but unfortunately the acting fell flat.

照相 zhào = xiàng take a photograph of；have one's photograph taken

照相馆 zhàoxiàngguǎn 【名】photo studio

照相机 zhàoxiàngjī 【名】〔架 jià〕camera

照样 zhàoyàng 【副】still；as before；as usual：虽然天气很冷,大家～干得热火朝天。Although it was bitterly cold, they all pitched into the work with their usual enthusiasm.

照样 zhào = yàng following a model or pattern：照这个样做一件上衣 have a jacket made according to this pattern 照着样儿写,别写错了。Follow this model when you write, and don't make any mistakes.

照耀 zhàoyào 【动】shine

照应 zhàoyìng 【动】❶ look after：列车员对老人和小孩～得非常周到。The attendants took excellent care of the old people and children on the train. ❷ coordinate；correlate：写文章要前后～。In writing an article one must pay attention to the relationship among its different

parts.

罩 zhào 【名】(～儿) shade：这盏灯有～没有? Does this lamp have a shade? 【动】cover：闹钟上～了个玻璃罩儿。The alarm clock was protected by a glass cover.

罩子 zhàozi 【名】cover；shade；hood

肇 zhào

肇事 zhào = shì　cause an accident；make trouble

肇事者 zhàoshìzhě 【名】one who causes an accident，trouble-maker

zhē

折 zhē 【动】❶ turn over：～了个跟头 turn a somersault ❷ pour from one container to another：用两个碗～一～,开水就凉了。If you use two cups and pour the boiling water from one to the other and back again a few times, you can cool it down.
另见 zhé；shé

折腾 zhēteng 【动】❶ toss about：他睡不着,在床上来回～。He tossed about in bed, unable to fall asleep. ❷ do sth. repeatedly：这个收音机他拆了装,装了拆,整整～了一天。He spent a whole day repeatedly dismantling and assembling the radio.

遮 zhē 【动】❶ cover from view；screen：云把月亮～住了。Clouds obscured the moon. ❷ ◇ cover up；conceal：～丑 conceal something ugly ～人耳目 pull the wool over people's eyes

遮蔽 zhēbì 【动】block：前面的楼房～了我们的视线。The building in front blocked our view.

遮盖 zhēgài 【动】❶ cover up：大雪～了田野。Heavy snow covered the fields. ❷ conceal；cover up：～缺点 conceal one's short-comings

遮羞布 zhēxiūbù 【名】fig-leaf

遮掩 zhēyǎn 【动】同"遮盖"：身体有残疾要敢于正视,不要～。When one has a disability, one should face it squarely, not cover it up.

zhé

折 zhé 【动】❶ break off；break in two：～断 break in two ～一枝柳条 break off a willow branch ❷ turn back；change direction：他刚走不远又～回来了。He hadn't gone far before he turned back. ❸ fold；bend：把信～好 fold the letter carefully ❹ convert into：～价 convert property into money 【名】discount：打七～ give a 30% discount
另见 zhē；shé

折叠 zhédié 【动】fold

折叠床 zhédiéchuáng 【名】〔张 zhāng〕folding bed

折叠椅 zhédiéyǐ 【名】〔把 bǎ〕folding chair

折合 zhéhé 【动】convert into：一英镑～多少美元? How much does one British pound amount to in US dollars? 五十公斤～一百市斤。50 kilos is equal to 100 *jin*.

折回 zhéhuí 【动】turn back（halfway）

折价 zhé = jià　calculate in terms of money；convert into money

折旧 zhéjiù 【动】depreciate

折扣 zhékòu 【名】discount

折磨 zhémo 【动】afflict；inflict on；cause to suffer 【名】affliction

折扇 zhéshàn 【名】〔把 bǎ〕folding fan

折射 zhéshè 【动】(phys.) refract

折算 zhésuàn 【动】convert

折衷 zhézhōng 【动】compromise；eclectic 也作"折中"。

折衷主义 zhézhōngzhǔyì 【名】eclecticism

哲 zhé

哲理 zhélǐ 【名】philosophic theory

哲学 zhéxué 【名】philosophy

zhě

者 zhě 【尾】❶ -er;-ist (person)：文艺工作～ literary worker or artist 医务工作～ medical worker 唯物主义～ materialist ❷ *indicates a thing*：前～ the former 后～ the latter 二～必居其一 either this or that

褶 zhě

褶子 zhězi 【名】pleat

zhè

这（這）zhè 【代】❶ this (*as opp. to* 那)：～本词典 this dictionary ～个地方 this place ～是办公室。This is an office. ❷ this moment; right now：请你等一等，他～就去。Please wait a minute. He is going right now. 听了他的话，我～才知道他们不来的原因。Only after he had explained did I realise why they couldn't come. ❸ act in this way *used as a part of the predicate of a sentence and usu. in conjunction with* 就 *or* 可：你～就不对了，怎么能骂人呢! If you act this way, you are to blame. You mustn't call people names! ❹ *used with* 那 *meaning "this and that"*：说～道那 talk about this and that 他参观工厂的时候，看看～，看看那，觉得都很有意思。During his visit to the factory, he looked at this and that, and found everything very interesting.

这个 zhège 【代】❶ this (person)：～是二年级学生，那个是三年级学生。This student is in 2nd year, that one in 3rd year. ❷ this (thing)：～就是我们常说的工艺美术工厂。This is the Arts and Crafts Factory we've talked about so much! 你说的是～呀，大家早就知道了。So this is what you were talking about! We knew it long ago!

这会儿 zhèhuìr 【名】〈口〉at the moment：我～忙着哪，待(dāi)会儿再去。I am very busy at the moment; I'll go later.

这里 zhèlǐ 【代】同"这儿"，*but not as colloquial*

这么 zhème 【代】❶ so; such; like this *always used as an adverbial adjunct*：他就是～刚强。He was as firm as that. 这张桌子原来就～放的。The table has always been placed like that. 这口井～深哪! This well is so deep! 屋子里就～几个人。There are only these few people in the room. 你～一讲，我就懂了。Now that you have explained, I understand it. ❷ *used before an approximate number to stress indefiniteness*：他推荐的参考书也就～六、七本。He recommended only six or seven reference books.

这么着 zhèmezhe 【代】like this; so：我看，～大家会满意的。If we do it this way, everybody will be satisfied, I think.

这儿 zhèr 【代】here：到～来 come here ～是百货大楼。Here is the department store. 你告诉他上我～来一趟。Tell him to come to my place.

这些 zhèxiē 【代】these

这样 zhèyàng 【代】so; such; like this：❶ *used as an attributive*：像《红楼梦》～的小说才不愧为世界第一流的文学作品。Only novels such as *A Dream of Red Mansions* deserve

to be called classics of world literature. ❷ 同"这么" ❶（*usu. in written language*）：你～做就可以节省时间。If you do it like this, you'll save time. ～小一件事不要去麻烦他了。We'd better not bother him with such a trifle. ❸ *used as a complement*：你做什么去了,累得～? What have you been doing that made you so tired? ❹ *stands for a certain action, used as a predicate*：你应该～：先打个电报,再写一封信说明详细情况。This is what you ought to do：send a telegram first, and then write a letter to explain in detail how things stand. 先把路垫平,～,后边的车就可以顺利通过了。We must make the road level first, then trucks will be able to travel along it without any problem. 人人出主意想办法,～,一定能完成任务。If everybody contributes his energy and know-how, we will certainly finish the task.

zhe

着 zhe 【助】❶ *indicates action in progress*：走在游行队伍前面的人都举～红旗。Those who walked at the front of the parade were holding aloft red flags. 他笑～说："谢谢!""Thanks very much!" he said with a smile. 他们说～说～就争论起来了。They were talking when gradually it turned into an argument. ❷ *indicates a static state*：桌子上放～闹钟。An alarm clock was on the table. 墙上挂～一张世界地图。A world map hung on the wall. 天还黑～他就走了。He left while it was still dark. ❸ 着 *can be added to some prepositions*：向～胜利前进! March towards victory! 他对～我笑了笑。He smiled at me.

另见 zhāo；zháo；zhuó

着呢 zhene 【助】*used after an adj. to show a high degree*：这个电影好～! This film is excellent! 这花香～。How sweet the flower smells!

zhēn

针（針） zhēn 【名】❶〔根 gēn〕needle：穿～ thread a needle 毛衣～ knitting needle ❷ stitch：这儿开线了,缝几～吧! That seam is going to come apart；you'd better put in a few stitches. ❸ injection：打防疫～ give a preventive inoculation 一天打两～ have two injections daily

针刺麻醉 zhēn cì mázuì acupuncture anaesthesia

针对 zhēnduì 【动】be directed at；point at；be aimed at：～这个问题发表意见 express one's opinions on this question ～儿童的特点组织课外活动 organize extracurricular activities keeping in mind the special characteristics of children

针对性 zhēnduìxìng 【名】with a clear aim；with clear implications

针锋相对 zhēn fēng xiāng duì tit for tat

针剂 zhēnjì 【名】injection

针灸 zhēnjiǔ 【名】acupuncture and moxibustion【动】cure by acupuncture and moxibustion

针织品 zhēnzhīpǐn 【名】knitted goods；knitwear；hosiery

侦（偵） zhēn

侦查 zhēnchá 【动】investigate；look into（a case）

侦察 zhēnchá 【动】scout；reconnoitre 【名】reconnaissance

侦察兵 zhēnchábīng 【名】scout

侦察机 zhēnchájī 【名】〔架 jià〕reconnaissance plane；scout

侦破 zhēnpò 【动】detect，investigate and uncover

侦探 zhēntàn 【动】detect；spy on 【名】detective；secret agent

珍 zhēn

珍爱 zhēn'ài 【动】treasure；love dearly；be very fond of

珍宝 zhēnbǎo 【名】jewellery；treasure

珍本 zhēnběn 【名】rare edition；rare book

珍藏 zhēncáng 【动】treasure

珍贵 zhēnguì 【形】valuable，precious

珍品 zhēnpǐn 【名】treasure

珍奇 zhēnqí 【形】rare；precious

珍视 zhēnshì 【动】prize；value

珍惜 zhēnxī 【动】treasure and avoid wasting

珍重 zhēnzhòng 【动】❶ take good care of（one's health）：望～身体。I hope you'll take good care of yourself. ❷ hold dear；treasure and value：～历代的文化遗产 value the cultural heritage of the past

珍珠 zhēnzhū 【名】〔颗 kē〕pearl

真 zhēn 【形】❶ real；genuine；true：～话 the truth ～事 real event ～金不怕火炼。Genuine gold fears no fire；the real thing can stand any test. ❷ really；truly；indeed：好 really good ～有办法 really resourceful ❸ clear：听得～，听不～？Can you hear clearly? 远处的字我看不～。I can't see those characters clearly. They're too far away.

真诚 zhēnchéng 【形】honest；earnest；sincere

真空 zhēnkōng 【名】vacuum

真理 zhēnlǐ 【名】truth

真面目 zhēn miànmù one's true self；true features；true colours

真凭实据 zhēn píng shí jù factual evidence；indisputable evidence

真切 zhēnqiè 【形】distinct

真情 zhēnqíng 【名】❶ actual state；real situation；facts ❷ real emotion or feelings；～实感 real feelings ～流露 unintentionally reveal one's real feelings

真实 zhēnshí 【形】real；true；actual

真相 zhēnxiàng 【名】truth；true state；facts：不明～ be ignorant of the facts 也作"真象"。

真相大白 zhēnxiàng dàbái the actual state of affairs has been made clear

真心 zhēnxīn 【名】〔片 piàn〕wholehearted；heartfelt；sincere

真心实意 zhēnxīn shíyì genuinely and sincerely；truly and wholeheartedly：他～地为大家办事。He works sincerely and whole-heartedly for all of us.

真正 zhēnzhèng 【形】real；genuine：～的茅台酒 genuine Maotai（spirits）～地拥护 truly support ～是这样的。It really is this way.

真挚 zhēnzhì 【形】sincere；cordial；genuine

斟 zhēn 【动】pour（wine or tea into a cup）

斟酌 zhēnzhuó 【动】weigh and consider；deliberate upon；think over：～字句 weigh one's every word 这件事情～～再定。Think over the matter and then make a decision.

甄 zhēn

甄别 zhēnbié 【动】screen；investigate and examine sb.'s past history

zhěn

诊（診）zhěn 【动】diagnose；consult；examine：～脉（of Chinese traditional medicine）diagnose by feeling the pulse

诊断　zhěnduàn　【名】diagnosis【动】diagnose

诊疗　zhěnliáo　【动】diagnose and give medical treatment

诊所　zhěnsuǒ　【名】clinic

诊治　zhěnzhì　【动】同"诊疗"

枕　zhěn　【动】rest one's head on：～着一个枕头 rest one's head on a pillow　～戈待旦 with one's spear for a pillow, waiting for the dawn；(fig.) maintain fighting vigilance

枕巾　zhěnjīn　【名】〔条 tiáo〕towel on top of pillow case

枕木　zhěnmù　【名】sleeper

枕头　zhěntou　【名】〔个 gè〕pillow

zhèn

阵(陣)　zhèn　【名】❶ battle formation；troops in battle array ❷ battle-field；position：上～杀敌 go to battle to wipe out the enemy 【量】for wind, rain, applause, etc.：一～～的凉风 gust after gust of cool wind　今天下了好几～雨。There were several rain showers today.

阵地　zhèndì　【名】position；battle field；front

阵地战　zhèndìzhàn　【名】〔场 cháng〕positional warfare

阵脚　zhènjiǎo　【名】forefront；position (usu. fig.)：稳住～ secure one's position 这个意外事件搅乱了我们的～。This accident upset our plans and threw us into confusion.

阵容　zhènróng　【名】❶ line-up；battle array ❷ strength displayed by troops or athletes：～整齐 a well-balanced line 这个水球队～很强。This water polo team is a strong one.

阵势　zhènshì　【名】❶ formation ❷ situation

阵亡　zhènwáng　【动】be killed while fighting in war

阵线　zhènxiàn　【名】battle front

阵营　zhènyíng　【名】camp

阵雨　zhènyǔ　【名】shower

振　zhèn　【动】◇ ❶ raise；shake：～臂高呼 raise one's arm and call for action 小鸟～翅高飞。The bird fluttered its wings and soared. ❷ rise；be moved to action：精神为(wéi)之一～ feel one's spirit soar (as a result of sth.)

振动　zhèndòng　【动】oscillate；vibrate

振奋　zhènfèn　【动】inspire；stimulate：～人心 raise people's morale

振兴　zhènxīng　【动】rejuvenate

振振有辞　zhèn zhèn yǒu cí　plausible；speak plausibly

振作　zhènzuò　【动】pull oneself together：～起来 bestir oneself；pull oneself together ～精神 brace up

震　zhèn　【动】quake；shake；vibrate：～碎了一块玻璃。A windowpane shattered. 声音太～耳朵了。The sound was deafening.

震荡　zhèndàng　【动】shake；tremor

震动　zhèndòng　【动】❶ vibrate；tremble；quake ❷ (of an event, news) alarm；shock：～全国 reverberate throughout the nation ～人心 make a great impact on people

震撼　zhènhàn　【动】shake；shock

震惊　zhènjīng　【动】shock；alarm；be alarmed

镇(鎮)　zhèn　【动】❶ repress；keep down：～痛 kill pain ❷ guard：坐～ (of a garrison) assume command ❸ cool (using ice)：把汽水用冰～一～ put soda water on ice 【名】country town：小～ small country town 到～上去办些货 go to town to do some purchasing

镇定　zhèndìng　【形】unperturbed；composed

镇静　zhènjìng　【形】keep one's head；unruffled

镇静剂　zhènjìngjì　【名】tranquilizer；sedative

镇压　zhènyā　【动】repress；suppress；put down；quell

zhēng

争　zhēng　【动】❶ quarrel；dispute；argue：为这个问题大家～得面红耳赤。They argued over this issue until everybody was flushed crimson with anger. ❷ strive for；contend for；compete for：～冠军 compete for the championship ～着发言 vie with each other to speak

争辩　zhēngbiàn　【动】argue；debate

争吵　zhēngchǎo　【动】quarrel；squabble

争持　zhēngchí　【动】disagree；dispute

争端　zhēngduān　【名】contention；dispute

争夺　zhēngduó　【动】strive for；fight for；contend for

争分夺秒　zhēng fēn duó miǎo　seize every minute and every second；(fig.) race against time

争光　zhēng = guāng　win honour

争论　zhēnglùn　【动】argue 【名】controversy；dispute

争气　zhēng = qì　try to bring credit to；strive to live up to；work hard to win honour for：为祖国和人民～ win honour for the country and the people 我们一定要争一口气，把学校课程设置上这项空白填补上。We are determined to bring credit to our school by filling this gap in our curriculum.

争取　zhēngqǔ　【动】strive for；endeavour to：～时间 race against time ～胜利 strive for victory ～群众 try to win over the masses

争权夺利　zhēng quán duó lì　struggle for power and profit

争先　zhēngxiān　【动】contend for first place；compete to be the first

争先恐后　zhēng xiān kǒng hòu　struggle to be at forefront and not willing to lag behind

争议　zhēngyì　【动】argue；dispute；debate：～不决 argue without reaching a decision 【名】controversy：在那件事上有～。There is controversy over that issue. 对候选人～不大。There wasn't much controversy over the candidates.

争执　zhēngzhí　【动】dispute with；contend with；be at odds with：双方～不休。The two parties were engaged in endless disputes.

征　zhēng　【动】◇ ❶（徵）summon；call；recruit ❷（徵）levy；collect：～税 levy a tax ～粮 collect grain ❸（徵）request；ask for；solicit；seek：～文 solicit articles (for a magazine etc.) ～得同意 seek and obtain sb.'s agreement ❹ start military campaign：～战 go to battle；go on an expedition

征兵　zhēng = bīng　conscription；recruit；draft

征服　zhēngfú　【动】conquer；overcome：～水患 conquer flooding

征稿　zhēng = gǎo　solicit contributions (to a journal, etc.)

征购　zhēnggòu　【动】purchase by the state

征候　zhēnghòu　【名】sign indicating that sth. is going to happen

征婚　zhēng = hūn　advertize for a marriage partner

征集　zhēngjí　【动】collect；gather

征求　zhēngqiú　【动】ask for (opinion)；solicit

征收　zhēngshōu　【动】levy and collect; impose (a duty) on

征税　zhēng = shuì　levy (or collect) taxes; taxation

征途　zhēngtú　【名】long journey

征象　zhēngxiàng　【名】同"征候"

征询　zhēngxún　【动】ask for; seek the opinion of

征用　zhēngyòng　【动】make a requisition for

征兆　zhēngzhào　【名】sign; indication

挣　zhēng

另见 zhèng

挣扎　zhēngzhá　【动】struggle: ～在死亡线上 struggle to barely make a living ～着起床 struggle to get up 敌人在投降前进行了最后的～。The enemy put up a final desperate struggle before surrendering.

峥　zhēng

峥嵘　zhēngróng　【形】〈书〉❶ (of mountains) lofty and steep: 山势～ steep and towering mountains ❷ (of a period of time) outstanding; extraordinary: ～岁月 eventful years

狰　zhēng

狰狞　zhēngníng　【形】hideous; ferocious

症(癥)　zhēng

另见 zhèng

症结　zhēngjié　【名】crux: ～所在 where the crux of the matter is 找出问题的～ find out the crux of the matter

睁　zhēng　【动】open (eyes)

蒸　zhēng　【动】❶ steam ❷ evaporate

蒸发　zhēngfā　【动】evaporate

蒸馏水　zhēngliúshuǐ　【名】distilled water

蒸汽机　zhēngqìjī　【名】steam engine

蒸蒸日上　zhēng zhēng rì shàng　ever flourishing; become more thriving with each passing day

zhěng

拯　zhěng

拯救　zhěngjiù　【动】save; rescue

整　zhěng　【形】❶ whole; entire; complete; overall: ～天～夜 all day and all night ～年～月 throughout the years ～套设备 a complete set of equipment 两个人～干了一天。It took two men a whole day to do it. ❷ ◇ orderly; neat; tidy: 衣帽不～ untidily dressed 【动】❶ pack; put in order; arrange: ～装待发 pack and get ready for the journey ～旧如新 repair sth. old and make it as good as new ❷ make sb. suffer; punish: 他这是～人, 而不是帮助人掌握技术。What he did just to humiliate her and did not help her to master the technique.

整编　zhěngbiān　【动】reorganize (troops)

整党　zhěng = dǎng　consolidate the party organization; party rectification

整顿　zhěngdùn　【动】rectify; reorganize; readjust; put sth. in good order

整风　zhěng = fēng　rectify the style of work; rectification of an incorrect style of work

整改　zhěnggǎi　【动】rectify and reform

整个　zhěnggè　【形】(～儿) whole; total; entire: ～晚上 all evening ～城市 the whole city ～的苹果 a

whole apple 这部小说写的是石油工人，歌颂的是～工人阶级。Although this novel is about oil workers, it really extols the virtues of the working-class as a whole.

整洁 zhěngjié 【形】neat and tidy

整理 zhěnglǐ 【动】put in order; straighten out：～行装 pack things ready for a journey 把书～一下 put the books in order ～文化遗产 sort out and select from our cultural heritage 把材料～出头绪来 sort out the material

整流 zhěngliú 【动】(electr.) rectify

整流器 zhěngliúqì 【名】(electr.) rectifier

整齐 zhěngqí 【形】❶ tidy; orderly; in good order：～的队伍 orderly ranks 服装～ neatly dressed 工具摆得整整齐齐 The tools are laid out neatly. ❷ neat and kept in good repair：这一带的工人宿舍都很～。The workers' houses in the area are all kept in good repair. ❸ uniform in size：这几行字写得多～! How uniform these lines of characters are! 麦苗出得～。The wheat is sprouting very evenly.

整容 zhěng = róng ❶ tidy oneself up (i.e. have a haircut, a shave, etc.) ❷ face-lifting

整数 zhěngshù 【名】whole number; (maths.) integer

整套 zhěngtào 【名】a complete set of; a whole set of：～房屋 a suite of rooms

整体 zhěngtǐ 【名】whole; as a whole; entity

整形 zhěng = xíng plastic

整修 zhěngxiū 【动】renovate; repair; restore; put in order：～房屋 renovate houses 梯田～得很好看。The terracing of the fields has been beautifully repaired.

整训 zhěngxùn 【动】train and consolidate

整整 zhěngzhěng 【形】exactly *used before a numeral to indicate a fairly large round number*：～一百亩水稻 exactly a hundred *mu* of paddy fields ～一个春天没下雨。It didn't rain at all the whole spring.

zhèng

正 zhèng 【形】❶ straight; upright：他用手指着～北方。He pointed due north. 纪念碑在广场的～中央。The monument was right in the centre of the square. ❷ the right side (*as opp. to* 反)：这块布看不出～反来。I can't tell the right side of this cloth from the wrong side. ❸ ◇ correct; right：不～之风 an incorrect trend ❹ (of colour or flavour) right; pure：这种红颜色不～。This kind of red isn't quite right. ❺ principal; chief (*as opp. to* 副)：～副连长都来了。Both the company commander and the deputy company commander have arrived. ❻ (maths.) positive (*as opp. to* 负)：～负数 positive and negative numbers 负乘负得～。When a negative number is multiplied by another negative number, the result is a positive number. ❼ (of figures, designs, etc.) regular：～三角形 an equilateral triangle 【动】rectify; correct; set right：～一～帽子 straighten one's cap 【副】❶ *indicates action in progress*：他们～开会，你一会儿再找他吧! They are in a meeting, you'd better come to see him later. 我～等着他的电话呢! I'm waiting for his phone call. ❷ *used before an adjective to indicate the state sth. or sb. is in*：我睡得～香，一声雷把我惊醒了。I was sound asleep when a thunderbolt wakened me. 他～年轻，应该在基层

多锻炼锻炼。He is young and ought to be toughened by more experience at the grass roots. ❸ 同 "正好"【副】

正本清源 zhèng běn qīng yuán radically reform

正比 zhèngbǐ 【名】(maths.) direct ratio

正常 zhèngcháng 【形】normal：情况很～。Things are quite normal. 机器～运转。The machines are operating properly.

正常化 zhèngchánghuà 【动】normalize；bring back to normal：两国关系～。The relations between the two countries have been normalized. 突击阶段过去以后，一切又～了。Things returned to normal after the rush job was over.

正大光明 zhèngdà guāngmíng open and aboveboard；just and honourable

正当 zhèng dāng at a time when；just when；when；while：～同学们热烈讨论的时候，老师进来了。The students were in the midst of a lively discussion，when the teacher came in.

正当 zhèngdàng 【形】proper；legitimate；rightful；due：～要求 reasonable request ～的理由 sound reason ～行为 proper conduct

正点 zhèngdiǎn 【形】(of train, aeroplane etc.) on time

正电 zhèngdiàn 【名】positive electricity

正法 zhèngfǎ 【动】execute (a criminal)

正方体 zhèngfāngtǐ 【名】(maths.) cube

正方形 zhèngfāngxíng 【名】(maths.) square

正告 zhènggào 【动】inform in all seriousness；warn sternly

正规 zhèngguī 【形】regular；standard：～学校 a regular school ～方法 standard method

正规军 zhèngguījūn 【名】regular army；regular forces

正轨 zhèngguǐ 【名】the right track：纳入～ bring onto the proper path 工作走上～。The work has developed along the right lines.

正好 zhènghǎo 【形】just right；just in time；just suit the purpose：这件衣服他穿～。This jacket fits him perfectly. 你下班时坐这趟车～。When you knock off work，you'll be just in time to catch that bus. 你来得～，我们正等你帮忙呢！You've come just at the right moment. We've been waiting for your help. Note：*the adjective* 正好 *cannot be used attributively，nor can it be modified by a negative adverb or any adverb of degree，and it cannot be reduplicated.* 【副】❶ happen to；as it happens，球一踢，球一掉到井里。He kicked the ball and as it happens，kicked it right into the well. 我一觉醒来，钟～打十二点。At the moment the clock struck twelve，I chanced to wake up. 我去找他，他～出差了。When I went to see him，he happened to be away on business. ❷ exactly：他们弟兄两个脾气～相反，一个爱动，一个好静。The two brothers are exactly opposite in temperament：one likes to be active while the other tends to be quiet and reserved.

正号 zhènghào 【名】(maths.) positive sign

正经 zhèngjing 【形】❶ respectable；honest；decent：～人 a decent person 假～ feigning respectability ❷ proper；serious (*as opp. to* frivolous *or* trivial)：～事 a serious matter 我说的是～话，不是开玩笑。I was not joking. I meant business. ❸ official；standard：～货 standard products

正面　zhèngmiàn　【名】❶ front；facade；frontage：～进攻 frontal attack 大楼的～朝南。The building faces south. ❷（of cloth, paper, etc.）the right side（*as opp. to* 背面 *or* 反面）：这种纸～是红色的。The right side of this kind of paper is red. ❸ positive（*as opp. to* 反面）：～教育 educate by encouragement and example ❹ the more obvious aspect：问题的～反面都要看到。Both the obvious and the more subtle aspects of the problem should be taken into consideration. ❺ direct：～提出问题 put forward questions in a direct way

正面人物　zhèngmiàn rénwù　positive character

正派　zhèngpài　【形】upright；honest；decent

正品　zhèngpǐn　【名】quality goods；certified products

正气　zhèngqì　【名】healthy tendency；open and above-board way of doing things

正巧　zhèngqiǎo　【形】in good time；by（a happy chance）；by coincidence：你来得～，我正想去找你。You came just at the right moment. I was just going to look for you. 这一球～踢到守门员胸前，让守门员给抱住了。Luckily, the ball fell right in front of the goal keeper, who caught it just in time.

正确　zhèngquè　【形】correct；right

正式　zhèngshì　【形】official；formal；full

正视　zhèngshì　【动】face squarely：～现实 face reality squarely 敢于～工作中的问题 dare to face squarely the problems that arise in one's work

正事　zhèngshì　【名】one's proper business

正数　zhèngshù　【名】（maths.）positive number

正统　zhèngtǒng　【名】orthodox

正文　zhèngwén　【名】text；the main body（of a book, etc.）

正义　zhèngyì　【形】just；righteous：非～战争 unjust war 【名】justice：主持～ uphold justice 伸张～ promote justice

正音　zhèng＝yīn　correct pronunciation

正在　zhèngzài　【副】同"正"【副】❶

正直　zhèngzhí　【形】just；upright

正宗　zhèngzōng　【名】genuine；authentic；orthordox

证（證）　zhèng　【名】◇❶ evidence；proof：以此为～ take this as evidence ❷ certificate；card：会员～ membership card 工作～ employee's identity card

证词　zhèngcí　【名】testimony

证件　zhèngjiàn　【名】papers；certificates

证据　zhèngjù　【名】evidence；proof

证明　zhèngmíng　【动】prove；certify；testify；confirm：我～他当时不在场。I testified that he was not on the scene at that time. 事实～他是对的。Facts proved that he was right. 【名】proof；certificate：出个～ issue a certificate 此～无效。This certificate is invalid.

证券　zhèngquàn　【名】〔张 zhāng〕bond；security：有价～ negotiable securities

证人　zhèngren　【名】witness

证实　zhèngshí　【动】confirm；corroborate；verify；testify

证书　zhèngshū　【名】〔张 zhāng〕certificate；testimonial

证物　zhèngwù　【名】exhibit（produced in court as evidence）

证言　zhèngyán　【名】testimony

证章　zhèngzhāng　【名】badge

郑（鄭）　zhèng

郑重　zhèngzhòng　【形】serious；sol-

emn

政 zhèng 【名】◇ politics；certain administrative aspects of government

政变 zhèngbiàn 【名】coup d'état

政策 zhèngcè 【名】policy

政党 zhèngdǎng 【名】political party

政法 zhèngfǎ 【名】 *short for* 政治 *and* 法律

政府 zhèngfǔ 【名】government

政纲 zhènggāng 【名】political programme；platform

政绩 zhèngjì 【名】achievements in one's official career

政见 zhèngjiàn 【名】political view

政局 zhèngjú 【名】political situation

政客 zhèngkè 【名】politician (*derog.*)

政论 zhènglùn 【名】comment on politics

政权 zhèngquán 【名】political power

政体 zhèngtǐ 【名】system of government；form of government

政委 zhèngwěi 【名】 *short for* 政治委员 political commissar

政协 zhèngxié 【名】 *short for* 中国人民政治协商会议 the Chinese People's Political Consultative Conference

政治 zhèngzhì 【名】politics

政治避难 zhèngzhì bì nàn （political）asylum

政治家 zhèngzhìjiā 【名】statesman

政治经济学 zhèngzhì jīngjìxué political economy

政治局 zhèngzhìjú 【名】the Political Bureau

政治性 zhèngzhìxìng 【名】political nature (e.g. of one's work)；political content (e.g. of a textbook)

挣 zhèng 【动】❶ struggle to get free from：骡子～开了缰绳。The mule got rid of its bridle. ❷ earn：～钱 earn money

另见 zhēng

挣命 zhèng = mìng struggle for one's life

挣脱 zhèngtuō 【动】struggle to free oneself；shake off；get rid of：～枷锁 rid oneself of one's shackles 从苦难中～出来 struggle to shake off one's misery

症 zhèng 【名】illness；disease

另见 zhēng

症状 zhèngzhuàng 【名】symptom

zhī

之 zhī 〈书〉【代】it *always in the objective case*：战而胜～ struggle against and defeat it 广大群众无不为（wéi）～欢欣鼓舞。There isn't anybody who isn't delighted over the news. 【助】❶ *connects the modifier and the word it modifies, equivalent to* 的 ① *indicates the possessive case*：旅客～家 "Travellers' Home" 大海～滨 shore of the vast sea ② *indicates a descriptive modifier*：光荣～家 a glorious family 必经～路 an inevitable road ❷ *used between the subject and the predicate of a S-P construction to turn the subject into the modifier and the predicate into what is modified*：这次活动规模～大，范围～广，参加人数～多都是空前的。The scale, the scope and the number of people taking part in this extra-curricular activity were all unprecedented.

之后 zhī hòu （*usu. in written language*）❶ after (*referring to time*)：三天～ after three days 打败对手～ after defeating his competitors 继成昆铁路通车～，湘黔铁路又通车了。

After the Chengdu-Kunming Railway was opened to traffic, the Hunan-Guizhou Railway was also completed. ❷ behind (*referring to locality, less frequently used*)：房屋～有一片果园。 At the back of the house is an orchard. ❸ then：会议总结了今年的生产情况，～，又讨论了明年的生产计划。 In the meeting they summed up this year's production and then they discussed the production plan for the next year.

…之际 …zhī jì 〈书〉 at the time when：两国建交～ at the time when diplomatic relations between the two countries were established 值此国庆十周年～ on the tenth anniversary of the founding of our Republic

…之间 …zhī jiān ❶ between：来往于北京上海～ come and go between Beijing and Shanghai 在图书馆和礼堂～ between the library and the auditorium 三十岁到四十岁～ between 30 and 40 years old 三点至四点～ between 3:00 and 4:00 朋友～ between friends 逐步缩小城乡～的差别 gradually narrow the gap between the city and the countryside 搞好婆媳～的关系 deal with the relationships between mother-in-law and daughter-in-law 发展各国人民～的友谊 develop friendship among the peoples of various countries ❷ *used after a word or phrase denoting a period of time, to show that the speaker thinks the time is very short*：那把钳子怎么转眼～就不见了？ How did the pliers manage to disappear from one moment to the next? 院子里的桃花一夜～都开了。 The peach blossoms in the courtyard burst into full bloom overnight. 这个工厂两年～就建成投产了。 This factory was built and went

into operation in only two years.

…之类 …zhī lèi *used after the enumeration of things to mean "and the like"*：菜市场里摆满了黄瓜、西红柿～的新鲜蔬菜。 The market was bursting with vegetables such as tomatoes and cucumbers.

…之流 …zhī liú (of persons) and the like (*derog.*)：希特勒、墨索里尼～ Hitler, Mussolini and the like

…之内 …zhī nèi within：两天～ within two days 校园～ on the campus 方圆百里～ within a radius of 100 *li* 职责～的事 a matter of duty

…之前 …zhī qián before；in front of (*usu. in written language*)：天亮～ before day-break 临走～ before departure 年底～力争完工 strive to finish construction before the year is out 钟楼～有几棵古柏。 There are a few ancient cypresses in front of the bell tower.

…之上 …zhī shàng above；over：不能把个人利益放在集体利益～。 Personal interests must not be placed above the interests of the collective.

…之外 …zhī wài ❶ beyond：我的老家在千里～。 My hometown is over a 1000 *li* away. 工程进展的速度出乎人们意料～。 The rate of progress has certainly exceeded our expectations. ❷ 同"除了…以外"chúle…yǐwài：他（除了）完成本职工作～，还常去帮助别人学习技术。 As well as taking care of his own responsibilities, he often helps others to acquire new techniques. （除了）这块地～，别的地都种油菜。 All the fields will be sown with rape except this plot.

…之下 …zhī xià under；below：在反吸烟运动影响～，她毅然停止吸烟。 Under the influence of anti-smoking campaigns, she quit smoking

for good.

…之一 … zhī yī one of the…：这个公司是先进单位～。This company is one of the most advanced. 空气是生物生存的必要条件～。Air is one of the conditions necessary for the existence of living things.

…之中 … zhī zhōng within (a process)；among：这个地方一天～气温变化很大。There are great changes in temperature within 24 hours here. 我们几个人～，小王最年轻。Among the handful of us, Xiao Wang is the youngest.

支 zhī 【动】❶ support；prop up；raise；erect：把帐篷～起来 pitch a tent 她手～着头坐着。She sat with her chin propped on her hands. ❷ sustain；bear：头疼得实在～不住 a headache which can't be borne 体力不～。One's physical strength has been strained to the limits. ❸ send (away)；order about：把他～开 send him out of the way ❹ pay out or withdraw (money)：～款 pay out or withdraw cash 【量】❶ *for stick-like things*：三～枪 three rifles 两～铅笔 two pencils 十～香烟 ten cigarettes 五～蜡烛 five candles ❷ *for army units*：这～部队 this army unit ❸ *for songs or melodies*：两～歌 two songs 一～新乐曲 a new melody ❹ watt：二十五～光的灯泡 a 25-watt bulb ❺ (of textiles) count：六十～纱 60-count yarn

支部 zhībù 【名】branch of an organization

支撑 zhīchēng 【动】❶ prop up；support：这棵松树的一个横枝用一根柱子～着。A horizontal branch of the pine tree was supported by a prop. ❷ barely maintain；sustain：～着病体 struggle on despite poor health ～门面（*fig.*）keep up ap-

pearances

支持 zhīchí 【动】❶ support；sustain；back：工作上互相～ support each other in working ～孩子们的首创精神 support the initiatives of the children ❷ 同"支撑"❷ 【名】support

支出 zhīchū 【动】pay；disburse 【名】expenditure；outlay

支架 zhījià 【名】support；stand

支解 zhījiě 【动】dismember

支离破碎 zhīlí pòsuì shattered；splintered；split

支流 zhīliú 【名】❶ tributary ❷ secondary aspect；minor aspect：小李主流是好的，缺点只是～。Xiao Li is basically a good man with some minor weaknesses.

支配 zhīpèi 【动】❶ allot；allocate；arrange：合理～时间 a reasonable allocation of the time available ❷ control；dominate；manipulate；guide：受人～ be controlled by others 思想～行动。Thinking guides action.

支票 zhīpiào 【名】〔张 zhāng〕cheque

支书 zhīshū 【名】*short for* 支部书记 secretary of a party branch

支吾 zhīwu 【动】stall；equivocate；prevaricate：～其词 speak evasively 一味～ keep on equivocating

支援 zhīyuán 【动】support；aid；hold up；help；back 【名】support；help

支支吾吾 zhīzhīwūwū 【形】be humming and hawing：别～，有看法就开门见山地说嘛！Please don't hesitate. If you have differing views, speak up!

支柱 zhīzhù 【名】mainstay；brace

只（隻） zhī 【量】❶ *for one of a pair*：两～手 two hands 一～鞋 a shoe ❷ *for certain animals, boats or containers*：三～母鸡 three hens 一～小船 a small boat 一～箱子 a suitcase

另见 zhī

汁　zhī　【名】juice

芝　zhī
芝麻　zhīma　【名】〔粒 儿〕sesame

枝　zhī　【名】branch；bough；twig【量】❶ *for sth. on a branch*：一～花 a spray of flowers ❷ 同"支" zhī【量】❶
枝节　zhījié　【名】❶side issue；minor issue：不要抓住一些～问题不放。Don't dwell on minor issues. ❷ unexpected trouble；obstacle deliberately put in one's way：横生～ raise unexpected difficulties
枝叶　zhīyè　【名】leaves and branches；foliage

知　zhī　【动】◇ know；be aware of
知道　zhīdào　【动】know；be aware of
知己知彼　zhī jǐ zhī bǐ　know the enemy and know oneself
知觉　zhījué　【名】consciousness
知名　zhīmíng　【形】(usu. of persons) well-known；celebrated；famous：～人士 a well-known public figure　这位作家是全国～的。This writer is famous throughout the country.
知名度　zhīmíngdù　【名】popularity；celebrity status：茅台酒的～相当高。Maotai liquor has a great reputation.
知难而进　zhī nán ér jìn　push on in spite of difficulties；advance despite difficulties
知情　zhī＝qíng　know the details of an incident
知趣　zhīqù　【形】know how to please；have a sense of propriety
知识　zhīshi　【名】knowledge
知识产权　zhīshi chǎnquán　intellectual property rights

知识产业　zhīshi chǎnyè　the intellectual industry
知识分子　zhīshi fènzǐ　intellectual；the intelligentsia
知识青年　zhīshi qīngnián　educated youth；middle school graduates
知无不言，言无不尽　zhī wú bù yán，yán wú bù jìn　speak up and speak without reserve
知心　zhīxīn　【形】understanding deeply；bosom (friend)
知足　zhīzú　【形】be happy with one's lot

织（織）　zhī　【动】knit；weave
织补　zhībǔ　【动】do invisible mending

脂　zhī
脂肪　zhīfáng　【名】fat；grease

蜘　zhī
蜘蛛　zhīzhū　【名】〔只 zhī〕spider

zhí

执（執）　zhí　【动】〔书〕❶ hold；carry：手～教鞭 hold a pointer in one hand ❷ persist in；stick to；adhere to：～意不肯 stick to an idea and be unwilling to give it up
执笔　zhíbǐ　【动】do the actual writing (of a collective statement)
执法　zhífǎ　【动】enforce the law
执教　zhíjiào　【动】be a teacher：李老师已～三十多年。Mr. Li has been teaching for more than 30 years.
执迷不悟　zhí mí bù wù　persist in error；refuse to come to one's senses；refuse to mend one's way
执拗　zhíniù　【形】pigheaded；wilful
执行　zhíxíng　【动】carry out；put into effect；execute：～政策 put the policy into effect ～命令 carry out orders 一切按原计划～ do every-

thing in accordance with the original plan

执行主席 zhíxíng zhǔxí executive chairman

执照 zhízhào 【名】〔张 zhāng〕license

执政 zhízhèng 【动】be in power; be in office

直 zhí 【形】❶ straight (*as opp. to* 弯):马路又宽又～。The road is both broad and straight. 这条线划得很～。This line was drawn very straight. ❷ straightforward:这个人很～。He is very straightforward.【动】straighten:他笑得～不起腰来。He doubled up with laughter. 你～着脖子看什么呢? What are you rubbernecking at?【副】❶ 同 "一直" yìzhí *usu. used in conjunction with* 到 *or* 至:会议～至深夜才结束。The meeting lasted well into the night. 公路～伸到山脚下。The road runs straight to the foot of the mountain. ❷ keep on:风吹得树～摇晃。The tree kept on swaying in the wind. 我在后面～喊他,他就是听不见。I kept on calling him from behind, but he simply couldn't hear me.

直拨 zhíbō 【动】direct dial:～电话 a direct dialing phone

直播 zhíbō 【动】live broadcast; live television transmission:现场～ broadcast live

直达 zhídá 【动】through (train)

直到 zhídào 【介】❶ until *emphasizes that there has been no change up to a certain time or that there is no exception*:～天黑他才回来。He didn't come back until it was dark. ～现在还没消息。There has been no news up till now. 他一家失散十几年,～现在才团聚。His whole family had been separated for over ten years and have just been reunited. ❷ to:这次大扫除

从教室、宿舍～食堂,都彻底清扫了一遍。In this general cleaning, every corner from classrooms and dormitories to the dining hall, was thoroughly cleaned. 从学生～校长都参加了今天的植树活动。Everybody, from students to the president of the institute, took part in tree-planting today.

直观 zhíguān 【名】direct perception through the senses; audio-visual

直角 zhíjiǎo 【名】(maths.) right angle

直接 zhíjiē 【形】direct; immediate; first-hand (*as opp. to* 间接):～经验 first-hand experience ～联系 direct contact 姑母从上海～去天津,不准备在南京停留。My aunt will go directly to Tianjin from Shanghai, not stopping over in Nanjing.

直接宾语 zhíjiēbīnyǔ 【名】direct object

直截了当 zhí jié liǎo dàng outspoken; straightforward

直径 zhíjìng 【名】diameter

直流电 zhíliúdiàn 【名】(electr.) direct current

直升飞机 zhí shēng fēijī helicopter

直属 zhíshǔ 【动】be directly under...:中央～单位 unit directly under the central government ～机关 department directly under... 这个出版社～教育部。This publishing house is directly under the Ministry of Education.

直率 zhíshuài 【形】frank; straightforward; plain spoken; outright

直爽 zhíshuǎng 【形】同"直率"

直挺挺 zhítǐngtǐng 【形】straight and stiff

直系亲属 zhíxì qīnshǔ immediate relative

直辖 zhíxiá 【动】exercise direct jurisdiction over

直辖市 zhíxiáshì 【名】municipality under central authority

直线 zhíxiàn 【名】〔条 tiáo〕straight line

直销 zhíxiāo 【动】direct sale：厂家 ～ direct sale by the producer

直言不讳 zhí yán bù huì speak without reservation；not mince words：请你 ～ 地指出我们工作中的缺点。Please point out the shortcomings in our work frankly.

直译 zhíyì 【动】literal translation；word for word translation

直音 zhíyīn 【名】use one Chinese character to indicate the pronunciation of another

侄 zhí 【名】◇ nephew (brother's son)：叔 ～ 二人 the uncle and his nephew

侄女 zhínǚ 【名】niece (brother's daughter)

侄子 zhízi 【名】nephew (brother's son)

值 zhí 【名】❶ ◇ price；cost ❷ (maths.) value 【动】❶ cost；be worth：这套茶具 ～ 多少钱？How much does this tea-set cost？❷ ◇ happen to be：时 ～ 佳节。It happens to be festival time. ❸ ◇ worth (usu. in the neg.)：不 ～ 一提 not worth mentioning

值班 zhí = bān be on duty

值得 zhíde 【动】worth；worthwhile used as the predicate：只要对大家有益，多费点儿力气也 ～。As long as it benefits all of you, it is worthwhile even if it costs a lot of effort. 为这点儿小事，花这么多时间不 ～。It isn't worthwhile to spend such a lot of time on such a trivial matter. Note：It can also be used with a verb, verb phrase or S-P construction, the subject of the sentence being the recipient of the action：这双皮鞋很好，～ 买。This pair of shoes is of very good quality and worth buying. 这个词的用法 ～认真讨论。The usage of this word merits serious discussion. 这个问题 ～我们研究。It is worthwhile to investigate this problem.

值钱 zhí = qián valuable

值勤 zhíqín 【动】(mil.) be on duty

值日 zhírì 【动】(of school children) be on duty

职（職） zhí 【名】◇ ❶ duty ❷ position；post

职别 zhíbié 【名】official rank

职称 zhíchēng 【名】professional title

职工 zhígōng 【名】staff and workers

职能 zhínéng 【名】function

职权 zhíquán 【名】authority of office

职守 zhíshǒu 【名】post；duty：忠于 ～ be devoted to one's duty

职位 zhíwèi 【名】position；post

职务 zhíwù 【名】duty (one's professional duty)

职业 zhíyè 【名】occupation；profession；vocation

职业病 zhíyèbìng 【名】occupational disease

职业学校 zhíyè xuéxiào vocational school

职员 zhíyuán 【名】staff member；office worker

职责 zhízé 【名】responsibility and duty

植 zhí 【动】◇ plant；grow；cultivate：～ 树造林 plant the land with trees

植被 zhíbèi 【名】vegetation

植物 zhíwù 【名】plant

植物人 zhíwùrén 【名】a vegetable

植物学 zhíwùxué 【名】botany

植物园 zhíwùyuán 【名】botanical garden

殖 zhí

殖民地 zhímíndì 【名】colony

殖民主义 zhímínzhǔyì 【名】colonialism

zhǐ

止 zhǐ 【动】❶ stop；put a stop to：～痒 stop the itching 她的眼泪～不住地往下流。She could not stop the tears from trickling down. ❷ to：参观时间自上午八时起至下午五时～。Opening hours：8：00 a. m. to 5：00 p. m.

止步 zhǐ＝bù stop；halt

止境 zhǐjìng 【名】limit；boundary

止痛 zhǐ＝tòng assuage pain；stop pain

止血 zhǐ＝xuè staunch；stop bleeding

只（祇） zhǐ 【副】only ❶ *used before a verb to restrict the scope of the verb or the quantity of the object*：我～刮脸，不理发。Shave only, no hair-cut. 教室里～剩下三个人。Only three students were left in the classroom. ❷ *used before a noun or pronoun which is not the object, usu. followed by a numeral plus measure word*：我们新开的菜地～白菜一项就收了两万多斤。In our newly-made vegetable fields, we harvested 20000 *jin* of cabbage alone (to say nothing of other vegetables). ～他一个人坐车,我们都骑车去。He is the only one going by bus；the rest of us are all going by bike.

另见 zhī

只得 zhǐdé 【副】同"只好"

只顾 zhǐgù 【副】simply；merely *used in a compound sentence*：他一往前走,别人喊他都没听见。He simply rushed ahead and didn't hear the people calling him. 他们俩连饭都忘了吃,～下棋了。The two of them were completely absorbed in chess and even forgot about supper.

只管 zhǐguǎn 【副】by all means：你有什么话～说吧！If you have anything to say, by all means speak up. 这件事我去办,你～放心。I'll see to this matter, don't you worry about it.

只好 zhǐhǎo 【副】have to：等了半天他不回来,我～走了。I had waited for a long time, but he didn't show up and I finally had to leave. 河上没有桥,我们～涉水过去。There wasn't any bridge on the river so we had to ford it.

只见树木,不见森林 zhǐ jiàn shùmù, bùjiàn sēnlín fail to see the forest for the trees；(*fig.*) have only the part in mind but ignore the whole

只是 zhǐshì 【副】❶ merely；only；just：我～做了一点儿应该做的事,不值得表扬。I just did what was expected of me；it isn't worth mentioning at all. 我的意见很不成熟,～供你参考。My opinion hasn't been well thought out and is only for your reference. ❷ simply：大家都劝他回去,他～摇摇头,不肯走。Everybody tried to persuade him to go back, but he simply shook his head and refused to leave. 你不能每天晚上～看电视,要首先把功课做好。You can't spend all your evenings watching TV. You must finish your homework first. 【连】but；only：他的汉语学得不错,～发音还不太好。His Chinese is not bad, but his pronunciation isn't too good. 这本书我看过,～时间久了,内容记不清了。I have read this book, but it was a long time ago and I don't altogether remember its contents.

只许州官放火,不许百姓点灯 zhǐ xǔ zhōuguān fàng huǒ, bù xǔ bǎixìng diǎn dēng the magistrates were allowed to burn down houses, but the common people were forbidden even to light lamps; (*fig.*) the privileged can get away with anything while ordinary people have no freedom at all

只要 zhǐyào 【连】 as long as *often used with* 就:为这么点小事他不会怪你的,～你道一下歉就行了。He won't be really offended at such a trifle as long as you apologize. ～你有问题,什么时候问我都可以。Whenever you have a question just ask me any time. 张师傅～一听声音,就知道机器有没有毛病。Lao Zhang, a veteran worker, can tell whether the machine is working properly just by listening to it. Note: *the clause with* 只要 *can also be the second clause in the sentence*:你一定能学好,～你努力。I'm sure you can do well in your studies, provided you make an effort.

只有 zhǐyǒu 【副】❶同"只好":票不够,我 ～ 不去了。There aren't enough tickets to go round; I had to give up. 大盆的月季都卖完了,他～买小盆的了。All the bigger pot roses were sold out; he had to buy small ones. ❷ only *used to limit the subject*:别人都坐车,～他坐船。All the others are travelling by train; he is the only one going by boat. 我们公司～他会法文。He is the only one who knows French in our company. 【连】 *indicates a necessary condition, usu. used with* 才:～农业发展了,工业才有足够的原料和市场。Only when agriculture is fully developed, can industry have sufficient materials and markets. 要想今天晚上赶到,～坐飞机。If you want to be there on time this eve-

ning, the only way is to go by plane.

只争朝夕 zhǐ zhēng zhāo xī seize every minute; race against time

纸(紙) zhǐ 【名】〔张 zhāng〕 paper

纸币 zhǐbì 【名】 bank note; paper currency

纸上谈兵 zhǐ shàng tán bīng an armchair strategist

纸张 zhǐ zhāng 【名】 all sorts of paper

指 zhǐ 【名】◇ finger:天黑得伸手不见五～。It was so dark that one couldn't see one's hand. 【动】❶ 用手一 ～ point at something with one's finger point at; point to:时针～着三点。The hour hand of the clock pointed to three. ❷〈口〉count on; rely on:光～着他一个人不行,要大伙一起干。We can't rely on him alone; we must all work together. ❸ aim at; be meant for sb.:这句话主要是～他说的。These words were aimed primarily at him.

指标 zhǐbiāo 【名】target; objective (set for production etc.)

指出 zhǐchū 【动】point out; indicate:不周到的地方,请你～。Please point out any omission part. 大会主席～,会议开得很成功。The chairman pointed out that the conference was a success.

指导 zhǐdǎo 【动】instruct; guide; direct

指导员 zhǐdǎoyuán 【名】political instructor

指点 zhǐdiǎn 【动】❶ instruct; show how:师傅～我学开车床。A veteran worker showed me how to operate the lathe. ❷ advise; give guidance; point out; indicate:哪些地方用词不当,请给～～。Please point

out any words inappropriately used and tell us how to use them properly.

指定 zhǐdìng 【动】appoint；assign；name

指挥 zhǐhuī 【动】❶（mil.）command；conduct；direct：他一生～过许多次有名的战役。During his lifetime, he conducted many famous campaigns. ❷（of an orchestra）conduct：～大合唱 conduct a choir 【名】（mil.）commanding officer；（of orchestra）conductor：工地～ foreman of a construction site 乐队～ orchestra conductor

指挥棒 zhǐhuībàng 【名】〔根 gēn〕baton

指挥部 zhǐhuībù 【名】headquarters

指挥员 zhǐhuīyuán 【名】commander；commanding officer

指甲 zhǐjia 【名】nail

指教 zhǐjiào 【动】instruct；give advice：请多多～。Please give us your advice.

指控 zhǐkòng 【动】accuse；charge

指令 zhǐlìng 【名】order；instruction

指名 zhǐ = míng point out sb.'s name；mention sb. by name

指明 zhǐmíng 【动】clearly point out

指南 zhǐnán 【名】guide book

指南针 zhǐnánzhēn 【名】compass

指日可待 zhǐ rì kě dài the day is not far off；just round the corner：这条铁路全线电气化已经～了。We expect the whole length of this railway line to be electrified soon.

指桑骂槐 zhǐ sāng mà huái revile the locust while pointing to the mulberry；(fig.) make oblique accusations

指使 zhǐshǐ 【动】instigate；incite

指示 zhǐshì 【名】instruction；directive：领导的～ instructions from the leadership 【动】instruct；indicate；direct：县委～要集中力量搞好夏收。The County Party Commit-tee instructed us to concentrate our manpower on the summer harvest.

指手画脚 zhǐ shǒu huà jiǎo order (others) about with wild gestures

指数 zhǐshù 【名】❶ index number ❷（maths.）index

指头 zhǐtou 【名】〔个 gè〕finger

指望 zhǐwàng 【动】look forward to；expect；pin one's hopes on；count on：农民们都～今年有个好收成。The peasants are all looking forward to a good harvest this year. 【名】hope：很有～ very hopeful 你要的戏票这星期没～啦! There's no hope of your getting a ticket to the play this week.

指纹 zhǐwén 【名】❶ loop and whorls on a finger ❷ fingerprint

指引 zhǐyǐn 【动】guide；conduct；lead

指印 zhǐyìn 【名】fingerprint；finger mark

指责 zhǐzé 【动】censure；blame；denounce；charge；accuse

指战员 zhǐzhànyuán 【名】commanders and fighters；officers and men

指针 zhǐzhēn 【名】❶ pointer；indicator ❷ guide；guiding principle

指正 zhǐzhèng 【动】*polite way of asking for others' comments on one's work*：不妥之处请～。Please point out anything that is not quite right.

趾 zhǐ 【名】◇ toe

趾高气扬 zhǐ gāo qì yáng give oneself airs and swagger about；cocky

zhì

至 zhì 【动】◇ to；till：营业时间自早九时～晚八时。Business hours are from 9 a.m. to 8 p.m. 长城东

起山海关,西～嘉峪关,全长约五千公里。The Great Wall starts at Shanhaiguan in the east and ends at Jiayuguan in the west and has a total length of about 5000 km. 【副】◇ the most; 这本书～迟下星期一还你。I'll return the book to you next Monday at the latest.

至多 zhìduō 【副】at most; 看样子他～不过三十岁。He looks to be thirty at most. 我～能跟你去看看,长期住下去不行。I can at best go there with you to have a look, but I won't be able to stay. 这辆摩托车你～骑三天,下星期我要用。You can use the motorcycle for three days at most because I'll need it next week.

至高无上 zhì gāo wú shàng most lofty; supreme; paramount

至关紧要 zhì guān jǐnyào the most important; of the utmost importance

至今 zhì=jīn up to now; until now; hitherto

至少 zhìshǎo 【副】at least; 这座建筑物～有五百年的历史了。This building is at least 500 years old. 文章写好后～要看两遍。After you have finished a piece of writing, you must read it at least twice. 你如果不去看他,～托人带信去。If you can't go to see him in person, the least you can do is to send him a message.

至于 zhìyú 【连】as to; 我要出差去,～什么时候走,还没定。I'm going on a business trip, but it hasn't yet been decided when I'll go. 我只知道他是个著名的物理学家,～他有什么著作,我就不清楚了。I only know that he's a well-known physicist. I'm afraid I don't know anything about his publications. 【副】implies "to a certain extent", used only in the negative or in a rhetori-cal question; 你工作虽然很忙,但总不～连写信的时间也没有吧! I'm sure you are very busy, but surely not so busy that you can't write a letter. 一点儿小事,～这么着急吗? It's a very trivial matter. How can it possibly worry you as much as that? 夏天刚过,你就穿上了毛背心,～吗? Summer is just over. Can it possibly be so cold that you have to wear a wool vest?

志 zhì 【名】◇ ❶ will; goal; ～大才疏 not have the ability to achieve one's goal ❷ record; 县～ county annals 地理～ local geographical records

志哀 zhì=āi indicate mourning

志气 zhìqi 【名】ambition; aspiration

志趣 zhìqù 【名】aspirations and interest

志士 zhìshì 【名】people with lofty ideals

志同道合 zhì tóng dào hé cherish the same ideals and follow the same path

志向 zhìxiàng 【名】what one wants to do in the future; aspiration; ideal

志愿 zhìyuàn 【名】desire; wish; will; 祖国在发展中医学方面的需要就是我的～。My wish is to do what my country needs most in developing Chinese medicine. 【副】of one's own free will; voluntarily; ～参加边疆建设 volunteer to participate in the construction in the border regions

志愿书 zhìyuànshū 【名】application form

制(製) zhì 【动】manufacture; make; create; ～版 make printing plates ～革 process hides ～药 pharmacy 【名】◇ system; 八小

时工作～ an eight-hour work-day system

制裁 zhìcái 【动】apply sanctions against

制定 zhìdìng 【动】enact; work out

制动器 zhìdòngqì 【名】brakes

制度 zhìdù 【名】system; institution

制服 zhìfú 【名】〔件 jiàn〕uniform: 一套新～ a new uniform 他穿着一件～上衣。He is wearing a uniform jacket.

制服 zhìfú 【动】subdue; bring under control: ～敌人 conquer the enemy 石油工人～了井喷,保住了油井。The oil-workers managed to bring the blowout under control, thus saving the well. 也作"制伏"。

制品 zhìpǐn 【名】products; goods: 橡胶～ rubber products

制胜 zhìshèng 【动】come out victorious; gain mastery over

制图 zhì = tú make charts or blueprints

制约 zhìyuē 【动】restrain

制造 zhìzào 【动】❶ manufacture; make: ～拖拉机 manufacture tractors ～出新型小轿车 manufacture a new type of small sedan ❷ fabricate; create: ～分裂 foment disunity ～紧张局势 create a tense situation ～谣言 fabricate rumours

制止 zhìzhǐ 【动】stop; check; prevent

制作 zhìzuò 【动】manufacture

质(質) zhì 【名】❶ nature; character; quality: 由量的变化到～的变化 from quantitative to qualitative change 不同的事物有不同的～。Different things differ in nature. ❷ quality; degree of goodness: 产品的～和量都不可忽视。Neither quantity nor quality of products can be ignored.

质变 zhìbiàn 【名】(philos.) qualitative change

质地 zhìdì 【名】texture; grain: ～坚韧 strong but pliable in texture ～优良 very fine in texture

质量 zhìliàng 【名】❶ (phys.) mass ❷ quality: 提高教学～ improve one's teaching 产品的～很好。The quality of the products is very good.

质朴 zhìpǔ 【形】simple and unadorned; plain

质问 zhìwèn 【动】query; interrogate; question

质疑 zhìyí 【动】call in question; query

质子 zhìzǐ 【名】proton

治 zhì 【动】❶ ◇ govern; administer; rule; run: ～国 govern a country ❷ ◇ (of a river) harness; control: ～黄工程 the project to control the Yellow River ❸ cure; heal; treat: 他的病还能～好吗? Is there any hope of his being cured? ❹ (of pests) exterminate: ～蝗 exterminate locusts

治安 zhì'ān 【名】public security; public order

治本 zhì = běn treat the underlying cause; effect a permanent cure (as opp. to 治标)

治标 zhì = biāo give symptomatic treatment; bring about a temporary solution (as opp. to 治本)

治病救人 zhì bìng jiù rén cure the illness and save the patient; (fig.) point out someone's weaknesses only in order to help him

治理 zhìlǐ 【动】❶ govern; manage; run: ～国家 govern a country ❷ harness; tame; bring under control: ～荒山 transform barren mountains ～淮河 harness the Huai River

治疗 zhìliáo 【动】remedy; cure; treat; heal

治丧 zhìsāng 【动】take charge of a

funeral service

治山 zhì = shān transform mountains

治水 zhì = shuǐ tame a river

治外法权 zhìwàifǎquán 【名】extraterritoriality

治装 zhìzhuāng 【动】make preparation for a long journey; buy things necessary for a long journey

治罪 zhì = zuì punish sb. (for a crime)

桎 zhì

桎梏 zhìgù 【名】shackles; yoke

致 zhì 【动】❶ pay; send; extend (respects, congratulations, greetings, etc.); ～电吊唁 send a cable of condolence ～欢迎词 make a speech of welcome ～以热烈的祝贺 extend warm congratulations 此～敬礼 respectfully yours... ❷〈书〉incur; result in; 学以～用 learn in order to use one's knowledge

致哀 zhì'āi 【动】pay one's respects to the deceased

致癌物质 zhì'ái wùzhì carcinogen

致词 zhì = cí make a speech; address

致富 zhìfù 【动】get rich; make a fortune; 发家～ build up a family fortune

致敬 zhìjìng 【动】salute

致力 zhìlì 【动】devote oneself to; make efforts in; concentrate effort on

致命 zhìmìng 【形】fatal; vital; lethal; mortal

致使 zhìshǐ 【动】cause; result in (some undesirable consequence)(usu. in written language): 由于调拨不当,～物资积压。Because of improper allocation, a lot of goods and materials were overstocked. 连日暴雨,～水位猛涨。Successive days of heavy rain caused a sudden rise in the water level.

致死 zhìsǐ 【动】cause death; cause to die; 迫害～ die from persecution

致谢 zhìxiè 【动】extend thanks to

致意 zhìyì 【动】send one's regards to; give one's compliments to; extend greetings to

秩 zhì

秩序 zhìxù 【名】order

掷(擲) zhì 【动】throw; cast

室 zhì

窒息 zhìxī 【动】stifle; smother; suffocate; choke

智 zhì 【名】◇ wisdom; intelligence; wit

智慧 zhìhuì 【名】wisdom

智力 zhìlì 【名】intelligence

智力竞赛 zhìlì jìngsài intelligence contest

智谋 zhìmóu 【名】wit; resource

智能 zhìnéng 【名】intelligence; 提高～ raise level of intelligence

智取 zhìqǔ 【动】outwit; take by strategy

智商 zhìshāng 【名】IQ (intelligence quotient): ～高 high IQ ～比较低。Sb.'s IQ is relatively low.

智育 zhìyù 【名】intellectual training; intellectual education

滞(滯) zhì 【动】stagnant; sluggish

滞留 zhìliú 【动】be detained; be held up

滞销 zhìxiāo 【动】unsalable; unmarketable

置 zhì 【动】❶ ◇ place; put; set aside: 漠然～之 apathetically set sth. aside ❷ purchase; buy; ～几件家具 buy some furniture ～装 buy clothes

置办 zhìbàn 【动】buy

置换 zhìhuàn 【动】(chem.) displace

置若罔闻 zhì ruò wǎng wén ignore completely; take no notice of; turn a deaf ear to: 对这种恶意攻击，绝不能～。We simply cannot ignore this sort of malicious attack.

置身 zhìshēn 【动】place oneself in; put oneself in: ～事外 stay out of the matter ～于群众之中 be one with the masses

置于 zhìyú 【动】put in; place in: ～通风阴凉处 store in a cool, well-ventilated place

置之不理 zhì zhī bù lǐ ignore; pay no attention to

置之度外 zhì zhī dù wài not take into account

zhōng

中 zhōng 【名】◇ ❶ center; middle: 位置居～ situated in the centre ❷ short for 中国 often in contrast with 外: 闻名～外 well-known both at home and abroad ❸ inside; among; in: 家～ at home 心～ in one's heart 山～ in the mountains ❹ in the process of; during: 发展～国家 developing countries 研究～的问题 problems under study 在干～学 learn while working
另见 zhòng

中波 zhōngbō 【名】medium wave

中餐 zhōngcān 【名】Chinese meal

中草药 zhōngcǎoyào 【名】Chinese traditional medicine

中常 zhōngcháng 【形】average

中档 zhōngdàng 【形】medium grade: ～服装 medium grade clothes

中等 zhōngděng 【形】average; moderate; medium

中等专科学校 zhōngděng zhuānkē xuéxiào secondary specialized school; polytechnic school

中点 zhōngdiǎn 【名】(maths.) midpoint

中断 zhōngduàn 【名】break off; interrupt; come to a stop

中古 zhōnggǔ 【名】the middle ancient times; medieval times

中国工农红军 Zhōngguó Gōng Nóng Hóngjūn the Chinese Workers' and Peasants' Red Army

中国共产党 Zhōngguó Gòngchǎndǎng the Communist Party of China

中国画 zhōngguóhuà 【名】traditional Chinese painting

中国人民解放军 Zhōngguó Rénmín Jiěfàngjūn the Chinese People's Liberation Army

中国人民志愿军 Zhōngguó Rénmín Zhìyuànjūn the Chinese People's Volunteers

中和 zhōnghé 【动】neutralize

中华民族 Zhōnghuá Mínzú the Chinese nation

中华人民共和国 Zhōnghuá Rénmín Gònghéguó the People's Republic of China

中级 zhōngjí 【形】middle rank; secondary

中坚 zhōngjiān 【名】pillar; backbone; mainstay

中间 zhōngjiān 【名】❶ centre; middle: 院子～是一棵核桃树。There is a walnut tree in the middle of the courtyard. ❷ among: 我们几个人～，小李最高。Xiao Li is the tallest among us. ❸ in the process: 从一个普通战士成长为一个优秀指挥员，～不知要经受多少考验。The process of development from ordinary soldier into outstanding commander involves countless trials. ❹ between: 地球运行到太阳和月亮～，就发生月食。When the Earth passes between the Sun and the Moon, an eclipse of the moon occurs.

中间派 zhōngjiānpài 【名】 middle-of-the-roaders; middle elements

中间人 zhōngjiānrén 【名】 middle-man

中介 zhōngjiè 【名】 intermediary; medium

中立 zhōnglì 【动】 remain neutral; observe neutrality

中立国 zhōnglìguó 【名】 neutral country

中立化 zhōnglìhuà 【动】 neutralize

中流砥柱 zhōngliú dǐzhù firm rock in midstream; mainstay

中年 zhōngnián 【名】 middle age

中农 zhōngnóng 【名】 middle peasant

中篇小说 zhōngpiān xiǎoshuō novelette; novella

中秋节 Zhōngqiūjié 【名】 Mid-Autumn Festival; the Moon Festival

中山装 zhōngshānzhuāng 【名】 a kind of man's jacket; Chinese tunic suit

中世纪 zhōngshìjì 【名】 the Middle Ages

中式 zhōngshì 【形】 Chinese-style: ～服装 Chinese-style suit ～家具 Chinese-style furniture

中枢 zhōngshū 【名】 axis

中途 zhōngtú 【名】 midway

中外 zhōngwài 【名】 Chinese and foreign: ～记者 Chinese and foreign correspondents

中文 Zhōngwén 【名】 Chinese language

中午 zhōngwǔ 【名】 midday; noon

中西医结合 zhōng xī yī jiéhé combination of both traditional Chinese and Western medical treatment

中线 zhōngxiàn 【名】 ❶ (maths.) median (of a triangle) ❷ (of basketball, volleyball) centre line; (of football) halfway line

中心 zhōngxīn 【名】 ❶ centre: 湖～有个亭子。There is a pavilion in the centre of the lake. 天安门位于北京的～。Tian'anmen is at the centre of Beijing. ❷ (of matter, etc.) core; key: ～环节 key link ～任务 key task ❸ (of cities, regions, organizations) heart: 政治～ political centre 文化～ cultural centre

中心语 zhōngxīnyǔ 【名】 word modified (by some modifier)

中型 zhōngxíng 【形】 medium-sized

中性 zhōngxìng 【名】 neutral character; neutral

中学 zhōngxué 【名】〔所 suǒ〕 middle school; secondary school

中旬 zhōngxún 【名】 the second ten days of a month; mid-month

中央 zhōngyāng 【名】 ❶ centre: 花园～有一个喷水池。There is a fountain at the centre of the garden. ❷ the central authorities: ～机关 central organizations 中国共产党的各级组织都必须服从～的领导。The various levels of organization of the Chinese Communist Party are subordinate to the leadership of the Party's Central Committee.

中央集权 zhōngyāng jíquán centralization; centralization of authority

中央委员 zhōngyāng wěiyuán member of the central committee

中央委员会 zhōngyāng wěiyuánhuì central committee

中药 zhōngyào 【名】 traditional Chinese medicine

中叶 zhōngyè 【名】 middle period (e. g. of a certain dynasty, century)

中医 zhōngyī 【名】 ❶ doctor of the traditional Chinese medicine ❷ traditional Chinese medical science

中游 zhōngyóu 【名】 ❶ (of a river) middle reaches: 长江～ the middle reaches of the Changjiang River ❷ ordinary; mediocre: 要争上游,

不能甘居～。One should aim high and never be reconciled to just being mediocre.

中原　zhōngyuán　【名】the Central Plains of China

中止　zhōngzhǐ　【动】discontinue；suspend；break off：～谈判 suspend (or break off) negotiations

中专　zhōngzhuān　【名】short for 中等专科学校

中子　zhōngzǐ　【名】neutron

忠　zhōng　【形】loyal 【名】loyalty；faithfulness；devotion

忠诚　zhōngchéng　【形】loyal；faithful：对人民的事业无限～ utterly loyal to the cause of the people 为人要～老实。One should be loyal and honest in one's dealings with people. 教师应该～于教育事业。A teacher should be utterly devoted to the cause of education.

忠告　zhōnggào　【名】sincere advice；admonition：这是对你的～。This is honest advice and is for your benefit. 【动】counsel；admonish；advise：一再～ advise time and again

忠厚　zhōnghòu　【形】honest and kindly：为人～ honest and kindly

忠实　zhōngshí　【形】❶ reliable；devoted；faithful：～的朋友 devoted friends ❷ truthful：～地记录下来 faithfully record

忠心　zhōngxīn　【名】loyalty；faithfulness；devotion

忠心耿耿　zhōngxīn gěnggěng　infinitely loyal；most faithful and true

忠言逆耳　zhōngyán nì ěr　honest advice is hard to take；sincere advice jars on the ears

忠于　zhōngyú　【动】be loyal to；be true to；be faithful to：～祖国 be loyal to one's country ～人民 be true to the people

忠贞　zhōngzhēn　【形】loyal and steadfast

终（終）　zhōng　【名】◇ end；finish：自始至～ from beginning to end 【副】in the end；我们～将胜利。We will win victory in the end.

终点　zhōngdiǎn　【名】terminus

终端　zhōngduān　【名】terminal

终归　zhōngguī　【副】❶ eventually；in the end：不管技术多复杂,只要肯努力,～会掌握的。No matter how complicated a technique may be, provided that you try hard enough, you will master it in the end. ❷ 同"究竟"jiūjìng【副】❷：事实～是事实,谁也否定不了。A fact is, after all, a fact, and nobody can deny it.

终极　zhōngjí　【形】ultimate

终结　zhōngjié　【动】wind up；end up

终究　zhōngjiū　【副】同"终归"

终了　zhōngliǎo　【动】be over；be finished；come to an end

终年　zhōngnián　【名】❶ the whole year round；all year round：～辛劳 work hard all year round 山顶积雪～不化。The snow on the peaks of the mountains doesn't melt the whole year round. ❷ die (at the age of...)：～七十九岁 die at the age of 79

终日　zhōngrì　【名】all day long

终身　zhōngshēn　【名】one's whole life；all one's life：～的事业 lifelong cause ～总统 life-time president

终身制　zhōngshēnzhì　【名】lifelong tenure

终审　zhōngshěn　【动】last instance；final judgment：～判决 final judgement

终生　zhōngshēng　【名】life-time；one's whole life：奋斗～ struggle throughout one's life ～难忘 not to be forgotten as long as one lives

终于　zhōngyú　【副】at (long) last；finally：经过几个月的紧张劳动,这出

戏～排演出来了。After several months of hard work, the play was finally ready for public performance. 她期待很久的这个宝贵时刻～来到了。The precious moment which she had looked forward to for a long time came at long last. 由于身体的原因,他想当飞行员的愿望～没能实现。Owing to his health, his wish of becoming an aviator was never realized.

终止 zhōngzhǐ 【动】stop; cease; put an end to; conclude

衷 zhōng

衷情 zhōngqíng 【名】heartfelt emotion; inner feelings

衷心 zhōngxīn 【形】heart-felt; sincere; from the bottom of one's heart: 表示～的感谢 express one's heart-felt thanks ～祝贺 sincerely congratulate (sb. on sth.) ～拥护 support wholeheartedly

钟(鐘) zhōng 【名】〔座 zuò〕

❶ bell: 敲～ ring a bell ～响了。There goes the bell. ❷ clock ❸ time as measured in hours and minutes: 八点～ eight o'clock 十分～ ten minutes

钟爱 zhōng'ài 【动】be devoted to (a child); cherish

钟表 zhōngbiǎo 【名】general term for clocks and watches

钟头 zhōngtóu 【名】〔个 gè〕hour

zhǒng

肿(腫) zhǒng 【动】swell; be swollen

肿瘤 zhǒngliú 【名】tumour

肿胀 zhǒngzhàng 【动】swell; swelling

种(種) zhǒng 【名】❶ seed:

白菜～ cabbage seeds 撒～ sow seeds ❷ race: 黄～人 the Asiatic race 【量】kind; class; variety; species: 两～情况 two kinds of situations 好几～花布 several kinds of printed cloth 三～颜色 three different colours 作了～～努力 make all sorts of efforts

另见 zhòng

种类 zhǒnglèi 【名】class; kind; variety; species

种子 zhǒngzi 【名】seed

种族 zhǒngzú 【名】race

种族歧视 zhǒngzú qíshì racial discrimination

种族主义 zhǒngzúzhǔyì 【名】racialism; racism

zhòng

中 zhòng 【动】❶ hit on sth.;

fit; suit: ～意 be to one's liking 击～要害 hit on the most vulnerable spot ❷ be struck by; suffer: ～弹 be struck by a bullet ～了坏人的奸计 be caught by a villain's treacherous plot

另见 zhōng

中标 zhòng=biāo win the bid

中毒 zhòng=dú be poisoned: 药物～ chemical poisoning 食物～ food poisoning

中计 zhòng=jì be trapped: 中了坏人的计 be trapped by a rogue

中奖 zhòng=jiǎng draw a prizewinning ticket in a lottery: 中了大奖 get the winning number in a bond

中肯 zhòngkěn 【形】(of remarks or writing) pertinent; to the point: 他的意见很～。His opinion is very much to the point. 他在讨论会上提出的几个问题都十分～。The questions he raised during the discussion were all very much to the point.

中伤　zhòngshāng【动】slander；hurt with slanderous remarks

中暑　zhòng=shǔ suffer heatstroke

众（眾）zhòng【形】〈书〉numerous；many（human beings only）

众多　zhòngduō【形】numerous（human beings only）

众叛亲离　zhòng pàn qīn lí opposed by the masses and deserted by one's followers；be isolated

众人　zhòngrén【名】everybody

众人拾柴火焰高　zhòngrén shí chái huǒyàn gāo the fire burns high when everybody adds logs to it；(fig.) the more people, the greater strength

众矢之的　zhòng shǐ zhī dì be the target of attacks from all sides

众说纷纭　zhòng shuō fēnyún many different opinions

众所周知　zhòng suǒ zhōu zhī as all know；it is known to all

众志成城　zhòng zhì chéng chéng a united people is like a strongly fortified city；(fig.) unity is strength

重　zhòng【形】❶ weight：这包大米有五十公斤～. This bag of rice weighs 50 kilos. ❷ heavy：箱子很～。The trunk is very heavy. ❸ serious：伤势很～ seriously wounded 灾情不～. The damage done by the disaster was not serious. ❹ of more than usual size, amount, force, etc.：任务～ an enormous task 他担负最～的工作. He took on the most difficult job. ❺ important；weighty：友谊～于比分. Friendship is more important than the final score. 【动】place value upon：～男轻女是封建思想. Considering men superior to women is a feudal concept. 写文章不能只～形式而不～内容。In writing, one mustn't pay attention to form only and overlook content.
另见 chóng

重兵　zhòngbīng【名】strong forces

重大　zhòngdà【形】important；great；vital；major

重担　zhòngdàn【名】heavy burden；heavy load；heavy responsibility

重地　zhòngdì【名】important place

重点　zhòngdiǎn【名】❶ stress；main point；key-point ❷ weight（of a lever）

重读　zhòngdú【动】pronounce with stress

重工业　zhònggōngyè【名】heavy industry

重活　zhònghuó【名】heavy work

重力　zhònglì【名】gravity；gravitational force

重量　zhòngliàng【名】weight

重任　zhòngrèn【名】a task of importance；prime task；a task of great significance

重伤　zhòngshāng【名】a severe injury

重视　zhòngshì【动】pay great attention to；take sth. seriously；attach importance to

重武器　zhòngwǔqì【名】heavy weapons

重心　zhòngxīn【名】❶ centre of gravity：物体的～ the centre of gravity of an object ❷（maths.）centre ❸ key point：问题的～ the crux of a problem 工作的～ the main emphasis of the work

重型　zhòngxíng【形】heavy-duty；heavy（e. g. machine, weapon, etc.）

重要　zhòngyào【形】important；significant；essential；major

重音　zhòngyīn【名】stress；accent

重用　zhòngyòng【动】put sb. in an

important position

重油　zhòngyóu　【名】heavy oil

重镇　zhòngzhèn　【名】place of strategic significance; strategic post

种（種）　zhòng　【动】plant; grow: ～树 plant trees ～花 grow flowers

另见 zhǒng

种地　zhòng = dì　do farm work

种痘　zhòng = dòu　vaccinate; vaccination 也作"种牛痘".

种瓜得瓜,种豆得豆　zhòng guā dé guā, zhòng dòu dé dòu　plant melons and get melons, sow beans and get beans; reap what one has sown; as you make your bed, so you must lie on it

种田　zhòng = tián　farm; go in for farming

种植　zhòngzhí　【动】plant

zhōu

舟　zhōu　【名】boat

周　zhōu　【名】week: 上～ last week 下～ next week ～末 weekend 学期考试要用一～时间. This semester's examinations will last for a week. 【形】◇ ❶ thoughtful; considerate: 招待不～ not be attentive enough to the guests 计划不～. The plan is not well thought out. ❷ all over; whole: 喝酒以后～身发热. After drinking some wine, I feel warm all over. 【量】circumference; circle; circuit: 绕地球一～ circle once around the earth; be equal to the circumference of the earth 运动员绕场一～. The athletes marched once around the arena.

周报　zhōubào　【名】weekly

周长　zhōucháng　【名】perimeter; circumference

周到　zhōudào　【形】thoughtful; considerate

周而复始　zhōu ér fù shǐ　go round continuously

周刊　zhōukān　【名】weekly magazine

周密　zhōumì　【形】circumspect

周末　zhōumò　【名】weekend

周年　zhōunián　【名】anniversary

周期　zhōuqī　【名】cycle; period

周期表　zhōuqībiǎo　【名】(chem.) periodic table

周期性　zhōuqīxìng　【名】periodicity

周岁　zhōusuì　【名】one full year (of age); years of age

周围　zhōuwéi　【名】around; round: 关心～的群众 be concerned about the people around you 注意～的情况 pay attention to what is going on around you 广场～新种了不少树. Recently, lots of trees have been planted around the square.

周详　zhōuxiáng　【形】detailed and complete

周旋　zhōuxuán　【动】❶ treat; deal with: ～到底 fight to the bitter end ❷ mix with other people; socialize

周游　zhōuyóu　【动】tour

周折　zhōuzhé　【名】twists and turns; tortuous course

周转　zhōuzhuǎn　【动】(of funds, etc.) turnover

洲　zhōu　【名】continent: 地球上有七大～. The Earth is made up of seven continents.

洲际导弹　zhōujì dǎodàn　intercontinental missile

粥　zhōu　【名】gruel; porridge

粥少僧多　zhōu shǎo sēng duō　little gruel for many monks — not enough to go around

zhóu

轴（軸） zhóu 【名】❶ axis；axle：自行车的中～出了毛病。Something has gone wrong with the axle of the bicycle. ❷（～儿）scroll；spool：线～ a spool for thread 画～ scroll painting 【量】*for things rolled around a reel*：一～线 a spool of thread 一～画 a painting mounted on a scroll

轴承 zhóuchéng 【名】bearing；axle bearing

轴心 zhóuxīn 【名】axis；axle centre

zhǒu

肘 zhǒu 【名】the elbow

zhòu

咒 zhòu 【动】curse；abuse 【名】incantation

咒骂 zhòumà 【动】curse；abuse；vilify

昼（晝） zhòu 【名】daytime

昼夜 zhòuyè 【名】day and night；round the clock

皱（皺） zhòu 【动】wrinkle；crease；knit（brow）

皱纹 zhòuwén 【名】wrinkle；crease

骤（驟） zhòu 【形】〈书〉sudden：形势～变 a sudden change in the situation

骤然 zhòurán 【副】suddenly；unexpectedly（*sometimes also* 骤然间）：气温～下降。The temperature suddenly dropped. ～间狂风大作。Suddenly a gale started to blow.

zhū

朱 zhū

朱红 zhūhóng 【形】vermilion；scarlet

珠 zhū 【名】◇❶ bead；pearl ❷（～儿）a bead-like thing：水～ drops of water 泪～ tear drops

珠宝 zhūbǎo 【名】jewelry

珠算 zhūsuàn 【名】calculation with an abacus

珠子 zhūzi 【名】〔颗 kē〕bead

株 zhū 【量】*for trees*：两～柳树 two willow trees

株连 zhūlián 【动】implicate；involve in a criminal case

诸（諸） zhū

诸侯 zhūhóu 【名】feudal princes

诸如 zhūrú 【动】such as（*usu. in written language*）*used before the enumeration of illustrations to show that there are more than one*：她很喜欢中国古典文学，～唐诗、宋词等都涉猎过。She is very fond of Chinese classical literature and is familiar with such works as Tang and Song poetry, etc.

诸如此类 zhū rú cǐ lèi　and so on and so forth；et cetera；things like this；this kind of things：～不胜枚举。Things like this are too numerous to mention. 妈妈每天下班回家，不是洗菜做饭，就是洗衣服打扫卫生，～的事没完没了。Once home from work each day, Mother either washes vegetables and does the cooking, or does the washing and cleaning up , or endless other

things of this sort.

诸位 zhūwèi 【代】 *polite form of addressing a group of people*

猪 zhū 【名】〔头 tóu〕pig

猪肉 zhūròu 【名】pork

蛛 zhū

蛛丝马迹 zhū sī mǎ jì spiders' webs and horse's tracks;(*fig.*) traces;clues

蛛网 zhūwǎng 【名】spider web;cobweb

zhú

竹 zhú 【名】◇ bamboo

竹竿 zhúgān 【名】〔根 gēn〕bamboo pole

竹笋 zhúsǔn 【名】bamboo shoot

竹子 zhúzi 【名】bamboo

逐 zhú 【动】◇ drive out;expel;～出门外 drive sb. out of the door

逐步 zhúbù 【副】step by step;bit by bit;by degrees;gradually;～解决 solve it step by step 工作正在～开展。Our work is progressing gradually.

逐个 zhúgè 【副】one by one 对有困难的学生,教师～进行辅导。The teachers give individual tutoring to students who are having difficulties.

逐渐 zhújiàn 【副】gradually;little by little;～发展 develop gradually 天气～变暖。The weather is gradually getting warmer.

逐年 zhúnián 【副】year by year;产量～上升。The output is increasing year by year. 职工人数～增加。The number of workers and staff members has increased year by year.

逐一 zhúyī 【副】one by one;报告人对这些问题～作了说明。The speaker answered these questions one by one.

逐字逐句 zhú zì zhú jù word for word;literal;literally;word by word and sentence by sentence

zhǔ

主 zhǔ 【名】◇ ❶ possessor;owner;master;房～ owner of a house 物归原～。The thing has been returned to its owner. ❷ host (*as opp. to* 宾 *or* 客);～队以五比二取胜。The host team carried the day with a five to two victory. ❸ principal;main;这个地区的牧民以肉食为～。Meat is the staple food for the herdsmen of this region. 【动】◇ have a definite view;advocate;stand for;力～改革 strongly advocate reform

主办 zhǔbàn 【动】sponsor;be responsible for;be in charge of

主编 zhǔbiān 【名】editor-in-chief;报纸～ editor-in-chief of a newspaper 【动】edit;那本诗集由他～。He edited that anthology of poems.

主持 zhǔchí 【动】❶ manage;direct;preside over;～会议 preside over a meeting ～日常工作 be in charge of routine work ❷ uphold;stand for;～正义 uphold justice

主次 zhǔcì 【名】primary and secondary (e.g. importance)

主导 zhǔdǎo 【形】dominant;leading;～思想 dominant thinking 占～地位 occupy a dominant position 【名】leading factor;以农业为基础,以工业为～ take agriculture as the base, industry as the leading factor

主动 zhǔdòng 【形】initiative;争取～ try to gain the initiative 他工作

很～. He displays great initiative in his work.

主动脉 zhǔdòngmài 【名】aorta

主犯 zhǔfàn 【名】prime culprit

主妇 zhǔfù 【名】housewife; hostess

主攻 zhǔgōng 【动】launch the main attack

主顾 zhǔgù 【名】customer; client; patron

主观 zhǔguān 【名】subjectivity; ～认识 subjective understanding ～努力 one's own personal efforts 【形】subjective: 看问题要避免～片面. Try to avoid being subjective and one-sided when looking at problems. 你对这件事的看法太～了! You are too bigoted as far as this matter is concerned.

主观能动性 zhǔguān néngdòngxìng subjective initiative

主观世界 zhǔguān shìjiè subjective world

主观唯心主义 zhǔguān wéixīnzhǔyì subjective idealism

主观性 zhǔguānxìng 【名】subjectivity

主观主义 zhǔguānzhǔyì 【名】subjectivism

主管 zhǔguǎn 【动】be responsible for; be in charge of

主见 zhǔjiàn 【名】one's own idea; definite view; one's personal judgement

主将 zhǔjiàng 【名】commanding general

主角 zhǔjué 【名】leading actor or actress; main role; title-role

主力 zhǔlì 【名】main forces

主力军 zhǔlìjūn 【名】the main force; principal force

主流 zhǔliú 【名】❶ main stream; main current ❷ main trend; principal aspect: 分析形势, 要看清～和支流. In analysing a situation, it's essential to distinguish the main aspect from the minor ones.

主谋 zhǔmóu 【名】chief instigator

主权 zhǔquán 【名】sovereignty

主人 zhǔrén 【名】❶ host ❷ master; owner; proprietor; possessor

主人公 zhǔréngōng 【名】hero or heroine (of a literary work)

主人翁 zhǔrénwēng 【名】❶ master: 国家的～ masters of the country ❷ 同 "主人公"

主任 zhǔrèn 【名】chairman; director

主食 zhǔshí 【名】staple food

主使 zhǔshǐ 【动】instigate

主事 zhǔ = shì be in charge; take charge

主题 zhǔtí 【名】main theme

主题歌 zhǔtígē 【名】〔首 shǒu〕theme song

主体 zhǔtǐ 【名】main body; essential part

主席 zhǔxí 【名】chairman

主席台 zhǔxítái 【名】platform; rostrum

主演 zhǔyǎn 【动】be the main performer; play the main role

主要 zhǔyào 【形】main; principal; essential; leading; important; major; key

主意 zhǔyi 【名】❶ opinion; decision; idea: ～已定 have already made up one's mind ❷ method; idea: 出～ have an idea; work out a method 这个～不错. That's not a bad idea.

主语 zhǔyǔ 【名】(gram.) subject

主宰 zhǔzǎi 【动】dominate; master; control; dictate

主张 zhǔzhāng 【名】proposition; opinion; assertion: 好～ a good proposal 自作～ make a decision without being authorized to do so 【动】maintain; advocate: 我～你在苏州多呆几天. I would suggest that you stay a few more days in Suzhou.

主旨 zhǔzhǐ 【名】purport; sub-

stance；gist

主治　zhǔzhì　【名】indications

主治医生　zhǔzhìyīshēng　【名】physician-in-charge；attending doctor

主子　zhǔzi　【名】boss；master (*derog.*)

煮　zhǔ　【动】cook；boil

嘱(嘱)　zhǔ

嘱咐　zhǔfu　【动】bid；enjoin；direct；instruct

嘱托　zhǔtuō　【动】entrust；require (sb. to do sth.)

zhù

助　zhù　【动】◇ help；assist；aid：～我一臂之力 lend me a helping hand

助产士　zhùchǎnshì　【名】midwife

助词　zhùcí　【名】(gram.) particle

助动词　zhùdòngcí　【名】auxiliary verb

助教　zhùjiào　【名】assistant (in a university or college)

助理　zhùlǐ　【名】assistant；helper

助理研究员　zhùlǐyánjiūyuán　【名】assistant research fellow

助燃　zhù＝rán　help combustion

助人为乐　zhù rén wéi lè　find pleasure in helping others；ready to help others

助手　zhùshǒu　【名】helping hands；assistant；helper

助威　zhù＝wēi　to encourage (by cheers or applause)

助兴　zhù＝xìng　add to the fun；liven things up

助学金　zhùxuéjīn　【名】student subsidies；student grant

助长　zhùzhǎng　【动】encourage；foster (*derog.*)：歪风邪气不可～。Bad tendencies should not be encouraged.

住　zhù　【动】❶ live；make one's home at；stay：你～在哪儿？Where do you live? 他～的地方离这儿不远。The place where he lives is not far from here. 你到天津去～旅馆还是～朋友家? When you go to Tianjin, are you going to stay in a hotel or with a friend? ❷ ◇ stop：雨～了。The rain has stopped. Note：住 *is used after some verbs as a complement* ① *indicates a standstill, stagnation, etc.*：拿～ hold it tight 把～方向盘 hold firmly to the steering-wheel 他把球接～了。He's caught the ball. 一句话把他问～了。That question left him speechless. ② *used with* 得 *or* 不 *to indicate whether or not one can stand sth. physically*：坚持不～ unable to stick it out 我虽然有点儿头痛，还支持得～。Though I have a slight headache, I can still hold out.

住处　zhùchù　【名】residence；dwelling；lodging

住房　zhùfáng　【名】housing；living quarters

住户　zhùhù　【名】inhabitant

住口　zhù＝kǒu　shut up；keep (one's) mouth shut

住手　zhù＝shǒu　Stop! Hands off!；stop

住宿　zhùsù　【动】stay for the night

住所　zhùsuǒ　【名】lodgings

住院　zhù＝yuàn　be hospitalized

住宅　zhùzhái　【名】residence；house；dwelling

住址　zhùzhǐ　【名】address

贮(贮)　zhù　【动】◇ store up；keep；reserve

贮藏　zhùcáng　【动】hoard；save

贮存　zhùcún　【动】stock；store up

注　zhù　【动】◇ pour：大雨如～ a downpour 【名】notes；annotations；

加～ annotate

注册 zhù＝cè register

注定 zhùdìng【动】be doomed to (e.g. failure)；be bound to

注解 zhùjiě【动】explain with notes；～古书 explain the classics by annotation【名】explanatory notes；加上几条～,这首诗就容易懂了。Add a few notes and you will make this classical poem much easier to understand.

注目 zhùmù【动】focus attention；gaze at

注入 zhùrù【动】instil；inject；empty into

注射 zhùshè【动】inject；injection

注射剂 zhùshèjì【名】injection

注射器 zhùshèqì【名】injector

注视 zhùshì【动】watch attentively；watch with concern

注释 zhùshì【动】annotate【名】annotation

注销 zhùxiāo【动】write off；cancel

注意 zhùyì【动】pay attention to；be attentive；take notice of【名】attention

注意力 zhùyìlì【名】attention

注音 zhù＝yīn（use symbols to) indicate pronunciation

注音字母 zhùyīnzìmǔ【名】the national phonetic alphabet

注重 zhùzhòng【动】attach attention to；pay great attention to；lay stress on

驻（駐）zhù【动】stay；be stationed；各国～华使节 diplomatic envoys from various countries to China 部队～在海岛上。Troops are stationed on the island.

驻地 zhùdì【名】place where troops are stationed

驻防 zhùfáng【动】garrison；be on garrison duty

驻军 zhùjūn【名】garrison (troops)

驻守 zhùshǒu【动】defend with stationed troops；garrison

驻扎 zhùzhā【动】encamp；be stationed

柱 zhù【名】◇ pillar

柱石 zhùshí【名】column and its base；(fig.) pillar (of a state)

柱子 zhùzi【名】〔根 gēn〕pillar

祝 zhù【动】offer (one's) compliments to；wish；greet；congratulate

祝词 zhùcí【名】congratulations；congratulatory speech

祝福 zhùfú【动】bless；blessing

祝贺 zhùhè【动】congratulate；～两国建立外交关系 offer congratulations on the establishment of diplomatic relations between the two countries ～你获得百米赛跑第一名。Let me congratulate you on your winning first place in the 100 metre dash.【名】congratulations；请接受我衷心的～。Please accept my heartiest congratulations.

祝酒 zhù＝jiǔ drink a toast

祝寿 zhù＝shòu congratulate on one's birthday (for an aged person)

祝愿 zhùyuàn【动】wish；～您健康、幸福。I wish you good health and happiness.～贵国日益繁荣昌盛。We wish your country ever-growing prosperity.【名】wish；致以良好的～ with best wishes

著 zhù【动】compose；write 鲁迅～《阿Q正传》"The True Story of Ah Q", written by Lu Xun ～书立说 write a book to propound a theory

著称 zhùchēng【动】〈书〉be noted for；be known for；桂林以山水～于世。Guilin is known throughout the world for its scenery.

著名 zhùmíng【形】famous；well-

known；celebrated

著作 zhùzuò 【名】works；writings

著作权 zhùzuòquán 【名】copyright

蛀 zhù 【动】(of moths etc.) eat into

蛀虫 zhùchóng 【名】moth：毛衣让～咬坏了。The sweater is moth-eaten. 贪污腐化是国家的～。Corruption is a corrosive to the country.

铸(鑄) zhù 【动】(metal) cast：～成大错 make a grave mistake 这些古兵器都是用青铜～成的。These ancient weapons are all cast out of bronze.

铸工 zhùgōng 【名】foundry worker

铸件 zhùjiàn 【名】foundry goods

铸造 zhùzào 【动】cast

筑(築) zhù 【动】build：～路 build a road ～堤 build a dam

zhuā

抓 zhuā 【动】❶ clutch；grab：～一把米 grab a handful of rice 他～起皮包就走。He grabbed his briefcase and left. ❷ catch；arrest：～麻雀 catch sparrows ～小偷儿 catch a thief ❸ scratch：～痒痒 scratch an itch ❹ pay special attention to；grasp firmly：～先进典型 find and make full use of advanced models 做工作要善于～重点。One must be good at grasping the essentials in doing any kind of work. ❺ attract：这部小说一开始就～住了读者。This novel catches the attention of its readers from the very beginning. ❻ be responsible for；be in charge of：这位同志是～宣传工作的。This comrade is in charge of propaganda work.

抓耳挠腮 zhuā ěr náo sāi twist one's ears and rub one's face as a sign of perplexity：他急得～想不出办法来。He scratched his head but failed to think of a way out.

抓工夫 zhuā gōngfu find time to do sth.

抓获 zhuāhuò 【动】arrest：主犯已被～。The principal criminal has already been arrested.

抓紧 zhuā // jǐn take a firm hold on；attend most closely to；grasp firmly

zhuān

专(專) zhuān 【形】special；for a particular person or purpose：～款 money set aside for a particular purpose 这位大夫～治眼病。This doctor specializes in eye diseases. 这所学校是～为培养少数民族干部而建立的。This institute was established especially to train national minority cadres. 【名】◇ speciality：一～多能 expert at one skill and able in many

专案 zhuān'àn 【名】special case；one that needs thorough investigation

专长 zhuāncháng 【名】professional ability；technical skill；speciality；specialized skill

专车 zhuānchē 【名】special train

专程 zhuānchéng 【副】be on a special trip to

专横跋扈 zhuānhèng báhù tyrannical；despotic；ride roughshod over

专机 zhuānjī 【名】special plane

专家 zhuānjiā 【名】specialist；expert

专刊 zhuānkān 【名】special issue

专科学校 zhuānkē xuéxiào technical college；vocational school

专栏 zhuānlán 【名】(newspaper) special column

专利 zhuānlì 【名】patent

专门 zhuānmén 【形】❶ specialized：～人才 specialists ～研究文学 specialize in literature ❷ specially：～拜访 make a special visit to someone

专名 zhuānmíng 【名】proper name

专区 zhuānqū 【名】special administrative district

专题 zhuāntí 【名】special theme

专心 zhuānxīn 【形】whole-hearted；attentive

专心致志 zhuānxīn zhì zhì devote oneself to；set one's heart on；wholehearted and exclusive

专修 zhuānxiū 【动】specialize in

专修科 zhuānxiūkē 【名】special course

专业 zhuānyè 【名】special line；speciality；profession

专业户 zhuānyèhù 【名】specialized household：养猪～ pig-raising specialized household

专一 zhuānyī 【形】single-minded；concentrated

专用 zhuānyòng 【动】(reserved for) special use

专员 zhuānyuán 【名】❶ (administrative) commissioner ❷ person specially assigned for a job

专政 zhuānzhèng 【名】dictatorship 【动】exercise dictatorship over

专职 zhuānzhí 【名】full-time post

专制 zhuānzhì 【名】autocracy：君主～ an autocratic monarchy 【动】tyrannize；be autocratic

专注 zhuānzhù 【动】concentrate one's attention on；devote one's mind to

专著 zhuānzhù 【名】〔部 bù、本 běn〕monograph

砖（磚） zhuān 【名】〔块 kuài〕brick

砖头 zhuāntóu 【名】〔块 kuài〕fragment of a brick

zhuǎn

转（轉） zhuǎn 【动】❶ change direction；turn：～过身来 turn around 向左～ turn left ～败为胜 turn defeat into victory 天气由阴～晴。The weather has turned fine. ❷ transfer；pass on：请把信～给他。Please pass this letter on to him. ❸ transfer：这个学生是从别的学校～来的。This student has been transferred here from another school.

另见 zhuàn

转变 zhuǎnbiàn 【动】change；be transformed；remould：～看法 change one's views 态度～了。His attitude has changed. 【名】change；transformation；alteration：思想感情来一个彻底的～ effect a thorough change in one's thinking and feelings

转播 zhuǎnbō 【动】relay (radio)

转产 zhuǎn = chǎn change the line of production

转车 zhuǎn = chē change train or bus half way

转达 zhuǎndá 【动】pass on (another's message)；convey

转动 zhuǎndòng 【动】turn (from one direction to another)

转告 zhuǎngào 【动】pass on to sb.：请你把明天出发的时间～给小王。Please pass on to Xiao Wang the time to leave tomorrow.

转轨 zhuǎn = guǐ change track；re-orient

转化 zhuǎnhuà 【动】transform；change；turn into；transmute

转换 zhuǎnhuàn 【动】change；convert；transform

转机 zhuǎnjī 【名】a change for the better；favourable turn

转嫁 zhuǎnjià 【动】shift；transfer；

厂家不能把本厂的损失～给消费者。Producers should not shift their losses to consumers.

转交 zhuǎnjiāo 【动】forward; hand over sth. for one person to another

转口 zhuǎnkǒu 【动】transit: ～贸易 entrepôt trade

转卖 zhuǎnmài 【动】resell

转念 zhuǎnniàn 【动】be on second thoughts; reconsider (and give up an idea)

转让 zhuǎnràng 【动】transfer one's claim or right to sth.

转入 zhuǎnrù 【动】switch to; change over to: 由防守～进攻 switch from defensive to offensive 由公开～地下 shift from open to insidious tactics

转身 zhuǎn = shēn （of a person） turn round

转手 zhuǎn = shǒu ❶ pass on: 请你把东西直接交给他吧，别转我的手了。Please hand it over to him directly, don't ask me to relay it. ❷ sell what one has bought: 这批货他一～就赚了一大笔钱。He made a killing by reselling this batch of goods.

转述 zhuǎnshù 【动】tell sb. what another person said

转瞬之间 zhuǎnshùn zhī jiān in the twinkling of an eye

转弯 zhuǎn = wān （～儿）turn a corner: 汽车向右～。The car made a right turn. 商店离宿舍很近，～就到。The shop is quite near our dormitory, just round the corner. 他脑子还没转过弯儿来。He still hasn't got his mind around the problem.

转弯抹角 zhuǎn wān mò jiǎo ❶ be full of twists and turns: 这条路～的，很难走。This path is full of twists and turns and hard to follow. ❷ beat about the bush: 他有意见就坦率地提出来，从不～。He is frank and out-spoken and never beats about the bush. 也作"拐弯抹角"。

转危为安 zhuǎn wēi wéi ān turn a dangerous situation into a secure one

转学 zhuǎn = xué transfer to another school

转眼 zhuǎnyǎn 【副】in the twinkling of an eye; quickly: 时间过得真快，～又是一年。Time passes so quickly that another year will be over in a flash. ～间,他就把自行车修好了。He fixed the bike in the twinkling of an eye.

转业 zhuǎn = yè change one's occupation or profession

转移 zhuǎnyí 【动】❶ shift; divert; transfer: ～目标 distract people's attention from sb. or sth. 部队～了。The troops have been transferred. ❷ change: 社会发展的规律是不以人的意志为～的。The objective law of social development is independent of man's will.

转院 zhuǎn = yuàn transfer from one hospital to another

转运 zhuǎnyùn 【动】transship; transport

转载 zhuǎnzǎi 【动】republish (sth. which was published elsewhere)

转战 zhuǎnzhàn 【动】fight from place to place

转折 zhuǎnzhé 【动】❶ a turn in the course of events: ～时期 a transitional stage 历史的～ a turning point in history ❷ shift in meaning as indicated by a conjunction

转折点 zhuǎnzhédiǎn 【名】turning point

zhuàn

传（傳） zhuàn 【名】biography
另见 chuán

传记 zhuànjì 【名】biography

传略 zhuànlüè 【名】(short) biography

转(轉) zhuǎn 【动】❶ turn；rotate：车轮飞~。The wheels turn rapidly. ❷ revolve：~圈子 circle (around sth.) 九大行星围绕着太阳~。The nine planets revolve around the Sun. ❸ stroll along；saunter：到街上~~，买点东西。Take a stroll along the streets and do some shopping.

另见 zhuàn

转动 zhuàndòng 【动】turn；rotate；revolve

转炉 zhuànlú 【名】converter

转门 zhuànmén 【名】revolving door

转圈 zhuàn = quān　turn round

转向 zhuàn = xiàng　lose one's bearings

赚(賺) zhuàn 【动】make (money)

撰 zhuàn

撰文 zhuàn = wén　write an article

撰写 zhuànxiě 【动】write (usu. short articles)

篆 zhuàn

篆刻 zhuànkè 【名】seal cutting 【动】inscribe in seal characters

篆书 zhuànshū 【名】seal character (a style of Chinese calligraphy, often used on seals)

zhuāng

庄(莊) zhuāng 【名】village

庄稼 zhuāngjia 【名】crops

庄严 zhuāngyán 【形】solemn；august

庄园 zhuāngyuán 【名】manor；estate

庄重 zhuāngzhòng 【形】grave；not frivolous

桩(樁) zhuāng 【名】pile；stake；post：木头~ a wooden post 打~ drive a stake into the ground 【量】for event, matter, case, etc.：一~事情 an event 一~案件 a lawsuit；a legal case

桩子 zhuāngzi 【名】〔根 gēn〕stake；pile

装(裝) zhuāng 【名】◇❶ clothing；outfit：春~ a spring outfit ❷ theatrical costumes and make-up：上~ dress and put on make-up 卸~ take off one's stage make-up and costume 【动】❶ pretend；feign：~样子 make a pretence of ~聋作哑 play deaf and dumb ❷ dress up as：这个小孩最爱~解放军。What this child likes best is to dress up as a P. L. A. man. ❸ load；fill；pack：~箱 pack a box 把啤酒~进瓶子 fill bottles with beer 木材都~上了汽车。The timber has all been loaded onto the trucks. ❹ install；fit：~电灯 install electric lights ~了一台机器。A machine was installed.

装扮 zhuāngbàn 【动】dress oneself up as；guise；make up

装备 zhuāngbèi 【动】equip；furnish with；install；fit out：这支部队是用现代武器~起来的。This unit is equipped with up-to-date weapons. 【名】equipment；installation：技术~ technical equipment 军事~ military equipment

装点 zhuāngdiǎn 【动】decorate：各色花朵，把大自然~得生机勃勃。Dotted with flowers of every possible hue, the wilderness setting was bursting with life.

装订 zhuāngdìng 【动】bind (book)

装潢 zhuānghuáng 【动】decorate：
~门面 decorate the shop front 这
个橱窗还需要～一下。This shop-
window still needs to be dec-
orated. 【名】decoration；mounting：
这种座钟～相当讲究。The casing of
this kind of table clock is exquisite. 也作"装璜"。

装甲兵 zhuāngjiǎbīng 【名】ar-
moured corps

装模作样 zhuāng mó zuò yàng 同"装
腔作势"

装配 zhuāngpèi 【动】assemble（ma-
chine）

装腔作势 zhuāng qiāng zuò shì pose；
give oneself airs；behave in an affected manner

装饰 zhuāngshì 【动】decorate；
adorn；embellish：节日的公园～得
很美丽。During festivals，the
parks are all beautifully decora-
ted. 【名】decoration；adornment：
民族文化宫的～充满了民族色彩。
The decorations of the National
Minorities Cultural Palace are suffused with local colours.

装饰品 zhuāngshìpǐn 【名】decora-
tions；adornment

装束 zhuāngshù 【名】dress；attire：
看他的～，还以为是个华侨呢! One
would think from the way he is
dressed that he is an overseas Chinese.

装卸 zhuāngxiè 【动】❶ load and
unload ❷ assemble and dismantle

装修 zhuāngxiū 【动】furnish：～房子
furnish a house

装运 zhuāngyùn 【动】load and
transport；ship

装载 zhuāngzài 【动】load

装置 zhuāngzhì 【动】install；furnish
with；equip with：～天线 install an
antenna ～通风设备 install ventilation equipment 【名】installation；
device：自动化～ automatic device

zhuàng

壮（壯） zhuàng 【形】ro-
bust；strong；stout；healthy：年轻
力～ young and strong 身体真～
physically robust 【动】◇ strength-
en：～声势 lend strength and impetus ～胆子 lend courage

壮大 zhuàngdà 【动】become big
and lusty；strengthen；grow in
strength

壮观 zhuàngguān 【形】look magnificent and impressive；grand-look-
ing

壮举 zhuàngjǔ 【名】a great under-
taking；heroic undertaking

壮阔 zhuàngkuò 【形】grand and ex-
pansive

壮丽 zhuànglì 【形】grand-looking；
magnificent

壮烈 zhuàngliè 【形】courageous；
heroic

壮年 zhuàngnián 【名】prime of life；
one's prime

壮志 zhuàngzhì 【名】lofty ambi-
tion；great aspiration

壮志凌云 zhuàngzhì língyún soaring
aspiration

状（狀） zhuàng 【名】◇ ❶
form；shape：这种动物～似小狗。
This animal resembles a small dog
in appearance. ❷ condition；state
of affairs：病～ the condition of
the patient ❸ a lawsuit；a legal
case：告了他一～ sue him；lay a
charge against him

状况 zhuàngkuàng 【名】conditions；
state

状态 zhuàngtài 【名】state

状语 zhuàngyǔ 【名】（gram.）adver-
bial adjunct

撞 zhuàng 【动】❶ collide；

bump into：二人～了个满怀。The two of them bumped into each other. ❷ strike with force：～钟 strike the bell ❸ rush in；intrude：外面～进一个人来。A man rushed in from outside.

撞车 zhuàng＝chē collision of vehicles：出了～事故。There happened a collision of cars.

撞击 zhuàngjī 【动】ram；dash against

撞锁 zhuàng＝suǒ ❶ be locked out on a visit；find sb away from home ❷ spring lock

zhuī

追 zhuī 【动】❶ chase after；pursue：你～我赶 compete with one another 奋起直～ try hard to catch up with those who are advanced 他们已经走了半小时了，现在去～，还得上吗？They left half an hour ago. If we run after them now，do you think we can possibly catch up with them？ ❷ search for；investigate：～根究底 investigate the ins and outs of something

追捕 zhuībǔ 【动】pursue and capture：～案犯 pursue and capture the offender

追查 zhuīchá 【动】investigate；inquire；search into；find out

追悼 zhuīdào 【动】grieve over (sb.'s death)

追肥 zhuī＝féi additional fertilizer；additional manuring

追赶 zhuīgǎn 【动】chase after；run after；race with

追击 zhuījī 【动】pursue and attack

追加 zhuījiā 【动】add to (original amount)

追究 zhuījiū 【动】get to the roots of；find out (cause, etc.)

追求 zhuīqiú 【动】❶ pursue；seek；

～真理 seek truth ～进步 seek after progress 不能盲目～数量。Don't try simply to increase quantity (at the expense of quality). ❷ woo；run after；pursue

追认 zhuīrèn 【动】❶ confer posthumously ❷ subsequently confirm or endorse：～他为烈士。He was recognised posthumously as a martyr.

追溯 zhuīsù 【动】trace back；investigate into the origin of

追随 zhuīsuí 【动】follow；go after；tail behind

追问 zhuīwèn 【动】get to the bottom of

追赃 zhuī＝zāng recover stolen goods or money

追逐 zhuīzhú 【动】chase after；pursue

追踪 zhuīzōng 【动】trace

锥（錐）zhuī 【名】◇ awl；drill 【动】drill：～个窟窿眼儿 drill a hole

锥子 zhuīzi 【名】〔把 bǎ〕awl

zhuì

坠（墜）zhuì 【动】❶ ◇ fall：～马 fall off a horse ❷ weigh down：苹果把树枝～弯了。The apples weighed down the branches.

坠毁 zhuìhuǐ 【动】(of aeroplane) crash

坠落 zhuìluò 【动】crash；fall

坠入 zhuìrù 【动】fall into

zhūn

谆（諄）zhūn

谆谆 zhūnzhūn 【形】〈书〉earnest (instruction, advice, etc.)；earnestly and repeatedly

zhǔn

准 zhǔn 【名】(準)◇ accepted standard；criterion：以此为～ take this as the criterion 【形】accurate：枪打得～ shoot accurately 看～目标 take careful aim 发音有不～。His pronunciation of this word is not accurate. 【动】allow；permit：～他三天假 grant him three days' leave 工程重地不～随便进入。Construction site! Unauthorized persons not admitted. 【副】(準) definitely；certainly；sure：大坝～能按时合龙。The dam can definitely be completed on schedule.

准备 zhǔnbèi 【动】❶ prepare；pave the way for；get ready：～发言 prepare a speech ～行装 get ready for a trip ❷ plan：暑假你～去哪儿？Where do you plan to go during the summer vacation? 【名】preparation；preparedness；readiness：事前作好～ make preparations in advance 毫无～ without the slightest preparation

准确 zhǔnquè 【形】accurate；exact；precise

准绳 zhǔnshéng 【名】criteria；accepted standards

准时 zhǔnshí 【形】punctual；on time

准许 zhǔnxǔ 【动】permit；allow；consent；approve of

准予 zhǔnyǔ 【动】give permission to；permit

准则 zhǔnzé 【名】guiding principle；norm；standard

zhuō

拙 zhuō 【形】◇ ❶ stupid；clumsy；dull：勤能补～。Diligence can make up for a lack of proficiency. ❷ a polite self-deprecating way of referring to one's own work, opinion, etc.：～作 my writing ～译 my translation ～见 my opinion

拙笨 zhuōbèn 【形】clumsy；awkward

拙劣 zhuōliè 【形】clumsy and inferior

捉 zhuō 【动】catch；capture；seize；arrest：～住一个小偷 catch a thief 猫～老鼠。A cat caught a mouse.

捉摸 zhuōmō 【动】fathom；ascertain：不可～ impossible to ascertain ～不定 unable to predict 这个人到底想些什么，真是难以～。It's really hard to fathom what's going on in his mind.

捉拿 zhuōná 【动】arrest：～凶手 arrest the murderer

捉弄 zhuōnòng 【动】play trick upon sb.

桌 zhuō 【名】◇ table；desk

桌布 zhuōbù 【名】〔块 kuài〕tablecloth

桌面儿上 zhuōmiànrshang 【名】on the table；aboveboard：有意见应该摆到～来谈，不要背后议论。If you have any views (on this subject), please put them on the table. Don't talk behind people's backs.

桌子 zhuōzi 【名】〔张 zhāng〕table；desk

zhuó

灼 zhuó

灼热 zhuórè 【形】scalding hot

苗 zhuó

苗壮 zhuózhuàng 【形】sturdy；

healthy and strong：禾苗～ sturdy rice seedlings 儿童～成长。The children are growing up healthy and strong.

卓 zhuó

卓见 zhuójiàn 【名】excellent opinion；brilliant idea

卓绝 zhuójué 【形】extreme；unsurpassed；outstanding：英勇～的事迹 outstandingly brave deed 艰苦～的斗争 extremely bitter struggle

卓有成效 zhuó yǒu chéngxiào extremely effective

卓越 zhuóyuè 【形】prominent；brilliant；distinguished

卓著 zhuózhù 【形】outstanding；distinguished

浊（濁） zhuó 【形】❶ muddy；turbid ❷（of voice）deep and rough：～声～气 deep-voiced

浊音 zhuóyīn 【名】（phonetics）voiced sound

酌 zhuó 【动】〈书〉❶ drink（wine）：独～ drink alone ❷ deliberate；weigh and consider；consider：～办 deliberate, and then act accordingly 妥否请～。Please consider whether or not everything has been properly done.

酌量 zhuóliàng 【动】deliberate；consider

酌情 zhuó ＝ qíng deliberate on the actual situation and then decide；use one's discretion

啄 zhuó 【动】peck

啄木鸟 zhuómùniǎo 【名】〔只 zhī〕woodpecker

琢 zhuó 【动】chisel

琢磨 zhuómó 【动】（of jade, etc.）carve and polish
另见 zuómo

着 zhuó 【动】❶ touch：不～边际 not to the point；irrelevant ❷ apply；use：～色 apply color ～墨 apply ink 不～痕迹 without a trace ❸〈书〉dispatch；send：～你部速去桥头镇。Dispatch your unit immediately to the town at the bridgehead.
另见 zhāo；zháo；zhe

着陆 zhuó ＝ lù land；landing

着落 zhuóluò 【名】❶ whereabout：丢失的东西已经有～了。We have already discovered the whereabouts of the things that were lost. ❷ assured source：经费还没有～呢！We don't know yet where the funding is coming from.

着手 zhuóshǒu 【动】begin；set about；get down to：～准备 begin to prepare 从何～? Where should we begin? 开始编纂 begin to compile

着想 zhuóxiǎng 【动】bear sth. in mind；consider the interest of；think of

着眼 zhuóyǎn 【动】see from the angle of；have sth. in mind：大处～，小处着手。Keep the major issues in mind, but begin with the minor ones. 这个城市搞建设～于就地取材。We must keep local materials in mind in the construction of this city.

着重 zhuózhòng 【动】make a special effort to；stress

着重号 zhuózhònghào 【名】emphasis mark

ZĪ

孜 zī

孜孜不倦 zīzī bù juàn diligent；persevering；indefatigable：～地工作 work indefatigably 学习～ study diligently

咨 zī

咨文 zīwén 【名】❶ official communication between government offices of equal rank ❷ report by the head of the government on affairs of state

咨询 zīxún 【动】seek advice；consult；seek the counsel of；consult

姿 zī

姿势 zīshì 【名】gesture；position；gesticulation；posture

姿态 zītài 【名】❶ posture；carriage：～优美 elegant posture ❷ attitude：以主人翁的～出现 appear in the role of master ❸ style（of persons，writing）：高～（show）magnanimity 低～（display）meanness

资（資）zī

资本 zīběn 【名】capital

资本家 zīběnjiā 【名】capitalist

资本主义 zīběnzhǔyì 【名】capitalism

资产 zīchǎn 【名】❶ assets；property；estate ❷ capital

资产阶级 zīchǎnjiējí 【名】bourgeoisie

资产阶级民主革命 zīchǎnjiējí mínzhǔ gémìng bourgeois-democratic revolution

资方 zīfāng 【名】agent of a capitalist

资格 zīgé 【名】qualifications

资金 zījīn 【名】funds；capital

资力 zīlì 【名】financial strength：～不足 insufficient financial strength

资历 zīlì 【名】curriculum vitae and qualifications

资料 zīliào 【名】❶ materials for some specific purpose ❷ material；data：参考～ reference material 积累大量的～ accumulate a wealth of data

资源 zīyuán 【名】resources

资助 zīzhù 【动】subsidize；assist financially；give financial backing to

滋 zī

滋 zī 【动】grow：～事 create trouble 豆子～芽儿了。The beans have sprouted.

滋补 zībǔ 【动】nourish：～身体 be nourishing ～品 nourishing food

滋润 zīrùn 【动】moisten：河水～着两岸的杨柳。The river waters the willows on both banks. 【形】moist：土地～。The soil is moist.

滋生 zīshēng 【动】❶ multiply；flourish；thrive：草木～。The vegetation is flourishing. 搞好环境卫生，防止蚊蝇～。Improve environmental sanitation and prevent the breeding of mosquitoes and flies. ❷ stir up；incite：～事端 create trouble

滋事 zīshì 【动】stir up a disturbance；start trouble；make trouble：球迷～。The soccer fans created a disturbance.

滋味 zīwèi 【名】（～儿）taste；flavour

滋长 zīzhǎng 【动】grow；develop：有了成绩要防止～骄傲情绪。When one has made some achievement，one must guard against arrogance and conceit.

zǐ

子 zǐ

子 zǐ 【名】❶ ◇ son：父～ father and son ❷（～儿）seed：黄瓜～ cucumber seeds 菜～ vegetable seeds 花～ flower seeds ❸ egg：鱼～ fish roe 虾～ shrimp roe 鸡～儿 hen's eggs ❹ ◇ something small and hard：棋～儿 chessman 石头～儿 pebble 枪～儿 bullet

另见 zi

子弹 zǐdàn 【名】[发 fā] bullet；shell

子弟 zǐdì 【名】❶ sons and younger

brothers ❷ general term for young generations

子弟兵 zǐdìbīng 【名】troops made up of the sons and brothers of the people, usu. referring to the local population

子宫 zǐgōng 【名】womb

子女 zǐnǚ 【名】sons and daughters

子孙 zǐsūn 【名】❶ children and grand-children; sons and grand-sons ❷ descendents

子音 zǐyīn 【名】consonant

仔 zǐ

仔细 zǐxì 【形】❶ careful; attentive：观察得很 ~ observe very closely ~研究 study carefully 这人做事很~。He is very careful in whatever he does. ❷ cautious; careful：看照片的时候一点儿，别弄脏了。When you look at the photographs, please be careful and don't smudge them.

姊 zǐ 【名】◇ elder sister

姊妹 zǐmèi 【名】sisters; elder and younger sisters

紫 zǐ 【形】violet; purple

紫红 zǐhóng 【形】purplish red; the colour of red wine

紫外线 zǐwàixiàn 【名】ultra-violet rays

zì

自 zì 【代】self (usu. in written language)：~言~语 talk to oneself ~作~受 As you make your bed, so you must lie on it. ~相矛盾 self-contradictory ~找苦吃 ask for trouble 【介】❶同"从" cóng 【介】❶：~古以来 since ancient times ~下而上 from bottom to top ❷ from used after a verb：来~远方的朋友 a friend from afar 选·鲁迅全集第三卷 taken from vol. 3 of the Complete Works of Lu Xun 【副】naturally：~当珍惜 Of course I'll treasure it! 他来问我，我 ~ 有话回答。When he comes to confront me about it, I have my answer ready.

自白 zìbái 【名】written statement making clear one's position and views

自暴自弃 zì bào zì qì give up hope and deliberately go to the bad; give oneself up as hopeless

自卑 zìbēi 【形】having inferiority complex

自吹自擂 zì chuī zì léi brag and boast; blow one's own trumpet; self-praise

自从 zìcóng 【介】since Sometimes it is used in conjunction with 以来：他~出生就没见过他父亲。He has never seen his father since his birth. ~实行新的管理制度以来，这个厂的生产有了很大发展。Since the new management system was put into effect, the production of this factory has increased tremendously.

自大 zìdà 【形】self-important; arrogant; conceited

自动 zìdòng 【形】❶ voluntary; of one's own accord：王大妈盖新房，村民们~来帮忙。When Aunt Wang was building her new house, many villagers came of their own accord to help her. ❷ spontaneous：~燃烧 spontaneous combustion ❸ automatic：~流水线 automatic assembly line

自动化 zìdònghuà be automated; be automatized; automation

自动控制 zìdòng kòngzhì automatic control

自动铅笔 zìdòng qiānbǐ propelling pencil

自动线 zìdòngxiàn 【名】automatic

production line；transfer machine

自发 zìfā 【形】spontaneous：～倾向 spontaneous trend ～地组织起来 organize spontaneously

自费 zìfèi 【形】at one's own expense

自封 zìfēng 【动】proclaim oneself：～为专家 be a self-proclaimed expert 他这个"理论家"是～的。He is a self-proclaimed "theoretician".

自负 zìfù 【形】conceited

自高自大 zì gāo zì dà full of vainglory；vainglorious；self-important

自告奋勇 zì gào fènyǒng volunteer one's service；willingly take the responsibility upon oneself

自供状 zìgòngzhuàng 【名】confession

自顾不暇 zì gù bù xiá unable even to fend for oneself

自豪 zìháo 【形】taking pride in；proud of

自己 zìjǐ 【代】❶ oneself：学习主要靠～努力。Success in study mainly depends on one's own efforts. 门怎么～开了？How did the door open by itself? ～的衣服～洗。Everybody washes his own clothes. 房间我～收拾吧！I'll tidy up the room by myself. ❷ of one's own side；closely related：都是～的弟兄，不必客气。We are all brothers, please don't stand on ceremony.

自己人 zìjǐrén 【名】one of us

自给 zìjǐ 【动】be self-support；self-sufficient

自给自足 zì jǐ zì zú self-sufficient；able to support oneself

自救 zìjiù 【动】provide for and help oneself：生产～ provide for and help oneself by engaging in production

自居 zìjū 【动】consider oneself to be usu. in the structure "以…自居"，(derog.)：以功臣～ consider oneself to be someone who has

rendered great service 以学者～ be a self-styled scholar

自觉 zìjué 【动】be aware of usu. used in the negative：这个青年受坏人引诱，开始堕落而不～。This young man was under bad influence and became corrupt without being aware of it. 【形】conscientious；of one's own free will：～遵守各项规定 observe all regulations of one's own free will 他虽年轻,但工作、学习都很～。Though he is still young, he works and studies on his own initiative.

自觉性 zìjuéxìng 【名】the state of being aware of the importance of sth. and so quite willing to do it

自觉自愿 zìjué zìyuàn of one's own accord；willing；be ready to

自绝 zìjué 【动】cut oneself off from

自夸 zìkuā 【动】boast

自来水 zìláishuǐ 【名】running water；tap water

自来水笔 zìláishuǐbǐ 【名】fountain pen

自力更生 zì lì gēng shēng rely on one's own efforts；self-reliant

自立 zìlì 【动】support oneself；rely on oneself

自流 zìliú 【动】❶ (of water) take its own course：～灌溉 gravity flow irrigation ❷ (of things) take their own natural course：对青年既不能约束过严，又不能一切任其～。We mustn't be too strict with young people, nor can we let them do whatever they like.

自留地 zìliúdì 【名】plot for private use；plot for personal needs

自满 zìmǎn 【形】complacent；self-satisfied

自命不凡 zì mìng bù fán think of oneself as being superior to others；consider oneself no ordinary person

自欺欺人 zì qī qī rén　try to deceive others only to end in deceiving oneself；deceive oneself and others；sheer hypocrisy

自然 zìrán　【名】nature：征服～ conquer nature【形】❶ natural：她说汉语,语调很～。She speaks Chinese with a very natural intonation. 她没有什么舞台经验,动作不够～。She doesn't have much stage experience, so her acting isn't natural enough. 看他那自自然然的样子,不像有什么大事。From the relaxed way he is behaving, I think nothing serious can have happened. ❷ something to be expected；natural：他第一次跳伞,有点害怕,这是～的事。This is the first time he has done parachute jumping and it is only natural that he should be a bit nervous.【副】naturally：你就是太累了,没别的毛病,休息两天～会好的。You are just overtired. There is nothing wrong with you. You'll be all right after a couple of days' rest. 他看到这些革命文物,～地就想起了过去的战斗生活。When he saw these objects from the revolutionary war period, he naturally thought of his past fighting life.

自然辩证法 zìrán biànzhèngfǎ　natural dialectics

自然而然 zìrán ér rán　naturally

自然规律 zìrán guīlǜ　natural law；law of nature

自然界 zìránjiè　【名】natural world；nature

自然科学 zìrán kēxué　natural science

自然灾害 zìrán zāihài　natural calamity

自然主义 zìránzhǔyì　【名】naturalism

自燃 zì rán　self-ignite；spontaneous combustion

自如 zìrú　【形】with facility；freely：运用～ use with facility

自杀 zìshā　【动】commit suicide

自身 zìshēn　【名】oneself；self

自食其果 zì shí qí guǒ　reap what one has sown；be made to pay for one's evil doing

自食其力 zì shí qí lì　earn one's own living；live on one's own toil；self-supporting

自始至终 zì shǐ zhì zhōng　from beginning to end：～不变 no change at all from beginning to end ～跑完全程 run the whole course from beginning to end

自首 zìshǒu　【动】give oneself up (to law)

自私 zìsī　【形】selfish；egoistic

自私自利 zìsī zì lì　selfish；selfishness

自投罗网 zì tóu luówǎng　walk straight into a trap

自卫 zìwèi　【动】defend oneself；self-defence

自卫战争 zìwèi zhànzhēng　war of self-defence

自慰 zìwèi　【动】console oneself

自我 zìwǒ　【代】oneself；self：～介绍 introduce oneself ～牺牲 self-sacrifice

自我批评 zìwǒ pīpíng　self-criticism

自习 zìxí　【动】study by oneself；review one's lessons

自信 zìxìn　believe in oneself：～能胜任这项工作 believe in one's own competence for the job【形】self-confident：他很～。He is full of confidence

自行 zìxíng　【副】❶.by oneself，～处理 settle (the matter) by oneself ～安排 make arrangements by oneself ❷ of one's own accord：～退出 withdraw of one's own accord；back out willingly

自行车 zìxíngchē　【名】〔辆 liàng〕bicycle；bike

自修 zìxiū　【动】❶ review one's lessons by oneself ❷ study on one's

own; teach oneself

自诩 zìxǔ 【动】brag and boast

自选商场 zìxuǎn shāngchǎng supermarket

自学 zìxué 【动】study by oneself

自以为是 zì yǐ wéi shì consider oneself in the right

自由 zìyóu 【名】freedom; liberty 【形】free; liberal: ～活动 (a time for) free activities ～参加 optional attendance

自由竞争 zìyóu jìngzhēng free competition

自由恋爱 zìyóu liàn'ài free to choose one's spouse

自由落体 zìyóu luòtǐ (phys.) free falling body

自由市场 zìyóu shìchǎng free market; open market

自由体操 zìyóu tǐcāo free callisthenics; free exercises; floor exercise

自由王国 zìyóu wángguó (philos.) the realm of freedom (as opp. to 必然王国)

自由泳 zìyóuyǒng 【名】(swimming) freestyle

自由职业者 zìyóuzhíyèzhě 【名】professional man

自由主义 zìyóuzhǔyì 【名】liberalism

自圆其说 zì yuán qí shuō make one's argument consistent and not self-contradictory; justify oneself

自愿 zìyuàn 【动】of one's own free will; voluntarily: 本人～ of one's own free will ～报名 enter one's name voluntarily 出于～ on a voluntary basis

自在 zìzài 【形】free; unrestrained: 逍遥～ at leisure and free from care 燕子自由～地飞翔。Swallows fly about, carefree and at liberty.

自在 zìzai 【形】comfortable; at ease: 主人太客气了,反而使大家觉得不太～。The excessive hospitality of our host made us feel rather uncomfortable.

自知之明 zì zhī zhī míng (have) the wisdom to know oneself

自治 zìzhì 【动】exercise autonomy; autonomous rule

自治区 zìzhìqū 【名】autonomous region

自治权 zìzhìquán 【名】autonomy

自治县 zìzhìxiàn 【名】autonomous county

自治州 zìzhìzhōu 【名】autonomous district

自主 zìzhǔ 【动】be on one's own; be one's own master: 在封建制度下,婚姻不能～。Under feudalism, young people could not marry the person of their own choice.

自助 zìzhù 【动】help oneself: ～餐 buffet

自转 zìzhuǎn 【动】revolve on its own axis

自传 zìzhuàn 【名】autobiography

自尊心 zìzūnxīn 【名】self-respect

自作聪明 zì zuò cōngmíng consider oneself clever and act accordingly

自作自受 zì zuò zì shòu suffer from one's own action; stew in one's own juice

字 zì 【名】❶ character; word ❷ pronunciation (of a character or word): 她唱歌吐～很清楚。When she sings, she pronounces every word very distinctly. ❸ style of a written or printed character ❹ wording: 用～讲究 very exact in wording 这篇发言～～都有份量。Every word in this speech carried great weight. ❺ ◇ written pledge: 立～为凭 give a written pledge

字典 zìdiǎn 【名】〔本 běn,部 bù〕dictionary

字画 zìhuà 【名】calligraphy and painting

字迹 zìjì 【名】handwriting

字据 zìjù 【名】signed paper (e. g.

receipt；IOU）

字里行间 zì lǐ háng jiān　between the lines

字面 zìmiàn　【名】literal（sense of the word）

字母 zìmǔ　【名】letter；alphabet

字幕 zìmù　【名】caption；subtitle

字体 zìtǐ　【名】❶ specific style of calligraphy ❷ typeface

字帖 zìtiè　【名】〔本 běn〕samples of the calligraphy of a master calligrapher reproduced for use as a copybook

字斟句酌 zì zhēn jù zhuó．weigh every word；choose one's words carefully

zi

子 zi　【尾】❶ *put after a noun morpheme*：叶～ leaf 儿～ son 房～ house 椅～ chair 帽～ cap 车～ vehicle 瓶～ bottle ❷ *put after an adjectival or verbal morpheme to make a noun*：胖～ a fat person；fatty 瘦～ a thin person；skinny 垫～ cushion 铲～ spade

另见 zǐ

zōng

宗 zōng　【量】（*for a large sum of money，goods，etc.*）：一～买卖 a transaction；a deal

宗教 zōngjiào　【名】religion

宗派 zōngpài　【名】faction；group；sect

宗派主义 zōngpàizhǔyì　【名】factionalism；sectarianism

宗旨 zōngzhǐ　【名】aim；intention；object（of an organization，institution etc.）

宗族 zōngzú　【名】clan

综（綜） zōng

综合 zōnghé　【动】synthesize；sum up；comprehensive：把各方面的意见～一下 sum up various opinions ～利用 comprehensive utilization ～大学 university

综述 zōngshù　【动】summarize；sum up

棕 zōng　【名】❶ palm ❷ palm fibre；coir

棕色 zōngsè　【名】brown

踪 zōng　【名】◇ trace；footprint

踪迹 zōngjì　【名】trace；footprint；track

踪影 zōngyǐng　【名】同"踪迹"（*usu. in the negative*）

zǒng

总（總） zǒng　【动】sum up；assemble：～起来说 sum up 【形】general；total：～的情况 the general situation ～产量 total output ～动员 general mobilization ～罢工 general strike 【副】❶ always；invariably：这孩子可好啦，～来帮我干活儿。This child is certainly very good. He always comes to help me with my chores. 这儿春天～刮风。It's always windy here in the spring. 他～觉得时间不够用。He finds that he never has sufficient time. 这个词我念了好几遍～记不住。I've studied this term repeatedly but I just can't remember it. ❷ eventually：正义的事业～会胜利的。A just cause will eventually prevail. 你这种合理要求～会得到满足的。Your request is reasonable and will eventually be granted. ❸ at least：长城他～去过三四次了吧！He must have been

to the Great Wall 3 or 4 times at least. 参加大会的～有一万多人。There must have been at least 10000 people at the rally. 这件事～该商量商量再办。Others must at least be consulted before the matter is finalized. 这个连队种的蔬菜虽然不多，～够吃了。Though the company has not planted a large quantity of vegetables, they are at least enough for the company's own consumption.

总编辑 zǒngbiānjí 【名】〔位 wèi〕editor-in-chief

总产值 zǒngchǎnzhí 【名】total output value

总得 zǒngděi 【助动】have to; must

总动员 zǒngdòngyuán 【名】general mobilization

总额 zǒng'é 【名】total amount; total sum; total

总而言之 zǒng ér yán zhī in a word; in short; to put it briefly

总纲 zǒnggāng 【名】general programme

总工程师 zǒnggōngchéngshī 【名】engineer-in-chief

总共 zǒnggòng 【副】altogether; in all; 这个学校～有两千名学生。There are altogether two thousand students in this school. 这几样东西～五块钱。These articles cost five *yuan* in all.

总归 zǒngguī 【副】同"终归" zhōngguī

总和 zǒnghé 【名】sum; sum total

总机 zǒngjī 【名】telephone exchange; switchboard

总计 zǒngjì 【动】amount to; total

总结 zǒngjié 【动】sum up; ～工作 sum up one's work ～经验教训 sum up one's experiences and lessons 【名】summary; 年终～ annual report 这份～写得很全面。This summary covers every aspect (of the problem).

总括 zǒngkuò 【动】sum up; put in a nutshell

总理 zǒnglǐ 【名】premier; prime minister

总量 zǒngliàng 【名】total amount

总是 zǒngshì 【副】*about the same as* 总【副】❶❷:他～那样谦虚。He is always very modest. 每天上班她～来得很早。She always comes to work very early every day. 这种试验～会成功的。This kind of experiment will eventually succeed.

总数 zǒngshù 【名】total amount; sum total

总算 zǒngsuàn 【副】❶ 同"算"【副】*but more emphatic*:坐了三天的火车，～到家了。After travelling by train for three days we finally got home. 真不容易，～把你找到了。What a lot of trouble it was, but we've finally found you after all! ❷ could almost be regarded as; 我虽然不是他的亲姐姐，但我们～一家人。Although I'm not his sister, we could almost be regarded as members of the same family.

总体 zǒngtǐ 【名】totality; entirety

总统 zǒngtǒng 【名】president

总务 zǒngwù 【名】service work of an institution (e. g. care of grounds, dining room etc.); general affairs

总则 zǒngzé 【名】general rules; general principles; general provisions

总之 zǒngzhī 【连】❶ in a word; 篮球、排球、乒乓球，～，很多球类运动他都喜欢。Basketball, volleyball, table tennis, in a word, all sorts of ball games appeal to him. ❷ *when it is impossible or unnecessary to explain in detail, one can use 总之 to convey the main idea in a nutshell*:记不清是谁了，～有人找过你。I can't remember who it was; any-

way, there was someone looking for you.

zòng

纵（縱） zòng 【名】❶ from north to south：这条铁路～贯南北。This railway line runs from north to south. ❷ vertical：～切面 vertical section 【动】❶ let go；set free：欲擒故～ set the enemy free in order to catch him ❷ indulge in；let oneself go：～声大笑 indulge in hearty laughter ～目瞭望 look as far into the distance as possible ❸ jump；leap forward or upward：身子一～ 就跳过了壕堑。He jumped across the ditch. 【连】〈书〉even if；though

纵队 zòngduì 【名】(mil.) column

纵横 zònghéng 【形】vertical and horizontal；lengthwise and crosswise：铁路～ with railway lines criss-crossing (the country) ～数十里都是稻田 paddy fields for scores of *li* in all directions 【动】〈书〉move about freely：武工队～于敌后。The guerrillas manoeuvred freely behind enemy lines.

纵横交错 zònghéng jiāocuò criss-cross

纵虎归山 zòng hǔ guī shān allow a tiger to run back to the mountain；(*fig.*) allow a dangerous person to return to his haunts

纵火 zòng = huǒ set on fire；commit arson：～犯 arsonist

纵情 zòngqíng 【副】to one's heart's content：～歌唱 sing to one's heart's content ～欢呼 cheer as much as one likes

纵然 zòngrán 【连】even if：～有雨，也不会很大。Even if it rains, it won't rain very heavily.

纵容 zòngróng 【动】indulge；pamper

纵身 zòngshēn 【动】leap forward or upwards

纵深 zòngshēn 【名】(mil.) depth

纵使 zòngshǐ 【连】同"即使" jíshǐ

zǒu

走 zǒu 【动】❶ walk：你～得太快了，我跟不上。You are walking too fast; I can't keep up with you. ❷ leave；depart：～了几个人。Several people have left. 今天别～了，住下吧。Don't leave today! Stay here over night! ❸ run；move：这块手表～得很好。This watch runs well. ❹ go；make a trip：麻烦你一一趟吧。May I trouble you to go there? ❺ go by way of：～东门出去吧。Let's go by way of the east gate. 你去大连是～水路还是～旱路? When you go to Dalian, will you go by sea or by land? ❻ leak；let out：～了消息 leak the news ～了风声 let out a secret ❼ go and pay a call on (relatives)：姥姥～亲戚去了。Granny has gone to pay a call on her relatives. ❽ depart from the original：他唱歌总～调。He tends to sing out of tune. 烟搁得太久，就要～味儿。If cigarettes are kept for too long, they will lose their flavour.

走动 zǒudòng 【动】❶ walk about；stretch one's legs：手术后要少～。One mustn't move about too much after an operation. 出去～～，别总坐在屋里。You ought to go out and walk about occasionally and not sit in your room all the time. ❷ socialize with relatives or friends：我们两家常～，关系很好。Our two families often visit each other, and are on good terms.

走读 zǒudú 【动】attend a day school：～生 day student

走访 zǒufǎng 【动】interview

走狗 zǒugǒu 【名】lackey；running dog

走过场 zǒu guòchǎng make a sham of sth.；reduce to a mere formality：开讨论会要注意实效，不要～。A discussion is held to bring about some actual result, and it is not merely for show.

走红 zǒuhóng 【动】be very popular

走后门 zǒu hòumén get in by the "back door"；secure advantage through influence；a backdoor deal

走火 zǒu=huǒ (of a gun) fire accidentally

走廊 zǒuláng 【名】corridor

走漏 zǒulòu 【动】leak；let out；disclose：～消息 leak a piece of news

走路 zǒu=lù walk

走马观花 zǒu mǎ guān huā look at the flowers while riding on horseback；(fig.) make a cursory investigation (of some situation)：了解情况要深入，不能～。In order to understand a situation, one must go into it deeply, not just skim the surface. 也作"走马看花"。

走俏 zǒuqiào 【动】sell well

走私 zǒu=sī smuggle

走投无路 zǒu tóu wú lù find oneself cornered

走向 zǒuxiàng 【名】(of veins in ore，mountain ranges, etc.) alignment；trend

走形式 zǒu xíngshì stress the formality：只～，不重内容，不会有效果的。If one stresses form only and neglects content, nothing will be achieved.

走穴 zǒuxué 【动】(of a performer) moonlight

走样 zǒu=yàng deviate from the original model

走运 zǒu=yùn be lucky；have good luck

走卒 zǒuzú 【名】underling；pawn

zòu

奏 zòu 【动】play（music）

奏鸣曲 zòumíngqǔ 【名】sonata

奏效 zòu=xiào show results；prove effective

奏乐 zòu=yuè play music；strike up a tune

揍 zòu 【动】hit；beat；strike

zū

租 zū 【动】rent；hire：～了一套房间 rent a suite of rooms ～车 hire a car 【名】rent

租界 zūjiè 【名】concession；foreign settlement；leased territory

租借 zūjiè 【动】lease

租金 zūjīn 【名】rent；rental

租赁 zūlìn 【动】rent

租用 zūyòng 【动】rent；take on lease

zú

足 zú 【名】〈书〉foot：赤～ barefoot 【形】enough；sufficient：吃饱了，喝～了 have had enough food and wine 信心很～ with full confidence 这工作他～能胜任。He is fully qualified for this job. 哥哥～有一米八高。My elder brother is fully 1.8 metres tall. 我们～～等了一个钟头，他也没来。We had waited for fully an hour, but he didn't show up.

足够 zúgòu 【动】sufficient；adequate；enough：给予～的重视 attach sufficient importance to 时间～了。There is enough time. 这些稿

纸～我用的。There is sufficient paper for my purpose.

足迹 zújì 【名】trace; footprints

足球 zúqiú 【名】❶〔个 gè〕football ❷ football game

足岁 zúsuì 【名】actual age

足以 zúyǐ 【副】enough; sufficient: 举了这么多例子，～说明问题了。You have cited quite enough examples to illustrate the problem. 这些理由不～说服他。These reasons are not sufficient to convince him. 仅仅这几个例句，不～讲清楚这个词的各种用法。These few sentences are not enough to illustrate the different usages of the word.

zǔ

诅（詛）zǔ

诅咒 zǔzhòu 【动】curse; abuse

阻 zǔ

阻碍 zǔ'ài 【动】obstruct; hinder; hamper; impede: ～交通 obstruct traffic 旧思想意识的统治会～社会的发展。An outmoded ruling ideology often hampers the development of a society. 【名】obstruction: 冲破～ break through an obstruction

阻挡 zǔdǎng 【动】block; hold up

阻击 zǔjī 【动】(mil.) block; check

阻截 zǔjié 【动】stop; intercept

阻拦 zǔlán 【动】hinder; obstruct; stop

阻力 zǔlì 【名】resistance

阻挠 zǔnáo 【动】hamper; hinder

阻塞 zǔsè 【动】block; obstruct

阻止 zǔzhǐ 【动】prevent; obstruct; stop; hold back

组（組）zǔ 【名】group; section; unit: 科学考察～ scientific investigation team 五十人分成五个～。The fifty people were divided into five groups. 【动】◇ organize; form: 用下列单字～词。Form words using the following characters. 【量】group; set: 一～电池 a battery

组成 zǔchéng 【动】constitute; be composed of; make up

组歌 zǔgē 【名】group of songs on one theme; suite of songs

组阁 zǔ=gé form a cabinet

组合 zǔhé 【动】make up; compose: 青山、绿水、各色的鲜花～成一幅美丽的图画。Green hills, blue rivers and flowers of various colours make up a beautiful picture. 【名】combination: 词组是词的～。A phrase is a combination of words.

组建 zǔjiàn 【动】set up; form: ～少年足球队 form a juvenile soccer team

组曲 zǔqǔ 【名】(mus.) suite; pieces of music (on one theme) for a certain instrument

组诗 zǔshī 【名】group of poems on one theme

组织 zǔzhī 【动】organize: ～一次讨论会 organize a discussion ～起来力量大。Organization means strength. 这篇文章～得不错。This article is well-organized. 【名】❶ (physiol.) tissue: 肌肉～ muscle tissue ❷ organization: 学生组织 student organization; student body 学校的体育～很关心你们的健康。The school sports organization is very concerned about your health.

组织性 zǔzhīxìng 【名】sense of organization

组装 zǔzhuāng 【动】assemble: 进口零件，国内～ import spare parts to be assembled domestically ～车间 assembling workshop

祖 zǔ

祖父 zǔfù 【名】grandfather (father's father)

祖国 zǔguó 【名】motherland

祖母　zǔmǔ　【名】grandmother（father's mother）

祖先　zǔxiān　【名】forefather；ancestor

祖宗　zǔzōng　【名】ancestry；ancestor

祖祖辈辈　zǔ zǔ bèi bèi　for generations in the past

zuān

钻（鑽）　zuān　【动】❶ bore；drill：～孔 drill a hole 钢板～透了。The steel plate is drilled through. ❷ go through；make one's way into：～山洞 go into a cave in the mountain ～进森林 go deep into the forest ❸ probe into a subject；make a penetrating study of：死～书本不行，必须联系实际。It's no good just burying oneself in books, one must also apply what one learns to practical work. 他有一股～劲儿。He is very persistent in probing into things.
另见 zuàn

钻劲儿　zuānjìnr　【名】〔股 gǔ〕studiousness；spirit of studying intensively

钻空子　zuān kòngzi　avail oneself of loopholes：决不让坏人钻我们的空子。We must leave no loopholes for bad people to exploit.

钻探　zuāntàn　【动】drill for exploratory purposes

钻研　zuānyán　【动】make a penetrating study of

钻营　zuānyíng　【动】curry favour with person in power with an eye to personal gain

zuàn

钻（鑽）　zuàn　【名】❶ drill；auger ❷ ◇ diamond；jewel：十九～的手表 a 19-jewel watch
另见 zuān

钻床　zuànchuáng　【名】driller；drilling machine

钻机　zuànjī　【名】drilling rig

钻戒　zuànjiè　【名】diamond ring

钻石　zuànshí　【名】diamond

钻头　zuàntóu　【名】bit

攥　zuàn　【动】clasp；clutch；clench

zuǐ

嘴　zuǐ　【名】〔张 zhāng〕mouth

嘴巴　zuǐba　【名】❶ mouth：把～张开 open your mouth ❷ cheek；side of the face：打～ slap sb. in the face 给了他一个～ slap his face

嘴唇　zuǐchún　【名】lip

嘴快　zuǐ kuài　have a loose tongue：这个人～，什么话也藏不住。This person has a loose tongue and can't hold back anything.

嘴脸　zuǐliǎn　【名】（hideous；ugly）features（fig. only）

嘴贫　zuǐ pín　garrulous：奶奶嘴太贫，说起来没完没了。Granny is very garrulous and once she starts she will go on and on.

嘴甜　zuǐ tián　smooth-tongued；honeymouthed：小兰这孩子～，见人就叫。Xiao Lan is a smooth-tongued child and greets everyone she sees.

zuì

最　zuì　【副】indicates the superlative degree：～了解情况 be best acquainted with the situation ～说明问题 can best illustrate something ～根本的原则 the most fundamental principle ～本质的东西 the

essential matter 这样讲～清楚。It is clearest if explained this way.

最初 zuìchū 【名】at first；at the very beginning；original；initial

最多 zuìduō 【副】at most

最好 zuìhǎo 【副】had better；it would be best：这块地～种花生。It would be best to plant peanuts in this plot of land. 这种菜～吃生的。This vegetable is best eaten raw. 用不着的东西～先别买。You'd better not buy things you don't need right away.

最后 zuìhòu 【名】the last；final；ultimate；eventually：～一个座位 the last seat 我的名字排在～。My name is the last on the list. ～的胜利属于人民。The final victory belongs to the people. ～我想讲一讲自己的感想。Finally, I'd like to say a word or two about my own impressions.

最后通牒 zuìhòu tōngdié ultimatum

最惠国待遇 zuìhuìguó dàiyù most-favoured-nation status；MFN status

最近 zuìjìn 【名】of late；lately

最少 zuìshǎo 【副】at least

最终 zuìzhōng 【副】in the end；eventually：～，冠军仍属红队。In the end, the championship still went to Team Red.

罪 zuì 【名】❶ guilt；crime：有～ be guilty of a crime 判～ pass sentence on ❷ hardship；suffering：年轻时,他受了不少～。He suffered a lot when he was young.

罪大恶极 zuì dà è jí commit most heinous crime

罪恶 zuì'è 【名】evil；crime：～极大 monstrous crime

罪恶滔天 zuì'è tāotiān monstrous crimes

罪犯 zuìfàn 【名】criminal；convict

罪过 zuìguò 【名】offence；fault；sin

罪魁祸首 zuìkuí huòshǒu chief criminal；arch-criminal

罪名 zuìmíng 【名】charge；accusation

罪孽 zuìniè 【名】sin；iniquity

罪人 zuìrén 【名】sinner；guilty person

罪行 zuìxíng 【名】criminal act；vicious act

罪证 zuìzhèng 【名】evidence of crime

罪状 zuìzhuàng 【名】actual facts of a crime

醉 zuì 【动】be drunk

醉鬼 zuìguǐ 【名】drunkard；sot；inebriate

醉心 zuìxīn 【动】have a strong affection for (a specific branch of study, kind of work, etc.)；be bent on

醉醺醺 zuìxūnxūn 【形】tipsy；intoxicated

醉意 zuìyì 【名】signs of inebriation；feeling tipsy

zūn

尊 zūn 【动】◇ respect；esteem；revere：～师爱徒。The students respect the teachers and the teachers love the students. 【量】for statues：一～佛像 a statue of the Buddha

尊称 zūnchēng 【名】respectful form of address

尊崇 zūnchóng 【动】hold in esteem

尊贵 zūnguì 【形】respectable；honourable

尊敬 zūnjìng 【动】respect；esteem；revere

尊师 zūnshī 【动】respect teachers：～爱生 students respect teachers and teachers cherish students

尊严 zūnyán 【名】dignity：维护民族～ uphold national honour 失掉～

lose one's dignity

尊重 zūnzhòng 【动】(of opinion, work, person, etc.) treat with due respect

遵 zūn 【动】◇ abide by; observe; obey

遵从 zūncóng 【动】obey; follow

遵命 zūn=mìng be in compliance with the order

遵守 zūnshǒu 【动】observe; adhere to; abide by

遵循 zūnxún 【动】follow; abide by; comply with; act in accordance with

遵照 zūnzhào 【动】同"遵循"

zuó

昨 zuó

昨天 zuótiān 【名】yesterday

琢 zuó
另见 zhuó

琢磨 zuómo 【动】ponder; turn sth. over in one's mind; 这首诗越～越有味儿。The more you ponder over this poem, the more interesting you'll find it to be.
另见 zhuómó

zuǒ

左 zuǒ 【名】left; the left side 【形】left; radical

左边 zuǒbiān 【名】left side

左面 zuǒmiàn 【名】同"左边"

左派 zuǒpài 【名】leftists

左倾 zuǒqīng 【名】❶ left-leaning ❷ "left" deviation

左手 zuǒshǒu 【名】〔只 zhī〕left hand

左翼 zuǒyì 【名】left wing; left flank

左右 zuǒyòu 【助】*used after a numeral and measure word to show an approximate number*; 二百吨～ about 200 tons 【动】hold (sb.) under one's thumb; manipulate; ～战局 be master of the war situation

左…右… zuǒ... yòu... *an emphatic expression indicating repetition of an action*; 左顾右盼 look this way and that 左思右想 keep turning sth. over in one's mind 左说右说 say sth. over and over again 左一趟右一趟派人去请 keep on sending people to invite him over 左一句右一句说个没完 keep on babbling

左右逢源 zuǒ yòu féng yuán things are getting on smoothly whichever way they go; find a smooth path whichever way things go

左右为难 zuǒ yòu wéi nán be in a dilemma; 这件事让他～。This affair put him in a dilemma.

zuò

作 zuò 【动】❶ ◇ rise; 枪声大～。Bursts of heavy gun-fire broke out. ❷ do; make; ～画 draw a picture ～计划 make a plan ❸ pretend; be affected; ～鬼脸 make faces 故～姿态 behave in an affected manner ❹ be engaged in; busy oneself with; ～斗争 be engaged in struggle ～报告 make a report

作案 zuò=àn commit a crime

作罢 zuòbà 【动】call off; cancel

作弊 zuò=bì practise fraud; cheat

作对 zuòduì 【动】be antagonistic to (sb.).

作恶多端 zuò è duō duān have done a lot of evil

作法 zuòfǎ 【名】method; way of doing things

作废 zuòfèi 【动】become invalid; make null and void

作风 zuòfēng 【名】style of work;

working style

作梗 zuògěng 【动】obstruct；impede；hamper；hinder

作怪 zuòguài 【动】make trouble；play tricks；be a nuisance；do mischief

作家 zuòjiā 【名】writer；author

作假 zuò=jiǎ cheat；play tricks。严防～ take strict precautions against cheating

作价 zuò=jià fix a price on sth.；evaluate：他把房子卖给邻居，～两千元。He sold his house to his neighbor，fixing the price at 2000 yuan.

作茧自缚 zuò jiǎn zì fù weave a cocoon and get imprisoned in it；(fig.) be caught in one's own trap

作客 zuò=kè be a guest

作料 zuòliao 【名】seasoning；condiment

作难 zuònán 【动】put obstacles in the way；make it difficult for

作陪 zuòpéi 【动】be invited along with the guest of honour at a banquet

作品 zuòpǐn 【名】a literary or artistic work；composition

作曲 zuò=qǔ compose；musical composition

作曲家 zuòqǔjiā 【名】composer

作数 zuò=shù 同"算数" suànshù

作祟 zuòsuì 【动】make mischief；cause trouble

作威作福 zuò wēi zuò fú abuse one's power；ride roughshod over；play the tyrant

作为 zuòwéi 【动】use as；regard as usu. used in 把 sentences or sentences where the subject is acted upon：他可以～我们学习的榜样。He could be regarded as a model to follow. 我们想选这篇文章～阅读材料。We are thinking of using this article as reading material. 很多青年把报效祖国～努力的方向。Many young people regard building up

their motherland as their goal. 【名】◇ conduct；accomplishment；action：有所～ accomplish something 这人很有～。This person has really accomplished a lot. 【介】as：你～一个领导应该关心工人的养老金问题。You，as a member of the leadership，ought to be concerned about the old-age pension of your workers. ～一件艺术品来说，这个雕刻还有些粗糙。As a work of art，this sculpture is a bit crude.

作文 zuòwén 【名】composition；exercise in writing

作物 zuòwù 【名】crop

作息 zuòxī 【动】work and rest

作业 zuòyè 【名】❶ actual work arranged for a worker ❷ training arranged for soldiers ❸ homework

作用 zuòyòng 【名】❶ function；role：发挥～ play a role in；fulfil a function ～很大 have a very important role in ❷ action；effect：同化～ assimilation 化学～ chemical action 【动】affect；act on：一个物体～于另一个物体。One substance (object) acts on another.

作用点 zuòyòngdiǎn 【名】(phys.) point of action

作用力 zuòyònglì 【名】(phys.) applied force；action force

作战 zuòzhàn 【动】fight；make war

作者 zuòzhě 【名】author (of a book)

坐 zuò 【动】❶ sit：请～。Please sit down. ❷ travel by；go by：～车 travel by car ～船 go by boat ❸ (of a building) face away from：礼堂～北朝南。The auditorium faces south. ❹ place on a fire：把锅～到炉子上。Put the pot on the stove. ❺ (of guns) kick；recoil：让枪托～了一下 be kicked by (the recoil of) the rifle ❻ (of a building) subside；sink：房基～下去十毫米。The foun-

dation of this house has subsided 10 mm.

坐班 zuò = bān keep office hours: ~制 a practice of keeping office hours

坐标 zuòbiāo 【名】(maths.) coordinate

坐标轴 zuòbiāozhóu 【名】coordinate axis

坐井观天 zuò jǐng guān tiān see the sky from the bottom of a well: (fig.) have a very narrow view of things

坐牢 zuò = láo be put in prison: be imprisoned: be sent to jail

坐立不安 zuò lì bù ān restless: on pins and needles

坐落 zuòluò 【动】(of building, house) be located: be situated: 职工疗养院~在风景秀丽的湖滨。The sanatorium for the workers and staff members is situated on the shore of a beautiful lake.

坐山观虎斗 zuò shān guān hǔ dòu sit on top of the mountain and watch two tigers fight: (fig.) watch two parties attack each other and wait to get the spoils when both sides are exhausted

坐视 zuòshì 【动】look on with indifference: sit by and watch

坐卧不宁 zuò wò bù níng unable to sit down or sleep at ease: be very uneasy

坐享其成 zuò xiǎng qí chéng sit by, and enjoy the results of others' labour without doing a stroke of work

座 zuò 【名】(~儿) ❶ seat: 这个礼堂有两千个~。This auditorium has two thousand seats. ❷ pedestal: stand: 塑像的~ pedestal for a statue 花盆的~ stand for a flower pot 【量】for mountains, bridges, tall buildings, reservoirs, etc.: 两

~大山 two huge mountains 一~小桥 a small bridge 一~古城 an ancient city 一~宝塔 a pagoda

座次 zuòcì 【名】order of seating

座谈 zuòtán 【动】have a discussion meeting

座谈会 zuòtánhuì 【名】forum: symposium: discussion meeting

座位 zuòwèi 【名】seat (usu. in public place): 在公共汽车上青年人应该给老年人让~。When riding on buses, the young ought to give up their seats to seniors. 剧场里已经没~了。There wasn't an empty seat left in the theatre.

座无虚席 zuò wú xū xí no empty seat

座右铭 zuòyòumíng 【名】motto: maxim: "为人民服务"是我们的~。"Serve the people" is our principle.

座子 zuòzi 【名】❶同"座" ❷ stand: base: 钟~ a stand for a clock ❷ saddle (of a bicycle, etc.): 自行车~ a bicycle seat

做 zuò 【动】❶ make: do: ~点心 make pastries 猪皮可以~箱子。Pig skin can be used to make suitcases. ❷ write: ~诗 write poems ~文章 write articles ❸ do: engage in: ~事 work ~买卖 do business ❹ be: become: ~教员 be a teacher ~个好工人 be a good worker ❺ be used as: 拿稻草~造纸的原料 use rice straw as the material for making paper

做伴 zuò = bàn (~儿) keep sb. company

做法 zuòfǎ 【名】way of making things: ways and means: tactics

做饭 zuò = fàn prepare meal: cook

做工 zuò = gōng do (manual) work

做客 zuò = kè be a guest

做梦 zuò = mèng dream: have a dream

做人 zuò = rén ❶ conduct oneself; behave; ～要光明磊落。One should be open and aboveboard in dealing with people. ❷ be an honest person; 痛改前非，重新～ correct one's errors and turn over a new leaf

做手脚 zuò shǒujiǎo cheat; juggle with things

做寿 zuò = shòu (of elderly people) celebrate birthday

做学问 zuò xuéwen devote oneself to scholarly research; be engaged in scholarship

做贼心虚 zuò zéi xīn xū a thief is bound to be nervous

做主 zuò = zhǔ decide (things) for oneself; take (matters) into one's own hand

做作 zuòzuo 【形】 affected; unnatural; pretentious; 这个人说话～得很。That fellow has a very affected way of speaking.

附 录 （Appendices）

（一）汉语拼音方案
Scheme for the Chinese Phonetic Alphabet

一、汉语拼音字母表
Table of the Chinese Phonetic Alphabet

字母 (Letters)		字母的名称 Names	字母 (Letters)		字母的名称 Names
印刷体 Printed Form	书写体 Written Form		印刷体 Printed Form	书写体 Written Form	
A a	*A a*	[a]	N n	*N n*	[nɛ]
B b	*B b*	[pɛ]	O o	*O o*	[o]
C c	*C c*	[tsʻɛ]	P p	*P p*	[pʻɛ]
D d	*D d*	[tɛ]	Q q	*Q q*	[tɕʻiou]
E e	*E e*	[ɤ]	R r	*R r*	[ar]
F f	*F f*	[ɛf]	S s	*S s*	[ɛs]
G g	*G g*	[kɛ]	T t	*T t*	[tʻɛ]
H h	*H h*	[xa]	U u	*U u*	[u]
I i	*I i*	[i]	*V v	*V v*	[vɛ]
J j	*J j*	[tɕiɛ]	W w	*W w*	[wa]
K k	*K k*	[kʻɛ]	X x	*X x*	[ɕi]
L l	*L l*	[ɛl]	Y y	*Y y*	[ja]
M m	*M m*	[ɛm]	Z z	*Z z*	[tsɛ]

* V 只用来拼写外来语、少数民族语言和方言。
  V is used only to transcribe foreign words, words of national minority languages and local dialects.

二、汉语拼音方案、国际音标、威托玛式注音法

声韵母对照简表

Initials and Finals of the Chinese Phonetic
System，and Their Corresponding International
Phonetic Symbols and Wade System Symbols

一、声母表　Table of Initials

汉语拼音 Chinese Phonetic Symbol	国际音标 International Phonetic Symbol	威托玛式 注音法 Wade System Symbol	汉语拼音 Chinese Phonetic Symbol	国际音标 International Phonetic Symbol	威托玛式 注音法 Wade System Symbol
b	[p]	p	shi	[ʂʅ]	shih
p	[pʻ]	pʻ	r	[ʐʅ]	j
m	[m]	m	ri	[ʐʅ]	jih
f	[f]	f	j	[tɕ]	ch
d	[t]	t	ji	[tɕi]	chi
t	[tʻ]	tʻ	ju	[tɕy]	chü
n	[n]	n	q	[tɕʻ]	chʻ
l	[l]	l	qi	[tɕʻi]	chʻi
z	[ts]	ts	qu	[tɕʻy]	chʻü
zi	[tsʅ]	tzǔ	x	[ɕ]	hs
c	[tsʻ]	tsʻ	xi	[ɕi]	hsi
ci	[tsʻʅ]	tzʻǔ	xu	[ɕy]	hsü
s	[s]	s	g	[k]	k
si	[sʅ]	ssǔ, szǔ	k	[kʻ]	kʻ
zh	[tʂ]	ch	h	[x]	h
zhi	[tʂʅ]	chih	半元音	semi- vowels	
ch	[tʂʻ]	chʻ	y	[j]	y
chi	[tʂʻʅ]	chʻih	w	[w]	w
sh	[ʂ]	sh			

二、韵母表 Table of Finals

汉语拼音 Chinese Phonetic Symbol	国际音标 International Phonetic Symbol	威托玛式 注音法 Wade System Symbol	汉语拼音 Chinese Phonetic Symbol	国际音标 International Phonetic Symbol	威托玛式 注音法 Wade System Symbol
a	[a]	a	iu	[iou]	iu
o	[o]	o	ian	[iɛn]	ien
e	[ɤ]	ê	in	[in]	in
ê	[ɛ]	—	iang	[iɑŋ]	iang
er	[ər]	êrh	ing	[iŋ]	ing
ai	[ai]	ai	iong	[iuŋ]	iung
ei	[ei]	ei	u	[u]	u
ao	[au]	ao	ua	[ua]	ua
ou	[ou]	ou	uo	[uo]	uo
an	[an]	an	uai	[uai]	uai
en	[ən]	ên	ui	[uei]	ui
ang	[ɑŋ]	ang	uan	[uan]	uan
eng	[əŋ]	êng	un	[uən]	un
ong	[uŋ]	ung	uang	[uɑŋ]	uang
i	[i]	i	ü(yu)	[y]	ü(yü)
ia	[ia]	ia	üe(yue)	[yɛ]	üeh(yüeh)
ie	[iɛ]	ieh	üan(yuan)	[yɛn]	üan(yüan)
iao	[iau]	iao	ün(yun)	[yn]	ün(yün)

三、声调符号　Tone Marks

阴平	阳平	上声	去声
-	´	ˇ	`
1st tone	2nd tone	3rd tone	4th tone

声调符号标在音节的主要元音上。轻声不标。例如：

Tone marks are put above the main vowel of the syllable. The neutral tone is not marked. Thus：

妈 mā	麻 má	马 mǎ	骂 mà	吗 ma
（阴平）	（阳平）	（上声）	（去声）	（轻声）
1st tone	2nd tone	3rd tone	4th tone	neutral tone

四、隔音符号　The Dividing Sign

a，o，e 开头的音节连接在其他音节后面的时候，如果音节的界限发生混淆，用隔音符号（'）隔开，例如：pí'ǎo, hǎi'ōu, míng'é。

When a syllable beginning with a, o, e is immediately preceded by a syllable such that it is likely to be confused with another syllable, the dividing sign （'） is used，e. g. pí'ǎo, hǎi'ōu, míng'é.

（二）常用标点符号用法简表
Common Punctuation

名　称 Name	符　号 Punctu-ation Mark	用 法 说 明 Usage	举　例 Example
句　号 Period	。	表示一句话完了之后的停顿。 indicates the end of a sentence	虚心使人进步,骄傲使人落后。
逗　号 Comma	,	表示一句话中间的停顿。 indicates a pause within a sentence	对于北京,他并不陌生。
顿　号 Pause Mark	、	表示句中并列的词或词组之间的停顿。 indicates a short pause between items of a series	中国古代有许多重要发明,比如指南针、造纸、印刷术、火药等。
分　号 Semicolon	;	用于分句之间,表示大于逗号而小于句号的停顿。 indicates a longer pause than comma between coordinate clauses	语言,人们用来抒情达意;文字,人们用来记言记事。
冒　号 Colon	:	用以提示下文。 introduces a quotation, explanation, etc.	各位代表:现在会议正式开始。
问　号 Question Mark	?	用在问句之后。 used at the end of an interrogative sentence	刚才谁来了? 这个问题是怎样解决的?
感叹号 Exclamation Mark	!	表示强烈的感情。 used at the end of an exclamatory sentence	啊!多美呀! 我多么想看看她呀!

名　称 Name	符号 Punctu- ation Mark	用法说明 Usage	举　例 Example
引号 Quotation Marks	"　" '　'	1. 表示引用的部分。常用的是双引号（"　"）。引号中再用引号时，用单引号（'　'）。 Double quotation marks are used to indicate a quotation or direct speech. If there is a quotation within a quotation, single quotation marks are used.	小王说："我同意大家的意见。" 　老师问学生："你们懂得'青出于蓝'的意思吗?"
		2. 表示特定的称谓或需要着重指出的部分。 distinguish a term or phrase from the rest of the text	"教师"是个光荣的职业。 　"有物有序"是古人对于写文章的两个基本要求。"有物"就是要有内容，"有序"就是要有条理。
		3. 表示讽刺的意思。 used with an ironic implication	这样的"聪明人"，实在还是少一点好。
括　号 Parentheses	（　）	表示文中注释的部分。 mark off explanatory or qualifying remarks	中国猿人（全名为"中国猿人北京种"，或简称"北京人"）在我国的发现，是对古人类学的一个重大贡献。
省略号 Suspension Points	……	表示文中省略的部分。用六个圆点，占两个字的位置。 six dots, indicating the omission of a word or words	菜市场里，蔬菜很多，有白菜、黄瓜、西红柿、豆角儿……真是琳琅满目!

名　称 Name	符　号 Punctu- ation Mark	用　法　说　明 Usage	举　　例 Example
破折号 Dash	——	在文中占两个字的位置。 1.表示下面是解释说明的部分,有括号的作用。 a line occupying a space of two characters, sets off a parenthetical phrase or clause	世界闻名的伟大建筑——万里长城,在两千多年前的秦代已经建成。
		2.表示意思的递进。 indicates a progression in meaning	某种理论认为:认识世界要经历实践——认识——再实践——再认识的过程。
		3.表示意思的转折。 indicates a shift in meaning	海上的渔船可以随时了解风情,及时避入渔港——不过,有时意料不到,也会出事。
连接号 Hyphen	—	1.表示时间、地点、数目等的起止。在文中占一个字或两个字的位置。 indicates beginning and end, used between places, times, numbers, etc. It takes the space of one or two characters	1949年—1979年 "北京—上海"直达快车
		2.表示相关的人或事物的联系。 indicates some relationship between persons or things	我国秦岭—淮河以北地区属于温带季风气候区,夏季高温多雨,冬季寒冷干燥。

名　称 Name	符号 Punctu- ation Mark	用法说明 Usage	举　例 Example
书名号 Title Marks	《　》 〈　〉	表示书籍、文件、报刊、文章等的名称。 used around titles of books, articles, newspapers, journals, etc.	《红楼梦》 《人民日报》 《〈中国工人〉发刊词》
间隔号 Separation Dot	·	1. 表示月份和日期之间的分界。 separates the day from the month	十·一
		2. 表示有些民族人名中，名、父名、姓等的分界。 separates the different parts of some foreign full names	列奥纳多·达·芬奇 爱新觉罗·努尔哈赤
着重号 Mark of Emphasis	·	放在文中需要强调部分的每个字下面。 a dot under each character of the part of text which needs to be emphasized	工艺美术应在保持传统特色的基础上，进一步革新和提高。

（三）繁简体字对照表
List of Simplified Characters and Their Original Complex Forms

七画
〔車〕车
〔夾〕夹
〔貝〕贝
〔見〕见
〔壯〕壮
〔妝〕妆

八画
【一】
〔長〕长
〔亞〕亚
〔軋〕轧
〔東〕东
〔兩〕两
〔協〕协
〔來〕来
〔戔〕戋
【丨】
〔門〕门
〔岡〕冈
【丿】
〔侖〕仑
〔兒〕儿
【乛】
〔狀〕状
〔糾〕纠

九画
【一】
〔剋〕克
〔軌〕轨
〔庫〕库
〔頁〕页
〔郟〕郏
〔剄〕刭
〔勁〕劲
【丨】
〔貞〕贞
〔則〕则
〔閂〕闩
〔迴〕回
【丿】
〔俠〕侠
〔係〕系
〔鳧〕凫
〔帥〕帅
〔後〕后
〔釓〕钆
〔釔〕钇
〔負〕负
〔風〕风
【丶】
〔訂〕订
〔計〕计
〔訃〕讣
〔軍〕军
〔衹〕只
【乛】
〔陣〕阵
〔韋〕韦
〔陝〕陕
〔陘〕陉
〔飛〕飞
〔紆〕纡
〔紅〕红
〔紂〕纣
〔紈〕纨
〔級〕级
〔約〕约
〔紇〕纥
〔紀〕纪
〔紉〕纫

十画
【一】
〔馬〕马
〔挾〕挟
〔貢〕贡
〔埡〕垭
〔華〕华
〔萊〕莱
〔莖〕茎
〔莧〕苋
〔莊〕庄
〔軒〕轩
〔連〕连
〔軔〕轫
〔劃〕划
【丨】
〔鬥〕斗
〔時〕时
〔畢〕毕
〔財〕财
〔覎〕觃
〔閃〕闪
〔唄〕呗
〔員〕员
〔豈〕岂
〔峽〕峡
〔峴〕岘
〔剛〕刚
〔剮〕剐
【丿】
〔氣〕气
〔郵〕邮
〔倀〕伥
〔倆〕俩
〔條〕条
〔們〕们
〔個〕个
〔倫〕伦
〔隻〕只
〔島〕岛
〔烏〕乌
〔師〕师
〔徑〕径
〔釘〕钉
〔針〕针
〔釗〕钊
〔釙〕钋
〔殺〕杀
〔倉〕仓
〔飢〕饥
〔脅〕胁
〔狹〕狭
〔狽〕狈
〔芻〕刍
【丶】
〔訐〕讦
〔訌〕讧
〔討〕讨
〔訕〕讪
〔訖〕讫
〔訓〕训
〔這〕这
〔訊〕讯
〔記〕记
〔凍〕冻
〔畝〕亩
〔庫〕库
〔浹〕浃
〔涇〕泾
【乛】
〔書〕书
〔陸〕陆
〔陳〕陈
〔孫〕孙
〔陰〕阴
〔務〕务
〔紜〕纭
〔純〕纯
〔紕〕纰
〔紗〕纱
〔納〕纳
〔紝〕纴
〔紛〕纷
〔紙〕纸
〔紋〕纹
〔紡〕纺
〔紐〕纽
〔紓〕纾

十一画
【一】
〔責〕责
〔現〕现
〔匭〕匦
〔規〕规
〔殼〕壳
〔堊〕垩
〔掗〕挜
〔捨〕舍
〔捫〕扪
〔摳〕抠
〔堝〕埚
〔頂〕顶
〔掄〕抡
〔執〕执
〔捲〕卷
〔掃〕扫
〔萵〕莴
〔乾〕干
〔梘〕枧
〔軛〕轭
〔斬〕斩
〔軟〕软
〔專〕专
〔區〕区
〔堅〕坚
〔帶〕带
〔厠〕厕
〔硃〕朱
〔麥〕麦
〔頃〕顷
【丨】
〔鹵〕卤
〔處〕处
〔敗〕败
〔販〕贩
〔貶〕贬
〔啞〕哑
〔閉〕闭
〔問〕问
〔婁〕娄
〔啢〕唡
〔國〕国
〔喎〕㖞
〔帳〕帐
〔崬〕岽
〔崍〕崃
〔崗〕岗
〔圇〕囵
〔過〕过
【丿】
〔氫〕氢
〔動〕动
〔偵〕侦
〔側〕侧
〔貨〕货
〔進〕进
〔梟〕枭
〔鳥〕鸟
〔偉〕伟
〔徠〕徕
〔術〕术
〔從〕从
〔釬〕钎
〔釩〕钒
〔釧〕钏
〔釤〕钐
〔釣〕钓
〔釹〕钕
〔釵〕钗
〔貪〕贪
〔覓〕觅
〔飥〕饦
〔貧〕贫
〔脛〕胫
〔魚〕鱼
【丶】
〔詎〕讵
〔訝〕讶
〔訥〕讷
〔許〕许
〔訛〕讹
〔訢〕䜣
〔訩〕讻
〔設〕设
〔訪〕访
〔訣〕诀
〔產〕产
〔牽〕牵
〔烴〕烃
〔淶〕涞
〔淺〕浅
〔渦〕涡
〔淪〕沦
〔悵〕怅
〔鄆〕郓
〔啟〕启
〔視〕视
【乛】
〔晝〕昼
〔張〕张
〔將〕将
〔階〕阶
〔陽〕阳
〔隊〕队
〔婭〕娅
〔媧〕娲
〔婦〕妇
〔習〕习
〔參〕参
〔貫〕贯
〔鄉〕乡
〔紺〕绀
〔紲〕绁
〔紱〕绂
〔組〕组
〔紳〕绅

〔紳〕绅
〔細〕细
〔終〕终
〔絆〕绊
〔紼〕绋
〔絀〕绌
〔紹〕绍
〔給〕给

十二画
【一】
〔貳〕贰
〔預〕预
〔堯〕尧
〔揀〕拣
〔馭〕驭
〔項〕项
〔賁〕贲
〔場〕场
〔揚〕扬
〔塊〕块
〔達〕达
〔報〕报
〔揮〕挥
〔壺〕壶
〔惡〕恶
〔葉〕叶
〔貰〕贳
〔萬〕万
〔葷〕荤
〔喪〕丧
〔葦〕苇
〔葒〕荭
〔葤〕荮
〔棖〕枨
〔棟〕栋
〔棧〕栈
〔椏〕桠
〔極〕极
〔軲〕轱
〔軻〕轲
〔軸〕轴
〔軼〕轶
〔軫〕轸

〔軺〕轺
〔畫〕画
〔腎〕肾
〔棗〕枣
〔硨〕砗
〔硤〕硖
〔硯〕砚
〔殘〕残
〔雲〕云
【丨】
〔覘〕觇
〔睏〕困
〔貼〕贴
〔貺〕贶
〔貯〕贮
〔貽〕贻
〔閏〕闰
〔開〕开
〔閑〕闲
〔間〕间
〔閔〕闵
〔悶〕闷
〔貴〕贵
〔鄖〕郧
〔勛〕勋
〔單〕单
〔喲〕哟
〔買〕买
〔剴〕剀
〔凱〕凯
〔幀〕帧
〔嵐〕岚
〔幗〕帼
〔圍〕围
【丿】
〔無〕无
〔氫〕氢
〔喬〕乔
〔筆〕笔
〔備〕备
〔貸〕贷
〔順〕顺
〔傖〕伧
〔傴〕伛
〔傢〕家

〔鄔〕邬
〔衆〕众
〔復〕复
〔須〕须
〔鈃〕钘
〔鈣〕钙
〔鈈〕钚
〔鈦〕钛
〔鈍〕钝
〔鈔〕钞
〔鈉〕钠
〔鈴〕铃
〔欽〕钦
〔鈞〕钧
〔鈎〕钩
〔鈧〕钪
〔鈁〕钫
〔鈕〕钮
〔鈀〕钯
〔傘〕伞
〔爺〕爷
〔創〕创
〔飩〕饨
〔飪〕饪
〔飫〕饫
〔飭〕饬
〔飯〕饭
〔飲〕饮
〔爲〕为
〔脹〕胀
〔腖〕胨
〔腡〕脶
〔勝〕胜
〔猶〕犹
〔貿〕贸
〔鄒〕邹
【丶】
〔詁〕诂
〔詞〕词
〔評〕评
〔詛〕诅
〔詞〕词

〔詐〕诈
〔訴〕诉
〔診〕诊
〔詆〕诋
〔詘〕诎
〔詔〕诏
〔詒〕诒
〔馮〕冯
〔痙〕痉
〔勞〕劳
〔滇〕滇
〔測〕测
〔湯〕汤
〔淵〕渊
〔渢〕沨
〔渾〕浑
〔愜〕惬
〔惻〕恻
〔惲〕恽
〔惱〕恼
〔運〕运
〔補〕补
〔禍〕祸
【乛】
〔尋〕寻
〔費〕费
〔違〕违
〔韌〕韧
〔隕〕陨
〔賀〕贺
〔發〕发
〔綁〕绑
〔絨〕绒
〔結〕结
〔綆〕绠
〔經〕经
〔絎〕绗
〔給〕给
〔絢〕绚
〔絳〕绛
〔絡〕络
〔絞〕绞
〔統〕统
〔絕〕绝

〔絲〕丝
〔幾〕几

十三画
【一】
〔頊〕顼
〔琿〕珲
〔瑋〕玮
〔頑〕顽
〔載〕载
〔馱〕驮
〔馴〕驯
〔馳〕驰
〔塒〕埘
〔塤〕埙
〔損〕损
〔遠〕远
〔塏〕垲
〔勢〕势
〔搶〕抢
〔搗〕捣
〔塢〕坞
〔聖〕圣
〔蓋〕盖
〔蓮〕莲
〔蒔〕莳
〔蓽〕荜
〔夢〕梦
〔蒼〕苍
〔幹〕干
〔蓀〕荪
〔蔭〕荫
〔蒓〕莼
〔楨〕桢
〔楊〕杨
〔嗇〕啬
〔楓〕枫
〔軾〕轼
〔輕〕轻
〔輅〕辂
〔較〕较
〔竪〕竖
〔賈〕贾
〔匯〕汇

〔電〕电
〔頓〕顿
〔盞〕盏
【丨】
〔歲〕岁
〔虜〕虏
〔業〕业
〔當〕当
〔睞〕睐
〔賊〕贼
〔賄〕贿
〔賂〕赂
〔賅〕赅
〔嗎〕吗
〔嗶〕哔
〔嗊〕唝
〔暘〕旸
〔閘〕闸
〔黽〕黾
〔暈〕晕
〔號〕号
〔園〕园
〔蛺〕蛱
〔蜆〕蚬
〔農〕农
〔嗩〕唢
〔嘩〕哗
〔嗚〕呜
〔嗆〕呛
〔圓〕圆
【丿】
〔筧〕笕
〔節〕节
〔與〕与
〔債〕债
〔僅〕仅
〔傳〕传
〔傾〕倾
〔僂〕偻
〔賃〕赁
〔傷〕伤
〔傭〕佣
〔裊〕袅

〔顧〕顾
〔鈺〕钰
〔鉦〕钲
〔鉗〕钳
〔鈷〕钴
〔鉢〕钵
〔鉅〕钜
〔鈳〕钶
〔鈸〕钹
〔鉞〕钺
〔鉬〕钼
〔鉭〕钽
〔鉀〕钾
〔鈾〕铀
〔鉑〕铂
〔鈴〕铃
〔鉛〕铅
〔鉚〕铆
〔鈰〕铈
〔鉉〕铉
〔鉈〕铊
〔鉍〕铋
〔鈮〕铌
〔鈹〕铍
〔僉〕佥
〔會〕会
〔亂〕乱
〔愛〕爱
〔飾〕饰
〔飽〕饱
〔飼〕饲
〔飴〕饴
〔頒〕颁
〔頌〕颂
〔腸〕肠
〔腫〕肿
〔腦〕脑
〔魛〕鱽
〔鳩〕鸠
〔獅〕狮
〔猻〕狲
【丶】

〔誆〕诓
〔誄〕诔
〔試〕试
〔詿〕诖
〔詩〕诗
〔詰〕诘
〔誇〕夸
〔詼〕诙
〔誠〕诚
〔誅〕诛
〔話〕话
〔誕〕诞
〔詬〕诟
〔詮〕诠
〔詭〕诡
〔詢〕询
〔詣〕诣
〔該〕该
〔詳〕详
〔詫〕诧
〔詡〕诩
〔裏〕里
〔準〕准
〔頏〕颃
〔資〕资
〔羥〕羟
〔義〕义
〔煉〕炼
〔煩〕烦
〔煬〕炀
〔塋〕茔
〔熒〕荥
〔煒〕炜
〔遞〕递
〔溝〕沟
〔漣〕涟
〔滅〕灭
〔溳〕涢
〔滌〕涤
〔滻〕浐
〔塗〕涂
〔滄〕沧
〔愷〕恺
〔愾〕忾

〔憺〕怕
〔憫〕悯
〔窩〕窝
〔禎〕祯
〔禕〕祎
【乛】
〔肅〕肃
〔裝〕装
〔遜〕逊
〔際〕际
〔媽〕妈
〔預〕预
〔彙〕汇
〔綆〕绠
〔經〕经
〔綃〕绡
〔絹〕绢
〔綉〕绣
〔綏〕绥
〔綈〕绨

十四画

【一】
〔瑪〕玛
〔璉〕琏
〔瑣〕琐
〔瑲〕玱
〔駁〕驳
〔摶〕抟
〔摳〕抠
〔趙〕赵
〔趕〕赶
〔摟〕搂
〔摑〕掴
〔臺〕台
〔摘〕抟
〔墊〕垫
〔壽〕寿
〔摺〕折
〔摻〕掺
〔摃〕㧏
〔勩〕勚
〔蔞〕蒌
〔蔦〕茑
〔蓯〕苁

〔蔔〕卜
〔蔣〕蒋
〔薌〕芗
〔構〕构
〔樺〕桦
〔榿〕桤
〔覡〕觋
〔槍〕枪
〔輒〕辄
〔輔〕辅
〔輕〕轻
〔塹〕堑
〔匱〕匮
〔監〕监
〔緊〕紧
〔厲〕厉
〔厭〕厌
〔碩〕硕
〔碭〕砀
〔颯〕飒
〔盦〕盦
〔爾〕尔
〔奪〕夺
〔殞〕殒
〔鳶〕鸢
〔甄〕甑
〔僕〕仆
〔僑〕侨
〔僞〕伪
【丨】
〔對〕对
〔幣〕币
〔彆〕别
〔嘗〕尝
〔嘖〕啧
〔曄〕晔
〔夥〕伙
〔賑〕赈
〔賒〕赊
〔嘆〕叹
〔暢〕畅
〔嘜〕唛
〔閨〕闺
〔聞〕闻
〔閩〕闽
〔閭〕闾
〔閥〕阀
〔閤〕合

〔閡〕阂
〔闍〕阇
〔閿〕阌
〔嘔〕呕
〔蝸〕蜗
〔團〕团
〔嘍〕喽
〔鄲〕郸
〔鳴〕鸣
〔幘〕帻
〔嶄〕崭
〔嶇〕岖
〔罰〕罚
〔嶁〕嵝
〔幗〕帼
〔圖〕图
【丿】
〔製〕制
〔種〕种
〔稱〕称
〔箋〕笺
〔僥〕侥
〔債〕债
〔僕〕仆
〔僑〕侨
〔僞〕伪
〔銜〕衔
〔鉶〕铏
〔鋅〕锌
〔銬〕铐
〔鉺〕铒
〔鉻〕铬
〔銠〕铑
〔鉿〕铪
〔銪〕铕
〔銍〕铚

〔鉻〕铬
〔錚〕铮
〔銫〕铯
〔鉸〕铰
〔銥〕铱
〔銃〕铳
〔銨〕铵
〔銀〕银
〔銣〕铷
〔餓〕饿
〔餌〕饵
〔蝕〕蚀
〔餉〕饷
〔餄〕饸
〔餎〕饹
〔餃〕饺
〔餏〕饻
〔餅〕饼
〔領〕领
〔鳳〕凤
〔颱〕台
〔獄〕狱
【丶】
〔誡〕诫
〔誣〕诬
〔語〕语
〔誚〕诮
〔誤〕误
〔誥〕诰
〔誘〕诱
〔誨〕诲
〔誑〕诳
〔說〕说
〔認〕认
〔誦〕诵
〔誒〕诶
〔廣〕广
〔麽〕么
〔廎〕庼
〔瘞〕瘗
〔瘍〕疡
〔瘋〕疯
〔塵〕尘
〔颯〕飒
〔適〕适

〔齊〕齐
〔養〕养
〔鄰〕邻
〔鄭〕郑
〔燁〕烨
〔熗〕炝
〔榮〕荣
〔縈〕萦
〔犖〕荦
〔熒〕荧
〔漬〕渍
〔漢〕汉
〔滿〕满
〔漸〕渐
〔漚〕沤
〔滯〕滞
〔滷〕卤
〔漊〕溇
〔漁〕渔
〔滸〕浒
〔滻〕浐
〔滬〕沪
〔漲〕涨
〔滲〕渗
〔慚〕惭
〔慪〕怄
〔慳〕悭
〔慟〕恸
〔慘〕惨
〔慣〕惯
〔寬〕宽
〔賓〕宾
〔窪〕洼
〔寧〕宁
〔寢〕寝
〔實〕实
〔鞁〕鞴
〔複〕复
【乛】
〔劃〕划
〔盡〕尽
〔屢〕屡
〔獎〕奖
〔墮〕堕
〔隨〕随

〔皸〕皲
〔墜〕坠
〔嫗〕妪
〔顒〕颙
〔態〕态
〔鄧〕邓
〔緒〕绪
〔綾〕绫
〔綺〕绮
〔綫〕线
〔緋〕绯
〔綽〕绰
〔緄〕绲
〔綱〕纲
〔網〕网
〔維〕维
〔綿〕绵
〔綸〕纶
〔綬〕绶
〔綳〕绷
〔綢〕绸
〔綹〕绺
〔綣〕绻
〔綜〕综
〔綻〕绽
〔綰〕绾
〔綠〕绿
〔綴〕缀
〔緇〕缁

十五画

【一】
〔鬧〕闹
〔璡〕琎
〔靚〕靓
〔輦〕辇
〔髮〕发
〔撓〕挠
〔墳〕坟
〔撾〕挝
〔駔〕驵
〔駛〕驶
〔駟〕驷
〔駙〕驸
〔駒〕驹

〔駐〕驻
〔駝〕驼
〔駘〕骀
〔撲〕扑
〔頡〕颉
〔撣〕掸
〔賣〕卖
〔撫〕抚
〔撟〕挢
〔撳〕揿
〔熱〕热
〔鞏〕巩
〔摯〕挚
〔撈〕捞
〔穀〕谷
〔慤〕悫
〔撏〕挦
〔撥〕拨
〔蕘〕荛
〔蕆〕芨
〔蕓〕芸
〔蕢〕蒉
〔蕒〕荬
〔蕪〕芜
〔蕎〕荞
〔蕕〕莸
〔蕩〕荡
〔蕁〕荨
〔樁〕桩
〔樞〕枢
〔標〕标
〔樓〕楼
〔樅〕枞
〔麩〕麸
〔賫〕赍
〔樣〕样
〔橢〕椭
〔輛〕辆
〔輥〕辊
〔輞〕辋
〔槧〕椠
〔暫〕暂
〔輪〕轮
〔輟〕辍
〔輜〕辎

〔輻〕辐
〔甌〕瓯
〔歐〕欧
〔毆〕殴
〔賢〕贤
〔遷〕迁
〔鴉〕鸦
〔憂〕忧
〔碼〕码
〔磑〕硙
〔磣〕碜
〔確〕确
〔賚〕赉
〔遼〕辽
〔殤〕殇
〔鴉〕鸦
【丨】
〔輩〕辈
〔劌〕刿
〔齒〕齿
〔劇〕剧
〔膚〕肤
〔慮〕虑
〔鄴〕邺
〔輝〕辉
〔賞〕赏
〔賦〕赋
〔腈〕腈
〔賬〕账
〔賭〕赌
〔賤〕贱
〔賜〕赐
〔賙〕赒
〔賠〕赔
〔賧〕赕
〔嘵〕哓
〔噴〕喷
〔嘩〕哗
〔噠〕哒
〔噁〕恶
〔閫〕阃
〔閬〕阆
〔閱〕阅
〔閾〕阈
〔數〕数
〔踐〕践
〔遺〕遗

〔蝦〕虾
〔嘸〕呒
〔嘮〕唠
〔噷〕唑
〔嘰〕叽
〔嶢〕峣
〔罷〕罢
〔嶠〕峤
〔嶔〕嵚
〔幟〕帜
〔嶗〕崂
【丿】
〔頲〕颋
〔篋〕箧
〔範〕范
〔價〕价
〔儂〕侬
〔儉〕俭
〔儈〕侩
〔億〕亿
〔儀〕仪
〔皚〕皑
〔樂〕乐
〔質〕质
〔徵〕征
〔衝〕冲
〔慫〕怂
〔徹〕彻
〔衛〕卫
〔盤〕盘
〔鋪〕铺
〔鋏〕铗
〔鋱〕铽
〔銷〕销
〔鋰〕锂
〔鋇〕钡
〔鋤〕锄
〔鋯〕锆
〔鋨〕锇
〔銹〕锈
〔銼〕锉
〔鋒〕锋
〔鋅〕锌
〔銳〕锐

〔鋃〕锒
〔鋥〕锃
〔鋼〕钢
〔鋦〕锔
〔賡〕赓
〔慶〕庆
〔廢〕废
〔敵〕敌
〔頦〕颏
〔劍〕剑
〔劊〕刽
〔鄶〕郐
〔餑〕饽
〔餓〕饿
〔餘〕余
〔餒〕馁
〔膞〕䏝
〔膠〕胶
〔鴇〕鸨
〔魷〕鱿
〔魯〕鲁
〔魴〕鲂
〔潁〕颍
〔颳〕刮
〔劉〕刘
〔皺〕皱
【丶】
〔請〕请
〔諸〕诸
〔諏〕诹
〔諾〕诺
〔諑〕诼
〔誹〕诽
〔課〕课
〔諉〕诿
〔誶〕谇
〔談〕谈
〔誼〕谊
〔諒〕谅
〔諄〕谆
〔誶〕谇
〔廟〕庙

〔廠〕厂
〔廡〕庑
〔瘞〕瘗
〔瘡〕疮
〔導〕导
〔瑩〕莹
〔潔〕洁
〔澆〕浇
〔澾〕达
〔潤〕润
〔澗〕涧
〔潰〕溃
〔潿〕涠
〔潷〕滗
〔澇〕涝
〔潯〕浔
〔潑〕泼
〔憤〕愤
〔憫〕悯
〔憒〕愦
〔憚〕惮
〔憮〕怃
〔憐〕怜
〔寫〕写
〔審〕审
〔窮〕穷
〔褸〕褛
〔褲〕裤
〔誰〕谁
〔論〕论
〔諗〕谂
〔調〕调
〔諂〕谄
〔誶〕谇
〔談〕谈

〔駕〕驾
〔嬋〕婵
〔薑〕姜
〔嬌〕娇
〔嫵〕妩
〔嬀〕妫
〔駑〕驽
〔犛〕牦
〔緙〕缂
〔緗〕缃
〔緹〕缇
〔緲〕缈
〔緝〕缉
〔緼〕缊
〔緦〕缌
〔緞〕缎
〔緱〕缑
〔編〕编
〔緡〕缗
〔緯〕纬
〔緣〕缘

十六画
【一】
〔璣〕玑
〔墻〕墙
〔駱〕骆
〔駭〕骇
【乛】
〔遲〕迟
〔層〕层
〔彈〕弹
〔選〕选
〔槳〕桨
〔漿〕浆
〔險〕险
〔嬈〕娆
〔嬌〕娇
〔嬙〕嫱
〔壇〕坛
〔擁〕拥

〔據〕据
〔薔〕蔷
〔薑〕姜
〔薊〕蓟
〔薦〕荐
〔蕭〕萧
〔頤〕颐
〔曇〕昙
〔鴣〕鸪
〔薩〕萨
〔蕷〕蓣
〔嘵〕哓
〔踴〕踊
〔螞〕蚂
〔螄〕蛳
〔樸〕朴
〔橋〕桥
〔機〕机
〔輳〕辏
〔輻〕辐
〔輯〕辑
〔輸〕输
〔賴〕赖
〔頭〕头
〔醜〕丑
〔勵〕励
〔磧〕碛
〔磚〕砖
〔磽〕硗
〔歷〕历
〔曆〕历
〔奮〕奋
〔篳〕筚
〔篩〕筛
〔舉〕举
〔興〕兴
〔嶨〕峃
【丨】
〔盧〕卢
〔曉〕晓
〔瞞〕瞒
〔縣〕县
〔膃〕腽
〔瞜〕䁖
〔鴨〕鸭

〔閫〕阃
〔鬮〕阄
〔閶〕阊
〔閿〕阌
〔閣〕阁
〔閡〕阂
〔曇〕昙
〔噸〕吨
〔鴞〕鸮
〔曄〕晔
〔踹〕踹
〔螞〕蚂
〔噹〕当
〔罵〕骂
〔噥〕哝
〔戰〕战
〔噲〕哙
〔鴦〕鸯
〔曖〕暖
〔嘯〕啸
〔還〕还
〔嶧〕峄
〔嶼〕屿
【丿】
〔積〕积
〔頹〕颓
〔穇〕穇
〔墾〕垦
〔餞〕饯
〔餜〕馃
〔餛〕馄
〔餡〕馅
〔館〕馆
〔頷〕颔
〔鴒〕鸰
〔膩〕腻
〔鷗〕鸥
〔鮁〕鲅
〔鮃〕鲆
〔鮎〕鲇
〔鮓〕鲊
〔穌〕稣
〔鮒〕鲋
〔艙〕舱
〔錶〕表

〔鍺〕锗
〔錯〕错
〔錨〕锚
〔錛〕锛
〔錸〕铼
〔錢〕钱
〔鍀〕锝
〔錁〕锞
〔錕〕锟
〔鍆〕钔
〔錫〕锡
〔錮〕锢
〔鍋〕锅
〔錘〕锤
〔錐〕锥
〔錦〕锦
〔鍁〕锨
〔錇〕锫
〔錠〕锭
〔鍵〕键
〔錄〕录
〔鋸〕锯
〔錳〕锰
〔錙〕锱
〔錩〕锠
〔艦〕舰
〔餳〕饧
〔餶〕馉
〔餒〕馁
〔餜〕馃
〔餛〕馄
〔膾〕脍
〔鴟〕鸱
〔鮐〕鲐
〔鮒〕鲋
〔鮃〕鲆
〔鮑〕鲍
〔鴿〕鸽
〔膕〕腘
〔臉〕脸
〔鮊〕鲃
〔卿〕卿
〔鮑〕鲍

〔鮁〕鲅
〔鮊〕鲃
〔鴝〕鸲
〔獷〕犷
〔穎〕颖
〔獨〕独
〔獫〕猃
〔獪〕狯
〔鴛〕鸳
【丶】
〔謀〕谋
〔諶〕谌
〔諜〕谍
〔謊〕谎
〔諫〕谏
〔諧〕谐
〔謔〕谑
〔謁〕谒
〔謂〕谓
〔諤〕谔
〔諭〕谕
〔諼〕谖
〔諷〕讽
〔諮〕谘
〔諳〕谙
〔諺〕谚
〔諦〕谛
〔謎〕谜
〔諢〕诨
〔諞〕谝
〔諱〕讳
〔憑〕凭
〔鄺〕邝
〔瘻〕瘘
〔瘮〕瘆
〔親〕亲
〔辦〕办
〔龍〕龙
〔劑〕剂
〔燒〕烧
〔燜〕焖
〔熾〕炽
〔螢〕萤
〔營〕营

〔縈〕萦
〔燈〕灯
〔濛〕蒙
〔燙〕烫
〔澠〕渑
〔濃〕浓
〔澤〕泽
〔濁〕浊
〔澮〕浍
〔澱〕淀
〔懞〕蒙
〔懌〕怿
〔憶〕忆
〔憲〕宪
〔窺〕窥
〔窶〕窭
〔褸〕褛
〔禪〕禅

【フ】
〔隱〕隐
〔嬙〕嫱
〔嬡〕嫒
〔縉〕缙
〔縝〕缜
〔縛〕缚
〔縟〕缛
〔緻〕致
〔縋〕缒
〔縫〕缝
〔縐〕绉
〔縭〕缡
〔縑〕缣
〔縊〕缢

十七画

【一】
〔耬〕耧
〔環〕环
〔贅〕赘
〔璦〕瑷
〔覯〕觏

〔黿〕鼋
〔幫〕帮
〔騁〕骋
〔駸〕骎
〔駿〕骏
〔趨〕趋
〔擱〕搁
〔擬〕拟
〔擴〕扩
〔壙〕圹
〔擠〕挤
〔蟄〕蛰
〔縶〕絷
〔擲〕掷
〔擯〕摈
〔擰〕拧
〔轂〕毂
〔聲〕声
〔藉〕借
〔聰〕聪
〔聯〕联
〔艱〕艰
〔藍〕蓝
〔舊〕旧
〔薺〕荠
〔薟〕蔹
〔韓〕韩
〔隸〕隶
〔檉〕柽
〔檣〕樯
〔檟〕槚
〔檔〕档
〔櫛〕栉
〔檢〕检
〔檜〕桧
〔麯〕曲
〔轅〕辕
〔轄〕辖
〔擊〕击
〔臨〕临
〔磽〕硗
〔壓〕压
〔礄〕硚
〔磯〕矶

〔鴯〕鸸
〔邇〕迩
〔尷〕尴
〔鷙〕鸷
〔殮〕殓

【丨】
〔齔〕龀
〔戲〕戏
〔虧〕亏
〔斃〕毙
〔瞭〕了
〔顆〕颗
〔購〕购
〔賻〕赙
〔嬰〕婴
〔賺〕赚
〔嚇〕吓
〔闌〕阑
〔闃〕阒
〔闆〕板
〔闊〕阔
〔闈〕闱
〔闋〕阕
〔曖〕暧
〔蹕〕跸
〔蹌〕跄
〔蟎〕螨
〔螻〕蝼
〔蟈〕蝈
〔雖〕虽
〔嚀〕咛
〔覬〕觊
〔嶺〕岭
〔嶸〕嵘
〔點〕点

【丿】
〔矯〕矫
〔鴰〕鸹
〔簣〕篑
〔簍〕篓
〔輿〕舆
〔歟〕欤
〔鵂〕鸺
〔龜〕龟
〔優〕优

〔償〕偿
〔儲〕储
〔魎〕魉
〔鴿〕鸽
〔禦〕御
〔聳〕耸
〔鵑〕鹃
〔鍥〕锲
〔鍇〕锴
〔鍘〕铡
〔錫〕锡
〔鍶〕锶
〔鍔〕锷
〔鍤〕锸
〔鍾〕钟
〔鍛〕锻
〔鎪〕锼
〔鍬〕锹
〔鍰〕锾
〔鎩〕铩
〔鍍〕镀
〔鎂〕镁
〔鎇〕镅
〔斂〕敛
〔鵠〕鹄
〔懇〕恳
〔館〕馆
〔鍚〕钖
〔餳〕饧
〔餶〕馉
〔餿〕馊
〔膿〕脓
〔臉〕脸
〔膾〕脍
〔膽〕胆
〔臏〕膑
〔鮭〕鲑
〔鮚〕鲒
〔鮪〕鲔
〔鮦〕鲖
〔鮫〕鲛
〔鮮〕鲜
〔颶〕飓
〔獷〕犷
〔獰〕狞

【丶】
〔講〕讲
〔謨〕谟
〔謖〕谡
〔謝〕谢
〔謠〕谣
〔謅〕诌
〔謗〕谤
〔謚〕谥
〔謙〕谦
〔謐〕谧
〔褻〕亵
〔氈〕毡
〔應〕应
〔癘〕疠
〔療〕疗
〔癇〕痫
〔癉〕瘅
〔癆〕痨
〔鵁〕鹪
〔齋〕斋
〔鮺〕鲝
〔糞〕粪
〔糝〕糁
〔燦〕灿
〔燭〕烛
〔燴〕烩
〔鴻〕鸿
〔濤〕涛
〔濫〕滥
〔濕〕湿
〔濟〕济
〔濱〕滨
〔濘〕泞
〔澀〕涩
〔濰〕潍
〔懨〕恹
〔賽〕赛
〔襇〕裥
〔襖〕袄
〔禮〕礼

【フ】
〔蟎〕蟎
〔繭〕茧

〔屨〕屦
〔彌〕弥
〔嬪〕嫔
〔嚮〕向
〔績〕绩
〔縹〕缥
〔縷〕缕
〔縵〕缦
〔縲〕缧
〔總〕总
〔縱〕纵
〔縴〕纤
〔縮〕缩
〔繆〕缪
〔繅〕缫

十八画

【一】
〔耮〕耢
〔閿〕阌
〔瓊〕琼
〔攆〕撵
〔鬆〕松
〔翹〕翘
〔擷〕撷
〔騏〕骐
〔騎〕骑
〔騍〕骒
〔騅〕骓
〔擾〕扰
〔擼〕撸
〔擻〕擞
〔攄〕摅
〔擺〕摆
〔贄〕贽
〔燾〕焘
〔聶〕聂
〔聵〕聩
〔職〕职
〔藝〕艺
〔覲〕觐
〔鞦〕秋
〔藪〕薮
〔薑〕姜
〔蠒〕茧

〔藥〕药
〔蕘〕荛
〔蟶〕蛏
〔櫝〕椟
〔櫃〕柜
〔檻〕槛
〔櫚〕榈
〔檳〕槟
〔檸〕柠
〔鵓〕鹁
〔轉〕转
〔轆〕辘
〔醫〕医
〔礎〕础
〔殯〕殡
〔霧〕雾

【丨】
〔豐〕丰
〔覷〕觑
〔懟〕怼
〔叢〕丛
〔矇〕蒙
〔題〕题
〔韙〕韪
〔瞼〕睑
〔闖〕闯
〔闔〕阖
〔闐〕阗
〔闕〕阙
〔顒〕颙
〔曠〕旷
〔蹣〕蹒
〔嚙〕啮
〔壘〕垒
〔蟯〕蛲
〔蟲〕虫
〔蟬〕蝉
〔蟣〕虮
〔嚕〕噜
〔顓〕颛

【丿】
〔鵠〕鹄

〔鵝〕鹅
〔穫〕获
〔穡〕穑
〔穢〕秽
〔簡〕简
〔簀〕箦
〔簞〕箪
〔雙〕双
〔軀〕躯
〔邊〕边
〔歸〕归
〔鏵〕铧
〔鎮〕镇
〔鏈〕链
〔鎘〕镉
〔鎖〕锁
〔鎧〕铠
〔鎸〕镌
〔鎳〕镍
〔鎢〕钨
〔鎿〕镎
〔鎦〕镏
〔鎬〕镐
〔鎊〕镑
〔鎰〕镒
〔鎵〕镓
〔餼〕饩
〔餾〕馏
〔饈〕馐
〔臍〕脐
〔鯁〕鲠
〔鯉〕鲤
〔鯀〕鲧
〔鯇〕鲩
〔鯽〕鲫
〔颼〕飕
〔觴〕觞
〔獵〕猎

〔雛〕雏	〔鵡〕鹉	【丨】	〔鯪〕鲮	〔鶯〕莺	〔韶〕韶	〔齠〕龆
【丶】	〔鵑〕鹃	〔贈〕赠	〔鯫〕鲰	〔顙〕颡	〔獻〕献	〔黷〕黩
〔謹〕谨	〔鬍〕胡	〔闞〕阚	〔鯡〕鲱	〔繮〕缰	〔黨〕党	〔贍〕赡
〔謳〕讴	〔騙〕骗	〔關〕关	〔鯤〕鲲	〔繩〕绳	〔懸〕悬	〔饑〕饥
〔謾〕谩	〔騷〕骚	〔嚦〕呖	〔鯧〕鲳	〔繾〕缱	〔饒〕饶	〔臚〕胪
〔謫〕谪	〔壢〕坜	〔疇〕畴	〔鯢〕鲵	〔繰〕缲	〔饋〕馈	〔朧〕胧
〔謬〕谬	〔壚〕垆	〔蹺〕跷	〔鯰〕鲶	〔繹〕绎	〔饌〕馔	〔騰〕腾
〔癧〕疠	〔壞〕坏	〔蠐〕蛴	〔鯛〕鲷	〔繯〕缳	〔饑〕饥	〔鰭〕鳍
〔雜〕杂	〔攏〕拢	〔蠅〕蝇	〔鯨〕鲸	〔繳〕缴	〔臚〕胪	〔鰣〕鲥
〔離〕离	〔擻〕擞	〔蟻〕蚁	〔鯕〕鲯	〔繪〕绘	〔朧〕胧	〔鰨〕鳎
〔顏〕颜	〔難〕难	〔嚴〕严	〔鯔〕鲻	〔闥〕闼	〔鰵〕鳘	〔鰥〕鳏
〔糧〕粮	〔鵲〕鹊	〔獸〕兽	〔繪〕绘	〔闡〕阐	〔鰷〕鲦	〔鰟〕鳑
〔燼〕烬	〔藶〕苈	〔嚨〕咙	二十画	〔鶡〕鹖	〔鰜〕鳒	〔鰩〕鳐
〔鵜〕鹈	〔蘋〕苹	〔羆〕罴	【一】	〔矓〕昽	〔鰟〕鳑	〔鰮〕鳁
〔瀆〕渎	〔蘆〕芦	〔羅〕罗	〔瓏〕珑	〔蠣〕蛎	〔獼〕猕	〔鰳〕鳓
〔瀦〕潴	〔鵓〕鹁	【丿】	〔驁〕骜	〔蟶〕蛏	〔觸〕触	〔鰾〕鳔
〔濾〕滤	〔藺〕蔺	〔氌〕氇	〔驊〕骅	〔蠑〕蝾	【丶】	〔鱅〕鳙
〔鯊〕鲨	〔蘄〕蕲	〔犢〕犊	〔騶〕驺	〔蠐〕蛴	〔護〕护	〔鰼〕鳛
〔濺〕溅	〔勸〕劝	〔贊〕赞	〔騮〕骝	〔嚶〕嘤	〔譴〕谴	〔玁〕猃
〔瀏〕浏	〔蘇〕苏	〔穩〕稳	〔攖〕撄	〔鶚〕鹗	〔譯〕译	〔觼〕觖
〔濼〕泺	〔藹〕蔼	〔簽〕签	〔攔〕拦	〔髏〕髅	〔譫〕谵	〔韃〕鞑
〔瀉〕泻	〔蘢〕茏	〔簾〕帘	〔攙〕搀	〔鶪〕䴗	〔議〕议	〔韉〕鞯
〔瀋〕沈	〔顛〕颠	〔簫〕箫	〔聹〕聍	【丿】	〔癥〕症	〔歡〕欢
〔竄〕窜	〔櫝〕椟	〔牘〕牍	〔顢〕颟	〔犧〕牺	〔辮〕辫	〔權〕权
〔竅〕窍	〔櫟〕栎	〔懲〕惩	〔驀〕蓦	〔鶩〕鹜	〔襲〕袭	〔櫻〕樱
〔額〕额	〔櫓〕橹	〔鏌〕镆	〔蘭〕兰	〔籌〕筹	〔鐝〕镢	〔欄〕栏
〔襧〕袮	〔櫧〕槠	〔鏗〕铿	〔蘞〕蔹	〔籃〕篮	〔競〕竞	〔轟〕轰
〔襠〕裆	〔櫞〕橼	〔鏢〕镖	〔蘚〕藓	〔譽〕誉	〔贏〕赢	〔覽〕览
〔襝〕裣	〔轎〕轿	〔鏜〕镗	〔鶘〕鹕	〔覺〕觉	〔鐨〕镄	〔酈〕郦
〔禱〕祷	〔鏨〕錾	〔鏤〕镂	〔飄〕飘	〔罌〕罂	〔鐳〕镭	〔飆〕飙
【乛】	〔轍〕辙	〔鏝〕镘	〔櫪〕枥	〔薟〕莶	〔鐿〕镱	〔殲〕殡
〔醬〕酱	〔轔〕辚	〔鏰〕镚	〔櫨〕栌	〔艦〕舰	〔寶〕宝	【丨】
〔輻〕辐	〔繫〕系	〔鏞〕镛	〔櫸〕榉	〔鐃〕铙	〔騫〕骞	〔齜〕龇
〔隴〕陇	〔鶇〕鸫	〔鏡〕镜	〔攀〕攀	〔鐝〕镢	〔寰〕寰	〔齦〕龈
〔嬸〕婶	〔麗〕丽	〔鏟〕铲	〔麵〕面	〔鐐〕镣	〔襬〕摆	〔歔〕歔
〔繞〕绕	〔厴〕厣	〔鏑〕镝	〔櫬〕榇	〔鐦〕锎	二十一画	〔矓〕眬
〔織〕织	〔礪〕砺	〔鏃〕镞	〔櫳〕栊	〔鐧〕锏	【一】	〔囁〕嗫
〔繕〕缮	〔礙〕碍	〔辭〕辞	〔礫〕砾	〔鐫〕镌	〔耀〕耀	〔齕〕龁
〔繒〕缯	〔礦〕矿	〔饉〕馑	【丨】	〔鐠〕镨	〔瓔〕璎	〔闢〕辟
〔斷〕断	〔贋〕赝	〔饅〕馒	〔鹹〕咸	〔鐒〕铹	〔鰲〕鳌	〔囀〕啭
十九画	〔願〕愿	〔鵬〕鹏	〔鹺〕鹾	〔鐋〕铴	〔攝〕摄	〔顥〕颢
【一】	〔鵪〕鹌	〔臘〕腊	〔齟〕龃	〔鐓〕镦	〔騾〕骡	〔躊〕踌
	〔璽〕玺	〔鯖〕鲭	〔齡〕龄	〔鐠〕镨	〔驃〕骠	〔躋〕跻
	〔豶〕豮		〔齣〕出	〔鐥〕䦅	〔驄〕骢	〔躑〕踯
			〔齙〕龅	〔鐔〕镡	〔驂〕骖	〔躋〕跻
				〔饒〕饶	〔釋〕释	〔躍〕跃
					【乛】	
					〔鷓〕鹧	

（四）中国行政区划

Administrative Divisions in China Including Municipalities Directly under the Central Government, Provinces, Autonomous Regions and Special Administrative Regions

名　称 Name	简　称 Abbreviation	省会（或首府） Seat of the Local Government
北京市 Beijing	京 Jing	北京市 Beijing
上海市 Shanghai	沪 Hu	上海市 Shanghai
天津市 Tianjin	津 Jin	天津市 Tianjin
重庆市 Chongqing	渝 Yu	重庆市 Chongqing
河北省 Hebei	冀 Ji	石家庄市 Shijiazhuang
山西省 Shanxi	晋 Jin	太原市 Taiyuan
内蒙古自治区 Nei Mongol 　Autonomous Region	内蒙古 Nei Mongol	呼和浩特市 Huhhot
辽宁省 Liaoning	辽 Liao	沈阳市 Shenyang
吉林省 Jilin	吉 Ji	长春市 Changchun
黑龙江省 Heilongjiang	黑 Hei	哈尔滨市 Harbin
山东省 Shandong	鲁 Lu	济南市 Jinan
河南省 Henan	豫 Yu	郑州市 Zhengzhou
江苏省 Jiangsu	苏 Su	南京市 Nanjing
安徽省 Anhui	皖 Wan	合肥市 Hefei
浙江省 Zhejiang	浙 Zhe	杭州市 Hangzhou
江西省 Jiangxi	赣 Gan	南昌市 Nanchang
福建省 Fujian	闽 Min	福州市 Fuzhou
台湾省 Taiwan	台 Tai	
湖北省 Hubei	鄂 E	武汉市 Wuhan

名 称 Name	简 称 Abbreviation	省会（或首府） Seat of the Local Government
湖南省 Hunan	湘 Xiang	长沙市 Changsha
广东省 Guangdong	粤 Yue	广州市 Guangzhou
海南省 Hainan	琼 Qiong	海口市 Haikou
广西壮族自治区 Guangxi Zhuangzu Autonomous Region	桂 Gui	南宁市 Nanning
甘肃省 Gansu	甘 Gan 陇 Long	兰州市 Lanzhou
青海省 Qinghai	青 Qing	西宁市 Xining
宁夏回族自治区 Ningxia Huizu Autonomous Region	宁 Ning	银川市 Yinchuan
陕西省 Shaanxi	陕 Shan	西安市 Xi'an
新疆维吾尔自治区 Xinjiang Uygur Autonomous Region	新 Xin	乌鲁木齐市 Ürümqi
四川省 Sichuan	川 Chuan 蜀 Shu	成都市 Chengdu
贵州省 Guizhou	贵 Gui 黔 Qian	贵阳市 Guiyang
云南省 Yunnan	云 Yun 滇 Dian	昆明市 Kunming
西藏自治区 Xizang or Tibet Autonomous Region	藏 Zang	拉萨市 Lhasa
香港特别行政区 Hong Kong Special Administrative Region	港 Gang	
澳门特别行政区 Macao Special Administrative Region	澳 Ao	

（五）中国国家机关
China's State Organs

1. 全国人民代表大会	**National People's Congress (NPC)**
主席团	Presidium
常务委员会	Standing Committee
办公厅	General Office
秘书处	Secretariat
代表资格审查委员会	Credentials Committee
提案审查委员会	Motions Examination Committee
民族委员会	Ethnic Affairs Committee
法律委员会	Law Committee
财政经济委员会	Finance and Economy Committee
外事委员会	Foreign Affairs Committee
教育、科学、文化和卫生委员会	Education, Science, Culture and Public Health Committee
内务司法委员会	Committee for Internal and Judicial Affairs
华侨委员会	Overseas Chinese Affairs Committee
法制工作委员会	Commission of Legislative Affairs
特定问题调查委员会	Committee of Inquiry into Specific Questions
宪法修改委员会	Committee for Revision of the Constitution
2. 中华人民共和国主席	**President of the People's Republic of China**
3. 中央军事委员会	**Central Military Commission**
4. 最高人民法院	**Supreme People's Court**
5. 最高人民检察院	**Supreme People's Procuratorate**

6. 国务院	**State Council**
(1) 国务院部委	**Ministries and Commissions Directly under the State Council**
外交部	Ministry of Foreign Affairs
国防部	Ministry of National Defence
国家发展计划委员会	State Development Planning Commission
国家经济贸易委员会	State Economic and Trade Commission
教育部	Ministry of Education
科学技术部	Ministry of Science and Technology
国防科学技术工业委员会	Commission of Science，Technology and Industry for National Defence
国家民族事务委员会	State Ethnic Affairs Commission
公安部	Ministry of Public Security
国家安全部	Ministry of State Security
监察部	Ministry of Supervision
民政部	Ministry of Civil Affairs
司法部	Ministry of Justice
财政部	Ministry of Finance
人事部	Ministry of Personnel
劳动和社会保障部	Ministry of Labour and Social Security
国土资源部	Ministry of Land and Resources
建设部	Ministry of Construction
铁道部	Ministry of Railways
交通部	Ministry of Communications
信息产业部	Ministry of Information Industry
水利部	Ministry of Water Resources
农业部	Ministry of Agriculture
对外贸易经济合作部	Ministry of Foreign Trade and Economic Cooperation
文化部	Ministry of Culture
卫生部	Ministry of Public Health
国家计划生育委员会	State Family Planning Commission
中国人民银行	People's Bank of China

国家审计署	State Auditing Administration
(2)国务院办事机构	**Offices under the State Council**
国务院办公厅	General Office of the State Council
侨务办公室	Office of Overseas Chinese Affairs
港澳事务办公室	Hong Kong and Macao Affairs Office
台湾事务办公室	Taiwan Affairs Office
法制办公室	Office of Legislative Affairs
经济体制改革办公室	Office for Economic Restructuring
国务院研究室	Research Office of the State Council
新闻办公室	Information Office
(3)国务院直属机构	**Departments Directly under the State Council**
海关总署	General Administration of Customs
国家税务总局	State Taxation Administration
国家环境保护总局	State Environmental Protection Administration
中国民用航空总局	Civil Aviation Administration of China (CAAC)
国家广播电影电视总局	State Administration of Radio，Film and Television
国家体育总局	State Physical Culture Administration
国家统计局	State Statistics Bureau
国家工商行政管理局	State Administration of Industry and Commerce
新闻出版总署	Press and Publication Administration
国家版权局	State Copyright Bureau
国家林业局	State Forestry Bureau
国家质量技术监督局	State Bureau of Quality and Technical Supervision
国家药品监督管理局	State Drug Administration (SDA)
国家知识产权局	State Intellectual Property Office (SIPO)
国家旅游局	National Tourism Administration
国家宗教事务局	State Bureau of Religious Affairs

| 国务院参事室 | Counsellors' Office of the State Council |
| 国务院机关事务管理局 | Government Offices Administration of the State Council |

(4)国务院直属事业单位 **Institutions Directly under the State Council**

新华通讯社	Xinhua News Agency
中国科学院	Chinese Academy of Sciences
中国社会科学院	Chinese Academy of Social Sciences
中国工程院	Chinese Academy of Engineering
国务院发展研究中心	Development Research Centre of the State Council
国家行政学院	National School of Administration
中国地震局	China Seismological Bureau
中国气象局	China Meteorological Bureau
中国证券监督管理委员会	China Securities Regulatory Commission (CSRC)

(5)部委管理的国家局 **State Bureaux Administered by Ministries or Commissions**

国家粮食储备局(国家发展计划委员会)	State Bureau of Grain Reserve (under the State Development Planning Commission)
国家国内贸易局	State Bureau of Internal Trade
国家煤炭工业局	State Bureau of Coal Industry
国家机械工业局	State Bureau of Machine-Building Industry
国家冶金工业局	State Bureau of Metallurgical Industry
国家石油和化学工业局	State Bureau of Petroleum and Chemical Industries
国家轻工业局	State Bureau of Light Industry
国家纺织工业局	State Bureau of Textile Industry
国家建筑材料工业局	State Bureau of Building Materials Industry
国家烟草专卖局	State Tobacco Monopoly Bureau

国家有色金属工业局(以上由国家经贸委管理)	State Bureau of Nonferrous Metal Industry (all under the State Economic and Trade Commission)
国家外国专家局(人事部)	State Bureau of Foreign Experts Affairs (under the Ministry of Personnel)
国家海洋局(国土资源部)	State Oceanic Administration (under the Ministry of Land and Resources)
国家测绘局(国土资源部)	State Bureau of Surveying and Mapping (ditto)
国家邮政局(信息产业部)	State Post Bureau (under the Ministry of Information Industry)
国家文物局(文化部)	State Cultural Relics Bureau (under the Ministry of Culture)
国家中医药管理局(卫生部)	State Administration of Traditional Chinese Medicine (under the Ministry of Public Health)
国家外汇管理局(中国人民银行总行)	State Administration of Foreign Exchange (under the People's Bank of China)
国家出入境检验检疫局(海关总署)	State Administration for Entry-Exit Inspection and Quarantine (under the General Administration of Customs)

（六）中国的民族
Nationalities in China

汉 族	Hànzú		柯尔克孜族	Kē'ěrkèzīzú (Kirgiz)
蒙 古 族	Měnggǔzú (Mongol)		土 族	Tǔzú
回 族	Huízú		达 斡 尔 族	Dáwò'ěrzú (Daur)
藏 族	Zàngzú		仫 佬 族	Mùlǎozú (Mulam)
维 吾 尔 族	Wéiwú'ěrzú (Uygur)		羌 族	Qiāngzú
苗 族	Miáozú		布 朗 族	Bùlǎngzú (Blang)
彝 族	Yízú		撒 拉 族	Sālāzú (Salar)
壮 族	Zhuàngzú		毛 难 族	Máonánzú
布 依 族	Bùyīzú (Bouyei)		仡 佬 族	Gēlǎozú (Gelo)
朝 鲜 族	Cháoxiǎnzú		锡 伯 族	Xībózú (Xibe)
满 族	Mǎnzú		阿 昌 族	Āchāngzú
侗 族	Dòngzú		普 米 族	Pǔmǐzú
瑶 族	Yáozú		塔 吉 克 族	Tǎjíkèzú (Tajik)
白 族	Báizú		怒 族	Nùzú
土 家 族	Tǔjiāzú		乌孜别克族	Wūzībiékèzú (Ozbek)
哈 尼 族	Hānízú		俄 罗 斯 族	Éluósīzú
哈 萨 克 族	Hāsàkèzú (Kazak)		鄂 温 克 族	Èwēnkèzú (Ewenki)
傣 族	Dǎizú		崩 龙 族	Bēnglóngzú
黎 族	Lízú		保 安 族	Bǎo'ānzú (Bonan)
傈 僳 族	Lìsùzú		裕 固 族	Yùgùzú (Yugur)
佤 族	Wǎzú (Va)		京 族	Jīngzú
畲 族	Shēzú		塔 塔 尔 族	Tǎtǎ'ěrzú (Tatar)
高 山 族	Gāoshānzú		独 龙 族	Dúlóngzú (Drung)
拉 祜 族	Lāhùzú		鄂 伦 春 族	Èlúnchūnzú (Oroqen)
水 族	Shuǐzú		赫 哲 族	Hèzhézú (Hezhe)
东 乡 族	Dōngxiāngzú		门 巴 族	Ménbāzú (Moinba)
纳 西 族	Nàxīzú		珞 巴 族	Luòbāzú (Lhoba)
景 颇 族	Jǐngpōzú		基 诺 族	Jīnuòzú

（七）中国的主要姓氏
Common Chinese Family Names

二画	仉 Zhǎng	巩 Gǒng	陈 Chén
卜 Bǔ	**五画**	关 Guān	迟 Chí
刁 Diāo	艾 Ài	华 Huà	狄 Dí
丁 Dīng	白 Bái	吉 Jí	杜 Dù
三画	包 Bāo	纪 Jì（Jì）	贡 Gòng
弓 Gōng	边 Biān	江 Jiāng	谷 Gǔ
马 Mǎ	冯 Féng	匡 Kuāng	何 Hé
千 Qiān	甘 Gān	刘 Liú	花 Huā
上官	古 Gǔ	吕 Lǚ	来 Lái
Shàngguān	弘 Hóng	米 Mǐ	劳 Láo
万 Wàn	邝 Kuàng	那 Nà	冷 Lěng
卫 Wèi	乐 Lè	年 Nián	李 Lǐ
习 Xí	厉 Lì	农 Nóng	连 Lián
于 Yú	龙 Lóng	朴 Piáo	陆 Lù
四画	卢 Lú	齐 Qí	麦 Mài
贝 Bèi	宁 Nìng	祁 Qí	闵 Mǐn
卞 Biàn	皮 Pí	乔 Qiáo	邱 Qiū
车 Chē	冉 Rǎn	曲 Qū	芮 Ruì
从 Cóng	司 Sī	全 Quán	沙 Shā
邓 Dèng	司马 Sīmǎ	任 Rén	邵 Shào
方 Fāng	司徒 Sītú	戎 Róng	佘 Shé
丰 Fēng	申 Shēn	阮 Ruǎn	沈 Shěn
公孙	石 Shí	师 Shī	时 Shí
Gōngsūn	史 Shǐ	孙 Sūn	宋 Sòng
孔 Kǒng	帅 Shuài	汤 Tāng	苏 Sū
毛 Máo	田 Tián	邬 Wū	邰 Tái
牛 Niú	叶 Yè	伍 Wǔ	佟 Tóng
区 Ōu	印 Yìn	向 Xiàng	汪 Wāng
仇 Qiú	乐 Yuè	邢 Xíng	沃 Wò
水 Shuǐ	左 Zuǒ	许 Xǔ	巫 Wū
王 Wáng	**六画**	延 Yán	吴 Wú
韦 Wéi	安 Ān	伊 Yī	肖 Xiāo
文 Wén	毕 Bì	阴 Yīn	辛 Xīn
尹 Yǐn	成 Chéng	仲 Zhòng	轩辕
尤 Yóu	池 Chí	朱 Zhū	Xuānyuán
	达 Dá	**七画**	严 Yán
		岑 Cén	杨 Yáng
			应 Yīng

余 Yú	**九画**
张 Zhāng	柏 Bǎi
邹 Zōu	种 Chóng
八画	段 Duàn
法 Fǎ	费 Fèi
范 Fàn	封 Fēng
房 Fáng	革 Gé
国 Guó	宫 Gōng
杭 Háng	郝 Hǎo
季 Jì	贺 Hè
金 Jīn	洪 Hóng
经 Jīng	侯 Hóu
居 Jū	胡 Hú
郎 Láng	宦 Huàn
林 Lín	姜 Jiāng
罗 Luó	荆 Jīng
茅 Máo	柯 Kē
孟 Mèng	柳 Liǔ
宓 Mì	娄 Lóu
苗 Miáo	骆 Luò
欧 Ōu	饶 Ráo
欧阳	荣 Róng
Ōuyáng	施 Shī
庞 Páng	闻 Wén
屈 Qū	郗 Xī
单 Shàn	项 Xiàng
尚 Shàng	胥 Xū
武 Wǔ	宣 Xuān
冼 Xiǎn	荀 Xún
易 Yì	姚 Yáo
郁 Yù	俞 Yú
岳 Yuè	禹 Yǔ
郑 Zhèng	查 Zhā
周 Zhōu	赵 Zhào
竺 Zhú	钟 Zhōng
卓 Zhuō	祝 Zhù
宗 Zōng	祖 Zǔ

十画				十五画
敖 Áo	桑 Sāng	寇 Kòu	稽 Jī	蓝 Lán
班 Bān	谈 Tán	隗 Kuí	蒋 Jiǎng	雷 Léi
柴 Chái	唐 Táng	梁 Liáng	焦 Jiāo	廉 Lián
晁 Cháo	陶 Táo	隆 Lóng	景 Jǐng	路 Lù
党 Dǎng	铁 Tiě	鹿 Lù	鲁 Lǔ	蒙 Méng
恩 Ēn	翁 Wēng	麻 Má	彭 Péng	蒲 Pú
高 Gāo	奚 Xī	梅 Méi	覃 Qín	裘 Qiú
耿 Gěng	席 Xí	盘 Pán	舒 Shū	筱 Xiǎo
顾 Gù	夏 Xià	戚 Qī	粟 Sù	解 Xiè
郭 Guō	徐 Xú	萨 Sà	覃 Tán	雍 Yōng
海 Hǎi	晏 Yàn	盛 Shèng	逯 Tí	虞 Yú
姬 Jī	殷 Yīn	屠 Tú	童 Tóng	詹 Zhān
贾 Jiǎ	袁 Yuán	隗 Wěi	温 Wēn	甄 Zhēn
晋 Jìn	原 Yuán	尉 Wèi	谢 Xiè	
凌 Líng	诸 Zhū	续 Xù	游 Yóu	十四画
栾 Luán	诸葛 Zhūgé	阎 Yán	越 Yuè	蔡 Cài
秘 Mì		章 Zhāng	曾 Zēng	管 Guǎn
莫 Mò	十一画			廖 Liào
倪 Ní	曹 Cáo	十二画	十三画	蔺 Lìn
聂 Niè	常 Cháng	程 Chéng	鲍 Bào	缪 Miào
浦 Pǔ	崔 Cuī	储 Chǔ	楚 Chǔ	裴 Péi
钱 Qián	符 Fú	董 Dǒng	褚 Chǔ	谭 Tán
秦 Qín	龚 Gōng	傅 Fù	窦 Dòu	熊 Xióng
容 Róng	扈 Hù	富 Fù	靳 Jìn	臧 Zāng
	黄 Huáng	葛 Gě	蒯 Kuǎi	翟 Zhái
	康 Kāng	韩 Hán	赖 Lài	

十六画
薄 Bó
霍 Huò
冀 Jì
穆 Mù
薛 Xuē
燕 Yān

十七画
戴 Dài
鞠 Jū
糜 Mí
魏 Wèi

十八画
瞿 Qú
鄞 Fēng

上官
公孙
司马
司徒
东方
欧阳

诸葛
轩辕

8个 两字姓

（八）中国亲属关系简表
Family Relationships

名　称 Name of Relationship	性别 Sex	亲属的关系 Relationship	称　呼 Form of Address
祖　父 zǔfù	男	父亲的父亲 father's father	爷爷 yéye
祖　母 zǔmǔ	女	父亲的母亲 father's mother	奶奶 nǎinai
外祖父 wàizǔfù	男	母亲的父亲 mother's father	外公；姥爷 wàigōng; lǎoye
外祖母 wàizǔmǔ	女	母亲的母亲 mother's mother	外婆；姥姥 wàipó; lǎolao
父　亲 fùqin	男	father	爸爸；爹 bàba; diē
母　亲 mǔqin	女	mother	妈妈；娘 māma; niáng
公　公 gōnggong	男	丈夫的父亲 husband's father	爸爸；爹 bàba; diē
婆　婆 pópo	女	丈夫的母亲 husband's mother	妈妈；娘 māma; niáng
岳　父 yuèfù 老丈人 lǎozhàngren	男	妻子的父亲 wife's father	爸爸；爹 bàba; diē
岳　母 yuèmǔ 丈母娘 zhàngmǔniáng	女	妻子的母亲 wife's mother	妈妈；娘 māma; niáng

名　称 Name of Relationship	性别 Sex	亲属的关系 Relationship	称　呼 Form of Address
伯　父 bófù	男	父亲的哥哥 father's elder brother	伯伯；大爷 bóbo；dàye
伯　母 bómǔ	女	伯父的妻子,父亲的嫂嫂 wife of father's elder brother	大娘；大妈 dàniáng； dàmā
叔　父 shūfù	男	父亲的弟弟 father's younger brother	叔叔 shūshu
婶　母 shěnmǔ	女	叔父的妻子 wife of father's younger brother	婶婶；婶娘 shěnshen； shěnniáng 婶子；婶儿 shěnzi；shěnr
姑　母 gūmǔ	女	父亲的姐姐或妹妹 father's sister	姑姑；姑妈 gūgu；gūmā
姑　父 gūfu	男	姑母的丈夫 husband of father's sister	姑父 gūfu
舅　父 jiùfù	男	母亲的哥哥或弟弟 mother's brother	舅舅 jiùjiu
舅　母 jiùmu	女	舅父的妻子 wife of mother's brother	舅母；舅妈 jiùmu；jiùmā
姨　母 yímǔ	女	母亲的姐姐或妹妹 mother's sister	姨妈；姨 yímā；yí
姨　父 yífu	男	姨母的丈夫 husband of mother's sister	姨父 yífu
妻　子 qīzi 爱　人 àiren 媳妇儿 xífur	女	wife	

名　称 Name of Relationship	性别 Sex	亲 属 的 关 系 Relationship	称　呼 Form of Address
丈　夫 zhàngfu 爱　人 àiren	男	husband	
亲　家 qìngjia	男	儿子的岳父或女儿的公公 son's or daughter's father-in-law	亲家 qìngjia
亲家母 qìngjiamǔ	女	儿子的岳母或女儿的婆婆 son's or daughter's mother-in-law	亲家 qìngjia
兄 xiōng	男	elder brother	哥哥 gēge
嫂 sǎo	女	哥哥的妻子 elder brother's wife	嫂子;嫂嫂 sǎozi; sǎosao
弟 dì	男	younger brother	弟弟 dìdi
弟　妹 dìmèi 弟媳妇 dìxífu	女	younger brother's wife	弟妹 dìmèi
姐 jiě	女	elder sister	姐姐 jiějie
姐　夫 jiěfu	男	姐姐的丈夫 elder sister's husband	姐夫 jiěfu
妹 mèi	女	younger sister	妹妹 mèimei
妹　夫 mèifu	男	妹妹的丈夫 younger sister's husband	妹夫 mèifu

名 称 Name of Relationship	性别 Sex	亲 属 的 关 系 Relationship	称 呼 Form of Address
堂 兄 tángxiōng 叔伯哥哥 shūbai gēge	男	伯父或叔父的儿子(比自己年龄大的) son of 伯父 or 叔父 (older than oneself)	哥哥 gēge
堂 嫂 tángsǎo	女	堂兄的妻子 wife of 堂兄	嫂嫂;嫂子 sǎosao; sǎozi
堂 弟 tángdì 叔伯兄弟 shūbai xiōngdi	男	伯父或叔父的儿子(比自己年龄小的) son of 伯父 or 叔父 (younger than oneself)	弟弟 dìdi
堂弟妹 tángdìmèi	女	堂弟的妻子 wife of 堂弟	弟妹 dìmèi
堂 姐 tángjiě	女	伯父或叔父的女儿(比自己年龄大的) daughter of 伯父 or 叔父 (older than oneself)	姐姐 jiějie
堂姐夫 tángjiěfu	男	堂姐的丈夫 husband of 堂姐	姐夫 jiěfu
堂 妹 tángmèi	女	伯父或叔父的女儿(比自己年龄小的) daughter of 伯父 or 叔父 (younger than oneself)	妹妹 mèimei
堂妹夫 tángmèifu	男	堂妹的丈夫 husband of 堂妹	妹夫 mèifu
姑表兄 gūbiǎoxiōng	男	姑母的儿子(比自己年龄大的) son of 姑母 (older than oneself)	表哥 biǎogē
姑表嫂 gūbiǎosǎo	女	姑表兄的妻子 wife of 姑表兄	表嫂 biǎosǎo

名　称 Name of Relationship	性别 Sex	亲属的关系 Relationship	称　呼 Form of Address
姑表弟 gūbiǎodì	男	姑母的儿子（比自己年龄小的） son of 姑母（younger than one- self)	表弟 biǎodì
姑表弟妹 gūbiǎodìmèi	女	姑表弟的妻子 wife of 姑表弟	表弟妹 biǎodìmèi
姑表姐 gūbiǎojiě	女	姑母的女儿（比自己年龄大的） daughter of 姑母（older than oneself)	表姐 biǎojiě
姑表姐夫 gūbiǎojiěfu	男	姑表姐的丈夫 husband of 姑表姐	表姐夫 biǎojiěfu
姑表妹 gūbiǎomèi	女	姑母的女儿（比自己年龄小的） daughter of 姑母（younger than oneself)	表妹 biǎomèi
姑表妹夫 gūbiǎomèifu	男	姑表妹的丈夫 husband of 姑表妹	表妹夫 biǎomèifu
舅表兄 jiùbiǎoxiōng	男	舅父的儿子（比自己年龄大的） son of 舅父（older than oneself)	表哥 biǎogē
舅表嫂 jiùbiǎosǎo	女	舅表兄的妻子 wife of 舅表兄	表嫂 biǎosǎo
舅表弟 jiùbiǎodì	男	舅父的儿子（比自己年龄小的） son of 舅父（younger than one- self)	表弟 biǎodì
舅表弟妹 jiùbiǎodìmèi	女	舅表弟的妻子 wife of 舅表弟	表弟妹 biǎodìmèi
舅表姐 jiùbiǎojiě	女	舅父的女儿（比自己年龄大的） daughter of 舅父（older than oneself)	表姐 biǎojiě

名　称 Name of Relationship	性别 Sex	亲属的关系 Relationship	称　呼 Form of Address
舅表姐夫 jiùbiǎojiěfu	男	舅表姐的丈夫 husband of 舅表姐	表姐夫 biǎojiěfu
舅表妹 jiùbiǎomèi	女	舅父的女儿（比自己年龄小的） daughter of 舅父（younger than oneself)	表妹 biǎomèi
舅表妹夫 jiùbiǎomèifu	男	舅表妹的丈夫 husband of 舅表妹	表妹夫 biǎomèifu
姨表兄 yíbiǎoxiōng	男	姨母的儿子（比自己年龄大的） son of 姨母（older than oneself)	表哥 biǎogē
姨表嫂 yíbiǎosǎo	女	姨表兄的妻子 wife of 姨表兄	表嫂 biǎosǎo
姨表弟 yíbiǎodì	男	姨母的儿子（比自己年龄小的） son of 姨母（younger than oneself)	表弟 biǎodì
姨表弟妹 yíbiǎodìmèi	女	姨表弟的妻子 wife of 姨表弟	表弟妹 biǎodìmèi
姨表姐 yíbiǎojiě	女	姨母的女儿（比自己年龄大的） daughter of 姨母（older than oneself)	表姐 biǎojiě
姨表姐夫 yíbiǎojiěfu	男	姨表姐的丈夫 husband of 姨表姐	表姐夫 biǎojiěfu
姨表妹 yíbiǎomèi	女	姨母的女儿（比自己年龄小的） daughter of 姨母（younger than oneself)	表妹 biǎomèi
姨表妹夫 yíbiǎomèifu	男	姨表妹的丈夫 husband of 姨表妹	表妹夫 biǎomèifu

名　称 Name of Relationship	性别 Sex	亲 属 的 关 系 Relationship	称　呼 Form of Address
内　兄 nèixiōng 大舅子 dàjiùzi	男	妻子的哥哥 wife's elder brother	哥哥 gēge
内　嫂 nèisǎo	女	内兄的妻子 wife of 内兄	嫂嫂；嫂子 sǎosao； sǎozi
内　弟 nèidì 小舅子 xiǎojiùzi	男	妻子的弟弟 wife's younger brother	弟弟 dìdi
内弟妹 nèidìmèi	女	内弟的妻子 wife of 内弟	弟妹 dìmèi
大姨子 dàyízi	女	妻子的姐姐 wife's elder sister	姐姐 jiějie
襟　兄 jīnxiōng	男	大姨子的丈夫 husband of 大姨子	姐夫 jiěfu
小姨子 xiǎoyízi	女	妻子的妹妹 wife's younger sister	妹妹 mèimei
襟　弟 jīndì	男	小姨子的丈夫 husband of 小姨子	妹夫 mèifu
儿　子 érzi	男	son	
儿媳妇儿 érxífur	女	儿子的妻子 son's wife	

名 称 Name of Relationship	性别 Sex	亲 属 的 关 系 Relationship	称 呼 Form of Address
女 儿 nǚ'ér 闺 女 guīnü 姑 娘 gūniang	女	daughter	
女 婿 nǚxu 姑 爷 gūye	男	女儿的丈夫 daughter's husband	
侄 儿 zhír 侄 子 zhízi	男	哥哥或弟弟的儿子 brother's son	
侄媳妇儿 zhíxífur	女	侄儿的妻子 wife of 侄儿	
侄女儿 zhínǚr	女	哥哥或弟弟的女儿 brother's daughter	
侄女婿 zhínǚxu	男	侄女儿的丈夫 husband of 侄女儿	
外 甥 wàisheng	男	姐姐或妹妹的儿子 sister's son	
外甥媳妇儿 wàishengxífur	女	外甥的妻子 wife of 外甥	
外甥女儿 wàishengnǚr	女	姐姐或妹妹的女儿 sister's daughter	
外甥女婿 wàishengnǚxu	男	外甥女儿的丈夫 husband of 外甥女儿	

名 称 Name of Relationship	性别 Sex	亲 属 的 关 系 Relationship	称 呼 Form of Address
内 侄 nèizhí	男	内兄或内弟的儿子 son of 内兄 or 内弟	
内侄女儿 nèizhínür	女	内兄或内弟的女儿 daughter of 内兄 or 内弟	
孙 子 sūnzi	男	儿子的儿子 son's son	
孙媳妇儿 sūnxífur	女	孙子的妻子 wife of 孙子	
孙女儿 sūnnür	女	儿子的女儿 son's daughter	
孙女婿 sūnnǔxu	男	孙女儿的丈夫 husband of 孙女儿	
外孙子 wàisūnzi	男	女儿的儿子 daughter's son	
外孙媳妇儿 wàisūnxífur	女	外孙子的妻子 wife of 外孙子	
外孙女儿 wàisūnnür	女	女儿的女儿 daughter's daughter	
外孙女婿 wàisūnnǔxu	男	外孙女儿的丈夫 husband of 外孙女儿	

注：① 本表"名称"栏内的名称，只用于书面或间接称呼，一般不作口头直接称呼。
　　② 本表"称呼"栏内的名称，用于口头直接称呼，也可用于书面或间接称呼。对自己的晚辈或同辈但比自己小的人，一般多直呼其名。

Notes：
① The forms listed in the "Relationship" column are used in the written language or when the person is referred to and not as forms of address.
② The terms listed in the "Form of Address" column are used as forms of address, and they are also used in the written language or when the person is referred to. For people of the same generation but younger than oneself or younger generations, personal names are usually used as forms of address.

（九）中国历代纪元简表

Chronological Table of Chinese History

原始社会 Primitive Society			约公元前 2600 年—约公元前 1600 年 C. 2600B. C. —C. 1600B. C.
奴 隶 社 会 Slave Society		夏 Xià	约公元前 2100 年—约公元前 1600 年 C. 2100B. C. —C. 1600B. C.
		商 Shāng	约公元前 1600 年—约公元前 1100 年 C. 1600B. C. —C. 1100B. C.
		西　周 Xīzhōu	约公元前 1100 年—约公元前 771 年 C. 1100B. C. —C. 771B. C.
		春　秋 Chūnqiū	公元前 770 年—公元前 476 年 770B. C. —476B. C.
封 建 社 会 Feudal Society		战　国 Zhànguó	公元前 475 年—公元前 221 年 475B. C. —221B. C.
		秦 Qín	公元前 221 年—公元前 206 年 221B. C. —206B. C.
	汉 Hàn	西　汉 Xīhàn	公元前 206 年—公元 25 年 206B. C. —25A. D.
		东　汉 Dōnghàn	公元 25 年—公元 220 年 25—220

封 建 社 会 Feudal Society	三国 Sānguó	魏 Wèi	公元 220 年—公元 265 年 220—265
		蜀汉 Shǔ	公元 221 年—公元 263 年 221—263
		吴 Wú	公元 222 年—公元 280 年 222—280
	西晋 Xījìn		公元 265 年—公元 316 年 265—316
	东晋 Dōngjìn		公元 317 年—公元 420 年 317—420
	南北朝 Nán- běi- cháo	南朝 Nán- cháo	宋 Sòng 公元 420 年—公元 479 年 420—479
			齐 Qí 公元 479 年—公元 502 年 479—502
			梁 Liáng 公元 502 年—公元 557 年 502—557
			陈 Chén 公元 557 年—公元 589 年 557—589
		北朝 Běi- cháo	北魏 Běiwèi 公元 386 年—公元 534 年 386—534
			东魏 Dōng- wèi 公元 534 年—公元 550 年 534—550
			北齐 Běiqí 公元 550 年—公元 577 年 550—577

		西魏 Xīwèi	公元 535 年—公元 556 年 535—556
南北朝 Nán- běi- cháo	北朝 Běi- cháo	北周 Běi- zhōu	公元 557 年—公元 581 年 557—581
封 建 社 会 Feudal Society	隋 Suí		公元 581 年—公元 618 年 581—618
	唐 Táng		公元 618 年—公元 907 年 618—907
	五代 Wǔdài	后　梁 Hòuliáng	公元 907 年—公元 923 年 907—923
		后　唐 Hòutáng	公元 923 年—公元 936 年 923—936
		后　晋 Hòujìn	公元 936 年—公元 946 年 936—946
		后　汉 Hòuhàn	公元 947 年—公元 950 年 947—950
		后　周 Hòuzhōu	公元 951 年—公元 960 年 951—960
	辽 Liáo		公元 916 年—公元 1125 年 916—1125
	北　宋 Běisòng		公元 960 年—公元 1127 年 960—1127
	金 Jīn		公元 1115 年—公元 1234 年 1115—1234

	南　宋 Nánsòng	公元 1127 年—公元 1279 年 1127—1279
封建社会 Feudal Society	元 Yuán	公元 1279 年—公元 1368 年 1279—1368
	明 Míng	公元 1368 年—公元 1644 年 1368—1644
	清 Qīng	公元 1644 年—公元 1840 年 1644—1840
半殖民地 半封建社会 Semi-colonial and Semi- feudal Society		公元 1840 年—公元 1911 年 1840—1911
	中华民国 Zhōnghuá Mínguó	公元 1912 年—公元 1949 年 1912—1949
新民主主义社会 New-democratic Society 社会主义社会 Socialist Society	中华人民共和国 Zhōnghuá Rénmín Gònghéguó	公元 1949 年建立 founded in 1949

（十）计量单位简表
Weights and Measures

	市 制 及 进 位 法 Chinese System	折 合 公 制 Metric Value	折 合 英 美 制 British and U. S. Value
长　度 Length	1 分（10 厘） 1 寸（10 分） 1 尺（10 寸） 1 丈（10 尺） 1 里（150 丈）	 3.3333 厘米（cm.） 0.3333 米（m.） 3.3333 米（m.） { 0.5000 公里（km.） 0.2700 海里（nauti- cal mile)	 1.3123 英寸（in.） 1.0936 英尺（ft.） 3.6454 码（yd.） 0.3107 英里（mi.）
面积和 地　积 Area	1 平方尺(100 平方寸) 1 平方丈(100 平方尺) 1 平方里(22500 平方丈) 1 分（6 平方丈） 1 亩(10 分) 1 顷(100 亩)	0.1111 平方米 （sq. m.） 11.1111 平方米 （sq. m.） 0.2500 平方公里 （sq. km.） { 6.6667 公亩（a.） 0.0667 公顷（ha.） 6.6667 公顷（ha.）	1.1960 平方英尺 （sq. ft.） 0.0965 平方英里 （sq. mi.） 0.1644 英亩（a.）
体积和 容　量 Physical Volume and Capacity	1 立方尺(1000 立方寸) 1 立方丈(1000 立方尺) 1 合 1 升（10 合） 1 斗（10 升） 1 石（10 斗）	0.0370 立方米 （cubic m.） 37.0370 立方米 （cubic m.） 100 毫升（ml.） 1 升（l.） 10 升（l.） 100 升（l.）	1.3078 立方英尺 （cubic ft.） { 1.7598 品脱(英) （pt.） 0.2200 加仑(英) （gal.） 2.7498 蒲式耳(英) （bu.）
重　量 Weight	1 钱 1 两（10 钱） 1 斤（10 两） 1 担（100 斤）	5 克（g.） 50 克（g.） 0.5000 公斤（kg.） 0.5000 公担（q.）	 1.7637 盎司(常衡) 1.7637 oz. （Avoirdupois) 1.1023 磅(常衡) 1.1023 lb. （Avoirdupois)

（十一）常用量词表
Common Measure Words

	说　　明 Explanation or English Equivalent	例　子 Examples
bǎ 把	名量：(1)用于有柄的器物 *for things with a handle* (2)用于成把的东西 bunch；bundle (3)用于一手抓拢的数量 handful (4)用于某种人物 *for leadership，with ordi-nal number only；for peo-ple with special skill* 动量：用于同手有关的一些动作，或抽象事物的形象说法 *for actions done with hand or some abstract nouns*	一～刀子(斧子、胡琴、伞，扫帚、钥匙、椅子) 一～菊花(菠菜、萝卜、筷子) 两～豆子(花生、米) 第一～手｜一、二～手｜一～好手 擦一～脸｜拉他一～｜一～攥住｜加一～劲儿
bān 班	名量：(1)用于学习、工作等组织 class (2)用于人群 bunch (of people) (3)用于军队的编制单位 squad (4)用于定时开行的交通运输工具 *scheduled service of transportation*	两～学生 咱们村里这～年轻人真不错。 两～战士 一～车｜今天最后一～飞机
bàn 瓣(～儿)	名量：用于果实、种子等分开的小块 segment or section (of a tan-gerine)；piece	两～橘子｜把苹果切成几～。

	说　　　　明 Explanation or English Equivalent	例　子 Examples
bāng 帮	名量:用于人 bunch (of people)	一～孩子
bāo 包	名量:用于成包的东西 package; bundle	一～点心(礼品、香烟)
bèi 倍	名量:用于倍数 -fold	二的五～是十。|产量增长一～。
běn 本	名量:(1)用于书籍簿册 　　　*for books, etc.* (2)用于电影胶片的盘数 　　　reel (of cinema film)	两～书(杂志、账、字典) 这部电影一共七～。
bǐ 笔	名量:(1)用于书画艺术 　　　*for handwriting or painting, used only with numeral* 一 *or* 几 (2)用于款项等 　　　sum	一～好字|他能画几～山水画。 两～钱(贷款、经费)
biàn 遍	动量:用于动作次数 time	那本书我已经看了一～。
bō 拨	名量:多用于分批的人 batch (of people)	一～参观的人|分两～出发
bù 部	名量:(1)用于电影、书籍 　　　*for films, books, etc.* (2)用于车辆、机器 　　　*for vehicles, machines, etc.*	一～电影(纪录片、小说) 两～汽车(机器)
cān 餐	名量:〈书〉用于饮食顿数 *for meals*	一～饭|一日三～
cè 册	名量:用于书等 volume	一～书|藏书三万多～。|这部书共六～。
céng 层	名量:(1)多用于建筑物、建筑部件等分层物 　　　storey; layer (2)用于分项、分步的事物(多为文章、思想等) 　　　*for a component part in a sequence (referring to writing or thought)* (3)用于物体表层物 　　　sheet; coat	两～玻璃窗(楼、台阶) 去了一～顾虑|还有一～意思 一～薄膜(水、灰、皮、漆、土、油)

	说　　　　明 Explanation or English Equivalent	例　子 Examples
chá 茬(～儿)	名量:用于同一块土地上作物种植的次数 crop	一～庄稼
cháng 场	名量:用于事物的经过 *for the process of a matter or an occasion*	一～大病(风波、争论)|一～雨(雪)
	动量:用于某些行动 *for certain actions*	哭了一～|闹了一～
chǎng 场	名量:用于文娱、体育项目的场次 *for recreational activities or sports*	一～电影(戏、篮球、球赛)
chóng 重	名量:用于门、山等 layer, *for door, mountain, etc.* (*implying the sense of obstacle*)	两～门|万～山|冲破一～又一～困难
chū 出	名量:用于戏剧等 *for drama*	一～喜剧(丑剧、京剧、戏)
chuàn 串	名量:用于某些连贯起来的事物 string; cluster	一～珠子(烤肉、钥匙)
chuáng 床	名量:用于被子等 *for quilt, sheet, etc.*	一～被子
cì 次	名量:用于事情经过的次数、届次等 *for events*, No.; session, *etc.*	一～试验(事故、手术)|十二～列车|二～会议
	动量:用于行动的次数 time	来过两～|进了一～城
cù 簇	名量:多用于聚集成团成堆的花卉、植物等 cluster; grove	一～鲜花|两～竹子

	说　　　　明 Explanation or English Equivalent	例　子 Examples
dá 打	名量:十二个叫一打 dozen	三～铅笔（乒乓球、毛 巾、手套）
dài 代	名量:用于表示辈分 generation	一～新人
dàn 担	名量:用于成担的东西 *for things that can be carried on a shoulder pole*	一～水（柴）
dào 道	名量:(1)用于某些长条形物 *for things in the shape of a line*	一～缝｜一～光线｜几 ～皱纹
	(2)用于门、墙等 *for door, wall, etc. (as a barrier)*	一～门（围墙、防线、铁 丝网）
	(3)用于命令、题目等 *for orders, questions, etc.*	一～命令（禁令、算术 题、手续）
	(4)其他 course, etc.	上了好几～菜｜上了三 ～漆
dī 滴	名量:用于成滴的少量液体 drop	几～眼泪（汗、水、眼 药）
diǎn 点	名量:(1)用于事项等 point; item	几～注意事项｜两～意 见｜几～内容
	(2)时间单位 o'clock	五～钟｜四～三刻
dǐng 顶	名量:用于帽子以及有顶的东西 *for hats and things with a top*	一～帽子（钢盔、草帽）｜ 一～轿子（帐篷、蚊 帐）
dòng 栋	名量:用于房子（多为整座的） *for buildings*	几～房子（楼房、平房）
dǔ 堵	名量:用于墙 *for walls*	一～墙
dù 度	名量:用于有周期性或间隔性的事项 *for occasions*	两～会谈｜一年一～的 中秋节｜这个剧曾两 ～公演。

	说　　　明 Explanation or English Equivalent	例　子 Examples
duàn 段	名量:(1)用于长条物分成的部分 　　　　section; segment	一～木头(管道、绳 子、铁轨)
	(2)用于时间、路程等的一定 长度 period; length	一～时间(路程、距 离、经历)
	(3)用于语言、文字等的一部分 paragraph	一～话(台词、文章)
duī 堆	名量:用于成堆物 　　　　pile	一～石头(垃圾、书)
duì 队	名量:用于行列 　　　　troop	一～士兵(民兵、人马)
duì 对	名量:用于成对的人、事、物 　　　　pair	一～夫妻|一～矛盾| 一～花瓶
dùn 顿	名量:用于饮食 　　　　*for meals*	一～饭(晚饭、早餐)
	动量:用于批评、斥责、劝说、打骂等 行为 *for criticism, reproach,* *beating, etc.*	批评了一～|骂了一 ～|打了一～
duǒ 朵	名量:多用于花朵、云彩 　　　　*for flowers, clouds, etc.*	几～花(白云)
fā 发	名量:用于枪弹、炮弹 　　　　round (of shells)	十～子弹(炮弹)
fān 番	名量:(1)常用于费时、费力、费心或 过程较长的行为。前面常 加数词"一"或"几" *for the course of any ac-* *tion which takes time,* *usu. used with numeral* 一 *or* 几	一～心血(唇舌、工 夫、周折)
	(2)略同于"种",前面常加数 词"一" kind, *usu. used with nu-* *meral* 一	别有一～风味|别有 一～天地|完全是 一～好意

	说　　明 Explanation or English Equivalent	例　子 Examples
	(3)用在"翻"后,表示倍数 *used after* 翻 *to mean -fold*	翻了一～|翻了几～
	动量:用于行动,前面常加数词"一" *for certain actions, used with numeral* 一	打量一～|研究一～|整顿一～
fāng 方	名量:〈书〉用于少数方形物 *for things in a square shape*	一～砚台(图章)
fēn 分	名量:(1)货币单位 *unit of currency*	二～钱|五角三～
	(2)时间单位 *minute*	八点三十五～|五十～钟一节课
	(3)把一个整体分做十分(常用于抽象意义),"十二分"表示超出一般的 $\frac{1}{10}$ (for abstract things); 十二分 means more than usual amount	九～成绩,一～缺点|十～指标,十二～措施
	(4)评定成绩或胜负的记数单位 *point*	甲队胜了十～。|他数学考了八十～。
fèn 份	名量:(1)用于搭配成组的东西 *portion; share*	两～菜(点心、礼品)
	(2)用于报刊文件等 *for papers, periodicals, manuscripts, etc.*	两～报(文件)
fēng 封	名量:用于信件等 *for letters, etc.*	一～电报(信)
fēng 峰	名量:用于骆驼 *for camels*	两～骆驼
fú 幅	名量:用于布帛、字画等 *for cloth, calligraphy, painting, etc.*	一～布|一～挂图(山水画、宣传画)
fù 副	名量:(1)用于成对或成组的东西 *set; pair*	几～扑克牌(对联、耳机、眼镜)

	说　　　　明 Explanation or English Equivalent	例　子 Examples
	(2)用于面部表情 *for facial expressions*	一～笑脸｜一～凶相｜ 一～严肃的表情｜ 两～不同的面孔
	(3)用于中药(同"服") dose (of traditional Chinese medicine)	三～药
gǎn 杆	名量:用于长形有杆的器物 *for things with a stick*	一～枪(秤、旗、烟袋)
gè 个	名量:应用范围很广,可代替一般名量词 *the most extensively used measure word which can take the place of many measure words*	一～杯子(苹果、鸡蛋、故事、节目、人、国家、钟头)
gēn 根	名量:用于细长物 *for long and slender things*	几～火柴(钉子、粉笔、绳子、竹竿、香肠)
gǔ 股	名量:(1)用于成条物 *for things in the shape of a stream*	一～清泉｜一～暖流｜ 一～逆流｜山上有 两～小道
	(2)用于气味、气体、气力等,前面常加数词"一" *for smell, gas, strength, etc., usu. used with numeral 一*	一～香味(臭味、烟热气、劲儿)
	(3)用于成批的人,多含贬义 gang, horde (usu. derog.)	一～土匪｜两～敌军
háng 行	名量:用于成行的东西 line	两～字(热泪、诗、手迹、小树)
hù 户	名量:用于人家、住户 household	那里有几～人家。｜ 这个合作社是三～ 贫农办起来的。
huí 回	名量:用于旧长篇小说的章回 chapter (of traditional Chinese novel)	《红楼梦》第六十～
	动量:用于动作次数 time	去过一～长城｜我再试一～。

	说　　明 Explanation or English Equivalent	例　子 Examples
huǒ 伙	名量:用于人群,有时有贬义 group; band（usu. derog.）	一～人｜一～流氓
jí 级	名量:(1)用于台阶、楼梯等 step; stage	十多～台阶｜这个楼梯有十三～。
	(2)用于等级 grade; class	八～风｜三～工｜八～工资｜一～运动员
jiā 家	名量:用于家庭或事业、企业单位等 for families, enterprises, etc.	一～人家｜一～报纸（银行、饭馆)
jià 架	名量:(1)用于机器、机械等多带支架的物体 for machines with sup- ports	一～飞机（显微镜、照相机)
	(2)用于有架的植物等 for plants on a trellis	一～葡萄｜两～黄瓜
jiān 间	名量:用于房间 for rooms	一～屋子（病房、会客室)
jiàn 件	名量:用于衣服、家具、事情等 for clothes, furniture, af- fairs, etc.	三～衣服（皮袄、家具、事情)
jiǎo 角	名量:货币单位 unit of currency	两～钱｜三元四～
jié 节	名量:(1)用于带节的植物,或可连续的物体的一部分 for plants with joins; length; section	一～竹子｜两～甘蔗｜三～电池｜两～车厢
	(2)用于诗文、课程等的部分 section	第三章第八～｜这首诗有四～。
jié 截	名量:用于长条形物体的部分 section; chunk; length	一～木头｜两～粉笔
jiè 届	名量:用于定期的会议、运动会、毕业班级或政府的任期等 for regular conference, sports meet, graduating class, term of office, etc.; session	第三十～联合国大会｜第三～运动会｜第三～毕业生｜美国第三十九～总统

	说　　　明 Explanation or English Equivalent	例　子 Examples
jú 局	名量:用于比赛(排球、乒乓球、棋类等) *game; set; innings*	第三～他以二十一比六取胜。
jù 句	名量:用于语言、诗等 *for sentences or lines of poem*	一～话(歌词、诗)
jù 具	名量:用于尸体、棺木等 *for corpses, coffins, etc.*	一～尸体
juǎn 卷	名量:用于卷成筒状的东西 *roll; scroll; spool*	一～报纸(画、胶卷)
juàn 卷	名量:用于书(现在多为整部书所分成的单册) *volume*	《鲁迅全集》第五～|两～本
jūn 军	名量:用于军队的编制单位 *army*	调来了一～人
kē 棵	名量:用于植物 *for plants*	一～树(草、牡丹、庄稼)
kē 颗	名量:用于颗粒状或球形物(一般比"粒"大) *for small and roundish things (bigger than* 粒*)*	一～珠子|几～豆子|一～红心|一～人造地球卫星|两～炸弹
kè 刻	名量:时间单位 *quarter of an hour*	三点一～|一～钟
kè 课	名量:用于课文 *for lessons*	第三～|两～课文
kǒu 口	名量:(1)用于人 *for human beings*	一家五～人
	(2)用于猪 *for pigs*	两～猪
	(3)用于有口或有刃的器物 *for things with an opening or edge*	一～井(缸、锅、剑)
	(4)用于语言,前面用数词"一" *for languages, usu. used with numeral* 一	一～北京话|一～流利的英语

	说　明 Explanation or English Equivalent	例　子 Examples
kuài 块	名量:(1)用于块状物 　　piece；cake (2)用于片状物 　　*for things in the shape of* 　　*a sheet* (3)货币单位,同"元" 　　*unit of currency,same as* 　　元	一～肥皂(糖、石头、 手表) 三～毯子(木板、手 绢、秧田) 两～钱|两～三毛钱
kǔn 捆	名量:用于捆起来的东西 bundle	一～稻草(柴火、旧 书)
lèi 类	名量:用于种类 sort；kind	两～矛盾(情况、问 题)
lì 粒	名量:用于颗粒状物(一般比"颗" 小) grain	一～米(药、子弹)
lián 连	名量:用于军队的编制单位 company	两～战士
liàng 辆	名量:用于车辆 *for vehicles*	三～车(轿车、坦克、 自行车)
liè 列	名量:用于成行列的人、物 *for things in a series*	一～横队|一～火车
lún 轮	名量:(1)〈书〉用于太阳、月亮 　　*for sun or moon* (2)用于比赛、会谈 　　round（of games, con- 　　tests，talks，etc.）	一～红日|一～明月 比赛进入第二～。| 第二～会谈
lǚ 旅	名量:用于某些军队的编制单位 brigade	一～骑兵
máo 毛	名量:货币单位 *unit of currency*	两～钱|三块一～
méi 枚	名量:用于圆形或圆锥形物等 *for small roundish things*	一～纪念章(棋子、硬 币、导弹)

	说　　　　明 Explanation or English Equivalent	例　子 Examples
mén 门	名量:(1)用于亲事、亲戚 　　　　*for marriages, relatives* 　　(2)用于炮 　　　　*for cannons* 　　(3)用于课程、学科、知识等 　　　　*for courses in a school,* 　　　　*disciplines, etc.*	一～亲戚(亲事) 几～大炮 一～功课(科学、学问)
miàn 面	名量:用于有扁平面的东西 　　　*for flat things or things* 　　　*with a flat surface*	一～旗子(锦旗、镜子、鼓)
miǎo 秒	名量:时间单位 　　　second	几～钟|三分二十～
míng 名	名量:(1)用于人 　　　　*for people* 　　(2)用于名次 　　　　*for place in a competition*	一～学生 第一～|前八～
mù 幕	名量:(1)用于景象,前面常加数词"一" 　　　　*for scenes, usu. used* 　　　　*with numeral 一* 　　(2)用于戏剧 　　　　*act*	一～动人的景象 五～话剧|第二～|一～丑剧
pái 排	名量:(1)用于成排的人、物 　　　　*row* 　　(2)用于军队的编制单位 　　　　*platoon*	小朋友站成了一～。|一～座位|一～果树 两～战士
pài 派	名量:(1)用于派别、流派 　　　　*school; faction; clique* 　　(2)用于景象、语言等,前面只 　　　加数词"一" 　　　　*for scenes or speech, used* 　　　　*only with numeral 一*	分成几～ 一～新气象|一～胡言
pán 盘	名量:(1)用于盘状物或绕成盘状的 　　　物件 　　　　*for things of a plate-* 　　　　*shape or coiled* 　　(2)用于棋赛或某些球赛 　　　　*game; set*	一～磨(电线、铁丝、绳子、磁带) 一～棋|今天的男子乒乓球单打,每一～都打满了五局。

	说　　　明 Explanation or English Equivalent	例　子 Examples
pī 批	名量:用于较多数量的人、动物、东西 batch; lot	代表们一～一～到达。｜进了一～货
pǐ 匹	名量:用于骡、马、布等 *for horses*, *mules*, *etc.*; bolt	三～马(骡子)｜一～布
piān 篇	名量:(1)用于文稿 *for writings* (2)用于本册零页或纸张,常儿化 sheet, *often retroflexed*	一～论文(稿子、日记、社论) 这本书缺了一～。｜给我几～纸
piàn 片	名量:(1)用于片状物,有时儿化 piece, *often retroflexed* (2)用于地面、水面 stretch; sheet; expanse (3)用于景象、声音、语言、心意等,前面只加数词"一" *for scenes*, *sound*, *speech*, *intention*, *etc.*; *used only with numeral* 一	几～饼干(面包、药片) 一～绿色的原野｜这两～麦子长得真好。｜一～汪洋 一～大好形势(丰收景象、欢腾、哭声、胡言乱语、好心)
piě 撇	名量:用于像撇儿的东西 *for things like the left-falling stroke of a Chinese character*	两～胡子｜他有两～漆黑的眉毛。
qī 期	名量:用于分期的刊物、班级等 *for periodicals*, *training-course*, *etc.*; issue	第三～《英语世界》｜咱们是同一～毕业的。
qǐ 起	名量:(1)用于事件 case (2)用于人的分拨 lot; batch (of people)	一～案件(车祸、事故) 今天来参观的已经有好几～了。

	说　　　明 Explanation or English Equivalent	例　子 Examples
qǔ 曲	名量:用于歌曲 *for songs or musical pieces*	一～悲歌
qún 群	名量:用于成群的人、动物等 group; flock; crowd	一～人(学生、孩子)│ 一～鸽子(牛、羊)
shàn 扇	名量:用于门、窗等 *for doors , windows , etc.*	一～门(窗户、屏风)
shī 师	名量:用于军队的编制单位 division	一～民兵
shǒu 首	名量:用于诗词、歌曲 *for poems , songs , etc.*	两～诗(歌曲)
shù 束	名量:用于某些顺着捆、放在一起的 东西(多为花、文稿等) bunch; sheaf	一～鲜花(诗稿、文 件)
shuāng 双	名量:用于成对物 pair	几～袜子(鞋)│一～ 手
sōu 艘	名量:用于船只(较大者) *for ships*	一～轮船(货轮、军 舰)
suì 岁	名量:用于年龄 *for age*	十八～
suǒ 所	名量:用于成栋的房屋、建筑等 *for houses , buildings*	三～房子(楼房、医 院、住宅)
tāi 胎	名量:用于人和哺乳类动物怀胎、生 育的次数 birth; litter	第一～│一窝三～
tái 台	名量:(1)用于某些机器 　　　*for machines* (2)用于戏曲演出等 　　　performance	几～机器(车床、发电 机、收音机) 一～戏
tān 摊	名量:用于摊开的糊状物 puddle; pool	一～血│一～泥
táng 堂	名量:用于课时 *for classes*	一～课

	说　　　明 Explanation or English Equivalent	例　子 Examples
tàng 趟	名量:用于班车等 *for scheduled service of transportation*	还有一～车|今天最后一～班机
	动量:用于来往、走动的次数 *trip*	走一～|白跑了一～
tào 套	名量:用于成套成组的事物等 *set*	一～规矩(制度)|一～课本(丛书、邮票)|两～衣服(房间、家具)|一～班子
tiāo 挑	名量:同"担"(dàn)	一～谷子
tiáo 条	名量:(1)用于长条形物 *for anything of a long narrow piece*	一～带子(管子、街、裤子、口袋)
	(2)用于某些动植物 *for some longish animal or fruit*	两～鱼|三～狗|三～黄瓜
	(3)用于肢体器官 *for limbs*	一～胳臂(腿)
	(4)用于消息、办法等 *for news, method, etc.*	一～消息(新闻、办法、定律、路线、纪律、意见)
	(5)用于以固定数量组合成的某些长条形物 *for bar-like things*	一～肥皂(两块)|一～香烟(十包)
	(6)用于人命 *for human lives*	四～命
tiē 贴	名量:用于膏药 *for medicated plaster*	一～膏药
tǐng 挺	名量:用于机枪 *for machine guns*	两～机枪
tóu 头	名量:(1)用于某些牲畜 *for some domestic animals*	一～牛(驴、猪、羊)
	(2)用于大蒜等 *bulb*	一～蒜

	说　　　明 Explanation or English Equivalent	例　子 Examples
tuán 团	名量：(1)用于成团物 　　　　　ball (2)用于其引申义，前面只加 　　数词"一" 　　*for some abstract things,* 　　*used only with numeral 一* (3)用于军队的编制单位 　　regiment	两～毛线｜一～纸 一～漆黑｜心里一～ 火 一～军队
wán 丸	名量：用于中药丸 *for rather big pills of tradi-* *tional Chinese medicine*	两～药｜每次服一～
wěi 尾	名量：〈书〉用于鱼类 *for fish*	一～鲜鱼
wèi 位	名量：用于人（较客气的说法） for people (*polite term*)	两～客人｜各～代表
wèi 味	名量：用于中药配方 *for ingredients of a Chinese* *medicine prescription*	十几～药
wō 窝	名量：(1)多用于一个窝里的小动物 　　　　*for small animals or in-* 　　　　*sects in a nest* (2)用于一胎所生或一次孵出 　　的动物 　　litter; brood (3)用于坏人的集团 　　*for a group of bandits,* 　　*rascals, etc.*	一～蚂蚁 下了一～小猪（狗） 一～贼（坏蛋、流氓、 土匪）
xí 席	名量：(1)用于整桌的筵席 　　　　*for banquet* (2)〈书〉用于谈话，前面只加 　　数词"一" 　　*for talk, used only with* 　　*numeral 一*	一～酒｜一～酒筵 　　　　（jiǔyán） 一～话

	说 明 Explanation or English Equivalent	例 子 Examples
xià 下	动量:用于动作次数 time	打了几~|敲了三~门
xiàng 项	名量:(1)用于文件、工作等 for manuscripts, work, etc. (2)用于事物所分的项目 item	一~指示(声明、决 定、工程) 三~议程(决议、内 容)
xiē 些	名量:用于不定的数量,前面常加数 词"一" some, used only with numeral —	一~日用品|一~作 家|一~时候
yǎn 眼	名量:多用于井 for wells	一~井
yàng 样	名量:用于事物的种类 kind	两~礼物|几~菜
yè 页	名量:用于书页 page	一~稿子
yíng 营	名量:用于军队的编制单位 battalion	两~战士
yuán 元	名量:货币单位 unit of currency	一~钱|三~五角
yuán 员	名量:用于武将 for generals	一~猛将(女将、闯 将)
zāo 遭	动量:用于行动的次数,或表示周、 圈儿 trip; round	到外面转了一~|去 过一~|用绳子绕 了两~
zé 则	名量:〈书〉用于寓言、随笔、题目、新 闻等 for fables, notes, news, etc.	一~寓言(试题、新 闻)|随笔二~
zhǎn 盏	名量:用于灯 for lamps	一~灯(电灯、煤油 灯)
zhāng 张	名量:(1)用于平面物体或有平面的 物体 for flat things or things with a flat surface (2)用于少数能张开的物 for bows and mouths	一~纸(票、扑克牌)| 两~桌子(皮、饼、 床) 两~弓|一~嘴

	说　　　明 Explanation or English Equivalent	例　子 Examples
zhāng 章	名量:用于文章、歌曲的段落 　　　chapter; movement	第二～
zhèn 阵	名量:用于段落,前面常加数词"一" 　　　spatter; gust; fit, etc. 动量:用于动作段落,前面常加数词 　　　"一" 　　　*for actions that last for* 　　　*sometime , used only with nu-* 　　　*meral 一*	一～风(雨)｜一～枪 声(掌声、骚动) 打了一～｜闹了一～｜ 说笑了一～
zhī 支	名量:(1)用于队伍等 　　　　*for troops* 　　　(2)用于歌曲、乐曲 　　　　*for songs , melodies, etc.* 　　　(3)用于杆状物 　　　　*for stick-like things*	一～队伍(部队、舰 队) 一～歌(民歌、曲子) 一～铅笔(香烟、蜡 烛)
zhī 只	名量:(1)用于某些成对物的一个 　　　　one of a pair 　　　(2)用于某些动物 　　　　*for some animals* 　　　(3)用于某些器具、工具 　　　　*for some utensils*	两～耳朵(脚、鞋) 一～羊(猫、猴子) 一～箱子｜一～船
zhī 枝	名量:(1)用于带枝的花 　　　　spray 　　　(2)用于杆状物(同支(3)) 　　　　*for stick-like things*	一～梅花 一～香烟(钢笔、蜡 烛、枪)
zhǒng 种	名量:用于人、事、物的种类、样式 　　　kind, type	两～人(人物、动物、制 度、习惯、思想、意见、 颜色、东西)
zhōu 周	动量:用于绕行次数 　　　circuit	绕场一～

	说　　　明 Explanation or English Equivalent	例　子 Examples
zhóu 轴	名量:用于卷在轴上的线,或装裱的带轴字画 spool; scroll	一～线（丝线）｜一～山水画（中国画）
zhū 株	名量:〈书〉用于植物 *for plants*	一～松树｜一～玫瑰
zhuāng 桩	名量:用于事项 *for matters, affairs, etc.*	一～喜事（大事、心事）
zōng 宗	名量:用于货物等 *for goods, etc.*	一～货物（款项、生意）
zǔ 组	名量:(1)用于成组事物 　　set; series	一～电池｜两～仪器
	(2)用于学习、工作等组织 　　group	一～学生
	(3)用于成组的文艺作品 　　*for literary or musical compositions made up of several parts*	一～诗｜一～歌｜两～画
zuò 座	名量:用于较大、较稳固的物体 *for big buildings, structures, etc.*	一～山（碉堡、宫殿、楼房、纪念碑、石雕、桥梁、大钟）

（十二）化学元素表
Chemical Elements

原子序数 Atomic Number	元素名称 Names of Elements	符　号 Symbols	英文名称 English Names
1	氢 qīng	H	hydrogen
2	氦 hài	He	helium
3	锂 lǐ	Li	lithium
4	铍 pí	Be	beryllium
5	硼 péng	B	boron
6	碳 tàn	C	carbon，carbonium
7	氮 dàn	N	nitrogen
8	氧 yǎng	O	oxygen
9	氟 fú	F	fluorine
10	氖 nǎi	Ne	neon
11	钠 nà	Na	sodium
12	镁 měi	Mg	magnesium
13	铝 lǚ	Al	aluminium
14	硅 guī	Si	silicon
15	磷 lín	P	phosphorus
16	硫 liú	S	sulphur
17	氯 lǜ	Cl	chlorine
18	氩 yà	Ar	argon
19	钾 jiǎ	K	potassium
20	钙 gài	Ca	calcium
21	钪 kàng	Sc	scandium
22	钛 tài	Ti	titanium
23	钒 fán	V	vanadium
24	铬 gè	Cr	chromium
25	锰 měng	Mn	manganese

原子序数 Atomic Number	元 素 名 称 Names of Elements	符 号 Symbols	英 文 名 称 English Names
26	铁 tiě	Fe	iron
27	钴 gǔ	Co	cobalt
28	镍 niè	Ni	nickel
29	铜 tóng	Cu	copper
30	锌 xīn	Zn	zinc
31	镓 jiā	Ga	gallium
32	锗 zhě	Ge	germanium
33	砷 shēn	As	arsenic
34	硒 xī	Se	selenium
35	溴 xiù	Br	bromine
36	氪 kè	Kr	krypton
37	铷 rú	Rb	rubidium
38	锶 sī	Sr	strontium
39	钇 yǐ	Y	yttrium
40	锆 gào	Zr	zirconium
41	铌 ní	Nb	niobium
42	钼 mù	Mo	molybdenum
43	锝 dé	Tc	technetium
44	钌 liǎo	Ru	ruthenium
45	铑 lǎo	Rh	rhodium
46	钯 bǎ	Pd	palladium
47	银 yín	Ag	silver
48	镉 gé	Cd	cadmium
49	铟 yīn	In	indium
50	锡 xī	Sn	tin
51	锑 tī	Sb	antimony
52	碲 dì	Te	tellurium
53	碘 diǎn	I	iodine
54	氙 xiān	Xe	xenon
55	铯 sè	Cs	cesium
56	钡 bèi	Ba	barium

原子序数 Atomic Number	元素名称 Names of Elements	符号 Symbols	英文名称 English Names
57	镧 lán	La	lanthanum
58	铈 shì	Ce	cerium
59	镨 pǔ	Pr	praseodymium
60	钕 nǔ	Nd	neodymium
61	钷 pǒ	Pm	promethium
62	钐 shān	Sm	samarium
63	铕 yǒu	Eu	europium
64	钆 gá	Gd	gadolinium
65	铽 tè	Tb	terbium
66	镝 dī	Dy	dysprosium
67	钬 huǒ	Ho	holmium
68	铒 ěr	Er	erbium
69	铥 diū	Tm	thulium
70	镱 yì	Yb	ytterbium
71	镥 lǔ	Lu	lutetium
72	铪 hā	Hf	hafnium
73	钽 tǎn	Ta	tantalum
74	钨 wū	W	tungsten，wolfram
75	铼 lái	Re	rhenium
76	锇 é	Os	osmium
77	铱 yī	Ir	iridium
78	铂 bó	Pt	platinum
79	金 jīn	Au	gold
80	汞 gǒng	Hg	mercury
81	铊 tā	Tl	thallium
82	铅 qiān	Pb	lead
83	铋 bì	Bi	bismuth
84	钋 pō	Po	polonium
85	砹 ài	At	astatine
86	氡 dōng	Rn	radon
87	钫 fāng	Fr	francium

原子序数 Atomic Number	元 素 名 称 Names of Elements	符 号 Symbols	英 文 名 称 English Names
88	镭 léi	Ra	radium
89	锕 ā	Ac	actinium
90	钍 tǔ	Th	thorium
91	镤 pú	Pa	protactinium
92	铀 yóu	U	uranium
93	镎 ná	Np	neptunium
94	钚 bù	Pu	plutonium
95	镅 méi	Am	americium
96	锔 jú	Cm	curium
97	锫 péi	Bk	berkelium
98	锎 kāi	Cf	californium
99	锿 āi	Es	einsteinium
100	镄 fèi	Fm	fermium
101	钔 mén	Md	mendelevium
102	锘 nuò	No	nobelium
103	铹 láo	Lr	lawrencium
104	𬬻 lú	Rf	rutherfordium
105	𬭊 dù	Db	dubnium
106	𬭳 xǐ	Sg	seaborgium
107	𬭛 bō	Bh	bohrium
108	𬭶 hēi	Hs	hassium
109	鿏 mài	Mt	meitnerium

图书在版编目(CIP)数据

简明汉英词典/《简明汉英词典》编写组编.—修
订版.—北京:商务印书馆,2002
　ISBN 7-100-02109-X

　Ⅰ.简… Ⅱ.简… Ⅲ.①英语-词典 ②词典-汉、英
Ⅳ.H316

中国版本图书馆 CIP 数据核字(2001)第 073560 号

JIĂNMÍNG HÀNYĪNG CÍDIĂN
简 明 汉 英 词 典
修 订 版

编著者　《简明汉英词典》编写组

修订人　王　还　赖汉纲　田万湘

　　　　许德楠　张　维　王升印

商 务 印 书 馆 出 版
(北京王府井大街36号　邮政编码 100710)
商 务 印 书 馆 发 行
北 京 冠 中 印 刷 厂 印 刷
ISBN 7-100-02109-X/H·604

1982年9月第1版　　　开本 787×1092 1/32
2002年1月第2版　　　印张 32 1/8
2002年1月北京第6次印刷

定价:40.00元